A HISTORY OF THE SIKH PEOPLE

(1469-1988)

BY

DR. GOPAL SINGH

ALLIED PUBLISHERS PVT. LIMITED

NEW DELHI MUMBAI KOLKATA CHENNAI NAGPUR
AHMEDABAD BANGALORE HYDERABAD LUCKNOW

ALLIED PUBLISHERS PRIVATE LIMITED

1/13-14 Asaf Ali Road, **New Delhi**–110002
Ph.: 011-23239001 • E-mail: delhi.books@alliedpublishers.com

Khasra No. 168, Plot No. 12-A, opp. Wisdom Academy School, Kamta, Surendra Nagar, **Lucknow**–227105
Ph.: 09335202549 • E-mail: lko.books@alliedpublishers.com

17 Chittaranjan Avenue, **Kolkata**–700072
Ph.: 033-22129618 • E-mail: cal.books@alliedpublishers.com

15 J.N. Heredia Marg, Ballard Estate, **Mumbai**–400001
Ph.: 022-42126969 • E-mail: mumbai.books@alliedpublishers.com

60 Shiv Sunder Apartments (Ground Floor), Central Bazar Road, Bajaj Nagar, **Nagpur**–440010
Ph.: 0712-2234210 • E-mail: ngp.books@alliedpublishers.com

F-1 Sun House (First Floor), C.G. Road, Navrangpura, Ellisbridge P.O., **Ahmedabad**–380006
Ph.: 079-26465916 • E-mail: ahmbd.books@alliedpublishers.com

751 Anna Salai, **Chennai**–600002
Ph.: 044-28523938 • E-mail: chennai.books@alliedpublishers.com

5th Main Road, Gandhinagar, **Bangalore**–560009
Ph.: 080-22262081 • E-mail: bngl.books@alliedpublishers.com

3-2-844/6 & 7 Kachiguda Station Road, **Hyderabad**–500027
Ph.: 040-24619079 • E-mail: hyd.books@alliedpublishers.com

Website: www.alliedpublishers.com

First edition : 1979

Second (revised and updated) edition : 1988

Latest Reprint 2015

ISBN : 81-7023-139-6

PRICE : ₹ 925.00

This edition of *A History of the Sikh People* is published by Allied Publishers Private Lir
by arrangement with World Book Centre, New Delhi

Published by Sunil Sachdev and printed by Ravi Sachdev at Allied Publishers Private Limited, Printing Division, A-104 Mayapuri Phase II, New Delhi 110064

4/2015

Dedicated

to

INDIA, the Mother,

for whose freedom and integrity

countless Sikh heroes

laid down their lives

TABLE OF CONTENTS

Part II

Abbreviations

GSG	Gur Partap Surya Granth (also called Suraj Parkāsh)(Bhāi Vir Singh's edited edition has been used)	by Bhāi Santokh Singh
Mk	Mahān Kosh (Gur Shabad Ratnākar Mahān Kosh) 1st ed.	by Bhāi Kāhan Singh
PPP	Prāchin Panth Parkāsh (verse) (1953 edition)(Published by Khālsā Samāchār, Amritsar)	by Bhangu Rattan Singh
SBM	Sikhān di Bhagat Mālā Published by Khālsā Samāchar Amritsar	by Bhāi Mani Singh
Adi Granth	Guru Granth Sahib (Sikh Scripture) standard edition, Published by SGPC	All translations by the author
GR	Gyān Ratnāvali (Guru Nānak's Biography)	by Bhāi Mani Singh

Note 1 : *Unless otherwise indicated, only first editions of reference works have been used. The Mahātamā is by G.D. Tendulkar, published in 8 volumes, by Govt. of India. Quotations from* **"A HISTORY OF THE SIKHS"** *by J.D.Cunnigham are from the 1915 edition revised by* **HLO** *Garret and reprinted in Delhi by S. Chand and Company, though the first (1849) edition has also been used for comparisons and corrections."The Oxford History of India" by Vincent Smith refers to the 1958 edition, as published in the revised/rewritten form by the Clarendon Press, Oxford. "Autobiography" of Master* Tārā Singh refers to the book, "Māster Tārā Singh, Jiwan te Sangharsh" (Panjābi) as edited and published by his son, Jawant Singh, at Amritsar (1972). *"Panjāb, past and present" is a six-monthly Journal edited by Dr. Ganda Singh and published by the Panjābi University, Patiālā. Extracts from the Rehat nāmās are taken from Bhāi Kāhan Singh's standard work, "Gurmat Sudhākar."*

Note 2 :— *No separate bibliography is given at the end, as each Chapter contains in the footnotes the names of the authorities and the books and the editions used. An exhaustive bibliography by Dr. Gandā Singh is also available in print.*

PART I

CHAPTER I

THE BACKGROUND

Sikhism has been defined by most historians—otherwise well-meaning and scholarly, though casual in their treatment of this dynamic faith—as an offshoot of the Bhakti movement, the Hindu mystic renaissance of the Middle Ages, emphasising the oneness of God and man's direct emotional relationship with His Personal or Absolute Reality, irrespective of caste or creed. But, as we shall see, the scriptural authority the Bhaktas built their thesis upon was the Veda (except for Karma Kānda), and the loving adoration *(Bhakti)* of God was to be offered to any one of the incarnations of Vishnu, both of which doctrines Guru Nānak, the founder of the Sikh faith, repudiated. There are other fundamental differences also like the Bhakta emphasis on renunciation, contempt for women, spiritual indifference to, not total repudiation of, caste as a social force and non-involvement with a dynamic, purposeful life, in all of which Guru Nānak took a different and a more earth-aware course.

Others even more superficial have looked upon this movement as a synthesis of the fundamentals (whatever the term might imply) of Hindu Bhakti and Muslim Sufi-ism. If anything, Nānak's basic inspiration was indigenous, even pre-Āryan, and he, as we shall see, either rejected or wholly gave a different meaning to the basic concepts and doctrines of both Hinduism and Islām. "My God is neither in the Veda nor in the Semitic texts, for He is beyond both, being a living Presence."

Still others, more recent though most casual and ignorant both of the Sikh Scriptures and the original historical records, have interpreted Sikhism as a kind of "Panjābi nationalism" which lies today in a shambles before our very eyes. Incidentally, Guru Nānak (nor any other of the Sikh Gurus) ever so much as mentioned the word

"Panjāb" in his extensive writings. Though born in the Panjāb, his tours took him not only to the entire sub-continent of India but also to Ceylon, Tibet and the Middle East. Certainly he wasn't out to propagate "Panjābi nationalism" there! But, even statesmen of great vision like Mahātmā Gāndhi and literary geniuses like Rabindra Nāth Tagore have seen in the evolution of the Sikh movement from Guru Nānak to Guru Gobind Singh a degeneration of the world of the spirit (of which Nānak was such a superb expression) into the "cult of the sword" in the hands of the tenth and the last Guru. Tagore, however, wrote his thesis before he witnessed the horrors of the two world wars in the present century, and Mahātmā Gāndhi lived to repudiate his own thesis of "non-violence in all circumstances" by blessing the defence of Kashmir, through armed resistance, and the "brave and selfless" resistance of the Poles to Hitler's onslaught in 1939 as "non-violent", being offered in self-defence.* As we shall see, it is to the eternal glory of the Sikh movement that the sword was drawn only when all other means had been exhausted, and under the leadership of the Gurus, always in self-defence. Victories were won, but their fruit was never claimed in the form of territory or reparations. And even when a sovereign empire was created, its fruits were shared equally with all, and religion was separated from the affairs of the State.‡

---

* See on Poland, "Non-violence in Peace and War," by M. K. Gāndhi (P. 240 —Navjivan Publishing House); On Kashmir, ibid, Vol. II (pp. 321, 363). Almost every Gāndhite of note in India, led by the Sarvodaya leader, Jaya Prakāsh Nārāyan, and the spiritual heir of Mahātmā Gāndhi, Shri Vinobā Bhāvē, cried out for armed help to the forces of liberation in East Bengāl in 1971, when neither appeal to the conscience of the world nor to the conscience of their persecutors was of any avail. Ultimately what led to the freedom of Banglādesh was the resort to a clash of arms, when all other choices were closed upon India and Banglādesh.

‡ Asoka's renunciation of war after the bloody battle of Kalingā is cited often enough to emphasise India's faith in non-violence since time immemorial. This is, however, historically not true, though India has seen, as Mr. Nehru rightly points out in his "Discovery of India" far longer periods of peace, and her wars may have been far more humane, than in other parts of the world in the corresponding periods. But, it must also be remembered that the supreme Rig Vedic god, Indra, is a warrior-god; so also are Shiva and his consort, Kāli or Chandi, and the heroes of Mahābhārata and Rāmāyana worshipped by the Hindus through the ages as the incarnations of Vishnu. Indeed, except for the Buddha, who learnt all the arts of war (being a Kashatriya Prince) but never practised them, all the other nine incarnations of Vishnu (including the one, Kalki, who is yet to appear to destroy evil) are involved in a gigantic war or bitter struggle against injustice

No notice, however, need be taken of those who have termed Sikhism as a Hindu challenge to the growing might of Islām, both political and military, during the Moghal period, as the Gurus at no time accepted this as one of their social or religious aims. On the contrary, Muslims fought along with the Hindus as the supporters of the Sikhs, throughout history, for the ideals their Gurus cherished and proclaimed. And those eminent historians like J. N. Sarkār who see nothing unique or original in this movement and dismiss it as a casual aberration on the historical process are better left unanswered. From the fruit only can one judge the quality of the seed. And, in the present as much as in the past, the significant Sikh contribution in spite of their small numbers, (they were 13 million out of 665 million Indians, according to the Census of 1981), to the integrity, the polity and the economy of the Indian sub-continent and the religious idea of the world is there for all to see.*

However, at times a historian (not necessarily a Sikh) with a perceptive vision has risen to point to the basic uniqueness of the Sikh movement. One such was Qāzi Noor Mohammed, a bitter enemy of the Sikh creed, who in his eye-witness account of the Sikh struggle against the Afghāns of the eighteenth century, in his *Jangnāmā*, has paid tribute to the Sikh ideals such as only a man of far-seeing and catholic mind alone could do. Another distinguished name is that of Joseph D. Cunningham (1812-1851), the author of "A History of the Sikhs" (1848), who was an eye-witness to the first Anglo-Sikh war. Still another was the well-known philosopher-poet of the present century, Dr. Sir Mohd Iqbāl, the dream-builder of

---

and oppression. As for Asoka, the following opinion by a well-known scholar of India's ancient past, Dr. A. L. Basham, may be of interest to the reader:

"It is clear that Asoka was not a complete pacifist. The wild tribesmen of hill and forest were a constant source of danger to the more settled parts of the empire...Asoka clearly tried to civilise them, but it is quite evident that he was ready to repress them by force if they continued their raids. He made no mention of reducing the army. Despite his remorse at the conquest of Kalinga, he was too much of a realist to restore it to its original rulers. For all his humanitarianism, he maintained the death penalty, which was abolished by some later Indian Kings...Though Buddhist tradition records that he abolished judicial torture, this is not clearly stated in his edicts." ("The Wonder that was India," pp. 54-55).

* Their population (1981) was over one crore in Panjab out of a total population of 1 crore, 68 lakhs, (or, about 60%), and over 3 million in the rest of India. (See table at the end). They should be about 2 million abroad. Their population at present (1988) should be about 16 million in India.

Pākistān.* And mention must also be made of the Emperor Jehāngir, the persecutor of the fifth Guru, Arjun, who also though unexpectedly, understood the basic significance of the Sikh movement and hence tried to destroy it as soon as possible.

Qāzi Noor Mohammed accompanied Ahmad Shah Abdāli in his invasion of India in 1764. This is what he has to say about Sikhs who fought bitterly against his master :

"Do not call Sikhs 'dogs' (*sag*) because they are brave like lions on the battlefield. If you want to learn the art of war, then learn it from them on the field of battle......When engaged in giving charities they surpass even Hātim. When they take the sword in hand, they gallop from Hind to the country of Sind and nobody, however strong and substantial, can dare oppose them. The body of each of them looks like a mountain and in grandeur excels fifty men.

"If their troops take to flight, do not consider it a defeat. It is a trick of their mode of war. May God forbid the repetition of such a fraud. They resort to such deception in order to make the angry enemy grow bold and to run in their pursuit. When they find them (the pursuers) separated from their main body and cut off from all help and reinforcement, they at once turn back and give them the hardest time possible."

What is, however, more significant is the following observation of his, which, according to him, distinguishes the Sikh warrior from the usual run :

"In one thing they excel all other warriors. They never kill a coward and do not obstruct one who flees from the field. They do not rob a woman of her gold, may she be a queen or a slave-girl. Adultery does not exist among these 'dogs.' None of them is a thief."**

---

* Here it must be said to the credit of Iqbal's vision that in his address to the Allahabad session of the All India Muslim League in 1930, he enunciated the conception of Pākistān (though he did not give it that name) as consisting only of Panjāb, Sind, the Pathānland, Baluchistān and Kashmir. The idea of a second, eastern wing (of East Bengāl) was an imposition of Mr. Mohammed Ali Jinnāh in the Muslim League session of 1940, though he too visualised two "sovereign, independent and autonomous entities of the two wings," which they have now become, thus defeating the forced union between the two wings solely on the basis of religion.

**"In Manu Smriti" such a code is also enunciated : "A warrior fighting from a chariot might not strike one on foot; an enemy in flight, wounded or asking

Joseph D. Cunningham was a rare—and perhaps the first European—who, inspite of the many mistakes of fact he commits in delineating the lives of the Sikh Gurus (though his account of the first Anglo-Sikh war is the most authoritative), had grasped the fundamentals of the Sikh faith, not as a mere movement of reform or an offshoot of Bhakti, but as something more cataclysmic :

"It has been usual to regard the Sikhs as essentially Hindu, and they doubtless are so in language and everyday customs, for Gobind did not fetter his disciples with political systems or codes of municipal laws; yet in religious faith and worldly aspiration, they are wholly different from other Indians, and they are bound together by an objective unknown elsewhere. But the misapprehension need not surprise the public nor condemn our scholars, when it is remembered that the learned of Greece and Rome misunderstood the spirit of those humble men who obtained a new life by baptism. Tacitus and Suetonius regarded the early Christians as a mere Jewish sect; they failed to perceive the fundamental difference, and to appreciate the latent energy and real excellence of that doctrine which has added dignity and purity to modern civilisation."

He continues: "The last apostle of the Sikhs (Guru Gobind Singh) did not live to see his own ends accomplished, but he effectually roused the dormant energies of a vanquished people, and filled them with a lofty though fitful longing for social freedom and national ascendancy, the proper adjuncts of that purity of worship which had been preached by Nānak. Gobind saw what was yet vital, and he reillumined it with promethean fire. A living spirit possesses the whole Sikh people, and the impress of Gobind has not only altered the constitution of their minds, but has operated materially and given

---

** *F. N. (Contd.)*

quarter might not be slain; the lives of enemy soldiers who had lost their weapons were to be respected; poisoned weapons were not to be used. Homage and not annexation was the rightful fruit of victory." But as Dr. Basham has pointed out ("The Wonder that was India," p. 126), this code "was not always kept." "The heroes of Mahābhārata infringed them many times, even at the behest of their mentor, Krishna, and the infringements are explained and pardoned by recourse to causistical arguments of expediency and necessity......... The rules of war could only be maintained strictly by a King certain of victory or certain of defeat." In the later and more popular *Arthshāstra* of Kautilya, however, we hear nothing of these rules. According to Elphinstone, "A Marāthā thinks of nothing *but* the result, and cares little for the means." (See also part II)

amplitude to their physical frames.* The features and external form of a whole people have been modified, and a Sikh chief is not more distinguishable by his stately person and free and manly bearing than a minister of his faith is by a lofty thoughtfulness of look, which marks the fervour of his soul, and his persuasion of the near presence of the Divinity."‡

Emperor Jehāngir (1526 - 1627), who had the fifth Guru, Arjun, executed in 1606, had also seen in the Sikh movement something more than a mere movement of religious reform or a novel spiritual adventure. Though he cites the "help" (in the form of a blessing) given by the Guru to his rebel son, Khusrau, as the main cause of the Guru's execution (which excuse as we shall discuss later, is wholly spurious), he lets himself out on a more fundamental reason in his autobiography "*Tuzak-i-Jehāngiri*," when he writes :

"At Goindwāl, on the bank of the river Beās, lived a Hindu, Arjun by name, in the garb of a Pir or Sheikh. *Thus, many innocent Hindus and even foolish Muslims he brought into his fold who beat the drum noisily of his self-appointed prophethood.* He was called Guru. From all sides worshippers came to offer their homage to him and put full trust in his word. For three or four generations, they had warmed up this shop. For a long time I had harboured a wish that I should set aside this shop of falsehood or I should bring him into the fold of Islām." (P. 35)

So that it was not a mere Hindu reformer who was being put to death by an orthodox Muslim emperor, but one whose instruction even "foolish" Musalmāns were also accepting (and for which reason Jehāngir's father, Akbar the Great, the founder of *Din-i-Illahi*, had come personally to pay homage to the Guru at Goindwāl). This is what made Sikhism a "shop of falsehood," for it was being acknowledged *by both Hindus and Musalmāns.* Not for nothing had Guru Nānak raised his unusual slogan : "There is no Hindu, no Musalmān," when he entered first upon his divine mission, late in the fifteenth century.

Some influential leaders of Muslim sects, like Mirzā Ghulām Ahmad of Qadiān (1835-1905 A. D.), head of the Ahmadiyā or the

*This physical change, adds Cunningham, was noticed also by Sir Alexander Burns (Travels, I,285, and II, 39), by Elphinstone (History of India, II, 564) and it also slightly struck Malcolm (Sketch of the Sikhs, p. 129).

‡"A History of the Sikhs," pp. 84-85.

Qadiāni sect, have tried to establish that Nānak, the founder of Sikhism, was a devout Muslim. (How else, he argues, could he visit the Meccā, or accept a robe of honour in Baghdād on which is inscribed the entire text of the Qurān, and how otherwise would Muslims argue and fight for claiming his dead body, etc.?) ("*Sat Bachan*," Urdu, second edition, 1902, pp. 4377-4504). On the other hand, some scholarly Hindu historians, like Dr. Indu Bhushan Banerjee, have claimed that Nānak was as good a devout Hindu as any other Bhakta and that he challenged, and changed, nothing in their way of life, neither caste, nor the sacred thread, nor the authority of the Hindu scriptures, or the efficacy of pilgrimages, etc. ("Evolution of the Khālsā," Vol. I. pp. 114-145) !

But, a far more perceptive philosopher-poet of India, Dr. Sir Mohd. Iqbāl (1876-1938 A. D.) asserts in his *Bang-i-Darrā* that "when our nation did not heed the illuminating message of Gautam the Buddha and recognised not the worth of this unique jewel of a man, rose Nānak, the complete man, in the Panjāb, to proclaim the message of *Tauhid* (the oneness of God)."

Iqbāl could well have added that while the oneness of God was proclaimed by many before Nānak, not so the oneness of man which was the more distinctive contribution of the founder of the Sikh faith. Perhaps, sensing the ample distinction, Iqbāl did not attribute Nānak's emergence as a great world-teacher to the influence of Islām, but to a far older order, that of Gautam the Buddha, who even though he did not believe in God as Person or the human soul* partaking of His essence, yet preached the gospel of one man ‡, not through Sanskrit, "the language of the gods or his chosen priests," but of common speech—Pāli—cutting through all intermediaries, the sacred texts, sacrifices and rituals, the myth and the miracle and the interventionist role of the gods and goddesses. It is also significant that the Hinyāna or Therāvādin (which is supposedly the original teaching

*It has been suggested that the *Nirgun* (attributeless) God of the Upanishads and the *Shunya* (Void) doctrine of the Buddha are closely inter-linked, and that as the Buddha believes in transmigration, what is it that transmigrates if not the soul, which he describes as sense-impressions; that the philosophical side of Buddhism is built on the *Sānkhya* school of Hindu philosophy and it is only in ethics that Buddhism is original.

‡However, the Buddha kept the women by and large out of the monastic order and did not attack caste with the ruthlessness of Nānak and the succeeding Gurus.

of the Buddha) was accepted less and less by the people (more particularly its emphasis on self-culture—*Arhathood*—and withdrawal from the secular world, its teachings directed more to the monks than to laymen) and it was the Mahāyāna, or the great vehicle, which was accepted by most people in Asia. This latter doctrine transformed the great Buddha himself into a god whose compassion could not only be invoked through prayer, worship and meditation, but even more through good works for others (as embodied in the ideal of the *Bodhisattva*), thus bringing it more and more in line with the later-day Sikh thought. For, no other religion—bar the Christian—emphasises so much the ethical conduct being a necessary adjunct of spiritual life as the Buddhist and the Sikh. As in Buddhism, directives in such minute details** are given in the Sikh Scriptures and other derivative texts, as also the biographies of the Sikh Gurus and their devout followers, that the discerning eye of Mohammed Iqbāl could not but visualise a closeness between the two faiths, as casual observers would indeed fail to mark.

Another similarity may also be of interest to the students both of religion and history. Though the Buddha was born on the borders of Eastern India, and for a time (i. e. after a lapse of about three centuries after his death during the reign of Asoka and for some two centuries afterwards) spread to the whole of India, its so-called original doctrine was soon lost, and with the Buddha being accepted as one of the ten incarnations of Vishnu, it became a part of the all-absorbing Hindu belief and ritual. It was, however, in the North-West of India—the Valley of Gandhār—where, since the beginning of the Christian era, the purity of the doctrine was preserved and preached. It was at the University of Taxilā, where scholars and pilgrims came from Afghanistān, China and Tibet, Ceylon, Thailand Turkistān, Malaysia and Cambodiā to drink deep at the fount of the Buddhist doctrine in its true manifestation. Also the Gandhāra

**See Appendices. Also see the *Vārs* and *Kabits* of Bhai Gurdās; *Sikhān di Bhagat Mālā* by Bhāi Mani Singh; *Rahitnāmās* of Bhāi Nandlāl, Bhāi Dayā Singh and Bhāi Chaupā Singh; *Hukamnāmās* of Gurus Tegh Bahadur and Gobind Singh; *Prem Sumārag: Janam Sākhis* of Mehervān and Bālā and India Office, London; *Gur-Partap Suryā Granth* and *Dabistān-i-Mazāhib*, etc. "Dabistān" quotes such fantastic stories about the compassion and charitable nature of the Sikhs of the Guru period that though they seem shocking to the common moral code, they reveal a people prepared to share their all with the needy even if he were a thief or a thug in the garb of a Sikh.

School of Art developed here (no doubt under the influence of the Greeks) to take the highly intellectualised message of the Buddha to the common mass through an emotional and aesthetic approach, which did much to propagate the Buddha's message to far off lands, including China and Japan. It must be remembered that it was under Kanishaka, the ruler of the North-Western India of the first century A. D., that a great assembly of the world Buddhists was held at Peshāwar to bridge the growing cleavage between the various schools of Buddism, notably between Hinayāna and Mahāyāna and it was the latter doctrine that ultimately triumphed.

This is also the land where the nomadic Aryans, from Central Asia first found their village-settlements on the ruins of an older city-civilisation and the Hindus of later days found their name (from "Sindhu" or the inhabitants of the land of Sind and its tributaries), their basic religious doctrines and their civilisation which have stood the test of several millennia. It is here that the Rig Veda, the main corpus of the Brahminic faith, found its first utterance, as also the Bhagvad Gitā, which reconciled various modes of attaining to the Supreme. But, strangely enough, though the Buddha calls his religion "Āryā Dharma" and was himself an Āryan prince, he derived his main inspiration from the pre-Āryan civilisation, now called the Dravidian, whose main contributions have been monism as against the Āryan polytheism, secular more than ethereal, spiritual more than metaphysical. And those were also the traits that centuries later, when whatever was left of Buddhism had degenerated into Tāntric ritual in India and the main body was driven out of here to find its home elsewhere and when Hinduism—or more specifically Brahminism—had become a matter of form rather than inner illumination, and could no longer face the challenge of Islām at the spiritual even more than the political level that there arose "a complete man," called Nānak, to challenge the Semitic as much as the Āryan view of life.

One of the more significant matters in which Guru Nānak and his successors derived inspiration from their pre-Āryan past was their repudiation of the village-culture, propagated by the Āryans, as against the city-civilisation of the Harappā-Mohenjodaro period which the Āryans from Central Asia had uprooted and destroyed. It is in this part of India that most of the Gurus were born and their instructions struck firm roots. Historians have uptodate taken no notice whatever of this significant fact that no Guru settled down in his ancestral village and more often than not built a new model town for his family and followers to move to and farm or trade in. As we shall see later on, these townships were not founded by the Guru to escape the wrath or jealousy of the relations of their predecessors, as has been suggested by most historians, but to give a new and fuller content to the secular living of their people. The towns of Kartārpur, Taran Tāran, Khadur, Goindwāl, Amritsar, Sri Hargobindpur, Kartārpur, Anandpur, etc, in the Panjāb owed their origin and prosperity to the Sikh Gurus. Again, as in the Harappā culture, the growth of the cities founded by them was pre-planned and not haphazard, and stone, brick and lime, instead of mud, were used as building materials. Furthermore as time passed, these cities were girdled with forts and fortresses (as at Mohenjodaro and Harappā) from the time of the sixth Guru onwards. Why Guru Gobind Singh invokes the supreme God as Shiva and his consort, Chandi, as the destroyer of evil, are not accidental. Without any belief in gods and goddessess other than the one God, the Guru is using the pre-Āryan, Dravidian symbols to point out where his main inspiration lay. The Sikh temples rising smoothly in the midst of the sparkling water-tanks and the pilgrim-stations being built not on the banks of the rivers or over the mountains (as the Āryans did) but on the trade-routes, also point to the same conclusion. And Guru Nānak is perhaps the first North Indian to try his hands at the Southern musical notes (rāgas).

2

What is the type of the people among whom the Sikh Gurus were born and who were the first to accept whole-heartedly their doctrines both of spiritual regeneration and moral and social hope? As is well known, the part of Hindustān that the Gurus were born into was first the seat of the Indus Valley iron-walled, city-civilisation of Mohenjodaro and Harappā, replaced later by the war-like, nomadic Āryans (lit. noblemen) from Central Asia, by village-culture.*

*Comments Prof. Basham ("The Wonder that was India," pp. 16-17):—

"Obviously there were numerous well-to-do families in the Indus cities, which perhaps had a middle-class larger and more important in the social scale than those of the contemporary civilisations of Sumer and Egypt" (a tendency that still marks out the Panjāb from the rest of Hindustān).

That the indigenous black aborigines were defeated in long-term engagements is clear both from the war-like qualities of the Vedic gods, like Indra, and also from the relics and ruins of the civilisation they displaced. The new waves of migrating Āryans also tussled with the older settlers, one clan with another, thus making the people of the North-west both aggressive and tough, the extremes of heat and cold in summer and winter also contributing their own share to the same effect. Alexander the Great of Macedonia found the resistance to his march into the Panjāb (lit. the land of the five rivers, the tributaries of the river Indus or Sind) so over-powering that he had to return, frustrated, in his grand design as a world-conqueror. Even a defeated Porus of Western Panjāb, when asked by Alexander what kind of treatment he would like to receive, defiantly answered "As behoves one King to treat another." The Panjābi men of arms fought in Persia in the armies of King Darius, five centuries before Christ. Horse as a weapon of war as against the elephant which later became India's military curse was known to the Panjāb even in pre-Āryan times. "Flaming thunder-bolts" were hurled at Alexander by the Panjābi men of arms and it is the opinion of many scholars that gun-powder was invented not in China but in the North-West of India. The cow, so revered in later Hinduism, is nowhere depicted in pre-Āryan seals, though the bull is (and which later became the mount of the god Shiva). Phallic worship (or worship of the procreative faculty) was an important element of the Harappā religion, and burial (not cremation) was the usual rite. It was a meeting place of many races, and cotton (as against the bark of trees) was first used by the Harappā people, two to three thousand years before it became current in Europe. Not only several weapons of war like the sword and the axe (employed also for peaceful purposes) were extensively known, but also life here had a gaiety and an abundance which the exclusive Āryan tribes (which exclusiveness was based on colour, profession or time of migration) later frowned upon, as they moved farther into the Indo-Gangetic plains or the heartland of Hindustān. Influenced by long-term peace, the over-productive earth, and an enervating climate, the Āryans began to speculate, as time passed, more on the other world and the nothingness of life, than the joys and the beauties of here and now. Most scholars are of the opinion that the dark-coloured aborigines of the Indus Valley civilisation (now known as Dravidians and mostly inhabiting Southern India), like the Jāts of the Panjāb, are Scythians in origin and came from

Central Asia, whose one branch migrated as far south in Europe as Bulgaria.*

The aborigines observed no caste (e.g. in the South, even now, there are no Kashatriyas or Vaishas) and upto now, among the Panjāb aboriginies, like Sānsis, no ceremony is complete without drinking and dancing. There was no priestly class among them. Upto the time of the Rig Veda (composed mostly in the Panjāb), the culture of the pre-Āryans is sought to be assimilated, by and large, by the immigrants, especially the love of life and its secular joys, but is later looked upon for the same reason with scorn. ‡ The Panjāb, the first home of the Āryans, is now termed "an impure land where Vedic sacrifices are not performed." The magnificent hair-styles of women on the Mohenjodaro seals, the urbane living standards, the building of structures for the convenience of the citizens rather than the temples for gods and palaces and tombs for Kings as in contemporary Egypt, reveal that it was a predominantly secular civilisation, "advanced and singularly uniform, closely akin, but in some respects even superior to that of contemporary Mesopotamia and Egypt." "Their public baths, municipal Government and drainage system are still the marvel of the Sumerian civilisation of that period." writes Jawāharlāl Nehru, "and their manufactures reached even the markets on the Tigris and Euphrates. Trade was not confined to raw materials, and luxury articles, and fish, regularly imported from the Arabian sea-coasts augmented the food supplies of Mohenjodaro."**

"Nothing," says Sir John Marshall, "that we know of in other countries at this period bears any resemblance, in point of style, to the faience models of rams, dogs and other animals, or to the intaglio engravings on the seals, the best of which—notably the humped, short-horned bulls—are distinguished by a breadth of treatment and a feeling for a line and plastic form that have rarely been surpassed in glyptic art, nor would it be possible, until the classic age of

---

*The language of the Gypsies in Bulgaria is very similar to the language of the hilly areas of the Panjāb, and the traditional customs, folk-tunes and costumes of the Bulgarians resemble those of the hilly areas of the Panjāb, now called Himāchal Pradesh, and Kashmir.

‡ "The Aryans called them Pālikās, i.e. 'excluded,' and Vratyas or heretics. "Their women," said they, "wandered through the streets and fields adored with garlands, intoxicated and undraped. With cries like the neighing of horses, they run to the bathing places." (History of the Panjāb, S.M. Latif, p. 34).

** Discovery of India, J. L. Nehru, p. 70

Greece, to match the exquisitely supple modelling of the two human statuettes from Harappā." All that was beautiful or useful and even dreadful (for it was supposed to blight the enemy) became sacred for the sensitive people of the Panjāb, and fine jewellery, with semi-precious stones set in gold filigree, has been unearthed from the ruins of Taxilā. A vigorous school of sculpture developed here—the Gandhāra School of Art—and also a mixed culture as a result of the inter-action on the Panjābis of the various races like the Greeks, Chinese, pre-Muslim Turks, the Iranians and the Scythians upon each other. These fiercely independent people were governed neither by the King nor the priest, but by their duly-chosen representatives. The idea of Kingship is Āryan in origin and is of later growth. The worship of images and idols in the post-Buddha period is also a Greek influence ('but',* as the idol is called in Hindustāni, itself is a derivative of 'Buddha'), and purdah among women was introduced by the far later Muslim conquest. Nowhere were the women honoured so much as in the early Āryan and the pre-Āryan civilisations. She is "the light of the dwelling." She makes her own choice of the husband and gaily dressed women "with their hair in four knots" are coveted. Even the Āryan gods live in the snowy cool of the Himalayas or beyond. They dig canals for irrigation and sow corn, beans, barley and sesame. They know the use of medicinal herbs, of weaving and spinning, and also make fine leather goods. They have among them smiths, carpenters, carriage-makers, ship-builders, goldsmiths and other artisans.

Says Arrian, the Greek Historian of Alexander's campaign in the Panjāb, "no nation is fonder of singing and dancing than the Indian" (meaning thereby, as is obvious, the people of Panjāb). Except for domestic servants, slavery was unknown here, as it was in Greece or Rome. Northern India (or North-Western to be precise) was famous for her weapons of war, especially for her quality of steel, her swords and daggers. When Alexander invaded Persia, it is stated by Firdausi, the Persian poet, in his "Shāhnāmeh" that swords and other weapons were hurriedly sent for by the Persians from India. This is not all. The University of Taxilā, which was the capital seat of the North-Western province of Ashoka's empire, became first for the Brahmins and later for the Buddhists a foremost seat of higher learning in the whole of Asia, not only in the arts and religion, but more espe-

* 'u' pronounced as in 'bull.'

cially in science and medicine. The grammarian Panini, the author of the "Yoga Sutra," Pātanjali, the physician Charak, the surgeon Sushruta and the political theorist, 'Chānakya, to name only a few of the world-renowned masters, were all the products of the University of Taxilā. The study of astrology and astronomy was pursued here as much as the study of pure mathematics, algebra and geometry. As Jawāharlāl Nehru puts it, "Banāras has been a centre of learning and even in Buddha's days it was old and known as such, but Banāras does not appear to have been at any time anything like a University such as existed then and later in other parts of India. There were numerous groups there, consisting of a teacher and his disciples, and often between rival groups there was fierce debate and agrument. But in the north-west, there was an ancient and famous university at Takshashilā or Taxilā.........noted for science, especially medicine, and the arts and to which travelled sons of nobles and Brahmins, unattended and unarmed, to be educated. Probably, students came also from Central Asia and Afghanistān. It was considered an honour to be a graduate of Taxilā.........Physicians who had studied there were highly thought of and it is related that whenever Buddha felt unwell, his admirers brought to him a famous physician who had graduated from Taxilā."*

Thus, neither the pre-Āryans nor the early Āryans of the Rig Vedic period discarded the secular in preference to the spiritual. It was the Buddha, who attacked the concepts of God and soul, so majestically expressed in the Upanishads, and the gods and goddesses of the Rig Veda identified with the forces of nature (both good and beautiful, or terrible, but by far more the former than the latter), priesthood, sacrifice, and the desires of the flesh and emphasised renunciation ("for all life is pain ") and non-injury to living beings, and who for a thousand years after his demise continued to influence the thought and history of Hindustān. He also attacked caste** at least

* Discovery of India, p. 117

** Comments S.M. Latif, the noted Muslim historian of the Panjāb, in his "A History of the Panjāb" (P. 45): "The caste system is only technically bad. It may be said to be morally bad if it created hatred and abhorrence of one another. But generally speaking, it has not that effect in India. The distinction observed by the ancient Romans between patrician and plebeian was essentially a caste distinction. The hereditary distribution of employments among the ancient Egyptians bore a close analogy to caste. Everybody in Europe, everybody in Persia and Arabia set up his separate table. Persons of a certain standing in

in the monastic order, if not generally. It is no marvel, however, that Buddhism was uprooted from the soil of its birth and struck its roots in other countries like China, Korea, Japan, more as Mahāyāna (a modified form of Hinduism or Brahminism) than in its so-called original doctorine of Hinayāna, whose self-negating philosophy made it unpopular for the people of India, given to the joy and beauty of life, to music and dance, sculpture and painting, urbane living and believing in life not only on the earth, but in the life ever-lasting. The rise of neo-Hinduism under Shankara, with his doctrines of Māyā and the attributeless (*Nirgun*) God who was indeed identified with the individual soul accepted, by and large, the main thesis of the Buddha. Coupled with this was the need of medieval India to arm itself and fight the invading marauders as much as local adventurers. All these factors gave a death-blow to the existence of Buddhism in India.

However, the brief interludes of foreign attacks by the Egyptians, the Persians, the Scythians or the Tartars, followed by Alexander the Great, made the Panjāb not only the battle-ground but also opened its civilisation to European and Central Asian influences, and to trade and commerce abroad, and the mixing of blood. But when the foreign hordes were finally expelled, we come to certain well-known names of history whose fortune is connected vitally with the Panjāb. Apart from the heroes of the war of Mahābhārata, which was fought at Kurukshetra to the south-east of the Panjāb, we come across such remarkable figures as Chandragupta Mauryā, his grandson Asoka (Governor of Taxilā, before becoming emperor in the third century B.C.), Kanishka, with his headquarters at Peshāwar, Chandra Gupta (who, driven from Pātliputra, took refuge in the Panjāb and helped by Panjābi men of arms became a great empire-builder in the fourth century A.D.), till the Huns almost shook the Gupta empire, and the rival dynasties within India through their internecine warfare opened the door for her conquest by the forces of Islām, or more particularly those claiming to act on its behalf to give an idealistic edge to their own personal ambitions.

As is well-known, the invasions of the Muslims started with the seventeen-year old Mohammad-bin-Kāsim, an Arab general, in 711

** *F. N. (Contd.)*

society ordinarily marry only among people of position equal to their own. Only the Hindus have carried their system too far, (but) caste, properly speaking, is not peculiar to India."

A.D. This, however, was not meant originally to be a war of conquest but a limited engagement to rescue an Arab vessel detained at the mouth of the Indus by a Hindu Prince, Dāhu, but the initial success attending upon Kāsim and the enormous booty he received as a result, emboldened him to bring the whole of Sind, including Multān, under his sway, though only for a very short period. For Kāsim was killed and sewn in raw hide under the orders of his master (on account of the suspicion sown in his mind about Kāsim's character by the two beautiful daughters of the conquered Hindu Prince, who had been offered by Kāsim to his master for his harem). Over two centuries later (977 A.D.), when Jaipāl ruled in the Panjāb, Sabuktagin, a slave of Turkish extraction, assuming sovereign authority at Ghazni, attacked the Panjāb but met with little territorial success, and returned with a large booty though leaving a few mosques behind. However, his heart was inflamed with thoughts of revenge, for he believed to have been tricked into a withdrawal by Jaipāl whom he considered he had shown magnanimity. He returned again, defeated Jaipāl and annexed the western parts of the Indus, exacting a heavy price for his victory. On his death, his thirty-year old son, Mahmud, made it a habit to invade India for loot, his thirteenth invasion being in 1027, only three years before his death at the age of sixty-three. Acknowledged by the entire Muslim world as its chief, and apart from the staggering booty in gold and jewels he acquired in India, his sway extended from Kashmir to Isfahān and from the Caspian Sea to the Ganges. The Indian part of the Ghaznavi empire lasted for over two centuries among the descendants of Mahmud, though bitter fights raged frequently, entailing large massacre of men and destruction and looting of property, as the throne of Ghazni changed hands or the local Hindu rājās raised their rebellious heads as they indeed did at frequent intervals. For the first time during this period, large-scale conversions of Muslims through force became the hall-mark of the onslaughts, besides the destruction and desecration of their temples and the carrying away of Hindu women and children as slaves.

It is not worthwhile to dwell in any detail on those succeeding to the throne of Ghazni, like Muhammed Ghori, who was assassinated in the Panjāb; Kutab-ud-din-Aibik, the first Muslim king to be crowned at Lāhore, and who later occupied Delhi and commemorated its conquest by the erection of the huge, smooth, tapering *Qutab-Minār*, in red stone, on which were inscribed the verses from the Holy

Qurān—a marvel still of architectural daring, beauty and design. He was followed by the slave dynasty brought about both by merit and marriage into the royal household, though during this period Delhi became the chief centre of learning and the resort of holymen, including Farid-ud-Din, Ganj-i-Shakar (whose work is included in the Sikh Scripture) and Khwājā Qutab-ud din Bakhtiār Kāki, and others. Ghazni was now more an appendage of Delhi than vice versa. Once the Panjāb had fallen, as it did finally in 1001 A. D., the way was now open for the conquerors from the North-West, to bring the entire of North, West and East India, if not also substantial parts of the South, under their sway.

For a time, Persian became the language of the court and the elite, and a new hybrid language, Urdu, (or the language of the camp or the army built originally on Panjābi* but later on *Khari Boli*, or the dialect of the country around Delhi and Mathurā, but with a liberal admixture of Persian and Arabic vocabulary) started being evolved. The Sufi orders of Islām, accepting much of Hindu thought and practice, did much to popularise Islām, especially among the lower and untouchable classes of the Hindus. Meantime, Chengiz Khān, the Mongol pagan (1221-22), his grandson Halāku, and various other descendants of Chengiz invaded the Panjāb, one after another, late in the thirteenth and early fourteenth century A. D., but were invariably defeated. It was, however, the descendants of Chengiz's son-in-law, Khalij Khān, who becoming a convert to Islām and settling down with a large number of families in the mountainous west of the Panjāb (where their progeny still remains) rose in the favour of the Ghazni Kings, usurped the throne of Delhi, and founded the dynasty of the Khaljis. They were followed by the Tughlaks, their founder, Ghias-ud-Din, taking his name from his father, a Turkish slave of India's Slave-king, Balban. They halted the attacks of the Mongols (or Moghals) and even attacked them in their own country. The invasion of Timur or Tamarlene of Samarkand, also of Mongol blood, in 1398 A. D., however, brought about their downfall, accompanied by savage butchery, plunder and devastation, the worst sufferers again being the people of the Panjāb, notably at Tulambā, Dipālpur and Bhatnēr. The whole districts of Multān and Lāhore were totally ravaged. Delhi especially was deluged in blood. All prisoners of war, numbering a hundred thousand, were put to the

* See "*Panjāb main Urdu*" by Dr. Mahmud Shairāni.

sword. Hindu women were outraged in large numbers by Timur's soldiery and the city of Delhi was set upon fire. Soon, however, he was on his way back home, though he committed much pillage and wholesale slaughter on the way, compelling many people, including the Rājā of Jammu, to embrace Islām.

The Tughlaks, who built an empire as extensive as that of Asoka, including parts of the South, were followed by the imbecile Sayyads (1414-50 A. D.) from whom the throne was captured by the Lodhis under Bahlol (1451-88 A. D.), Governor of the Panjāb, whose ancestors were from a commercial Afghān tribe and who won, through both personal chivalry and intrigue, the throne of Delhi, the titular King adopting him as his son. He was, however, a mild and just Prince, treating his courtiers as his friends and seldom mounted the throne "in order to avoid display of authority". In his early days, he was even fond of visiting the darveshes and claimed his throne being the blessings of one of them. His son, Sikandar Lodhi (1488-1517), from a Hindu wife, was also a man of literary and religious disposition and distributed alms to the needy Muslims every Friday, though, being a bigot, he demolished many Hindu temples of historic import, as at Mathurā, and raised mosques on their ruins, "considering this as an act of piety". He prohibited their bathing at the sacred ghāts. The shaving of beards and heads by the Hindus at the pilgrim-stations was forbidden, and a Brāhmin of Kanēr who had declared Islām and Hinduism, both, to be true religions, was ordered to be beheaded on his refusal to accept Islām. Otherwise, he was "a good and capable ruler" and cared deeply for the welfare of his subjects, taking personal pains in the matter of prices, weights and measures, and charities to the poor. He never changed an established custom and deprived no one of his Jāgir. Ibrāhim Lodhi (1517-1526), his son, who succeeded him, imprisoned his own brother and later put him to death. He was an extremely cruel and a vicious man and created many enemies among the Afghān nobles, including Daulat Khān Lodhi, the Governor of the Panjāb (of whom we shall have to speak much later on). His uncle, Alā-ud-Din, fled to Kābul and collecting a body of 40,000 horse attacked him, joined by Daulat Khān. Though defeated in the war, Ala-ud-Din escaped to the Panjāb and egged on by him, Daulat Khān sent his agents to Kābul to urge Bābur, the Moghal ruler there, and a great-grandson of Timur, to invade India, whose throne after three or four partial attempts, he finally won in 1526, and established the Moghal dynasty which lasted a little over three hundred years, and seven generations.

Nānak was a contemporary of the Lodhi dynasty, and of Bābur, whose descendants, as we shall see, had much to do with the house of Nānak, and who, with a very few exceptions, kept themselves on the best of terms with the Sikh Gurus for a period extending to about two centuries.

3

Here we must pause to deliberate upon the socio-political conditions of the age which witnessed also the birth of Nānak, the Guru, as to how far they affected his life and message and also vice-versa.

Much has been written about the Muslim violence and tyranny, the bigotry, the forced wholesale conversions of the subject peoples, the destruction of Hindu temples and total denigration of their religion and age-old customs and beliefs, the imposition of jezia, a discriminatory religious tax, the denial to them of public service, and the dishonouring and carrying away as slaves of Hindu women and the imposition of Purdah on the rest, etc., etc.* But, much should not be read into this wholesale condemnation of the conquering faith of Islām. It must be noted that in the medieval ages wars in Europe, even between the Christians of various denominations, were far more violent. It may be true that during the Hindu period of Indian history or whatever is known of it, from the rule of Asoka (he came to the throne in 273 B.C.) to the death of Harsha (647 A.D.), the wars were more humane and the various religions—Brahminism, Buddhism, Jainism, Tantarism or animism—as much as the various races, Āryan and Dravidian, Scythian and Mongolian, Greek and Persian, all coexisted side by side in comparative peace or coalesced with each other, unobtrusively, as time passed. But, instances are not unknown in which bloodshed, cunning and intrigue, wholesale conversions, destruction of each other's temples, and looting and burning of property and carrying away of women as the war-booty or dishonouring them were the order of the day. To cite only a few examples:

* For details see Shri Rām Sharmā's "The Crescent in India" and "The Religious Policy of the Moghals"; also "The History and Culture of the Indian People" Volumes 6 and 7 (Bhāratiya Vidyā Bhavan).

The Āryans destroyed not only the well-built walled cities but uprooted wholesale the culture of the pre-Āryan Dravidians, through war and violence, and treated the aborigines as second-class citizens, if not as pariahs, as references to them in the Rig Veda amply testify. Later, the Āryans clashed with each other, and the wily intrigues of a woman, Kaikei, at the court of Ayudhyā, which led to the banishment of Sri Rāma, the noble rightful heir to the throne, the abduction of his wife, Sitā, and the resultant war with and utter rout of Rāvana, a Brahmin King of Lankā, through the defection of his own brother, Bibhishana, as much as the superior, death-dealing arms of Shri Rāma's forces have so impressed our race that upto date we do not cease to re-create, year after year, in song and stagecraft, the bloody drama with all its attendant violence and vileness. The war of Mahā-bhārata is even a more classic example of brother shedding the blood of brother and reckless killings, the dishonouring of the enemy's womenfolk, including Draupadi, who was stripped naked in the open court of Dusāsana, and the practicing of various deceptions forbidden by religion but sanctified by expediency. Reference has already been made to the terrible carnage in the war of Kālinga waged by the later-day pacifist Asoka, "in which 1,500,000 persons were carried away captive, 1,00,000 were slain on the battle-field and many times that number died." The last of the powerful Hindu Kings, Harsha (died 647 A. D.), according to the Chinese pilgrim, Huan Tsang (or Yuan Chwang) "went from east to west subduing all who were not obedient. His elephants were not unharnessed nor his soldiers unhelmeted." He kept a force of 60,000 elephants, 1,000,000 cavalry and 50,000 infantry, and except for the Panjāb, subjugated the whole of upper India, not excluding Bihār and a large part of Bengāl.

When the Muslims appeared finally on the soil of India, at least for three centuries in the beginning (900 A.D, to 1200 A.D.), the Hindu India, divided into caste and clan, was fighting grim battles, one with the other, and quite often siding with the invader rather than with each other to contain the foreign onslaughts.

It was a Hindu general, who fought along with Mohd-bin-Kāsim against his own King. The Jāts of Sind governed ruthlessly by the Brāhmin usurper refused to be on the ruler's side. The story of Jai-chand of Kanauj (who extended his dominion from Kanauj to Bihār) siding with Alā-ud-Din Khalji against Prithvirāj Chauhān of Delhi due to a family feud is well-known though what is less known is his invasion of the territory of Chandels and the defeat of their king,

Paramardi. According to Kalhana's *Rājtarangni*, "Harsha (a ruler of Kashmir from 1089 to 1109 A.D.) displayed in his chequered life a strange combination of cruelty and kindheartedness, liberality and greed, violent self-willedness and reckless supineness, cunning and want of thought."

King Sankravarnan of Kashmir (883-902 A.D.) made himself notorious by his extortionist greed, oppressive taxation and *temple-looting*. The great and wise King Bhoja of Mālwā (1010-1065 A.D.) "carried on incessant warfare with all the surrounding (Hindu) Kingdoms—Chedi, Lata and Karnata. While Bhima I, King of Gujarat, invaded Sind, Bhoja attacked Gujarat. He, in turn, was attacked by a Southern Chalukya King, Someshwara II. Mulrājā of Gujarat became a great ruler by attacking Cutch, Kāthiāwar and Ajmer. For long years, a three-cornered struggle began between the Gurjars, the Pālās of Gujarat and the Rashtra-Kutas of the Deccan for the overlordship of North India. The Cholās, the Pāndavas and the Cherās in the South repeated this performance.* How could any composite culture or political stability or a soulful religion flourish in such a state of affairs?

No wonder, the Muslims soon filled this vacuum in an atmosphere of cultural decadence, internecine warfare and religious confusion. But once the Muslim power settled itself in the throne of Delhi, it is one Muslim race fighting against another of their own faith, Turk against the Arab, Afghān against the Turk, Persian against the Mongol, Pathān against Pathān, Sunni against Shia and Hindus were only incidentally involved. Initially, there was bound to be large-scale tyranny, loot, bloodshed and discrimination, but once the throne of Hindustān was assured to a Muslim dynasty, it is the Sufis who propagated the cult of Islām (which did not negate higher Hinduism, and indeed assimilated many local customs and beliefs), and not the fire and the sword.** Individual marauders and sectarian monarchs can not be picked upon to make out a general case against the recklessness of Islām as such. The Islām that came to India, or took root in its soil, was only a name and a form. The content, to all intents and purposes, had been Indianised (if not Hindu-ised)

* For the internecine warfare between the Marāthās & Rājputs in the 17th & 18th centuries,see part II.

**It is infact the Moghals, who, after after about a thousand years, dreamt and actualised the dream of Akhand Hindustan, making even Afghanistan a part of it.

and used persuasion rather than coercion upon the subjects to join a society more egalitarian than their own. Were it not so, the Hindus would not be a majority people to this day after a thousand years of Muslim rule. What saved them was not their resistance (for, they actively collaborated with the state apparatus after a time, for long years, *as Hindus*), but the Islāmic society itself had become, as time passed, permissive and the rulers, though nominally Muslim, became interested more in the safety and splendour of their dominions and good and easy life of court, than in spreading the exclusive gospel of Islām, in return for a promised heaven in the Hereafter. Music and dance and drinking bouts, painting of the court's splendour and intimate lovelore, erotic poetry (much of which under the guise of mystic symbols also challenged the exclusive doctrines of Islām), harems and howries, self-aggrandisement and palace intrigues, the deification of the King as *Zil-e-ilāhi*, and the denigration of the ulemā, became the rule rather than the exception. It may all have been against the orthodox precepts of the Prophet Mohammad and the practices of his Caliphs, but who cared? Life in the here and now was more precious and its rewards more immediate and alluring than the pledges to be redeemed in the Hereafter. For both sides, Muslim as well as Hindu, therefore, the game was not worth playing. The prize had lost all its original glitter and glory. The hardy desert-man and the mountain-warrior had now tasted civilisation. And the Hindu did not lag behind to respond.

As will be seen later, though Nānak's contemporary Afghān King, Ibrahim Lodhi, was reckless, and thus invited the wrath of his own nobles and a successful Moghal invasion, not so, by and large, the contemporary Kings of Nānak's birth and youth—Bahlol and Sikandar Lodhi. Nawāb Daulat Khan Lodhi, Governor of Panjāb, in fact became a near disciple of Nānak, all of whose early companions, including the village chief, Rai Bulār and Bhāi Mardānā, his life-long companion, were Muslims. If it be some kind of a synthesis between the two creeds that he is claimed to have attempted, then Kabir and a host of his near-contemporaries, like Tukārām, Chandidās, Ravidās, etc., had certainly preceded Nānak in preaching the gospel of one God (which doctrine, it is stressed by many, was under the influence of Islām, as if the concept was not known to the Hindus for at least two millennia before the birth of Prophet Mohammad), castelessness, and the cult of Bhakti (loving adoration of God), etc. The Muslim Sufis were stressing the same ideals no less. And, though the basic doctrines of Nānak's faith were essentially Hindu—the belief in Karma, transmigration and Nirvāna or Moksha being the end of all life-activity, —as we shall see, he wholly transformed the meaning of these concepts. And yet he was accepted as Guru by the Hindu no less than the Muslim. He did the same in respect of almost every basic doctrine of Islām, including that of Tauhid, to which we have already referred. Whosoever compares with some seriousness and study the spiritual discipline propounded by Nānak and the one propagated by the Sufis would find more to differentiate than to obviate all distinctions between the two. To take only one instance, Nānak's five *Khands* (or stages, as enunciated in his composition, the *Japji*) and the Sufis' seven stages of spiritual evolution have practically very little in common.

The basis of the uniqueness of his message lies, therefore, not in the synthesis of the two 'warring' creeds, but in giving a new depth and dimension to the basic concepts of both, while denouncing their outer manifestations in each case. To take only a few examples: while both Hindus and Muslims stressed the concept of one God, it was Nānak who proclaimed the concept also of one man. While to the Muslim Sufi, as much as to the Hindu Vedāntist, only a particular path alone could lead to man's salvation, according to Nānak, all paths that led to the same goal were sanctified and worthy of man's highest attention and esteem. According to both, the final revelation had either been made by God through the Veda or the Qurān, according to Nānak, God revealed himself from age to age, and though the Truth did not change, its interpretations and media did, according to the demands of the times. The world may have come into being in a single atomic explosion but its age couldn't be finally determined. Perhaps, it evolved from one stage to another, through aeons of years. Says Nānak :— "God first created the air, from the air came water and from water throbbed the three worlds into being, including the world of man." "God does not shower His gifts on the chosen races but on all men at all times." "He has put into the world whatever He had to, once and for all." "It is man who has to search out, analyse and make compounds of God's elements, exploit them and distribute them in equity and in good faith." It is not God, therefore, who is to be blamed for our misery, but man. God is to be praised for His having blessed us with all that we would ever need—and with a mind, for its wholesome exploitation and equitable distribution, and a Soul to dispel the ego as much in individuals as in societies and nations, and to find eternal repose, thus rising above the limitations of Time.

"There are myriads upon myriads of universes," proclaims Nānak, "and the suns and the moons, the spheres and the stars, the worlds and the underworlds," and "their count cannot be made by the Qāzis or the utterers of the Purāns." "Heaven is not only in the Hereafter, but also here"—so is hell. *Moksha* or redemption can also be attained here by man, with an integrated mind. Life is transitory, and all-too-brief, and the ideal is to merge one's Time-sense with the Timeless, but it is not by denying or renouncing life that the ideal can be attained, but by grappling with it, in all its fury and fantasy, not for oneself, but for the others, and, what is even more important, in the name and for the sake of the ideal that is God. For, "man's world is the battle-ground of God" and "it is to express and justify His existence, His moral Law, His Compassion as much as His retribution that he created the earth" and in it the man "whose destiny is not to identify himself with the animal, but with the spiritual, within him and in the universe, if also not beyond." "He who flouts God's Moral Law finds God—and man—arrayed against him in a myriad ways." "Only man has the possibility to evolve into a superman, the angel," not Niétzsch's ideal to overpower others, but to overpower himself, endowed as he is with a mind and a Soul. Hence the life of man—and equally of woman—is sacred, and neither it originates in sin, nor waits till the doomsday or a day of judgment upon its chosen Prophet to bestow upon it a life of eternal bliss, or to burn ever thereafter in the fires of hell. To avenge in the way of God is not by killing the opponent—(the infidel or the *Malechha*)—but by converting him to his own essential self. It is not by gathering goods but gathering God that one can find rest for the Soul, not by building empires but by building hearts. All rituals and institutions, and all taboos of dress and diet and social behaviour—divorced from the life of the Spirit are false, and can please not God, nor bring quietude to the Soul, only the inner illumination and the compassion of the heart can. God is not in the books—sacred or profane. He is a realisation, not through belief in a particular dogma, but through experience of His all-pervading Presence and Grace at all times everywhere. His Word too is echoed through the universe—and in man's soul—age after age.

How vast was the conception of Nānak, therefore, in respect as much of man and his universe as of God and His revelation, and how much different from the current coin, can be seen here, in howsoever brief a manner. But, of this, more later. Suffice it to say that Nānak's spiritual—and social—ideas contradict not a whit either the discoveries of science or the ever newly-propounded economic theories. For, according to him, God reveals himself through man and nature in a myriad ways through each of His facets—good as well as bad—He being a God of wonder, but he alone attains unto Him who does not hand himself over, body and soul, to the merely material, and though the material indeed is the expression of the spiritual, the spiritual alone is the justification for the material. And not by unnatural miracles is the spiritual in man to be judged. For, every facet of life is miraculous, every particle of nature, all laws of the universe (how uniform, never arbitrary, governed timelessly, by the never-changing rule of God's law). Every other miracle is a trick of the muscle or the psyche, and is not worthy of a serious man's attention. The only miracle Nānak claimed for himself, therefore, was that he would teach man not how to overcome others, but how to overpower himself. And Nānak did not believe in a sectarian, self-contained state, based on geography, race, language or even a particular religion. He believed in the universal man and the universal state, both man and his universe being the creation (or expression) of a universal Soul. If he denounced the "kings as butchers" and the "courtiers as the running dogs," he was denouncing absolute and reckless personal power as such for all times, and not in a particular age, including his own. It is only in this context that Nānak's uniqueness both as a Prophet and as a man of history can be ascertained and certified. His greatness lies therefore not in his followers creating a secular empire in the North-West, two hundred and fifty years after his demise, and the successful military challenge they offered to the later Moghals* (thus turning the tide of invasions from the West to the East after a lapse of a thousand years and the throne of Kābul, for long years the arbiter of India's destiny, exchanging hands at the mercy of the Sikh monarch at

*The much-esteemed Dr. Arnold Toynbee in "A Historian's approach to religion" like Gāndhiji and Tagore before him, while bemoaning the transformation of the Sikhs from a peaceable community into a war-like sect ascribes the political success of the Sikh-Khalsa to having "fought the Moghal ascendancy with its own weapons" (A Study of History, Oxford, Abridgement, p. 745), a precedent which, according to him, the All-Union Communist Party also employed

Lāhore), but to the ideal of the one man and one God that he preached, of the living man and the living God. Not that his followers fought and won, but how cleanly they fought and for what purpose they won? It is Nānak as an original, idealistic thinker that should claim the attention of history, not merely the conquests or the material achievements of his race.

Before we conclude this chapter, it is but necessary that we enunciate the Sikh view of history. Lately, attempts have been made to separate the Nānak of history from Nānak, the founder of a world faith, and thus a man also of legend, myth and miracle. And, though the latter attempt has been lauded by the ignorant even among the Sikhs as being in conformity with the "spirit" of modern, scientific age, it has served more to confuse than to illuminate Sikh history. For the Sikh Gurus have always claimed that though they were born in time, the message they had come to declare and impart was eternal and had come from God. "I know not how to utter, for all that I deliver unto you is the command of God," says Nānak, though he never claimed that he was either the first or the last Guru, Prophet or the Messiah. The Guru, according to him, was God the eternal, who always was and will always be. His Word also, therefore, was heard by and communicated to mankind, age after age, by prophets and seers and will continue to be so done, though the essential core will remain the same as ever. The Sikh theory thus gives both a continuity to history as well as a uniqueness at given periods, when history ceases to move except in narrow, selfish, status-quoist grooves, devoid of purpose and meaning, and a man of spiritual vision and moral daring rises on the scene and history pulsates with a dynamism unknown before.

---

* *F. N. (Contd.)*

to its advantage, under Lenin. But the distinction between the Sikh ideal of war and the other empire or idea-builders, as stated above, has always to be taken into account if we are to do justice to their entire history and not merely lean upon casual or ill-assorted episodes to read in it a meaning not intended by its makers. Not one of the wars that the Sikh Gurus fought was to carve an independent territory for themselves, nor did they impose their way of life upon others through force or fraud. Their small numbers (13 million in 1981) are due not merely to the strict religious discipline enjoined upon them but also because proselytisation has never been practised by them even in the hey-days of their empire.

4

The Sikh view of history, therefore, is that devoid of meaning (a meaning, that is, which corresponds to the purpose of God in Creation as enunciated, in eternal terms, by the Gurus), history is a sordid record of man's brutalisation of his inner self, tyranny and bloodshed, exploitation and war. Instead of movement, it is the stultification of all that is ennobling and eternal in man. Man the individual as much as part of the social whole, is the primary test of history's worth. Nānak and his followers thus can be studied as part of history only as its redeemers, and not as its victims.

Understood thus, it is easy enough to dismiss out of account, without impairing the faith of a Sikh, any event, no matter how significant in secular terms, which measures not upto his standard of judgement. Defeat, for instance, in the cause of God, if crowned by martyrdom, becomes glorious and success attained at the expense of God's moral law becomes repugnant to the Sikh mind. That God intervenes in the affairs of the world on the side of those who fight, detachedly, for its secular welfare and moral health is a miracle of human history in which the Sikh has firm faith. But that miracles in the form of happenings in defiance of God's natural—and eternal—laws, should determine a man's spiritual prowess or God-awareness is denounced vehemently by the Sikh Gurus as the work of mountebanks and charlatans. That devout chroniclers have associated miracles with the Gurus and the mass of people believe in them as an act of faith cannot lead us to conclude either, that such "blind" faith is born out of ignorance and superstition (let alone man of every religious faith, even the Marxists dogmatically "believe" in the ultimate victory of their idea and any experimentation with or improvement upon the "original doctrine" is considered a sacrilege, a heresy and a deviation), or that once we separate the Nānak (or his successors) of flesh and blood from the Nānak of faith and prophecy, we shall have a true glimpse of Sikh history. For, as we have said, Nānak can lay claim, unlike Bābur, his kingly contemporary, to history, as understood by the Sikhs, only if he continues to move men's minds and souls (and for this reason remains an object of worship and prayer) throughout history, rather than at a given moment to become a mere sporadic event in the relentless march of time. Nānak must remain the conquerer of time in order to claim our allegiance, and not as a plaything of history.

Unlike Islām, Sikhism did not start with a political success, but like Christianity, as a protestor against it and a martyr at its hands. But, when, ultimately, there was no choice left but to fight the imperial rule with its own weapons and create an empire, no one's social norms or spiritual beliefs were tampered with. The Sikhs chose to remain a minority people, fighting not against but on behalf of the majority, and sharing political and military power with the others even on a more generous scale than they would have even under their own dispensation. Whether it was Bandā Singh Bahādur or Ranjit Singh, Mahārāja of the Panjāb, who led them to political victory and national self-assertion, the personal conduct of each one of them was made a subject of public scrutiny and if it did not accord with the Guru's mandate, it was publicly censured and even punished.* For, to the Sikh, though earthly prosperity is sacred, not so at the expense of the moral health of the individual or the state, and those alone are fit to lead and rule who willingly submit themselves to the rules of good conduct as enunciated by the Gurus. Everyone else may be forgiven, but not the ruler of men. He must answer—and pay—for his deeds (and misdeeds). This is what has made the leadership of the Sikhs, whether spiritual or political, such a hazardous and tortuous task. No one can remain at the pinnacle for long. Time and again it has made the Sikhs leaderless, or a victim of intriguing gangsters or ignorant maglomaniacs, or sly sycophants of the powers that be, but their days have always been numbered. But, let it be also recorded that Sikh history not only demolishes reputations, it also builds them as speedily.

And this brings us to another vital point. The Sikhs do not build their peoplehood, like the Christians, or the Arabs or even the Hindus either on the basis of territory or language, race, colour or caste, custom or tradition, but on the basis of religion in its widest possible sense. That is how, it is the Saint, the martyr and the man of compassion who has always elicited their soulful

*Bandā, as we shall see later, was disowned by the Sikhs, by and large, it is said, for his assuming the airs of a Guru and flouting several other commandments of the tenth Master in the midst of a life-and-death struggle, (though some recent historians like Dr. Gandā Singh, do not corroborate this thesis). So was Ranjit Singh, the founder of the Sikh empire in the entire North-West of India, reputed to have been censured publicly for laxity of private morals, by the then custodian of the Akāl Takht, Akāli Phoolā Singh, who, as a general, also fought in many of Ranjit Singh's fiercest battles and even laid down his life in one of them.

allegiance and not the man of power, or self-centred affluence. The means for any acquisitions are for the Sikh more important than the ends. This trait in the Sikh character nurtured for two centuries by the Gurus, and employed as a measuring rod ever thereafter has led also to some unfortunate consequences. Firstly, time and again it has tied down Sikh political life to the Sikh temples and their custodians (no matter how they attained their authority over them) and secondly, it has kept out of of the political arena some of the best and most sensitive minds of the community who have refused to be subjected to the vicious orthodoxy of the ignorant which was more often employed to keep the saner rivals out than to promote the ideals of the faith. The Gurus never intended—or propagated—such a self-stultifying view of the Sikh way of life as has, in recent times, been the community's misfortune to witness.*

However, this trait has given the Sikhs an edge over the other communities as well, though in another not wholly unexpected way, which is generally passed over by the historians. As their religion is bound not to any particular geography, culture (in a limited sense), race or caste, they are easy to spread out and integrate themselves with other societies the world over. Believing as they do in the

---

* However, this point should not be laboured too much, as it is more an aberration on the life-current of the Sikhs than a permanent feature of their life. True, that even after the demise of the tenth and the last Guru, Gobind Singh (1708 A.D.); the community for a time took its inspiration from the Gurdwārās, when they were fighting their life-and death battle, as under Bandā Singh (1710-1716 A.D.), and during the Misal period immediately thereafter (upto 1800 A.D., the year of Ranjit Singh's rise to power). The latter, however, after acquiring his kingdom, very wisely separated the church from politics (which is not the same as separating religion from politics) and instead of the *Gurmattās* (edicts) being issued from the holy *Akāl Takht*, at Amritsar, the highest seat of Sikh religious authority, a cabinet decision was instituted by him instead, and was accepted without demur by the Sikhs at large. Moreover, the Sikhs have never, except during the periods of stress, accorded to their historic places a superstitious sanctity whcih would make totems of them. An arid desert-place, now called Damdamā Sāhib, was blessed by the tenth Guru as Guru's Kāshi (Kāshi is considered the holiest of Hindu pilgrim-stations).

The wars of the Cross that figured in history for the possession of Jerusalem by the Muslims and the Christians alike have never been thought of for Nankānā Sāhib, the birth-place of the founder of Sikhism, which is now in the territorial and political jurisdiction of Pākistān, though managed nominally by the Sikhs, while several other historical shrines have been allowed to decay or to remain closed both in India and Pākistān, depending upon their importance and income.

universal state and the universal man (and it is their religion that teaches them this), they have been and may well again be, the spearheads of many progressive movements the world over. As we shall see, early in the present century, the freedom movement of India took its roots in the most dedicated (even violent) form in some of the Sikh temples (as in Californiā, Vancouver, Malāyā and Hong Kong) that the Sikh colonists had established abroad. The Gurdwārā reform movement of the 1920's merged itself entirely with the non-violent struggle for freedom led by Mahātmā Gāndhi and Jawaharlāl Nehru. So did the Kookā movement, though in a limited way, immediately after the revolt of 1857 had been crushed.* Even the Communist Party of India has often enough participated on behalf of their official nominees, in the Gurdwārā elections, and departure

* The Kookās (or the Nāmdhāri Sikhs) under Bābā Ram Singh, their pious leader, have laid rightful claims for being the initiators of the freedom movement in the country. Bābā Rām Singh, once a soldier in the Sikh Army, became the spearhead of a movement initiatally of spiritual regeneration among the Sikhs after their defeat and loss of empire in 1847 at the hands of the British. But it is also a fact of history that under the inspiration of the revered Bābā, his followers refused to have any truck with the English education and the British-founded institutions, including the law-courts, the railway trains and the post office, etc. They even boycotted the tap-water for its being polluted with the animal skin which allegedly lined the metal tubes! The Nāmdhāris also wore the home-spun cloth long before Mahātmā Gāndhi initiated the movement of Swadeshi. Sixty-six Kookās were blown from the mouth of the canon at Malerkotlā and Bābā Rām Singh himself was deported to Rangoon where he died in incarceration, even though his deportation and arrest or the martyrdom of the 66 Kookās were concerned primarily with the murder of a few Muslim butchers, and not consciously with the freedom movement, (however much anti-British they were culturally & spiritually). However, Baba Ram Singh's preference for the rosary as against the sword, his emphasis on vegetarianism, his revival of various Hindu rituals and customs, like havan and yognas, etc., and his followers' strict observance of an exclusive kitchen for their own sect, as in the case of the Brāhmins, were repugnant equally to the doctrines of Guru Nanak and Guru Gobind Singh. They do not look upon the Granth Sahib as "Guru", like the other Sikhs & believe in a personal Guru. The boycott of English education and such useful institutions as the law-courts, the post office, the railway train and tap-water made the Kookās a revivalist rather than a progressive movement, even though later the Kookās under Gandhiji's leadership suffered much, along with other Sikhs, for the cause of the country's freedom. They are also said to have established some contact with the Russian Govt. through one of their "Subās" for the overthrow of the British Govt.

Contd.

from or denunciations of the Sikh injunctions the matter of form by their membership has been officially frowned upon!

Time and again, the community was almost wiped out either physically or economically in the middle of nearly every century, (the last being in 1947) during the last half a millennium, and yet it rose again from its ashes, reinforced in its belief in the never-dying laws of God and the Guru. For, just as the Sikhs look to the past to be inspired by its martyrdoms, suffered for eternal values (and not for secular profit or dominions), they look forward to the future, to give a meaningful direction to history and not to become the willing or unwilling victims of its ever living-and-dying process.

CHAPTER II

GURU NĀNAK

(1469-1539 A. D.)

Guru Nānak*, the founder of the Sikh faith, was, according to his oldest extant biography, born on April 15, 1469 (Vaisākh sudi 3, 1526 Bikrami)**, at Talwandi Rāe Bhoē, a village about 40 miles to the south-west of Lāhore (now in Pākistān). His father, Mehtā Kālu, a Khatri of the Bedi (Vedi) clan, was a Patwāri or accountant, to the Muslim landlord of the village, Rāi Bulār by name, a Bhatti Rājput by caste, and of intense religious disposition. His mother, Triptā, bore a daughter five years before the advent of Nānak and was named Nānaki, who later married a revenue official of high standing, Jairām, a pious Khatri of Uppal caste.

---

* Lit. he in whom duality *(Anik)* is not *(Na)*. It is suggested by some who want to be 'original' or 'different' from all others that Nānak was born in his mother's hometown, *Kāhnā Kachhā* (in the district of Lāhore), and hence was called Nānak (from Nanakē, mother's home). But Sikhs have never accepted this conjecture and Nankānā Sāhib has continued till this day as the only recognised place of his birth. The only person who first propounds this theory is Meharvān (of whom we shall have to speak much, later in this chapter), only at one place in the Damdamā Sāhib version of his *gostis*, though elsewhere and in the Khālsā College version (now published) it is Rae-Bhoe-Di-Talwandi that is credited with Nānak's birth. Meharvān gives the name of Nānak's mother's hometown as *Chahalvālā* and not *Kahnā Kāchhā*. The latter theory is supported about 400 years after Nānak's birth (during the disintegration of the Sikh empire, when all Sikh institutions were under attack and suspicion was being sown about them), by the court physician of Ranjit Singh, W.L.M. M' Gregor (History of the Sikhs), who, however, identifies the mother's village as *Māree*, near *Kutchwa*. But he is unreliable in most of his details, including the date of Nānak's birth which he places

F. N. Contd.

in 1468 and not 1469 and in his suggestion that Nānak's father being childless had become a holy mendicant till Nānak arrived (as a result of a faqir's blessings, a story which he quotes but repudiates), and his father again resumed the occupation of a 'merchant'. *Kānhā Kāchhā* is mentioned also by Cunningham (History of the Sikhs, P. 35 f.n.) because "*One* manuscript account (which he does not name) states this". But what about the other, and more reliable manuscripts and the acceptance, without question, by all Sikhs, of Talwandi being the birth-place of Nānak which Cunningham himself accepts (ibid), besides Malcolm (Sketch of the Sikhs, P. 78) and Forster (Travels, i, 292-93). According to several old manuscripts, the Sixth Guru, Hargobind, visited Nanakānā Sahib on his way to Kashmir, and this visit is commemorated in the form of a shrine. Ranjit Singh himself endowed this place with a liberal *Jāgir* and not any other. May be, some vested interests intent on making the mother's birth-place (which is differently quoted by different writers) famous, circulated this theory, or just to create confusion in Sikh ranks, and to denigrate the importance of Nanakānā Sahib.

It is strange that the ***Purātan Janam Sākhi***, and ***Gyān Ratnāvali*** both do not give any name for Nānak's mother and wife and it is from Bālā that the names now accepted are derived. Meharvān gives Tipārā as Nānak's mother's name and Ghumi for his wife. The name of the sister also is not mentioned by the tradition earlier than *Gyān Ratnāvali*, pointing to the insignificance of female entities in Nānak's times.

** Though the oldest chronicles, like the ***Purātan Janam Sākhi***, Meharvān's *Janamsākhi*, and *Janamsākhi* of Bhāi Mani Singh, corroborate this date, the later biographers like Bhāi Santokh Singh (1788-1843 A. D.) give the full moon-night of ***Kārtik*** (November) as his birthday. The latter's ***Nānak Parkāsh*** (1823 A. D.), however, gives the age of Nānak to be 70 years, 5 months and 7 days, which also brings us back to April as his birth-date (though Bhai Vir Singh points out in his edited edition of "Nānak Parkāsh" (P. 1255) that several manuscript copies omit this reference, and thus it may be an interpolation). Says Macauliffe : "As late as Sambat 1872 (1815 A. D.), it was in *Vaisākh* (April) that the anniversary fair of Guru Nānak's birthday was always celebrated at Nanakānā." According to him, Bhai Sant Singh Gyāni a Sikh divine held in high esteem by Maharājā Ranjit Singh, first initiated the move to celebrate Guru Nānak's birthday in *Kārtik* at Amritsar, in order to wean the Sikhs away from attending a Hindu fair held at the same time at Rām Tirath nearby. But, he does not quote any authority for this. See also "*Katik Ke Vasākh*" by Karam Singh, and "A Short History of the Sikhs" by Ganda Singh (P. 2). But, in spite of this evidence, it is really strange that Maharājā Ranjit Singh should have authenticated the Nānakshāhi Samvat from *Kārtik* and not *Vaisākh*. And, why have Sikhs so tenaciously stuck to the former date of Nānak's birth and discarded altogether the latter one? If it is suggested that the Sikh farmers found *Kārtik* more convenient than *Vaisākh* for celebrations of the Guru's birthday, the latter date coinciding with the cropping season, then *Kārtik* is similarly the sowing season for the farmer. And if this be a valid reason, why did Guru Gobind Singh deliberately choose *Vaisākhi* (April 13) for the birth-date of the Khālsā ? It is very naive to suggest that the fiat of a single Gyāni Sant Singh ran with the whole community three ceturies after the birth of Guru Nānak to accept whole-heartedly a sudden shift in the date of his birth! Why does Bhai

Kālu had one brother, Lālu, but the historians are silent about his occupation or the course of his life. It appears (from the discourses he is reported to have had with his son) that Nānak's father, besides his official position, was a landlord of substance, and kept a large stable.* The village of Talwandi, now called Nankiānā, popularly NANKĀNĀ SĀHIB** after the name of Nānak, was situated deep in a forest "girdled by a broad expanse of aborescent vegetation which, when not whitened by the sand blown by the winds of the desert, wears through all seasons a cheerful appearance".

** *F. N. Contd.*

Gurdās become lyrical in his praise of the full-moon night of *Kārtik* (Kabits 343, 44, 45, 48)? *Kārtik mās, rut Sarad pooranmāshi, āth Jām, Sāth ghari, āj teri bāri hai"* (i. e. In the cool season, of the month of Kārtik, on this day of eight watches and sixty gharis, it is thy turn to appear) – (Kabit 345). Is he merely giving a free play to his poetic fancy? But, he does not do so in respect of any other date. If it is suggested that Gurdās could have been more explicit by crediting this date positively with the birth of Guru Nānak (which he doesn't), then, it must also be seen that he makes a very veiled reference even to the martyrdom of Guru Arjun (vār 24, Pauri 23), to which he was himself an eye-witness. And this is so because in the Sikh credo, it is not the dates of birth and death that are of prime importance, but what they signify and impart to the historical process. Or, is it that as Meharvān's own father, Prithi Chand, was November-born, he could not detract from its importance by giving about the same birth-date to Guru Nānak? And, if Meharvān's is to be accepted as the most authentic of Nānak's biographies, then he ascribes names to both his mother and wife which no other chronicler does. Says Cunningham: "The accounts agree as to the year of Nānak's birth, but differ with regard to the *day* of the month on which he was born. Thus, one narrative gives the 13th and another the 18th of the month *Kārtik* of the year 1526 of Vikramājit" (p. 35 f.n.). If the Sikhs had abandoned the April date only in the days of Ranjit Singh, as Macauliffe suggests, then Cunningham being a contemporary must have known about it and made reference to it. All this leads one to conclude that much more research is necessary to disprove the prevalent date of Nānak's birth.

* Says the *Siyar-ul-Mutākhrin* (Briggs' translation, i.110) that he was a grain merchant.

** Lit. The only home (*ain*) of Nānak. Several shrines commemorating his birth and the doings of his childhood stand to this day at Nankānā Sāhib, the more important being Gurdwārā *Janam Asthān* (in memory of his birth); *Kiarā Sāhib* (where his cattle grazed another's farm); *Tambu Sāhib* (see p.38f. n.); *Patti Sāhib* (in memory of his school days); *Bāl-lilā* (commemorating his childhood pranks); and *Mālji Sāhib* (where he grazed the cattle). These were liberally endowed by the Sikh Misals and later by Ranjit Singh, which endowments have continued to this day and are now being administered by the Government of Pākistān.

Towards the end of his life, Guru Nānak composed a Calender poem BARA MĀ'H (expressing his deep anguish at his separation from GOD and also his ecstacy at the unitive experience) in which he gives us some idea of the natural beauty by which the countryside of his birth—the Bār—was surrounded:

> "*Blessed is the month of* **Chaitra**
> *when the black bee hums with joy.*
> *The woods are in bloom and I long for my love.*
> *The beauteous* **Koel** *sings in the mango-tree........*
> *Blessed is* **Vaisākh** *when the trees are draped in green leaves.*
> *The bride sees it all and prays:*
> *'O Lord, have pity, and come into my home.*"
>
> (*Ādi-Granth, P. 1108*)

At the age of six, Nānak was put to school first with a Hindu Pandit who taught him the rudiments of arithemetic and reading and writing in Devnāgari, Gurmukhi, and Sanskrit or Sāstri. Later, he studied with a Maulvi, who instructed him in the Muslim literature—both secular and spiritual. After a few years, they seems to have exhausted their store of learning for Nānak, as he seems to have despaired of them both, and wandered in the woods nearby to meet and discourse with the holy men of various faiths, who abided there, on religion, philosophy and ethics.

According to *Sair-ul-Mutākhrin*, Nānak was educated by one Sayyed Hassan*, a neighbour of his father's who conceived a regard for him and who was wealthy but childless. "He was instructed in the most approved writings of the Mohammedans." In his "Sketch of the Sikhs", Malcolm reiterates several Muslim writers' contention

* Some scholars like Bhāi Kāhan Singh give the name of his Muslim teacher as Qutab-ud-din, with whom he studied Persian in 1482 A.D., i.e. at the age of 13. At the age of 6, he is said to have studied, according to them, with Pandit Gopāl who taught him Hindi (or was it Gurmukhi ?) and three years later with Pandit Brijlāl from whom he learnt Sanskrit. This makes for an approximately 8-year schooling period. According to the *Purātan Janam Sākhi*, Nānak was sent to learn 'Torki', (i.e. the Muslim tongue, Persian, and perhaps also Arabic) at the age of 9, and Sanskrit two years earliar (p. 6) (See also Kāhan Singh's *Gur Shabad Ratnākar Mahān Kosh, P. 2073*).

that "Nānak had learnt all the earthly sciences from Khawaja Khizar, i.e. Prophet Eliās."*

While studying with a Hindu Pandit, Nānak is credited with having questioned his learned teacher on the inner meaning of each letter, and on the wise one being non-plussed at such an unusul enquiry, he himself gave the answers in a poem of exquisite beauty, called *Patti* (included in the Sikh Holy Book), the Ādi-Granth.**

---

* It has been fashionable for some historians to aver that, as Guru Nānak was not "long" at school, he must have remained illiterate. But the 976 hymns, notably in Punjābi and Hindui interspersed liberally with Persian and Arabic vocabulary, that he wrote and which have come down to us in their original purity, are of such excellence both as poetry and religious philosophy that they debunk altogether the theory of Nānak's "illiteracy". They reveal such deep and searching study especially of the Vedas, the Shāstras, the Purāns, the Qurān, the Yoga Sutra of Pātanjali, etc., and such sure use of their technical terms in a language of such maturity and with their lyrical cry so intense and the handling of metre and rhyme so perfect that one is amazed at the ignorance of our "historians". Compared to our modern curricula of liberal education where words are memorised and facts never experienced - education in medieval times confined itself only to the basic instruction in three 'Rs and basic religious and secular literature, the candidate later learning on his own, through experience and travel, and not through the printed word which was nowhere available. Even the most "learned" of the monarchs and seers could not boast of any learning other than this.

** The poem emphasises the uncompromising unity of God who is all-powerful, all-pervading, the creator, sustainer and destroyer of all, who keeps detached and is yet involved in every detail of His creation, for nothing happens which is not in accord with His Divine Order. He apportions to each his lot according to his deeds. So, he who dwells upon Him, and looks upon good and bad alike, is released from the endless cycle of 'coming-and-going' and merges in Him, the eternal Truth.

Nānak, in this poem, calls himself a poet (Shāir), and gives it the title of '*Patti-likhi*' (i.e. this acrostic or alphabetical poem, was written out (*likhi*) on a wooden tablet (which to this day is called *Patti*).

Whether he wrote this poem at the young age of about 12 or 13 years, or later, one significant fact that emerges out of it is that the letters Guru Nānak uses are not of the Nāgri script, but of Gurmukhi - all 35 of them, and including the typical Gurmukhi letter of 'ੜ' (ṛ). The pronunciation of the letters is also not according to the Nāgri but Gurmukhi characters (*sassā, khakhā, gāggā*, etc., and not *sā-khā-gā*). So, the thesis held by some biographers that he was taught only Nāgri and not Gurmukhi as well, is knocked out. This also establishes clearly that it was not the second Sikh Guru - Angad - who should be credited (as many biographers suggest) with the "invention" of the Gurmukhi script which must have existed as indeed it did before Guru Nānak. (See the author's "*Panjābi Sāhit Dā Itihās* and G. B. Singh's *Gurmukhi dē Janam tē Vichār*.)

After the completion of schooling at the age of 13, Nānak's father arranged for his son's *Yagyopavit* ceremony, when all Hindu male children of higher castes wear the Sacred Thread (symbolising re-birth or initiation into the faith) and hear the Word of the Veda from the family priest. A great feast was arranged and, as is usual, relations and friends from far and near gathered to participate in the auspicious occasion. But, to the chagrin and dismay of all, Nānak refused to wear the Sacred Thread saying, "I shall wear a Thread which will be soiled not, nor broken nor burnt, nor worn out, and will accompany a man into the beyond." When asked lothingly by Pandit Hardyāl, the family priest, what kind of Thread he would wish to wear, he answered serenely:-

"*If compassion be the cotton,*
And contentment the thread,
And continence the Knot,
And the Truth the twist,"

it would make an ideal Thread for one's Soul, which would even defy death. Nānak continued : "What is the meaning of the Sacred Thread when a man who wears it holds not his hand from theft, fornication, falsehood and deceit ? Our hands that kill wear not the thread, nor the feet which rush out to commit evil, nor the tongue which slanders, nor the eyes which covet another's beauty or riches. Himself the Brāhmin goes about without a thread like this, but insists that the others wear it. Hear ye people : this is a wonder of wonders. His mind is blind and his name is wisdom!"*.

This audacity the father could hardly bear. He was put to great ridicule and shame by his young son. So, he gave him some cattle to graze. It is said while he put the cattle to the pasture, he himself

---

* Women and untouchables are prohibited from wearing the sacred thread, or hearing the Vedas. According to *Manusmriti*, a Brāhmin should wear the thread of cotton, a Khatri of jute, and a Vaisha of sheep's wool. A Brāhmin should wear, at this ceremony, black deer-skin, a Khatri red deer skin, and a Vaish a he-goat's skin. They should also hold in their hands staffs made out of different kinds of wood. For a Brāhmin, according to Nārada, this ceremony should be held in spring; for a Khatri in summer and for a Vaisha in winter. A Brāhmin should be initiated at 8, a Khatri at 11 and a Vaisha at 12 years of age. From this, one could safely infer that Nānak's age at this time could not be less than 11 years. Normally, the sacred thread is worn just before marriage and if that were so, this ceremony would have taken place when Nānak was about 16.

sat composed, under a banyan tree, meditating on God. The cattle browsed through the standing crop of a farmer and despoiled it. The farmer complained to Rai Bulār who seems to have made good the loss.* Such was the devotion that young Nānak evoked from his surroundings.

Several other similar episodes are also narrated in the idiom of the devout to prove that Nānak had shown sure signs of divinity even in the early years of his life. Most exquisite verses are weaved round such incidents. Many historians doubt if these verses were uttered, spontaneously, on such occasions. But, their authenticity is not in doubt, and hence it is immaterial even if they were composed by Nānak later in life: what is significant is the grandeur of the vision they reveal.**

It appears, despairing of Nānak as a farmer or a herdsman, his father gave him some money to buy merchandise from the market of Chuharkhānā nearby. But Nānak gifted away this money to the poor who accosted him on the way. When he came back empty-handed, his father went out to meet him outside the village where he sat under a tree,† and asked what had become of the money he was entrusted with. Nānak replied: "Father, you had asked me to do a

---

* According to the *Purātan Janam Sākhi* (p. 7) a miracle was wrought by Nānak at this time and when they all went out to visit the grazed farm, it seemed to stand intact.

** For instance, when asked by his father to farm, he is reported to have said:—

"In my body's farm, my mind is the ploughman and right conduct the cultivation. I water it with humility and sow in it the seed of God's Essence. Contentment is my harrowing of it, and Poverty its fence. Tended by love, the seed will sprout and fill my granary." (Sorath M. 1). He continued: "I'll grow so much in my farm that it will be sufficient not only for me and my family, but the whole world. And after one has eaten out of my hands, he will crave no more. It will settle the accounts of everyone whether these be of this birth or the previous ones. And the Man for whom I till my land protects me from drought as from floods and whatever I ask and whenever, he gives so much that I entreat: "Enough, no more." (*Purātan Janam Sākhi*, P. 9)

When asked what his Master was like, he is believed to have said:— "Everyone hears of Him as great, and calls Him so, but he alone knows His worth who sees Him. O Father, my Master's worth can be measured not, for he who loves Him merges in Him. One would compare Him if there were one to compare with Him. So everyone who knows Him says: 'O God, Thou art only what Thou art." (Āsā M. I, Chaupadē).

† This aged tree is still preserved with a wall built round it for protection. It is known as *Tambu Sāhib*, or the holy trunk.

"profitable bargain" (*Sachā Saudā*),* what better profit could one have in this world and in the next than being blessed by feeding the poor and the holy?" Kālu was naturally enraged and spanked his son for his recklessness.

It is said, Nānak would now keep to himself for long hours and take little interest in the affairs of the world. He would sit listless in long and deep meditations. The father fearing that Nānak perhaps had been gripped by some mysterious malady called in a physician to examine him. The physician felt his pulse, but the 'patient' smiled and said :

"O innocent one, feel not my pulse, for my malady is not of the body but of the Soul. Take not care of me. O wise one, but of thyself, for he who is not himself would respond not to thy cure. The malady I'm blest with is that I'm in love and he alone whose lover I am knows how to get me over it."**

When the physician, wonder-struck, asked Nānak what the malady of his Soul was like, he answered in most profound terms :-

> "*My one malady is that I live separated from myself.*
> *And the other that I seek to be what I ought to be.*
> *And the third that I'm in the eye of the all-powerful*
> *Angel of Death.*
> *And, then, there is pain to suffer and man comes only*
> *to pass away.*
> *O worthy physician, which of these maladies would you*
> *cure, yea, which indeed?*" †

He emphasised that while the maladies of the body could be cured, the maladies of the Soul could not be, unless it found its identity with the Oversoul. And this one could not do unless he forsook his selfhood (*haun-main*) and identified himself with the whole creation by making its pain one's own.

His father and mother tried hard to bring him round to the ways of the world, but Nānak felt called upon to perform a mission for

---

* The main Gurdwārā in the memory of this event is still known *Sachā Saudā* (now in West Pākistan, in the district of Sheikhupurā).

** *Malhār Ki Vār*, M. 1.

† Malhār M. 1

which he felt acutely he had been entrusted with by God. He told them :-

"I know not who's my father, who my mother, and from where I came :
And why have fire and water blended to make of me what I am.
Within me there's something that gnaws at my heart as if my soul is on fire.
And I feel only if I submitted to my Lord's Will, there'll be peace for me." †

Despairing, the parents thought of marrying him off. Perhaps, they thought, he might feel settled in the ways of the world after his marriage. So, possibly at the age of 16,* he was married to Sulakhani, daughter of Moolā, a pious Chonā Khatri merchant of

---

† Gauri M. 1

* There is some difference of opinion regarding the age of his marriage. Bhāi Mani Singh in his *Gyān Ratnāvali* avers that Nānak married at the age of 14, when he was still at Talwandi (P. 123). Gandā Singh (A History of the Sikhs) suggests 18 to be his age at marriage, when he had, according to him, shifted to Sultānpur. Says the *Purātan Janam Sākhi* "at the age of 12, Nānak was married" (P. 6). Meharvān's *Janamsākhi* gives the date of the betrothal ceremony as the first day of the dark half of Vaisākh (Vaisākh Vadi Ekam), Samvat 1542, i.e. "when he was 15-16 years of age", and that the marriage took place at Talwandi (P. 33). If Nānak finished his schooling at 13, it must have taken quite some time for his parents to persuade him to marry. And, knowing as we do his predispositions in his early days, it is unthinkable that he would have accepted the Nawāb's service (rejecting all other avocations) before his marriage. If it is suggested that an early marriage was popular, and must have been insisted upon by his parents before he grew into an adult and could become more difficult, the natural answer would be that in that case we shall have to dismiss all stories (let alone miracles) about his 'unusual' and 'other--worldly' utterances and behaviour right from his school-days. What is the authority of the historians for their conjectures about the age of marriage, joining the Nawāb's service and later abandoning it is not known. Meharvān makes such a graphic account of this marriage and makes it such a fabulous affair that, it appears, both parties were extremely well-to-do. Meharvān gives the name of Nānak's mother as *Tipārā* and of his wife, *Ghumi*. Malcolm quoting some nameless Sikh authors, gives the date of marriage as Āsārh (June-July) of Samvat 1545, i.e. at the age of 19.

Batālā (now in the district of Gurdāspur). He had two sons from this marriage—Srichand and Lakhmi Dās.*

Now that he had somehow accepted to enter into matrimony and had two sons and a wife to look after, it was but natural that a man of Nānak's sense of natural responsibility looked out for some employment. So, according to all reliable accounts, he accepted the suggestion of his parents to join the service of Nawāb Daulat Khān Lodhi (later Governor of Panjāb) at Sultānpur, then the capital of Jullundhur- Doab. This appointment obviously was secured for him by his brother-in-law, Jairām, who already was employed with the Nawāb and was held by the latter in high esteem for his honesty and piety. After a while, Nānak was joined by his wife and two sons, as according to most early accounts of his life, he stayed here for about ten years.• Here he was also joined by Mardānā, a Muslim drummer

---

* No one is clear about the dates of their birth, though both were alive at the time of their father's demise. *Meharvān* gives their dates of birth when Nānak was 27 and 28, i. e. in 1496 and 1497 A.D., i.e. twelve years after his marriage according to this author when Nānak was still at Talwandi (P. 66). According to Kāhan Singh, Lakhmi Dās was born on 19 *Phagun*, Samvat 1553 (1496 A.D.) at Sultānpur and died on 13 *Vaisākh*, Samvat 1612 (1555 A.D.) at Kartārpur (Mahān kosh, P. 3162). The dates for Sri Chand given by him are :- Birth : Bhadon Sudi 9, Samvat 1551 (1494 A.D.) at Sultānpur and death on 15 Asuj, Samvat 1669 (1612 A. D.) at the age of 118 years. Lakhmi Dās was a married householder and the Bedis of the present day claim their descent from him, even though, as we shall learn later, he was disinherited by his father for his impudence and excessive display of worldly outlook. Sri Chand became an Udāsi recluse, and his *Akhārās* or *Maths* did a lot to propagate the faith of Nānak in their own Vedantic light even during the darkest days of the persecution of the Sikhs by the Moghals. The orthodox Sikhs, however, have never identified themselves with the Udāsis, calling them a heretical sect, disapproved of by Guru Nānak himself.

• "A History of the Sikhs", by Gandā Singh and Tejā Singh affirms that Nānak was married at the age of 18, while in the employ of the Nawāb at Sultānpur, and left service at the age of 27 to launch upon his divine mission. The *Purātan Janam Sākhi* is silent as to how many years Nānak stayed at Sultānpur. However, it is stated here that *after* his marriage *and* the birth of his two sons, at Talwandi, Nānak joined the service at Sultānpur, leaving his family behind and assuring them that he would call them when he felt settled. From the respect and trust of the Nawāb that he enjoyed, it can be safely conjectured that it must have been a reasonably long period of stay here. Meharvān, however, says Nānak went to Sultānpur at the age of 35 years, 6 months and 15 days, and stayed there only for 2 years. According to him (P. 73), Mardānā accompanied him along with ten servants and that Nānak rode on a horse-back, took another one also along, together with two camel-loads of goods, tents, clothes, linen carpets and furniture (a paraphernalia wholly alien to Nānak's way of life).

(*doom or Mirāsi*) of Talwandi, who seems to have developed a special liking for Nānak from his very early days and played deftly on the rebeck (*rabāb*), as Nānak sang his hymns.* From his masterly compositions in verse for which detailed instructions are given as to their *rāga* and *tāla*, one can safely deduce that Nānak was a man of great sensibility and a lover and practiser of fine arts, particularly classical music and poetry. Mardānā too seems to have secured the employment of the Nawāb** through the intervention of Nānak.

According to all reliable records, Nānak became extremely popular with the Nawāb and his servants to whom he would issue rations from the imperial stores. "He worked so well that everyone was pleased with him and said, 'What a man, what a man". Everyone commended him to the Nawāb who also greatly admired him. Whatever rations (*aloofa*) he got for himself, he would offer these to others in the name of God, himself being content with the barest

---

* According to the *Purātan Janam Sākhi* (P. 14), he and several other companions of Nānak's childhood came here to seek employment with the Nawāb and secured it through the intervention of Nānak. And when Nānak sat to eat, he would always share his food with all his companions. Till late into the night, they would all sing the praises of God, and during the last watch of the night (about 4 A.M.) Nānak would go out to the river and bathe to participate again with his companions in devotional singing till the morning rose, and he would dress himself in proper form "anointing his forehead with a saffron-mark" and leave for the office, an account book in his hand.

** All historians are agreed that Nawāb Daulat Khān Lodhi (died 1526) was appointed Governor of Panjāb by Ibrāhim Lodhi in or about 1502 A.D. and remained at his post for over 20 years, giving the Panjāb comparative peace and prosperity. But, later, due to the maltreatment of himself and his son, he turned against Ibrāhim and invited Bābur to invade India in 1523 (Oxford History of India, V. Smith, third edition, P. 321). Later on he turned against Bābur as well, for the emperor not having kept his word for restoring Panjāb's Governorship to him (which he had lost in an expedition against him by Bihār Khān, a general of Ibrāhim Lodhi) but instead arrested him, though he was later released and put in charge of Sultānpur (Bannerjee, Evolution of the Khālsā, P. 39), which, according to Kāhan Singh, was his ancestoral estate (Mahān Kosh, P. 1958). Sultānpur then was also the capital of a province - Jullundur-Doab. So we know that Daulat Khān had something to do with Sultānpur, where the ruins of his fort can still be seen. Bābur in his *Bābur-Nāmā* mentions Daulat Khān's father, Tātār Khān, "as having been appointed by Bahlol Lodhi to the Governorship of a country north of Satlej (?) and Sarhind, and that on his death, Sikandar Lodi took-over these territories and gave only Lāhore to Daulat Khān one or two years before I came into Kābul (910 A.H., i.e. in 1502 or 3)". (A.S. Beveridge's translation, Vol.I, P. 383).

minimum for his upkeep."* It is also said when he would weigh up the stores and reached the figure '13' (in Hindustani *Terā*, which also means Thine), he would enter into an ecstasy and continue endlessly to repeat : "*Terā, main Terā*" (Thine, O God, I am Thine"). **

One morning, as he had gone to the river as usual "along with an attendant", he entrusted his clothes to the latter and himself entered into the water of the river *Vaēn*, "but did not come out". Says the *Purātan Janam Sākhi* he was in the meanwhile "ushered into the God's Presence in the True Court. Lord-God offered him a cup of nectar saying, 'drink thou it, Nānak, it is the nectar of My Name.' Nānak bowed down to His God, drank the cup and was blessed by God. Said God, 'Nānak, I'm with you. My blessing is upon you. I've emancipated you and whosoever will utter thy name will also be blessed. Keep detached from the world of 'coming-and-going', and dedicate thyself to Nām (identication with the totality of existence), Dān (charity of heart) and Isnān (purity of conduct), *sevā* (selfless service) and *simran* (meditation on God). I have blessed thee with My Name. So, commit thou thyself only to this task."†

The same source states that Nānak was asked by God to utter what he had experienced of God, and Nānak uttered "in the

---

* *Purātan Janam Sākhi*, P. 13

** Says Malcolm in his "Sketch of the Sikhs" (P.15) that on reports reaching the Nawāb that Nānak was squandering his stores on unauthorised persons, he arrested Jairām. But, on the account being taken, a balance was found in his favour on which Jairām was not only released but re-instated in the employment and the favour of his master.

† As this is the most decisive and turning point in the life of Nānak, we have quoted at some length from the original sources as to the nature of his experience which finally settled for him the course of his future life. It must be mentioned here that taking out all that is mystical from the life of a prophet and the founder of a world faith and to bring him down to the level of a mere historical person would NEVER yield the whole man to us. Moses, Jesus, Mohammad, Gautam the Buddha and other prophets and mystics of repute all had this kind of spiritual experience which words might express in myth, or symbols, unintelligible to the merely secular, but which is nonetheless most significant to understand and appreciate the meaning of their life and message.

strains of the "Unstruck Melody" (*Anhad dhuni*) the following hymn:—

"If aeons were my age
And air my food and drink ;
And I caged myself in a cave
Where entered neither the sun nor the moon,
And, were I not to sleep even in dream,
I'll still not be able to value Thee, nor Thy Name, O Lord.
The True Lord has His Seat in Himself:
I only hear of His Merits.
If I were to be pressed like a reed-mat, or ground
Like grain in a mill :
If I were to burn myself in fire,
And mix with the ashes,
I'd still not be able to value Thee, nor Thy Name, O Lord.
If I were a bird and trailed across a hundred skies,
And remained unseen, and ate nought nor drank,
I'd still not be able to value Thee, nor Thy Name, O Lord.
If I were to read through millions of pages
If I were to write with an ocean of ink with the speed of winds,
I'd still not be able to value Thee, nor Thy Name, O Lord."

(Sri Rāg M.1, 4:2)

Lord-God then said: "Nānak, you have realised My *Hukam* (The Divine Order, or Will). Whomsoever you will bless will also be blessed by Me. My name is the Transcendent God (*Parbrahma-Parmeshwar*), thy name will be Guru-God (Guru-Parmeshwar)." Nānak then prostrated at God's Feet, and was blessed by God with a Robe of Honour. The same source says that Nānak uttered the *Japji* (Sikh morning prayer) and the *Ārti*• at this time in the presence of God.

When Nānak did not appear for a considerable time, the attendant, disappointed, rushed back to report to the Nawāb. A great search was conducted, divers tore through the waters but could find no trace of Nānak. "After three days," he appeared at the same spot from where he had disappeared. On his return to the town, "he distributed all he had".*

• *Purātan Janam Sākhi* P. 15. It is also stated here that the Guru sang his morning prayer, the *Japji* in Rāg Āsā, though the Ādi Granth contains no such direction.

*Ibid, p. 15.

Many people gathered round him. The Nawāb also came to see him and asked: "Nānak, what has happened to you?". The people said to him; "Sir, he has been for three days in the river. It appears his "mind seems to have been affected." The Nawāb said: "It is most heartbreaking for me." Nānak now wore only a loincloth. The rest he had gifted away, and went out into the wilderness to join the faqirs along with Mardānā.

For a whole day, Nānak would utter not a word. The next day, he made an unusual utterance: "There is no Hindu, no Musalmān *(Nā Ko Hindu, nā Musalmān)** and would utter nothing else. People reported this to the Nawāb who said: "Do not disturb his way of life, for he is a faqir." But the Qāzi would not be silenced and prevailed upon the Nawāb to ask Nānak into his presence. But Nānak refused to go, saying: "What do I care for the Nawāb?" The Nawāb sent his men again who pleaded : "Nānak, the Nawāb wants to see your holy face (*didār*). In the name of God, please do bless him." Nānak thereupon went to the court, wearing a *muktā* (black string, made of wool or silk, which the faqirs wrap round their turban or cap or wear across their chest denoting renunciation and abandonment). The Nawāb asked him to remove it and wear a *Kamarband* (a soldier's or an official's belt) instead. It is said, Nānak did as he was bidden. The Nawāb then asked the Qāzi to question Nānak on anything he wanted to. The Qāzi naturally asked him to explain what he meant by the unusual utterance he was making—"*nā ko Hindu, nā Musalmān*". The Guru replied:

> "It is far too hard to be a Muslim: only if one has an implicit faith in the religion of God, and purges oneself of the scum of ego with the scraper (of truth) and submits to the will of God, obliterating his doubts about life and death, and is compassionate to all life; then alone one my be called a true Muslim."

(Mājh M.1. Shaloka)

---

* How revolutionary this utterance then was (as it still is even among the most enlightened communities) would be clear from the treatment meted out to a contemporary Brahmin sage, Budhan of village Kaner (according to Firishtā, Kataen, near Lucknow), whom Ibrāhim Lodhi, the Emperor of Delhi, put to death on the *fatwā* given by two Qāzis. The only crime he was charged with was that the Brahmin had proclaimed in the hearing of some Muslims that "the religion of both Hindus and Muslims, if practised with sincerity, was equally acceptable to God". (Elliot's translation of *Tārikh-i-Daoodi*", Vol, 4, pp. 464-65).

Elaborating further his point, he said : "The true mosque for a Muslim should be compassion; his prayer-mat implicit faith in God, and the right livelihood his Qurān; humility his circumcision, and continence his fasting, good deeds his Kāāba, and Truth his prophet and the dependence on God's Grace his *Kalimā* and the *Nimāz*."

It is said the Qāzi was non-plussed and the Nawāb stopped him from further argument saying: "There is no occasion now to question him further." But the Qāzi was persistent and wanted Nānak to perform the Nimāz with him and see if it made any difference to him. Nānak accompanied him to the mosque, but stood aloof and just smiled. The Qāzi, full of wrath, reported the matter to the Nawāb saying: "You say that he is a good man, but see how he, a mere Hindu, laughed and ridiculed me when I was offering my prayers in the mosque." When the Nawāb questioned Nānak, he replied: "I smiled not to ridicule him but because the prayers of the Qāzi were not accepted by God, for while he prayed, his mind was in his mare which had given birth to a foal this morning, lest the young one fall into the well nearby. It is said the Qāzi, amazed at Nānak's intuition, bowed down to Nānak in reverence, saying: "He is the blessed of God." And, says the *Purātan Janam Sākhi*, all Sayyads, Sheikhs, Qāzis, Maftis, Khāns, Mehrs and Muqqadams were similarly impressed by his perceptive vision. To whichever side he turned, people greeted him with utter reverence. The Nawāb said: "Nānak has attained the Truth. It would be a sacrilege to question him." He too bowed at Nānak's feet—an unusual gesture by an autocratic official of middle ages but revealing also the the catholicity of his outlook and his spiritual leanings. Then, whosoever came to the Nawāb said: "God speaks through Nānak." The Nawāb persuaded him to stay back saying: "All the kingdom and the possessions and the authority I have is yours. It is my misfortune that a *Vizier* of mine like yours should turn a faqir."* But Nānak left for the wilderness, saying: "God will bless you, but I shall stay not here. The world and all its pleasures and possessions are yours. I have abandoned them from this day."*

* It is an amazing fact of history that though Guru Nānak had to say quite a few bitter things later on about the kings, courtiers, Qāzis, and Mullāhs, his first admirers were all Muslims – Rai Bulār, Mardānā, Nawāb Daulat Khān Lodhi, and his Muslim teachers of Arabic & Persian. In all the three biographies, called the *Janamsākhis*, written about a hundred years after Nānak, possibly in the regimes of Shāh Jahān and Aurangzeb, the biographers paint a picture of communal

* *F. N. (Contd)*
tolerance (if not of harmony), not only on the part of Muslim divines, sufis, etc., but even political dignitaries. This point has to be emphasised due to the confusion created by interested historians of later days picking upon only casual and stray incidents or one or two bigoted Muslim monarchs like Aurangzeb, who was tyrannous not only to the Hindus, but also to his father and brothers and sons and daughters, but of this later.
Mehervān (1581-1640 A.D.), nephew of Guru Arjun, writes in his *Janamsākhi:* "In the days of Nānak's marriage, grain was cheaper a hundred times and the land-revenue much less. The officials did justice; the subjects were religious-minded. Everyone was happy and the days were good" (P. 29, Khalsa College, Amritsar, ed., 1962). This is corroborated by contemporary historians as well, though religious bigotry on the part of *some* Muslim rulers or Mullāhs and Qāzis in the days of transition is duly emphasised by others. For a fuller view of Nānak's times, see Chapter I.
** At this point, we must consider Nānak's treatment of his family. Undoubtedly, in an Indian household upto very recent times (on the countryside this is still the case) no man ever took into consideration the views of his wife, or even of grown-up children, about his career. Only the parents counted (as they still do) and with them dialogues and discussions of Nānak are frequently mentioned, in detail, by all his biographers, though Nānak is reported always as totally engrossed in the world of the spirit to whom the reactions of the family—even his parents—are of no account.

But, Nānak who insisted on a life of the household and glorified womanhood and painted such sensitive accounts of woman's physical charm and beauty, identifying her with the awakened human soul, could not have treated his wife and children casually. He may have been averse to marriage initially, but once he entered into matrimony, he would have spared nothing to keep them happy. It can, therefore, be safely surmised that he took up service with the Nawāb only for fourteen years after which the sons could look after themselves. What is more, he came back to them after his long journeys and visited his family after the conclusion of every single tour, even as the *Janamsakhi* tradition testifies.

His love for his sister 'Nānaki' is referred to in most touching terms in some of the Sākhis, and equally so for his mother. When Nānak met his mother on his return from his very first tour, and she wailed : "Sacrifice, O son, to thee: Sacrifice a million times. Blessed is the earth thou walkest upon, blessed the people thou meetest", Nānak could not restrain himself, and wept. *(Purātan Janam Sākhi* P. 49).

And, whenever even a casual mention is made of his wife, as when he departed for Sultānpur, Nānak treats her with great affection and consideration. On seeing her cry, he said: "O my innocent one, what use I was to thee here?" She said: "While you were here, I felt blest as if with the rule of the world. Without you, the world is no use to me." Nānak was greatly moved and said: "Do not worry. Let me go now and if I can find employment, I shall call thee," (*Purātan Janam Sākhi*, P. 13), which he did. That such words are put in the mouth of Nānak by the devout biographers who delineate him at the level of a myth and a legend, if not God Himself, speaks much about Nānak's attachment to his family.

CHAPTER III

THE SOURCES OF GURU NANAK'S BIOGRAPHY

As we have seen, there is a still a dispute as to the exact date of Nānak's birth, and some may argue about Nānak's total years of schooling or the exact date or the occasion when a particular verse of his was composed or uttered, but no one has disputed his highly inquisitive and cultured mind* or the authenticity of his compositions included in the Ādi-Granth. There are differences of opinion about the age and place of Nānak's marriage, but none whatsoever about the fact that he was married and had two sons. The service with Nawāb Daulat Khān Lodhi as a store-keeper is also conceded by all biogra-

* Swāmi Dayānand, founder of the Ārya Samāj, did attack Nānak's learning (vide Satyāra'h Parkāsh's Chapter on the Sikhs), but for wrong reasons. He says the Guru knew little of Sanskrit and yet tried to pretend that he did. As an illustration, Dayānand accuses Nānak of having corrupted many Sanskrit words like 'Bhai' (fear) which Nānak changes into "Bhau." Being ignorant of how the Prakrits and the spoken tongues like Panjābi, even though derived from Sanskrit, underwent changes and *tatsam* words became *tadbhav*, the Swāmi did not know that "bhai" of Sanskrit always changes into "Bhau" in Panjābi, 'Khai' into 'Khau' and so on. Then, Nānak was writiting not in Sanskrit but in Panjābi or Hindi, though, at other places he also uses the *tatsam* form of 'Bhai' as well (see Āsā di Vār, M. 1). Again, the Swāmi's charge that the Guru reviled the Vedās, without having read them, is based on ignorance. The Guru did criticise, like the Buddha before him, the Vedic pantheism, ritualism, formalism, the hierarchy of caste with the Brahmin at the top, but he never reviled any religion as such. The quotation on which the Swāmi bases his argument *('Ved Parhē Parh Brahmā mooā, Charon Ved Kahāni'')* does not occur in the Ādi-Granth.

phers, though not at what age he was engaged in or abandoned this service. That most of the time Mardānā, the Muslim drummer, accompanied him on his divine mission is also corroborated by most of the early biographers, though the name of Bālā, a Hindu Jāt of Sandhu clan, is also suggested by one or two later biographers as being his companion at the time of "*Sachā Saudā*" (or, the True Bargain) and then later also as a travelling companion. His "first" biography called *Bhāi Bāle Wāli Janamsākhi* (a tell-tale biography full of myth and miracle which became the last and not the first of Nānak's biographies) is also ascribed to him. *

The names of his father, mother, sister, wife, sons, as of the village chief are identical in most of the biographies. That Nānak was a precocious child, given to questioning and with a perceptive mind and intense spiritual disposition is also illustrated at great length even by those Muslim historians unfavourably disposed to the house of Nānak. That he was a classical musician and poet of great excellence is also not in dispute, nor the fact that he evoked reverence of both Hindus and Muslims from his early days, and that the first slogan of his mission was: "*Nā Ko Hindu, Nā Musalmān*" (There is no Hindu, no Musalmān).

But, when Nānak enters upon his divine mission after abandoning service with the Nawāb, quite a few of his journeys and incidents connected with them become the subject of controversy.

First, let us state on the authority of contemporary evidence, which incidents and places in the life of Nānak are part of the Sikh heritage. For this, we have to rely mainly on the following sources :

I. *Bhāi Gurdās* (Died 1637 A.D.). A near relation of the third Sikh Guru, Amar Dās, who lived in the court of the third, fourth, fifth and the sixth Gurus, was a devout Sikh, and a poet and philosopher of a high order. He gives us in his Vārs (ballads, which are 40 in all), a few major incidents in the life of Guru Nānak (Vār 1) and the names of a few of his choice disciples (Vār 11).

---

* The fact that Bhāi Bālā did not accompany the Guru in most of his travels and that his name is neither mentioned by Bhāi Gurdās (in Vār 11) nor by any of the older chronicles of Guru Nānak should not oblige us to dismiss him out of account. The relics associated with him, like *Bhāi Bāle Dā Khooh*, in Nankānā Sāhib itself and the very strong and persistent tradition associating his name as a companion of Guru Nānak at least in his earlier travels also point to the same conclusion.

He was also the scribe of the Ādi-Granth and his work, according to an accepted tradition, was described by the fifth Guru, Arjun, to be the 'Key' to the understanding of the Sikh ethos and doctrine Being so close to the four Gurus who succeeded the second Nānak, his word cannot but be accepted as the most authoritative the more so because the charge of interpolation has never been levelled against his work.

But then, he is also a poet, given to flights of imagination. Also he is writing as a missionary and not as a historian. Moreover, he is writing about 80 years after the demise of Guru Nānak when the latter had already become a legend and a god. But making allowance for all these facts, one cannot but accept as truth the outlines, if not the trappings, of Nānak's life as revealed by him. He does not write a detailed account of Nānak's life but only refers to what he considers to be the most significant events of his later life. In particular, he mentions (*after referring briefly to his visit to "all" the pilgrim-stations*), Nānak's sojourn to Meccā and Baghdād to have a dialogue there with Muslim divines; to the Sumeru (or Kailāsh) mountain to converse with the Yogis; to Multān to have a discourse with the Sufis there, and to Achal Vatālā to debunk the commonly-held yogic belief that it is through miracles that a man of God establishes his claim to spirituality. Finally, Bhāi Gurdās refers to Guru Nānak's settled life as a house-holder, at Kartārpur (now in Pakistān), a township he himself founded on the left bank of the river Rāvi, where passing on his throne to Bhāi Lehnā, his devotee, in preference to his sons "who were bad of mind and rebellious of conduct and followed not the Master's commands," he left for the heavenly abode.

In fact, these are indeed the most significant events of Nānak's life. About Nānak's visit to Meccā, Medinā and Baghdād, we have referred at some length later in this book. A significant fact that emerges out of Nānak's discourse with the Yogis at Achal Vatālā is that when asked to perform a miracle, Nānak refused to, saying, in the words of Bhāi Gurdās :—

> "*bājhon sachē nām de,*
> *hor Karāmāt asāthē nāheen.*"

and :-

> "*gur sangāt bāni binān,*
> *dooji ot naheen hāi kāi.*"

i. e. "Apart from the True Name (of God), I have no other

miracle to show", "and but for the companionship of the Guru and the Word (of God), I lean on no other support."

Elaborating it further and basing his argument on a similar hymn by Guru Nānak, Bhāi Gurdās puts these words in the mouth of the Guru:—"Even if I were to wear the robes of fire and abide in the house of snow; even if I were to eat iron and drive the whole world before me: even if I were able to weigh up the earth and the sky in a balance with a mere *tanka* (an insignificant weight) and had so much (spiritual) power that I could ferry anyone across (an ocean) merely by wishing it, it would be all vain without the illumination of the True Name, as the shade of a cloud.'

And yet, Bhāi Gurdās seeks to establish the identity of the Guru through the miracles which he, according to Gurdās, performed at Meccā and in Baghdād!

Again, on the one hand, Bhāi Gurdās makes Guru Nānak laud unmistakably the life of the household in his dialogue with the yogis at Achal Vatālā,* and yet prefaces the life of Nānak with statements which are not corroborated by the Word of the Guru anywhere in the Ādi Granth. For instance, his statements, that when the Guru ventured out on his journeys, "he (Nānak) having *first* attained the grace of God, later entered upon a life of extreme austerities," and that "he lived on sand and *akka* (swallow-wort) and slept on bare hard ground, littered with gravel (*rorān ki gur kari vichhāi*)", cannot be taken in their literal sense:

Bhāi Gurdas mentions only the name of Mardānā, and not of Bālā or any other as having accompanied the Guru on his journeys.•

* Asked Bhangarnāth the yogi: "Why you have poured *Kānji* (an alkaline liquid) in the 'milk' and soured it, so that now when you churn the stuff, you gather no butter?" (i.e. by donning a householder's robes and involving yourself with the world, you have lost the merit of holiness). The Guru replied: "O Bhangarnāth, your mother (i.e. your Guru) knew not the way. She "washed" not the "churn" (i.e. the body) and thus through ignorance burnt down the 'flower' (of the soul). For, what kind of holiness is this that you abandon the world and yet beg at the door of the householders for alms? Without giving, one receives nothing."

• Other Sikhs of Guru Nānak that Bhai Gurdās mentions without any details regarding their lives are:-

Tāru Popat, Prithā Khērā, Mardānā, Prithimal, Daulat Khān Lodhi, Mālo Māngā, Kālu Khatri, Bhagtā Ohri, Sihān Gajjan, Chaudhri Bhagirath, Ajitā Randhāwā, Boora Buddhā, and Phirnā Khēhrā. Bhāi Mani Singh, who writes in some detail about them in his *Sikhān di Bhagatmālā*, has not much to say about their lives either and weaves round them only the message of the Guru.

His description, however, of the state of affairs at the advent of Guru Nānak, though given to poetic fancy, is at the core substanti true. Says he:-

In the age of Truth (*Sat-yug* or the ideal state) people believed in in one God and not another. Rising above attachment and Māyā, they performed *tapas* [austerities] in the forests and lived on the vegetation that grew around them. They lived for a hundred thousand years and built not (for their glory or comfort) mansions, forts and decorative houses (*mandir*). In the *Tretā* age of the Suryavanshi Kings, men got involved with Māyā, attachment and ego (and so) their span of life declined to one-tenth. In the *Duāpar* age of the Yādvas, men's span of life and character, both, had a steep fall. But in the Kāli age (i. e. the present times), men have assumed a wholly evil mind. People hesitate to practise the conduct of the three earlier Vedas (Rig, Yajur and Sam), and are being licked by the flames of atred and ego. No one acknowledges another as worthy of worship The Kings are unjust. The age is like the knife and the courtiers are like butchers (an echo of Guru Nānak's own words). Justice has become a thing of the past (three yugas); in the fourth yuga (i. e. the present times) it is a question of give-and-take. And men are evil in their deeds. No caste likes another and they clash with and burn each other like bamboos on fire. Though the Buddha took birth in this very age, people discriminate not between wisdom and ignorance. No one listens to another and does what is in his mind. People revile the Vedas, and worship the dumb stocks and stones or tombs and graves. Some believe in *tantras* and *mantras* and the world is full of disputation, wrath and contention. Everyone is for himself and each one follows a different religion. Some but worship the sun and the moon, others deify the earth or the sky, or water, air, fire and (even) the Angel of Death. Hatred, strife, ego and slander have torn the world. There are four religions, and four castes, each at daggers drawn with the other. There's but one Name (of God) and yet the Hindus and Muslims are estranged from His Path by their own different ways. The Hindus have abandoned the Vedas, the Muslims the Katebs (Qurān, etc.) and the Mullās and the Brāhmins fly at the throat of each other, leaving Truth (of God) alone."

Gurdās continues; "In this age of total darkness, Nānak rose like the sun when all the stars sink in the skies, or like a lion who when he roars puts to flight all the other life in the forest. Wherever the Bābā (i. e. Guru Nānak) set his foot, it became a place of worship. Every household became the house of God where men sang the praises of the Infinite. The *four* continents (*chak*), and nine divisions (*khand*) of the earth he himself visited to their last limits."

Speaking of the transformation wrought by Nānak, Bhāi Gurdās affirms that "*the Guru brought together all the four Varnas [castes] into one fraternity and all the four religions he made the four pillars of one religion. He brought on the one platform of equality the king and the beggar and* lo, the proud heads he made to bow down at the feet of the poor. He saved the whole age of Kaliyuga through the *mantram* of the True Name. Each one of his disciples had to drink the wash of his feet. The Guru having visited the [Hindu] pilgrim-stations came to the conclusion that the rituals and beliefs of the past were of no avail without the loving adoration (of God). *He read the four Vedas and the* (*six*) *Sāstras*, but found that Brahmā (who is believed by the Hindus to have revealed the Vedas) had written not the word "love" in his texts. Nānak proclaimed to the world, that one could attain not God by assuming religious garbs. He said, the God-man (*Gurmukh*) should transcend his caste, and become casteless, and live the life of innocence and humility. He found not religion either in the siddhas, or the nāthas, the long-lived ascetics and celibates and their so-called gurus, the gods and goddesses, and Kāli, or the pirs and prophets of the Turks (i. e. the Muslims). It was like the blind leading the blind."

This should give us a most authoritative and almost contemporary view of Nānak's life and philosophy in howsoever meagre a detail.

II. Another contemporary of Bhāi Gurdās was the Muslim historian and mystic, Mohsin Fāni, the author of the Persian ms. *Dabistan-i-Mazāhib*,* who met the sixth Sikh Guru, Hargobind, (1595-1644 A.D.) in person and had several discourses with him on religious subjects. Though his work is not free from errors in details (he

* Translated into English by Gandā Singh (1940). The David and Shean translation (1843) is most inaccurate.

Originally a resident of Persia, Fāni, a great traveller and mystic, later passed many years of his life in Kashmir. Fāni was his pseudonym, his actual name being Sheikh Mohd. Mohsin. His birth-date is believed to be 1615 A.D. and he wrote this book probably round 1645 A.D. He died in 1670. The chapter on Sikhism is only one out of many devoted to various faiths then practised in India. According to Kāhan Singh (Mahān Kosh, P. 1856, f. n.), the author of this book, according to some historians, is Mir Zulfikār Ali alias Mubidshāh.

regales us with many juicy stories about the innocence and the unquestioning faith of the Sikhs and their desire for service and sacrifice in the name of the Guru), in bare essentials his is one of the more dependable works for a historian.

Says he: "*Nānak-Panthis* who are known as Guru-Sikhs or disciples of the Guru have no belief in idols and idol-temples. Nānak is from the Bedis—a sub-caste of the Khatris. In the reign of Emperor Bābur, he became famous. Before the victory of the late Emperor (Bābur), he was a *Modi* to Daulat Khān Lodhi, who was one of the high officials of Ibrahim Khān, Emperor of Delhi and *Modi* is an official incharge of the granary.

"Once a Saint came to him and captivated his heart so much that Nānak, going to his shop, gave away all his own and Daulat Khān's grain he had in the stores. He severed his connection with his wife and children. Daulat Khān was astonished to hear this. As he saw signs of saintliness in Nānak, he refrained from punishing him. Nānak underwent severe austerities. At first, he reduced his food and, after some time, he depended upon drinking a little of cow's milk. After that he lived on *ghee* and then on water. Lastly, he lived on air like those who in Hindustān are called *Pavan Ahāris* or consumers of air alone.*

"Some people became his disciples. Nānak believed in the unity of God as it is laid down in the tenets of Mohammed. He also believed in the doctrine of transmigration. Holding wine and pork unlawful, he abstained from animal food** and enjoined against cruelty to animals. After his death, meat-eating became common among his disciples.†

"Just as Nānak praised the Mohammedans, he also praised the incarnations and the gods and goddesses of the Hindus. ‡ But he knew them all to be the creation (of God) and not the Creator. He

---

* We have already written about it before, doubting the authenticity of this belief. That he must have been very frugal and disciplined in his food-habits, however, must be conceded.

** A hymn of Guru Nānak (Vār Malhār M.1, Ādi-Granth, P. 1289) repudiates this thesis.

† How could this happen unless Nānak enjoined upon his followers to make no distinction as to the nature of the food. As he says in his Word, "only that food is to be avoided which leads to physical pain or thoughts of sin in the mind." (Sri Rāg M. 1).

‡ This too is incorrect, as the Word of Nānak (quoted elsewhere in this chapter) testifies.

denied the doctrines of *Halool* (incarnation of or direct descent from God) and *Iitihad* (direct union of the All-pervading God with any particular body). They say that he had the rosary of the Mohammedans in his hand and the sacred Brāhminical thread round his neck.

"His disciples narrate so many of his miracles which cannot find room in this brief sketch. One of these is that Nānak, having been displeased with the Afghāns, deputed the Moghals over them. So, in the year 932 (Hijri, 1526 A.D.), His Majesty the late Emperor Zahir-ud-din Mohammed Bābur gained victory over the Afghān (King) Ibrāhim.*

"The *Bāni* (Word) of Nānak comprises of prayers, admonitions and counsels and most of his sayings are on the greatness of God Most Holy. And all that is in the language of the Jāts. A Jāt, in the vocabulary of the Panjāb, is a villager and a peasant. Nānak's disciples have no regard for the Sanskrit language......

"The 'sons' (i.e. disciples) of Nānak are in the Panjāb. They are called *Kartāris* (i.e. the worshippers of Kartār, the Creator). But according to the opinion of some, his sons did not inherit his spiritual office. They say that by his order, Guru Angad from the caste of *Trehan* Khatris sat in place of Nānak.........

"They say that in ancient time Bābā Janak was Rājā Janak.** In the opinion of his disciples, Guru Nānak, in a previous life having been Rājā Janak, had accomplished spiritual work along with his temporal Kingdom and called mankind to God......

"I have also heard it said from a Sikh who called Nānak a near-slave of God that when Nānak severed his bodily connection, his Soul reached a point from where issued forth two roads, one leading to

---

* Macauliffe in his "Sikh Religion" narrates a similar though fantastic prophecy having been made about the coming of ferangis by Guru Tegh Bahādur (Vol. IV P. 381), being dissatisfied with the Moghals. *The Purātan Janam Sākhi*, in its Hafizabādi version, also refers to Nānak having blessed Bābur with a long rule for his progeny (PJS, P. 67. f.n.), but this is contradicted by the hymns of *Bābur-vāni* (Āsā M. 1 and Tilang M. 1). It is, however, a fact of history that Nānak's first employer and admirer (whom Bhāi Gurdās includes among his disciples), Nawāb Daulat Khān Lodhi, did invite Bābur to invade India, though being dissatisfied with him later, he turned against him. May be, the earlier association of Nānak with Daulat Khān Lodhi has given currency to this story.

** King Janaka, father of Sitā, the consort of Rāma. Janaka is known for his just rule, piety and spiritual prowess.

heaven and the other to hell. Nānak chose the road to hell and brought the inhabitants of hell out of the infernal region. The God Most High said to him: "These sinners cannot enter heaven. So you should go to the world and liberate this multitude." Nānak consequently came to the world. And now those inhabitants of hell are the multitude of his disciples. And the Guru comes to this world and returns back till all of that sect (i.e. the sinners) obtain salvation. Other than this man, no one is seen among the Sikhs who holds Bābā Nānak to be God......

"During the time of each *Mahal* (Guru), the Sikhs increased till in the reign of Guru Arjan Mal, they became numerous, and there were not many cities in the inhabited countries where some Sikhs were not to be found. There is no restriction among them that a Brāhmin may not become the disciple of a Khatri, for Nānak is a Khatri and no Guru amongst them is from the Brāhmins. Similarly, they placed Khatris under the authority of the Jāts, who belong to the lower caste of the Vaishas, as the big *Masands* † of the Guru are mostly Jāts. And the Sikhs consider the Gurus *Sachā Pādshāh* (the True King) and their agents *Masands*. They call them Rāmdās (or the servants of God) also.

"They have so decided that an *Udāsi*, that is a renouncer of the world, is not praiseworthy. Therefore, some Sikhs of the Guru do agricultural work and some trade, and a multitude takes up service..." etc. etc.

From this long but pertinent quotation, several vital conclusions emerge, namely, that

(i) Nānak believed in the unity and not the plurality of God, nor in incarnations, nor pantheism, nor in the Vedāntic creed "That art Thou." He reviled not any religion in its essence, but its ritual and outer exhibitionism he criticized severely, including identification of God with an idol, and making the inner illumination, humility and piety of conduct the test of the God-awakened, and not the denomination they professed.

† The word is a corrupted form of *Masnad* (Persian), or the seat of authority. This title was bestowed on several Sikhs of repute in various parts of the country, whose function was to collect the offerings of the devout and remit these once every year to the Guru and to preach the gospel to the Guru's disciples. After sometime, they became very powerful and corrupt and so this institution, now held in contempt, was abolished by the tenth Guru.

(ii) Nānak abolished caste, making not only the lowest equal in all respects to the highest in spiritual hope as in secular power, but put the lowest in caste in authority over the highest.

(iii) He brought religion into the ken of everyone—the Brāhmin as much as an untouchable, man as well as woman. Every dress, every kind of diet, all ways that lead not only to the one God but also to one man were sanctified by him.

(iv) Nānak and most of his disciples following him did not consider him to be God, but only "servant of God Most High," and the Guru—the illuminator—refused to enter heaven until all humanity is redeemed.

(v) Nānak's service with Nawāb Daulat Khān—as a Modi (store-keeper) and the reason for its abandonment are confirmed by this author as also the fact that Nānak's relations with Bābur were not casual but intimate, even though no reference is made here to their actual meeting. Another fact of importance that emerges out of this book is that the Moghals brought order in our land and were popular by and large, as the Afghāns were not, due to their tyrannous ways.

III. Another, and the most reliable, account of Nānak's life in its barest outlines is to be culled from the Ādi Granth, compiled by the fifth Guru Arjun, in 1604, whose authenticity has never been challenged. There are in this holy book Guru Nānak's references to Bābur's invasion (perhaps the third invasion, in 1521) and the devastation and bloodshed caused by it in his address to Lālo* (of whom we shall hear more later in this chapter). Then there is the Coronation Ode (or *Vār Sattā te Balwand***), in Rāg Rāmkali, making clear why Nānak

* Mcleod's thesis that 'Lālo' is not a proper name, but only means "beloved" (Guru Nānak and the Sikh Religion, P. 87) is far-fetched. Nowhere in the Ādi Granth is "Lālo" used in this sense, while "Lāl" and "Lālan" are. It is is true, in Bhāi Gurdās (Vār II) or even in the *Purātan Janam Sākhi*, there is no reference to the story connected with Bhāi Lālo, but to doubt what is not included here, and to doubt even more what is included (as the unmistakable reference to Nānak's visit to Meccā) is to destroy all basis of research on the life of Guru Nānak, as on the life of all founders of world religions.

** The internal evidence of their ballad (Vār) reveals that these two brothers, claiming descent from Mardānā, were musicians in the Court of the second Sikh Guru, Angad, though some believe that they were in the employ of the fifth Sikh Guru, Arjun. (Mahān Kosh, Kāhan Singh, P. 448). It is said, they wanted a

passed on his Throne to Angad and a few other relevant hints about Sikh beliefs and practises in his time. The inclusion in the Ādi Granth of a hymn by Mardānā, Nānak's Muslim companion, and direct references to a few other episodes by or about Nānak also add to our knowledge about his life or life of the other Gurus and their times. The eulogy of Guru Nānak by Poet Kal, as included in the Ādi Granth, reveals that by the time of the Granth's compilation (1604 A.D.) the devotees looked upon Guru Nānak as the incarnation of God (he is identified with Rāma and Krishna by the poet). In his autobiographical poem, *Bachittar Nātak*, Guru Gobind Singh makes only observations of spiritual import about Guru Nānak and the only historical references are (i) that he was born into the house of Bedis and (ii) that the Bedis, or thc Veda-learned, derive their lineage from Sri Rāmchandra.

From the Coronation Ode*, however, we come to know that :—

(i) Nānak passed on his Throne, "while yet alive to Angad" in whom burnt the same light, though the "body was different. Lo, the one became the other. Over his head waved the God's 'canopy' (*Chhat* i.e. *Chhatar*) and he occupied the 'Throne' (*takht*) of Guruship. Nānak disinherited his sons, "for they obeyed not the command of the Master:" *so also the other Sikhs*, "whom he put to a hard test."

(ii) The institution of the community-kitchen (*langar)* had become an established fact in the time of Guru Nānak and was continued by the other Gurus.

(iii) Upto the time of the fifth Guru, the emphasis was on meditation on the one God, and *the Way of the Name* was

** F. N. (Contd.)

large sum of money from the Guru to meet the expenses of their daughter's marriage, namely, all the offering made to the Guru on the Baisākhi day, when Sikhs from far and near would come to visit the Guru, which request the Guru conceded, but the offerings not being large enough, they wanted more. The Guru tried to oblige them with a reasonable sum, but they refused to be reconciled and withdrew from the Guru's Court, in spite of the persuasion of various well-known devotees and a visit to their house of the Guru himself. Puffed up by pride in their professional skill, they insulted and abused the house of Nānak. Later, they were struck by pestilence and wanted forgiveness from the Guru which through the medium of Bhāi Ladhā, a devout Sikh, was granted to them. They lived to a ripe old age upto the time of Guru Arjun and wrote a ballad in praise of the first five Gurus which includes some of the salient features of the Sikh philosophy.

* Ādi Granth, P. 966-68.

inculcated among the householders, and woman had come into her own in the Sikh society. The wife of Guru Angad, Khivi—"the noble one"—is mentioned with great reverence as being the support of the earth "who gives enormous shade to the multitude" and "who distributes rich food to the disciples (*langar daulat Vandiey, ras amrit Khir ghiāli).*

(iv) The words of royalty like '*takht*' (Throne), *chhat* (canopy), *Sachā Pādshāh* (True King), *dohi* (Proclamation), *rāj* (rule), *Kharaj* (sword) etc., though used in spiritual terms, have become common usage. This is important to state here because their use later on led to a misconception that there was a conscious departure from the fifth Guru onward from pacificism to building state power.

One more important historical reference to Guru Nānak's life in the Ādi Granth is about the date of Bābur's (third) invasion which made such a powerful impact on his sensitive mind: *ān athatrē, Jān satānvē, hor bhi uthsi mard kā chelā* which is interpreted to mean that the Moghals would come to India in Samvat 1578 (1521, A.D.) and leave in 1597 (i.e. 1540 A.D.) This refers, it is said, to the flight of Humāyun from India (in 1540) and to the emergence of Sher Shāh Suri, liberal Pathān King, who is referred to here as the "Disciple of Man" (*mard ka chelā*)*. It is common knowledge that Sher Shāh established peace disturbed initially by Moghal occupation and his catholicity of outlook and consideration for the poor earned him the gratitude of his subjects, Hindus as well as Muslims.

And now we come to the *Janamsākhis*, or hagiographies, several of which have been unearthed and are available either in manuscript or as published works edited carefully in recent times by Sikh scholars. Some of the more reliable are :—

1. *Purātan Janam Sākhi* or *Vilāyat Vāli* or *Colebrooke's Janam Sākhi.* Presented by Mr. Colebrooke (who found it in the Manuscript form in India) to the East India Co., who deposited it in the India Office Library, London, it was first published in 1883 in Lāhore from a photostat copy, under Government authority, at the request of prominent Sikhs of Lāhore & Amritsar. In 1885, another *Janamsākhi* (similar in

---

* Tilang M.1. For interpretation of this verse, see Bhāi Kāhan Singh's Mahān Kosh (P. 320-21), and also the author's English version of the "Guru-Granth Sahib" (f. n. P. 692). Some scholars are of the opinion that the phrase "Disciple of Man" refers to Guru Gobind Singh, the tenth Sikh Guru.

every respect to the above, with a few verbal changes here and there) was published by Bhāi Gurmukh Singh of the Oriental College, Lāhore, from a manuscript he found at Hāfizābād (now is Pakistān) and called it "*Hāfizābād Vāli Janamsākhi*." Mr. M.A. Macauliffe, author of the "Sikh Religion," based his account of Guru Nānak's life on this manuscript. Bhāi Karam Singh, a modern historian, claims to have seen a copy of it with a bookseller of Lahore dated Samvat 1790 (1733 A.D.) (with illustrations) and another copy made in Samvat 1787(1730 A.D.) which claimed to be the copy of an earlier manuscript of Samvat 1787 (1730 A.D.) written by a scribe of Burhānpur. He also claims to have seen several other copies of it as well—one in Hyderābād (Sind) whose scribe was from Shikārpur (Sind) & another at Bahāwalpur. Mr. Mulk Rāj Bhallā had seen a copy of it whose scribe was from Burdwān and is dated Samvat 1824 (1767 A.D.)

As this *Vilāyātvāli Jānamsākhi* seems to be the oldest record and, therefore, more reliable—of Guru Nānak's life—it is but proper to discuss its date of origin and contents in some detail.

First, as to its date of composition. As there are hymns of the fifth Guru, Arjun (died 1606), included in its text, it is fair to conclude that it was first written out about 80 to 100 years after the demise of Guru Nānak.* The only objection to this thesis is that once Guru Arjun compiled the Adi Granth and separated the apocryphal literature from the genuine one, it was hardly possible for any devout Sikh to have taken the liberty of incorporating apocryphal hymns ascribed to Guru Nānak, as this Janamsākhi does on occasions. Thus, one can fairly surmise that though this hagiography was written out in the time of Guru Arjun, it must have been before the compilation of the Ādi Granth (1604 A.D.), as its spellings also differ from those of the authorised version of the Granth.

The writer uses the *lagas* and *matras* even in his prose version as employed in the writing of old Panjābi which makes it a genuinely old manuscript. The margins are drawn with hand and the caligraphy is inartistic in an age known for this art. But, as some of the phrases are confusing and letters and words are either missing or mis-spelt which confusion is not as apparent in the *Hāfizābād Vāli Janamsākhi*, it appears the manuscript of the India Office Library is not the original one, but a copy of the original (which has so far not been traced) or a copy from a copy.

Again, this is a manuscript on which all the later biographies of Guru Nānak were based, as for instance, the supurious *Bāle Vāli*

Janamsākhi (see below) which repeats verbatim some of the Sākhis (episodes) included in the *Purātan Janamsākhi*. Even Mehervān draws upon it for facts, if not for their interpretation.

And, what is most, this is a manuscript which though repeating some of the miracles attributed to Guru Nānak yet, on the whole, keeps it free from the merely miraculous and is nearest to the original doctrine of the Master.

The incidents connected with the life of Guru Nānak's (dateless) travels after he abandons service at Sultānpur, as given in this biography, are:—

First Journey:

(1) Tulambā (Multān; conversion of Sheikh Sajjan), though in this biography, the place-name is not given.

(2) Pānipat (discourse with Shāh Sharaf).

(3) Delhi (brought a dead elephant to life, and met Sultān Brahm (Ibrāhim? Beg).

(4) Meeting with Sheikh Wajid.

(5) Banāras (discourse with Pandit Chatur Dās)

(6) Nānakmatā (discourse with the Yogis)

(7) Kāmrup (Assam: emacipation of Nur Shāh)

(8) Back to Talwandi, twelve (?) years after leaving Sultānpur, and meeting with the parents.

(9) Goindwāl (healing of a leper)

(10) Saidpur (Eminabād; arrested by Bābur)

(11) Lāhore (emancipation of Dunichand, the millionaire)

(12) Back to Talwāndi.

(13) Founds Kartārpur.

All through this journey, he is accompanied by Mardānā, the Muslim low-caste drummer.

Second Journey.

Guru Nānak's second journey is to the South of India right upto Ceylon and he is accompanied by Saido and Gheho, according to one version, and according to others by Saido and Siho or Saidā, Gheo and Siho or Saido, Siho and Mardānā. Conversion of Rājā Shivnābh of Ceylon is the main incident of interest in this journey (see below).

Third Journey

His third journey is to the north acccompanied by Hassu, a *Lohār* (blacksmith) and Sihān, a *chhimba* (calico-printer), which takes him to:

(1) Kashmir (discourse with Pandit Brahm Dās)

(2) Mount Sumeru (discourse with the Siddhas)

(3) Back to Kartārpur.

(4) Achal Vatālā (discourse with the Yogis).

Fourth Journey

Is to Meca (discourse with Qāzi Rukundin),

Fifth Journey

Is to Gorakh-hatri, near Peshāwar, a popular centre of the Nāth Yogis.

Back to Kartārpur, he puts his sons and disciples to severe tests and finding a devout disciple, Lehnā, as the genuine coin, passes his spiritual Throne on to him, and calls him Angad.

Passes his Book of hymns also on to his successor (P. 114).

Breathes his last on Asu Vadi 10, Samvat 1595 (1538 A.D.).

The date of Nānak's birth as given in this manuscript is the 3rd day of the light-half of the moon in Vaisākh of Samvat 1526 (April 15, 1469 A.D.). He goes to school at the age of seven to read and write the 35 letters (of Gurmukhi, as Nāgri letters are 52) with a Pandit (name not given) and at the age of nine with a Māulvi (name not given) to study *Torki* (Persian ?). He marries at the age of twelve and has two sons, Sri Chand and Lakhmi Dās, before proceeding to Sultānpur.

It seems odd that this biography omits the account of Bhāi Lālo, and Guru Nānak's visit to Baghdād, Jagannāth Puri and Hassan Abdāl (Panjā Sāhib).

As we have already seen, the name of the incident connected with the life of Bhāi Lālo is not mentioned even by Bhāi Gurdās, nor the incidents at Puri or Panjā Sāhib.

II. And, now, we come to the Janamsākhi of Meharvān, nephew of the fifth Guru, Arjun, and the only son of Prithi Chand of whose wild hostility to his younger brother we will have much to say in the text of this book. Though this hagiography is full of fantastic details (as whenever Guru Nānak is called into the presence of God), and apocryphal hymns composed by Meharvān himself are ascribed to Nānak, his general approach to the life and teachings of the Master is one of supreme devotion.*

---

* On several occasions, Meharvān (1581-1640 A.D,) excels every other interpreter of the Sikh faith in the mystic interpretation of the Guru's Word. Even if we do not accept as historically true some of the incidents narrated by him, we cannot but be inspired by the insights he offers into the mysteries of the Guru's Word. Which shows that he was a man of profound spiritual learning and experience. At times, his explanations of the Sikh theology are relevant to modern thinking than of some of his more orthodox contemporaries as when he defines the nature of heaven and hell. ("He who commits sins, goes to hell and he who practises virtue goes to heaven. The world engages itself in the deeds of hell and heaven, and so the sinners are born in the world in the lower echelons of society and the virtuous in the higher ones. This is the way of the Veda. But the way of Wisdom is different, for the wise one commits neither good nor bad of his own volition, and prides not on his self nor believes in the doctrine of Karma, but in the Will of God who is the dispenser of both good and evil. Heaven and hell are only for those who believe that they did what they did. But he who is detached from both good and evil and acts as God bids him do will belong only to God and God to him." (P. 145).

His original name was Manohar Dās and according to Bhāi Santokh Singh (Gur-Partāp Surya Granth, Rās 2, Ansu 29, P. 1763), the fifth Guru was very fond of him and treated him "like his own son." He was an extremely devout person, given to much meditation, "reading the Japu of Guru Nānak 21 times in the day and prostrating before the Book after each reading." He was married and had three sons. Bhāi Gurdās who has in his Vārs (see Vār 26) denounced all detractors of the Gurus, particulary Srichand and Lakhmi Dās (sons of Guru Nānak), Dāsu and Dātu (sons of Guru Angad), Mohan and Mohri (sons of Guru Amar Dās), and Prithi chand and Mahādev (sons of Guru Ram Dās), has not at all mentioned the name of Maharvān. Kesar Singh Chhibar, author of Bansālvināmā, however, suggests that Meharvān also compiled a Granth of his own in opposition to the one compiled by Guru Arjun, in which he included only the hymns of the first four Gurus but not of the fifth one, the inference deducible therefrom being that he did not acknowledge Arjun as the fifth Guru. However, he is supported by no other evidence. Bhāi Santokh Singh makes no

Some of the episodes which are not included in the *Purātan Janam Sākhi*, but find a conspicuous place in Meharvān's version, are :—

First Journey :

From Sultānpur (where according to this *Janamsākhi*, Guru Nānak went at the age of thirty-five years, six and a half months and stayed for two years), the Guru, accompanied by Mardānā proceeded to Delhi, at the time of Salim Shāh* Pathān, (but there is no refe-

---

* *F. N. Contd.*

mention of it and in the ms. called *Goshtian Meharvān*, Guru Arjun's name as the fifth Sikh Guru is mentioned in succession to the previous four Gurus.

Dabistān-i-Mazāhib, a contemporary work, says clearly that "Meharvān called himself a Bhakta" (and not Guru), though when the sixth Guru, Hargobind, was put into prison by Jehāngir, Meharvān used to discourse to the Sikh congregations on spiritual matters, thus giving currency to the misconception that he had become a Guru. In fact, on the very first page of his Janamsākhi, Meharvān styles himself as the "sevak (servant) of Nānak."

Apart from the fact that Meharvān being so closely related to Guru Arjun, was well conversant with the Sikh historical lore, his biography is a store-house of folk cultural traditions as practised or believed in those days. As one of the oldest styles of Panjābi (Lehndi and Mājhi) and Hindvi prose interspersed liberally with Persian and Arabic vocabulary, it is a most valuable document. The prose has a natural and yet a disciplined rythm. Its vocabulary and imagery like those of the *Purātan Janam Sākhi* have not only an appeal for the ear and mind, but more so for the soul. The details in which this biography revels and the mysteries of the spirit it unravels move even the most inhibited mind. It has reason in it, besides faith and high imagination, a strong dramatic undertone, and a vast knowledge particularly of the Hindu scriptures and mythology, besides the ways of the world and even the underworld. His verbal pictures are superb, whether he is detailing a ceremony or an event or a spiritual non-verbal evperience of the soul.

At various places (for instance, the dialogue between Nānak and his wife at the time of Nānak's departure for Sultānpur, P. 74), Meharvān is so close to the *Purātan Janam Sākhi* in his phraseology and argument that, it seems, he has based his factual data (though not always his spiritual interpretation of the Guru's Word) on the former.

If Meharvān's version was written out before the 1st Vār of Bhāi Gurdās, as is indirectly testified by the Janam Sākhi of Mani Singh (P. 1), then the *Purātan Janam Sākhi* being more austere in its details, must have preceded even Meharvān's.

* It could not have been the period of Salim Shāh (son of Sher Shāh Suri), because before his rule (1545-1553 A.D.), the Guru had breathed his last.

rence to the dead elephant being revived, only that from the king's kitchen alms were then being distributed to the poor, though the king was a tyrant).

Hardwār, Prayāg (Allāhābād), preaches against hattha yoga and giving pain to the body to secure 'release'.

Banāras (discourse with the Pandits on pure and impure food, virtue and sin, heaven and hell, and against caste and mere book-knowledge).

Meeting and spiritual discourse with Rājā Harināth (no place given).

*Meeting with Kabir.**
Enters again into the presence of God.
Hājipur, Patnā (discourse on the nature of God).
Ayodhyā (dialogue with God).

Jagannāth Puri (meeting with Rājā Bharthari†, but no mention of the 'Ārti' incident).

For three years, the Guru was in eastern India and then he proceeded to the South (P. 203), visiting Rameshwaram (uttered the *Ārti*) and from there to a Vilāyat *whose language he did not understand* (P. 217), and from thence to another place *with a different Rājā* and *speaking a different tonuge*, but *all believers of one and the same God*.

Meets with Kalyug.

Then, he goes far into a 'land of darkness,' then on the sea-side; faces a mountain-like thing, with the body of glass (i. e. impermanent), a burning torch in hand and raw meat in his mouth. It is the country of the Rākshasas (it appears, due to their dark colour and Shāktic beliefs like human sacrifice, etc. it was called the land of Rākshasas, as the Āryans did before, as stated in the Rig Veda).

---

* If the dates of Kabir's birth (1399 A.D.) and death (1518 A.D.) are as accepted by most of his followers, there is a possibility of their having met at Banāras, but no historical record suggests this thesis, nor any other *Janam Sākhi* or chronicle dealing with the life of Kabir. Recent researches, however, reveal that Kabir lived only 50 years and died in 1450 A. D., i. e. 19 years before Nānak's birth. [Kabir by Dr. P.N. Tiwāri, N.B.T., P. 47]

† He should not be confused with the ancient author of "Vairāg Shatak" etc.

Then he goes all through the southern country or *Sadik Desa* (the land of Belief?) and lands in the country of the thugs. (The incident of Sajjan, the thug, given in the *Purātan Janam Sākhi* as having happened at Tulambā, near Multān, is repeated here).

(Discourse with God).
Meeting with Rajā Jagannāth of the South.

Meeting with Vaishnavas, who greet him always with "Rām-Rām" or "Jai Rām-Krishan."

Discourse on death in another place in the South.
(Meeting again with God, and again).
Ujjaiṇ
Vijhāvani (Vindhya mountains?)
On the bank of the Narbadā river.
Again meets with the thugs.
Ujjain (discourse with Rājā Bhārthari).
(Meets again with God).
Meets several Rājās on the way.
Bikāner.
Sorath Desa (Saurashtra?)

After five years in the South, *Nānak proceeds back to Sultanpur via Mathurā (spiritual discourses).*
Kurukshetra (discourse against pilgrimages, but **not** *on meat-eating).*
Sultānpur (meets with Nawāb Daulat Khān and has long discourses with him on spiritual matters).

Second Journey :

Mount Sumeru (dialogue with the Siddhās).
(Dialogue with God).
Gorakh Hatri (Dialogue with a Yogi).
Multān (dialogues with the grandson of Pir Bahāvdi(n) (and others).
(Dialogues with God, a faqir and a Mullāh).

Meccā (accompanied by two Muslim faqirs, Rahim (ud) di (n) and Karim (-ud) di (n); stays there 12 months. No mention is made here of the well-known incident of Guru

Nānak having spread his feet towards the Kaabā or of the Kaabā moving to whichever direction his feet were dragged. The first of these incidents, however, is narrated in a mosque in Multān. (P. 449).

Hinglāj

The Guru returns after a stay of three years in the western countries and on this journey also visits *Rome*, *Shām* (Syriā), Kābul, Peshāwar, and reaches Saidpur-Saloi, accompanied by Mardānā.

Tillā Bālgudāi (dialogue with Yogis, Bābur's arrival and massacre of Yogis and others is mentioned, but not of Nānak's meeting with Bābur).

Talwandi (meeting with the parents). Then, travelling through Mana Gopāla, Jodhki, Khānpur, Mithā Arāin, Satgharā, Mājhā, he reaches—

Pāk Pattan (Meeting with Sheikh Brahm or Ibrāhim).

Dipālpur

Khokhovāl

Kiri Pathānān

Pakhoki Randhāwi (meeting with Karoriā) and founds Kartārpur.

There are, says the copyist of this ms., 14 *Sākhis* missing in his version, and he has narrated only 153 *Sākhis*, though there are according to him, 167 Sakhis in the *Pothi Sach Khan*d (containing Guru Nānak's biography). According to Meharvān, moving out of Sultānpur in 1506 A.D., at the age of 37½ years, the Guru is back after 14 years to settle down at Kartārpur in 1520 A.D. (the year of Bābur's sack of Saidpur).

The Guru, according to this version, was 3 years in the east, five years in the south, one year in the north, 3 years in the west, i.e., 12 years in all. Perhaps, he took two years initially in wandering through the Panjāb on his way to the eastern country.

As would be seen, this version makes no mention of the Guru's visit to Kāmrup (Āssām), Baghdād (though Rome, Shām, or Syriā and Kābul are mentioned in passing), or Hassanabdāl (Panjā Sāhib). And Ceylon, though indicated, is not mentioned by name.

Nānak's date of birth is given as the 3rd day of the light half of the moon-month in Vaisākh, samvat 1526 vikrami, at Chāhal Vālē (though at other places, he mentions only Talwandi as his place of birth, as in the Khālsā College version and also in *gost* 17 of the Damdamā version) in the house of Kālu; of Bedi Khatri caste, and resident of Rāi Bhoē Ki Talwandi. His mother's name is given as Ṭipārā. Rāi Bhoē is the landlord of the village Talwandi. At the age of 7, he starts reading with a Pāndhā (Hindu Pandit, name not given). One year later, he is put to school with a Mullā (*Makhdum*) to study *Torki*. He is an unusually intelligent student and in a few days, "grasped arithmetic (*Jama-Kharach*), account-keeping of an office (*daftar dā hiseb*) and became well conversant with Persian, Arabic and Turkish."

At the age of 9, is arranged the sacred-thread ceremony, at the age of 15-16 his marriage with Ghumi, daughter of Mulā, Chonā Khatri of Batālā. Two sons are born to him, Lakhmi Das and Sri Chand, when he is twenty-seven and twenty eight years of age respectively, at Talwandi.

At the age of 35 years and 6½ months, he goes to Sultānpur and gets into the employ of Daulat Khān Lodhi on the recommendation of his sister's husband, Jairām, an Uppal Khatri (already in the service of the Nawāb), as a store-keeper. He stays here only for two years and then ventures out on his journeys.

III. The three later accounts of Guru Nānak's life, are: Santokh Singh's *Nānak Parkash*, Mani Singh's *Gyān Ratnāwali* and *Bhāi Bālā's Janamsākhi*. Bhāi Bālā's biography need not detain us here, as firstly it was produced at a much later date and secondly there is so much of the imaginative and the miraculous in the episodes given here that they are better classified as poetry or mythology than history. All internal evidence goes to prove that Bālā either did not exist (Bhāi Gurdās does not mention his name among the Sikhs of Guru Nānak detailed in his Vār 11, nor does any of the *Purātan Janam Sākhis* refer to him even by implication), or if he did, the version in his name was written out in comparatively recent times, that is not earlier than the later part of the eighteeth century. Its language and mythological approach to the life of Guru Nānak betray its recent origin. It sounds strange that (as his Janamsākhi points out in the very beginning) he did not know who the successor of Guru Nānak was, nor Guru Angad had ever heard of his association with his Master! It cannot also be believed that Bālā knew more about the details of

Guru Nānak's life than Guru Angad himself, who was for several years serving him with unquestioning devotion in the later part of the Master's life. The whole story seems to be a concoction to establish its bonafides. Several episodes in this book, of which several versions are now available in print, are, however, either a verbatim or a condensed copy of the *Purātan* tradition.

As Bhāi Santokh Singh (1788-1843 A.D.) whose poetic faculty is comparable only to Tulsidās's, bases his whole argument on Bālā, as a historian he too cannot be taken too seriously. Moreover, his *magnum opus* was written out in 1823, that is, about three centuries after Guru Nānak's demise. And, as is very obvious from the tone and the atmosphere created throughout by this venerable poet, his objective is more to evoke the feelings of worship and awe by invoking the miraculous and the spiritual in the life of the founder of his faith than to be true to the bare facts of his mundane life.

As for Bhāi Mani Singh's Janamsākhi, it is apparent from its very beginning that it was not written by him but uttered and then taken down by one of his hearers. Bhāi Mani Singh (died 1737 A.D.) who was a devout Sikh of the tenth Guru and, after his demise, became the custodian of the Hari-mandir (later known as the Golden Temple) at Amritsar, and a martyr, is believed also to have compiled the Book of the Tenth Master *(Daswin Pādshāhi Dā Granth* or the *Dasam Granth)*. He it was to whom the Tenth Guru is said to have dictated the whole of the Ādi Granth at Talwandi Sābo when access to the original copy was denied to him by its custodians. His is, therefore, a venerable name as an exponent of the Sikh doctrine and his *Sikhān di Bhagat Mālā* (or, the life-stories of the devotees of the first Sikh Guru whose names are mentioned by Bhāi Gurdās in his Vār 11) is considered to be an authentic exposition of the Sikh way of life. Its style resembles that of his Janamsākhi; and the scholarly way in which the Sikh doctrine is expounded in the latter title leave little doubt in one's mind as to its association with a man as learned and devout as Bhāi Mani Singh. But, the fantastic (apart from the spiritual) is so much mixed up with the factual that it is difficult to accept the whole as authentic history. Malcolm, in his "Sketch and History and present state of the Sikhs" (1812), however, bases his account of Guru Nānak on this as well as earlier records, which shows that its authenticity had come to be accepted by then. Whatever is not recorded in the earlier manuscripts and first comes to light in this book or in similar other works we have made use of after careful sifting. Sarup Dās Bhallā's Mahimā Parkāsh in verse (1776 A.D.), (*) Ghulam Hussain's *Siyar-ul-Mutākhrin* (1785 A.D.), Sewā Dās's *Parchian* in prose (1588 A.D.) and Bhangu Rattan Singh's *Panth Parkāsh* in verse (written in 1809 A.D. and published in 1841 A.D) also we have drawn upon, besides other secondary sources quoted in the footnotes.

There is a *Mahimā Parkāsh Vārtak* (in prose) as well, which is larger in size than the one is verse, but its authorship is still in dispute, though modern scholars, like Dr. Ganda Singh and Bhāi Vir Singh ascribe its authorship to Kirpāl Singh Bhallā and Bawā Kirpāl Singh respectively. The dates of Nānak's birth and death are given differently in the two mss. Its date of writing is variously given as 1741 and 1773 A. D., and is a beautiful specimen of Panjābi prose of the 18th century. From internal evidence, it seems to be based on the *Kavitā* version which is definitely older, but strangely enough, it omits the stories of Sajjan the thug and Guru Nānak's meeting with Rājā Shivnābh (of Ceylon). It also states that a competitor to Guru Nānak's throne alongwith Bhāi Lehnā was Bābā Buddhā. Also that the Guru's body was cremated on the banks of the Rāvi but that no remains were found "when a search was made for the ashes to be consigned to the Gangā." No dispute between the Hindus and Muslims over his dead body is indicated here. A ms. copy (No. SHR: 2308) copied in 1932 from the one in the possession of Bhāi Vir Singh can be seen at the Khālsā College, Amritsar library.

CHAPTER IV

GURU NANAK'S TRAVELS

WALKING THROUGH THE WILDERNESS, along with Mardānā, Nānak covered much territory to the south-west of Panjāb. But he stopped nowhere. Whenever a habitation stood on the way, he passed it by. He would pick wild berries or fruit and satisfy his hunger. But, his companion grumbled that he was treating him to no feast as was usual for them who accompanied the pious. But, the Guru reprimanded him, saying that if a person chose the way of God, he should be self-dependent and not live on the charity of the community. But Mardānā, it seems, was not at all convinced of the reasonableness of his Master's advice.

One day, Nānak allowed him to visit a habitation. There, when it became known that a man of God had entered their village, men and women swarmed round him asking for his blessings. Mardānā blessed the folks profusely, and they brought him not only delicious foods of various kinds, but also offered him robes of silk, wool and cotton, and also scents of many varieties. Mardānā was very pleased at this consideration, and, carrying his bundle, hastened back to the Guru's repose in the wilderness. When Nānak saw his companion loaded with so many gifts, he smiled, and asked why he had disobeyed his command. Mardānā felt uneasy, but said he could not disappoint his devotees, and so he carried the bundle along. Nānak asked him to throw it away, which he did with a heavy heart. Then, Mardānā asked him whether what one gave away, in charity, to the needy reached the Guru and pleased God. Nānak said, "Yes, to feed the hungry and cover the naked brings God's mercy upon the giver, but one must give out of one's honest earnings"; and "he who receives it must receive only in accordance with his need and no more."*

As they travelled along, on the way, they came across a pious-looking thug, Sajjan (meaning gentleman) by name.† He was sitting by the road-side, rosary in hand, his catty eyes opening only occasionally to look at the passing travellers. He had not only built a mosque, being a Muslim Sheikh, but also a temple for the Hindus and he would not allow any traveller of whatever community to pass by without offering him hospitality. He would plead with him to stay for the night, treat him with utmost courtesy, and then as the night grew, rob him of all he had and cut his throat and throw his dead body into the well nearby. In the morning, he would come and sit as if in a trance, reciting the beads of a rosary, waiting patiently for the next victim of his foul designs.

When he saw Guru Nānak, he said to his followers, "Treat him well. This seems to be a rich person. His face sparkles with affluence." And so they did. But, when night came and they asked him to retire, Nānak said he would first sing a song in praise of God and then go to sleep. When all his men had gathered, with Sajjan seated in front of Nānak, Mardānā took out his rebeck and applied his deft fingers to its strings to emit pious notes in Rāg Suhi. And Nānak sang :

"Bright sparkles the vessel of bronze, but rub it and its inner soil comes off. They who call themselves our friends aren't so, unless they stand by us in the Court of God where all our accounts are settled.

---

* The "*Purātan Janam Sākhi*" here inserts erroneously a hymn of the fourth Master. We have, therefore, based the reply of Nānak on his own words as given at various places in the Ādi Granth.

† This place is identified by most Sikh scholars as Tulambā, near Multān, in the south-west of Panjāb (M. K. P. 433) and is now called Makhdumpur. At nearly a mile's distance, there is a Gurdwārā in the memory of Guru Nānak. *Purātan janam Sākhi* does not name any place, and Meharvān's account places this episode late in Guru Nānak's life in his journey towards the south, on the banks of the river Narbadā (P. 294) though the factual details are about the same as in *Purātan*, and even the words put in the mouth of the thugs (Sajjan is mentioned nowhere) are an echo of the *Purātan Janam Sākhi*, though the hymn said to have been uttered by the Guru at this time is different from the one given in the *Purātan* version. Bhāi Mani Singh's *Janamsākhi* places this episode (it names Sajjan, the thug, also) outside Hastināpur (Delhi?), from where, according to to this source, the Guru proceeded to Kāshi (Banāras or Vārānasi).

What worth is a ruin, even if it be plastered and decorated from without? The cranes live by the river-banks, like the devotees, but their eyes are set ever on the victims of their never-ending hungers. The Simmal-tree is full of leaves and flowers and fruit, but its fruit has no flavour, and the flowers have no fragrance, and the leaves give no shade.

"The blind man carries the bundle on his head and walks up a mountain, steep and of long distance, but how can he scale the heights without eyes? O Nānak, of no avail is our cleverness and our feigned goodness. Only His love saves and cuts the fetters off our feet."

When Sajjan heard this heart-searching hymn from Nānak, something stirred within him. His Soul was awakened, and, much ashamed at his foul past, he fell at the feet of Nānak, hugged them warmly, and wept, saying: "O Master, you have found me out. Now tell me, how am I to be redeemed? How are my sins to be forgiven?" Nānak said, "It is only in two ways that God forgives the past of a man: to confess one's guilt and to expiate for them." Sajjan cried, "I confess to my shame that I have robbed many people, and cut their throats and amassed a fortune thereby, pretending all the while my devotion to God. But, how am I now to expiate for my sins?" The Guru replied: "Bring out all you have and distribute it among the poor and the holy in the name of God." Sajjan, in a moment of supreme transformation, did all that he was bidden to, and thereafter became a great devotee of God. Nānak made him the first high priest of his mission. Everyone who heard of this remarked, "Nānak has indeed performed a miracle!"

From here, Nānak and his companion went to Sayyadpur (now called Eminābād, in the district of Gujranwala) and stayed at the house of a low-caste carpenter, Lālo by name.* This soon became the

* This episode is not given either in the *Purātan Janam Sākhi*, or by Mehervān or Mani Singh. Nor does Bhāi Gurdās mention the name of Lālo among the devout Sikhs of Guru Nānak in his Vār 11. This has led Macleod *(Guru Nānak and Sikh Religion, P. 87)* to conclude that the episode is "most improbable". He has even tried to render the words "Ve Lālo" (Ādi Granth, Pp. 722-23) as "O beloved", thus contradicting the traditionally-accepted belief that the hymn is addressed to the Guru's disciple called Lālo. As we have said earlier (p.25 f.n.), in the whole of the Ādi Granth, the word 'Lālo' is nowhere employed to mean 'O beloved', as 'lāl' and 'lālan' are. The episode (commemorated in the form of a Gurdwārā) also does not contradict the Guru's philosophy, if we separate the factual from the miraculous part of it. It is first mentioned in Bālā's *Janam Sākhi*. As for its

talk of the town that a holy man of Kshatriya descent had accepted the hospitality of an untouchable. This talk also reached the ears of Malik Bhāgo, a local official of high caste. He had arranged a great feast to which he invited holy men from far and near. Hearing that Nānak was a great devotee of God, he called him also to partake of his food. But Nānak refused to participate, saying:

"There are the lowest of the low-born and the lower still and the least of these. Nānak is only a companion of them and has no desire to compete with the great."

The Malik was greatly incensed at this reply and asked his servants to force Nānak into his presence if he would not come of his own accord. The Guru seeing the haughtiness of his emissaries at first refused to budge, but then thinking that this might be a good occasion also to teach him a lesson, agreed to go. When he reached the palatial residence of his host and was offered food, he declined to eat. When asked why he was insulting the Chief thus in the presence of the whole assembly when he had felt no qualms in partaking of a low-caste carpenter's food, the Guru replied calmly: "Your food reeks of blood, while that of Lālo, the carpenter, tastes like honey and milk." When asked how he came to this impertinent conclusion, the Guru replied: "Lālo earns with the sweat of his brow and out of it offers whatever little he can to the wayfarer, the poor and the holy, and so it tastes sweet and wholesome, but you being without work, squeeze blood out of the people through bribery, tyranny and show of authority. Such food cannot but be stained with the blood of the weak, the innocent and the poor,"*

Bhāgo was much ashamed at this and became speechless. News travelled like wild fire in the countryside that a Guru of men had appeared who could challenge caste and authority with a fearlessness unknown before.

F. N. Contd.

omission in the *Purātan Janam Sākhi*, we must take note of the fact that the episode of Baghdād which is so elaborately detailed in Bhāi Gurdās is also omitted in the former. And, the tradition in regard to Bhāi Lālo is as strong as the prevalent birth-date (Kārtik) of Guru Nānak.

* According to Bālā, a miracle was performed by Guru Nānak at this place. When challenged by the arrogant Malik to prove his charge, the Guru took the food from his house in his one hand and from that of Lālo in the other, and when he squeezed the two, blood issued forth from the former and milk from the latter. (Also see Macauliffe, Vol. 1, Pp. 43-44).

From there, the Guru proceeded to Kurukshetra, a great centre of Hindu pilgrimage, where a big fair was being held on the occasion of the solar eclipse.

It is said that here, a follower of his offered him deer-meat to eat. The Guru who had never made any distinction between one kind of food and another and took whatever was offered to him, did not refuse the courtesies of his devotee. And, he allowed him to roast it for his food.* The local people who normally abhorred meat-eating, more so on 'auspicious' days like those of the lunar and solar eclipses, were much incensed at this. Whoever heard of this sacrilege, became furious. Some of them ran towards him with their clubs; others wanted to stone him to death. When Nānak saw an excited mob coming upon him, he asked them: What makes you rush upon me like mad? What wrong have I done you?" Looking at his serene, gentle face, and his soothing voice, the mob was exercised all the more. "You cook meat at a place of pilgrimage and on an auspicious day, and, then, you plead innocence as if nothing has happened?" Nānak replied: "Only they who have never seen flesh are exercised at its sight, but why should man who's conceived in flesh, and is himself nothing but flesh and bones; who is fed on the mother's breasts, who is with the tongue of flesh; whose mouth is of flesh, who marries flesh, who produces flesh and breathes in flesh. Is there a man or woman who deals not in flesh?" †

His detractors persisted that even when man dealt with flesh and was conceived in and made up of flesh, it was a sin to eat it. The Guru replied: "Do we not all take water from which springs all life? It gives life to man, as to the animal and to vegetation. Shall we

---

* This episode, again, is not mentioned in *Purātan Janam Sākhi* or in Mehervān's version. It first occurs in Bhāi Mani Singh's *Gyān Ratnāvali* (P. 123) which mentions Nānak having been engaged here in debate with a Pandit, called Nānu Chand. The deer-meat was, according to this version, brought to him as an offering by a Prince and his consort, who, having been dispossessed of their realm, came to him for a blessing. In the dialogue that followed with the Pandit, he is not only convinced of Nānak's logic, but persuades also the fellow-Brāhmins, basing his argument on the Veda, the Purānas and even the Qurān, saying that even the Hindu gods could be propitiated since the earliest times only through *yagnas* in which meat was invariably served, and that it has been the *dharma* of the Kashatriya Kings since ages to hunt. If, argued the Pandit, such activities of the rulers were impious, why did the Brāhmins accept their offerings, etc.? (P. 128)

† *Ādi Granth* (*Vār Malhār*, P. 1289)

then shun water because it produces life, is life? And, don't the plants have life? They breathe, they love, they live and they die. And, what is one to say of those who do not eat animal flesh, but devour men and suck their blood?"*

Most of his detractors knowing him to be lost left him in disgust, while some others, more sensitive, were convinced that what he was saying was after all not without reason. Then the Guru addressed the converts thus: "O men, I do not eat for relish of the palate, but take whatever is offered to me in good faith by one who has earned with the sweat of his brow. It would be ungodly for me to refuse to eat what comes to me in God's Will."

From here, Guru Nānak proceeded to Pānipat, where a great Muslim Sufi, Abu Ali Qalandar, also known as Shāh Sharaf† had established a spiritual centre in the late thirteeth century. Here he met with one of his descendants also called by the same name. At first, the Sufi Saint wanted to know why Nānak was wearing the dress of a householder, so unusual for a faqir, and why he had not shaven his head. Nānak answered: "It is the mind that one must shave, not one's head. And to be humble like the dust is the true way to shave one's mind." As for his dress, he explained: "One must abandon pleasures and egotism and surrender one's head to one's God. Then, whatever dress one wears is sacred."

Nānak continued: "One must submit to the instruction of the Wise, and to cherish God in the heart should be the gown and the cap of the holy. He who holds his mind and relishes the fare of both pleasure and pain alike, and lives, composed in utter poise, for him, it matters not what dress he wears."

When asked to what sect and caste he belonged and how he lived, Nānak replied, "I belong to the sect of the Right Way. My caste is that of fire and wind. I live in the manner of the tree and

---

* *Ādi Granth*, Ibid.

† Shāh Sharaf died on August 30, 1332 A.D. Originally a resident of Persia, he had settled at Pānipat probably late in the preceding century. It is one of his descendants, also called by the same name (as is usual in such orders) that Guru Nānak must have met. It is erroneous for the writer of the *Purātan Janam Sākhi* to indicate the ensuing dialogue as having been held with Shāh Sharaf, the founder of the House. The name of the disciple who first met the Guru outside the town and conveyed the presence of Nānak to Shāh Sharaf is given in the *Purātan Janam Sākhi* as Sheikh Tatihar.

the earth, for, like them, I endure being cut or dug into. Like a river, I care not whether one throws flowers into me or dust. Like the sandalwood, I consider that alone to be living with is fragrant."

His host then asked him what a dervish should be like. Nānak answered: "He who while alive is dead; while he wakes is asleep, and who knowingly gets robbed of himself. He alone is a dervish who welcomes both joy and pain, alike, and sorrows not, nor is angered, and covets nothing and has no pride. Who sits composed in God, hearing nought but what God utters and beholding Him alone in everything that is, and is not."

Shāh Sharaf was so pleased at these replies that he bowed at his feet and kissed his hands, saying: "O man of God; to question thee was a sacrilege on my part. Even to behold thee is to behold the vision of God."*

And, now the Guru proceeded towards Delhi. On the outskirts of the imperial city, it is said, an elephant belonging to the emperor had died. Its keepers were very sad, fearing loss of employment. When they heard of the Guru's arrival, they entreated him to bring it back to life. But the Guru said, "Life and death are in the hands of God. No man can intervene in His Mysterious Play. It is best to rejoice in whatever comes from Him. So long as there's life in man, one prays for the best to one's God; but once He wants to take life, man should submit to His Will cheerfully."†

---

*The words quoted throughout this episode are from the *Purātan Janam Sākhi* and not from the Ādi Granth.

†This version is based on Guru Nānak's sayings incorporated in the Ādi Granth, as interpreted in Mani Singh's version of this account. (P. 164-65). While Mani Singh's version does, (though after a great deal of argument and hesitancy), Meharvān's account of the Guru's Delhi visit does not mention the miracle associated with this story by the *Purātan Janam Sākhi* (P. 114-15). The *Purātan Janam Sākhi* version narrates that the Guru, taking pity on the *mahouts*, brought the dead elephant back to life. When the King, whose name is given as Brahm Beg (Ibrāhim Beg, according to the Hafizābādi version), heard of this, he came to see the Guru and asked him if it was he who had resurrected the elephant. The Guru replied: "It is God who gives life to all and it is He again who takes it back. I have only prayed for its revival." At this stage, the King asked him to perform another miracle and make the elephant die, which the Guru did. When, however, he was asked to revive it again, the Guru replied, "Your Majesty, the iron when put in fire becomes red-hot and if some one touches it, he only burns his fingers. Similarly, the *faqirs*, who are inflamed by God's fire, are not to be played

P. T. O.

From here, the Guru proceeded to Hardwār.* On the banks of the holy Gangā, he saw many people throwing water towards the east. When questioned, they said they were offering water to their dead ancestors in the high heavens for the peace of their Souls. Nānak smiled, and without a moment's hesitation, started throwing water towards the west. The devout were much amused at this unusual gesture of his, so they asked him what he was doing. Nānak replied: "I come from the north-western part of India. I keep a farm in my birth-place. I seek to water it from here, for I wonder if there has been sufficient rainfall since I came!" The pilgrims laughed at his innocence, and said, "You certainly are grown up and mature enough to understand that your water cannot reach that far to be of any use to your farm." Nānak replied: "You are strange creatures. My offering cannot reach a few hundred miles away, while yours can even get to the other world?" The questioners became speechless, perplexed both at his impertinent questioning of their faith and the irrefutable logic behind it. Nānak made many converts here to whom he preached: "He who keeps God in the mind and does right, which is also good, his Soul is ever in peace both here and in the Hereafter. He need perform no other ritual to please his God."

At another place, he entered the cooking-square of a devout Brāhmin who was wild with rage and demanded his explanation for defiling his kitchen. The Guru said, his kitchen-square was already polluted by the angry man, who harboured so much of hatred for his fellow-men of lower castes, that at their mere presence, his place was defiled. This made the Brāhmin even more angry. The Guru thereupon said, "Ignorance is the low-caste drummer-woman; cruelty the butcheress; a slanderous heart the sweepress, and anger that ruins the

---

with. God's Word His lovers can change, but their Word can be changed not." (p, 24-25). These are rather unusual utterances for a man of Nānak's inborn humility, besides the miracles which he has denounced throughout his works. Hence, we have narrated the story shorn of its miraculous trappings. There is a Gurdwārā, called Nānak Piao, about 3 miles outside Delhi, commemorating this event. Mehervān gives the name of the King as Salem Shāh Pathān (son and successor of Sher Shāh) but his reign began 6 years after the death of Nānak.

*The story connected with Hardwār is not mentioned in the *Purātan Janam Sākhi* but Meharvān refers to it at great length (P. 117-18). So does Mani Singh, though the latter interprets the Guru's water-throwing to the West as a symbolic act, signifying that "the farms and gardens of the Guru whom he irrigates are his disciples and the water is his instruction in God's Wisdom." (P. 175)

mind is like a *chandāla.* O Brāhmin, it avails not if one draws the lines of one's kitchen-square, when all the four low-castes defile one's within."*

He, then, asked him to "make truth, self-restraint and good deeds his 'lines,' and the utterance of God's Name his ablution,"‡ so that he became acceptable to his God.

When, on his way, the Guru visited Vrindāvana, another great centre of Hindu pilgrimage, he saw some showmen enact Krishna-Lilā (the dramatic performance representing the life of Lord Krishna). The Guru was dissatisfied at this dramatic show staged by people who did so not as an act of piety or dedication, but to earn their living by amusing the crowd. Said he:

"The disciples play, while the Gurus dance.
Nimble the movements of their feet, their heads,
And, lo, they throw dust in their hair, like mad.
All this is but to amuse the crowd!
And they beat time only to satiate their hungers.
They perform the parts of gopis and Krishnas,
And Sitās and Rāmas.
But he alone serves God on whom is God's Gace,
And, in the dewy morn rises with zeal in the mind,
And dwells on the Wisdom of the truly Wise.
Else, do not the oil-presses dance, and the spinning wheels?
And the hand-mills and the potters' wheels?
And the incessant whirlwinds in the deserts, and tops?
And, the churning-sticks, and the threshers,
And, the birds whose flying knows no rest?
Endless are those who tumble and dance,
Bound by the writ of their habits.
They who dance thiswise to amuse themselves, only wail in the end.
For they fly not into the yond, nor become the miracle men.
Such of them who dance (this way) only recreate their minds, (but attain not unto God).
For, he alone, O Nānak, loves God who fears Him."†

---

*Ādi Granth, Sri Rāg, p. 91.
‡Ādi Granth, Sri Rāg, P. 91.
†Ādi Granth, Vār Āsā, M. 1

THE GURU and his companion now started on their journey towards the east. Says the *Purātan Janam Sākhi*: "Nānak's dress now was a strange motley: a mango-coloured jacket, over which he threw a white sheet; the hat like that of a Muslim anchorite (Qalandar), with a necklace of bones upon his neck, and a frontal mark of saffron, imprinted on his forehead in the style of the Hindu devout." This dress was in part Hindu, in part Muslim. But, never had anyone donned it before.

On the way, they saw a Muslim notable, Sheikh Wajid (or Bajid) alight from a palanquin. The carriers of his palanquin and other attendants soon started fanning him; two of them kneaded his body to relieve him of fatigue. Mardānā, the Guru's companion, was greatly agitated at this and questioned his Master: "O beloved of God, pray tell me, is there no justice in this world? The man who has travelled in a palanquin feels tired and his fatigue is being relieved by those who carried him on their shoulders! Is it that he has a different God?" The Guru replied: "Mardānā, it is all the result of one's deeds. God creates all men equal and blesses them with human birth, when one has the opportunity to become what one may. Some avail of this opportunity, others don't. This is how some have joy on the earth while others suffer. But, do not mistake, O Mardānā, the earthly joys to be a means to spiritual satisfaction, or even a contented life. For, in the ultimate analysis, it is spiritual fulfilment that brings real happiness and inner integration. He who is happy now, may be unhappy tomorrow; but a spiritually awakened and integrated mind would keep ever in joy, ever in the peace of poise."

From here, the Guru proceeded towards Pilibhit and arrived at Gorakhmatā,* a great centre of Yogis, about twenty miles away. Here, he sat under a pipal tree which had long withered with age. It is said, this tree became green soon after, much to the wonderment of the people around. The Siddhas of this place engaged Nānak in a religious discourse asking him who he was, and whose disciple. The Guru asked Mardānā to play on the rebeck while he himself sang the following hymn of his :

"O God, is there a scale or a weighman, or a measure,
or a tester of Thee ?
Is there an evaluator to put value on Thee ? Is there
a Guru to make me wise in Thee ?

* This place is now called Nānakmatā and has a Gurudwārā commemorating the memory of Nānak's visit. The sixth Guru, Hargobind, also visited this place.

O love, I know not Thy limits.
For, Thou it is who pervadest the earth, the waters,
the underworlds and the skies and art contained
*in all that is.**

Asked, how then one was to know God, to see Him, and to realise Him, the Guru replied :

The mind is the scale, understanding the weight, and His service the weighman. And within the heart is He to be weighed and seen and dwelt upon.

"Nay, He Himself is the balance, His tongue, His weight, His weighman. And Himself He sees Himself, and realises too, and deals in Himself.

"But, he who's blind, and of low disposition, and a stranger to His ways and ever wobbles in the mind, how can he and those who seek his company ever know the state or extent of God ?" *

The Yogis said what he had uttered may be true, but Realisation came only through their way. They, therefore, asked him to adopt their dress and the yogic discipline to obtain emancipation from the snares of life and to enter into the super-conscious state of "*Samādhi*" where there is all bliss and joy. The Guru replied :

"Yoga consists not in a patched gown, nor in the Yogi's staff, nor in smearing one's body with ashes, nor in the ear-rings, nor a shaven head, nor in the blowing of the horn.

"He alone knows the way who abides amidst the impurities of the world and yet remains detached and spotless.

"Yoga consists not in words:
For, he alone is a Yogi who looks upon all men as equal;
And dies while yet alive,
And hears the Unstruck Melody, and enters into the state
of Fearlessness, when one's Doubt is dispelled, and
cease the outgoings of his mind:
And Nectar rains upon it and oozes the music
of equipoise within one,
And one comes to know oneself." *

---

* Suhi M. 1.

It is said, the Yogis were now completely won over and paid homage to the Guru.

From here, Nānak and his bard, Mardānā, proceeded to Banāras, far-famed as the holiest of Hindu centres of pilgrimage. This birthplace of Kabir and Ravidāsa, two renowned devotees of God, and a great centre of Sanskrit learning, housed a learned Pandit, Chatur Dāss† by name. While going towards the Gangā for a holy dip, he saw the Guru in his unusual dress and said with a sneer: "What kind of a holy man are you? You neither wear the necklace of Tulsi, nor have a rosary in your hand, nor possess a *saligrāma* (the sacred quartz stone representing the god Vishnu). How will you be emancipated ?" The Guru answered:

> *"He who waters a barren land wastes his life.*
> *O Brāhmin, make God the object of thy worship, and*
> *Right conduct the necklace of Tulsi, and ride the boat*
> *of God's Love with prayer in the heart for His*
> *Mercy and you will be ferried across."* *

The Guru continued :

> *"He who seeks to belong to the Master of the Garden, makes good deeds his well, the necklace and the waterpots, and yokes his mind, like an ox, to draw water from the well, and thus irrigates his farm with the Lord's Nectar and fulfils himself."**

The Brāhmin said :

"What you say may be true, but how is one to overcome one's mind which is full of lust and wrath ?" The Guru replied: "Lust and wrath too can be beaten into a ploughshare, being nothing but energy. Instead of their riding the man, man should ride them." *

---

† This shows that Guru Nānak never met Kabir, as is alleged by several European historians, nor accepted his influence upon him, otherwise even if dead, the places or people connected with him must have been visited by Guru Nānak. Dr. P, N. Tiwāri, quoting a report in the Archaeological Survey of India says that Bijli Khān got a tomb of Kabir erected on the right bank of the river Ami (in the Basti Distt. of U.P.) in 1450 A.D., i.e. 19 years before Guru Nānak was born. (Kabir by P.N. Tiwari, National Book Trust, P.47)

* Basant Hindol, M. 1.

The Brāhmin then asked: "Can a crane be changed ever into a swan? How can a man, who is ill-destined due to his past Karma, turn the course of his life?" The Guru replied : "If God's Grace be upon one, one's past is totally obliterated. And Grace comes to all who seek it in humility, through self-surrender, and the knowledge of, and obedience to, the Will of God."

The Pandit said, "But how can knowledge come without learning?" The Guru answered: "Knowing is not understanding, intellect does not always lead to wisdom, for the body is too weak and the heart too young to resist evil. That is how one acquires two mothers (hope and desire), and two fathers (attachment and envy)."

Chatur Dass questioned; "If that be so, what is the hope for man's redemption?" The Guru replied: "Know you not that while the vegetation is in bloom, it yet has fire within it? The earth is bounded by the sea and yet is not washed away ? The sun and the moon reside in the same sky. But, the one does not imbibe the characteristics of the other." The Pandit then asked: "What are the qualities of the God-awakened being." The Guru replied: "He who knows God to be all-pervasive, and eats up the illusion that surrounds us all. And the hallmark of such a one is that he always has compassion is his heart." *

The Pandit then inquired if his learning and teaching would be of any avail to him in the realisation of the Ultimate Reality. The Guru uttered 54 stanzas on the nature of Knowledge and of God, reiterating his belief that there was nothing that did not come from God: the gods, angels, mind, wisdom, the universe, man, good and evil. "Why, therefore, get involved with the Other; one must write out and reflect upon God's Name."* When asked how was this God to be realised, the Guru said, "Through love. For he who loves God knows not another: he looks upon all alike, has compassion for all life, and illusion lures him not, and he is content to be himself."

The Pandit was greatly impressed by the Guru and became his disciple.

The Guru, then, proceeded to Gayā, the far-famed place where Gautama, the Buddha, had performed his penances. This place was now taken over by the Brāhmins who asked Nānak to perform

---

* Rāmkali M. 1. † The place where the Guru stayed in Banaras (now, Varanasi), is now known as "Guru kā Bāgh".

the customary ceremonies for the spiritual comfort of his dead ancestors. The Guru replied:

> *"God's Name is my earthen lamp, and sorrow is the oil that burns therein. The more I light the lamp, the more my sorrows are consumed, and lo, I suffer not the agony of death thereafter.*
> *"God's Name, again, is the rice-balls, the leafy bowls, and obsequies and the holy rivers and the ablutions.*
> *While men offer gifts to the gods, it is the Brāhmin who eats them. Instead, one must beg of God to grant peace to his Soul both here and in the Hereafter, for there's nothing like His love."* †

As they proceeded further,* they passed through a town in which celebrations were being held on a lavish scale on the birth of a child in the house of a rich merchant. Next morning, the child passed away and there was much wailing and crying. Mardānā asked the Guru, "O Master, why is man afflicted by joy and sorrow, almost by turns, and how is one to find peace in this world where men are born only to pass away?" The Guru replied: "It is only one's lack of understanding which makes one indulge in the joys of life excessively, and when these pass away, man suffers. If one were to meditate on God Who goes not and keep oneself even-minded, both in joy and pain, taking both to be the blessings of God, one stays in poise and does not suffer." He, then, uttered a hymn giving the four stages of man's life: childhood, youth, old age and death, comparing them with the four divisions of night which make one forget oneself, as in sleep, and then when one wakes up, one repents.

---

† Āsā M. 1.

* The Guru in this journey is also said to have halted at Patnā where he converted a jeweller, Sālis Rāi, to his faith. The story is told that the Guru sent Mardānā to the town with a jewel he had found on the way to sell and buy some food for him. While others put a ridiculously low price on it, Sālis Rāi gave away a sizeable sum merely for having the privilege of such a precious sight. Mardānā, however, did not accept the money in exchange for nothing. This so impressed Sālis Rāi that he came to visit the Guru and after a discourse with him became his disciple. The story, however apocryphal, is meant to convey the moral that the worth of a thing as much as an ideal is in the eye of the knower and not the charlatan.

On the way, the Guru halted at a place where he was visited regularly by a devotee of his. Another man wanted to follow suit, but falling in love with a woman of ill-repute, he forsook the Guru's path and indulged in revelries. After some time, this man on his way to the house of his paramour once found what he thought was a pot full of gold mohurs, but when he opened the treasure, there was only one gold coin and the rest all coals. The devotee of the Guru on the other hand, ran a poisonous thorn in his foot. He reported this to his Master, saying "O Guru, he who comes thy way is punished, while he who visits the house of evil is rewarded with a gold coin! Strange are the ways of God!" The Guru remarked: "My son, ask thy heart if it feels contentment and bliss within, by sticking to the way of God and ask also the other man if he has the same inner peace and poise, or burns ever in the fire of desire and lust. It is not one's worldly affluence that makes for a happy and contented life, but what gives one's mind and heart stability and equilibrium. Your friend will grieve the moment his joys are snatched away, but you possess riches that would go not, nor be burnt nor drowned, and would stay with you. Men who go for the pleasures of the moment lose the joy of the ever-lasting." *

The Guru now came to a village where men and women served him with all their heart. The Guru blessed them saying: "May ye all scatter." At the next village he was very poorly received. The Guru cursed them saying: "May ye remain where ye are!" Mārdāna was greatly preplexed at this. He asked: "O Master, strange are thy ways. They who serve you, you want them to scatter, while the others who

---

* The *Purātan Janam Sākhi* version narrates the Guru's reply thus. Said the Guru: "The treasure which was struck by your companion was indeed full of gold mohurs, but due to his being addicted to vice, he got only one gold coin, the rest having turned to coals. He had, in his earlier life, given away, in charity, to a Sādhu, a gold mohur as a result of which he was to have received a pot full of them. But the more he ran after evil, the more his reward was turned to dust. You had to suffer being nailed to the cross, but due to your devotion to God, your suffering was reduced to a mere pricking of the thorn." Which only shows that according to the Guru, it is one's own deeds that lead to worldly affluence or misery. However, in the hymn quoted at the end of this incident (Māru M. 1.), it is also pointed out that "the more one is involved in his craze for worldly pleasures the more is one trapped" and that "the rusted iron becomes gold (i.e. one finds one't true self in equipoise) if one meets with the True Guru and sucks-in the Nectar-Name" (P. 31-32). We have depended, therefore, more on the Guru's own words than the narration of the *Purātan Janam Sākhi*.

treat you ill, you want them to stay in their homes, secure and whole?" The Guru replied: "O Mārdanā, if those that serve others scatter, they would, by their example, make others also likewise; while if those that are inhospitable to the wayfarers and the holy, stay where they did, at least they wouldn't corrupt others by their bad manners."†

The Guru now reached Dhubri in Kāmrup (Assam)*, via Bengāl. The women of this region were famous for their feminine charm and in enticing men. Nur Shāh was the queen of this haven of beauty.@ Mardānā, as usual, stung by hunger, asked the Guru's

---

† Here, the *Purātan Janam Sākhi* again confronts Nānak with three thugs who wanted to murder and rob him, but seeing his holy face and a miracle (by which the thugs saw the couriers of Death and angels fighting over a burning corpse which was to have been taken by the former to hell, but owing to Nānak's vision falling on it, the angels now wanted to remove it to heaven), they fell at his feet and distributed all their ill-gotten wealth to the poor. It appears, this and the story of the Kāli-yuga which follows Nānak's visit to Assam, should be placed either in Assam or in the land of the nearby man-hunting Nāgās.

* *Purātan Janam Sākhi* calls it "Kauru Des", which is only a corrupted form of Kāmrup (lit. the land of lust and beauty). The State of Assam was known as Kāmrup since ancient times (vide Oxford History of India, P. 195) and its women were known for their beauty and free ways. Aurangzeb's general, Mir Jumlā, who invaded Assam in 1662, calls it a "wild and dreadful country,..... whose people are reputed to be expert magicians" (Talish, as translated by J.N. Sarkar in Bihar and Orissa Research Soc. Journal, Vol. 1, Pp. 179-95). That Guru Nānak visited Assam and met Shankar Deva, the renowned Hindu Vedantist of this period, is corroborated by contemporary evidence. He too was against shāktism & tantrism, and believed in samyavād (equality). (*Guru Teg Bahadur* & Assam, p. 48)

He is said to have visited Dāccā on the way back from Kāmrup. This seems quite likely, as at the time of the ninth Guru's visit to Dāccā, such was the enthusiasm exhibited by the local Sikhs that the Guru called it the "Home of Sikhism". The name of the Dāccā *masand*, Bulāki, who sent a golden palanquin for Guru Gobind Singh in his childhood to travel back from Patnā to Ānandpur, is well-known in Sikh history. In several of his *Hukam-nāmāhs*, (or edicts), Guru Gobind Singh also calls East Bengal "the Home of Sikhism". Dāccā then was not as famous as now and was only the seat of a *Thānedār*, but it was a trading centre of great importance and the Guru possibly on his return from Kāmrup and going south towards Puri must have stayed here. Out in the waste, near Jāfarābād (now called Dhanmandi) is a well dedicated to Guru Nānak's visit, which is one of the oldest monuments of the town. In the month of *Chaitra*, a fair is held here and miraculous properties are ascribed to this water. (See Dāccā Review, Vol. V. Oct-Nov. 1915).

@ It is not necessary that Nur Shāh should have been a sovereign or a chieftain, but merely a famous sorceress, and queen of beauty. The reference to the "women's

permission to visit the town. When he reached the palatial abode of the queen of beauty, she called him in, taking him to be an innocent creature on whom she would work her charms. Mardānā, seeing her dazzling figure and much pleased with her courtesan manners, was completely possesed by her. When, for quite some time, he did not return, the Guru went after him, and finding him a virtual prisoner in the hands of a handsome maiden, tried to persuade her to let his companion out. But she was adamant saying the man had chosen her out of free will and so she would not let him go. She even tried to entice the Guru by her charms and suave manners. But, the Guru spurned her advances, saying: "She who sells dust cannot exchange her goods with musk. Without worthy deeds, one finds not the True Spouse."

Nūr Shāh then tried to dance her way into the approval of Nānak. She made such graceful and tender gestures, so nimble of feet was she and so exquisite in her make-up and expression that it was impossible for the usual run of men to resist her charm. But the Guru sat unmoved and sang:

"The desires of the heart clang like cymbals and the ankle-bells, and the world's drum beats with them to keep the time. Such are the times that even the sages dance to their tunes. O God, where are the men of continence to plant their feet? All joys, all blessings, are bought and sold, but how long is one to enjoy and forsake his inner being and God? Men are without compassion and kings without justice. Their appearance is human but their doings are those of curs. But, he alone is approved, who thinks himself to be a guest in this garden of beauty and is not enticed away from God!"*

Then Nur Shāh asked her companions to corrupt Nānak with their riches. Thereupon they brought gold, jewels, scents, dresses and

rule" only signifies the matriarchal society of this tribe which Guru Nānak visited. That Mardānā, according to *Purātan Janam Sākhi*, was transformed into a ram or lamb by Nur Shāh by tying a thread or an amulet to his wrist should not be taken literally. It only signifies that he became spell-bound by her beauty. As Sir Vincent Smith rightly points out: "The contact (between the Mongolian and the Indian idea's) has resulted in the evolution of a peculiar *Tāntric form of Hinduism which offers special honour to female forms of the deity called Sakti*. All the processes by means of which Hindus and strange tribal gods are converted into respectable Brāhmanical deities, may be illustrated in Assam." (Oxford History of India, P. 196).

Whether Nūr Shāh was the actual or a corrupted name of a follower of goddess *Kāmakshya* or only signified her Kingly (or Queenly) beauty, as the name literally implies, is of not much significance.

* *Ādi Granth* Āsā M. 1.

delicacies to please him and make him stay with them as their master and slave. But, the Guru was not at all impressed and uttered the following hymn:

"O ignorant woman, why are you proud of your beauty, your riches? Why not relish the spouse of your heart within, He who is nearer than near, but Whom you search without and after? Let His fear be the collyrium for your eyes and your decoration be of His Love. But if you love Him not, and play clever with Him and try to please Him through courtesan manners and have greed in your mind, then you please Him not. If you surrender to His Will with all your heart, and be yoked ever to His Feet and offer your body and mind to Him, then your Lord loves and owns you as His very own. Says Nānak: she alone is beauteous and meritorious and clever and wise who merges her whole being in her Love."*

It is said, Nūr Shāh was deeply moved by the soul-stirring message of Nānak, and stood before him with joined palms, beseeching him to forgive her past and to accept her as his disciple. This the Guru did, saying "If you keep God in your mind in whatever you do, you will be blessed and emancipated." She also released Mardānā who sought Nānak's benediction so that he remained steadfast in the Guru's Path.**

From here the Guru and his associate proceeded towards wilderness.† A strong wind was howling in the wastes, uprooting the age-

---

*Ādi Granth; Tilang M. 1.

**From here, the writer of the *Purātan Janam Sākhi* takes the Guru to a place called 'Kiri Nagar' (lit. the city of ants), "black and dreadful like the devil", where, it appeared, no one had set his foot before. But the Guru told Mardānā that "a powerful rājā had come here before but was humbled by the ants." May be, it is a mere setting for the hymn of Guru Nānak included at the end of this episode (*Sihān, Bājān, Chargān, Kuhian, tinā Khavālē Ghāh*........ Adi Granth, Vār Majh), or a warning that before a determined multitude of the poor and the downtrodden, even the mightiest tyrants are humbled. It has also been suggested that perhaps some incident connected with a place called *Kiri-nagar* in the Shivālik Hills has been associated in the *Purātan Janam Sākhi* with what is popularly known to have happened to Suleiman, the just, the celebrated king of fable and myth.

Later, the Guru is said to have met Sheikh Fārid in Āsā (Āssām) Des. May be, there was a *gaddi* of Farid in Āssām as well in those days, but lacking historical confirmation, we have placed this story later, on the Guru's return to the Panjāb.

† This appears to be the land of the man-hunting Nāgās, to the North-East of Assam. Even Mir Jumlā, Aurangzeb's general, who led an expedition against

old trees. Soon, there was torrential rain and thunder and lightning. The sky became murky and dreadful with streaks of fire and blood. Mardānā was struck with terror and said, "O Guru, strange are thy ways. You've brought me to wilderness where, if I die, there'll be no one even to bury me gracefully and, may be, my flesh becomes a prey for wild animals." Nānak smiled and said, "Mardānā, life and death are in the hands of God whose fear fills the earth, the sky and all the elements. So, whosoever is attached to His fearless and eternal Master, he comes not to grief."

As they were discoursing thus, it is said, they saw a wild being, half-human in form, but very dreadful of features and demeanour approach them. The Guru said, "Brother, who are you? Why have you come to us at this unearthly hour?" He replied: "I am the spirit of the Kāli age and have come to entice you. All the dreadful things you have seen happen before you this day were my doings. But, as you weren't afraid, now I've come to offer you gold and jewels and palatial mansions and houris of exquisite beauty for your pleasure, so that you may follow my way, and so too others seeing thy example."

The Guru asked Mardānā to play upon the rebeck and uttered the following hymn:

> "*Were there a mansion of pearls inlaid with gems, and perfumed with musk, saffron, fragrant aloes and sandalwood...*
>
> *Were the earth to be studded with diamonds and rubies:*
>
> *Were houris of exquisite beauty shining like a bead*
> *to please me with their delicate gestures, I'd leave not*
> *the hand of my God, nor abandon the support of His Name!*
>
> *Were I to become a Siddha, seated in a holy trance, and*
> *work miracles,*

**F N. Contd.

Assam in 1662, expresses the horror with which the country and the people were regarded by outsiders. Writes he: "Assam is a wild and dreadful country abounding in danger. Its roads are frightful like the path leading to the nook of Death. Fatal to life is its expanse like the unpeopled city of Destruction. The air and water of the hills are like the destructive Simoom and deadly poison to natives and strangers alike. (The inhabitants) resemble men in nothing beyond this that they walk erect on two feet......Every caravan that set foot on this land deposited its baggage of residence in the halting place of Death." ("Talish", as translated by J.N. Sarkar, in the Journal of Bihār and Orissā Research Soc., Vol. I, pp. 179-95).

And could become now manifest, now hidden, at will,
and people were to acclaim me for this,
I'd leave not the hand of my God, nor abandon the support of His Name:
Were I to become a monarch, seated on a throne, with large armies to obey my commands,
O Nānak, all that would be vain like wind.
*For, I'd ask God still to give me His Hand."**

It is said, the demon on seeing Nānak thus spurn his offers fell at his feet and said, "O Nānak, I may bless him who follows thee with the world's riches, but would disturb not the peace of his mind."

The Guru now returned via Dacca, 24 Parganas and Cuttack and proceeded towards Puri, on the Bay of Bengāl, where Vishnu is worshipped as Jagannātha, or the Lord of the universe. When, in the evening, the priests started performing the Ārti, going round and round the idol of Jagannātha, with earthen lamps placed in salvers of silver, and burnt incense to make the atmosphere fragrant, the Guru asked: "What's this all about?" The priests replied: "This is how one pays homage to the Lord of the universe. You should also participate in the service as do the others." The Guru thereupon uttered a hymn, one of the most beautiful in the whole gamut of Indian mystic poetry:

"The sky is the salver, the sun and the moon are the lamps,
with the spheres of stars studded in it like jewels:

---

* Sri Rāg, M. 1. It is quite likely that this devilish-looking man has been identified by the imaginative writer of the *Purātan Janam Sākhi* with the spirit of the Kāli yuga, (or the dark, present age) and that the hymn of Guru Nānak, as included in the Ādi Granth (Sri Rāg, M. 1) is given here to portray his utter contempt of the earthly riches. The appearance of Mārā to the Buddha and of Satan to Jesus to tempt them away from the path of God have a striking similarity to the above incident, but it does not mean, therefore, that a man of God, each in his own way, does not pass through such an experience at one stage of his life or another, and that if a particular experience happened in the case of one, it cannot happen to another, or that the pious biographers of such men are looking out for such stories to be incorporated in the lives of their Divine Masters in order to prove their prophethood by conforming such incidents to the accepted norms or experiences of those gone before.

The sandalwood of the Malai mountain scatters fragrance across, and the winds waft the scents of all the flowers of the earth:

Thus is Thy Worship performed, O Thou destroyer of fear.

Thousands are Thy eyes, yet **hast Thou eyes?**

Thousands are Thy forms, **yet hast Thou a form?**

Thousands Thy feet, **yet hast Thou feet?**

Thousands Thy noses to smell, **yet hast Thou a nose,**

O Wonder of wonders?

Thou art the light that lights all hearts, and which becomes manifest through the instruction of the Guru.

O men, that alone is worship which pleases my God!

Like thebumblebee, my mind craves for the honey of His Lotus-feet,

And cries:

'O God, bless Nānak, the Cuckoo, with the rain of Thy Mercy,

*That he merges in Thy Name!'"**

The priests of the temple found it profitless to argue any more with him and left him alone.

At Puri†, Nānak also met a Brāhmin who kept his eyes and nose closed so as to deny himself the pleasure of the senses. It was his

---

* *Ādi Granth, Dhanāsri*, M. 1. According to Mehervān, this hymn was uttered by Guru Nānak at Rāmeswaram (South India).

* According to Kāhan Singh, Guru Nānak visited Puri in 1566 Vikrami (April 1509-March 1510) (MK, P. 1497). Dr. B. Majumdār, in his *Chaitanya-Charitar Upādān* tells us on the authority of Ishwardāsa's *Chaitanaya Bhāgvat* (Oriyā) that at Puri, Guru Nānak met the famous Vaishnava Saint, *Chaitanya Mahāprabhu,* and that he participated in Kirtan with him, along with Sārang (which Dr. Gandā Singh identifies as *Sarangiā* or Mardāna, the rebeck-player), Rupa and Sanātana (once ministers of Allāuddin Hussain Shāh of Bengāl (1483-1559) who left royal service and became the followers of Chaitanya), Jagai and Madhai, two ruffians converted by Chaitanaya, Jangali and Nandini, two Vaishnavites, who went about dressed as women or Lord Krishnā's gopis, Gopal Guru and Mattā Balrām, and Nāgar Parshotamdāsa. This manuscript, *Chaitanaya Bhāgvat*, according to available researches could be placed either at the end-part of the 16th century or early part of the 17th. Our information is based on the illuminating article of Dr. Gandā Singh in the "Sikh Review", Calcuttā, of October-November, 1969(Pp 58-61).

claim that thus he achieved much mental concentration and could divine the secrets of others. The Guru put his claim to the test. He took away the jug of water lying in front of him, placed it behind his own back and asked, "Could you find out where's your jug?" After making many guesses, the Brāhmin gave up. The Guru thereupon uttered the following hymn for his instruction:

> *"Men know not the spirit of the times, nor the essence of Yoga, nor the way of Truth.*
>
> *The holy places have been corrupted and defiled; lo, the whole world is drowned thus.*
>
> *In the Kāli age, the way to man's Release is through God's love.*
>
> *In vain do men hold their nose and close their eyes and claim that they see the three worlds,*
>
> *But they see not what's behind them. O, what a miracle is this?"**

The Guru now returned to the Panjāb. He dressed himself like a householder and visited the shrine of Sheikh Farid-ud-Din, Ganj-i-Shakar, a great Muslim Sufi of the 13th century, at Pāk Pāttān. The custodian of the shrine, Sheikh Brahm (Ibrāhim?), seeing him robed like a householder, said:

> *"Either one should covet the world, or God,*
>
> *But, one must place not one's feet in two boats, lest one be drowned."*%

Nānak answered:

> *"Why not make use of both: have one's goods in one, and one's soul in the other?*
>
> *For such a one, there's no wreck, no loss: neither one sees the boat, nor the water!*
>
> *He cherishes only the goods of God which's True and pervades all, all-too-spontaneously."*†

**Dhanāsri* M. 1.

†The verses whose translations are given here are not from the Ādi Granth, but from *Purātan Janam Sākhi* and ascribed to Farid and Nānak (P. 41).

Ibrāhim then engaged him in a spiritual dialogue, employing various metaphors and symbols to convey his belief about God, man and the world. He said: "The whole world is enamoured of the 'witch' (i.e. Māyā) which is false from within, and as one looks on, one's 'farm' (i.e. life) is ruined!"

The Guru answered back in the same metaphor: "Men have been in love with the 'witch' since the begining of Time. But he who keeps a watch over his 'Farm' will never see it ruined."

Said Ibrāhim: "My strength is gone, my mind is torn, my body ceases to function. O love, bring me a medicament that may cure me of my ailment."*

Replied Nānak: "Thy physician is Truth, and is within thee, not without. To utter Him or to call Him from without is false: one must Realise Him within one's Soul."**

Sheikh Ibrāhim wailed: "When there was time to construct a boat, I did't. And, now when the river is in flood, how can I carry myself across? O love, touch not the safflower, its colour will fade away. The soul is weak, and the command of the Beloved hard to bear. As the cow once milked yields not again, so also our single life. The call from beyond calleth, and the swan-soul is sad that it has to pass and dust return to dust."†

Nānak replied in a most optimistic tone: "If one constructs the boat of meditation and self-discipline, the crossing is easy enough. Then, one meets not with an angry river, and the path is all-too-smooth. He who gathers merit in his skirt, the God of Himself owns him and forsakes him never, if he gives up ego and evil."‡

Sheikh Ibrāhim then said: "I seem to agree with you. But, the tree of life yields flower in the first part of the night, and it fruitions in the morn. And he alone is blessed who keeps awake through the night."††

Nānak replied: "The bounties are in the hands of God, the Giver. Some He passes by, even though they are awake, others He wakes out of sleep and blesses."*

**Ibid (P. 42).

† *Ādi Granth*, Rāg Sūhi, Farid.

‡ *Ādi Granth*, Rāg Sūhi, M.1.

††Ibid, *Shalokas* of Farid.

* Ibid.

Explaining his point further, Nānak said, "If man were to receive Bliss only as a result of his own efforts, what need, then, is there of God and His Grace? Effort one must make, but the fruits thereof must be surrendered to God. Only thus does one's ego depart and one merits the Grace of God. Else, the realm of the spirit also degenerates into a market place of give-and-take." And, then, he uttered the following hymn:

> *"When Thou, O God, art with me, I have everything,*
> *For, thou, O love, art my capital -stock.*
> *When I abide within Thee, I am at peace and feel blessed.*
> *In Thy Will Thou blessest man with a throne and glory.*
> *In Thy Will Thou makest man a beggar, sad at heart.*
> *In Thy Will do rivers flow across the deserts.*
> *In Thy Will doth the lotus flower in the (mind's) sky.*
> *In Thy Will do we cross the impassable sea (of material existence).*
> *In Thy Will are we drowned in the midstream.*
> *In Thy Will Thou seemest pure and beauteous, and one is imbued utterly with Thy Praise.*
> *In Thy Will Thou seemest dreadfuland one exhausts oneself coming and going.*
> *O Love, Thou art unfathomable, incomparable, without an equal,*
> *And saying thus, I surrender myself to Thee.*
> *O God, I ask nought from Thee, but for Thy Vision †*
> *I crave."*

It is said Sheikh Ibrāhim, like his illustrious teacher, Bābā Farid, Ganj-i-Shakar, used to fast for as many days as he possibly could. This he did in order to obtain religious merit and purge his mind of desire even for bread. Whenever anyone would bring offerings to him, more often than not, he would refuse it saying, "I've already eaten". He did this once in the presence of the Guru. The giver, much offended, taunted him: "Do you also imitate the ways of Farid who even when he fasted used to fasten on his

† *Ādi Granth*, Sūhi, M.1.

stomach a wooden cake in order to give him false comfort of bread, and used to pretend that he had eaten even though his mind always craved?" Sheikh Ibrāhim's heart was much touched at this reproach and he said to the Guru: "Pray tell me why I should lie to the people that I have indeed taken my food, while my mind craves."

The Guru replied: "It is a sin to deny oneself the necessities ef life. One must not crave for pleasures, but whatever comes from God,one must accept with good grace and thankfulness. Starvation never leads to "spiritual bliss." And he quoted Kabir in support of his argument: "He who forsakes bread and pretends God's love, has neither the merit of a wedded spouse nor of a chaste widow." Nānak added: "Without a well-nurtured body, God could not be cherished or realised." The essentials on the path of spiritual ascent were not fasting or self-denial, but self-surrender, contentment, compassion and humility.

The Sheikh was much pleased with this discourse.

From here, the Guru and Mardānā ventured through a small desert where they could find nothing to eat. Mardādā, much distressed, asked his Master: "Pray, tell me what is to become of me? I came out with you in the hope that at least you wouldn't starve me to death. Now, hunger gnaws at my heart, and there is nothing I can find to have my fill." The Guru pointed to some wild berries and asked him to satisfy his hunger with these, but not to carry any with him. Mardānā ate his heartful, but disregarding the instructions of the Guru, put some in his pockets and as he felt hungry next morning partook of them with utter abandon. Soon after, he felt pain in his stomach and became miserable. Being asked, he told Nānak that disregarding his advice he had brought some wild berries with him also and eaten them while he felt hungry that morning.

The Guru smiled and said, "Mardānā, that is how man suffers. He not only demands what he needs now, but also what he needs for the morrow, depending not on God but on himself. And, the food he thus accumulates and deposits gets stale, even if it is not stolen or does not create jealousy in the minds of others. And so whosoever feeds himself on the left-overs suffers." Mardānā was soon well, but expressed a wish to go back home. "I can suffer hunger with thee no more," he wailed. Nānak said: "Mardānā, I bless thee. You are saved both in this world and the next. You gave me devotion before any other and this I value more than my life. You may now proceed to your home in peace." Mardānā touched the feet of his Master, and Nānak hugged him to his bosom, saying to his utter delight: "You go and I follow you, but tell no one of my whereabouts."

When Mardānā reached Talwandi, Nānak's mother greatly overwhelmed with emotion asked: "Where have you left my son? Pray tell me, when shall I see his holy face again?" Mardānā kept silent, and after meeting his people, soon left the village.

Nānak's mother followed him, believing that his sudden departure must be at the bidding of Nānak who might be somewhere nearabout. At only three miles from the village, Mardānā halted and so did Nānak's mother who, to her utter delight, saw her son face to face after several years. Nānak, seeing the sight of his mother, rushed to touch her feet. The mother embraced him and terderly caressing his forehead, sobbed: "Sacrifice to thee, O son, blessed is the ground thou treadest, blessed the people thou meetest, thy mother is blessed for having brought thee forth. Thank God, I have seen thee again."

Nānak was also much overcome with emotion and wept. The mother offered him some sweets, but Nānak said, "Mother, I'm already satisfied." The mother inquired: "O son, what have you eaten and when?" Nānak asked Mardānā to play on the rebeck while he sang a hymn which said, "He who believes, tastes all that's sweet; he who hears His Word tastes all that's saline. He who utters His Name, tastes all the sour foods, and he who sings His Praise tastes all the condiments. All the thirty-six delicacies that the tongue relishes are his who loves God, and whose love my God approves. All other tastes are vain, O mother, for they bring evil to the mind and to the body pain."*

Then, his mother said, "My son, remove the beggar's gown you've put on and wear the clothes I've brought thee." Nānak replied: "The joy of wearing red is his who is imbued with the colour of God, of wearing white his who lives in Truth and gives away whatever he has. The joy of wearing blue is his who rids his interior of the dark spots, and of the cosy footwear his who stands ever in the Presence of God."*

Soon, his father got scent of Nānak's coming, and he rushed to the spot on the horseback. Seeing Nānak robed like a faqir, he said,

*Ādi Granth, Sri Rāg, M. 1.

"Son, take my horse and ride back to thy home. I'm much distressed at your sight, the son of a proud householder wandering like a beggar." Nānak fell at the feet of his father and said, "Father, the horses are no use to me. He who knows His Way, goes not another. He whose glory shines in the Presence of God by His Grace feels himself to be the king of the world."† Kālu, then, asked him to visit at least his people back home and comfort his bones for some time in the family house. Nānak replied, "The pleasure of uttering His Name is my home; my family is my God's Grace. And only that I obey which my Master ordains."†

Kālu was much distressed to hear these words and said, "Only if I knew what has disappointed you in life, I would set things right. If you want to marry another woman, I'd get you one, if another house, I'd provide you with it." Nānak replied: "God alone I have married. He it is who orders me about, as the whole world he yokes, each to his own task. And whosoever else errs, my God errs not." Nānak then asked his parents' permission to depart: "I had promised to come and see you. That promise I have kept. Now I beg of you to grant me leave that I do what God bids me do." Finding any further argument fruitless, his parents departed, sad at heart.

Once again, the Guru went to see Sheikh Ibrāhim at Pāk Pattan. Outside the town, the Guru sat along with Mardānā, singing a hymn which said: "Thou art the tablet, O God, Thou the pen, Thou also the writing. Yea, Thou art our only God, why therefore think of another?† This utterance a follower of Sheikh Ibrāhim heard and reported to his master that Nānak had arrived again in the neighbourhood. Sheikh Ibrāhim went out to receive him and after paying courtesies to him, asked, "Nānak, you say there is but one God; true, but there are two ways: which one must one adopt and which reject?" The Guru replied: "If there is one God, then, there is only His way to attain Him, not another. One must follow that way and reject the other. Worship not him who is born only to die, but Him who is eternal and is contained in the whole universe."

Ibrāhim quoted Farid-ul-Din,Ganj-i-Shakar,to convey that without abandoning the world, one couldn't go the way of God. Nānak replied that he whose mind was clean,would attain God wherever he

† Ibid, Āsā M. 1.

be. The Sheikh then asked, "What is that word, that virtue, that spell, which captivates the heart of the Beloved?" Nānak replied: "Humility is the word, forbearance the virtue, civility the spell which charms the heart of our Master." Ibrāhim asked, "How can a man of affairs who lives on the blood of others be approved by God?" Nānak replied, "If one keeps the 'knife' of Truth in the 'scabbard' of Merit, and then cuts one's 'throat' with it, the 'blood' of greed will be shed and one shall be approved by God."* Asked Ibrāhim, "Is an intercessor necessary to meet with God?" Nānak replied, "The pure Soul is the intercessor. God Himself is the Guru and he who surrenders his Soul to God becomes like unto Him." The Sheikh then asked for his blessings and Nānak said, "God will bless thee, and thy goods will arrive safe home," meaning thereby that his devotion would be accepted by God.

On the way, the Guru was met by a recluse who asked him to define the word "Udās" (Abandonment). Nānak answered: "He who makes use of everything but deems not any as his own has abandoned the world. Such a one meets with God."

At Goindwāl, he visited the house of a leper whom everyone had discarded and left to live on the outskirts of the village. Nānak stayed here for some time, nursing the ailing man who was in utter distress. The leper asked him, "O Guru, how does man contract disease?" The Guru replied, "By forgetting God, for the malady is not in our body but in our Souls. While man can cure his body's ailments, only God can cure our Souls. He whose Soul is in health, minds not the body's pain, but he who leans only on the body, keeps his Soul ever in pain."‡ It is said, the leper recovered soon thereafter, and became a great devotee of God.**

CONTINUING HIS WANDERINGS through the central parts of the Panjāb, Nānak arrived at Sayyadpur and visited his devotee, Bhāi Lālo, a second time. Lālo complained to the Guru of the oppression of the Pathān rulers. Nānak replied, "When goodness departs from men and nations, they invariably come to grief."† The end of

---

**Rāmkali ki Vār* M. 1, Shaloka.

‡*Ādi Granth, Dhanāsri* M. 1.

**From here, the Guru is said to have passed once again through Sultānpur and from thence to Vairowāl, Jalālābād, Kiri Pathānān, Batālā, etc; (*Purātan Janam Sākhi*, P. 57-58).

†*Āsā* M, 1.

the Pathān regime, he said, was at hand. And, on this occasion, he uttered a prophetic hymn pointing to the advent of Bābur who was soon to occupy the throne of Delhi after bitter fighting in the Panjāb. Addressing Lālo, Nānak sang:

"O Lālo, I utter as is revealed unto me the Word of God.

With the marriage-procession of sin, Bābur hastens hither and asks for the hand (of the bride, our motherland) at the point of the sword.

Men have lost religion, nay, even the sense of shame, and falsehood walks abroad.

Not the Brāhmins and the Qāzis, but the Devil-incarnate conducts the 'marriage'.

Women, Hindu or Muslim, sing the 'marriage-songs' through their wails.

And men sing of their killers, and anoint their foreheads with the saffron-mark of blood.

Nānak hymns the praises of God in the city of the flesh.

And proclaims that He whose justice is ever true and who assigns to each man his task, He sits apart and watches over us all.

*And, lo, our bodies will be torn into shreds, and, then, Hindustān will know the intent of what I utter."**

A few days later, Bābur invaded this place, sacked the town, put many men to the sword, and captured others, including Nānak and Mardānā.• While the Guru was made to carry a heavy load on the head, Mardānā worked as a groom. Later, Nānak was asked to grind

---

**Ādi Granth*, Tilang, M. 1.

•Mālcolm, in his *Sketch of the Sikhs,* thinks Nānak's interview with Bābur must have taken place in 1526 or 27 during his travels, but makes no mention of his imprisonment. Mohd. Latif, in his *History of the Panjāb*, says he was imprisoned by Ibrāhim Lodhi for nine months due to the vast influence Nānak was gathering and that he was released by the orders of Bābur, but what source he bases this information upon is not known.

As is well-known, Bābur invaded India four times (twice in 1519, and once in 1520 and 1524 A. D.) before he finally settled on the throne of Hindustān, in 1526 A.D. It was during his third attack in 1520 that while upto Siālkot, there was practically little resistance to his onslaught, the people of Sayyadpur (or Saidpur,

F.N. Contd.

now called Eminābād, in the district of Gujranwālā, West Panjāb) put up a stiff fight and there was a large-scale massacre of the people at the hands of Bābur's armies (vide Sharmā's "The Crescent in India", P. 217). It may have been here and during this expedition that Guru Nānak witnessed the depredations wrought by Bābur's hordes (to which elaborate references are made by him in the Ādi Granth, in Rāgas Āsā and Tilang). However, there is another equally gruesome, though one-line reference, also in the Ādi Granth, about Lāhore: *Lāhore Shahr, Zahr Kahr, savā pahr* (e. i. for 1 1/4 quarter of the day, i. e. for four hours, a deadly curse descended on the city of Lāhore). This happened, according to historical records, in 1524, again at the hands of Bābur. But, the reference by Guru Nānak to the Lāhore episode is so slight that his meeting with the emperor at Lāhore or having witnessed the massacre there at first-hand is remote, for the tragic scene he writes about is the most vivid, passionate and intimate account of a regular battle. But, if the verses included in the Ādi Granth and quoted in this anecdote by the writer of the *Purātan Janam Sākhi* refer to the sack of Saidpur, who then are the princes "who were hacked to pieces or starved to death, for Bābur's authority now reigns supreme"? (Āsā M. 1, Ashtapadis). Again, it is a battle in which "one side fired artillery guns (*tupak*), while the other side employed war-elephants." These references suggest that it may not have been the siege of a small town like Saidpur.

But, when we read in Guru Nānak that the Moghals would come to India in '78 (i e. Samvat 1578 or 1520-21 A. D.) and quit in '97 (i.e. Samvat 1597 or 1539-40 A. D., when Sher Shāh Suri took over in mid-1539 from Humāyun, (vide Tilang M. 1), it seems that in the Guru's far-seeing eyes, the Moghal regime, though not yet settled on the throne of Delhi, in 1521, was unmistakably on the way to it. It can safely be assumed, therefore, that the occurrence of a firm date (1520-21 A. D.) as the coming of the Moghals into India in the hymn addressed to Bhāi Lālo of Saidpur refers to the grim fight that the inhabitants of this town under their Pathān princes and commanders put up against Bābur. It is quite likely that the use of the artillery by Bābur may have taken place in the battles of 1520, as according to available records, "between the years 1514 and 1519, Bābur profitting by the example of Shāh Ismāel was determined to possess effective artillery, and secured the services of an ottaman Turk, named Ustād Ali, who became his Master of Ordnance." The two earlier expeditions of Bābur in 1519 also witnessed gruesome massacres resulting in the total submission of the people of the North-West of India, upto Bherā, and it was only due to the critical situation at home – and not the resistance in Indiā – that Bābur had to march back to Kābul. That Daulat Khān Lodhi, Governor of Panjāb, with whom Guru Nānak had intimate personal relationship had, around 1524, invited Bābur to invade India and was in communication with him even before, may have tempted Bābur to meet the Guru at Saidpur, the more so when we find that even though a grim warrior, Bābur at heart was a sensitive person with a highly-developed religious bent of mind. He is referred to as a *Qalandar* in one of the legends described in *Tārikh-i-Dāudi*. During his attack in 1519, he gave strict orders to his troops "to do no hurt or harm to the flocks and herds of the people (of Bherā) nor even to their cotton ends and broken corn at a hand-worked stone-mill.* But, Nānak at heart was pleased, it appears, for his firm belief in God's unfailing justice had been redeemed. The cruelty and viciousness of the Pathān regime had been

---

needles" (Memoris of Bābur, Beveridge's translation, Section II, P. 377). Again in 1524, even when Daulat Khān Lodhi had rebelled against him, he intervened personally and killed one of the high officers of Humāyun in order to save the family of Daulat Khān from dishonour (Briggs, History of the Rise of the Mohammedan Power in India, Vol. II, P. 42). The magnanimous way in which he treated the family of the dead and the defeated Ibrāhim Lodhi also supports this view. In the face of a crisis at the battlefield of Chitaur, he forswore drinking and broke up all his gold and silver goblets and "distributed them to the faqirs." His prayer to God "to transfer the rest of his years to his ailing son," Humāyun, and the fact that he died in the process, reveals nothing less than a very sensitive and religious nature. For such a one, therefore, to have sought the blessings of the man of Nānak's spiritual station and fame (who was reputed to be the mentor and friend of Nawāb Daulat Khān Lodhi, Governor of Punjāb), does not seem to be either out of place or highly improbable. It is irrelevant to suggest that in such an event Bābur should have mentioned this episode in his *Memoris*, which are indeed very sketchy and give no account of his adventures between 1620 & 1626. As to why Bhāi Gurdās should not have made an elaborate reference to this is also beside the point, as Bhāi Gurdās's account of Guru Nānak's life is in bare outlines of what the former considers to be the most significant from the point of the Sikh doctrine. However, Bhāi Gurdās, in the same Vār I, has much to say about the tyranny of the Kings which Guru Nānak had to contend with and comment upon. It is also true that Mehervān makes no mention of Guru Nānak's meeting with Bābur (though he refers to the presence of Guru Nānak at the sack of Saidpur) nor of his utterances in this context referred to above. This, however, may be due to Mehervān's general character and the tone of his *Janamsākhi*. to write nothing against the rāj. In any case, it has to be stated that at no time does Guru Nānak compromise his basic ideals in his hymns known as "Bābur-Vāni" (Rāg Āsā Āshtapadis). If anything, they reaffirm Nānak's conviction that God's retribution must befall those who deflect from the path of justice and moral rectitude and that while Bābur may have saved India from the Afghān tyranny and chaos, it in no way justified his own barbarities. Whether, therefore, Guru Nānak physically met Bābur or not (and this is the least important in the whole episode), the fact stands out that Nānak was no mere pacifist interested only in the inner life or the life beyond, but that he was an earth-aware prophet of the living humankind, who was daring enough to speak out against tyranny in the language of blood and tears and even to court imprisonment as a consequence thereof. This fact is significant from the historical point of view, as the thesis is often preferred that while Guru Nānak, like Kabir, was interested only in the life of the spirit, it was the later Gurus, notably the sixth and the tenth who gave a militant turn to the community.

* The broken stones of this hand-mill said to have been worked by Guru Nānak we saw at the house of a Sikh in Kābul.

ended as if by the inexorable Will of God. So while other prisoners cried and groaned as they laboured, Nānak sang hymns in praise of God, one of which said :-

> "*O God, I am Thy bond-slave: How fortunate am I that Thou hast bought me over*
> *At Thy shop; and, in return, blessed me with Thy Word.*
> *Now, I serve Thee as Thou wantest me to serve.*
> *O God, how can Thy slave play clever with Thee ?*
> *There is no choice for him but to submit to Thy Will, and never to say, Why ?*
> *O Love, my father is also Thy slave, so also my mother: I am the offspring of Thy slaves:*
> *And as my mother dances, and my father sings, I, too, pay my devotions to Thee.*
> *O Master, if Thou art thirsty, I bring Thee water; if hungry, I grind corn for Thee,*
> *And wave the fan over Thee, and caress Thy feet, and utter ever Thy Name.*
> *O God, I have betrayed Thy salt, but, Thou forgivest and blessest me with glory.*
> *For, Thou art ever compassionate, the great Giver, since the beginning of Time; and no one hath found Release without Thee.*"

When this was reported to Mir Khān, the army General, that a faqir was dancing for joy over the labour he was entrusted with, he conveyed it to Bābur. The Emperor, much impressed, said he would like the faqir to be brought to his presence and expressed distress that such a one should have been put to hardship. When Nānak was presented to Bābur, and the latter asked for his forgiveness, Nānak sang:

> "*They whose tresses shone with lustre, their partings lined with vermillion,*
> *Their locks were sheared, and dust was thrown on their head:*
> *They who lived in the palaces do not find a place now in the common.*
> *O God, greetings to Thee,*

O Primal Being, no one knoweth Thy limits;
Thou donnest as many garbs as there are.
Beauty and riches which led men to much revelry, now have turned their enemies.
If only one were to forethink, one would come not to grief!"

Then Bābur said, "I've come to invade India, to release people from the oppression of the Pathāns." The Guru replied, "True, but you will go the same way if you oppress your subjects. These riches and lust for power have wasted away many people before. They come not without sin, but they keep no one's company for ever. And whoseever loses goodness of heart, him my God destroys."* Bābur was

---

* Ādi Granth, Āsā M. 1, Ashtāpadis, As the two hymns said to have been uttered by Guru Nānak at this time are of quite some historical importance, we quote them here in full. They not only reveal Nānak's anguish at human suffering, but also his acute observing eye and his tender sensitiveness to the objects of physical beauty. However, it is not necessary that all the hymns connected with the invasion of Bābur may have been composed or uttered at this stage. May be, they were composed after the battle of Pānipat (in 1526 A.D.), when there was much bloodshed and the suffering of the native princes as well as of common people was much more pronounced.

"They whose lustrous hair shone in plaits and were filled with vermillion in the parting,
Their hair was sheared with the scissors and their mouths were chocked with dust.
Yea, they who revelled in their palaces, now find not a seat even in the common.
Hail to Thee, O Lord, All-Hail:
O Primal Lord, I know not Thy end for Thou Changest the scene of Thy play many many times.
When these beauties were married, their glamorous spouses sat by their side,
They were carried in palanquins *and the bangles inlaid with ivory dangled round their arms.*
(In greetings), water was waved over their heads, and they were fanned with glass-studded fans.
A hundred thousand coins were offered to them when they sat and also when they stood.
And they chewed nuts and dates, and enjoyed the bridal couch.
(But), today round their necks is the noose, and their necklaces of pearls are broken into bits.
Both riches and beauty have become their enemies,
Which had lured them away to enjoy life's manifold pleasures.
Now, the soldiers have been told to dishonour them and carry them off,

F, N. Contd.

If the Lord Wills, He Blesses with Glory, if He so Wills, he punishes man.
But, if one were to foresee and fore-think, why would he be punished thus?
The kings had lost their heads and indulged in revelries.
But now that the writ of Bābur prevails, not even the princes get their bread to eat.
The Muslims have lost their prayer-time and the Hindus of their worship.
And, how can the Hindu women without a bath and plastering their kitchen-square, anoint their foreheads with the saffron-mark?
They who remembered not Rām, in their time, are now accepted not even if they shout "Allāh".
Some (warriors) return to their homes and from them others ask about the welfare of their kins (on the battle-field).
In the lot of some it is so writ, that (with their spouses gone) they will wail in anguish their whole lives.
Says Nānak: "That what the Lord Willed has come to pass, else what could the man do of himself?" (7–11)
"Where are the stables now, where the horses, where are the drums, where the flutes?
Where are the sword-belts, where the chariots, where the red dresses (of the soldiers), pray?
Where are the looking glasses, where the beauteous faces, no, I see them not before me.
This world belongs to Thee, O Lord: Thou art its Master,
And Thou Establishest and Disestablishest in a moment,
And through the lure of riches dividest brother from brother.
Where are the homes, where the mansions, where the magnificent sarais?
Where are the beauteous brides lounging on a cosy bed, seeing whom one would get no sleep.
Where are the betel-leaves and their sellers, where the harems—all have vanished like the shadow.
Many, O many, have been consumed and wasted away by their riches,
Which one gathers not without sinning, nor carries along when dead.
He whom the Lord wishes to destory, his goodness he destroys first.
Hearing of the invasion of Bābur, millions of Muslim divines prayed for his halt,
But, he burnt all the age-old temples and the resting places, and the princes, cut into pieces, were thrown to the winds.
And, not a Moghal was blinded.
And, no miracle, no charm, saved the man from disaster!
The Moghals and the Pathāns grappled with each other and the swords clanged on the battle-field.
And while the Moghals fired their guns, the others put their elephants forth.
But they whose fortunes were the losers at the Lord's Court, death forsure was in their lot.
The Hindu and Muslim and Rājput women had some their veils torn off from head to foot, while others were licked by the flames.

much moved by these words and said, "O man of God, forgive my sins. I promise not to commit oppression on the poor any more." The Guru took leave of him, saying, "Let God be thy light."*

As they came to the town of Sayyadpur, Mardānā heard much wailing of men and women for their dear ones who had been massacred by the hordes of Bābur. He asked the Guru why so many innocent men were done to death along with those few who were guilty. The Guru asked Mardānā to relax under a banyan tree, and after a while when he would come back he would answer him. As Mardānā reclined under the tree, he dozed off. And, then, suddenly, the bite of an ant awakened him. In one sweep of the hand, Mardānā rubbed off his feet as many ants as he could find, thus killing several of them. Nānak saw this, and before Mardānā could ask for the answer to his question, Nānak said to him: "You now know, Mardānā, why do the innocents suffer along with the guilty ?" Mardānā said, "O Master, thou alone knowest thy mysteries." Seeing much distress all round, Nānak asked Mardānā to play on the rebeck and himself sang the following hymn:

"O God, Thou protected Khurāsān, and brought terror to Hindustān.

But thou takest no blame for this, and sent the Moghals to bring ruin and death unto us.

And they whose loved ones returned not to their homes,
O, how did they pass their nights ?

The Lord Himself is the Doer and the Cause, so who it is that one may go to ask ?

For all joy and sorrow comes from the Lord.
Who other than Him can one go to wail ?
The Lord of Command yokes all to His Will and is thus pleased,
And, Nānak, we gather what is writ in our Lot. (7.12)"

* According to Latif, it was not Bābur, but Ibrāhim Lodhi, who ordered him to be kept in close confinement for seven months where he had to grind corn the whole time. This the emperor of Delhi did on receiving reports that "a faqir whose tenets were different both from the Korān and the Vedas was openly preaching to the people and the importance which he was assuming might in the end prove serious to the state". "His (Nānak's) distress came to an end in consequence of the victory gained by the emperor Bābur over Ibrāhim." (History of the Panjāb, P. 245). But, this incident is corroborated by no other source.

O God, when men are punished thus, and wail, Thou feelest no pain?

O Creator, Thou belongest to all.

If the powerful duel with the powerful, one minds it not.

But, if a ravenous lion pounces upon a herd of cows, the Master must answer for it.

They who have spoiled the priceless jewel (of India) and behaved like curs, will be wiped from memory after they are gone.

O God, Thou Thyself unitest and then separatest men from Thee. For such is Thy glory.

If someone has a great name, and enjoys himself to his heart's desire,

He is treated by Thee like a worm, who eats well (but thinks not).

*But he who dies while yet alive and lives in Thy love alone wins."**

It is said when Bābur heard of this, he once again invited the Guru to meet him, and offered to grant him anything he asked for. Nānak replied, "Your Majesty, it's only fools who ask anything from one other than God." When Bābur pressed his request several times, in great humility, Nānak asked him to release the prisoners he had taken. This, it is said, the Emperor did. Now, Bābur offered him wine. But, the Guru refused it, saying, "That which intoxicates a man for a little while and then leaves him cold and frustrated is of no use to me. I'm inebriated with something more enduring than this." Bābur misunderstood him, and offered him hashish (Indian hemp) instead. The Guru, much amused, sang the following hymn to explain himself:

"Love is my hemp, my heart its pouch:

O God, I'm mad after Thee, estranged from the rest.

With prayerful hands as the bowl, it is for the Vision of Thee I beg at Thy door,

O love, grant me the alms I ask for.

Saffron, flowers, musk and sandal make everyone fragrant,

* Āsā M.1.

So do the Saints with the fragrance of their souls,
No one says butter can be defiled, or milk,
So also the soul of the devotee whichever caste houses it.
O God, grant Nānak the alms of Thy Mercy,
That he may ever be imbued with Thy Name and Forsake
*Thee never."**

The Guru then took leave of the Emperor saying that if he would be just and revere the holy and indulge not in pleasures and be merciful to the poor and remember God in everything he did, he would come not to grief and his rule would last long.**

---

* Tilang M.1.

** In the Hāfizābādi version of the *Purātan Janam Sākhi*, it is said, Bābur promised to release the prisoners "if the Guru would bless him with rulership over India for many generations." The Guru blessed him likewise and Bābur released the prisoners he had taken" (in Saidpur). (*Purātan Janam Sākhi*, foot-note P. 67). "According to one of these reports," says Mohsin Fāni, "Nānak being dissatisfied with the Afghāns, called the Moghals into the country, so that in the year 932 of the Hejirā (A.D. 1525-26), Zāhir-ud-Din Bābur Pādshāh gained victory over Ibrāhim, the King of the Afghāns". This confusion may have arisen due to Guru Nānak's intimate friendship with Nawāb Daulat Khān Lodhi who in fact invited Bābur to invade India. Two of the explanations offered by recent historians or biographers of Nānak for the absence of any reference to Guru Nānak by Bābur in his memoirs are: (I) "Nānak was not at that time a man of sufficient note and importance to attract the attention of the Emperor when engaged in drawing up an account of his own life and exploits" (History of the Punjāb, Mohd. Lātif, P. 249, though the fact of his having met and conversed with Bābur is admitted by this historian). (2) "It has to be noted with regret that among the gaps which occur in the memoirs of Bābur as recorded by himself, one is about the period 926 to 932 A.H. (or 1520 to 1526 A.D.). These gaps have been filled up by the translator with the historical supplements, based on other books about the period. If Bābur had left a record of the events of this period, he would surely have mentioned his meeting with the Guru" (*Life of Guru Nānak*, by Kartār Singh, P. 224, f.n.). This last is a very pertinent and valid explanation though the fact must be noted that apart from a few general and not very laudatory observations about India's cultural ethos, Bābur, as was natural for an empire-builder, confines himself to the description of his military exploits in his memoirs and not of *any* spiritual personage whom he may have encountered, or discoursed with. But, the fact of meeting with Bābur is the least significant, the more relevant point being Nānak's active protest against his initial orgies and his enunciation of the eternal moral truth that "injustice cannot go unpunished", whether it is practised by the Lodhis, the Moghals or anyone else. *Prachin Panth Parkash* says the Guru blessed Bābur with seven generations of rule (p. 284). Both Rattan Singh (Ibid p. 277) & Osborne say the Guru was received kindly by Bābur to whom he was introduced by Daulat Khān (Ranjit Singh, p. 7).

The Guru now proceeded towards Sialkot via Pasrur. Here he rested under a wild caper tree which still stands to his memory.* He told Mardānā to go to the town and offer a penny twice at every shop and ask: "My Master wants to buy a penny worth of truth, and a penny worth of falsehood." Mardānā was much amused at this strange request, but did not cross the Master believing that he might be wanting to teach him some new aspect of Truth. Going from shop to shop, he put this question. Some considered him insane, others that he was trying to make fun of them. But one shopkeeper, Moolā by name, was much overwhelmed with this kind of questioning and said, "Go and tell your Master that life is false, and death is true." When Mardānā brought this answer to his Guru, Nānak said, "Such a sensitive soul I would like to see. It appears he knows the Reality." Moolā was brought to the presence ot the Guru who wanted him to accompany him on his travels. This he did for some time and returned to his home soon thereafter. But when the Guru visited his town a second time and asked for his whereabouts, Moolā's wife fearing that he might leave her again lied that he had left for a distant land. Moolā too, it appears, had despaired of his wanderings which were full of hazards and did not even bring him the daily bread to eat. Than to die in wilderness, he seems to have thought, it was better to stay at home in comfort with his family. The Guru sensing that he was being cheated, said, "This man used to protest that life is false and death is real, but now he too

---

* The tree now known as *"Bābē Di-Bēr"* is held sacred by the Sikhs and a beautiful Gurdwārā stands in memory of the Guru's visit to this place. It is said that here the Guru also shattered the pride of a Muslim Peer, Hamzā Ghaus, who was performing penances to invoke God's wrath upon the city, one of whose childless Hindu inhabitants had pledged to him that if as a result of his blessings he was blessed with a son, he would make an offering of him to the faqir. The man got three sons, but refused to honour his word. The faqir, much enraged, embarked upon a 40-day fast "in order to invoke God's curse upon the city of liars" and to destory it. But even though the forty days of his self-mortification passed, nothing happened to the city. This made the faqir even more furious and he came to call upon the Guru sensing that perhaps it was on account of his holy presence that his (evil) prayers were not answered by God. The Guru shamed him saying that, firstly, a man of God must not be wrathful or vengeful and even wrong-doers and sinners should be reclaimed and not destroyed. And, then, to destroy a whole town for the omission of one person and to seek God's intervention for a personal wrong was the height of churlishness.

seeks to cling to falsehood. So, let it be. But who can escape death ?"*

Travelling thence to Mithankot, Nānak came to meet Mian Mitthā (lit. the sweet one), a great Muslim Sufi, who contrary to what his name implied was very proud of his station. When told of the arrival of Nānak, he said to his followers: "I'd go to see him, and squeeze him dry like a lemon." When he came, Nānak greeted him with much courtesy. Mian Mitthā asked haughtily: "O Nānak, there are only two things which if a man accepts he is approved by God: one, God Himself and the other, the Prophet. But you accept not the second, nor read the Qurān. How are you then to be redeemed ?" Nānak replied, "It is the Qurān of the Right Conduct that I read, and as I live in God, I lean not on another. For, he who is in love with the One, loves not another."

Mian Mitthā than asked, "How can a lamp be lighted without oil ?" Meaning thereby that without the aid of the Muslim holy book, the Qurān, how could one's interior be illumined ? Nānak answered: "The (body's) lamp, if in it be the oil of wisdom, and the wick be of God's fear, and if it be lighted with the torch of Truth, its light illumines our within, and we see God. He who while he is in life serves the others of his kind, he gets a seat in the Presence of God."†

Then, Mitthā asked, "What is Wisdom ? How is one to fear God ? How is the torch of Truth to be lighted ? What indeed is Truth ?" Nānak answered: "To love is to be wise; to surrender to it, in all humility, is to fear God, to believe in it is to light the torch, and to know that He alone is in everyone and everything is to know the only Truth one ought to know."

Then Mian Mitthā asked, "What is the name of God that is most sacred to Him, which pleases Him most ?" Nānak replied, "Any with which one can be involved. For Thee, it is Allāh." And uttering "Allāh" thrice to him, Nānak took his leave, leaving Mitthā a much chastened man.

The Guru now visited Lāhore. Here, a multi-millionaire, Duni Chand by name, had planted scores of flag-staffs in front of his door.

---

*It is said that as a result of the Guru's 'curse', Moolā died soon thereafter, bitten by a snake (GR, P. 348). But from what the Guru is said to have preached to Hamzā Ghaus, it is highly improbable that the Guru himself indulged in cursing individuals who could not afford to keep his company for long.

† Sri Rāg, M. 1.

When asked what they stood for, someone explained that each flag denoted a hundred thousand rupees that the rich man possessed. Duni Chand heard of the arrival of the holy man and wishing him to partake of the feast he had arranged in honour of his dead father, requested him most profusely to grace the occasion. Nānak agreed, but said, "I would come if only I received an answer to my query from you." What is that ?" inquired Duni Chand in all humility. Nānak said, "I would partake of your feast if you take from me a small needle I have cherished all my life and deliver it safe to me in the after-life." "How can that be ?" asked Duni Chand, "how can one carry things of this world into the beyond ?" Nānak asked, "Then, why have you made such a display of wealth at your door if you cannot take even a little needle along with you into the beyond ?" Duni Chand was much ashamed at this reckless advertisement of his riches and, as directed by the Guru, distributed all he had to the poor and dedicated himself to meditation and service of the poor.

The Guru now came to what is now known as Kartārpur on the western bank of the Rāvi and not only stayed here for some time but founded a settlement.* A young boy, seven years of age, used to visit the Guru every morning and evening. One day, Nānak asked him what made him come to him at such an early age. The boy replied: "I have seen my mother lighting firewood. And it is the little sticks that burned first. That made me realise that one knows not when one's life comes to an end. So, one must start on God's

*According to the *Purātan Janam Sākhi,* it was a multi-millionaire Muslim called Karoriā (he is also addressed as Diwān in the *Purātan Janam Sākhi,* meaning chief or Sikdār, Sardār—according to Mehervān), who incensed by the Muslims as much as the Hindus following Nānak, went out to arrest him, but, says the *Purātan Janam Sākhi*, 'he fell from the horseback, and was smitten with blindness." His pride thus humbled, he later came on foot to visit the Guru and gifted away the site for the settlement at Kartārpur (P. 74). According to Mehervān, the township was founded at the end of his journeys, some time in 1526-27 A. D. as the Guru, according to this narrative left Sultānpur in 1506 A.D., (after a stay here of only about 2 years) on his first journey at the age of 37 years. According to *Purātan Janam Sākhi*, the Guru's travels started about 1500 A. D. and extended to over two decades in all. However, the latter source places the founding of Kartārpur before his second journey to the South, sometime in 1512-13, which seems improbable. Mehervān's chronology, otherwise, may not be acceptable, but it seems more likely that Kartārpur may have been founded at the end of the Guru's tours. And yet, as has been pointed out earlier, it is rather surprising how in factual details and even in vocabulary, Mehervān follows the *Purātan* version even in this *Sākhi.* According to Mahān Kash (P. 902), the city was founded in 1504 A. D., & the Guru settled here in 1522.

way soon enough." Nānak was much pleased at this reply. This boy, who lived to a hoary age, and became a renowned savant and later anointed the five successors to the Throne of Nānak, has since then been known as "Bābā Buddha" (the revered old one), due to his maturity even at his tender age.

Hearing of the Guru's settlement at Kartārpur, householders as much as the seekers of God, the rich as well as the poor, came from far and near to pay their homage. His fame had by then spread to the four corners of Hindustān and it is not unnatural that he attracted large crowds. Even his father came with all his people, his wife, and two sons, and his mother and other relations. Nānak took off his unusual robes and dressed himself in the way of the world, a turban on his head, a sheet of cloth over his shoulders, and a cover round his waist. Morning and evening, religious services were performed. He also started cultivating a farm and out of its produce, food was offered to whosover came to see him. Thus was laid the foundation-stone of a community-kitchen in which everyone, high or low, caste or no caste, and men of all creeds were made to eat together, perhaps for the first time in our history.

One day, a Brāhmin came to the Guru and asked for alms. He was directed to take food in the community-kitchen along with others. But, he refused, saying unless he cooked himself what he ate, he would be defiled. First, he would dig up the earth, then mark off and plaster the kitchen-square with cow-dung, wash the firewood so that no insect be burnt with it, and then cook his food. The Guru promised to give him uncooked food-stuffs that he needed after he had dug up and found no life coming out of the earth's womb ! But the more he dug up, the more insects he saw coming out of the earth. Nānak told him, "It is not through food that we are defiled, but through an evil mind."

Two Sikhs, Mālo and Bhāgo, asked the Guru if any good attached to the practise of penances. The Guru replied: "To practise penances is to reject the goodness of God. If we put to deliberate pain the body which is the temple of God, how are we to please Him? One should burn one's craving, not one's body. The mind can be steadied not by tearing it away, under compulsion, from the activity of life, but by yoking it to God in whatever one does. Holy is he whose mind is holy, who does injury to no one, and serves everyone, minding not the coat he wears, and remaining humble and giving up desire even in the midst of the work-a-day world."

It is here, it is said, that the Guru composed one of his masterpieces, the Bārā-Māha, in which he expresses his utter devotion to his one God, like a wedded spouse pining for her lord and master who has gone abroad. The changing moods of nature from month to month are reflected here in superb poetry, making more and more intense the lover's sense of separateness and lodging for union with the beloved.

A Sikh came to the Guru asking for help to marry off his daughter. The Guru sent one of his devotees, Bhagirath by name, to fetch him some gold ornaments from Lāhore, but not to stay there overnight. The devotee carried out the instructions with such devotion that the jeweller also liked to accompany him to the Guru. Here, he was overwhelmed with the piety and wisdom of Nānak and became a devotee of his. It is said, from here he went to Ceylon, distributing all he had to the poor, in order to propagate the message of his new faith and even converted Rājā Shivnābh of Ceylon to Nānak's way.

2

The Guru now decided to take a journey to the South. His companions were two Jāts, Saido and Gheeho. Seeing the Guru rise very early in the morning, and bathing at the river, they thought the Guru worshipped the god of water, Khwājā Khizar. It is said, "one day they had a vision of Khwājā Khizar who told them that while he was water, Nānak was the air in which water is contained". Their doubt thus dispelled, they yoked themselves to the service of the Guru with more sensitive devotion.

On their way to the South, they came across a famous Jain temple. Its custodian, Anbhi*, came to visit the Guru and asked, "Do you take old corn or new? Do you shake trees to get fruit? If so, then you destory life and are not worthy to be called a holy man."

*The Hafizābādi version of the *Purātan Janam Sākhi* calls him Narbhi. According to the *Purātan Janam Sākhi*, "the Guru used to live now-a-days on a handful of sand. With the sandals of wood on his feet, and a staff in one hand, he had twisted ropes round his head, arms and legs, and on his forehead was stamped a saffron mark" (P. 78). It seems obvious that his food must have been very sparse. Though Bhāi Gurdās also refers to his having lived on *Akka* and sand (Vār 1), for some time, it may not be taken to be literally true, as the Guru has denounced such yogic austerities in severe terms.

Nānak answered: "From water came the fourteen gems; on the river-banks are all the Hindu places of pilgrimage; water washes us clean; how can one despise the cool, flowing water, which gives life to us all. As for destroying life, is there anything that has no life, flowers and leaves have life, so has water life, so has corn, so have milk and curds. It is through wisdom that one is emancipated, not by shunning food that God has blessed us with, in any form.†"

As they passed through wilderness*, a devilish-looking man (whose name in some of the Janam-Sākhis is given as Kaudā), used to eating human flesh, barred their way. The Guru was accompanied by another Jāt also this time, Seeho by name. Seeing them, he wanted to spear them to death and then eat their flesh. Saido and Gheeho were much anguished at this, and started wailing The Guru stood composed, and sang the following hymn:

"If God be merciful, He'd cause the devotee to do as he is bidden,

And worship Him in whatever comes to his lot.

Such a one is then acceptable to my God."

Seeing his serene and holy face in the face of utter danger, the tyrant, it is said, was transformed, and became a devotee of God.

On the way, he met a Muslim Pir, Makhdum Bahaudin Qureshi, who was very proud of his spiritual attainments and renown. Many of his miracles he advertised to the Guru. Nānak said to him, "You are a spiritual person, and yet so proud of your station? The way of God is the way of humility. He who becomes fond of his own praise, loses God." The Pir took this censure to heart, and asked Nānak to stay with him for some time more to instruct him back to God's path. The Guru replied:

"Who can stay at a place, when nothing stays?

I would stay only, if that where I am, were to stay with me.

Yea, God alone stays: so I'd bide with Him,

---

†Mājh Ki Vār, M. 1.

*"An island in the ocean", says the *Purātan Janam Sākhi* (P. 81) in the Dhanāsri (Tanasirim ?) Desa. This must, however, be the territory of the aborigines of the Gond (or Bhil) tribe (now included in Madhya Pradesh). And Kaudā may be a corrupted from of Gonda, once a wild tribe.

For, the world stays not, nor the sky, nor day, nor night, nor moon, nor sun, nor the stars,

Nor Kings, nor pirs, nor angels, nor ascetics, nor men, nor books, nor rituals:

Yea, God alone stays, or His Word."*

Much humbled, the Pir asked "Whom am I to adopt as my Guru?" Nānak replied. "He who is the Guru of us all: thy God."

From there, the Guru proceeded towards Ceylon.† *On being* told that a great faqir had come from India to visit his land, the King, whose name is given in the Sikh chronicles as Shivanābh, (the name may have been Shivānābham)

---

*Sri Rāg M. 1.

†According to Mehervān also, Guru Nānak journeyed towards the South. He does not mention Ceylon by name, though he records his visits to river Kāveri and Rāmeshwaram, "from where he went to one *Vilāyat* after another, whose language and customs and rules were all different, but they all worshipped one and the same God." His visit to the South, according to Mehervān, took place immediately after his visit to Puri. There are several references in the Ādi Granth also which confirm the view that Guru Nānak was intimately conversant with the cultural ethos of the South — or Dakhan, as in his use of certain typical South Indian (Dakhni) variations of the Hindustāni musical system. The hymn in Rāg Dhanāsari (known as *Ārti*, and said to have been composed or uttered by him at Puri, or Rāmeshwaram, according to Mehervān) contains a reference to the sandal-scented winds from the Malai Mountain (in the State of Madrās) which is famous for its sandalwood. Lankā (Ceylon) is also mentioned by name in several of his hymns and the dominant southern cult of Shiva is commented upon at innumerable places by Guru Nānak in the Ādi Granth.

Though in the early part of the 16th century, Ceylon was divided into three independent kingdoms—Jaffnā, Kotte and Kandy – the latter two states were Buddhist, peopled by the Sinhalese. Only Jaffnā was inhabited by Tāmil Hindus, and may be, due to its proximity to the Mālābār Coast and the constant flow of Indian immigrants and merchants even from north India into this region, it was this part of Ceylon which Guru Nānak visited. It is true that history does not record any King or Chieftain of the name of Shivārābh at this or any other time who may have ruled anywhere in Ceylon. However, the tradition of Guru Nānak's visit to Ceylon was so persistent that a century after his death, the fifth Guru, Arjun, is said to have sent one of his devotees, Bhāi Pairā, to Ceylon in search of a copy of the "*Prān Sangli*" which Nānak was said to have composed and left with a devotee there. (SP, Rās 3, Ānsu 32). What Pairā brought back with him, however, the fifth Guru found to be spurious. It is stated in a prose-piece called "*Haqiqat Rāh Mukām Shivnābh Rājē Ki*", as appended at the end of the Bano recension of the Ādi Granth (see Chapter III) that Bhāi Pairā met the grandson of Rājā Shivanābh

F. N. Contd.

named Māyādunne, who is a historical figure, and fought the Portuguese as a Chieftain of a portion of the State of Kotte. But, Pairā could not have met Mayādunne, as the uprising against his brother with which he is connected and as a result of which Kotte was split up, occured in 1521 A.D. May be, he was one of his descendants, also called Māyādunne, whom Bhāi Pairā may have met. Historical evidence is, however, clear on the point that the cult of Shiva was extermely popular among the Tāmils of Ceylon upto the 16th century, thus making it obvious that the Guru met a Saivite King or Chieftain whose name may not have been Shivanābh, but only connoted his being the follower-king (Nābh) of Shiva.

However, in a paper entitled "Guru Nānak and Ceylon", delivered at a However, in a paper entitled "Guru Nānak and Ceylon", delivered at a Seminar in the Panjābi University, Patiālā, Dr. Saddhamangla Kārunāratna of Ceylon, basing his argument on a Sanskrit inscription on an old slab preserved in the Archaeological Museum at Anurādhpur (No. in the Museum Register, M. 111, confirms the visit of Guru Nānak to Ceylon. "The inscription scribbled in very small characters on the original writing, it is said, had been written on the orders of King Dharma Parākramabāhu, who came to the throne in 1493 A.D. In the fifteenth year of King Parākarmabāhu (i.e. Dharma Parākramabāhu IX), a religious teacher named Jnānak-ācharya (i.e. J-nānak-Ācharya) is said to have come to Jayawardhna from a village in the vicinity of Sāmantapattānā (Samaniurai). He met the King and expounding the doctrines of his faith, requested him to embrace it. The King, however, said he would do so if Nānak-Āchārya would defeat in a public debate the powerful Buddhist hierarch, Dharmākriti-Sthāvira, on the subject of a Supreme Personal Deity. This J-Nānak-ācharya did to the great satisfaction of the Brāhmin advisers of the King, the majority of whom voted in favour of Nānak's exposition of his doctrine, as they were very averse to the rising influence of the Buddhist monk. But, when they learnt that Nānak insisted on the acceptance of monotheism and rejected image-worship and the supremacy of Brāhmins in the hierarchy of caste, they invited him to meet the challenge of a more adroit and well-informed debator called Dharma-rājā-pandita, father of the poet Alāgiyavānnā. The subjects for debate this time were image-worship and the Brahmins' pretensions. As was the custom, a vote was taken at the end of the debate and this time the Brāhmins saw to it that the majority voted against Jnānakācharya who left Jayavardhna-pura soon thereafter. Thus, the Brāhmins re-established their supremacy by getting rid of both the Buddhist monk and by manoeuvring to make Guru Nānak also leave the country.' No mention is made here if the King accepted Nānak's faith or didn't, or whether for fear of the powerful hold of the Brāhmins in the court, he kept the fact of his conversion only to himself.

Prof. Kirpāl Singh of the History Research Depārtment of the Panjābi University, Patiālā, who visited Ceylon in this connection in 1968, in his report to the University has said that ten miles to the south of Batticaloā, formerly Mattakallāpo, in the east of the island, there is a small village called Kurukā Mandal (or Guru-Kā-Mandal), in which there is an old temple whose priest told him that it was named after a Jagat-Guru (world teacher), who visited that site some 450 years ago. Writing late in the nineteenth century, Gyāni Gyān Singh also mentions the name

sent beautiful damsels to tempt him with their charm. But Nānak took no notice of them. Then the King himself came and asked: "What's thy name, thy caste? Are you a yogi?" Nānak replied, "A yogi is he whose interior is cleansed with the discipline of God's love, and who is ever imbued with His Truth and whose comings and goings are ended. O God, what is Thy Name, Thy caste? When thou callest me into Thy Presence, I would ask Thee to answer the questions of my mind."

Then the King asked, "Are you a Brāhmin?" Nānak answered: "A Brāhmin is he who bathes in the waters of God's Wisdom, and knows the One alone whose light permeates the three worlds."

The King asked, "Are you a Khatri, a shopkeeper?" The Guru replied: "My tongue is the beam, my heart is the scale, and I weigh therewith the Essence of the Unknown. There is but one shop, and one merchant and the customers too are all of the same type."

The King asked if he was a Hindu or a Muslim. Nānak replied: "The True Guru has resolved the differences for him of the two ways who is yoked to the One alone: he cherishes His Word and dispels his Doubt."

The King was much impressed by these answers, and asked about the stage of a being such as the one Nānak had described to him. Nānak answered in most subtle terms: "The man of God lives in a state of super-consciousness, a Void it is, where there's neither joy nor sorrow, hope nor desire, caste nor castemarks, no sermons, no hymning of hymns; seated in himself, man meditates, composed like the sky, and knows himself."

F. N. Contd.

of the place where Guru Nānak met Rājā Shivānabh as Māttiākalām (or Mattakallappo). But this place is in the east, while *Haqiqat Rāh Mukām* (British Museum, UR. 1125) mentions the Guru as having visited Jaffnā in the north. According to the route given in the Haqiqat, the Guru took a boat from Nāgāpatnam at the mouth of the river Kaveri.

Says Kirpāl Singh: "The location of Gurdwārās - and Udāsi Mutts - at Rāmeshwaram and others at Guntoor, Kānchipuram, Trinmalai, Trichanāpali, built under the orders of Chandulāl Bedi (a descendant of Guru Nānak and then Prime Minister of Hyderābād) in the early part of the 19th century show that the Guru may have taken the old pilgrim-road to the South from Puri to Trichnapalli, visiting Guntur, Kānchipuram, and Trinamalai on the way and returned via Rāmeshwaram, Tilaganji (near Trivandrum), Nānak-Jhirā (Bidar), Nander, Broach, etc, the road that Malik Kāfur took in the 14th century for his expedition." (Sikh Review, Calcutta, October-November, 1969). In Tamil Nadu, there are still Gurdwaras in the memory of Guru Nanak, at Rameshwar, Salaur, Bhakkar and Shiv Kanji. Colombo also has an old Sikh temple and Guru Granth's old rescentions are found at Burhānpur (M.P.), Surat, Bombay (Mahalakshmi), Amravti, and Nirmal (Hyderabad, now Andhra Pradesh).

This composition, consisting of 40 stanzas and known as "Prāna-sangli" is no longer extant.* It is said the King was extremely pleased with him. The Guru blessed† him and said, "Thy devotion will be approved by God."

On his return to the Panjāb, the Guru went to a fair of the yogis in Achal-Vatālā† on the occasion of the Shivrātri fair. He was wearing the dress of a householder. There was such a vast crowd wanting to see and pay homage to him that the yogis grew jealous and their leader, Bhangarnāth, asked, "O boy, why have you made the 'milk sour (by wearing the robes of a householder while claiming to be an ascetic)? No butter (of wisdom) is thus churned." Nānak replied, "He whose 'mother' (i.e. the Guru) is unwise,makes the 'milk' sour by washing not the 'churn' (of the mind). He who abandons family life and curses it, shouldn't go out to beg at the door of the house-holders (as the yogis do). He who does nothing here, will get nothing hereafter."

The yogis were much taken aback at this curt though straight answer. So, they tried, it is said, to overwhelm him with a show of their occult powers. They assumed many fearsome and odd forms, but the Guru was unmoved and when they asked him to show them a miracle, in order to establish his identity as a man of God, the Guru replied, "All miracles are a negation of God. I believe in no miracle but God's Word and the companionship of the holy*", "Were I to put

* From the fragments now available of this metrical composition, it is obvious that the poem deals with the state of "super-consciousness" (*unmana)* and the method of attaining it, the nature of the soul and the body and the state of Void (*Shunya*) where the Absolute God abides. The excessive yogic terminology employed here makes it clear that is is the handiwork of some yogi, and not of Guru Nānak. Guru Arjun seems to have rejected it for inclusion in the Ādi Granth for the same reason.

@ *Purātan Janam Sākhi* refers to Guru Nānak having discoursed at this stage with the Siddhas not at Achal-Vatālā, near Gurdāspur, Panjāb, but at the Sumerū (or Kailāsh) mountain. But, according to Bhāi Gurdās, this conversation occured at Achal-Vatālā, after the Guru had settled finally at Kartārpur. We have placed it here on his return to the Panjāb from the South and before he leaves for Kashmir, as it seems natural that before he ventured out on another journey, he could not but have halted for a little while in the Panjāb before leaving for Kashmir, and from thence on to the Sumerū (Kailāsh) mountain. If, as the version of Bhāi Gurdās implies (Vār 1), the Guru went to Achal-Vatālā from Kartārpur and if we are to accept the thesis of Mehervān that Kartārpur was founded at the end of the Guru's tours, this episode will have to be placed later in his life.

* Bhāi Gurdās, Vār 1.

on the dress of fire, bide in a house of snow and eat iron, and eschew all my pain, and drive the earth before me, and weigh the whole firmament with a mere trifle, and perform the impossible, all that would be vain, if God blesses not me with His Grace and the joy of ever living in Him."@

It is said Nānak was now offered a cup of home-made liquor by the yogis in order to induce *samādhi* (the state of super-consciousness). The Guru refused the offer, saying, "He who has the Knowledge of the Divine, and meditates upon it, and does only what is good, and loves God, keeps ever intoxicated."

The Yogis asked, "Who, in your opinion, is a hermit?" Nānak replied, "He who with the 'sword' of Wisdom wrestles with the five passions, and knows how the ten organs of action and five of perception function, whose mind is ever filled with the Divine, and who makes pilgrimages, within, all the year round, and washes the pride of his heart, is indeed, a hermit."†

The Yogis then asked him to join their ranks without which no one could find Release. The Guru said, "Not through a patched coat, nor ear-rings nor wallet, nor the yogi's staff, nor a deer's horn can one become a true yogi. For me, he alone is a yogi who controls his five passions, sleeps little and eats but sparingly, and keeps devoted to God, restrained in desire, uttering wisdom, thus making his body and mind holy, and accepting as good whatever comes from God, the Good. Then, the Uustruck Melody of God's Word will fill one's being."*

In his third round of travels, Nānak proceeded to Kashmir. It is said, he wore in his journey "leather on his feet and on his head, twisted a rope round his body, and on his forehead stamped a saffron-mark like a devout Hindu." He was accompanied by Hassu, a blacksmith, and Sihān, a calico-printer. In Srinagar, they met a Brāhmin of repute, Brahm Dās was by name, who, in order to show off his learning, came with two donkey-loads of Sanskrit works to greet him. As a mark of piety, he wore a Shaligrām (stone-idol) upon his neck. Seeing the Guru robed in an unusual dress, he asked, "What kind of a faqir are you? You wear leather which is forbidden

---

@ *Sri Rāg*, M. 1.

† *Āsā*, M. 1.

* Sūhi M. 1.

to the holy. Why do you twist a rope round your body? What is your way?"

Nānak replied, "There is but one Road which leads to the only Door. The True Guru's Wisdom teaches everyone the Way."

Brahm Dās then asked, "Know you how the world was created? What was in the beginning and what was not?" The Guru replied:

"In the beginning was utter darkness and chaos upon chaos.
Then, there was neither earth, nor heaven, nay nothing,
but God's indescribable and wondrous Will.
Neither day there was, nor night, nor sun, nor moon,
only God reflecting on Himself in the Void.
There was neither wind nor water; nor the sources of
creation, nor speech,
Neither creation, nor destruction, neither coming nor going.
No seas, no rivers, no continents, no hells there were.
Nor paradise, nor world, nor underworld, there was,
Nor Brahma, nor Shiva, nor Vishnu, but my only God.
No rituals there were, no penances, nor the sacred books,
nor incantations, nor charms, nor the many, many ways.
No caste then was, nor pride, nor death, nor life, nor man,
nor soul, nor subject, nor king.
And when and how He pleased, He created the world and all
*we see and believe."**

The Pandit was still so proud of his learning that in spite of his being impressed by the Guru's instruction, he would yet feel hurt if the new teaching went against his own. Nānak feeling the inner state of his mind asked him to accept a Guru. "Who could be my Guru?" he asked, "I know everything I ought to know." Nānak then directed him to a wilderness where in a house he would find four faqirs who would tell him who his Guru could be. The Pandit said,

---

**Māru Sohile*, M. 1. This hymn has often been compared to the hymn of creation in the Rig Vedā (X. 129, 1-2), but the emphatic denunciation that Nānak makes here of the Vedic pantheon and rituals, charms and incantations, karma and what evolved out of it and disrupted the Hindu society—caste or varnāshrama dharma—makes it a thing apart from the original hymn. This also refutes the thesis of Swāmi Dayānand that the Guru "criticised" the Veda without knowing its contents.

"May it be so," and went to the place he had been told. The faqirs pointed towards a temple where they said he would meet his Guru. When Brahm Dās went there, he saw a beautiful, but nude, damsel who instead of greeting him crossed and insulted him. When he narrated the story to the faqirs who had directed him to her, they said, "this woman is MĀYĀ. Your heart is in her, and that is how you cannot find peace of mind." This led to much heart-searching on the part of the learned Brahmin who came to Nānak to ask for instruction. The Guru said to him, "Learning is not Wisdom. Wisdom comes through experience: experience through spiritual discipline which, if disinterested and grounded in humility, invokes the Grace of God." The Brahmin, purged of ego, dedicated his life to contemplation and disinterested service of others.*

The Guru, now scaling peak after peak, reached Mount Sumeru (or Kailāsh). There he met some renowned Siddhas whose fame as miracle-men and ageless ascetics had travelled through the country. They asked him in what state he had left his country, how the people lived. The Guru replied :

"*The Kāli age is the knife, kings are butchers,*
and justice has taken wings.
The darkness of falsehood is abroad,
And one knows not if ever there will rise
the moon of Truth.
The subjects are blind, and submissive, being
unwise, and live on falsehood.
The teachers dance to the tune of the disciples:
The Qāzis do justice if their palm is greased,
And what bind men and women to each others is
greed, not love."†

---

*The *Purātan Janam Sākhi* here narrates the story of a poor *bādhi* (carpenter) who gave shelter to the Guru in his thatched hut. In the morning, the Guru felled his hut and broke the string-bed in which he had passed his night. When Mardānā asked the reason therefore, the Guru said, "I have blessed him with a palace whose four pillers hide beneath them vast treasures." Such symbolic stories only reveal how distressed Nānak was at the sight of poverty of the honest, diligent and self-effacing workers and how, at every opportunity, he would inspire them to better economic and secular life.

†*Ādi Granth*, P 145,

Then, the Siddhas asked, "What is thy name, thy sect, thy object of contemplation? Where do you come from, where do you dwell and whither are you bound?"

Nānak answered: "I dwell in God who has his seat in every heart. I act as I'm bidden by God, the True Guru. I came in accordance with God's Will and will depart when He so ordains. To reflect upon my only God is my prayer. He who knows himself acts thiswise and is absorbed in the True One."*

The Siddhas asked,"Know you not that the world is like an ocean and is impassable. He who escapes it not, is drowned."

Nānak replied, "Like a lotus or as the water-fowl, I live in the water, so I'm drowned not. He who meditates on God's Word and lives, desireless, in the midst of desire, he remains unaffected by sorrow For him, there is neither coming nor going."**

The Siddhas, it appears, acknowledged, however grudgingly, the truth of what he said and greeted him with "*Ādēs-Ādēs*". It is said that here the Guru composed his philosophical composition, called the *Siddha Goshti*, through which are expounded the basic doctrines of his faith.†

On the way back, the Guru visited a place called Hassan Abdāl, the seat of a Muslim divine, which was then occupied by a person known as Vali Kandhāri, or the mystic from Kandhār. He was a person proud of his station and occult powers. Mardānā felt very thirsty, but there was no water around except on top of the hillock where lived the great Valı. Mardānā trekked upto him and asked for water which was refused to him because he was a kāfir (an infidel) and yet pretended that he was accompanied by a great Hindu Saint! "If he has no supernatural powers, why call your Guru a Saint?

**Sidha-goshti*, Rāmkali M. 1.

***Sidha-goshti*, Rāmkali M. 1.

†According to Gyāni Gyān Singh (Twarikh Guru Khālsā, p. 450), Guru Nānak visited Khatmandu in Nepāl. His visit to Tibet, though not confirmed by the present Dalai Lāmā in his communication to us is, however, affirmed by several rceent Buddhist Bhikhshus (who do not belong to the Dalai Lāmā's sect). They assert "that Guru Nānak is revered in Tibet as an emanation of Guru Padamsambhava". Bhāi Vir Singh's information based on eye-witness accounts is that several monastries contain his image and there he is worshipped as Bhadra Guru, or the Great Master, and that the followers of this sect visit Amritsar as pilgrims, and have belief in the Ten Sikh Gurus. (Nānak Parkāsh, Vol. II, edited by Vir Singh, pp. 690-93).

And if he has any, then, he should get water wherever he needs it." Mardānā, greatly distressed, reported the matter to the Guru, who, after a moment's thought, asked his follower to dig up the earth. He had hardly pushed aside a huge boulder, assisted by his Master, that sparkling water gushed out. The Muslim divine was greatly irked at this, and it is said threw a huge boulder towards them. This the Guru halted with the palm of his right hand. In memory of this event, a stone carrying the impression of his hand in recession (and not in relief as is given in earlier books) still stands at Hassan Abdāl, known popularly as Panjā Sāhib (or the Sacred Palm), at the head of a spring of lustrous water, about thirty miles from the present capital of Pākistān.* It is held in great reverence by all communities and is believed to be the hand-impression of Guru Nānak himself and is a centre of pilgrimage to this day. A great fair is held here on the day of Baisākhi (13th of April) to which people repair from long distances.

4

THE LAST—and the fourth—trip NĀNAK made was to Meccā, Medinā and Mesopotamia. In this trip he was accompanied by Mardānā. According to Bhāi Gurdās, "Nānak dressed himself in blue robes like a Muslim hājji. In one hand, he carried an earthen goblet for ablutions, and in the armpit the 'holy book' and a prayer-mat. Whenever occasion arose, he performed his prayer in the orthodox Muslim way",† and disclosed his identity to no one lest he be prevented from making this sacred journey which was permissible only to men of the Muslim faith.‡

---

*This episode is not included in the *Purātan Janam Sākhi* nor in Mehervān. Bhāi Gurdās makes no mention of it nor does Mani Singh, and it is included only in Bālā's *Janam Sākhi*. Sardār Hari Singh Nalwā built a temple here in 1833 to commemorate the event. Mahārājā Ranjit Singh first visited it in 1818. Moorcraft mentions a visit to it in 1823. (Travels in Panjāb etc. 319-320) & Shahamat Ali in 1839 (Sikhs & Afghāns, Pp. 158-59)

† Bhāi Gurdās, Vār I. According to "*Twārikh Guru Khālsā*" by Suraj Singh (1913), the Guru travelled through Mithankot, Sukkur, Rohri, Shikārpur, Larkānā, Hydrābād, Thattā, Hinglāj and Karāchi from where he took a boat for Aden (Pp. 114-16). Says Sewārām Singh in his "Divine Master" (P. 145) that passing through Sind, he boarded the ship at Dwārka.

‡It is stated by some biographers that a certain Muslim faqir (Shāh Sharaf) had a long spiritual discourse with him at Aden (Twārikh Guru Khālsā, Suraj Singh, p. 116). This is now preserved in a prose-piece called "*Hāzar nāmā*" (Panjāb University, Lāhore, manuscript Nos. 421 and 1091). The dialogue may have occur-

When he arrived in Meccā, * tired and footsore, it is said, he slept at night, with his feet towards the holy Kaabā. This was

---

F. N. Contd.

red elsewhere, but its incisive, terse style and singular content are something unique in mystic literature. A few quotations will suffice :

Q: Where is your home ?
A: In care-freeness.
Q: What is happiness ?
A: To be absorbed in His Vision.
Q: What is your wear ?
A' To die while yet alive.
Q: What is your body ?
A: Love for all.
Q: What is the nature of Paradise ?
A: Living in Truth.
Q: What is Hell ?
A: To be involved with the contingent.
Q: What is knowledge ?
A: Humility.
Q: What is renunciation (asceticism) ?
A: Patience (contentment).
Q: Who is one's friend ?
A: Right intention.
Q: Who is a dervish ?
A; He who is compassionate.
Q: Who is a King ?
A: He who is never unjust.
Q: Who is an *Auliā* (seer) ?
A: He who is desireless.
Q: What is emancipation ?
A: Conforming to an ideal.
etc. etc.

*Did Guru Nānak actually visit Meccā or is it the figment of a fertile though pious imagination ? If we are to believe that he did, how could he, the non-Muslims being strictly forbidden from entering its exclusive precincts ? If he assumed the garb of a Muslim hājji, as all Sikh authorities, including Bhāi Gurdās, afflrm (Vār 1), did his movements or his name not betray him on the way and was Guru Nānak capable of such a deliberate 'deception' ? No historical evidence, in spite of our best efforts, could be unearthed from the archives of Saudi Arabia, nor any local tradition commemorating his visit. How are then we to account for it as a fact of history and not a pious lengend ? Mehervān, for instance, places the facts of the episode (the Guru turning his feet towards the Kaabā, though not the mirculous incident of his feet being dragged to the other side and the Kaabā moving along with it) in a Mosque near Multān, in Panjāb, and not at Meccā, though he admits the fact of his having visited Meccā, as do all other near-contemporary Sikh

* *F. N. Contd.*

records. Some versions of the *Bālā Janam Sākhi* place this incident at Medinā which, of course, is a place not forbidden to the non-Muslims.

But, we must also take into account the fact that Nānak's visit to Meccā has not at all been contradicted to this day by any Muslim historian from Mohsin Fāni to Mohammad Latif and Mohd. Iqbāl. Says Latif: "He travelled over the whole of India; visited Persia, Kābul, and other parts of Asia, and it is said even Meccā. A story is related *by both Hindus and Mohammedans* in connection with Nānak's visit to Meccā......" Latif even takes the Guru from here to Istanbul, "where he met the Sultān of Turkey who was noted for his cupidity and extreme oppression. Guru Nānak's admonitions had a great effect on the Sultān who is said to to have distributed his hoarded treasures to the faqirs and the needy and to have discontinued oppressing his people" (History of the Panjāb, P. 245). Says Dr. Sir Mohd. Iqbāl, the noted poet-philosopher and one of the founders of Pākistān: "He is also said to have travelled through Persia and to have visited Meccā and Baghdād. In Persia and Afghānistān, he gained converts and established dioceses notably at Bushahr and Kābul" (Encyclopaedia of Islām, Vol. 4, London, 1934, under the entry "Sikhs").

Leaving the miraculous part aside (a cloud shading him on the way, his miraculous arrival at Meccā, the turning around of Kaabā, or the water-level rising in the wells of Meccā on his arrival, etc.), we must consider the fact of his visit to this holest of Muslim shrines from the historical point of view. First, of course, are the near- contemporary, written Sikh records all of which invariably affirm his visit to Meccā. Again, all of them are unanimous in their view that the Guru was dressed as a Muslim hājji. The *Purātan Janam Sākhi* even says that in spite of his assumed garb, a Muslim Darvesh, who accompanied him, identified him as a Hindu and said: "No Hindu has so far gone on a pilgrimage to Meccā. You also travel not along with me; either you go a little ahead of me or follow me." But, he does not ask him to desist from this venture, nor makes any fuss about it to the fellow-pilgrims, indicating thereby that the strictness with which non-Muslims were debarred from visiting Meccā in the recent times was not then enforced to the total exclusion of non-Muslims. It must also be noted that while all Sikh chronicles record the fact of Nānak having slept at Meccā at night with his feet pointing towards the Kāābā, except for Bhāi Gurdās, no one gives the location of his rest as a mosque, much less the most sacred of them. One Qāzi Rukun-ud-Din (vide 'History of the Panjāb' by S. M. Latif, P. 243. Bhāi Gurdās called him 'Jiwan' which is an Indian name) sees him in this position, but takes no serious offence, as he addressed him most politely: "O man of God, you are pointing your feet towards the House of God. Why do you do so?" (Bhai Gurdās says, 'Jiwen' kicked him). Similarly, according to Mehervān, the Guru's identity was revealed to two of his follow-pilgrims, Rahim Din and Karim Din. They asked him, "Are you the same Nānak who distributed all his belongings to the poor at Sultānpur (P. 451)?" And when they were convinced that it was he who had declared 'There is no Hindu, no Musalmān", they treated him as did the Muslim villagers on the way—with utmost consideration and respect, though they warned him also that as no Hindu had gone before him to Meccā, he should not

considered to be an act of great sacrilege as no Muslim ever does so. An Arab priest, much incensed at this impertinence, kicked him saying, "You infidel, know you not you've turned your feet towards the house of God?" The Guru answered: "you turn my feet towards a direction in which the house of God is not." The Mullā dragged his feet in the opposite direction, but, it is said, he saw the Vision

---

also accompany them. The Guru agrees but on reaching Meccā, they find that he has been there long before them and that the divines of Meccā have received him with great warmth after their spiritual discourses with him (P. 453). The voluminous "*Makkē Di Gosht*" (discourse at Meccā) with Qāzi Rukun-Din, in ms., (a copy of which is also with the author) is another pointer to the fact that Nānak's journey to Meccā had become the subject of wide discussion at home.

Secondly, as it has been stated earlier, no Muslim historian to date has contradicted the fact of this visit, nor called it impossible or even improbable.

Again, in line with the doctrine that Guru Nānak preached, it seems natural that after visiting all the Hindu shrines in India, he should have proceeded to Meccā as a *Hājji*. In the present century, the great Hindu savant, Swāmi Rāmakrishna Paramhansa, took habitation in a mosque for a time to identify himself with the Supreme Reality through a path different from his own. It is also well-known that at least three Christian adventurers, the most recent being T. E. Lawrence, visited Meccā in the garb of Muslims without being molested or spied upon as suspects. The gown with the verses of the entire Qurān woven into it and said to have been gifted to Guru Nānak at Baghdād (and till the partition of India in 1947 was lying at Derā Sāhib, Kartārpur) is another testimony of Nānak's intimate relationship with the spiritual world of Islām. Mirzā Ghulām Ahmed, head of the Muslim Ahmadiyā (Qādiāni) sect, not only admits in his numerous writings about Guru Nānak the fact of his visit to Meccā, but deduces therefrom that he was in fact a Muslim ! (vide *Sār Bachan*", Urdu, second ed , 1902, pp. 4377-4504). Says Sujān Rāi in his "*Khwāsautul-Tawārikh*" that the main incident narrated here occurred at Medinā. It may also be mentioned here that the devout Muslims, however, believe that the Kaabā moved several times from its place to offer its *Didār* (sight) to the holy saints and mystics who could not visit it owing to illness or the hazards of the journey or otherwise to pay homage to them. *(See Tārikh-i-Farishtā* (Persian) Vol. ii 416, etc., as quoted in Panjāb past and present", Vol. III, intr.)

If Guru Nānak's visit to Baghdād has now been established from the inscription found there in the early part of this century, a fact discussed later in this chapter, there is every reason to believe that Guru Nānak could not have missed the opportunity of a visit to Meccā. Not for nothing did the Hindus and the Muslims both lay claim to his dead body. That he attracted Muslims as much as the Hindus as his followers or admirers from Mardānā and Rāi Bulār to Daulat Khān Lodhi, points only to one conclusion, namely, that the Guru was accepted not as the prophet of an exclusive religion or sect, but as a mystic whose vision transcended the arbitrary limitations of sect, creed, colour, caste and geography.

of God in that direction also. This amazed the Muslim divine and saying, "Allāh, Allāh, this is a miracle-man; he makes men see." He repeated the incident to several of his colleagues. "A great Teacher has come from Hind exuding divinity and performing miracles," he said. They flocked to him in large numbers and one of them asked, "Pray tell us, which of the two is greater: Hindu or Musalmān?" The Guru replied, "He who does good and lives in God, for without doing good, both will come to grief."

They then asked him if he kept a fast in the month of Ramzān. Nānak replied, "I keep the fast every day: I fast by turning away from the Other and fixing my gaze on the One alone. I treasure compassion and abandon craving: thus do I fast."

Then, they asked, "Do you read the holy book, the Qurān?" The Guru replied, "I do not read, I do what is bidden by God. He who reads, but stills not his mind, his anxiousness goes not. But, he who loves, all that he does is worship. But how will they attain God whose Gods quarrel with one another."

It appears that several Muslim Saints who had come from India and had met Nānak before, among them Sheikh Ibrāhim Makhdum Bahāudin, etc., also came to know that Nānak was in their midst. So they told men of their faith about his unorthodox ways and mystic approach to the problems of spiritual life. They also came to pay their homage to him and asked other people to learn from him and not to argue with him. Then, they all asked how God's pleasure was to be attained by men of the world? Nānak replied: "By submitting, in all humility, to whatever comes from God."

After some time, the Guru went to Medinā and from there to Baghdād.* There, he sat outside the city and shouted his own prayer which said, "There are millions of nether and upper regions, and no one has found their limit. Only my God knows how vast is His expanse."† The Muslim priests were greatly enraged, for they had been instructed that there were only seven upper regions and as many nether worlds. But Nānak argued that a mortal who wanted to find the limits of God's power would only weary at the end. To

*"After visiting Meccā and Medinā, the Master travelled northwards through Jerusalem, Damascus and Allepo, and turning to the South-East, stayed for some time in Baghdād", says Sewārām Singh in his "Divine Master" (P. 145).

†Ādi Granth, Japji.

his memory, a shrine still stands in Baghdād, looked after by a devout Muslim.*

---

*An inscription in Turkish dated 912 Hijrā (1505-6 A. D.) first chanced upon by a Hindu ascetic, Swāmi Ānandācharya, before the first World War "outside the town of Baghdād", inspired the Swāmi to write a poem on the incident, later published in his volume of verse, called "Snowbirds" (Macmillan; 1919). The poem refers to the Guru having instructed and illumined the heart here of an Irānian disciple, the saintly Bahlol "for eight fortnights" who lived for "sixty winters" thereafter "resting on the Master's Word like a bee poised on a dawnlit honey-rose". (To suggest that Ānandswāmi must have seen the inscription some time after the Sikh soldiers invaded the city in March 1917 and unearthed another inscription whose details follow in this footnote, seems incredible, as no private traveller like the Swāmi could have been allowed entry into Baghdād during the period of hostilities, between 1914 and 1918). The date on this inscription, however, has been misread, it appears. For the other inscription in Ottaman Turkish gives a more reliable date—927 Hijri (1520-21) which should corresspond to the Guru's visit to Baghdād. Its translation, however, has been variously made by different scholars, as follows :

(1) "In memory of the Guru, that is the Divine Master, Bābā Nānak Faqir Auliā, this building has been raised anew, with the help of the seven Saints." And the chronogram read : "The blessed disciple has produced a spring of Grace—year 927 H. (History of the Sikhs, by Gandā Singh, P. 12).

(2) Guru Murād died. Bābā Nānak Faqir helped in constructing this building which is an act of grace from a virtuous follower - 927 A. H. (I. B. Banerjee, *Evolution of the Khālsā* Vol. I, P. 73). (Bannerjee even throws up a fantastic theory here based on his above translation, namely, that Nānak had a Guru in the person of one Murād at Baghdād !)

Bhāi Vir Singh in his *Nānak Chamatkār* (Vol. II, P. 664, f, n. follows in essentials the first version.

But, Macleod *(Guru Nānak and the Sikh Religion*, Pp. 130-32) secured the following from Dr. V. L. Menage, Reader in Turkish at the School of Oriental Studies in London :

1. See what the Glorious Lord proposed.
2. ( ) that the building should be new.
3. The seven having given help, there came for the chronogram of it :
4. 'The blessed disciple performed a meritorious work; may He recompense it.'

Year 917 A. H. (A. D. 1511-12).

His arguments are (i) that the word "Guru" is a misreading of Turkish 'gor' in line 1, meaning 'see', (ii) Murād (in line 1) is not a personal name, but bears its usual lexical meaning - 'desire', 'wish" (iii) the experssion Glorious Lord (of line 1) could not be applied to a human being, however saintly, but must refer to God. But, while the Turkish scholar admits the words in line 2 to be Bābā Nānak Faqir (or Bābā Nānak-i-Faqir) he avers that it does not fit the metre - and if it does, it does

The Guru then returned to his country, presumably via Kābul. On the way, he also halted at Multān, which was much frequented by faqirs in those days. The faqirs sent him a cup of milk, full to the brim, signifying that the place was already full of them and another like him could not be contained. The Guru placed a jasmine flower on top of the milk, suggesting that just as that flower with its weightlessness floated on the surface and displaced not the milk, so would he live in their midst, with the burden only of fragrance !

And, now, the Guru, far-famed and aging in years, though not in spirit, settled down at Kartārpur, on the right bank of the river Rāvi. He discarded the pilgrim's dress and donned the robes of a

---

not make sense ! And further that though the figures on the inscription 'certainly' appear as 917 Hijrā (A.D. 1511-12), the chronogram, according to his reading would indicate 1226 A.H. (1812 A.D.) - and this he says in order to conform to another thesis of his, namely, that the riddling chronogram of this nature, 'so far as he knows', do not make their appearance until the eighteenth century and that it would be 'surprising' to find an Ottaman Turkish inscription of this date in Baghdād (first occupied by the Ottamans only in 1534 A.D.).

One cannot but agree with the learned scholar that the first line should be read as he has deciphered, that the epithet "Glorious Lord" could not be applied to a human being in the primary seat of Islāmic theology. But, it must be conceded that he is stretching the argument a little too far by asserting that as the words 'Bābā Nānak Faqir' though clearly discernible do not fit with the metre, they should be left out of account. Also, that though the figures 917 Hijrā appear 'certainly' on the inscription, they should be made to conform to the chronogram in accordance with *his* calculations based on *his* reading of line 4 ! It is obvious that it is the figures which are in such cases more reliable and that the chronogram must agree with them, as they do, (according to the experts whom we have shown the inscription) rather than vice-versa.

Dr. J. Tekin, Lecturer in Turkish at the Harvard University has, however, interpreted it thus: "(i) Look what was wished by the Glorious Lord in His Majesty, (ii) that a new establishment he built for the Saint Bābā Nānak, (iii) the Seven gave help and there came this chronogram, (iv) the blessed disciple performed a meritorious work. May He then recompense it." According to him, the words "Bābā Nānak" fit in with the measure he has worked out, (⏑ - / - ⏑ ⏑ - / - ⏑ - / - ⏑ ⏑ - /) but thinks that the inscription could not be older than the year 1700 or so, for the letter 'P' used in the word "yapadi" in line 4 had not come into use in Turkish by that time (*Guru Nānak and the Origins of the Sikh Faith*, by Harbans Singh, P. 228). The same author is of the opinion that the figure 927 as shown in earlier photographs now reads as 917 H, as the figure 2 has since been mutilated and now reads more like the figure 1. (Ibid).

householder. As has been stated before, his wife was already here, looking after a farm along with her son, Lakhmi Dās, the other, Sri Chand, having become a recluse (*Udāsi*). Hearing that the Guru had come back, men and women flocked to him from the four corners of India to pay him homage and receive instructions from him.*

It is here that Mardānā, his life-long musician companion, breathed his last.† The Guru took his son, Shāhzādā, into his household and he played the rebeck like his father to the holy congregations, while Nānak sang his hymns. It is still a tradition that the Muslim Rabābis (rebeck-players) perform devotional music (*Hari Kirtan*) in the Sikh temples, with as much zest, and are revered as much, as the Hindu and Sikh musicians.

It is here that Bhāi Lehnā, later known as Angad, became a great devotee of the Guru and succeeded him to his spiritual Throne. Lehnā was going, as usual, on a pilgrimage to the temple of Vaishno Devi, the goddess he worshipped. On the way, he was persuaded by one of the Sikhs to stop over for the night and meet Nānak, the Guru. This Lehnā did, and was so impressed with the piety and searching wisdom of Nānak that he became his disciple and served him most faithfully till the end of his days.

---

* Says Mohd. Latif of these days: "Though a faqir in name and appearance, he exercised great influence over vast numbers who looked upon him as their spiritual leader. His expenses were like those of a King and he established an alms-house where thousands of helpless and poor people were fed." (History of the Panjāb, P 245-46).

† GR. P. 497: "His body was consigned to the river Rāvi". According to Mohd. Latif, who obviously bases his account of Mardānā's demise on Bālā's *Janam Sākhi*, places it in Khulm (which fact is also referred to in GR. P. 497, though the place named is Khurmā-Des) in Afghānistān where he was cremated according to his own wish (History of the Panjāb, P. 245). Kahan Singh (MK P. 2856) supports the thesis that Mardānā died on the banks of the river Kurram, in Afghānistān, at the age of 75 (1459-1534 A.D.). *Purātān Janam Sākhi* makes no mention whatever of Mārdāna's end, nor of any of Nānak's parents or relations, though, according to Mohd. Latif, his father and Rai Bulār had died before Nānak ventured out on his travels to Ceylon and the countries of the Middle East. Though completely in line with the Indian tradition, it is rather strange that no account should be given by the more authentic and earlier Sikh biographers of any of Nānak's parents, or of his disciples, or even of his loved sister's end, and only the later Bālā tradition or Mani Singh should have filled this serious lacuna in the case of Mardānā, Mehtā Kālu and mother Triptā (See GR, Pp. 505-6)—who all died at Kartārpur, though the events are not sensitively portrayed and made only an occasion for an unusual and casual metaphysical instruction.

One day, in order to put his followers to a test, the Guru assumed the garb of a wild man. Donning a tattered gown, an open knife in hand, and taking some hunting dogs with him, he proceeded towards the forest. Seeing him dressed thus, many of his followers fled in terror. Others who went a little further found some copper coins scattered on the road and picking them they, too, hastened back. Some who remained found a few silver pieces further ahead, and picking these they too returned home. Only two of his Sikhs and Lehnā remained. The party now approached a burning pyre, beside which lay a dead body, covered with a white sheet and emitting foul smell. The Guru, his eyes wild, thundered: "Whosoever desires to remain with me, let him eat this corpse." The other Sikhs fled in horror, but Lehnā remained and said, "I would obey my Master." And, as he proceeded towards it, the Guru stopped him, saying, "That's enough. I now know how many have the moral strength to follow my Path."

Lehnā not only worked on the farm, but devoted his entire spare time to the contemplation of God's Name. Nānak put him along with others to several more tests, but whereas his sons always disobeyed him, and his other followers shirked work or did it grudgingly, Lehnā never wavered in his faith. Divining his end to be near, the Guru anointed him as his successor, placing five paisas and a coconut in front of him and going round him four times.* Bhāi Buddha, his other devoted Sikh, applied the tilak (saffron-mark) to his forehead as a mark of approval. Such was Nānak's humility that he considered the ceremony incomplete without its being approved by his devout followers.

---

* Guru Angad served his Master for at least six years at Kartārpur, (he is said to have met Guru Nānak in Samvat 1589 or 1532 A.D. - M. K, P. 333), and it is impossible that within this period, he should not have learnt all about the Guru's travels and experiences from him personally. We cannot agree with Bālā's *Janam Sākhi*, therefore, that after the demise of Nānak, his successor was in search of a man who should have accompanied him on his travels and known intimately the facts of his life, and thus he chanced upon Bālā - a Sāndhu Jāt - of whom he had not at all heard earlier! Or, that Bālā's biography of Nānak was written out by one Pairā Mokhā of Sultānpur, at the behest of Guru Angad, as dictated by Bālā. In the first place, Bālā is not at all mentioned by any of the earlier Janam-Sākhis or by Bhāi Gurdās (in Vār 11), though the strong and persistent tradition about his association with Guru Nānak at least in his early life cannot be lightly brushed aside. But, if Bālā were such an intimate associate of Gurū Nānak, to the exclusion of others, including Bhāi Buddhā, Gurū Angad would have known all about him. If

The Guru's wife protested: she brought to him his two sons and said, "What is to become of me, of them?" Nānak replied, "God is your refuge. I have done what God in His Will bade me do." The Guru then sang the following hymn:

"Hail, my True King, hail, Thou who createst and yokest each to his appointed task.

And, then, when one's days are over and the cup is full, Thou separatest the body from the soul.

When the hour striketh, the soul is led away and the dear ones wail in sorrow.

Remember God, O my loved ones, for all must depart.

The world is but for a few brief days and then we part.

Like a guest we should bide here, and be not vain.

For, in the other world, only the deeds are reckoned, and God accepteth only those who have lived in his love :

O father, they alone mourn us truly, who mourn in love for our good, not goods.

*O love, they alone weep for us, who weep for love."**

Then the Guru asked his followers to sing the composition called "Sohilā" (or God's Praise), which he had enjoined upon them to sing before retiring to bed, and which says:

"Sing the Praises of my Lord seated in the house of Poise.

Yea, of my fearless God, whose Song brings the mind home.

He whose gifts cannot be evaluated, how can one evaluate Him, the Giver ?

F. N. Contd.

a biography of Gurū Nānak was, therefore, ever dictated in the life-time of Gurū Angad, it must have been by the latter himself, though it seems now lost to posterity.

* Vadhans M. 1. It is given in the *Purātan Janam Sākhi* (P. 111) that the Bārā Māh (or his well-known calendar poem) was also uttered by Guru Nānak at this time.

The year, the month, the hour of 'marriage' is fixed. Pour oil on the threshold, my mates, and bless me that I meet with my love.

*In every home, today or tomorrow, cometh from beyond the call. So assemble your God in the heart, for the day must come for us all."**

After this, Nānak bowed before Guru Angad and entrusting his "Book of Hymns" to him,** entered into *Samādhi*, and was no more. Now, it is said a quarrel ensued between Hindus and Muslims whether Nānak should be buried like a Muslim or cremated like a Hindu. Both claimed his body with equal vehemence. The wise of the two communities decided that flowers be kept by both, overnight, on his body and the flowers of whomsoever withered first should give in to the other. But in the morning, the flower-offerings of the one party remained as fresh as those of the other. But, says the devout chronicler, when they lifted the cotton sheet from his body, they found not the body, only silence and flowers! They then decided that they would divide the cotton sheet into two equal halves, one burying it and the other consigning it to fire. This happened on Asu Sudi 10, Samvat 1596 (or, Monday, September 22, 1539 A. D.).***

---

* Sohilā, Gauri Deepaki, M: 1. It is also stated in the *Purātan Janam Sākhi* (P. 114) that Gūru Nānak sang his *Ārti (Gagan mahi thāl...........)* also before his demise, and ended his recitations with the last *slokā* of the Japji.

***Purātan Janam Sākhi* (p. 114). This incident throws significant light on some of the controversial corners of Sikh history. The fact that a book of hymns, written (obviously in Gurmukhi characters) by Gurū Nānak himself was handed down to Guru Angad debunks the thesis held so far, namely, that (1) it was not the first Guru but the second who gave vogue to the Gurmukhi characters. In fact as we have said before, these characters were current even before Guru Nānak: (2) that the fifth Guru had to hunt up material for the compilation of the *Ādi* Granth from [illegible]'d sources. I fact, the earlier Gurus' compositions must have been before him in his own house, which fact is also corroborated by various hymns of the 2nd, 3rd, 4th and 5th Gurus, following closely not only the content but also the style, metre, musical measure and even the vocabulary of the earlier masters. For details, see Sāhib Singh's "*Kujh hor Dhārmik Lekh*" (First ed., Pp. 9-45).

***"*Gurpurab Nirnay*", by Karam Singh, (p. 57). Most Sikh authorities support this date, though *Purātan Janam Sākhi* gives Asu Sudi 10, S. 1595 (1538 A.D.) as the date of his demise. However, one of its ms. copies lying at the Khālsā College, Amritsar Library, corroborates our view, though [illegible] supports the former date of 1538 A.D. (Sikh Religion, Vol. 1, p. 191). "A Short History of the Sikhs" by Gandā Singh (p. 17) also supports our view; so do Bhāi Kāhan Singh (MK.

Thus ended the life-story of this unusual and mysterious man who became a legend in his own life-time and for whom his life—nay all life—was one single experience of Truth, and who lived that he may suffer and see, and who saw a Beyond that is here, within us, within the reach of us all, and yet so distant and unreal to many. He gave meaning to life by integrating it with the total self, by taking out of it what was not life, by dying while alive and yet living the life, whole and entire, which makes man both happy and free.

F. N. Contd.

p. 2074), and Bhāi Mani Singh (Gyān Ratnāvali, p. 587). The ms. copy of the Ādi-Granth at Kartārpur places this date ten days earlier, namely, at Asu Vādi 10, but in the same year (Sāmvat 1596 or 1539 A.D.).

CHAPTER V

GURU NĀNAK AS A PHILOSOPHER AND A POET

Guru Nānak's philosophy of life has been set forth in the preceding pages through his life-story, though it must be emphasised that in no single composition of his, an integrated pattern of his doctrines can be sought. And this is as it should be, for, according to Nānak, religion is an experience, not a matter of set beliefs, dogmas or rituals. This, however, does not mean that he is confused, obscure or inconsistent, or has no specific ideas or concepts about the religion he seeks to expound. It only means that while the highest end of man's earthly existence, according to Nānak, is God-realisation, that is, a total integration of the personal ego with the Creator of the universe of virtue and wonder, the state one enters upon as a result of such unitive experience is ineffable and cannot be expressed in verbal terms. Again, while man is helpless before God, the all-powerful, and cannot storm his citadel solely by his own efforts and must, therefore wait upon His Grace, he yet is endowed with a free will with which he can prepare the ground for invoking the Grace of God. For this, the path is of self-discipline (the discipline that is of both mind and heart) through self-surrender and self-denial, spontaneously (through *sahja*) not through self-torture or forced body-postures (*hatha yoga*), customary rituals (*karam kanda*), or even intellectual analysis or mental acceptance of God, or His Truths, for to enter upon the state of Grace, all of man's faculties, mind, emotion and will, have to come into play. Only a house-holder—man as well as woman of every caste and creed—could experience this state, though not the one who is self-indulgent, but the one who keeps detached in the midst of attachments, "like the lotus flower sticking out its head proudly through marsh and mud," "as a duck floats, care-free, in the stream." Thus, Nānak is both a supreme mystic and a prophet of secular hope.

According to him, one must participate in the activity—every activity—of the world, not to gather, but to share the fruits thereof. But sharing itself leads not to the integration or the illumination of man unless it is dedicated to God, the ideal Good, through whose Grace, we are endowed with the human birth and an opportunity to work and to share in the name of the ideal in whom alone we can find both a kind of peace *(sahja)* and joy *(ānand)* that passes understanding (and which is termed 'heaven'). Why man should embark upon this idealistic adventure is because he who doesn't, burns ever in life (which is 'hell'), and his mind is ever restless and its coming-and-going (Āvāgavan) is never ended.

Were it not so, man wouldn't be in perpetual misery, age after age, no matter what the state of his material health. Only if man learns to awaken himself to the *Hukam* (Divine Order) of God, which the Guru's Word echoes in the inner recesses of man, *time after time*, and which is writ large in the nature of both man and all creation of God, he finds perpetual repose. It is to the eternal credit of Nānak that he neither identified God with a particular religion or region (celestial or otherwise), nor the Guru with a person or a time-cycle. The Word also is eternal, like the Guru and God, and cannot be identified either with a particular language or specific concepts. The Name (Nām) which he enjoins time and again for man to meditate upon is also not a particular name of God or Guru, in a given language, but every notion, aspect and idea that expresses His virtue and wonder. "As much has God created, that much is His name" (Japu). Utterance, therefore, of the Word or the Name is not enough, it is its realisation that matters. Love is its language and the whole creation is its form. This is not the voice of a mere Bhakta, for unlike a Bhakta, Nānak believes not in the worship of God's incarnations *(Avtārvād)*, nor drives man out of his earthly activity *(Vairāg)*.

Religion has thrived mostly on the fear of nature and the miracles of the Prophets. Nānak is emphatic that nature acts according to fixed laws or what he calls Hukam, (the Divine Order), that it is essentially moral and if one must fear anything, one must fear oneself, one's own ego, which flouts this moral Order, and hence comes to grief. "He alone is afraid who sins: the man of God is ever in joy," for the awakened one attunes himself to the Divine Order and nothing that comes from God he takes as evil. The only miracle Nānak claimed to perform was to make man able to transcend himself. "Except for the Guru's Word (i.e. the eternal truths) and the companionship of the holy (which makes one understand its import), I have no other miracle to show."*

Guru Nānak, like the Hindus, believed in *Karma*, transmigration of the Soul and the end of all human activity being to find release from "coming-and-going" (*Āvāgavan*). But, as we shall see later in this chapter, he transformed the meaning of all these terms. He has referred copiously to Hindu mythology, not to imply his belief in it but in illustration of a moot point. It has been suggested that his strict monotheism is a direct influence of Islām. His insistence on *Sangat* is said to be derived from Muslim *Jamāt* or Buddhist *Sangha*. His doctrine of Divine Grace, it is surmised, is derived from the Christian creed. His total dedication to the loving adoration (*Bhakti*) of God makes him in the eyes of the casual observer a follower of Hindu *Bhakti*, and Muslim Sufi-ism, or both, whose synthesis, it is suggested, he attempted. But, for the perceptive minds, he reinterpreted both Islamic *Sufi-ism* and Hindu *Bhakti* and instead of making an amalgam of the two, asked man to rise above both. The Divine Will (*Razā or Hukam*) is not arbitrary, according to Nānak, as it is in Islām, nor his God is exclusively the God of his own followers, nor his heaven a stage in the Hereafter, nor does he divide mankind into Momins (Believers) and Kāfirs (Unbelievers). His monotheism also is not a belief only in the transcendental aspect of God, as in Islām, but also in His immanence and His Presence here before us. "Neither the Vedas nor the Semitic texts know His Mystery, for, He is outside of them, both, and is a Presence for us all to see." (Māru Sohila, I).

In respect of the Hindu influence, the basic doctrines of Hinduism Nānak rejects out of hand (the belief in the *Vedas* and the *Purānas*, the Trinity of Godhead, identification of God with the forces of nature, the incarnations of Vishnu, the belief in caste, *hatha yoga* and *vairāga* or renunciation of the world, the degradation of the women (according to *Manu-Samiriti*) *Karma-kānda*, (or ritual, etc.) As a Bhakta too, as has been pointed out (and will be elaborated later on),

* Bhāi Gurdās, Vār 1.

his difference with the cult of *Bhakti*, as enunciated by Rāmānuja, Vallabhāchārya and Rāmānanda, are fundamental. With the Alwār Saints of the South, he has a certain affinity, but only to a small extent (in their emotional, mystic approach to reality). Nānak bases his religion on something more solid and earthly, as well as more idealistic.

As we have already seen, wherever Nānak went, he challenged superstition, formalism in religion (both Hindu and Muslim), caste-consciousness, separateness or superiority born of creed, sex or colour and awakened men to their inner self which, indeed, had, in the words of Pipā, emanated from a Universal Self :

> "*That what is in macrocosm is also in microcosm*
> *and he who searcheth, findeth too.*" (*Ādi Granth*)
> **(Jo brahmandē, soee piṇdē,**
> **Jo Khojē so pāvēy).** (Pipā, Dhanāsari)

For this, it wasn't necessary to deny the world, but to actively engage in honest secular activity, not only to earn one's bread, but to have the privilege of sharing it, and this, not to pamper one's ego or to earn other men's favour or gratitude, but as an offering to the Divine within us and beyond. And what is more, according to Nānak, the merit of a devoted life of the spirit was not to be had merely in the Hereafter, but also in the here and now. If on account of our own delusion (Māyā)—of getting involved with the unreal taking it to be real—we fall in bondage and experience misery, then deliverance (*Jiwan Mukti*) is also here in the living life :

> "*Why blame others, blame your own deeds.*
> *For one receives the fruit of what one sows.*"
> **(Dadē, Dos na Deu Kisey, Dos Karamān āpnian:**
> **Jo men kiā, so men pāyā, dos na deejē avar janā).** (Āsā, Patti, I)

Thus, although Nānak accepts the validity of the Hindu view of Karma (the law of cause and effect on the moral plane) leading to transmigration, and the end of life being the attainment of *Moksha* (*Mukti*), *Nirvāna* (*Nirbān* in the Guru's terminology), or deliverance from a mere coming and-going (*Āvāgavan*), he entirely invests their meaning with a new significance. This human birth is not a punishment for our sins committed in an unknown past, but a stage in man's evolution from which there is only but one higher state, that of the superman (*Gurmukh*, or the God-man), of an angel's, not Neitschze's man of power to overpower others. Hell is here and also heaven. "In ego," says Nānak, "does one experience heaven or hell." (*Haon wich narak surag avtār*—Vār Āsā). "O father, my coming-and-going have ended. The fire that burnt within me is cooled with the nectar of Thy Name."

Man is not born in sin, nor is the world false; even though transitory, it is the abode of the True One. "Precious is the human birth," says Nānak, "only those turned Godwards attain to it." (*Mānukh Janam dulambh, Gurmukh pāyā*). Again, says he: "Implanting His Name within us, God has made our body the expression of His law." (Vār Āsā),

"True are Thy worlds, True Thy Universes," though "false are the kings and those that subject themselves to their authority and also they who come here merely to go out, build castles of dust but not hearts of men !" (Vār Āsā), says Nānak. "Wondrous are sounds and sights and the wisdom of men and the distinctions they cultivate, *and even their separate ways*. Wondrous are those who walk on Thy Path *and also those who are strayed away*. O God, I'm wonderstruck on seeing all Thy wonders." (Vār Āsā).

So that, according to Nānak there is nothing inherently sinful. "Whom shall I call bad when there is not another without Thee ?" (*Mandā Kisnun ākhiyē, Jān tis bin nāhin Koey*) proclaims he.

But, still there is sin and pain in the world. "The world was created for the Saint," says Kabir, "but thieves have taken it over, though the earth minds not their weight and even brings them profit." Such, however, is not the reaction of Nānak. Not only did he court imprisonment at the hands of Bābur, but uttered some of his most patriotic verses at this time, full of not only anguish but an appeal to act and rebel:

"Nānak: now is the time to sing the wedding-songs of death,
And anoint our foreheads not with saffron, but with blood."

"Pain is the cure: pleasures are the malady," proclaimed he as a medicament for the state into which his countrymen had fallen. Was the God of men (both Personal and Absolute, transcendent as well as immanent, who belongs to all, everywhere, and at all times, who's without fear and without hate, is not only the God of Grace and the source of all good, but also the punisher of evil), to blame for this? Apparently yes, but in reality no. "For he whom God wishes to waste away, He takes away his goodness first." Thus the response of Nānak to the political challenge to his country is not merely socio-political but basically religious and moral. A morally weakened man and society fall a prey also to secular ills. But, it is given also to man, says Nānak, to restore his inherent goodness by attuning himself to his God, through constant self-denial and living for causes and ideals higher than himself, judging every deed he does by the standards of the absolute, and not personal pelf or profit.

This one remarkable feature in Nānak's message transformed our whole society whereever his holy name travelled : that the body, the temple of the God of Truth, was to be yoked to find out and attune ourselves to this Truth, not merely for the sake of individual salvation, but for uplifting a whole corporate society. "Nānak: he who is redeemed redeems others too by his presence." (Japu). And redemption comes through the discipline of a type of what Sri Aurobindo has lately termed "Integral yoga," (or *Sahj Yoga*), which is a combination of the Bhakti-yoga, Karmayoga, and Gyan-yoga, but *not* of Hathayoga, maceration or burning-awáy of the body.

It is thus highly unjust and both metaphysically and historically incorrect to classify Nānak or his movement as an offshoot of the Bhakti cult. The Bhaktas, though they denounced, by and large, the distinctions of caste* and station and even creed, ritual and formalism in religion and insisted on redemption being attainable to everyone, through the loving adoration of the one God — whether of His Absolute (Nirgun or attributeless) self, or more particularly of the incarnations of Vishnu — Nānak was emphatic that there was but one God, formless (*Nirankār*, though not attributless), unborn, and not incarnated, both absolute and personal (personal not as a Person, but as Light and Love, expressed through His Word, or the Unstruck Melody which resounds at the heart of every particle of the universe), transcendent (i.e. unknowable and indescribable) as well as immanent

* However, Rāmānuj, the 11th/12th centuary South Indian Brāhmin, who gave an intellectual basis to the cult of Bhakti, as against the emotional mystic tone of the Alwār Saints, proclaimed that *Bhakti* could be practised only by the twice-born, i.e. the three higher castes, excluding the Sudras and women. It was his cult that was propagated by Rāmanand, Kabir, etc , in the North, though it was also emphasised that *Prāpati* (God's Grace) could be depended upon by everyone.

(as in nature). His second vital departure from Bhakti was the reality he gave to the world of form. He agreed not with the Bhaktas that it was Māyā—an illusion or delusion—though in the time-sense it was temporal and transitory, but in its being the abode of God, his battle-field, the expression of His moral Law, and partaking wholly of His essence, it was real. It is thus that against the prevailing trend in the Bhakti movement, Nānak sanctified the life of the household and gave woman a status equal in every way to man. He thus spiritualised secular life and to the earthly life he gave spiritual sanctions and moral hope. For Nānak, without ethics a spiritual life could not be consummated.

And not only does he sanctify the life of the earth, but also rejecting out of hand all the theories about the origin of the world which reason will not accept. For him, the origin of the world is a mystery, though he makes references to God first creating air, then water, and out of water all life. He also avers that man is the acme of the animal life, nay, God's own image, and that whosoever wants to attain God will find Him in his within and not without, that God was and will be at all times and so also the Guru and His Word, That the only speech He appreciates is that of love. Thus, according to Nānak, to identify God only with particular religions and Truth to be the monopoly of a few messengers or prophets at a given time is wholly irrelevant, so also the coats and foods and languages and forms of worship sanctified by different creeds. Neither God is anthromorphic nor His heaven or hell definite places to which man repairs in the Hereafter. God is within us all—and yet beyond all—He is both in Time and beyond Time. And, He is a Presence, for His moral and spiritual laws whosoever accepts, finds not only quietude (*Sahaj*) but also joy (*Ānand*) here and now, and he who doesn't, burns in the fires of his own creation, here before us.

It is thus to the eternal glory of Nānak that whereas before him look into the books of India's history as well as you may, you do not come across a whole man for centuries before him. With his rise, arises also a galaxy of Saints who are also warriors, poets and musicians, builders and organisers and men dedicated to service of the others, irrespective of caste or community, and a new socio-spiritual order comes into being which gathers high and low (more low than high) Hindu and Mohemmedan, the Āryan and the Semitic, on a single platform, and ultimately welds them into a formidable social force. Foreign imperialism is ended, and even more than that the tyranny of one way of life upon another. The earth becomes more productive, women become equal, if not superior of men. Not only is caste-exclusiveness wholly obliterated, but also caste-consciousness. And men grow not only in the soul, but become more broad of limb, more full of defiance against earthly odds, and fighting not for the self, or an exclusive group, but for values, and against tyranny, whether spiritual or social, from whatever quarter it comes. They do not suppress their desires through an ascetic discipline, but express them through song and rythm and the dance of the soul, which is Ānand (or Bliss).

That Nānak, disinheriting his sons, could find a successor as worthy of him as Angad and that this could continue for about two centuries thereafter is another tribute to his insight into the character of men and his power to reshape and rebuild them after his own image. Everyone of them was not only an awakened soul, but a man of action ever-ready to do or die, and often-times a poet and a philosopher, if not also a builder and an organiser of cities and commerce and peoples.

Guru Nānak as a Poet

Nānak, as is well-known, was a poet of great excellence, and was conscious of it. (He calls himself "*Shair*" - poet - in one of his hymns). One may even make bold to say that he was the father of modern Indian renaissance. He writes in a language which is not always Panjābi, as is now understood, but in a mixed language, which for want of a better name, we may call "*Sadhu bhāshā*" (or Sadhukri), understood then as now all over North India. His sentiment is essentially Indian : and never for once does he so much as mention the name of Punjāb in his extensive writings. He accepts the basic tenets of the Indian view of life — self-surrender against self-assertion; idealism against mere existentialism; a democratic spiritual temper so as to not only to tolerate, but appreciate and, if possible, integrate another's point of view; spiritualism against materialism, though the house of Nānak emphasises that the spirit and the matter have emanated from and submerge in the same source. ("Nānak: The subtle and the apparent are, indeed, identical"), which is a revolutionary doctrine though, today, in the age of modern science, it seems so natural and so true.

But, what distinguishes him from the run of other poets is that Nānak is less metaphysical and more mystic, more lyrical and less discursive or didactic, more personal than formal.

He gives not so much the philosophy as the psychology of love. John Donne's famous lines, "For God's sake hold your tongue, and let me love," aptly describes the prevailing mood of Nānak's poetry. But love is nowhere affected as in much of Vaishnava poetry, but is always a spontaneous, intimate experience. The gymnastics of metres and words, the calculated subtlety, rhetoric of wit, the poetic conceit, are not his, as one finds in most metaphysical poetry. It is the heartful expression of an innocence that is born of an inner heartfelt experience.

Nānak employs speech-rythms extensively in his poetry and not the conventional metres, many of which he uses and yet subtly transforms so as to conform to the mood and the sentiments and the feeling than to the set patterns of Hindi prosody. He is perhaps the first Indian poet to have experimented with free verse and blank verse. And so many variations does he introduce into the age-old measures that it is wellnigh impossible to designate them, even if all these could be delineated through laborious research. And that is what he does also with his words. He uses them for their inner meaning, their feel, their sound correspondence with the prevailing mood rather than their correct, accepted notations as found in a lexicon. That is how one finds that Nānak is more than any other poet of modern Indian renaissance the harbinger of a new freedom in the style of poesy. One should not call it a style, for Nānak is inimitable and never stylish.

And, so also with his subject-matter. His main theme and its treatment is so modern that Pearl S. Buck was constrained to remark that of the moderns in letters, Guru Nānak is one of the most modern. For, when asked about the origin of the universe, he said, "When one thinks of the beginning, one is lost in a sense of wonder."* He calls the world "egg-shaped," visualises a time "when there was chaos upon chaos and God alone was seated in His absolute Trance, when there was no sin and no virtue, no heaven or hell, no earth or sky, air nor fire. And when it pleased Him, He caused the universe to come into being, not only the universe of man, but also many

* "*Ād Ko bichār bismād Kathialē*"—Sidha Goshti - M. 1.

other universes."* "There are myriads of the under-worlds and the skies," says he but they are all strung upon the One alone and obey fixed laws, ever the same for everyone, in all ages and climes. The age of the world and man is known to Him alone who caused them.• For us, it is a mystery. And He created them for His play, for expressing His power, His virtues and His Grace. All that He had to give man He has already given and if only he knows how to harness and distribute it, he it is who'd say, "Enough, no more!"

What is the nature of this God—the Creator and the Destroyer of all, the giver of pain and pleasure, "to whom if one's inself attuneth, he asketh for nought but for Him alone?" Says Nānak: "I know not how to describe him, for He can be compared to Himself alone. So I submit to Him: O God, Thou are what only Thou art."

It is not for any reward in the Hereafter that one becomes His devotee. "The wise one," says the fifth Nānak, "abandons even the *desire* to be emancipated.@ For, emancipation, according to Nānak, is not to be released into the emptiness of the void, but into the rythms of love. And who that has loved craved ever for his release? Loving is itself emancipation.

Of the nine Rasas or moods, into which Indian literary tradition has categorised poetry, there is not one in which Nānak's poetry does not excel—*Srinagār* or *Shānt*, *Karunā* or *Rodra*, or *Bhayānak*, *Adbhuta* or *Vira*, *Hāsya* or *Bibhatsa*. But nowhere is the expression of joy exuberant, nor of sadness unalloyed. It is mellowed, seasoned wood out of which the words and moods are carved. The sentiment and the mood are always spontaneous, intimate and heart-felt and the words and images which echo them are equally so. The transitoriness of life, and man's indulgence to the detriment of his inner growth is expressed not in words but in feeling. Rendered literally, it would read—

"O black deer, hear thou, why art thou attached to the beauty
of the garden ?
The fruit of vice is sweet for a day, and then it giveth pain.
The world is like a sea-wave, like lightning's flash,

---

* Māru Sohilē, 1

• Jāpu, 1.

@ "*Kai baikunth nahin lavē lāgē: Mukat bapri bhi gyani tyāgē.*" (Māru, M. 5)

It cometh and it goeth......

Nānak speaketh the truth, dwell thou on thy Lord in the mind,
for tomorrow thou diest, O black deer.

O black bee, thou that hoppest from flower to flower......
O my stranger soul, thou that art involved in strife......

O fish, separated (from the sea) with a tear staying still
in thy eyes ......

O split stream, thy Union is rare with thy source!"

Nānak is very aesthetic in the delineation both of his objective, the unitive experience of God, and the path that leads to it. "My God," he says, "is ever-fresh, ever-new, ever-beneficent."

What is he like? "Of beauteous eyes and sparkling teeth, of sharp nose and luxurious hair, of a golden body and alluring gait, of steps like a peacock's, of flowering youth, whose speech is ever sweet and full of melody like a koel's in a mango-grove!" Again, he compares the soul of the seeker to "a young bride, drunk with her beauty of sharp features whom the beloved also seeks to enjoy."

That is why the symbol of the bride and the groom is represented over and over again to express the pain of separation, the ever-fresh joy of intimacy, the spontaneity of self-surrender, and the cool comfort of the seeker being also the sought-after.

And the world and all the elements like the God who created them are a sheer wonder:

"The earth is studded with six jewels, where one is sent out to love." "The God is like a tree in fruit, of deep and cool shade, ever-green, whose sap gives eternal life." If it is a forest, "it is of the fragrant sandal-wood, even though girt by snakes." "Blessed, blessed are my beauteous doors (i.e. the body) through which enters my love, and I'm cooled."

Says Nānak: "God is like a beauteous temple, studded with rubies and jewels and pearls and pure diamonds. He is the enticing fortress of gold." "No, no, my God is not in the books, neither in the Veda nor in the Semitic texts. There is nothing like unto Him in the world. But, lo, my King is here before me, for, verily, He is a Presence!"

What is good? "That what pleases my God." Where is God? "Where one's good heart is." What is Truth? "That which goes not and is valid wherever and by whomsoever tested." What is beauty? "Which makes one lose oneself in its ecstasy and wonder and stays whole and forever."

For Nānak, Truth is not an abstraction, nor is beauty, nor goodness. It is live and active and is seen, felt and experienced. Says he: "Truth is above everything, but higher still is the living of Truth." It is only by emptying our within of our self, that we enter into the realm of Truth, but this self-surrender should be inborn and heart-felt. For, "do not the hunters of deer also bow down?" "A sinner, indeed, bows down twice as much as a lover!" What is worship? It is not a formalistic ritual, but a hearty self-denial. "Whatever a God-conscious being does, is worship!"

How is one to keep detached in the midst of the world? "Like the lotus, its roots in mud, but its flower above the surface of the water: like the duck in a stream." How is one to love? "Like water loves the milk. The heat it suffers upon itself, but the milk it allows not to burn."

Guru Nānak in his style is so pithy and direct that his words have entered into our folklore. There is no verse of his which does not contain one or two enunciations of Truth with the discipline, spontaneity of utterance and meaningfulness of a proverb. Only a few examples will suffice:

1. Truth is never too old.
2. He who loses God loses himself.
3. Heaven is attained not through words,
   but through the practice of Truth.
4. What kind of wisdom is this that nourishes
   within us ego or greed?
5. What kind of love is this which makes us
   not fear-free of the beloved?
6. He who conquers himself, conquers the whole world.
7. Not through knowledge one knows, but through realisation.
8. Pain and pleasure are the two garments that one wears.
9. Dust returns to the dust; air blends with the air.
   Who is it, then, that dies?
10. What shall I do in the forest when the spring is here
   within me?

11. Nānak : each one that I have seen is in pain,
except the one who is awakened like the Guru, etc. etc. . . .

Nānak never used the word "I" in his entire writings except in a spirit of deep humility. "I'm the lowest of the lowborn, what have I to do with the high and mighty? God's Grace is only where the poor and the lowly are cared for." In humility that is born of self-confidence and thus is natural and spontaneous, there are very few in the history of man to compare with Guru Nānak.

For him, there were no final truths except those that answered the questioning of man—every man—through the ages. He never considered himself either the final messenger of God, or an exclusive one. And therein lies his eternal glory.

CHAPTER VI

GURU ANGAD DEV

(1504 — 1552 A.D.)

The nomination of a successor by Guru Nānak as worthy as Guru Angad has been described by historians as one of the most significant events in the evolution of the Sikh faith into a dynamic society. It is suggested that if Guru Nānak would not have continued the line of succession, his doctrines, whose fundamentals he had clearly enunciated, would not have been put to the test of living life over a long period so as to burn them into the soul of a people. There was so much in the writings of Guru Nānak on which a cult of asceticism could also be built (as his son, Sri Chand, indeed did). And, then, Hinduism itself being not a fixed dogma like Islām but a parliament of religions (due to the sanctity it allowed to every kind of ritual and belief, from idol-worship to the belief in the Formless and the Absolute, from a materialistic faith like Sānkhya's to the Soul being the only Real and its total identity with the Oversoul, as in Vedānta) could easily have absorbed the new faith as one of its many diverse sects. Moreover, in spite of the best spiritual instruction (as in the case of Kabir), men do not easily give up their caste and custom and merge in a new society unless there is a strict guidance over a long period, not only in words but also through deeds. And this is what Guru Nānak intended and Angad fulfilled with such high distinction. Sikhs were now held together not by the commonality of certain doctrines and beliefs about God, Karma, Soul and Transmigration, but assumed the form of a society expressing its doctrines through a living, dynamic social life.

Born in Mattē-di-Sarāi, about six miles from Mukatsar (in the present district of Ferozepur in the Indian Panjāb), in the house of Bhāi Phēru, a Trehan Khatri merchant, of the womb of Rāmo, on the 11th of Baisākh of Samvat 1561 (1504 A.D.), Angad, whose earlier name was Lehnā,* was a man of extreme religious bent of mind. His father changed his place of residence several times from Mattē-di-Sarāi to Harikē and from there back to his original home, which too he abandoned once again to settle in Khadur, now Khadur-Sāhib, in the present district of Amritsar. Lehnā seems to have married early in life a pious and devoted woman called Khivi and had two sons, Dātu and Dāsu, and one daughter—Amro—from her.@

While living in Khadur, Lehnā used to visit Jawālāmukhi, a famous temple of the goddess Durgā, in the Shivālik hills, where the fire emitting from the volcano mountain-top is worshipped by the devout Hindus. Year after year, he made this pilgrimage and with bells and drums performed a ritual-dance before his idol. One morning, however, he heard his neighbour, Bhāi Jodhā, recite a hymn of Guru Nānak, saying:

"Serving whom one attains Beatitude, in-gather Him,
the Lord, thou.
The deeds that fruition into evil, why do such evil deeds ?
Do no evil and cultivate foresight, looking far into the future
And go the way that makes thee not lose face with thy Lord.
*And strive only for that which brings thee (true) profit.***

*Guru Angad's biography we have based mostly on writings either his own, or about him, in the Ādi-Granth (like *Sattē-di-Vār*, Swayyās, etc.), the *Janam Sākhis* of Guru Nānak, *Dabistān*, Vārs of Bhāi Gurdās (1. 11, 26), Sarup Dās Bhallā's *Mahimā Parkāsh*, Sevā Dās's *Parchian*, Bhangu Rattan Singh's *Panth Parkāsh*, and a judicious selection from *Suraj Parkāsh*, as edited by Bhāi Vir Singh, etc.

@ Some of the points of historical importance as revealed in his own writings or the writings about him and included in the Ādi Granth (especially the *Sattē-di-Vār*, p. 967) are: (1) He is called the True King (*Sachā Pādshāh*), and a canopy (*Chhatar*) waves over his head. (2) Guru Nānak's sons did not obey him and turned their back also on Guru Angad, and that they were considered 'evil-minded' by the devout. (3) Guru Angad lived like a Dervish, with unparalleled humility. (4) Khivi, his wife, served in the free Community-Kitchen, whose institution is continued. (5) Angad, the son of Phēru, came to live in a village called Khadur and brought it back to life and prosperity. (6) Lehnā was given the name of Angad, being the limb of Nānak's limb (*ang*).

**Āsā-di-Vār, Pauri 21.

It appears the words affected the sensitive mind of Lehnā so much that he implored his companions to break their journey that year* at Kartārpur to call upon Guru Nānak, on their way to Jawālāmukhi. The Guru received Lehnā with great affection and courtesy and instructed him in the way of the one God. The more Lehnā heard the Guru's discourses, the more he was convinced of their meaningfulness and decided after a few days' halt to discontinue his journey, and bidding farewell to his old associates, settled in the service of the Guru. On the latter's advice, he visited his family who seeing his determination let him go back to live with Guru Nānak. Here, he served the Guru with such single-minded dedication that the sons of Guru Nānak as much as the other devout Sikhs were put in the shade beside him. He would work on the farm as a labourer, wash the Master's clothes, repair or reconstruct fallen mud-houses, hail or sunshine, at the dead of night as in the scorching heat of the day, no matter how long it took to please his Master who was in the meantime putting all his associates to the test and was indeed hard to please for that reason. One day, when he was carrying three bundles of grass, dripping with mud, he spoiled his new wear. The Guru's wife was much distressed and said to Nānak: "This is how you treat those who come to receive spiritual instruction from you? Look at the huge load he carries and the way his clothes have been fouled by mud!" The Guru replied: "O innocent one, it is not mud that sticks to him, it is saffron with which he is being anointed. And as for the load, he has to carry a burden which no one else could carry."

Seeing him separated from his family for long, the Guru asked Lehnā to go back to Khadur for a while and instruct people in his way. Lehnā did as he was bidden. Here, he converted Takht Mal, the headman of the village, and many others. A community-kitchen was also initiated and men from far and near started pouring in to receive spiritual instruction from him. Even Guru Nānak visited him here twice and on his second visit, seeing his never-failing devotion to God and man, took him back to Kartārpur.

As has been stated before, the Guru put Lehnā and others, including his sons, to further tests and finding only Lehnā equal to the honour, anointed him as his successor, on July 14, 1539 A.D., only about three months before his demise, and called him Angad (he who's born of his own limbs). As both Bhāi Gurdās and the "Coronation Ode" (vide Ādi Granth, PP.* 967-68) testify, Guru Nānak ins-

*1532 A. D.

tructed his followers that "though the body had changed, it was the same spirit that animated him as well as Angad".

It is said, the shock of his Master's separation, however, was so overwhelming for Guru Angad, that he shut himself up in a secluded spot at Khadur and lived on a little quantity of milk provided him by a devout woman disciple, Nihāli by name. It was after a great struggle by several well-known leaders of the Sikh church led by Bhāi Buddhā that the Guru agreed to come out of his seclusion. But once he decided to do so, he threw himself heart and soul into his divine mission.*

He would rise three hours before daybreak, wash himself with cold water, and then perform meditation and recitation of the Guru's Word. Then the musicians, Sattā and Balwand, would sing the Word in his presence to large audiences. He would personally treat the sick, particularly lepers, and early in the day, his wife would distribute food to all who had come to visit the Guru, irrespective of caste, creed or station. The children would be specially cared for and instructed by the Guru himself. He would organise wrestling bouts for the youth and various sports for children. In the evening again, devotional hymns would be sung before everyone retired to his repose.

The Guru was the very embodiment of humility. When a few renowned yogis came to visit him, they attempted to win him over to the way of yoga through renunciation of the world, donning of a special yogic garb and breath-control and other yogic exercises to awaken the serpentine-power• with which, they claimed, man could not only live long but also perform miracles. The Guru quoting his Master replied: "Why live long if we are no use to the society and have to roam about as recluses? Why perform miracles which transform not the man's within but only overawe others and increase one's ego? Miracle-making is the work of charlatans, not of men of God who live ever in His Will and try to transform their natures and those of others. This is the miracle one must perform through the yoga of equipoise(*sahj-yoga*), whose essence is that man must live and work in the world but dedicate himself and the fruit of his efforts to

* Some historians aver that the Guru accepted seclusion to avoid hostility on the part of Guru Nānak's sons, others that he wanted to test the faith of his Sikhs. One is strongly tempted to agree with the latter view, as withdrawal from the world either on account of hostility of rivals, or grief, would not be in keeping with the spirit of the Guru. • Kudalini

God and God's men. A yogi is he who considers everyone as his equal and has compassion in the heart and who controls his desires and not his breath, and finds illumination in the natural, spontaneous way (*sahja*) and not by forcing one's will or the God's." The head of the yogis was so pleased with his piety and innocent wisdom that he urged him to ask for a favour. The Guru replied: "I live as my God and Guru direct me and I have no other desire to fulfil, but if you are insistent, be ever so kind as to bless me with humility."

It is said that Bābur's son, Humayun, having been defeated by Sher Shāh, was fleeing India via Lāhore and hearing the repute of the Guru came to call upon him at Khadur for his blessings, with a good number of presents. The Guru was absorbed in his meditation, and no one dared disturb him. The fugitive King waited so long that he was enraged and put his hand to the hilt of his sword to strike the Guru. The consternation that ensued among the devout shook the Guru out of his trance and seeing what was happening reprimanded the royal visitor saying: "It is unchivalrous for a King to flee from the battle-field and vent his wrath upon men of God." Humayun begged his forgiveness. The Guru in his compassion granted him pardon and, it is said, blessed him saying that though his path may be arduous and long, he would win back the throne of Hindustān. When after a time, Humayun succeeded to the throne of Delhi again, he wanted to do some favour to the Guru. By this time, Guru Angad was no more and his successor, Guru Amar Dās, sent back the reply to the emperor that the only favour the Guru's house asked of him was that he be just to all people alike.

Several stories are told by the Sikh chroniclers of how austere was the personal life of the Guru. Believing in the precepts of Guru Nānak that one should live by the sweat of one's brow and share it with others and look upon the offerings of the devout as poison for personal use, the Guru would earn his daily bread by twisting *moonj* and not partake of the considerable offerings, these being wholly surrendered for the community-kitchen. Apart from his never-failing humility and dedication to the cause, he was very meticulous in imparting the same qualities to his followers. A Sikh, called Mana, worked in the Guru's kitchen, but he became so proud of this office that he refused to serve or obey anyone but the Guru. "I shall do anything for you," he would protest, "but I cannot go about serving every kind of man." The Guru was alarmed at such haughtiness in his disciple and said to him, "If that be so, such a one as yourself should burn himself alive." The disciple had no opportunity now to retrace his steps and, disgusted, went out into the forest, collected some firewood and wanted to cremate himself. But, as the tongues of fire leapt into the sky, he became afraid. A robber passing by asked him the reason for raising the fire and standing by it, naked and afraid. Mana narrated the whole story. The robber had already heard of the Guru's repute and said: "Not you but I shall carry out the command of the Guru in order to wipe off my sins. You take these jewels from me which I have recently stolen. They are so precious that you could live on their proceeds all your life in utter prosperity." Mana was extremely happy over this bargain and came to the town to dispose off the jewels. But, he was arrested for the theft and hanged. When the news reached the Guru, he said: "The egotists and the perverts lose the merit of both this world and the next, even if they live in the presence of the Guru."

Sattā and Balwand were two musicians in the Guru's Court, whose greed resulted in their deserting the Guru and denigrating the House of Nānak by saying: "It is we whose superb music attracts people to the Guru and his house gathers large offerings. And now when we demanded money for a daughter's marriage in the family, he obliges us not.* No one would have cared even for Nānak but for Bhāi Mardānā, the ace musician." The Guru did not mind his own insult but could hardly bear the uncharitable remarks about his Master, whereupon he refused to see them thereafter in spite of their wailings and protestations. They tried to attract people to their music at their own dwellings, but no one turned up. They became very miserable and desti-

*Santokh Singh (GSG Rās 3) places the incident in the time of Guru Arjun among whose Sikhs alone, Bhāi Ladhā is mentioned by Bhāi Gurdās. But, it appears from the internal evidence that the *Vār* contains more elaborate details about Guru Angad than any other Guru. As for Ladhā, he might have lived right upto the days of Guru Arjun, though why should his name not be included among the second Guru's Sikhs is a factor which throws doubt on Bhāi Ladhā's part in the whole story. It is said, no matter how much money the Guru offered them for the marriage of a daughter in their family, they would ask for more. Ultimately, they settled for the entire offerings on the day of Baisākhi the annual festival on which large crowds visited the Guru from far and near. But, that year, the pilgrims were far fewer and the expectations of the musicians were not fulfilled, at which they asked for more money. The Guru expelled them from his court saying, "The offerings are not my personal property but a trust for the poor. In the interest of a single family I cannot sacrifice the interest of the whole community."

tute, and seeing no other way out implored Bhāi Ladhā, a great devotee of the Guru at Lahore, to intercede in their behalf. Bhāi Ladhā, known as *Paropkari*, or the helper of the poor, was much over-whelmed by their entreaties and rode to Khadur on a donkey, his head shaven and his face blackened, as a sign of penitence on their behalf. The Guru pardoned the musicians whereupon they uttered what is known as *Sattē-Balwand-di-Var* (the Coronation Ode) in which they praised the House of Nānak for its charity, humility and dedication to God. They lived to a ripe old age into the days of Arjun, the fifth Guru, and added a verse in praise of each succeeding Guru upto the fifth. This Ode in incorporated in the Ādi Granth and, as we have seen, is a reliable source-material for constructing this period of Sikh history. The Guru on this occasion, said: "There are only two things which subserve man in the end—one, the constant remembrance of God, and the other, selflessness. If a man thinks not of the others but only of himself, his devotion and customary penances and charities also are of no avail, for they are not dedicated to God, but to one's own salvation, or pampering of one's ego."

Guru Angad's repute had by now spread far and wide. This led to much jealousy and heart burning, firstly on the part of a *tapā*, or a Hindu recluse, and secondly among the high castes and the men of substance. The recluse thought, and perhaps rightly, that no one paid him obeisance because of the preachings of the Guru against asceticism, while the men proud of their caste and station in life felt humiliated at the course the Guru's instructions were leading the people on : "there is no high or low; all men are equal in the eyes of God." So, they conspired to get rid of him and once when there was no rainfall, the *tapā* told the leaders of the village that unless Guru Angad left the village, there would be no rains that year. The Jāt farmers, much distressed at the sight of the withering crops, came in a deputation to the Guru and laid bare the intent of their visit with tearful eyes. The Guru replied : "Nature cannot bend to your will merely by human sacrifice to the gods, or by injuring someone's heart. But, if your rain-god is satisfied by my quitting this village, I shall do so without a moment's hesitation."

The Guru left the village, but the rains did not come. People were so furious with the recluse that they wanted to do him to death, when a devout disciple of the Guru, Amar Dās (of whom we '' ll hear more later on) interceded and grievously incensed as ' the insult offered by the villagers to the Guru at the behest of the wily *tapā*, asked them instead to yoke the latter to their ploughs, instead of their bullocks, and as they would drag him through their farms, rain would fall. In despair, the farmers carried out, in letter and spirit, what Amar Dās had enjoined, and lo and behold, the rains came in all their might and fury!

The villagers now waited in a deputation on the Guru and implored him to come back to his old habitation. But when the Guru heard of the severe punishment meted out to the *tapā*, his heart was much distressed, the more so because his own devout disciple, Amar Dās, had inspired or condoned it. Addressing Amar Dās, he said: "You should have shown endurance, in the face of adversity, like the earth, steadfastness like a mountain and compassion like a river. For the wise and the holy, it is unforgiveable if they practise not humility and remain not even-minded in weal or woe." Amar Dās felt much distress in the heart over what he had done and so the Guru forgave him.

Again, when Amar Dās blessed Khiwān, a devotee of the Guru with the boon of a son, the Guru warned him : "Do not go about disbursing your blessings and curses without due deliberation. God is merciful to all men of prayer and good intentions, and one need not exhibit one's spiritual prowess by such showmanship."

But, such was the devotion shown by Amar Dās to the Guru that neither the Guru's sons nor other disciples could come up anywhere near him. Though fairly old, he would bring water from the river Beās nearby, even on the days of severe cold and lashing winds. Once when the Guru's foot caused him much pain on account of a sore, Amar Dās sucked the poisonous matter out of it which gave immediate relief to the Guru. And such was his innocent devotion, that while the Guru presented him with a turban each year as a badge of honour and approval, he would for twelve years remove not one, but wrap one around the other, in spite of the fact that people ridiculed him for his blind faith and said: "It is age that has turned the old man's head."

In the meantime, the Guru allowed one of his rich disciples—Gobind—to build a township on the bank of the river Beās, but refused to call the new settlement after his own name and called it Gobindwāl (now, Goindwal), to commemorate the memory of the disciple instead. Amar Dās was asked by the Guru to repose here for the night and come to the Guru by day-break. Amar Dās's family joined him there and due to his presence, the colony was soon inhabited and became not only prosperous but also holy. A Sikh temple was also erected here, which resounded with the Guru's Word night and day. But, such was the reverence he showed to the Guru that he would walk back to Gobindwāl from Khadur every night with his face ever turned towards the Guru. But, as it often happens, some people would jeer at him for his oddities and say to themselves: "But, where should now the man go? He is aged and helpless, homeless and without honour!"

When the Guru heard this, he embraced Amar Dās before the whole congregation and said: "He whom you call homeless and without honour and support will be the home of the homeless, the honour of the unhonoured and the support of the supportless." And soon after, on the day of his demise, he bowed before him, placing five *paisās* (copper coins) and a coconut before him signifying as Guru Nānak had done before, that from now on Amar Dās will succeed to the Guru's throne and not his sons or other devotees. This time too, Bhāi Buddhā, the devout Sikh, was asked by the Guru to anoint his forehead with saffron-mark (*tilak*). This was on Chet Sudi 4, Samvat 1609 (March 29, 1552, A.D.), when Guru Amar Dās was over 72 years of age.

GURU AMAR DĀS

(1479—1574 A.D.)

In the hands of Guru Amar Dās, three significant events took place. (1) He analysed and indeed enlarged the Sikh doctrine so as to distinguish it from a similar terminology amongst the Hindus and Buddhists, and for that purpose also paid acute attention to the preservation of the original writings of his Masters placing them side by side for comparison and contrast with some other Hindu Bhaktas and Muslim Sufis whose popularity was then attracting large masses of people. (2) He emphasised strongly the new status accorded to women by the Sikh society by deprecating their seclusion through *Purdāh* and the cruel custom of *Sati.* (3) And, he innovated new and more sensitive and inexpensive ceremonies for marriage and death.

Amar Dās* was born in a village called Bāsarkē, near Amritsar, on Vāisakh Sudi 14, Samvat 1536 (May 5, 1479 A. D.) in the home of Tej Bhān, a Bhallā Khatri, who lived both by agriculture and trade. Tej Bhān had four sons from his wife, Bakht Devi, the eldest of them being Amar Dās. Though Amar Dās became a householder like his father and from his marriage to Mansā Devi, he had two sons—Mohri and Mohan—and two daughters—Dāni and Bhāni—he was a

* The life-story of Guru Amar Dās is constructed here primarily from the original sources like the Ādi Granth. Some contemporary sources like Bhāi Gurdās (Vārs 1, 11 and 26) and *Dabistān-i-Mazāhib,* and secondary sources like *Parchis* of Sevā Dās and Rattan Singh's *Panth Parkāsh* have also been consulted. The gaps are filled up by a judicious selection from *Mahimā Parkāsh* of Sarup Dās Bhallā and Santokh Singh's *Guru-Partāp Surya Granth* as edited by Bhāi Vir Singh, besides Mani Singh's *Sikhan di Bhagat Mālā, etc.*

man of intensely religious dispoistion. He was a strict Vaishanavite and made several pilgrimages to the Gangā for twenty years, fasted on all auspicious days, and lived in every way a clean and pious life. But, there was some spiritual anxiety tugging ever at his heart. He was not at peace with himself and was in search of a teacher (Guru) who could give his mind rest. Once when returning from a pilgrimage, a Hindu Sādhu refused to partake of the food served him by Amar Dās, "as he was a Guruless egotist", his search for a spiritual guide became even more intense.

Deeply impressed by Guru Nānak's hymns sung in his brother's home (to whose son the daughter of Angad, Bibi Amro, had recently been married), he prevailed upon her to accompany him to her father-Guru's abode at Khadur, and after a brief time, had his wish fulfilled. His mind was greatly calmed on meeting the Guru and on hearing his words how "dross could be transformed into gold by the true Guru". But being a Vaishanavite, he recoiled in the mind from taking meat- dishes which, according to Macauliffe, were served on that day in the Guru's kitchen†. The Guru told him that the meats one should avoid are—envy, greed, ego, slander and usurpation of others' rights. He repeated to him the hymn of Guru Nānak in this connection and this satisfied the questionings of his mind.

We have already narrated the sense of utter dedication with which Amar Dās served his Master, even though he was aging in years. Though no definite period of time is given about his entry into the Guru's sanctuary, it could not have been earlier than his middle fiftees, and, as we have seen, he succeeded to the Throne of Nānak when he was over seventy-two. The "Coronation Ode" in the Ādi Granth testifies that he was accepted, like Guru Angad before him, as the embodiment of the same spirit which animated Guru Nānak:

> "*Anointed the same way, seated upon the same Throne, in the same Court*
> *Was Guru Amar Dās, approved like his sire and grandsire.*"*.

---

† "The Sikh Religion", Vol. II. Pages 32,-33, However, now-a-days in the Community-Kitchen attached to the Sikh temples, and called the Guru's Kitchen (or, Guru-kā-langar) meat-dishes are not served at all. This may be because various types of people eat in the Guru's Kitchen, nothing that is not [illegible] to everyone is served,

* In spiritual, not physical, pedigree.

He made Bāsak-Nāgā† (of Contemplation) the churning-string
and of his (spiritual) prowess
The churning-pot. And made the Sumeru mountain
(of consciousness) the churning stick,
And thus churned the Ocean (of the Word). And lo,
He obtained the fourteen gems (of Wisdom) with which the
whole world was illumined.
He rode the steed of Equipoise, saddled with chastity,
And made Truth his bow and the arrows of the Lord's praise.
How dark was the Kāli age ? How it dazzles now after the
(Guru's) sun
Has blazed forth with its myriad rays. Truth grew in his
farm-land.
He shaded the whole world with (God's) Truth. O, what
a nectar-sweet feed
He fed us on: ghee, refined flour and sugar. Within his
mind rang
The approved Word and He knew the inmost state of the four
corners (of the world).
He stamped each and all with his Grace and rid everyone of
his coming-and-going.
(Through him), God Himself took on a human form — He,
the Wise **Purusha**,
Standing firm like the Sumeru mountain, was shaken not
by the winds (of Desire).
He knew the inmost state of all, yea, he the inner-knower
of all hearts.
O True King, how am I to praise thee, thou, who art so utterly
wise.
Nānak's canopy waved (over Amar Dās) and the whole following
*was struck with wonder."**

---

† The references here are all to the mythical Pauranic story of the churning of the ocean by the angels in their elemental fight against the demons. They found fourteen gem-like substances, in this process, including nectar and poison and with the former revived all their companions and with the latter slew all the demons.

*Ādi-Granth, Pp. 967-68.

The long quotation gives a clue to the historian to several pertinent keypoints of Sikh history. (1) The Sikhs had a firm belief that Amar Dās, though different in body, had the same spirit informing him as had Nānak, the first Guru, a fact to which Mohsin-Fāni also makes a reference in Dabistān. (2) Guru Amar Dās was noted for his spiritual prowess and illumination so much that even though the Sikh doctrine forbids belief in God incarnating Himself as man, the devout Sikhs by now had come to believe (as this Ode and the Swayyās of the bards in the Ādi Granth, Pp. 1392-96 testify) that God Himself had indeed taken a human birth in the Gurus. (Also see *Dabistān*) (3) The institution of the community-kitchen initiated by Guru Nānak was continued by Guru Amar Dās and that rich food was served therein and not coarse bread, which also shows that there were devouts in sufficient number to support his free kitchen. (4) In offering his instructions, he made no distinction between one caste, creed or station and another. "He stamped each and all with His Grace." (5) The symbols of royalty like *Sachā Pādshāh* (True King), *Takht* (Throne), *Chhatar* (canopy), *Darbār* (court), etc., though used for their spiritual import, had freely come to be associated with the Gurus. This last point needs to be emphasied, as in the days of the later Gurus, these terms were utilised by the emperors and others inimically disposed towards the Guru's house to malign them and bring them into conflict with the Moghal authorities. A plea has been made that whereas in the days of the first five Gurus, the emphasis was on spiritual matters, it was from the sixth Guru onwards that the terms associated with royalty like Sachā Pādshāh, takht, chhatar, darbār, etc., had come into vogue, and hence a conflict between the Gurus and the emperor had become inevitable. As would be seen from this quotation, these terms had become household words with the Sikhs from the days of Guru Nānak himself and secular activity (which included passive resistance to the imperial authority) was as much a part of their teaching as the spiritual awakening of man.

However, the Guru was so frugal in his personal habits that he would himself only take coarse bread and never care to possess more than one set of clothes. Whatever offerings came on a single day were spent the same day, depending for the morrow upon the good God Men frequented Goindwāl in large numbers, both as visitors and settlers. The Rājā of Haripur, in the Kangrā Valley nearby, was so impressed by the piety of the Guru's nephew, Sāwan Mal, who visited his state for timber, that he made a gift of all his requirements for the development of Goindwāl and himself came to call on the Guru. But the Guru insisted that he would see the Rājā only after he had partaken of the food in the community- kitchen. Though highly caste-and-class-conscious, he could not but submit to the Guru's wishes. Thereafter, the Guru received him with utmost affection, but not one of his queens who had refused to lift the veil from her face. For, Guru Amar Dās not only preached the equality of man, irrespeetive of caste or station, he also tried to liberate womanhood from the evils of *Purdāh* and *Sati* (self-mortification on the funeral pyre of her dead husband), and encouraged women to participate in social and religious life.

As the repute of the Guru grew, Dātu, the eldest son of Guru Angad, was stung more and more by jealousy and set himself up as Guru at his father's seat in Khadur. Once when a party of Sikhs came here from afar to visit Guru Amar Dās in the mistaken belief that the Guru still kept his residence in Khadur, they refused to see Dātu and proceeded to Goindwāl instead. This hurt him so much that he himself set out for the Guru's place, and seeing him seated on a high pedestal surrounded by royal splendour and a large flock of devout devotees, could not contain his wrath and abused him as a 'usurper' and a 'wretched servant of their household', and advancing furiously towards him, kicked him off his throne. The Guru, however, in his utter humility, started pressing the feet of the offender saying, "I'm old. My bones are hard. You may have been hurt." And not wanting to give the least offence to his detractor, left Goindwāl the same evening for Basarkē—his native village. Here, he shut himself in a small house for quiet meditations, repeating to himself the words of Kabir :

"*He who has claims upon the world, only burns his heart.*
But he who surrenders all his claims, is care-free
And shames even a King."

Dātu now occupied the Guru's place, but very few devotees would come to pay him homage. After amassing a little fortune, he left for his native place, Khadur. It is said, on the way he was met by robbers who not only divested him of his treasure, but also struck Dātu on the foot with which he had kicked the Guru. On the other hand, the Sikhs led by Bhāi Budhhā, started a frantic search for the Guru. They put the Guru's mare in front of the search party and praying to

God for success in their mission followed her to Basarkē, where she brought them in front of a deserted house on the front door of which was written in the Guru's own hand, "whosoever opens this door, him I'll own not as my follower". It was an injunction hard to disobey, but Bhāi Buddhā said to his associates : "The Guru being a supreme yogi, cares for nothing in the world — neither fame, nor riches nor a following. But we cannot live without his guidance. Guru Angad enjoined upon us to hold on to his skirt. How can we now abandon him, even if he wishes in his superb act of renunciation, to be left alone." And saying this, he broke into the house from the back door without touching the lock on the front-door, thus also fulfilling the command of the Guru in letter, if not in spirit. When the Guru saw some of his most devoted Sikhs entreating him with tearful eyes not to abandon them like this saying, "If a child errs, the mother minds it not, if a man errs, God disowns him not", the Guru was overwhelmed by their devotion and accompanied them back to Goindwāl. A festival is held every year on the full-moon day in the month of *Bhādon* at Basarkē in commemoration of this event.

Many Sikhs now thronged to the Guru's place for spiritual instruction. Some were deprived of their riches and, frustrtated with life, came to his abode for the quietude of their mind. Others who had all, but were anxious due to their search for something higher they could not grasp or understand, came for spiritual solace.

This induced some Muslim Pathāns also to live at Goindwāl for business or other avocations. But they grew fiercely jealous of the Guru's repute and as time passed,picked up one quarrel after another with the Sikhs. The Guru instructed his followers in humility and forbearance. But, when a group of war-like Sanyansis came to visit the Guru and the pellet of a Muslim boy knocked out the eye of a Sanyāsi, the others of his company beat the boy to death. A fierce fight ensued between the local Muslims and the Hindu recluses, resulting in much bloodshed on both sides. On another occasion, when an imperial treasure was being carried through Goindwāl, one of the mules laden with cash strayed into the Pathān quarters which they appropriated. On being found, the imperial troops gave them examplary punishment, thus giving the Guru and his followers a long period of respite. The Guru told his Sikhs : "In God's house, justice is sure. Only it is a matter of time. The arrows of humility and patience on the part of the innocent and the peaceful never fail in their aim".

One day, the Guru was riding by a wall which he saw was on the verge of falling. He galloped his horse past the wall at which the Sikhs questioned him : "O Master, you have instructed us, 'fear not death, for it comes to all' and 'the Guru and the God-man are beyond the pale of birth and death', why did you then gallop past the collapsing wall ?" He replied cooly, "Our body is the embodiment of God's light. It is through the human body that one can explore one's limitless spiritual possibilities. Even the gods envy the human frame. One should not, therefore, play with it recklessly. One must submit to the Will of God, when one's time is over, but not crave death, nor invite it without a sufficient and noble cause. It is dying while yet alive — that is, self-surrender for the good of man — that one should seek, not physical annihilation".

Once the Sikhs asked the Guru : "What is the most auspicious time for launching out upon a journey, or a new undertaking, a marriage or a festivity, and how, if not through astrology, one is to avoid misfortune in the future", the Guru replied : "Every time and place is sanctified by God for the man of prayer. Only, he is affected by good and bad omens who cherishes not God. To consult the movement of the stars or future-reading is a pastime of the ignorant or the charlatans. That what is in the lap of God must remain a mystery and no one can escape the result of his deeds (*karma*) except through prayer and self-surrender. Life would be far more miserable if we knew what was to happen to us on the morrow, or even the next moment. It is, therefore, best that we leave to our God what must remain a mystery for us human beings. For, while our best calculations can fail, not so the mercy and compassion of God."

The ascetic son of Guru Nānak, Sri Chand, though disinherited by the father, was still alive and preaching his gospel of renunciation as an *Udāsi*, though he was mature and disinterested enough not to come actively in the way of the third Guru. But, it was really hard for the common run of the Sikhs "to choose between Guru Nānak's son and the nominee of his nominee". The message of Nānak was spreading far and wide through various sources and to protect its pristine purity and to reach the largest number of seekers in the vast land of India, Guru Amar Dās divided the whole country into twenty two dioceses, called *manjis* (or seats of spiritual authority, on the analogy, it is said, of Akbar's division of the country for administrative purposes into as many administrative units) and gave charge of each to a devout follower of his.* This not only spread the gospel far and wide and increassed considerably the number of the Guru's followers, all over India, it also gave, as we shall see, the Sikh church an organisation that was to contribute in due course both to its initial strength and ultimate weakness. At this time, however, it led to a great mass-awakening and upsurge among the people and the Guru's central treasury also benefitted greatly from the contributions collected through these, new viceregents (later known as Masands†) of the Guru.

The more the Guru's influence grew, the more intense also became jealousy against him. For instance, when he visited Kasur, the Governor of the city, a Hindu Khatri, refused to offer him a place to pitch his tent in his garden, in spite of oppressive heat and he sought shelter with a poor Pathān. But, the Guru never lost his compassion. It is said, whenever he would hear the cry of woe from any quarter, wherever he lived, he would immediately start praying for those in distress, heal and succour the sick and the wounded, and go out personally in spite of his age to console the bereaved.

Hearing his repute, a Muslim of Delhi, Ala-Yār, who used to trade in horses between Kābul and Hindustān, came to see him and was so bewitched by his humility, spiritual illumination and moral fervour that, abandoning his trade to his son, he became a devout follower of the Guru. Later, he was appointed a Masand for the diocese of Delhi.

It is said it was Guru Amar Dās who first named Baisākhi (April 13), Māghi (1st day of Magha, *mid-January*) and Diwāli (the festival of lights in October/November) as the three days for his followers to

---

* These twenty-two disciples were mostly Jāts, though they also contained a Muslim, namely (1) Alā-yār. His other appointees were: (2) Sachnasach of Sheikhpur, (3) Sādhāran, (4) Sāwan Mal, the Guru's nephew, (5) Sukhan, (6) Handāl, (7) Kedāri, (8) Khedā, (9) Gangu Shāh, (10) Darbāri, (ii) Pāro of Dallā, (12) Pherā, (15) Buā, (14) Beni of Dāu, (15) Maheshā of Sultānpur, (16) Māi Dās (17) Nānak Chand, (18) Murāri, (19) Rājārām, (20) Rang Shāh, (2I) Rang Dās of Thattā, (22) Lālo of Dallā.

† The word is a corrupted form of *Masnad-i-Ālā* (or the seat of high authority). In due course, the Masands became very powerful and corrupt and not only lost moral health and appropriated the Guru's money, but some of them even defied his authority. The tenth Guru abolished this institution. Now-a-days, it is a word of contempt.

congregate from far and near at the Guru's place, thus formally founding an organised Sikh church.

In the meantime, the Guru married off his daughter, Bibi Bhāni (who was given to prayer and meditation and was the most beloved of the Guru's children) to a very pious and diligent young follower of his, Jethā by name, who though born in Lāhore, had come with a party of pilgrims to visit the Guru and was so enchanted by the holiness of the atmosphere at Goindwāl that he decided to stay here. He would earn his living by selling boiled and sweetened whea (*ghungniān*), and in his spare time would attend to the service of the Guru, or meditate on God. Finding him to be worthy in every way, and knowing the dedicated disposition of his daughter, the Guru blessed her marriage. It was to prove a most worthwhile union, for Jethā, as we shall see, was later also to assume the Throne of the Guru.

As the Hindu belief of man incarnating himself in eighty-four hundred thousand species was still very strong among his followers, who mostly came from the Hindu stock, the Guru ordered a well (*Bāwali*) being dug up with 84 steps and enjoined that whosoever will bathe in it and recite at each step the whole composition of *Japji* by Guru Nānak, his "coming-and-going" (transmigation) will end. The belief is still firmly held by the devout and twice in the year, large crowds make a pilgrimage to Goindwāl.

In the year 1567 A. D., when Akbar visited Lāhore, he made a call on the Guru at Goindwāl. His fame as a great spiritual leader had already reached the ears of the emperor, but when he saw the non-sectarian, though earth-aware atmosphere of the holy sanctuary, he was deeply impressed. On being told that the Guru would see no one, high or low, till one had partaken of the food from the common kitchen (*langar*), Akbar, a man of broad sympathies and high culture, welcomed the idea and partook of the food distributed there, sitting in a row with his subjects of humble origin. Before departing, Akbar wanted to endow this unique institution (where all men, irrespective of creed, caste or station, could satisfy their hunger in such large numbers) with the revenue of several villages. But the Guru refused to accept any imperial offerings saying that the Guru's kitchen must be self-supporting and depend only upon the small offerings of the devout. According to some historians, the emperor not willing to disregard the Guru's wishes in this behalf, bestowed the *Jāgir* on the Guru's daughter, Bhāni, instead, which fact is, however, not substantiated by the imperial records.*

A reference is made in the Ādi-Granth† to another tapā (Hindu recluse) who due to the arrogance of caste and wild jealousy, used to slander the Guru. Once, even though invited on a festive occasion, he decided not to partake of food from the Guru's kitchen, but when he learnt that the Guru was also offering money to the participants, he sent in his son, surreptitiously (who, it is narrated by the Sikh choroniclers, broke a leg while scaling the wall of the kitchen). It is also given in the same hymn that "what he committed at home (it is said he committed adultery with the landlord's wife) became known to the elders" and so was severely punished by them. On this occasion, Jethā (later Guru Ram Dās) laid down the attributes of a mendicant or a faqir :

> *"An ascetic is not he who's filled with greed, and*
> *like the cursed ones, craves for Māyā.*
>
> *But, here is an ascetic whom I invited to a feast*
> *and he refused, but, later, in remorse, (surreptitiously)*
> *sent in his son. The leaders of men*
> *all laughed, and said :- "This man is fired by greed.*
>
> *Wheresoever he sees not enough, he goes not, but*
> *seeing more, he forsakes all his vows.*
>
> *He slanders the saintly beings to earn applause, but*
> *for this sin, he is destroyed by God. Among the people*
> *he passes for an ascetic but, within,*
> *he commits sin. But, lo,*
> *the Lord has exposed his evil nature*
> *to the whole world."*‡

Similarly, when a devotee made an offering of a precious necklace of pearls and rubies to the Guru, the latter put it on the neck of his son-in-law, Jethā. But Jethā was so disinterested and so much absorbed in the thoughts of God that he bestowed it on a Muslim faqir of

* According to the Gazetter of Amritsar (1883-84). it was Guru Rām Dās who first settled near the tank (of Amritsar) about 1547 A.D., and obtained a grant of the site with 500 bighas from Akbar in 1577, and paid to the Zamindārs of Tung who owned the land a consideration of Rs. 700 Akbari.

† *Ādi Granth*, P 315, Gauri Ki Vār M. 4.

‡ Ādi Granth, P. 316, Gauri Ki Vār, M. 4.

Goindwāl, who complained to him that though he was poor, he had received no bounty from the Guru's house !

Seeing the Guru's instruction cutting across the barriers of caste and creed, and his influence spreading far and wide, the high-caste Khatris and Brāhmins of the neighbourhood, supported by a rich Marwāhā Hindu merchant, resolved to wait in deputation upon Akbar, to plead against the Guru corrupting their age-old traditions and religious beliefs. They even instigated the Muslim owners of the land where the Guru had dug up the *Bāwali* to complain to the royal court that the full price of their land had not been paid to them and that they were driven out of their hearths and homes by force. A servant of Marwāhā even blackned his face and put on tattered clothes to bewail before the emperor the lot of the "oppressed" made miserable by the disciples of the Guru. But, this man with his entourage came back utterly disappointed from the royal court, and they were ill-received even by their own folk when they returned home. A reference to their abject humiliation is made in the Ādi Granth.*

But, when the Brāhmins entered their complaint and said that the Guru's novel preachings would lead to disorder in the realm, as he wanted to shape the society anew and to break up all that was hallowed by custom and usage, both by the Hindus and the Muslims, the emperor decided that he would summon the Guru to ask for his explanation to the charges. A royal courier was immediately despatched to Goindwāl. The Guru politely excused himself on account of old age, but sent out Jethā to answer the charges levelled against the Guru's house. Jethā was received by the emperor with great courtesy and he explained his viewpoint so ably that the emperor was deeply impressed. "Birth and caste are of no avail before God", Jethā said quoting Guru Nānak, "It is deeds which make or unmake a man. To exploit ignorant people with superstitions and to call it religion is a sacrilege against God and man. To worship the infinite, formless and absolute God in the form of a totem, an image or an insignificant or time-bound object of nature, or to wash one's sins not through compassion and self-surrender, but through ablutions; to insist upon special diets, languages and dresses, and fads about what to eat and what not, and to condemn the mass of human beings, including women, to the status of sub-humans and to deny them the reading of the scriptures and even work of every kind is to tear apart man from

---

† Gauri Ki Vār, M. 4.

man. This is not religion, nor it is religion to deny the world through which alone man can find his spiritual possibilities."

Akbar, it is said, was so overwhelmed by the exposition of his faith by Jethā, that he not only dismissed the plaint of the Brāhmins but called upon them to ask his forgiveness. As all historians are agreed that Akbar had long thought of evolving "God's religion for all men," (*Din-i-Ilāhi*) and that he had discourses, among others, with the exponents of the Sikh doctrine as well, the expositions of Jethā must necessarily have influnced him a great deal*, as Sikhism in those days was the only faith in India not only vigorously propagating but practising these tenets.

Following in the footsteps of Guru Nānak, the third Guru also now undertook a tour of all the Hindu places of pilgrimage• in order, as Jethā (later Guru Rām Dās) writes in the Ādi-Granth (*Turkhāri Chhant*) "to instruct and emancipate the people at large". And, as is given in the same composition, "anyone who crossed over with the Guru paid no charge to the tax-gatherers," 'as the emperor had excused the toll-tax on the followers of the Guru. Seeing this, large masses of pilgrims declared themselves to be the Guru's disciples and the tax that year from the pilgrims, it is said, came to nothing. The Guru visited Kurukshetra and the holy places on the banks of Yamunā and the Gangā. Declares the Ādi Granth : "The ignorance of those who saw the Guru was dispelled and light dawned on their hearts. Religious services were held every day and people came to behold the Guru in large numbers. The Yogis, digambars, sanyasis and men belonging to all the six schools (of Hindu religion) conversed with him. All who meditated on the one God and repeated the Guru's name were exempted from the collection of toll-tax. The Guru, quoting from the Smiritis and Shāstras, proved to all the existence of the one God and the efficacy of dwelling on God's Name. He said, "the Purānas commend alms-giving, but from Nānak's Words one attains the service of God." "Many people took shelter in the

---

* Ishwari Parsad, "A Short History of the Muslim Rule in Indiā", Vol. II, Pp. 366-368.

• According to Macauliffe, it was at Akbar's suggestion to Jethāji that the Guru undertook this pilgrimage in order to pacify the enraged Hindu sentiments (Sikh Religion, Vol. II, Pp. 108-9). This is not corroborated by the authentic sayings of Guru Rām Dās in this context (Tukhāri Chhant) and incorporated in the Ādi Granth to which reference has been made in the text.

True Guru". This shows that the Guru, as has been alleged by some, did not go out on a pilgrimage, but for the propagation of his faith to rid people of their superstition and cant.

These days, a Khatri merchant, named Gango, came to visit the Guru and placing a penny-worth of brown sugar as an offering bemoaned to him about his tragic loss in trade and implored him to accept him in his service, so that he attained deliverance. The Guru replied : "It is no use running away from life. One can attain emancipation even in the household through disinterested service of the others. You go and open a bank at Delhi and serve the holy and the needy, and pray for the success of your clients." Gango adopted this suggestion and soon became a thriving banker. In order to put his faith to test, the Guru sent a poor man to him with a letter that he be given some help. Gango disregarded the Guru's letter, thinking that if he honoured his instructions once, the Guru would make recurring demands on him in behalf of one poor man or another, and sent back the man disappointed. The Guru himself fulfilled his need but said, "he who in power and affluence can remember not God or his own fellowmen and becomes egotistical and selfish, he invariably comes to grief." And so it happened. The tide of fortune turned and Gango became bankrupt again. Now, he had no other support but the Guru's and came back to him as a penitent, and performed penances, or was seen absorbed in God. Seeing his helplessness and genuine sense of regret, the Guru not only forgave him but appointed him a messenger of his faith.

Not only did the Guru's kitchen serve the poor, night and day, but he personally attended to the cure and nursing of the sick and the aged. A leper (who had lost all his relations in his childhood) he loved and nursed so well that giving him the name of Murāri (the destroyer of the demon, *Mur*, one of Krishna's epithets), he persuaded one of his disciples, Seenha, to give his daughter in marriage to him. When Seenha's wife heard about it, she was greatly upset, and asked : "What is the caste of this man, of what parentage is he and of what station ?" The Guru told her : "I am his God-father. My caste is his caste, your daughter will come to my home after her marriage." The mother's feelings soothed thus, the Guru appointed him one of the twenty-two messengers of his faith. Similarly, purging two Brahmins, called Khedā and Beni, of their pride of book-knowledge and caste-consciousness, the Guru blessed them too with the same position as Murāri. Two other Khatris, Phiriā and Katārā of Delhi (their names are also given as Pherā and Kedāri), also were blessed similarly, on account of their devotion. They did much to demolish people's beliefs in the yogic miracles and incantations.

When a Brāhmin, proud of his book-knowledge and learning in Sanskrit questioned the Guru, "Why do you impart instruction to your disciples not in Sanskrit, the language of gods in which all the Hindu lore is written, but in their mother-tongue, like Panjābi, the the language of the illiterate mass", the Guru replied, "Sanskrit is like a well, deep, inaccessible and confined to the elite, but the language of the people is like rain water—ever-fresh, abundant and accessible to all." He said : "I want my doctrines to be propagated through every language which the people speak, for it is not language but the content that should be considered sacred or otherwise."

As has been pointed out, while the Sikhs were served rich meal from the Guru's kitchen, the Guru himself lived on coarse bread. Bhāi Buddhā and other devout Sikhs were greatly pained at this. The Guru replied : "The Guru's kitchen is for the poor and the needy,run with the small offerings of the devout. I cannot appropriate to myself, the custodian, anything more than what might keep me barely alive. So should the leaders of the faith. They should eat but sparingly and devote themselves ever to the disinterested service of the others and make not their good acts known merely to earn the people's applause. They should abandon avarice, lust, pride and wrath and maintain their mental equipoise, so that they participate in the joys and sorrows of others at all times, and as for themselves, submit ever to the Will of God. This is how they could instruct others also in the same way".

Now, the Guru asked Jethā to found another city, and first to dig up a tank there and to build a house for himself. This Jethā did on the lands bought by him from the Zamindārs for a price of 700 Akbari rupees.* This tank came to be known as Santokhsar and the place as *Guru's chak* (later Rāmdāspur, the present Amritsar) which in course of time became—and still is — a great centre of commerce and place of holy pilgrimage with its Golden Temple and the "Pool of Nectar", and also had to play a most significant and vital part in Sikh history.

* According to Suraj Parkāsh, Rās 2, Chapter 11, these lands were given as a gift to Jethā by Akbar. But, says the Gazetter of Amritsar (1883-84) that Jethā purchased them for 700 Akbari rupees from the Zamindārs of Tung. The length of the Amritsar tank is 500 ft., its width 490 ft., and depth 17 ft. It is now fed by Bāri Doab Canal through a pipeline, so that the water remains fresh. Earlier, water was brought from the river Rāvi, a rare feat in those days.

The Guru seeing his end near, put his two sons and another son-in-law, Rām, to the test along with Jethā and finding the latter upto the mark in every way†, appointed him his successor, in the same way as he had been by Guru Angad, on Asuj 2, Samvat 1631 (September 1, 1574), and re-named him Rām Dās (Servant of God). The Guru's eldest son, Mohan, refused to pay homage to him, but the younger one, Mohri, accepted the Guru's verdict with good grace. So did all other devout Sikhs, led by Bhāi Buddhā, who also anointed his forehead with a saffron-mark.

Acting as Guru for about twenty two years, Amar Dās breathed his last on the full moon day of Bhadon, Samvat 1631 (1574 A. D.) at the ripe old age of 95 years. In a composition, called "Sadd' (or the Call), his grandson, Sunder, has given an account of his death and how the Guru forbade his followers from observing the ancient customs of mourning the dead, and to make it an occasion for the recitation of God's Name, and submit to the Will of God as an act of faith.‡

It is said, before his demise, the Guru dictated to his elder son, Mohan, the compositions of himself and the two earlier Masters and adding the Word of the Hindu and Muslim mystics of the middle ages preserved them, in two volumes, for posterity. It is claimed that the fifth Guru, Arjun, made use of them for the compilation of the Adi-Granth. However, as we have said earlier, it is not unreasonable to suppose that the written record of their compositions was handed down from one Master to the other at the time of succession.

---

† It is said, on the orders of the Guru, Jethā built and demolished a platform seven times, without demur, while all others abandoned the work in disgust.

‡ Ādi-Granth, Sadd, Sunder, Rāg Rāmkali.

GURU RĀM DĀS

(1534—1581 A.D.)

Guru Rām Dās ascended the spiritual Throne of Nānak at the age of almost forty years and breathed his last, according to the authentic Sikh records, exactly seven years after. But, during this brief period, he achieved considerable progress in expanding the activities of the Guru's House. He sent out many of his devout disciples called Masands or, the Guru's Agents, even to the neighbouring countries like Afghānistān to spread the gospel and also to collect the offerings of the devotees which he needed more than ever not only to run the community kitchen, but also to complete the excavation of the second tank (later called Amritsar)* and to expand the activities of the city of Rāmdāspur he had founded in the life-time of the third Guru.

Born at Lāhore in the house of Hari Dās, a Khatri of the Sodhi clan, of the womb of Anup Devi, on Kārtik Vadi 2, Samvat 1591 (September 24, 1534, A.D.), Jethā (later known as Rām Dās), as we have seen in the earlier chapter, was married to the younger daughter of Guru Amar Dās, Bibi Bhāni, and had three sons from her—Prithia (or, Prithi Chand), Mahādev and Arjun Dev. It has also been narrated how due to his unflinching devotion to God and disinterested

* Medicinal properties were and are ascribed to the water of the tank. It is said, a leper who fell in it by chance, became whole. To the memory of this event stands a *ber*-tree and the portion of the tank near it is called "*Dukh-bhanjani*" (or, the destroyer of sorrows).

service to the Guru, he was appointed to succeed Guru Amar Dās.† From his lyrical compositions, included in the Ādi Granth, it is evident that he was a man of great sensitivity, devotion and spiritual fervour and peerless humility, besides being a successful builder and an organiser of the Sikh Church. So touching was his humility that when Bābā Sri Chand, the aging ascetic son of Guru Nānak, came to visit him and asked him why he kept such a long beard, he answered : "To wipe the dust off the feet of holy men like yourself," and he proceeded to perform this supreme act of devotion to the honoured guest. But, Sri Chand held his hand and embraced him saying: "It's enough. This is the kind of character by which you have deprived me of my ancestoral heritage. Now, what more is left with me that I could offer you for your piety and goodness of heart?"

It appears that by now the opposition to the Guru's House both by the relations of the first three Gurus and the jealous monks, ascetics and yogis had almost died down. Large numbers of men and women came from far and near to receive spiritual instruction and also to participate in the excavation work of the second tank and the building of the city of Rāmdāspur, as the Guru emphasised time and again to the Sikhs that one could fulfil one's life not merely by quiet meditations but in actively participating in the joys and sorrows of others. This is how one could also rid oneself of the prime malady—Ego—and end his spiritual loneliness.

---

† The popular reason ascribed for this accession, possibly, is based on Bhāi Gurdās's version (Vār 1) - *Jān nā desān Sodhion, horas ajar nā Jariā Jāi* (I will not let go the Guru's throne out of the clan of Sodhis, as the others will not be able to bear the unbearable). These words are put into the mouth of Bibi Bhāni, daughter of Guru Amar Dās, who it is said, once saw one of the legs of the stool, on which the Guru was seated, absorbed in meditations, giving way, and utterly devoted as she was to her father-Guru, she put her fist beneath it to keep it even. This hurt her hand grievously and when the father opened his eyes and saw what had happened, he was overwhelmed with emotion and asked her to ask for a favour. At this time, she is reported to have said: "Master, if you are merciful, let not the Guru's throne hereafter pass out of the house of Sodhis" to which belonged also her husband. The Guru granted her wish, but said: "You've asked for a boon which will lead to much trouble and disputation." And so it did, but Bhai Gurdās, who wrote this verse probably after the martyrdom of Guru Arjun, saw in this the unfailing vision of the third Guru and of Bibi Bhāni who had, both, foreseen, according to Gurdās, what dangerous times were ahead to meet whose challenge much sacrifice and daring were necessary, besides spiritual awakening, and that Bibi Bhāni sought this high honour not for the glorification of her husband's caste but for her progeny to dare and die for a great cause.

One of the high acquisitions of the Sikh church in these days was the entry into it of Bhāi Gurdās Bhallā, a relation of the third Guru, a superb poet and scholar of comparative religion, who was to become a great exponent of the Sikh credo in course of time. He was deputed to preach at Āgrā where he, with his deep knowledge of Hindi and Sanskrit and the Hindu scriptures, spread the gospel of the Guru with great success.

But another trouble nearer home was brewing for him, which, in course of time, was to involve the imperial authority against the Guru's house. It is said, the Guru's first cousin, Sahāri Mal, came from Lāhore to invite the Guru to his son's marriage. The Guru being tied down to the work he was executing, expressed his inability to do so, but promised to send one of his sons instead. He tried hard with the eldest son, Prithi Chand, but the latter was apprehensive that during his absence, his coveted position might be entrusted to someone else. Mahādev was a recluse and excused himself on the ground that he was not at all interested in the affairs of the world. The Guru thereupon asked his youngest son, Arjun Dev, to proceed to Lāhore which he agreed to do with such grace and humility that the Guru's heart was filled with gladness.

But, a month passed and the Guru did not call him back from Lāhore. Arjun Dev wrote two epistles in verse, one after another but these were intercepted by Prithi Chand and never reached the Guru. Thereupon, Arjun wrote a third epistle and, as a precaution, numbered it 'three' and gave strict instructions to the messenger to hand it over personally to the Guru. This was done, and the Guru, seeing the number of the letter and sensing who might have intercepted the previous two communications, asked Prithi Chand to produce them. At first, Prithi hesitated a good deal but seeing the insistence of the Guru and the consequences of refusal to comply with his wishes, he brought them to the Guru. Arjun had written (and here are quoted two verses of his from the Ādi Granth):-

"My mind longs to have the sight of the Guru.

With tearful eyes, it wails like the Chātrik-bird.

My thirst goes not, nor peace I find, without the sight of the beloved Saint. (1)

Sacrifice, O Sacrifice am I unto the sight of the Saint, my Guru, my beloved.

Pray tell me, how long, how long, is to be my separation from the Lord of the earth.
*Blessed, blessed is the land where thou livest, my friend and Master. (2)"**

When the Guru read them, he was moved to tears by the innate humility and sincerity of Arjun's utterance. He called him back at once and when the two met, Arjun is said to have uttered the following verse :

"*By great good fortune, I have met the Guru-Saint,*
And found the eternal Lord in my own home.
I serve him ever and go not from him for a moment.
*Says Nānak, thy servant, "I am Thy slave, O Lord."**

The story may be apocryphal, because before a person ascended the *gaddi* of the Guru, he could not have used the appellation of ' Nānak", as Arjun does in this verse. It may only be indicative of the intensity of his love for the eternal Guru (i.e. God).

The Guru was now confirmed in his views that it was his youngest and not the eldest son who deserved to succeed to the throne of Nānak. And, so he duly appointed him as Guru on Bhādon Sudi 2, Samvat 1638 (September 1, 1581), when Arjun was only about eighteen years of age, the day when his father breathed his last.

* Mājh M 5, Chaupadās.

CHAPTER VII

GURU ARJUN DEV

(1563—1606 A.D.)

A poet of supreme sensitivity and divine inspiration, a philosopher in his own right, a builder of cities and international commerce and the first martyr of the Sikh faith, with whom we enter into the main-stream of history, and who centralised the Sikh church and made Sikhs the people of the Book — this was Guru Arjun. His span of life was a mere two score years and three and yet such was his organisation of the Sikh church that from a society of spiritually-awakened householders, the Sikhs staked their claim for peoplehood, who could withstand the challenge not only of the spirit, but also of a firmly-rooted imperial power.

Born at Goindwāl, on Vaikāsh 19, Samvat 1620 (April 15, 1563 A. D.), in the house of Guru Rām Dās, of the womb of Bibi Bhāni, Arjun was the youngest of the Guru's three sons, the eldest being Prithia (or Prithi Chand), a recklessly ambitious and vicious person (of whom we shall have to write at length presently), followed by Mahādev, who had become a recluse in the lifetime of his father. His sensitivity as a poet, his devotion to God and his Guru-father, the possessiveness of Prithi Chand and the renunciation of world by Mahādev had made him a natural choice for the Guruship even at the young age of eighteen. And, like his illustrious predecessors, he fully justified the choice. In due time, he was married to Gangā, daughter of Kishan Chand of village Meo in the present district of Jullundur.*

---

* It is said this was the Guru's second marriage, his first wife, Rām Kaur, having died childless soon after their marriage.

But as soon as Guru Arjun ascended the throne of Nānak, Pithia started a wild compaign of vilification and hostility against him, and even provoked the wrath of Sulhi Khān, a high Government official of Jullundur-Doāb. Guru Arjun tried to pacify him by alloting all rents from the house property to him, and the income accruing from a surcharge on businessmen which came to him as the owner of the property, he gave to Mahādev, himself depending only on the voluntary offerings of the community. But as we shall see, far from giving him any satisfaction, Prithi Chand or Prithia as he is contemptuously called, became even more vile and vengeful.

The Guru in the meantime completed the tanks of Santoksar and Amritsar under his personal supervision and applied himself whole-heartedly to the extension of the city of Rāmdāspur. In the middle of the tank of Amritsar, the Guru laid the foundation of the Hari-mandir (later known as the Golden Tample).* He enjoined on all Sikhs to contribute one-tenth (Daswandh) of their income for community purposes. As large sums of money were required, the Guru sent out missionaries to make collections from the devout from the other parts of the country. One Bhāi Kalyānā volunteered to go to the city of Mandi, the citadel of the Hindu Rājputs, and by his piety and dedication to the cause, he converted many people to the faith of Nānak, including the Rājā himself, who came with large presents to visit the Guru.

Such was the innate humility of the Guru that when the Sikhs represented to him that the Hari Mandir to be built in the middle of the tank of Amritsar should be raised on such a high pedestal that no other building in the town might equal its stature, the Guru replied that the House of God is exalted because it believes in humility. "So, I would rather keep it a few steps down from each side of the city-level" and so he did. In order also to shed the superstitious

* The British named it Golden Temple. Its foundations were laid on January 13, 1588. According to tradition, the Guru invited Hazrat Mian Mir (Born in Sistān, Iran, in 1553, died at Lahore on 11 Aug. 1635 A. D., according to MahānKosh, p. 2912) then a well-known Muslim divine of Lāhore, to lay the foundation-stone. But this fact is not supported by any other historical evidence, though Mian Mir seems to have met the Guru and developed an extreme liking for him. And according to all Sikh records, he wailed miserably on witnessing the tortures heaped on the Guru. Jehāngir, in his Tuzak, writes with utmost reverence and humility about this great Sufii Saint and mentions his visits to him, "to seek his blessings". It is said, he tried to intercede with the emperor on the Guru's behalf during his incarceration but could not succeed. According to Mahān Kosh (P. 228), Guru Arjun himself laid the foundation-stone of the Darbar Sahib, and its tank was named "Amritsar". It was gold plated by Maharaja Ranjit Singh, and has exquisite workmanship in designs beaten into it. It is a marvel of engineering skill in its structure.

belief of the Muslims that God's House is in the West and of the Hindus that it is in the East (where the sun rises), he kept the Hari Mandir open on all sides. "My faith is for the people of all castes and all creeds from whichever direction they come and to whichever direction they bow." It is said, a mason accidently displaced the foundation-stone, whereupon the Guru prophesied : "Never mind, it will be built again." As we shall see later, the Guru's prophecy was duly fulfilled. Ahmad Shāh Abdāli destroyed the temple and filled the tank with rubbish in 1762 A. D., but the Sikh army two years later recovered its possession and rebuilt it.

When the tank was complete in all respects, the Guru wrote many hymns of thanksgiving,* some of which said : "God Himself has come to accomplish my tasks. He it is who has helped in the construction of the tank. He who bathes in it, earns the merit of ablutions at all the sixty-eight (Hindu) pilgrim stations, and (customary) charities. The sinners are purified here as they reflect here on God's Name." "He who bathes in the tank of Rāmdās, his Soul shall be saved and his heart's desires fulfilled. He shall become eternal and his comings-and-goings will end."†

The joy of the Sikhs knew no bounds. They came from far and near to visit the Guru and the new centre of their faith. Many tradesmen came to settle in Amritsar and increased its popularity and prosperity. But this also ignited further jealousy not only in the heart of Prithia, but also among the imperial governors and courtiers, one of them being Rājā Birbal, an extremely influential Minister in the Court of Akbar, who was stung by the Guru's influence among both the Hindus and the Muslims and was on the look out of an opportunity to curb it.‡ While marching against the Yusafzais (1586) at the head of a punitive expedition, he had levied, with the permission of the emperor, a one-rupee tax on the head of each Hindu household and asked his agents to collect it from the citizens of Amritsar. The Khatris there refused to pay and complained to the Guru who represented to the Rājā's agents that they being a community other than

* In Rāgas Sorath, Bilāwal and Suhi, included in the Ādi-Granth.

† These lines have been interpreted in spiritual terms also by those who see a contradiction in the Guru's injunction against pilgrimages and the lyrical praise bestowed upon a visit to the tank and temple at Amritsar. But, those who know the distinction between pilgrimage as a holy ritual and one that is undertaken to rekindle one's faith in God and man are afflicted by no such doubts.

‡ "Akbar did not agree with Birbal." To him, the Sikh doctrines "seemed deserving of high commendation." (V.A. Smith, *Akbar*, P. 171).

the Hindus should be exempt from the tax, as was done by the emperor before when Guru Amar Dās and his entourage were exempted from the pilgrim-tax. "Ours is a trust property, and all its incomes are utilized on public works or running a free kitchen open to all. How can we be subjected to a tax", the Guru is reported to have said. Birbal was furious on hearing such a reply and asked his men that the Guru be brought into his presence by force, should he be unwilling to come otherwise. The Guru, unperturbed, sent back the imperial soldiers with a polite but firm reply that he was afraid of no persecution for a just cause and refused to answer the summons. Birbal theatened that unless the tax was paid, he would raze the city of Amritsar to the ground, but no one paid and before he could do any harm, he received royal orders to march expeditiously towards the frontier, where he was killed in a battle with the Yusafzais. Prithia, however, continued to cause annoyance to the Guru by making false reports to the King-emperor or by provoking the authorities of Jullundur-Doāb, notably Sulhi Khān, but fortunately another Minister, Wazir Khān, deeply impressed by the Guru's gentle piety and his followers' dedication to God, interceded, it is said, on his behalf, and a collision was somhow avoided, but the atmosphere remained charged with tension. Round 1590 A.D., the Guru set out, along with some of his devotees, like Bhāi Gurdās and Bidhi Chand, on a tour of Mājhā, the country between the rivers Rāvi and Beās. He visited Khadur, Goindwāl, Sarhāli, and Khānpur, where he was received not by the rich headman, on account of his caste-consciousness and the Guru's preaching of equality between all men, and given no shelter in spite of heavy rains and he had so seek accommodation in the tattered hut of one Hemā who served the Guru with extreme devotion.

It was during this tour that the Guru bought some land in the village of Khārā and laid the foundation of another now well-known city of Tarn Tāran, and started the work of digging a tank, even more spacious than at Amritsar (1590)*. On seeing burnt bricks and lime-

* Sikh chroniclers and following them Mr. Macauliffe adduce every time some kind of hostility of the near relations of the earlier Gurus so that the Gurus one after the other are obliged to leave their habitual abode or abandon the cities founded by their predecessors and even by themselves. Though some jealousy and intrigue was inevitable in a situation in which the Gurus flouted the law of pomegeniture and natural succession, the main reason why the Gurus never stuck to one place and built new towns and habitations seems to be that they wanted their followers

kilns being built by the Guru, the local Governor, Nur-ud-Din, seized them for the building of a Serai after his own name. The Guru. however, did not provoke a clash and merely said, "He who annoys the poor will forsure come to grief. The thing will come back to where it belongs." In the year 1775, two Sikh generals, Khushāl Singh Faizalpuriā and Jassā Singh Rāmgarhiā, pulled down Nur-ud-Din's serai and used its bricks in the construction of the tank.

From there, the Guru visited the Jullundur area where he purchased more land to build the now well-known town of Kartārpur. As was usual with him and his House, he dug up a well here—calling it Gangsar (or, the source of Gangā, the holy river of the Hindus) both for meeting their needs of water-supply and for their clean, healthy living. He made a large number of converts and passing through Khem Karan and Chunian, visited Lāhore on the invitation of the Sikhs. Here, again, he constructed a well, now called Bāoli Sāhib, in the area of Dabbi Bazār. Here, he met some well-known Muslim Saints like Shāh Hussain, Shāh Suleiman, Shāh Ināyat Qādri, Sheikh Wali Shāh, Yogis like Shambhunāth and Bhaktas like Kāhnā and Chhaju and had long spiritual discourses with them, befriending every one of them and influencing their thoughts a good deal, as we find particularly in the verse compositions of Shāh Hussain (and later of Bullah Shāh, the devout disciple of Shāh Ināyat Qādri). It is said, even the Viceroy of Lahore was deeply impressed by his preachings and paid all expenses for the construction of the *bāoli*.

From here, the Guru proceeded to visit Derā Bābā Nānak at Kartārpur (on the western bank of the Rāvi, now in Pākistān) and later visited Barāth where he met Bābā Sri Chand, the ascetic son of Guru Nānak. On being questioned, the Guru told him about the hostility of Prithia. Sri Chand replied : "This will be his undoing and ruin both in this world and the next".

F, N. Contd.

not only to reconstruct the country and add to its affluence, but also not to stick to particular places as exclusive symbols of spiritual pilgrimage or sanctity. It is in line with what the Gurus did in respect of inheritance, language, choice of dress and food, the first manuscript of the Ādi Granth, weapons and clothes used by them personally, particular directions and postures in which men might pray and the sanctity of fixed days and auspicious moments for penance, prayer and the starting of ventures, etc. The Gurus sanctified the whole earth and all its activities in their every manifestation if dedicated to God. [See also Chapter i]

*In Samvat 1651 (or, 1594 A. D.)

The Guru now returned to Amritsar but only to find the jealousy of his eldest brother even more accentuated. But Parithia consoled himself and his wife with the thought that as the Guru was childless, the *gaddi* would pass on to their son, Mehervān. Guru Arjun's wife was much exercised on this account and implored him to grant her the boon of a son. This wish of hers was fulfilled when on June 14, 1595 A.D. a son was born to their house,* and was named Hargobind after great festivities and functions of thanksgiving.

The birth of a son to the house of the Guru finally dashed the hopes of Prithi Chand and he resolved to leave no stone unturned in order to finish both the father and the son. At first, he provoked an attack on Amritsar by Sulhi Khān. This the latter did on the pretext of levying and collecting a tribute. The Guru left Amritsar with his family and entourage and settled at Wadāli, a few miles away, and from there went to a barren tract of land called Raur where a Gurdwārā still stands to his memory. Later, he came back to live at Wadāli which had long been subjectd to dacoities and plunder due to its prosperity. With the arrival of the Guru, however, calm prevailed. Finding scarcity of water, the Guru dug up a well here also worked by six persian wheels (*chhe-hartā*) and the village is since then known as Chhē-hartā Sāhib. A yearly fair is held here in January. Sulhi also hearing that the Guru had abandoned the town with his treasure before his arrival went back disappointed, and waited for another suitable opportunity.

Though the Guru had left Amritsar, and Prithia for a time tried to convince the Guru's followers that it was he and not Arjun who should be looked upon as Guru, no one put trust in his words and

* The Sikh chroniclers, in order to establish the innate humility of the Guru, narrate an interesting incident in this context. They say the Guru said to his wife, "If you need a boon, ask not me but a pious Sikh like Bābā Budhā, the aged seer and devout disciple of Guru Nānak." This she did first going to him with a large entourage, seated in a high carriage, with large presents of delicacies etc., which Bābā Budhā resented and said: "What stampede has occured in the Guru's house that his wife comes to me with such a confusion of men and goods"? The Guru's wife had to return, much humbled, and later took a trip to him on foot, carrying his sparse daily food of bread, butter-milk and onions. The Bābā was deeply pleased and breaking an onion with his fist prophesied: "A son will be born to thee who will crush the enemies of Nānak's house, just as I have crushed this piece of onion with my hand." It is said, Bābā Budhā's chance remarks regarding the 'stampede' were also fulfilled later by Sulhi Khān coming to plunder Amritsar and the Guru's taking refuge in a village nearby.

continued to flock for the Guru's vision wherever he was. Prithia, however, did not lose hope and tried first through a wet-nurse and then through a Brahmin male-nurse to poison the new-born child of the Guru. But, he failed grievously on both occasions. The Brahmin, as the Guru testifies in the Ādi Granth (Bhairo M. 5), died of colic, while the female nurse exposed the vile design of Prithi Chand to the Guru. It is said, thereafter, a snake charmer was employed by Prithia for the same end, but he too failed, and exposed Prithia to much ridicule and shame among the people. On the entreaties of the inhabitants, the Guru now returned to Amritsar, when his child was only two years of age. Later, when Hargobind got small-pox, Prithia's hopes again rallied, but to his never-failing misfortune, the child recovered completely after a while.*

Undaunted in his foul designs, in spite of his exposure, Prithia again consulted with his friend, Sulhi Khān, and decided to approach the emperor at Delhi in order to lodge a complaint against the Guru. His younger brother, Mahādev, tried to bring about harmonious relations in the family but failed. The Guru also sent Bhai Gurdās to conciliate him but to no effect. At this, the latter composed a verse denoucing Prithia's vileness, which said :

"The crane may live at a pilgrim-station, but it finds no peace.
It may rain all over, but the Chātrik drinks not a drop.
The bamboo may live near the sandal tree, yet it catches not its perfume.
The musk is in the navel of the deer, yet he runs out and afar in its search.
Arjun, the Guru, remains the True King, while the face of the minā† is blackened."

---

*Such tender feelings of filial affection are expressed by Guru Arjun at the birth of Hargobind and his recovery from small-pox as well as the failure of the Brahmin male-nurse to poison the child that there is no doubt left in one's mind as to how much the Gurus cared for and rejoiced in the life of the household. Though the Guru rejected the advice of the orthodox to propitiate the Hindu goddess of small-pox, Sitala, or Durga, etc., constant prayers were addressed to God to save the life of Hargobind, and when this happend, the Guru composed many hymns of thanks-giving. (See Āsā M. 5, Bilāwal M. 5, Sorath M. 5, Gujri M. 5, Bhairo M. 5, etc.)

†Minā, literally means a mean wretch. This epithet is employed for Prithia and his progeny and the *Rahit-nāmās* ascribed to the devout Sikhs of Guru Gobind Singh warn the Sikhs not to have any dealings with them and the *Masands* and those who killed their daughters, etc. But it is also enjoined that those who seek forgiveness or are not actively hostile are to be forgiven.

Sulhi wrote to the imperial court at Delhi for an audience with the emperor and on receipt of a favourable reply proceeded to Delhi along with Prithia. But the emperor refused to give a sympathetic hearing to the memorial presented to him on the plea that it was not proper for a King to interfere in the affairs of holymen. Utterly demolished, Prithia fell ill. The Guru composed a hymn of thanksgiving to commemorate this occasion :

"The memorandum against the Guru proved false.
And the slanderers have come to a grievous loss. .
He whose support is Govind, the supporter of the earth,
Him the Yama comes not near.
......
Nānak sought the refuge of the (True) Court.
*And so his honour was saved by Lord the God."**

Meanwhile, the Guru applied his mind to the training of Hargobind not only in languages and religious philosophy, but also in riding, the use of weapons, astronomy and medicine, agriculture and public administration and even chemistry and other known sciences. Much of the religious education was imparted by Bhāi Budhā, but, it appears, various experts were employed to equip Hargobind to meet the challenge of the times. Himself the Guru kept to imparting spiritual instruction to the large number of the disciples who came to him from far and near, listened to or performed the devotional music in the *Hari Mandir*, he himself being a great instrumentalist and a vocal singer. The Guru's absorption in God and his never-failing faith pulled him through all the machinations that were engineered against him by his adversaries.

After giving the Sikhs a central temple for pilgrimage, the Guru now proceeded to collect the sayings of his predecessors so that an authenticated version of these be kept in the form of a book, and to separate it from apocryphal literature then considerably on the increase on account of Prithia's own and his son's compositions in the name of Nānak. Finding his popularity widspread, some yogis, sanyasis, udāsis, sufis, etc., had also floated verses in the name of Nānak in order to corrupt his doctrine. On being told that there

* Gauri M. 5.

was a verse-composition of Guru Nānak, called Prān Sangli, deposited with the royal household of one of Ceylon's principalities, the Guru, it is said, sent Bhāi Pairā to collect it from there. But the version that Pairā brought back after a long and arduous travel, the Guru did not accept as genuine, as it was obviously a treatise on *hatha-yoga* in verse, by a clever recluse who tried to pass it on the Sikhs in the name of Nānak. The Guru also is said to have despatched Bhāi Gurdās and later Bābā Budhā to Goindwāl to persuade Mohan, the elder son of Guru Amar Dās, to part with the copy of the two-volume book of the Guru's hymns* that he was reputed to have compiled under the personal supervision of his father and in which were also included the selected works of the Hindu Bhaktas, like Kabir, Ravidās, etc.

But, Mohan, it is said, refused to oblige, more so because he was ever absorbed in meditation and no one dared disturb him. Bābā Buddhā, the Jāt, even broke open the door behind which Mohan had locked himself in, but on the advice of Mohri did not awaken him out of his trance. Thereupon, Guru Arjun is said to have gone personally and sat in the street outside his house, singing a hymn to his praise with such profusion as to compare him to God himself (*Gauri chhant* M. 5). Mohan was much softened by this exemplary humility of the Guru and parted with his treasure (though in our view the story is rather far-fetched.) On the way back, the Guru also called on Dātu and Dāsu, Guru Angad's sons, and after a dialogue with them on spiritual matters, came back to Amritsar.

The Guru now pitched a tent for himself in a quiet corner near a grove and on the one hand started sifting the material for the compilation of the *Granth*, and on the other set upon the excavation of another tank, called Rāmsar, on this site. Bhāi Gurdās was entrusted with the task of the scribe of the Granth, while during his absence the Guru appointed Bābā Buddhā to minister to the need of imparting religious instruction to the never-ending stream of pilgrims to the Hari-Mandir. As the work of compilation was nearing completion,

---

* Of these two volumes, or *Sanchiān*, only one is now extant and is the property of one Bhagat Singh Bhallā, a refugee from West Pākistān, now resident of Patiālā. On Page 215, it is stated in the margin : "*Guru Angad Gurmukhi Akhar banai*", which seems to be a clear case of after-thought and interpolation by someone. However, as started elsewhere, the Guru had in fact most of the compositions of the earlier Gurus already with him, though he may have searched for other sources as well. The Guru is said to have visited Bābā Mohan in 1603 A. D.

the Guru prohesied, according to *Gurupartap Surya Granth* that "this great work will be translated into Indian and foreign languages by men of learning and dedication so that the Gospel spreads the world over as oil spreads over water."*

Not only were the works of all the five Gurus, including Guru Arjun, included in the Granth, but also the select verses from Hindu Bhaktas like Kabir, Jaidev, Nāmdev, Dahnnā, Ravidās, Pipā and Rāmānand, (which are indeed the most authentic of their writings now available, as since 1604 no one has been able to make any changes in their texts), but also Muslim divines like Farid and Mardānā, Sattā and Balwand, the Guru's minstrels, and several bards (Bhatts).† Bhāi Gurdās's verse was also invited for inclusion

* The first-ever complete English version was published, in four volumes, by the present author between 1960 and 1962, in fulfilment of the Guru's injuctions and prophecy.

† The Granth is arranged not subject-wise, but according to the musical measure (Rāga) in which a hymn is meant to be sung. There are in all 31 such measures (or rāgas), namely, Sri, Mājh, Gauri, Āsā, Gujri, Devgandhāri, Bihāgrā, Vadhans, Sorath, Dhanāsari, Jaitsiri, Todi, Bairāri, Tilang, Sūhi, Bilāwal, Gond, Rāmkali, Natnārain, Māligaurā, Mārū, Tukhāri, Kedārā, Bhairo, Basant, Sārang, Malhār, Kānrā, Kalyān, Parbhāti, and Jaijai-vanti. As would be seen from this catalogue, the Guru rejected the measures which were expressive of excessive exhuberance or unalloyed sadness. Besides the compositions of the first five Gurus, the sayings of Guru Tegh Bahādur, the ninth Guru, were added by Guru Gobind Singh but nothing of his own except a Dohā ascribed to him (*bal hoā, bandhan chhutē, etc.*), though included in the *Shalokas* of the 9th Master.
The book contains 5894 hymns in all, out of which the largest number is by Gurū Arjun (2216). Gurū Nānak has 976 hymns to his credit, Gurū Angad 61, Gurū Amar Dās 907, Gurū Rām Dās 679, Gurū Tegh Bahādur 118 and Bhaktas and bards, 937. The Bhaktas and Sufis included in the Granth are—Kabir, Rāmānand, Ravidās, Surdās, Pipā and Bhikhan from U.P., Jaidev from Bengāl, Nāmdev, Tirlochan and Parmānand from Mahārāshtra, Pipā and Dhannā from Rajasthān, and Beni, then popular all over North India. The writings of five Muslims—Bābā Farid, Bhikhan, Sattā, Balwand and Mardānā are also incorporated in the Granth. No other religion has perhaps shown this catholicity of outlook in bringing together views of such diverse hues and even when they are diametrically opposed to the tenets of the faith of whose Scripture they now form an integral part. The language of the Granth is mostly Hindi and only in parts Panjābi, though some Persian verses are also included in the Rekhtā (broken) form, thus signifying that it is not the language but the content that matters for spiritual illumination. It is well-known that most of the Bhaktas included in the Granth belonged to the lower castes & were householders. A hymn in Rāg Māru by Mirā Bāi is included in the original copy lying at Kartārpur. but is crossed out with the same pen.

(Contd.)

but, in his extreme humility, he begged to be excused on the plea that it was not fit and proper for him to be treated on a par with the Gurus and other Saints of high esteem. It is said, Guru Arjun thereupon ramarked, "Your works I bless as the 'Key' to the understanding of these scriptures". And so indeed they are.

Several other Hindu and Muslim divines, like Kahnā, Chhaju, Shāh Hussain and Peelu—all of Lāhore—volunteered their compositions for inclusion in the Granth, but the Guru declined the offer

said :

"I am He, Yea, no other but He,
Of whom sing the Vedas and the Purānas,
But reach not His limits."

This the Guru rejected as raising man to the status of God. Their essence was identical, he said, and the man's Soul merged in the Oversoul as a drop in the ocean, but the drop could not claim to be the sea, but only a part of the whole. Chhaju similarly decried women as evil and was rejected. Peelu denounced the human birth and was considered unacceptable. Shāh Hussain came very near acceptance, but the Guru excluded him too for the reason that he had enjoined man to keep silence and not to share with others the mystery of God. The Guru said, "This is against our mission Whatever man has, he must share—God's mysteries as much as secular well-being."

Known initially as *Pothi Sāhib*, the Guru was immensely pleased when the work was completed and he installed it at a high pedestal, on Bhādon Sudi 1, Samvat 1661 (August, 1604 A.D.) seating himself at a much lower level and instructing everyone to bow before it, not as an idol, but as the Book of divine inspiration which instructed

F. N. Contd.

So also a hymn by Kabir beginning with the words "Dekho Logā" is crossed out. To suggest as some do, that the word "Khālsā" in Kabir's hymn in Rāga Sorath originally was Khulāsā and was changed to "Khālsā" by Guru Gobind Singh is also a mis-statement, as the word Khālsā occurs in the original Kartārpur version as well. It is also not true that Guru Arjun left a few blank pages for Guru Tegh Bahādur's writings, as wherever pages are left blank, the word of the 9th Marter could not have been inserted, according to the scheme of the Granth's composition.

living men in the ways of God and dedicated secular life. Bhāi Budhā was appointed the first Custodian (Granthi) of the Book and the Guru enjoined that it was open, unlike the Hindu Scriptures, to men of every caste and unlike both the Hindus and the Muslims and indeed every known creed till then, even women could become the priests or minstrels of the new faith and lead the congregations. Nothing has made the Sikh faith more live and dynamic than this that its scripture is in the spoken language of the people and is available to all, including women, for imbibing and even ministering its instructions.

Bhāi Banno, a devout Sikh of Māngat (Distt. Gujrāt, now in Pakistān) was entrusted with getting the copy of the Book bound at Lāhore, as speedily as possible. But, he took his own time and had another copy made of it, adding some apocryphal literature also at the end. This, it is said, was considered highly objectionable by the Guru who ordained that Banno's recension was to be looked upon as spurious (*Khāri Bir)*. Others, however, aver that as Banno belonged to the village Khārā, Banno's recension is called Khāri Bir and that the Guru who wanted the Scripture to be as widely spread as possible, could have no cause of complaint if another copy had been made out. Of course, the apocryphal writings included by Banno in his copy must have annoyed the Guru and the book rejected as unauthorised.

It appears, the Sikhs had to deal with Kābul as traders in horses and also, may be, in fruits, and hence a sizeable Sikh community grew up in Afghānistān of whose devotion to the Guru many stories are narrated in the Suraj Parkāsh and how the Guru, through his occult powers, helped them in the days of their distress. The Guru also sent out his missionaries to other parts of the country, including Kashmir. The hill Rājās of Kulu, Suket, Haripur and Chambā also became his devotees like that of Mandi had done before.

A village chaudhari, called Chuhar, asked the Guru how could he follow his instruction of speaking the truth at all times when for the men of affairs, it was impossible to do so. The Guru asked him to keep an account of his daily lies and to make a confession of them before the whole congregation *(Sangat)* on the first of every month. To his surprise, Chuhar saw his conduct improving day by day. As has been said, his missionaries were also asked to collect the offerings of the devout and a tithe (one-tenth of his income) every Sikh had to set apart for communal work. But his preachers, the Guru warned : "He who instructs others but not himself, is greedy or jealous and does not look upon the offerings made in the name of the Guru and God or the Sangat as poison for himself, is unfit to preach and will be damned. If pious conduct, honest living and dedication to God and his men is enjoined by me for every householder, these injunctions are to be followed by the leaders of the community even more, who should set an example of clean living and high purpose."

In the same year, Hargobind was married to the daughter of Narāin Dās, a grandson of Bhāi Pāro, a well-known missionary of Guru Amar Dās. In these days, it was not unusual for devout householders to pledge their daughters to the progeny of the Guru, or the daughters or their mothers themselves taking such a vow in their behalf. It was like a vow to remain virgin and the Lord's bride, even if the other party was already married. Another Sikh, Hari Chand's daughter also had made a similar pledge and on Hari Chand's entreaties, the Guru had no choice but to accept his offer as well.* Those who criticise the Gurus having married within their own castes, have also to keep this fact in view that the choice was made often enough by devout Sikhs and not by the Gurus or their parents.

But the Guru's detractors would allow no peace to him. When Akbar had called on the Guru (1598) at Goindwal, Prithia represented that in the Granth, (then in preparation), the Guru had reviled the religion both of Hindus and Muslims. The emperor who was trying his every nerve to evolve a single religious platform for both (though, some of the ulema were calling him an 'enemy of Islam' and an'infidel') could hardly bear this. He wished to hear a few verses from the book. The Guru asked Bhai Gurdas to do the reading

* The story of Chandu, a Diwān (Finance Minister) of Akbar at Delhi (Macauliffe, the Sikh Religion, III, Pp 70 - 76) whose daughter had been refused by the Guru for his son, for he had spoken some derogatory words about his house which the Sikhs of Delhi resented, and linking up of this family feud with the subsequent martyrdom of Guru Arjun by the Sikh chroniclers seems to be a pure forgery and a fantasy. In the first place, as we shall see, Jehāngir himself admits his total responsibility in his *Tuzak* (memoirs) for the Guru's martyrdom. Secondly, there is no historical evidence of a Chandu having been the emperor's Diwan at Delhi or even at Lahore. Possibly, this story was given currency by clever sycophants of the emperor' name. According to Mahan Kosh (P. 1441), Chandu was a revenue official at Lahore, and being inimical to the Guru, had also reported against him to the emperor'. (See also P. 195).

Akbar shuffled a few pages and asked a particular hymn to be read to him.* Bhāi Gurdās duly read it out. It said:

"My God has breathed His Light into the dust
And so brought the world into being.
He it is who created the sky, the earth, the waters and all vegetation.
O man, whatever one sees, passes away.
But, the world usurps another's due and is forgetful of God.
It is the world of the animal, nay, of ghosts and goblins.
It eats the forbidden fruit, usurping what belongs to another.
Hold thy mind, O man, or God will burn thee in the fire of Hell.
Thy benefactors, thy brothers, thy courts and kingdoms and thy homes
Are of no avail to thee, when siezes thee the Angel of Death.
My Lord, purest of the pure, knows all that is within thee.
Nānak: pray thou to His Saints (that they lead thee on to the True Path.)"†

But Prithia was not to be beaten. He pointed out that Gurdās might be reading some special compositions from memory in order to please the emperor. At this, he got commissioned the services of another Gurmukhi-knowing reader, called Sāhib Dyāl. When the emperor asked him to read from another page at random, the following hymn rang out :

"Man sees not the Lord within himself,
And displays the stone-god upon his neck.
The worshipper of Māyā wanders about, deluded by doubt,
And churns the waters (for butter) and so wastes his life away.
The stone that he calls his god,
Drowns the man along with itself.
O God, I am a great sinner who has betrayed Thy salt.

* According to "A History of the Sikhs" (Ganda Singh & Teja Singh) the meeting took place at Goindwāl in 1598, when the Granth was still under preparation. Giani Gian Singh says the meeting took place at Batālā (Twarikh Guru Khalsa, P. 81), in 1604. Akbar was not in the Panjāb at this time. In GoindwVl the Guru met Akbar in 1598 personally. If the Book was taken to him after its completion it could have been only in Agra, where the emperor then was, which seems highly improbable.

† Tilang. M. 5.

I ride the boat of stone and seek to reach the far end.
Meeting the Guru, I knew my Lord,
And saw the Perfect Builder of our Destiny
*Pervade the earth, the waters and the interspace,"**

On his request, still another hymn was read out to him :-

"Some call Thee **Rām**, *others* **Khudā**,
Some serve Thee as **Gosāin**, *others as* **Allāh**.
But, O beneficent God, Thou art the only doer and the cause.
So bless me Thou with Thy Mercy, O Compassionate One.
Some go to the (Hindu) holy places, others to perform **hajj**,
Some offer Thee oblations, while others bow down before Thee.
Some read the Vedas, others the **Semitic texts**:
Some are robed in white, others in blue.
Some are called Turks, others are termed Hindus,
Some seek the (Hindu) heaven, others the (Muslim) paradise.
Says Nānak, 'He who realises the Will of the Lord,
He alone knows the Mystery of the one, all-powerful God."†

The emperor who had already visited the the Guru before and accepted his hospitality ‡ was so pleased that he said:- "Excepting love & devotion to God, I so far find neither praise nor blame to any one in this Granth. It is a volume worthy of reverence".**

He wanted to offer the Guru a suitable gift for the huge expenditure he was incurring on the welfare of the people, but the Guru is said to have replied : "The house of God and the Saints must be self-supporting and not depend upon the imperial gifts. But if Your Majesty be so pleased, then the land-revenue of the farming community for this year be remitted for the Panjāb, for due to shortage of rain, there

---

* Suhi M.5.

† Rāmkali, M.5.

‡ According to Badauni, on the 13th of the month of Azur (1595 A.D.), Akbar, with a large military contingent, crossed the Beās and called on Guru Arjun at Goindwāl "whose character and teaching he appreciated". He also states that the people paid obeisance to the successive Gurus as spiritual leaders and solicited their benedictions. According to *Akbar Nāmā* by Abul Fazal (Part III, P. 745, trans. by Beveridge) "On the way (from Lāhore from where he started out for Āgrā on Nov. 6, 1598 after a stay of over 13 years in the Panjāb) the emperor accepted an entertainment at the house of Arjun Kuru, a notable *Brahmin* (sic) chief, at Govindwāll on the Biās.".

**Bannerjee & Hayland, the Commentary of Monserrate (Intr. V, VII).

are near famine conditions in the land." The emperor complied with the wishes of the Guru and this not only brought much-needed solace to the peasantry but also increased considerably the Guru's influence and fame among all communities, and his slanderers were humbled.

This, however, had not disheartened and he kept on plotting against the Guru with his friend, Sulhi Khān. The latter on the pretext of collecting land-revenue, proceeded to attack the Guru at Amritsar. Some interested people tried to instil fear in the mind of the Guru, but he refused either to change his place of residence or to ask for a compromise with the marauder and offered prayers to God for his protection, as the Ādi Granth testifies (Āsā M.5). Fortunately, on the way, Sulhi's horse bolted and he was burnt in a brick-kiln. There is a hymn by Guru Arjun commemorating this occasion, included in the Ādi Granth (Bilāwal M. 5), which says:

> *"The Lord has protected me from the attack of Sulhi;*
> *For, he could carry not out his foul design and he, the defiled one, died in disgrace.*
> *The Lord chopped off his head with His mighty axe,*
> *And lo, in an instant, he was reduced to the dust.*
> *He thought evil of me and evil consumed him in its fire.**
> *And He who created Him destroyed him too.*
> *Nothing of him remained—neither sons, nor friends, nor riches, nor kinsmen.*
> *Says Nānak: I'm a Sacrifice unto that Master, who has fulfilled the Word of His slave!"*

But on October 17, 1605, Akbar died and was succeeded by Jahāngir, notorious for his lax moral life which he tried to get condoned by the ulemā by dancing to their orthodox views on Islām.† Reports were reaching his ears through Sheikh Ahmad Sirhindi,

---

* Also see Todi M.5 in this context.

† His first wife, daughter of Rājā Bhagwan Dās & mother of Khusru, took opium & died on account of his ill-treatment of her, though in his *Tuzak* he blames her death (1604) on Khusru's attitude towards him (!) [vol. I, pp 55–66 tr. by Beveridge). Akbar wanted to disinherit him in favour of Khusru for his disloyalty (& his wanton cruelty & excessive use of opium & liqour) arrested him & put him in chains, for ten days, slapped & abused him (Nov. 1604), but later reconciliation was affected through Akbar's mother & his wives. (Abul Fazai's *Akbar Nāmā*, Tr. Beveridge, III, P. 1244).

popularly known as Mujadid Alif Sāni, an extremely bigoted and well-known Sunni divine of Sirhind, of the growing influence of the Guru, particularly among the Muslims. The Sheikh, therefore, might also have urged the King-emperor to counteract and destroy him.*

Jahāngir was therefore looking out for a suitable opportunity firstly to please the orthodox ulemā, and secondly to remove a source of potential rival power in the most sensitive region of India. And this he got when his son, Khusro, rebelled against him and was marching through the Panjāb towards Afghānistān. Jehāngir admits as much in his memoirs, called *Tuzak-i-Jehangiri.* Writes he: "At Goindwāl, on the bank of the river Beās, lived a Hindu, Arjun by name, in the garb of a Pir or Sheikh. Thus, many innocent Hindus and even foolish and ignorant Musalmāns he brought into his fold who beat the drum noisily of his self-appointed prophethood. He was called Guru. From all sides, worshippers came to offer their homage to him and put full trust in his word. For three or four generations, they had warmed up this shop. For a long time I had harboured the wish that I should set aside this shop of falsehood or I should bring him into the fold of Islām."

He writes further :

"In these days, Khusro passed through this way.† This foolish person resolved to call on him. Khusro halted for a time at this place and this man came to see him and discoursed with him on many matters and also applied with saffron to his forehead what the Hindus

---

* In his letter to Sheikh Farid Bukhāri, alias Murtazā Khān, Governor of Lāhore, the Mujaddid approves gleefully of the execution of the Gurū in these words :- "The execution at this time of the accursed Kāfir of Goindwāl ....with whatever motive........ is an act of highest grace for the followers of Islām." (Maktubāt-i -Imam Rabbāni, Vol. I, Part iii, letter No. 193).

† That Guru Arjun received & honoured Khurso in his Court was not without reason. The British Ambasador in the court of Jahāngir, SIR Thomas Roe (in his *Embassy*, ed. by Foster, 1889, 2 vols) has this to say of him :- "Sultān Khusrū, the eldest brother of Prince Khuram, (later Shāh Jahān) is both extremely beloved & honoured of all men (almost adored & very justly) for his noble parts. If he prevails in his rights, his kingdom will be a sanctuary for Christians, whom he loves & honours, favouring learning, valour, the discipline of war, and abhoring all covetousness. If the other (Khurram) win(s), we shall be the losers. He is a hater of all Christians, proud, subtile, false & barbarously tyrannous".

call *Kashkeh* (*Tilak*) and consider as a good omen. When I heard this account personally, I already knew about his false pretences. So I ordered that he be brought into my presence, that his property be confiscated and his sons and other possessions be made over to Murtazā Khān and he be dealt with (put to death) in accordance with the political (siyāsat) and the common law of the land (Yāsā*)."

This unassailable evidence makes three things obvious:

(1) That the Guru's "political crime" of "calling upon" Khusro and applying a saffron-mark to his forehead, was an after-thought on the part of Jahangir who had already made up his mind either to put the Guru to death or to bring him into the fold of Islām, not because he was a political rebel, but because innocent Muslims as much as Hindus were accepting him as their spiritual leader.

(2) There is no mention in the King's memoirs of any heavy fine having been imposed upon the Guru who being unable to pay was put to death, or his son later put into prison for that reason. *Dabistān*, however, mentions a fine having been imposed, though all Sikh historical records are silent about it.

(3) The story of a Chandu having anything to do with this martyrdom is a concoction of the Sikh chroniclers, like the authors of *Mehmā Parkāsh* and *Gurpartāp Surya Granth*. It may be that some Hindu employee of Murtazā Khān called Chandu may have been associated with the process of extreme tortures inflicted for five

---

* Yāsā is a Turkish word, meaning pact, law, code (of laws) – (Turkish-English Dictionary by Wahid Morān, published by Turkish Ministry of Education, p. 1382). It does not mean, as Kapur Singh has suggested," a law applicable to holy-men whose death was brought about without spilling blood." Nor does it mean "vengeance, murder or robbery" as Bhāi Vir Singh opines, (*Asht-Gur Chamatkār*, Part II, P. 89), though as the word is of central Asian origin and was first used by Chengiz Khān for his laws which were extremely cruel, its connotations might be these. "Siyāsat", according to V. A. Smith means "capital punishment" (Oxford History of India, p. 258) and was employed in this sense in the days of the Tughlaqs.

It is recorded by the Sikh chroniclers that the Guru was given extreme tortures. He was seated on a red-hot iron pan and burning sand poured over his head. He was then boiled in a kettle. (Some even go so far as to suggest that he was later unsuccessfully sought to be sewn up in cow's hide) and when his body was full of blisters, he was consigned to the river Ravi for further torture or was just drowned-(Dariye-Boreo). (See Panth Parkāsh, B. Rattan Singh and *Bansāwali nāmā* by *Kesar Singh Chhiber*).

consecutive days on the Guru (May 24 - 29) which led to the currency of the story in order to mitigate the wrath of the people against the emperor and his regime.

Moreover, we are aware that Jahāngir followed closely on the heels of Khusro and, according to his own account, he crossed over to Goindwāl on the afternoon of April 15, 1606, where he learnt that Khusro had been arrested. Now, he takes it easy and roams about in the territory of Mājhā for twelve days and reaches Lāhore on April 27. Upto then, he hears nothing of the part played by Guru Arjun in the affairs of Khusro, who is brought into his presence at Lāhore on May 1. The emperor inflicted severe punishments on his 700 accomplices upto May 7, but there is no news yet of Guru Arjun's involvement. Another fortnight passes and suddenly on or immediately after May 20, he is informed of the Guru's such serious misdemeanour that he orders him to be put to death! On the other hand, when, during his pursuit of Khusro, Jahāngir learnt of the blessings the former had received from Sheikh Nizām of Thānesar, the emperor immediately called him into his presence and providing him with the necessary expense, expelled him out of the realm, and sent him out to Meccā (as a punishment!)

Even the rebel-prince, Khusro, himself was not put to death. His vision was blinded (though partially) and six months later the father relented so much that he employed a skilled Persian physician to restore his eye-sight. On his success to a great extent, the physician was rewarded with the title of *Masih-ul-Zamān*. (Elliot, VI, Pp. 448-49).

It is clear, therefore, that the Guru was tortured to death not so much for political as for religious reasons. While saying so, one cannot be oblivious of the fact that Jahāngir who in the initial stages (he succeeded to the imperial throne on Nov. 3, 1605) acted as a fanatic (due possibly to the hostility of the Muslim orthodoxy his father had generated against himself for his *Din-i-Ilāhi*), later turned very sympathic to other religions, particulary Hinduism & Christianity. SIR Thomas Roe (who was accredited to him as a British envoy) considers him an atheist when he met him first in 1616, others that he became somewhat of a *Deist*, Sufi or Vedāntin. But when hostilities began with Goa, then a Portugese settlement, he got all Christian churches which he favoured earlier (possibly to secure Portugese trade & their support against the British) closed down. He also passed severe orders against the Jains of Gujarat "but that was because he considered them to be seditious." All Sikh historical records confirm his having befriended Guru Hargobind later in life. His differences with Guru Arjun came too early in his reign & political motives got mixed up with religion. The blessings offered to Khusro by the Guru were usual in the case of all visitors, big or small, and even the application of a saffron-mark on his forehead (which was wholly unusual for the Guru's house), was a religious ceremony and not a material help to the rebel prince. He may have, like his grand-father, Akbar, before him, and indeed like every other visitor, even partaken of food in the Guru's free kitchen. But that he should have been offered monetary assistance or that the emperor should have imposed a heavy fine on the Guru which he failed to pay (as J. N. Sarkār and Mohsin Fāni allege) seems to be untrue. Even the emperor himself does not give any indication about it in his *Tuzak*. How, then, does the Guru become a political rebel or 'a revenue-defaulter' (as J. N. Sarkār puts it) passes one's comprehension, and the only reason one can deduce from the King's own version is that it was a most callous case of religious persecution* The Guru incurred the wrath of the sovereign not only because "innocent" Hindus but also "misguided" Muslims were accepting him as their religious leader, and the movement of synthesis which Akbar† had set his heart upon and which collapsed immediately on his death and in which the Guru's movement was proving such a solid success became an eye-sore to Jahāngir and his orthodox *ulemā*, and the Guru became the first martyr for religious freedom of *all* men, not only in Sikh history, but in the entire annals of Hindustān till then.

The emperor's orders were carried out, in every detail, on May 30, 1606 A.D.

---

* A Jesuit missionary, Father Ferdinand Guerreiro S. J. (died, 1617) in his letter published in 1609 in Lisbon in the Annual Relations, 1706-1607 (Part IV, Book III, Ch. V, of 138-151/r) & reprinted in Coimbra in 1931, Vol II, pp. 366-370 confirms this. Inter-alia, the letter reads :—

"When the Prince (Khusru) was flying from Āgrā, he passed through a place where was living a man they call the Guru of the gentiles (heathens) as amongst us the Bishop and Pope, of theirs. He was held as a Saint and venerated as their universal head, and the Prince went to meet him. He asked for some good omen. He gave it to him for the newly reigning Prince and put a *tikka* on his head, although this one (the Guru) was a gentile and the Prince a Moor (i.e. a Muslim), yet the Prince was the son of a gentile woman. Thus, owing to the opinion (the

F. N. Contd.

Prince) had of the Saintlines of that (Guru), he took that mark as a sign of the good success of his undertaking.

"When the King had the Prince in his hands, he sent for the said Guru, held him prisoner, and some gentiles interceded for thair Saint. Finally, he was condemned (to pay) more than 1,00,000 *cruzados*, and a rich gentile begged the mercy of the King, coming forward to stand credit for the said Guru, I say for that money; the King handed him (the Guru) over to him (the rich gentile). It appears the rich gentile hoped for some interventions to succeed in remitting also the fine. He was mistaken...he gave every day new torments to this Saint. He ordered to give him much torture... he took away his food, he did him thousand and one dishonours. In that way their good Pope died, overwhelmed by the sufferings, torments and dishonours..."

This letter mentions two additional items of information, such as we do not find in the *Tuzak*. One, that he was fined, and secondly that some rich Hindu had pledged to pay the fine and the Guru was handed over to him for some time to extract this fine, but later as perhaps the money could not be raised and hopes for the remittance of fine were not fulfilled, the Guru was tortured to death. Who this rich Hindu was? Was he Chandu ? Why the whole community was not able to collect this sum for the release of the Guru, we are not told. The latter part especially is hard to believe. Possibly, the emperor in order to soothe the feelings of the Sikhs had agreed to release the Guru, on payment of a fixed sum, but later changed his mind. His own writing is explicit on the point why he wanted to put the Guru to death : *his universal religious appeal*. The "help" rendered to Khusro by the Guru was only an excuse to do him to death. It also becomes clear that being the son of a Hindu mother, Khusro may himself have requested the application of a Tikka to his head by the Guru as a good omen, and not that it was a general practice in the Guru's house.

+ Such is the quirk of history that a rare synthesiser like Akbar, was not allowed rest even in his grave, at Sikandra, near Agra. The Jāts in the neighbourhood who revolted in the days of Aurangzeb (in 1688) "dugup, in 1691, Akbar's bones from his grave, threw them into fire and burnt them!" (Oxford History of India, P. 336) Today his name is totally forgotten. While orthodox Muslims have treated him as a renegede from Islam, Hindu India honoured a Rājput princeling of Mewār, Rana Partap, who fought against him, as their national hero, not Akbar who brought Hindus & Muslims on a single spiritual & political platform.

CHAPTER VIII

SOCIO-POLITICAL CONDITIONS OF INDIA AS DEPICTED IN THE ĀDI GRANTH

No historian of the Sikhs has cared to cull out of the voluminous Sikh Scripture, THE ĀDI GRANTH, the socio-political conditions of the middle ages in India. Of course, these are not gathered in any single chapter of the Granth, but have to be garnered through careful and laborious research from the idioms, metaphors and similes pertaining to such conditions. But this is a source-material whose authenticity has never been challenged, and yet no historian to date has gathered this, both to reveal the social ideals of the Sikh Gurus as well as to pinpoint the social conditions of their age. Occasionally, there is a direct reference to such conditions, as, for instance in the poetry of Guru Nānak where he denounces with extreme passion the cruelty, the bigotry and the extortionist ways of the kings and their courtiers :

> *"The Kāli age is the knife; kings are butchers, and righteousness has taken wings.*
>
> *Where can one find the moon of Truth in this dark night of falsehood, O where ?"*

Nānak calls kings 'tigers' and their courtiers 'running dogs,' "who wake people out of their beds." The "king's servants tear their nails into the bodies of the subjects and suck their blood." "The Qāzis who sit in the courts to minister justice, rosary in hand and the name of *Khudā* on their lips, commit injustice if their palm is not greased. And if someone challenges them, lo, they quote the scriptures!" "Greed is the King and Sin the Courtier, Falsehood is their honoured official, Lust their assistant. And lo, they all assemble each day to confer on the matters of state!"

The society is divided into the extremely rich and gruellingly poor. "The rich enjoy themselves to the full, drunk with their youth and beauty. Their beds are soft; they wear silk, their tresses are smoothed behind their ears. Proud in their minds, they ride elephants, with golden canopies over their heads. And their harems are full of choice beauties."

The revenue officials (Patwāris) in the village with whom the peasantry had to come into direct contact, every day, "sting like snakes." "The officials of the state are great deceptors. They trap even their own mothers, fathers and friends." The Chaudhries (headmen) of the village are also corrupt and tyrannous, and "they report on and get their kinsmen bound down". "The officials are like the hawks and deer, who are out to trap their own caste." "The subjects are blind and pay willing obedience like the dead." "The wise ones dance and make music, and deck themselves like players on the stage to please the crowd." "They call each other Miān (title of Muslim nobles) and speak the tongue of the foreigner." "The temple-gods have been taxed, and even God wears the Muslim blue." "The Khatris have abandoned their religion and hold fast to the *Malechhas*" (foreigners). "People are not averse to the eating of meat over which has been breathed the foreign tongue (or Kalimā, as the Muslims do)."

"Greed is like the dark prison-house: unrighteousness is like the fetters on one's feet. Money-gathering is like being constantly hammered. Sin is like the overpowering *Kotwāl*" (Police chief).

Slavery is also rampant though it is not dehumanised. Slavery is denounced vehemently, though the ungrudging loyalty to the master is quoted as a fitting example for man's devotion to God. The slaves are bought and sold; and a stamp is burnt into their forehead to indicate to whom they are obligated in debt or otherwise. "How fortunate am I that God has bought me over for a price, like a slave. My wages are the Guru's Word and I do whatever I'm bidden to." "My father is a slave (of God), so also my mother. I'm the offspring of slaves. My mother dances and my father sings and in their company, I too sing the praises of God, my King." "I'm The slave of my Guru, and lo, he has inscribed his insignia on my forehead, for I have to pay off a great debt to him." "He who obeys his master, gets double wages: he who doesn't, gets a beating of shoes." Who will honour the poor in such a society? "No one looks upon the poor with favour. The man of poverty may try as hard as he would, but the rich look not towards him. If the poor one goes to the rich, the rich man turns his back upon him."

The poor wander from place to place. "The calves, the poor, the slaves and the wayfarers are separated from their kins even in the rains, when the snakes, the deer, the fish and the bride in bed with her spouse are in utter joy." The rich are drunk with pride and power. "He who has ten maunds of grain and four *takkās* in his purse, he walks not straight. He is puffed up that he has an estate of a hundred villages or is endowed with a Jāgir of two lakh *takkās*." Nānak calls the rich, "blind and deaf" and "confused in mind". The account-taking of the Yama (Angel of death) is compared (and not unjustly) to the extortionist village-bania, when he comes to ask of the debtor the account and faces him with his debts. "The debtor is pressed as the sesame seeds are in the oil-press." "Friendship with a moneylender (Kirār) is false, and leads only to falsehood." "He who has turned his back upon God gathers debts like poison."

The villages are, therefore, depleted of their men-folk at regular intervals, though not on account of political upheavals; but due to extortionist *baniās*, taxes and tax-gatherers. "O father, I shall bide not in this village, for the *Kāyath*, (*Kāyastha* or *Baniā*) like my conscious mind, makes demands upon me every hour (*ghari*)." "And when the balance becomes unbearable, the five peasants desert their farm, and lo, their master like the soul, is bound down."

The Hindu society is divided rigidly into four castes. But certain startling revelations are made about the private, lechrous lives of the Brāhmins. "The dancing girl sings in the home of the Brāhmin." "They who wear the sacred thread have sharp knives in their hands." "He marries off the daughter of his client with due ceremony only if he gets his wages. And so also when he shows the Path to the devotees." "His mind is blind, but he calls himself the wise one." "The speech of the Brāhmin is in Sanskrit, of the Sudra in Prākrit (or, the people's tongue)." "He wraps round himself a *dhoti* of three and a half yards and he has three bands to his sacred thread. But, call him not the Saint of God; he is but a thug of Banāras." (Kabir). Was Banāras a well-known centre of the thugs in the days of Kabir? "He (Nāmdeva) was driven out of the temple for they called him an untouchable (sudra)!" That is why, in the words of

Kabir, "though the world is like a house of wood on fire, it is the 'wise' Pandits who'd be consumed by it, while the innocents will be saved."

In the hierarchy of castes, the sweepers (*chuhrās*, or *chandāls*) are considered by the society to be the lowest. Those who compete with them in this honour are dogs and thugs. The drummer or the drummer-woman (*doomani*), is comparable only to the butcher. The greatest transformation that a devotee of God can hope to attain in human life is "to be transformed from a sweepress to a Brāhmin woman!"

Not only are the Sudras denied the reading (or even the hearing) of the Hindu Scriptures, but even women are denied this privilege. They are innocent playthings of man, fit only for a hunt by man, 'the eternal hunter'. They are to keep their faces covered even before their spouses, and burn themselves alive when their husbands die. The imagery of a devoted, unquestioning, mute and humble woman of sweet speech, her breath sweetened with the chewing of the betel-leaf and five nuts, of utter beauty, decked with sixteen kinds of embellishments, who is redeemed only if her spouse is pleased with her (he may yet be displeased even after all her efforts, for, his love, like God's, is *his* prerogative—he may deny this to a seeming lover and enjoy another woman's bed not so wise and clever and beauteous and ostentatious), is employed extensively in the Ādi Granth to denote the human spirit in love with the eternal spouse of us all, our God. "One wife, one man" applies only to the woman and not to the man who may enjoy whomsoever he chooses if he has the means and the capacity to. A widower will certainly re-marry, but the widow never. "She will wear black, keep her hair dishevelled, appear not in public or on an auspicious occasion even before the family, like the one whom her husband has deserted."

An acceptable bride must have "sons as her off-spring, should be of unblemished character, of fine chiselled features, white of colour, robed in red, of eyes like a deer's or the lotus flower, expert in many fine arts, from a good, large and prosperous family, obedient, ever-content ("even if she is starved or served unbuttered bread and has the hard ground to sleep on"), an expert cook, stitcher, handicrafter and spinner at the spinning wheel, a watchful supervisor of the household, who should accommodate every wish of the joint family." For a virgin, or for one whose spouse is abroad, all decorations are a taboo. A woman, though necessary for every household, is yet an expendable commodity. Daughters are considered inauspicious and even murdered at birth, or if found in illicit relationship.

The curse and the oppression of the joint family, however, finds expression through the ever-suffering bride: "My mother-in-law is my enemy, my father-in-law is garrulous. My husband's elder brother (*Jeth*) burns me at every step." "How cursed is my mother-in-law who permits me not even to meet with my spouse." "How happy I am that my spouse has separated me from my mother-in-law's house, and his brothers and their wives are as dead to me. Now no longer I'll suffer their tyranny."

As the arts—like dancing, music, etc.,—were tied down to religious ritual, those who performed them did so merely to amuse the crowds and collect coins rather than express their inmost selves through them. To dramatise the lives of Rāma and Krishna, through *lilās* and Rāsas, for popular amusement, seems to be common at the hands of folk dancers and performers who are not held in high esteem. The theatre-houses are no other than the temple-halls or the courts of the Kings. But, open-air improvised theatre is the most common. The players deck themselves with many kinds of fine dresses and headgears, paint their arms and faces, and to amuse the crowd even throw dust in their heads and roll in the dust, or strike their heads against the hard ground (see Āsā di Vār, M. 1.) Kabir has compared God with a painter (chitrakār) and there is a mention also of an Art gallery (chitrashālā). The houses of the rich are painted with many kinds of motifs from the *outside* (a typical Indian habit for outer exhibitionism and inner loneliness) !

There are various kinds of ritualistic practises indulged in to trap the unwary. "Some keep their eyes closed and hold their nose (i.e. breath)." "Others live in silence, deck themselves with leaves or wander about naked." "Some practise six kinds of works." "The *Kāprias* carry their begging bowls (*Kamandal*) in their hands and beg from door to door." "Some shave their heads, others wear matted hair or keep a tuft." "They (Yogis and Sādhus) wear the ochre robes." "Some live in the crematoriums or in the wastes or woods and eat dirt and throw ashes in their heads." (Āsā di Vār M.1.). "They wear not cotton, but leather." "The *Srevrās* (Jainas) dread clean water, do not bathe themselves and drink mud. They beg for the left-overs from door to door. They pluck their hair and search for worms in their excreta (in order to save their life). They march in a line, one after the other." (Mājh-Ki-Vār, M. 1.). "Then there are the Kanpāttā Yogis, with their torn ears and large ear-rings, with a horn to blow, their bodies smeared with ashes, wearing a beggar's robes, a staff in one hand and a begging bowl in the other, with deer-skins to squat on to meditate." "They show miracles to the people like flying in the air, disappearing at will, living buried in snows or underground, and eating iron and other uneatables, cursing or blessing people with boons." "Some ascetics put their bodies to great torture, and even immolate themselves by being sawn alive, or sleep on iron nails, walk barefooted, remain naked, do not accept cooked food and live on milk or vegetables, and perform extreme austerities." On the other hand, the *Chārvākiyas* or Vām-mārgis drink wine, eat meat and indulge in sex as a matter of ritual. The ways of the Yogis and their 12 sects, the ten divisions of the Sanyāsis, and of a myriad other sects like *Avadhuts*, *Maunis*, *Bhagautis*, *Tantrics*, *Jangams*, *Jyotshis*, *Jainas*, *Brahmins*, and various types of Muslim ascetics, sufis, pirs, etc., are detailed in the Ādi Granth at great length.

The Brāhmins perform yagnas and other rituals, read the Vedas and Sāstrās—all for wages—bathe themselves at or visit (like other caste Hindus) sixty-eight Hindu pilgrim-stations in India, notably Triveni (the confluence of the three sacred rivers—Gangā, Jamunā and Saraswati—at Prayāg or Allāhābād), Gangā (at Haridwār) and Gangā again at Kāshi (Banāras). "They wash the wood before they raise fire," "do not accept food cooked by another," "dig up their hearths rather than use the one built upon the earth," "plaster their homes and their kitchen-squares with cow-dung which is considered most sacred." Birth and death are both considered inauspicious and the woman especially is not allowed to touch anything or anyone for forty days after its occurrence, till, after due ceremony and expense, her "impurity" is washed off. Even menstruation makes a woman "impure" during that period. (Āsā di Vār, M.1.).

There are so many rituals to be performed by the house-holder over which only the Brāhmin can preside, and so much is to be offered to him and to the relations and caste-men on all occasions—birth, marriage, initiation (for men), death, new business, good or ill-fortune befalling the household (the birth of a daughter, for instance, was a misfortune), propitiation of the dead ancestors on several occasions (especially on auspicious days) every year, etc. etc. that one becomes afraid of life.

But, the Brāhmin had also by now compromised, though surreptitiously, with the ruling class of Muslims. "They accept their money, and even mimick their ways, and are instrumental in levying taxes on the Hindus and all they consider sacred (like the Brāhmin and the cow)." "The Brāhmin blows his conch and presides over the ceremonies at the houses of tyrants and blood-suckers." "Even the thieves give away in charity to the Brāhmins to propitiate their dead ancestors!"

Instead of an inner spiritual realisation or the identity of the God and the Soul, the common run of Hindus are inspired not so much by the Opnaishadic ideals of a Universal God but the Vedic ritual, or Karma Kānda, and by the mythological Paurānic tales. The Sikh Scriptutures reveal a most remarkable and wide knowledge of the Hindu pantheon and their religious beliefs, superstitions and practices. Some of the names of the mythological figures which occur, by way of illustrations, in the Ādi Granth are: Rāma and Sitā: Radhā and Krishna; Lakshman (Lachhman), Rāvana; Indra; Parsurāma; Ajay; Pāndavas; Janmejā: Chanderhāns; Dhrishat-Budhi; Umā (Pārvati); Janaka; Dhoma (the rishi); Dhruva; Kapila; Oodho; Akruru; Ugarsen; Sukhdeva; Parikhat, Mandhātā; Bhabikhan; Bharathri; Durbāsā; Hanumān; Rājā Puru; Angrā (the rishi), Ajāmal; Bālmik; Kavaliapir; Ganikā; Gaja; Sudāmā; Kubijā; Bidar; Prahlāda: Daropadi; Sandāmarkā; Pingalā; Shivji (Shiva); Vishnu; Brahmā; Sanaka; Sanadan: Sanat Kumār; Suras; Sidhas; Gandharvas; Apasharās; Mohinis: Kinaras; Yakshas; Kansa; Vyāsa; Nārada; Arjuna; Madhu; Kaitabh; Mehkhaja; Harnākasha (Harna Kashyap); Jarāsindh: Kaljaman; Rakatbeej; Kālnem; Daryodhana, Kesi, Chanur, etc., etc.

Eighty eight crores of Sheikhs, fifty six crores of Musāhibs, and 1¼ lakhs of prophets are sunk in the psyche of the Muslim populace.

The various professions of the people referred to in the Ādi Granth are : farming *(Kirsān)*, Carding, weaving *(Julāhā)*, washing (dhobi); sewing *(Darzi)* extraction of oil from oil-seeds *(Teli)*, pottery-making *(Kumihār)*, shopkeeping *(baniā)*, gardening *(Māli)*, retail or wholesale trade *(Banjārā, Saudāgar)*, Usury *(Shāh)*, fighting *(Kashatriyas)*, reading and teaching of the Vedas and presiding over religious ceremonies *(Brāhmiṇs)*, shoe-making *(chamār)*, fortune-telling

(*Jotshi*), Jeweller (*Sarāf*), broker (*dalāl*), goldsmith (*Suniāra*), iron-smith (*Lohār*), carpenter (*tarkhān*), Singer (*dhādi*), dancer (*Rāsdhāri*), groom (*Sāis*), drummer (*doom*), watchman (*Pahruā*), magician (*Bājigar*), barber (*Nāi*), Government or private service (*Chākri*), hunting (*shikāri*), fisherman (*Māhi*), boatman (*Khevat*), butcher (*Kasāi*). cowherd (*gawālā*), sweeper (*chandāl*), etc., etc.

The farms are irrigated through Persian wells, or depend upon rainfall. The rainy season is expressed almost in symbols of ecstasy. "The rains have come; I've found my God." It is the season of the union of the separated couples, and those whose grooms are not at home in this season of coolth and verdure ("when the peacocks dance," and "everyone's shame is covered through abundance of food, fodder, cotton and sugarcane", and "the bride weaves her hair in smooth plaits and saturates the parting with vermillion") writhe in anguish.

Some of the metals whose use is extensive at this time are : gold, silver, copper, brass, bronze, glass, iron, coal, rubies, pearls, diamonds, and various other precious metals. A mythical stone—"The philosopher's stone" (*pāras*) — is mentioned over and over again whose very touch transmutes the eight *baser* metals into gold.

Out of the colours, red is considered the most auspicious. The newly-wedded bride is draped in red, so also the man of God when he has the unitive experience. Black colour, significantly enough, is looked upon as most inauspicious, being the colour of one "who is separated from the spouse" or has gathered infamy. Ochre is patronised by the (fake) Sādhus of various denomintions. But, white is the colour of the swan, the Saint, and also of age. Yellow is both auspicious, being the colour of spring, as also of the one estranged from God (*Manmukh*). The four Vedas also have a colour associated with each, according to their importance. Muslims wear blue, the Sufis black, the Hindus white. Green being the colour of verdure (and hence of inner illumination) is also auspicious.

Some of the eatables mentioned in the Ādi Granth are : milk, (buffalo's milk has a preference over cow's); wheat-flour; rice; lentils; ghee; salt; sugar; betel-leaves; various kinds of nuts; goat-meat and fish; banana; mango; cocoanut; berries; raisin; cloves; refined sugar; molasses; grapes; honey, etc. Indian hemp and wine are in use both with the yogis and the householders; the rich especially indulge in wine (and women). But, tobacco is not mentioned, its use having become prevalent only in the days of Jahāngir. The home-made wine is prepared (especially by the yogis) through fermentation of molasses to which are added the *Mahuā* flowers and the bark of *Kikkar*, and it is distilled through a funnel like an *Araq*.

Silks and woollens are worn by the rich, cotton by the poor. Thirty six kinds of delicious foods are mentioned. Paper is indigenously prepared from the *tār* tree and ink either from charcoal or the lamp-black. The earthen lamp is the only means of lighting. The sun and the moon are also compared to two "earthen lamps (*dipak*)." Thefts and dacoities by thieves and highwaymen are also mentioned time and again. The thugs minister a potion to the wayfarers (it is called *thagauri*) which makes their victims lose his consciousness. Prostitutes and procurers are also mentioned with contempt.

Sixteen kinds of womanly embellishments are mentioned — weaving of hair in smooth plaits; parting the hair in the middle; saturating the hair-parting with vermillion (a sign of the wedded state); chewing of betel-leaf and nuts to sweeten one's breath; wearing of silks and jewellery of various kinds (hand-rings, bracelets, necklace, nose-ring, ear-rings, etc.). The dried skin of walunt is rubbed on the lips to dye them red. A (round or vertical) frontal-mark on the forehead (*tikkā*) is considered auspicious. Scents of various kinds are also used, as is soap. "The bed of the wedded bride is (figuratively) decked with jewels, rubies and diamonds !" They wear bangles of ivory. Shirts and blouses (*chola-choli*), Shalwār and ghagrās (bell-bottom trousers) are mentioned, but not (*dopattās*) (as head-cover), though references to the veiling of the face (*ghund*) show clearly that this is the one thing women couldn't do without. Men probably wear their hair long and keep untrimmed beards and moustaches* as signs of piety, and the head is shaven clean only on the death of the father, (*bhadrā*) by the Hindu males, or by sanyasins. The Muslims, of course, did not let their beards grow beyond a handful and trimmed their moustaches in the middle, but the Sufis didn't. Turban is very much in vogue and beard and the turban are considered to be the symbols of honour.†

Hindu women especially wear their hair long and it is a sign of dishonour for them to shear their locks, or even to exhibit their tresses in public. The custom of dowry is universally prevalent and

* "*Sir paliā, dārhi pali, muchhān bhi paliān*" (Shalokas of Farid).

† "*Main bholāwā pag dā, mat meli hoe Jāe.*" (Shalokas of Farid).

is approvingly quoted in the Ādi-Grandh, even though symbolically : "O God, grant me the 'dowry' of Thy Name", though it is also stated that dowry of other kinds is "false."

The word city or town (*Shahr*) is mentioned by Guru Nānak only once in the Ādi Grandh, but all other poets (except Ravidās) refer only to the village (*pind* or *giraon*). Guru Nānak calls his country "Hindustān," but never for once does he mention "Panjāb" in his extensive writings, nor does any other poet of the Granth. The villages are surrounded by high mud-walls with a few outlets. Apart from the poorer sections (who herd together), the richer classes do not mix freely, nor are they neighbours to each other. Even the money-lenders (*Shāhs*) and the traders (*Vyapāris*) live apart.

The bāzārs are covered and the village streets reasonably wide for human and animal traffic. For, a narrow street is compared to "the streets of hell", or the bridge leading to it, according to the Muslim faith (*Pursalāt*) (*Shalokas* of Farid). The streets are muddy which shows that they are not paved. (Ibid). Village Panchāyats are held in great esteem. Stones and burnt bricks are used as building material (possibly by the rich). The rich even decorate their buildings with carvings and paintings.

The Hindus are subject to *Jezia*. Even the Brāhmin and the cow are taxed (and why not ?). The sign of holiness is expressed through miracles. The Qāzi confronts Nāmedeva with two alternatives : "Either accept Islām and uttar "*Khudā*", abandoning the name of Rām, or perform a miracle and bring to life a dead cow !" "He refused to perform the miracle to save his life, and was ordered to be trampled by an elephant, but lo, the elephant made him obeisances and thus God intervened to save the honour of his devotee." But, the Sikh Gurus denounce miracle-making as the work of mountebanks and showmen.

The royal army has four kinds of fighting forces — elephant divisions; cavalry, camel corps and infantry. Guru Nānak has mentioned the use of "*tupak*" (a small artillery gun) by Bābur's men. The royal forts have a double wall and are surrounded by three dykes. The armies normally use arrows, spears, swords and double-edged daggres in war, but the royal camp moves with large harems and kitchens, tents, flags, drums and pipes, precious carpets, canopies, etc., and the officers are richly dressed. Even their bodyguards with their red tassel and decorated kammarbands are a sight to see.

Hunting expeditions are highly popular with the royalty and feudal gentry.

Some of musical instruments mentioned in the Sikh Scripture are: *Sitār*, *Sārangi*, *ik-tārā* (one-stringed instrument), *tuti* (pipe), *singi* (horn), rabāb (rebeck), *bansri* (lute), the hand-drums (jori and dholak), *chhainē* (cymbals), war-drum (dhol), jhānjar (ankle-bells), *sankh* (conch), *kingri* (fiddle), *bheri* (a small drum), *shahnāi*, etc. Out of the trees and flowers, *Chandan* (Sandal), *simmal*, tulsi, *baint* (reed), *Arind* (castor-oil tree) *Kasumbha* (safflower), *Akka* (swallow-wort), *Chaupati* (water-lily)are mentioned again and again. Some of the birds, animals and worms referred to in the Ādi Granth (more for their inborn habits which they cannot overcome than their mere description) are: pig, dog, donkey, cat, jackal, crane, swallow, camel, horse, elephant, ant, bumble bee, deer, hawk, *garura*, sparrow, parrot, mouse, snakes of various kinds, fish, leopard, lion, tiger, sheep, charag (kind of hawk), kuhi (kind of hawk), crow, koel (cuckoo), chātrik, peacock, tandua (shark?), ox, cow, bull, crocodile, swan, frog, kirli (lizard), cock, buffalo, honey-bee, goat, eagle, monkey, etc.

Eighty four lakhs of species are mentioned, half in the waters and half on land. Four sources of creation (*Khānis*) are emphasised, namely, *Andāj* (egg-born), *Jairaj* (foetus-born) *Utbhuj* (earth-born), and *Setaj* (sweat-born). The earth is supposed to have nine divisions (Khand), though they are not named. The whole universe is divided into three parts (the world, the underworld or the world under water, and the heavens), and fourteen spheres (*lokas*). Human speech is divided into four categories—*Madhamā*, *Baikhri*, *Parhā*, *Basanti*, as it progresses from the throat, tongue, teeth and finally is uttered with the lips. Seven continents (*dipas*) and seven seas are referred to, but not by name. The popular Hindu belief that the earth is supported by a mythical Bull is ridiculed by Guru Nānak, saying "there is earth upon earth." (Japu, M. I). That the sun illumines the moon first occurs in the word of Nānak ("*sas ghar sur samāendā*").* Nānak also rejected the Muslim thesis that there are only seven heavens and seven under-worlds by his declaring emphatically: "There are myriads of heavens and underworlds." (Japu, M.I.). And also that ours is not the only sun. "There are myriads of suns and moons and *Indras* and spheres." (Ibid). He also emphasises that they

* Bhāi Jodh Singh thinks this only refers to the yogic practice of breath-control.

traverse endless miles without end, "though one day all will come to an end," to be reborn again. Ours is not the first creation, "there have been many creations and dissolutions before"—all through the Will of the One and only God who ever was and will for ever be. "In the beginning, there was nothing but chaos—neither sun there was, nor moon, neither earth nor waters nor stars. Man there wasn't nor woman, neither trees, nor birds." (Māru, M.1). So, the thoughts about "virtue" and "sin" are also time-bound and change from age to age and people to people. (Gauri, Sukhmani, M.5). Matter and energy are also interchangeable, for, in essence, they spring from the same source. * These last two are indeed revolutionary doctrines, one in the sphere of ethics and the other in the sphere of physical science. That the universe came into being in a single atomic explosion (*Eko Kwāo*) is mentioned by Guru Nānak (Japu).

The fifth Guru, Arjun, refers to human evolution through a very slow process, from the worm to tree and bird and animal resulting, finally, in the human form.†

That the seasons (six of these are mentioned) were the result of the changing position of the sun in relation to our earth is also mentioned (*Suraj ēko, rut anēk*"). That life is all-pervading, in the plants as much as in water—"which gives life to all"—is emphasised. (Āsā Vār, M.1). As for creation, Guru Nānak has this to say: "First God created air; from air was water and from water evolved the three worlds and God pervaded all that was." When and at what period of the evolution all this happened is, however, not mentioned.

Many other customs are also referred to. The dead are bathed and draped in silk. Woman beat their breasts in mourning crying "hāi-hāi." Some are cremated (Hindus), some are buried (Muslims), some are cast into the waters (holy men), some are torn by dogs and eagles (Pārsis). The dead are propitiated by the Hindus in the belief that their Souls are still alive.

It is the groom who, accompanied by a marriage procession, musicians and drummers, would go to the bride's house to solemnise the wedding ceremony. The bride is brought to the groom's house in a palanquin (*doli*) where she is initially received with great courtesy. The mother-in-law waves water over her head and drinks it. Oil is poured on the threshold (as an auspicious omen) before she crosses it.

---

* *Nānak, so sūkham, soi asthūl.* (Gauri Sukhmani, M.5)

† Ādi-Granth, Gauri Guareri, M.5.

To go abroad, that is, to go out of one's own village, is a source of great anguish to the bride left behind with her in-laws. To cross the seas was considered extremely treacherous. Perhaps that is how the world is often compared to an "impassable sea," though it is often mentioned that ships, boats and rafts carry one across to the other shore.

Cow is considered sacred by the Hindus, and pork is forbidden to the Muslims. To appropriate another's due is like tasting "the forbidden meats." With temperate or cold weather is associated also spiritual poise, and with the heat of the summer months "the agony of separation." How sensitive!

Sixty-eight places of Hindu pilgrimage are mentioned time and again. Some of the places sacred to the Hindus which are mentioned by name are: Jagannāth puri, Hardwār, Kāshi, Kedāra, Kurekshetra, Mount Kailāsh, Gayā, the rivers Gangā, Saraswati, Jamunā, Godāvari and Gomti, Prayāg (Allāhābād), Dawārkā, Bindrabān, lake Mansarovar, Rikhikesh and Mathurā. As for the Muslims, only Kaabā is mentioned as their most sacred place of pilgrimage, though the common mass also pay homage to the tombs of pirs and faqirs. Other name-places mentioned in the Ādi Granth are: Hindustān, Orrisā, Kābul, Lankā, Kartārpur, Khadur, Khurāsān and Beas. Which shows clearly that except for the river Godāvari in the south, Hindustān is identified by and large with northern and eastern India.

The guests and holymen are treated with great consideration. As a sign of reverence, the dust of a holy man's feet anoints the devotees' forehead. The seekers (like the young in relation to the old) fall at the feet of the revered one. Money (*damrā*) is freely in use as an item of exchange. The miserly bury their treasures underground, and are very often deprived of them by thieves, or worms (or women). The poor do not normally eat the buttered bread and live in improvised mud tenements, as against the luxurious foods and decorated palaces (*dhaular*) of the rich.

CHAPTER IX

BHĀI GURDĀS

And The Sikh Way Of Life

Bhāi Gurdās, a Bhallā Khatri, was a near relation of the third Guru, and was converted to Sikhism in 1579 A.D. by the fourth Guru, Rām Dās. A great scholar of Persian and Sanskrit and of comparative religion, he is a poet of superb beauty, his most famous compositions being *Vārs* in Panjābi (ballads, 40 in number, the 41st being by another poet, Gurdās Singh, a contemporary of the tenth Guru) and *Kabits* and *Swayyās* in Braj Bhāshā, Through these works, he offers a most authoritative interpretation of the Guru's Word. Guru Arjun, it is said. wanted to incorporate some of his works in the Ādi Granth, but, in his humility, he declined the honour. The Guru thereupon blessed his work as the "key to the understanding of the Sikh Scriptures." He was the scribe of the Ādi Granth, preached the Sikh doctrine far and wide from Kābul to Kāshi, and died at Goindwāl in 1637 A.D. A socio-economic history of the times could be culled from his works.

It would be worthwhile to quote briefly from his writings as to what was his understanding of Sikhism in his times.

(1) Salutations to the Guru who blessed us with the *mantram* of the True Name (Sat Nām), and emancipated us, ferrying us across the Sea of material existence. Lo, the fear of birth-and-death for us is no more, nor doubt, nor separation. Everyone comes here to go out, and thus suffers pain in the midst of a world of illusion. The punishment of death hangs over the head of the evil-doers, for they waste away their human birth. But they who hold fast to the feet of the Guru are emancipated through the True Word. They confirm

their faith in meditation of the Name (Nām), compassion (Dān) and inner purity (Isnān), and with devotion, they celebrate the Guru's Deeds. As one sows, so one reaps.

(2) Out of the eighty-four lakhs of species, the human birth is the most sublime. So one must devote it to pious works and share the fruit of one's toil with others. One should make content his fellow-beings and drink the wash of their feet. One should abandon not humility and fall at the feet of the others. One should emancipate not only oneself, but also the other men of faith.

(3) There are four sects of the Muslims and four castes of the Hindus, but due to ego, they slander and tussle with each other. The Hindus consider Gangā and Banāras to be sacred, the Muslims look upon Meccā and Kaabā as the abode of God. The Muslims stick to circumcision, the Hindus to the sacred thread and the frontal mark. Some call their God Rām, others Rahim. The two names are of the same God, but these divide them into two separate ways. They care not for the *Vedas* or the *Katebs* (Semitic texts), for the devils are enticed by the greed for worldly goods. Truth is now the concern of no one: the Brāhmins and the Mullāhs are interested only in dissentions. And so the world comes and goes.

(4) One becomes a disciple (i.e. a Sikh) not through talk, but by dying in life. Illuminated by faith and contentment, one becomes a martyr to the cause, dispelling one's doubts and fears. One slaves for the Master and does as he is bidden, caring not for hunger or sleep. He brings water and grinds corn for the others, washes their feet and waves fan to them. At peace with himself, he neither weeps nor laughs. He who becomes such a perfect *Dervesh,* he alone tastes the nectar of love, and is blessed and fulfilled like the new moon of the *Id.*

(5) He who loses, wins: he who wins is the loser in the end.

(6) The humble are forever victorious: the egotists always lose.

(7) Of all ways, the way of the householder is the best.

(8) All rituals are false—yagnas, the raising of the sacred fire, *Japa, tapa,* continence and forced discipline, customary charities, pilgrimages, asceticism, belief in *tantra* and *mantra,* yogic postures, fasting and worship, blessing and cursing, miracle-making and other such deceptions, belief in tombs and crematoriums and yoginis and saviours, Shiva and Shakti, gods and goddesses. Only the Guru's Word saves, or the companionship of the holy.

(9) Belief in omens, good and bad, leads one to disillusionment.

(10) The path of the Guru's Sikh is like a razor's edge, finer than the hair, and to taste what is tasteless, for one must abandon one's cravings, and the love of the Other, and yoke oneself to the service of the One alone.

(11) In power, to become powerless, in honour to feel humble, being wise and to remain innocent and to submit ever to the Will of God—such a one is approved both in this world and the next.

(12) Sacrifice I am to the one who is humble from within, who touches not another's woman nor wealth, who slanders no one and returns good for evil, who eats little and sleeps little, who serves his fellowmen, who gets cheated (of his self) but cheats not another, who looks upon all alike, who lives in the world but is not of it, who disciplines his outgoings, and is devoted ever to the Guru's feet.

(13) Of all persons, the most abominable is an ungrateful wretch.

(14) One must love the Guru as a *Chakori* loves the moon, as a *chakvi* craves for the sun, as lotus flowers in the love of water, as a peacock dances at the sight of the clouds, as is the longing of the wife for her spouse and of the mother for the child.

CHAPTER X

GURU HAR GOBIND

(1595—1644 A. D.)

Guru Hargobind was only eleven years when his father became a martyr. According to the orders of emperor Jahāngir, the Guru's son must have been put under arrest along with his father, and there is no reason to suppose that it was not so. The Sikh [illegible] are, however, unanimous that it was not his son but five other Sikhs who were arrested and tortured to death along with the Guru. They assert that it was six years later that the sixth Guru was confined by the emperor in the fort of Gwalior for charges other than those levelled against his father, for a period which varies from forty days to twelve years ! It may be, argue some others, that the very young age of Hargobind made the emperor relent from putting him into prison earlier, but this is hardly a sufficient explanation.*

---

* If we are to go by the dates of the Guru's marriage and the birth of his sons and daughter, it becomes obvious that the Guru's incarceration must have been along with his father's or immediately thereafter. All Sikh chroniclers are unanimously of the view that Guru Arjun died in 1606, when Hargobind was only 11 years of age and that the latter's eldest son, Bābā Gurdittā, was born in 1613 followed by Suraj Mal (1617), Ani Rāi, (1618) and Atal Rāi (1620). And if he was married a year before the birth of his first son, i e. in 1612, the Guru's incarceration could not have been but from 1606 to 1612 A.D. And, if the same writers are to be believed and Jehāngir developed a friendship with the Gurū and had spiritual discourses and went out hunting with him, he could not have done so before 1619 (when he returned to Āgrā after his expeditions in Rajputānā and Gujrāt and before 1627 when he died) and by which time he must have clearly known the intentions and the effect of the Guru's Mission.

According to the chronology of Sikh sources, which, as we shall see, is not trustworthy, Hargobind was invested with his high office immediately the news of Guru Arjun's martyrdom was received by his followers in Amritsar. Like always, it was Bābā Buddhā who performed this most significant ceremony, and, according to custom, wrapped a turban round his head signifying that the office of the father (symbolised by the headgear) had descended upon the son. The young Guru, however, refused to accept a *Seli* (woollen cord worn as a necklace or round the head by the earlier Gurus as a symbol of their spiritual station) and wore two swords instead, one on each side—one to signify temporal power (*Miri*) and the other spiritual (*piri* or faqiri).* He also gave instructions to the *masands* and to the large gathering assembled on this occasion from far and near to make offerings in future in horses and weapons, and not in cash. Along with the devotional music, the Guru made martial music popular among his followers (the *Dhunis* or martial tunes suggested for the various ballads—Vārs—included in the Ādi Granth, however, are erroneously said to have been appended by Guru Hargobind)† and encouraged physical culture and training in weapons of offence and

---

* It is ridiculous for the Sikh chroniclers to associate casualness or chance with such a deliberate choice of the Gurū. It is said that Bābā Buddhā while decking the young Guru with a sword put it on the right (i.e. the wrong) side, and later tried to shift it to the left side. But, the Guru said, "Do not shift what you have put on me already. Bring me another sword that I dangle from the other side too. The one sword shall signify *miri* (secular power) and the other *piri or faqiri* (renunciation and spiritual station)." Were it so, Guru Arjun would not have himself trained his son, unlike the earlier practice, in the art of warfare.

†It is interesting to note in this connection that several of the noted warriors of Guru Hargobind, including Bidhi Chand, were Sikhs of Guru Arjun. According to Mani Singh's *Sikhān di Bhagat Māl,* (based on Bhāi Gurdās's Vār 11), Guru Arjun, in his life-time, had enjoined upon two renowned soldiers, Bhāi Sigārā and Bhāi Jaitā, to take to the service of his son, Hargobind, "in whose form we shall take up arms." "Through skill in the knowledge of arms, we shall wrest the sovereignty of the Kings and through attachment to the (Guru's) Word, acquire the knowledge of Divinity. One person fights for the King as a mercenary, but in your case you will find worldly affluence along with redemption, and be released while yet alive". To other soldiers also, who came for spiritual instruction, Guru Arjun gave similar advice : "Fight only for what is morally justified against the tyrants who tyrannise over the poor. Think of God while fighting and share with the needy all that you earn." (SBM, stories of Bhāi Partapu and Aditi Soini). May be, Bhāi Mani Singh is using his hind-sight, a century after the event, to attribute to Guru Arjun the genesis of what happened in later times.

defence. The spiritual side was also not neglected and services were held, morning and evening, attended by the Guru personally for the inner enlightenment of his people so that his greater emphasis on the temporal may not detract his followers from the spiritual ideal to defend which a warlike posture had now become essential. The Guru soon had about one thousand horse under him and many Jāts of Mājhā, Doābā and Mālwā, including Muslims, joined his ranks, on one of whom, Paindē Khān, he showered special affection. He also kept a body-guard of 52 horse.*

Against this new stance of the Guru (though the force he raised was of modest strength) the Masands (or the Guru's agents)

* According to Bannerjee (Evolution of the Khālsā, Part II, pp, 30-40), so long as the Sikh Gurus took to peaceful ways of the spirit, it is the trading classes, mainly Khatris, who followed them and as is the peace-loving and docile nature of the commercial classes, the internal feuds in the Guru's camp or the external threats from the empire did not take place. But, after the Sixth Guru had recruited the Jāts of Mājhā and Mālwā in his camp, to meet the challenge of the times, the Guru's house was riven by faction and feud and he was involved in several engagements with the imperial forces, as the Jāts since time immemorial have been a clannish people given to tribalism, war and plunder even among their own castes. This, however, cannot be accepted as the whole truth. It is true, just as the conversion to Christianity of the Romans, the Greeks, the Germans and the Anglo-Saxons each gave a distinct characteristic to Christianity as did the inhabitants of Persia, Mongolia and Turkey give each a distinctive turn to history on their conversion to Islām, some of the Jāt tribal characteristics also could not but have influenced the course of events in Sikh history. But, this influence should not be exaggerated all on the negative side. Just as the Khatris brought their sharp intellect, sense of economic and socio-political organisation, and love of the fine arts like music and poetry and an idealistic view of life into the mainstream of Sikh history, so the Jāts contributed their vigour, sense of heroism and sacrifice and independence of character. If the Sikh Gurus were all Khatris, and Banda Singh a Rajput, General Jassā Singh an Ahluwalia and another General name-sake of his a Rāmgārhiā, and Hari Singh Nalwā (the C-in-C of the Army during the days of the Sikh empire) a Khatri, the Jāts not only contributed great warriors and empire-builders like Ranjit Singh, but also scholars like Bhāis Mani Singh and Kāhan Singh, poets like Bhāi Santokh Singh and devotees like Bābā Buddhā and Sant Attar Singh. It must be mentioned here that the 22 Masands appointed by Guru Amar Dās for the propagation of the Sikh faith were mostly Jats, though one was also a Muslim. As for feuds and intrigues, the Khatri relations of the Gurūs — notably Bedis and Sodhis — stopped short at nothing to harm the interests of the Gurūs themselves. It is thus to the eternal credit of the Gurus that they tried to create a single civilised society out of a mass of feuding castes, tribes and clans. If a few individuals or moments of history have failed to come upto their ideals, such failures cannot be generalised.

became very apprehensive, as did the household of the Guru. Even a man of such dedication as Bhāi Gurdās had to enunciate elaborately the wild talk against the Guru by his own followers and his own explanation thereof. Writes Bhāi Gurdās :—

> "*(The earlier Gurus) sat in their temple, but the present one roams from place to place.*
>
> *Earlier, the kings came to pay homage to the Gurus; now our forts are attacked by the kings.*
>
> *The followers too find no peace, for (the Guru) is ever on the go, and is terrified by nothing.*
>
> *The earlier Gurus ministered instructions in the arts of peace from their couch; the present one keeps hunting dogs and loves the chase.*
>
> *The earlier ones composed and sang devotional hymns, the present one neither instructs in, nor hears nor sings the hymns.*
>
> *He keeps not the devout with him, but is happy in the company of our wretched enemies:*
>
> *(But) one can hide not the Truth (of his being), and the Sikhs, like the bumble-bee, crave his lotus-feet.*
>
> *He suffers the insufferable and asserts not his self.*"[1]

That the transformation was marked and was of such a nature as to create consternation even among the devout and the members of his family is thus apparent from this authentic eye-witness account. In mid-1606 (i.e. immediately on ascending the *gaddi*), he is said to have laid the foundation-stone of the Akāl-bungā (or Akāl Takht) facing the golden temple and, when built, the Guru held his court here to minister to secular matters.* Some of his devout followers like Bidhi Chand, Pirānā, Jethā, Pairā, and Langāhā, he made commanders of one hundred horse each. It is said, he would go out hunting with his

---

[1] Var 26 Pauri 24.

* That a separate place was necessary for secular deliberations, seems to be the reason behind the building of the Akāl Bunga. This tradition has continued ever since, and no political or secular matter is discussed within the Hari Mandir. (See Miri and Piri in the Appendices).

followers each forenoon, accompanied by hounds and hawks. But these events, it appears, are predated by Sikh historians by five to six years.

The Guru was now in the prime of his youth. According to the Sikh chroniclers, reports of the Guru's activities reached the ears of the emperor, and he called him into his presence.* The Guru assigned the secular duties of the Hari Mandir (like the collection of the offerings, etc.) and the community kitchen to Bhāi Buddhā and the spiritual instruction to Bhāi Gurdās, and set out for Delhi, in mid-January, 1612 A. D.* (i.e. when he attained his majority), accompanied by three hundred horse, and halted outside the imperial city at a site known as Majnun-kā-tillā@, on the bank of Yamunā. Many followers called on him here as well as on the way and expressed apprehension as to the result of his present meeting with the emperor but the Guru gave them heart saying, "My life is dedicated to God. Whatever He Wills, I must accept with all my heart and soul, and so should you. He who has faith in the utlimate justice of God and fights not for aggression or the gratification of his ego, wins in the end. The temporary ebb and tide in the life of an individual or a nation must not affect the tranquility of one's mind. The one thing our Gurus have rid us of is FEAR. We should, therefore, trust in God, never aggress against anyone in word, though or deed, remain humble and do our secular jobs whatever they be, with honesty and diligence, and share with our fellow human-beings what we earn, and hate or be envious of no one, but if for the sake of *Dharma*, or

* Macauliffe, leaning heavily on the legend-loving Sikh chroniclers again brings in Chandu (who still pleads with the Guru for the marriage of his daughter), and Prithiā's son, Mehervān, etc., being instrumental in poisoning the ears of the emperor against him, as if the emperor was interested only in the match-making of a petty official, Chandu's, daughter, or settling a family feud between Prithiā (later his son, Mehervān) and the Guru's house. Bhāi Gurdās while reviling every enemy of the Guru's house, including Prithiā, does not mention Mehervān, who seems to have been much liked by Guru Arjun himself and who, unlike his father, was a man of quiet and highly sensitive and spiritual disposition. Nor does Bhāi Gurdās mention the name of Chandu at any place or in any context whatsoever.

@ As we have shown above, in 1612 A.D., the Guru should have come out of the prison rather than enter it.

the moral law, we have to suffer or sacrifice our all, we must not hesitate. For, ultimately, all that we are and have, belongs not to us, but to God. We enjoy His bounties but when He demands their surrender we should willingly offer them at His altar. My father did likewise. So shall I. So should you." These words of high wisdom and chivalry from the young prince gave his Sikhs much confidence in the future of their faith.

The Sikh chroniclers here narrate at great length the Guru's visit to the emperor and the spiritual discourses he had with him. But, it seems rather odd that a man of Jehāngir's disposition would have indulged in this kind of pastime with a person he had called to question on the matters of state. But, if we accept the thesis that this happened after the Guru's release sometime between 1611 and 1612, then everything falls into its place and it appears the emperor was now seriously trying to befriend him. Also, it seems reasonable that the Guru must have been asked searching questions on the fundamentals of his faith to satisfy the King as much as the *ulemā* that no serious harm was intended to Islām by the propagation of the Sikh doctrine. It is also unreasonable to believe (as the Sikh historians would have us believe) that the Guru was initially received with great courtesy at the royal court, and that he stayed in Delhi as a free citizen for quite some time without any harm or threat of molestation, much less of imprisonment. It is also recorded by them that the emperor took great fancy to his youthful and yet serene looks, his magnificent prowess (he is said to have accompanied the emperor on a chase and saved him from an attack of a tiger with one stroke of his sword)*, but becoming ill and being told by an astrologer (who, it is said, was bribed by Chandu !) that a holyman should do "penance" for

* Though the story may be apocryphal or embellished to heighten its dramatic effect, it is said a poor grass-cutter follower of the Guru once came to see him while he was camping just facing the emperor's tent. The grass-cutter, crying that he wanted to see the vision of the True King, was led by the royal attendants into the camp of the King-emperor. The grass-cutter put a paisā (copper-coin) before him and stood, with folded hands, praying, his eyes filled with tears and his throat choked with emotion. The King was overwhelmed with the devotion of a loyal subject, and offered to make him a large present. The Sikh replied, "O True King, if you are so pleased, bless me with the glory of God's Name that I be emancipated." When the devotee was told he had come to the wrong camp, and that the one who granted redemption was housed in the opposite camp, the devotee unhesitatingly picked up from the presence of the emperor his humble offering saying :- "Then, this too is meant for him, not your Majesty."

him, "in confinement", in order to save the emperor's life, Jehāngir "persuaded" the Guru to enter the fort of Gwalior and remain there a virtual prisoner for twelve years doing "penance" for his "recovery"! In the first place, the emperor was not seriously ill these days, and from 1613 to 1619 was engaged in the battles of the Deccan, Rājputānā, Gujarāt, etc. This also makes it probable that it is at the end of his incarceration, sometime in 1611-12, that the emperor met him and not before sending him to prison.

Troyer's English translation of the *Dabistān-i-Mazāhib* made such a mess that for a long time, wrong reasons were adduced for the Guru's confinement. He writes :

"Hargobind became involved in many difficulties; one of them was that he appropriated to himself the pay due to the soldiers in advance; he carried also sword against his father; he kept, besides, many servants and was addicted to hunting. Jehāngir, on account of the money due to the army and of the mulet imposed upon Arjun Mal, sent Hargobind to the fort of Gwalior.", etc.

But in the original Persian, there is not a word either about the money due from the Guru to his soldiers nor any hint of his having carried the sword against his father. The exact translation is : "He (Guru Hargobind) had to contend with numerous difficulties. One of them was that he adopted the style of a soldier (*wazhāi-sipahiān pesh grifi*), wore a sword contrary to (the custom) of his father (*barkhilāf-i-pidar shamsher bast*) maintained many servants (*Naukran nigāhi-dāsht*) and went out hunting. His late Majesty (Jehāngir)—may he abide in paradise—in order to extort from him the balance of fine imposed upon his father, Arjun Mal, imprisoned him in the fort of Gwalior......on scanty rations......for a period of twelve years."*

The only charge brought forth against Guru Hargobind by the author of *Dabistān* is that Jehāngir sought to realise the balance of the "fine" imposed upon his father. This also is contrary to facts, as Jehāngir himself in his *Tuzak* makes no mention whatever of any fine levied upon Guru Arjun. His property was to be confiscated and his 'sons' taken into custody. It is, therefore, safe to assume that Guru Hargobind was arrested along with his father in pursuance of the emperor's *firmān* and kept in the Gwalior fort where

---

* *Dabistān,* Vol.II, P.274. *Dabistān* also states that the incarceration of the Guru took place in 1616 A D., which is contrary to all other authoritative evidence.

several other Hindu princes, inimical to the rāj, were also confined.

The Sikhs, according to *Dabistān*, however, showed their utter fidelity to the Guru. "They came from far and near and circumambulating round the fort, with eyes filled with tears of affection and reverence, would go back home praying for his early release." The Guru also conducted himself with such pious and dedicated routine that Jehāngir was convinced of his innocent intentions, and seeing the devout feelings of his followers towards him, released him much before his term of imprisonment. It is said the Guru insisted on his fellow-prisoners also being set free before he would agree to walk into freedom aud that Jehāngir was so moved by his piety that he agreed to do so, though there is no historical evidence to substantiate this. The Guru is for this reason called *"Bandi Chhor"* (the emancipator of the captives), but this indeed is a spiritual apellation and has been invariably applied to God and the Gurus (as in the *Ādi Granth*) throughout.*

At this point, it is possible to accept the uniformly-held traditional version that after the Guru's release, the emperor tried to befriend him, and both might have gone together hunting or otherwise entered into spiritual and secular discourses, and even travelled or camped together on some journeys.† It may also be, as Macauliffe

---

* The Sikh chroniclers have given a free rein to their imagination in this context, as at many other such periods of crisis, for they would not let their Gurus and heroes suffer deliberately, for a great cause, without showing a miracle to escape tragedies! In this case, Bhāi Jethā, a devout Sikh, is said to have secured the Guru's release in a matter of 40 days "by soothing the emperor who was troubled by fearful visions", through his occult powers! The Guru was displeased with him, it is said, for his exhibiting miracles, saying, "If the ocean does not speak, why should a drop be so pretentious?" (Macauliffe, Vol. IV. P.25, etc.)

†It is said, Jehāngir now handed over Chandu to Guru Hargobind, according to the then-prevailing law, for a fit punishment for the tortures he had inflicted on the Guru's father and that the Sikhs put a chain round his neck and dragged him all along the way from Delhi to Lāhore via Amritsar, people spitting in his face and throwing dust on his head. At last, he gave up his ghost at Lāhore when a person struck him with a red-hot iron ladle. This seems highly unlikely to have been condoned either by the compassionate Guru or by his sensitive Sikhs. Moreover, according to all available historical evidence, the episode of Chandu seems to be the product of some fertile imagination.

To suggest, however, as Mohsin Fāni, and following him Cunningham have done, that the Gurū accepted the employment of Jehāngir is neither corroborated by

narrates, that Nur-Jahān with the other ladies of the harem came to call on the Guru one of these days. But, this conciliation was soon coming to an end, not on account of the hostility of Mehervān, son of Prithiā, and such other hostile factors, but for more solid political reasons, though it never resulted in a head-on clash during the life-time of Jahāngir.

These days, a Sikh Masand, Sujān, resident of Kābul, brought a most precious race-horse as a present for the Guru. While passing through Lāhore, it was captured by the Moghal authorities or a Qāzi who refused to part with it except for a consideration. This was

Tuzak-i-Jāhāngiri nor by any contemporary Sikh records. That Jahāngir may have been influenced by the Guru's piety, or by Mian Mir's intervention (to whom he makes most reverent references in the *Tuzak*) is quite in keeping with his dual character. Forster, in his Travels (p. 259) refers to a Moghal officer, called Mahābat Khān, having interceded on behalf of the Guru. The *Tuzak*, however, which makes detailed mention of all appointments and dismissals and sketches intimately the character of his nobles (and religious discourses with the Jesuit fathers and Jains, yogis, Vaishanavas and Muslims like Sheikh Ahmad Sirhindi (the detractor of Guru Arjun, whom he had at first imprisoned at Gwalior for two years for his heresies- he claimed to be Imām Mehdi--and later regretting the incident honoured him with royal gifts and left him alone) makes no mention whatever of Guru Hargobind. Mohsin Fāni's assertion that "the Guru attached himself to Yār Khān, the eunuch, who held the office of a Faujdār in the Nawābi of the Panjāb and whom he assisted in the administration" (Dabistān. Vol II, P. 274) is thus patently absurd, so also similar statements of *Panth Parkāsh* (P. 107) and *Itihās Guru Khālsā* (P. 128) that "the Guru was given a command of 700 horse, 1000 foot and 7 guns". On the other hand, Mohsin Fāni also states that "the Guru had 800 horses in his stable, 300 cavalry, and 60 men with firearms were always in his service" "And whosoever was a fugitive from his home, took refuge with the Guru" (*Dabistān*, II. P. 277), A person in the employ of the emperor could not have given refuge to the fugitive princes, without incurring his active hostility. It appears that the diplomatic truce that occurred from 1612 to the death of Jahāngir between the emperor and the Guru has been seized upon by interested writers to create an impression of the Guru's total surrender and employment in the imperial forces as a petty official. According to Nārang, "Rām Partāp, the fugitive Rājā of Jaisalmer, took refuge with (Guru) Hargobind and Yār Khān and Khawāja Sarāi, dismissed commanders of the Moghal army, entered the Guru's asylum (Transformation of Sikhism, p. 106 f.n.). Also that two nobles, Anwar Khān and Hassan Khān left the service of Government and took refuge with (Guru) Hargobind." (Macauliffe, Vol.IV, p. 100).

[1] On his own admission, Fāni's acquaintance with Guru Hargobind came about towards the end of the Guru's life, sometime in 1640 A.D. (1053 Hijri), and Cunningham not unjustly dismisses him, "as a gossiping and credulous person" even in the eyes of the contemporary Sikhs. (pp. 59-60 f.n.)

promised to him and the horse got released and presented to the Guru, but the ransom money was never paid and this led to the Qāzi lodging a complaint with the emperor, or his Viceroy at Lāhore. Meantime, the Qāzi's daughter, whose name the Sikh chroniclers give as "Kaulan" (lit. lotus, which may be an assumed name, on account of her lotus-like eyes or tender body) fled her home, both on account of her father's tyranny over her and her spiritual disposition acquired from her preceptor, Hazrat Mian Mir—and sought refuge with the Guru. It is said, she made large presents to the Guru but the latter did not accept them for the Guru's treasury, and instead dug up a tank at Amritsar—now colled Kaulsar—to commemorate her memory before she died not long after. But, the Guru remained most solicitous of her feelings and comfort to the end of her days.* The Guru also dug up another tank at Amritsar called Babeksar (the pool of enlightenment), thus bringing their total number to five. Meantime, it is said, the Qāzi's complaint was dismissed by the higher authorities, thus giving the Guru the much-needed breathing-time for the propagation of his faith, but, as we shall see, only for a brief spell.

The Guru now proceeded to Pilibhit to help one of his devotees, Almast†, who was being deprived by the yogis of the possession of a

---

* According to Sir G.C. Narang, Kaulān (or Kamlā) was a Hindu forcibly converted to Islām and kept as a concubine by the Qāzi (Transformation of Sikhism, P. 62). Cunningham is also of this view who bases his information on un-named Mohammedan authors (History of the Sikhs, p, 58).

† Almast, the Udāsi Sikh priest (either he or his name-sake) was also, it is said, deputed by Guru Hargobind to go to Shujātpur, near Dāccā, and take charge of the *Sangat* there. This Sangat was known after Nathā Sāhib, third in succession to Almast, and according to the inscription on the well, its founding is ascribed to Almast, and its priests were appointed and removed by the High Priest of Nānakmatā (vide G.B. Singh's article, "Sikh relics in Eastern Bengal", Dāccā Review, 1916, p. 228). Thus, under Guru Hargobind, the seats of Sikhism were consolidated from Kābul on the one hand to Dāccā on the other, first sanctified by the visit of Guru Nānak. Under his son, Bābā Gurdittā, the system of Sangats and Masands was supplemented by four Dhuāns (hearths or consecrated seats supervised by Bālu Hasnā, Almast, Phūl Shāh and Gondā) under the Udāsi Sikhs who, though living celibate and ascestic lives, as enjoined by Bābā Sri Chand, their founder, in no other way departed from the Sikh doctrine. The Guru's eldest son, Bābā Gurdittā, father of the seventh Guru, was adopted and appointed successor by Bābā Sri Chand and in token thereof "put on Gurdittā's head a Persian hat (topi) and on his neck a string of lotus seeds". Under Gurus Hari Rāi, Teg Bahādur and Gobind Singh, six Bakhishes (Bounties)

temple sacred to the memory of Guru Nānak, earlier called Gorakhmatā, but which the Sikhs had re-named Nānak-matā. He travelled extensively through this territory and many other places on the way giving spiritual instruction to his followers. In 1613 A.D., a son was born to his wife, Dāmodri, who was named Gurdittā and whose features, it was believed, very much resembled those of Bābā Nānak. Later, he visited Nanakānā Sāhib and other places associated with the name of the first Guru, and went also to Kashmir to meet his devotees, especially Sewā Dās, a Brāhmin convert to his faith and his mother, Bhāgbhari, who had spun a robe with great dedication for the Guru to wear. An important shrine dedicated to this visit still stands near Srinagar. It is said, so overwhelmed was Bhāgbhari on seeing the Guru that she started blurting out incoherent and importunate talk: "O Guru, you are the sinner, I your redeemer. You are the captive, I your deliverer", etc. The Sikhs flew into rage, but the Guru said, "I understand fully the intent of what she means. She is in a state of ecstasy where words lose their habitual meaning."

Later, during his visit to Srinagar in Garhwāl, the Guru met Swāmi Ramdās Samrath, a great spiritual teacher of Mahārāshtra and later the instructor of Shivāji, the founder of the Marāthā Empire. Rāmdās was at first greatly shocked on seeing the Guru riding a horse and sporting royalty in his dress and manners, accompanied by a huge and armed bodyguard and following the chase. He said to the Guru, "You are on the spiritual throne of Guru Nānak, a great Saint. How does it fit you, his successor, to sport regalia like this?" The Guru replied, "*Zāhir amiri, bātan faqiri : Guru Nānak ne Māyā tyāgi thi: Sansār nahin tiāgyā thā.*" (I display royalty only from the

---

F. N. Contd.

were added to their order, which included the Suthrāshāhis, Sangat Sāhibis, Jitmalias, Bakhatmalias, Bhagat Bhagwāniās and Mirānshāhis. The Udāsis have played a most notable part for the propagation of the Sikh faith in times of worst crises in its history, but the Akāli movement of the present century for the control of the Sikh historic shrines (See Part II) has disrupted the existing cordial relations almost permanently between the two. Earlier, the Udāsis wore a crown of long hair on their head, covered by a tall, cony cap, but many of them are now shaved and though the majority still wear the ochre robes (earlier they wore deep red), some even smear their naked bodies with ashes and even wear matted hair. However, they all believe in the Sikh Scripture, the Guru Granth Sāhib.

outside; inwardly, I'm detached like a faqir. Guru Nānak had abandoned Māyā (i.e. attachment to the world), not the world itself.) Swāmi Rāmdās was much pleased at this reply and said, "*Yeh* (*bāt*) *hamāre man bhāvti hai.*" (This reply satisfies us). And, he changed thereafter the course of his intruction and on his return to Mahārāshtra, instructed Shivāji, his pupil, that the age-old lesson of renunciation imparted by our ancient teachers had been misconstrued by the Hindu race, thus leading to their political and moral slavery of foreign hordes. It was time to re-discover it as the Guru had so inimitably explained.

In 1617 A.D., another son, Suraj Mal, was born to Marwāhi or Mahādevi, the other wife of the Guru, whom he had wedded on the entreaties of a devoted Sikh, called Dwārā of the village of Mandıāli. From this third wife, Nānaki, he had another son, Ani Rāi, a year after, and in 1820, she bore him yet another son, called Atal Rāi. The Guru also had a daughter—Viro—from his first wife and her he married to a very poor, though bright boy who had come to pay him a visit along with his father. Both the father and son were stunned to be honoured thus, but the Guru said, "Such is the custom of my house. Here, the poor are exalted and if they remain humble, dedicated to the disinterested service of God and man, they become prosperous and renowned." Nānaki gave birth to another son, Teg Bahādur, in 1622 A.D.

On October 28, 1627, Jahāngir died and Shāh Jahān ascended the throne of Delhi. It was being daily reported to the Guru that his growing strength among the people and more especially his raising of an army, howsoever small, was causing consternation in the imperial quarters. The Guru took all precautions to safeguard his honour, but warned his followers never to precipitate a fight, for his intention was neither to wrest a dominion for himself nor glory as a warrior, but the protection of the self-respect of his followers. So much was the Guru attached to his Sikhs that when a party of Sikhs came to visit him at Amritsar from a great distance, reaching at midnight, and the Guru insisted that they be fed properly before he could see them, every one around, including his immediate attendants, expressed their inability. The Guru thereupon said, "There are baskets of sweets in the household kept for the marriage of my daughter. Let these be distributcd among the visitors." To this his wife, Dāmodri, objected. The Guru thereupon uttered a curse, "If the guests go away hungry from my door and the sweets lying in my house are no use to them, then, these will not be tasted also by the bridegroom's party, but looted by the Moghals."

According to the Sikh chroniclers, this very year, i.e. 1628 A.D., Shāh Jahān, the new emperor, was on a hunting expedition nearby and a white hawk, presented to him by the Shāh of Irān, flew into the Guru's camp at Amritsar in pursuit of a duck. The Guru flew a hawk of his own which seized the duck and on the emperor's hawk joining in the seizure, the Sikhs caught them both. The emperor's huntsmen, accompanied by troopers, remonstrated with the Sikhs to return the hawk, but they refused to part with their booty. There was a brief altercation and several of the imperial troops lost their lives, the rest hastening back to report to Lāhore to the King-emperor where he had halted by now. The emperor was enraged on this insolence and show of authority by the Guru's followers and sent one of his generals, Mukhlis Khān, with 7000 cavalry to bring both the Guru and the hawk into the presence of the King. The Sikhs of Lāhore getting scent of the news apprised the Guru of the impending danger. The Guru offered prayers to God and assembled his forces in a fortress, called Lohgarh, he had built earlier and put them in battle array. He even improvised a cannon out of the hollow trunk of a tree to discharge stones with a deadly effect. The imperial forces reached the outskirts of Amritsar at the dead of night and were engaged in a furious battle. Many heroes were killed on both sides, including Shams Khān, and Sultān Beg, two well-known generals in the King's army, and Singhā, Mohan and Gopālā, valiant warriors, on the Guru's side. The Guru also fought in the thick of the battle-field and claimed countless heads with his never-failing arrows. Bidhi Chand and Paindē Khān also fought recklessly on his side. Swords flashed and clanged; lances and arrows pierced the hearts of the enemy or their horses; matchlocks rained hell-fire. Finding no hope for victory after a fight for several days, Mukhlis Khān challenged the Guru to single combat. The Guru galloped quickly to his side and shouted at him, "You strike first, so that you have no regrets. In my house, this also is the rule. We do not invite the battle, nor strike the first blow."

Mukhlis Khān waved his sword twice with great skill at the Guru's person, but every time missed his aim. The Guru gave him no further opportunity and struck him with such a masterly skill that his head was cleaved in two. This created utter confusion in the remaining Moghal ranks and they fled in disarray. A shrine, called

Sangrānā Sāhib, commemorates the Guru's first decisive victory against the Moghal army.*

The Guru immediately thereafter solemnised the wedding of his daughter at Jhabāl nearby, where his family had been sent earlier for safety. Here a Moghal soldier tried to take the Guru's life, but his musket burst and killed the soldier instead. The Guru thereafter visited the shrines at Tarn Tāran, Goindwāl and Kartārpur along with his family to pay homage to God. It is in these days that he killed another tiger with his sword and shield, thus adding to his repute as a man of singular courage, and many more warriors enlisted themselves for service in his ranks. More and more arms, ammunition, horses and gold came to him from his devotees from far and near. But, Paindē Khān, the Muslim general in his ranks, meanwhile was becoming a source of great concern to the Guru by his arrogance and overbearing manners, and as the Guru tried to curb his haughtiness, he grew even more resentful. The growing might of the Guru also brought about tranquillity in the region; travel became safe and thefts and robberies on the highways or in the towns and villages under his influence became a thing of the past. He also founded another city on the banks of Beās, called Sri Hargobindpur.† But the chaudhri of the village, Bhagwān Dās, a

* Some say, the Moghal force did not consist of more than 700 horse. According to *Dabistān* (Vol. II, p, 275), the Moghal forces plundered the city and looted the Guru's property, and that the battle was not decisive. The genesis of the battle, however, was not as petty as the refusal of the Sikhs to release an imperial hawk. It was a question of the self-respect of a living people who were once again being subjected to dishonour and severe persecution. According to *Badshāhnāmā* of Lāhori, Shāh Jahān had ordered early in his reign that all Hindu temples which were then under construction should be demolished. Repairs of old temples were also prohibited. According to Qazvini, Muslim girls married to Hindus were forcibly snatched away. "General orders were issued to scour the Panjāb and put down this practice by force". The *bāoli* of Guru Arjun at Lāhore was filled up with earth, and a mosque raised upon its site. It was also proclaimed that "no conversion from Islām were to be permitted and a special department under a "Superintendent of Converts of Islām" was created "for the special purpose of making converts". "Any crime could be expatiated if the criminal was willing to be converted to Islām."

† Also called Gobindpur, which, according to GSG, was established by the sixth Guru. But, Bhāi Kāhan Singh, quoting the Kartārpur recension of the Ādi Granth, credits Guru Arjun with having established this city in 1587 A.D. (MK, P.750). Macauliffe supports GSG's version (Vol. IV, P. 105).

Khatri of the Gherar tribe, fell foul of him and though he was killed in a clash with the Sikhs, his son, Rattan Chand, vowed to avenge his father's death and sought the assistance of the Subedār of Jullundur, who attacked the Guru's forces at Hargobindpur with a force of ten thousand. The Guru was equipped with a force only half as much.

At first, a message was sent to the Guru by the Moghal commander to abandon the town and thus to avoid a clash. But the Guru rejected the offer with contempt, as he said, he was being forced into a fight, when he desired to acquire neither dominions, nor wealth. The Guru advised his followers not to fire the first shot, but also not to turn their back on the enemy if a fight became inevitable. "Let no one kill a fleeing soldier nor the one who has surrendered. And no woman's honour should be molested, nor women or civilian property captured in reprisals or as booty." "We are fighting for a righteous cause—our right to live with honour and in peace—and not for the sake of self-glory, or rule over others," he said.

A bitter fight ensued. It is said the battle was also joined by Karam Chand, son of Chandu, and Rattan Chand, son of Bhagwān Dās, both of whom wanted to avenge their fathers' deaths. The latter was shot by the Guru himself, but Karam Chand was captured by Bidhi Chand after a close fight and brought before the Guru. Bidhi Chand wanted to put him to death but the Guru ordered his release, saying, "It is not manly to strike at a defenceless person." But, the thankless wretch came back to battle with the Guru. His horse fell dead and his sword was broken into two, and the Guru wanting not to take advantage of this, dismounted his horse, threw away his sword and challenged him to a wrestling bout. In the very first go, the Guru lifted him up with his powerful arms and dashed his head to the ground, killing him instanteously. Most of the Moghal forces, including their many-splendoured generals, licked

absolute and undisputed victory over the Moghals. The Guru now ordered the Masands to go ahead with the construction of Sri Hargobindpur. Here, to the wonderment of all, the Guru also constructed a mosque for his Muslim labourers and soldiers.

Now, the Guru attended to the spiritual instruction of his followers. One day, as he was discoursing on the study of the Scriptures, he said, "Everyone who reads the Word of the Guru should do so with deliberation and understanding and try to live it in his own life. But, how many there are who could even utter correctly and with faith the first composition in the Granth Sāhib—the Japji of Guru Nānak?" It is said, a pious Sikh, called Gopāl, came forth and with bowed head and joined palms volunteered to do so only if the Guru would be pleased to bless him. The Guru welcomed the quiet self-confidence of this devotee and allowed him to exhibit his performance. So perfect was his delivery and his utterance so charged with devotion that it affected powerfully the Guru's heart and mind and he decided to transfer the Guruship to him. But, the reciter when he reached the end of his performance, wished in his heart that if the Guru be merciful, he should reward him with a choice horse. The Guru reading his mind granted him the wish he had harboured in his thoughts and said, "But for the craving of your mind for an earthly object of life, I would have surrendered my Throne to you. But, it is hard to concentrate on God for His own sake, dismissing out of account the pleasures of life."

After some time, the Guru visited Kartārpur, Khadur and Goindwāl to call upon the descendants of the first four Gurus and offered them large presents. He also met Bābā Sri Chand, the ascetic son of Guru Nānak, in his retreat in a deep forest. When the Bābā complimented him on his chivalry and piety, the Guru replied with profound humility, "It is all the result of your blessings." Meantime, his great devotee, Bābā Buddha, who had served six Gurus, in succession, passed away, ripe in years and glory, leaving his son, Bhānā, in the Guru's service. Bābā Gurdittā, who was by now married to Natti, got a son, named Dhir Mal who, as we shall see later, was to prove a great source of strife in the Guru's house. But Bābā Gurdittā himself was a man of great piety and detachment, and when Bābā Sri Chand asked the Guru's permission to adopt one of his sons, he made for him the choice of Bābā Gurdittā to whom Sri Chand "gave away his own Persian cap and put on his neck a string of lotus seeds", as if to transfer his *gaddi* to him. Taking his instruction from his father, Bābā Gurdittā also founded the city of **Kiratpur.** * (or the city of God's praise), a place hallowed by a miracle-making Muslim devotee of Guru Nānak, Budhan Shāh, at

* The land for the place was purchased by Guru Hargobind in 1626 A,D. from Rājā Tārāchand of Kahlūr, but the city was actually built with the help of Bābā Gurdittā. (MK, P. 992).

the base of Shivālik hills, and propagated the Guru's faith here with great devotion and steadfastness.

The other son, Atal Rāi, though much beloved of the Guru, it is said, started performing miracles and once is said to have revived Mohan, a seemingly dead playmate of his. The Guru, however, showed his utter displeasure and said, "My son has started dissipating his spiritual powers without discrimination. Shall our occupation now be to revive everyone's dead son and interfere ever in God's Will, we who are enjoined to accept whatever good or bad comes to us in His pleasure." Bābā Atal took the reproof so much to heart that he gave up the ghost soon thereafter while yet he was only in his ninth year. This led to great sorrow and lamentation in the family, but the Guru said, "Atal has become, like his name, immortal, for he has obeyed the Will of God willingly. He will be the guardian-angel of the city of Amritsar and no one will turn away from his door hungry or empty-handed." A nine-storeyed structure, called the Bungā of Bābā Atal was also erected later (1778-1784) to commemorate this nine year wonder of a child and to this day the poor are constantly fed, night and day, at this beautiful shrine chiselled in cool marble.

In those days, as more and more of his disciples came to visit the Guru, Bhāi Gurdās used to expiate on the mysteries of the Guru's Word through his superb verse. One day he wrote:

> "*If a mother becomes unchaste, it does not befit the son to disgrace her.*
>
> *Nor should a Sikh lose his faith, even if the Guru enacts a play to his detriment.*"

The Guru thought Gurdās had become egotistical and too proud of his never-failing faith. He, therefore, put him to a test and sent him out to Kābul to purchase horses, but there he misplaced his money and ran back for shame. Thus humbled, he had no heart to face the Guru and took refuge at Banāras where he discoursed with the learned Brāhmins on the merits of the Guru's Way, and later wrote to the Guru to forgive him his impertinence, saying:

> "*If a mother poisons her son, there's no one to save him.*
>
> *Nor, if the fence devours the crop.*
>
> *Or, if the guide misleads the wayfarer into a wilderness.*

Or, if the Guru enacts his play to instil doubt in the mind of the follower.
It is he alone who could pull him out of his delusion."

The Guru was much pleased at his regained humility and brought him back to his presence, but soon thereafter he breathed his last, in the year 1629 A.D., full of glory and becoming immortal for his profound exposition of the Sikh way of life, In 1630 A.D., another grandson of the Guru was born at Kirtarpur in the house of Bābā Gurdittā. He was called Hari Rāi. After touring many places sacred to the Gurus' memory in Panjāb, the Guru also joined his son at Kirtarpur, along with his family, establishing another township, Bhāi Rupā, in the year 1631, in honour of a devotee of his.*

These days two masands of Kābul, Bakht Mal and Tārā Chand, brought considerable presents for the Guru, including two choice steeds of high pedigree, on behalf of the Sikhs of Afghanistān. But, as in the past, these horses were forcibly taken away from them by the imperial officials at Lāhore and presented to the emperor Shāh Jahān who was then camping there. The Guru on learning this repeated affront was much distressed and asked Bidhi Chand, formerly a highwayman and now a staunch follower of the Guru, to rescue his treasure. Bidhi Chand wormed himself into the confidence of the Keeper of the royal stable at Lāhore, Sondhā Khān, becoming first a grass-cutter and then a magician and rode both the horses by turns safe to the Guru's sanctuary.

This naturally incensed the emperor so much that he despatched a sizeable force under Lālā Beg to punish the Guru. The Guru, on hearing the news of the army's advance against him, retired to a thick forest by the side of a tank, now called Gurusar, in the distsict of Nabhā. The battle was joined for eighteen hours on Maghar 16, Samvat, 1688 (1631 A D.), but such was its fury and disaster that the Guru's side suffered twelve hundred soldiers dead or wounded, though almost every Moghal general of consequence also lay on the battle-field. The loss of the enemy in dead was several times the Guru's and the remainder of the troops fled in terror and shame. All war-booty was distributed among the poor and when a Sikh, a descendant of Mahārāj, the Guru's devotee, kept to himself a pre-

* The present Bhāi Sāhib of Bāgrian traces his origin to Bhāi Rupa.

cious sword of a fallen Pathān general and lied about its possession to the Guru, the latter prophecied, "He who keeps this sword shall also perish by it with all his family." And so it happened in the same year. Due to a family feud, the sword was employed by its keeper against his adversaries and the whole family perished through mutual slaughter.

The Guru on the way back from the battlefield stopped for a while at Kangar, the place of Rāi Jodh, who had fought valiantly on the Guru's side. He also celebrated in 1632 A.D. the marriage of his other son, Teg Bahādur, to Gujri, daughter of Lāl Chand and Bishan Devi. In the same year, he is said to have allowed Bhāi Bidhi Chand to make a third copy of the Granth Sāhib, the original being with him and the other one at Māngat, as has already been referred to in the last chapter. It is said, the Guru also permitted a young artist to draw his picture in pure white muslin dress, riding a white steed, a white hawk on his hand and shaded by a white canopy, but the same is no longer extant.

Now, there appeared dissensions in the Guru's troops mainly due to the avaricious and overbearing nature of Painde Khān. Once the Guru honoured him with costly presents, including a *Khilat* (robe of honour) and a choice horse. These he transferred to his son-in-law who also seized a white hawk, much beloved of the Guru's, from the Sikhs. When the Guru asked for an explanation, Painde Khān answered in rude and intemperate language. The Guru dismissed him from his service and he caused the defection also of of five hundred other Pathāns as well, and went to complain to his cousin, Qutab Khān, then the Governor of Jullundur, who at first refused to help an ungrateful wretch, but thinking that the emperor might be pleased at such a venture, asked Paindē Khān to make his complaint to the King-emperor in person at Lāhore where he would join him. The emperor saw in this a fit opportunity to humble the Guru and sent a force of fifty thousand under Kāle Khān, brother of the deceased Mukhlis Khān. At first, they tried to trick the Guru into their trap or slay him through an emissary of peace, but he went back humbled and crest-fallen as none of his trickeries yielded any result. The battle was now joined at Kartārpur. It is said, on the eve of the battle, Dhirmal sent a secret letter to Paindē Khān pledging his support to him.

But the Guru's son, Teg Bahādur (so called because of his skill in swordsmanship) wielded his sword with great skill, as did Bābā Gurdittā. Many warriors of renown fell on the bettlefield and the remaining Moghal generals taunted Paindē Khān to exhibit his prowess of which he was so proud and boastful. There was no choice for him now but to advance and he shouted arrogantly at the Guru, his former benefactor and Master, "Come out of thy hiding, O Guru. Why do you cause innocent blood to be spilled ? Either surrender, or I take you to the emperor to forgive you your many wrongs, or face the challenge of my never-failing sword which is thirsting for revenge." The Guru leapt out of his ranks and coolly advancing towards Paindē Khān said, "I am here before you. I have built you up, an orphan, into a warrior of rank, like my own child. Now, you strike first so that you have no regrets later on". Paindē Khān struck twice first at the Guru's leg, but only to cut the stirrup. The next stroke he received on his shield. Paindē Khān now tried to catch hold of the Guru's bridle, but the Guru gave him a kick so staggering that he could assemble himself only after some time. He made another attempt, but this time his falchion split from the handle and fell to the ground. The Guru alighted from the horse and said, "I will not take advantage of your adversity. Come, Let's fight in single combat." Painde Khān again tried his luck with his sword, mocking all the time at the Guru, "If you have the power, why don't you take your chance" ? The Guru replied, "Because I'm still hesitating to take a life that I have loved, but lest you deem it my cowardice, here goes." And saying this, with a single flash of his double-edged scimitar, cleaved his body into two.

Seeing his body roll in dust, the Guru was so much filled with compassion that he put his shield on the fallen warrior's face in order to shade his face from the scorching sun, and clasping him to his bosom, wept, as one crics over a dead child and prayed that God grant him forgiveness and a place in the heaven.

Bābā Gurditta's arrows pierced the head of another general, Asmān Khān. Seeing him dead, the Bābā also wept bitterly and when the Guru asked him why, he replied, "We were both playmates. He tried to kill me but failed, and I succeeded, but what a success ! Here lies a man, an old friend, dead at my hands never to rise again. Such is the result of bearing arms. Here I surrender them to you. Let me go home and die in peace." Thus saying, he is said to have retired from the field of battle, being convinced that the Guru's victory was assured now, anyhow.

The Moghal forces were completely demoralised over the death of two of their most competent generals. But retreat in such a situation was also impossible as they had no face to show to the King-emperor. So they made one more desperate attempt. In this fight the other two valiant generals, Qutab Khān and Kālē Khān, the commander-in-chief, tasted death at the hands of the Guru in single combats, one after the other. It is said when Kālē Khān failed in his many attempts at the Guru's body, the latter flashed his double-edged scimitar with such dexterity, that it severed the head of his adversary in one go, the Guru shouting, "Not this way, but this." Says Mohsin Fāni of this incident that the Guru "had killed his enemy not out of hostility, but being a Guru (or Teacher), was merely instructing him in sword-play."*

Hardly about a thousand of the Moghal troops remained to flee the battlefield. The Guru also lost seven hundred of his choice warriors, but the battle ended in his total victory on 24th day of Hār, Samvat 1691 (1634 A.D.).

The Guru now proceeded to Kiratpur near where an old Muslim devotee, Budhan Shāh, was waiting anxiously to receive him at his death-bed. It is a fascinating fact of the Guru's life that neither the fatigue of battle nor the joy of victory withheld him from attending to the welfare of his meanest devotees. But, while every one accompanied the Guru, not so Dhirmal and his mother who, ashamed of their collaboration with the Moghals, chose to remain behind and even kept with them a large property of the Guru's, including the original copy of the Granth Shahib, refusing to part with it even for a while for Bhāi Bindhi Chand to complete his copy which he had brought to more than half the original.

Reaching Budhan's abode, the Guru blessed him and was with him till he breathed his last. Later, he arrived in Kiratpur. From here, he sent out Bidhi Chand to Bengāl on the pressing requests from his devotees that they wanted to see him. As the Guru had much work to attend to at Kiratpur, he sent Bidhi Chand instead. Such was the devotion the Guru evoked from his Sikhs that, according to Mohsin Fāni, when he commissioned a follower, called

* *Dabistān* II, Pp. 279.80.

Bāsava, to go from Balkh to Iraq to buy horses, he proceeded there immediately even though his son was on his death-bed and died on his return. But so full of humility and communal spirit was he that when asked whom are the Sikhs to recognise as Guru if the Guru was far away, he replied, "Any Sikh who comes to you with the name of the Guru on his lips." Fantastic stories are given by Mohsin Fāni as to how far one Sikh would go to serve another in the name of the Guru and how they would help and pray for the success of the less fortunate in the community. "The Guru himself also does the same."

Fāni further comments, "The Guru believes in one God. His followers put not their faith in idol-worship. They never pray or practise austerities like the Hindus. They believe not in their incarnations, or places of pilgrimage nor the Sanskrit language which the Hindus deem to be the language of the gods. They believe that all the Gurus are the same as Nānak. The Sikhs are not restricted in the matter of eating or drinking. A learned Hindu, Partāp Mal, told a Hindu youth who felt caste restrictions irksome and consequently desired to embrace Islām, 'why not turn a Sikh and eat and drink as you will !' The Sikhs under all the Gurus have increased so much that even in the days of Guru Arjun, one or more representatives of Sikh religion could be found in every Indian city. To such an extent was caste disregarded that the Brahmins became the disciples of the Sikh Khatris, for none of the Gurus was a Brahmin. And Khatris paid homage to the Jat masands who were a low section of the Vaishas. Guru Hargobind, (also) gained a large following at Kiratpur. He kept 900 horses in his stables and always entertained three hundred horsemen and sixty gunners (artillery men)."

The Guru was extremely fond of humour. It is said, he brought up an orphan, called Suthrā, whom he gave all liberties to crack jokes with him. Once, the Sikhs complained to the Guru that while a devotee was reciting the first verse of the evening prayer — *Rahirās* — which said, "O God, sing to thee the Mohinis, the agels, the heavens, the underworlds," Suthrā butted in, at the end of every line with a caustic remark saying, "So what ?" The Guru asked for Suthrā's explanation. He replied, "O Master, every one recounts the good deeds of others. So I said to the devotee, 'What is it to you if others sing God's praise, you yourself also should'." Similarly, according to Mohsin Fāni, when a Brahmin, called Deva, expounded the doctrine of Vedanta to him, the Guru, pointing to an ass, said, "When all is Brahm (God), what is he ?" The Brahmin replied, "You are God and you are the too."* The Guru had a hearty laugh at this.

Bābā Gurdittā, who, as we have seen, had preceded the Guru to Kiratpur with his family, died here at the age of twentyfour, having taken to heart, it is said, the reproach of the Guru, like Atal Rāi, before him, for having shown a miracle and re-animating the dead cow of a farmer friend. The Guru sent for his son, Dhirmal, and asked him also to bring along with him the copy of the Granth Sahib so that it may be read on the solemn occasion of his father's demise. He was also told to receive the customary turban on this occasion and other property of his father lying at Kiratpur. But, knowing that his was not an honourable name in the Sikh fraternity and that he might be deprived of a valuable possession, like the original copy of the Granth Sahib, (on which he thought he would build his own *gaddi*), he refused to go. His younger grandson, Hari Rai, the Guru loved with all his heart and initiated him to all instruction, spiritual as well as secular, to fit him for the high office of Guruship which his grandfather wanted to transfer to him. For, Teg Bahadur, his son, had retired into solitude, and Ani Rai and Suraj Mal were too worldly, even though of great religious disposition.

Not only was Hari Rai being well-trained in the use of arms and other secular duties, but he was spiritually most awakened. So sensitive he became to pain that when once passing through a garden on a wintry day, the loose flaps of his long garments struck a flower off its stem, so full of remorse was he that he kept the fold of his gown tucked in his arms ever thereafter. When his grandfather heard about it, he remarked, "It behoves God's servants to be tender to all things." The Guru passed the last ten years of life in prayer and meditation at Kiratpur.

In March, 1644, Hari Rai was consecrated as Guru, seventh in succession to Guru Nānak, on the eve of the Guru's demise, at the age of fourteen years. The Guru put five paisas and a coconut before him, circumbulated him four times, bowed to him and after Bhāi Buddhā's son, Bhānā, had anointed his forehead with a saffron-mark, he was declared to be the Guru. Everyone assembled on the occasion now bowed to him and made their offerings.

On Chet Sudi 5, Samvat 1701 (1644 A. D.), Guru Hargobind breathed his last. Such was the devotion he had evoked among his

---

* *Dabistān*, II, Pp. 279-80.

followers that according to Mohsin Fāni, an eye-witness, two of them Rajārām, a Rajput, and a Jāt servant of his son-in-law, jumped into his funeral pyre and placing their faces on his feet, consigned themselves to the flames along with him. "Many others wanted to follow suit, but the new Guru forbade it."

CHAPTER XI

GURU HARI RĀI

(1631—1661 A. D.)

Born in Kiratpur in the house of Bābā Gurdittā, the eldest son of Guru Hargobind, Guru Hari Rāi, as we have seen, came to occupy the throne of Nānak at the age of fourteen. Like his grand-father, he too kept a cavalry of 2200 horse in his employ and went out hunting. But so compassionate was he that he would capture but never kill a bird and would feed and keep them in the zoo. He was particularly fond of deer and kept a large number of them. He also saw to it that he never employed his retinue in warfare against the Moghals or any other element hostile to him. It is also said that when Dārā Shikoh, eldest son of Shāh Jahān, who, like Akbar, was the most beloved both of his father and the people at large fell seriously ill, as his cunning younger, Aurangzeb, had administered to him tiger's whiskers in a dainty dish, and no remedy could be found for his recovery, the Guru, hearing about it, sent him a herbal medicine which cured him completely. He would pass by the hutments of the poor and accept their food and eat it in their company to their utmost pleasure.

Morning and evening, he would listen to the devotional music in the company of his followers and then discourse on the Guru's Word. However, he would miss no opportunity to inculcate in his disciples the noble sentiments of humility and disinterested service without which, he said, mere knowledge of the Divine or belief were of little avail. Once he chanced upon a serpent in a forest whose skin sparkled in the warm sunshine of winter. Pointing to it, the Guru said, "This serpent might as well have been a pandit in his previous life —

beautiful to behold in his dress, but the only knowledge he has is, to bite. Men also bite others through jealousy; even when they teach about God it is not through love or self-surrender, but through the sharp wits and the poisonous fangs of controversy and argument."

And so attached was he to his loving devotees that when once he would not be awakened out of his trance for hours and the Sikhs became anxious for his life, he explained as he opened his eyes : "A devout Sikh of mine, Gondā by name, is meditating upon me at Kābul and much as I would like to shake myself off his sight, he would cling tenciously to my feet. I had, therefore, no choice but to remain seated, unmoved and absorbed in his thought."

Once he asked some of his Sikhs who had boasted to him that they never turned away hungry from their doors anyone who came to them at the meal time, and even dusted their shoes and washed their feet, the Guru said, "This is not enough. Anyone may come to you at any time and should go back satisfied. But do service in such a way that the poor guest may not feel he is partaking of some charity but as if he had come to the Guru's house which belonged to all in equal measure. He who has more should consider it as God's trust and share it in the same spirit. Man is only an instrument of service : the giver of goods is God, the Guru of us all." The Guru concluded, "The temple and the mosque may be repaired or rebuilt, but not a broken heart."

And the Guru himself acted on this precept. Once in 1650 A.D., when on a visit to the Mālwā territory of Panjāb, two brothers, Kālā and Karam Chand of the Mahrāj clan, representated to him at a place near Naṭhānā (lit. placeless) that the people of the Kaura tribe would not let them settle in their midst, the Guru personally interceded in their behalf with the head of the tribe, Chaudhry Jait Pirānā, but the latter remained adamant and would not even give the poor of the other caste even five ploughs of land for their bare sustenance. The Guru asked Kālā and Karam Chand to leave the place next morning with him and take possession of the land wherever night overtook them. This they did but their adversaries came soon upon them with all their fury and might to drive them out. The Guru advised them to offer resistance and seeing their hopelessness in a struggle with their superiors, decided to throw in all his strength on their side, and Jait Pirānā was killed in the engagement, thus leading to the establishment of an estate for the dispossessed. Later again, when they complained that no one in the surrounding areas would intermarry with them, the Guru instructed all his followers who came to visit him here to shed their tribal prejudices and form alliances in marriage with the Mahrāj people.

The Guru stayed on this settlement for some time. Once when Kālā brought to the Guru his two nephews, Sandali and Phul, sons of Rupchand, Phul, it is said, put his hand on his belly. The Guru asked Kālā why he did so. Kālā replied, "Master, the young ones are hungry." The Guru is said to have prophecied, "I have banished their hunger as of all the poor of my land.* They who shall fight not only for themselves but for all the others taking everyone to belong to the same one God, irrespective of caste or creed, shall prosper. For such is the will of God and those who shall oppose this eternal will shall perish."

On his way back to Kiratpur, the Guru's wives@who were some distance behind, were waylaid by an officer of the Moghal army who was marching at the head of a column from Lahore to Delhi. It is said, his grandfather, Mukhils Khān, had been killed in a battle with Guru Hargobind and he thought it to be a fit occasion for revenge. But, the Sikhs fell upon the Moghal forces like lightening and scattered them. One of the persons who led the assault on Guru's behalf was Gaura, a powerful zamindār, who had, out of pique, killed a Sikh bodyguard of the Guru's once, and was all the time thereafter lurking around his camp,pleading for forgiveness. He fought, along with his men with such exemplary courage that the Guru again brought him into his fold.

---

* The erstwhile rulers of the Phulkian States –Patiālā, Nābha and Jind - trace their origin to Tilokā, eldest son of Phul. At one time, they played a notable part in the Sikh fight against the Moghals, but later became their vassals (and sometime after, of the British), and falling a prey to luxury, intrigue and jealously, they lost the iufluence they had in the community thus also fulfilling the Guru's prophesy.

It is said, when Kālā returned home, his wife felt jealous of the Guru's blessing bestowed on the nephews of her husband, and compelled him next morning to take his own sons along, which the man dutifully did. His sons too enacted the same part as Phul had done the day before, but not with the same results. The Guru is said to have blessed them only with a small jāgir, called Bāhia, on which till lately they paid no land-revenue. The Guru obviously saw that the parents of the children were alive and had an estate, and that Kālā had only been goaded by his wife's jealousy and greed to ask for more.

@The Guru was married twice. From one, Kotkalyāni, was born Rām Rāi & from the other, Krishana Kaur, was born Hari Krishan.

In the meantime, Shāh Jahān fell seriously ill and Aurangzeb, his second son, by aligning himself with his younger brother, Murād, marched on Dārā Shikoh, his eldest brother and defeated him. He imprisoned his father at Agra along with Murād who had earlier assisted him in his struggle for the throne of India, and pursued Dārā Shikoh who was by this time fleeing to the Panjāb with depleted forces. Dārā, as has been pointed out earlier, was known to be a great liberal like his great grand-father, Akbar, and was much beloved of the people. According to a legend, already quoted, the Guru had him recovered from a serious illness before. And in his utter distress when he called on the Guru on the right bank of the Beas, the Guru arrayed his entire, though modest, force; to halt the march of the pursuing troops till Dārā had fled to safety, though, it appears, there was no occasion for the Guru's forces to clash with the Moghals.* Unfortunately, Dārā was captured after a while and put to death. That in accordance with the tradition of his House, the Guru offered this help to Dārā Shikoh inspite of his otherwise pacifist role in life is 'because Dārā was the beloved of all the communities in India.' It is said by his critics that "he was violent of temper and arrogant of manner". But in the same breath it is confirmed that "he was deeply imbued with pantheistic mysticism of the Sufis. He associated gladly with Hindu philosophers and went so far as to take part in producing a Persian version of some of Upanishads which he declared to be a revelation earlier than the Qurān".

The news, however, reached Aurangzeb, who now declared himself emperor, that the Guru had blessed and assisted the escape of Dārā. So, he was summoned to Delhi. The Guru did not go himself but sent his son, Rām Rāi, instead. It appears, Rām Rāi, with his courtly manners and high intellectual and spiritual attainments was able to satisfy the emperor of the essentially peaceful and all-embracing nature of the new faith, and was accorded much honour by the Court. But, once in his sycophancy, he went so far as to misinterpret a verse of Guru Nānak which said, "God alone knows who burns in hell (the Hindu or the Muslim), for (like the Hindus whom fire consumes here), the earth of the Muslim graves also suffers being fired by the potter who fashions bricks and vessels out of its clay." (Āsā Vār M. 1). Rām Rāi, when asked to explain why the Muslim religion had been reviled thus in the Granth of the Sikhs, he replied, "The words of Guru Nānak are misquoted by his detractors. The

* The Guru is said to have kept a force only of 2200 horse for self-defence.

original word refers not to the 'Musalmān' but to 'Baimān' (the faithless)".

Though Aurangzeb and his *ulemā* were satisfied, the Guru on hearing the reports from the Sikhs of Delhi, was much upset. He said, "Rām Rāi was a genuine claimant for my throne. But the Guruship is like the milk of a tigress which can be contained only in a cup of gold. Now, Rām Rāi shall never see my face again."

And so it happened. Rām Rāi never met his father again in the latter's life-time and with his new-found affluence and friendship with the emperor, he left for Dera Doon to found his own *gaddi*.@

The Guru breathed his last on the ninth day of the dark half of Kārtik, Samvat 1718 (1661 A. D.), bequeathing his throne to his six-year old son, Hari Krishan.

@ The *gaddi* continues upto this day, worshipped by a large number of Hindus. The present holder of the office is Mahant Sri Charan Dās. The followers of Rām Rāi are called Rām Raias. Guru Gobind Singh, as we shall see later in this book, reconciled them to his house by helping the widow of Rām Rāi at a time of acute difficulty for her.

GURU HARI KRISHAN

(1656—1664 A.D.)

We have seen how the seventh Guru, Hari Rāi, disinheriting his elder son, Rām Rāi, appointed his six-year old child, Hari Krishan, the Guru in succession to himself. Like the founder of their house, Guru Nānak, Hari Krishan also was absorbed in meditation from early childhood and was treated by the Sikhs with great affection and esteem. But, his elder brother learning of his father's decision to disinherit him lodged a complaint with the King-emperor, who had by now, it is said, become his great admirer and friend.

Aurangzeb, cunning that he was, saw in this a golden opportunity to destroy both, by first summoning the child Guru to Delhi, and then doing nothing about it, and thus prolonging the family feud to mutual recrimination through the King's balancing tricks and eventual exhaustion and destruction of both. This he did through Rājā Jai Singh of Amber (Jaipur), a great Rajput general in the imperial army, who was asked to conduct the Guru to Delhi with all the courtesies due to his station. At first, the Guru's mother and his masands were much perturbed over these sudden and uncalled-for summons, for they suspected that Rām Rāi's close association with the King and the latter's notorious cruelties heaped upon his own father and brothers and conspicuous partiality to Islām must bring certain harm to the Guru, but Rājā Jai Singh seems to have convinced everyone that no evil was intended and that the emperor, in view of the petition preferred against the Guru, wanted to hear the other side so that no miscarriage of justice took place. He pleaded that it was in the Guru's own interest to place his case before the emperor if not personally, then, through his trusted followers. Rājā Jai Singh also promised to keep the Guru as his own guest in Delhi and to stand surety for his safety.

The Guru came to Delhi with his mother and masands. He was kept in the bungalow of Rājā Jai Singh as a royal guest and from that day the hallowed spot is called Banglā-Sāhib where a beautiful Gurdwārā now stands to his sacred memory. Large crowds of people came to pay him homage, both on the way to Delhi and in the imperial capital itself. This not only frustrated the hopes of Rām Rāi, but also assured the emperor that the Sikhs by and large were satisfied with the present succession. The emperor must have thought that it would not be before a decade that the Guru would attain his majority and till then at least the Sikhs would leave him in peace. To intervene in a family feud which would bring no benefit to the state and might alienate a militant section of his subjects and create religious unrest during the early part of his regime, would be highly impolitic. On the other hand, if he took no notice of the plaint, the Sikhs would feel gratified and beholden to him. And so, after hearing both parties, the Guru being represented through Rājā Jai Singh and some well-known masands, the emperor announced that he would not intervene in a family dispute of a religious nature—a very unusual decision for him to take! This, however, gave joy to the hearts of the Guru's followers.

It is said, by now the repute of the Guru had spread so widely that the Brahmins grew jealous of it and taunted the Sikhs, "Your Guru is called Hari Krishna, a mere child of eight years! Krishna, the incarnation of Vishnu, uttered the Gita which is the repository of all the eternal truths, If your Guru also calls himself Krishna, let him expound the truths of Gita to us". It is said, a seemingly innocent-looking Sikh and a poor grass-cutter by profession stood up in the assembly and said, "Let alone the Guru, even I could expound the truths of the Gita if only the Guru were to favour me with his Grace." The Guru, thereupon, it is said, touched him with his cane as a token of his benediction and the Sikh dilated upon the truths of Gita so well that it humbled the pride of the learned pandits.* Which shows that no matter what his station, the Gurus had made inter-religious instruction a part of every Sikh's curriculum

---

* According to *Gur-Tirath Sangreha,* by Pt. Tārā Singh Narotam, the incident occurred at Parigkhara, near Ambālā, while the Guru was on his way to Delhi.

so that they understood the truths of their own religion better and accepted them with a whole mind and heart.

Unfortunately, the Guru contracted small-pox here and merged in the infinite at the age of nearly eight years, on the 14 th day of the light half of Chetra, Samvat 1721 (1664 A.D.). His young body was cremated at Tilokhari, in the South of Delhi, on the bank of the Yamuna.

Before, however, the Guru breathed his last, he pointed to his followers that the next Guru (Bābā) would be found at Bakālā.

CHAPTER XII

GURU TEGH BAHĀDUR

(1622—1675 A.D.)

Guru Tegh Bahādur was the youngest son of the sixth Guru, Hargobind, and his wife Nānaki. Born in Amritsar, he was a trained rider and a marksman, and for showing great feats of swordsmanship in the battles that his father fought, he was known as Tegh Bahādur (Hero of the Sword). But, early in his youth and especially after his father's settlement at Kiratpur, he seems to have accepted voluntarily a life of retirement and contemplation. His verses included in the Ādi-Granth bear ample testimony to his contempt for earthly joys and riches and even active involvement with the secular world. That is how he was passed over earlier by his father and the succession fell upon his nephew. It is in this context that he was even earlier known as Tyāg Mal (the Master of Renunciation).

But now that Guru Hari Krishan had pointed out before his demise that the Bābā (Guru) would be found at Bakālā, the Sikhs repaired to this resort in large numbers. Seeing a vast opportunity to delude the masses and attain riches and glory, it is said, a few other claimants to the throne also set up their gaddis at this place, each with his agents (or Masands) to attract the unwary devotees to his own master. Confusion prevailed for a while till a Sikh merchant, Makhan Shāh, on putting each to the test, is said to have found the True Guru in Tegh Bahādur—a decision which many other devout Sikhs also participated in and hailed. This thus seems to have been an election by consensus—the first-ever in Sikh history in the case of a Guru. Some eye-witness accounts however discount this theory.*

The ascension to the gaddi by Guru Teg Bahādur perturbed Dhirmal, his nephew, so much that he decided to make a murderous assault on him and rob his property. A Masand of his, Sihān by name, aimed with a gun at the Guru one night and though it wounded him, the shot did not prove fatal. The Guru's movable property was [illegible] kept serene and calm at this tragedy. When the Sikhs came to know of it in the morning, in spite of the Guru's protests, they broke open the door of Dhir Mal, took possession of all the looted property, and binding Sihān hand and foot presented him to the Guru. The Sikhs also looted the original copy of the Granth Sāhib, a possession which Dhir Mal always utilised for extorting presents from the devout and proclaiming that it was indeed he who being the custodian of the original Granth deserved to be worshipped as Guru.

Sihān pleaded to the Guru most humbly for a pardon. Seeing his distress, the Guru ordered his release and forgave him his sins. "The Guru must be compassionate, like the mother, in all circumstances" he said. He also asked the Sikhs to return the copy of the Granth Sāhib to Dhir Mal. "I will want my Sikhs to inscribe the instructions of the Granth Sahib in their minds and souls and not permit them to believe a particular copy of the Granth or any other symbol or totem or sacred spot as conferring any special privilege on its custodians. For, once religious institutions are exploited as

---

* The Sikh chroniclers, as usual, cite a miracle which settled the issue. Makhan Shāh fearing a shipwreck of his merchandise on the high seas, vowed to offer five hundred gold mohurs to the "True Guru" if his goods reached home in safety. On his wish being fulfilled he came to Bakālā, but finding 22 claimants to his gift, he placed only one gold mohur before each saying to himself, "the True Guru will himself ask for the whole sum," which only Tegh Bahadur did. At this, Makhan Shāh proclaimed with the beat of drum : "I've found the Guru, found the Guru "(*Gur Lādho re, Gur Lādho re*)." Bhāi Vir Singh, the Sikh savant of the twentieth century, is of the opinion, however, that the number of claimants to Guruship could not have been 22, but two only, namely Dhir Mal and Rām Rāi. (GSG, annotated by Vir Singh.) However according to *Bhatt Vahi of Tomar-Bijloton*, Makhan Shāh met the Guru about 2 months later than his assumption of the *gaddi*. It is said the Guru asked his being called "Deg Bahādur" (the Master of Bounties or the Supporter of the poor instead of Teg Bahādur (Master of the sword). (See Mohd Latif. History of the Panjāb, P. 259). But this appellation does not seem to have got currency, even though the suggestion shows (as is clear from his edicts or Hukamnāmās) that he got completely over his earlier mood of renunciation & took interest in the affairs of the household as well as the secular needs of his congregations. Most Persian records written about a hundred years after his demise repeat the story of Makhan Shāh Lobānā. See Umdat-ul-Tawārikh (Sohanlāl). Khālsā nāmā (Bakhat Mal), Ibrat Nāmā (Ali-ud-Din) etc.

property, the soul of religion will vanish." The Sikhs had no choice but to return this precious possession to its owner.

How farsighted the Guru was in this injunction was proved once again when he went to visit the Hari Mandir at Amritsar. He bathed in the tank, but when he tried to enter the temple, its doors were closed upon him by the Sodhi custodian (Harji, grandson of Prithiā and son of Sodhi Mehervān) and he came out, in disgust, to rest at another spot outside, now called Damdamā Sāhib. The Guru at this time said to his much-chagrined followers: "This is what comes of treating the soul as a commodity and exploiting the holy places as a means of one's economic advancement. Such men and communities perish by the roots."*

Though after a while, the Guru returned to Bakālā, he decided to move to Kiratpur. Once again, the Sikhs flouted the injunction of the Guru, and it is said looted the copy of the Granth Sāhib from Dhir Mal's household, this time with the blessings of the Guru's mother. But, when the Guru heard about it, it is said, he ordered that the book be thrown into the river, Beas, which he was crossing at that time. "It is a bone of contention, a raging fire which is consuming us all. Why can't we get rid of it?" The Sikhs did so with a heavy heart. Dhir Mal, who was following on the Guru's track, got it soon thereafter out of the shallow river-bed and returned back home satisfied with the recovery of his precious treasure.†

As was the tradition of the Guru's house, he too instead of settling down at Kiratpur, founded a new city, called chak Nānaki (later Ānandpur) in the year 1665 A.D., on the site of an old dilipidated village called Mākhowāl, in the former state of Kahlur (Bilāspur) by purchase of land from the Rājā.‡ After a while, in the same year,

* The present-day litigations, intrigues, mutual jealousies and black-mail, electoral manipulations, and even violence over the possession of the Sikh Gurdwaras (which have vast incomes to corrupt the custodians with money and power of religious institutions) and politics based on a religious platform are the result of the present-day Sikhs having forgotten the instructions of their Guru in this behalf. It is sad to note that while every attempt, noble and ignoble, is made to ensure one's control over a Gurdwara with property and income, very few persons are coming forward to manage the lesser-endowed shrines which are falling into ruins.

† This copy is now in the possession of the Sodhis of Kartārpur, who claim to be the descendants of Dhir Mal.

‡ According to *Guru Kiān Sākhiān*, Rāni Champā Devi gifted three villages to the Guru to establish the new township. (Sākhi 22).

he left on his missionary tours, accompanied by his mother and wife and an entourage of devout disciples. After traversing the south-eastern tract of Panjāb, he visited the Bāgar territory, now comprising the State of Haryānā. Finding scarcity of water, he got wells dug up everywhere he halted, preached to the people the lessons of hard, honest work, coupled with charity, weaning them away from the scourge of tobacco and other intoxicants, healing the sick and converting those committed to crime and sin to a cleaner and more wholesome way of life. It is certainly a fact to marvel at how a former warrior turned a recluse now again participated in secular life with such zeal and dedication. No wonder, he created a stir wherever he went and gathered a large following. It is said, he also hunted on the way.

During this tour, he visited Kurekshetra, Āgrā, Ittāwa and Priyāg (modern Allāhābād), where he stayed for six months preaching his gospel. Wherever he went, he distributed all the offerings he received form the devout among the poor and the holy and fed the hungry from his never-failing community-kitchen. At Priyāg, his wife, Gujri, conceived a child. From here, he went to Banāras where his shoes and coat are still preserved in the Gurdwārā Bari Sangat later built in his memory. As he proceeded further, he came to a river called Karam-nāsh (destroyer of good deeds) which the Hindus considered inauspicious to bathe in, due to a Pauranic superstition. The Guru had a hearty bath here saying in the words of Guru Amar Dās, "Omens, good and bad, affect only those who cherish not God in their heart."

From here, he proceeded to Gayā and from thence to Patnā, preaching the Gospel of Nānak all through, and ridding the people of their caste-consciousness, sectarianism, cupidity of the Brāhmins and manifold superstitions of the common mass. Though he was pressed hard by the custodians of various temples to make offerings or suffer penances and perform other rituals and ceremonies for the repose of his own soul or that of his ancestors in the other world, the Guru refused to pander to their beliefs, and said, "He who trusts in God and makes an honest living to share with others and injures no one, nor harbours ill-will against another need perform no other rituals. His soul ever stays in health. And, as for the ancestors, they gather the reward of what they themselves have sown and no one can bless or curse them after they are gone,"

Staying at Patnā, for some time, the Guru set out on a tour of Kāmrup (Assam) via Dācca, where the local Sangats were eagerly waiting to have him in their midst. These were the spots hallowed by Guru Nānak and no other Guru after him had visited the north-eastern part of India.* He left his family at Patnā to the care of his brother-in-law, Kirpāl.

At Dācca, he was received most warmly by a very pious and devoted Masand, Bulāki, along with the local devotees, which included Bulāki's mother who had vowed that if the Guru visited them, "she would seat him on a beautiful couch she had prepared and dress him with the cloth she had spun herself and treat him to a meal cooked with her own hands". It is said, she also had a picture painted of him to be hung in her room.

The Guru now reached Kāmrup and preached to the people for about 2 years the gospel of his house at various places. Here, he also brought about a compromise between the forces of Rājā Rām Singh, a Rājput general of Aurangzeb, (who had led an expedition against Assam), and the local King to the satisfaction of both in 1670. He had met the Rāja, a year earlier (Feb. 1669) at Rangmati in Assām.

* These sangats or congregations were established right from the days of Guru Nānak who travelled widely, from Kathiawār to Assam & Kashmir to Ceylon. Outside India too, Kābul always had a sizeable *sangat*. These were increased in the days of the succeeding Gurus & most of them put in charge of the *Masands* (or deputies) both to collect the offerings for the Guru & to minister to the day-to-day spiritual needs of the devotees. However, the eastern parts were visited personally after Guru Nānak only by Guru Tegh Bahādur after a century and a half. In the days of the 6th Guru, sangats had been firmly established at Ālamganj, Binā, Mongher, Ujjain, Bruhānpur, Gujrāt, Lucknow, Patna, Agra, Prayag, Jaunpur, Raj Mahal & Dācca.

† The Sikh chroniclers suggest that the Guru came to Assam along with Rājā Rām Singh. One of his *Hukamnamahs* also suggests that he was following the camp of a Rājāji (Hukamnama, 16). Knowing the sad fate of ealier expeditions, particularly of Mir Jumlā, it is said, Rām Singh pleaded with the Guru at Patnā to go along with him so that the magic charms of the Assamese have no effect on him ! It is said, however, that the Guru brought about a compromise between the two parties, dividing the land of Kāmrup into two portions, one for the local King and the other for the emperor of Delhi. But the expedition of Rājā Rām Singh was undertaken in 1668, while according to the Sikh chroniclers, the Guru got the news of his son's birth either at Dācca or in Assam. The birth of his son took place in December 1666 A.D. Unless the Guru visited Assam after the birth of his son, Gobind Dās (Rāi), (which is not supported by most Sikh records), he was already in Assam when the expedition took place and participated in bringing about a com-

At Dhubri, where Guru Nānak had stayed, he asked the soldiers on both sides to build a huge mound in memory of the first Guru's visit. Every soldier contributed a shieldful of earth till the mound was raised to an imposing height. The Guru also had a pavilion erected on the top. By his peaceful ways, he brought many people into his fold and some of his entourage also were left behind whose lineage still inhabit these parts of Assam and are highly respected by their local compatriots for their industry, integrity and charity of heart, besides chivalry which they have exhibited on many an occasion in defence of their acquired homeland.

Though the fact of the Guru having accompanied the expedition of Rājā Rām Singh may be dismissed (in spite of the best relations of the family with the Guru's house) both as unhistorical and also being not in keeping with the Guru's spiritual temper, besides Aurangzeb's own tyrannous and bigoted ways with which the Guru was all-too-familiar by now, the Guru seems to have been deeply impressed by the affection and esteem so overwhelmingly shown him by the people of East Bengāl and Assam, and helped them overcome their predicament. Not unnaturally, therefore, he called Bengāl "the home of Sikhism".

It appears, either the Guru heard the news of his son's birth on December 22, 1666 A.D. at Patnā, during his eastern tours which must have begun in the middle of that year and continued for three years or more, or he began his tour only after the birth of his son, which seems less likely.* But, he must have been touring Assam (besides Eastern Bengāl) for quite some time and made a considerable impact on the people there, so that when Assam was attacked so powerfully and with internal dissensions raging in his kingdom, the

---

F. N. Contd.

promise, as a true Saint should have done. According to *Bhatt Vahi Talaoda, Pargna Jind*, the Guru was interned twice at Delhi for brief periods of one to two months, first on Nov. 8, 1665 A.D. & then on April 7, 1670 A.D. & on both occasions, it was the Jaipur ruler, Mirza Rājā Jai Singh, who interceded on the Guru's behalf & that it was during his second eastern tour that he accompanied the Rājā ji (i.e Rājā Rām Singh, his son) to Assam.

* According to *Bhatt Vahi Poorbi Dakhni*, the Guru went out on his first tour to the east on June 9, 1656 & that his only son, Govind Dās, was born at Patna on 18 Dec., 1661 A.D. about three years before he ascended the *gaddi*. This however is not supported by other records.

Ahom King sought the Guru's intervention for a peaceful settlement honourable to both sides.†

After his return to Patnā sometime in 1669-70, where he seems to have stayed for one to three years, he took care to arrange for the instruction of his young son not only in the Sikh religious lore, but also in Persian and Sanskrit, and in the manly sports like riding, hunting and swordsmanship, as Guru Gobind Singh himself testifies in his Bachittar Nātak.

Some time between 1671 to 1673, the Guru returned to Ānandpur in the Panjāb, preaching on his way back, the gospel of the Gurus and bringing large persecuted Hindu masses into his fold and even influencing considerably the Muslim popular opinion in his favour.*

---

† In November 1661, an extremely vicious attack was launched against Assām by Mir Jumlā, the Moghal Governor of Bengāl but due to incessant rains, epidemics and exhaustion of supplies, a treaty was signed with the Ahom King in December through the mediation of Dilir Khān, according to which the Rājā agreed to pay, 1,20,000 *tolās* of silver, 2000 *tolās* of gold and 50 elephants and offered ***an ugly daughter*** to the emperor and fifteen elephants and another daughter with cash and goods to the Khān-Khānān. Of the conquered places, a few forts and towns in cultivated districts near the frontier of Bengāl were to be attached to the imperial dominions. "But at the close of the next four years (1666), the Moghals had lost much (of their gains). Gauhāti fell in 1667. But then the Ahoms fell on evil days, Kāmrup having become a prey to civil war. During the eleven years, 1670-81, seven kings sat on its throne and only one of them died a natural death." The Moghals naturally profitted by this situation and the expedition of Rājā Rām Singh in 1668 and the mediation sought by both sides of a holy man trusted by both in such circumstances would seem quite probable and likely. This is further corroborated by the fact that after the escape of Shivaji from his custody, Rām Singh was in disgrace at the imperial court for two years prior to this expedition, his son was kept a hostage at the court (and later killed by making him wrestle with a tiger when his father was still in Assam) and this expedition was entrusted to humiliate or get rid of him than to let him succeed in his mission and be honoured. Rām Singh, therefore, was in desperation to succeed, no matter how.

* Basing their information on *Padshāh Burānji*, the well-known modern Sikh historian, Gandā Singh also states that the Guru's activities of even earlier days (1664-65) had created such a stir that he was hauled up before the emperor and on the surety of Rājā Rām Singh, son of Mirzā Rājā Jai Singh, the trouble came to an end. (A Short History of the Sikhs, Part I, P. 53). Malcolm & Forster attribute this arrest to the machinations of Rām Rāi. But, it is hardly feasible that during the very first year of his Guruship (1665 A.D.), when the Guru was busy building the township of Ānandpur, he became a suspect and was put

He continued to do so at Ānandpur which people from far and near visited to pay him homage.

By now, the religious persecution of the Hindus at the hands of Aurangzeb was in full swing. He ascended the throne in mid-1658, though the formal accession took place a year later. All historians are agreed that one of the major causes of his success in the war of succession over his brothers was "due to his avowed solicitude for Sunni (orthodox) interests". His father, Shāh Jahān, was equally confirmed in orthodoxy and even early in his reign, "had ordered the demolition of 76 new Hindu temples in the district of Banaras alone" and "the wonderful temple of Orchhe was razed to the ground". "Hindus were forbidden to dress in the Muslim style." "The women of Bir Singh Budhela were treated in a manner which shocks our sense of decorum." "He hated the Christians and waged war against them." "To the Shias,he was equally hostile and his wars against them were undertaken not merely for conquest,but for the extripation of heresy and the triumph of the true doctrine." He abolished mixed marriages and ordered "that no Muslim girl should remain in the house of a Hindu unless he embraces Islam". The Hindus of the Panjāb were severely punished for marrying Muslim women who were snatched away from them and made over to the Muslims. A Hindu who was believed to have insulted the holy book " was put to death. About seven mosques were redeemed and three temples turned into mosques."* But, let it be said to his credit that compared to Aurangzeb, Shāh Jahān was an emperor of great nobility and sensitiveness, otherwise he would not have sponsored and supported even in the face of his failure and weakness, Dārā Shikoh, a liberal Sufi, as his heir-apparent, and spurned and humiliated Aurangzeb time and again. And, as Lane-Poole remarks, "Shāh Jahān was too prudent a king to let religion override statesmanship" and patronised many

F N. Contd.

under arrest. Later that year, he set out on his tour of the pilgrim-stations and Guru Gobind Singh's own account of these days in his *Bachittar Nātak* says nothing of this arrest or custody. May be, Guru Hari Kishan's coming to Delhi to see the emperor and his stay with Rājā Rām Singh are being confused with the ninth Guru's stay with him by the English historians.

* For details, see Qazwini's *Padshāhnāmā*, A. U. Ms. J. N. Sarkar's "History of Aurangzeb", Vol. I, Manucci's *Storia do Mogor*, Bernier's *Travels*, Sri Rām Sharma's "*Religious Policy of the Moghals*", etc. For further references in this context, see Lane Poole's *Aurangzeb*, and especially Khāfi Khān's *Muntakhabul-Lubāb*.

Hindus in his magnificent court, besides several noted Hindu musicians, like Jagannāth (who was favoured with the title of Mahā-Kavi Rāi), and Hindi poets, like Sunder Dās.

But, when Aurangzeb came to the throne in 1657, though the personal life of the emperor became outwardly extremely abstemious and (as compared to the pomp and splendour of Akbar and Shāh Jahān) frugal, his religious policy became extremely severe and punitive, as time passed, inspite of the Hindu blood in his veins and those of his progeny.* At first, he forbade the building of new temples by the infidels. Then, all temples built recently were to be demolished and old ones not allowed to be repaired. In a general order issued in April 1669, he called upon "all governors of provinces to destroy with a willing hand the schools and temples of the infidels; and they were strictly enjoined to put a stop to the teaching and practising of idolatrous forms of worship. This applied especially to the provinces of Banāras, Thattā and Multān". Even earlier, when he was the Governor of Gujarāt, in 1645 "he had converted the temple of Chintāman into a mosque and ordered a cow to be slaughtered in the shrine". The building was, however, restored to the Hindus by the orders of Shāh Jahān, but when Aurangzeb came to power, he issued a firmān (dated November 20, 1665) that "his earlier orders be carried out." The famous temples of Somnāth in Kathiāwār, in Banāras and the fabulous derā of Keshav Rāi at Mathurā were destroyed". "There was also wholesale demolition of temples in Kutch-Bihār, Ujjain, Udaipur, Jodhpur, Golkandā, Bijāpur and Mahārāshtra."

According to *Ma'asir-i-Alamgiri*, "the richly-jewelled idols (of Hindus) taken from the pagan temples were transferred to Āgrā and there placed upon the steps leading to the Nawāb Begum mosque, in order that they might ever be pressed under foot by the true believers." Similar 'honour' was bestowed upon the "cartloads of bejewelled Hindu idols" captured from Jodhpur which were kept under the steps of the Jumā Masjid for being trodden upon. In November 1665, he forbade the illuminations made by Hindus at the Diwāli festival and the playing of Holi throughout Gujarāt. In

---

* Aurangzeb's grand-mother (Shāh Jahān's mother) was a Hindu. Akbar's mother too was a Hindu. One of Aurangzeb's several queens, Nawāb Bāi, mother of his successor, Bahādur Shāh, was also a Hindu Rajput princess from Rajauri in the Kashmir state. His favourite concubine, Hira Bāi, was also a Hindu.

1668, he forbade Hindu *Jatrās*. In 1671, it was laid down that all rent-collectors in crown lands must be Muslims. The provincial Viceroys and *talukdārs* were called upon to dismiss their Hindu *peshkārs* (clerks) and *diwāns* (accountants). In 1674, lands held by the Hindus in Gujarāt, in religious grants, were all confiscated.*

According to Khāfi Khān "Aurangzeb ordered the temples of Sikhs also to be destroyed and the Guru's agents (*masands*) for collecting the tithes and presents of the faithful to be expelled from the cities."

So that only within a few years of the assumption of power, Aurangzeb had exhibited an extremely perverse and bigoted frame of mind and its intensity had almost reached its zenith during the eleven-year tenure of his spiritual office by Guru Tegh Bahādur (1664-1675). As a consequence, the Jāts had rebelled in 1669 round Āgrā and Mathurā but were crushed with great severity, 5000 being killed and 7000 forcibly converted. In March 1670, the Moghal general, Hassan Ali Khān, was engaged in slaying and capturing the rebels, plundering their houses and dismantling their strong forts.

The Hindu sect, called Satnāmis, also called Mundilis (or clean-shaven ones), whose strongholds were Nārnaul and Mewāt, on the borders of the Panjāb, rebelled in May 1672. They were householders by and large, and even though they dressed like dervishes, they carried on small trade and agriculture and many of them bore arms. They were not more than four to five thousand in number, but they fought savagely, and gave cause of much alarm to the emperor. After a few engagements, however, they were finally crushed.

Rājput resistance, except in minor revolts here and there, had long been silenced by the ancestors of Aurangzeb and Rājās Jaswant Singh of Jodhpur and Jai Singh of Amber (Jaipur) commanded Moghal armies against the Marāthas, though both shared an equally

* Five years later (April 2, 1679), Jeziā was again imposed upon the Hindus after a lapse of a century when it was abolished by Akbar. (But this was done four years after the death of Guru Tegh Bahādur). Similarly, in 1695, Hindus were forbidden to ride well-bred horses, elephants or *palkis* (palanquins) and to wear arms. Certain modern Sikh writers have given these firmāns also as reasons for Guru Tegh Bahādur's taking up cudgels on behalf of Hindus, but these steps, as we have seen, were launched by Aurangzeb *after* the martyrdom of the ninth Guru. May be, they helped the tenth Master to formulate his policies.

disastrous fate, later, at the hands of Aurangzeb. It was Mirzā Rājā Jai Singh, who had, during his ruthless campaign against Shivāji in 1665, concluded a treaty with the latter so favourable to the King-emperor that Shivāji accepted to become a *mansabdār* in the Moghal army and even to go to Delhi along with his eight-year old son, Sambhāji (who was also made a *Panjhazāri*) to wait upon the emperor with large presents and even to assist the Moghals in the invasion of Bijāpur. It is to the glory of Shivāji that after being humiliated by Aurangzeb at the court, he and his son escaped from the custody of the Rājput general, but the whole drama disheartened the Hindu masses that those who were expected to lead them in their fight against tyranny were themselves becoming collaborators and even helping the Rāj to trap those heroes on whom the masses had pinned their hopes.

And, to crown all, came the untold tyranny heaped upon the Brāhmins of Kashmir. When the rulers forced the large masses of Hindus to embrace Islām, they pointed out that their spiritual leaders were Brāhmins and unless they took the lead, their followers would not desert their age-old faith. So, a concerted attack was launched against the Brāhmins of Mathurā, Banāras and other holy places who, in turn, pointed to the Brāhmins of Kashmir, who due to their learning in the Hindu sacred literature and high sense of moral duty had indeed assumed the spiritual leadership of all Hindus, Brāhmin or non-Brāhmin, everywhere. Thus the Kashmiri Pandits became a special target of attack. Iftikhār Khān, the Moghal Viceroy in Kashmir, set about converting them to Islām by the sword and killing those who refused. Others fled the country in terror. The Muslims who espoused the cause of the Hindus were mercilessly put to death.

In such a period of crisis, a deputation consisting of 500 Brāhmins from Kashmir under the leadership of one Kirpā Rām*, a famed Brāhmin of Mattan, waited upon Guru Teg Bahādur at Ānandpur and acquainted him with their tragic fate and implored him to take a lead in order to save them from certain disaster. The Guru after a thought said to them, "You go and tell the Moghal Viceroy that the Brāhmins will gladly accept to embrace Islām if

*This Kirpa Rām later became the teacher in Sanskrit of Guru Gobind Singh, became a Khālsā and died fighting at Chamkaur. (See *Bhansāvlināmā* of Kesar Singh). See also P.N.K. Bamzai's "History of Kashmir", P. 571.

Teg Bahādur, whom we revere as our Guru, is persuaded to do so." The Guru thus took upon his person the challenge of an empire on behalf of a whole persecuted humanity. How, at crucial times, a single man's soul with nobility of ideals to inspire him even to death, can turn the course of human history, no matter how staggering the odds, is best illustrated by the exemplary manner in which Guru Tegh Bahādur stood up to the challenge of the times.†

The reply of the Guru was duly conveyed to the emperor, through his Viceroy in Kashmir, which must have poured oil on the fires raging in the heart of Aurangzeb, and orders were issued for his immediate arrest.

However, the none-too-reliable Muslim historians like Ghulām Hussain, author of *Siyar-ul-Mutākharin*, suggest that the emperor was informed that the Guru was "gathering many followers. Thousands kept him company wherever he went. While Sheikh Ahmad Sirhindi made forcible exactions from the Musalmāns, Tegh Bahādur did so from the Hindus, and that if their influence was allowed to grow, it might lead to trouble"*. "Hence", the Guru, according

---

† The Sikh chroniclers here narrate a story saying that when Guru Tegh Bahādur was ruminating over the sad plight of the Kashmiri Brāhmins, in came his nine-year old son, Godbind Dās (Rāi), and asked his father for the sudden and unnatural gloom over his countenance. The Guru replied, "Unless a holy man lays down his head for the sake of the poor Brahmins, there is no hope for their escape from imperial tryanny." Gobind replied, "Revered father, who would be better equipped for this than yourself?" The Guru hugged his son to his bosom and wept for joy. "I was only worried about the future, for you are far too young". "Leave me to God", Gobind replied, "and accept the challenge of the Moghals."

According to *Suraj Prakāsh*, Guru Tegh Bahādur did not meet his son after he left Patnā. But, this cannot be true, as according to the *Bachittar Nātak* of Guru Gobind Singh, when he was taken to the Panjāb, he was "fondled by all sorts of nurses" and "received instruction of various kinds". He could only have been put to the care of nurses when he was very young and received instruction under his father's guidance. It is also natural that before taking the final plunge, the Guru must have brought his family back to their home. See also Sukhā Singh's *Gur-Bilās* (which corroborates our statement) and also Guru Gobind Singh's own words, "*Jab ham dharam karam mo āē, devlok tab pitā sidhāē*" (when I was able to attend to the affairs of the secular and spiritual world, my father repaired to the abode of gods). (*Bachittar Nātak*).

* A grossly misleading English translation of this book, written about a century after the event, by Raymond and Briggs, has this to say about Guru Tegh Bahādur: "This man finding himself at the head of so many thousands of people, became

to this author, was arrested by the Governor of Lāhore and executed *at Gwalior* and his body, cut up in four parts, was hung at the various gates of the Gwalior fortress, while the Muslim faqir was allowed to proceed to Afghānistān".*

It appears, the large offerings made by the devout to the Guru were miscontrued as "forcible exactions" and his peace-loving disciples as an "army of plunder".

But, another earlier historian, Bakht Mal, who uses contemporary records for his materials in his *Twārikh-i-Sikhān* (*Ms*), has this to say about the reasons of the Guru's arrest:

"Now that Guru Tegh Bahādur had come to power, his faithful disciples came to his help and increased his influence. He lived a hard life. He was, however, very independent. Whatever his disciples brought to him, he distributed and kept nothing for himself. In a short time he acquired mastery over all his subjects (i.e. disciples). When Aurangzeb heard about the Guru, he summoned him to Delhi from Lāhore. He was brought to Delhi. He did not mind the troubles he encountered on the way and travelled with an easy mind. When he reached Delhi, his disciples came and gave him valuable offerings. The Guru did not accept anything. When the Sultān heard of this, he was upset and requested him to perform a miracle. The Guru said, "Miracle is the head of the lovers, place the sword on my neck". The emperor was angry at these words and ordered his execution. The Sikhs say that the executioner felt

---

F. N. Contd.

aspiring; and he united his concerns with one Hafyz Ādam, a Mohamedan fakir. These two men no sooner saw themselves followed by multitudes, implicitly addicted to their chief's will, then, forsaking every honest calling, they fell to subsisting by plunder and rapine, laying waste the whole province of Panjāb." (Pp. 84-86). This became a bedrock for later English historians like Cunningham, otherwise a very judicious and sympathetic writer, to aver that "the Guru was more of a kingly than priestly spirit". (Pp. 157-58). It came handy to biased missionaries like Dr. Ernest Trumpp to malign the Gurū (*Ādi Granth*, translation, introduction, page 89). Sir J.N. Sarkār, the eminent modern historian, also echoes this sentiment without reference even to the correct translation of the original.

* P. 392. This shows the unhistorical sense of the writer. No other record supports him. On the contrary, all available evidence shows that the Guru was beheaded at the Chāndni Chowk of Delhi and his body cremated in the same city where stand two historic shrines to his eternal memory, respectively called Sisganj and Rakābganj.

himself almost incapable of touching the head of the Guru. Before he died, the Guru requested a Sikh who was in attendance to carry away his head after his execution.

"A liberty-loving faqir happened to pass where the corpse of the Guru lay and said, 'the Sultān has not done well. Such things will lead to great rebellion and Delhi will become utterly desolate' "

"The Sikhs brought the Guru's head to Ānandpur and kept it. The body was cremated at Rakābganj. The places of execution, of cremation and the burial of the head have become places of pilgrimage for the Sikhs. This happened in 1732, Vikrami, Samvat, (1675 A.D.) in the month of Maghar, the fifth day of the bright-half."†

According to some historians, before the orders of the emperor for his arrest could be carried out, the Guru had, after girding upon his nine-year old son the sword of Guru Hargobind and hailing him his successor and Guru of the Sikhs, set out for the countryside of southern Panjāb and Haryānā, preaching his gospel and donating whatever offerings came to him for digging up wells, building poor houses, healing the sick and starting community kitchens. Wherever

---

† This not only tallies with the contemporary Sikh records like Mani Singh's "*Sikhān di Bhagat Mālā*", but also with Guru Gobind Singh's own version in the *Bachittar Nātak* that when his father was asked to show a miracle, he said, "this is the work of charlatans and mountebanks, for to the men of God, it is shameful to display their occult powers". That there was no political reason for the Guru's arrest is also testified by Guru Gobind Singh in the same verse :

"My father sacrificed his life,
To protect the religion of the Hindus—
Their sacred thread and their frontal mark.
In this dark Kāli age,
He performed this supreme act of sacrifice
For the sake of *Dharma*.
He gave away his head,
Without a sigh on his lips.
Lo, he surrendered his life—
But not his resolve."

According to Latif, the emperor had many religious disputations with Guru Tegh Bahādur and asked him to show miracles if he was a true Guru or to embrace Islām ....."The Guru being unable to satisfy His Majesty one way or the other was by the King's order thrown into prison and on his persistently refusing to become a convert, was subjected to bodily tortures ....."(A History of the Panjāb, p. 260).

To suggest that Rām Rāi was in any way responsible for his arrest and execution **is a pure myth, though several Muslim historians (See later) refer to it.**

he went, large masses of people, Hindus as well as Muslims, came out to greet him and pay him homage. A large number of places, now held sacred to his memory, which he visited during these tours, are dotted all through these tracts, especially in the erstwhile State of Patiala like Gurdwarās *Dukh niwāran* and *Moti Bāgh*. According to earlier Sikh chroniclers (like Santokh Singh and Gyani Gyan Singh) it was only at Āgrā that he surrendered himself to the imperial authority, and was presented to the King at Delhi.† But modern researches show that he was arrested three or four days after his coming out of Ānandpur (at Malikpur Ranghrān near Ropar, according to Kesar Singh Chhibar's *Bansavalinama* and *Bhatt Vahis* and at Dhamdhān, according to Sarup Dās Bhallā) and kept in prison at Sirhind for about four months before being sent to Delhi.

The king, it is said, questioned him either personally or through the Qāzis about his activities which had been conveyed to him by the provincial authorities and may be also by some Muslim zealots and orthodox Hindus, as Bakht Rāi testifies. He was also asked why he was hailed as the Guru or prophet and called "*Sachā Pādshāh*" (the True King) and if he really believed in his being one, he should perform a miracle to justify his claim.

The Guru repudiated any insinuations of his political activities, but reprimanded the emperor severly for his blind orthodoxy and persecution of faiths other than his own. "Hinduism may not be my faith, and I may believe not in the supremacy of Veda or the Brāhmins, nor in idol-worship or caste or pilgrimages and other rituals, but I would fight for the right of all Hindus to live with honour and practise their faith according to their own lights."

This was a staggering reply for Aurangzeb to hear from a man fighting for upholding a religion other than his own.*

---

† A fantastic story is told by Sikh chroniclers that at Āgrā the Guru sent a boy with some money to buy sweets for him and gave him a costly shawl to wrap it. The boy was arrested as a thief and on being questioned, led to the arrest of the Guru. How he whom thousands were coming forth to worship all along the way, suddenly became an unknown quantity at Āgrā, passes one's wits.

* According to *Padshāh Burānji*, an Assamese account of Aurangzeb's regime, "a saint of the faith of Guru Nānak became the Guru of a large number of Brāhmins and Kshatriyas The Brāhmin Bhattāchāryās or the Hindu priests and Kāzis of the Musalmāns reported to the Pādshāh, "this man does not belong to any particular school of faith, he goes about ravaging the country". The empero

As for his being called a "*Sachā Pādshāh*", he answered: "Every ruler of the world must pass away, but not the Word of God or His Saint. This is how people not only call me a True King but have done so through the two centuries before me in respect of my House and also in respect of others who preceded them and who identified themselves not with the temporal and the contingent, but with the eternal and the never-dying." And, he refused to perform a miracle saying "this is the work of charlatans and mountebanks to hoodwink the people. Men of God submit ever to the Will of God."

At this, he was asked to embrace Islām, "the only true religion" according to Aurangzeb. But, the Guru replied, "For me, there is only one religion — of God — and whosover belongs to it, be he a Hindu or a Muslim, him I own and he owns me. I neither convert others by force, nor submit to force, to change my faith."

Naturally, this was too much for Aurangzeb. He ordered that the Guru be tortured. It is said, he was removed to an iron cage and kept hungry for days and subjected to many other humiliations. A story (it may be apocryphal but is significant nonetheless) is told that when these days a Sikh, in agony, asked the Guru if they would rebel and despoil the cities of Delhi and Lāhore, he answered coolly "you have only received a drop of Grace from the ocean of God, and

asked the Guru to appear before him but he did not come. On the other hand, he defied the authority of the Pādshāh and roamed about plundering and destroying the country attended by thirty-thousand Nānak-panthi *sepoys*. The Pādshāh became indignant and he deputed Alo Khān Pathān who captured the Guru. The Padshāh ordered the Guru to be executed, who for fear of his life, sought the protection of Rājā Rām Singh, who became surety for the leader. But the Nānakpanthi Guru also made his escape. The Padshāh accused Rām Singh saying, 'How is it that you have allowed the Guru to flee, though you yourself stood surety for him?' To this Rām Singh replied, "What is he? Only a Rājā or a Nawāb is worthy of your vengeance. He is only a mendicant fakir." (Translation by S.K. Bhuyān p. 163), But this is full of mis-statements. Perhaps, Shivāji's escape in 1666 A.D. from Rām Singh's custody is being mixed up with the Guru's escape. His father, Jai Singh, alto had stood surety for Shivāji, but due to the Marāthā hero's escape, Rām Singh was disgraced and kept out of the Court for two years, after which, as we have seen, he was sent on a treacherous expedition to Assam during which period his own son was got killed by the emperor. At the time of the Guru's martyrdom, Rām Singh was still in the eastern regions.

So, the question of his standing surety for the Guru does not arise. Perhaps, the earlier stay at Delhi of Guru Hari Krishan with Rājā Jai Singh is being confused by the author with Guru Tegh Bahādur's staying in the custody of his son.

you feel such power in your veins, but he who is at one with the Ocean, he too must possess some spiritual power. If he uses it not, you also submit to His will."*

When nothing availed, Aurangzeb ordered that he be executed.† First his three companions were put to death with extreme tortures. These three martyrs were—Bhāi Mati Dās (who was sawn alive), Bhāi Dyālā (who was boiled to death) and Bhāi Sati Dās (who was burnt alive). The emperor's orders about the Guru were carried out on November 11. 1675 A. D,, and he was beheaded in the Chandni Chowk of Delhi. He lay there dead the whole afternoon, but no one dared to pick up his body for fear of the King's reprisals. But, it is said, a severe storm swept through the city and the sky became murky. Under cover of darkness, two Sikhs, both of lower castes, one a *Lobānā* (lit. a water-carrier or a petty travelling salesman), carried off his severed body and the other, a Rangrettā (calico-printer) carried off his head to Ānandpur where his son was. The body was cremated the same evening by the devotee by setting fire to his straw-hut in the Rāisinā village to avoid detection. His ashes were buried in the same ground where now stands a tall, domed temple in smooth marble, called Rakābganj. The place of his execution, also swathed now in white marble with golden domes and known as *Sisganj*, is situated in the heart of old Delhi.‡ His life was gone, but his glory was writ large across the skies.

---

* The stories, narrated by Macauliffe, and based mostly on *Suraj Prakāsh*, of the Guru's escape from and entry at will into his prison-house and other miracles may be dismissed as not in keeping with the Guru's thought, otherwise there was no reason for him to suffer at all. But, he deliberately chose suffering in order to identify himself with the sorrows of the common mass.

† "Tegh Bahādur, the ninth sixth Guru, was executed because he refused to accept Islām," (Oxford history of India by V.A. Smith, p. 409).

‡ Some historians like J. N. Sarkār have doubted that Auranzeb ever met the Guru, as according to them, he was not present at Delhi and since *June 1674* was at Hassan Abdāl, midway between Rāwalpindi and Peshāwar, *personally directing operations for a year and half against the Afghāns* and that the warrants for the Gurū's execution were issued by the emperor from there. The Guru was executed at Delhi on November 11, 1675, and it is quite likely that the emperor had a month or two earlier returned from his expedition victorious. According to Khāfi Khān, the emperor returned from Hassan Abdāl in May 1672, when the Satnāmis rose in rebellion and distributed charms and amulets to his soliders to reinforce their flagging morale, but he may have returned to Hassan

F. N. Contd.

Abdāl two years later. But Latif (History of the Panjāb, p. 260) corroborates the Sikh chroniclers and states that "the emperor had many religious disputations with Tegh Bahādur and asked him to show miracles if he was a true Guru, or embrace Islām."

Says Cunningham (A History of the Sikhs, p 65) that in reply to the emperor's demand for working a miracle, the Guru had replied that "the duty of man was to pray to the Lord, yet he would do one thing. He would write a charm and the sword should fall harmless on the neck around which it was hung. He placed it around his neck and inclined his head to the executioner: a blow severed it, to the surprise of a court tinged with superstition, and upon the paper was found written *Sir diā, sirar nā diā* (he had given his head, but not his secret); his life was gone, but his inspiration or apostolic virtue still remained in the world." (Bhangu Rattan Singh in his PPP also narrates a similar story, p. 38). Expiating on it, Cunningham comments: "Such is the narrative of a rude and wonder-loving people yet it is certain that Tegh Bahādur was put to death as a rebel in 1675, and that the stern and bigoted Aurangzeb had the body of the unbeliever publicly exposed in the streets of Delhi."

Cunningham obviously has picked up the above dramatic story from the Sikh chroniclers and the fact of the Guru being hauled up as a rebel from the Muslim sources like Ghulām Hussain, etc., adding in the foot-notes that the Guru, during his incarceration, also prophecied to Aurangzeb "about the coming of the white race from the West and reducing his empire into the dust". This "fact" has been reproduced by various English authors like Rawlinson *(Indian Historical Studies)*, Macauliffe *(The Sikh Religion)*, V.A. Smith *(Oxford History of India)*, etc. But, this is a later invention, and was made a battle-cry for the Sikh soldiers from the princely Phulkian states during the mutiny of 1857, when they helped the British against the titular Moghal emperor in the assurance that they were thus avenging the blood of their martyrs from the Moghals. (For further details of the Sikh part in the Mutiny of 1857, see part II.) That the Guru sacrificed his head to protect the honour of the Kashmiri Pandits & refused to show a miaracle saying it is the work of magic men & is a violence against the laws of God, is supported by all reliable Sikh historians like Santokh Singh, (*Guru Partap Surya Granth)* Kesar Singh Chhabera (*Bansāvlināmā)*, Bhangu Rattan Singh (*Panth Parkāsh*) Giani Gyan Singh (Panth Parkāsh)& others. P.N.K. Bamzai in his "History of Kashmir" also supports this thesis. (P. 371).

According to *Ibrat Nama* of Ali-ud-din, the Emperor Aurangzeb, called Guru Tegh Bahadur to Delhi on a complaint lodged by Rām Rāi, and asked the Guru to show a miracle, On his refusal to do so, he was beheaded.

***Tawarikh-i-Punjab*, by Bute Shah, says the Guru was called to Delhi by Aurangzeb on a representation of some *Amirs* as well as Rām Rāi who accused the Guru of usurpation (of the *gaddi*) and temporal ambition.**

***Zikr-i-Guruan* by Ahmad Shah repeats this assertion of Ram Rai's complicity**

CHAPTER XIII

GURU GOBIND SINGH

(1666-1708)

That a fatherless child of nine*, surrounded by the hostility of a powerful empire as much as the viciousness of relations and the covetousness and cruelty of the deputies (*the masands*), who were expected to bring spiritual solace to the world and promote their secular welfare, should think of making a clean sweep of these formidable odds is a miracle of the human soul. And, what is more, the Guru realised in a single life-time, whose span was all-too-brief, what he had dreamed to do. The wish became father of the thought and the thought was actualised into a living reality.

While the Guru had such a formidable array of hostile forces against him, he also had many positive assets. His followers were

---

* Says Cunningham (*A History of the Sikhs,* pp. 66-83) that Guru Gobind was in his fifteenth year when his father died, that for another twenty years (upto 1696 A. D.), he lived in "obscurity" (hunting, acquiring knowledge, writing, etc.), when the goddess, Durgā, was "invoked" by him through the "sacrifice" of a disciple and also the Khālsā initiated. According to him, the Guru breathed his last at the age of 48. All these dates have, however, been proved wrong, as also the "invoking" of the goddess, and his living in "obscurity" for twenty years (see below).

Cunningham makes an interesting observation that the term "Rāi" used by Guru Gobind as his surname before the birth of the Khālsā is derived from the Marāthā "Rāo", just as the appellation of "Singh" used later on by him was derived from the Rajputs. Others give his earlier name as Gobind Dās.

spread far and wide throughout India, Ceylon, Afghanistān, and Central Asia to wheresoever the holy name of Nānak and his successors had travelled. All his followers were extremely devoted to his house, made their offerings regularly, no matter what their station in life, visited him at least once every year, and no sacrifice was too great for them in the Guru's cause. Mostly small peasants, artisans and traders (though occasionally these also included sovereigns of states and rich merchants), their one aim in life was to attain salvation through the Guru's door by seeking his benediction. It is them that the Guru wanted to organise into a more cohesive, more determined, more self-sacrificing group, and infusing in them the spirit of nationhood as much as spiritual hope.

He, therefore, sent word to all his followers to make offerings to the Guru's house direct, at the time of their visits to the Guru. They were asked also to offer, if they could, arms and horses instead of cash and grain. He accepted professionals also into his small army that he started to raise. He made it obligatory for those that lived with him to exercise their muscles along with their souls. He gave orders for the construction of a huge war-drum (called "Ranjit Nagārā, or the drum of victory) which was to be beaten, morning and evening, as a symbol of royalty. Hunting expeditions became an everyday feature of the Guru's life who also got himself trained in all the weapons of war. But, the fact must be emphasised that he did not for one moment neglect either his followers' spiritual education and discipline, or his own. Himself he got extremely well-versed in Sanskrit, Persian, Arabic and Panjābi, and read through all the ancient and current lore in these languages. He inspired his followers also to do likewise.* Morning and evening, religious

---

* The Guru was also, it appears, well-versed in playing on the rebeck (*Sirandā*), *mirdang* and the hand-drums. A rebeck said to belong to him is still preserved at Rawālsar (in the Himachal Pradesh). As soon as Aurangzeb banished music in his realm, musicians of repute flocked to the Guru's Court, so also poets, 52 of whom are well-known. He treated them with utmost consideration and kept gold *mohurs* or shawls under their pillows while they were asleep so that their sensitivity was not hurt. The Guru had initiated a mass education programme at Ānandpur. According to GSG, he had resolved "that not one of my Sikhs shall remain illiterate, whether young or old."

Every description of Guru Gobind Singh's person delineates him as a very handsome, sharp-featured, tall and wiry man, immaculately and richly dressed as a prince. Decked with a crest upon his lofty, cone-shaped turban with a plume

services would be held to keep the minds attuned to the Supreme Being so that whatever secular activity was undertaken must be yoked and dedicated to His purpose.

According to the traditional (though not very accurate) Sikh records, which we summarise here, "some of the chiefs of the Shivālik hill states, particularly Rājā Bhim Chand of Kahlur (Bilāspur), got scared at the activities of Guru Gobind.* Sensing this, the *masands* approached the Guru's mother entreating her to ask the Guru to desist from his warlike activities, the beating of the war-drum, the recruitment of professionals in his army, etc., and to devote his entire time to the spiritual education of his followers. The *masands* were also apprehensive that these activities of the Guru could one day be a menace to their own existence. Hence, their advice was not wholly selfless.

F.N. Contd.

suspended behind from the top, he was ever armed with various weapons, including a bow and a quiver of arrows, a sword, a discus, a shield and a spear. His choice steed was of bluish-grey colour and on his left hand always perched a white hawk when he sat on the throne or went out hunting.

* Though in the absence of more reliable data, we have given in the text the traditional account of the Guru's own life of these days (as given in the GSG and other Sikh texts, like *Gur-Bilās* and followed meticulously by Macauliffe), not much reliance can be placed on its accuracy in every detail. For, the Guru, in his own *Bachittar Nātak* (or Autobiography) makes no mention of the hostility of Bhim Chand leading to a clash with him later at Bhangāni. In fact, it is Fateh Shāh, the Rājā of Srinagar (Garhwāl) who, according to the Guru, "became angry for no reason" and along with several other Rajās of the hill-states supported by Muslim Khāns (possibly of their own armies) attacked the Guru. It appears that although Bhim Chand might have become apprehensive of the Guru's rising power and even felt jealous, he did nothing to provoke a clash. Instead, as the Guru himself testifies, "in these days, I tried to spread religion to the best of my ability", "and also hunted game." "I left my home and proceeded towards Pauntā." The Guru came to succeed his father at the young age of nine (1675 A. D.) and the battle of Bhangāni was fought most probably in 1688 A. D. (Sunder Singh in his "Battles of Guru Gobind Singh", P. 11, places it in 1686 A.D.) It appears, therefore, that the Guru was left unmolested, (Aurangzeb too was engaged in his battles in the Deccan) till he came to maturity, when he left for Pauntā and stayed in the state of Nāhan for about three years. The voluminous literature created by the Guru and attributed to these years also corroborates this thesis. Fateh Shāh, being inimical to the Rājā of Nāhan, must have felt perturbed at the fortifications being made by the Guru on his borders.

"But, the Guru ignored the pleadings of his mother. Meantime, a Sikh from Assam, Rattan Rāi, brought some very precious gifts for the Guru, including an elephant trained to do many kinds of tricks*; a weapon which could serve the purpose of five kinds of different arms, five horses with golden trappings, a throne-shaped device from which puppets would emerge to play chess, and several costly jewels and dresses". The Sikh chroniclers record this "Rattan Rāi to have been born to the home of a chieftain of Assam, Rājā Rām, who had become a great devotee of Guru Tegh Bahādur during his visit to Assam. It is said he had asked the Guru to bless him with the boon of a son which wish of his was granted. After the demise of his father, the young prince came to pay homage to the Guru and brought these valuable presents as a token of esteem in which his family held the Guru's house.

"Although the growing influence and power of the Guru gave the Rājā of Kahlur much cause for alarm, his courtiers advised him to be on good terms with him. The Rājā, therefore, went to call on the Guru. But when he saw the splendour of his court†, the dedication of his large following and his increasing military strength, he was burnt with jealousy. Reaching home, he thought of grabbing his precious possessions or, failing this, to go to war with him to curb his rising influence. He, therefore, sent word to the Guru through an emissary to lend him the presents he had received from Assam as his son was being engaged to the daughter of Rājā Fateh Shāh of Srinagar (in Garhwāl), and he wanted to make a display of his possessions. The Guru, however, refused to oblige him, knowing the treacherous state of his mind. The Rājā repeated the request through another state official who was also to threaten the Guru in case of refusal. But, the Guru dismissed him also with contempt. The *masands* tried to put fear of a war with the Rājās in

* Some historians suggest that it was a war-elephant and that it may have been the gift of Rājā Mānik Rāi of Chittāgong, through the Sikh *Sangat* of Dāccā, at the Guru's own behest, as is evident from his second letter (*Hukamnāmā*) to the Sangat of Dāccā. The gift is acknowledged in a subsequent letter of the Guru.

† A reference is made by some Sikh writers in this connection to a visit to the Guru of a few *Sanyasis* (recluses) who made disparaging remarks about his claim to being a God's man and yet rolling in splendour. The Guru said : "My Sikhs shall not deny themselves the joys of the earth, though they will remain detached in their inner core."

the mind of the Guru through his mother. But, they too failed in their attempt.

"The other hill chiefs tried to accentuate these differences by pretending loyalty on either side and encouraging either party to settle with the other through a clash of arms. Inflamed, the Rājā made a final bid to hook the Guru's possesions and sent word through a brother-prince that a refusal would mean a challenge to his sovereign authority with its attendant consequences. The Guru replied to him in the same tone, and started preparations for a show-down with him.

"In these days, an invitation came to the Guru from the Rājā of Nāhan to pay him a visit and hunt game in the Doon valley. It is said, the Rājā invited the Guru as he was inimical to Rājā Fateh Shāh of Srinagar and wanted the Guru's assistance, should he be attacked. The Guru accepted the invitation and set out with his family and five hundred armed men, mostly Udāsis. For the defence of Ānandpur, he left a sizeable garrison behind. The meeting was very fruitful. The Guru was very pleased with the natural scenery and set up his camp on the banks of the Yamunā, near Paontā*.

* According to the Sirmur Gazetteer (pp. 15 & 51), the Guru halted first at Tokā where the spot is marked by a Gurdwārā. Thence he was brought to Nāhan by the Rājā and later proceeded to Paontā, 26 miles away, on the bank of the river Yamunā (or Kalindri). Paontā is so called because the Guru made it his footstool (*paontā*) or resting-place. The *Sirmur Gazetteer* states that the Guru stayed here for 3 to 5 years (two differnt periods of stay are given on pages 51 and 112). The period of 3 years (1685-86 to 1688-89 A. D.) seems reasonable, as voluminous and soul-stirring heroic and spirirual literature by the Guru is attributed to this period, besides the ruins and relics of the fort he built here. If the Sikh records are to be believed, the Guru came to Paontā shortly before the marriage of Bhim Chand's son and left immediately after the event which period resulted also in the battle of Bhangāni. This sudden movement to and fro cannot be justified on any account.

A recent writer's assertion that the Guru was removed to Paontā by the "leaders" of the Sikh community "for his safety, for the possibility of his being taken to Delhi as a hostage could not be ruled out", is ridiculous in the extreme. In the first place, Nāhan was the most loyal tributory of Delhi and the Rājā did not help the Guru, as we shall see later, even at Bhangāni, though the Guru was fighting Fateh Shāh, his Rajput rival and adversary. Secondly, Aurangzeb had left the young Guru alone, being engaged in the battles in the Deccan; and all of the engagements prior to 1695 were primarily with the hill chiefs, and not with Aurangzeb, whose help was occasionally sought by the Hindu Rājput princes against the Guru.

The Rājā was so much impressed by his bearing and valour, the discipline and dedication of his Sikhs and their unswerving faith in God that he requested the Guru to stay there for a longer period. He promised to assist in the construction of the fort for housing the Guru and his men. The Guru was persuaded by his followers to agree to the proposal, their idea, it is said, being to get rid of the hostile atmosphere around Ānandpur.

"Meanwhile, Rājā Fateh Shāh of Srinagar heard of the Guru's repute and paid him a visit. As has been pointed out, he and the Rājā of Nāhan were not on good terms. The Guru mediated between the two and brought them close to each other. The Guru hunted big game in the surrounding forest, and once killed a tiger with a sword and shield. This greatly impressed both the Rājās. It was here that Sayyad Badruddin, popularly known as Budhu Shāh of nearby Sadhaura, a man reputed for his saintly disposition and of whom we shall hear more later on, came to call on the Guru and also sent five hundred Pathāns who had been discharged from the Moghal army to serve under Guru Gobind Singh.*

---

* It is really strange that the Guru in his autobiographical poem, called the *Bachittar Nātak*, should not mention even once the name of Budhu Shāh who is said to have offered 500 Pathāns for his army and who are reported later to have deserted him, as a consequence of which Budhu Shāh is said to have come to the Guru's rescue with 700 followers of his, including his four sons, two of whom are said to have lost their lives in the battle of Bhangāni. On the other hand, the Guru makes a mention of several Muslim *Khāns* opposing him in this battle on the side of the hill chiefs. But as the tradition about Budhu Shāh's association with the Guru is extremely strong and several facts of later Sikh history are associated with his house, it seems possible that he offered his help at a much later date and in another battle whose account is not rendered by the Guru in this poem, which deals only with his encounters, prior to the birth of the Khālsā (1699 A. D).

According to Bhāi Kāhan Singh, the three Pathān generals—Bhikhan Khān, Najābat Khān and Hayāt Khān—whose names are mentioned by the Guru in his *Bachittar Nātak*, as opposing him in the battle of Bhangāni, were the ones recruited at the instance of Pir Budhu Shāh and only one of them, namely Kālē Khān, did not prove a traitor to the Guru's cause (MK. P. 2641). The Sikh historians are unanimous that Sardār Usmān Khān of Sadhaura got the Pir executed for his help to the Guru and that, as a reprisal to it, Bandā Bahādur attacked Sadhaura in 1709 A. D. and hanged Usmān Khān. Unless, however, Budhu Shāh's execution came in the days of the Guru's own grim struggles after 1704, the Guru must have done something himself to punish the culprits or gone to his family's help. Moreover, the assistance rendered in an engagement in which the Moghals were not

It was here, at Paontā, that the Guru wrote much of his chivalrous and devotional verse, which was later collected in a single volume called Dasam Granth (the Book of the Tenth King) or whatever of it was available after his death. He employed 52 poets also to render into Hindi the classical Purāntic tales of chivalry, notably of Chāndi, the goddess of war, who destroyed the demons, and of the heroic exploits of Rāma and Krishna. He rewarded the poets with utter munificence. It is said in order not to hurt their sensitive pride, the Guru would cause costly shawls and gold mohurs, etc, to be placed under their pillows as rewards for their creative work. His *Bachittar Nātak*, sort of autobiography, gives many interesting and inspiring details of his life here, and a little later at Ānandpur. In Riti Kāvya, or traditional poetry, the Guru's poetry is unexcelled in the sweep of imagination, choice of word and phrase, and mastery over metre. There is no metre known to Indian prosody that has not been employed by this great Master (he experimented with over 250 metres), nor a mood that he has not captured. Such is the power he communicates that it is sheer excitement even to utter or listen to it. His war-poetry especially occupies a unique place in Indian letters.*

F. N. Contd.

directly involved and only the Hindu hill chiefs were, could not have provoked the excessive wrath of the Pir's co-religionists. This also shows that the Pir helped the Guru later, possibly during the worst days of his crisis at Ānandpur.

* The *Dasam Granth* consists of 1428 pages. According to all available evidence, it was compiled by Bhāi Mani Singh, the devout and learned Sikh custodian of the Golden Temple (who later became a martyr) 26 years after the death of Guru Gobind Singh, at Damdamā. But, some historians assert that it was not the *Ādi Granth*, but his own Book that the Guru dictated to Bhāi Mani Singh. However, much of its secular portion is the subject of great controversy even amongst the Sikhs who ascribe its authorship not to the Guru, but to some of his 52 poets who lived at his court.

The contents of this Granth, which is mostly in Braj Bhāshā, are : (1) Jāp, or meditations, (2) *Akāl Ustati*, or the praises of God and the denunciation of ritual, superstition and cant, (3) *Chandi Charitra*, I and II, or the life of Chandi, the goddess of war, (in Braj) (4) *Vār*, or ballad of Durgā, the exploits of the goddess ef war (in Punjabi), (5) *Gyān Prabodh*, or the sayings of Wisdom, which also include some tales from Mahābhārta, (6) *Chaubis Avtār*, or the life-stories of the incarnations of Vishnu, according to the Hindus, and *Brahmavatār* and *Rudravtār*, (7) *Shabd Hazārē*, or devotional hymns, (8) Thirty-three *Swayyās*, or the praises of the one immortal, unknowable God of wonder and grace, (9) *Khālsā Mahima*, or words

F. N. Contd.

in praise of the Khālsā, (10) *Shastra Nām-Mālā,* verses in praise of many arms, (11) *Charitropkhyān* or 404 tales of the wiles of women, (12) *Zafar Nāmā* (in Persian), or letter of victory, addressed to Aurangzeb, (13) *Hikāyats,* or legends and tales, also in Persian, including some stories on the lines of *Charitropakhyān.*

As soon as the *Dasam Granth* was compiled, it led to a great controversy among the Sikh divines, especially in relation to its secular portions and more notably in regard to the *Charitro-pākhyān* and *Hikāyats.* It was decided to divide the book. Bhāi Mehtāb Singh of Mirankot (who was charged by the *Panth* to capture or assasssinate Masā Ranghar who had then planted himself in the holy Golden Temple at Amritsar and was desecrating its sanctity) suggested to the leaders of his community that if he came back victorious in his mission, the book should be preserved in one volume, otherwise it may divided into two. Mehtāb Singh was successful in putting Masā Ranghar to an ignoble death and hence the volume was preserved as it now is. This, however, as the Sikh savant, Bhāi Kāhan Singh points out, (See *Gurmat Sudhākar,* second edition, P. 35) is a most arbitrary way of settling a point of such literary and theological significance. Morover, a single man's point of view should not have prevailed, especially of a military hero, or even a *Jathēdār* in search of martyrdom, in preference to the viewpoint of the theologians and scholars who were still discussing the point. Several recensions of this volume are now current, some of which contain some extra hymns also. Though it is a pity that the text of the *Dasam Granth* has yet to be fixed by scholars and theologians, it is our considered opinion that the secular portion of what is now available in print is also the creation of the Guru himself, not only because of the internal evidence of style and diction, but also because the secular portion, including *Charitro-pākhyān* does not, by any chance, contradict the Guru's philosophy of a full-blooded, though detached life in all its manifestations. A supreme artist that the Guru was, he could not ignore to write about the seamy side of life, though he does not commend it anywhere.

To pick up on the Guru's extensive use of Hindu mythology, or the praises of Krishna's scintillating play on the flute, or the most sensitive protrayal of feminine beauty and charm, the inclusion of certain erotic scenes, or how, in the days of Rāmāyana, the Kashatriyas worshipped the Brahmins, of the call of the heroes in some of the *Hikāyāts* to bring them a cup of intoxicating wine, etc , and to dissociate the Guru from their authorship would be the height of artistic sacrilege. The Guru who, in his *Akāt Ustat* (whose authorship anyhow is beyond doubt) can write this about God : "Now you are a beggar, now a King; now the reciter of the *Gayatri,* now the *Muezzin* giving call to prayer; now the lover of own wife, now the lover of another woman; now you are the strong drink, now the drunkard," (6:16) could not but be a man of superbly catholic mind, seeing the variegated manifestation of God in everything and everywhere. And was it not Guru Nānak who said : "O God, wondrous are those who tread Thy path and wondrous are those who are strayed away." (Vār Asā). It is very difficult however, for puny, hidebound minds to appreciate this grandeur of spiritual and aesthetic vision.

"One of these days he heard that Rām Rāi, son of Guru Hari Rai, and a cousin of Guru Gobind (who, as we have seen, had fallen out with his father on ministerpreting a verse of Guru Nānak to the emperor Aurangzeb in order to seek his favour and had set up a *gaddi* of his at Dehra Doon)*, had been cremated by his deputies, the masands, while he was in a trance, and yet not dead. The *masands* wanted to usurp his huge property themselves and the more ambitious even sought to claim succession to him. This tragedy was reported to the Guru at Paontā and his assistance was sought by Panjāb Kaur, the widow of Rām Rāi, to curb the *masands.* The Guru, forgetting his differences, immediately set out for Dehrā Doon. When he heard of the lascivious life of the *masands*, and their other crimes, he gave them suitable punishment. Some escaped; those that had stood loyal to Panjāb Kaur he rewarded.

"Now approached the marriage of Bhim Chand's son with the daughter of Rājā Fateh Shāh. The latter invited the Guru also to

*1. This beautiful district town in the valley (*Doon*) is called Dera-Doon for housing the tomb (*Dehrā*) of Rām Rāi, which reveals the high esteem in which he was held by the local populace. On the one hand, this incident clears Rām Rāi of the charge of any complicity in the earlier arrest, if not the ultimate martyrdom of Guru Tegh Bahādur, as alleged by Malcolm, Forster and Cunninghum, (besides establishing the compassionate and catholic nature of Guru Gobind Singh's character). On the other hand, it gives us a further clue to the period of the Guru's stay at Paontā, for Rām Rāi died in 1687 A. D. (MK, P. 3101), and if, as is almost certain, the Guru came to the rescue of his widow from Paontā, he must have come to the latter place some time earlier, and consolidated his position there before he was able to render any effective assistance to her. Again, in the voluminous verse-composition, *Krishnavtār* (verse 2490) ascribed to the Guru, it is stated that this piece was finished at Paontā, in the month of Sāvan of Samvat 1745 (i.e. mid-July to mid-August 1688 A. D.). Thus, the Guru's stay at Paonta could be safely deduced as from 1685-86 to 1688-89 A.D. Thus unless the battle of Bhangāni took place in 1688 and not in February 1686 A.D. (Gur-Bilās places it in 1689, though GSG refers to it as having taken place nine months before the birth of the Guru's first son, Ajit Singh, which it says took place at Ānandpur on November 9, 1686), the Guru left Paontā for Ānandpur two years after the battle and not immediately thereafter. In which case the birth of his first son must have taken place at Paontā (as Bhagat Lakshman Singh's "Life of GGS" testifies, though he places it in the year 1685 A. D., P. 66). The *"Mahān Kosh"* also corroborates the date, though the place of his birth is not mentioned by the auther (P. 142), who gives the date of the battle at Bhangāni as Vaisakh 18, Samvat 1746 (or late April, 1689 A D. p. 2774). Dr. Kirpal Singh places, in our view rightly, the battle of Bhangāni in September 1688 (Sikh Review, January 1967).

his house to participate in the celebrations. But the Guru sent his emissary, Diwān Nand Chand, with precious presents, accompanied by five hundred horse. He was received with utmost consideration at Srinagar. When the groom's party arrived near Paontā, they found the Guru's camp right in their way. Rājā Bhim Chand sensed danger, and so he sent an envoy to the Guru to allow him safe passage. The Guru said he had no grudge against the bridegroom who could pass safely through, along with some attendants, but the rest of the party, including Rājā Bhim Chand, should take another available route, so that men were not provoked on either side. The Rājā acquiesced in this arrangement, but was greatly stung and pledged to take revenge, once the marriage was over. When the groom's party reached Srinagar, they objected strongly to any presents of Guru Gobind being accepted by the bride's house. Fateh Shāh was also told that unless he joined hands with his brother princes to fight the Guru, the marriage of Bhim Chand's son to his daughter would be cancelled. The Guru's party had, therefore, to leave in disgust. On the way, Bhim Chand's forces tried to intercept and dispossess them, but the Guru's troops soon put the enemy to rout with their accurate and devastating gunfire. They reached Paontā safe, but soon received news that the hill chiefs were preparing for a major attack on their way back home. When the Guru heard of this, he marched his troops six miles ahead, towards a place called Bhangāni, to wait for the combination of the hill chiefs come to battle with him.

"When the Sikh troops got orders for the march, they were exceedingly excited over the news. But the Pathāṇs, thinking that the Guru's main dependence at this time was upon them, decided to desert to the enemy who would reward them with much cash at this critical moment. The Guru tried to dissuade them against this treachery, but they were adamant.* The Guru sent word to Budhu Shāh

---

* That there were desertions in the Sikh camp at this time is testified by the Guru himself in the *Bachittar Nātak* :—"They who fought not for me I expelled from the town" (of Ānandpur, where the Guru came after the battle of Bhangāni). But, there is no indication that these were the Pathāns recruited on the recommendation of Budhu Shāh. According to Bannerji (Evolution of the Khālsā, Part II, P. 74) "there was a party in the Guru's camp who cared little for his cause and who had joined him merely for the sake of personal profit. Perhaps these were the people who were primarily responsible for these repeated outrages on the subjects of the hill chiefs, of which we get many indications in the Sikh records. Indeed, the marauding instinct was characteristic of the Jāts who formed the bulk of the Guru's followers and whom, it seems, the influence of Sikhism never completely chastened."

also to tell him how his men had misbehaved. The Muslim divine was so shocked that he presented himself for service along wiih his four sons and a brother and seven hundred followers.† According to *Bachittar Nātak*, the chiefs of Dadhwār and Jaswāl, Ghazi Chand of Chandel and Gopal (Rājā of Guler) and Hari Chand fought on the side of Fateh Shāh, besides many others.

"The Guru also gave command to the Udāsis, five hundred of whom were accompanying him, to prepare for the battle. But, except for their leader, Kirpāl, everyone fled to safety. The battle which was soon upon the Guru raged with utter fury. Budhu Shāh's men and relations fought with as much valour as the Sikhs. Mahant Kirpāl, the Udāsi, fought with his club and made mincemeat of the enemy including a deserter Pathān general, Hayāt Khān. The Guru even employed a cannon built by one of his Sikhs from Banāras, Ram Singh by name. A confectioner, named Lāl Chand, who had never learnt how to handle arms, fought with such bravery that even the trained Pathāns were taken by surprise. He killed several of them. One of the bravest of Rājās, Hari Chand, fell in the battle-field.* The Guru lost his cousin, Sango Shāh. Pir Budhu Shāh

† The battle of Bhangāni was fought only for one day, and the Guru's version of it corroborrates it. We also learn from his account that the news of the projected attack was suddenly conveyed to him and was provoked by Fateh Shāh without cause. Unless the Pathāns had established their contact with Fateh Shāh much earlier and the desertions also come about not on the eve of the battle, but some time before, the story of Budhu Shāh being shocked by the Pathāns' desertion and his own joining the Guru's forces with his followers and sons from a distance of about 100 miles must be dismissed as unreliable.

* According to *Sirmur Gazetteer*, both Hari Chand and Fateh Shāh fell in the battlefield (P. 15) and the Rānis of both the leaders became *Sati* and their eight tombs are still seen at Bhangāni. The Sikh records, however, tell us that "Fateh Shāh had fled when he found his cause hopeless". The Guru does not call Hari Chand "*Kror rāyān*" (or "the chief of Karor", as Mecauliffe translates, or a "multi-millionaire" as Bannerjee does). The correct translation of this verse would be: "Hari Chand too fell at my hands and many other princes of untold riches." According to Bannerjee (Evolution of the Khālsā, Part II, P. 76), "we nowhere find it mentioned that the chief of Karor had anything to do with Guru Gobind Singh", that "Hari Chand was a rich and powerful chief, but not the ruler of Handur (Nalgarh)", among whose long line of princes, the name of Hari Chand does not occur. (See "Simla Hill States Gazetteer", Nalgarh, P. 60). It was Dharam Chand who ruled in Nalgarh from 1618 to 1701, succeeded by his son, Himmat Chand. But, as the Sikh tradition persistently connects Hari Chand with

lost two of his sons. But the losses of the enemy were so colossal that they fled in disarray. The Guru blessed Pir Budhu Shāh with a Kirpān (small, Sikh dagger), and a comb, with some broken hair of his, and a turban in remembrance of his services to the Guru's cause. These were secured for a high consideration from his family by the Mahārāja of Nābhā and are still preserved as sacred relics in the erstwhile princely state of Nābhā."@

After a stay, most probably of three years at Paontā (1685-86 to 1688-89 A.D.), the Guru now returned to Ānandpur. On the way, it is said, even the Rājā of Nāhan did not come out to greet him, as he was expected to, fearing the wrath of his brother princes who had been trounced and mauled badly by the Guru's forces, though this seems highly improbable. But, he was very warmly received by the inhabitants of Ānandpur. The Guru built a fortress here, with strong and lofty battlements around it.

The Sikhs came to visit the Guru from far and near. His fame as a warrior-saint attracted to him many a chivalrous youth, besides poets, musicians and men of religious disposition. The hunting expeditions were resumed as usual, and occasionally the Sikhs who strayed from his train would also exhibit some more exuberance than was expected of them. They were flushed with recent victory and howsoever the Guru might instruct to restrain them, they did, on occasions, it seems, transgress limits of worthy behaviour, especially when they could not get fodder for their horses even on payment, nor goats for meat. This would distress the Guru greatly.

Rājā Bhim Chand must have been greatly perturbed by the defeat of his brother-princes at Bhangāni (even if he, himself, as the Guru testifies, did not participate in it), and felt jealous over the Guru's growing power, but he was more apprehensive of maintaining his position as an independent ruler against the Moghals who were seeking to curb his power, he being the most notable of the hill

---

F. N. Contd.

Nalgarh, "Hari Chand might have been a younger son who had been sent by his father to assist Fateh Shāh, the chief himself being too old to join personally." (Evolution of the Khālsā, Part II, P. 76).

@ A letter said to be in the handwriting of the Guru dated Phagun Sudi 12, 1743 BK (February 25, 1686) and still preserved by the descendants of the Pir is referred to by the modern historians as decisive (a) for determining the date of the battle of Bhangāni and (b) the Pir's own part in it. But, if the Guru's *Bachittar Nātak* is to be believed, both these assertions fall to the ground.

chiefs. He, thereupon, took counsel with his advisers as to the best course he might adopt to make up with the Guru's house. He was very wisely advised by his counsellors to seek a rapprochement with the Guru, both in the interest of peace within his dominions and to put up a joint front against the Moghals.

An envoy was sent accordingly to sound the Guru, who responded generously, as was expected from his station and spiritual temper. He said, "I have no quarrel with anyone. I want only to be left in peace to propagate the cause of *Dharma*. My father gave his head to protect the religion of the Hindus. But here am I, trying to infuse a new spirit in this dying race, being refused cooperation by the Hindu chiefs, and even resisted and attacked without cause. My followers cannot even buy for cash what they need from the surrounding villages. Such is the hostility generated against us. We have not aggressed against any one even once. But, certainly, we mean now to defend our honour."

The envoy, however, beseeched the Guru to forget the past, and to consider the Rājā's territories as his own. The Guru replied, "In my house whosoever comes with friendly intent and in humility is received with open arms. We do not harbour grudge against those who seek to be friendly." Rājā Bhim Chand was much pleased on hearing this report and prepared himself to call on the Guru with large presents. The Guru also bestowed upon him a robe of honour. It appeared there was now complete understanding between the two.

In these days, emperor Aurangzeb ordered the Governor of Jammu, Mian Khān, to advance upon the hill chiefs to gather tribute, which, according to several historians, they had refused to pay, inspired by the Guru. Accordingly, the Governor sent his Commander-in-Chief, Alif Khān, to do the job. The other hill chiefs said to Alif Khān that as Rājā Bhim Chand was the greatest of them all, he should be asked to pay first. If he did so, everyone else would follow suit. An envoy was sent by the Moghal warrior to the Rājā, demanding tribute under threat of war. Rājā Bhim Chand told the imperial envoy that he would much rather fight than pay the tribute. He also sought the immediate assistance of the Guru at this critical moment. For, he thought, once the Moghals were given a fitting reply in war, they would leave them in peace for long. Otherwise, their demands would know no end. This would also cement the relations between the house of the Guru and their own, thus making Bilāspur the unchallenged leader of all the hill chiefs.

When the Prime Minister of the Rājā appeared in the presence of the Guru with a request for assistance, he made such courtesies that the Guru could not refuse him. "We are under the protection of the house of Nānak. So there is nothing that the Moghals can do to us if only you were to be our guide and light." The Guru granted his prayer and alerted his troops. Meanwhile, Alif Khān had gathered tribute from some of the hill chiefs, notably from Kāngrā and Bijharwāl who became his allies, against the combined forces of the Guru, Rājā Bhim Chand and others. By common consent, the Guru was given the command of the Allied forces. The enemy was obliged to come out of his fortresses and challenge the Allies on open ground. He showed exemplary valour so that Rājā Bhim Chand wanted to beat a retreat. At this, the Guru personally took the field and challenged one of the Rājās, Dayāl, chief of Bijharwāl, and pierced his heart with his bullet. His arrows created such havoc amongst the enemy forces and the Sikhs fought with such reckless courage that the enemy fled the field, under cover of darkness. This is known as the battle of Nadaun and was fought probably late in 1690.‡

The Guru then returned to Ānandpur and the Rājās, it appears, decided to reconcile themselves to the payment of tribute to the emperor, in spite of the Allied victory. Perhaps, they thought that any long drawn-out resistance would not be feasible for them. On the way back to his home-town, therefore, the Guru again encountered the hostility of the villagers who refused to sell fodder and grain to his troops, most surely under the inspiration of their chiefs. Thereupon, the Sikh troops took what they needed by force, "but not without making due payment", according to some historians like Macauliffe, and by looting the village of Aslun, according to others. When the Guru reached Ānandpur and saw a brief period of peace, his forces grew in strength so much that the Governor of Panjāb, Dilāwar Khān, was also scared. So, late in 1694, he sent

‡ According to Gandā Singh, about 1687 A. D. (*A History of the Sikhs*, p. 64, f.n.), but as we have seen, the Guru was still at Paontā in the middle of 1688 A. D., finishing his composition, *Krishnavtār*. His sudden departure for Ānandpur can thiswise be more suitably explained as also why Bhim Chand received him with open arms at Ānandpur.

an expedition, 11,000 strong, under his son, Khānzādā, to force the Guru to pay tribute, or to sack the city of Ānandpur. After him, every other hill chief was also to be served with a similar notice, or humbled through war. Sensing the approaching storm, however, many people left Ānandpur. But the Guru's forces met the advancing Moghal troops on the bank of the Satluj, and inflicted a crushing defeat on them. Thereupon, Dilāwar Khān, Governor of Kāngrā, sent another expedition, this time under a slave-general of his, Hussain by name. Hussain plundered village after village with great rapacity and alarmed Rājā Bhim Chand so much that he thought it would be better to become an ally of his than the Guru's. He, therefore, paid whatever tribute he was asked to, and so did the other princes. Not only this, they made common cause with him and advanced with their troops along with the Moghals on Ānandpur.*

On the way to Ānandpur, the Moghal general wanted to settle accounts with Rājā Gopāl, chief of Guler, who had refused to fall in line with his brother princes, as the sum of tribute demanded from him was not within his means. He sent his envoy to the Guru for assistance. The Guru at first tried to bring about a reconciliation between him and the other hill chiefs, so that they could together face the Moghal onslaught. But this did not work. One of his brother princes even tried to trap and kill him, but he escaped and was now left with no choice but to give battle to the combined forces of the Moghals and the Rājās of Kāngrā and Bilāspur. The Guru sent some troops for his help, several of whom were slain on the battlefield. But, in the battle also fell the Moghal general and the Rājā of Kāngrā. Bhim Chand fled with his army, and Gopāl was victorious. He came to pay tribute to the Guru with large offerings. This was, however, not the end of their troubles. Aurangzeb, greatly incensed, sent his son (later Bahādur Shāh) to bring the hill chiefs to book. He in turn sent out Mirzā Beg and later four other renowned generals to subdue them.† This they did with utter callousness, inflicting

* This is called *Hussaini Yudh*, having been fought against the slave-general, Hussain Khān.

† The statement of the eminent Sikh historians, Dr. Gandā Singh and Tejā Singh, basing their argument on a verse of the *Bachittar Nātak* (see next page) that some kind of understanding had been reached between the Government and the Guru through the intercession of a Sikh, Bhāi Nand Lāl, who was the *Mir Munshi* at

crushing defeats on them, plundering and burning their territories, and clean-shaving and parading the prisoners on donkeys through the villages. Some of these included those who had deserted the Guru and took shelter in the hills with all their treasures, though the Guru was left severely alone.*

F. N. Contd.

Multān for 30 years and also served as such under Prince Muazzim, (later Bahādur Shāh, but who in fact took over as Governor of Kābul, Multān and Lāhore only in 1696 A.D.) as a result of which while the hill Rājās were severely punished, the Guru was left alone, is highly controversial. In the first place, the verse in question cannot by any stretch of imagination be construed to mean what it does to the learned authors of "A Short History of the Sikhs" (P. 65), especially in the context in which it is written, and secondly it goes against the whole philosophy of the Guru's house. All his future struggles against Aurangzeb become devoid of purpose or at least of moral significance, and makes the birth of the Khālsā only three years later, to be an event of little social or political import. The reasons for the Guru's help at a later date to Bahādur Shāh in his fight for succession are discussed towards the end of this chapter. Why Bahādur Shāh left the Guru alone may be on account of the personal assessment of the situation, even against the advice of his father, as he did earlier in respect of the Shīa Kingdoms of the South, even though he had to suffer incarceration for seven years for his courage of convictions. Thus, it appears, Bhāi Nandlāl's part in this affair seems not to be of much consequence, assuming that he did, or could play such a vital role in his position. As we shall see later, Bhāi Nandlāl had to leave his service soon after Bahādur Shāh assumed the Governorship of Multān and to seek refuge in Ānandpur with the Guru.

* In his *Bachittar Nātak*, the Guru makes very caustic references to the deserters who were looted by the Moghal forces and had no face even to come back to the Guru. In the end, he makes these prophetic remarks :—

"*Bābē kē, Babur kē Do-ou.*

Āp karē Parmēshar So-ou.

Dinshāh in ko anmāno,

Dunishāh un ko Pahchāno.

Jo bābē kē dām na de-hai

Tis tē geh bābur kē Lē-hai."

"The house of the Bābā (Nānak) and of Bābur, both, are the creation of God, the one in the realm of the spirit and the other in the domain of the secular world. And (such is God's law) that he who denies his allegiance and support to the Bābā (Nānak), him the house of Bābur seizes, robs and destroys." This verse has been employed by some historians to misinterpret the Guru's intentions in that he sought to justify the rule (even misrule) of whosoever was in the seat of political power. The whole tenor of the Guru's life was against this defeatist and

It may be stated here that in the meantime the Guru had married twice, while still young, as he had no issue from the first one for seven years. The second one, Sundari, gave birth to one son, Ajit Singh (1686). The other, Jitoji, later also brought forth three sons, Jujhār Singh (1690), Zorāwar Singh (1696) and Fateh Singh (1699).*

One day, a Brahmin of great repute, Kesho Dās by name, came from Banāras to visit the Guru. He claimed that if he were helped with the wherewithals for a *homa* (sacrificial fire), he could make visible the goddess of power, Chandi or Durgā, also known as Kāli. He said it was through extreme austerities and *tapas* that the goddess would appear, and only if a man like him were to be the master of ceremonies. He harangued the followers of the Guru also on the great blessings that the goddess would bestow on whosoever could invoke her grace. Such a one could never be defeated in war. He attributed the successes of the ancient Hindu heroes like Bhim and Arjun to their being the votaries of Durgā.

The Sikhs were much impressed with his talk and supported his request to the Guru. The Guru replied: "Even gods and goddesses are subject to the Will and Authority of the one God who is supreme over all creation. He it is from whom we should seek all boons and

---

F. N. Contd.

morally-degrading tendency. The verse, therefore, if read in its proper perspective and context, can only mean that he who, out of fear or expediency, flouts God's Moral Law, becomes a victim to God's wrath through the tyrannisers of the world, who too reflect the opposite (though inevitable) part of God's Moral Law.

@ Jeetoji, daughter of Harjas, a Khatri of Lahore, was married to the Guru in the year 1677 A. D., when he was only 11 years old. But upto the year 1684, he had no issue from her, when on the insistence of his mother, he was married again in that year to Sundri, daughter of Ram Saran, another Khatri of Lāhore. She gave birth to Ajit Singh, the first son of Guru Gobind Singh in the year 1686. Later, however, Jeetoji gave birth to the three other sons of the Guru, the last, Fateh Singh, in 1699, and died soon thereafter (in January 1701). In the same year, Rāmu, a Khatri of Rohtās, District Jehlum, offered his daughter, Sāhib Kaur, to him, pleading that his daughter had pledged herself to be the bride of the Guru even if she had to remain a virgin after the wedlock, as the Guru had insisted. The Guru could not resist his entreaties and married her. She is referred to by all historians as *Kavārā dolā* (virgin wife). The Guru later blessed her as the Mother of the Khālsā. That is how when an orthodox Sikh is asked about his parentage, he invariably refers to Guru Gobind Singh as his father, Sāhib Kaur as his Mother and Ānandpur as his place of birth or residence.

benedictions. He gives man the power to make and unmake his destiny if man surrenders himself to Him and fights only for his causes." But, it appears ever though the devout, Sikhs were convinced with these arguments, not so the hillfolk in whose midst the Guru now lived and who were only grudgingly being drawn towards his instruction, which were wholly opposed to their age-old traditional beliefs. So, as Dr. Gokal Chand Narang rightly points out (Transformation of Sikhism, pp. 85-86), in order to convince them of the futility of their beliefs, "the Guru ordered a great sacrifice (homa) to be performed with the ostensible object of making the goddess appear. The ceremony is said to have lasted for a year. At the end of that time, when Durga Ashtami came round again, the Guru asked the presiding priest when the goddess would make her appearance. The Pandit said that the goddess would reveal herself only if a pure and holy man of noble lineage sacrificed himself at the altar, and had his head flung into the fire. The Guru was apparently pleased, and said to the Pandit with a smile of sarcasm on his lips, 'Where shall we find, revered sir, a holier man than yourself whose head could form a fitting offering to the goddess.' The Pandit was struck dumb and decamped on a false pretext. The Guru flung all the remaining material into the fire and came out from behind the screens with a drawn sword flashing in his hand. The large quantity of the homa material thrown in a lump into the fire blazed forth in a large flame which being on a lofty hill was seen for miles around, and was taken as a sign of the propitiation and appearance of the goddess."

The Guru, then, walked down the hill of Nainādevi, a drawn sword in his hand, and said to the crowd waiting breathlessly for his vision: "This is the true manifestation of the goddess of Power, the shining steel with which evil is punished and virtue protected and rewarded. He who is willing to taste its baptism for a righteous cause invokes indeed the blessings of God."*

* The *Gur Bilās* of Sukhā Singh (completed in 1797 A, D. when the Sikhs were once again coming under the away of the Brāhmins) gives the name of the Brāhmin as Dattānand and makes him a resident of Ujjain. It is also stated here that the Brāhmin needed an expense of Rs. 1,25,000/- and a period of four years for the manifestation of Devi, that the Guru himself undertook the Devi's worship under Dattānand's directions and when the period of austerities and worship was drawing to a close, the Brāhmin wanted one of the Guru's own sons to be offered as a sacrifice before the Devi could make her appearance, but the Guru refused to accept this demand and a Sikh's head was offered instead. The Pandit now left

The Guru thereafter, recited a few couplets to show that the power resided in the people themselves and not in the gods and goddesses. Pointing to his followers, he said: "It is through ye that I have won battles; through your favour that I have distributed bounties to the poor. Through ye it is that all my woes are past, through your favour that my house is overflowing with material possessions. Through your kindness have I overpowered my enemies; through your favour am I instructed in wisdom. I'm exalted because ye, O people, have exalted me, else there were many poor ones like me wandering luckless and friendless."

He continued: " One who serves the people, pleases me. Nothing else is pleasing to my mind. Offer gifts to them if you may, for no one else is worthy to receive them. To show favour to them bears

---

F. N. Contd.

the Guru alone and asked him to wait for the manifestation of Devi. After some terrible experiences—the raging storms, earthquakes, devastating rains, etc...—the Devi appeared and gave him her own sword at which there were great rejoicings, etc. Rose (in his Glossary of Panjāb Tribes and Castes, Vol. I, p. 695) and Cunningham (in his History of the Sikhs, p. 70) repeat this story, though with the addition that the Guru was prepared to offer his son as a sacrifice, but his wives and mother would have none of it which compelled the Guru to choose a Sikh instead. Cunningham makes another fantastic statement that when the Devi appeared, the Guru, terror-stricken, closed his eyes, at which the Devi ordained that he would have no success in his lifetime and that his sect would flourish after him! Malcolm in his "Sketch of the Sikhs" (pp. 49-50) repeats this story on the authority of "one of the most respectable and best-informed authors of that sect", but chooses to keep his name anonymous.

But, it is clear from the own writings of the Guru ("I propitiate neither Ganesh nor Krishna, nor Vishnu. I*'ve heard of them, but recognise them not*. It is God's Feet alone that I adore"—Krishnāvtār), as well as the whole tenor of his life and the teaching of his house that the above story is nothing but a concoction, cleverly circulated first during the early part of Ranjit Singh's reign and seized upon by some of the drama-loving British historians thereafter. For a fuller and correct version of the whole incident, see Bhāi Vir Singh's *Devi Poojan Partāl.* It must be emphasised that though the Guru, in his verse-compositon, *Chandi di Vār,* eulogises Chandi or Durgā, the goddess or war, over much, he makes her a creature of God (or Bhagauti) like Brahma, Shiva, Rām, Krishan, etc. He never even once identitifies Durgā with *Bhagauti* which he renders in his own special vocabulary as God, the All-Powerful, *Kāl, Mahākāl, Kharagket, Tegh, Sri Kharag, Khandā, Sarabloh,* etc., which only can be interpreted as Time, All-time (or Timeless), the Holy Sword, the double-edged (and so, discriminating) weapon, All steel, etc, which only signify the omnipotence of God, the sure destroyer of evil. In the *Chandi-di-Vār*", the phrases like *"Lai Bhagauti Durgshāh*" (Durga took up the Bhagauti, i e. the sword in her hands), make obvious the meaning of the term.

fruit here and hereafter, for any other service is of no avail. My possessions, my body, my soul are at the disposal of my people. For, nothing else avails, nay, nothing."

The Guru writes that hearing these words, the Pandit was much grieved and wept.*

II

March 30,1699.† It was on the first day of Vaisākh, mid-spring, and the beginning of the Hindu new year, that Guru Gobind Singh, after a great thought, decided finally to evolve a new order. Upto now, everyone, Hindu or Muslim, was welcome to the portals of the new faith, if he pledged to forego his caste exclusiveness, interdine, serve man irrespective of his creed or position, to be pure in word, thought and deed, and to believe only in one God, and discard all cant, supserstition and ritual. It was a society of the peaceful and the holy. The fifth Guru, Arjun, had even given up his life without demur, in a most non-violent way, at the behest of the empror Jehāngir. His son, Hargobind, the sixth Guru, wore arms, however, and kept a small force with which he fought the forces of Shāh Jahān in self-defence several times, and always won. Guru Hari Rai, who succeeded him, also maintained a cavalry of 2200, though he never used it. The eighth Guru, Hari Kishen, died very young, at the age of 8, and the ninth Guru, father of Gobind, was beheaded in Delhi under orders from Aurangzeb, but no fight followed, no rebellion

* In these days, when the Guru was holding a Darbār at Ānandpur, some itinerant players, staged a drama to highlight the misdeeds of the *Masands,* how they literally robbed the poor Sikhs and led a most corrupt and lecherous life. It is said, the Guru, already incensed with the immorality and exploitation of the *Masands* was now confirmed in his resolve to abolish this institution altogether which had been in existence for over a century (from the days of Guru Rām Dās to the year 1698). He collected the *Masands* from far and near and punished them according to their deserts. "Some were flogged; others were made to part with their ill-gotten wealth to the owners. The few who were found innocent were released and sent back rewarded. But the order of the Masands ceased to exist from that date."

† According to Bhangu Rattan Singh's *"Panth Parkāsh"* (pp. 43-44), the Guru initiated the Khālsā on a Wednesday (after consulting the pandits for an auspicious day (!) in the month of Baisākh, in the year 1752 (Vikrami) or 1695 A. D. But no other historian corroborates this date, or his consulting the Pandits for an auspicious day.

raised its head.† Guru Gobind Singh had seen how he himslf was being pursued by the surrounding hill-chiefs, even though they claimed to be Hindus, in collusion with the Moghal emperor, Aurangzeb, for the mere fact that he wanted the people of all religions to co-exist and not to be coerced to accept a way of life which they did not voluntarily choose. He had no territorial ambitions, and meant harm to no one. Yet, he hardly found peace for himself or those who belonged to him.*

---

† It is pointed out in this connection, however, that the courage of the two Sikhs who carried away, one the head and the other the body of the martyred Guru kept under strict surveillance by the Moghal forces, in the heart of the town of Delhi, was no mean achievement. It is also stated in *Maasir-i-Ālamgiri* (P. 94) that seven or eight months after this incident (June-July 1676 A. D.) "an aggrieved person (identified later as a Sikh) flung a stick at the emperor (Aurangzeb) in the compound of the *Diwān-i-Ām*, as he was mounting his horse", and "on October 27 of the same year, another "ill-starred disciple of Guru Tegh Bahadur threw two bricks at the emperor one of which reached the chair (in which he was seated)." In both cases, the persons charged with the crime were handed over to the *Kotwāl* (and most surely executed). But, these acts of individual heroism, though highly commendable in themselves, made no impact either on the fortunes of the Moghal empire or in arousing the masses to a concerted action.

* That Aurangzeb had by this time got scared of the successes of the Guru is obvious from the orders he issued on November, 20, 1693 A. D. "News from Sarhind. Gobind declares himselself to be Guru Nānak. Faujdārs ordered to prevent him from assembling (his forces)." (*"Akhbārāt-i-Darbār-Mualla"*, Vol. I, 1677-95 R. A. S., London version). It was after this that the Guru was attacked by the combined forces of the hill chiefs and the Moghals in 1695 and later even the emperor's eldest son, Bahādur Shāh, was asked personally to march against him. By this time, Aurangzeb had shown himself to be highly bigoted and insensitive to the feelings of the Hindus who constituted the majority of his subjects. In 1690, he issued an edict prohibiting the Hindus from being carried in palanquins or riding Arab horses. According to Khāfi Khān's *"Muntakhab-ul-Lubāb"* (Vol. II, P. 278), Aurangzeb (himself a Sunni) went out to invade Deccan's Shia Kingdoms in order to punish the 'infidels' (i.e. the Shia Muslims). According to *Maasir-i-Ālamgiri*, jezia (poll-tax) was reimposed on the Hindus in 1680 A. D. (according to others in 1697). They had to pay double duty on their goods. And, when the Hindu shop-keepers and workmen of Delhi protested in mass, he got them trampled under the elephants (Khāfi Khān's ML, Vol. II, P. 252). According to the same author, not only Hindu temples of great eminence were ordered to be destroyed, but also the Sikh temples, and the Guru's agents were expelled from the cities (ibid, pp. 651-652).

On the defeat and capture of Sambhāji, son of Shivāji, in 1689 A. D., Aurangzeb ordered that the tongues of both Sambhāji and his Vizier Kabkalas (or Kavi-Kalas) be cut out, so that they might no longer speak disrespectfully

The Guru, therefore, decided to evolve an order which would keep as its ideal of life nothing but sacrifice for the cause of *Dharma*, and would not accept either for themselves nor for others slavery,

---

F. N. Contd.

(against the emperor and the Prophet). After that, their eyes were to be torn out. Then, with ten or eleven other persons, they were to be put to death with a variety of tortures (for 24 days, according to the Cambridge History of India, Vol. IV, P. 284), and lastly that the skins of the heads of Sambhā and Kabkalas be stuffed with straw and exposed in all the cities and towns of the Deccan with the beat of drum and sound of trumpet. (Khāfi Khān, Muntakhabal Lubāb, Vol. II, P. 383).

That Aurangzeb had ordered the Hindu idols to be removed from the historic temples (and trodden under foot on the footsteps of the mosques at Āgrā and Delhi) has already been mentioned in the previous chapter. Music, a necessary part of Hindu, Sikh and Ṣufi ritual, was bañished from the realm in 1669. No Hindu was allowed to wear arms and the beards, longer than four fingers, even of the Muslims (as prescribed by the Muslim Shariat) were cut down to the religiously permissible limits. According to Manucci, one Qumir was beheaded by Aurangzeb's orders "for his writing a work with Christian tendencies which none of his Muslim divines could refute". In 1669, he stopped the celebration of Muharram, sacred to the Shias. Sarmad, the great Sufi, was beheaded publicy as a heretic. According to *Ahkām-i-Ālamgiri*, Aurangzeb forbade the employment of even the subsmissive Rajputs as faujdārs or provincial governors. The employment of Hindus in their age-old occupations of revenue and clerical assistants was also forbidden, according to *Maasir-i-Alamgiri* and *Muntakhab-ul-Lubāb.* Many Hindus were forced to change their religion in order to retain their appointments. Successive expeditions were led against the Marāthas, the Rājputs, the Jāts, the Satnāmis and the Shias, and no quarter was allowed to anyone not adhering to the orthodox Islamic Sunni creed.

When the earlier order (of November 20, 1693) to curb the activities of Guru Gobind Singh and his Sikhs, did not produce much effect, "a general order was issued for their massacre" (*Maasir-i-Ālamgiri*, P. 153). "In the Sarkār of Sirhind, a Sikh temple was demolished to give place to a mosque. The Sikhs, in their turn pulled down the mosque and killed the *imām*." (*Kalim-i-Tayyibat*, P. 115, as quoted by S. R. Sharma in his "Religious Policy of the Moghal Emperors P. 141).

"Some time after, when 20,000 Sikhs, (obviously unable to suffer persecution) were proceeding towards the country of Bārakzai Afghāns, their Muslim escorts fell upon them in co-operation with other Muslim fanatics and killed them." (Ibid, P. 141-142). According to *Ahkām-i-Ālamgiri* (2a), "Aurangzeb issued orders to prince Shāh Ālam (later Bahādur Shāh) to imprison the Sikhs and expel them from the districts under his command."

It is, therefore, not unnatural for the tenth Guru to have made a final bid to embark on the course of a total, violent resistance to the regime of Aurangzeb, though not to Islām as such.

either political, or social or economic. And, if for this they had to fight their way through, they wouldn't shirk the use of arms; in fact, arms would be an instrument for the achievement of an ideal world-order in which no one sat upon another's rights or ideas and each individual was free to pursue any path of life so long as he did not come in the way of another.

"The Hindus," at this stage, as Dr. Gokal Chand Narang has aptly remarked, "were too mild by nature, too contented in their desires, too modest in their aspirations, too averse to physical exertion and terror-stricken and demoralised, even though strongly attached to their religion. They had religion, but no national feeling. (So) Guru Gobind Singh sought to make nationalism their religion."*

Several events that stood out in the Guru's mind had perhaps influenced this decision. His father, Guru Tegh Bahādur, had been beheaded in a public square of Delhi, but no one had come forward, except two low-caste Sikhs in disguise and under cover of darkness, to claim his body. One Hindu chief was fighting with another, and even asking for assistance against his co-religionists from the emperor Aurangzeb. Even though the Guru had helped the Rajput hill chiefs as often as they needed his help against the Moghals, they ultimately came to terms with them and left the Guru alone to fend for himself.

Caste had so much divided our race† that when Guru Gobind Singh wanted some Sikhs to learn Sanskrit, the Pandit, whose name

---

* *Transformation of Sikhism*, p. 79. Nationalism, however, was encouraged by the Gurus as a stage in man's socio-political evolution and not as an ideal, which was to be a world-order, of which a nation, freely constituted by its people through democratic expression (and not being a mere geographical expression or a historical accident) was to form an integral, though inter-dependent, part.

† Such was the tyranny of caste that when in the year 1674 A. D. Shivaji, the great Marāthā hero, wanted to get himself crowned as a Hindu King, no Brāhmin priest would come forward to annoint him, he being the son of a farmer and hence a *Vaisha*, and not of the Kashatriya or the warrior class. For six months, Shivāji entertained thousands of Brāhmins and gifted away tons of gold and silver to them but even though they accepted his bounties, they refused to accede to his wish. Ultimately, a famous Pandit from Banāras, Gangā Bhatt by name, agreed to do so for a heavy bribe on the express condition that when at the coronation ceremony he would read out **the Vedic text**, he would do it so rapidly that Shivaji would not be able to discern the correct text, the hearing of the Veda being forbidden

is given as Raghu Nāth, refused to teach them as they belonged to the lower castes.* Daughters were murdered at birth and a women was so downgraded and secluded as to deny her all the rights and privileges of a living, human being.† Even though a large number of Sikhs followed the teachings of the Guru and accepted him in every way as their spiritual guide, they were far too involved with their household and environments to be ever prepared to answer the

---

F. N. Contd.

for the low castes, (which included women). (For details, see 'Aurangzeb' by Sir J. N. Sarkār, Vol. III.)

Caste, however, has very deep-rooted causes, and cannot be abolished by merely legal or social pressures, unless it is replaced by an ideology which gives an indivdual a sense of better belonging. Today, no matter how low one's caste, one finds one's identity at least within that caste. Beginning as *varna* (or colour-consciousness) with the white Āryans against the black aborigines, it gradually became identified with one's hereditary profession. Ultimately, anyone who worked for a living with his hands—farmer as much as the sweeper or the tanner, barber or a washerman, drummer or butcher, oilman or weaver—became a low-caste. As the workers were recruited by the land-owners, princes (Kashatriyas), merchants (Vaishās) and priests (Brāhmins) only from the aborigines, on account of their black colour, one finds even to date a most distinctive difference between the skin-colours of the lower classes, or untouchables, and the three higher castes. It is, however, the lower castes of the socially-persecuted humanity that flocked to the standard of an egalitarian Islām, Sikhism, Christianity and Buddhism. However, these communities themselves falling a prey to sect and caste have, by and large, betrayed their original doctrine of castelessness. It appears, moreover, that so long as the institution of marriage persists, the question of colour, of blood and race and therefore of caste would continue to dominate men's minds. Love, they say, knows no caste, but certainly it is very partial to colour—the whiter the better.

* The Guru thereupon sent five of his devout Sikhs—Karam Singh, Gandā Singh, Vir Singh, Sainā Singh and Rām Singgh—to Banāras where, assuming the robes of Hindu Brahmachāris, they learned Sanskrit and became well versed in all its ancient literature. They were honoured by the Guru with the title of "Nirmalās" (or, the Pure ones") and their sect to this day has done much to illumine men's minds by the interpretation of the Sikh sacred writings, though in a special Hindwi language. But, as time passed, they interpreted the Sikh theology more and more in terms of the Hindu Vadāntic tradition.

However, it seems surprising that the Guru, himself a householder, should have sanctioned the Nirmalās remaining ascetics or out of wedlock ?

† When Alā-ud-Din Khilji attacked and conquered Chittor in 1303 A. D., the great citadel of Rajput resistance, 13000 of choice Hindu brides instead of taking to arms and pouncing upon the enemy as women under the leadership of the tenth Guru did, leapt into flames to perform *Sati* when their spouses fell in the battle.

call of supreme sacrifice for the sake of *Dharma*. They were a spiritual and a social entity but not a politically dynamic or decisive force. And, into this the Guru wanted to convert them now, if there was to be a future for them also as a people, each one of whom was not merely free but equal in all ways.

Were the people willing to go through fire? This the Guru wanted to put to a test. So, on the first day of Vaisākh, when men and women had gathered as usual, from far and near, at Ānandpur, to pay homage to the Guru, he stood up in the assembly, of a sudden, naked sword in hand, and thundered, "I want a Sikh who can offer his head to me, here and now. My sword is thirsting for the head of one who had learnt the lesson of surrender to me."

There was a hush in the whole congregation. What did the Guru mean? No one before him had asked any follower of his to offer this supreme sacrifice. And, for what reason? No one could divine what was behind this play of the Master, who had ever bestowed supreme affection and care on them. The Guru, his eyes flashing like lightning, roared again, "Is there no one in this whole assembly who would stand up and say, 'Here I give myself up to you'. You who've always chimed: 'He who loves the God's way offers his head to Him on the palm of his hand'?" There was utter silence even now. When, for the third time, the Guru asked, "Is there not one who could prove his faith in me?" a Sikh from Lāhore, Dayā Rām, a Kharti, came forward, slowly, his head bowed and his palms joined in prayer: "O King of kings, here I offer my head to thee. It was always thine. If it can be of any use to thee, I would deem it the greatest privilege, and feel redeemed."

The Guru, says the tradition, took him into an enclosure, and slaughtering a goat there, came back, his sword dripping with blood, his eyes redder and fiercer than before. Many in the congregation fled in terror. Others bemoaned in their thoughts that the Guru had perhaps lost reason. But, when the Guru asked, "I want another head. Dharma cannot be protected now except by those who are prepared to make the supreme sacrifice of their lives", another person, Dharam Dās of Rohtak answered to his call the same way. He was also taken to the enclosure, another goat slaughtered and the Guru came out before a fear-stricken audience, his sword drenched in blood. At this point, many Sikhs rushed to the Guru's mother, asking her to intervene, or to depose him from the spiritual Throne of Nānak. For, wasn't he shedding the blood of innocent followers of his merely to satisfy his whim? The mother, it is said, sent word to the Guru, but he was adamant in carrying out his will.

This time, and another two times, came forward three more persons, Mohkam Chand of Dwārkā, Sāhib Chand from Bidar, and Himmat of Jagannāt Puri, to offer their heads, one by one. After the five had thus surrendered themselves to the Guru, the Guru put a stop to further demands. Meantime, he brought out the five Sikhs he had taken into the tent, dressed in fresh garments, blue-turbaned, with loose, long, yellow shirts, a waist-band round their waists, with sorts of nicker-bockers worn as under-wears, and with swords dangling by their sides, they looked not only smart, but soldier-like, inspiring and dedicated. These the Guru called his *Panj-pyārē* (the five beloveds). The whole assembly thereupon resounded with the shouts of "Sat Sri Akāl" (Immortal is God), and entreated the Guru to bless them likewise. It would be of interest to note that out of the five, four belonged to the depressed classes.*

---

* Dayā Rām was a Khatri from Lāhore, Dharam Dās, a jāt from Rohtak, Mohkam Chand, a washerman of Dwārkā (in Gujarat), Himmat, a water-carrier of Jagannāth Puri (in eastern India) and Sāhib Chand, a barber from Bidar (in South India). Thus, they not only represented the five parts of the Indian subcontinent, but also their names symbolised the five great virtues of the Sikh religion, namely, *Dayā* (compassion), *Dharma* (moral righteousness), *Himmat* (courage), *Mohkam* (fortitude) and *Sāhib* (mastery over the self). It is perhaps for the same reason that the Guru sanctified the figure 'five' (as Gurū Nānak also did before him in his hymn, '*Panch Parwān*', etc.,), to accord with the five directions (including space) and embracing thus the whole universe. He established the five *takhats* or the seats of Sikh spiritual authority (three in the Punjāb, namely, the *Akāl Takhat* at Amritsar, the two at Ānandpur Sāhib and Damdamā Sāhib, the fourth in the east of India at Patnā (eastern India) and the fifth at Nāndēd in the South). It is said that just as there are five *Karamindriyas* (working faculties) and five *Gyānindriyas* (knowing faculties), five passions to be controlled, and five negative injunctions to be obeyed (namely, to have no dealings with the *Masands*, *Minās* (i.e. the progeny of Prithi Chand), the descendants of Dhirmal and those who kill their daughters (*Kurimārs*) or smoke tobacco (Panth Parkāsh by B. Rattan Singh P. 44), the Guru also enjoined the five symbols (K's) to be observed. Later, he also said that anyone who wishes to see him in person would have his vision wherever "the five pure ones" are assembled. (GSG, 2, 23). Cf. *Panch-Shabad*" of the yogis and the first five disciples of the Buddha. It is said, the Guru made all Sikhs, no matter what their stature, equal, like the five fingers which are equally useful but still dependent one upon the other. Panchāyat (or the Assembly of Five select elders to adjudicate upon disputes) has been a well-known social institution in India. So, the figure '5', it is surmised, has a socio-religious significance.

The Guru now asked for a steel bowl filled with water, and started stirring it with a steel double-edged dagger, reciting all the while the five compositions one by one, composed by himself or the earlier Gurus.* As this was being done, his wife, Jeetoji, came with some sugar-bubbles (Patāsās). The Guru asked her to sweeten the water in the bowl with these. "It is a very happy coincidence", he said, "the Khālsā shall not only be warlike, but also sweeten the life of those whom he is chosen to serve." When the readings were finished, the Guru administered what he called "A*mrit*" (nectar) as Pahul to his beloved five, and then asked them to partake of it from the same bowl by turns. This done, he now stood before them with folded hands, entreating them to administer the "*Amrit*" to him likewise.

This almost stunned them, as also the rest of the assembly. "You are the Guru, our spiritual guide, for both here and the hereafter, our redeemer and our saviour, unto whom we have delivered up also our lives. How can we administer '*Amrit*' to you, O King of Kings ?" The Guru said : "It is a new order I have evolved from this day, where there shall be no high and no low. I want to establish this fraternity on the basis of utter equality by asking to become your disciple now." On his refusal to take back his words, the Guru was administered "*Amrit*" the same way, much to the wonder of his devout followers. It electrified the atmosphere as nothing else could. It is said many thousand persons were baptised thus on that day at

* These are - the *Jap* of Guru Nānak, *Jāp*, *Benati Chaupai* and ten *swaiyyas* of Guru Gobind Singh, and *Ānand* of Guru Amar Dās. According to the "*Panth Parkāsh*" of Bhangu Rattan Singh (P. 43), the Guru first read out the invocation (Ardāsā), then 32 (33 ?) *Swaiyyas* (his own composition in praise of God the immortal) and *Chandi di Vār*, and later distributing the holy pudding (*Karāh Parshād*) among them instructed them to (i) submit to the Word of the holy Guru Granth, (ii) to wear arms, (iii) follow the chase, and not to taste the Kosher (halāl) meat, (iv) wear unshorn hair and (v) to abandon the ways and customs of the ancestors (P. 44). According to *Gur Sobhā* of Sainapat (1711 A.D.), the Guru at this time instructed that the Sikhs should (i) hymn the Praises of God in the society of the holy, (ii) should not use tobacco, (iii) keep unshorn head-hair and beard, (iv) to discard the company of five kinds of people (see text), (*Gur Sobhā*, Verse, 30 : 146), (v) abandon greed and be compassionate to all. Bhāi Santokh Singh (in his GSG, rut 6, Ansu 20, Ank 16-19) also adds that co-habitation with the woman of a Turk (i. e. a Muslim) was also considered a grave sin by the Guru, so that in the fight with the Muslims, the Sikhs should not succumb to abduction or rape of the enemy's womenfolk, even when the enemy did not observe this code.

their request, their number rising to eighty thousand in two weeks' time. The Guru called them the *Khālsā,* the pure and his very own ideal (*Isht Suhird*).

The Guru then addressed them thus : "From now on, you have become casteless.* No ritual, either Hindu or Muslim, will you perform, and believe in superstition of no kind, but only in the one God who is the Master and the Protector of all, the only Creator and Destroyer. In your new order, the lowest will rank equal with the highest and each will be to the other a *Bhāi* (brother).‡ No pilgrimages for you any more, nor austerities, but the pure life of the household, which you should be ready to sacrifice at the call of Dharma. Women shall be the equal of men in every way. No *purdāhs* for them any more, nor the burning alive of the widow on the pyre of her spouse. He who kills his daughter, the Khālsā shall not deal with him. Five K's you will observe as a pledge of your dedication to my ideal. You will wear your hair unshorn *(Kes)*† like the ancient sages or Kashatriyas (warriors), a comb (*Kanghā*) to keep it clean, a steel bracelet (*karā*) to denote the universality of God, an under-

---

* Though caste was altogether abolished by the Gurus, the present-day Sikhs observe this rule more in its breach. Not only have they themselves become an exclusive caste, but inter-marriages between the Jāts (who incidently derive their origin along with the Khatris and the Rājputs from a common Khashatriya ancestory) and the non-Jāts are becoming more and more rare. The treatment meted out to the converts from the *Chuhrās* (sweepers, called Mazabhi Sikhs) and the *Chamārs* (termed *Rāmdāsias*) does little credit to this fraternity which rejects caste in its religious philosophy. It must be emphasised that in the army of today, the latter two classes have proved their mettle like the Khatris and the Jāts; and some of the known fighters of Guru Gobind and of later days came from these classes who formed the vanguard of the Sikh fight for freedom against the Moghals. Unfortunately, the all-pervasive Hindu influence in the matter of caste has left no community untouched, including Muslims and Christians. The Sikhs being socially far more akin to the Hindus have accepted their influence in this context the most.

‡ This word is used nowadays for the officiating Sikh priest. The Sikhs, however, have no priestly class and any lay person of character, *whether man or woman,* can lead the congregation and baptise others into the faith. The ceremony of initiation earlier was to drink the wash of the Guru's feet and to greet each other by touching the other's feet. A Sikh, no matter what his status, is nowadays addressed as "Sardār" (lit. chief). In the days of Ranjit Singh, they were addressed as Singhji and even the Mahārāja himself was called "Singh Sāhib".

† That human hair is the biggest source of vitamin-D is claimed by a well-known doctor, Chandā Singh of Faridkot, who has submitted his scientific researches to W. H. O. at Geneva for scrutiny and dissemination if proved worthwhile.

wear (*Kachhā*) to denote chastity and a steel-dagger *(Kirpān)* for your defence. Smoking being an unclean habit and injurious to health you will forswear.† You'll love the weapons of war, be excellent horsemen, marksmen, and wielders of the sword, the discus, and the spear. Physical prowess will be as sacred to you as spiritual sensitiveness. And between the Hindus and the Muslims, you will act as a bridge, and serve the poor without distinction of caste, colour, country or creed.* My Khālsā shall always defend the poor and *Deg* (the community kitchen) will be as much an essential part of your order as *Teg* (the sword). And from now on, Sikh males will all call themselves 'Singh' (lions)@ and women 'Kaur' (Prince) and greet each other with *Wāhēguru Ji Kā Khālsā, Wāhēguru Ji Ki Fateh* (the Khālsā belongs to God : Victory be to God)."‡

---

† It is stated that though fond of liqour, Jahāngir, like his contemporaries, James I of England and Shāh Abbās of Persia, believed tobacco to be a noxious drug & forbade its use (Oxford History of India, V. A. Smith, P. 373)

* See Appendix. "The Cambridge History of India" (Vol. IV, p. 245) has cited no reference to support its unusual thesis that the Gurū "organised the (Sikh) sect into the most dangerous and implacable enemy of the Moghal Empire and *of the Muslim faith*". Cunningham and J. N. Sarkar also echo this viewpoint. The tenor of the Guru's life and instruction as of his whole house was against religion being the basis of a state or the difference in religion being made an excuse for oppression, domination or war. The Guru's hostility was not to Islām as such, nor even to the whole house of the Moghals, but to a particular tyrannous regime. The Guru, indeed, forgetting the wounds inflicted upon him by Aurangzeb and his agents, helped his son, Bahādur Shāh, to gain the imperial throne in the war of succession. In every battle of his, the Hindus fought as much on his side as the Muslims, however few they might have been. In the midst of his worst crisis, it is two Muslims, Nabi Khān and Ghani Khān, who escorted him to sefety or harboured him against the pursuing Moghal forces. The man who wrote: "The same are the temple and the mosque" could hardly be termed anti-Hindu or anti-Muslim.

@ Rājpūt Hindus have always called themselves Singhs. It is from them that this appellation has been taken, though not 'Kaur' for women which is typically Sikh. A whole beard and turban are (or, at least were) also worn by the Rājputs and a sword was their constant companion, till its use, as also of the beards and the turbans was forbidden to them by Aurangzeb, to which most of them submitted, while the Sikhs took up the challenge and made these an inseparable part of their religion. The meaning of the word 'Kaur' (Kanwar or Koer) is Prince, not princess, as the Guru wanted to give women the dignity of the male.

‡ See *Rahitnāmās* in the appnedix. It is true the Rahitnāmās, & other such works ascribed to the *hazuri* (intimate) devotees of Guru Gobind Singh, have not been historically authenticatad, yet the beliefs that Singhs held immediately after the

As the word went round the countryside that the Guru had created a new order with the mission of "do or die", it infused a new spirit in the Hindu citizenry, as it struck terror in the hearts of his adversaries.

According to a later Muslim historian, Ghulām Mohyiuddin, the emperor was duly informed by the news-writer of the address given by Guru Gobind Singh to his followers on the birth of the Khālsā. "He has abolished caste and custom, old rituals, beliefs and superstitions of the Hindus and banded them in one single brotherhood. No one will be superior, or inferior, to another. Men of all castes have been made to eat out of the same bowl. Though orthodox men have opposed him, about twenty thousand men and women have taken baptism of steel at his hands on the first day. The Guru has also told the gathering : 'I'll call myself Gobind Singh only if I can make the meek sparrows pounce upon the hawks and tear them; only if one combatant of my force faces a legion of the enemy'."* Because the Sikhs even under Bandā believed these to be the basic injunctions, their authenticity cannot be doubted.

F. N. Contd.

Master's demise and are corroborated by eye-witness accounts, both British & Muslim (see later), leave no one in doubt as to the basic principles enunciated by the Guru at the time of initiation. For later versions, see Latif's "History of the Punjab" (p. 271); Cunningham's "History of the Sikhs (pp. 73-74): "Panth Parkāsh" of B. Rattan Singh (p. 44); "Transformation of Sikhism" (pp. 81-85): *Tarikh-i-Panjāb* by Butē Shah, 4th edition (pp. 405-6). *Gur Sobhā* by a contemporary poet of the Guru, Sainapat, mentions the following injunctions (1) Meditation on God (2) Overcoming of five passions (3) Unshorn head-hair & beard (4) rejection of tobacco (5) compassion to all (p. 33)

* It is really strange that though the later historians (Sikh as well as non-Sikh) and the authors of the *Rahitnāmās* (Codes of Conduct), write, in detail, about the Guru's commandments to the Sikhs, he himself nowhere does so, even though he had a long spell of peaceful time twice after the birth of the Khālsā, to incorporate his commandments in one of his compositions. The only verse he has left to posterity enunciating the Code of Conduct for the Khālsā proclaims: "He who meditates on the Supreme Light, night and day, and believes not in another, has perfect love in the heart and puts not his faith in fasting, tombs, graveyards and convents, and for whom the pilgrimages consist in being compassionate, charitable, chaste and self-disciplined and who recognises in all no one but the One alone and whose heart is illumined with the Divine Light is a Khālsā, purest of the pure." (Guru Gobind Singh, 33 Swaiyyas). In fact, the Guru never forced his new discipline on all Sikhs, even some of the most devout being allowed not to be baptised, like Bhāi Nandlāl and Bhāi Kanihyiā. Thus, a distinction was permitted to remain between a Sikh (disciple) and a baptised Singh, and this is how till lately a large

The hill chiefs were also greatly scared. While the Guru one day went out hunting in the Doon Valley, two of them, Balia Chand and Ālim Chand, challenged him with a large detachment. Though the Sikhs were few in number, they gave an excellent account of themselves. The Guru's arrows brought havoc in the enemy's camp. Balia Chand was shot dead; Alim Chand lost one of his arms and fled. With many dead left on the battlefield, the hill armies beat a retreat, humbled and in disarray.

When the other Rajput hill chiefs heard of this encounter, they were gravely alarmed. Finding themselves weak, if not helpless against the Guru, they decided to approach the emperor at Delhi through a petition. The emperor was in the Deccan, engaged in grim battles. So, in his absence, the Subedār of Sirhind received their representatives. The memorandum said, "The present Guru is tenth in succession to Nānak, the Guru who preached the gospel of peace and human brotherhood. That is how we raised no objection to his finding residence in our midst. But, his ideas and intentions are different from Nānak's. When we tried to curb his rising power with which he aims to challenge even the emperor himself, he repaired to the Nāhan state, made friends with the Rājā there, and then came into conflict with him and Rājā Fateh Shāh of Srinagar. A battle was fought between us and him at Bhangāni where human blood flowed in abundance. Then, he returned to Ānandpur, and established a new order, called the Khālsā, which is contrary to all our cherished beliefs and customs. He says his religion is distinct as much from the Muslim, as from the Hindu faith. And, yet he wanted us to join hands with him to fight our emperor against whom he harbours profound grudge. This we have refused to do, much to his annoyance and discomfiture. He is now gathering men and arms

F. N. Contd.

body of the Sikhs, called *Sahjdhāris*, though outwardly not conforming to the symbols of the Khālsā, yet accepted the spiritual and social code of the Gurus and remained an inalienable and worthwhile part of the Panth. The word Khālsā, it may be pointed out, has been used by Kabir (*Kaho Kabir, ham bhaē Khālsē*, Rag Sorath), as also by the earlier Gurus, notably the 6th & the 9th, in their Hukamnāmās to denote the Sikhs who were the special charge of the Guru as against *Sahlangs* whose spiritual instruction was in the hands of the Guru's deputies (or *Masands*). Guru Gobind Singh himself employed the word *Khālsā* in his *Hukamnāmās*, even after 1699, for the entire Sikh *Sangat*, not only for the initiates or Singhs.

from all over the country to challenge the Moghal empire. We cannot restrain him, but as loyal subjects of your Majesty, we seek your assistance to drive him out of Ānandpur and not to allow grass to grow under your feet. Otherwise, he would become a formidable challenge to the whole empire, as his intentions are to march soon upon Delhi itself." This representation was duly forwarded by the Viceroy of Sirhind to the emperor.

After some time, the imperial Government replied to this representation,saying that the hill chiefs could be assisted by imperial troops if their expenses were paid for. To this,the hill Rājās readily agreed. Accordingly, the Moghal generals, Painde Khān and Din Beg, were despatched to help the Rajput princes with a force of ten thousand troops under both. At Rupar, they were joined by the hill forces under direct commands of their rulers. The purpose of this assault, as advertised, was to drive the Guru out of Ānandpur, but if he promised to live as a loyal subject, then, he would be allowed to abide there on payment of a tribute.

When information reached the Guru that a strong force was advancing against him, he organised his men also in battle array. He appointed the five Beloved ones as five generals of his army, and himself also decided to fight along with his troops. The fire-power of the Sikhs inflicted heavy losses on the enemy. Though the Moghal forces on the one hand and the Rajputs on the other were haranguing their troops separately that it was a *Jehād* (religious war), nothing availed them. At last, General Paindē Khān decided to engage the Guru in single combat and thus determine the result of the battle. He challenged the Guru to come out and face him personally. Hearing this, the Guru galloped his steed towards him and roared, "I'm Gobind Singh come to settle accounts with you". Paindē Khān taunted the Guru, "Why don't you settle with me then? Strike first, so that you have no regrets." The Guru smiled and said, "It is not the custom of my house to fire the first shot. You have aggressed against me. So, I give you the privilege!"

Paindē Khān moved his horse around the Guru in many positions to strike him with the sword, but the Guru was so swift with the movements of his horse, that the Pathān general felt helpless. He, then, discharged an arrow which whizzed past the ear of the Guru. The Guru taunted him, "Your archery is perfect!" Paindē Khān discharged another arrow which also missed its mark. Upon this, he hastened to retreat, but was challenged by the Guru: "You dirty coward, why don't you let me have my chance also?" Saying this, the Guru aimed an arrow at the ear of Paindē Khān which was the only part uncovered by armour. The aim was so sure that Paindē Khān fell off the horse-back and died. The other general, Din Beg, now took the command. The Moghal troops fought desperately, while the hill troops fled in disarray, seeing the battle going in favour of the Sikhs. Din Beg was himself badly wounded and seeing no chance of victory beat a retreat. He was pursued by the Sikh forces upto Rupar, but the Guru advised them not to harass them any further. The Sikhs captured a large booty from the battle-field and having wrought much destruction on the enemy troops, were greatly enthused over this decisive victory.

The Guru now sent instructions to his Sikhs that whosoever came to see him must bring either an arm or a horse. When the news of the Guru's victory reached far and near, many people came to join the ranks of the Khālsā. The Guru employed armourers to make muskets, swords and arrows and collected a large quantity of gunpowder and lead.

Some of the hill-chiefs felt panicky and decided once again to approach the emperor for assistance, and make valuable presents to him. One of their number advised them not to do so, and to muster their own forces, surround Ānandpur from all sides and starve its occupants to death or submission. This advice was later accepted. Each hill chief, among them, the Rājās of Jammu, Nurpur, Mandi, Bhutān, Kulu, Kainthal, Guler, Chambā and Srinagar, contributed his contingent. Rājā Ajmer Chand, son of Bhim Chand of Bilāspur, was to be in overall charge of the invading force and everyone agreed to submit to his decisions. Ajmer Chand first sent an emissary to the Guru asking him either to abandon Ānandpur or pay them the arrears of yearly rent on the land on which the city stood. Failing this, the town was to be blockaded from all sides.

The Guru spurned this demand with the contempt it deserved adding, that as the site of the Ānandpur town was bought as freehold by his father for cash, no one could claim from him a rent on it. And if it was the desire of the hill chiefs to deprive him and his followers of their lawful habitation through force, then the Guru had no choice but to fight back in self-defence. The Guru said he meant no harm to them whatever, if only they would let him in peace and not join forces with the Moghals against whose tyranny he was preparing to fight. Indeed, he sought their help and assistance in this holy war.

The Rājās were furious at this reply. They were convinced that the Guru would not buy peace at the cost of honour, and would much rather fight than surrender or sue for peace. Thereupon, they collected a large army contributed by every chief of the hill states. There were not many Sikhs residing in Ānandpur at this time. But, they were joined soon by the devout from many corners of the Panjāb. The Guru's eldest son, Ajit Singh, now in his teens, was also permitted to command a company of one hundred. The two forts at Ānandpur—Lohgarh and Fatehgarh—were put in charge of two separate commanders with a force of one thousand to guard each fort. The Guru advised his forces not to move beyond the town, but to remain on the defensive.

The Sikh chroniclers say the hill forces swarmed in like the locusts. But, though outnumbered and outweaponed, the Sikhs fought with such bravery and self-assuredness that the enemy was thrown into confusion and the Ranghars and Gujars sought to flee. These two castes were known for their fighting qualities, and bearing a grudge against the Guru over an earlier fight in which they had lost and their towns of Nuh and Sajpur had been sacked, had mustered a strong force under their leader, Jagatullah. But nothing availed them against the accurate marksman-ship and death-daring chivalry of the Sikhs. Jagatullah was shot dead and the Sikhs would not even allow the enemy to remove his dead body. The Guru himself, seated on a mound, aimed his deadly arrows at the enemy accounting for innumberable heads.

At this, the Rājās decided to make one final assault from three directions. But, even this did not yield any result. Jagatullah's body lay on the cold dust, but in spite of determined attacks of the enemy, the Sikhs made it a point of prestige not to let it fall into their hands. After bloody skirmishes, the enemy retired to their camp. Here, they were counselled by some, like the Rājā of Mandi, to sue for peace with the house of Nānak, there being no dishonour involved in approaching a high spiritual personage with a petition for peace. But some of the Rājās thought this would further embolden the Guru, that he was not as strong as he was feared and that if they did not lose heart, they would soon gain an upper hand. So, they made a desperate try again. This time they concentrated all their forces on a single point. The Guru's son, Ajit, showed exemplary courage. His horse was wounded, so he fought on foot. The Sikhs fought with their backs to the wall and wroght havoc in the enemy's forces. In the end, the hill chiefs thought it was useless to continue the fight any longer and after a siege of two months, they withdrew. But, before they did so, they tried another method of breaking through the defences of the fort. They sent an intoxicated elephant to make a breach in the walled defences. Seeing this, a Sikh, Duni Chand, who had brought a detachment of five hundred from the Central Panjab to aid the Guru, fled in terror, secretly. The Guru on hearing of this remarked, "He who flees from death in the face of danger to his nation finds death awaiting him in another garb." It is said when Duni Chand reached Amritsar and his foul deed was known to the community, he was ostracised from society and died a lonely man soon thereafter, stung by a cobra.

The elephant, except for his trunk, was covered with a steel coat-of-mail. He had to make an assault on the front door of the Lohgarh fort with a spear stuck in his forehead. The hill forces were to march in his rear so that when the front gate was breached, they would storm the troops within and a great massacre would follow. The fort would thus fall into their hands. The Guru appointed one of his valiant soldiers, Bachittar Singh, to pierce the elephant's trunk with a lance. Another Sikh, Udē Singh, was appointed to chop off the head of Rājā Kesari Chand who was leading this assault.

Bachittar Singh was successful at the very first go, in driving his lance into the head of the mad elephant advancing menacingly towards the fort. The animal got furious in his rage, turned back and trampled many of his own troops to death. Udē Singh challenged Kesari Chand in single combat and cut off his head. After much massacre of their men, and abandoning much war-booty, the hill chiefs took to their heels in the dead of night, losing the most prominent of their ranks, Rājā Ghummand Chand, also on the battlefield.

However, they decided to give no peace to the Guru and made frantic appeals to the emperor to assist them in their designs. On hearing of it, the Guru this time decided to meet the enemy on open ground, some distance ahead of Ānandpur. Seeing the Guru thus exposing himself to attack, the hill chiefs advanced upon him. The Guru's forces took positions on an elevated ground, and soon beat them back. Then, a Muslim guuner was employed for a high reward to get the Guru. But in this also they failed. With one shot, the gunner killed a servant of the Guru, but the Guru employed his skill in archery to devastating effect and killed both the gunner and also his brother who had the same mission on hand.

Meantime, the imperial army under the Subedar of Sirhind, Wazir Khān, reached the spot. Though the Guru was advised to hasten back into the fort of Ānandpur, he refused to budge from his ground and advanced with about five thousand men, in three detachments, the Guru commanding the rear and his son, Ajit, with another four, the vanguard. There was desperate fighting right upto the bank of the Satluj which the Guru crossed along with his troops to take positions on the other side. But, the losses of the imperial and the hill armies were so colossal that they decided to retreat, and, offering presents to the Moghal Viceroy, entreated him to go back and not to pursue the battle any more. The hill-chiefs were happy that the Guru had left Ānandpur, but their satisfaction was short-lived, as after a brief while the Guru returned with the beat of drum. Now Rājā Ajmer Chand, who was his prime enemy, sued the Guru for peace and sent him costly presents aud a very conciliatory communication. The Guru replied in the same friendly tone. The other hill chiefs also followed suit, and peace reigned for some time in this battle- scarred region.

During the brief period of peace that followed, the Guru instructed his followers in the finer, spiritual or social aspects of Sikh life. Men and women trekked long weary distances to have his sight, and, as was the Guru's injunction, made offerings of arms or horses to him. Congregations would assemble, morning and evening, in which besides the chanting of the Guru's Word by the musicians, the Guru would minister instructions on dedicating one's life and all one had to the Supreme Being, to keep Him ever in one's remembrance and to do everything in His name and for His pleasure. The Guru also enjoined upon his followers to serve each other, irrespective of any distinctions, and to look upon the whole humanity as one.

One day, the Guru feeling thirsty asked some water to be brought to him. A young boy obeyed the command, but when the Guru looked at his soft, feminine hands, he said to him : "Your hands are so tender that I wonder if you have ever used them!" The boy said this was true. He was born to rich parents who wouldn't permit him any manual work. The Guru threw away the water he had brought, saying, "I wouldn't accept any offering from a hand that has not served another."

Every Sikh was expected to make an offering of the tithe, each year, to the Guru. This the Sikhs did with utmost devotion, taking this to be a favour of the Guru. They came from all over the country, not only from the Panjāb, but from as far away as Kābul and Kandhār. One day, a Sikh came to him in quest of peace. "I've earned enough," he said, "now I want to be at your feet to listen to your instructions and redeem myself." The Guru put him under a tutor to teach him reading and writing so that he could read the Guru's Word himself and write it for others. But, when the tutor uttered to him the first stanza of Guru Amar Dās's composition, *the Ānand*, beginning, "I'm in bliss, for I've attained unto the Guru," he refused to learn any more! The tutor complained to the Guru of the apathy of the learner. On being questioned by the Guru, the Sikh replied, "What more is there for him to teach and me to learn when I've found the Guru and feel blessed. This is what I came here for!" The Guru embraced him saying, "Blessed are you who have found the Guru that soon, and so well."*

A Sikh, Kahan Singh by name, was greatly devoted to the Guru. He was once plastering a wall when a splash of mud fell on the Guru's dress as he was passing by. The Guru humorously remarked: "Such a one should get a slap in the face!" Many Sikhs rushed forward and gave the poor man a hearty drubbing. The Guru who was witnessing the scene felt distressed and asked, "You have carried out my instructions very thoroughly indeed! Now I ask: is there one who would marry his daughter to him? He is so devoted to my work and ought to be rewarded with a suitable match." Most Sikhs became utterly mute, but a man from Kandhār immediately offered his daughter to the poor man.

Hearing that his kitchen was not well served, the Guru one day visited it in disguise, and asked for food. Those in charge made

* Another story is also recounted by the Sikh chroniclers of a handsome rich youngman who having read in the Adi-Granth that "as the world is a passing show one must not get involved in it", refused to marry. On his parents' pleas, the Guru instructed the young sensitive mind thus: "He who does right in the world and is dedicated to the good of others and God, for him there is no involvement. He lives like the lotus in mud." The youngman was greatly impressed by the Guru's words and accepted his advice to rear the family.

refusals on various grounds, some that the food was not yet ready, others that the Guru must eat first. He then went to the house of Nandlāl, the poet, and asked for something to eat. The poet immediately brought some uncooked eatables and offered them to the needy. The Guru recounted this episode in one of his gatherings, saying, "When a hungry man asks you for food, do not make excuses. Give away whatever you have, and you will be blessed. A poor man's mouth is indeed the Guru's treasury."

One day, finding the rations in the Guru's kitchen dwindling, his mother stopped the Sikhs from serving food to others. The Guru was greatly distressed on hearing this and pronounced a curse: "Those who have given this evil advice to my mother, may the Turks destroy them!" The mother tearfully begged of her son to pardon her and those that had given her false reports of the dwindling rations. The Guru said, "O mother, the Guru's kitchen will never be empty, nor my Khālsā's, so long as it is meant to serve others." And, he forgave those who were responsible for this misdemeanour.

In the meantime, Rājā Ajmer Chand sent a Brāhmin to the Court of the Guru in the garb of a devotee but indeed to keep a watch over his activities, and the size of his treasury. By giving secret information, he was responsible for two of the finest horses being stolen from the Guru's stable. One day, he suggested to the Guru to grace the fair at Rawālsar, near Mandi, where the hill chiefs also gathered each year. He said this would be an ideal opportunity for a rapproachement between the two sides.

The Guru agreed on the entreaties of his mother and a large number of the devout. The Guru received the Rājās in his camp with great warmth and they and their queens were literally charmed by his manners and sweet speech. They implored the past to be forgiven to which the Guru said: "In my house, we do not store up the past, only the present and the future." The Guru arranged a big feast in honour of his visit and invited high and low to partake of it. But the high-caste Brāhmins refused the invitation, saying, "He has corrupted the religion of our fore-fathers. How can we interdine with men of low castes or give up our age-old beliefs in our gods and rituals by following his way of life?"

Knowing that the hill-folk were very superstitious and believed in astrology, the Guru said: "My Sikhs will never be a prey to superstitions. For them, one moment is as good as another. He who has faith in God will not like to divine His secrets through astrology or such like superstitions."

It is said a Vaishnava, Har Gopāl by name, being influenced by his father's newly-awakened faith in the Guru, came to visit him with a handsome offering, but he felt disgust in his mind on seeing the Guru taking a meat diet. Though he pretended to the Guru that he had utter faith in him, and was blest by the Guru who also offered him a steel bracelet, on way back home he confided to a Sikh that he had wasted his money on the Guru who was a meat-eater. The Sikh asked him to transfer to him the Guru's blessings and the steel bracelet in return for the money he had offered to his Saviour. The Vaishnava was much pleased with the deal and received his money back from the Guru's devotee with great joy. But after some time, he incurred such heavy losses in his trade that he had neither the money, nor the peace of mind. So, he went back to the Guru to ask forgiveness. The Guru said to him, "I eat whatever comes to me from God. I eat not for the taste of the palate, but to keep myself a fit and a worthy instrument of God's mission. Men quarrel over diet, dress and ritual and over caste, community and creed, and have thus torn man from man. My mission is to restore mankind to a single brotherhood. So, how can I love one kind of man and hate another? They whose lives and deeds are dedicated to God find everything that comes from Him sacred and good. My Sikhs shall never live on charity or religious offerings, but through honest means earn to live *(Kirat Karni)* and live to share *(Wand Chhaknā)*, and will ever keep God in their hearts (*Nām japnā*) in whatever they do. All else is secondary and of little consequence."

A Brāhmin complained to the Guru that some Pathāns had abducted his bride. The Guru sent an expeditionary force of one hundred cavalry under his young son, Ajit Singh, to restore the Brāhmin's bride. Ajit Singh fell on the Pathāns in the night like lightning and produced the culprits along with their booty before the Guru. The woman was restored to her husband and the Pathāns punished for their misdeed.

The Guru's fame was now spreading far and wide, thus giving alarm to the hill chiefs. In these days, two Muslim generals, Sayyad Beg and Alif Khān, were marching from Delhi to Lāhore. Rājā Ajmer Chand thought this an excellent opportunity to ask for their assistance which was agreed to on payment of one thousand rupees a day. Sayyad Beg, on hearing of the Guru's holy character, refused to fight and indeed joined the Sikh ranks. Together, they gave a hot chase to Alif Khān and his forces and made them retreat with heavy losses. Sayyad Beg transferred all his wealth to the Guru and decided to cast his lot with him in future.*

After a brief period of peace, the hill chiefs with a force of ten thousand attacked Anandpur again. The Guru had only eight hundred men with him, but he asked them to meet the enemy in the open this time, and not from behind the battlement. A great carnage followed. The Guru instructed the Khālsā army to aim their arrows and guns from positions of vantage and not to pursue the enemy nor charge him with swords hand to hand. But when the Sikh troops saw the enemy retreating, they pursued him. The Guru was much displeased at this for, as he had visualised, the enemy finding them hopelessly outnumbered fell upon them and inflicted heavy losses. The Guru now himself took the field and this enthused the Khālsā so much that they routed the enemy.

However, the respite after this victory also turned out to be all-too-brief. For, on insistent entreaties from the hill chiefs, the imperial troops soon advanced against the Guru's house under a Moghal general, Sayyad Khān. The Guru had only five hundred men at this disposal, at this time. He put them in battle-array under General Sayyad Beg and Maimum Khān, another devotee of his. At first they were disheartened to hear of a large army advancing towaads Anandpur, but the Guru gave them heart and said, "In the final analysis it is man's heart that leads one to victory, not numbers or arms. And he who has a moral cause to fight for always has God on his side." Sayyad Beg engaged himself thereupon in a single combat with a hill chief and killed him. Seeing this, a Moghal general, Din Beg, filled with hatred against Sayyad Beg for having deserted the Moghal army, struck him from behind and killed him. Maimun Khān fought with great bravery, as did other Sikhs and took a huge toll of life of the enemy's hosts.

Seeing such fantastic deeds of valour, General Sayyad Khān himself advanced towards the Guru on horseback. But, on beholding his serene and holy face said to him, "You strike first. I do not have the heart to take the initiative." The Guru replied, "In my house, we never fire the first shot. If you wouldn't strike me, I wouldn't strike you either." The General was so much overcome

* "Sikh Religion" Macauliffe, Vol. V. P. 163.

by emotion on hearing these words that he dismounted and fell at the Guru's feet. The Guru blessed him with the Name of God and said, "You are saved in both the worlds." Sayyad Khān, however, could not restrain his troops who continued to war with the Sikhs. But, he retired to a distance, when another commander, Ramzān Khān, took the field against the Guru. The Guru aimed his arrow and killed his horse. But his forces were far too few to be able to romp victory home this time. The Guru, therefore, decided to leave Ānandpur which was captured and looted by the Moghal army. The Sikhs were so much exercised over this defeat that they wanted the Guru to permit them to pursue the enemy and to die fighting rather than suffer humiliation of a defeat. The Guru permitted them to do so. They gave a hot chase to the enemy and not only killed a large number of them but also relieved them of much of their booty. Many lost their lives but those that remained brought the Guru great joy and he came back to Ānandpur with them much relieved.

The emperor was greatly exercised over this debacle of his huge army. The Qāzi advised that the Guru be brought to the presence of the emperor. Aurangzeb is said to here agreed with this and sent a message to the Guru saying, "Your religion and mine believe in the unity of God. Why should there be any misunderstanding between us? There is no choice for you nor for any one else but to acknowledge my sovereignty which I have obtained from Allāh, the Almighty. If you have any grievance, come and see me and I shall treat you as a holy man, but do not challenge my authority, else I shall have to march personally against you."

To this the Guru replied, "There is only one Sovereign, God the All-powerful, to whose Will both your Majesty and I are subject. But you recognise this not and discriminate against and pursue those who differ with you in faith and bring harm to their person and religion. God has sent me with a mission—to restore righteousness on the earth. How can I be at peace with you so long as our ways are different?"* The Guru, however, treated the emperor's envoy with great courtesy, and bestowed a robe of honour on him.

---

* Though this letter of the King and the Guru's reply have not been traced in the original, the Guru's reference to it in his *Zafarnāmā* makes it clear that correspondence to this effect had been entered into between him and the emperor. Also see "Sikh Religion" Macauliffe, Vol. V, P. 165, and "A History of the Panjāb", Latif, P. 267. For a translation of the entire *Zafarnāmā,* see the author's "*Thus spake the Tenth Master.*"

The Sikhs from various parts of the country, notably the central Panjāb, came to visit the Guru in large numbers. They brought offerings of horses or arms as was the Guru's bidding. They learnt the lessons of warfare at Ānandpur. The Guru, however, felt that even though calm prevailed around him, it was a lull before the storm. So, he must not be caught unprepared if the challenge came from any source, at any time.

The hill chiefs were also secretly planning to have a show-down with the Sikhs in one final, decisive bid in collaboration with the imperial forces. They, therefore, sent another emissary, this time in the person of Rājā Ajmer Chand to the Deccan where the emperor was waging war against the Deccan Sultanates. The Rājā met the emperor, personally, and presented a petition on behalf of his fraternity detailing "the anti-state activities of the Guru's house for the last over one century which resulted in the martyrdom of his father and great grand-father." The emperor was told that "the Guru who had founded a new religion wanted all Hindus to embrace it and to wage war on the Moghal empire." The emperor, alarmed at these reports, ordered the despatch of all available troops at Delhi, Sirhind and Lāhore to march on Ānandpur, under the supreme command of Wazir Khān, Subedār of Sirhind. These were joined by the hill troops. The Guru got information from his devout followers from Delhi and elsewhere of the approaching storm. Though troops from the imperial capital could not be spared, those from Sirhind and Lāhore made a formidable combination for the far fewer men the Guru had under arms with him.

When the enemy's hosts reached the outskirts of Ānandpur, the Sikhs discharged their artillery fire with such venom and accuracy that it took a great toll of the enemy's life and horse. The Guru's army was shelling from within the forts, while the enemy was without any such cover and was on a lower ground. Two of the Guru's generals, Udē Singh and Dayā Singh, were ordered at the close of the day's battle to charge the enemy in a single combat. They with their storm-troopers rushed into the enemy's ranks and inflicted heavy losses on the enemy. After a reorganisation of forces, the enemy was compelled, as we shall see, to pursue a different strategem. The fear lurking in everybody's mind that the Guru was a performer of miracles was coming true. Macauliffe records nine hundred dead on the enemy's side on the first day of the battle.

Next day, the Guru himself took the field on a charger. He showed magnificent skill in archery and his men fired with deadly precision. All attempts to capture the Guru alive or to kill him failed. So, it was decided to change the tactics and to cut off outside supplies from the fort so that the Guru and his men be starved into submission. The Guru asked his followers not to venture forth, but to hold the forts put under the charge of different commanders, including his son, Ajit Singh. The enemy cut off all supplies. The Sikhs in the dark of night pounced upon the enemy and created havoc and looted much booty. At day-break, another assault from the enemy followed, but to no avail against the Sikh guns.

These days, a Sikh, called Bhāi Kanihyā, was reported to the Guru as ministering water to the fallen in battle, irrespective of friend or foe. The Guru called him to his presence and asked him why he was offering water to the enemy's wounded. Kanihyā replied, "Since you've taught me to make no distinction between man and man, I do not see amongst the wounded any but you." The Guru was so pleased with this reply that he blessed him with salvation. His followers, the Sēwāpanthis, whose one aim in life is SERVICE (*sēwā*), are an honoured part of the community to this day.

The hardships of the beleaguered troops increased with each day. Inspite of the night sorties of the Sikhs, it was becoming nearly impossible to subsist on the meagre rations left within the fort. Even water supplies were running out. Starvation stared everyone in the face. Some of them complained to the Guru's mother that their hardships were being unnecessarily prolonged, for the Guru would not let them venture out, except occasionally and at night, but the booty they got was not enough to sustain them for long and their losses in such assaults were also heavy. For some time, they lived on the leaves of trees and bark ground into flour. Hundreds of Sikhs sought the permission of the Guru to leave him. The Guru was much distressed, but said he would permit them to do so only if they denied him in writing. Even this forty of them did, saying, "Neither you are our Guru, nor we Thy Sikhs." But, as we shall see later, when they returned home, they were so shamed by their womenfolk that they returned to battle at Mukatsar and each one of them died fighting for the Guru.

Seeing the Sikhs not surrendering, even though by all estimates their resources were totally exhausted after a siege of seven long months, the hill chiefs hit upon another plan. They sent an emissary, a Brāhmin, who said both the Hindus and the Muslims promised on oath that if the Guru would only leave the fort of Ānandpur, the enemy's forces would retire and the Guru might return to his fort, later, at his pleasure. The Sikhs could even take all their movables with them. The Guru saw in this proposal a trick to drive him out of his entrenchments, and so did not agree. But the entreaties of his mother and devout followers left no choice for him. However, to put the bonafides of the enemy to the test, he asked for pack bullocks to convey his property first. This was immediately complied with. The Guru, however, sent out only the useless and waste material, covering it with brocade. This caravan was to move out at the dead of night with the help of torch lights. When this procession reached the enemy's camp, they pounced upon it with great ferocity, throwing all their oaths and solemn commitments to the winds. But, when, on day-break, they found to their shame the contents of their booty, they knew that they could not trick the Guru being caught in their trap.

The Guru now reminded his followers of what he had told them beforehand. But, meantime, the Moghals sensing the Guru's reactions at their foul deed, sent in another emissary, this time with a message, in the emperor's name, expressing regret at the misbehaviour of the imperial troops and promising safe conduct, should the Guru condescend to quit Ānandpur. The Sikhs were in dire straits. The Guru's mother also joined hands with them in making entreaties to accept the emperor's offer and not to let his innocent followers die of starvation. Even if the imperial troops were to betray their trust, it would be better, it was argued, to die fighting than through hunger. The Guru accepted the latter alternative, and so set fire to his possessions: those that could not be disposed off thus, were buried in the ground. The Guru's mother, with the two youngest sons of the Guru, aged 6 and 8, and his two wives (Sundri and Sāhib Kaur) were to go first, while the Guru with five hundred of his followers was to move out along with his two elder sons, at the dead of night. It was the bitingly cold month of December of the year 1704 A.D.

On reaching Sirsā, the Guru met his mother and his two younger sons and entrusted a devout Sikh to take them to Delhi, to where his wives had already left. But, he took them instead to Rupar to a relation of his. Here, the Guru's mother met a Brāhmin, Gangu, who was once their cook, who later took them to his village, Kheri, near Sirhind, and betrayed them to the Nawāb of Sirhind in order to usurp the considerable cash and jewellery the mother had on her. The Nawāb offered them the choice between Islām and death. "We are the sons of Gobind Singh who knows not defeat, nor surrender," the elder one is reported to have said, "our grandfather laid down his life, but gave up not his faith. So shall we." When asked to bow before the Nawāb, the little heroes kept their backs straight, and refused to pay obeisance to the vicar of tyranny who was after the blood of their father and his peace-loving followers. When told that their father was dead and so there was no more any earthly hope for them, they are said to have replied: "Our father is deathless. He can never die." Realising that even though tender of age, they were resolute of will and firm in faith, they were ordered to be bricked up alive.*

Historians have gone lyrical over the manly and fearless ways of the innocent ones, but what else could one expect from the offspring of Guru Gobind Singh ? However, for the aged mother of the Guru, the shock was too overwhelming and, on hearing of the heart-rending news, she collapsed. @

---

* Some historians say they were executed.

@ Latif explains away this gruesome tragedy thus:— "His (Guru Gobind's) mother, Gujri, and his two sons, Zorāwar Singh and Fateh Singh, effected their escape to Sirhind, where they concealed themselves in the house of a Hindu disciple, Kuljas, the Dewān of Wazir Khān, the governor of the province. Kuljas produced them before the governor, who, being an orthodox Mohamedan, spared their lives, in accordance with the Mohamedan law, which forbids the slaughter of unbelievers who are minors or belong to the female sex. The Dewān bore some personal grudge to Gobind Singh, and repeatedly entreated Wazir Khān to kill the widow and the two sons of the object of his envy, reminding him that they were the offspring of one who was the inveterate foe of all Mahomedans, and were sure to follow the footsteps of their father. Wazir Khān told him that he would on no account violate the rules of his religion, which prescribed that a son must not suffer for the wrongs done by his father, and that every one was responsible for his own actions. One day, as the two sons of the Guru were sitting in the governor's *darbār*, he was much pleased with their graceful appearance and seemingly good looks, and said to them with kindness: 'Boys! what would you do if we were to give you your liberty ?' The boys answered, 'We would collect our Sikhs, supply them with implements of war, fight with you and put you to death.' The governor said: 'If you were defeated in the fight, what would you do then?' The boys replied: 'We would collect our armies again and either kill you or be killed'. The governor was enraged at this intrepid and haughty reply, and ordered Kuljas to remove the boys from his

The Moghal authorities conducted a search in the Brāhmin's house, suspecting that he had kept to himself the jewellery and other valuables of the Guru's mother. On his refusal to divulge where he had buried the treasure, they tortured him to death. The only one to protest against this heinous crime against the Guru's sons was the Nawāb of Malerkotla who said, "The sins of the father should not be visited upon the tender sons. If we could not defeat the Guru, why wreak vengeance on these poor little ones." But, his pleas went unheard. The Sikhs under Bandā Singh Bahādur kept this act of grace on the part of Malerkotla's house so much in their memory that whereas they destroyed Sirhind utterly, and butchered Wazir Khān and his entire family, they spared the state of Malerkotla altogether.*

The Guru was in the meantime being pursued by the Moghal army. He took shelter in an improvised mud fortress at Chamkaur, where a bloody battle ensued, resulting in the loss of all but five of

---

F. N. Contd.

presence and to despatch them at his home. The boys were accordingly put to death by Kuljas. Some say he put the children under the foundation of a wall and closed the place up, and thus buried them alive. Gujri died of grief at the sad end of her grand-children." (*History of the Panjāb*, p. 265). However, the part that Kuljas (or Suchānand as some call him) played in this tragic drama is not supported by any reliable source, nor that the Nawāb was inclined at any stage to spare the life of the young ones. *Akhbārāt-i-Darbār-i-Mualla* (of 25 Rabi-ul-Awal, in the fourth year of Bahādur Shah's reign) states clearly that "the Sikh Khālsā are inimically disposed whole-heartedly towards Wazir Khān, because *he* has killed the (two) younger sons of Guru Gobind Singh."

* Even during the worst communal holocaust of many centuries that occured in 1947, when Hindu, Sikh and Muslim populations of the divided Panjāb migrated *en masse* to their respective homelands amidst much carange, no Muslim of Malēr-kotlā was touched, and they were pathetically persuaded to stay back in India along with the Nawāb, which they did. The present Nawāb of Malerkotla cherishes a letter said to have been written by his ancestor, Nawāb Sher Mohd. Khān, to Āurangzeb in this behalf, in which the Nawāb undertakes to keep the young ones in his custody or send them over to the emperor for him to make them his wards in order to keep them out of the harm's way. But, it appears, no reply to this communication was ever received. Later, however, the Nawāb of Malerkotlā played a significant part in resisting the Sikh rise to power under Bandā Singh Bahādur & later (see vol. II), but the Sikhs have kept in their racial memory only the Nawāb's compassion for the young sons of Guru Gobind, and not his armed resistance to them at a later date.

the forty Sikhs† who were now with the Guru, the rest having been left at Sirsa to withstand the Moghal assault till the Guru had crossed to safety. The Guru's two elder sons, Ajit and Jujhār, also died fighting valiantly at Chamkaur in single combats. The Guru had insisted, much to the anguish of his followers, that if not the first, his sons must not be the last to die. Seeing them fall before his very eyes, he offered prayers of thanksgiving to God: "O God, I've surrendered to Thee what belonged to Thee."

Now, the Guru's own life was also in danger. But, he refused to leave the five who were still with him. They did their best to prevail upon him saying if he were to keep alive, the faith would grow once again into a formidable force. But the Guru said, "My life is not more sacred then a devoted follower's. I'm going to die in battle along with you, if there's no other choice." Hearing this, the Sikhs were much distressed. So, they hit upon a plan. The five gathered together and passed a *Gurmattā* (resolution) and presented it to the Guru thus: "You have always said that wherever there are five of you, dedicated to me, there I shall also be, and whatever you ask, that shall be granted unto you. Now, we command you, as your Guru, to leave the fort post-haste, and let's deal with the enemy later as best as we can." The Guru felt so helpless. His own injunctions were being quoted against him! He decided to obey, and after hugging each of them to his bosom and saying, "God be with you, you are redeemed both in this world and the next," he left. Two of them remained behind to lay down their lives next day, one of them being Sant Singh who wore the Guru's crest to masquerade for him. The Moghals were greatly disappointed to find, on inquiry, that the man of mistaken identity was not Guru Gobind Singh, but one of his followers. But before the Guru left, he discharged two arrows which struck the torches in the hands of the Moghal bodyguards, and then pierced through their bodies. Under cover of darkness he walked, through the forest, and lay down tired at Māchhiwārā, between Rupar and Ludhiana, where the other three Sikhs also joined him as directed.

---

* Some say, it is these forty martyrs that the Guru blessed as the *Muktās* (or, the Saved ones), mention of whom is made in the Sikh prayer. Bhāi Jodh Singh does not agree with this. His contention is that it is the 40 deserters of Ānandpur who came to battle at Mukatsar, shamed by their women folk, and died fighting that earned them this title'. In "Zafarnamah", the Guru mentions the 40 Companions who sacrificed their lives in the battle at Chamkaur & not any others.

On being informed that a detachment of the Moghal army was still pursuing him, it became incumbent on him to escape to safety soon. But his feet were blistered, and he could hardly walk. At a Sikh's house where he was putting up now for a day, he met two Pathāns, Nabi Khān and Ghani Khān, who had visited his court earlier also, and had sold Arab horses to him. They offered their services to the Guru. It was decided that the Guru would be carried on a cot by the two Pathāns and two Sikhs, while the fifth one would serve as an attendant. The Guru was to disguise as a Muslim Pir from Uch†, recently returned from Hajj, and fasting. The scheme saw them safely through the Moghal troops who were camping on the way.

It is said the Moghals would offer them safe conduct only if the "Pir" would eat with them along with his followers. The Guru, however, excused himself saying he was on fast, and would touch nothing but raw barley. His three Sikhs were, however, advised to eat whatever was served with God's name uttered over it. When the two Pathāns took leave of the Guru after seeing him to safety, he offered them several presents and a certificate which is still preserved by their descendants and whenever it is shown to a devotee, he invariably makes an offering to this family of noble lineage.

On the way, he met Mahant Kirpāl who had fought on his side so valiantly in the battle of Bhangāni, but Kirpāl would not keep him for fear of the Moghals. The Guru went thence to Jagraon and Raikot and met the Muslim *chowdhry* of these towns, Rāi Kalhā by name, who offered him great courtesies at his village, called Jātpurā. Him the Guru blest with the gift of a sword. From here, he proceeded to the Lakhi forest where he encamped for some time in the midst of great natural scenery. Whoever heard of the Guru's coming, came

---

* *Uch* was then a famous centre of Muslim divines, or "Pirs", 38 miles south-west of Bahāwalpur (now in West Pakistān). Among the Muslims, it is known as *Uch-Sharif* (or, the holy Uch). According to the Sikh savant, Bhāi Vir Singh, (vide his annotated edition of *Nānak-Parkāsh*, Chapter 59, Verse 36, f. n.) Uch used to be the seat of a well-known Muslim Pir, Jalal Sāni Makhdum Rukunuddin, Abdul Fateh, originally from Arabia, and his descendants claim that it is he who met Guru Nānak at Meccā and discoursed with him. Another Sikh divine of the present century, Sant Sangat Singh of Kamālia had visited his *durgāh* which had in its possession a wooden footwear (*Kaus*, or *Kharanv*, to which Bhāi Gurdās refers in Vār 1) said to have been gifted by Guru Nānak to Pir Rukunuddin at Meccā. Inspite of the offers of large sums of money and land, the descendants of the Pir have refused to part with this holy relic.

to him overcome with emotion. The Guru himself writes: "When they heard of their Shepherd, they were full of gratitude to God. The flocks would touch not grass nor water, and no one waiting for the other ran to have a sight of the Master and be blest by him." It is here that the Guru received the heart-rending message from Sirhind about the martyrdom of his two young sons and mother. The Guru, composed as ever, bent upon his knees and lifting his hands to God in prayer uttered: "These too, Thy trust, I have rendered unto Thee", and digging up a shrub with his knife he made this prophecy: "Just as I' ve torn this shrub by its roots, so shall this tyrannous empire be destroyed, root and branch, and much too soon."

From Jātpurā, the Guru proceeded to Dinā. A Sikh had presented his horse to him on the way and this facilitated his march away from the Moghal forces than was possible otherwise. The Guru halted at Dinā for some time. It is here that he wrote his Persian composition, *Zafarnāmā* (or, the Letters of Victory) in the name of Aurangzeb. This letter breathes defiance and contempt for an earthly power which is yoked to tyranny and sin, and lays down the eternal rule that he alone wins in the end whose cause is just. That he alone does good who is right.

The Guru says in this epistle, inter alia: "O king, I have no faith in your oaths. You vow to go one way and follow another. I would not have withdrawn my forces from Ānandpur if I hand't put my faith in what you pledged to me. When there is no other course open to man, it is but righteous to unsheath the sword. When your forces advanced against me, I gave them a taste of my arrows. Some of your men fled, others were sent to the other world. And, I escaped, unhurt, by God's Grace. Not a hair of my head could all your forces touch.

"I protest that you believe neither in God, nor the Prophet. You keep not your word, and lie, putting faith in worldly weal and power, and not your God. You know not the value of an oath on the Qurān. If the prophet Mohammed were here, I would present to him this foul deed of your envoy and the Qāzi vowed before me on your behalf, and then you betrayed my trust! If even now you repent and come to see me here in this territory of the Bairārs, who are all my followers, they shall give you safe conduct and you shall not be harmed. I wish I could speak to you face to face.

"I owe allegiance to only God, my King, If He so desires, I might come to you. But, did your God ask you to tyrannise over others? Fie on your regard for God and Religion ! But, hear me : do not employ your sword to murder the innocent, for the God on high would for sure punish you. Fear God, therefore, who is the Master of the earth and the heaven, and whose vengeance is terrible, who fears no one and is the protector for ever of the poor.

"What if you have killed my four sons ? Remember, the coiled snake is still alive. By putting out a few sparks, you have quenched not the fire thereby. Your troops plundered the goods I had sent out (of the Ānandpur fort) believing their oath to be true. But just as you have forgotten God, God will now forget you and you will be punished for your evil deeds. But I wonder if you know God. You have an empire, wealth and pomp, a generous disposition, warlike qualities, but far from you is Religion.

"My protection is God than whom there is no one better, nor higher. He who acts honestly, him the God saves to perform His service. How can an enemy touch his person of whom God on high is the friend and refuge ? Life is but for a brief few moments. Change is the law of life. Whoever comes here, also quits the scene. So, whatever one's strength, one must annoy not the weak and thus destroy one's roots."

This unnsual letter the Guru sent in 1706 A. D. through two of his trusted Sikhs, Dayā Singh and Dharam Singh. The letter was duly delivered to the emperor, personally, in the South at Ahmadnagar, and the emperor expressed a wish that the Guru might come and see him, but before the two could meet, news was received that the emperor was dead.*

---

* That Aurangzeb, in his last days, had become so much conscious of his barbarous and bigoted ways is borne out by the letters he addressed to his sons from his death-bed, which said, inter alia: "I know not who I am, where I shall go and what will happen to this sinner full of sins. My years have gone by profitless. God has been in my heart but my darkened eyes have recognised not His light. There is no hope for me in the future. When I have lost hope in myself, how can I have hope in others. I have greatly sinned and know not what torment awaits me (in the Hereafter)." (History of India, Vincent Smith, Oxford, 1920, p, 448).

The Sikh historians aver that this change was wrought after Aurangzeb had received the letter of Guru Gobind Singh which detailed his excesses and those of his viceroys in a language which he understood and coming from a holy man affected much his mind and heart.

(Contd. on next page)

In the period that intervened, the Guru travelled through the Mālwā country. Some easy-going Sikhs of the central Panjāb (Mājhā) hearing of the Guru's nearness waited upon him and implored him to return to the peaceful path of Nānak.

They promised to intercede on his behalf with the emperor, so that further animosities between the two houses might cease. But the Guru refused to listen to them saying, "I'm fighting for a cause, not for myself. I have sacrificed my sons, my father and my mother for this cause. And, now you come to ask me to withdraw from the fight to save my person ? This will never be. Whosoever wants to live in ignoble peace may compromise with tyranny. I wouldn't, till I have breath in me, nor one who will choose to follow me." These men then left for their homes, disappointed, but when they reached their destinations and told the people of the Guru's determination to continue the fight, hundreds of them resolved to fight on the Guru's side led by a woman, Māi Bhāgo, who donning a man's dress, shamed and censured them back to the path of suffering and sacrifice. Some of them were those who had earlier denied the Guru at Ānandpur and eacaped from the battle.

The Guru now got news that he was being pursued by the imperial troops, at least ten thousand strong, under Wazir Khān, Subēdār of Sirhind. He, therefore, proceeded towards Khidrānā, in the district of Ferozepur. In the meantime, the large contingent of Sikhs from Mājhā (whose strength some historians like Latif have put at 12,000, though the Sikh chroniclers say they were far fewer, some say as few as forty) saw a huge force advancing towards the Guru who was sheltered by a forest only a short distance away. They engaged the Moghal hosts so recklessly that everyone of them including the brave heroine, Māi Bhāgo, fell on the battlefield. It is said they attracted the Moghal forces towards themselves by spread-

---

(F. N. Contd. from P. 311)
At this time, it is said, the Guru started out for the Deccan to meet the emperor possibly in response to his invitation. Otherwise, there was no reason for the Guru to proceed to the South so suddenly. Some verses, especially 53-54, of the Zafarnāmā also hint at such a possibility. But, the thesis of some other historians that possibly the Guru wanted to enlist the support of the Marāthās and the Rājputs may not be untenable either. Though Shivāji had died in 1680, his son Sambhāji was put to death in 1689, by Aurangzeb, with horrid tortures and the latter's son, Sāhuji, was taken under protection by the emperor, yet among the Marāthās there was quite some fire still left, and so also among the Rājputs. Moreover, the Guru's appeal was to be to the Marāthā and Rājput peoples, and not only to their rulers

ing their white cotton sheets on the trees and shrubs all around. The Moghals seeing a huge Sikh camp pounced upon it and after a fierce battle, killed everyone of their number. The Moghal forces thinking that the Guru also must be one of the slain, retired from the field quite some distance behind, as they could not find water for their troops. When the Guru went to the scene of the battle to find out wherefrom had that timely contingent arrived to assist him, he found one of the Sikhs, Mahā Singh by name, still a little conscious. The Guru took him in his lap, wiped his face, and with tears of joy in his eyes, said : "Ask whatever you may and I grant you that. You have redeemed yourself both here and in the Hereafter." The devotee, his breath choked with emotion, sobbed : ' Master, if you are in mercy, forgive me and my companions our earlier betrayal of you at Ānandpur. Pray tear up the piece of paper on which, to our shame, we wrote : we acknowledge you not as our Guru. We have tried to wipe our treachery to you with our blood. Now own us if you may in your Mercy and bless us that we die in peace." The Guru blessed him profusely, tore up their collective letter of apostacy and said, "You are all saved by God in whose cause you have laid down your lives. God's mercy shall be upon you and upon those who'll choose to follow you." Māi Bhāgo who showed signs of life was picked up by the Guru from the battle-field and taken with him for treatment. He got all the dead bodies collected and cremated with due honours.

The Guru now proceeded to Talwandi Sābo (in the erstwhile Patiālā state) and now called Damdamā Sāhib (or the place of the Guru's rest). Here, he stayed for quite some time* dictating the Ādi Granth to a devout Sikh of his, Bhāi Mani Singh, and adding to it his father's hymns and, according to tradition, one verse of his own.‡ He did so because, it is said, the original copy was with his cousin, Dhirmal, who refused to part with it. And, the Sikhs wanted an edition certified by the Guru. He also made additions to his

* Some historians like I. Bannerjee in his *Evolution of the Khālsā* (Part II) think the Guru stayed here for three years.

‡ This edition was later kept in the Golden Temple, Amritsar, but was either destroyed or taken away during the desecration of the Temple by Ahmad Shāh Abdāli in 1762, but inspite of the best efforts of researchers, the original copy has not been traced in Kābul or elsewhere. However, several copies of this edition had been made before the loss of the original.

own compositions. Here, he was also joined by his wives, Sundri and Sāhib Kaur. When they asked the Guru where the young sons were, the Guru replied, pointing to his followers : "For these thousands, I sacrificed the other four. So long as these sons of mine are alive, I will not consider the death of my four sons in vain !"

The Guru blessed this part of the land saying instead of coarse grain and shrubbery, it would yield wheat and fruit, which it does now, and scattering his reed-pens in all directions he said, "This will one day be a place of great learning." It is now known as the the Guru's Kāshi. The Guru, according to Dr. Ernest Trumpp, made 1,20,000 converts during his stay at Damdamā. The old glory of Anandpur, it appears, had returned and Sikhs thronged here from far and near. Now, the Guru decided to depart along with five others towards the Deccan via Rajputānā, in spite of the beseechings of his devotees. "My message of hope must spread from one corner of this land to the other," he said: "I cannot sit back and relax, when my nation is on fire." It appears, he wanted the Rājputs and the Marāthās fighting sporadically and individually, and even divided among themselves, to join hands with him to give a decisive bettle to the Moghals.*

While the Guru was yet on his way, at Bhagaur, in Mārwār, he heard of the death of Aurangzeb on February 20, 1907. His eldest son, Bahādur Shāh, was engaged in a military expedition in Afghanistān at that time. Taking advantage of this, his younger brother, Moham-

* In one of his letters to his followers in Dāccā, the Guru called Bengāl his 'spiritual homeland,' which shows that he was inspired in his fight, contrary to the usual run, by the distress of his entire country and not merely of Panjāb. It may be of interest to remark that in the Ādi Granth, no Guru ever so much as mentioned the name of Panjāb in his writings. It was always 'Hindustān'—a concept which was then a very vague geographical expression for most of our people. However, Dr. Gandā Singh thinks the Guru had received a communication from the emperor Aurangzeb to see him, and he was going South for that purpose. He says the Guru had already sent a reply through Bhāi Dayā Singh in his letter called "Zafarnāmā", but Daya Singh had not yet returned home with the emperor's reply. In the Zafarnāmā itself, there is a casual hint that if the king would not come to see him, he himself might call upon the king to apprise him of his misdeeds and those of his agents. However, this is a letter of defiance, not of reconciliation. And, how could the Guru proceed to the Deccan without waiting for the king's reply? The reasons must therefore be sought elsewhere for his abandoning the mission of consolidation in the Panjāb of a sudden, & leaving for the Deccan,

mad Āzam, usurped the throne. Bahādur Shāh hastened back home to fight his way to his legal heritage. He had often heard of the heroic exploits of Guru Gobind Singh, and, also, that being a man of spiritual disposition, he harboured grudge against systems, not men. He, therefore, took a chance and appealed to Guru Gobind Singh, through an intermediary, to forget the past and bless and help him gain possession of the imperial throne.* He promised to look into, and redress, any grievance the Guru might have against his house.

Though the Guru wasn't sure of Bahādur Shāh keeping his word once victory was his, he had heard of his catholicity of outlook as against the bigotry and one-track mind of his father. So, he decided to give his offer a trial and sent a detachment of two to three hundred horse, under one of his trusted disciples, Dharam Singh, to render whatever assistance they could to Bahādur Shāh in his hour of crisis.†

* This intermediary is said to have been Bhāi Nand Lāl (born 1633) of Multān (some say he was born at Ghazni in Afghanistān, e.g. MK, p. 2164; others aver that he was born in Āgra), who became a Sikh of the Guru in 1682. According to some authorities, Nandlāl being a great scholar and poet of Persian, was employed as *Mir Munshi* with Prince Muazzam, even before he became the Governor of Multān in 1696 A.D. According to "Mahān Kosh," he was employed at Āgrā by the Prince in 1683, through the recommendation of the Guru (!) but that he left his service due to the pressure of Aurangzeb to convert him to Islām in 1697, and came to live at Ānandpur. But if Bhai Nandlāl died in 1705 (See "A Short History of the Sikhs," Ganda Singh, p. 65 f.n. Also Mahān Kosh (P. 2165), the question of his mediation at this time should not arise. However, in later works Dr. Gandā Singh credits him as having completed his ***Rehatnāmā*** in 1712 A.D. (Guru Gobind Singh's death at Nanded, P. 124). Nandlāl's Persian works in verse (under the pen-name of Goya) especially *Zindgināmā*, Diwan-i-Goyā, *Tansifo-Sanā*, are read with great veneration, like the works of Bhāi Gurdās. A Rahit-nāma (the Code of Sikh Conduct) is also ascribed to him (see Appendix VI). It would be a significant sign of the Guru's catholicity if he authenticated the "Code of Conduct" for the Khālsā by one who had not himself joined it formally.

Nandlāl had two sons—Lakhpat Rāi and Lilā Rām. The former died childless, while the latter's progeny used to live in Multān and Bahāwalpur before the partition of the country in 1947 and were still called "Bhāis."

† Why Bahādur Shāh made, and the Guru accepted, the request for assistance is amply justified by the character of the former as evidenced by historians of the time. Contrary to his father's Sunni creed, Bahādur Shāh was a Shia, and a liberal Sufi like his uncle, Dārā Shikoh, who too was on the best of terms with

A bloody battle was fought near Dhaulpur for three days, early in June 1707, in which Mohammad Āzam, along with several of his principal officers, was killed, his army scattered and Bahādur Shāh proclaimed himself the emperor of India. He was extremely grateful for the token assistance that the Sikh detachment had rendered him and sent Dharam Singh to express heartfelt gratitude to the Guru.* He also made a request to the Guru to see him, saying he himself would have paid a visit to the Guru, but this gesture might be misconstrued by some of his bigoted followers.

F. N. Contd.

the Guru's house and was offered material help and a robe of honour by the seventh Guru, Hari Rai, when Dārā was a fugitive after the battle of Samugarh, and which so much annoyed Aurangzeb that he called the Guru to his presence to answer for it. Dārā, it may be recalled, was a great votary of Hazrat Mian Mir of Lāhore, a renowned Sufi, who, according to tradition, had been called upon by fifth Guru, Arjun, to lay the foundation stone of the now famous Golden Temple at Amritsar. Thus the relations of Sikhism particularly with the Muslim Sufis and Shias, both persecuted by Aurangzeb, were most cordial, as they also were during the days of Akbar, the Great.

According to Mohd. Latif (A History of the Punjāb, Calcutta, 1890, pp. 181-182), "Bahādur Shāh was a generous, munificent and extremely good-natured prince. His tolerance and amiability were in great contrast to the bigotry and hypocrisy of his predecessor, Aurangzeb. Brought up in the school of adversity (he was kept in confinement for seven years by his father charging him with softness to, and hobnobbing with, the Sultans of Bijapur and Golkanda whom he was asked to subdue but with whom he wanted to make rapproachement of the king-emperor) he had grown up mild and affable to such a degree that the people called him the saint-king."

Latif continues: "According to the historians, his gifts in jewels and rich dresses were truly royal. In his dress he was plain like a devotee. He tried at Lāhore to introduce the *Khutba*, according to the Shia creed, but on being opposed by the Sunnis abandoned the idea, a singular sign of his liberal outlook. Fond of the society of learned men, he took great delight in discourses on topics of law and divinity. He was most popular in Panjāb and one of the gateways of Lāhore (Shāh-Ālmi) was named after him......"

It may also be that perhaps, because, inspite of his father's instructions, Bahādur Shāh had refused to molest the Guru in 1695 and instead of advancing against him, sent his forces to crush his enemies, the Guru, as a mark of gratefulness, lost no time in accepting his plea for help, while he was passing through the Panjāb to join the battle of succession.

* Says *Gur Sobhā* it was a Sikh soldier who shot Tārā (Mohd.) Āzam and this fact impressed the Shāh most. (P. 115)

When this invitation was received in the Guru's camp, the Sikhs would not advise the Guru to accept it. They feared there might be some catch in it. The Guru's wives also entreated him likewise. But the Guru said, "Life and death are in the hands of God at all times. Hence, one cannot be too careful in avoiding danger." He accepted the invitation and accompanied by one of his wives, Sāhib Kaur, and leaving the other one, Sundri, in Delhi, (the third one had died in 1701) he marched towards Āgrā where the emperor had encamped himself. On the way, he halted at Mathurā and Vindrā-vana and held discourses to the people.*

When he reached Āgrā on August 2, 1707,† the emperor received him with great courtesies, and presented him with a jewelled dagger (*dhuk-dhukhi*)‡ and a robe of honour and thanking him profusely for the moral assistance he had rendered him requested him to spend some time with him. The Guru gladly accepted this invitation. He thought it would be a good opportunity to bring to the emperor's notice the tyrannies heaped upon his followers by the imperial rule, notably the Nawāb of Sirhind, who had ordered his two young sons to be bricked up alive, and had perpetrated untold tyrannies on the people.

This nearness of the Guru became an eye-sore to many of his courtiers, and some of them decided to embarrass the Guru. One day, as he was conversing with the king in the presence of some courtiers, one of them, said to be a learned Sayyed from Sirhind, made a request thus : "O Guru, we have heard of the great house of Nānak. You are the tenth in succession to the founder of your religion. We consider only him to be divine who can perform miracles. It would give us great satisfaction if you too could allay our

---

* Thus says *Tārikh-i-Bahādurshāhi*, a source book, of this incident "At the time the (emperor's) army was marching towards Burhānpur, Guru Gobind, one of the descendants of Nānak, had come into these districts to travel, and accompained the royal camp. He was in the habit of constantly addressing assemblies of worldly persons, religious fanatics and all sorts of people." (*As quoted in History of India As* Told by Its Own Historians, Vol. 7, page 566). Khāfi Khān, a contemporary of Aurangzeb, and no friend of the Guru's house, in his "*Muntakābul-Lubāb*" corroborates this view that the Guru accompained by some 200 *sowars* became a "companion" of the emperor for some time, on his march to the Deccan. It was not an employment as Commander, as Forster and Cunningham wrongly insinuate.

† According to *Akhbārāt-i-Darbār-i-Muallā*, this meeting took place on July 23, 1707.

‡ The word has also been rendered as 'scarf' and 'necklace.'

doubts in this behalf." The Guru sensed clearly what lay behind this seemingly innocent request. But in order to put his questioner in the wrong, he aswered : "Why, the emperor himself is the miracle-maker. He can raise high who's humble, and demolish those that are high and mighty." The questioner was, however, persistent. "Sir, what you speak is truth but I want to know if there's a miracle your Holiness can perform." The Guru thereupon took out a gold coin and said, "Look, what a miracle is this ? It can buy anything in the world, any person, any value. Isn't ?" "Yes, your Honour, but we would be pleased to know what miracles can *you* perform. That is what will allay our doubts." The Guru, thereupon, drew his sword and thundered : "This is the miracle I can perform. I can chop off the head of anyone who dares challenge me. Here is the final arbiter for the destinies of men and nations."

The questioner became speechless. The emperor, who was listening to the questions and answers with great interest before, reprimanded the questioner for his impudence. "No, no, Excellency," he said, "You shouldn't mind this impertinence on the part of my courtier." As this news travelled, everyone was amazed at the fearlessness of the Guru even in the presence of the emperor of the land, in whose presence it was just not possible for anyone to appear armed, much less to draw the sword.*

One day the emperor said to the Guru, "There is no faith better than ours. Why shouldn't those who want to escape hell embrace it." The Guru replied, "Your Majesty, it is not the stamp but what is inside it that makes a coin worthwhile. Even if a counterfeit coin has Your Majesty's creed imprinted upon it, no one will exchange it with goods in the market place. So also in the case of faith. It is not the label, but the content that is pleasing to God, and which determines who is to be consigned to hell, who to heaven. I believe in one God, not two or three, and for me no one is an infidel save one who denies His Presence."

One day, the Guru made known to the emperor the desire he had harboured for some time. This was to dismiss and prosecute Wazir Khān, Subēdār of Sirhind, who had heaped untold tyrannies on the people. The emperor was taken aback at this demand, but

* That the Guru was permitted to go, armed, and escorted by five Sikhs, also armed, into the presence of the emperor is supported by Mohd. Latif in his "History of the Panjāb" (Calcutta, 1891, p. 273).

did not refuse it at the moment. He said he would consult with his ministers and would tender a reply later. He requested the Guru to wait for a year till his rule was firmly established and invited him to accompany him on his march towards Jaipur and other places. The Guru, though annoyed at the emperor's hesitancy, still did not want to break off his relations suddenly and agreed to accompany the emperor on his march, starting early in November 1707, to see if given a further chance, he would meet with his demand which was legitimate and in accordance with the Qurānic injunctions and equity.

The Guru, however, waited for some time more at Āgrā, addressing the holy congregations every morning and evening. Meantime, the emperor marched towards Jaipur. Later, the Guru's camp followed his, and soon overtook the emperor and visited Jodhpur and Chitaur along with him. The Rājput princes of these places paid homage to the Guru, who continued his march southwards along with the emperor till he reached Burhānpur where a devout Sikh had prepared a house for the Guru. The Guru honoured him with his visit and stayed in the house for some time. The emperor in the meantime had left and later wrote to the Guru to join him. The Guru accepted his request and both proceeded towards the South. The Guru had with him some infantry and two to three hundred cavalry equipped with lances.* They travelled together upto Nānded, where they reached in mid-September, 1708.

When he reached Nānded, the visited the house of a *Bairāgi*, Mādho Dās by name. The Guru had heard earlier in Rajasthān that the *Bairāgi* could perform miracles and had such skill in magic that he could overthrow any one who sat on his couch, merely by wishing it. The Guru thereupon went into his hut, and lay on his couch in his absence. When Mādho Dās came and saw a stranger occupying his couch, unharmed, he couldn't believe his eyes. The Guru, he was told in advance by one of his followers, had also slain one of his goats and cooked and eaten its meat. This sacrilege and affront the *Bairāgi* could not bear, and demanded an explanation from the intruder. The Guru replied that he was too fatigued and having come upon the hut of one who was known for his hospitality,

* Here the Guru seems to have parted company with the emperor who, according to Daulat Rām's *Life of Guru Gobind Singh,* wanted the Guru, now, to help him against the Marāthās which the Guru refused to do and finally broke off from him.

he could not but recline on the couch and eat whatever was available. The Guru also told him that he had come to reclaim him from the life of a recluse. When Madho Dās looked into his eyes and at his figure and saw something unusual in his charming, fearless manners, he asked who he was. When told that he was Guru Gobind Singh in person, he fell at his feet, and said, "O Master, I'm thy slave (Bandā). You have honoured me by your visit and emancipated me. Pray tell me if there is any command of yours I can carry out. You are the saviour of our race."‡

The Guru was deeply touched at this homage. When asked, Mādho Dās narrated his whole story to the Guru. Born in Poonch, near Rajauri (Kashmir) in 1670 A. D., he farmed for some time, practised firearms and went on hunting expeditions. One day, he had killed a she-deer and found, to his utter distress, two young ones in her womb. This shocked him so much that he renounced the world and became a recluse, settling later at Nanded and practising austerities. Here, he had also learnt the practice of Yoga, and some magic. The Guru liked his sensitive nature, but reminded him that when tyranny had over-taken men, it was the duty of the more sensitive to fight against it and even to lay down their life in the struggle. Mādho Dās, who now called himself the Master's slave, (Bandā), offered to do as he was bidden.* The Guru thereupon

---

‡ It is surmised by some recent historians that the Guru had not only heard of his repute during his recent travels, but known him also at an earlier date. Otherwise to appoint a stranger to lead the Sikhs in the Panjāb in a struggle of life-and death even temporarily till the Guru joined him later, seems a little improbable. But, no prior contact has to date been historically established.

* The following dramatic dialogue (which may be the result of the author's imagination as well) is recorded by Ahmed Shāh of Batālā in his *Zikar-i-Guruan-wa-Ibtida-i-Singhan-wa-mazahab-i-eshan:*

Madho Dās: Who are you ?
Guru Gobind Singh: He whom you know.
Madho Dās: What do I know ?
Guru Gobind Singh: Think it over.
Madho Dās: (after a pause): So you are Guru Gobind Singh ?
Guru Gobind Singh: Yes.
Madho Dās: What have you come here for ?
Guru Gobind Singh: I have come to make you my disciple.
Madho Dās: I submit. I am your Bandā (slave).
See also "*A Short History of the Sikhs*" by Teja Singh and Gandā Singh Vol. I. Part 2, p. 80, f,n.; Ali-ud-Din's Ibratnāmā, P. 93; Browne (Tracts), P. 9.

baptised him‡ and named him Bandā Singh (though he continued to be known popularly as Bandā Bahādur or Bandā, the Brave). The Guru also presented him with a sword and five arrows from his quiver and instructed him to remain chaste, not to turn away from battle, to remain humble in victory, not to found a sect of his own, to look upon his associates in this mission as comrades and equals, as the principles of the Khālsā brotherhood enjoined, and never their superior, and to take counsel with them at all times.

The Guru blessed him that so long as he carried out the Guru's mission in the spirit in which it was intended—punishing the evil-doers and raising the poor and the down-trodden in a spirit of dedication and detachment, with God in the heart, ever and at all times, the Guru's hand will always be at his back.* Bandā bowed at the Guru's feet and promised to do as he was instructed and never to depart from the path set out for him by the Master.

Thereupon, the Guru gave him detailed instructions to proceed to the Panjāb along with some other Sikhs,† Binod Singh, Kāhan Singh and Bāz Singh, etc. and to wait at a point near Buria (in Ambālā) for reinforcements which the Guru would get him sent. Thereafter, he was to attack a place nearby, called Sadhaurā, where his devout Muslim follower, Budhu Shāh, had been executed along with his disciples by his co-religionists for helping the Guru's cause. Later, he was to march on Sirhind, lay seige to the city and seize and personally execute Wazir Khān, the Subēdār, whose prosecution the Guru had demanded earlier from the emperor but was disappointed by the latter's evasive replies. Later, he was to settle accounts with the chiefs of the hill states adjoining Panjāb some of whom had been inimical, without cause, to the Guru's house and had even joined hands with the Moghal emperor to attack and harass him at a time

---

‡ For references on this point see under the chapter of Bandā Bahādur.

Also, Ahmad Shah (*Ibid* P. 11) *Ibrat nāmās* of Ali-ud-din (P. 39), etc., and Gandā Singh's "Bandā Singh Bahādur" (Panjābi, P. 20)

* It cannot be, as is suggested by some historians, that the Guru enjoined upon him not to marry. Himself a householder, the Guru could not have preached him celibacy. If he was asked to remain chaste, it is a different matter altogether.

†Dr. G.C. Narang puts this figure at 25. So does H. R. Gupta (History of the Sikhs, Part II, P. 6)

when he needed and had asked for their help to defeat the common enemy. The Guru said, he too would join him soon.*

Bandā left Nānded soon after, with a letter from the Guru in the name of the Sikhs to flock to his banner. The Guru stayed here for some time more. He would meditate on the bank of the river Godavari at a secluded spot. While here, many Sikhs came from far and near to visit him and make him presents. A Sikh once presented to him a valuable diamond ring. The Guru was sitting by the riverside, absorbed in the thought of the Divine, and threw the ring into the river. The Sikh was greatly disappointed. He entreated the Guru to tell him about where he had thrown the ring so that he could dive into the river and search for it, for it was such a precious thing. The Guru smiled and throwing another precious ring (which, it is said, the emperor had gifted him) into the river, he exclaimed, "There, I threw it there !" The whole congregation was amazed at the detachment of the Guru from the possessions of the world.

The Guru after some time seems to have sent away his wife, Sāhib Kaur, who had accompanied him to the Deccan, to Delhi, where his other wife, Sundri, was. She was not willing to part, as she had taken a vow that without seeing the Guru each day, she would not partake of food. But the Guru prevailed upon her and blessing her with five different weapons told her to look at them whenever she desired to behold him. Bhāi Mani Singh, a great divine and learned follower of the Guru, was also made to accompany her.†

---

* This fact, and the letter the Guru wrote to his followers at Dhaul, dated October 2, 1707, reveal that the Guru had every intention of continuting the fight against tyranny and to go back to the Panjāb.

† Sāhib Kaur accompanied Bandā Bahādur upto Delhi and lived there for quite sometime. She died before Mātā Sundri (but the exact year is not known. However, according to one of the Hukamnāmās she issued to the Kabilā of Bhāi Rāmā of Phul Vansh (*vide* Hukumnāmās ed. by Dr. Gandā Singh) she harboured a grievance that she was being discriminated against in the matter of offerings & Mātā Sundri was being preferred in this behalf. Both lived separately but when she died (upto 30 Dec. 1734 A. D. her Hukamnāmās are available and those of Mātā Sundri upto 10 Aug. 1730), she handed over the weapons of Guru Gobind Singh in her custody to Mātā Sundri, co-wife of Guru Gobind Singh, who exercised considerable influence on the Panth after the demise of the Guru. She lived most of the time in Delhi, but also for a brief while at Mathurā where she was endowed with a

Soon after, one night, as the Guru was retiring to his bed in his camp, a young Pathān, Gul Khān (according to Santokh Singh, and Jamshed Khān, according to *Akhbārāt-i-Darbār-i-Mualā*) entered into his presence. The man had visited the Guru earlier also during the last few days, claiming to be his devotee. As this visit was not considered unusual, no one stopped him. The Guru offered him *prasād* (sanctified food) which the rascal devoured at once. Then, as the Guru was bidding him good-bye and in the process of reclining on his bed, he plunged a dagger into the Guru's illustrious body twice. The Guru jumped from his bed with the speed of an angry lion, drew his sword and chopped off the head of the fleeing assassin.

All evidence now goes to prove that the murderer was a hireling of the Subedār of Sirhind, who, fearing reprisals from the Guru for

---

F. N. Contd.

small *Jāgir* by the royal house of Jaipur. Her residences both at Delhi and Mathurā are still preserved in the form of Gurudwārās. She had adopted a son called Ajit Singh, but seeing his crude and haughty manner and his proclaiming himself Guru, she disowned him. (Ajit Singh later killed a mendicant & was charged with murder and dragged to death, being tied to the tale of an elephant.) After the martyrdom of Bandā, when Sikhs were riven by faction and feud, Mātā Sundri appointed Bhāi Mani Singh as the Granthi (lit. keeper of the Book or custodian) of the Golden Temple. She died in 1747 A.D. The five weapons are still preserved at Gurdwārā Rakābganj at Delhi.

‡ Says the *Gur Sobhā*, written by the Guru's court poet, Saināpati, that there were two conspirators, the other one being caught and killed by the Sikhs. Some Sikh historians also assert (See *Gur-Bilās*, by Sukhā Singh, Chapter 29: 47-48, GSG of Bhāi Santokh Singh etc.) that the emperor, who was now camping near Nanded on hearing of it was much distressed and is reported to have sent his personal surgeons (one of them said to be an Englishman) to treat the wound. Later, when he learnt of the Guru's demise, the emperor sent a robe of honour for the deceased's (adopted) son (Ajit Singh) and ordered that the Guru being a *darvesh*, his considerable movable property should not lapse to the state but be handed over to his next of kin. (*Akhbārāt-i-Darbār-i-Muallā*, Rajasthān State archives, dated the 9th day of Ramzān and in the 2nd of of Bahādur Shah's reign corresponding to Nov. 11, 1708). It is said, before the Guru's demise, the emperor sought to round up about 700 Pathāns of the area and punish them for harbouring a criminal who had assaulted the Guru, but the Guru asked him not to punish the innocents. On the other hand Dr. Gandā Singh in his *Guru Gobind Singh's Death at Nanded* (p. 20), says the king "ordered the grant of a dress of honour to the son of Jamshed Khān Afghān who had died at the hands of the Guru !" The emperor is here seen to be playing a double game ! Incidentally, the *Khilat* to the murderer's son was awarded earlier and to the Guru's heir about three weeks later !

his dastardly deeds despatched this hired assassin to put an end to the Guru's life at the first opportunity.*

The wound was treated immediately and stitched up. On the fourth day (according to Bhāi Santokh Singh), the Guru appeared in his *Darbār* and it was considered he was well on the way to recovery. But in the middle of the night, when he stretched a little, the wound again gaped open.† The Guru sat up, in pain, and thinking his journey's end to be near, he called aloud some of his immediate followers. By the time they arrived, the Guru was absorbed in meditatton, but the Sikhs were at once apprehensive that something dreadful was in the offing. His face was serene and calm, as usual, and he betrayed no signs of a sinking man, but of one utterly composed and withdrawn in his own inner being, his eyes quietly closed, like petals of lotus at sundown. As soon as the prayer was over, some of them choked with emotion, could not resist expressing their deep anxiety at what they feared was in the womb of the future. But, the Guru, collected as ever, replied in subdued tones : "The one thing men dread most is death. I have always lived in its nearness and looked it in the face. So should every one of you who claims to follow me. I'll ride to my death as a bridegroom does to the house of his bride. So, do not grieve for me. For wheresover are the five pure ones of you dedicated to God, there my presence shall also be."‡ Asked who was to succeed him to the spiritual Throne

* According to the *Khālsā Nāmah* of Bakht Mal, Bahādur Shāh had granted a *firmān* in favour of the Guru upon Wazir Khān for the payment to him of Rs. 300 a day. It is natural, therefore, that on account of this close association of the Guru with the emperor, Wazir Khān should have been in fear of his life unless he removed the Guru from his way. According to the same source, (pp. 19-22), Wazir Khān had got an attempt made earlier also on the life of the Guru, but it had failed.

† Some chronicles, like *Mahmā Parāksh* (1774) suggest that he was trying a heavy bow, when the stitches gave way. *Mahmā Parkāsh* also confirms the Guruship having been passed on to the Guru Granth by the tenth Master on the eve of his death.

‡ GSG, Ain 2, 23. (.) According to the contemporary *Gur Sobhā,* the Guru said :— "I have bestowed the physical (or secular) Guruship on the Khālsā"— and "The True Guru is the infinite Word whose contemplation enables one to bear the unbearable." (41-43): For more references, Dr. Gandā Singh's book *"Guru Gobind Singh's Death at Nanded"* may be consulted. That the main difference between the *Tatt*

of Nānak, he replied, "The Word as enshrined in the Granth Sāhib. Whoever searches me here, finds me. You shall hereafter look upon it as the visible embodiment of the Gurus.@ I had come to establish God on earth, and so I entrust you to Him. He will ever be your Guide, Protector and Refuge, so long as you keep to His Path."

The Guru, with quiet, graceful movements, put on a clean and pleasing dress. He, then, stood to perform the *Ardāsā* (closing prayer). According to Koer Singh's *Gur-Bilās* (XXI, 99-102, P. 284) the Guru circumambulated four times round the Ādi-Granth, and making an offering of five *paisas* and a coconut, as was customary at the time of the succession of the new Guru, bowed before it, thus formally declaring the Holy Book to succeed him as the "True Guru." He then put on a waistband, as was usual with him while going on a battle, slung a bow on his shoulder, and taking his musket in his right hand, uttered to those around him in a final salutation : "*Waheguru ji kā Khālsā, Waheguru ji ki Fateh !*" (The Khālsā belongs to God; Victory be to God), and breathed his last. Before he did so, however, he asked his followers not to mourn for him nor to erect a shrine commemorating his death.* The Guru in his humility wanted his own name to be effaced utterly and sought merely to be followed as life, not worshipped as a tomb. But, the Sikhs after the cremation next morning, gathered his sacred ashes† and built a platform on it. The Khālsā whom the Guru had declared as his successor in secular matters resolved that the memory of such a great one as Guru Gobind could not but be commemorated.‡

F. N. Contd.

Khālsā and the followers of Bandā was based on his alleged assumption of the Guru's role (see later) shows that the Sikhs by and large firmly believed the tenth Guru to have ended succession after him.@ See *Umdatul Twarikh* by Sohanlal Suri, Vol. I (64-65); *Sketch of Sikhs* by Malcolm, P. 76, Forster, Vol. I. P. 263 (*Travels*)

* GSG, Ain 2, 24. † According to Koer Singh's *Gur Bilās*, a small dagger was also found in the ashes.

‡ The stories regarding the the Guru having walked to his funeral pyre and having disallowed anyone to go near it or having disapppeared on a horseback in which state he was "seen" by some persons should be dismissed out of account, according to the present researches. Says Gur Sobha :— "the Guru was well on the way to recovery in about four days. But on the last day, while he was trying a heavy bow, his wound gaped open. The Guru breathed his last four gharis after midnight and was cremated before dawn." (P. 131). It is said, the bow was presented by an emissary of Bahādur Shāh for sinister reasons !

An estimate of his character

Thus ended, at the young age of 42, an amazing character in the history of the human race. Assuming secular and spiritual responsibilities for not only his immediate followers, but for human freedom in this sub-continent, for man's dignity and his right to his personal beliefs and ways of life, at the tender age of 9, fatherless, surrounded by jealous and intriguing members of his ancestral family, by the hill chiefs around, and above all, the Moghal emperor and his viceroys, he gave a new secular hope and spiritual dynamism to a whole people. He moulded out of sheer clay men and women of steel, sparrows who could pounce upon the hawks and tear them open. Only three years after his death, the Sikhs under Bandā were the masters of a large portion of territory in central and south-east Panjāb and were threatening Delhi. Fifty years after, they were the masters of the Cis-Satluj states, and a major power in the territories lying between the Gangā and the Yamunā, after a life-and-death struggle which, in its heroism and sacrifice, has few parallels in the history of mankind. The Guru had made death for a cause so popular that even when price was put on the head of every Sikh, and the whole community was hounded out of its habitations and lived for years in the woods and hideouts, not one surrendered or accepted defeat. By the end of the century, they had established their rule over the entire Panjāb, and later also in Kashmir, Ladākh and the Pathānland right upto the Khyber pass. For the first time in a thousand years of India's history, the tide of invasions had turned west-wards. This was nothing short of a miracle.

But this was not all. He composed poetry that has few peers in the annals of literature; so vast is its canvas and imaginative sweep. The Guru created not merely a community of warriors, but men who would, even during war-time, never forsake God, and whose victories would be for the sake of Dharma, not for self-glory or greed. This is why while Guru Gobind Singh fought and won many battles, he never claimed the fruits thereof. Because, according to Guru Gobind Singh, it was not power, but ethics and open diplomacy that must determine the polity of a nation. And a nation must consist of a whole people, not a society broken up by caste, colour, creed or ideas of a superior race. This democratic spirit which the Guru infused in the Khālsā brotherhood, in which the highest was equal to the lowest, and where a small, well-knit, idea-inspired band of men and women fought and acted in the name, and for the sake, of a whole people, with the same weapons as employed by the enemy, has made Arnold Toynbee remark that he had anticipated Lenin by two centuries.* He abolished succession to Guruship knowing what abuses an office by heredity can lead to He even proclaimed, as has been pointed out that "whosoever calls me God would be consigned to hell." (See *Bachittar Nātak*). The Sikhs had to turn in secular matters to the whole Khālsā for a unanimous resolution, or the consensus (the *Gurmattā*), which was obligatory for everyone to follow. And, though he fought both with the Moghals and their vassals, the Hindu hill chiefs, he inculcated nothing but respect for the other man's faith. "Men are the same all over, though each hath a different appearance," he preached in his *Akāl Ustāt*.

For the first time, our race was given the message of the whole man. The same person was to be the devotee of God, as much as a warrior, tiller of the soil as well as the performer of menial duties. *Seva* (Community service), and *Langar* (Community kitchen) have since been the *sine-qua-non* of the Sikh fraternity. The taboos of dress and diet no longer were important for a spiritual life. Nor any profession was forbidden to a Sikh. But, all that he did was to be in the name of God. For, the Guru said, "The Khālsā belongs to God, and so victory also, in every field, is God's." He who only earns but does not share, he who only gathers joys but does not sacrifice, he who runs after the transitory allurements of life but is not dedicated to God for ever and at all times, could not claim the Guru as his own.

The distinct contribution of Guru Gobind Singh thus lay in organising a socio-political body of spiritually-awakened, but earth-aware people who were to spearhead the movement for the liberation of a whole society, and not merely remain content with the self-sufficient peace of the spirit, or the material well-being of an individual. In the transformation of whole corporate society through a well-knit, dynamic, conscious, and frontal organisation deriving its authority from, and working solely in the interest of the whole people, in every detail of their life. In making the baptism of steel and fire a necessary adjunct of a dedicated life. In making democratic temper permeate every layer of a man's being as much as of a society of which man is but a portion and a limb. And, yet in making a universal

* *A Study of History* (Oxford, Abridgement, 1960, p. 745).

God both the inspiration and the ideal of social and individual activity. In short, it may be said, that whereas Guru Nānak gave meaning to life, Guru Gobind Singh invested death with a new purpose.

We have already taken note elsewhere of the view-points of various historians, European and others, of the past centuries, about the mission of Guru Gobind Singh. A few quotations, more recent, and mostly from the non-Sikh sources may be of interest to the reader.

Writes Sayyad Mohd. Latif, eulogising the merits of Guru Gobind's contribution : "He was a lawgiver in the pulpit, a champion in the field, a king on the *masnad* and a faqir in the society of the Khālsā."* When Swami Vivekānanda was asked how very remarkable it was that Guru Gobind Singh could unite both Hindus and Muslims and lead them, both, towards the same end, he remarked that such an example in Indian history was indeed very rare.† Similar tributes have been paid by another modern Savant, Shri Aurovindo Ghosh "for the novel direction and form given to Sikh religion by Guru Govind Singh in the democratic institution of the Khālsā".**

Dr. Sir Gokal Chand Nārang is in our view quite justified in saying that "though he did not actually break the shackles that bound his nation, he had set their souls free, and filled their hearts with a lofty longing for freedom and ascendancy. He had broken the charms of sanctity attached to the lord of Delhi and destroyed the awe and terror inspired by Moghal tyranny."‡

In the words of Prof. Bannerjee, "It is undeniable that Guru Gobind Singh must be counted among the greatest of Indians of all ages. The object he attempted was great and laudable; and the means which he adopted were such as a comprehensive mind could alone have suggested. (And) it will not do us to forget that whatever else he might have been, Guru Gobind Singh was first and foremost a religious leader. None but a person of a saintly disposition, highly spiritual and with a complete resignation to the Will of God could

---

* *History of the Panjāb*, Calcutta, 1890, P.

† *Vivekānand's Works*, Vol. VI, p. 469.

** *Foundations of Indian Culture* by A. Ghosh, P. 132.

‡ *Transformation of Sikhism*, Delhi (1960), p. 98.

have behaved as he did during the acute crisis of his life. Leaving home and everything in the hands of the enemy, he bids farewell to Ānandpur, and with his ranks depleted and his family dispersed, his wives going in one direction and his mother with his two younger sons he knew not where, he arrives at Chamkaur and is at once surrounded by the Moghals and the hill chiefs. After a superhuman fight against the heaviest of odds, in which he sees his two dearest sons and his chosen companions fall one after another before his very eyes, he stealthily leaves the place and for some time is hunted like a wild animal, now escaping in one disguise, now in another, when news arrives of the barbarous and brutal murder of his two younger sons. He faces all this with a supreme composure and goes on with his work as if nothing has happened. He compiles a new recension of the Granth Sahib, adds to his own compositions and busies himself in laying strong the foundations of Sikhism in the Mālwā tract. Certainly, no mere politician or soldier could have done it. It is significant that after a very close contact with the Guru for more than a year, Bahādur Shah treated him as a *dervesh* and considerable moveable property left by him to be relinquished to the heirs, though, according to rule, it ought to have been confiscated. A man who preached that 'the temple and the mosque are the same,' could not have been the enemy of a community or a class. There is nothing in the Guru's life and writings to support any such conclusion. He had left the leadership to the collective wisdom of the community knowing full well that it would throw up its own leaders as need arose, and that the Guru's hopes were not belied is shown by the part that even such obscure men as (Nawāb) Kapur Singh and Jassā Singh Kalāl played in the Sikh war of independence. (They) blunted the edge of Abdāli's aggressive power which even the Marāthās failed to resist, and turned his great triumph at Pānipat into a barren victory."*

Bhangu Rattan Singh, whose family had seen or participated in the Sikh struggle for freedom in the eighteenth century, sums up neatly the purpose of the Guru Gobind Singh in creating the Khālsā : "The Guru created the Khālsā, for he wanted to transfer sovereignty to the poor of our land, so that they might remember in the days to

---

* *Evolution of the Khālsā* (Part II) by Prof. I. Banerjee, Calcutta, 1962, pages 156-169.

come that there was also in history a Guru by the name of Gobind Singh."†

† *Prāchin Panth Parkāsh*, by B. Rattan Singh, P. 41 :—

"in gariban haon deon pādshāhi,
yeh yād karen meri guriāyee."

PART II

CHAPTER XIV

BANDĀ SINGH BAHĀDUR

(1670 — 1716)

It has already been stated in the previous chapter how Guru Gobind Singh had met Bandā, converted him to his faith,* and despa-

* Dr. H. R. Guptā (History of the Sikhs, Part II, pp 2-6) rejects various views about his place of birth which have been offered, namely, that he was a native of South India (Cunningham) or born in Jullundur-Doab (James Brown, India Tracts, II, 9), or in Rajouri in the Poonch distt. of Kashmir (as Dr. Gandā Singh and other Sikh sources assert). He thinks, his place of birth was in the Sirmur state, as during his battles, he traversed the hill-states like one born to them. But this is not a conclusive evidence. Warriors get help from agents or their own followers from the unknown areas to show them the tracks and routes of adventure and escape.

Dr. Guptā also thinks, Bandā was not baptised (Bhangu Rattan Singh, Karam Singh Historian, and Suraj Paṛkāsh of Santokh Singh, also support this view). Dr. Guptā thinks, the Tenth Master did so deliberately so that powerful, spiritually-awakened and renowned that Bandā was, he may not stake his claim to Guruship after his death. This is a fantastic viewpoint. If the Guru would not have baptised him, how would he have been accepted by all the devout and orthodox Sikhs as their leader, especially when he wore the Sikh symbols. Says Syed Mohd. Latif (who is bitterly opposed to all his activities) that "he was initiated into the *Pāhul*" (by the tenth Master). (History of the Panjāb, p. 274). According to Malcolm, narrating Bandā's excesses in the territories he conquered," "life was only granted to those who conformed to the religion and adopted the habits of the Sikhs." Says M'gregor :—"Bandā received *Pahooldee* and became a Sikh" (History of the

tched him along with 25 others to the Panjāb posted with letters in the names of some of his devout Sikhs. (†) His immediate mission was to collect as much of the war-material and as many of the Sikhs round him as possible when the Guru was also to join him, (‡) if he could not setue his affairs with Emperor Bahadur Shāh. The negotiations with the Emperor, as we have seen, fell through, but before the Guru could move back to the Panjāb, he was assassinated.

At the time of Bandā's departure for the Panjāb, somewhere around September-October of 1708, the Guru, according to the Sikh chronicles, had instructed him "not to forget himself on attaining power" and to "keep chaste and disciplined in war as in peace and not to set himself up above the people, and keep the fear of God and Guru always in his mind." He was also assured by the Guru that "whenever he was in need or distress, he should assemble five Sikhs and offer prayers along with them and his desires would be fulfilled."*

Bandā,who took nearly a year to reach the Panjāb,lacked neither prowess nor character and was determined to carry out in letter and spirit the behests of the Guru. But he neither had money on him,

---

F. N. Contd.

Sikhs, vol. I, p. 106). Butē Shāh's evidence (Zikr-i-Gurān etc.) that Bandā was so called because he deposed before the Tenth Master as his slave (Bandā) has already been quoted. Bandā's *Hukamnāmā* (dated Dec 12, 1710) addressed to the Sangat of Jaunpur says, inter alia : "Call upon the Guru's name. The Guru will protect you." This proves clearly that he was a devout Sikh. That he died as a devoted Sikh, and looked like the Tenth Master is corroborated by Khāfi Khān's *Muntakhabul-Lubāb*, vol ii p. 761. (See also Irvine and J. N. Sarkārs "Later Moghals"). And, did not Bandā issue his coins in the names of Gurus Nānak and Gobind Singh? "Bandā was administered *Pāhul* by the Tenth Master," says the Mahān Kosh (p. 2676). Dr. Gandā Singh in his *Banda Singh Bahadur* quotes many other references as well to support our view' (Panjābi version, P. 20). MK says the Guru named him Gurbakhsh Singh (P. 267)

† According to "*Prāchin Panth Parkāsh,*" (p. 82) the Guru had specifically given orders to Bandā to invest Sarhind and murder Wazir Khān, its Nawāb, and then to attack and defeat the Panjāb hill-chiefs, who had been inimical to him.

‡ See the "*Hukamnāmā*" of Guru Gobind Singh, dated Oct. 2, 1707 addressed to the Sangat of Dhaul.

* Bandā, according to "*Prāchin Panth Parkāsh,*" (P. 83) put this to the test, and on his very first march towards Sirhind prayed, alongwith five others, for money to wage the impending warfare. At that very moment, a rich Lubānā (merchant) Sikh brought several thousand rupees as his tithe in offering, thus establishing Bandā's faith even more firmly in the Guru's word.

nor weapons. But, on his way to the Panjāb, he was met with in Rajputānā as also in and around Delhi by men of his fath who honoured the Guru's word in everyway and soon money became of little consequence to him. Being of a very charitable disposition, whosoever came to work for him even as a menial was offered a gold *Mohur* as a gift, whether he was a potter or an oil-man, a sweeper or a mere beggar. (*) This created not only an extremely favourable impression of him on the poor, but also attracted to him robbers and thugs whom he punished ruthlessly. Some of these had even to shake off whatever they had accumulated in their exploits of a whole lifetime. This also gave heart to the people of the South-eastern Panjāb which his ever-increasing force was now marching through, as the free-booters had made life in this frontier province rather hazardous and insecure. As soon as the devout Sikhs received the edicts of the Guru, they abandoned their hearths and homes in their hundreds especially in Majhā, Mālwā and Doābā, and marched out to join Bandā's forces. The Phulkiān chiefs did not themselves join in, but they seemed to have helped him with cash and mercenaries.

The news of the Guru's assassination set the Panjāb Sikhs literally on fire. The cold-blooded murder of his two young sons at Sirhind only a few years ago was still rankling in their minds and hearts. Therefore, when they heard of Bandā's coming, they gathered round him from all sides, irrespective of the difficulties put in their way by the local administrations. Of course, they knew what formidable force they were fighting against. According to J.N. Sarkār,† Aurangzeb had left an army of 1,70,000 men with ten times that number as non-combatants. No doubt it had to look after and keep order in a vast empire, also that Aurangzeb had greatly exhausted his resources in men & money in the Deccan wars. However, the resources of the empire were also vast. Yet such was the terror created by Bandā's call that the Subēdār of Sirhind, Wazir Khān, was unnerved, the moreso because it was he who had on his hands the blood both of Guru Gobind Singh and his two innocent sons.‡

---

* "*Prāchin Panth Parkāsh*"—p. 83.

† History of Aurangzeb, P. 420.

‡ Though this fact may not have been clearly established at that time, the suspicion in the minds of the Sikhs must have been strong that it was the Nawāb, who fearing the Guru's nearness to the Emperor must have deputed hired assasins to put an and to the Guru's life. Dr. Hari Rām Guptā is of the view that the emperor himself had organised the assassination of the Guru.

The primary aim of Bandā at this time was to attack Sirhind, not only to punish the Nawāb's dastardly acts,but to establish with his people as much as the Government of the day that the Sikhs wouldn't put up with this kind of humiliation and tyranny any longer, no matter what the price.

But, Sirhind was not an easy target to capture. It was the seat of the provincial capital. Its Nawāb was one of the pillars of the Moghal empire with a huge army under his command. He had been in power for long years and had accumulated considerable wealth and position. It is true that Bahādur Shāh was still waging a war with his brother, Kām Bakhsh, at this time, in the South of India, but he could still send considerable help to him from Delhi and the imperial armies stationed in the surrounding areas. So, Bandā decided wisely that he would first attack small citadels of power nearby, firstly to create a general disorder and contempt for imperial authority and secondly, to put to the test his own forces regarding their capacity for warfare, sacrifice and hardship. He was in the meantime hopeful of attracting a larger force from the Central Panjāb, the heartland of the Sikhs, and gather more money and equipment for waging a tough, and maybe, long drawn-out war with Sirhind. He, therefore, decided to attack, and destroy, its right and left flanks.

Near Kaithal, he successfully attacked an army detachment which was carrying the revenues of this area to the imperial treasury at Delhi. In the scuffle that followed, he captured not only cash but also a large number of horses which he needed badly, for upto now his force consisted only of infantry. He shared this loot with his forces, who were drawing no regular pay but fighting only a holy war, so as to convince them that he personally was above temptation.

On Novmber 26, 1709, Bandā fell on Samānā, to which belonged Jalāl-ud-Din, the executioner of the ninth Guru, Tegh Bahādur, and the two killers of Guru Gobind Singh's young sons, Shāshal Beg and Bāshal Beg. It was also a very prosperous town, built like a fortress. He attacked it from all sides and though fired on ceaselessly from the ramparts of the fortress of the Faujdār and by other notables from their roof-tops, Bandā and his men cut through all resistance, set fire to the mansions of the nobles and put to the sword whosoever came in their way. About ten thousand people are estimated to have lost their lives, including the Faujdār and the three executioners above-named, besides many other notable Sayyads and Moghals. The booty was extensive and the victory decisive. Bandā appointed one of his notable officers, Fateh Singh, to be the Faujdār of this town and nine other surrounding parganās.

Than Kaithal, the victory at Samānā was in every way much more rewarding and of far greater significance. His soldiery received a substantial share of the booty, leaving a sizeable sum also for future warfare. The victory at Samānā also unnerved the Subedār of Sirhind and he tried desperately to strengthen his defences and gather and put his entire force on the alert.

But Bandā was wise enough to be patient for a time and avoided a head-on clash with him till the forces from Mājhā and Doābā could join him who, as he learnt now, were being detained on the other side of the Satluj river by the Pathāns of Malerkotlā and Rupar.*

So, Bandā turned the course of his march and instead of proceeding towards Sirhind, fell upon Ghuram, Thaskā and Mustafābād. The first two small towns he took easily, but at Mustafābād he was met by heavy gun-fire and a trained force of nearly two thousand under its seasoned Faujdār. Some of Bandā's force, which consisted only of free-booters, deserted him at this stage, but others fought valiantly and won the day.

Now, Bandā advanced towards Sadhaurā, an extremely prosperous town, whose chief, Usmān Khān, was held in great dread by his subjects due to his tyrannous ways. What had irked the Sikhs even more about him was that he had got Sayyad Badruddin (alias Buddhu Shāh) tortured to death for the help he had rendered Guru Gobind Singh in one of his battles. (†) Usmān had made the life of the Hindus particularly miserable and did not allow them even to cremate their dead and would butcher cows, held sacred by the Hindus, in public streets. Many Hindus had deserted the city for these

* "*Prāchin Panth Parkāsh,*" P. 87.

† Sikh historians, besides Macauliffe and others, are unanimous that this help was rendered in the battle of Bhangāni, the very first the Guru fought against Fateh Shāh, the Rājā of Srinagar and his collaborators. But, as we have said before, the Guru in his autobiographical poem about his early life, called *Bachittar Nātak*, makes no mention whatever of Budhu Shāh's help. May be, Budhu Shāh helped the Guru in a later fight, possibly in the more gruesome and decisive battle at Ānandpur.

reasons, and a large body of them represented to Bandā Singh that they be rescued from his never-ending tyranny.

However, before Bandā launched his attack on Sadhaurā, he fell upon another quarry on the way, namely, the township of Kapūri which he set fire to, and possibly killed the chief, Kadmuddin, son of a high-ranking noble during the reign of Aurangzeb. He had not only inherited a huge fortune from his father but also became a tyrant and especially a women-baiter. No Hindu woman of beauty and charm was safe from him. Bandā divested him of his father's ill-gotten treasures and made the township safe for a time for honourable living.

When Bandā was about to enter Sadhaurā, many of the persecuted poor joined his ranks who, it appears, avenged on their age-old persecutors with extreme cruelty. A spot where most of the killings took place, is still called '*katal-garhi*' (the murderous fortress). Sadhaurā fell after a cruel battle, though the total loss of life on either side has never been reliably estimated. However, the whole town was burnt to ashes incuding also, unfortunately, a place of veneration for the Muslims, namely, the masoleums of *Ganj-i-Ilm* and *Kutab-ul-Aktāb* which were partially smoked.*

Meantime, the Sikhs, detained on the other side of the Satluj found an opportunity to cross the river, but before they could join Bandā's ranks, they had to contend with a large, highly-disciplined and trained force of Sher Mohd. Khān, Nawāb of Malerkotra, who was egged on by the Nawāb of Sirhind to halt the march of this reinforcement. The Nawāb's force was not only far more numerous but was equipped with pieces of artillery and large quantities of ammunition. The Sikhs, mere peasants turned soldiers of faith, had to fight with swords, arrows and small fire-arms—besides of course their spirit of revenge and an undying faith in their ultimate victory. Sher

---

* Earlier than Sirhind, Khāfi Khān does not mention the names of any other battle-fields except for saying that "he (Bandā) fought with two or three *Faujdārs* who went out to punish him, defeated them and killed them. In many villages which he plundered, he appointed *Thanādārs* and *Tahsildārs* to collect the revenues of the neighbourhood for him and matters came to such a pass that with three or four thousand infidels (i.e. Sikhs) who were leagued with him, he wrote orders to the Imperial Officers and the managers of the *Jagirdārs* calling upon them to submit to him and to relinquish their posts." (*Muntakhābul Lubāb,* Vol. ii, P. 653). We have, therefore, based our account on the Sikh sources, notably "*Prāchin Panth Parkāsh,*" for details of these earlier battles.

Mohd. Khān was badly wounded, his valiant brother and nephew fell in the battlefield along with hundreds of others and the Sikhs tore their way through to join hands with Bandā at a place midway between Banur and Kharar where Bandā came out personally to receive them.

Reinforced thus, Bandā was in no mood to lose time for his final assault on Sirhind. Fearing this, the Nawāb of Sirhind caused the nephew of his Hindu vizier, Suchānand. to force his way alongwith a thousand trained men into Bandā's camp pretending loyalty to him, but to put him to death at the earliest possible opportunity. Bandā, a man of simple faith, put trust in his word and accepted him and his force. Meantime, the Nawāb had gathered round him all his tributaries and proclaimed a *Jehād* (holy war) against the Sikhs. Of course, he lacked neither ammunition nor men disciplined by training and by war. According to Khāfi Khān, Wazir Khān was leading a force of 15,000 men,* including seven to eight thousand musketeers, and five or six thousand horse, besides an elephant corps, several pieces of artillery and trained body of gunners to man them.

Khāfi Khān's estimate of Bandā's forces seems to be extremely exaggerated. If he is to be believed, Bandā "in the course of three or four months had gathered four or five thousand pony (Yābu)-riders and seven or eight thousand motley footmen. His numbers daily increased and much plunder fell into his hands, until he had eighteen or nineteen thousand men under arms and carried on a predatory and cruel warfare." By the time he invaded Sirhind, according to Khāfi Khān, "there were thirty to forty thousand men with him !" But, according to Sikh accounts, they couldn't be more than fifteen to twenty thousand. Moreover, Bandā had neither any elephants, nor artillery and did not even have enough horses for his soldiery. Most of his men couldn't be employed on a regular basis. They were either fighting a battle of freedom, without expecting any reward (though their number was limited), or they were mercenaries (like the ones sent by the Phulkian chiefs) or plain marauders who, thrilled by Bandā's successes, had joined his ranks to reap a rich harvest of loot, if successful, or to desert their chief if faced with an impending defeat.

* According to Gandā Singh and Tejā Singh ("A Short History of the Sikhs", p. 83), Wazir Khān's force, combined with those of his collaborators from Hissār and its neighbourhood and of Lāhore, Eminābād, etc. could not have been less than 20,000.

But their leadership by and large was in the hands of the tried and devout followers of Guru Gobind, like Bāj Singh, Fateh Singh, Karam Singh, Dharam Singh, Shām Singh and Ali Singh (the last one having joined him after abandoning the service of the Nawāb of Sirhind).

Wazir Khān marched personally about ten miles out of Sirhind to give battle to the advancing enemy and the battle was joined on May 12, 1710, on the plain of Chapper-Chiri. Wazir Khan's troops fought with their backs to the wall and initially such was the consternation in Sikh ranks that the men who had joined them lured only by loot, fled the battle-field. They were followed by a thousand others who had been smuggled in by Wazir Khān earlier. Seeing this, Bandā himself leapt to the forefront and led the attack. The contemporary Muslim accounts of this battle are full of invectives against the Sikhs who are called 'wretched and worthless dogs,' 'hellish infidels,' 'fanatical ruffians,' and their leader a 'veritable monster,' and yet they do not fail to admire their reckless courage and spirit of sacrifice. Says Khāfi Khān, "when the battle began, great bravery was shown on both sides but especially by the confederate sectarians. They advanced sword in hand against the elephants and brought two of them down. Many Musalmāns found martyrdom and many of the infidels (i.e. the Sikhs) went to the sink of perdition. The Musalmān force was hardly able to endure the repeated attacks of the infidels when a musket-ball made a martyr of Wazir Khān and they were put to flight."*

"Money and baggage, horses and elephants fell into the hands of the infidels, and not a man of the army of Islam escaped with more than his life and the clothes he stood in. Horsemen and footmen in great numbers fell under the swords of the infidels who pursued them

* According to S. M. Latif (*History of the Panjāb,* P. 274) Wazir Khān was killed by an arrow, but another Muslim source describes his death thiswise :—"Wazir Khān came face to face with Bāj Singh, shouting 'be careful, you dirty dog,' and rushed upon him with a lance. Bāj Singh snatched the weapon from Wāzir Khān and struck it on the head of his horse and wounded it. After a while, Wazir Khān pulled out an arrow and thrust it at the arm of Bāj Singh. Then drawing his sword he sprang forward to make an end of him. Fateh Singh who was standing nearby, took his sword and struck Wazir Khān with it so strongly that it passed through his shoulder down to his waist and his head fell to the ground." (*Ahwāl-i-Salātin-i-Hind,* folio 35b-36b).

as far as Sirhind." The city of Sirhind was taken two days later. Continues Khāfi Khān, "in this opulent town full of wealthy merchants, bankers and tradesmen, men of money and gentlemen of every class...no one found the opportunity of saving his life, wealth and family. When they heard of the death of Wazir Khān, they were seized with panic. They were shut up in the town and for one or two days, made some ineffectual resistance, but were obliged to bow to fate." Khāfi Khān here charges the Sikh forces with extreme cruelty, sacrilege and rapacious appetite for blood-letting, carnage and loot. According to him, "they tore open the wombs of pregnant women, dashed every living child upon the ground, set fire to the houses and involved rich and poor in one common ruin. Whenever they found a mosque or a tomb, they broke it to pieces, dug it up and made no sin of scattering the bones of the dead." But, such a strong statement from a Muslim writer, highly partial to his own regime and distressed at its shake-up, can only be taken with a pinch of salt.

Of course, the hearts of the Sikhs were burning with revenge against Sirhind and its ruler. It was the determination of the Sikhs, therefore, to punish this accursed city,* and especially its wily Nawāb (and his accomplices like Suchānand, his Brāhmin Vizier) from whose abandoned treasures they extracted a booty of over twenty to thirty million rupees, besides vast military stores and equipment. But the city was saved from complete ruin at the intervention of local Hindus against the payment of a large ransom.

As for committing sacrilege against the mosques and tombs, it is a negation of the whole tenor of the Sikh movement for liberation which was being supported not only by the Hindus (save for those in the imperial employ or otherwise afraid) but also by a sizeable number of Muslims. Though many Muslims were converted to the Sikh faith at this time (including Dindār Khān, ruler of a neighbouring area and Mir Nasir-ud-Din, the official reporter of Sirhind), some even out of fear or to win his favours, Bandā never brought pressure to bear on

* According to traditional belief, the Guru (Gobind Singh) on hearing of the tragic murder of his young sons at Sirhind had pulled a shrub from its roots and prophesied :—"thus will this tyrannous rule be destroyed, root and branch. The city of Sirhind will be completely ruined, brick clashing with brick." Since then, devout Sikhs, whenever they visit Sirhind, pull out a brick or two from its ruins and throw them into the waters of the nearby rivers. A Sikh railway contractor, during the early British rule, got the bricks of its ruins crushed under a railway line that he was charged to build.

anyone to accomplish his conversion. From a report made to Emperor Bahādur Shāh by an official news-writer, it appears that during Bandā's stay at Kalānaur in April 1711 (i.e. a year after the battle of Sirhind), he (Bandā) had assured the Mohammedans that they would not be interfered with in any way, and that all those who came to join his ranks...would enjoy full religious liberty, including that of saying *Namāz* and *Azān*." As a result of this, five thousand Muslims joined his army and their number, says another report, "went on increasing daily."†

Now, Bandā turned to administering the territory that he had brought under his control. He appointed Bāj Singh, who had accompanied him from Nānded, as one of the Guru's chosen ones, Governor of Sirhind, with Ali Singh as his deputy and gave charge of Samānā and Thānēsar to his other confidants. On the fall of Sirhind, the entire territory with a revenue of Rs. 36 lakhs a year between Karnāl and Ludhiānā lay at his feet.

Such was the awe he inspired throughout the occupied territory that, according to Irvine, "it led to a complete and striking reversal of previous customs" in our caste-ridden land. "A low scavenger or a leather-dresser, the lowest of the low in Indian estimation, had only to leave home and join the Guru (i.e. Bandā), when in a short time he would return to his birth-place as its ruler with his order of appointment in his hand. As soon as he set foot within the boundaries, the well-born and wealthy went out to greet him and escort him home.

"Arrived there, they stood before him with joined palms, awaiting his order...Not a soul dared to disobey an order and men who had often risked themselves in battle-fields, became so cowed down that they were afraid even to remonstrate. Hindus who had not joined the sect were not exempt from these."*

What is even more significant, Bandā, for the first time in India's memorable history, abolished the corrupt and extortionist intermediaries, called the Zamindārs (absentee landlords) and distributed land to the tillers of the soil, thus creating peasant properietors—a class

† *Akhbār-i-Darbār-i-Muallā* (Jaipur) dated April 28, 1711 A. D. and another undated report from the same source, as quoted by Dr. Gandā Singh in "Panjāb, past and Present," Oct 1970 (Pp 223-231) in which other useful material has also been collected about Bandā Bahādur.

(*) "Later Moghals," I, p. 98-99.

which has been the backbone, since then, of all movements of religious and political freedom in the Panjāb.

Muslim historians credit Bandā even with supernatural powers. Says Khāfi Khān, "with jugglery, charms and sorcery, he pretendad to perform miracles before credulous people and gave himself the name of Sachā Pādshāh (True King)"* Other yogic feats he was believed to possess were, that he could "go without sleep indefinitely", "could foretell the future", "assume the garb of another—animal or man", "could walk in or out of an assembly at will, without being recognised," "could emit fire from his mouth," and "was immune to the effect of arms and could even fly in the air." "He could turn a bullet from its course and could work such spells that spear and sword had little or no effect upon his followers."† All this shows that he had impressed the contemporary political and religious scene in no insignificant way.

Bandā now gave a new capital to his realm. Instead of Sirhind, he chose Mukhlispur, a hilly place near Sadhaurā, and rebuilt its old fortress calling it Lohgarh (or the Fortness of Steel). He also started a new Era, beginning wirh the date of his conquest of Sirhind. He assumed royal authority and struck coin not in his own name but in the name of the True Guru. The inscription on one side of the coin read (in Persian, then the court-language) :

Sikkā zad barhar do ālam
Tegh-i-Nānak Wāhib Ast
Fatah Gobind Singh Shāh Shāhan
Sacha Sāhib Ast.

"This coin is struck for the two worlds to commemorate the pious Sword of Nānak, and also the victory that (Guru) Gobind Singh, the True King of Kings,brings".

The reverse of the coin had the following words inscribed in praise of the new capital :

Struck in the City of peace, signifying the
good fortune of man and the magnificence
of the blessed Throne.

(*) Muntakhabul-Lubāb, vol. ii, p. 651.

(†) Later Moghals, I, p. 111.

His official seal similarly contained no reference to his person, but was dedicated to the eternal glory of the Gurus. It read :

> *"Dēg-o-Tēgh-o-Fatah-o-Nusrat-bēdrang*
> *Yāft Az Nānak-Guru-Gobind Singh*

(The Sword, the worldly treasures, victory and unalloyed power I've found from Gurus Nānak and Gobind Singh).

Bandā, however, was not the man to rest on his laurels. He knew that as soon as the Emperor was free from his expedition in Rajputānā (he had already defeated his brother in the Deccan), he would march against him. Moreover, if he let the grass grow under his feet, it would give a much sought-for opportunity to his adversaries to rise against him. He also did not want his soldiery to indulge in ease and comfort and thus become an easy prey to the enemy who surrounded them on all sides. So he fell upon Sahāranpur which was easily taken after a show of resistance. From there, he advanced on Jalālābād and sent his emissaries in advance with a letter asking Jalāl Khān, the Faujdār, to surrender, without bloodshed. Infuriated, Jalāl Khān paraded Bandā's emissaries through the streets on donkeys and turned them out of the town in disgrace. Hearing this, the march on Jalālābād was speeded up, defeating all resistance on the way. The city was besieged but continuous rainfall obliged him to raise the siege and to retire to Jullundur—Doab to where they were urgently summoned by the leaders of the local community. The Sikhs had risen as one man against the tyranny of Shamas Khān, the Faujdār of Jullundur, who had raised an enormous force of *Jehādis*, estimated at a hundred thousand, against them. Five thousand well-trained horse and thirty thousand infantry were pressed into service. Upto this time, the Sikhs had gathered seventy to eighty thousand soldiers—both cavalry and foot—according to Muslim sources. After a game of hide-and-seek, both Jullundur and Hoshiārpur were occupied by them without striking a blow.

Meanwhile, the Sikhs of Mājhā also rose in revolt and with a small irregular force of seven to eight thousand captured Batālā, Kalānaur and Pathānkot, and even threatened Lāhore in whose surroundings there were bitter fights with the irregular *Jehādis*, even though the Governor of Lāhore, Aslam Khān, terror-struck, did not venture out of the town. The Sikhs were by now masters of the entire Panjāb east of Lāhore. "And if Bahādur Shāh had not quitted the Deccan in 1710, there is every reason that the whole of Hindustān would have been subdued by these invaders."*

The Emperor was greatly alarmed by these reports and on June 27, 1710, he suddenly left Ajmer and marched in person towards the Panjāb, with a huge army, at least sixty thousand strong, including some Rājput troops, avoiding even Delhi and Āgrā. He also gave orders that the Commanders of Delhi, Oudh, Moradābād and Allāhābād join him there. So unnerved was he by reports of the Sikh terror that on September 8, he enjoined, through a royal edict, on "all Hindus employed in the imperial offices to shave their beards"—a symbol of both religion and royalty for the Sikhs. Most of the Hindus obeyed the command, even though grudgingly, but a small number committed suicide at this dishonour, the beard even for them, till then, being a badge of respectability and honour.

The Sikhs could not possibly resist the imperial onslaught on the main highways. So they evacuated Thānēsar and Sirhind and retired into the fort of Lohgarh. From here they fell upon the Emperor's forces encamped at Sadhaurā on December 4. Even their muskets and arrows created such a devastation that, according to Khāfi Khān, "they in their fakirs' dresses, struck terror into the royal troops. The number of the dead and the dying was so large that for a time it appeared as if they were going to lose."† But soon the Sikhs retired to their fort. The Emperor, though reinforced, did not dare attack them in their stronghold and decided instead to lay a long siege to the fort and starve them to death. The scheme worked and the Sikhs had soon to kill their horses and other animals to keep body and soul together. At last, there was no choice but to break through the siege, at any price. One Gulāb Singh, a Sikh official, who resembled Bandā, offered to impersonate him, and

---

* Malcolm, "Sketch of the Sikhs," P. 99

† One of the reasons of the low morale of the imperial forces may also be the declining resources of the empire due to continuous warfare in the Deccan and Rajputānā. According to Khāfi Khān "it was a treasure of only 13 lakhs to which Bahādur Shāh had succeeded and that too had been given away. The income of the empire during his reign was insufficient to meet the expenses." (*Muntakhabul Lubāb*, Vol. ii, P. 683). This cannot be true however.

on December 10, Bandā made good his escape with his men in the dark of the night and made for the hills of Nāhan.*

When the Moghal forces took the fort next morning, they found that the "promised prize had escaped without leaving a trace behind him" and in his place was an impersonator and the bodies of a few Sikh soldiers, dying or dead. So infuriated was the Emperor that he ordered the Moghal general, Hamid Khān, to pursue Bandā and bring him into his presence, dead or alive. If not, the Rājā of Nāhan, Bhup Prakāsh, was to be arrested and carried alongwith Gulāb Singh, in an iron cage to Delhi. Hamid Khān, however, could not lay his hands upon Bandā and thus only the other order of the Emperor could be carried out. "However, two million coins were dug out of Lohgarh", besides "the capture of three cannons and seventeen light pieces."†

Bandā sent out *Hukamnāmās* to Sikhs all over to join him at once in this holy war. A large number of them gathered at Kiratpur in response to this call and Bandā now marched upon the Rājās of the hilly areas in the Panjāb including Kahlur (Bilāspur),‡ Mandi, Kulu and Chambā, some of whom, as we are aware, had given much discomfort to the last Guru. They all submitted to him, with good grace, without even a show of fight, except for Bilāspur which was attacked and its forces destroyed or scattered. Rājā Udè Singh of Chambā even offered Bandā in marriage a girl from the royal family. Bandā married her and had a son, Ajai Singh, from her.

Bandā bided his time in the hills for a while, though only six months later he over-ran Raipur, Behrāmpur, Kalānaur and Batālā.

---

* Says *Tārikh-i-Irādat Khān*: "Who can relate his (Khān-Khānān's or the supreme Moghal commander's) weight of grief and disappointment on finding that his promised prize had escaped......He for an instant lost almost the use of his faculties, which were absorbed in the dread of the Emperor's anger and not without reason. This grief......stuck like a poisoned arrow in his breast. He lost all satisfaction in worldly enjoyments, and from the day of his disgrace declined in health, so that not long after...(he) resigned his soul (Elliot and Dowson translation, Pp. 555-6 in the "History of India as told by its historians," Vol. VII).

† *Cambridge History of India,* Vol. IV, P. 323.

‡ Gandā Singh and Tejā Singh in "*A History of Sikhs,*" (P. 95) say that the Sikhs fought first with Rājā Bhim Chand of Kahlur. This is incorrect, as due to a mental disorder, Bhim Chand had abdicated in 1692 A.D. in favour of his son, Ajmer Chand.

But pursued by the imperialists, he had again to retire in the hills of Jammu whose topography as a young person he knew too well. As a result of his expeditions, the Emperor issued orders 'to kill the Sikhs wherever found.' Some of the civilians were also caught for no other reason than that they belonged to this faith and 'sold to the Moghal soldiers in the horse-market of Lāhore.'

Meantime, Emperor Bahādur Shāh died a mental patient on February 18, 1712. He was succeeded by a licentious weakling son of his, who was dethroned by his nephew, Farukh Siyar, early in 1713, his father, Azim-u-Shāh having already been killed in a battle of succession with his brothers. This confusion offered a golden opportunity to Bandā to come out into the open again and recapture Sadhaurā and Lohgarh, which once more became the Sikh capital. The new Emperor was a petty tyrant and his little over six years' reign was marked by intrigue, the rise of low sycophants to power and tyranny of the worst kind. In the Panjāb, however, his Governor, Abdus Samad and his son, Zakariā Khān, Faujdār of Jammu, carried out implicitly the royal behests to destroy the Sikhs, root and branch. In October 1713, Bandā was obliged to evacuate his newly-acquired territories, including Lohgarh,and again retire to the Jammu hills.* Here, he is said to have married a second time which

* According to "Prāchin Panth Parkāsh," (pp. 128-150) "by this time, Mātā Sundri, the widow of Guru Gobind Singh had turned against Bandā. It is stated that she had received a message from Farukh-Siyar, through Bhāi Nandlāl, (a devout Sikh of the Guru who is reported to have mediated and brought about a rapproachement between Bahādur Shāh and Guru Gobind) to intercede on his behalf with Bandā. The Emperor, it is said, gave the assurance that whatever Bandā had done so far would be forgiven and he would not only be granted a *Jāgir* but also a reconciliation would be affected between the Hindu hill-chiefs and the Guru's House. Mātā Sundri is said to have done as she was told, and addressed him a communication, but Bandā ignored her message saying "after all, she is a woman and doesn't know that the Turks (i e Moghals) wouldn't spare my life once I fell into their hands." "When, however, Bandā did not agree, both Mātā Sundri and Sāhib Devi were arrested by Farukhsiyar to put pressure on Bandā. Even while incarcerated, Mātā Sundri tried her best to bring Bandā round to conciliation with the king." It is also stated that" Bandā was greatly incensed at this intervention and sent word to her saying "I am no longer your Sikh, but a *Bairāgi* and a Vaishnava. I shall now abolish the war-cry of "Victory to the True Guru" ('Wāhiguru-ji-ki-Fateh') and substitute instead "Victory to the Presence" ('Fateh Darshan'). It is said when this message was conveyed to the king-Emperor, he asked Mātā Sundri to remove from Bandā's ranks the true Sikhs of the Guru

F. N. Contd.

Mātā Sundri, it is stated, not only sent out Hukamnāmās (edicts) to the followers of the Guru to desert and denounce Bandā, but also uttered a curse that 'if he wouldn't desist from his destructive path, he would lose all his prowess and power which were the gift of the Guru's".

According to the author of this story, as Bandā still ignored the wishes of Mātā Sundri, her curse befell him and he started losing ground, day by day. He married twice at Chambā and "thus lost his chastity." "His head turned" and he quarrelled often with the devout Sikhs saying, "it is I who have brought you a dominion and rule, otherwise you were no better than mercenaries." The true Sikhs then began deserting him, and taunted him that if it were so, he should start his own Panth and see the result! "Bandā indeed did so, and started a sect in his own name. He discarded the blue of the Khālsā and donned red robes, gave up the meat diet and insisted on strict vegetarianism." "He even styled himself Guru." But as he advanced to capture Lāhore, many devout Sikhs of Guru Gobind refused to participate in the venture and the Panth was divided between the *Tatt* (i.e. orthodox) Khālsā and the Bandai Khālsā (i.e. the followers of Bandā). Thus, Bandā could not capture Lāhore and in frustration left for Gurdāspur, etc. It is also stated that, Bandā threatened to start his own Panth after Mātā Sundri had intervened in his affairs. Before that when a Sikh, named Bulākā Singh (P. 98) complained about the ridicule heaped upon the Sikh-Khālsā and Guru Gobind Singh by the followers of Rām Rāi at village Ghudāni, near Pāyal, Bandā ordered that the latter should be severely punished, their *masands* arrested, looted and driven out of the village. The orders were immediately carried out. (Ibid 99).

At this time it is said, "Fārukh Siyar tried to win over the Tatt-Khālsā to his side, by making to them offers of office, money, *Jāgir*, remission in land-revenue, duty-free trade, etc. But when he failed in his attempt, the same trick was played on Bandā and his men. But they too did not fall into the trap. "The division in his ranks, however, had weakened Bandā much more, as he was still on the war-path and the *Tatt Khālsā* from now on did no more than watch on the side-lines" etc. The whole story seems fantastic, as it has many weak links. Bhāi Nandlāl, the Emperor's so-called emissary, had died at least a decade before this event. Even if he were alive, as some historians assert, it is highly unlikely that the widow of Guru Gobind Singh, egged on by an Emperor, totally hostile to her race, would deliberately create divisions in the Panth, when they were fighting a life-and-death battle. She had personally also nothing to gain as she (along with Mātā Sāhib Kaur, the other widow of the Guru) was being comfortably looked after by the offerings from the devout. She had no family save an adopted son, Ajit Singh, whom she had later disowned. If a serious rift would have occurred and that as a result of her intervention on behalf of the Emperor, the Muslim (and other) historians would certainly have made good use of it. But not a word occurs in any of the contemporary records about what, on every count, must be termed a decisive turn of events.

It is likely, that certain differences may have arisen during the life-time of Bandā, which after his death did lead to a schism in the Panth on the lines above stated.

resulted in the birth of another son of his, Ranjit Singh by name, and waited patiently for his opportunity.

Early in 1715, Bandā again appeared on the scene, and after a fight took over Kalānaur and Batālā. Farukh Siyar admonished his

---

F. N. Contd.

The Sikhs, by and large, may not have acquiesced easily in the change of the war-cry, (which was subsequently abandoned), nor in his being lauded as "Guru" by his courtiers and immediate followers, though at no time did he condone it, and struck coins and issued his edicts in the name of the Guru. The use of the word, "Sachā Sahib', as Dr. Guptā points out (History of the Sikhs, part II p. 4) was in reference to the true God and not his own person. "Fateh Darshan" is always preceded by IK-Onkār," (one God). Hence, it may also be interpreted to mean:— "Victory to those who believe in the God's Presence." Some sycophants and disruptionists might have tried to puff up his ego. His vegetarianism also may have irked some Sikhs, and that for reasons of warfare and expediency rather than as a matter of doctrine, as Bhangu Rattan Singh clearly points out. "How could vegetarianism work in the midst of warfare ? (p. 133)". His two marriages also were not in defiance of any Sikh religious code which sanctifies the life of the household. Guru Gobind Singh, while emphasising chastity, was certainly not asking Bandā to keep out of wedlock all his life. Even the author of "Panth Parkāsh" cites the instance of only 500 of the *Tatt Khālsā* to have deserted him at a single point. Even if they were more, one of them being Binod Singh who left him at Gurdās-Nangal, it might have been more as a result of differences in tactics of warfare, than on matters of religious principle. To the end, according to all Muslim and European eye-witness accounts, Bandā claimed to be the Sikh of the Guru, and not one of those arrested and beheaded alongwith him denounced him as an imposter. This legend should, therefore, be dismissed out of account. Possibly, the charge that Bandā didnot take the *pāhul* also was circulated at this time by his enemies, inorder to discredit him in the eyes of the devout. However, the contemporary Muslim historians, fanatically opposed to his exploits and character which they decribe as extremely "barbarous" yet credit him with a likeness to Guru Gobind Singh. (See Khāfi Khān's *Muntakabul Lubāb* and Mohd. Qāsim's Ibrat Nāmā). May be, their describing him (and following them the Europeans calling him) "Bandā Guru" may only mean the Guru's Bandā (or slave), as Bandā always chose to describe himself.

May be, (as has happened often enough before and after this event in Sikh history) the whole episode of the schism was the result of jealousies and intrigues, born out of the success of Bandā and the envy of others who could not be generous enough to give him credit for superb leadership in times of an acute crisis in the affairs of the community. Or, the Sikhs were too shocked at the defeat of one who was succeeding all along the line so well, and they could not find any other explanation for this except that he had deviated from the True Path of the Guru, a statement wholly unwarranted on every material count. Or may be, Bandā had developed an overbearing attitude towards his followers and thus gone against the Guru's teachings leading to protest and murmur, if not the actual schism.

Governor at Lāhore, Abdus Samad Khān, and reinforcing his troops by those of some Hindu hill-chief like the Rājās of Kāngra and Jasrotā, asked him to pursue the Sikh forces relentlessly. This order was carried out. Bandā gave an excellent account of his knowledge of warfare. However, the odds were heavily against him and he had to retreat to a fort he had recently improvised at the village of Gurdās-Nangal, very near the town of Gurdāspur. He dug up a moat around it and flooded it and the surrounding areas with water by diverting a nearby canal. But by now he was surrounded on all sides by the imperial troops. Nothing from without could find its way in. Often,the Sikhs would sally forth in small groups, gather grass for their animals and foodstuff for the besieged warriors and return to safety in the midst of a hail of bullets and arrows, leaving several of their ranks behind, wounded or dead. But this also could not last for long. They had to fall back "on oxen, and horses and other animals, and in the absence of fire-wood, were obliged to consume flesh raw, thus leading to dysentry and privation". "After a time, they stripped the bark of the trees, and their small shoots and thus filled their bellies." "Some of them are believed even to have cut flesh from their own thighs, and eaten it".

And yet, but for Binod Singh (who had developed differences with Bandā over his tactics and wanted the Sikh forces to cut through the siege and face the enemy in the open), no one deserted his camp, and for several months (according to some historians, nine whole months) Bandā resisted the pressure of all the military power that the mighty Moghal empire could muster against him.

According to Khāfi Khān, the fort at Gurdāspur (possibly he means Gurdās-Nangal) "was capable of holding fifty to sixty thousand horse and foot soldiers" and though trapped in the fort with little means of escape, "the infidels (i.e. the Sikhs) fought so firecely that the army of Islām was nearly over-powered. Over and over again,they showed the greatest boldness and daring and made nocturnal attacks upon the imperial forces. Abus-Samed Daler Jang, while lying in front of their poor (?) fortress was obliged to throw up an intrenchment for the defence of his force. He raised batteries and pushed forward his approaches. The siege lasted a long time, and the enemy... frequently made sallies into the trenches and killed many of the besiegers. To relate all the struggles and exertions of Abdus Samad and his companions in arms would exceed our bounds. Suffice it to say that the royal army in course of time succeeded in cutting off from the enemy his supplies of corn and fodder and the stores in the fort were exhausted."*

Eight thousand soldiers are reported to have succumbed to hunger and disease, thousands had been killed in daily clashes, the others were on the verge of collapse. In this condition, Bandā decided to throw open the gates of the fortress which the imperial forces occupied on December 7, 1715, and Bandā and his few hundred surviving stalwarts walked into captivity without any resistance or sign of regret. "Such was the will of the Guru," opines a Sikh chronicler. "The man of miracles had been reduced to miserable straits, for he had set himself up above the heads of his people—a posture that went totally against the grain of Guru Gobind's teachings."

According to Khāfi Khān, about three to four thousand of them were put to sword there and then (others say they were far fewer which is more believable) and their heads, stuffed with hay, and stuck upon spears, were taken out in a procession, led by Bandā, dressed in a mock regal dress, seated on an elephant, and confined in an iron cage. He was followed by 740 of his devout followers (Khāfi Khān puts their number at 1000) including his wife and 3 year old son, Ajai Singh (Khāfi Khān puts his age at 7 to 8 years which shouldn't be correct) on saddleless camels. And yet such was still Bandā's dread "that a Moghal officer was tied to him to plunge his dagger into his body if he tried to escape." First, they were paraded through the streets of Lāhore to the wild jeers and taunts of the crowd, throwing upon them heaps of dust and rocks from the house-tops and then taken to Delhi for presentation to the King-emperor.

Says Khāfi Khān, "In the month of Moharram (Feb. 29, 1716) the prisoners and the stuffed heads arrived at Delhi. The Bakshi, Itimadud-Daula Mohd. Amin Khān received orders to go out of the city, to blacken their faces and put wooden (mock) caps on the heads of the prisoners...to give a warning to all spectators." All eye-witness accounts, however, are unanimous in proclaiming that "they (the Sikh prisoners) showed not the slightest sign of dejection or humiliation on their faces." As they were taken out in the mock procession, "they seemed to be happy and cheerful, merrily singing their sacred hymns." After the procession had passed before the

* *Muntakhabul-Lubāb*, ii, P. 761.

Emperor, orders were given for confining the Guru (i.e. Bandā), his son (and wife) and two or three of his principal companions in the fort... Two or three hundred...were to be put to death every day* before the Kotwāl's office† and in the streets of the bāzār." Adds the author, "The men of Khatri caste, who were secretly members of the sect, and followers of the Guru, sought by the offer of large sums of money to Mohd. Amin Khān and other mediators to save the life of the Guru (i e. Bandā), but they were unsuccessful."

Every one of them was offered mercy if he would renounce his faith in favour of Islām, but not one son of Gobind betrayed the religion of his forefathers and to a man "underwent their fate with wonderful patience and resolution." They even vied with one another for priority in death.‡ Khāfi Khān narrates the story of a young Sikh boy, who was forgiven by the emperor on the entreaties of his aged mother that her son was not a Sikh, but was driven into their camp by force and compulsion. But when the executioner, just about to sever his head, was handed over the orders of his release, the boy remonstrated angrily :—"My mother is a liar. I wish heart and soul to join my follow-beings in devotion to the Guru : send me quickly after my companions." And so the young hero met with a a martyr's death.

Three months later, on June 9, 1716 came Bandā's turn. "His life and that of his 26 companions had been spared for so long in order to get some intelligence about their treasure." As if the humiliation to which an erstwhile mighty enemy had been subjected was not enough for a crude and uncivilised regime, he and his companions were again paraded through the streets of Delhi and taken to near Qutab Minār to circumambulate the tomb of Bahādur Sháh as if in a homage. First, all of his choice companions, including Bāj Singh and Ali Singh, were executed, one by one, in his presence. And last of all came his turn. "He was dragged from his iron cage, like a wild beast, and then dressed in a (mock) princely robe, embroidered with gold and a scarlet turban. The heads of his followers were paraded on pikes all around him." He was given the usual choice

* According to *Ibrat-nāmā* of Harisi, their bodies were hung up on trees on the outskirts of Delhi.

† Near the present day Hardinge Library and very close to the Chāndni Chowk of Delhi.

‡ *Ibrat-nāmā* of Harisi, P. 35-a.

between Islām and death, and Bandā with all his heart chose death. "His (3-year old) son, Ajai Singh, was placed in his lap and he was asked to cut his throat." Bandā, it appears, refused.* "The executioner, thereupon, cut the child to pieces and thrust the quivering young heart into the father's mouth, who stood unmoved, like a statue, completely resigned to the Will of God."

According to *Siyar-ul-Mutākharin*, Mohd. Amin Khān, one of the Tribunal, struck by Bandā's extraordinary appearance, asked him why "a man who shows so much acuteness in his countenance and has displayed so much ability in his conduct should have been guilty of such horrid crimes." Bandā replied with the greatest composure :— "Whenever men become so currupt and wicked as to relinquish the path of equity and to abandon themselves to all kind of excesses, then the Divine Avenger never fails to raise up a scourge like me to chastise the race become so depraved; but when the measure of punishment has been filled, then he raises such a man as you to punish him in return."

Bandā's execution is narrated by contemporary records as the most horrible of all. "His eyes were cut out of their sockets, one by one. His hands and feet were then chopped off. His body was then torn by red-hot pincers and finally his head was executed."† But, according to all historians, Muslim and other, he bore his tortures with utmost equanimity and poise of the mind and soul. All the four brothers of Bāj Singh died with him, as also Ali Singh and the other devout and choice Sikhs of Guru Gobind, and not one deserted his camp in the face of sure death.

---

* "*A History of the Sikhs,*" by Tejā Singh etc. P. 79. *Siyar-ul-Mutākharin* (P. 80), Griffin, Cunningham and Latif (*History of the Panjāb*, P. 280), however, assert that Bandā complied with the command without the slightest hesitation. Khāfi Khān, however, leaves an alternative for the executioner. (*Muntakhabul Lubāb*, Vol. ii, P. 761).

† According to Prāchin Panth Parkāsh (p. 159), Bandā was kept blinded for many days after which he was dragged behind a horse-carriage and thus gave up the ghost, proclaiming all the while that "whoever kills me in whatever way will meet with the same fate", and "this prophecy was fulfilled." (As is well-known, Farukh-Siyar also was blinded by the Sayyad brothers soon thereafter (1719), kept in a dungeon for two months, with a bow strung round his neck to torture him and at last strangled to death). P.P.P. gives, however, a wrong date for Bandā's execution (Samvat 1778, i.e. 1721 A D.) which does not tally with any of the eyewitness accounts. Fārukh Siyār's death is also placed by this historian three years later (i.e. 1724 A. D.) which is wrong.

Bandā's Character

Bandā's role in the Sikh struggle for freedom has been the subject of severe controversy. It is a fact that in the brief span of seven years, he had shaken a rule as vast and as firmly-rooted as the Moghal empire. From Karnāl to Lāhore, an area of over 25000 square miles, was liberated, even though for a brief period of time. He had put to the sword atleast 50,000 people in battle. (History of the Sikhs, part II, H.R. Gupta, p. 37). In the history of the world, according to the same author, "he should not rank less than Alexander the Great, Changiz Khān, Nādir Shah, Ahmad Shāh Abdāli, or Napolean Bonaparte". He was the first empire-builder for the Sikhs and a great national hero for the Hindus, a scourge for the tyrants (but a man of compassion and generosity for the Muslims who supported his political cause, not his religion). Bandā struck coins and proclaimed the sovereignty of the people in the name of the Guru. Such was the consternation that the King-emperor, Bahādur Shāh, had to march in person against him, finding most of his subedārs and generals in the area east of Lāhore either murdered, displaced or cowed down. It is true that much devastation of village and town also took place in the process, people abandoned their hearths and homes in panic, blood flowed in torrents and excesses must have been committed by Bandā and his men to settle scores of a whole century of persecution and humiliation not only heaped upon the Sikhs, but the majority people of Hindus and even a sophisticated liberal minority of the Muslims as well, like the Sufis and the Shiās. And, after all, it was a war and a war between two unequals, the one side backed by the resources of a mighty empire, and the other supported only by the common, untrained and unequipped masses, though with a burning zeal of a newly-sprung and yet a persecuted faith. The Hindu civilians helped Bandā with money secretly, whenever they could, but they never joined his ranks in any large numbers. (In fact some of the Jāts, Rājputs and Bundhelās fought against him along with the Moghal forces). Nor did the Muslims, except for some adventurers, inspired more by a desire for loot than to establish a soverign dominion of the entire people, irrespective of caste and religious faith. His excesses against the Muslim nobility and his partiality towards the Hindus and the cow may also have aliented their sympathies. And above all, the Moghal empire, inspite of all its weaknesses, still had large enough resources to crush a sporadic rebellion confined to a comparatively small part of Hindustān.

But it was Bandā who, for the first time after Guru Gobind Singh, made his people taste the fruits of political freedom. But, it appears, he did not wholly imbibe the spirit with which the Gurus had invested the whole people with sovereignty, also making each of the constituents a full and equal partner in spiritual hope as much as in social and political ascendency. And for this reason, he could not keep in check some of his enthusiastic followers from building a personality cult around him, in spite of, as seems likely, his own aversion to it. It is a fact of history that though he may have discouraged it, and he died the noble death of a hero and martyr, disowning neither the Guru nor his faith to the last, the Muslim historians, one and all, call him 'Bandā-Guru'. The report of Englishmen attached to the Moghal court also refer to him as the "rebel Gooroo". It was believed also in the common mass, according to Khāfi Khān, that he (Bandā) "gave out that in the course of transmigration, which the Sikhs believe in and call avatār, he had taken the place of the murdered Gobind, who had come to life in his body for the purpose of taking revenge." But, these historians never suggest that he deliberately did so in order to divide the community or that it had any such effect on most of his followers.

However, it must be conceded that something did happen somewhere which must have irked the devout Sikhs of the Guru like, for instance, his innovation of a new war-slogan, "*Fateh Darshan*" (or 'Fateh Daras' as the Muslim historians point out, meaning "Victory to the Presence") though as we have pointed out, it might have meant nothing more than "Victory to God's Presence" or "to those who believed in God's Presence." Binod Singh's desertion from the besieged fort of Gurdās Nangal may have been as a result of tactical differences, and Mātā Sundri, the widow of Guru Gobind Singh, may have played no part in bringing about the schism (much less on the behest of the Emperor Farukh-Siyar). But that immediately after Bandā's death, a serious sectarian cleavage should divide the Sikhs in his name, also cannot be explained away by the mere zeal of a few of his fanatical followers. Or may be, they did so for their own reasons and not for any lapse on Bandā's part. It has happened in history many times before: the followers misinterpreting the original creed after the death of a hero or prophet, and using it for their own political advantage.

Again : one can understand the vicious attacks of the Muslim historians, mostly courtiers of the empire or in the imperial pay, on the character of Bandā, but why should the Sikh chroniclers, beginning with the most authentic Rattan Singh Bhangu do so, attributing his downfall 'to the different and new turn he was giving to the Sikh movement, notably in regard to doctrine."* May be, it was only the difference of temperament which was being exaggerated, Or, perhaps, this was the best way to explain away his defeat.

And yet, when all is said, the same Sikh chroniclers credit him, to the end, with the forbearance, the patience and the religious zeal of a true Sikh and even with the miraculous powers bestowed upon him, according to them, by Guru Gobind Singh, on his decision "to stake his all in the name of his new faith and in defence of all the poor and the persecuted of our land." If he had deviated in any material respect from the chosen path of the Gurus, the Muslim historians would not only have recorded it with the greatest glee, but the Moghal rulers themselves would have also spared his life and even forgiven and honoured him to push further the division among the Sikhs. On the other hand, according to Rattan Singh himself, when finally surrounded on all sides in the fort of Gurdās-Nangal, Bandā spared himself no hardship, thus inspiring the rank and file with his utter devotion to the cause. "No one knew when did Banda drink water or eat food. Whenever asked, he replied he was on a fast. Some thought he had spirits in his possession, others that he had disciplined his body through yogic austerities, or taken some such herb that he had controlled his appetite"* (and thus could live without eating). What is equally amazing is that when he asked his followers to lay down arms, not one disobeyed him and piled up their arms before him, and doors were opened unto the enemy to face a sure death. "All of them," continues Rattan Singh, "were reciting the hymn of the Guru saying, ' this world is transitory, the city of the dead. He alone lives in truth, who lives in faith, contented and patient. Thus they considered pain as pleasure, determined on giving up life, unafraid and with good cheer. But they also pronounced curses on the vile Turks

* One of the charges of a Sikh historian against Bandā's diet and dress is not only that he was a strict vegetarian, but also that he did not take wine. (Suraj Parkāsh, Uttar Ain, Ans. XIII, p. 374) and did not wear black !

(i.e. the Moghals) saying this rule will soon end, and that wherever the Khālsā will arise, they will depend only on God, be firm of faith and be afraid of no one."

Even the miserable death of Farukh-Siyar is attributed by the Sikh historian, Rattan Singh Bhangu, and others who follow him, to the prophecy uttered by Bandā that "whosoever kills me and in whatever way will meet with the same fate." Some of these chroniclers even resurrect him to live a much longer and twice-wedded life. All this in Bandā's favour certainly would not have been said by the same Sikh historians who allege that Bandā had, in the hour of victory, turned his face against the Guru and the Sikh doctrines. If so, why didn't any of his immediate successors (he left behind a wife and a son, called Ranjit Singh) stake his claim to Guruship after Bandā was no more, and why was it left to the others, far less known in the battle of freedom under Bandā's flag?

Not only did Bandā rouse the latent energies of his long suffering people to bid finally for total sovereignty, he also tried even within the brief period allotted him by fate to ameliorate the lot of the poor, both through his charitable disposition and through the abolition of Zamindāri. He also gave heart to the people to strike against an oppressive minority rule, by concerted action, daring and sacrifice. A small incident in this context may reveal how much he dared to transform the psychology of a sullen, terrified people. When a deputation of Hindus called upon him at Sadhaurā, complaining against the tyrannies of Muslim landlords, he asked his bodyguard to shoot the complainants. When questioned respectfully as to how the aggrieved deserved such a bloody treatment, he answered:—"You are so many and your oppressors so few. Is it not a shame that instead of dispossessing them, through a common, even if violent action, you should make a grievance of your own helplessness?" The complainants did as they were bidden to. And their example spread like a wild fire to other areas as well.

Bandā also was assured in his mind that the Sikhs, even though themselves in a minority, would win, because they would fight, as the Gurus had enjoined upon them to fight, in the name and on behalf of the whole people. His successes can be seen and appreciated only in this light, and also his humiliation and defeat. It is not necessary, as it often happens in the annals of the oriental peoples (the Sikhs not excluded) to look for extraneous causes either in a nation's periods of glory and pride or privation and suffering. It may be that the Sikhs were rudely shaken by Bandā's total downfall as they must not unnaturally have been over-elated on his sudden, meteoric rise, thus crediting success to his miraculous powers and his defeat to their loss.*

Perhaps it was the Guru, who, in his wisdom, had blessed Bandā and his followers with both, the first to inspire the long-suffering people with a new moral hope of political ascendency and the second, to warn them unmistakably against an easy victory before receiving the baptism of fire and paying the full price for social and political liberty in blood and tears. For, the nations that all the time are looking out for miracles without preparing themselves to become their worthy recipients, come to grief all-too-soon. To material success, as much as to spiritual illumination, there is no short-cut or an easy way out.

---

* It is nowhere related what happened to the wife of Bandā who was arrested with him. Possibly, she was executed. Dr. Guptā says, she was admitted into the harem of Durbār Khān Nāzir (History of the Sikhs, Part II, P. 34). But as has been said above, he had married another wife, Sāhib Kaur, who was left behind with his son called Ranjit Singh (some call him Ajit Singh). They both retired into their original place in the Jammu mountains and seemed to have lived a pious, religious life. Ranjit Singh was succeeded by his son, Jujhār Singh and Zorāwār Singh. The older Jujhār Singh assumed the pontiffship after his father and he was succeeded by Fateh Singh with whose death the pontiffship passed on to the descendants of Zorāwar Singh, whose descendants, after a time, resorted to litigation to settle the problem of succession which, ultimately, went to Teja Singh, to be succeeded after a time by Sardool Singh who died on April 6, 1948. His son, Jitendrapāl Singh (born october 2, 1944) now lives at Rohtak. The Derā of Bābā Bandā Singh is situated about seven miles from Riāsi in the province of Jammu and has a small jāgir attached to it. The Derā is run strictly according to Sikh religious custom and ritual.

CHAPTER XV

LIFE-AND-DEATH STRUGGLE

(1716—1768)

The gruesome death of Bandā left the Sikhs leaderless for a time. They could not believe how a man of his daring, sacrifice and near-miraculous deeds could come to such a tragic end. The shock was too overwhelming for some who, it appears, tried to explain it away by attributing his ultimate failure (if one may call it such) and brutal death to his having abandoned the true path of Guru Gobind Singh. This naturally led to a schism in the community, Bandā's immediate followers, now called Bandais, defending their hero to the hilt. Of course, when nations fail to achieve their objective with their outside adversaries, they are usually torn by civil strife and mutual recriminations, instead of taking a dispassionate, rational, long-range and overall view of momentary defeat and preparing for success with renewed vigour, unity and resourcefulness.

On the occasion of Diwāli of the year 1720, the matters came to such a pass that there were open fights in the holy precincts of the Harimandir in Amritsar*, between the more numerous followers of

* According to Rattan Singh, the feud between Kāhan Singh and the Bandais originated in the division of income of the Harimandir for the ten days of the fair that the former had organised on a payment of Rs. 10,000/- to the Moghal authorities. The Bandais had, he says, decided to pay more to the Moghals if they would permit them to hold the fair. According to him, the *Panth* was not only divided among these two factions but several other minor sects as well, like the

the Tatt Khālsā (the orthodox believers of Guru Gobind) led by Kāhan Singh, son of Bābā Binod Singh, and Bandais, the stray though fanatical followers of Bandā, led by Mahant Singh and Lāhorā Singh Kalāl. However, the matters were settled through the intervention of the elders in an unusual—and amusing—way which for a leadership fighting for statehood was, to say the least, primitive. Instead of thrashing out and resolving the differences of doctrine, (which it is stated had divided the two factions) through expert advice and mature deliberation, it was decided that a wrestling bout be organised between Miri Singh, son of Kāhan Singh, and Sangat Singh, son of Lāhorā Singh, and whosoever floored the other would be considered to have won the doctrinal point! Perhaps, when passions were rising high in a militant people, this was the best way to laugh out the whole episode (which also shows, because both parties agreed to this queer arrangement, that the differences were not fundamental, but only superficial and temporary). But it so happened that although Miri Singh threw Sangat Singh on his back, the other party did not acknowledge defeat. The atmosphere became even more tense and so it was resolved to cast lots (again a strangely irrational way of settling a dispute of doctrine) to see whom the Guru favoured in this factional dispute. Two pieces of paper, one bearing the words, "Fateh Darshan" (Bandā's innovation) and the other carrying "Wāheguru-ji-ki-Fateh" (the orthodox Sikh war-cry) were cast on the waters of the holy pool at Har-ki-Pauri in Amritsar. For a time, to the consternation of all, both of them seemed to sink, but suddenly the one bearing "Wāheguru-ji-ki-Fateh" rose to the surface and amidst shouts of Sat Sri Akāl, the Tatt Khālsā won the day. Some of the Bandais accepted this as the verdict of the Guru from on high, and led by Lāhorā Singh joined their ranks. But the others indulged in a free fight in which their leader, Mahant Singh, was killed and the rest left the scene in disgust.

F. N. Contd.

followers of Gulāb Rāi, Gangu Shāh, Bābā Hindāl, etc. who were either followers of the various *masands*, or derived their lineage from the Gurus' clans like Sodhis, Bedis, Bhallās and Trehans. Others like Minās (descendents of Prithi Chand) and Dhir Maliās had already been ex-communicated by Guru Gobind Singh. Hence their influence was minimal. Rām Rāiyās were ex-communicated before, but on Rām Rāi's death, Guru Gobind Singh himself helped his widow get rid of her *Masands* and a rapporachement was arrived at.

It appears that in this state of confusion of ideals and lack of purpose, many Sikhs went back to their age-old profession of farming, some entered state service or got their land-revenue excused. Some even were granted jāgirs by the state, though the true followers of Guru Gobind Singh gathered under the banner of the Tatt Khālsā, refused to give up arms and lived either on loot or temple-incomes, or possibly on the secret help given them by the civilian Sikhs (called Khulāsās*, or easy-going,) who didn't observe the discipline of the Khālsā or the chosen ones of Guru Gobind Singh.

It is, therefore, evident that it is the roaming armed bands of the Khālsā whose activities attracted the adverse notice of the authorities. Wearing blue, decked with all kinds of weapons, and not afraid to lay down their lives for the cause, they kept aloft the banner of resistance to the Moghal authorities, though from Bandā's death to about four years later, we do not hear of any major activities on their part either. Hearing of the feuds, Mātā Sundri, the widow of Guru Gobind Singh, then residing at Delhi, deputed Bhāi Mani Singh, highly-respected in the community for his devotion and learning, to be the head-priest (*granthi*) of the Harimandir at Amritsar (1721)† who managed the affairs of the temple diligently and with great sense of devotion. With the income of the temple, he ran a free kitchen for the upkeep of the aged, the infirm and the handicapped and religiously kept all the savings with the local bankers. The factional strife came to an end and more and more people visited the sacred temple, especially on Baisākhi (April) and Diwāli (in October) in peace and harmony.

But the troubles of the Sikhs outside did not cease, even though their activities at this time were sporadic. The Sikhs were also watching for an occasion for the Moghal power to be weakened further in order to bid finally for their sovereign

* They were later called *Sahjdhāris*, a term still used for all Sikhs who do not conform to the orthodox discipline of the Khālsā, but believe in the ten Sikh Gurus and the Guru Granth Sahib and conduct themselves socially and spiritually like any other Sikh.

† A letter whose authorship is credited to him was written from Amritsar to Mātāji in 1716, in which he gives a tragic picture of the disturbed conditions & the Sikhs having fled to the jungles and wastes of the Panjāb. If that be so, he must have been appointed to this post five or six years earlier.

power.† It will thus be interesting to know what was happening in Delhi at this time.

As we have seen, after the deposition and death by torture of Farukh-Siyar (1719 A. D.), a 20-year old grandson of Bahādur Shāh, Rafi-ul-Darajat, then held in prison, was proclaimed King, though the real power remained with the two Sayyad Brothers. The puppet-King, however, died within three months of "consumption" and his younger brother, Rafi-ul-Daulā, came to the throne, under the title of Shāh Jahān II. He too was held almost like a captive by the Sayyad Brothers, and neither allowed to go to the mosque for Friday prayers, nor to go out hunting or talk to any of his courtiers except in the presence of one of the Sayyads, or the guardian appointed to keep a watch over him. In this climate of humiliation, he too passed away in a little over three months, of "dysentry" and "mental disorder." A grandson of Aurangzeb, Neko Serā, proclaimed himself emperor, but was defeated and made prisoner and vast treasures of the Moghals fell into the hands of the Sayyad Brothers, though the division of spoils led to a bitter feud between them. On the death of Rafi-ud-Daulā, the Sayyad Brothers called in another 18-year old grandson of Bahādur Shāh (in October 1719) to become King, under the name ofMohammad Shafi, who after assuming power got rid of one of the Sayyad Brothers, through murder, and the other one was taken prisoner after a fight and the King became a free sovereign to act on his own.

If, therefore, we do not hear of any serious onslaught on the Sikhs at this time, it was not only because they needed time to reorganise their forces after a serious debacle, but also because the Moghal throne of Delhi itself had become a plaything in the hands of clever manipulators and naturally they could settle accounts with the Sikhs and others only after an emperor could consolidate his own position against his royal rivals and wily courtiers who had made him a helpless victim of their designs all these four years.

---

† Abus Samad Khān, a Turāni nobleman & a great general, was appointed by Fārukh-Siyar Governor of Panjāb, to fight the Sikhs. According to a Persian chronicler, "he filled the extensive plain (of the Panjāb) with blood as if it were a dish." He carried the title of "the Sword of the State." He continued is his position upto 1726, was awarded "a *mansab* of 6000, a bedecked *pālki*, elephants, horses, ornaments of gold, jewels worn in the turban, a turban bedecked with gold, a pearl necklace & some parganas in the Panjāb as *Jāgir*" for his excellent services. *Hakikat Binā*, as quoted by N. K. Sinha in his *Rise of the Sikh power*, P. 3 fn).

Moreover, the powerful Governor of the Panjāb, Abdul Samad Khān Dilerjang,* was required by the Sayyad Brothers to take the field against the Pathāns of Kasur, who had rebelled against the Moghal regime under Hussain Khān. With a force of eight to nine thousand horse under his command, he had expelled all officers of the Crown and levied contribution on the neighbouring territories. The General, Kutab-ud-Din, sent against him by the Panjāb Governor was killed, his cavalry was dispersed, and all his baggage looted. The Governor, thereupon, marched personally against Kasur and scattered the Pathān forces. But, hardly peace was restored that there were religious disturbances in Kashmir organised by a Mullāh, Abdul Nabi, who demanded that henceforth "no Hindu be allowed to ride a horse, to wear white robes or turbans or bear arms, to visit gardens and fields except on stated hours or to bathe on certain days." Many Hindus were mercilessly killed and their houses set on fire. Many had their noses and ears cut off; others were forcibly converted to Islam. Several thousand Shias were also killed and a large number of women taken away. Looting was also indulged on an extensive scale. Even the Governor, Ahmad Khān, who did not meet with the Mullāh's wishes was attacked and his nephew and some of his other important officials done to death. The Mullāh thereupon proclaimed himself ruler of Kashmir under the title of Dindār Khān. Delhi had to fight this fanatic usurper with great vigour, and it was after much bloodshed that the imperial forces could restore peace in Kashmir.

---

* According to Princep, not only was reward offered for Sikh heads, by Abdul Samad but there was sure death for all persons invoking the name of Guru Gobind (*Origin of Sikh power*, p. 4). Says M'gregor (History of the Sikhs vol. II, p. 113), "strict orders were issued to kill everyone bearing the name of Sikh, and rewards offered for their heads. In order to distinguish the Sikhs from the other inhabitants of the Panjāb, all Muslims and Hindus were strictly enjoined to cut off their hair and beards." The emperor's edict "applicable to all parts of India, was to arrest every Sikh, wherever found, and if he didnot accept Islām to kill him. For every Sikh head, a reward of Rs. 25/- was to be given and for his capture alive, a sum of Rs. 100/-. Their pretty girls were to be reduced to concubines and others to be made servants. When a Muslim died, his grave was to be dug by a Sikh or his Hindu sympathiser. For *begār* (forced labour) in place of cobblers, Sikhs were to be employed," etc. See also the letter of Bhāi Mani Singh to Mātā Sundri. "The Sikhs have repaired to the woods and wastelands. The *Malechhas* dominate the country. In all habitations, no young woman is safe. The Guru's enemies have also joined hands with them. *Hindāliās* report to Govt. on their movements

Though the emperor was trying to assert himself, he was weakened considerably by the jealousies and mean intrigues at the Court, the rampant corruption and the rebellious attitudes of the Viceroys of Deccan, Ajmer and Gujarāt, and the rising demands of the turbulent and powerful Marāthās on the Emperor.

It was, therefore, left to the ingenuity of each provincial Viceroy to keep his own authority intact by whatever means available at his disposal. In a situation like the one now obtaining at the imperial capital, every provincial Governor tried to, if he could, fish in the troubled waters, and with this end in view, would not like to take chances, within his own territory, with any of the trouble-makers.

In 1726, Abdul Samad Khān was replaced as Governor of the Panjāb by his more ruthless son, Zakriyā Khān, also known as "Khān Bahādur." And the first task under instructions of the emperor he undertook himself was to show his utter callousness and contempt for the Sikh life. It appears, the Sikhs had, in the intervening decade of peace (1716 26), reorganised their forces and harassed the Moghal authorities from their hide-outs in the forests and the bushy wastes of the Central tracts. Sometimes, they would fall upon the Government treasury, at other times on the rich Zamindārs and other notables. But the Hindus were generally spared from these drepidations, as also women of every community. And the poor, if not helpled, were never touched.

The Khān Bahādur now gave orders that the Sikhs be hunted out wherever they be. A price was put on the head of each Sikh, and whosoever was captured from country or town was put to death in *Nakhās*, the horse-market of Lāhore. Their severed heads were exhibited in pyramids to put terror into the minds of the onlookers. The Sikhs called them "Shahid Ganj" or, the "Treasure-trove of Martyrs." In this atmosphere of ruthless persecution, the Sikhs had no option but to leave their hearths and homes and retire to the woods, subsist on roots and grass, or whatever vegetation they could lay their hands upon. The only redeeming feature was the

F. N. Contd.

etc. (As quoted in Trumpp's *Ādi Granth's* translation, edited by Giani Harnām Singh Ballabh, intr. XIX, 1960), though it is dated Amritsar, April 1716, while according to all reliable authorities, Bhāi Mani Singh took over the custodianship of the Amritsar temple in 1721.

help the peasantry by and large rendered them secretly by giving them individual refuge or sustenance in times of dire need.

It is in these days that the stirring couplet "*Rāj karegā Khālsā, Āki Rahē Nā Koē : Khuār hoē sab milēngē, bachē sharan Jo hoē* :* (recited in all Sikh congregations upto the present day) came into vogue. The continuous, uninterrupted reading of the Guru Granth, called the *Akhand Pāth* also was resorted to in these days of stress (it has now become a part of the Sikh ritual). A new, manly vocabulary was given currency† among the Sikh guerrillas which showed with what brave face and heart they had accepted the challenge of their persecutors.

In the year 1726, a Sikh of high religious repute, Tārā Singh, who had fought several battles under Bandā and rendered whatever assistance he could with his small band of 22 volunteers to his community in distress, was pounced upon by a large Moghal force, sent by Zakriyā Khān from Lāhore, and he alongwith each one of his associates was done to death. The Sikhs lost no time in taking revenge. Royal troops carrying revenue chests to Govt. headquarters at Lāhore were looted in the Mājhā area for several years. These attacks were carried on relentlessly, much to the discomfiture and humiliation of the Govt. caravans bringing horses for Govt. troops from Kābul were pounced upon and the horses snatched for the use of the Sikh free-booters. These actions were, however, so sudden and swift that before the attackers could be confronted by Govt. troops, they had already vanished into the forests or the hills and dunes.

* It means: "The Khālsā shall rule, and no one will challenge their authority. Humiliated in defeat, all will join their ranks and he alone will be saved who seeks their refuge." It is a part of *Tankhāh Nāmā* by Bhāi Nandlāl, the well-known court-poet of Guru Gobind Singh. [Also see last Appendix]

† Parched grams (*chholē*) were called "almonds"; onions were termed "silver coins" (rupā), stale hard loaf was called "sweet bread" (*mitthā parsādā*), to go hungry was "to be intoxicted", to die was to "invade" (the citadel of Death) (*charhāi karnā*), a young Sikh was called "a snake" (*bhujangi*); to fine a man was "to employ him for wages" (*Tankhāh lagāni*); to ride a donkey was to "ride the back of the police-chief" (*Thānēdār*). A single person became *sawā lākh* (1,25,000), and feminine names and concepts were changed into masculine (Holā for Holi etc) and contempt for money expressed by calling it *Māyā* and a silver-rupee coin as *damrā* (petty penny). Now these terms are used mostly by the free-lance Nihangs.

Frustrated, the Government tried to buy peace. The Lāhore Governor sent his emissaries, in March 1733, in their hide-out at the foothills of the Shivālik range to offer a *Jāgir* and a Nawābship to the Sikhs. The first reaction of the Sikhs was to reject it unceremoniously. But later, after a hot discussion, it was agreed to take the Govt. at its word and try the pursuits of peace for a while.

But now, the trouble arose as to which person should be invested with the honour. Such was the urge for self-effacement in those days that one after the other, everyone rejected the offer. Darbārā Singh, their Chief, refused it saying, "the Guru promised us sovereignty. We cannot be content with a mere Nawābi." Others said it was a trick of the Moghal to divide the fraternity where all were equal and no one was superior to the other. All eyes were now riveted on one Kapur Singh, a devout and self-effacing Sikh, who was waving a large fan over the assemblage at this time. "Why not elevate him, our faithful and humble associate, if no one else is willing to accept the offer," the leaders yelled with one voice. But Kapur Singh stood adamant, saying, "I would not give up the privilege of serving my fellow-men. What is a Nawābi before the honourable occupation I'm already engaged in ?" When pressed hard on all sides, he agreed, but on the condition that five Sikhs should touch with their sacred feet the Royal Command, both in order to reject it with contempt and also to sanctify it for acceptance.* This was done, and Kapur Singh became a Nawāb,† and, as will be seen, proved his

* Prāchin Panth Parkāsh, P. 214

† Born in 1697, Kapur Singh, a Virk Jāt of Faizalpur, had developed martial qualities from an early age. Even before he was invested with Nawābship, he had shown his mettle as a leader (next only to Darbārā Singh whose Jathā or band he had joined) and distinguished himself both as a warrior and as peace-maker. Such, was, however, his humility that even after he was made the Nawāb, he continued to serve in the community-kitchen. Kapūr Singh died in 1753, appointing Jassā Singh Ahluwāliā to succeed him as the Jathēdar (leader) of the Panth. Kapūr Singh was later known as the founder of the Faizalpuriā or Singhpuriā *misal* as well. It is said by Sikh historians that "there was not a part of his body two inches wide which did not bear the mark of a wound suffered in battle". According to Latif, "he was undoubtedly the most distinguished of the Sikh leaders who paved the way for the greatness of the nation as an indigenous ruling power............He converted a large number of people, jats, carpenters, weavers, chhatris and others to the persuation of Govind and the religious aspect in which he was held was so great that institution into the *Pāhul* of the Guru with his hands was considered a great distinction. It was he who first organised the Sikh forces into Buddhā Dal

mettle and sagacity as the supreme leader in peace as much as on the field of battle. However small the significance of this episode, it nonetheless gave a chance to the Sikhs to go back to their homes and settle down in their age-old occupations of agriculture or trade. But the fire once lit to become a sovereign people did not die in the hearts of the vanguard, who utilised the brief opportunity of peace to organise themselves under Nawāb Kapur Singh into an army of elderly veterans called the *Budhā Dal*. The young Sikhs, however, organised under their own banner and were called *Tarunā Dal*. Being raw and inexperienced though full of zeal for the faith and the spirit of adventure, it was hard to maintain discipline among them. Hence it was decided a year later (1734) to establish five centres (*) for them at Amritsar, each with its own drum and flag, and composed of not more than 2000 men. Anyone could join any of these bands and also leave it at will and join another. No one was given any salary and all dined in a common kitchen. The discipline was strict. No one could leave for home, without due leave, and whatever was brought in (either through temple-offerings or the Jāgir or the help rendered by civilians) was kept in the common treasury. Nawāb Kapur Singh was in the over-all charge of both the Dals, and such was his awe and respect that his word was law for everyone.

It appears, soon the young soldiers became restive and started marching not only through Bāri-Doab, but also went right upto Hānsi and Hissār levying taxes and gathering tribute. Zakriyā Khān tried to prevail upon Nawāb Kapur Singh to get the Singhs recruited in the imperial army or to let them settle down in the

---

F. N. Contd.

and Tarunā Dal and later welded them both into Dal Khālsā but for which the Sikhs would have been scattered into insignificant splinter groups. Inspite of all this power and prestige, he always remained humble and considered himself only one among the many illustrious sons of the Guru. This is no better exemplified than in his refusal to make his leadership hereditary. After him he appointed Jassā Singh Kalāl to lead the Panth, he being considered the ablest of them all.

* The five bands of the youth were led by (1) Deep Singh Shahid (II) Prem Singh and Dharam Singh Khatris (iii) Daswandhā Singh (iv) Bābās Kāhan Singh and Binod Singh and (iv) Bir Singh and Amar Singh, both Mazhabi Sikhs. They were headquartered in Amritsar at Rāmsar, Bibeksar, Lachhman-sar, Kaul-sar and Santokh-sar. It will be seen that leadership of every caste was represented in these *Jathās*, including the so-called untouchables.

revenue-free lands in the villages. Both the suggestions were spurned by the community at their Diwāli get-together in 1735. The Government, therefore, cancelled their Jāgir, and both sides came in conflict with each other. Lakhpat Rāi, the Chief Minister of the Khān Bahādur, dispersed the Budha Dal from Bāri Doab and it was obliged to take shelter in the Mālwā region. Here they punished Sirhind once more, and helped Ālā Singh (the founder of the Patiālā state) to extend his territory. On their way back, however, they were attacked by Diwān Lakhpat Rai, at Basarkē, near Amritsar, with a force of seven thousand, and defeated. This brought the Tarunā Dal into action, who pursued the victorious Moghal army and engaged them in a grim battle near Lāhore, inflicting heavy losses and killing two important Commanders and a nephew of Lakhpai Rāi.

The Lāhore Government was so much alarmed as a result of this action that they took possession of the Central Temple of Amritsar and no Sikh was allowed to visit or go near it. Large-scale arrests of Sikhs were also affected and a proclamation issued that no one should offer them shelter or help of any kind, and whenever a Sikh is found, he should be handed over to the Government. Thousands of Sikhs fell victim to this compaign of genocide.

But the gruesome martydom of the venerable Bhāi Mani Singh,* the pious and learned custodian of the Harimandir at Amritsar inflamed the passions of the Sikhs as perhaps nothing else could. Mani Singh had taken permission from Government to celebrate the Diwāli festival on a payment of Rs. 5,000 for a ten-day fair. The Sikhs trekked in large numbers from all over to gather at their holy shrine, but the Government in the meantime changed its mind and tried to molest and terrorise the pilgrims on the way, by sending out a strong force under Lakhpat Rāi, the Diwān. The fair was, there-

* Born in Kaibowāl near Sunām in the Patiālā distt, he was entrusted to Guru Teg Bahādur's care when he was only five. He look *Pāhul* at the hands of Guru Gobind Singh. In 1704, Mātā Sundri and Sāhib Devi were escorted by him to Delhi when the tenth Guru abandoned Ānandpur. In 1705-6, he brought them back to Damdamā Sāhib where he wrote the new recension of the Ādi Granth, as dictated by Guru Gobind Singh. In 1721, he was appointed the custodian and head priest of the Amritsar central temple by Mātā Sundri. Latif gives 1728 A. D. as his date of martyrdom, Gyāni Gyān Singh & Dr. Gandā Singh place it in Nov. 1738, Bhāi Kāhan Singh in 1737. His age at martyrdom is given by some writers as ninety, and his date of birth placed in 1544, and death in 1634.

fore, very thinly attended and Bhāi Mani Singh, it is said, not being able to gather enough offerings, after defraying the expense of the fair, could not pay the Government dues. He was, therefore, arrested and on his refusal to accept Islām (a choice that was offered to him) was cut up limb by limb (1738). (*) A companion of his, Diwān Singh, was broken on the wheel. So much was the shock of this gory event felt in the community that they pledged to avenge it on the state apparatus on a scale that would shake it to its roots. Their choice forces retired to the Lakhi forest, the sandy dunes of Rājasthān, or the Shivālik hills and waited for their opportunity.

And this opportunity they got early next year (1739) when Nādir Shah, the ruler of Persia, invaded India via Kābul. All through the Panjāb upto the gates of Lāhore, Nādir's armies savagely ravaged the country freely using both fire and sword at all places. A bitter fight ensued at Eminābād between Kalandar Khān, the deputy to the Viceroy of Lāhore, commanding a force of ten thousand horse and Amir Khān, a dependent of Nāsir Khan, Moghal Governor of Peshāwar, who had submitted earlier to Nādir Shāh. Kalandar Khān

* As the Sikhs to date repeat in their congregational prayer (see Appendix) all the terrible events of carnage at this time ("remember those who were cut up limb-by limb, were sawn alive or broken on the wheels... "etc), there is no reason to disbelieve that Bhāi Mani Singh was tortured to death. But that he couldn't gather a paltry sum of Rs. 5,000/- if not from the fair, then from his bankers or otherwise, or refused to pay Government dues which brought about his horrible end cannot be believed in good conscience. Sohan Lāl's evidence that he was punished for converting other people (possibly including Muslims) to his faith may be more nearer the truth. The Sikh version (see Prāchin Panth Parkāsh, P. 223) that Mani Singh was cut up limb-by-limb because of a curse that the Sikhs had pronounced upon his head, years ago, when he tried to re-arrange the contents of the Guru Granth and separate the Guru's Word from that of the Hindu and Muslim Bhaktas, is also a very facile explanation. Though such a copy accredited to Bhāi Mani Singh is lying at Nānded, it should also be noted that there is no place for curses or omens in the Sikh credo. Even if the copy accredited to Mani Singh is genuine, it didnot find acceptance of the Panth and the matter ended there. Ultimately, it was not their curses on the Moghals or the Afghāns but their sufferings and mighty endeavour that brought the Sikhs to power. This episode is a further witness to the fact that being unable to explain the death, by torture, of a highly pious leader of their faith, the Sikhs have invented the unbelievable theory of the Guru's or the Sikhs' curse (just as in the case of Bandā Singh) having brought about his death by torture. Martyrs suffer and sacrifice their life not because they are cursed, but because they are blessed by God to blaze the trail for others. through their high idealism and nobility of character, for which they deliberately invite suffering on their heads for a great cause.

was killed and much carnage ensued. Zakriyā Khān was so much demoralized and terror-tricken by this episode that after having advanced about fifteen miles outside Lāhore, he hastily retreated to his capital with all his force of twenty thousand horse. The Persian army pillaged all the towns and villages on its way to the Panjāb capital and massacred the inhabitants. When they met the armies of the Lāhore Governor after fording the Rāvi, a grim battle ensued in which the Lāhore Chief was "completely routed and repulsed with great slaughter". After putting up a half-hearted defence, the Governor sent an emissary to Nādir Shāh, begging for clemency. The latter agreed to receive the Governor personally and the deal was settled for Rs. 20 lakhs (raised both from the State treasury and rich citizens of Lāhore) besides a large number of elephants. Lāhore was thus saved from massacre and spoilation. Zakriyā Khan was confirmed as Governor of Panjāb and his brother accepted in Nādir's employment. The Shāh also struck a gold coin at Lāhore, and thus adding the Panjāb to his realms, marched towards Delhi, desolating the Panjāb all along the road.

What happend later—the utterly humiliating defeat at Karnāl of the Moghal army consisting of 1,50,000 horse, 500 pieces of artillery and vast numbers of irregulars and a huge elephant corps at the hands of the far less numerous though better-trained and more hardened in battle Persians—is well-known to the students of Indian history. The Moghal Commander-in-chief, Khān-i-Dauran Khān. died in action. Saadat Khān, the Viceroy of Oudh, was taken prisoner. At least ten Indian Princes of eminent rank, with one hundred nobles and thirty thousand soldiers,lay dead on the battle-field. Three days after the defeat of his armies, the Moghal emperor of India marched in a procession to the victor's camp to offer his formal submission. This pleased Nādir Shah so much that as his intention seemingly was not to seat himself on the throne of Hindustān but according to his letter sent to Emperor Mohammad Shāh of Delhi on the eve of his attack 'to drive the infidels (i.e. Marāthās) to the abyss of hell' (for having imposed tribute on the dominions of the King of Musalmāns), he agreed to confirm the Emperor of Delhi in his dominions on payment of 250 million rupees as indemnity for the war. And so long as this payment was not made, he was to remain in honourable confinement in his *zenānā* (or the harem) guarded by the Persion soldiers.*

* Says Mohd. Latif : – "Poets, musicians and nautch girls took up more time of the emperor (Mohammed Shāh) than affairs of the state. Nādir's letter was not ans-

In the meantime, the Indian army was to remain without its officers and the Persians were allowed to remove every piece of ordnance, and seize the jewel office, including the world-famous *Koh-i-Nur*,* and the jewel-studded Peacock-Throne, besides the precious royal wardrobe. The keys of the Red Fort were also demanded and obtained by the Persians, thus putting themselves in control of all that the Moghal King could call his own, including his life and numerous wives.

After conducting the King to the royal palace in a procession and welcoming him profusely, the Emperor laid at Nādir's feet all that the Moghals had accumulated in gold, silver and precious stones through generations. His Ministers and courtiers followed suit. Nādir paid his soldiery their arrears of pay and gratuity lavishly (though cunningly enough in his own coin). It appears all would have gone well but for the massacre of some of the Persian soldiers (their number is put at 3000) by a Delhi mob. Even Nādir Shāh himself was fired upon. This so infuriated the victor that unsheathing his sword, he ordered a general massacre of all its citizens—men, women and children—till in half a day the streets of all of Delhi were drenched with blood, and the city littered all over with corpses. Every building of consequence was destroyed or set upon fire. About 1,50,000 people were killed by the early afternoon like dumb sheep. Thousands of Hindus killed themselves along with their whole families to escape dishonour. Thousands threw themselves into the wells.

F. N. Contd.

wered for full two years; he sent another while on his way to India. The emperor threw it into the wine (he was drinking then), quoting a line from Hāfiz, "let this meaningless document be drowned in the sparkling wine". "His son from a Hindu dancing girl, (who succeeded him later) was (also) a true son of his parents .....He extended his Zenānā (harem) so that it occupied a space of a mile. He lived in gardens for one or two months at a time and would remain without sseing the face of any male being for a week together".

——History of the Panjāb, P. 220

* Lit. the mountain of light. This world-famous diamond, originally of 139 carats, is said to have been the property of warrior Arjun of the Mahābhārta fame and of the Mahārājās Karan and Vikramaditya of antiquity. But, it surfaces in history in 1628 A.D. when Mir Jumlā of Golcandā presented it to Shāh Jahān. (Possibly it was mined in Golkandā itself). It continued with the Moghal Kings thereafter, till it was looted by Nādir Shāh by a trick of exchanging turbans with Mohammad Shāh, (the defeated Moghal King of Delhi). The latter had pretended its having been lost, but Nādir Shāh coming to know that he kept it always tucked in his

Nothing precious that the Persians could lay their hands upon was spared. It is only after he was implored most abjectly by some of the Moghal king's courtiers, rubbing their noses in the dust that Nādir Shāh put his sword in the scabbard and the general massacre was stopped.‡

But such was the carnage that when Nādir was implored to put an end to it by the Moghal emperor and his courtiers, they said to him :—"Not a soul has been spared by your Majesty's avenging sword. If it be your wish to carry on the destruction any further,

---

F. N. Contd.

turban, exchanged turbans with him and thus appropriated the *Koh-i-Nur* as well. Through Nādir's grandson, Shāh Rukh Mirzā, it fell into the hands of Ahmad Shāh Abdāli and from him it came to Shāh Shujāh, King of Kābul. Mahārājā Ranjit Singh acquired it from the latter on promise of aid to recover his throne, (which promise, as we shall see later, was kept). When the British conquered the Panjāb, they appropriated this jewel also for the British Crown. It was cut into four pieces and still decorates the crown of the *feringi* monarchs. Its value was once reported to be half a day's expense of the whole world. According to Osborne, originally it was one and a half inches long and an inch wide. (Ranjit Singh, P. 13).

The Peaccok Throne (*Takht-i-Tāoos*) studded with very large and precious stones which is now lying in the imperial treasury in Tehrān is claimed by the Irānian Govt. as the replica of the throne looted by Nādir Shāh, and not the original one, whose whereabouts they claim not to know. This may, however, just be a ruse for the unwary to escape its return to the Indian people, otherwise it is hard to believe that a highly-prized and sought-for treasure like this should go untraced for two centuries after its being looted by Nādir Shāh and taken back to Irān with great care and precaution.

‡ Lest it be construed that we in India, given the opportunity, were not capable of meting out this kind of treatment to our Hindu co-religionists within India, the following account, only five years later (1744), of the Marāthā invasion of Bengāl may be cited. Says the Bangāli Poet Gangārām:— "The *bārgis* (Marāthā horsemen or *bārgirs*) came up and encircled them (the fleeing villagers) in the plain. They snatched away gold and silver, rejecting all else. Of some people they cut off the hand, of some the nose and ears; some they killed outright. They dragged away the beautiful women, tying their fingers to their neck with ropes. After looting in the open, they entered the villages; after burning the villages, they roamed on all sides, plundering. Some victims they tied with their arms twisted behind them. Some they flung down and kicked with their shoes. They constantly shouted "give us rupees, give us rupees". When they got no rupee, they filled their victims' nostrils with water and drowned them in tanks. Some were put to death by suffocation. Those who had money gave to the *bārgis*; those who had none gave their lives." (Oxford History of India, P. 466)

infuse life into the dead and renew the slaughter." Nādir stopped further bloodshed in Delhi immediately but "on some trivial pretext put to the sword six thousand inhabitants of Moghalpurā and thousands were slain in the villages adjoining Delhi. In the royal market, where the tumult had first arisen, he had the noses and ears of seven hundred persons, seized indiscriminately, cut off."

Not content with what he had been offered voluntarily, Nādir now proceeded to plunder every valuable still left in the personal possession of the king, in his treasury or with his nobles, courtiers and wealthy citizens, no matter what methods he had to employ. Threats, torture and intrigue were fully pressed into service to disgorge priceless treasures of great beauty, value and antiquity. Fear, death and shame stalked the imperial city as never before.

Large contributions were levied also on the governors of provinces and the total wealth carried back by Nādir has been estimated variously between seven and seventy crores of money, besides jewels, furniture, rich dresses, and a very large number of elephants (1000), horses (7000), and camels (10,000). As has been stated already, every soldier was rewarded and all their arrears paid to the tune of Rs. 20 crores. His officers carried away treasures worth about 10 crores, (though the Shāh while crossing the Chenāb on the way back home caused every soldier and officer to be searched and to seize all the valuables they were carrying with them). 100 eunichs, 130 writers, 200 smiths, 300 masons, 100 stone-cutters and 200 carpenters, besides many beautiful women, were also carried back home.

A treaty was drawn up between him and the Moghal king ceding all the territories north-west of the Indus, including Kābul, Sind, Thattā, and the four districts of the Panjāb, Chahār Mahal, lying near the Jehlum river, to the King-emperor of Persia. At Lāhore, he collected a crore of rupees from Zakriyā Khān, the Governor of Lāhore.*

In the confusion caused by the invasion of Nādir Shāh, the Sikhs built a mud-fortress at Dalēwāl to the north-west of Amritsar on the banks of Rāvi, in the midst of thick forests, for refuge and retreat at the time of need. The whole of the upper Bāri Doāb was by them

* It may be of interest to note that the same Nādir Shāh, the terror and scourge of Asia, became mad a few years later, got the eyes of his own son torn out of their sockets in a fit of rage, and was assassinated by his soldiers, at the instigation of his own nephew !

asked to pay tribute. When Nādir's forces, carrying enormous booty passed though these areas on their way back home, marching slowly due to the heat of May, the Sikhs pounced upon them, time and again, and divested them of a sizable amount of their treasures. They also rescued many women and artisans whom the invaders were taking alongwith them.

A little later, the rear of the Nādir's forces was attacked on the Chenāb, during the days of heavy rainfall. The Sikhs pursued them right till the day they left the shores of India. Nādir was much perturbed to hear of all this and asked Zakriyā Khān, Governor of Lāhore, (who was escorting him out of the Panjāb) where from had these "barbarians" descended, who could dare challenge his might with such impunity. Replied Zakriyā Khāni:—"They are a group of faqirs, founded by Nānak, a miraculous man, who come to visit their sacred tank at Amritsar twice a year and then disappear into nowhere. "Where do they live?" demanded Nādir Shāh, "On the saddles of their horses," replied Zakriyā Khān. "Be warned, therefore," said Nādir perceptively, "For, they seem to smack of sovereignty. They might occupy your lands before long."*

Zakriyā was much incensed at this rebuke and took redoubled measures to suppress the rising force of the Sikhs as hard as he could.‡

Immediate orders were issued to all headmen of the village communities not to allow refuge to the Sikhs on any pretext. Their

---

* Also see Foster, Travels, I, 272.
According to Prāchin Panth Parkāsh (pp. 231-32), the reply of the Khān Bahādur was :— "We donot know where to find them ? They eat as they run, and sleep on galloping horse-backs. We tyrannise over them, they find peace in it. They seem to need no water in summer nor warm their limbs in winter. They grind not their corn, nor know the taste of salt or butter. A single man fights like a hundred and they fear not death for the sake of their faith...And though founded by Nānak as a sect of faqirs, they seek to avenge themselves on all who they think have brought harm to their 9th Guru and the four sons of the last one. Nādir said, "you are getting only what you deserve. But such people cannot live without sovereignty".
According to M'gregor (part II, p. 115), the conqueror (Nādir) after hearing the report smiled and said— "They ought to be destroyed and their country seized."

‡The British historians are of little use for this period (1716-38). They seem to have heard little or nothing of them for a whole generation. The Muslim historians also by and large skip this period. So our account is based mostly on Sikh sources, the most reliable of which is Rattan Singh's Panth Parkāsh, or accounts based on it, or on Ibrat Nāmā by Ali-ud-din.

hide-outs were combed mercilessly time and again to hunt them out. Men, women and children were butchered in large numbers anywhere they were found, for no other reason but the fact of their being Sikhs.

A price was put on their heads. Anyone giving reliable information of their whereabouts was paid Rs. ten, but this prize was increased five times if a Sikh was brought to the Qāzi's court, dead or alive. Anyone could plunder their homes. Anyone giving them shelter was punished with death. Anyone giving them food was forcibly converted to Islam. They were hunted like wild beasts; thousands who refused to be converted to Islam were put to death.* Many Hindu and Muslim *chaudhris* earned a name for themselves with the administration for their merciless slaughter of the innocent Sikhs. Notable among these were Karmā of village Chinnā, Rāmā Randhāwā of Talwandi, Sāhib Rāi of Nowsherā Dhalā, and Massā Ranghar of Mandiāli. Some of them brought cart-loads of Sikh heads to the Governor at Lāhore.

But, the worst and most heinous crimes were committed by Massā Ranghar. He was put incharge of the sacred Sikh temple at Amritsar by the Governor, and he converted the holy of the holies into a dancing hall. He smoked and drank within the precincts of the inner sanctuary and converted its surrounding precincts into a stable.

When this heart-rending news spread, two devout Sikhs from Jaipur, Mehtāb Singh (originally of Mirankot) and Sukhā Singh of Māri Kambo took upon themselves to avenge this gross insult to their cherished faith.

In August, 1740, they reached Amritsar and under the disguise of Muslims come to pay their land-revenue, they entered the precincts of the temple and made straight for the sanctuary where they saw Massā being entertained to music by a nautch-girl. While Sukhā Singh guarded the entrance, Mehtāb fell like a wounded tiger on Massā with his drawn sword and chopped his head off. Before the royal guards could recover from the shock, the assailant and his companion had fled.

Zakriyā Khān was cut to the quick on hearing this and he collected all the chowdhries of the parganās round Amritsar to help him trace the culprits in return for a high prize.

* Gordon, *History of the Sikhs* P. 50., Prāchin Panth Parkāsh, pp. 232-33,

It was left to Harbhagat, the leader of the breakaway Niranjani sect of Jadiālā, to volunteer to accomplish this job. He had helped the Government earlier also in this treacherous activity. Mehtāb Singh's village, Mirānkot, was surrounded under the command of Nur-ud-Din. He could not be found there but his child-son, Rāi Singh, was wounded in a combat between Harbhagat and Nathā Khairā, who tried to intercede on behalf of the innocent child. The child was left for dead, but he later revived and became the father of Rattan Singh Bhangu (author of Panth Parkāsh in verse) whose record of Sikh history is about the most reliable about this period, being based on eye-witness accounts.

The timely assassination of Massā gave heart to the Sikhs, and though they refused to oblige the enemy by venturing out of their hide-outs in large numbers, individual Sikhs made history by challenging governmental authority in the open.

One of them was Botā Singh, a Sandhu Jāt of Bharānā, who alongwith a Ranghretā Sikh, Garjā Singh, brought much ridicule on the head of the administration. Inspite of the Government's ban on the Sikhs to visit Amritsar, these two would time and again come to have a dip in the holy tank and then disappear into the bushes near Taran Tāran. Not content with this hide-and-seek affair, Botā decided to plant himself on Grand Trunk Road, near Serāi Nūruddin, and started collecting tolls from all the passersby. He charged one *ānnā* per cart and *one* paisā per donkey-load. And such was the fear he had instilled in the people's minds that no one dared refuse. When no one stopped him, he informed the Governor, through a comtemptuous letter of his new avocation.† The Governor, highly incensed, sent a force of one hundred horse to arrest him. But, the two Sikhs refused to surrender and died fighting.

Two other notable martyrdoms at this time also lighted new fires in Sikh hearts. One was the martyrdom of Bhāi Tārū Singh and the other of Bhāis Subeg Singh and Shāhbāz Singh, father and son.

Tārū Singh, a young lad of 25 and a cultivator who helped men of his faith with foodgrains and shelter in times of stress, was accused of treason, arrested and brought to Lāhore for execution.

† In the Panjābi folklore, this letter is still commemorated as follows :—"*Chithi likhai Singh Botā, hath hai sotā; vich rāh khalotā; ānnā lāyā gaḍē nū, paisā lāyā ḳhotā: Ākho Bhābi Khānon nū, yun ākhē Singh Botā.*"

He was asked to embrace Islām and on his blunt refusal, couched in impertinent and contempuous terms, it was ordered that his hair be scraped off his scalp. "But the determined votary of Guru Gobind" says Cunningham, "would neither yield his conscience nor the symbol of his conviction, and his real or pretended answer is preserved to the present day.The hair, the scalp and the skull, said he, have a natural connexion, the head of man is linked with life and he was prepared to yield his breath with cheerfulness."

The orders of the Governor were, however, carried out in full. His hair was mercilessly scraped off along with the scalp, but he stood the torture manfully, reciting the Word of the Guru all along. He died in July, 1745. It is said the man responsible for this torture died a few hours later, struck by a disease which stopped his urine.

Meantime, Mehtāb Singh, the assassin of Massā Ranghar, was also arrested. It was ordered that his body be broken on the wheel. A similar fate awaited Subeg and Shāhbāz Singh. The latter, a mere lad of 15, studied in a Muslim school and was once reported to have used intemperate language about Fātimā, the daughter of Prophet Mohammad. To atone for this, he was asked to embrace Islām. On his refusal, his father, an influential Zamindār and contractor of the Government,* was also arrested on the charge of being a spy of the Sikhs and condemned to death, unless he chose to accept Islām, an offer he rejected with contempt. Thereupon, both father and son were broken on the wheel. "They bore their torture with great patience shouting 'Akāl, Akāl'. "When, it is said, after a time, the boy could bear the torture no longer and was almost prepared to yield, the father looked furiously into his eyes and the boy's spirit revived." Along with his father, he went down the valley of death, shouting 'Akāl, Akāl,' the name of the immortal God.

* He is said to be the man who had earlier brought about a rapproachement between Govt. and the Sikhs, when a *Jāgir* and Nawābship were accepted by the latter and peace between the two parties ensured atleast for a year. (Gandā Singh and Tejā Singh, History of the Sikhs, vol. I, p. 121.) These authors (Ibid, p. 130) as well as Sikh tradition testify to their being broken on the wheel. The Sikhs recount this valiant deeds in their daily prayer.

More, next page]

The death of Zakriyā Khān and the fact of his son, Yāhyā Khān having succeeded him six months later (July I, 1745-Jan 3, 1646) gave some respite to the Sikhs, due to the confused state of affairs in the Panjāb. But the murder at the hands of the Sikhs of Iaspat Rāi, Faujdār of Eminābād and brother of the Lāhore Nawāb's Diwān, Lakhpat Rāi, aggravated the situation for them much more than the facts of the case warranted. A Sikh force (some put their number at 2000) had gone to visit Eminābād, (Rori Sāhib), a place sacred to the memory of Guru Nānak. A letter was sent to the Faujdār that they be allowed to buy up rations from the town as they had been without food for days on end during their travels. The Faujdār threatened them that if they did not move out of his sphere of authority immediately, he would forcibly drive them out. The Sikhs, according to a Muslim historian, Ali-ud-din, author of *Ibrat Nāmā* took away a large herd of sheep for slaughter without payment and were in the process of their meals when the Faudjār fell upon them. The Sikhs offered stiff resistance and one of them—a Rangrettā Sikh, Nirbhau Singh, climbing up the tail of the elephant which Jaspat Rāi was riding, chopped his head off. Finding their leader dead, the Moghal forces were thrown is disarray and Sikhs looted the city of Eminābād with full abandon. It was after a payment was made that they even allowed the head of Jaspat Rāi to be handed over to his heirs for cremation.

The author of the *Prāchin Panth Parkāsh,* however, states that according to the story as narrated to him by his father, as extreme tortures had produced little effect on both Shāhbāz and Subēg, the Nawāb ordered their being taken off the wheel and put into prison. A few days later, the Nawāb felt seriously ill and asked for pardon of them both and offered them whatever they wanted. He also released them forthwith, but Subeg said he could not forgive the Nawāb, only the *Panth* could. He was thereupon sent to contact the Khālsā in the woods, but he was told that as the Nawāb was cursed by Tāru Singh, the martyr, unless he (the Nawāb) agreed to receive seven strokes with the martyr's shoes, he could not be cured. Such was the distress of the Nawāb that he even agreed to this punishment. He got temporary relief but died four days later... For two days, Subeg Singh was allowed even to strike a coin in his own name! (pp. 267-68 and 292-300). The story seems fantastic. However, some Muslim and Hindu historians aver that inspite of his having massacred about ten thousand Sikhs during his regime, Zakraiyā Khān was also an able and just ruler who commanded respect from Hindus and Muslims alike. His death plunged the whole country into grief. Zakriyā Khān is also credited by them with having secured from Nādir Shāh the liberation of thousands of captives, both Hindu and Muslim. (Hari Rām Gupta quoting various authorities in his *History of the Sikhs* II, pp. 68 and 55 supports this view).

Hearing this, his brother was inflamed with rage. He wept bitterly before the Nawāb, threw his turban on the Nawāb's feet and vowed that he would call himself the son of a Khatri only after extirpating all traces of the Sikhs from the pages of history.* The Nawāb was, it seems, himself waiting for such an opportunity. He, therefore, got all the Sikhs of Lāhore arrested and executed on March 10, 1746, inspite of the intercession of some Hindu leaders with the Diwān on their behalf.

According to Ibrat Nāmā, the people were warned with the beat of drum that no one should read the Sikh Scripture and anyone taking the name of the Gurū be arrested and his belly ripped open. Says Rattan Singh that even the word '*Gur*' (jaggery) which sounded like 'Guru', was not to be uttered, nor the word *pothi* (as it reminded the Sikhs of their Scripture). Many volumes of the Holy Granth were collected and thrown into rivers and wells. The holy tank of the Amritsar Sikh temple was filled up with the earth.

A huge army scoured the entire countryside in search of the Sikhs under the personal command of the Nawāb, Yāhyā Khān, and his Hindū Diwān, Lakhpat Rāi. The Sikhs, about fifteen thousand in number, had taken refuge in the reedy marshes of Kahnūwān. With the help of guns, the Sikhs were hounded out of their hide-outs and forced to proceed towards the Rāvi. They tried to take shelter in the Basholi hills, but were refused refuge by the Hindu populace due to the fear of the Moghal reprisals. Food and ammunition were both exhausted and the Rāvi was in flood and could not be crossed with their half-starved horses. In utter desparation, some were asked to escape to the mountains of Mandi and Kulu, and to rejoin the forces of the Khālsā at Kiratpur. But the main force, under Sukhā Singh, pounced upon and tried to cut through the Moghal forces. In the process, hundreds had to sacrifice their lives, some were taken prisoners, others escaped into a jungle where they were mauled both by the army and the local populace. About two thousand of them were able to cross the Rāvi and enter the Riārki part of Gurdāspur. It was the beginning of June (1746) and to march long sandy distance on naked, blisering feet, was an unbearable ordeal. Crossing the Beās, at Sri Hargobindpur, they had hardly settled down for a while to cook their mid-day meals, when a body

---

* *Ibrat Nāmā*, Pp. 229-231.

of the local Pathāns fell upon them. They could not but run for their lives, as Lakhpat Rāi was also reported to be on their heels. They crossed the Satluj at Aliwāl and escaped into Mālwā.

Atleast seven thousand Sikh men were killed in this campaign and another 3000 arrested and brought to Lāhore in mock-dresses on camel-backs to be executed with great torture at Lāhore.* Their heads were piled up to make pyramids and their bodies buried under the walls of a mosque.

In no earlier single campaign had so much loss of life been suffered by the Sikhs. Hence, they called it a Ghalughārā (The Holocaust). But sixteen years later in 1762, they had to suffer a worse disaster at the hands of Ahmad Shāh Abdāli, the Afghān conqueror. This incident, therefore, later came to be known as 'Chhotā Ghalughārā' (the small Hollocaust). But suffering did not cow down their spirits, instead it inspired them to bid for sovereign power. All history is witness to the fact that unmitigated tryanny or uncompromising hostility against a person, a principle or a people have led only to one result—revolution. And no matter how long drawn-out the struggle (for one must wait for the right opportunity) if the cause is just, the result has always been a sure victory for the seemingly helpless victims.

* Hari Ram Guptā, History of the Sikhs, II, P. 77.

CHAPTER XVI

THE SIKH BID FOR PEOPLEHOOD

(1748—1764)

There was so much intrigue at the Delhi Court and the imperial power had been so much weakened by Nādir Shāh's invasion that anywhere the provincial satraps were powerful, they asserted their authority with impunity, as in Bengāl, Oudh and Hyderābad. But no matter how weakened, there was no question of Central Govt. loosening its grip on the affairs of the Panjāb —the gateway to Hindustān. Governors were changed often enough and rivalries among the claimants accentuated to the benefit of the emperor or his powerful courtiers in Delhi. As would be seen from these pages, in the course of about 50 years (1712 to 1767), the Governorship of the Panjāb changed hands *twenty* times. The Governors were, therefore. in mortal dread of the imperial power and never allowed the grass to grow under their feet. Unless they were ruthless with the rebels (or could affect a compromise with them without losing face) they could hardly command respect with the Delhi Court, or resist successfully the successive onslaughts of the Afghāns on the Panjāb.

The Sikhs, as we have seen, were fighting for their life, with backs to the wall. Their very existence was at stake. Hunted like wild beasts over the hills, as in the forests and plains, they had hardly any refuge to seek. But, the fire lit within them by Guru Gobind Singh and their own martyrdoms could not subside and they were prepared to compromise now on nothing short of sovereign power, no matter what price they had to pay in human suffering, and how long drawn-out was the struggle for power.

Meantime, circumstances helped them not a little when the Lāhore Governor, Yahyā's younger brother, Shāh Nawāz Khān, Governor of Multān, attacked Lāhore in 1745, and drove both him and Lakhpat Rāi out of power and expelled them from the province. Fearing that this usurpation of power will bring down upon his head the wrath of the Delhi Government, Shāh Nawāz invited Ahmad Shāh Durrāni (Abdāli) to invade India. He was promised submission of the Panjāb, if Shāh Nawāz was confirmed in his present position.

Much elated by this unexpected though highly welcome invitation, Ahmad Shāh Durrāni, the successor to Nādir's Kingdom, wasted no time and set off for Peshawar with a force of ten thousand. However, much to his discomfiture, Shāh Nawāz had in the meantime been promised confirmation of his office by the Delhi emperor (through his Prime Minister who happened to be maternal grandfather of Shāh Nawāz), on the condition that he opposed the progress of the invading Durrāni.

On reaching the Khyber, Ahmad Shāh sent a courier to Lāhore to consult with Shāh Nawāz on the plan of the campaign. But Shāh Nawāz dismissed him with contempt. The Durrāni invasion, however, continued to progress. The Shāh sent another messenger later from Rohtās, near Jehlum. Shah Nawāz was even more reckless this time, and put the messenger to death by pouring molten lead into his mouth. The Abdāli warrior could not bear this insult. He soon marched on Lāhore and occupied it without much resistance. Shāh Nawāz fled to Delhi and the new ruler appointed Lakhpat Rāi as Governor of Lāhore with Jumlā Khān of Kasur as his advisor. However, soon thereafter, Ahmad Shāh was defeated by the Delhi forces at Sirhind and hastened back to Kābul.

This upheaval gave an opportunity to Sikhs to appear again on the plains and to start their guerilla activities once again with full force. They also laid their hands successfully on the receding forces of Abdāli and divested them of their belongings. Under the leadership of Sardār Jassā Singh Ahluwāliā,† they also built a small fort

† Jassā Singh Ahluwaliā was born (1718-1783) at a village called Ahlu or Ahluwāl near Lāhore, established by his ancestor, Saddā Singh, a devotee of the sixth Guru, Hargobind. Hence, the surname of Ahluwaliā stuck to him. His forefathers were Kalāls (or wine-merchants). Hence, he is also called Jassā Singh Kalāl.

called Rām Rauni (citadel of Guru Rām Dās) near Amritsar, capable of accommodating 500 soldiers. The decision was hailed by all the Sikh leaders assembled there at the time of the Baisākhi of 1748.

These included Sardār Shām Singh Karor-Singhiā, Sukhā Singh of Māri Kambo, Charat Singh Sukarchakiā, Khushāl Singh and Hari Singh Bhangi. The whole community participated in this venture on a voluntary basis and not a penny was spent on its construction.

Another notable event happened on the same day. The Sikhs passed their first historic Gurmattā (Holy edict) at the Akāl Takht in Amritsar.*

Upto now, the Sikh forces were divided into 65 *Jathās* (or bands). Nawāb Kapur Singh reorganised them into eleven large bands, each of course, with its own name, leader and flag. These bands or

---

F. N. Contd.

However, such was "the admiration he won of the whole Sikh community that Jassā Singh Kalāl came to be known as "Guru Kā Lāl" (the beloved son of the Guru). Son of Badar Singh, Jassā Singh was hardly 5 years when his father died (1723 A. D.) and his mother entreated Mātā Sundri, widow of Guru Gobind Singh, to take him into her care. Mātā Sundri agreed to do so, and lavished much affection on him, instructing him carefully in the arts of war and peace. He studied the Sikh Scriptures under Bhāi Mani Singh. Later, Mātā Sundri asked Nawāb Kapur Singh to take charge of the promising youth. Both he and his mother used to perform the Hari-Kirtan before the Nawāb who much pleased at his supreme devotion to the faith and sense of duty and humility, appointed him also a store-keeper with his forces. As was natural, he participated in many a combat as well where he displayed such qualities of leadership that Nawāb Kapur Singh appointed him his successor on the eve of his death in 1753. Elated at his successful helmsmanship, the Khālsā honoured Jassā Singh with the title of Sultān-ul-Qaum (King of the whole people), when they captured Lahore in 1761 (1758, according to M.K.) In 1774, he founded the Kapurthala State. He was also called "*Bandi Chhor*' (The Deliverer) for having rescued 2200 Hindu women made prisoner by Abdāli.

* Osborne thinks, "the *Gurmattā* (which he mistranslates as the State Council) was instituted by the Tenth Guru, by which he gave a federative form to the Sikhs." (Ranjit Singh. p. 7). This is not so. Five persons chosen for their integrity and piety by the community consensus were asked to pronounce their judgement on matters referred to them. Or, the whole congregation resolved on a matter of importance, whether secular or doctrinal. This was called the Gurumattā (the Guru's Edict), but it had nothing to do with a confederacy or the institution of kingship as such. The Tenth Guru has left no instruction in regard to this. The Gurus themselves were nominated by their predecessors, though it was always seen as to who would be more acceptable due to his character to the entire congregation. But at Chamkaur, the Guru was subjected to accept a Gurumattā of five Sikhs against his own judgement to escape from the fortress.

Jathās, which came to be known later on as *Misals* (lit. equal, also an example) together were, however, given the name of *Dal Khālsā* (or the Khālsā force), under the over-all charge of Sardār Jassā Singh Ahluwāliā. It is the miracle of Guru Gobind Singh that everyone irrespective of caste, region or station accepted the decision of their venerable old leader with a clean and good heart.*

The eleven bands were :—(1) Ahluwāliā (under Jasssā Singh Ahluwāliā) (2) Bhangi (under Hari Singh Bhangi) (3) Dalewāliā (under Gulāb Singh of village Dalewāl) (4) Faizalpuriā (under Nawāb Kapur Singh) (5) Kanaihyā (under Jai Singh Kanaihyā) (6) Karor-Singhiā (under Karorā Singh) (7) Nakai (under Hirā Singh Nakai) (8) Nishānwālā (under Dasaundhā Singh) (9) Rāmgarhiā (under Nand Singh Sanghāniā) (10) Sukarchkiyā (under Nodh Singh.) (11) Shahid.‡

It may be noted that these *Misals* were not founded on the basis of caste. Each *Misal*, as would be seen, took its name either from the name of its leader or his village. In one case, it was the addiction of the

* Says Bhangu Rattan Singh :— Āpē Rāj, āpē majdur, badē bhujangi, dil kē sur. Āpē pisēn, Āp Pakāwen, to to badē sardār Kahāwen. Koi Kare nā Kise shareekā; Koi nā sunawe nij dukh ji kā." (p. 326). Which means :— "They were all brave of heart. They themselves ground their corn and cooked their own food. It is through such dedicated service that they became great Sardārs. None felt jealous of another nor ever gave vent to his own privations or personal grief."

‡ The twelfth Misal of Phulkiān (founded after the name of Bābā Phul (1627-1690 A.D.), a devotee of Gurus Har Gobind and Hari Rai, consisted of the Cis-Satluj states of Patiālā, Nābhā, and Jind. They, however, could not play any significant part in the Sikh struggle for freedom and decided to side with the Moghals, the Afghāns and the British successively. Against the Dal Khālsā, they sought the protection of the Afghān King, Ahmad Shāh Abdāli, against Ranjit Singh that of the British. The help which the Sikhs rendered the British at the time of the Mutiny in 1857 largely came from the rulers of the Phulkiān states, as also at the time of the Akāli resistance to the British in the present century. They also fought among themselves to the detriment of each other. That is how, in the opinion of Dr. H. R. Gupta (History of the Sikhs, part III, p. 129) "they have not to date thrown up any great man of history." But it should not be forgotten that they have within them some of the finest soldiers in the country, and have thrown up in the present century patriots like Sardār Sewā Singh Thikriwālā (Patiālā), scholars like Bhāi Kāhan Singh (Nābhā), and Saints like Sant Attar Singh (Sangrur). At the time of India's partition, Patiālā played a most noble role of welcoming about half a million refugees from West Panjāb and Mahārājā Yadavinder Singh as President of the Chamber of Princes frustrated the designs of the Nawāb of Bhopal and others who wanted the Indian states to form either independent entities or an independent federation, besides India and Pakistān.

fore-fathers of a leader to *Bhang* (hemp) that his progeny also came to be known as *Bhangis*. Jai Singh belonged to village Kāhnā, near Lāhore, and was hence known as Kanaihyā. The Nakkāis inhabited a territory known as Nakkā, situated between Lāhore and Gogaira (in the direction of Multān). The Sukarchakiā leaders came from the village Sukarchak, near Gujrānwālā, the Shahids drew their name from one of their ancestors, Suddā Singh, custodian of the Sikh shrine of Talwandi Sābo (Damdamā Sahib) who was killed in a battle with the Moghal forces, thus becoming a *Shahid* (or, martyr). The Nishānwālās became so known as they were the standard (Nishān) bearers of the Dal Khālsā. The Ramgarhiās were so called because Sardār Jassā Singh, their leader, had extended the Sikh fortress of Rām Rauni (later called Rāmgarh) at Amritsar.†

Every member of the community could consider himself a part of the Dal Khālsā, and everyone was free to join any of these bands if only he could bring a horse for himself to ride. The Dal Khālsā was to meet atleast twice a year at Amritsar. Such meetings were known as *Sarbat Khālsā* (The Whole Community or the *Panth*).* This body was to resolve through a *Gurmattā* (lit. the Guru's Resolve) where and how a battle was to be launched and how, in the event of victory, its spoils were to be apportioned. (Generally, these were distributed in proportion to the strength of each band, and every soldier received an equal share). The leader of the Dal Khālsā was to be the head both of the Sikh state and church. Hence, it was incumbent on him to propagate Sikh religion as well and to live strictly in accordance with the Sikh Code of conduct. Disobedience was punished at these bi-annual gatherings. For day-to-day affairs, a person's allegiance was to be to his section commander, but no

† According to Cunningham, the Karorsinghiās were known after their third leader, Karorā Singh. The original founder dying issueless "was succeeded by his nephew who left his authority to Karorā Singh, a petty personal follower, who again bequeathed the command to Baghēl Singh, his own menial servant. (Cunningham History of the Sikhs, P. 97). This shows that succession was not always hereditary among the *Misals* and merit was more the determining factor, and even the meanest could rise to the highest position.

* *Panth* literally means a Path, the Way, or the Sikh Way of life. But, it is used, in political terms, now-a-days, for the collectivity of the community like *Sarbat Khālsā*. The word has been used in religious terms (The Way) both in the Ādi Granth (see Gurū Nānak's *Japu*) and the Dasam Granth of Guru Gobind Singh (see *Bachittar Nātak*).

Jathā was to act against the interest of the whole *Panth*, and they were to help each other whenever need arose.

This organization stood the community in good stead in times of stress and tribulations ahead, as from the year 1748, a new factor had been introduced into the body-politic of the Panjāb. Instead of its being confined to the Sikh-Moghal fight, the incessant invasions of Ahmed Shāh Abdāli, ruler of Afganistān, brought the Sikhs in conflict with the Afghāns. And it is from them that the Sikhs wrested most of the Panjāb and Kashmir, the Moghals having become only nominal rulers of Delhi, without military or political strength, moral fibre or the old crusading spirit.

It will not be out of place therefore to narrate all the invasions of Ahmad Shāh. He invaded India ten times in twenty years (1748-68). The Panjāb saw during this period the change of 13 Governors, from Mir Muin-ul-Mulk (or Mir Manu) (1748) to Gujar Singh Bhangi etc (1761). The success or failure of each Governor, therefore, rested upon how far he could keep the peace for the farmers to raise their crops and the state to earn its revenues, to curb the rising power of the Sikhs with that end in view, and also to meet the challenge of the merciless invader every two years (sometimes every year). He had also to keep on the right side of the authority in Delhi, howsoever powerless and incapacitated it was. To keep internal conditions tolerably peaceful in the Panjāb was therefore of paramount importance to each one of them. And for this, the Sikhs, now out for a final bid for political power, either had to be placated or resisted and crushed. As will be seen, both methods were tried alternately (sometimes together), but nothing availed. The Sikhs had taken the plunge, burning their boats behind them and with only one aim and resolution—Victory. Nothing short of total sovereignty over their homeland (which was also their holy land) could satisfy their urge for freedom.

Abdāli, as we have seen, was defeated in his first invasion. As Muinul-Mulk was responsible for the Moghal victory, he was immediately rewarded with Governorship of the Panjāb. The treasury at this time was empty. Confusion and sense of insecurity prevailed among the people as much as the nobility. And, to crown all, the new Prime Minister, Safdar Jang, was determined to see Muin-ul-Mulk, who belonged to his opposing Party, brought to degradation and ruin.

Sikhs had occupied Amritsar during the intervening period; they had built a fortress there and had laid waste a good part of the Bāri and Rachnā Doābs. They had laid their hands on the retreating forces of Abdāli as well, and helped themselves to a considerable amount of booty. Mir Manu's first task was, therefore, to meet their challenge and, if possible, to crush them out of existence.

According to Mohd. Latif, his (Manū's) first concern was to storm the fort of Rām Rauni which he captured and reduced. "He then stationed detachments of troops in all parts infested by the Sikhs, with stringent orders to shave their heads and beards, where-ever they might be found. He issued strict orders to the (Hindu) Hill rājās to seize the Sikhs and to send them in iron chains to Lāhore. These orders were obeyed and hundreds of Sikhs were brought daily to Lāhore and butchered at the *Nakhās* (or the horse-market), out-side the Delhi gate, in the sight of the multitudes of spectators. The young Manū became an irreconciable foe of the Sikhs and was determined to extirpate the nation."†

"His plans," according to the same author, "however, were secretly thwarted by Adinā Beg Khān, the artful Governor of Jullundur Doāb, who saw in the turbulent tribe a means of advancing his own interests, and took care not to reduce them altogether".

Another factor, according to Latif, was the part played by his Hindu Minister, Diwān Kaura Mal, who was sympathetic to the faith of Nānak.* Both these factors must have played some part, as Kaurā Mal (lit. the Bitter Hindu) was known among the Sikhs gene-rally as Mithā Mal (the Sweet one). Adeena Beg also got on occass-ions much help from the Sikhs to consolidate his own position. The Sikhs also utilised the wily Khān to secure their base of operation against the Lāhore authority.

Towards the end of the rainy season (1748), Ahmad Shāh again invaded India. In vain did Manū ask for help from Delhi. When the faction-torn imperial court did not make any move, Manu went out at the head of all the force he could muster to meet the advancing enemy on the southern bank of the Chenāb. Some small combats took place,

† Mohd Latif, History of the Panjāb, P. 221.

* Diwān Kaurā Mal humoured the Sikhs even by paying a fine of Rs. 5/- per day for smoking, but his friendship with the Sikhs was not without a motive. In the first place, he kept the Sikhs off their guard for quite a while and also enlisted their support for the sake of his master to finish off Manu's brother, his rival for power.

but seeing the superior forces of Abdāli, and the general consternation his advance was creating, Manu sued for peace, and agreeing to pay as tribute each year the revenues of the most fruitful districts of the Panjāb—Pasūr, Gujrāt, Sialkot and Aurangābād (as in the case earlier of Nādir Shāh), he made the Abdāli retrace his steps. He further agreed to hold the Govt. of the Panjāb in Abdāli's name.

For thus averting a disaster not only for the Panjāb, but also for Delhi, the Delhi Court reverberated with Manu's fulsome praise at the hands of the puppet king, Ahmad Shāh, and the Queen-Mother who virtually ruled the kingdom in his name. Formerly, a Hindu dancing girl, Udham Bāi (later known as Bāiji Sāhibā, or Sāhibji-Sāhiba, but who assumed the title of Nawāb Qudsiā Begum) ruled the country with the help of an eunuch, Jawed Khān, who could neither read nor write. Court-intrigue in such a situation could not be avoided, and so several powerful courtiers tried to cut the youthful Manu to his size. His nephew, Shāh Nawāz, whom he had earlier displaced at Lāhore was made the Governor of Multān, much to his chagrin. Seeing the imbecility of the Delhi Court, Manu decided to resist this appointment and sent out a formidable force under Diwān Kaurā Mal, his Minister, in Sept. 1750, to Multān to dispossess the new incumbent. For about six months, Shāh Nawāz held his ground, but was ultimately defeated in a major combat and killed. His force were scattered. In this war, Kaurā Mal was greatly helped by the Sikhs* contributing a force of 10,000 horse at his request. Struck by his prowess, loyalty and diplomatic skill in enlisting Sikh support for his cause, Kaurā Mal was honoured with the title of Rājā and made the Subedār of Multān. Kaurā Mal also secured for the Sikhs a *Jāgir* in the Lāhore district worth Rs. 1,25,000 which made them call him "Mithā Mal". Mir Manu was now at the height of his glory. He had militarily challenged the authority of Delhi with success, and warded off the danger of Abdāli through diplomacy. He had subdued the Sikhs through merciless persecution, and later through compromise brought about by his Hindu Diwān. Now, he thought he could take on the Abdāli as well, and so refused to pay him the contracted annual tribute. The Abdāli was not the person to take such an affront lying down. So, he again crossed the Indus in 1751-52, and devastated the land between the Rāvi and Chenāb. He tried

* Prāchin Panth Parkāsh, p. 330.

to extract his dues through the emissaries he sent to Mir Manu, but Manu pleaded inability to pay, one, because the original contract was made under duress and secondly, land-owners had all fled, owing to the dread and fear the Shāh's invasion had caused. The Shāh was much incensed on receipt of such an insolent and evasive reply. He surrounded Lāhore, which remained under seige for four months, until Mir Manu was forced out of his entrenchments, and an open battle was waged in which the Afghān forces won a decisive victory.

Even the help of the 20,000 Sikh horse, secured through the agency of Diwān Kaurā Mal, was of no avail. The Sikhs out of patriotic motives had agreed to help if they were allowed in return to occupy the hilly tracts of Parol, Kathua, Basholi and the surrounding valleys. But, in actual combat, they do not seem to have fought any significant engagement except in some small scout parties of the Nihangs and two of their leaders—Sukha Singh of Māri Kambo and Sangat Singh—were killed. Rājā Kaurā Mal also fell on the battle-field.*

Adeenā Beg, the Governor of Jullundar-Doāb, who had come to participate in the war, fled back in panic. Manu had no choice now but to sue for peace and himself led the negotiating party into the Abdāli's camp. He made an offering of Rs. 30 lakhs to the victor, besides other presents. The Abdāli was magnanimous to a fault, and received Manu with extreme courtesy, showering praises on him for his bravery, diplomatic skill and administrative abilities. He conferred on him a rich *khilat*, with a bejewelled sword and a horse, and re-instated him in his old position as his Viceroy at Lāhore and returned to Kābul.†

---

* Some historians are of the opinion that Kaurā Mal was not killed by the Afghāns, but by a gunner of Adeenā Beg in this battle, due to jealousy or sheer accident.

† Mufti Ali-ud-Din in his *Ibratnāmā* and others give a very intersting episode of this time. When Mir Manū presented himself before the conquerer, the Shāh asked him sarcastically :—"How come, you didnot come to pay homage to your lord and master earlier ?" "Because", said the youthful and proud Manū, "I had another lord to serve at that time?" "Why did he not come to your rescue in distress?" "Because his servant could look after himself". "Suppose I had fallen into your hands, what treatment would you have given me"? "I should have cut your Majesty's head off your body and sent it to my King". "And now that you are at my mercy, what treatment do you expect of me"? Said Manū:— "If you are a tyrant, kill me; if a merchant sell me; but if you are a King, be generous and pardon my life." "The Shāh was so much impressed by his address that he

During the same expedition, the Abdāli King also occupied Kashmir, driving out the Moghal Viceroy, and appointed a Khatri from Kābul, Sukh Jiwan Mal, in his place.

After the departure of Abdāli, the Sikhs took advantage of the unsettled conditions and created havoc in the territory lying between Amritsar and the hills. Manu asked Adeenā Beg to put down this disorder with an iron hand. But Adeenā tried to conciliate the Sikhs, inspite of small skirmishes and invited Jassā Singh Āhluwaliā to a conference. He could, he said, get them from the Delhi court a separate territory to rule, otherwise they should join hands with him to rule the country together. But, the Sikh chief replied : "Our Guru has promised us sovereignty. Nothing short of it will satisfy us. We shall meet you on the field of battle and not around a negotiating table." However, Adeenā's appeals seemingly sincere for conciliation led some of the Sikh notables—one of them being Jassā Singh Rāmgarhiā—and a few others to join his ranks. The Rāmgarhiā Sardār was in fact much enraged at being ostracised by the community for the murder of his infant daughter, which is a great taboo according to Sikh religion. He went away to the enemy's side in a huff, but his conscience never let him rest and he came back to the fold of the Khālsā as soon as opportunity offered itself. When Mir Manū attacked the Sikh fort of Rām Rauni and, after a seige of three months and losing 200 of their number, through starvation or through sallies conducted daily to bring food from outside, the remaining Sikhs decided to come out and fight the battle in the open, shouting their war-cry "Sat Sri Akāl", Jassā Singh Rāmgarhiā, who was on Adeenā's side, deeply moved by the distress of his brethren, walked over to their side with a hundred followers. He was forgiven and welcomed with open arms.

Adeenā Bēg again took the Sikhs by surprise at Mākhowāl (Ānandpur), where thousands of pilgrims had gathered at the time of the Baisākhi festival (1753), and slaughtered quite a few of them. But, instead of cowing them down, it fired their wrath all the more, and

---

F. N. Contd.

conferred on him the title of *Farzand-i-Khās, Bahādur, Rustam-i-Hind* (own son, the brave warrior, like Rustam, of Hindutān). But such is the quirk of history that while Manū got his own pardon, appealing to the sense of a conqueror's generosity, he himself gave no quarter whatsoever to his own adversaries like the Sikhs till it became impossible for him to contain them & came to terms with them for a. brief while, to be followed again by extreme persecution.

their attacks on Jullundur and Bäri Doābs increased in frequency as well as intensity. Two expedititions were led against them by the Afghāns of Kasur as well. But, the major offensive came from Mir Manū himself in the central districts of Mājhā. Hearing that the Sikhs had renewed their rebellious activities with redoubled force, he gave orders to seize them wherever they could be found, and put them to the sword without pity. About 900 of them were killed when the fortress of Rām Rauni was attacked and captured. The countryside was scoured and cartloads of them were brought to Lāhore each day and hammered to death. When Sikh homes were divested of men, their women were captured alongwith their children, and asked to change their faith on pain of extreme torture. Their children were cut up into pieces before their eyes and they were made to wear garlands of their severed heads, but not one of these determined women either abjured her faith due to filial affection, or showed any dread of a painful and merciless death.*

Hundreds were captured under the personal command of Mir Manu and put to death at the *Nakhās* (horse-market) of Lāhore, known by the Sikhs as *Shahid Ganj*. Wells were filled with their heads. But the Khālsā took it all stoically, reciting a verse which has now entered our folklore :

"*Manu asādi dātri,*
asi Manu dē soē,
Jeon Jeon Sānu wadhdā,
asi dun swāē hoē."

(Manu is like a sickle,
we are like the ever-green tree.
The more he chops the branches off,
the better we grow and be.)

* The supreme ordeals and sacrifices of these noble and heroic women of our race are remembered by the Sikhs in their daily congregational prayers to this day. This kind of persecution according to the *Ibrat Nāmā*, continued for about four years (1750-53). Their *Jāgir* was also confiscated. Says Princep:— "Mir Manu had given orders to detain all Sikhs and shave their heads and beards '. (*Origin of Sikh power* p. 7). Says Miskin in his *Tazikirā*:— "They (Manu's agents) ran after these (Sikh) wretches for upto 50 *kos* in a day and slew them wherever they opposed them. Everybody who brought a severed Sikh head was rewarded with Rs. 100/-. Any-

On Nov. 2, 1753, Manu died a miserable death. He was out hunting when his horse bolted at the sight of a vulture and threw the rider off his seat. However, he got his foot caught in the stirrup, and he was dragged for some distance before he could be rescued. He breathed his last two days later in severe pain.

The Delhi King, Ahmed Shāh, hearing the sad news appointed his two-year old son, Mahmud Shāh, "Governor" of the Panjāb and another two-year old child, Mohd. Amin Khān, son the late Mir Manu, his "Advisor."

This drama, however, lasted only four days when Mir Nizāmud-din, brother of Mir Manu, was installed as absentee Governor, though the actual power lay with Mir Momin Khān of Kasur, a life-long friend of Manu. The arrangement was got confirmed from the Abdāli King who was the acknowledged overlord of the Panjāb since April, 1752.

The baby-Governor, Mohd Amin Khān, died six months later and the power was captured by Manu's widow, Murād Begum (better known as Mughlāni Begum). She got her authority confirmed both by Delhi and Kābul. However, the King-emperor of Delhi was deposed by his *Vizier* and both he and his mother blinded and put in prison, where he died (21 years later in 1775). Such was the fate of this unfortunate prince for having occupied the rickety throne of Hindustān for a bare six years—loss of eyes and twentyone years in prison !

Though a new King, Ālamgir Sāni (II) duly took over and was a pious and abstemious man of 55, well-versed in theology and history and much devoted to the imperial cause, the country was in an extremely bad shape. "The Marāthās had become a terror as also a beacon throughout southern India; Oudh and Allahabad had become virtually indepedent; the country south of Āgrā had been seized by the Jāts; Bengāl, Bihār and Orrisa owed little allegiance to Delhi and the Panjāb had become a tributary of Ahmed Shāh Abdāli of Afghānistān."

Mughlāni Begum began well, but ended up miserably. The confidence she reposed in the trusted courtiers of her late husband and

F. N. Contd.
body who snatched a horse (from a Sikh) could keep the horse to himself. Whoever lost a horse in a fight (with a Sikh) got it replaced by another by Govt," (pp. 68-69).

the honours she bestowed upon them initially, won her their unalloyed allegiance. But, soon she became jealous and suspicious of most of them, and got one of the very senior courtiers, Mir Bhikhāri Khān (son of the Prime Minister to Mir Manu, Raushan-ul-Daulā) seized in the Zenānā and beaten with shoes and sticks to death by her female attendants ! (Latif says she did so for he had ignored her advances !) Other courtiers were also either dishonoured or ignored. They became afraid even of their life. Most of them, therefore, stopped appearing in the Court and petitioned the Delhi emperor to depose and punish her. Disorder broke out bordering on anarchy throughout the Panjāb. Not a penny could be realised in land revenue and the Sikhs, taking advantage of the situation, "laid waste the country, depopulating villages and carrying all flocks and herds. All order, both civil and military, was at an end." Mughlāni Begum was imprisoned by the Governor of Eminābād who attacked Lāhore and occupied it.

The emperor sent a force to restore her to power which was done, in April 1755, but two months later she was deposed and interned again, this time by her uncle, Ubaid Ullah Khān, a great tyrant and plunderer. The Delhi Court ultimately appointed Adeenā Beg to take over as Governor who left Lāhore in the charge of his deputy and himself returned to his own headquarters in the Jullundur-Doāb, pulling strings all the time from outside. In the meantime, the Begum had sent her messengers to Ahmad Shāh Abdāli to come to her rescue. Abdāli sent a force which occupied Lāhore without any resistance, on Nov. 25, 1756. The Afghān warrior personally invaded the country for the fourth time in 1757, not only on the entreaties of Mughlāni Begum but also of the Delhi emperor himself (who was sickned by the court intrigues, against himself) besides Najib Khān, the Rohilla Chief. The Afghān King entered Delhi on Feb 28, 1757, and declared himself to be a royal "guest". He did not molest the Moghal emperor in any way, who had illuminated his palace as a gesture of welcome to the Afghān Chief, but Abdāli spared no courtier and ransacked every noble's household and helped himself to their enormous accumulated wealth. Tributes was also extracted from every house in the capital. Many people were subjected to great torture in the process and some committed suicide to escape dishonour. Mughlāni Begum was very helpful to him in rendering reliable information as to the treasure of each noble and was, therefore, awarded the title of "Sultān Mirzā."

Mathurā and Virindāvan were also sacked by the Shāh's army and a large number of Hindu ascetics and others assembled for the Holi festival massacred indiscriminately. Severed heads of cows were tied to the mouths of the dead Bairāgis and Sanyāsis. A large number of women were driven away as slaves and both towns set on fire.

The Abdāli chief himself took to wife, Hazrat Begum, a 16-year old daughter of the late emperor, Mohd. Shāh. No protestations of her widowed mother were of any avail. A daughter of Ālamgir II was married to his son, Prince Taimur. Sixteen other ladies of the royal harem were also inducted into the *Zenānā* of Ahmed Shāh Abdāli along with 400 female attandants. The booty the Shāh took back to Afghanistān was loaded on no less than 28000 elephants. 80,000 cavalry horses also fell into his hands. Thus, the ruin which Nādir Shāh had commenced was pretty well completed by Ahmad Shāh.

The Shāh would have stayed a little longer in India (the booty of every kind and in abundance was forthcoming), but his forces were infected with cholera (choked as the water of Jamuna was with human carcasses) and so he had to hasten back, appointing his own nominee, Ghāzi-ud-Din, as the Wazir of Delhi, and appointing his son, Taimur, the Viceroy of Lāhore, Sarhind, Kashmir, Thattā and Multān. On the way back to Lāhore, "the Sikhs plundered his baggage and cut off the rear-force of his army."* Captive women were also rescued in large numbers and sent to their homes. "The Shāh was so much incensed that during his brief stay at Lāhore,he sent a large expeditionary force to Amritsar to chastise the Sikhs. The city was plundered, the sacred Temple was demolished and the holy tank filled with rubbish.*

---

* This insult was soon avenged. A grim battle was fought by the Sikhs with the forces of Taimur Shāh's general, Atāi Khān, inorder to restore the sanctity of the temple under the leadership of Bābā Deep Singh who, fully aware of the hazards involved, invited Sikhs from far and near to join him to celebrate the Diwāli festival of 1757, at Amritsar. He gathered one thousand people ready for the supreme sacrifice. They all dressed themselves like bridegrooms determined to wed death, their eternal bride. Most of the Sikhs had at this time taken shelter in the Shivālik hills or in the wastes of Mālwā, and Deep Singh himself was occupied with making a copy of the Ādi Granth at Damdamā Sāhib. But, the call of sacrifice to restore the honour of the Guru's temple was irresistible. When his band reached the outskirts of Amritsar, Hāji Atāi Khān, pounced upon them of a sudden. But such was the fury with which the Sikhs fought that the Lāhore army fled in panic. More reinforcements arrived and there was much carnage. Almost every companion of the Bābā lost his life. His own head had received a mortal wound, But as he had

His son, Taimur, also tried to punish the Sikhs as hard as he could for a year for their threat to the peace of the land. On hearing that two Afghān soldiers had been killed in its vicinity, the temple at Kartārpur (Jullundur) was ransacked and burnt down. The venerable priest, Sodhi Vadbhāg Singh, was clubbed to near death. The Sikhs took up this challenge of sacrilege to their temples and there was no peace thereafter for the Afghān usurpers. The Sikh insurgent forces were soon levying Rākhi (protection- money) on the whole country. (This was one-fifth of the land-rent, and was taken in lieu of the protection (Rākhi) of Zamindārs, both Hindu and Muslim, who sought their guardianship willingly in these days of chaos and open loot.)

Taimur, in trying to assert his authority, called Adeenā Beg to his presence in Lāhore, who had fled to Hānsi and Hissār, during the Shāh's last compaign and later to the Shivālik hills. Taimur asked him to take up his old assignment. The tricky Governor of Jullundur Doāb, suspicious of the Afghān's intentions, agreed to do so on condition that his presence at the Lāhore court would not be insisted upon. For, he said, the Sikhs would occupy his lands, in in his absence. They had already established, he said, their hegemony over large areas in various parts of the country.* For some brief time, this was agreed to, but later he was called to the court. On his refusal, Taimur sent out a large force under Murād to punish Adeenā Beg, who appealed to the Sikhs for help, and enlisted their support on payment of all their expenses and ample share in the loot. The Allied forces, about 25,000 horse, won a decisive victory (Dec. 1757) with heavy losses to Taimur's army. All their captains were killed and the Afghān camp and baggage looted. All the artillery left behind by Ahmad Shāh, was seized.† The Sikhs raided Lāhore

---

vowed not to lay down his life before visiting the precincts of the Temple, he cut through the enemy forces, bleeding profusely, and fell dead only after he had arrived in the holy sanctuary. His supreme sacrifice and noble daring are commemorated in the Parikarmā of the Golden temple to this day.

* Jassā Singh Ahluwaliā, for instance, had carved out a principality for himself in Jullundhur-Doāb; Jai Singh Kanaihya and Jassā Singh Rāmgarhiā in the Riārki area (around Batalā), and the Bhangi Sardārs in large parts of the Bāri and Rachnā Doābs. The Nakā area (between the Rāvi and Gharā) had been occupied by the Nakais. Sardar Charat Singh, head of the Sukarchakiyās, had appropriated lands around Gujrānwālā and "occasionally carried his arms beyond the Jehlum,"

† History of the Panjāb, Latif, page 229

and its environs with impunity each day, creating confusion all around. Under instructions from Sodhi Vadbhāg Singh, the city of Jullundur, the home of Nāsir Ali, was burnt. It was Nāsir Ali who had committed atrocities at Kartārpur. "Nāsir Ali's body was dug up from the grave," according to Muslim historians, "and several mosques defiled. Much massacre of Muslims followed and Muslim women enslaved." Adeenā Beg, though victorious, fled to the hills, fearing reprisals of the Afghāns and his place as *Faujdār* of the area was taken by Sarfrāz Khān. Such was the fury generated by the carnage and sacrilege committed by Abdāli that the whole Sikh people had now stood up in revolt, determined to uproot the tyrants with the help of the sword.

According to Latif, Sikhs had on their own at this time captured Lāhore in their onward march. Jahan Khān, the Vizier, who was leading the Afghān forces, was seriously wounded and barely escaped with his life.

The whole of the country east of Chenāb was literally on fire. The Afghāns attacked the Sikhs in the Jullundur-Doāb area, under the command of Sarfrāz Khān, but they were routed with heavy losses. Seeing all his attemps at the suppression of the Sikhs only adding daily to their zeal and strength, Taimur removed his headquarters from Lāhore and made such a hasty retreat towards the Chenāb that the royal family fell into the hands of the enemy, though they were subsequently released with honour. Even in war, the Sikhs had not lost their sense of chivalry and magnanimity of heart.

Adeenā Beg had in the meantime also sought the help of the Marāthās, who were lurking around Delhi, promising to pay them rupees one lakh per day of march and half the amount for a day of halt. The Marāthās couldnot resist this tempting offer, and enlisted the support even of Ālamgir Sāni, the Moghal emperor, by promising to pay him half the revenues of the Panjāb and agreeing to administer the state in his name by turning out the Afghāns. The Sikhs also agreed to join the combined force in their assault on Lāhore on agreed terms of share in territory and loot. The Marāthās marched towards the Panjāb under their leader, Ragunāth Rao, and on March 9, 1758, they reached Sirhind. The combined might of the three forces--Sikhs, Marāthās and Adeenā Beg—fell upon Sirhind, and the city was totally ransacked and looted by the Sikhs. So thorough was the loot that not a soul had even a cloth left to cover his or her nakedness. The city was razed to the ground and all treasures buried underground were dug up and seized. (According to Latif, this created some misunderstanding between the Marāthās and the Sikhs, the former contending that the loot was their exclusive prerogative. Latif says thereupon the Sikhs parted company with the Allied forces. But all contemporary historians like Miskin, Ahmad Shāh, Bakht Mal etc. assert that all the three forces combined continued their march towards Lāhore). The Afghān Governor, Abdus Samad Khān, fled in panic, but was taken prisoner after a hot chase. Now, they crossed the Satluj where they were met by the forces of Lāhore under Jahān Khān, the Prime Minister. Finding the enemy-force irrestible, Jahan Khān thought wisdom to be the better part of valour, and retreated hastily to Lāhore. On April 10,1758, the Marāthās and the Sikhs together entered Lāhore, and killed every soldier of the Afghān army found within its limits. They made many prisoners here, and "forced them to clean the sacred tank at Amritsar filled with earth and defiled under the orders of Ahmad Shāh Abdāli." "The Marāthā chiefs also went to pay homage at the Amritsar Temple along with the Sikh Sardārs and were much honoured." Adeenā Beg also welcomed the Marāthās publicly at Lāhore where, however, they stayed only less than a month. Their financial position at Poona was not very strong and they could not maintain their communications and garrisons in the distant land of Panjāb, the more so because the Sikhs were bidding for sovereign power with such stubbornness and sacrifice for about 50 years now that the Panjāb could not be kept by the Marāthās except after a final and decisive showdown with them for which they were not at all prepared. They, therefore, left Lāhore to Adeenā Beg against an annual tribute of 75 lakhs, leaving a few of their detachments at Multān and Attock which were, however, driven out next year by Abdāli.

Two major reasons, according to Prof. N.K. Sinhā for the sudden withdrawal of the Marāthās were that "the pay of their army had fallen into arrears. A debt of 88 lakhs was due to the army. In the Panjāb, they couldnot make war to pay for the war as was invariably their habit. And they were also recalled to make a grand attack on the Nizām, a great danger to their existence in the Deccan.*"

Whatever the gains of the Sikhs in this campaign, much of the advantage lay for the time being with the Marāthās who, as has been

* *Rise of the Sikh Power*, P. 27

said before, appointed Adeenā Beg to be their Viceroy. For fear of the Sikhs as well as the Afghāns, however, he built his capital at Adeenā Nagar near Batālā, where he died four months later. †

The Marāthās bent on bringing the whole of Hindustān under their hegemony had at this time almost succeeded in enlarging their empire to an extent that the prophecy of Shivāji of watering their horses in the Hoogli on the one hand and the Indus on the other was nearly fulfilled. They had become a formidable power in the country from the Deccan to the Indus, had over-run the metropolitan provinces of Delhi and Āgra and were now also masters of the Panjāb.* What a pity that these two formidable forces—the Marāthās and

† Adeenā Beg, son of Channu, of Sharakpur (Lāhore), rose from a humble position, He went to Allahābād to acquire knowledge early in life in revenue administration, but back in the Panjāb, he started life as a contractor. He was put in charge of Sultānpur by Zakriyā Khān, at the time of Nādir's invasion & charged with the task of subduing the Sikhs whom he fought & compromised with as the situation dictated. He was a master-diplomat. No matter how much the upheaval and who the master of the Panjāb, his interests were always well-served. "He amused the Sikhs, the Delhi court he despised, the Afghāns he bewildered, and the Marāthās he effectively used to break the power both of the Sikhs and Afghāns to obtain his own independence. He was unscruplous and sometimes cruel," and always led a dual life.

* After the death of Shivajee (1680), the unitary state he had created broke up. Aurangzeb murdered his son (1689) and destroyed, through his Deccan campaigns, the edifice built by that great hero. Shāhu, his grandson, accepted the Moghal paramountcy, having been brought up as a hostage in the Moghal Court. The dream of the Hindu Empire was lost. But when in 1714, Bālāji Vishvānāth Bhatt was appointed the Peshwā (or the Prime Minister, which office became hereditary and more powerful than the King's), things started looking up, and a programme of expanding northwards began. By 1750, the Marāthā empire had become a confederacy with the Peshwā at the head, the King being reduced to the position of a ceremonial head, without any effective power. Scindia (of Gwalior) and Holkar (of Indore), who were earlier subordinates to the Peshwā and carried the Marāthā flag to the north Bengal in 1744 and captured Orissa in 1745 (and interfered with or attacked every Rājput state) asserted their virtual independence. The Gaekwārs (of Baroda) and the Bhonslās (of Nāgpur) followed suit. In 1761, in the battle of Pānipat, the back of the Peshwā was broken. Both his son and cousin died in the battle and he himself died soon thereafter of a broken heart. And now followed total disintegration. Murder and intrigue and frequent change of sides followed. They intrigued with the English, the Nizām, the ruler of Mysore—all for personal benfit. Nānā Phadnvis made an alliance with Mysore's Hyder Ali and the Nizām together with the French against the English (1778-1782), but the English secured the support of the Peshwā's uncle, Raghunāth Rāo, the Gaikwād and the other Marāthā

Sikhs together with the Rājputs and other patriots in the South, could not combine for a common cause to write a new (and glorious) chapter in the annals of India. But such, indeed, is the quirk of history. Not all that should happen, happens—not at least at the right moment. And, so the nations rise and fall.

F. N. Contd.

nobles and defeated the Allied forces. In 1782, the Marāthās made peace with the English, and waged war together with them and the Nizām against Tipu Sultān, the son of Hyder Ali, till recently their ally. They jointly defeated him in 1792. Later, they pounced uppn the Nizām and defeated him (1795). Mahādji Scindia got his possessions confirmed by the Moghal king and was appointed Deputy Regent of the empire, the actual Regent being the infant Peshwā. It may also be noted that it was the Moghal king who alongwith Tipu Sultān, had invited Ahmad Shāh Abdāli to destroy the Marāthā power, later the virtual "Protectors" of the imperial throne (from 1772 onwards). Scindia and Holkar now organised their forces independently on European lines, officered by Europeans, mostly French, whom (unlike Ranjit Singh) they gave full powers of command and operation to their utter ruin. The more they succeeded (as against the Nizām in 1795) the more they disputed one with the other (and all with the Peshwā at Poona). Scindia, who had taken over Delhi in 1785 and had to fight the Sikhs, the Rājputs and the Moghal nobles later defeated also Holkar in 1792, but his death in 1794 restored the balance. The Swarajya (home-) land was thus confined only to Mahārāshtrā, the others being only tributaries paying Chauth, or formal courtesies. And, a Marāthā imperial authority or administration was never established. Holkar's success against the Peshwā (in 1802) attracted British intervention. The European officers, Perron and others, walked over to the British side and Holkar ran towards the Panjāb (about which we will refer later on), compromised with the British, and came back to be confined to his own ancestral heritage. The Marāthās rose as rebels against Moghal tyranny, but attacked the Hindu powers as much in Rājasthān as among themselves. They became a formidable power for a century, but by the time the Sikhs came as a political force on the scene, they had already passed into history. Due to incessant warfare, no administrative or cultural innovation could be expected from them, but their role in the political history of later Moghal India is glorious, and was responsible alongwith the Sikh struggle for freedom for its final break-up.

CHAPTER XVII

THE SIKH BID FOR PEOPLEHOOD (2)

Ahmad Shāh invaded India for the fifth time, this time to punish the Marāthās particularly. They had insulted and turned out of Delhi the Shāh's representative, Najib-ud-Doulā, who was being harassed by them near Pānipat. Certain Rājput rulers (like those of Jaipur and Mārwār) also took advantage of this incident and promised support to the Shāh, as their territories were also being attacked by the Marāthās. The Moghal king was none-too-happy with his overbearing Prime Minister, Ghāzi-ud-Din, and wanted to get rid of him through foreign intervention. He too let it be known secretly to Abdāli that his visit would be welcome to him. Abdāli would have been less than human if he would not have taken full advantage of such a propitious situation. He crossed the Indus with a force of 60,000 on Oct 25, 1759.

The Marāthās could offer no appeciable resistance and abandoned their posts in the Panjāb hastily. The Sikhs offered stiff resistance and in one severe battle, about 2000 Afghāns lost their lives and their general, Jahān khān, was wounded. However, the Shāh occupied Lāhore and appointed his son, Taimur, as Viceroy there. He attacked the Marāthās at Taraori, near Pānipat, and defeated their forces there. He defeated them again at Barāri ghāt, near Sahāranpur. It seemed there was no effective resistance anywhere now to the Shāh and he spent a year around Delhi, in peace, "except for a few skirmishes with the Marāthās". According to some other historians, a major battle also took place near Bādli, around Delhi, between the two forces and the Marāthās force, of 80,000, under Datāji Scindia, was completely destroyed, Datāji himself being killed in the battle. Malhār Rao Holkar fled and other generals were vanquished. Near Sikandrā, Malhār Rāo Holkar was also surprised by Ahmad Shāh who so effectually routed him that he had to flee naked from the battle-field.

Though the Marāthās had been humbled and routed in earlier engagements, their resistance was far from broken. Accordingly, a formidable army left the Deccan for the North led by Wiswās Rāo, heir-apparent to the Peshwā (or the Grand Vizier who actually ruled the empire, the Marāthā king being only titular). The Jāts with a force of 30,000 also joined them. All the Marāthā chiefs accompained them to the battle which was to be the final arbiter of their destiny. Their force is estimated at 3 lakh men, including cavalry, with 300 pieces of cannon. The troops Abdāli had were 40,000 Afghāns and Persians, 13000 Indian cavalry and 38000 Indian infantry with 70 pieces of canon "borrowed from Indian allies."

The Marāthās occupied Delhi easily, cutting to pieces the small Afghān garrisons. Kunjpurā, on the Jamnā, 60 miles north of Delhi, was besieged next and the whole Durrāni garrison wiped out. Hearing this, the Shāh who was camping on the left bank of the Jamnā was inflamed with rage and crossed the river, swollen by rains, after some losses. For a time, the Marāthās cut off the Shāh's supplies and his lines of communication, but this was soon over, and the Shāh made himself the master of the situation within three to four months. Lying in the vicinity of each other and forced by the exhaustion of supplies, * the guerilla activities engaged in so far were abandoned, and the Marāthās were obliged to come out in the open and attacked the Durrāni in the early hours of the morning of Jan 7, 1761, when the Shāh was fast asleep and was woken out of his bed to mount his steed, without even the change of dress. Canon-shot met canon-shot. The sky was rent by the shouts of, "Har-Har Mahādev", and

* It is said in these days of acute distress, Sardār Ālā Singh (founder of *Pati-ālā*, on Āla's territory, now known as Patiālā) helped the Marāthās with supplies from the rear. The fact being known, it was feared the Durrāni would punish the Sardār with extreme severity. His wife, Māi Fato, however, sought pardon of the Shāh through a mediator, and purchased his goodwill on payment of Rs. 4 lakhs, per year. This the Sikhs never forgave. The Dal Khālsā condemned his action and fined him. (Ganda Singh. History of the Sikhs, P. 164)

"Allān-hoo-Akbar". The Marāthās were attacking the flanks of the Shāh's army and literally mowing them down. Many well-known Afghān warriors fell on the battle field, including their generals, Atai Khān and his uncle, the grand Vizier. The Durrānis, hard pressed, had to give way, for a time.

The Shāh now advanced in person and so fierce was the attack by the forces under his command that the Marāthās had no choice but to retreat, leaving countless dead and wounded on the battlefield. They were pursued for fifteen to twenty miles. Much carnage ensued. Almost all the great Marāthā chiefs, including Vishwās Rao, and Bhāu were killed. Others were seriously wounded. The number of those who fell on the battlefield on the Marāthā side has been estimated at 2 lakhs. 25000 were taken prisoner along with 50,000 choice horses and immense booty.

So great was the carnage and so demoralising its effect on the Marāthās that they never recovered from its disastrous shock. Bālāji, their Peshwā, died of grief soon thereafter. They evacuated their possessions in Hindustān and retired beyond the Narbadā never to recover their power again. Almost the whole of Hindustān now lay at the feet of Abdāli. It was this formidable conqueror that the Sikhs had to contend with now.

The Afghān King showed no desire to occupy the vacant Moghal throne, and returned to his own kingdom by way of the Panjāb. The Shāh alongwith his Panjāb generals being occupied elsewhere, the Sikhs had a field day in their homeland. They ravaged the country far and wide. They formed a confederacy under Jassā Singh, Chet Singh Kanaihyā, Hari Singh Bhangi, Lehnā Singh and other Sikh chieftains to pillage Lāhore. The suburbs of Lāhore were attacked successively. Hundreds of enemy lives were lost and the loss to property was beyond estimation. The Naib Subēdār, Amir Mohd Khān, shut himself up in the city. The Sikhs surrounded Lāhore on all sides and demanded tribute from the Viceroy's representatives. The Naib Subēdar offered them Rs. 30,000/- for *Karāh Parsād* (holy pudding) and the Sikhs left him in peace for the time being, but only as long as the Shāh was around. They now spread out in the country, threw up new mud-fortresses everywhere, and occupied the surrounding areas. The local officials were helpless. Some of them like the Governor of Chār Mahal, Nawāb Mirzā Khān, who tried to challange them with his force of 1000, was himself killed & his entire force cut to pieces.

As the Shāh passed through the Panjāb, the Sikhs fell upon his rear, near Goindwāl, and relieved them of much of their booty. About 2200 Hindu women made captive by the Shāh, were released and escorted back to their homes. They cut off the retreating enemy's supplies at times "but never making a direct attack", and inflicted whatever damage they could upon them right upto the Indus.

When the Shāh left for Kābul in the spring of 1761, there was nothing to hold them back. With a force of about 40,000 horse, "they carried their arms through the central Panjāb, the Doāb, and even beyond upto Nadaun in the Shivālik hills." The Faujdārs of Jullundur-Doāb were thrown out "like a fly out of milk." They also attacked Sirhind once again. The accursed city was never to be allowed peace, though this time only a part of it was looted. Malerkotla was attacked and thoroughly ransacked. The Shāh hearing these alarming reports, instructed his general, Nur-ud-Din Bāmzai, with a force of 12000 horse to chastise the Sikhs. But, when he crossed the Chenāb, he was met by a strong Sikh force, under Charat Singh Sukarchakiā, and repulsed with heavy losses. The Afghāns ran in complete disorder and took refuge in the stronghold of Sialkot. The Afghāns were completely routed at Sialkot as well. Nur-ud-Din himself fled in terror, disguised as a beggar, leaving his enormous baggage to be plundered by the Sikhs. "This signal victory over the seasoned troops of the greatest conqueror of Asia of the times, placed Charat Singh and his Sukarchakia Misal in the front-rank of Sikh leadership."

Charat Singh returned to his fortress in Gujranwālā, highly elated at his success. But the Governor of the Panjāb, alarmed beyond measure at this, ventured out in September, 1761, to punish and defeat him. He even recruited some Sikhs in his troops, and surrounded Charat Singh's fort at Gujranwālā. The other Sikh Misaldārs hearing of this rushed out for his succour and about 4 miles from Gujranwālā surrounded the forces of Ubaid Khān. Even the Sikhs in the employ of Government walked over to the Sikh side. This unnerved the Khān so much that, without striking a blow, he escaped in the dead of night, leaving his troops to take care of themselves. The Sikhs pounced upon the Afghān forces in the morning from all directions. Their morale, already low at the flight of their leader, they fled in panic to wheresoever fate took them, leaving their arms and stores and even their horses behind. The Afghān Governor, after much travail, reached Lāhore somehow and shut himself up within the security of its walls.

Charat Singh was no longer a Misaldār. He had now become a national hero.

And from now on, "the most glorious chapter of Sikh history and one of the most glorious of Indian history was to begin. It is a record of the duel in which the all-powerful Afghān conqueror was worn out by an obscure people who successfully wrested from his closed fist that part of India which the house of Taimur had failed to preserve from him...He (Abdāli) was now to find that a fight with the Sikhs was not a matter of strategy or tactics, nor a matter of effective military combination or calculation. A defeat inflicted upon them would be (useless) like a sword slash through a pond. His name did not inspire terror in their bosom : his resounding victories only made them far more strong and stirred them into far more defiance."*

The Sikhs now attacked Lāhore in full force. The city-gates were opened to them and led by Jassā Singh Ahluwāliā, they entered the city triumphantly (Nov. 1761).† Jassā Singh was proclaimed King (*Sultān-ul-Qaum*) and for the first time the Sikhs struck their coin as a sovereign power in the name of the Guru, with the following inscription :

"*Deg-O-tegh-O-fatah-O-nusrat-bē-darang*
Yāft-az-Nānak-Guru-Gobind Singh".

* N. K. Sinha, Rise of the Sikh power, pp. 31-32

† Latif places the present Sikh victory over Lāhore much earlier, in 1758. However, modern reseachers attribute the earlier occupation of Lāhore to the combind forces of Adeenā Beg, the Marāthās and the Sikhs. It is also said the inscription on the first coin struck at Lāhore under Jassā Singh read :— *Sikkā zad az Jahān ba fazal-i-Akāl; Mulk-i-Ahmad, grift Jassā Kalāl.*" (By the Grace of the immortal God is this coin struck in the country of Ahmad, seized by Jassā, the Kalāl.") But this, according to some historians, like Griffin and Ganesh Dās, seems to be a forgery inorder to inflame Ahmad Shāh against the Sikh chief. They say that no such coin has been seen so far. On the other hand, Browne (India Tracts, p.vii) asserts these coin were definitely struck and were in vogue for 15 years when the Sikh chiefs through a *Gurmattā* withdrew them and decided to strike the coin in the names of Gurus Nānak and Gobind Singh. Other coins are dated Samvat 1822 (1765 A. D.), 1825 (1768 A.D.) upto Samvat 1834 (1777 A.D.), with only a two-year gap (Samvat 1823-24) due to Abdāli's invasions. (Vide G.L. Chopra, Panjāb as a Sovereign state, Appendix VI). These were called Gobind Shāhi Sikkās (coins). All these coins were struck at "Lāhore, the capital City." In 1778 A. D., another coin was struck bearing the name of Amritsar, Akāl Takhat, as the seat of Govt.

(Food for our life and the sure victory of our sword
We attained through (the Grace of) Gurus Nānak and
Gobind Singh)

But, they do not seem to have planted themselves here for long, for the Lāhore fort continued to be occupied by Ubaid Khān, the Afghān Governor.

However, they assembled the entire Dal Khālsā. and passed a *Gurmattā* to attack Jandiālā Guru, a place held by Mahant Āqil Dās of the Niranjani breakaway sect, who had rendered information and help against the Sikhs to the Panjāb Govt. and the Shāh at Pānipat.* The Chief of Malerkotlā, Hingan Khān, who had become an implacable foe of the Sikhs alongwith other Muslim chiefs, was also punished severely. Sirhind was invaded once again. They ravaged Jullundur-Doāb and its new Governor, Rājā Ghumand Chand Katauch, a nominee of the Shāh, fled to the hills.

Thus passed the entire Panjāb from the Satluj to the Indus into the hands of the Sikh people.

Hearing of these disorders, Ahmad Shāh again crossed the Indus. The Sikhs left Lāhore in a hurry and the Shāh established his headquarters there in January, 1762. He issued orders to all *Jāgirdārs* and chiefs to join with their contingents the Governor of Sirhind who was surrounded by the Sikh forces at this time. He himself also marched out on Feb 3, 1762, towards the same place. The Sikhs broke up their camp at Jandiala which they had invaded to punish Āqil Dās, and rushed out to reinforce their brethren at Sirhind. The situation for the Nawāb was very precariaus when the Shāh arrived with a formidable force. About 30,000 Sikhs were camping at this time with their families at a village, called Kupp, near Malerkotla, with a view to attacking Sirhind. The Shāh sent instructions to the Nawāb of Sirhind to attack from the front, while he would himself take care of the rear.

He surprised the Sikhs by his sudden appearance. The Sikhs fought recklessly, but thousands were killed. Others threw a ring around the remaining families and moved on fighting. Shām Singh

* It was on the information of a Narinjani that Bhāi Tāru Singh, the martyr, had been arrested (1746), Mahtāb Singh's family persecuted (1740) and Sukhā Singh captured (1753), etc.

Karorsinghiā, Jassā Singh Ahluwāliā, and Charat Singh Sukarchākiyā, led the main army. No one gave them shelter or food on the way. Fearing the Shāh's wrath, people in fact tried to attack them, killing many of them.

They were on their way to Barnālā where, they thought, they would perhaps be able to find refuge with Bābā Ālā Singh, in whose territory it was situated. However, before they reached there, their forces were attacked by the pursuing Afghāns and a wholesale massacre ensued. This terrible caranage occured on Feb 5, 1762 and is known as *Wadā Ghalughārā* (the Great Holocaust). Sardār Jassā Singh Ahluwāliā received 22 cuts on his body in this battle, but he fought on heroically. The sacred volume of their Holy Book, which they always carried with them on their march, was also lost in this battle.* Out of 30,000 persons, over 10,000 thousand Sikhs (mostly women, children and old men who couldn't escape in time) lost this lives in this terrible blood-bath.‡ Most of them belonged to the central districts (Mājhā) of the Panjāb. But the Sikhs refused to be beaten or lose heart. Whenever they were reminded of this carnage, they said "The gold remains now in its total purity, having been cleansed of all its dross."

The Shāh was in the meantime busy heaping more humiliations and insults upon their heads. The bungās (or rest-houses) around the Amritsar temple were destroyed. The holy tank was desecrated with the blood of kine and filled with mud and refuse. The temple itself was blown up with gunpowder.† But, as the sacred

* Called Damdamā Bir (or the Damdamā recension), it was dictated by Guru Gobind Singh personally to Bhāi Mani Singh. It was this version which was invested with Guruship by the Tenth Master on the eve of his death. Its search was lately made at Kābul, but no such copy has been found in any liberary or the imperial palaces. It is not lying in the main Gurudwārā at Kābul as suggested by H. R. Guptā (History of the Sikhs, II, 183). However, several copies of it were already in existence before the original was lost. One of these is with the author of this work.

‡ Siyar-ul-Mutākharin puts the figure of those killed at this time at nearly 20,000, Miskin and Forster at 25,0000. Cunningham's estimate varies from 12000 to 25000. Murray's estimate is 12000. Rattan Singh and Gandā Singh's estimate is 10,000. On the site of this holocaust now stands a village called Jeetwāl, near Malod (Malaud).

† Mohd. Latif, History of the Panjāb, p. 284. Latif justifies this on account of the "atrocities" committed (according to him) by the Sikhs against the Muslims and their sacred places. Moreover, he says, being an inconoclaust (or image-

temple was being blown up, a flying brick-bat struck the Shāh on the nose and inflicted a wound which later proved fatal for him.†

The Shāh stayed at Lāhore upto the end of the year (1762). The Governor of Kashmir, Sukhjiwan Rām Khatri, had become independent and had refused to pay tribute as earlier agreed to by him. Rājā Ranjit Deo of Jammu helped the Shāh's forces in his campaign against Kashmir considerably. Sukhjiwan was captured and brought in chains to Lāhore. His eyes were cut out and thereafter he was ingnobly put to death. Another Governor, Sar Buland Khān, was appointed in his place. According to Sir J. N. Sarkār, the Shāh "invited the Marāthā envoys at Delhi to meet him at Lāhore. Bāpu went there in March 62, and Parshotam some two months later, after securing the Peshwā's approval. The Shāh sent robes and presents and the *tikkā* of Rājāship (the impression of his palm dipped in saffron or *Kesar Panjā*) in recognition of the Peshwā, Mādhav Rāo, in his Deccan dominions, possibly in order not to antagonise every rising political force in the country of Hindustān (especially when he was negotiating from position of strength) and he wanted to concentrate his whole might against the Sikhs, they being his next-door neighbours and always ready to challenge his immediate authority. He also agreed to recognise Shāh Ālam II as emperor of Delhi, on payment of a tribute of Rs. 40 lakhs per year.

But the humiliation he had heaped on the whole Sikh people, was too much to bear. The Shāh was still at Lāhore, when they again attacked Sirhind (May, 62) and the Nawāb, Zain Khān, defeated and obliged to pay tribute. The Shāh dared not come to his rescue. On Oct 17, 1762, on the occasion of the Diwāli festival, about 60,000

F. N. Contd.

breaker)" he (the Shāh) acted in strict conformity with the law of his religion and was actuated by a sense of duty when he undertook the destruction of the sanctuaries of the Sikhs." A man as painstaking in research as Latif does not, however, realise that the Sikhs never believed in idol-worship, nor ever desecrated or pulled down the Muslim holy shrines as the Shāh, and before him some other rulers of his faith,had done. The Sikh tradition and religion were wholly opposed to this kind of unholy activity.

† He died in June, 1773, at Murghāb. The nose-wound became cancerous, and took his life. For more references on this and the above point, Dr. Gandā Singh's *Ahmad Shāh Durrāni* may be consulted. All the Indian campaigns of the Abdāli are given in minute detail in this remarkable work and supported by all conceivable historical records in Marāthi, Panjābi and English.

of them assembled at Amritsar and resolved to avenge the insults he had offered both to their religion and their sense of dignity as a people. The Shāh found himself cornered, not only because of the lack of sufficient armed strength but more because of the resilience and the undying determination of the new faith. They attacked the neighbourhood of Lāhore and ransacked the country from Sirhind to Siālkot.*

The Shāh, alarmed and perplexed, tried at first to negotiate peace with them through an envoy. The Sikhs insulted the Afghān emissary and "without listening to his proposals, plundered him and his followers and drove them away."

The Shāh was now left with no choice but to meet their challenge. He attacked Amritsar on Oct 16, on the day of the solar-eclipse, one day before Diwāli, but the recklessness and fervour with which the Sikhs fought compelled the greatest warrior of Asia to beat retreat and "escape to Lāhore under cover of darkness."

"He was an ideal Afghān genius fitted for conquest but incapable of empire," according to Cunningham, but he was no mere adventurer. He was also a great statesman capable of diplomacy and compromise, knowing his priorities & also his limitations, quitting the scene with honour when the going was not good for whatever reasons. Hearing of some disturbanes in Kandhār, the Shāh had suddenly to leave Lāhore on Dec. 12, 1762.

No sooner had the Afghān forces crossed the Chenāb than the Sikhs fell upon Kasur, a Pathān settlement, which they subdued and plundered.† Then, they sacked Malerkotla and slew its Nawāb, Hingan Khān, who had become notorious for Sikh-baiting. In Dec. 1763, they seized Sirhind with a force of 50,000. Its Governor, Zain Khān, was killed and the whole cursed city set on fire once again, to

* Forster, 100-101. Some historians say the Sikhs drove the Shāh from Lāhore also at this time, but Sir J. N. Sarkār doesnot agree. He is of the view that the Sikhs captured Lāhore after the Durrāni's departure, late in 1763. (Fall of the Moghal Empire, II, 352).

† The reason for attacking Kasur was the plaint of the Brāhmins before the *Sarbat Khālsā* gathering at the Baisākhi festival (April 10, 1763) that the Nawāb, Usmān Khān, had abducted the wife of one of them and converted her to Islām. Hari Singh Bhangi volunteered to lead the expedition in which the Nawāb together with 500 of his choice soldiers were killed. The Brāhmin's wife was restored to him and the city given over to plunder,

fulfil the Guru's prophecy.* Brick clashed with brick and the ruins were ploughed over by donkeys. The place where the two tender sons of Guru Gobind Singh, aged 5 and 7, were done to death was commemorated with a Gurdwārā, called Fatehgarh Sāhib, (or, the Fort of Victory). At Morinda, near Sirhind, where the Guru's sons were betrayed, the two persons most responsible for it, Jāni Khān and Māni Khān, were captured and butchered, along with their families. Āla Singh, Rājā of Patiala, bought over the ruins of Sirhind for a sum of Rs. 25,000/- from Bhāi Buḍh Singh, an old companion of Guru Gobind Singh, to whom the town had been assigned after its conquest by the Sikh forces.

The *Tarunā Dal* (or the youth force) under Charat Singh Sukarchakiā stationed itself at Amritsar. Early in 1764, they cleansed the sacred tank and rebuilt the historic temple, whose foundation stone was laid by Sardār Jassā Singh Ahluwāliā himself. The Budhā Dal (or the Veterans' army) under their Ahluwāliā Sardār ransacked the country, punished their age-old enemies and established their military posts everywhere.

Jullundur-Doab was captured next and the Governor driven out. Alarmed by these reports, Ahmad Shāh sent his general, Jahān Khān, from Kābul, to punish the Sikhs. Led by Charat Singh and aided by the Bhangi Sardārs, they joined battle with him at Sialkot and inflicted a crushing defeat on him. Jahān Khān fled back to Peshā-

* Prof. N. K. Sinha thus compares the Afghān, the Marāthā & the Sikh soldier of that time :— "The Sikhs with their endurance & rapidity of movement, the excellent size & swiftness of their horses, resembled the ill-clad but powerful troops of Shivajee. They were pre-eminently well-fitted for a guerilla method of warfare, being in this respect very much superior to the Marāthās.!' He supports H. G. Rawlinson (Account of the Last Battle of *Pānipat, Intr.*). where the author says that "the supposed superiority of the Marāthās in guerilla warfare was a myth; it was only in quick action that the Marathā cavalry with it superb elan never failed to rout their opponents," and suggests that if as a supplement to the Marāthā elan of action, there had been the Sikh scheme of skirmishing after the Pathān fashion behind the enemy, affairs (at Pānipat) might have taken an entirely different turn. "It has been said that even in contending hand to hand, he (the Sikh) was terrible. A Sikh soldier had really to be killed twice." Analysing why such a Marāthā-Sikh combination couldnot be forged, the author says it was on account of the "unbecoming pride & presumption of the Marāthās, their failure to grasp the realities of the situation, the proverbial Marāthā greed for plunder, the presence of the wily Adinā Beg (who kept the two divided), the prevalent Sikh view that regarded the Marāthās as marauders." (Origin of Sikh power, pp. 25-26)

war, leaving even his family to take care of itself. His ladies were captured by the Sikhs but much to their credit, the women were "sent safely to Jammu."*

The provinces of Sirhind and Jullundur-Doāb were parcelled out among the various Misals. Lāhore was threatened again in Feb. 1764.* They asked the Abdāli's Governor, Kabuli Mal, a Hindu, that all the butchers of the city be handed over to them and cow-slaughter forbidden. The Governor naturally hesitated being the servant of a Muslim overlord, but "when the Sikhs broke through the Delhi gate, he yielded, and and agreed to cut off the noses and ears of a few butchers and paid a large sum to the Sikhs as *nazrānā*."† He agreed also to have an advisor, Tek Chand, appointed by them to "assist" him in his work.

The youth-force under Hari Singh Bhangi now ventured out to the South-west, while another section under Charat Singh invested the North-West. Aided by the Nakāi leader, Hirā Singh, and his sons Jhandā Singh and Gandā Singh, the Bhangi Sardārs captured the whole region called Lamma and Nakka which was occupied by the Nakais. On the fall of Multān it was apportioned to the Bhangis. They crossed the Indus and occupied the Derājāt. Sardār Charat Singh took over Rachnā and Chaj Doābs right upto Rohtās across the Jehlum. The regions of Delhi, Pothohār, and Pind Dādan Khān were taken next.

Hearing of this, the Shāh decided to invade India, once again, in Oct. 1764.‡ His own force of 18000 Afghāns was augmented by the Baluch force of Naseer Khān and the Lāhore force of Kabuli Mal. The Sikhs vanished out of sight on hearing of this new invasion, and took refuge in the Lakhi jungle, in the Mālwā region, about 150 miles from Lāhore. A large body had also gone to assist Jawāhar Singh,

---

* Says Forster (i,279) "The Afghāns in chains were also compelled to excavate the reserviour at Amritsar, which in the preceding year they had filled up. Though the Afghān massacre and persecution must have been deeply imprinted on their minds, *the Sikhs did not, it is said, destroy one prisoner in cold blood*."

† J.N. Sarkar (Fall of the Mughal Empire, II, P. 352)

‡ Abdāli had this time, according to the *Jangnāmā* (intr) of Qāzi Nur Ahmad wanted diplomacy also to play its part. He wanted Najeeb Shuja, the chief of Delhi, the Jāts & the Marāthās to combine with him to fall upon the heads of these cursed curs (i.e. the Sikhs), because the hare of a country can only be caught by the dog of that country," but no one picked up his scheme not even his own generals,

the son of Suraj Mal, the Jāt hero, who was fighting a grim battle against the Rohilla chief, Najib-ud-Daula.*

On his onward march, the Shāh's forces were taken on by the Sikhs. Their guerilla tactics paid them rich dividends, as in an open combat, they would have lost heavily. And yet so stiff was the resistance that it took the Shāh four days to cover a distance of about 30 miles from Lāhore to Amritsar where the Shāh expected a large body of Sikhs, but he found none except about 30 of them who stood guard over the Akāl Takht. Everyone of them them died in the engagements that followed. However, the Shāh's forces destroyed the sacred buildings once again and returned to Lāhore.

His next move was to procceed to Sirhind and not only to attack the Sikh forces wherever he met them on the way, but to utterly devastate the lands which gave birth to and sheltered these reckless "infidels." This was done. The people were massacred in broad day-light. No distinction was made between Sikhs and non-Sikhs. No body can count the number of things which fell into the hands of the crusaders.* The Shāh's army crossed the Satluj in three days, but the Sikhs had been so hardened by warfare and made too determined by persecution to let the enemy get the upper hand this time. Their back may have been broken, but not their faith in the ultimate victory of their cause.

Frustrated, the Shāh left for home via Sirhind where he was received by Ālā Singh of Patialā. The Shāh treated him with great courtesy, and on being assured of his loyalty, conferred upon him the title of Rājā. In return for an annual tribute of 3½ lakhs, he was allowed the banner and drum as insignia of royalty. The Sikhs were furious on hearing this. They punished Ālā Singh for submission

---

* Jawāhar Singh was interviewed by a hundred Sardārs at Barāri ghāt. "After saying the *Ardāsā* (prayer) the chanter cried out, 'Jawāhar Singh, son of Suraj Mal, has come within the shelter of Khālsā Jee and become a Sikh of Nānak. He is demanding redress for his father's blood." As everyone's opinion in the assembly counted (though the Sardārs would speak secretly into the ears of the visiting Ambassador etc. whatever they wanted to,) they could not stop anyone from having his say, even if it was bitter. Jawāhar Singh's case was, however, considered with utmost sympathy by all & help offered in full measure." (Rise of Sikh Power, N.K. Sinha, P. 109).

* It is in these days that the popular saying came in vogue:—

"Khādā peetā Lāhē dā: Rahndā Ahmad Shāhē dā".

(That alone is yours which you can drink & eat, for the rest Ahmad Shāh will loot.)

to a foreigner who was their inveterate foe and was out to destroy them, root and branch, besides demolishing and desecrating their sacred places and challenging their human dignity.

On the way back, the Abdāli clashed with the Sikh forces in Doābā. All the Sikh leaders of note took part in this battle, which lasted for a week. So reckless were their attacks and so much was the indignity and loss suffered by the enemy forces, that the Shāh refused to fight a determined encounter anywhere and continued on his march. He even did not stop at Lāhore and made straight for Afghanistān. But, the Sikhs continued to harass him on his retreat, frequently attacking his rear, cutting out his baggage train and taking many prisoners and plundering his camp-followers.

As soon as the Shāh had left the shores of India by march-end, 1765, the Sikhs resolved, though a *gurmattā* at Amritsar, to recapture Lāhore. The Governor, Kābuli Mal, was away to Jammu. The Bhangi Sardārs, Lehna Singh snd Gujjar Singh, attacked Lāhore, and making a large hole in the Lahore fort, entered it, on the night of April 16. The nephew of the Governor, Amir Singh, was taken into custody. Next day, the Bhangi Sardārs were joined by Sobhā Singh Kanahaiya and the city and its neighbourhood were divided among the victors.

Ahmad Shāh was quick to recognise the change. He sent large baskets of choice fruits to Lehna Singh Bhangi. But the latter returned them politely saying, it was a luxury fit only for the emperor. For a humble peasant like himself, he said, the best food was food-grains. Inspite of this rebuff, the Shāh had no choice but to recognise the *de-facto* Bhangi dominion over Lāhore.

At the time of the Shāh's death in 1773, the possessions of the Sikhs extended from Sahāranpur in the east to Attock in the west, and from Multān and Sind in the south to Kāngrā, Jammu and Bhimbar in the north. For nearly a generation therafter, the Afghān invasions were a thing of the past. The Sikhs now turned their attention to the Gangetic Doāb. The Moghals had come to rule only in and around the city of Delhi even if that, and their glory and power were being rapidly usurped by the feringis from the West, the traders turned warriors, in the place of the Muslim warriors turned traders or traitors.

The Sikhs had also become a sovereign power in their own right, and not as a result of submission to a foreign conqueror or compromise of principle. A new dawn seemed to have broken for the people of Panjāb.

CHAPTER XVIII

THE MISAL PERIOD

(1764—1798)

We must pause here to consider a very valid point for students of the history of this period. The non-Sikh records as much the Sikh chroniclers talk of a fight to the finish between the Moghals and the Sikhs and then between the Afghāns and the Sikhs. Unbelievable carnage is recorded not only on the field of battle, but also against civilians. According to conservative estimates, a little less than quarter of a million people had been decimated to death in about half a century (1710-1767).* The Sikh Symbols, by which their religious view of life is sustained, were attacked again and again, without any sense of pity or shame. Their temples were destroyed and desecrated. The Muslim historians, on the other hand, see in this only a retributive justice for the "iniquities" committed by the forces of Bandā Bahādur at Sirhind and several other places. The Sikh leaders who followed him, it is claimed, did not spare either

* Besides about 5000 Sikhs killed during the campaigns of the Tenth Master, "atleast 25000 lost their lives under Bandā Bahādur." The Moghal Governor, Abdul Samad Khān (1713-26) killed not less than twenty thousand and Zakriyā Khān (1726-45), an equal number. Yahiyā Khān (1746-47) destroyed about 10,000 in the first Ghalughārā (holocaust). Mir Mannu (1748-53) slaughtered more than thirty thoussnd. Adeenā Beg (1758) put to death atleast five thousand. Ahmad Shāh Abdāli and his Afghān Governors butchered around 60,000. Abdāli's Deputy, Najib-ud-Daulā, slew nearly twenty thousand. Petty officials and the (Muslim) public must have cut to pieces another 4,000. This makes up a total of 2 lákhs. (H. R. Gupta, History of the Sikhs, part II, Pp. 255-56).

Muslim life or their religious sentiments whenever an occasion arose. That their ferocity was confined to a few points, like Sirhind (where an unbelievable tragedy had occurred in the massacre of the two innocent children of Guru Gobind Singh) or a few individuals who had personally participated in such iniquities or in demolishing or desecrating the holiest of the Sikh shrines at Amritsar does not mitigate in the eyes of the Muslim historians the Sikh crimes against the Muslims.* But, a note of caution must be sounded here. While on the face of it, it appeared to be a war between the faiths of the victor and the vanquished, if we look carefully beneath the surface, the view assumes a different perspective altogether. It is from the Muslim Afghāns that the Muslim Moghals wrested the throne of the Hindustān. And two centuries later, the Afghāns turned the tables on them.

The Sunni Muslims of the north fought the Shiā Muslim Kingdoms of the south. And not all the forces of either party were Muslims. The indigenous Hindus were also fighting on both sides. The Marāthās were fighting not only the Moghals and Afghāns, but also the Hindu Rājputs who, in turn had "invited" Ahmad Shāh to chastise the Marāthās. The Marāthās helpd the Moghals against the British (and also against the Sikhs for a time) and fought with each other also with equal zest, when the occasion arose.‡ It was

---

* Apart from the authors of *Ibrat Nāmā*, *Jang Nāmā*, *Siyar-ud-Mutākhrin* and other such records, even the modern and enlightened Muslim historians, like Mohd. Latif, cannot help such judgment. On Ahmad Shāh Abdāli's desecration of the holy tank at Amritsar and the blowing up with the gunpowder of the central temple itself, Latif has only to say that Abdāli acted "in strict conformity with the law of his religion and was actuated be a sense of duty." And further that "the sacrilegous outrages committed by the Sikhs on the Muslim mosques and shrines were now avenged and paid with compound interest." (P. 284). But no specific instances are offered by him as to which historic or sacred Muslim places were destroyed or desecrated by the Sikhs ? However, the Sikh "atrocities" are also justified by this historian by saying, that "the indignities suffered by them (the Sikhs) were not of a nature to be easily forgotten. Thirst for revenge rankled in their breast. It was now their (Muslims') turn to suffer, etc." (pp. 285, 291).

‡ Elphinstone has some very pertinent remarks about the Marāthās and the Rājputs. Says he:— "They (the Marāthās) are active, laborious, hardy and persevering. If they have none of the pride and dignity of Rājputs, they have none of their indolence or want of worldly wisdom. A Rājput warrior as long as he does not dishonour his race seems almost indifferent to the result of any contest he is engaged in. A Marāthā thinks of nothing *but* the result, and cares little for the

a Rājput prince of Jaipur, Rājā Jai Singh, who battled against Shivaji on behalf of Aurangzeb, defeated him and made him a Moghal vassal. The Rājput princes were a pillar of strength to the Moghal rule and were not favourably disposed to each other, clan clahing with clan and inviting strangers and aliens for help against their own people. The instances of the common mass of Hindus and Muslims staying in peace for centuries together in the innumerable villages and towns of Hindustān cannot also be brushed aside too easily. And what is one to make of the Hindu influences on Islām even in the matter of religion and vice versa.*

"A holy" war against the "others" may be justified for any other religious creed, but it never was for the Sikhs whose founder built the foundations of his faith on the premises: "there is no Hindu, no Musalmān". The fifth Guru included the utterances of the Hindu and Muslim divines, along with those of his own house in the *Ādi-Granth,* which is now worshipped as the "Guru" of all Sikhs.

F. N. Contd.

means if he can attain his object. For his purpose, he will strain his wits, renounce his pleasures, hazard his person, but he has not a conception of sacrificing his life, or even his interest for a point of honour.........". (Oxford History of India, Pp. 410-11)

* See also the introduction for more references and details. Writes Dr. Tārā Chand, the well known historian and author of the "Influence of Islām on Indian culture":- "The Muslim mystic (Sufi) who sets out upon the path of union (*wasal*) or absorption (fanā) always needs a spiritual guide or *Murshid*, for if a man has no teacher, his *imām* is Satan. The guide or the preceptor (Pir or Sheikh, corresponding to the Hindu Gurū) is the first round which the whole machinery of Sufi monachism moves. His authority is divine......Dhul Nun asserted that a true disciple should be more obedient to his Master than to God Himself......the discipline of the seeker is *dhikr* (zikar) which ordinarily means remembering God and repeating his name, but which includes all devotional practices which include ecstasy and trance...there are two kinds of it, dhikr-i-jali (reciting aloud or *japam*) and dhikr-i-khali, or reciting mentally (*ajapā jāp*)...There has been much dispute among theologians as to the lawfulness of music (Hindu and Sikh practices) and dancing (a typically Hindu practice) regarded as religious exercises...... The encouragement given by most Moghal rulers to painting, love-poetry or music is well-known, though orthodox Islām forbids both activities. "The style (in painting) created by the Hindu and Musalman artists of the Mughal Court, was copied with local variations by court artists of Jaipur, Jammu, Chambā, Kāngrā, Lāhore, Amritsar, and distant Tanjore. (As for architecture) the places whether built in Jāmnagar, or in Calcutta or in Panjāb by Sikhs or by Jains in Central India are all in the same style of Hindu-Muslim (or Indo-Sarcenic) architecture..." (pp. 81-83) The Indian classical music is still a rage even in Afghānistān.

According to a legend, a well-known Muslim Sufi Saint, Miān Mir of Lāhore, laid the foundation stone of the sacred Sikh temple at Amritsar. When they took to war (no choice was left to them), Guru Hargobind as much as Guru Gobind Singh recruited a sizeable body of Muslims in their armed ranks. And so did Bandā Singh Bahādur. Jehāngir martyred Guru Arjun, but befriended his son, Guru Hargobind, who built a mosque for his Muslim troops. Guru Gobind Singh proclaimed in his verses :—"The same to me are the temple and mosque." The life of the Tenth Master was itself saved by two Muslims, Nabi Khān and Ghani Khān, when he was being pursued and hunted from all sides by the Moghal forces. And Guru Gobind forgetting the atrocities and iniquities heaped upon his people and even his whole family—father, mother, and all the four sons—by Aurangzeb or his minions, helped Bahādur Shāh, his Sufi son, in the war of succession. And the Shāh honoured him publicly in the royal court. With the Hindus, the Sikh movement had the best of relations at all times. The Sikhs had sprung largely from them and at the time of stress, the Hindus by and large stood by them and served as their rear-guard. The Sikhs fought for them as much, and never for once injured their religious sentiments and susceptibilities. In fact, cow-slaughter by the Muslims became many a time an issue of great religious significance to the Sikhs as also the preservation of the sacred monuments of the great Hindu faith.

If political fights, therefore, assumed also a religious significance, the fault lies as much in the situation inherent in medieval times as the exploitation of religion by the war-mongers, whose real interest was loot and domination, but who wore the mask of religion to deceive the unwary.*

* While the liberty of outlook of Akbar the Great has been noted by all historians to the point of his being called anti-Muslim, Jehāngir has also been termed an atheist by Sir Thomas Roe. So did Mullā Ahmad. The contracting of marriages by Mughal kings into Hindu Rājput homes and the recruitment of the Hindus into high civil and military posts by most of them has been already referred to in the previous pages. Even the pre-Moghal Afghāns and Persian kings were more influenced by their desire to consolidate their rule among an overwhelming mass of Hindus than by their craze to promote Islām. As Zia-ud-Din Barni says:— "Between the *Sunnat* (tradition) of the prophet Mohammad and his mode of life, and having the customs of the Irānian emperors and their mode of life and ruling them is a complete and a total contradiction and total opposition". (*Fatwasi-Fahandari*).

If religion were the sole motivating force of this bitter and unending warfare between the Sikhs and Muslims as such, the Sikhs, after assuming power, would not have fallen apart as miserably as they did till the great Ranjit Singh rose to unify them through war, diplomacy, the bonds of matrimony or the sheer assertion of power, nor the Sikh power in the Panjāb would have been demolished so recklessly and so speedily after his demise, Sikh fighting Sikh. And the Mālwā Sikhs would not have stood so much aloof to preserve their own self-interests when the overwhelming majority of the Sikhs elsewhere were being persecuted *en masse* and fought to the finish, and religious sentiments of Sikhs everywhere were being wounded and attacked.

After having sounded this necessary note of caution, we revert to our story.

The Sikhs, as we have said in the previous chapter were now masters of the Panjāb, though divided in authority among the twelve Misals. "The possessions of the Bhangis extended north from their cities of Lāhore and Amritsar to the Jehlum and then down that river. The Ghanais dwelt between Amritsar and the hills. The Sukarchakias ruled South of the Bhangis, between the Chenāb and Rāvi. The Nakkais held along the Rāvi, south-west of Lāhore. The Faizulpurias possessed tracts along the right bank of Beas and the Satluj, below its junction. The Āhluwāliās similary occupied the left bank of the former river. The Dallēwālias possessed themselves of the right bank of the upper Satluj and the Rāmgariabs lay in between these last two, but towards the hills. The Karor-Singhias also held lands in the Jullundur-Doāb. The Phulkias were native to the country about Sunām and Bhatinda, to the south of Satluj,and the Shahid and Nishānias do not seem to have possessed any villages which they did not hold by conquest, and thus these two Misals, alongwith those of Mānjhā, who captured Sirhind, viz.., the Bhangis, the Ahluwāliās, the Dellēwālias, the Rāmgarhias and the Karosinghias, divided among themselves the plains lying south of the Satluj, under the hills, from Ferozepur to Karnāl, leaving to their

F. N. Contd.

Said Alla-ud-Din Khalji to Quāzi Mughis-ud-Din:— "Whatever I consider to be in the interest of Govt. I order. I do not know what the God will do to me on *Roz-i-Kiāmat* (Day of Judgement)."

allies, the Phulkias, the lands between Sirhind and Delhi which adjoined their own possessions in Mālwā."*

Their respective as well as total military strength has been variously estimated at this time. Forster says in his "Travels" (1783) that the Sikh forces were estimated at 3 lakhs, but might be taken at 2 lakhs. Browne estimates about the same period their strength to be around 73000 horse and 25000 foot. Twenty years later (1803), Col. Franklin said the Sikhs could muster 2,48,000 cavalry, and in another book

---

* J. D. Cunningham, "History of the Sikhs," pp 97-98. The presentday villages bordering Delhi called *Singhu, Singhora, Bad-Khālsā* etc. point to the stationing of Sikh troops here in these days. The attacks around Delhi and across the Jamnā right up to Oudh were made inorder to weaken both the Moghal and the Rohillā powers, the main props of the Afghān mercenaries in India. In his secret report of March 5, 1779 to Warren Hastings, Mr. Middleton, British Resident at Lucknow, has this to say:—"The (Moghal) king (however displeased at the delay which their differences occasioned, and at the same time) alarmed at the accounts he daily receives of the ravages of the Sikhs about the environs of Delhy (insisted preemptorily on their concluding the negotiations so that) he might immediately return to oppose the incursions of the Sikhs." Similar reports were being received by the British Governor-General from his other representatives as well. The Budhā Dal (or the army of veterans) had, in fact, started ravaging the Gangetic Doab since 1764. Shāh Ālam, emperor of Delhi, had to purchase his peace by payment of 11 lakh rupees to the Dal, in March, 1788. In 1784, both the Sikh Dals plundered Bharatpur and the Sikhs could be persuaded to retire only on receiving a tribute of Rs. 7 lakhs. The Bharatpur ruler, Jawāhar Singh, persuaded the Sikhs to attack the territories of his rival, Mādho Rāo, of Jaipur. The Sikhs complied with his wishes and the ruler of Jaipur had also to pay them a heavy subsidy. Jawāhar Singh also used the Sikhs against Dholpur. The Sikhs attacked right upto Oudh in the Gangetic Doab 17 times in 20 years (1763-1788), once (in 1710) under Bandā and thrice between 1795 to 1804, attacking and gathering tribute from the areas of Saharanpur, Meerut, Deoband, Derā Dun, Mathurā, Rohilkhand, Aligarh, Muzaffarnagar, Ghaus Garh etc. with an army of upto 50,000 horse and one lakh infantry. The Cis-Satluj Sikh Sardārs and chiefs participated actively in these compaigns. Though G. R. C. Williams offers them rich tributes for suffering and bravery, he also credits them with "deceitfulness, cruelty and wine and bhang bibbling." (For details see G.R.C. Williams' three articles in the *Calcutta Review* "Vols. LX and LXI, pp. 102-145).

* When the Sikhs marched towards Delhi in March 1776, Najib's son, Zābitā Khān, not only joined them in their march upon Delhi but also become a Sikh, and was named Dharam Singh. A well-known saying has entered our folklore about this incident: *Aisā EK Guru Kā Chelā, Ādhā Sikh, Ādhā Rohelā.* (Such is this singular disciple of the Guru who is half-Sikh and half Rohilla). Zābitā Khān, however, got reconverted to Islām due to strong opposition of his orthodox subjects.

that could lead into action not more than 64,000. George Thomas estimated their strength at 60,000 horse and 5000 foot.

Their individual strength is a matter of even acuter controvery. However, it is certain that the Bhangis were the most superior in strength (20,000 men) and far vaster in possessions. The strength at this time of the Sukarchakias, who became the supreme masters of the Panjāb under Ranjit Singh later on, was only about one tenth of it (i.e. about 2000 horse*) which makes one more thing clear. In a revolution, it is never the numbers that count, but the character of leadership. Even a good cause is not enough in the hands of a selfish, corrupt or a divided leadership, nor even the spirit of supreme sacrifice among their followers.

Each Misal, as has been stated, was the master in its own dominions. Their Government by any standards of that time was more humane, just and impartial as between one citizen and another, irrespective of creed. Most Muslim writers deprecate their rule at this time as "harsh and oppressive." But, according to impartial observers, the relations between the rulers and the ruled were intimate and cordial. "The Sikh chiefs regarded their subjects as members of their family, and the people paid them by their sincere devotion and

---

* It is stated in the Annual Register (1809) that they (the Sikhs) make good soldiers, and can march from 40 to 50 miles a day, for a month together." There was practically no drill or systematic training in shooting (for the principal weapons were the sword, the scimitar and the spear, besides bows and arrows and, a restricted use of matchlocks) or the European discipline which was subsequently introduced by Ranjit Singh. The place of discipline was supplied by enthusiasm or the war-cry of *Sat Sri Akāl* or *Wahiguru Ji Kā Khālsā, Wahiguru Ji Ki Fateh.*" There were no regular uniforms. "The common trooper was clad in a turban, a shirt with open sleeves, and a pair of short drawers with tight fitting slippers. But the chiefs were often seen in chain armour, steel helmet, breast-plate, back plate, wrist guards and greaves." Used to extreme hardship, they would, a little away from the battle-field, parch a little grain for themselves, and despised the comforts of a tent. In lieu of this, a horseman was furnished with two blankets, one for himself and the other for his horse placed beneath the saddle with a grain-bag and heel ropes. This in time of war was the whole baggage of a Sikh." (Choprā : *Panjāb as a Sovereign state* P. 52, quoting Francklin's *Memoirs of George Thomas*).

According to Osborne, the twelve Misals could bring into field 70,000 horse. (Ranjit Singh. P. 10). Princep gives their break-up as :—Bhangi (10,000), Rāmgarhiās (3000), Kanahiyā (8000), Nakkai (2000) Ahluwāliā (3000), Dallewāliā (7500), Nishānwālās (12000), Faizaipuriā (2500), Karorsinghias (12000), Shahid (2000), Phulkian (5000) Sukarchakariā (2500). (*Origin of Sikh power*, P. 25).

respect. Was it not a marvel to see the Sikh chiefs squatting on the ground in the midst of their subjects plainly dressed, unattended by an escort, without any paraphernalia of Government talking, laughing and joking as if with their comrades, using no diplomacy with them, but having straight-forward dealings, simple manners, upright mind and sincere language. If their rule was sometimes harsh, it was paternal; if it was occasionally strict, it was sympathetic; if at times it appeared crude and rough, it was mild and tender."*

As against one Englishman describing their rule as "an administration without law, an aristocracy without conscience, roads without traffic and fields overgrown by forest," the *Asiatic Annual Register* (1809), gives the following eye-withness account of a traveller, an Englishman, who travelled between Buriya on the Jamuna to Lahore in 1808. Says he :—

"I was much gratified with the general appearance of the country, then in a state of high cultivation. The people were well dressed and bore every appearance of health, ease and contentment—the effect of a just and good government. I heard not one cause of complaint.

"The cultivators are assessed to the amount of one-half of the produce of their crops, which is paid in kind to the chief, as money is limited in the Panjab. Every allowance is made to the cultivator for unfavourable seasons and every species of oppression carefully guarded against by the chief.

"Though invested with uncontrolled power, his administration of justice is mild and equitable. He seldom dooms to death for murder; so lenient is the system of policy that crimes of that nature are punished by the temporary imprisonment of the criminal, by corporal chastisement and confiscation of property of every denomination which the chief converts to his own use...The *Kotwāl* submits a detail of all causes before him to the chief by whom alone punishments are awarded. This system seems to have a happy effect in so much that crimes are rarely perpetrated...Persons of all nations enter the towns with confidence and meet with no molestation while they remain...the same attention is paid to an Englishman as in our own territory, by the *Kotwāl* who readily sends the usual supplies of provi-

* H.R. Gupta, *History of the Sikhs,* Part III. p. 130.

sions and *for which no payment is received.* He also furnishes a guard or *chaukidārs* at night...

"Their benevolence is not narrowed by bigotry and disclaims the distinctions of religion or complexion.

"The chief of every town makes a point of subsisting all poor and needy travellers from his own funds.†

"The inhabitants receive the stranger with an air of welcome that prepossesses him in their favour. Contrary to what the traveller experiences in Musalmān towns where he is looked upon with contempt and regarded as an unwelcome intruder.

"One quality particularly raises the character of the Sikhs above all other Asiatics and that is their high veneration for the truth. Both as a people and as individuals, they may be considered as much less addicted to the low artifice of evasion, lying or dissimulation than any other race of Asiatics. Implicit dependence may be placed on their promise in all matters, either of public or private concern..."

Eye-witness accounts of George Thomas, Malcolm, Col. Polier, James Rennell and others corroborate these statements. "They differ from most religionists in that like the Hindus, they are perfectly tolerant in matters of faith." "They preserve good order and a regular Government." "The Zamindars of that country may have found it convenient to place themselves under protection of the Seiks (Sikhs) in order to avoid the more oppressive rule of their former masters."

It is also stated that in famine of 1783, the Sikh chiefs continued their *langar* (free kitchens). In what later was called the Montgomery district and where Sardār Budh Singh ruled occured the famine of 1783. According to the district Gazetteer, "*he* is *said to have sold* all his property and to have fed the people with grain from the proceeds."*

---

† The same writer gives the following information about the prevailing rates of commodities :—

Wheat flour...one rupee a maund (about 40 kilos) rice, 1/2 maund for one rupee; gur (jaggery), 1 maund and 15 seers a rupee; gram, one rupee a maund; other lentils, 35 seers to 1 maund a rupee etc. But, the average incomes except in the case of big land-owners, traders and soldiers, who also helped themselves with loot at the time of war, ranged between two to three rupees per month.

* In fact *langars* for the poor being a part of the Sikh religious ethos, were open all the time by all Sikh chiefs.

Says Malcolm :— "In no country, perhaps, is the *Rayat* or cultivator treated with more indulgence." Trade was as much cared for, and the cities grew in riches and importance. According to the *Rāwalpindi Gazatteer*, "Milkha Singh, the warden of marches in the North-West invited traders from Bhera, Miani, Pind Dādan Khān and Chakwāl to settle in Rāwalpindi and under his auspices the town grew rapidly in importance".

"After the plunder of Lahore by Zamān Shāh, the principal bankers have considered Amritsar the safer place of the two and reside chiefly at the latter city". Deserted ruins like Kalanaur and small settlements like Jagādhri and Nirkoor (in the Sahāranpur distt) developed into flourishing centres of trade and banking.

In the administration of justice, the Panchayats "consisting of men of the best reputation" settled the ordinary affairs of the village. And Malcolm quotes with approval the statement of a Panjābi settler of Calcuttā, "its great superiority over the vexatious legal system of the English Government which was tedious, vexatious and expensive and advantageous only to clever rogues."

In cases of theft, the culprits were fined if the goods were recovered and imprisoned till the fine was paid. If a man persisted in his crime, his right hand was cut off. "The fines were imposed keeping in view the capacity of the offender." The most heinous crimes were punished with the loss of ears, nose, hands or eyes, "though it was rarely resorted to."

There was, however, no capital punishment even for murder. In such cases, either a daughter was offered in marriage or large sum of money paid or 125 bighas of land, if available, were surrendered to the aggrieved family.

Courts were held in towns by *Abdāltis* who were either Muslim Qāzis or Hindu Kāyasths rather than Sikhs. Under a big chief, *Jāgirdārs* were given civi , criminal and fiscal powers as well. In larger states, judges were employed. Bribery was also occasionally resorted to by them, "but the Sikh chief asked every judge, on his retirement, to surrender a part of this estate or money believed to be beyond his normal sources of income." *"In Kaithal and Patiālā, the judges passed as many days in prison as on the bench."*

Inter-state trade was encouraged, as it added to the custom-duties of every state, through which the caravans passed from Amritsar to Māchhiwārā and Patiālā, from where they went to Rājputānā in Hānsi and Rājgarh, or to the Gangetic Doab via Thānesar and Karnāl, or to Delhi via Kaithal, Jind and Rohtak. The caravans were never molested on the way and were given certain privileges. They generally belonged to the clan of Nānak (Guru Putras) or the clans of other Gurus.

The Trans-Satluj Sikh chiefs struck coins in the names of their Gurus, Nānak and Gobind Singh, while the Cis-Satluj Phulkian states in the name of Ahmad Shāh Abdāli.*

As described in the *Ludhiānā Distt gazetteer*, "The conditions of the people other than the cultivators was also of very considerable comfort. They possessed fine physique which showed that they did not suffer from deficiencies of nourishment. They were well-clothed and well-housed". "The Zamindārs were well-to-do. Their homes were generally found to contain valuable property in the way

---

* (i) The Persian inscription in the former case were those made current by Bandā Bahādur, or by Jassā Singh Ahluwāliā while occupying Lāhore. These have been given before. In the cases of Patiālā, Jind, Nābhā and Kaithal, the words on the coins read:—"*Hukam shud zan Kādir bechun ba Ahmad Shāh; Sikkā zan bar seem-o-zar az māhi ta ba māh...Singh Jaloos maimnat manus zarab*", (God the indescribable, commanded Ahmad, the King, to stamp silver and gold currency, from the pisces to the moon...In the year of the reign, associated with prosperity, struck at......).

(ii) The other Phulkian states of Jind and Nābhā were founded a little later than Patiālā, though they owe their origin to same ancestor, Bābā Phul, whose eldest son, Tilokā, is considered to be the founder of the Phulkian dynasty. Gajpat Singh, the grandson of Tilokā after the defeat by the Sikhs of Sirhind in 1763, occupied a large tract of the Cis-Satluj country including the districts of Jind and Safaidon which extended to Pānipat and Karnāl. But he became a vassal of the Delhi emperor, Shāh Ālam II, and started paying him an annual tribute of 3 1/2 lakhs. He was created a Rājā by a Shāhi firmān in 1772 A.D. and struck coin in his state thereafter. Jind, like Patiālā, sought the British protection against Ranjit Singh and helped the British loyally in 1857, and encouraged his troops through his personal presence for which he was munificently rewarded.

(iii) The Nābhā state also resulted in similar circumstances. The grandson of Tilokā, Hamir Singh, founded the town of Nābhā in 1755. He joined other Sikh forces in the attack on Sirhind in 1762 and after victory extended his territory. He struck his coin in 1776. Hamir Singh's son, Jaswant Singh, forged an alliance in 1804 with the British against Holkar, the Marāthā chief, during his advance towards Lāhore. He put himself under British protection against Ranjit Singh in 1809. One year later, the nominal Moghal King of Delhi titled him. He wanted to personally lead his troops at Delhi in 1857, but, the British prevented him on account of his youth, and were content to receive a contingent of 300 from him, He was duly rewarded for his services in the Mutiny.

of bronze and brass utensils, clothes, jewellery and some hard cash."

As between the Hindus and the Muslims living in the same village, descending from the same stock and living under the same conditions, the difference in affluence was marked. "The Musalmān seems to think that his duty is completely performed when he has proclaimed his belief in one God and it is the business of providence to see the rest. As we pass each village, each field, each house, we can tell the religion of its owner by the greater idleness, poverty and pretention which marked the Musalmān. It is difficult to suggest any explanation of the fact".*

The Sikhs were considered "the finest peasantry of India". "The Sikh is more independent, more brave, more manly than the Hindu, and no whit less industrious and thrifty, while he is less conceited than the Musalmān, and not devoured by that carking discontent which so often seems to oppress the latter".†

And yet there was no Hindu-Muslim-Sikh problem as such. "All the three communities as a rule lived peacefully and in social and religious matters they often followed the practices of others". This forsure was due to the all-pervading influence of Sikhism even on the non-Sikh societies. On the one hand, their liberality of outlook encouraged Brahminic ritualistic influences to take hold of the Sikh and even Muslim masses, and on the other made all the religious communities far freer in their food and caste habits and in mutual respect and bonhmoie.

"Except when a cow is killed or a similar outrage is committed upon the feelings of either, they live together in peace........." At some places as in Derā Ghāzi Khān where under the Muslim rule, "the Hindus were allowed to ride nothing but donkeys and were forbidden to wear turbans", the Hindu were so cowed down that unless "he be in Govt employment, he seldom wears anything but a skull-cap or rides anything but a donkey".**

According to the traveller quoted above, "a villager will rarely persist in a charge which he knows to be false...The village life is

* Census report, 1881, i. 103-4

† Ibid.

** *Gazetteer of Derā Ghāzī Khān 1893-97* P. 75, as quoted by Dr. H. R. Guptā (History of the Sikhs, Part-III, P. 159) (also) infinitely more pure in this (sexual) respect than that of an English agricultural village...The Hindus married their girls off at an early age, the Muslims a little later and the Sikhs last of the three". As regards food-habits, "cereals formed the chief article of food. Vegetables were not much in favour, their place was occupied by pulses. Local fruits were freely consumed. Meat was used by a large section of society" but not very regularly. The total consumption of foodgrains for a man per day was about a seer (about 1 kilo). The peasant woman ate as much as the man.

"The Singhs being generally devoted to pleasure, gave every encouragement to *nautch* girls......The Hindu Jāts were in the habit of using *post* and opium and the Sikhs consumed spirits, but the ordinary Hindu and Muhammedan considered it a sin to do so". However, it is also amply recorded that the Hindu and Muslim nobility and rulers (with rare exceptions) freely used liquor, and tobacco was the bane of the Muslim rich as well as poor. The Akālis or Nihangs used hemp (Bhang) freely as a beverage (and some still do.)

"The woman of the poorer classes, including Rājputs and Brāhmins went about unveiled. The shrounded Musalmanee stops, turns her back at our approach, while she giggles within her *chudder*." "The Sikh women, unveiled, rode on horseback and even led troops into the battlefield. Being fond of good food and open air, they were known for the beauty of their shape, their feet and their teeth". Women, with the exception of the wealthiest classes, attended to household work. In the hills, south-eastern and eastern districts, the jāt woman and of the same or lower social position worked in the fields, but not so in the western parts. In the remaining portion of the Punjāb, the Arāin and other lower classes took a hand in agricultural work. Young or old, they all ground corn, brought water from the well and spun in company where they had fun also at the expense of each other. Males being more numerous, polygamy was not common, except among Muslims, the Sikh chiefs and the rich Hindus. The widow of the elder brother would marry the younger one among the jāts, Sikhs as well as others, so that the property of the deceased may not be divided or jeopardised. Girls were favoured by the Hindus as being a favourable commodity for exchange or money, "though a large number of them was considered a curse. Such families and those among the Rājputs and Sikh chiefs whose arrogance and pride deterred them from becoming fathers-in-law," (son-in-law, *Jawāi*, and brother-in-law, *sālā*, is still a term of abuse or contempt among the Jāts) practised the heinous crime of female infanticide, "by strangling her to death at birth and destroyed with ceremony." The Sikh Gurus had strictly forbidden this as also the custom of *Sati*, then prevalent among the Hindu high castes. Dedicating beautiful girls to the temples (like at Jawāla Mukhi) was common among Hindus and frowned upon by the Muslims and Sikhs.

The largest majority spoke their mother-tongue (Panjābi) and wrote it in either the Persian Script (as in the case of Muslims,) or Gurmukhi (as in the case of Hindus and Sikhs). Accounts were also kept in Gurmukhi by the Sikhs. The Brāhmins only used the Nāgri script and the Hindu traders employed a script very akin to Gurmukhi called *Landā* (or mundē).

Arms were manufactured in the Panjāb at several places, but mostly in the Sialkot district. Iron was imported from Mandi and Peshāwar, considered to be the best in India. Matchlocks prepared at Kotli (Sialkot) were in great demand, at fifteen rupees a piece.*

On the Threshold of freedom

While individual Misal territories were internally well-governed, their external relations with the other Misals bordering their own confines deteriorated as time passed. Internecine warfare increased.†

* History of the Sikhs H. R. Guptā Part III, p. 170. The Sikhs employed, besides swords, pikes, *Khandās* (double-edged swords), spears, lances, bows and arrows, sabres and cutlasses, muskets, matchlocks and light artillery, all locally madc. The coat of mail was used by soldiers in warfare, and Bandā Bahadur's available portraits show him as wearing a steel-helmet over his headgear as well. (see the frontispiece in Bandā Singh Bahādur, by Gandā Singh).

† In an age when "each Zamindār who from the Attock to Hānsi—Issār (Hissār) and to the gates of Delhi, lets his beard grow, cries Wah-Gorow, eats pork, wears an iron bracelet and can command from ten followers on horseback upwards, sets up immediately for a seik (Sikh) Sardār" (letter of Col. Polier from Delhi to Col. Ironside at Belgram, May 22, 1776). The democratic message of Guru Gobind Singh was misunderstood and no one was ready to submit to the authority of another, now that the common danger from without had passed. Writes Foster in a smilar vein of an incident at Kheynāspur six years later :— "I saw two Sicque (Sikh) horsemen, who had been sent from their country to receive the Siringnaghur tribute. From the manner in which these men were treated, or treated themselves, I frequently wished for the power of migrating into the body of Sicque for a few weeks;

The heroic fight for half a century waged by the sons of Gobind was forgotten in a decade and all the sacrifices, which have few parallels in human history. Perhaps, the soil was not yet ready for the seed, or the climate unpropitious. When foreign danger no longer threatened their existence and there was no other power within India to measure swords with them, the Sikhs fell a prey to mutual recrimination and warfare.

A pure and unalloyed democratic faith, the Sikh religion admits of no distinction of caste or station. The Sikh Commonwealth to an eminent and sympathetic historian of the Sikhs, H.R. Gupta,* "these confederacies (†), provided ample material for the formation of a

---

F. N. Contd.

so well these cavalier fared. No sooner had they alighted than beds were prepared for their repose and their horses were supplied with green barley pulled out of field. The *Kāfilāh* travellers were contented to lodge on the ground and expressed their thanks for permission to buy what they required. Such is the difference between those who are in and those who are out of power." (Travels (i) 227-229)

* H. R. Gupta, *History of Sikhs*, part III, P. 33.

† One wonders why the Misals instead of being called free republics are called a confederacy. Some historians like Cunningham have called the system "theocratic, confederate feudalism." But the Sikh *Misals* had no characteristics either of theocracy, confederacy or feudalism. The *Misals* (lit. equal) were not founded on any religious or theocratic principle. One *Misal* did not owe any allegiance to the other, except when the *Sarbat Khālsā* through a *Gurmattā* resolved to attack a common target. The chief was elected by consensus and sometime his immediate heairs brushed aside in favour of a more competent hand. No subordinate chief "owed any military or fiscal obligation to his overlord. They could also transfer their allegiance from one chief to another". They fought in the name of God and Guru, each exacted his share of land from his chief in proportion to the services rendered. All that a follower had to bring was a horse and a matchlock. When the *Misals* waged a common compaign, they shared the booty in accordance with the troops each provided, and so also all along the line. But as Nārang points out "sovereignty of the nation rested in the general body or the nation itself", which had however no physical but only a mystic sort of control over them all. Writes Prof. N. K. Sinha :—"We must distinguish between the feudalism of the Sikhs and that obtaining in Europe or in Rājputānā. The Misals were the confederals of equals. A Sikh disdained to acknowledge any earthly Superior; there was, at no stage in Sikh feudal history, a haughty *noblesse* as in Rājputānā or medival Europe. In Rājputānā, the chiefs were divided into distinct grades, like medieval Europe. In Rājputānā vassal Chiefs derived their authority from blood-relationship with the sovereign, unlike among Sikhs and there were no elaborate lists of feudal obligations (except for military service). Gibbon has

mighty republic which might have been the pride of the East as was the one in the West which was founded about this time in the United States of America. But then there was a Washington to convert this idea into a reality. This hero and his comrades were inspired by feelings of law, liberty and love of their countrymen. The Sikhs on the other hand (i.e. the Sikh Misals or their chiefs) were impelled by motives of self-assertion, self-conceit and self-aggrandisement. The Panjāb consequently possessed neither such a man nor such a spirit. The principle of equality inculcated by Guru Gobind Singh was abused by the Sikhs. They degraded the noble teachings of the Gurus, and instead of merging their personality in the community, they considered that the community existed to serve their own selfish ends. This made each Sikh chief haughty, arrogant and egotistic Each Sikh Misal became a centre of rivalry, jealousy and controversy and a home of contention, conflict and collision. Thus, the Sikh democracy resulted in a provincial anarchy, which let loose the forces of disruption and dissolution".

In 1774, Charat Singh Sukarchakiya and Jai Singh Kanaihya together were arrayed against Jhandā Singh Bhangi at Jammu, the former helping the son and the latter the father in their dispute over succession to the rulership of Jammu. Charat Singh was killed by the bursting of his own gun. This loss was too much for the Allies to bear, for Charat Singh's son, Mahān Singh, was too young to be a match for Jhandā Singh Bhangi who had by now become a sworn enemy of the Sukarchakias. A conspiracy was hatched to get rid of the Bhangi chief. A servant in the latter's camp was hired to shoot him down while he was walking, unattended, in his own camp.

The Bhangis left the battle in disgust and the field remained with the Allies who asserted the right of the dissolute son, Brij Rāj Dev, as the rightful heir to the Jammu throne, and the father, Ranjit Dev, who wanted his younger son to succeed him, felt greatly humiliated.

Jhandā Singh's brother, Gandā Singh, who succeeded him, was now looking out for an opportunity to avenge this murder, and

---

F. N. Contd.

has described European Feudalism as the offspring of chance and barbariam. The all-pervading sense of brotherhood and a super-added theocratic outlook would not allow distinctions of rank (among the Sikhs)." (*Rise of Sikh power*, Pp. 110-111)

declared war on Jai Singh Kanaihya. The reason was that on the death of a Bhangi chief, Nand Singh (who held the estate of Pathānkot as a gift from Jhandā Singh Bhangi), his widow instead of marrying the deceased's younger brother, in accordance with Jāt custom, offered her daughter and the estate of Pathānkot to the son of the Kanaihya chief. Fearing repercussions, the Kanaihya chief himself declined the offer, but persuaded Tārā Singh, another notable Kanaihya leader, to marry her. But Tārā Singh turned out to be most unscrupulous. He appropriated the estate but murdered both the mother and the daughter in cold blood!

Gandā Singh, thereupon, demanded the restoration back to him of the estate, which was refused. He came to Amritsar and met Jassā Singh Rāmgarhia who incited him to go to war with the Kanaihyas and offered his own help. Ranjit Dev of Jammu and Pir Mohd. Khān Chathā also sided with them, and they marched together against the combined force of the Kanaihyas, the Sukarchakias and the Ahluwāliās. They fought at Deenanagar for many days, but to the great misfortune of the Bhangis, their chief, Gandā Singh, fell ill and died. Charat Singh, his nephew, who succeeded him, died in battle, and the Bhangis had to retreat to Amritsar.

By now, Sardar Jassā Singh Ahluwāliā and his namesake Rāmgarhia chief had become hostile to each other. The past campaign at Deenanagar had accentuated the animosity. In 1775, both fought each other out at Zahura on the river Beas, in which Sardār Jassā Singh Rāmgarhia was wounded by a gunshot, compelling him to withdraw from the battlefield. The day was won by the Ahluwāliā chief.

A little later, the Ahluwāliā Sardār, while out hunting with a party towards the village Nangal, fell into the hands of Māli Singh, brother of the Rāmgarhia chief. A bitter fight ensued in which several persons were killed, Sardār Jassā Singh Ahluwāliā was himself wounded. Māli Singh put him in a palanquin and brought him to Srigobindpur to be kept in his custody. The Rāmgarhia chief was much annoyed at this. It was preposterous & unchivalrous, he said, to avenge one's wrongs in this surreptitious way. He apologised to the Ahluwāliā chief, asked for his forgiveness and set him free, offering him a horse and a shawl as a gift and properly escorted him out of his territory.

However, this incident rankled in the heart of Sardār Jassā Singh Ahlūwāliā. Meantime, a quarrel ensued between the Kanaihyas and the Ramgarhia's over the sharing of revenues of some possessions which were claimed by both parties, their territories in upper Bārī and upper Jullundur Doabs intermingling with each other's. This was contested and a battle ensued. The Kanaihyā chiefs, Jai Singh and Haqiqat Singh,were helped by the Ahlūwāliā forces. The Rāmgarhia Sardār fought heroically, but was overpowered at Srigobindpur and his garrison was expelled from there. A similar fate awaited them at Batālā and Kalānaur. The Rāmgarhias had to seek refuge in Jullundur Doāb, and from there in the Hissār district which became their home for some time thereafter.

The Kanaihyās and the Bhangis again fought at Jammu on the invitation the new ruler, Brij Rāj Dev, who had killed his brother and one of his sons in 1782 and imprisoned his other nephew. He was extremely unpopular on this account. To divert people's attention, he raked up a controversy with the Bhangis (who had earlier annexed some of his territory) and sought the help of the Kanaihyas against them. The Allied forces won a victory and Jammū became a tributary of the Kanaihyās on payment of Rs. 30,000/- as annual tribute. Soon thereafter, however, the Kanaihyas made up with the Bhangis and occupied the disputed territory themselves. The Rājā of Jammu invited the Sukarchakia chief, Mahān Singh, to his help. The Ahluwāliā chief stood by the Bhangis and the Kanaihyās. However, after some fighting, peace ensued and on certain terms, the Jammu Rājā was allowed to retain the part while the surrounding territory was handed over to Haqiqat Singh Kanaihyā, who was also promised an annual tribute.

However, on demanding the annual tribute only after six months, a quarrel ensued between the Rājā of Jammu and the Kanaihyā Sardār. Mahān Singh who was a great supporter of the Rājā of Jammu and had in fact exchanged turbans with him as a mark of affection and togetherness, was also this time won over by the Kanāihyās.

The forces of both marched on Jammū from different directions, but Mahān Singh reached earlier and looted the city. The Rājā fled to safety in the hills and the terrified rich merchants, who being fabourably situated had accumulated much wealth, disgorged over rupees two crore to Mahān Singh. After depositing the money at his Headquarters at Rāmnagar, he visited Amritsar to pay his homage. There,he visited Jai Singh Kanaihyā also, now his ally, but he was very bitter over not sharing the spoils of the loot in Jammu. "Be off, you dancing boy (Bhagtia)," he shouted, "I have no time for you." Much angered, Mahān Singh left his place.

Jai Singh Kanaihyā now wanted to teach the young and ambitious Mahān Singh a few lessons who had thus played a trick on his old patron. He plundered a few places in Mahān Singh's territory, including Rasulpur and Mandiala. But Mahān Singh worsted Jai Singh at Majitha and he had to flee across the Beas.

Now a new combination of forces arose. Mahān Singh made friends with Rājā Sansār Chand of Kāngrā and Jassā Singh Ramgarhiā who was desperately wanting to get back his possessions. The Allies marched upon Batālā, the headquarters of Sardār Jai Singh Kanaihyā. The battle was joined at Achal, in which Gurbakhsh Singh, the only son of Sardār Jai Singh, was killed. The old veteran was so unnerved at this tragedy that he "burst into tears, emptied his quiver of its arrows and dismounting from the horse, exposed himself to the enemy's fire. Such was the respect the old man commanded, however, that no one touched him in his grief and all withdrew quietly." Sardār Jassā Singh Rāmgarhiā recovered his territory, however, and set up his headquarters at Batālā.

Jai Singh Kanaihyā could not sit idle for long. The loss of Batālā made him restless. He joined hands with the Sukarchakias and won over Rājā Sansār Chand as well. The Allies attacked Batālā. Though Sardār Jassā Singh Rāmgarhia gave a tough fight and foiled all attempts of the opposing forces, with the help of the inhabitants of the town who obviously liked him and gave him much cooperation, the Allies had to raise the seige of the fort after 21 days. But, the seeds of further bitterness had been sown.

Several other similar incidents took place to accentuate dissentions. Gujar Singh Bhangi's three sons fought among one another and killed Sukha Singh, the oldest amongst them. The father fought with Sāhib Singh, the aggressive son, was reconciled, and fell out again. The old man died broken-hearted in 1788 at Lāhore, leaving most of his possessions to Fateh Singh, the youngest among them. In the trouble which started among the two brothers, Sāhib Singh having seized all the possessions of Fateh Singh, the latter sought the refuge of Mahān Singh, who had earlier sided with the former. The hostilities continued for about two years. However, Mahān Singh, in the midst of a battle in 1791, while his forces had laid seige to Sāhib Singh's fort at Sodhra, fainted on the elephant and had to be rushed back to Gujrānwālā where he died two days later. Due to this calamity, the seige was raised, but Mahān Singh had died too early. For his son, Ranjit Singh, was only 12 years of age when he was called upon to rule over the extensive territories of his father, in the face of much hostility and another terrible Afghān invasion which followed.

After the death of his father, Taimur Shāh, in 1793, Shāh Zamān the grandson of Ahmad Shah Abdāli, who was only 23 years of age when he ascended the throne of Afghānistān, started cherishing hopes of an Indian Empire. He made some attempts but failed miserably, and he nearly lost his throne into the bargain. The situation in India was very favourable. His agents were received with great consideration both by Shāh Ālam II, Moghal Emperor of Delhi, and by the Marāthā chiefs who offered robes of honour and other rich presents and cash gifts for their master. The British Governor-General also had sent presents to Shāh Zamān, on his accession to the throne alongwith a conciliatory letter.

Receiving favourable reports from his agents and encouraged by some members of the royal family in Delhi and by Tipu Sultān, ruler of Mysore, Shāh Zamān marched upon India in Dec. 1793. But except for arresting the Governor of Multān and realising arrears of revenue from Sind, he could not proceed further on his expedition of conquest for fear of the Sikhs. He then returned to Kābul.

Meantime, the Moghal emperor, Shāh Ālam II of Delhi, besides the Rohillā chief of Rāmpur and others made a request to

---

* Mention must be mabe about the Karorsinghias in this context. Karorā Singh the founder of the *Misal*, died issueless and his place was taken by Baghel Singh, who is well-known in Sikh history for locating & erecting shrines in Delhi to commemorate the martyrdom of Guru Tegh Bahadur and the staying-places of Guru Harkishan and Mātā Sundri in the year 1788 A.D. What is little known, however, is that when after the sack of Sirhind, the Sikhs were ravaging the country near Delhi, Baghel Singh helped the Moghal emperor, Shāh Alam's forces against them in 1778. Ten years later, when the Marāthā chief, Ambā Rāo, alongwith Ghulām Kādir Rohillā, invaded the Panjāb, Bhagel Singh was the first Sikh chief to offer his submission aud support their expedition. The erstwhile Kalsiā state was founded by this *Misal*. Baghel Singh occupied Delhi also for a little while in March, 1733, but on payment of Rs 3 lakhs in cash & 3/8th of the revenues as tribute by Shāh Alam II, Moghal emperor, he vacated Delhi on the condition that some of his troops would stay back to raise monuments to the Sikh martyrs and heroes which was agreed to. Where his force of thirty thousand stayed in Delhi is still known as *Tees Hazāri*.

the Shāh to invade India. The Delhi King wanted to get rid of the Marāthā control over him. Others had their own scores to settle with their rivals for power. The Shāh, much inflated by these invitations, marched again upon India in Nov. 1795.

By this time, the disunity among the Sikh *Misals* had become sufficiently pronouced and the Shāh was banking upon this in his advance towards Delhi. Ranjit Singh, then only a sapling of 15, was the only exception who was detemined to frustrate his march and invited Daulat Rāo Scindiā, the most prominent Marāthā chief in the North, for assistance. He thought seeing this formidable combination, other Sikh chiefs would also be compelled to fall in line. But the negotitation with the Marāthās yielded no result. The Sikhs under Ranjit Singh did not offer any open resistance upto the river Jehlum. Rohtās,on the Jhleum, where Ranjit's men were holding the fort, was vacated under his instructions, and it was captured by the Afghāns. Hearing the fall of Rohtās, people took to flight from the plains,right upto Amritsar to the hills and other places of safety as speedily as they could. "The means of conveyance were so much in demand that a bullock-cart at Amritsar could not be hired even for a hundeed rupees". Fortunately, the Shāh heard alarming reports of an insurrection from Herāt and hastened back to Kābul from Hassan Abdāl, early in January, 1796. This problem for him was, however, soon settled on his arrival.

But, the idea of the Indian conquest was not banished from the Shāh's mind. He sent his emissaries to Daulat Rāo Scindiā, pretending friendship with the Marāthās. His representatives also waited upon Shāh Ālam II. To both the idea conveyed was that the Shāh was interested only in subduing his troublesome neighbours, the Sikhs in the Panjāb, and was not interested in any further conquests. Strangely enough, he started negotiating with the Sikhs also for a safe passage to Delhi !

The Cis-Satluj Sikh states—Patiālā and others—were favourably disposed towards the Shāh,being his tributaries.

The other Sikh *Misaldārs* were agreeable to give safe passage on the condition that the Shāh part with a sizeable part of his plunder in their favour. But when Ranjit was approached for help, and requested for some presents for the Shāh, he is reported to have said, according to the British records:—"My presents will be personally delivered to the Shāh on the field of battle".

The Marāthās, though the most powerful force at this time in India, were not only disunited, but extremely afraid of Zamān Shāh, who, according to the British Governor-General, "has ever been an object of terror to them." They were, therfore, negotiating with the British to form a joint front against the invader. The Muslims, however, throughout India were greatly enthusiastic and looked upon him as the champion of their faith, the deliverer of their counntry." Leading Muslim nobles of the Panjāb had, therefore, offered him all help, besides the Rohillās, Tipu Sultān and others.

Ranjit Singh was the only one left in the whole way from Peshāwar to Delhi to defend his nation as best as he could. He advanced to the banks of Jehlum with 10,000 horse. At this time, he was only sixteen years of age.

The Shāh crossed the Indus on Dec 6, 1796. The people of the Panjāb hearing of his advance, fled in utter panic to the hills. Lāhore and Amritsar were virtually deserted. Ranjit Singh himself sent his family to Patiāla. Sāhib Singh of Gujrāt and Lehnā Singh Bhangi, chief ruler of Lāhore, also sent away their families to safer places.

Lehnā Singh, the popular ruler of Lāhore, was again contacted by the emissaries of the Shāh, assuring him of the Shāh's good intentions towards him if he did not oppose his advance. Lehnā Singh may have fallen for the bait, but he sent word to he the Shāh that "his comrades were hostile to the suggestion". Later, he himself evacuated Lāhore as the Shāh's forces marched forward unobstructed, except for small skirmishes here and there. The Shāh addressed a letter to Ranjit Singh to the same effect. The proud Ranjit wrote back to say that "he would not shirk crossing sword with the Shāh" as, "through the Guru's Grace, every Sikh was bound to be victorious".

The Shāh's forces were instructed thereupon "to kill all Sikhs who resisted with arms but to spare the rest". And this was followed strictly in relation to other civilians as well. On Dec 31, 1796, his forces entered Lāhore, which they occupied, Lahnā Singh Bhangi, the ruler, having escaped earlier to safety. No engagement was sought with Ranjit Singh on the way, nor the Sikh chief gave the Shāh any occasion for one. Here the Shāh received an "*arzi*" (supplication) from Sāhib Singh, Rājā of Patiālā, "expressive of his perfect submission, and wishing to attend upon him wherever he might please to appoint him".

When, however, the Hindu shopkeepers at Lāhore failed to celebrate the Shāh's victory by illumination etc., the Shāh ordered that except for Muslims, everyone be charged a poll-tax. Much tyranny followed and every Hindu home was disgorged of whatever it had.

On hearing that the Sikhs were gathering at Amritsar in large numbers to oppose him, the Shāh atonce stopped all merry-making and proceeded towards the sacred Sikh city. But to his dismay, the Sikhs had by then fled to safer places. Disgusted, the Shāh had, therefore, to come back to Lāhore. A few days later, in a small skirmish, a cavalry detachment of the Afghāns attacked Amritsar, but were driven back in shame by the few Sikhs who were stationed there.

The Shāh was greatly incensed over this incident which became a matter of prestige for him. He attacked Amritsar personally with a large army. The Sikhs had also decided to take him on and had gathered in sizable strength. They fought with such determination and recklessness in a hand-to-hand fight that the Durrānis retreated in panic, losing a large number of men and horses, the Sikhs pursuing them right to the gates of Lāhore. It is estimated that the Shāh lost 20,000 of his choice soldiers in this single day's fight (Jan 12, 1797) and the Sikhs about 15,000. Ranjit Singh had not boasted in vain. He showed his mettle so decisively that with his 9000 troops he was made reponsible for the security of the sacred city.

The Shāh arrived late in the night at Lāhore and gave instructions for further vigorous preparations. The Muslim chiefs of Multān, Bahāwalpur, Sind and Kasur were all summoned to Lāhore for assistance.

On the Sikh side, Ranjit stood over Amritsar towards the North, Sardar Jassā Singh Ramgarhiā kept watch over Srigobindpur, Gulāb Singh another 20 miles away and Lahnā Singh on the other side of the Beas. However, no help came from the Sikh state of Patiālā, Jind, Nabhā or Kapurthalā. The Marāthā chief remained stuck in their principalities in the Deccan. The Rajputs wanted to get rid of the overlordship and frequent invasions of the Marāthās and would have welcomed any move of the Shāh to weaken them. Similar was the mood of the Moghal emperor of Delhi. The British were out to protect only their own dominions, though the Sikhs, according to the British sources,were desirous of an alliance with them even twenty years earlier. The Sikhs in the Central and the Western

Panjāb were thus left also to fend for themselves. India was a nation indeed !

The Sikhs harassed the Shāh desparately by cutting off his supplies and intercepting his messages. On the other hand, the Shāh's troops being not allowed to plunder were also discontended. He also heard of an insurrection by his brother at Herāt. So, inspite of the entreaties of the Moghal King, the Shāh could not proceed to Delhi and levying a forced contribution on the citizens of Lāhore and collecting 22 lakh rupees, he hastened back to Kābul. He appointed Ahmad Khān Shahānchi-Bashi Governor at Rohtās with 7000 troops to look after his possessions between the Jehlum and the Indus. But, he dared not appoint anyone to this position east of Jehlum.

The news of the Shāh's departure was conveyed to the British Governor-General by the Rāmgarhiā chief, Sardār Jassā Singh, and Rai Singh Bhangi, who received back very friendly replies from him. The tone of the correspondence shows that relations of some of the Sikh chiefs with the English had become rather intimate and they could share each other's confidence.

The Afghān Governor at Rohtās, fearing a Sikh rising against him, tried to forestall them and crossed the Jehlum reaching as far as Gujrat. Here the Sikh forces of various Sardārs, who had gathered to chalk out a plan of action to recover their trans-Chenāb territories, clashed with him so bitterly that over 3000 Afghāns fell in the battlefield. Ahmad Khān was himself killed, his head cut off and sent to Ranjit Singh at Rām-nagar.

Preoccupied with his own problems, the Shāh paid little heed to this grievous rebuff to his prestige at this time. For, he was waiting for a more propitious moment to launch his final attack on India.

About the middle of the same year (1797), the Shāh received through the agents of Tipu Sultān of Mysore gifts of horses, half a million rupees and a written request to invade India or help Tipu with 20,00 soldiers on payment of three crore rupees in addition to their expenses". The Rājās of Jammu and Kāngra likewise made similar requests through their agents. The Muslim chiefs of the Panjāb, including those of Kasur and Jhang followed suit. The dispossessed Nawāb of Oudh also sought his help against the British. The Shāh, in order to ascertain who infact would stand by him in case of a fresh invasion of India, sent out his agents with letters to the Moghal emperor, the British Governor-General, the Nawāb of Oudh, the

Rohillā Chief, Tipu Sultān and others "in which their help was sought to extirpate the Marāthās and the Sikhs."

The British were not very favourably disposed to the Shāh's overtures. Instead, they tried to cultivate the Sikhs, without forging a formal alliance with them for some sort of a common understanding ro repel the invader. How far the others, who had promised him help could render effective assistance to him, however, remaind to be seen.

The Sikhs, expecting the invasion in the winter of 1797, assembled at the Diwāli festival at Amritsar. Rājā Sāhib Singh of Patiālā, also invited to the conclave, refused to join. In fact "Sāhib Singh received letters (from Shāh Zamān) in full court and after applying them to his forehead (as a mark of respect) delivered them to his *Munshis* to be read out." The Sikhs could muster a lakh of soldiers, but, being divided among themselves, no one put trust either in the soldiers or the promises of the other.

The youthful Shāh, hardly 28, crossed the Indus on the Oct 19. Two Sikh posts at Sarāi Kālā (Taxila) and Rāwalpindi were evacuated in haste, after a brief fight. He reached Gujrāt and Wazirābād. The Shāh had warned the Rājās of Kangrā and Jammu not to give refuge to the fleeing Sikh civilians, as the countryside was being deserted right upto the river Satluj. Ranjit Singh sent desparate message to Gulāb Singh Bhangi and others, camping at Amritsar, to come to his aid. Sada Kaur, Ranjit's mother-in-law, who was also camping there coaxed them :—"If you are Sikhs, march out to relieve Ranjit Singh. Else, change your dress with mine and I will proceed against the enemy". Ranjit Singh also reached Amritsar and sought their assistance.

Hearing that the Sikhs were gathering at Amritsar, the Shāh sent forth a force of 10,000 to attack them. The Sikh forces under Ranjit Singh, Sāhib Singh, Gulāb Singh, Jodh Singh and Budh Singh, which were hardly one fourth of the Shah's, took the Afghans on, in the outskirts of Amritsar. After a bitter fight, in which about 500 men on each side fell on the battlefield, the Afghāns were obliged to beat a retreat to Lāhore.

Meanwhile, seeing more trouble ahead and everyone's future at stake, more and more Sikh forces started gathering at Amritsar, till they had collected a force of about 10,000 horse. Bābā Sāhib Singh

Bedi, claiming direct descent from Guru Nānak, also joined with his 4000 horse. As good fortune would have it, there were dissentions at this time in the Shāh's party as well, one of them, Sher Mohd. Khān, becoming an informer of the Sikhs. He advised the Shāh to conciliate the Panjāb, particularly the Sikhs, as fresh disturbances were expected at Herāt. The army was disaffected due to lack of resources. The people had fled from the plains with their precious belongings and so even plunder was not possible. The Sikhs were prepared to meet the Shāh on the field of battle, and would destroy his rear if he marched to Delhi. The Marāthās and the British had also united against him. Other generals, however, incited the Shāh to take a final, desparate plunge and march upon Delhi. But, the Shāh wisely decided on caution.

The Sikh troops under Ranjit Singh and six other chiefs, including his mother-in-law, Sadā Kaur, were becoming restive and decided to move towards Lāhore with a combined force of 11000 horse, with a view to cutting off the Shāh's supplies from Kasur and Amritsar. Several bloody engagements between various detachments took place, inflicting not only losses of men, weapons and horses for the Shāh, but making foodgrains scarce and extremly costly in his camp. The Sikh forces surrounded Kasur but soon raised the seige, after plundering parts of it, on the arrival of large reinforcements—around 24,000 in two detachments—from the Shāh. But, they were far from cowed and were threatening him from all sides. An Afghān detachment of 1500 coming from Kābul was waylaid, near Gujrānwālā, destroyed and relieved of all its baggage by Dal Singh, uncle of Ranjit Singh, and before the Shāh's reinforcements could join battle with him, he with his troops had reached Amritsar.

Dismayed, the Shāh again tried his hand at reconciliation, and sent costly presents through Diwān Atmā Rām to the Sardārs at Amritsar, inviting them to acknowledge him the overlord of the Panjāb, while he would leave the internal administration to the Sikhs. Some Sikh chiefs, due to personal rivalries, indicated secretly their desire to accept the Shāh's terms but,this move being discovered,was nipped in the bud, and every Sikh chief took a vow not to negotiate separately, and not to submit to the enemy under any circumstances though some minor chiefs did submit, as at Sheikhupura, and offered *nazarānā* to the Shāh. Efforts were,on the other hand,increased to surround and blockade the Shāh at Lāhore.

"There is no Hindu, no Musalmān"

GURU NANAKDEV with a disciple
(A 19th century painting)

*"When no other remedy is of any avail,
It is but righteous to unsheath the sword."*

GURU GOBIND SINGH (on horse back)
(A late 18th century painting)

"The Guru has p d us sovereignty"

BABA BANDA BAHADUR
(Founder of first Sikh Kingdom)

S. JASSA SINGH AHLUWALIA

"In victory magnanimity, in defeat defiance".

MAHARAJA RANJIT SINGH

SARDAR HARI SINGH NALWA
(C - IN - C of Sikh Kingdom)

RAJA DHIAN SINGH DOGRA
(Prime-Minister of Sikh Kingdom)

MAHARAJ CHARAN SINGH (Sant Mat)

BABA RAM SINGH (NĀMDHĀR

SANT ATTAR SINGH (Sikh Saint)

BABA RATTA
(Nirānkāri)

Prof. PURAN SINGH
(Writer - Philosopher)

BHAI VIR SINGH (Saint-Poet)

BABA KHARAK SINGH (Akali Leader)

MASTER TARA SINGH (Akali Leader)

SRI AKAL TAKHT (Amritsar)

GOLDEN TEMPLE (Amritsar)

GIANI ZAIL SINGH
(ex-President of India)

S. BALDEV SINGH
(Ex-Defence Minister of India)

S. SWARAN SINGH
(Ex-Foreign Minister of India)

S. PARTAP SINGH KAIRON
(Ex-Chief Minister, Panjab)

S. GURBAKHSH SINGH (Writer)

AMRITA SHERGIL (Artist)

S. HUKAM SINGH
(Ex-Speaker, Lok Sabha)

BHAI KAHAN SINGH
(Sikh Scholar)

SARDAR BUTA SINGH
(Ex. Home Minister India)

S. DARBĀRA SINGH
(Ex-Chief Minister, Panjab)

S. SURJIT SINGH (Barnala)
(ex-C.M., Panjab)

S. PARKĀSH SINGH BĀDAL
(ex-C.M., Punjab)

Gen. S.S. UBAN
(Hero of Bangladesh war)

AIR CHIEF MARSHAL ARJAN SINGH
(Hero of Indo-Pak war, 1965)

SANT H.S. LONGOWAL
(Akali Leader)

SANT FATEH SINGH
(Akali Leader)

SHRI G.S. TOHRA
(President. S.G.P.C.)

J.S. BHINDRANWALA
(Fundamentalist)

BHAI JODH SINGH
(Sikh educationist)

DR. GANDA SINGH
(Historian)

The Afghān King made auother attempt to conciliate them and sent an agent, Neki Singh, to Amritsar, for talks. But, the Sikh spokesman, Bābā Sāhib Singh Bedi,* refused to listen to him, saying "we have taken the country of our forefathers through suffering and sacrifice and mean to keep it free, under our charge, whatever the cost,"* though this also sowed dissentions in their ranks. Neki Singh was shown respect, *khilats* were exchanged, but he was also asked to persuade the Shāh to go back home. Two representatives of Ranjit Singh and Bābā Sahib Singh Bedi also accompanied the Afghān agent to the Shāh's camp. They were prepared to return the booty, if negotiations proceeded favourably. At the same time, the Sikh pressure on Lāhore was also increased so much that the Shāh kept all its gates but one closed, even in the day time, and strict vigilance was exercised at this gate too. "So acute was the distress in the Shāh's troops that they started selling their clothes to buy food."

The Sikh agents were, therefore, warmly received by the Shāh's Vizier. They were escorted to Lāhore for about 8 miles by an Afghān contingent of 1000 horse.

But, while the negotiations were proceeding, came the calamitous news for Zamān Shah that the King of Persia had invaded Afghānistān and the Shāh's brother had again raised his standard of revolt. The Shāh, therefore, ordered that his forces march quickly back to Kābul.

No sooner had the Shāh left than the Sikh Sardārs, Chait Singh and Milkhā Singh, entered Lāhore (Jan 5, 1799) and occupied it. The other Sikh chiefs went back to their own territories.† The Shāh was beset with many misfortunes on the way. Due to incessant rains, the roads were broken, the rivers were in flood. Most of the Shāh's

---

* Bābā Sāhib Singh Bedi, grandson of Bābā Kalādhāri and son of Bābā Ajit Singh, claiming a direct descent from Guru Nānak was a formidable spiritual leader of these days, highly venerated by all sections of the Sikh society. Besides being a well-known preacher of his faith, he was also a great warrior and conquered considerable territory with his headquarters at Unā (in the distt of Hoshiārpur). We shall come across his name later in these pages many times as a wise counsel, conciliator, fighter and a source of great spiritual comfort at the time of stress and crisis,

† It is in these times that the following saying became prevalent : "*Singh Guru dē chatthē: Khān Peen nū wakho wakhrē, Laran bhiran nū Katthē* (*i.e. The Guru's Singhs* are chivalrous warriors like the Chathās. They eat and enjoy separately, but when they have to fight (the enemy), they fight together).

baggage, including 12 pieces of artillery, were sunk, while crossing the Jehlum. Many war-weary soldiers, due to hunger or privation, fell on the way or deserted him. Wild Muslim tribes of the North-West plundered his rear. Thus depleted of men and resources, Shāh Zamān, King of Kābul, reached Peshāwar on Jan 30, 1799, and back home about two months later.

This was the last of the Muslim invasions upon the Panjāb, the gateway to Hindustān. The field was now free for the Sikhs to make or unmake their destiny. They decided on nothing but total sovereignty, and it was not before long that they accomplished their cherished dream under Ranjit Singh, 'lion of the Panjāb.' The hour was ripe and the man had arrived to fight both internal discord and external challenges. The seed of freedom in which everyone was an equal share-holder sown by Guru Gobind Singh was soon to blossom into flower and fruit, and no unfavourable wind or weather was to challenge its right to life and liberty under the sun.*

---

* That except for brief periods, when the Afghān attacks came from the North-West, the whole of upper India was under the sway of the Sikhs from 1765 onwards, is testified by no less a person than Warren Wastings, British Governor-General (1772-85). Writes he :— "The Sics (Sikhs) who may be considered as a sect of schismatics rather than a nation have for some years past taken advantage of the weakness of the (Moghal) King's administration to invade and possess all his northern dominions." (*Warren Hasting's Memoirs relative to the state of India*, London, 1788).

CHAPTER XVIV

THE PANJĀB AS A SOVEREIGN STATE

Ranjit Singh* was only twelve years of age when his father, Mahān Singh,died. The conduct of the Sukarchakia Misal was, therefore, left to the care of his mother, Māi Malwain and the Diwān or Prime Minister of her husband, Lakhpat Rāi, a Khatri from Nowsherā. But, soon, all the affairs passed into the hands of his mother-in-law, Sadā Kaur, widow of the Chief of the Kanaihyā

* Ranjit Singh was born at Gujrānwālā on Nov. 2, 1780, according to all reliable historians, including Lepel Griffin, Paine, Mohd Latif, Kanaihya Lāl, M'gregor, Gandā Singh, Hari Ram Guptā etc. A plaque is still fixed outside the room of his birth to this day which now forms part of the municipal offices at Gujrānwālā. His great grandfather, Budh Singh, it is said, was initiated into the Sikh faith by the Tenth Master himself.

* Several European writers of the 18th century, besides Latif, accuse Ranjit Singh of having murdered his mother either by throttling her or with the sword, after being assured of her sex-orgies with her Diwān, Lakhpat Rai and a Brahmin,, Laik Misser. The Diwān, sent out on an expedition, was killed, (it is suggested, through a conspiracy). But these scandals and canards are generally spread by the losers against a successful rival, inorder to sow the seeds of disaffection against him and to bring him down in public estimation. History is full of such instances and European writers particularly have given a clean chit to no one who stood in the way of their ambitions. Sohanlāl makes no mention of it, in his *Udmat-ul-Twārikh.* That Carmichael Smyth in his "*History of the Reigning family of Lāhore*" accuses Ranjit's father also with matricide for her mother's intimacy with Hakikat Singh shows how determined some of the British historians of the period were on the character assasination of the entire family of Ranjit Singh, their principal rival in India in the first half of the nineteenth century.

Misal, Gurbakhsh Singh. Ranjit Singh was married at a very early age to her daughter, Mehtāb Kaur, and before he was 18, also contracted another marriage with Rāj Kaur, daughter of Sardār Khazān Singh, the Nakkai Chief. Little care was lavished, it is said by some European and following them, Muslim historians, on any formal education being imparted to him (except in the arts of war) and he, it is said, was either deliberately or unconsciously allowed to dissipate and indulge himself to excess. The two marriages, however, can be seen in a different light also. This was the only way to forge a common front of the various Misals. The only other alternative was war and unending conflict, to the utter ruin of the dream Ranjit had cherished of a consolidated Sikh empire in the North-West of India.

Shrewdness of character, the correct timing for concrete and positive action and diplomacy seem to have been a part of his blood. As soon as he assembled himself and found his actions and ambitions thwarted by treacherous courtiers, or overbearing and self-centred relations, he shook himself out of their demeaning and debilitating influences, and became the sole master of his destiny. He used everyone to promote his interests, but trusted to his own counsels. Ingratitude was, however, not in his grain, nor cruelty or the assertion of undue authority. As we shall see later, in his whole lifetime, he committed no one to death, provided amply for anyone whom he had dispossessed even after a clean battle, and remained defiant in defeat but generous and humble in success, and was human to a fault.

Not very tall but otherwise well-built and highly imposing in address, dignity and appearance (except for the pock marks on his face and loss of the left eye on account of having been struck by small-pox at an early age), a young sapling who had participated in battles with his father from the age of ten, and took over complete power in his hands at the age of seventeen, was beset with all the obstacles that fight for sovereignty has ever been contended with by any one in history. His nation was riven by faction. The Afghāns and the Marāthās knocked at his door constantly. The Panjāb Chiefs following the Phulkian States, would have submitted easily to the British. The Moghals, though much weakened, were still occupying the throne of Delhi. "He found the military array of his country a mass of horseman, brave indeed but ignorant of war as an art", as, for example, his next-door powerful rivals—the English—were. And lastly, he had no large independent financial resources either, nor the latest mechanised arms which the British could field at any time in ample measure. Everything had, therefore, to be begun from the very beginning. The only asset he had was the spirit of dedicated sacrifice inculcated by Guru Gobind Singh and the longing he had planted in their hearts for freedom, in which everyone participated as a co-sharer and as an equal among equals. But what was most disconcerting was that his co-religionists constituted only about 1/10th of the population of the Panjāb he had set his heart to conquer, 80% being Muslims with whom the relations of his community were determined more by the past history of persecution and authority than the needs of the present times. Another 10% were Hindus and even if the two combined their resources, it was hard indeed, if not impossible,to elicit the heart-felt allegiance of the vast majority of the populace.

A fortuitous circumstance, however, had helped Ranjit. All the venerated Sikh Chiefs who had fought the wars of freedom before him either singly or together were dead—Jassā Singh Ahluwāliā, once the king of the whole Sikh people, and the veteran Bhangi Chiefs—Jhandā Singh and Gandā Singh among them. Jassā Singh Rāmgarhia was too advanced in years and Jai Singh Kanaihyā, besides being far from his old self, had now entered into a matrimonial alliance of his grand-daughter with Ranjit (though he too died in 1793).

Militarily, however, the passage to glory was far from smooth. Besides the English and the Marāthās threatening his eastern flank, Sansār Chand of Kāngrā was extending his hill-empire and the Gurkhās of Nepāl had conquered Kumāon, invaded Sikkim and threaened Tibet. The Simla hills were also under their sway. And, the Afghān terror was not yet a thing of the past, nor their low-profile could be taken for granted for good. The Cis-Satluj Sikh states had virtually become a protectorate of the British. The French were seriously contending with the English for supremacy in India. The French Revolution of 1778 in the name of "liberty, fraternity and equality" had, due to its excesses, resulted in arousing against it an all-round hostility, and national defeat and humiliation gave birth to a remarkable warrior-statesman of history, Napolean Bonaparte, who,after restoring order in France, was now seeking an empire for France abroad. He bestrode all of Europe, between 1799 and 1815,and was threatening India. The British had already become virtual masters of large parts of our land in the east, north, west and south. From miserably small beginnings in 1600 as a trading company to compete with the Portugese and the Dutch for trade first in silks and spices and then in saltpetre, silver and gold, they were still struggling a hundred years later with Farukhsiyar in 1715 for a few more small concessions. But, by the close of the 18th century, they were the masters of all they surveyed in India. Let us examine how it all came about.

It was not only their rise as the masters of the high seas, defeating all their European rivals, or their industrialisation, or advances in military science, their money-power through commercialisation which could absorb defeat that won the day for them. What ultimately made this small "nation of shopkeepers" the masters of India—(and indeed of the two-thirds of the whole world, including North America)—was discipline, patriotism and a type of top leadership *which also encouraged* both *a middle-rung leadership, and individual initiative and acted strictly in accordance with the law atleast where their own rank and file were concerned.* It is these qualities which were wholly lacking in their rivals, which enabled them to sweep before them the self-centred though singularly brave and chivalrous rulers, almost throughout India, but disunited in every detail one from the other. *A culturally decaying India, suspicious of each other's motives, where allegiance was totally personalised and leaders acted on personal whims and preferences rather than on the basis of institutions or a well-defined law was (and still is) the main bane of India's political life. The change in a single master's fortune changed a whole people's fortune, and therefore neither loyalty was safe, nor honour, nor property, and personal sycophancy, intrigue and blackmail determined (and still do) one's chances of success rather than individual merit or patriotism.* That is how inspite of many leaders of brilliance among the Marāthā Peshwas, in the Mysore Muslim dynasty, in Bengāl, and among the Rājputs, nothing availed and everyone collapsed before the onsurge of the British.

Ranjit Singh had, therefore, to be extremely conscious and cautious of this new power prowling round his very borders. Daulat Rāo Scindia and his French lieutenant, Perron*, who had established their power around Delhi, together with the British adventurer,

* Perron through his leiutenant, Bourquin, had levied a contribution on the Cis-Satluj states and even entered into an alliance with Ranjit Singh for a joint expedition to the Indus and dividing the country south of Lāhore with him, but later backed out of his promise. Soon after, he fled to British territory.

George Thomas,* were threatening and sharing power. In the same areas all had been swept away by the forces of the Company Bahādur in the early period of Ranjit's rise to power. As the Marāthās were constantly harassing the Phulkian states at this time, the Sikh rulers of these states helped Lord Lake with a force of about 5000 against the Marāthās, who were the virtual masters of Delhi as well, with the Moghal king remaining only a titular head.

Sardār Charat Singh, grand-father of Ranjit, with his Hqs at Gujrānwālā had, in his authority, the Wazirābād, Sialkot-Rohtās, Pind Dādan Khān, region of the Panjāb. Ranjit's father, Mahān Singh, extended his suzerainty southwards, captured Akālgarh and realised tribute from Jammu. According to the British sources, Ranjit Singh fielded ten to twelve thousand horse against Zamān Shāh, during his fourth and last campaign against India in 1798, and harassed the Afghān ruler almost every day. According to Sohanlāl, he even rushed upon the *Samman burj* of the Lāhore fort, in which Zamān Shāh was stationed, fired shots at it and killed a few Afghāns. In his forays, he used to taunt Durrāni with the shouts :— "Come into the open, you grandson of Ahmad Shāh, the grandson of Charat Singh has come to greet you with arms". The Shāh, as has been said before, tried to conciliate the Sikh chiefs and among those who were despatched *khilats* by him was also the young Ranjit Singh, head of the Sukarchakia Misal.

It has already been mentioned that Shāh Zamān had lost 15 pieces of guns, while crossing the Jehlum in flood, on his way back to Kābul. Many writers (European, Muslim and others) have mentioned

* George Thomas, a British adventurer, came to India in 1781. For some years, he took service with Begum Samru, a dancing girl who had married a European adventurer called "Samru" (real name Reinhard), on whose death she inherited his estates of Sardhānā and the leadership of his small army. But, on being demoted by her for misconduct, he got himself employed with a Marāthā chief, Khandi Rao, and taught European drill to his troops. The district of Jhajjar was awarded to him as Jāgir but finding the field rich for adventure, he became an independent ruler in the country about Hānsi and Hissār, where he came into conflict with the forces of the Dal Khālsā and the Karorsinghia and the Phulkiān Misals.

He attacked Patiālā, secured a tribute, and received the submission of Malerkotlā but was driven out of there by Bābā Sāhib Singh Bedi. He is said to have 10 battalions and sixty guns and to have possessed a territory yielding a revenue of 4 1/2 lakhs. He beat back the Marāthā force, under their French general, Perron, twice, but was compelled to surrender to him in 1802 and died the same year.

that as Ranjit Singh retrieved them and sent them back to the Shāh, the latter was so pleased that he sent him a *sanad* authorising him to occupy Lāhore. These conjectures, however, should be dismissed as not only being improbable, but also historically incorrect.

Ranjit Singh possibly did retrieve 15 pieces of cannon from the river Jehlum and, according to most historians, restored some of them to the *vakil* of Shāh Zamān. The Shāh also sent him a *khilat*. But this handing over of the guns was about nine months (March, 1800) *after* Ranjit Singh's conquest of Lāhore on July 6, 1799.*

---

* N. K. Sinha, Ranjit Singh, P. 12. The author states that Shāh Zamān sent *Khilats* not only to Ranjit Singh but also to the rulers of Jaipur and Delhi. (Poona Residency correspondence, Vol IX, No. 7, introduction), which shows Shāh Zamān had not abandoned his craze for the conquest of India and wanted to secure their help. This move on his part perturbed the British so much that they sent their agent, Yusaf Ali, to contact Ranjit Singh in order to dissuade him from any help he might choose to render Shāh Zamān. The British help was also offered to Ranjit to consolidate his power. But before Yusaf Ali could reach Lāhore, Shāh Zamān had already lost his throne. Why Ranjit Singh sent back the guns to Shāh Zamān assuming that he did so at all, may be on account of his deeire to keep his options open and to warn both friend and foe that he would not hesitate to come to an understanding with the erstwhile enemies of his forefathers, if the Sikh power was challenged from within India by any power. Also, possibly he wanted Shāh Zamān not to side with his enemies with whom the latter was in also in secret correspondence.

There is another side also of the story.

The King of Kābul who had literally fled the field in miserable haste and could not wait even for retrieving his guns can not be considered by any chance to be in possession of Lāhore which he could gift away to anyone else, much less to Ranjit Singh,who had challenged his authority at Lāhore valiantly, by firing shots at the Samman Burj where the Shāh was staying. His general, Shahānchi Khān, was killed by Ranjit's forces. Moreover, if he had accepted any such authority from a foreigner, the Sikhs would not have forgiven him as they did not Bābā Ālā Singh of Patiālā. Lehnā Singh Bhangi refused a similar offer from Ahmad Shāh Abdāli in 1767 on the same grounds, and even returned his gifts. According to Waheeduddin "Shāh Zamān (hearing of the capture of Lāhore by Ranjit) sent emissaries to the rival factions and also to him. Ranjit Singh received them with great ceremony, accepted the gifts they were carrying for him and sent them back with more precious gifts: thus forestalling his rivals' designs. Among the gifts he sent were pieces of artillery which the Shāh had lost in the river Chenāb during his retreat and which he had salvaged." (*The Real Ranjit Singh*, P. 66). This statement seems nearer the truth.

According to all reliable historians, Lāhore was governed about this time by the sons of the three Bhangi Sardārs—Lahnā Singh, Gujar Singh and Sobha Singh—by the names of Chet Singh, Sāhib Singh and Mohar Singh respectively. They were "unscruplous, profligate and tyrannical." The Muslims of the town exerted the greatest influence in Lāhore and in the neighbourhood. Two of the most powerful of them were Mian Ashaq Mohammad and Mian Mohkam Din. The former's son-in-law, Badr-ud-din, picked up a quarrel with the Khatris of the town who complained against him to Chet Singh, making even a false allegation that he was in correspondence with Shāh Zamān of Kābul. Chet Singh, without hearing him, seized him and cast him into a dungeon. All efforts to get him released failed. The Sardārs even insulted the mediators. The Capital-city had been devastated time and again by the Afghāns and now another three tyrants had taken over, even though Sikh in name.

Thereupon, the petition was addressed to Ranjit Singh signed by all the leading citizens, Hindu, Muslim and Sikh, including Mian Ashaq Hussain, Hakim Hākim Rāi, Bhāi Gurbakhsh Singh, Mian Mohkam Din, Mohd Bakar, Mohd Tāhir, Mufti Mohd Mokarram, Mir Shādi and others how the famous city and its environs had been plundered and devastated by the present rulers, inorder to satisfy their ever-increasing appetite for liqour, luxury and debauchery, how the citizens felt unprooted and abandoned, and how about half the city had already been deserted.

The young Sukarchakia chief (who had created a name for himself by challenging Shāh Zamān at Lāhore and pursuing him right upto Jehlum) was invited to come and occupy Lāhore. The petitioners pledged to do all that was necessary for securing the object in view. "A citizen personally presented the petition to him at Rasulnagar." Rāni Sadā Kaur, his mother-in-law and the head of the Kanaihya Misal, was similarly addressed. All this shows that Ranjit's repute as a most humane and powerful chief had travelled far and wide.

After satisfying himself that the petition was genuine and the signatories meant to honour what they had represented to do, he started preparing for war. Collecting all the troops he could muster, he left for Batālā where he was joined by his mother-in-law. The forces of both marched towards Amritsar on the pretext of having a dip in the holy tank. From Amritsar, Ranjit proceeded in one march to Lāhore—a distance of 32 miles—with about 5000 men, (chiefly stragglers, according to Latif). On hearing of his approach, all gates that were generally kept open—Delhi, Lāhori and Rashmai (the others having been bricked up) were closed, and put under day and night watch. However, a breach was made by his collaborators in the wall and Ranjit was asked to enter through it silently.

Ranjit Singh fearing treachery and also wanting to advance openly, refused to accept this advice. It was, therefore, arranged that he enter the Lāhori gate on the 13th. Saffar 1215 Hijri (or July 6, 1799) at 8 A.M. On his arrival at the head of barely 500 men, the gate was opened by his collaborators. Small resistance was offered by the troops of the Lāhore rulers, and barely 200 of them dared to cross swords with him. Five of them lay dead on the spot. The remainder of Ranjit's troops also poured into the gate like a torrent and mounted the ramparts of the city. Chet Singh was misinformed on purpose and while he rushed towards the Delhi gate with 500 horse, he learnt to his dismay that the enemy was already inside the city walls,and his safety lay only in running back to the fort where he shut himself up. The other two chiefs fled the city. For 20 hours, fire was exchanged between the defenders of the fort and the forces of Ranjit Singh. All communications to the fort were cut off. Seeing treachery on all sides, the Bhangi chief surrendered the next morning. He was allowed safe and unmolested exit out of the town and Ranjit even offered him a large village as *Jāgir* for his maintenance. Lāhore was occupied by Ranjit Singh exactly one hundred years after the birth of the Khālsā at the hands of Guru Gobind Singh (1699).

Strict orders were issued that no pillage or looting should take place and the citizens shown every respect and consideration to provide them work. The artisans were engaged promptly to repair the unserviceable guns stacked in the fort. The city returned to normal in a few days and never looked back either in prosperity or peace for about half a century thereafter.

Now started a period of unceasing conquest. The immediate target in view after Lāhore should have been Kasur, a prosperous Pathān settlement. Nizamuddin, its ruler, was scared. So he joined hands with the rivals of Ranjit Singh, like Gulāb Singh Bhangi, who controlled Amritsar, Sāhib Singh Bhangi of Gujrāt and Jassā Singh Rāmgarhia. The Nawāb and his Allies attacked Lāhore, from the eastern side of village Bhasin. For two months, they lingered there.

Gulāb Singh Bhangi, however, died of excessive liqour and the other two quietly dispersed. Ranjit, however, held his hand against these rivals and turned his attention for the time being against the other and easier targets, as the Marāthās were also prowling around in the Cis-Satluj states, and were levying contributions upon them. † The British too were watching the situation carefully, and shifting their stand in regard to them in accordance with their varying needs, especially against France under Napolean in Europe and elsewhere.

Ranjit, therefore, attacked Jammu (1800 A.D.), which on account of its safer position had accumulated riches enormously. Jammu submitted to become his feudatory. On the way back, he fell upon Dal Singh, an old lieutenant of his father, who had started intriguing against him and had joind hands with his inveterate foe, Sāhib Singh Bhangi of Gujrāt. Dal Singh was defeated at Akālgarh, taken prisoner but later released on the intervention of a holy man, Bābā Kesra Singh.‡

---

† During this period, the name of Rāni Sāhib Kaur of Patiālā became famous for her daring in battle and able administration. Daughter of Rājā Amar Singh of Patiālā and elder sister of Rājā Sāhib Singh (who had succeeded to the gaddi of his father at the age 6 in the year 1780 and died in 1813 at the age of 39), she fought the Marāthās in 1794 A. D. and suceeeded in consolidating and extending her imbecile brother's rule, who in turn rewarded her with ingratitude, egged on by his Prime Minister, Nānu Mal, and overawed by his queen, Hukman, (aliās Āus Kaur) with whom also he was squabbling all the time. The Marāthā chief, Jaswant Rāo Holkar, is said to have remarked to Amir Ali, the Pindāri chief, "God has sent us these two pigeons to pluck : you take up the cause of one, while I take up with the other." A weakling that Sāhib Singh was, he sought the protection of the British and though their timely intervention would have settled their quarrels, Lord Lake refused to intervene. Later, when the Cis-Satluj Sikh chiefs went to Delhi to ask for British help against Ranjit Singh, he again gave them a cold shoulder considering Jamunā to be the settled British boundary. But when Ranjit Singh actually started his campaigns across the Satluj, the British suddenly changed their front and cried halt to his advances under threat of war.

‡ Latif says that Ranjit Singh trapped him. He invited him cordially to Lāhore to talk peace but took him into custody in the night, marched upon Akālgarh where he was resisted by Dal Singh's wife, Teḥju, who herself led her troops to the battle-field. He further states that the result of the warfare was inconclusive, as Ranjit Singh left soon thereafter to chastise Sāhib Singh of Gujrat, his more powerful ally. On the intervention of the the Bedī Bābā, Sāhib Singh, he was forgiven on punishment of a heavy *nazrānā* and Dal Singh released who soon died thereafter.

He also gave a *Jāgir* to his widow. Sāhib Singh of Gujrat was also punished and but for the intercession on his behalf by Bābā Sāhib Singh Bedi, he would have been utterly ruined. When he returned to Lāhore, as a victor, he was visited by Yusaf Ali, an agent of the British Government, who brought a letter of friendship from his masters alongwith some presents. He was received with courtesy and due honours, presented with a *Khilat* and offered valuable presents for the British authorities.

In the February of the following year (1801), Ranjit Singh formally assumed the title of Mahārājā in a public Durbār and declared that henceforth he be addressed as "Sarkār". All the chiefs, who owed allegiance to him, the Sardārs, *Chaudhris*, the *ulemā*, poets and others, attended the Durbār and offered their allegiance and *nazrānā*. A mint was also established this year at Lāhore but the silver and copper coins struck therein were called "Nānak Shāhi" coins. On one side of the coin was the picture of Guru Nānak and Mardāna and on the reverse the words :— "Guru Nānak ji Sahāi (May Guru Nānak protect us). The words were both in Persian and Gurmukhi. On some other coins, the inscription was the same as on the coins of Bandā Bahādur and *Dal Khālsā* when they first occupied Lāhore, namely,

"*Deg-o-teg-o-Fatah-o-nusrat-bedrang*
Yāfat-az Nānak-Guru Gobind Singh".

In the reverse was the year and the place of coinage.* The first day's coins were all offered to the poor.

---

* In Samvats 1861, 62, 63, and 66 (i, e. 1804, 1806 and 1809, A. D.) coins were struck which were popularly called Morān Shāhi *sikkas*, named after, it is said, Morān, the Muslim singing girl, who captivated the heart of the Mahārājā during these early young days of the Mahārājā's rule and for which the Akālis are said to have refused his offerings at the Akāl Takhat and later levied a propitiatory fine (*tankhāh)* of Rs. 1,25,000/- on him publicly. But, on his pleading poverty, the "culprit" was let off only by paying Rs. 5000/-. (After this, Ranjit sent Morān away to Pathānkot). Choprā. Cunningham and Griffin all confim this story which is also now a part of the Panjāb folklore. But, there is no picture of Morān on this coin, and though one of these coins has an *Ārsi* or thumb-mirror on one side. while others have a peacock's (*Mor's*), tail, their name might have taken after the latter symbol. *MOR* is a national bird of India and its hunting considered a sacrilege by the peasantry. The use of *ĀRSI* also by no stretch of imagination can be

The ungrateful wretch, Sāhib Singh of Gujrat, had again started intriguing against Ranjit and joined hands with Nizāmuddin, the Nawāb of Kasur. Ranjit Singh sent an expedition against Kasur, under Fateh Singh Kalianwālā. Nizāmuddin surrendered after a bitter fight and even offered his brother, Kutubddin, as a hostage, as a pledge for his future good behaviour, and the promise of armed assistance in times of need to the Lāhore Darbār. Ranjit Singh marched personally against Sāhib Singh at Gujrāt, but on his offering *nazrānā* and promise of future good behaviour, returned to Lāhore.

Now, Ranjit clashed with Sansār Chand of Kāngrā, who was pursuing a policy of expansion in the Panjāb hills, and even took possession of some of Rāni Sadā Kaur's territories towards the hills. Sansār Chand was defeated and agreed to become his tributary. Meantime, Ranjit Singh secured the friendship of the Ahluwāliā chief, Fateh Singh, and exchanged turbans with him as a mark of abiding friendship. Now the four Misals—Sukarchakaya (his own), Ahluwalia, Kanihya and Nakai were arraigned behind him. Fateh Singh was apprehensive both of Sansār Chand and the Rāmgarhias. And, all of them were opposed to the Bhangis who at this time controlled Gujrat and Amritsar.

Chiniot was conquered next from Jassā Singh Rāmgarhia. Fateh Singh Ahluwāliā got Pindi Bhatian and Dhanna as his share in the campaign across the Jehlum. Early in 1802 (according to M'gregor in 1800) Prince Kharak Singh was born to Rāni Rāj Kaur and great rejoicings were made. Sensing trouble again at Kasur, the Allies now marched upon the town and brought Nizāmuddin to his senses. He agreed to pay a heavy fine. Ranjit Singh next turned attention to Multān, which was being ruled by Muzaffar Khān, an Afghān, who claimed common descent from Ahmad Shāh Abdāli, and coming from Kandhār had captured Multān during the disturbed period following Nādir Shāh's accession to the throne of Kābul.

Muzaffar Khān finding hostilities against the powerful Mahārājā fruitless, came out to receive him, and offered large

F. N. Contd.
considered an exclusive prerogative of MORAN. It was used (and still is) by every woman of the Panjāb (and indeed India). This insignia may, therefore, as well be a tribute to the entire womanhood of Panjāb, liberated by the Gurus from their age-old thraldom and who (like Sadā Kaur) were playing an active part even on the battlefield.

presents. Elated at this success, Ranjit Singh fell upon Jhang, where Ahmad Khān its, ruler, offered stiff resistance but ultimately submitted and offered to pay an annual tribute. In this advance, according to the British sources, the Mahārājā marched as far as Rāwalpindi* in the north-west. Sansār Chand was at this time feeling very apprehensive of the Gurkhas and needed all the support he could muster. He had, therefore, no opportunity to challenge Ranjit Singh and soon made a solemn request for assistance.

Ranjit Singh, however, could not rest till he captured Amritsar from the Bhangis where a minor, Gurdit Singh, son of Gulāb Singh Bhangi ruled, the actual authority being in the hands of his mother, Mai Sukhan. Ranjit Singh secured the active support of an Amritsar banker, Ruhr Mal and Sheikh Kamāl-ud-Din, Sardār Deori. An innocent request was first made by Ranjit Singh, late in 1802, for the return of *Bhangian di-top* (a famous gun named after the Bhangi chiefs) and called Zam-Zamā,† which was captured from the Abdāli by the Allied forces in 1764 and in which campaign his grand father had also participated actively and was apportioned this cannon, but which was later appropriated by the Bhangis themselves.

The request was seemingly inocuous, but became a matter of prestige for both parties, the moreso because neither trusted the real intentions of the other. The Mahārājā marched with his forces upon Amritsar, and after a fight lasting only about two hours, the mother

---

* So-called because it is established by the side of a rivulet called Rāval. Pindi is from Pind (or village). Now, this is the capital-city of Pākistān, though the actual secretariat buildings etc. are located at a small distance away towards the Musree hills and called Islāmābād. The town had a large & very prosperous Hindu & Sikh population upto 1947, but had to migrate to India due to communal disturbances. It also housed (& still does) a large & beautiful laid-out cantonment.

† This gun was first made in 1757. It is 14 ft long and of 9 1/2″ bore, and was forged under the orders of Ahmad Shāh Abdāli, after collecting brass & copper vessels from the homes of the Hindus of Lāhore as a punishment and also because there was nothing more left with the Hindus to offer. Abdāli could not take it back to Kābul. It is so-named because in 1762 (1764 according to others) the Bhangi chiefs seized it from Khwāja Ubēg Beg, Governor of Lāhore, after a bitter fight, and offered it to Sardār Charat Singh Sukarchakiya who had also participated in the campaign. Later, they took it back from him under a pretext and never returned it. Ranjit Singh secured it after the seizure of Amritsar. In their battle with the British, the Sikhs lost it to them at Pheru-Shahr (Feroze-Shāh) on Dec 21, 1845. Since then, it is being displayed at Lāhore in an open park midway between the museum and the Panjāb University, as a museum piece.

and the child-ruler both fled the field and Ranjit Singh walked in as a conqueror of the holy city of Amritsar, which besides housing the much venerated Sikh temple, also was perhaps the greatest centre of trade and commerce in the entire north-west. It is said, Akāli Phoola Singh brought about a compromise so that without blooshed, Ranjit captured the holy city.

But other momentous events were taking place elsewhere. In Kābul, Shāh Zamān had been deposed and blinded by his brother, Mahmud, only a little after his departure from the Panjāb. He, in turn, was overthrown by another brother, Shāh Shujā in 1803. This palace revolution, one succeeding the other, greatly encouraged the Mahārājā to levy tribute on Jhang and Multān, two Afghān strongholds, and to feel his ground as far Rāwalpindi. Kasur had already submitted, and after Lāhore, the town next in importance, Amritsar, had also fallen in his lap.

In 1804, the Mahārājā held a Durbār and appointed, among others, Sardār Desā Singh Manjithia to command 4000 horse, S. Nihāl Singh Attāriwālā 5000 infantry, S. Hukma Singh Chimni 2000 horse, besides being incharge of the artillery. Ghaus Khān was made a commander of artillery and 2000 horse. Ghaus Khān and Roshan Khān Hindustāni were also appointed Commanders of the Najib platoon. The Bhangi Sardārs, the Ahluwāliās, the Kanaihyas and the Hindu hill-chiefs all agreed to supply military contingents at times of need. All were endowed liberally with *Jāgirs*. But, the sudden advance towards the north of Jaswant Rao Holkar, the Marāthā chief, in collaboration with Amir Khān, the Pindāri, in 1805 (inspite of his earlier setback and defeat at the hands of the British) at Fatehgarh and Dig created a new situation. They had levied tribute on the Cis-Satluj Sikh states and proclaimed that they would be helped by Ranjit Singh and the Afghāns against the British. Holkar was marching at the head of an army estimated to be 15,000 to 40,000 strong (some estimates say it was around 2 lakhs) hotly pursued by Lord Lake. His agents called on the Mahārājā at Lāhore, with presents. Ranjit Singh, thereupon, personally went to Amritsar and received Holkar with full honours and held consultations with the chiefs of other Misals who looked upto him for guidance. While these confabulations were going on, Lord Lake had crossed the Beas, and Holkar still trying for peace through his agents, settled terms with the British. He renounced all his possessions in the North and left for Central India. The Mahārājā was prepared, it seems, to take the plunge and to forge a formidable Sikh-Marāthā alliance to the detriment of Britain, inspite of his courtiers' hesitancy. But, he was sorely disappointed with Holkar for seeking his assistance and at the same time surreptitiously trying to negotiate peace with the British. He is said to have called him "*Puccā Harāmzādā*" (confirmed scoundrel)†. The withdrawal of such an ally to a far-off land, was, therefore, a source of comfort to Ranjit. It also gave him an opportunity to cross the Satluj in seach of conquest, as the British had left not a battalion behind in that area, and had declared their intention to safeguard their own vast possessions across the Jamunā.

Meantime, a bitter quarrel ensued between Rājā Sāhib Singh of Patiālā and his ambitious Rāni, Āus Kasur. Sāhib Singh being imbecile and incompetent, the Rāni wanted to appropriate the rule to herself by putting her minor son, Karam Singh, on the throne. At the same time,Patiālā was having armed skirmishes with Nābhā, over the possession of a village, Dolādhi, spilling much blood. Once, the Bhāi Sāhib of Kaithal, Jaswant Singh, who had sided with Patiālā, also got killed which infuriated Rājā Sāhib Singh so much that he took the field himself against Nābhā. Rājā Jaswant Singh of Nābhā was defeated. An effort was, therefore, made for a rapproachment through Mahārājā Ranjit Singh, as due to the policy of non-interference beyond the Jamunā,enunciated by Lord Cornwallis, their help could not be sought. For some time, when Holkar, the Marāthā chief, was in Patiālā, his help was sought by the Rāni against her husband, but on account of his own troubles and later hasty withdrawal, his help could be no longer of any use.

Ranjit Singh crossed the Satluj with 20,000 horse, on July 26, 1806, alongwith Sardārs Fateh Singh Ahluwāliā and Gurdit Singh of Ladwā. On the way, he secured *nazrānā* from the Sikh chiefs of Jullundur, subdued Nakodar, and entered the Patiālā territory on the third day. He seized Dolādhi, the subject of dispute. Rājā Bhāg Singh of Jind, his maternal uncle, and Rājā Jaswant Singh of Nābhā who had invited the Mahārājā were also in his train. There was a

---

† N.K. Sinha, *Ranjit Singh*, Page 18, quoting Kanje's *Metcalfe* vol I, p 267.
Ranjit Singh, thereafter, became a party to the compromise and a treaty was signed by himself, Sardār Fateh Singh Ahluwāliā and the British representative on Jan 1, 1806, (called the treaty of Lāhore) whereby the Sikh representatives guaranteed the departure of Holkar's army and the British undertook to keep away from the Sikh territories.

brief skirmish with the forces of Patiālā, but on the second day peace was restored, Dolādhi was handed over to Patiālā and Nābhā paid a *nazrānā* of Rs. 50,000/- to Mahārājā Ranjit Singh. At Patiālā,he could not affect a compromise between the Rājā and the Rāni, both of whom offered him large presents to secure his goodwill. The British grew suspicious of the Mahārājā's intentions and decided to strengthen the British garrison in Karnāl.

On the way back, Ludhiana was attacked. Founded by the Pathān Lodhis in 1480 A. D. and then ruled by two widows of a Muslim Rājput, Rāi Ilias Khān, whose family had held it for two centuries, Ludhiānā was a key prosperous town on the grand Trunk Road. He expelled the widows and handed over its charge to the Rājā of Jind. Jandiālā, Ranikot, Jagrāon, Baddowāl, Talwandi, Dākhā and Basia were captured next and distributed among the rulers of Jind, Nābhā and Sardār Fateh Singh Ahluwāliā, Diwān Mohkam Chand,* Sardar Bhanga Singh of Thānesar, and others. He conquered also the district of Ghamgrama and distributed it among the chiefs of Nābhā and Lādwā. He made no advance further than Ambālā, in this campaign. On his way back, he halted at Jwālā Mukhi where he was approached by Rājā Sansār Chand's brother with an offer of a *nazrānā* to help them expel General Amar Singh Thāpā of Nepal who had invaded and conquered the hill states, including Garhwāl and Sirmur, and had laid seige to Kāngra itself.

Ranjit Singh promised help. Hearing of this, Gen. Amar Singh Thāpā also sent his agents to him with an offer of double the *nazrānā*, if Ranjit did not intervene in this affair. The offer of Thāpā was,

* Son of a Khatri shopkeeper, he had enlisted himself in the army first with Sāhib Singh Bhangi, ruler of Gujrāt. Seeing his prowess, Ranjit Singh recruited him in his own forces. He soon rose to the position of a general. He participated in many wars and won a resounding success every time. He was given Jullundur and Phillaur in *jāgir*. The fort at Phillaur was built by him and he died there in 1814 A.D. His son, Moti Rām, was much honoured by Ranjit Singh who appointed him Governor of Kashmir (See later). He also participated in many diplomatic negotiations on behalf of the Mahārājā. Moti Ram's sons, Rām Dyāl and Kirpā Rām also served Ranjit Singh loyally. The former died in a battle at the young age of 21, and the latter was appointed Governor of Kashmir. But the Prime Minister of the Panjāb, Dhian Singh Dogrā who was very jealous of the family, sowed the seeds of suspicion in the mind of the Mahārājā and both father and son had to leave the Panjāb to settle down at Banāras. Moti Rām died in 1839 and his son in 1842 in that city.

however, rejected for the reason that a commitment was already made, and also because Ranjit did not like the foreigners to occupy lands adjacent to his own. The Gurkha menace was, however, soon over. A pestilence broke out among the Gurkha troops, and they scattered in disorder with utmost speed.†

Meantime, Kasur had again become a trouble-spot. Nizāmuddin, the old Nawāb, was dead and his son, Kutub-ud-din, was giving the Mahārājā every cause of concern. He had joined hands with Nawāb Muzaffar Khān of Multān and was collecting a large force for attacking Lāhore, the new seat of an ever-growing Sikh power. A strong expedition was, therefore, sent (Feb 1807), led by himself and Sardār Jodh Singh, son of his father's ally, the well-known Sardar Jāssā Singh Rāmgarhia, who had now become a trusted friend and ally of Ranjit Singh and was much honoured and loved by him for his dedication, loyalty and bravery. A seige was laid to the town which lasted for about a month when all the provisions stored within the city and the fort were exhausted. The Mahārājā's artillery reduced the fortifications of the town to the ground and there was hand-to-hand fight for well over half a day, which resulted in a large-scale massacre of the Afghān soldiers. The Nawāb tried to escape, but was intercepted and put in chains. The city was given over to plunder. When Kutub-ud-din was presented to the Mahārājā, he had become an object of great pity, feeling humiliated in the extreme. Everyone thought he would be shot or imprisoned. He himself was trembling with fear. But to everyone's surprise, Ranjit Singh asked his soldiers

† About this time in 1807, a Gaur Brāhmin of village Ikiri (Distt Meerut) called Khushālā, was recruited by Ranjit Singh as an ordinary foot soldier in the regiment led by Dhaunkal Singh on Rs. 5/- a month. Ranjit, much impressed with his looks and bearing, gave him rapid promotions. He soon become a *Jemādār* (or, lieutenant). To further ingratiate himself in the Mahārājā's favour, he turned a Sikh (it is said, the Mahārājā himself gave him *Pāhul*), and was named Khushāl Singh and became *Sardār-Deohri* or Lord Chamberlain, without whose permission no one could see the Mahārājā. Khushāl Singh invited his nephew, Teju, also from the village, who soon become Tej Singh and from a soldier's position in which he was taken into the Sikh forces became their Commander-in-chief at the time of the Anglo-Sikh wars when through his treachery and incompetence, the Sikhs lost a winning battle. Khushāl Singh also got his son, Rām Lal, converted into Rām Singh who became a general and a Rājā. Khushāl Singh died in 1844. His family settled down at Sheikhupurā, with a Jagir worth about Rs. 4 lakhs per year. Khushāl Singh proved a very corrupt and rapacions officer, notably as Governor of Kashmir, but the Mahārājā always forgave him after showing some annoyance,

to release him. "He has fought like a hero. We shall honour him and offer him a *Jāgir* across the Satluj,† in perpetuity." In return, the Nawāb agreed to supply 100 horsemen to the Lāhore Durbār whenever called upon. To the nephew of the Kasur chief, Fateh Din, another *Jāgir* at Marno in the Gurgaon distt, was also offered on the same conditions. Kasur with its adjoining countryside was offered to Sardār Nihal Singh Attāriwālā who was incharge of this campaign. Much wealth and war-materials, including 8 cannons and 300 guns, fell into the hands of the Mahārājā and the signal victory was celebrated by illuminations at Lāhore and Amritsar. Sardār Hari Singh Nalwā greatly distinguished himself in this campaign and was awarded a Jagir worth Rs. 30,000/- per year. Another noted commander, Sardār Hukmā Singh Chimni, who was wounded in the battle, was similarly rewarded.

Nawāb Muzaffar Khān of Multān had not complied strictly with the terms of the agreement made with the Mahārājā in 1802 and renewed three years later. So, the Mahārājā was left with no choice but to march upon Multān. However, the Nawāb saw reason after his town being captured and gave up resistance from the fort. He offered a large tribute and the Mahārājā, much pleased, next turned his attention to his neighbour, Bahāwalpur. The Nawāb, Bahāwal Khān, sued for peace and the terms being settled, the Mahārājā returned to Lāhore. At the same time, the estates of the various Sikh chiefs in the foothills of the Kāngrā mountain were also invested, which gave some annoyance to Sadā Kaur, the Mahārājā's mother-in-law, whose territories also lay in this area.

Once again, in Sept. 1807, the Mahārājā had been called upon by the Rājās of Jind, Nābhā and Patiālā to intervene in the dispute between Rājā Sāhib Singh of Patiālā and his Rāni. He was received by everyone with great courtesy and honour. The dispute was settled in favour of the Rāni who offered a necklace of diamonds worth Rs. 70,000/- on behalf of herself and her minor son.

Now, Ranjit Singh left for Ambālā* then held by the widow of Sardār Gurbakhah Singh, who presented *nazrānā* to the Mahārājā.

† The Nawāb of Mamdot held this *Jāgir* right to the days of the partition of India in 1947. It consisted of 22 villages and yielded in those days a princely revenue of Rs. 50,000/- yearly.

* Named after Ambā Devi (another name for Kālkā, Chandi, Nainādevi etc. after whose names other towns also flourished nearby), the town and distt. of "Ambālā

Tributes were also paid by the Sikh chiefs of Kaithal, Shāhābāb, Buria, Kalsia and Sirhind. They were offered *khilats* in return. Naraingarh was reduced next, after a bitter fight, and handed over to Sardār Fateh Singh Ahluwāliā, on receipt of a *nāzrānā*.

On his return to Lāhore, in Dec. 1807, he was informed that twins were born to Mahārāni Mahtāb Kaur, daughter of Rāni Sadā Kaur, and named Sher Singh and Tārā Singh. Ranjit Singh was greatly elated at becoming father again at the age 27, though rumours had also been spread by some evil-tongued and jealous courtiers and some foreigners that the two sons were planted on Ranjit Singh by Sadā Kaur inorder to increase her power over him and that they were, infact, the sons of a weaver of Mukerian and a maid-servant of of Sadā Kaur. As we shall see, these rumours were employed later on by the British and other contenders of the Panjāb throne in the post-Ranjit Singh period to great effect, even though the Mahārājā showered all the affection he could on the new-born and brought them up, like prince Kharak Singh, with the care due to their station.

In the next year (1808), the Mahārājā employed Bhowāni Dās, once a high revenue official in the Kingdom of Afghanistān, which he had to leave in disgust. The Panjāb's revenues of about Rs. 30 lakhs at this time were being managed by an Amritsar banker who also held the lease of Pind Dādan Khān salt mines. Bhowāni Dās, now the head of the Finance Department, organised both the civil and the military finance in a systematic manner which brought much order to the confused mess into which the state accounts had fallen. His brother, Devi Dās, also a high official at Kābul, joined him next year. The seal of the Mahārājā was handed over to another celebra-

F. N. Contd.

was first conquered by Sangat Singh and later descended to his brother-in-law, Dhiān Singh. The latter appointed Gurbakhsh Singh and Lāl Singh as *Thānedārs* in charge, himself going to live at Singhwālā in Ferozepur distt. On his return, he saw Gurbakhsh Singh having become the owner, Lāl Singh having died in the meantime. Gurbakhsh Singh died childless and his widow, Dia Kaur, took over the rule in 1783 A.D. Ranjit Singh temporarily ejected her but she was restored by Gen. Ochterlony, and held it until her death in 1823, when the British occupied it. (Latif, History of the Panjāb, 369.)

ted Hindu, Karam Chand, father of the famous Rattan Chand Dārhiwālā.

In September, 1808, after a lapse of 8 years, Sir Charles Matcalfe, British Agent, suddenly arrived with presents for the Mahārājā from his Government, with a view to strengthening the relations between the two powers. This was, however, not a mere courtesy call. The British had been alarmed at the rapid advance and rise to power of Mahārājā Ranjit Singh and were waiting for an opportunity to cry halt to it.

This opportunity they got as if for the asking when, dreading the increasing power of Ranjit, the leaders of the Cis-Satluj Sikh states, including the rulers of Patiālā, Nābhā and Jind decided in a conclave to send a deputation to the British resident in Delhi, Mr. Seton. Consequently, a delegation consisting of the Rājā of Jind, Bhāg Singh, Bhāi Lāl Singh of Kaithal, the Diwān of Patiālā, Sardār Chain Singh, and the confidential agent of Nābhā, Ghulam Hussain, was despatched to Delhi, and presented their memorandum to the British Resident on April 1. They protested their loyalty to every succeeding power in Delhi, and now formally sought protection of the British. They were shown much sympathy and given a verbal assurance of protection, for the British were watching with anxiety the scene in Europe and didnot want to prejudice their chances of friendship. They were feeling their ground with caution vis-a vis Ranjit Singh. So they did not commit anything in writing, nor even through a proclamation. "But, as the scene changed in their favour in Europe, they changed their stand and decided with Ranjit Singh to take Cis-Sathuj Sikh states under their protection. "Thus Ranjit's aspiration to give unity and coherence to diverse atoms and scattered elements and to mould the increasing Sikh nation into a well-ordered state or Commonwealth as Govind had developed a sect into a people, and had given application and purpose to the general institutions of Nānak, was frustrated as far as Cis-Satluj Sikh States were concerned."*

---

* Cunningham: History of the Sikhs, P. 120.

Due to the Russo-French alliance, the British had in fact become unduly alarmed, especially on account of the possibility of their joint advance towards India. Irān had fallen to the Russians in 1805. Britain refused to intervene and so they turned to France for help. In 1807 a treaty of friendship was signed by Irān with France, which also stipulated that Irān would afford assistance and facilitate a possible French move against India. Turkey at this time also favoured France to Britain. This was also the condition in respect of the other states of Near and Middle East as well. Scared out of its wits, Britain was frantically in need of friends in the East and so despatched their embassies to Kābul, Tehrān and Lāhore. Fortunately for Britain, France became suspicious in the eyes of both Irān and Turkey as a reliable ally against Russia, their next door neighbour and formidable enemy, so they turned to the British for an alliance. Turkey signed a treaty with Britain in Jan. 1809 and Irān two months later. Spain had rebelled against the French hegemony. There was a definite change in the wind by late 1808 in favour of Britain thoroughout the Near and Middle East. And Lāhore lost the significance it had achieved in British eyes, due to an international threat to their Indian possessions.

Ranjit's estimation was that the British would pay his price in return for his support against Franco-Russian alliance, should they launch an offensive against India. So for a time he tried to be evasive to the overtures of Metcalfe, when he proposed to Ranjit that he limit his ambitions to this side of the Satluj only, and agree to honour the protection the British had offered to the Cis-Satluj States. He was received at Kasur with due honours, but the Mahārājā broke off negotiations with him to venture out into the Cis-Satluj territories once again, before finalising his deal with the British. He wanted also to see how violently they reacted to his advance, across the Satluj, at this time and also to present them with a *fait accompli*. He seized Faridkot and Ambālā, levied exactions in Malerkotlā and Thānesar and exchanged turbans with the Rājā of Patiālā. The British envoy, who was asked to follow in his train looked on in amazement and dismay, protested vigorously against these excursions, but was dismissed with the reply that it was too late for Britain to protest. He had laid tribute on these territories twice before, and Britain had not intervened. Why then this sudden upsuge of interest in the states which were the genuine field of operation for Ranjit in the interest of the consolidation of Sikh power,

The British envoy was, however, getting more and more aggressive and restless. He even intrigued with the relations of Ranjit and his trusted generals, including Fateh Singh Ahluwāliā and Sadā Kaur, both of whom, according to Metcalfe, wanted to have favourable terms for themselves in exchange for agreeing to the British terms alongwith the other chiefs (possibly, this was one of the reasons for Ranjit's own change of front.) To reinforce their arguments, the British despatched a contingent under Sir David Ochterlony to the Satluj in Jan. 1809. The General advanced via Buria and Patiālā and but for Sardār Jodh Singh of Kalsia, the head of the Karor Singhia Misal, other Sikh rulers welcomed him with open arms. Ranjit sent his emissaries also to the British Commander to cry halt to his advance. In the beginning of Feb. 1809, Ochterlony made an open declaration through an *Ittilah-nāmā* taking the Cis-Satluj states under British protection and to resist with arms any encroachment on them by Ranjit Singh*. News was also received from Europe that there was no immediate prospect of a France-Russian assault on India and, therefore, the treaty with Ranjit Singh should be limited only to extending the British domination to the Satluj and not to a comprehensive defensive treaty. Seeing the seriousness of the British and not willing or able yet to measure swords with the British power, he had no choice but to acquiesce.†

The following 4-article treaty was thus signed by both parties on April 25,1809 (and ratified by the Governor-General-in-Council in May 1809). The text of the treaty is as follows:-

---

* Its copy was provided to the Cis-Satluj chiefs on 3rd May, 1809.

† British writers of this period are categorical that the British authorities were determined to cry a halt to Ranjit's conquests across the Satluj at any cost. That Ranjit Singh resisted their overtures for a considerable time is also conceded by them. Says Osborne, Mily. Secy to the Governor-General, Lord Auckland:-"The conduct of Ranjit was so unsatisfactory and he evinced such a strong disposition to continue his encroachments, that it deemed expedient to advance a body of troops under Col. Ochterlony to enforce the demands and support the negotiations of our agent." (*Ranjit Singh*, p. 12). Says Princep:- "Had danger indeed from that quarter (i.e., Russia and France) been more imminent, it would have probably been deemed politic to extend our direct influence further into the Panjāb in reduction of the power of a chief who showed himself so unfriendly" (*Origin of Sikh power*, P. 54). Ranjit Singh, knowing his limitations at this time, was therefore left with no choice. The nationalist historians of today who criticise him for this and suggest he should have taken the British on,at this time,when he had still to plant his feet firmly on the ground, donot appreciate the reality of the situation.

Treaty between the British Government and the Rājā of Lāhore. (Dated 25th April 1809)

Whereas certain differences which had arisen between the British Government and the Rājā of Lāhore have been happily and amicably adjusted: and both parties being anxious to maintain relations of perfect amity and concord, the following articles of treaty, which shall be binding on the heirs and successors of the two parties, have been concluded by the Rājā Ranjit Singh in person, and by the agency of C.T. Metcalfe, Esquire, on the part of the British Government.

Article 1—Perpetual friendship shall subsist between the British Government and the State of Lāhore : the latter shall be considered, with respect to the former, to be on the footing of the most favoured powers, and the British Government will have no concern with the territories and subjects of the Rājā to the north-ward of the river Sutlej.

Article 2. The Rājā will never maintain in the territory which he occupies on the left bank of the river Sutlej more troops than are necessary for the internal duties of that territory, nor commit or suffer any encroachments on the possessions or rights of the Chiefs in its vicinity.

Article 3—In the event of a violation of any of the preceding articles, or of a departure from the rules of friendship, this treaty shall be considered null and void.

Article 4—is about its ratification within 2 months by the Governor general (which was done on May 21, 1809.)

Ludhiānā became a military cantonment of the British, and Ranjit was obliged to fortify his defences at Phillaur, on his side of the Satluj, just opposite Ludhiānā, and increase the strength of the Gobindgarh fort at Amritsar.

It is thus apparent that Ranjit Singh, though outwitted by the British as much as the circumstances of the day, secured firmly (atleast so he thought) his one major frontier against the British onslaught and left him free to expand towards the north and the north-west. *Secondly, it left in his possession the territories he had acquired in the Cis-Satluj areas during his first operations,* though he had to abandon the choice fruits of his labours and bloodshed twice thereafter.

According to Prof. Sinha, "his (Ranjit's) failure to absorb the Cis-Satluj states was a tragedy of Sikh militant nationalism and the success of the Cis-Satluj Sikhs with the aid of the British Govt. marked the disruption of the great creation of Guru Gobind Singh". †

But chance as much plays a vital role in the lives of individuals as of nations, and there are times when neither force of arms nor of arguments is of any avail. At such times, it is the "other factors" which determine our destiny.

As soon as the Cis-Satluj states were free from the fear of Ranjit Singh, they tried to demolish and rob each other. Hence, the British found another excellent opportunity to meddle in their affairs and issue another proclamation (dated Aug 22, 1811) to protect them againt each other as well. This increased their power of interference, patronage, reprimand and even armed intervention, so that these states, as time wore on, became absolute dependencies of Britain rather than independent rulers in treaty alliance with the British power, of equal rank in law if not in fact.

Ranjit Singh, howerver, kept scrupulously bound by his campaigns towards the north-west. The British records of this period (esp. the communications of Ochterlony to Govt in 1809-10) plant

---

† S. N. Sinhā, *Ranjit Singh*, p. 34. But says Sārdesāi, the well-known Marāthā historian, in his illuminating address on the *"Career of Ranjit Singh and his politics,"* (Sept 23, 1939, at Bombay), "When he (Ranjit) was just rising on the Indian horizon, he witnessed and possible deeply contemplated on the life and work of Tipu Sultān, the Tiger of Mysore. Tipu was quickly finished in two successive battles by the calculating might of the East India Company. Yashwant Rāo Holkar began his meteoric career just about the same juncture. His rapid brilliant victories and equally rapid downfall doubtless supplied Ranjit Singh with a more moderate outlook in his furture dealings with the British power and wisely refrained from espousing (his) cause .. The last Peshwā, Bāji Rāo II, and his firm friend, Daulat Rāo Scindiā, struggled in vain to overcome the British power by means of secret plotting, ill-supported by the strength of arms. The emperor of Delhi, now only a well-remembered phantom of departed glory, was Ranjit Singh's next door neighbour, and an object lesson in the art of Kingship. Ranjit also watched with ardent curiosity and deep interest the opposite endeavours of prominent thinkers like (Raja) Rām Mohan Roy (of Bengāl), who were fimly convinced that political freedom was unthinkable for India unless religion and society were thoroughly reformed to suit the changing conditions of the world's life and progress. It is this aspect of the (the practical blend of various remedies) which deserves to be commemorated in the history of India." (*Journal of Bhāratiya Vidyā Bhavan*, Vol I, Part II, May 1940).

many suspicions in the minds of the unwary as to the real intentions of Ranjit Singh. For instance, he is said to have made overtures to Scindia. Agents from Holkar, the ruler of Gwalior and Amir Khān, the Pindari chief, were received at Lāhore for years after the conclusion of this treaty. Ranjit is said to have incited the Cis-Satluj States to overthrow the British yoke in conjunction with him and Holkar. But, as time passed, both sides understood each other better, and no untoward incident happened between the two formidable powers till the last day of Ranjit Singh's own reign and life.

On Aug 24, 1809, on the request of Sansār Chand of Kāngrā, he occupied the Kāngrā fort, defeating after a bitter fight Amar Singh Thāpā, the Gurkha commander of Nepal, who had invaded this area and had become a terror to the local populace. Thāpā agreed to retire across the Satluj. The war of 1814-15, between the British and the Gurkhas sealed the fate of the Gurkhas within the bounds of Nepal. Sardār Desa Singh Majithia was appointed commandant of the Kāngra fort and also made Nāzim or governor of the hill states of Kangra, Chamba, Nurpur, Kotla, Shahpur, Jasrota, Basoli, Mankot, Jaswan, Siba, Guler, Kahlur, Datarpur and Mandi, Suket and Kulu. Having received *nazarānā* personally from the chiefs of the last three hill-states, the Mahārājā returned to Jullundur Doab where he wrested Hariana from the widow of Baghel Singh, who had recently died, giving her a *Jāgir* in return for her maintenance. In the same year, he received a tribute from Wazirabad, held by Ganda Singh, son of Jodh Singh, who had also died. The Mahārājā was satisfied with this arrangement and did not annex his territory and invested the young chief with a *khilat* and a turban.

Gujrāt was captured next, in the same year (1809) by Fakir Aziz-ud-Din, the Mahārājā's trusted friend, courtier, and Foreign Minister ,† from Sāhib Singh Bhangi. The Mahārājā was much

† The three brothers, Aziz-ud-Din, Nur-ud-Din, and Imamuddin, sons of a well-known Lāhore physician and man of God, Syed Ghulam Mohd. Bokhāri, played a most notable part in the affairs of the Sikh State. They were introduced by their venerable father when he treated the Mahārājā for an eye ailment soon after Ranjit's conquest of Lāhore. They traced their lineage to a holy man of Bokhara and hence were called Bokhāri, but since Ranjit Singh's time they were known as the Fakir family on account of their piety. Aziz-ud-Din was the Mahārājā's advisor during his delicate negotiations with the British envoy in 1808, and later in 1834 led the negotiations with Amir Dost Mohd Khān of Kābul (who has

F. N. Contd.

advanced on Peshāwar to recover it from Ranjit Singh). When Dost Mohd. taunted him for serving a *Kafir* & fighting his own co-religionists, the fakir replied :—
"Is it not my duty to defend my country against aggression and be true to my salt? You too are fighting for power and not for Islam."

When the Fakir met Lord William Bentick in 1831 on behalf of his master, and the British Governor-General asked him as a matter of information which of the eyes of the Mahārājā was blinded, he replied :— "The countenance of my Master is so dazzling like the sun that I have never looked him in the face. I know how his gracious feet look like, but not his eyes".

When Ranjit Singh had a paralytic stroke late in 1838 and became speechless, he was one of the two trusted courtiers who could interpret his language of signs. "Even a son could not have done more for his sick father."

His other brother, Nuruddin, was "the Home Minister, almoner, director of royal palaces and gardens, one of the three custodians of the Keys of the royal treasury, commandant of the arsenal at the fort, a judge extraordinary" etc. Though not a member of the Mahārājā's Council (Cabinet) like his elder brother he was very close to the Mahārājā and interceded successfully several times on behalf of the princes with the ruler, their father. He even supervised the Mahārājā's food which was tested for two hours by the professional tasters before being offered to the Mahārājā. It was certified by Nuruddin with his personal seal. The food itself was prepared under the supervision of Hakim Bishan Dās, a trusted Assistant of Nuruddin.

The third brother, Imāmuddin, also held important administrative and military posts. He was the custodian of the famous Gobindgarh fort at Amritsar and Governor of the country surrounding it. He also held charge of the magazines, arsenal and royal stables there. He fought in the battle against the Kanaihyās. After the first Anglo-Sikh war, he was one of the Council of Regency to administer the country during the infancy of Mahārājā Dalip Singh. (For more details of this family, see *"The Real Ranjit Singh", by Waheeduddin).*

Says N. K. Sinha:—

"With so much of power in their hands, had these Mohemmadan officers been so inclined, they might have added one more party to the list of three, that arose on the death of Ranjit Singh. In addition to the Dogra, Sandhānwāliā and the Court parties, there might have been a Mohammadan Party resting on the support of the Fakir brothers, the Mohammadan officers in charge of artillery and the Mohammadan population of the Panjāb (who constituted an overwhelming majority). To the honesty of Azizuddin and his younger brothers there is no better testimony than this that the confidence Ranjit Singh reposed in them was never misused." (Ranjit Singh, page 183). This speaks volumes by implication about Ranjit Singh's liberality of outlook as well as the secular character of his state. But this also is a fact that "It is not every king who is served or likes to be served by men of this character."

pleased, conferred a valuable *Khilat* on him and appointed his younger brother, Nur-ud-Din, Governor of Gujrāt.

An expedition was led to Multān on Feb 24, 1810, the fourth during the last six years, as the Nawāb, Muzaffar Khān, after making an agreement, always failed to pay the stipulated tribute-money every year. He broke every other term of the agreement as well and helped with money, arms and horses the Nawāb of Kasur during his resistance to the Lāhore Durbār. He had harboured Ahmed Khān, Rais of Jhang, an enemy of the Sikh rule, and offered him refuge and instead of showing loyalty had betrayed the trust of the Sikh ruler. The town was occupied the next day. The Bahāwalpur chief was scared so much on hearing this that through his emissaries, he bought peace for himself by offering 500 cavalry in the campaign at Multān, after his offer of tribute of one lakh was refused. Nawāb Muzzaffar Khān shut himself up in his fort which was besieged on all sides by the Sikh forces. Even heavy bombardment for several days created no effect on him. The famous cannon, Zamzama, with its ball of 80 lbs also could not make any appreciable dent in the walls of the fort. Several noted Sikh warriors were blown up by either the mines laid by the enemy, or by gun-fire. These included Attar Singh Dhāri, a close associate of the Mahārājā, who was one of the first to enter Lāhore alongwith his master during its capture in 1799. But the Sikhs kept up their advance towards the fort under a shower of bullets by the Nawāb's forces from the ramparts, and were able to lay mines to the walls of the fort. However, when the mines burst, a huge mound of masonery fell with such a great force that under it were buried several noted Sikh warriors, including Hari Singh Nalwā.* Sardar Attar Singh Attariwālā and S. Nihāl Nihal Singh were also brutally injured.

---

* Sardār Hari Singh Nalwā (Born 1791 A.D. at Gujranwala) was the son of Sardār Gurdial Singh of Uppal Khatri caste, who was a Kumedān with the Sukarchakiā forces. Seven years later, he lost his father and was brought up by his maternal uncle with great care and affection. He was taught Persian and became well-versed also in religious lore and the arts of war. Later, he acquired mastery over Pushtu as well. At the age of 14, he got recruited in Ranjit's army, soon caught the eye of his discerning master and became his aid-de-camp. While out hunting, he killed a lion by a single stroke of his sword and was hence called Nalwā. He participated in the most important and decisive wars of Kasur, Multān, Attock, Kashmir, Hazārā, and Peshāwar and finally fell fighting at Jamrud on April 30,

The enemy threw flaming torches from above. Sardār Hari Singh's uniform caught fire and he was badly burnt. He was evacuated to safety instantly by a soldier. Others were similarly rescued. The Sikh forces were successful in breaking through the walls of the fort and a hand-to-hand fight ensued. Such was the fury with which the Sikhs mowed down the enemy, that the Nawāb raised his flag of peace and surrendered himself. The fort was captured. The Nawāb asked for forgiveness, swearing on his long white beard that in future he would remain loyal, offer tribute on time and never encourage or assist the enemies of the Sikh rule. A sum of Rs. 28 lakhs and 25 choice horses were offered as yearly tribute and his brother-in-law (sister's husband) was given as hostage for good conduct in future. The Mahārājā not only spared his life and forgave him for his past offences, but restored his old position to him.

Writes Elphinstone—"Almost the whole of the Panjāb belongs to Ranjit Singh (in 1809) who in 1805 was but one of the many chiefs". This miracle had happened by the rise of a single powerful leader bent not only on conquest by war, but also through diplomacy, persuasion, negotiations, generosity of heart and liberality of religious and political outlook. And as we shall see, the poor had as much to gain from his rule as the powerful allies who assisted him in his campaigns, and the deadly enemies, who resisted him, but in good time submitted to him even after the clash of arms. For, Ranjit while fighting his adversaries bitterly never humiliated any of them after their defeat,and provided them with an honourable status and a liberal endowment to live a life of honour and peace.

In the beginning of 1812, Prince Kharak Singh, then aged 10, was married to Princess Chand Kaur, daughter of Sardār Jaimal Singh Kanaihyā. All the Sikh chiefs, including those from the Phulkian states, participated on this happy occasion and offered large presents, horses and cash. The hill rājās as much as the Muslim Nawābs came

---

F. N. Contd.

1837, at the age of 46, rising in the process to the position of Commander-in-chief of the Sikh forces, He was appointed for a time Governor of Kashmir, Hazārā, & Peshāwar & was allowed to strike a coin in his name twice at Kashmir & Peshāwar. He was given many diplomatic assignments as well which he accomplished successfully. He had become such a dread among the Pathāns that upto this day "*Haria Rāghle*" (Hari Singh has come) is used by the Pathān mothers to frighten their unruly children.

from far and near. Sir David Ochterlony represented the British authorities in India. The Sikh monarch utilised the occasion to also exhibit his military power (especially their accomplishment in the European method of warfare) to the visitors, including the British representative.

It may be mentioned here that since 1802, the Mahārājā had started training his troops on the European lines and this aspect he particularly wanted his guest to become duly aware of.

The Consolidation of Sikh Power

Ranjit Singh having conquered the Panjāb proper between the Satluj and Attock, now turned his attention to the remanants of the Afghān empire in India. Kashmir, Peshāwar, the gateway to Kābul, Kohāt, Bannu, Derā Ismail Khan, and Hazārā, (the gateway to Kashmir) etc. still remained with the Afghāns, who were also nominally still supreme in Sind and Multān. In 1809, Shāh Shujā had lost the Afghān throne and left for the Panjāb to seek, ironically enough, the help of Mahārājā Ranjit Singh, swallowing his pride and forgetting the centuries-old animosities between the Afghāns and the Sikhs. The turn of fortune makes strange bedfellows and in political life there are no permanent enemies or friends, but only one's interests.*

* About this time (in 1810), Gulābā of Jammu got himself recruited in Ranjit's army at Rs. 3/- per mansem. He later brought in his younger brothers, Dhyānā and Suchetu also, who were given similar positions in the Sikh army. Being experts in cajolery, and also good fighters, they received such rapid promotions that Dhyān Singh became *Sardār Deorhi* replacing the Mahārājā's great favourite, Jamādār Khushal Singh. All the three brothers were titled *Rājās* by the Khālsā Darbār. Dhyān Singh also later became the Prime Minister of the Sikh state. Gulāb Singh became Governor of Jammu, and kept most of the time away from Lāhore leaving the field free for his two younger brothers to exploit. The Dogrā family became so powerful in the later years of Ranjit's rule that Dhyān Singh used to hold his own court in his house and "referred only such matters to the *Sarkār* which he considered more significant." While Ranjit Singh was alive, they were reputed to be anti-British, but after he died, they were thoroughly exposed. Dhyān Singh, his son, Hirā Singh, and his brother, Suchet Singh, all were murdered at the hands of the army or their rivals who were disgusted with their ways. Gulāb Singh gave up his anti-British protestations altogether, and became so much in league with them that after the Anglo-Sikh war, the territory of Jammu and Kashmir was bestowed upon him

The Shāh met Ranjit Singh at Sāhiwāl, (Khushāb, according to Murray). But, the interview, except for the exchange of presents, produced no material result. With the armed assistance of the Afghān Kashmir Governor, his old Vizier's son, he secured Peshāwar but was soon displaced by the Governor's brother who ruled over Attock and who sent him to Kashmir, where he was made a prisoner. His blinded brother, Shāh Zamān, once the terror of Hindustān, sought refuge at Lāhore. Meantime, the powerful Vizier of Kābul, Fateh Khān, wanted to punish both the Governor of Attock and Kashmir who had become virtually independent of the Afghān monarchy, though they held their positions in its name. But, without Ranjit's help, the task was considered impossible. Fateh Khān, therefore, took no time in coming to the Panjāb to seek the Mahārājā's help and support. The two met at Rohtās.

The Mahārājā grasped this opportunity with both hands. Strangely enough, the Vizier, who was accompanied by all of his 18 brothers, had also conspired to finish off Ranjit Singh during the interview. The Mahārājā, suspicious also on his part, came prepared for any eventuality. But the mishap did not materialise. The Mahārājā agreed to the proposal of the Vizier, one to test the ground for his own future use in Kashmir, and secondly to secure the release of Shāh Shujā whose queen, Wafā Begum, had pleaded with the Mahārājā at Lāhore for intervention. As she and her family were in distress, she was offered a subsidy of Rs. 4000/- per month by the Mahārājā, a strange though noble gesture against the bitterest enemies of his race for centuries (†). The Begum promised also to hand over the famous *Koh-i-Nur* diamond to the Sikh King, once her husband was released. (*)

F. N. Contd.

by the British, and the Sikhs soon after lost their empire ! But solong as Ranjit was alive, they gave him loyalty. According to Cunningham, Ranjit used the Dogrā, Sikh and Muslim parties to balance each other.

† Sinha, Ranjit Singh, P. 45, quoting Zafar-nāmā-Ranjit Singh and Monograph of Sept. 17, 1812.

* But when the demand for the *Koh i-Nūr* was made after the Shāh's release, the Shāh started making excuses. He even pretended that it was lost. Some historians suggest Ranjit Singh having stopped his rations "for two days" and even given him physical torture to recover the highly-prized jewel, which was later handed over to the Mahārājā when he personally called on the Shāh and offered him three lakhs

Ranjit Singh offered 12,000 Sikh troops under Dewān Mohkam Chand to march alongwith the Afghān forces, under a joint Command, on the conditions that (a) One-third of the territory of Kashmir and (b) One-third of the war-booty would be handed over to the Lāhore Durbār. It was also stipulated that the Afghān pretentions over Multān would be ended and Shāh Shujā released. The terms were agreed to by the Afghāns at Rohtāsgarh. Kashmir was conquered after a hard fight, but the Afghāns refused to honour the terms. Their Sikh allies "left Kashmir in disgust". All the expense, effort and sacrifices of the Sikh kingdom had gone in vain. They had spurned the offer of the Kashmir Governor, Ata Mohd. Khan, who wanted to seek their protection and help, "in exchange for all the valuables and cash he had", just to honour their word given to the Afghāns. But, this probing of the country became extremely useful to the Sikh forces later on. And, Shāh Shujā was also released from prison and brought to Lāhore with great honour.

Another result was even more beneficial. Taking alarm at the deposition of his brother in Kashmir, the Governor of Attock, Jahāndād Khān, petitioned the Sikh ruler to send his forces and occupy the strategic fort of Attock. This was done with lightening speed. Jahāndād Khān was paid a lakh of rupees and the fort occupied (March 1813). Apart from foodgrains and ammunition, 70 guns, mortars and swivels also fell into the hands of the Sikh forces. It is said, Fateh Khān was so much disturbed on hearing of this loss when he reached Kābul that he wept bitterly, and swore not to honour the agreement he had made with the Sikhs over Kashmir. This, however, seems to be an excuse and an after-thought, for the Sikh forces had already returned empty-handed from Kashmir, through forced marches.

F. N. Contd.

in cash (Rs 50,000/— on the spot, as advance) and a *Jāgir* worth Rs 50000/—annually. On June 1, 1813 Kot Kamāliā, Jhang and Kalānaur were transferred to him through a *firman*. Word was also given that the Shāh would be helped whenever he decided in his wisdom to invade Kābul inorder to regain his throne. (This promise was also kept). Shāh Shujā with his family later left for Ludhiānā and sought protection under the British. But as he again requested the help of the Sikh monarch from there to recover his kingdom, (which was given), it shows clearly that the two parties were not estranged, as is commonly made out,

But, the Afghāns could not take this affront lying down either. While on their way back from Kashmir, Dost Mohd Khān, brother of the Kābul Vizier, with his 4000 horse, decided to attack the Attock fort. The Afghān troops stationed on the other side of the river Attock, could not cross over, as the boats were all in the hands of the Sikh forces. However, the Afghāns dispersed a Sikh contingent at Hassan Abdāl. Gen. Mohkam Chand was, therefore, ordered to the front immediately.

He made Hassan Abdāl (or the sacred Panjā Sahib, hallowed by the visit of Guru Nānak) the base of his operations, the enemy's base being Hazro, where Mahmud of Ghazni had in the year 1008 defeated for the first time the combined Hindu forces of North India. On his arrival, the battle was joined on June 26, 1813 (July 13, according to some). After a bitter engagement and losing over 2000 men, the Afghāns were routed and fled, many of them getting drowned in the river while on the run. In the words of Pof. Sinha, "a victory of the Afghāns in this battle would have been as important an episode in the history of Sikhs as the third battle of Panipat was in the history of the Marāthās in the north". Attock was now strongly garrisoned. Gurmukh Singh, Diwān Singh and Sarbuland Khān were appointed to guard it. Hazārā was also captured by the Sikh forces the same year.

Kashmir was also again probed through Rajouri a month later, under Gen. Rām Dyāl, the grandson of Diwān Mohkam Chand.

Dal Singh and Nāmdār Khān occupied Peer Panjāl. But due to rains, the Sikh guns didnot operate and Shupian could not be taken. Rām Dyal had to fall back and ask for reinforcements. As much troops as could be spared were sent under Bhāi Rām Singh. The Mahārājā himself was probing the country through another route via Poonch, treacherously suggested by the Rājā of Rajouri, and getting caught in rain and storm, turned to Mandi and Tosh-Maidan pass, only to find the enemy deeply entrenched there. So he had to retreat hastily reaching Lāhore in August, after much loss. Bhāi Rām Singh had also to retreat and so too Ram Dyal. It gave a rude shock to the Mahārājā. Especially he was hurt by the treachery of Rām Singh whose precipitate withdrawal without cause had depressed the morale of the Sikh forces and the prize which seemed to Ranjit Singh to be within reach, could not be attained. In the meantime, in Nov. 1814, Diwān Mohkam Chand died, and the next expedition to Kashmir, which was planned under his able generalship, had to be abandoned for the time being.

The defeat of the Gurkhas at the hands of the British brought Gen. Amar Singh Thāpā to ask for Ranjit's help against them. This was refused, however, on account of his treaty with the British but from this time onwards he allowed Gurkhās, who though defeated were fine soldiers, to be recruited liberally in his army. This was the first state in India to welcome the Gurkhas in its army.

Multān was giving trouble again. Two more expeditions were sent against it in 1816 and 1817. Every time, the Nawāb, Muzaffar Khān, yielded and offered *nazranas*, made solemn agreements and promises, but refused to keep any of them. It was, therefore, decided that a final assault—the seventh in succession—be made and Multān annexed to the Sikh rāj for good. This time, conquest was to be the clear and sole aim, and no *nazrānā* whatever was to be accepted from the Nawāb, nor any contractual obligations incurred. In Feb. 1818, a strong force under Prince Kharak Singh, assisted by Diwān Chand, Hari Singh Nalwā, and Sardār Shām Singh Attāri was sent to reduce Multān, along with the suicide-squads of the Akālis. Muzaffargarh, Khāngarh and the city of Multān were captured, but the Nawāb refused to yield, even after the walls of his citadel were battered. Sword in hand, he fought like a man to the bitter end, alongwith his choice and trusted soldiers, and left the fight only when he fell on the ground dead, alongwith his five sons. One of them was wounded and the eldest was captured and alongwith the youngest asked for asylum. The Mahārājā as usual was generous and offered each brother a *Jāgir* worth Rs. 30,000/-. The bodies of the Nawāb and his five sons were buried with military honours. In this battle, great bravery was shown on both sides and many Sardārs fell on the Sikh side as well. The Akālis, under Sādhu Singh and Phoola Singh Nihang* fought like dare-devils

* Born about 1761 A. D. at village Seehan in the country of Bāngar in the house of Sardār Ishar Singh, Phoolā Singh Akāli had a deeply religious bent of mind from the very childhood. He did not marry for life and settled down in Amritṣar, where a *burj* and a *dera* or *chhaoni* called *Nihangān di Ckhaoni* still stand to his memory. He was a fierce and selfless warrior who only knew how to give of himself and never to seek any favour or reward from the state. That is why his prestige was extremely high and he was loved and feared at the same time. He, it is said, once publicly reprimanded Ranjit Singh at the *Akāl Takht* for his intimacy with Moran, a dancing girl. Phoolā Singh participated in many battles of Ranjit, and everytime distinguished himself by his reckless courage and fearlessness against the heaviest odds as at Multān. He died fighting near Nowshera in 1823, where across the river Ḳābul, his tomb (*Samādhi*) still stands as a witness to his undying chivalry Though he became an honorary Jathedar of the Akal Takhat,he never interfered in matter of state, nor was he allowed to.

counting no cost in life or limb. He honoured & loved his generals, but Ranjit* disgorded all his soldiers and officers of their ill-gotten loot amounting to about Rs. 5 lakhs. All noted warriors who had distinguished themselves in the campaign were granted *Ināms, Khilats* and *Jāgirs.* Sardār Hari Singh Nalwa's *Jāgir* was doubled. Diwan Chand was titled "Zafar-Jang".

On April 20, 1819, Ranjit Singh personally marched on Kashmir, with a force of 30,000, having learnt all the lessons from his earlier fruitless campign. Food and ammunition were stored at Wazirābād and Gujrāt. The front-lines was made up of the forces of Prince Kharak Singh, Sardār Hari Singh Nalwā and Akāli Poola Singh, followed by Misr Diwān Chand "Zafar Jang", Sardār Shām Singh Attāriwālā and Sardār Hukma Singh Chimni. The rear was made up of the Mahārājā's own bodyguard of 10,000 choice men. Rajouri was reached on May 1, and captured. Its ruler, Aggar Khān, was arrested, while fleeing the field of battle. However, when he was presented before the Mahārājā the next morning at Bhimbar, the "Lion of the Panjāb" not only forgave him, but on his assurance of loyalty, he was also restored to his old position.

The Sikh forces now advanced towards the peak of Behrāmgala, about 25 miles away, which was captured. Every obstacle on the treacherous path gave way before the determined onslaught of the Sikh forces. The fort of Tarai also fell inspite of the stiff resistance offered by the Afghān *Kiledār*. Rajouri, Bhimbar and Poonch were now under the Sikh occupation. Very soon, the 1800 ft high mountain range of the Peer Panjāl was scaled, and after a brief rest, preparations were set afoot at the *Maidān* of Supayean, and the attack launched from three sides on July 3. Jabbār Khān, the Afghān chief, fought heroically at the head of 12000 troops. Both sides used artillery to the best advantage and there was much loss of life on either

---

* So great was the affection the Mahārājā elicited from his courtiers & chiefs that when he was seized by typhoid in 1817, & his life seemed in danger, Sardār Nihāl Singh Attāriwālia, circumambulating round his sick-bed prayed to God (as Bābur had done in respect of his son) to take his life & save that of Ranjit Singh. It so happened that Ranjit Singh recovered & Nihāl Singh fell ill & died. (Griffin, Panjāb Chiefs, I, P. 241).

‡ Under Diwān Sāwan Mal, who was made Governor in 1821, Multān made great progress. So just was he as Governor, that once he even imprisoned his own son for having grazed his horse in another's farm without payment.

side. At last, a hand-to-hand fight ensued. Sword clashed with sword, spear with spear, bayonets pierced through the hearts of many a brave warrior. Sardār Hari Singh Nalwā fought Jabbār Khān face-to-face, and when the Afghān aimed his sword menacingly at the Sardār, Nalwā made such a ferocious attack on him that the hand wielding the sword was chopped off. The Muslim chief fled the field, bleeding and woebegone, and escaped to Afghānistān via Muzaffarābād. Kashmir was now free of the foreign yoke for the first time in 500 years.

The Sikh forces entered Srinagar on July 4, 1819. It was announced by the beat of drum that no soldier will touch anyone's life or property, nor despoil their honour in anyway, irrespective of their creed or persuasion. This was a new experience for the people used to being plundered and their women dishonoured or carried away at the time of every victory. Ranjit Singh was conveyed this heart-warming news at Shāhābād which pleased him much. Soon therafter, he left for Amritsar to pay his homage at the Guru's temple and offered a lakh and a quarter of rupees for covering the temple with gold leaf.*

* It is since this time that the Amritsar temple has been known as the Golden Temple., As has been stated before, this temple was blown up by Ahmd Shāh Abdāli in 1762. The Sikhs got it erected afresh three years later, on April 24, 1764, when its foundation stone was laid by Sardār Jassā Singh Ahluwāliā. Mahārājā Ranjit Singh got it gilded in 1819, after the victory of Kashmir, according to some. But the *Mahān Kosh* suggests (P. 228) that it was in 1802, after the conquest of Amritsar, that marble work and covering the temple with gold leaf were commissioned by Ranjit Singh. There's a plaque on the front door of the Golden temple saying "Satguru Rām Dās has bestowed a great favour on his humble servant, Ranjit Singh, by taking this service from him." It is dated Samvat 1887 (1830 A.D.). May be, the work was completed in this year and took about 11 years to be accomplished, as the motifs beaten in the gold leaf are extremely exquisite. Ranjit Singh, in his humility, insisted that his offerings should not be advertised as those of a king, but commemorated as those of a humble devotee.

To commemorate this historic victory and the earlier victory at Multān, two newly-born sons of Ranjit Singh were named Kashmirā Singh and Multāna Singh. The former was born to Rāni Dayā Kaur and the latter to Rattan Kaur—both widows of the late Sāhib Singh Bhangi, ruler of Gujrāt—whom Ranjit had married in 1811. Later, another son was born to Rāni Dayā Kaur and after the victory of Peshāwar was named Peshāwarā Singh. Like usual, the British and Muslim historians, like Latif, call all of them "reputed" sons of Ranjit and cast doubts on their legitimacy. According to Latif, Rattan Kaur "purchased" Multānā

The parganas of Darband and Muzzffarābād were also captured the same year, after bitter fighting. After bringing order in the administration in these territories, and after securing a report from Fakir Aziz-ud-Din on the conditions in the area, Diwān Moti Rām was appointed the first Governor of Kashmir.

Diwān Moti Rām, however, was a mild-mannered administrator. Hence, within a year it led to insurrections and violence at several places by the disgruntled elements. The revenue collections fell in arrears. People flouted the Government edicts and laws with impunity. Crime had increased considerably. Hence it was decided to replace the Governor by Sardār Hari Singh Nalwā, who took over charge on Aug 24, 1820. His very name and prestige were enough to knock sense into the heads of the rebellious Kashmiris.

Order was soon restored, occasionally also through the show of necessary force. The revenue collections became normal. Sardār Hari Singh Nalwā even reduced considerably the land revenue. Compared to the Afghān's 60 lakhs, he brought it down to 13 lakhs, which was 8 lakhs less even than the sum fixed by his predecessor, Diwān Moti Rām. He also abolished *begār* which was prevalent in the valley for a thousand years. He gave every encouragement to the weavers of exquisite shawls, for which Kashmir is justly famous, and to the production of paper of various special kinds, including papier mache, and to the cultivation of saffron which had been

---

F. N. Contd.

Singh from a Mohammadan slave-girl" (P. 419), and "Kashmirā Singh was really the son of a Jammu Rājput." (Ibid). But, he also states that Ranjit Singh acknowledged them as his sons and gave a large *jāgir* worth Rs. 50,000/— (in Sialkot) and Rs. 20,000/— (in Ajnālā) for the upkeep of his three sons. As if Ranjit, who according to all authorities, was an extremely clever statesman to judge strangers' motives was foolish enough to be duped, time and again, by all his women (except one, the mother of Kharak Singh, about whose legitimacy also Griffin is doubtful) and he loved being surrounded all the time by scandal and shame in respect of his offspring. A similar canard was later invented and broadcast about Prince Dalip Singh as well. It may be, the rivalry among the Rānis also was responsible for spreading these canards inorder to promote the claims of their progeny to succession. The Maāhrājā seeing Kharak Singh's inability even to manage his own estates (whose income was being misappropriated by his agents), was leaning heavily towards Sher Singh, as time passed. But after some time, he was again rehabilitated in his royal father's eyes. The various court parties also tried to promote their interests by playing one Prince against another, and in the process denigrate their rivals as "bastards," a usual Jāt pastime.

reduced to an insignificant quantity over the past two decades, due to frequent upheavals in the country. Many more police posts were established all over the territory and serious crimes were attended to personally by him. Uniform weights and measures were also introduced.

Sardār Hari Singh Nalwā had to be recalled only after two years, as the administration now highly toned up and running very smoothly could be handled even by a lesser person. Thousands of people lined up to give him a touching farewell. When the Sadār met the Mahārājā, he was so pleased with his work that he offered him Rs. 2 lakhs in cash, a neklace of pearls, a pair of golden bangles, besides the district of Hazārā, recently conquered, in *Jāgir*. He was the only chief in the Sikh state to have been allowed, while in Kashmir, to strike a coin in his own name.*

On Feb 11, 1820, Kanwar Nannihāl Singh was born in the house of Prince Kharak Singh, and great festivities were held and charities distributed.

In March 1822, for the first time, some European officers who had fought under Napolean or in the Napoleanic wars, came to the Panjāb in search of employment and adventure. Among them were two French officers, Colonels Ventura and Allard. They were well-received and after examining their credentials for some months, appointed Generals in the Sikh forces, the former in the infantry and the latter in the cavalry. They were to be paid Rs. 2500/- each per month, on the following terms and conditions:-

(1) If a war ensues between the Khālsā Durbār and a European power, they will prove true to their employers.

(2) They will not enter into direct correspondence with any European power.

(3) They will keep their beards whole, and eat no beef, nor smoke tobacco.

General Court and Avitabile, an Italian, and 16 others (according to British records, and forty two, according to Col. Gardner's list)

* The coin (rupee as well as Pasiā) was called "Hari Singhiā". On one side was inscribed his name in Persian letters and the other side were the words, *Sri Akāl Sahāi* (May God, the immortal, protect us). It was first struck in Samvat 1878 (1821 A.D.).

were the European or Anglo-Indian officers who served Ranjit Singh after this date.

According to Carmichael Smyth, there were 12 Frenchmen, 7 Anglo-Indians, 4 Italians, 4 Germans, 3 Americans, 2 Spaniards, one Russian, one Scotch and 3 Englishmen (thirtyseven in all.)

It has been fashionable with some writers to attribute the Sikh successes to the leadership of the European officers. But, it is conveniently forgotton that except for Nowshera and Peshāwar, almost all the other territories that formed part of the Panjāb Kingdom (including Lāhore, Amritsar, Multān, Jullundur-Doāb, Sialkot, Wazirābad, Jehlum, Rāwalpindi, Attock, Hazārā, the Derājāts and Kashmir) had already been conquered by the Sikh forces under their own indigenous leadership, and even instruction in the European methods of warfare had been imparted to the Sikh forces since 1802.†

† According to Vincent Smith, "t visit of Holkar to Lāhore as a fugitive in 1805 (Oxford History of India, P. 611) marked the beginning of the disciplined Sikh army."

The descriptive payrolls in the Khālsā Darbār records prove that battalions trained in the European fashion existed since 1807. There were three battalions initiated in the methods of European drill in 1807. Ranjit went incognito to look at a review of Lord Lake's army (which in 1805 was pursuing Holkar who had sought shelter with Ranjit Singh but who later compromised with Lake). "Allard, Ventura and Court thus played the same part in Panjāb under Ranjit Singh as did Gordon and Lefort in Russia under Peter the Great. They were entrusted with the task of carrying out details. They did not originate any new idea or initiate any new scheme. They merely gave a moderate degree of precision and completeness to a system already introduced." (Sinha, *Ranjit Singh*, P. 161; see also Sitā Rām Kohli's *Army of Ranjit Singh*; and G. L. Chopra's *Panjāb as a Sovereign state.*) According to Bābā Prem Singh, (*Mahārājā Ranjit Singh*) some of the Mahārājā's men had joined the British forces in 1802 who left them later and trained their own soldiers back home. Ventura and Court also became Governors of provinces, besides being instructors in the artillery. Honigberger supervised a gunpowder factory and Ventura even constructed a steam-boat. There was some resistance initially by both officers and men, and even Gurkhas, to serve under the foreigners and they even threatened to resist this by force, esp. because the Europeans were not only highly paid but favoured with *Jāgirs* etc. Europeans from various nationalities, deliberately so recruited to keep them apart from each other, (and therefore loyal to the state) also decried one another's merits and repute. Ranjit Singh insisted that they settle down in Panjāb as householders and as married men, and should not look back towards their ancestral homes any more. But after the death of Ranjit, they were not well-treated, suspected and even looted. Ventura and

The regular army in which the Sikh soldiery was the least interested initially (especially in being foot-soldiers, for they liked being free horsemen) consisted only of 4061 men in 1811 (2852 infantry and 1209 artillery). In 1838, the regular army grew in strength to 38,242 men (29617 in infantry, 4090 in cavalry, and 4535 in the artillery) and the total monthly pay bill came to Rs. 3,74,101, a sepoy getting Rs. 7 to 8½ and a Commandant (Kumedān) receiving Rs. 60 to 120 per month. The forces of the tributaries, the *Jāgirdars* and free horsemen were over and above the regular force. Earlier, payments were made at the time of the harvest, every six months, or *Jāgirs* allotted in lieu of pay. But the harvest-system of pay was soon discontinued and regular monthly emoluments introduced.

Including the irregular army on the eve of Ranjit Singh's death, the total strengh of the Sikh forces was 1,23,800 (92000 infantry and

---

F. N. Contd.

Court had narrow escapes, when they were sought to be physically assaulted. Lt. Col Faulkes was murdered. So, they had no choice but to quit the Panjāb. Kharak Singh was especially allergic to the French officers and considered them as friends of his rivals, particularly Sher Singh.

The Marāthās had also introduced the European drill and methods of warfare late in the 18th century, but unfortunately the regular forces trained by the Europeans for the Peshwās consisted not of the sons of the soil, but Telingas, Najibs and Alygholes—all non-Marāthās—"whose morality was very low." Ranjit, however, made the system popular among the Sikhs. Upto 1813, "the bulk of regulars consisted of Hindustānis, Gurkhās and Afghāns", as the Sikhs were not happy to serve in a regular army, but, Ranjit enlisted recruits from different communities in such a balanced way that from the company to the corps, the spirit of togetherness and belonging prevailed. Communalism, tribalism or localism were not allowed to hinder or thwart the efficiency of the army.

As the European officers had betrayed the interest of the Marāthās at the time of war (e.g. in 1802) and they walked over to the English side, Ranjit Singh was very careful and choosey about their nationality and background and kept a strict watch on their integrity and loyalty. But, none betrayed him in his life-time. Which shows to solicit loyalty also, the man at the helm matters and not merely better emoluments.

Authoritative British historians of the period concede that Ranjit Singh had introduced the European drill, discipline and organisation in his army since 1809, after he had witnessed a small number of trained soldiers accompanying Metcalfe over-powering a much larger number of the Akālis at Amritsar (who it is said, objected to the Shiā soldiers of the company taking out their *tāzias* in the holy city at the time of Moharram and a fight ensued). (*Ranjit Singh* by Osborne, P. 12); (*Origin of Sikh power*, by Princep, p. 52-53), etc.

31,800 cavalry and artillery, which is almost equal in strength to the entire Indian army's strength on the eve of the Second World War in 1939. There were 384 heavy guns and 400 light guns with the artillery.† According to Prof. Sinha, "the artillery of the Sikhs was much better than that of the Marāthās who relied mainly on the rejected artillery of other powers." "It was the weakest branch of the Marāthā service!' But Ranjit Singh had foundries of his own, where guns were cast within the Lāhore Fort, as in other parts of the town at Shāh Dera. The artillery was moreover, unlike the Marāthās under Scindiā and other chieftains, for the Sikh arms and equipment were not of a hetrogenous character. "As a result of western discipline, the rank and file of Sikh army became some of the finest rank and file in the world. They wanted but officers to be invincible".*

After the success, which attended the Sikh arms in Multān and Kashmir, Monghyr acrosss the Attock was attacked. Monghyr was a tributary of Afghānistān with a revenue of about ten lakhs. The Nawāb, Hafiz Ahmad Khān, had 25000 men under arms with him.

Ten forts, highly fortified, guarded its frontiers on all sides. But, it took the Sikh forces only four days under the over-all command of Sardār Hari Singh Nalwā to capture it on Dec. 20, 1821. Other notable warriors, who participated in this compaign were Sardār Dal Singh, Jamādār Khushāl Singh and Generals Diwān Chand and Kirpā Rām. The Nawāb was arrested and presented to the Mahārājā who not only forgave him his life, but also endowed him with a liberal *Jāgir* in Derā Ismail Khān. He was also honoured with a

† The name of Sardār Lehnā Singh Majithiā, son of Sardār Desā Singh Majithiā, the Sikh general, is well-known in this context. It was under his guidance that the best guns of the realm were produced. He was also an astronomer, a linguist, well-versed in higher mathematics and produced a watch, which besides showing time and date, also gave the directions of equinoxes. According to Bābā Prem Singh (Ranjit Singh, p. 178), there were five foundries in the Panjāb to forge guns. The names of some of those who who supervised works at various centres were Miān Kādar Bakhsh, (Lāhore Fort) Miān Afzal Ali (Idgah, Lāhore) Jawāhar Mal, (Shāhderā) Khalifā Imamuddin (Nakodar). The fifth foundry was at Sheikhpur. Gen. Court was another officer who ably assisted in this task. There were four kinds of mounts or pullers for the artillery. Bullocks and horses were used to drive the guns. Lighter guns were mounted on the camels and heavier ones were driven by or mounted upon the elephants, especially in the hilly areas. In the last fight against Kashmir in 1819, the elephant artillery played a notable part.

* *Ranjit Singh*, p. 170.

khilat. The Sikhs captured much cash and war-materials from the fort of Monghyr, including 22 heavy and 70 light guns, besides a large number of rifles and swords.

If Kashmir had to be retained, the pathway to it passing through Hazārā had also to be kept under discipline. The Hazārā territory harboured many independent chiefs and Khāns, even after its capture by the Durrānis in 1752 A.D. Being the home of reputed soldiers, the Afghāns recruited a large force from here, but couldnot get any other advantage. No one paid the revenue and whenever an expedition was sent against them, it suffered humiliation and defeat. The district had been captured by the Sikhs in 1818, and a fort built at Sarāi Salah,* but the disturbed conditions continued. One of the commanders—Makhan Singh—sent to discipline them was murdered at Mohammadpur on the banks of the river "*Daur*". The culprits were soon punished by Sardār Hukma Singh Chimni†, Kiledār of Attock, who led an expedition against them. Later in 1820, Sardār Shām Singh Attāriwala, Sardārni Sadā Kaur, Prince Sher Singh and Diwān Rām Dyāl were sent to bring about order in this area. Though the plains and the mountaneous territory were both cleared of the rebels and disrupters of peace, Diwān Rām Dyāl was killed at a place called Nārā. For two years, the territory was governed thereafter by Sardār Amar Singh Majithiā, who too was murdered here. The Mahārājā

* The most successful President of Pākistān, (1958-69), Gen. Ayub Khān, belonged to this village three miles from Haripur. He studied at the Khālsā High school, Haripur. The writer also hails from a village, Serai Niāmat Khān (Hazārā) (earlier called "*Singh-garhi*" or *Singhri-di-Sārān*) 9 miles away from Haripur, where he got his schooling in the same institution. His great-grand father, Dāsu, an Aide-de-Camp of Nalwā, held a *Jāgir* in this area, after which he alongwith many other Hindus and Sikhs migrated from the countryside of Jehlum and Rāwalpindi to live here. The whole countryside of the Frontier province was peopled by Hindus and Sikhs during this period as a matter of policy, giving them not only protection in the remotest areas, but also through offers of *Jāgirs* and other incentives encouraging them to shift here. Prof. Puran Singh, the well-known Sikh poet of the present century was also born in this district at Salhad, near Abboṭabād, (a city named after Captain Abott, the British Vice-resident, in 1853). The biggest dam of Pakistān at Tarbelā is in the district of Hazārā. The district is so-named because it is said when Tamérlane left India in 1399 A.D., he was so impressed by the verdure and natural beauty of this region that he left a Turkish platoon consisting of a thousand (hazār) soldiers behind, to keep it under his control. From hazār, the name Hazārā is derived.

† He was called "Chimna" affectionately by Ranjit due to his short stature.

thereupon decided to appoint Sardār Hari Singh Nalwā as Governor, for no lesser person could restore order in this turbulent land.

Hari Singh, after inquiry, captured the assassins of Sardār Amar Singh and ordered that they be blown from the mouth of the cannon. This brought about a decided change in the attitude of the people.

In the heart of the plains, a fort called "*Harikishan-garh*" and around it a large town called Haripur* (after the Sardār's own name) were built. He also built a Gurdwārā here, called "Shahidganj" to commemorate the heroic deeds of the warriors who had fallen in the various battles in this area. A Hindu temple was also constructed, besides a Muslim mosque.† The city was surrounded by gardens and water-channels ran through every street, as they still do.

In the year 1821, Ranjit Singh had to take very severe notice of the mis-doings of his mother-in-law, Rāni Sadā Kaur. She was a very brave and chivalrous person and marched to battle alongwith Ranjit to capture Lāhore. She had helped him in some other major campaigns as well in the early years of his reign. But, then, her overbearing nature led to a tussle between the two. Suspicions deepened when she tried to negotiate a separate peace with the British in 1809, without the knowledge of Ranjit,and which in fact compelled Ranjit Singh to sign up the Anglo-Sikh treaty that year with Metcalfe. Even her daughter, Mahtāb, who bore Ranjit Singh the twins (named Sher Sihgh and Tārā Singh) got estranged from the Mahārājā and left to live at her mother's home. Fearing treachery again, Ranjit confiscated her property, except Batālā, which was given over to her grandsons as *Jāgir*. She was given a meagre pension which infuriated her so much that she tried to escape to the British territory and

* It is a very prosperous tehsil town now-a-days and the fort is still intact, surrounded on all sides by a wide ditch.

†Like his monarch, Mahārājā Ranjit Singh, Sardār Hari Singh Nalwā also got many Gurdwarās of historic import built in this area, the most famous of which is the Gurdwārā at Panjā Sāhib (Hassan Abdāl). Its first temple and tank with marble-steps were got constructed by Nalwā in 1832 and completed a year later. Exactly a hundred years later, it was rebuilt, alongwith a huge serai to house the visiting pilgrims,for which huge funds were collected by the author's father, Sardār Ātma Singh, a prosperous Hindu merchant who turned Sikh in 1910, (and participated in the *morcha* of *Guru kā bāgh*). Now, it is in the charge of the Pakistān Govt. and is visited each year by hundreds of pilgrims on the Baisākhi day (13th April).

seek their protection. However, she was apprehended and kept in protective custody (where she died in 1832).

Early in 1823, Sardār Hari Singh had to leave Hazārā, as his services were needed to fight against the Afghāns across the Attock, at Nowsherā. The Afghāns under Mohd. Azim Bārakzai were very restive, seeing the Sikhs expanding their empire across the Attock, besides the other Afghān strongholds like Multān, Monghyr, and Kashmir, and were planning to cross the river and attack Sikh territory with a very large force, consisting of about 45,000 men. They made fortifications near the Jahāngirā fort, and decided to resist the Sikhs crossing the Attock. Under a shower of bullets, they destroyed the bridge of boats over the river, so that no reinforcements could reach the Sikh forces immediately from the other side. The Muslims indeed had declared a *Jehād* (holy war) against the Sikhs, and the fear of a prolonged and tough battle brought the Mahārājā personally to lead his troops. To lead the various contingents were appointed the ablest and most powerful generals of the Sikh rāj, namely, Prince Sher Singh, Sardār Hari Singh Nalwā, Akāli Phoolā Singh Nihang, Sardār Desā Singh Majithiā, Sardār Rattan Singh Gharjākhiā and Sardār Amir Singh Suriānwālā. The first-named two generals had, however, already taken the enemy on, crossing the river before the bridge was destroyed. They were exerting powerful pressure on the enemy, but needed reinforcements which had arrived on the other side of the river, but couldnot wait for the bridge to be constructed under the ever-present threat of enemy-fire. Akāli Phoolā Singh's suicide-squad now took the lead, and, without a moment's thought, plunged their horses in the swollen and turbulent river. How could the others stay behind ? Every one followed suit, but before they crossed over, the enemy had taken flight from Jahāngirā, leaving even their dead or dying in the battle-field and saying in despair:—"Tobā, Tobā, Khudā Khud Khālsā shud." (God forbid, but it appears, God himself has turned a Khālsā !).

But, the war was not yet over. When Mohd. Azim Khān heard of this humiliating disaster from his nephew, Mohd. Zamān Khān, who had led the battle at Jahāngirā, he was beside himself with rage, and decided to gather all his forces at Nowshera. The Mahārājā was being informed through his network of intelligence of the rapidly rising force of the enemy at Nowshera, but decided to wait for his heavy guns to arrive which were due by mid-day (March 14, 1823). But, at the morning Sikh service, which was always held in times of war or peace, a *Gurmattā* had already been passed that the *Ghāzis* shall be attacked the same morning, before they could gather more force. The Akālis, therefore, refused to wait in view of the Holy Resolve (*Gurmattā*), and wanted the attack launched without delay. The Mahārājā had also to yield and ordered prince Kharak Singh to take the lead. Fortunately, the artillery also arrived before time under Gen. Allard. A furious battle raged. The Sikh guns rained death on the enemy lines and soon the warriors took to hand-to-hand fighting. After the loss of many thousand dead, Azim Khān fled the battlefield, and heart-broken, died, on the way to Kābul. His forces also losing heart abandoned the field in complete disorder. 14 large and 18 small guns were captured by the Sikhs. Across the river Kābul (Lundā) also, fierce battles were fought and the *Ghāzis* were cruelly beaten in their game there too. But, one of the most loved and fearless Sikh generals, Akāli Phoola Singh, also laid down his life in this battle. His horse was shot and dismounting it, he rode to battle on an elephant, where he was sighted by a *Ghāzi* and soon a hail of bullets pierced his body, and he fell down dead. His memorial still stands intact there*. For Ranjit Singh as much as for others, the joy of a superb victory was marred by this sad and heart-rending event.

From 1822 onwards, another dark force was gathering on the horizon for the Sikhs, in the person of Sayyad Ahmad Brelvi (born 1796 A. D. at Bareilley in U. P.) He had a large, fanatical Muslim following in North India. On his way to Meccā for a Hajj the same year, and on his way back in 1826, he called upon Dost. Mohd Khān, Amir of Kābul, and solicited his military and cash assistance to resist the growth of Sikh power which might otherwise engulf Afghānistān itself, if not also the Muslim lands beyond. It is said, he met the Sultān of Turkey as well, during his travels for the same purpose, but with what result is not clear. He declared his determination to declare a *Jehād* against the Sikhs. Dost Mohd. Khān agreed with this assessment wholeheartedly, and offered all possible help. He even wrote to his brothers, Sultān Mohd. Khān and Yār Mohd.

---

* This monument (now situated in the Frontier Province of Pakistān) on the bank of the river Kābul was endowed with a *Jāgir* by Ranjit Singh and a gurdwārā was also built on the site. Sardār Gurbaksh Singh, well-known Panjābi writer and editor of "Preet Lari", settled there in early thirties of this century, and tractorised the farm attached to this monument. The place is still called "Samādh Akāli Phoolā Singh."

Khān, Afghān Governors of Peshāwar, to render him every conceivable assistance. As the Sayyad was a highly respected personage, Muslims from all over India contributed money to his coffers*. The preparations were made for a year thereafter. Atlast in 1827, the Hydari flag was unfurled and thousands of *Ghāzis* gathered around it on the plains of *Akorā Khattak*. They first surrounded the Sikh fort at Khairābād, whose Kiledār, Budh Singh Sandhānwāliā, taken unwares with a small force, could hardly resist the massive onslaught. Sardār Hari Singh Nalwā who, with a force of 8000 was touring Chhachh nearby, was apprised of this treacherous situation and took only a day's time to arrive. Inspite of this, the Muslim forces exceeded the Sikhs twenty times, the *Ghāzis* numbering over 1,50,000. But though full of religious zeal and determination to die, they soon found that they were a mere disorganised rabble against the highly-trained and war-tempered Sikh army, heavily out-numbered though it was.

Leaving thousands dead (the *maidān* is still littered with Muslim graves over a vast area), the Ghāzis led by Sayyad Ahmad fled the field. The Sikh cavalry pursued the fleeing enemy for a long distance inflicting heavy losses on them. The Sayyad was hunted down in 1831 at Bālākot and killed, after his several attacks in 1830 at Peshāwar and nearby were foiled by Hari Singh Nalwā and Gen. Allard. The Ghāzis dispersed to their homes and the Sayyad's family took refuge with the Nawāb of Tonk in India.

In the summer of 1827, the Mahārājā sent Diwān Moti Rām and Faqir Aziz-ud-Din to call on Lord Amherst, the British Governor-General in India, at Simla. He was the first Governor General to

---

* Though the British authorities in India did not ostensibly lend any helping hand to Sayyad Ahmad Brelvi, they put no curbs on his activities in their territories. In fact, Captain Wade expressed pleasure in his communication to the Secretary to his Govt. (June 17, 1831) that for the last five years the Sayyad had offered "employment" to the Sikh arms, and now that this phase was over, they would look out for fresh fields of conquest! According to Metcalfe's communication (1927) as Resident at Delhi, the Delhi emperor is said to have encouraged this spirit of joining the *Jehād*, and numerous quitted their homes and marched to join them, including some who resigned the East Indian Company's service for the same purpose.

* It is said, the Sayyad offended his Yusafzai followers by asking them not only for 1/10th of their incomes for the *Jehād*, which they gave willingly, but also offering all their marriageable daughters to marry his Indian soldiers. Many Yusafzais deserted him over this injunction.

pass his summer in the cool heights of the newly-developed hill-station. They offered large presents to him on behalf of their monarch. These included a fine woollen *Shāmianā*, made in Kashmir, and of exquisite design and handiwork and some precious horses. A *Shamiānā* made up of shawls was also presented for the British King. The Governor-General received them with great honour and loaded them with valuable gifts for their Mahārājā, including English steeds, an elephant with a silver *howda*, a jewel-studded sword, a two-barrelled gun, a newly-invented pistol, 2 necklaces of pearls, 2 rolls of gold brocade etc. Rich *Khilats* were bestowed upon the two officials as well. The return visit to the Mahārājā was paid by Capt. Wade, Political Agent to the Governor General, accompanied by several other high-ranking officials. They reached Amritsar on May 31, and were very cordially received by the Sikh monarch there. The first-day payments and gifts made to them included Rs. 5000/— in silver coins, Rs. 5000/— in gold mohurs, and 2000 baskets of fruits and sweets! After a brief stay and a visit to the Golden Temple, the British party left for home, highly satisfied with the mutual trust and respect subsisting between the two nations. (*)

The British, however, were not the only power to seek friendship with the Sikh Kingdom. The Czār of Russia had sent his complimentary communications to the Sikh monarch in 1814 and 1822. The Nizām of Hyderābād sent his Vakil to the Lāhore Durbār in 1826, with large presents, including a bejewelled sword, one gun, several rifles, four Arab horses and an exquisite canopy. The canopy was so glamorous that Ranjit immediately ordered that it be presen-

* In this very year, Sardār Fateh Singh Ahluwāliā, ruler of Kapurthalā, escaped to the British territory due to a conspiracy hatched by his Vizier, Sher Ali, against him in collaboration with his agent at Lāhore, Kādir Baksh. The latter started sending false reports and the Vizier building his case on them scared the Sardār into the belief that his life was in danger at the hands of the Lāhore Durbār. Ranjit considered Fateh Singh to be like his brother and had exchanged turbans with him, as a token of affection and esteem. Both had together signed the Anglo-Sikh treaty of 1806 and Fateh Singh had fought heroically on the Mahārājā's side in many an engagement. However, when he fled to Ludhiānā, he was given no asylum by the British and had to return. He took the risk and suddenly appeared on March 11, 1827, in Ranjit's court, asking for forgiveness for his intemperate behaviour. He laid this sword at the Mahārājā's feet, who was so touched by this gracious gesture that he embraced him in the open court and awarded him a *khilat* and rich presents.

ted to the Golden Temple at Amritsar (where it was preserved in the *Toshakhana* but damaged in 1984—see later). The envoys from the courts of Herāt (1826) and Baluchistān (1829) and the King of France (in 1836, through Gen. Allard) sent him large presents and letters of friendship. The King of Great Britain, William IV, personally sent a special delegation in 1830 with presents for the Mahārājā (which besides choice horses, included a four-wheeled carriage)* and a letter of "abiding friendship." The Maharājā received them with great honour and sent many precious gifts for the British King. They inspected a parade in their honour and were highly impressed with the turn-out, discipline and efficiency of the Sikh forces. On their way back home, they made an offering at the Golden Temple as well and prayers were offered on their behalf "for permanent friendship between the Sikhs and the British," (though they were not admitted into the inner sanctuary of the *Akāl Takht* by the anti-*feringi* Akālis).

Later, the Mahārājā himself met the Governor-General at Rupar, after visits of high-powered delegations were exchanged to make suitable arrangements for the royal visit.† The two met on 26th October 1831, accompanied by a great display of pageantry and armed power on both sides. The Mahārājā was escorted from Amritsar for 11 days by a contingent of British forces led by Sir Claude Wade. He was assisted in his negotiations with the British by Kanwar Kharak Singh, Sardār Hari Singh Nalwā, Sardār Attar Singh

---

* Another (and more important) reason for the British King to send these large horses (or Trojan horses) was to explore the river Sind and the Chenāb for "trade" purposes. That the purpose was not merely commercial but also political can be seen from the treaty of "commerce" Col. Pottinger concluded in 1832 with the Amirs of Sind. "Sind is now gone, for the English have seen the river," said a Sindi Sayyad & this proved true, as in a decade, Sind was annexed. As for the horses they died of over feeding being larger than any breed known in the Panjāb.

† The Sikh delegation to meet the Governor-General at Simla at this time consisted of Sardār Hari Singh Nalwā, Sardār Lehnā Singh Majithiā, S. Ajit Singh Sandhānwāliā, Fakir Aziz-ud-Din, Diwān Moti Rām and S. Dhannā Singh Malwai. The British delegation was led by Capt. Wade, Political Agent to the Governor General. It was at one of these meetings that the Governor-General asked the fakir which of the Mahārājā's eyes was blinded and the fakir had replied:—"The countenance of my ruler dazzles like the sun. I've therefore never looked him in the face. How can I tell ?"

The Governor-General was highly pleased at this show of high personal regard for the Mahārājā by one of his trusted Muslim Ministers.

Sandhānwāliā, S. Shām Singh Attariwālā, Rājā Gulāb Singh and a few others. The meeting was extremely important for the British as the recent Russian occupation of the eastern part of Irān (which matter was under correspondence between the Governor-General and the Sikh Kingdom due to its repercussions on India, particularly the Panjāb) and the opening up of the river Sind for internal navigation were to be discussed. The British Govt. wanted to impress the world with the fact that the Sikh power stood by them in case of any Russian advance towards India. Ranjit also wanted to exhibit not not only the Crown-Jewels and other regalia, but also the discipline and the western training of his army which could now take on any power in the East. He also wanted to impress that he was the undisputed leader of the Khālsā, without a rival in its ranks. According to Capt. Wade, however, most of the Sikh chiefs were against this meeting They wanted the Mahārāja to bide his time, as nothing would be gained by the Sikhs under the then prevailing circumstances. An Akāli even tried to assault the Mahārājā. If he finally made up his mind to agree to a meeting, it appears more in a spirit of resignation than as a result of deliberate resolution, or obstinacy.

So while in the discussions on the important matters of state, the gains were all on the British side (whether it was navigation through the river Chenāb, thus offering a passage through a Panjab river for the first time for the British, and restricting Ranjit's options over Sind, which was virtually taken under British protection, or the advance of the Russians through the North-West in which case the Panjāb was to shed its blood first to safeguard British dominions in India), Ranjit used this historic occasion to press an inocuous and a natural desire on his part but which also put in motion a trend which ultimately was to prove ruinous to the Sikh state as much as to Ranjit's own family and progeny as well.

This was his desire to get the Birtish to know and to confirm the Sikh Kingdom's line of succession. Ranjit introduced his son, Kharak Singh, to the Governor-General as the chosen successor of the Mahārājā

Discussions of the Mahārājā did take place with the notable courtiers on the eve of this unfortunate announcement. But with the exception of Sardār Ha i Singh Nalwā, no one made a public protest, though Dhian Singh, who according to Osborne was more inclined towards Sher Singh was cautious enough not to press his views strongly or openly & to keep his options open. According to Cunningham, "he (Nalwā) was one of those most averse to the recognition of the right of the Prince Kharak Singh, and the heir-apparent himself would seem to have been aware of the feeling of the Sikh people, for he had a year before (1830) opened a correspondence with the British Governor of Bombay, as if to derive hope from the vague terms of a complimentary reply.". †

Captain Wade, writing from Ludhiānā (July 19, 1834) to Macnaughten, gives an extremely poor judgement of the character and competence of Kharak Singh in view of the problems confronting him in the event of Ranjit's death (which the British expected due to his excesses & various ailments in the coming few years). Says he:- "*Imbecile in character and degraded in intellect as Kharak Singh is*, it is a mistake to suppose that Sher Singh is better qualified to hold the reins of Govt. He is a man of dissolute and debauched habits and from a love of indolence, despises the chores of business. The

---

† With regard to this interchange of letters, see the correspondence of the Persian Secretary to the Political Secretary at Bombay, 6th July, 1830. Adds Cunningham:— "That Ranjit Singh was jealous, personally, of Hari Singh or that the servant would have proved a traitor to the living master is not probable, but Hari Singh was a zealous Sikh and an ambitious man and Kharak Singh was always full of doubts and apprehensions with respect to his succession and even his safety. Col. Wade has informed the author that the whole of the Sikh chiefs were said by Ranjit Singh himself to be averse to the meeting with the British Governor-General"(possibly for this very reason). (History of the Sikhs, P. 173-74). Why Ranjit Singh insisted on this meeting can only be his keen desire to clear the way of succession for his eldest son. Ranjit Singh took the criticism in his stride, but Kharak Singh on account of this impertinence and the Dogras (or account of their own rivalry with Hari Singh) never forgave this great hero. This becomes clear from the fact that after this strong expression of opinion, Hari Singh was always kept on the borders among the the turbulent Pathāns, his letters for help were intercepted by Dhiān Singh and delayed till he died, and Ranjit confiscated all his property and released a portion for his widow and four sons only after they had been sufficiently humiliated and deprived. Hari Singh's only fault was that he had publicly said to the Mahārājā : "This state belongs not to an individual, but to the Khālsā Commonwealth. It is the sacrifices of a whole people over a century, blessed by the Guru's Grace, that we have won an empire. Its leadership belongs to where it belongs—to the whole Sikh people. Let them choose who shall lead them by a consesus (*Gurmattā*). Kharak Singh is my friend, but not able to bear this great burden. Let's not fail our people when they need our dispassionate lead most." But such is the call of blood that this hero of many battles and great patriot was not heard. In fact he was charged with an ambition to succeed the Mahārājā and seeds of hatred were sown against him.

French officers were for Sher Singh, but despised by Kharak Singh (which may be a good reason for Capt. Wade's hostility to Sher Singh.) (After Ranjit's death) Muslim tribes will rebel between Jehlum and Peshāwar. The three Jammu Rajāhs,all raised to their high stations by the Mahārājā,will declare independent their territories between Kashmir and Rāvi, so also the hill-states between Rāvi and Satluj. Multān will continue to owe allegiance under the popular and intelligent Governor (Sāwan Mal). The Afghāns of Kālābāgh, Derā Ismail Khān, Tonk, Bannu and Senghir will rebel. We expect not much trouble in the territory affecting our interests between Ropar and Haree Ke Pattan (on both sides of the Satluj) except from some loose bands of plunderers". (But for these very reasons, Kharak Singh's succession was to be welcomed by the British, so that on the pretext of the ensuing anarchy, they might advance their own interests.) Adds Wade:- "With every diffidence, in my judgement, I beg leave to submit for his Lordship's consideration whether in the event of Ranjit's death, it would not be proper to adopt the precaution of advancing a part of the Ludhiānā force to Ferozepur backed by a regiment of cavalry from Karnāl", etc.

According to Wade, (in the same communication) "the feud will occur not only between Kharak Singh and Sher Singh, but by the revolt of numerous chiefs (as detailed above) who have been the victims of his ambition."

On Feb 14, 1838, Capt. Wade again wrote to W.H. Macnaughten Secy to the Govt of India on the issue of succession a long letter, 16 months *before* Ranjit's demise, assessing the relative merits of each contender or pretender to the throne. This will be reproduced later. But, in regard to Kharak Singh, his views are highly significant:-

"*Kanwar Kharak Singh, the heir, wants energy and his manners are not in his favour, nor his mind brightened by those beams of intelligence which appear both in the conduct and the ohservation of his young and active son (Nau Nihāl Singh).*" *However, Wade is diplomatic enough not to go too far in his harsh judgement and tempers his earlier remark by suggesting "but I'm not inclined to consider him so utterly destitute of intellect as is generally supposed...... Though not much feared, he is loved by his dependents while no one in the country bears ill-will to him for he has injured no one.*

"*With these qualities (sic), the Kanwar Kharak Singh is perhaps wanted by the British Govt to confirm its influence in the Panjāb, if,* *our interests point out to us which I think they do to preserve the Sikh nation, between the frontier and the Mohammedan powers west of the Indus".**

A weak ruler, lacking energy and strong character, poor of intellect, not feared by his people or others but loved by his dependents, that is, being a good-goody sort of a [illegible] must have been in the best interests of the British. And why not?

Kharak Singh, knowing his inherent weaknesses, as has been pointed out, was also in regular correspondence with the British, asking for their support.

In a letter from Capt. Wade to Machnaughtan dated 10 Aug. 1836, it is confirmed that overtures were made by Kharak Singh to him in his letter (April 30, 1836) taken by Maulvi Āzam Ali, a personal servant of his, "asking for British help for his succession and pointing to the ambitions of the Jammu Rājās (who were reported to be anti-British at that time). (A reply was also sent to Kharak Singh on July 19, 1836).

Thus, the self-same hero, the formidable conqueror and consolidator of the Sikh empire, who chose to rule always in the name of the Guru and the Khālsā, also became a victim of his overpowering affection for an imbecile son, and conspired himself for the destruction of a plant which under his superb and God-given intelligence and leadership, the whole Khālsā (indeed his whole country irrespective of caste or creed) had nurtured with their blood and tears. The handiwork of two centuries was sacrificed over a personal whim and a vain desire to perpetuate his line, unmindful of the tradition of his faith, whose last Guru had enjoined upon his followers not to commemorate his memory even by raising a small platform in his

---

* Not that Ranjit Singh was an unsophisticated man of no vision who did not see through the British game. When a Christian missionary, Dr. Joseph Wolff, visited him in 1832,he put the matter bluntly to him, though in a humorous vein. Said Ranjit :—"You say you travel about for the sake of religion. Why then do you not teach to the English in Hindustān who have no religion at all ?" (And it is to the credit of the British Governor-General, Lord William Bentick, that when this remark was quoted to him, he replied :—"This is alas ! the opinion of natives all over India"). When the missionary, however, persisted in his religious discourse and asked the Mahārājā "how may one come nigh unto God," the Mahārājā burst into laughter and said :—"By making an alliance with the British Govt. as I lately did with Lord Nawāb Sāhib Bahādur at Roopar." (Travels and Adventures of Rev. Joseph Wolff, p. 375).

honour. Nations are not so much destroyed by outsiders, as by their inner discords and personal vanities, whims and vainglorious ambitions of its rulers, while sacrifice and the vision of a common future crown their efforts forsure with victory and grandeur.

The die was, however, cast.

Both sides took leave of each other with "satisfaction". The British because they had got all they had wanted over Sind or the advance upon India of Russia, and Ranjit Singh, Mahārājā of the Punjāb, because his natural line of succession had been perpetuated! In the fulfilment of Ranjit's desire, the British, as we have seen, were also fully assured that it would not be before long that the Sikh empire will crumble in the hands of weak and incompetent successors and the last sovereign state in India fall into their lap, without much effort and sacrifice on their part. They had only to bide their time.

After this, a large expedition was sent out under Sardār Hari Singh Nalwā and Kanwar Nau Nihāl Singh to capture Peshāwar (lit. that which comes first) and annex it. This was done on May 6, 1834, in a lightening campaign. After 800 years of Moghal and Afghān rule, Peshāwar fell to the sword of the Khālsā army.* When Dost. Mohd. Khān, Amir of Kābul, heard about it, he collected a huge army and planned an attack upon Peshāwar. However, realising how formidable the Sikh army was, he despatched a Vakil asking for negotiations to settle the frontiers between the two states. The Maharājā, who had arrived in Peshāwar by now, readily agreed to send Fakir Aziz-ud-Din and an American officer, Harlon, to Kābul to conduct the negotiations. Dost Mohd proved treacherous and took both into custody. Ranjit Singh, on hearing this, was naturally beside himself with rage and ordered a march on Jalālābād, the first frontier post

* In this compaign, an old patriarch (Gen. Ram Singh), his son (Gurmukh Singh) and his grandson (Kumedān Sher Singh), all of the Hassanwāliā clan, surrounded Hāji Khān, one of the rulers of Peshāwar, who made desparate bids to flee, but was seriously wounded and his sword snatched by Sardār Rām Singh. All the three generations were represented together at the Court of Ranjit Singh. Sardār Rām Singh was highly revered by the Mahārājā due to his high character and piety. He it was who had initiated Ranjit's father, Mahān Singh, into the Khālsā fold by administering *Pāhul* to him. All the three participated in the battles of Multān, Kashmir and Peshāwar and showed great acts of daring. (Bābā Prem Singh, Hari Singh Nalwā, pp. 196-97). The author's wife is a direct descendant of Sardār Rām Singh Hassanwāliā.

within the kingdom of Kābul. When Dost Mohd. knew that his trick had misfired, he released both the officers of the Sikh state and sent them back with due honours on a promise that a reconciliation be brought about between the two parties. On his return, Fakir Aziz-ud-Din was able to dissuade Ranjit from advancing towards Kābul. Forts were ordered to be built at Michni and Qilā Shakargarh (or, Shabqadar, earlier known as Sikh-Dheri). Hari Singh was appointed the first Governor of Peshāwar, with Kanwar Nau Nihāl Singh as his under-study.

As was the Mahārājā's usual practice, he endowed all the dispossessed Muslim chiefs of the area with liberal *Jāgirs*. Sultān Mohd. Khān, the defeated Afghān Governor, of Peshāwar and a brother of Dost Mohd Khān was offered a *Jāgir* with Rs. 3 lakhs as revenue in the districts of Kohāt and Hashatnagar. Other Muslim Sardārs were similarly rewarded and honoured.*

In Oct 1836, Sardār Hari Singh captured Jamrud, overlooking the Khyber pass, and hence of great military significance. Its mud-fortress was replaced by a large, reinforced fort and named "Fatehgarh".

In early March, 1837, Kanwar Naunihāl Singh was married to to the daughter of Sardār Shām Singh Attāriwālā. It was a fantastic marriage and surpassed all the festivities hitherto celebrated in the Sikh kingdom. The Rājās of all the Cis-Satluj and hill states were invited and participated in the occasion. The Governor General was represented by Sir Henry Fane, the Commander-in-chief, who made an offering of Rs. 11000/-to the bridegroom. Rājā Dhiān Singh, Prime Minister, offered Rs. 1,25,000/-followed by others, according to rank. The *tambol* totalled Rs. 50 lakhs.

The ceremony of investiture of the bridegroom was held at the Golden Temple, Amritsar, on March 7, when a wreath (Sehrā) of diamonds and pearls was tied with gold thread to the head of the bridegroom by the Mahārājā himself, and offerings were made to the sacred temple and all the *bungās* by the Sikh monarch. In the afternoon, the procession headed by the Mahārajā started for Attāri.

---

* So much care was taken to protect the religious sentiments of the Muslims of this area that when "there was a great dispute between the Musalmāns and the Hindus (about a temple at Peshāwar within the enclosure of a square dedicated to Gorakhnath). Gen.Avitabile caused a mosque also to be built for the Musalmans close to the Hindu temple." (Shahāmat Ali, *The Sikhs and the Afghans*, p. 209).

Seated on the elephant, Ranjit threw silver coins generously on all sides to be picked up by the poor. The crowds lining both sides of the road were unprecedented, over half a million by conservative estimates. Next day, everyone of them who was present in the 5-mile enclosure was rewarded. A million rupees atleast were given away on that day in charity.

The dowry was also very elaborate. It consisted of 101 cows, 101 she-buffalows, 10 camels, 11 elephants, gold and silver ornaments and utensils, precious stones, rich stuffs, consisting of silks of Multān and golden and scarlet *Kinkhābs* (brocades) of Banāras and 500 pairs of Kashmere shawls, unrivalled in their texture and worksmanship. Rich gifts were offered also to the distinguished guests, and back at Lāhore, the military prowess of the Sikh rāj displayed before the C-IN-C which both dazzled and warned him.

But soon thereafter, came a most heart-rending calamity. Dost Mohd Khān of Kābul, greatly perturbed at the capture of Jamrud, sent his son, and Mirzā Sami Khān, to carry the castle by assault. Sardār Hari Singh was not in station, and the fort was held by Sardār Mahān Singh with a small garrison of 600. He fought as hard as he could, but was no match against the heavy odds he had to contend with. He, therefore, sent in the night an urgent communication for reinforcements through a Sikh woman of great daring, Harsaran Kaur, who in the garb of an Afridi woman conveyed the letter, next morning. On its receipt, the Sardār personally proceeded towards Jamrud, and the enemy, terror-stricken, took to flight. The fleeing *ghāzis* were pursued upto a distance, but when the Sikh contingent was returning to the fort, Sardār Hari Singh Nalwā, according to Sir Lepel Griffin, "was struck by two balls, one in the side and the other in the stomach. He knew he was mortally wounded, but fearing to discourage his men, he turned the horse's head and managed to ride as far as his tent. He swooned as he was taken from his horse and half an hour later, the bravest of the Sikh generals, the man with the terror of whose name Afghān mothers used to quiet their fretful children, was dead." According to another account by Capt. Wade, "he received four wounds and two sabre-cuts across his breast, one arrow was fixed in his breast which he deliberately pulled out himself, and continued to issue his orders as before, until he received a gunshot wound in the side,from which he gradually sank and was carried off the field to the fort where he expired." † It is to the eternal credit of the secular Sikh policies that a ballad in praise of this noble warrior dying while fighting againt a Muslim power, has been written by a noted Muslim poet, Qādir Yār.

The news of his death and cremation the same night (April 30,1837) was kept a closely-guarded secret so that the enemy may not feel emboldened and return to attack the Sikh garrison. News was immediately despatched through a courier to Lāhore which was received by the Mahārājā personally three days after the heart rending incident. The Maharājā was shocked beyond measure, and wept unashamedly in the open court. When he learnt from Rājā Dhian Singh that urgent communications for aid had been received from Sardār Hari Singh Nalwā, but the Mahārājā was not apprised of them (due, it was said, to considerable strain he had gone through at

† When he died, Hari Singh Nalwā had an income of three lakhs and sixty seven thousand annually from his *Jāgir.* He had accumulated about Rs. 90 lakhs in his lifetime, most of which was confiscated. The Bankers of Amritsar with whom he kept his money were tortured by Imamuddin to disgorge the treasure, (British intelligence, 23 June 1837), which seems a strange and tragic reward for the magnificent and unrivalled services he had rendered to the state. It is said the Dogrā party in the court wanted to overawe other courtiers, and their own rivals or perhaps, Prince Kharak Singh wanted to avenge himself on his detractor after his death, and had poisoned the ears of the Mahārājā. But sad though the episode is, more should not be read in this than is warranted. It was a matter of policy with Ranjit to confiscate either a large portion or the whole of the accumulated property of a dead chief. He did the same with his mother-in-law, Sadā Kaur, at her death, as we have seen, and also with his son and heir apparent, Kharak Singh, who was compelled to deposit in the Govt. treasury all his mother's treasures, ornaments and cash amounting to Rs. 50 lakhs. His mother's belongings (worth another Rs. 50 lakhs) were divided equally in three parts, one part going to the state, the other to Kharak Singh, and the third part to Prince Nau Nihāl Singh, his son. The idea was not to let unearned wealth in a large quantity fall into the hands of the descendants. This also kept the courtiers and high officials in check in their own lifetime who were obliged to keep within limits in the accumulation of property. The same thing was done to Sardār Fateh Singh Ahluwāliā, his turban brother, and S. Uttam Singh Majithiā. Not that Hari Singh's widow was made destitute. According to British intelligence reports (23rd to 29th June, 1837) the widow of Hari Singh was approached by Munshi Sardhā Rām and told, that if she would return a part of the property, she could retain the Gujrānwālā distt in Jāgir. She, however, wanted that her two sons-Arjan Siggh and Jawāhar Singh-be recalled from Peshāwar, "when *Nazrānā* either more or less would be offered." This was agreed to. "But the revenue of that year's harvest was collected by the state!"

the time of Kanwar Nau Nihāl Singh's marriage), the Mahārājā was furious over this deliberate negligence and callousness on the part of his Prime Minister. Though the pretentions were different, the intention of the Dogrā chief, it appears now, was to remove physically, if possible, all possible contenders to the throne after Ranjit's demise.* However, Ranjit lost no time in advancing upon Peshāwar and the advance contingent reached there only six days later, the Mahārājā himself halting at Rohtās and taking command of the entire operations. But by this time, the Afghāns had taken to their heels.

The conquest of the territory right upon Jamrud not only led to the tribal territories being peopled by Hindus and Sikhs as merchants and farmers in sizeable numbers, but it also made Kābul almost a dependency of the Panjāb, now that its gateway was occupied by the Sikhs. Many a time, the conquest of Kābul itself was envisaged (and Shāh Shuja helped as in 1834 by the Khālsā Durbar in his abortive attempt to conquer Afghānistan † but a direct assault on Kābul was never made, except on the eve of the Mahārājā's death. The long line of communications through the Khyher pass, broken by rivulet and stream, was not so hard to keep, after the conquest of Peshāwar, but it was also the desire of Mahārājā not to annoy the British whose interests, due to Russian and earlier French fears, did not coincide with those of the Sikhs at the appropriate times, though in the Sikh hearts always surged a desire to capture the country not for its revenues (which were very meagre) but for the sake of poetic

* Such was the terror of Hari Singh that when Abbās Mirzā of Persia asked Mohanlāl if the Sikh army could compare in courage and discipline with his, Mohanlāl's reply was :—"If Hari Singh Nalwā were to cross the Indus, His Highness would soon be glad to retreat to his original government in Tabriz." (Mohanlāl, Travels, P XIX intr.)

† The terms of the treaty suggested by the Mahārājā to Shāh Shujā were peculiar. (I) That cow-slaughter would be abandoned throughout Afghānistān. (2) The gates of the Hindu Somnāth temple, looted by Mahmud of Ghazni, a thousand year ago, would be returned to the temple. Though the Shāh did not agree to them, it shows how Ranjit's mind worked to assuage the feelings of his subjects, whom the Afghān warriors through a thousand years had robbed and humiliated. Later, when the combined forces of the Sikhs, the British and the Shāh marched upon Afghānistān and Shāh Shujā was seated on the throne of Kābul, the gates of Somnāth *were* brought back, and delivered with due cermony to the temple. The British writers, however, doubt if they were the same gates or only passed as such.

justice to serve notice on the persecutors of their race for a millenium how the wheel of fortune can turn a full circle. The following conversation (March 1831)—between the Mahārājā and Jacquemont with regard to the future fields of conquest is highly significant.

Mahārājā:—What conquests can I undertake at present ?

Jacquement : Any country of Asia not already occupied by the English.

Maharaja:—But what province shall I first think of taking ? Tibet ? You have been there.

Jacuqement: Your Majesty would have only to send your Gurkha regiment, but that country is very poor.

Mahārājā:—What is the use of conquering such a country ? I want lands which are rich and prosperous. Could I not have Sind ?"

Ranjit had tried many a time to capture Sind, but the British always outwitted him. After his first expedition to Multān, the Amirs of Sind had started communicating with him. After the annexation of Multān, their envoys regularly came to pay their respects, though no tribute was offered, inspite of Ranjit's demand in 1826 that as he had inherited most of territory occupied earlier by Kābul, it was his right to receive tribute from Sind, as successor authority. Sind did not pay any tribute to Kābul either, mostly by blackmailing Afghanistān that if it asserted its right, the Amirs would seek the protection of Ranjit Singh. In 1831, after Ranjit's hands were free from Sayyad Ahmad Brelvi's upsurge, he turned again to Sind. He invaded and captured Bahāwalpur. The Baluch areas of Herrand and Dalji were taken next. He annexed Dera Ghāzi Khān and laid claim to Shikārpur next door, the gateway to Khurāsān, which was a great centre of commerce for all of central Asia. It contained a majority of Sikh (Sahjdhāri) population—all followers of Bābā Nānak, only one-tenth being Muslims. In 1832, Shah Shuja had agreed through a treaty to cede half of Shikārpur to Ranjit Singh for a payment of Rs. 1,25000/-. After the conquest of Peshawar, Shikārpur, which was its dependency, should have paid tribute to him. But, the British stood adamant and encouraged the Amirs to defy his authority and to forge an alliance with the British inorder to thwart his designs. When the Mahārājā was at Rupar (1831), negotiating with the British Governor-General, Lord William Bentick, the British Agent, Pottinger, was negotiating a treaty with the Amirs of Sind for rights to use the river Indus for navigation. This fact was, however, kept from

Ranjit Singh, though he was being asked to be a party to the opening up of the river for international commerce. But, the treaty that he signed in this context later made him also helpless against Sind, though some of the Tālpur princes continued to seek his friendship. In 1835, a regular campaign was again envisaged, but Sind in the meantime had almost been taken under the protection of the British and Ranjit was in no mood to fight on two fronts. This attitude of the British was, however, against the letter and spirit of the Treaty of 1809. The Governor-General had assured Ranjit Singh at Rupar in 1831 that the terms of that treaty were final. How could they now oppose his advance towards Sind or take Sind under their own protection is beyond understanding. But might knows no rights, treaty or no treaty.*

The Mahārājā, therefore, advanced in another direction—Ladākh, the back-door to Kashmir, a prosperous centre of shawl-work and a neighbour of Tibet, Nepal and China. Zorāwar Singh, the Dogrā Commander in the employ of the Lāhore Durbār, captuerd it, after receiving instructions from the Mahārājā, in 1834. Ladākh agreed to pay tribute. Iskardu (or little Tibet) was suggested as the next target. But, the Mahārājā thinking that this might land him in a conflict with China did not encourage his overzealous deputies for any further advances in this region. Being a statesman of great vision and maturity in military & political matters, he knew where to draw the ine, and when. He did not want to overreach himself.

However, Nepal started cultivating Ranjit Singh. After the Nepalese defeat at the hands the British in their wars of 1814-16, they had been isolated and were on the look-out of friends. Gurkhās were already being recruited in the Sikh army. Amar Singh Thāpā's son was a general in the Sikh Army. The British were becoming overbearing. The conquest of Ladākh had made the Sikh kingdom neighbours of Nepal. Over the matters of Sind, the British had bypassed Ranjit. So an official mission from Nepal (May 1837) was received cordially at Lāhore. The mission described the Mahārājā

* That the British had done injustice both to Ranjit and their own sense of fairness is reflected by Lord Auckland, the Governor-General's letter to the Home Govt. on this subject (Oct 7, 1836) :— "Are we at liberty to put one construction of the treaty at one time, and another at another, as it suits our convenience? If not, we can hardly say that we have any right to interefere between Ranjit Singh and Sind." But, he was over-ruled.

as the "lamp of Hindus, an Avatar", etc., and made many presents on behalf of their ruler. The Mahārājā, contrary to his earlier stand, also sent a letter to the Ruler of Nepāl, expressing his desire to continue friendly communication.

In the British records are quoted instances of Mahārājā Ranjit taking interest even in the affairs of Burma. In 1814, a Burmese Mission had come to Chittagong confidentially en route to the Sikh country. In 1818, the Government of Burma asked for the permission of the Governor-General to permit some of their nationals to proceed to the Panjāb "to collect original sacred writings" (of the Bhuddhist faith). "In 1823, some Sikhs claiming to be agents of Ranjit Singh came to Amarapura, capital of Burmā, and proposed a treaty, offensive and defensive, to drive the English out." However, nothing came of it. The Burmese took great pride in Sikh victories, for, by so doing, they put heart into their own people that all was not lost for them.

Atlast, the dream to conquer Afghānistān and place Shāh Shujā on its throne also matured, but it came about for internationl reasons, not the wishes of the Sikh monarch or the legal rights of the deposed Afghān chief. It was the Russian threat again, and Dost mohd Khān's overtures to them. He might have forged an alliance with the British, but his demand was the transfer of Peshāwar to Afghān rule, which the British had no means of doing, except by breaking off with Ranjit which would have landed them in a war with the Sikh kingdom. So they made a treaty with Ranjit Singh to conquer Kābul with the object of putting Shāh Shujā as a puppet king, on the throne of Afghānistān. Ranjit Singh hesitantingly welcomed the idea† for, he refused to allow the British forces to pass through

† Though Ranjit acquiesced in the project, his heart was not in it, for the reasons publicly advanced for an attack on Kābul were different from the ones the Governor General had shared with the British Govt. The British intentions were three-fold (i) to instal a pliant and helpful Shāh Shujā on the throne of Kābul to check the Russian advance (which was real); (ii) To limit the options further of the Sikh kingdom westwards and to encircle it, a fact which Ranjit feared and expressed to the British representative, inspite of being told that the British forces would be withdrawn from Kābul as soon as their main object was accomplished; (iii) To use the authority of the Kābul monarchy (even though represented by a deposed King, Shāh Shujā) to occupy Shikārpur (to which Ranjit always laid a claim) and to make it ostensibly a base for military supplies, but indeed to open up British commerce with Central Asia, and to keep it as long as possible under British con-

F. N. Contd.

trol and keep the Amirs of Sind under their thumb and occupy Sind in due course. When Sind was cut off from both the influence and pressure of the Panjāb and the Afghāns, all these objective were fulfilled. The siege of Herāt was lifted by Persia. Shāh Shujā was placed on the throne of Kābul and British prestige established for the first time in the North-West, the Shāh naturally leaning on the more powerful, more distant and historically less inimical British power than on the Sikhs who could hardly derive any comfort from this success except to accentuate more harted against themselves in exchange for some horses and cash by way of yearly tribute. To Shāh Shujā's efforts to capture the Afghān throne with foreign arms, the fiercely independent Afghāns also reacted adversely. He was overthrown a year later and the entire British force on way back wiped out. To compensate for this loss of face in the entire East, the British annexed Sind in 1843, and started earnestly their preparations against the Sikhs. Col H.C. Cook (in his *Sikh Wars*) is grateful to providence (P. 21) that the Sikhs did not attack the British while they were engaged in Sind or when, next year, they were involved in the Gwalior war when they (the Sikhs) would have had every chance of winning against them.

However, when the Kābul project was placed before the Mahārājā by the British representative, Macnaughton, on May 31, 1938, this is how his consent was manipulated : "I then said, 'Your Highness sometime ago formed a treaty with Shāh Shujāhulmulk; do you think it would still be for your benefit that that treaty should stand good, and would it be agreeable to your wishes that the British Govt. should become a party to that treaty? ' "This", replied His Highness, "would be like adding sugar to milk." "If such be decidedly the wish of your Highness, I said, I did not think the Governor General would object to supplying Shāh Shujā with money and officers to enable him to recover his throne...I told His Highness, as were my instructions, that we did not covet one *bighā* of additional ground, that the benefit of the combined scheme would be almost exclusively *his*..." (Governor-General to the Secret Committee, August 13, 1838).

Another explanation for the Sikh hesitancy, inspite of their desire to conquer Kābul is offered by Mackson's Memo to the Governor General (Oct. 17, 1838) : "Their desire to add Kābul to their possessions is perhaps increased by the sanction it obtains from *Guru-Ka-Bachan* (Guru's prophecy) that they shall recover the sacred portals of Somnāth from Ghazni, an event to be followed by the immediate overthrow of their power, but as the same unnamed book contains a prophecy that the power of the Sikhs as a nation is to continue for many thousand years, we may draw the conclusion that the time is hardly yet considered ripe for engaging in an expedition which is to end so fatally." The reference is possibly to a Brāhmin-written "*Sāu-Sākhi*" which contains many such cock-and-bull stories and contains a prophecy also about the Russian invasion and occupation of the Panjāb, etc. (which later in the century the Kookās also relied upon to their own and the Sikhs' detriment). The Sikh hesitancy sprang in fact from the same causes which led later to the British disaster. "He (Ranjit) knew better than Auckland and

[Contd. on next page]

the Panjāb & they had to pass through Sind instead. Shāh Shujā had through the Tripartite treaty (26th June, 1838) abandoned his claim to Sind, if the Amirs paid him a sum to be determined by the British Govt who were now to take Sind under their virtual protection. Ranjit was to be paid only 15 lakhs as cash "compensation" by Shāh Shujā which too he had to realise from the Amirs of Sind. The Shāh had to abide by any decision arrived at between the other two parties (Sikhs & the British) regarding Shikārpur & other areas of Sind lying on the right bank of the Indus. But, later, neither cash was paid, nor the territory allowed to the Sikhs.*

The British had also decided to participate with men and not only with money as was at one time envisaged, inorder that the entire advantage may not accrue to the Sikhs. Two forces, each 15000 strong, (the Panjab force consisting mostly of Muslims under Sheikh Basāwan) were therefore to march on Kābul through two different routes—the Shāh himself was to advance on Kandhār, through Shikārpur and Quetta, and his son, Taimur, at the head of a Sikh force had to advance on Kābul via Peshāwar, though the actual command was to be in the hands of Kanwar Nau Nihāl Singh.* Kandhār was captured in April, 1839, but the fall of Ghazni and Kābul, and the tearing through the Khyber pass of the Sikh forces (which were to

F. N. Contd.

Macnaughten the difficulty of maintaining a permanent foothold in Afghānistān. He readily gave up his claim to Jalālābād in return for a subsidy of 2 lakhs from Shāh Shujā. For him, Afghānistān was far better as a buffer against attack from further afield, to be kept from dangerous strength by fomenting divisions. (Vincent Simth, *Oxford History of India*, p. 615).

* In these very days (4 Sept, 1838), another son, Ranjit's seventh, was born to Rāni Jind Kaur, named Dalip Singh. According to Mahān Kosh (p. 1871), he wās born in Feb. 1837. But most European writers, including Cunningham, assert that his birth was not known to British authorities before Dec. 1940. They also say (see Griffin & others) that the Mahārājā was incapacitated by paralysis to produce children. This is not true, for the earlier attack was not of such an acute nature. Ranjit went out for a ride & held court regularly after it. Says Osborne who saw him in 1838, "At fifty eight, he is still a hale and hearty old man, though an imaginary invalid. All weakness disappears when he is on horseback." (The Court and Camp of Ranjit Singh, PP. 81-83). The story of illegitimacy was accepted later by the British for political reasons. After accepting him king & his mother the Regent, there was no reason to doubt Daleep Singh's parentage. But if this was done after the annexation of the Panjāb (though a pension was also allowed to him as the deposed king and *legal* heir to Ranjit's throne), one can very well imagine why such a canard was invented.

come a little later) were not to add another glorious chapter to the magnificent life of this conqueror, consolidator and a unique warrior of history whose life, inspite of all its shortcomings, was a model of compassion, integrity, liberal outlook and humanism. For the lion of the Panjāb in the meantime was dead.

In 1826, Ranjit had a bout of malaria which took him several months to recover. In 1834, he was attacked by paralysis of the right side which somewhat affected his power of speech. Being averse to western medicines (and also suspicious of foreign doctors, though a British doctor M'gregor's electric treatment did him considerable good) he would accept only indigenous *araqs*, salts and precious metals. But, he never took disease seriously. He insisted on holding his usual Durbār and riding out in the morning in the midst of fever. He was soon cured, & his power of speech was restored. At Ferozepur where he met Lord Auckland (Dec. 1838), according to M'gregor, "his energetic spirit still remained unsubdued, though his arms were feeble and he required assistance in mounting his horse." The festivities that he indulged in at this time were enormous, but almost on the eve of the departure of the Governor-General & his party, the Mahārājā was again struck by paralysis and he started talking in the language of signs. He developed cold and cough. With the onset of the summer of 1839, he had started sinking, but according to Osborne, "he preserved his senses to the last & was obeyed to the last by all his chiefs." Prayers were continuously offered by all sections of the society—Hindus, Muslims and Sikhs—for his long life and speedy recovery in every conceivable place of worship. He himself visited the Golden Temple, at Amritsar, and offered heartfelt prayers. Large amounts were given away in charity to the poor, to the temples, Gurdwārās and mosques in the form of cows and elephants, and gold and silver amounting, it is said, to about Rs. 2 crores. An order was issued banning slaughter of all animals in the Punjāb. Showing little or no improvement, he issued a proclamation on June 21, appointing his son, Kharak Singh, as the Mahārajā of the Panjāb with Dhian Singh Dogra as his Prime Minister. He placed solemnly the hand of his son in that of the Dogra chief, with tear-filled eyes, and with his courtiers looking on dazed & stricken with grief. His last wish that the jewel, Koh-i-Nur, be presented to the Hindu Temple of Jagan-Nath at Puri or the Golden Temple at Amritsar, was however not fulfilled, the Koh-i-Nor being a crown jewel. His bejewelled horses, valued at 30 lakh English pounds, he gifted to the Sikh temple at Nanded. He called in each courtier, one by one, & gave away many of his weapons to his lifelong followers and the reputed comrades-in-arms in a salute of final farewell.

And on Thursday, June Twenty Seven, eighteen thirty nine, before sunset, Ranjit Singh, lion of the Panjāb, lay cold and dead. The whole of the Panjāb was plunged into unspeakable mourning and grief not only over the passing of a much beloved king, but over the passing of a dream & a hope, of the sudden stopping of time & the vacancy of the future whose shadows haunted every perceptive mind & soul. Dumb-founded people were left only with a past, not a future.

Finally, a quarter of a mile away, within the precincts of the palace, his golden palanquin, carried by his choice courtiers & followed solemnly by men of rank, all bare-footed & dressed in the mourning white, accompanied by the wailing airs of music, wended its way slowly to the place of cremation. The funeral pyre of fragrant sandalwood was soon raised & Ranjit's body draped in choicest silks & rich shawls was placed upon it, to the firing of guns and the shrieking of bugles and the wailing of a million men & women. One of his Rānis, Mahtāb Devi, quietly ascended the pyre,with all her dazzling beauty, and took his noble head into her lap. Three other Rānis, also, alongwith a few maid-servants clasped in an embrace his dead body, utterly composed, in a spirit of dedicated sacrifice.* The pyre was lit by Kharak Singh & soon the man who had symbolised in his person for half a century the hopes & ideals of his entire people along with his beauteous lovers was burnt tinder & ashes. India was not to see the like of him again.

* As the custom of the *Sati* was condemned by the Sikh Gurus, so it was only the Rānis from the Hindu homes in the hill-areas and their maid-servants who performed the rite in accordance with their religious beliefs. Mehtāb Kaur was the daughter of Rājā Sansār Chand of Kāngrā. According to Osborne, "everything was done to prevent it, but in vain. They were guaranteed in their ranks and in all their possessions, but they insisted upon it." No Sikh Rāni or maid-servant, committed this act, nor were they compelled to, although Ranjit had 21 regulai wives. (On the other hand, when Rājā Suchet Singh, younger brother of Rājā Dhiān Singh died, all his 10 wives and 300 unmarried ladies of the zenānā committed *Sati*.) It is said the Prime Minister Dhiān Singh, overwhelmed by grief tried many a time to plunge into the funeral pyre, but was prevented by friends and courtiers. Some eye-witness accounts say this was only a farce being enacted by the Rājā to exhibit his loyalty to the dead chief which he was soon to betray. (See Carmicheal Smyth's "History of the Reigning family of Lāhore").

Ranjit was dead—the man who used to proclaim he was but the nagārā (war-drum) of Guru Gobind, the victory or success not being his, but the people's or the Guru's.

The man who had found a rabble divided by tribe and clan, and welded them into a nation such as the Guru had envisaged, was dead.

The man who had for the first time in a thousand years of India's history turned the tide of invasions, finally, and taken the fight into the enemy's very home,was no more.

The man who in defeat was defiant, in success humble and generous in the extreme, who brought together under a single flag of the Sikh-Khālsā men and women of all castes and creeds, means and motives, as was the Guru's dream right from the inception of the faith—was now lying listless in the lap of history.

The man who brought peace and prosperity to the meanest in the land, who was a lover of beauty and civilisation, who was more governed by the spirit of forgiveness for the rivals and defeated warriors, and dispossessed no one of his means of livelihood commensurate with his status and dignity, who punished less and reclaimed more, who never acted out of vengeance and took no one's life throughtout his entire hazardous career of half a century, except in war, had now become only an example and a name.

The man who fought only when he must, and was honoured by the rulers of Europe, and looked upto with envy and pride by the rulers of Asia and his fellow princes in India, not only for his military successes, but for his statesmanship, and who had entered the annals of Time as a warrior in line with Alexander and Napolean and, as an integrator in line with Bismarck and Garibaldi, and as a man of devotion and charity like Harishchandra and Hātim Tāi of ancient lore,was no more.

What a pity, however, that the idea of the Commonwealth which he was pledged to build in reality was betrayed by him in his hour of total truimph, for the love of an imbecile son. What a pity! what a pity ! !

CHAPTER XX

RANJIT SINGH : AN ASSESSMENT OF HIS CHARACTER & ADMINISTRATION

Ranjit Singh was not only a great warrior and conqueror, but also a superb consolidator of an empire and a firm though extremely compassionate administrator. According to Cunningham, Ranjit Singh "found the Panjāb a warring confederacy, a prey to the factions of its chiefs, pressed by the Afghāns and the Marāthās and ready to submit to English supremacy. He consolidated the numerous petty states into a kingdom, he wrested from Kābul the fairest of its provinces and he gave the potent English no cause for interference."

Writes Mohanlāl Kashmiri, Secy. to Sir Alexander Burnes after his visit to the Persian Court, in 1831, "I had heard the Persian dynasty praised, but it appeared nothing on examination. I imagine that true regal pomp is only seen in the Court of the Panjāb ruler whose name struck my ears everywhere, even in the deserts of Turkistān. Many people imagined that Ranjit Singh was the only king of India," (Travels, page 180).

Says Osborne :— "He is mild and merciful as a ruler. By sheer force of mind, personal energy and courage, he has established his throne on a firmer foundation than that of any other eastern sovereign and but for the watchful jealousy (!) of the British Govt would long ere this had added Sind, if not Afghanistān, to his present kingdom." "The Mahārāja," believes Gardener, "was indeed one of those masterminds which only require opportunity to change the face of the globe." Victor Jacquemount thinks, "the most skilful of our diplomats is a complete simpleton (before him)." Marshan compares him to Shivajee and in Capt. Murray's opinion, "he is perhaps more remarkable than either (Nepolean or Mehmet Ali); he never punished a criminal with death. Tenderness for life was a trait in the character of Ranjit Singh." M'gregor credits him with "powers of mind rarely met with, either in the eastern or the western world." In battle, always at the head of his troops and foremost in combat, and successful almost in all wars in which he was engaged, he never even once humiliated or dispossessed his fallen adversaries of the means of livelihood, commensurate with their past dignity and status, a trait which eastern character has yet to imbibe. Apart from the Sikh and Hindu chiefs, the *Jagirs* he granted to the Muslim Nawābs—the Mamdots, the Tiwānās, the Sials, the Ghebas, the Kharrals, the Bārakzai Sardars and others were upto the time of our independence (1947) being enjoyed by them. And, he always kept his word. His contract with the British, for instance, inspite of severe strains and stresses and stern opposition from his own camp and made almost under duress, he honoured in letter and spirit till his last breath.

And, what a miracle that though he ruled in the name of the Khālsā, (or *Panth Khālsāji*) and struck coins in the name of the Gurus and was on all accounts a devout Sikh, he always sought and won the willing and affectionate cooperation of the men of every creed and clan within his realms, to an extent that some European writers were constrained to remark that though "a Sikh by profession, he is a sceptic in reality," "for he visited, venerated and endowed the Hindu and Muslim places af pilgrimage as much as the sacred spots of the Sikhs." This, however, was the Sikh heritage bequeathed by the Gurus and it is to Ranjit's eternal glory that he practised it, even in the most adverse of circumstances.

"The Panjāb state" (under Ranjit Singh), writes Vincent Smith, "was neither a traditional Indian territorial state and monarchy, nor merely a dictatorship of one community over another. There was an element of partnership with other communities. Ranjit didnot claim the despotic sway of a traditional monarch over his own Sikhs. He was in some sense, its elected chief, and, like Augustus Caesar, he was careful never to push his pretentions too far. To the end though taking the title of Mahārājā, he claimed to be no more than the general of the Khālsā". He compares his liberality of outlook as well as diplomatic guile combined with his military skill and immense curiosity of the mind to Akbar's. "He dominated his contemporaries by intellect as well as by craft," he adds.

Man Of Faith :-

And, yet his devotion to his own faith remained undiminished. His daily routine began with early morning prayers, and his listening to recitations from the Holy Granth. He never took any decision to launch a campaign, without seeking its guidance. He always carried on his tours the two Sikh Holy Books—Adi Granth and the Dasam Granth—for which a special military escort was provided, "each member of which carried a Sikh banner. Every regiment had its own volume of the two Granths & religious insignia. Even the ministers of state carried separate copies of the Granths on their journeys." His gifting away of the precious canopy, presented by the Nizām of Hydrabad, to the Golden Temple, is an instance of abiding love of his faith. So also his munificence in covering the central temple at Amritsar with gold leaf, and the large land-gifts he made to Nankānā Sāhib, the Golden Temple Amritsar and the temples at Nanded, Anandpur, and other places, sacred to the Sikhs worth about Rs. 20 lakhs per year. He named the Amritsar public Gardens after Guru Rām Dās (Rām Bāgh) and the fort there as "Gobind Garh." But he also abolished cow-slaughter throughout his realms in deference to wishes of the Hindus and asked for the return of the gates of Somnāth from Shah Shuja as a part of the treaty he sought to forge with him in 1833. (That the Shah didnot agree with these proposals at that time is beside the point). But his wish was fulfilled by his successors after their victory over Kābul. The Hindu places of worship,* he endowed liberally alongwith those of the Muslims and the Sikhs. He made offerings to the Brāhmins, the Sayyads and the Nihangs equally on festive occasions and while distributing charity, no discrimination was ever practised. That is how all communities looked upon him not only as their protector but as one of themselves. Whenever he fell ill, as in 1826, and several times afterwards, prayers were offered in the Sikh and Hindu temples as much as in the Muslim mosques. No Musalmān General or Courtier ever betrayed his trust. And the ballad written about the first Anglo-Sikh war, in which the *Sarkār* (Ranjit Singh) is referred to in most moving terms, is the workmanship of a Muslim bard, Shāh Mohammad.

A caligraphist of the Qurān, despairing of his experience with the Muslim nobility, approached Ranjit Singh. He was offered the wages he had asked for—Rs. ten thousand. If the Sikh nobility in his court and army were represented by such stalwarts as Sardārs Chattar Singh, Sher Singh, and Shām Singh, Attāriwālā, Hari Singh Nalwa, Fateh Singh Ahluwāliā, Rām Singh Hassanwāliā, Bābā Sāhib Singh Bedi, Desā Singh Majithiā & Lehnā Singh, Amar Singh Kalān, Jodh Singh Rāmgarhia, Nidhān Singh panj-hathā, Attar Singh Sandhānwāliā, Fateh Singh Kalianwālā, Hukma Singh Chimni, Bhāis

* Especially the Shiva Temple at Banaras and the Jwalamukhi temple at Kangra which were gifted large amounts of gold.

Rām Singh, Gobind Ram & Gurmukh Singh, Kāhan Singh Mānn, & others, the Muslims were represented by the Fakir brothers—Azizuddin, Nuruddin & Imamuddin, Generals Ghaus Khān & Illahi Bakhsh, the dogras like Rājās, Dhiān Singh, Suchet Singh & Gulāb Singh and the Brāhmins like Khushāl singh, Rām Singh & Tej Singh, Misser Beli Rām & his four brothers and Misser Diwān Chand. If after his death, some non-Sikh parties (mostly the Purbias and the Dogrās) betrayed the cause of the rāj, it must not blind us to the fact that the Sikh Sardārs did much worse to each other, if not also to the whole Sikh people. The initiative was taken by the Sikh nobles themselves. If the others exploited the situation, bordering on anarchy, their actions, though inexcuable, can atleast be understood in the prevailing context. Who also will or can save a nation bent on self-destruction ?

Though he is considered "illiterate", Europeans have paid a very high tribute to his "inquisitiveness" and fund of knowledge on matters military, administrative and diplomatic. He was constantly in touch with the affairs in Europe and in the states bordering his own. He knew by heart the names of all the important officials,throughout his vast empire, and personally read the reports and dictated (& corrected) orders on all vital matters of the state. Both in "illiteracy" and his knowledge of affairs, he can only be compared to Akbar, the great,

His Military Organisation :-

A reference has already been made to his military organisation. As Cunningham has rightly pointed out, "he found the military array of his country a mass of horsemen, brave indeed, but ignorant of war as an art, and he left it mustering fifty thousand disciplined soldiers, fifty thousand well-armed yeomanary and militia, and more than 300 pieces of cannon for the field."*

"Indeed, the impression Ranjit's army left of the Sikh soldier was that he was the best in the whole of Asia & comparable to the best in Europe."

It has already been stated that long before the coming of the European officers (1822), the regular units were raised right from the year 1802, since when several Poorbias & Muslims, leaving the

* Col. Steinbach ("The Punjab") says, his force consisted of 1,10,000 men, of whom 70,000 are drilled according to European system. The cavalry consisted of 13,000 & the infantry & artillery to 60,000 more. The irregulars were nearly 40,000 strong of whom 20,000 are cavalry, the remainder being infantry & matchlock men. He had 376 guns &

service of the East India Company, had started joining the Sikh army at Lahore. Some of the Panjabis also learnt the methods of organisation and warfare from the forces of the Company by joining their ranks, and then leaving them to come back home and training their own compatriots. Ranjit Singh had himself visited Lord Lake's Camp in disguise (in 1805, according to Moorcroft's Travels, I,P. 102), while he was pursuing Holkar and observed the drill of the company's troops. Holkar of course advised him about organising the treasury, constructing defensive fortifications & disciplining the forces (Ibrat Nama of Ali-ud-din, f. 226 as quoted by G.L. Chopra). Metcalfe himself saw (in 1808) five of the trained battalions in the service of Ranjit Singh at that time. Initially, the raising of the regular infantry battalions created complications, because the Sikhs were averse to being enlisted as foot-soldiers. They hated being drilled which they called "Raks-e-laluan" (dance of the street girls). The majority, therefore, came from the Afghans, the Gurkhas & the Poorbias, who had left the service of the East India Company. However, as time passed, the Sikhs offered themselves in large numbers in the infantry as well and there were more applicants than could be recruited.‡ The army was divided into infantry, cavalry and artillery. The *Fauj-i-Khās,* or the Model Brigade, was raised in 1822 by Gen. Ventura and Allard, which consisted of four battalions of infantry, two regiments of cavalry and one troop of artillery comprising 24 guns." The *Topkhana khās* (special artillery corps) was raised by Mian Ghuas Khan, the Commander, in 1810, and another by Gen. Illahi Baksh in 1814. The Fauj I-Khās had its own emblems, the eagle, the tricoloured flag, with an inscription—"*Deg, Teg, Fateh.*" (Victory to the Sword which feeds the poor). Their dress was modelled on the uniforms of the East India Company's forces, all provided by the state. These were highly attractive and in the case of Allard's dragoons, "the trooper's dress is red jacket and black belts, one of

---

‡ According to Capt. Burnes "There are few Asiatics more brave than the Sikhs. They are individually brave and will attack a tiger or a lion on foot with a sword. Their physical powers surpass much those of the natives of Hindustān." Says Charles Massen, "As soldiers they are extremely patient of fatigue and capable of making prodigious marches with apparent ease. "They were credited with iron legs," according to Burton. "Free from prejudice, they would carry 8 days' provisions on their backs, dig a well if water was scarce, build a fort if circumstances required it, a kind of service which he (Ranjit Singh) can not prevail on the natives of Hindustān to perform." (Burnes)

which supports a pouch, the other a bayonet. Their trousers are long, of dark blue cloth, with a red stripe, & the turbans of crimson silk. The officers are attired from top to toe in bright crimson silk, & they merely carry a sabre attached to the ornamented belt."

Besides the regular army, there was also the Fauj-i-bequaid (irregular army), mostly comprising of Ghorcharas (horsemen). The Akālis or Nihangs, constituted another factor, decked in their shiny blue robes who fought both as foot-soldiers and on horseback and who wielded their special weapon, the Chakra (quoit), a sharp-edged discus, which they could employ with a stunning effect from fifty to a hundred yards. Their dare-devilry & recklesness paid handsomely when all other means had been exhausted. The payment was made on a regular monthly basis as against the earlier *Shashmāhi* (six monthly or seasonal) payment of wages or the grant of land or share in the plunder as in the days of the *Misals*. It was much resented in the beginning & *Tankhāh* (wages) became a word of contempt, (which it still is, among the Sikhs, being synonymous with fine !) But, gradually it was accepted both by the infantry and the cavalry, though the latter took a little time in reconciling themselves to their new fate !

Both Lord Fane, the British C-N-C, (1837) and Lord Auckland (1838) paid magnificent tributes to the turn-out and the discipline of Ranjit's army. Lord Fane reviewed "four regiments of cavalry (2400), twenty eight battalions of infantry (14,000), and sixty pieces of cannon and expressed the opinon that "they were all well-clothed, armed, accoutred & completely organised and placed under proper officers, & their movements were as good as those of our troops could be." Lord Auckland reviewed another eight or nine thousand of his troops on his way to Amritsar and said:—"In equipment, in steadiness & in precision of manouveres, they seemed in no respect inferior to our own army." This is what Ranjit's masterly leadership had made of what was originally a disorganised rabble under the Misals.

In civil administration, he fared equally well. It is well-known that most of his time he was engaged in battles, but he never for that reason neglected the mass of the people whom he conquered. The Moghals had introduced an organised system of Government, but the invasions of Nādir and Ahmad Shāh Durrāni had completely disrupted every trace of it. Ranjit reorganised the Civil administration, the collections of land-revenue and the judicial system on lines which earned for him the esteem and affection of all the disparate elements of his subjects.

The State Economy.

In 1899, Ranjit Singh was a small chieftain. Forty years later, when he died, he had left behind an empire of 1,40,000 square miles, extending from the Satluj to the Khyber pass and the Sulaiman mountains, bringing in an annual revenue of over Rs.3 crores, (or thirty million, according to British agents, which though a considerable figure in those days (wheat selling for one rupee to a maund or about 40 kilos) is no indication of the total revenues of the state with an estimated population of 53 lakhs. (In 1857, India's total population was estimated to be only 15 crores). As the state was parcelled out to various *Jagirdārs* and Sardārs who paid only a fixed share to the state exchequer, keeping the rest with themselves not only for their own dignified upkeep and for their administrative expenses, but for the upkeep also of the irregular forces which they were obliged to contribute to the state-army in times of need. The precious jewellery and other assets (the *Koh-i-Nur* itself was priceless) which Ranjit bequeathed to the state on the eve of his death and the magnificent prizes and gifts he offered to the noted warriors and administrators thoughout his reign are a sure sign of the sound economic health of the state. No war was lost for lack of resources nor any engagement abandoned for that reason. Sardār Hari Singh Nalwa left properties worth Rs. 90 lakhs most of which the state took over on his death. The wealth accumulated by the Dogras, the Majithias and the Brahmin, Khatri, Christian and Muslim nobility, besides the princes and their relations was colossal. His nobility lived in extreme luxury (though the masses also never experienced less than plenty.) Gulab Singh acquired Kashmir from the British in exchange for the cash he had appropriated (after Ranjit's death) on a single occasion. Gulab Singh's brother, Suchet Singh, left a property of 2 crores on his death. Jam. Khushal Singh sent about Rs. 30 lakhs with his wife to his village of Ekri, in the Meerut district, distributed six lakhs in charity and held large estates. Diwan Sāwan Mal, Governor of Multān, left behind Rs. 70 lakhs worth of cash and jewellery and an equal amount worth of property. Sardār Lahnā

Singh Majithia went on a pilgrimage (March 1844) with a retinue of 2500 men and spent over a crore of rupees during his absence from the Panjāb.*

HIS CIVIL ADMINISTRATION.

But, according to all observers, European as well as local, his was a just and an even-handed rule. Captain Wade testifies to his Majesty's "anxiety to restrain his troops (cavalry) from destroying the crops in the line of march. He had the most prohibiting orders in force on the subject and took prompt and severe notice of any infraction of them. His attention to the preservation of crops from destruction is remarkable. Few chiefs exercise more rigid control over the conduct of his troops than he does."

The Governor of Multan, Sāwan Mal, had imprisoned even his son for despoiling the crop of a farmer without due compensation.

The Central civil administration was in the hands of Diwān Bhawāni Dās, assisted by Diwān Gangā Rām (replaced by Rājā Dina Nāth on his death in 1816). In addition to the royal seal on the documents for payment (from where they originated), the two officials also affixed their individual seals. This routine was followed by 13 other offices where copies of the order were made and kept on record. But at last only one seal remained—that of the keeper of the royal seal—and other cumbersome intermediaries were abolished.

According to Shahamat Ali, a British agent, the revenues accrued from four principal sources. The *Khālsā* (King's own) lands (Rs. 1,96,57,172), Jagirs (Rs. 87,54,590), *Khairājdārs* (tributaries) (Rs. 12, 86000) and custom duties (Rs. 5,50,000 -). But, other major sources of revenue are left out by him, namely, *nazrānās* (presents); *Zabti* (escheats), *Ābkāri* (excise) *Wajuhāt-Moqarari* (stamp-duties and court fees) and *Chaukiat* (or octroi), which should exceed the estimated annual revenue several times over. In the beginning, the traditional system of *batāi* (crop-sharing) on the Moghal lines was enforced, which continued upto 1823. Later, the Govenment share calculated on standing crops (Kankut) in money terms was collected in cash. The Govt. was no longer obliged to protect the crops, collect grain and sell their share in the fluctuating market. This system was again replaced in 1834, and large irrigated areas auctioned to highest

* (H. R. Guptā, *Panjāb on the eve of first Sikh War*, p. 118)

bidders for 3 to 6 years. Sometimes, whole villages were similarly auctioned to the villages themselves to eliminate middlemen. The revenue varied in accordance with the fertility of the soil, the means of labour and so on. According to British records of 1859-50, it ranged between 33 to 40 percent in all, including the collector's share, though the revenue was considerably less in the Pathan areas across the Indus and in Multan, where it could come down to even twelve to twenty per cent but never more than one fourth. Cash crops, like cotton, sugar cane and tobacco brought in richer dividends, as prices of the yields increased. But the welfare role of the state should also not be minimised. Land revenue was remitted and relief immediately provided in times of poor crops or famine, as in Kashmir. Seed and *taccavi* loans were liberally offered, inundation canals and wells were dug up, stud bulls provided for better breed, robbery severely curbed, serais built, way-farers and horsemen employed as *harkārās* to carry post from one station to another.

The Panjāb was divided into 4 provinces *(subas)*: Lahore, Multan, Kashmir and Peshawar. Each *suba* was, as under the Moghals, divided into *parganas*, *parganas* into *taalqas*, and *taalqas* into *mouzas* or villages (50 to 100 units). The court language and the language of records continued to be Persian.

Each *Suba* was under a *Nāzim* (Governor) and under him in each district (taalaqa) a Kārdār, who was an administrator and a revenue and Judicial officer rolled into one. Though their powers were wide, strict vigilance was exercised by the office of the *Nāzim* over them so that they did not become exacting, corrupt or oppressive. News-writers were attached to them as well as the *Nāzim*, who, besides keeping the Central Govt. informed of the day to day happenings, could and did submit secret reports also on the officials to whom they were attached.

So strict were the instructions the Mahārājā had issued for securing even-handed justice to all his subjects, that he even did not spare himself or his sons. The follwing Royal order, issued on 19 poh, Samvat 1888, (1831 A.D.) is a shining example of the kind of Government Ranjit Singh wanted to give his people.

"Ujjal Didār, Nirmal Budh, Sardār Amir Singhji and our sincere well-wisher, Faqir Nurruddin ji. May you live long, by the grace of Sri Akāl Purukh and enjoy the protection of Sri Akāl Budh.

"By the grace of Sri Satguruji, this exalted command is issued to you so that, deeming yourself to the security of Lāhore, you should take care of the duties pertaining thereto. Sri Satguru ji forbid, if His Majesty, his beloved son, Kharak Singhji, Kanwar Sher Singhji, the Rājā Kalān Bahādur, (i-e, Rājā Dhiān Singh, Prime Minister), Rājā Suchet Singhji or Jamādārji, should commit any inappropiate act, you should bring it to the notice of His Majesty. Secondly, you should send your trusted representative to the Sardārs with instructions to refrain from commiting inappropriate acts......Moreover, you should not permit forcible possession to be taken of any person's land or any person's house to be demolished. Nor should you allow any high-handedness to be practised upon woodworkers, fodder-vendors, oil-vendors, horse-shoers, factory-owners etc.........(you) should not permit any person to be treated harshly and should forward to His Majesty any petitions intended for him. Furthermore, you should send for Chāṇd Mal, Kotwal of the Royal court, and Baba Pāndā and obtain from them the news of all happenings so that every person's rights are secured & no person is oppressed......Hazara Sowars should be appointed to watch the roads."*

As for the administration of justice, the settlement of disputes in the villages rested with the Panchayats (assemblies of five elders elected by consensus for their standing and good repute.) They generally settled the matters though arbitration. But if rejected by either party, an appeal lay with the Kārdār. Kārdārs administered justice in the cities alongwith the *Nāzims* and *Adālties* (or paid Justices). As there were no set codes, both civil & criminal cases were decided on the basis of custom of both Hindus & Muslims. Capital punishment could be awarded only by the king himself, and he never even once condemned any one to death, for murder or robbery etc. Heavy fines were imposed (if the criminal could afford it), mutilation of limbs was seldom resorted to, but no one's life was taken.

Ranjit Singh had abolished the Gurumattā (edict issued from the *Akāl Takht* by the consensus of only the Sikh community) and substituted it by a decison of his Cabinet, consisting of people of all creeds and persuations.

---

* The Real Ranjit Singh, Pp. 32-33

To decry and denigrate a man of these exceptional qualities for his drinking bouts, several marriages & concubines, nautch-parties and such other frivolities, and pastimes and that too on the part of the Europeans, who have never left anything to chance in such matters, throughout their history, is the height of hypocrisy, meanness and chicanery. Nations which permit no relaxation to its rulers and path-finders are landed only with tyrants. Aurangzeb was extremely abstemious in his personal habits, but he ruined and disrupted the 200-year old Moghal empire.

Moreover, one does not find any palace-interference in the matters of state. Rāni Sadā Kaur tried to, but failed miserably, though she was a leader in her own right, not merely because she was Ranjit's mother in-law. If the Mahārājā were morally that lax and could exhibit himself in public, drunk and seated on an elephant with a street girl, Moran, as is suggested, what kind of respect or awe, much less affection, could he have elicited from his orthodox followers, no matter of what religion. If he won not only the physical control but also the heart-felt affection of the mass as well the nobility (as all records, including European, reveal that he did), then no one can doubt the high element of exaggeration indulged in by his detractors and rivals. The same is the case in respect of his progeny, all considered illegitimate (including Kharak Singh, though not quite, perhaps because he was both incompetent & an imbecile). That Ranjit opted for him as a successor is however the greatest tragedy of this otherwise magnificent man which destroyed his progeny and the Sikh empire, both, in a period of less than a decade and which was built by the blood and tears of the whole people,after about a century of struggle and sacrifice. But, then,such is the tragedy of history and of life.

Personal Characteristics

Though of medium stature whom nature had deprived of the light of his left eye,with his countenance all pock-marked, the light-brown skin of his face and the large rolling right eye set in a massive head with a flowing, well-kept beard made his presence prepossessing. Fond of swimming, riding and hunting, his body was all muscles and his wiry frame could take on the hardest fatigue. Most of the time leading an exacting camp life on the fields of battle (he hardly got, if ever, a respite of continuous two years of peace), he would give no chance to his body to relax,except when back home after a victory. He would accept any challenge from nature. Once, when he crossed the furious waters of the Attock, then in flood, on a horse back, the enemy fled, in terror, saying "*Khudā Khud Khālsā shud* (God himself has turned a Khālsā)!

But though a warrior of great eminence, he was unusually tender of heart. "He kept no eagles or hawks as a symbol of manliness. Even while hunting hares, the main objective was to exercise the limbs of the greyhounds. The horsemen accompanying the greyhounds were instructed never to chase and run down a hare. Should he happen to hear a fowl scream or a goat bleat piteously when taken for slaughter, the Mahārājā would at once order its release. He used to say it was uncowardly and unchivalrous to shoot a tiger, and it should be attacked only with a sword, lance or spear which would match the sharp nails of the wild beast.

"Once when he heard a tigress wail for her cub, which was captured and caged in the fort, he could not sleep the whole night and let the young one off in the morning, saying, "I cannot take the curse of a mother."

Ranjit was in the habit of listening to the plaints of his people, whenever they would deposit their written grievances in the box outside his chamber, or accept them in the open street when he was out riding. And, he would bring justice to the needy with utmost speed. Stories of his munificence have entered our folklore, like the one of a widow in distress who had heard that the Mahārājā was a "*pāras*" (philosopher's stone) and whichever metal received his touch turned into gold. She did the same with her iron cooking pot which she rubbed against the person of the Mahārāja when he was out once on a ride. When told why she had done so, he ordered her pot to be filled with gold mohurs !

Ranjit was a man of highly aesthetic tastes. He was extremely fond of beauty, whether male or female, animal or natural. He surrounded himself with the choicest soldiers and courtiers whose bearing and appearance dazzled the viewer. Himself dressed sparingly, without much jewellery on him (except for a necklace of pearls) and never sitting on the throne (but either in a chair with legs tucked in or on the cushioned carpet), he would insist on his courtiers decking themselves with precious jewellery. And, his Court in its glitter and majesty cast a spell on the foreign visitors. Once, when Sardār Shām Singh Attāriwālā came to the court without the necklace of rare pearls which he had worn a day earlier and had been much appreciated, the Maharājā questioned him. The Sardār replied that the jeweller had wanted seventy thousand rupees as its price while he could afford only half as much. The Mahārājā immediately ordered the full money to be paid to the Sardār so that he came next day bedecked with this choice necklace. For the sake of a famous horse—Laili—he is said to have fought a battle with the Bārakzai Sardārs of Peshāwar. He used to chuckle: "This rascal of an animal has cost me four lakhs of rupees and 12000 men." Laili, though, was not the only cause of the fight! No wonder, he was equally fond of good-looking brides and inmates for the *zenana.**

His love of the arts was equally well-marked. While invading Peshāwar, he gave special instructions to Sardār Hari Singh Nalwā to take every care to spare the library at Chimkini from destruction.† When the Moghal court at Delhi could no longer offer employment to the artists and the Panjab hill-chiefs had become mere tributaries of Ranjit, the well-known artists like Mohd Bakhsh, Kehr Singh, Purkhu etc. came to the Lahore Court and were offered patronage both by him and his sons and courtiers. G.T. Vigne made several

* The names of his 21 married queens are (i) Mehtāb Kaur, Daughter of Rāni Sadā Kaur and head of the Kanhiyā Misal. Married in 1796, she died in 1813. (ii) Rāj Kaur, daughter of S. Rām Singh of the Nakkai Misal. (iii) Rāni Jindān, daughter of Sardār Mannā Singh, in the employ of the Mahārājā (iv) Rāni Rattan Kaur and Dayā Kaur, widows of Sāhib Singh Bhangi of Gujrāt. From these wives, he begot seven sons. Other Rānis were : (vi) Mehtāb Devi (also called Guddan), (vii) Rāj Bansi (both daughters of Rājā Sansār Chand whom he married late in life and for whom he had to fight a battle, it is said); (viii) Bibi Moran (ix) Gul Begum (x) Rup Kaur (ix) Chānd Kaur (xii) Lachhmi (xiii) Rāj Devi (xiv) Har Devi (xv) Devno (xv) Ram Devi (xvii) Rāni Devi (xviii) Saman Kaur, (xix) Gulāb Kaur (xx) Bannat (xxi) Danno. Most of the marriages were, however, contracted for political reasons. A cultural troupe of 125 choice girls in the realm entertained him and his guests. Sometimes they were dressed in military uniform and asked to fight among themselves much to the amusement of the onlookers. Muslim writers say a mosque was named after Moran after her death near the Mati chowk at Lāhore, and a village in the Amritsar distt. also bears her name. Gul Bahār Begum also is said to have built a mosque at Lāhore which is still intact.

† An innocent Sikh leader of the present times, Sant Fateh Singh, (died, 1972) who leapt into political fame merely by fasting for a time over the issue of Panjābi Subā, however, caused some of the rarest manuscripts of the Sikh Scriptures consigned to the flames "as they had become too old"! He did not realise what was posterity losing thereby.

portraits of the Mahārājā. Osborne has left 16 excellent sketches of him and his sons and courtiers. Emily Eden, sister of Lord Auckland, and an expert painter, made an exquisite painting of Ranjit as well as others. A Sikh school of Art (mainly of portraiture of individuals or the court or love-scences modelled on the Kāngrā and Guler schools) came into existence.* The court historian, Sohan Lāl was munificenily rewarded. Bute Shāh, Khushwaqat Rāi, Kanaihyā Lāl and Amar Nāth also were engaged at this time in the writing of Panjāb or Sikh history, particulary of the reign of Ranjit Singh himself. Several Purānas, Yoga Vashishta, Rāmāyāna and the Bhagvad Gitā etc. were translated into Panjābi. Sikh murals and frescoes of this period were to be seen in the Māhārājā's palace, the Shishmahal at Lāhore, his residence at Rāmbāgh, Amritsar, and at the nobles' residences and the Golden Temple and Bābā Atal's temple at Amritsar etc. Ivory-disc miniatures had also become popular at this time. Ranjit got many of the dilipidated Moghal buildings and gardens restored and built new ones like the *Bārādari* of Hazoori Bāgh at Lāhore.

He endowed the *pāthshālās*, *Dharmshālās* and mosques—traditional centres of learning to spread literacy. He had invited a Christian missionary, Maj. Lourie, to teach English to the princes, but didnot agree to his teaching Christianity as part of the curriculum. However, he sent out some good Sardārs to Ludhiānā to be trained in English and French. A printing press was also sought to be installed and a person—Rām Singh—sent to Ludhiānā to be trained in printing technology. The Persion school of *Mian Wada* at Lāhore was liberally endowed. How he encouraged Lehnā Singh Majithiā and others to invent new types of guns has already been noted. The Mahārājā got several of his Sardārs trained by the Europeans in the art of surgery, electric treatment, engineering, arms manufacture and so on.

He got several of the Sanskrit, English and French works translated into Panjābi or Persian prose, and their authors were highly rewarded. The Panjābi poets like Hāsham were awarded Jāgirs.†

* For details, see Archer's volume on "Paintings of the Sikhs" (London), 1966,

† For details, see the author's "History of Panjābi Literature."

No wonder, there was no class of people in the Panjāb who didnot shed tears of anguish on the departure of so powerful and yet so sensitive and compassionate a ruler, a lover of beauty, and though a formidable warrior and conqueror, essentially a man of compromise, bonhomie and peace..

CHAPTER XXI

SUNSET OF THE EMPIRE

The very act of Mahārājā Ranjit Singh appointing an inefficient, imbecile and morally uninspiring son, Kharak Singh, as his successor against saner advice contained in it the seeds of civil warfare, and disintegration.* The British, who were not the unconcerned spectators they pretended to be, had visualised as much in supporting his claim.

Right from the days of Ranjit's rise to power, the British had reached a definite conclusion that an independent Sikh state was necessary only so long as it served as a buffer and a shock-absorber between Afghānistān and the European powers (particularly France and Russia). But the moment it showed its real independence and tried to keep its options open, it would be in British interests to occupy it or atleast to keep on its throne only convenient symbols who could be manipulated in times of need.

---

* It is said, the continuous and excessive use of opium and wine etc. had impaired his faculties so much that he could take no initiative or give judgement on any issue, these matters being left to his aide, Chet Singh Bājwā, his favourite relation. But, on the other hand, on assumption of power, he had dismissed Gen. Sultān Mahmood from the artillery for his confirmed drunkenrress. Though pleas were made on his behalf by Sardār Fateh Singh Mānn and Jamādār Khushāl Singh that "he had promised to drink no spirits in future," the Mahārājā refused to reconsider his decision till further proofs of his amendment were forthcoming" (*Lāhore Akhbār*, June 7, 1840).

That he was incompetent otherwise or lacked initiative and would lean on unsure advice or advisers etc., however, proved to be true.

On the eve of the signing of the Amritsar treaty (1809), as we have seen, troops were immediately pressed into service and the Cis-Satluj states taken into protective custody when Ranjit hesitated for a time to agree to a treaty of "friendship" between the two rival (though unequal) powers and refused to limit his ambitions only to his side of the river. Princep (in his *Origin of Sikh power*) makes it abundantly clear :- "Had danger from that quarter (i.e. France and Russia) been more imminent, it would probably have been deemed politic to extend our direct influence into the Panjāb in reduction of the power of a chief (Ranjit Singh) who showed himself so unfriendly"* (for taking an independent line). !

From 1827 to 1831, Sayyed Ahmed Brelvi had raised the standard of a holy war (*Jehad*) against the Sikhs. His fighters came mostly from British territories. The Lt. Governor of the N.W. provinces wrote to Ghulam Ali, *Rais* of Allahabad in reply to his memorandum, "that solong as the peace of their (British) territories was not disturbed, they had nothing to say, nor had they any objection to such prepartions". When the Mahārājā fell seiously ill for the first time in 1834, correspondence was exchanged between Capt. Wade, the British political agent at Ludhiana and Macnaughton, Secy. to the Governor-General, as to the attitude the British Govt. should adopt towards the Panjāb in the event of Ranjit's death.

He expressed an opinion that the feud (for successsion), would occur not only between princes (Kharak Singh and Sher Singh) but will be accompanied "by the revolt of numerous chiefs who have been the victims of his ambition," (including, according to him, the Muslim tribes between Jehlum and Peshawar). "The three Jammu Rājāhs, all raised to their high stations by the Mahārājā, will declare independent their territories between Kashmir and Rāvi, so also the hill-stations between Rāvi and Satluj. Multān will continue to owe allegiance (to the Lāhore Durbār) under a popular and intelligent Governor (Sāwan Mal). The Afghāns of Kālā Bāgh, D.I. Khān, Tonk, Bannu and Senghir will rebel . . . and with every diffidence, therefore, in my judgement, I beg leave to submit whether in the event of Ranjit's death, it would not be proper to adopt the precaution of advancing a part of the Ludhiānā force to Ferozepur, backed by a regiment of cavalry from Karnāl" . . . He also recommended the

* P. 54.

shifting of his own Headquarters to Ferozepur. Capt. Wade knew well indeed that Govt. had hitherto not done so "lest it should give umbrage to the Mahārājā" . . . but he is politically pragmatic enough to suggest that "there seems to be no obligation on our part to observe the same delicacy on his demise,when the interests of our Government and those who look to our protection are involved more than ever in *the military occupation of that place.*"†

We have already seen, how Ranjit Singh, strictly in accordance with the Amritsar treaty (1809), wanted to extend his territories to Sind in order to secure the Arabian sea-shores and engage in international commerce and acquire a sea-route to Europe, besides becoming a sea-power. But the British resisted all his plans to this effect and finally foreclosed his options at Rupar (1831) by signing a trade treaty (which was virtually a political treaty) with the Amirs of Sind in April, 1832. After they had obtained Ranjit's signatures against his better judgement for a joint expedition to Kābul in Dec. 1838, at Ferozpur, the encirclement of the Sikh kingdom was total and complete. When the Kābul expedition, at first successful, was undone by the Afghāns, the British made up with Dost Mohd Khān, who had again replaced Shah Shuja, on the condition that he would remain friendly with the British. The Sikhs, who were earlier a party to the expedition, were not even consulted, when the new understanding was arrived at between the British and the Amir of Kābul. (This was done, it is said, because Nau-Nihāl Singh himself had started negotiations earlier with Dost Mohd Khān which later proved to be false).

On the eve of Ranjit's death, Capt. Wade realised that between 1834 (when Wade had visualised the disintegration of the Sikh empire more easily) and 1838, the Mahārājā had done considerable spadework to consolidate the power of the thone vis-a-vis its rivals, both within and outside his realms. He had considerably increased the disciplined troops. He had withdrawn the trained troops from his feudal chiefs and started paying them regulerly from the State treasury. This formidable disciplined force "which represents the national interests of the Sikhs, has no attachment to any particular chief, and looks to the Mahārājā as the founder of their strength. The men have respect and attention for him and his family." The feudal

† Capt C.M. Wade's political despatch to W.M. Macnaughten, dated Feb. 14, 1838

armies of the various Sikh and Dogra chiefs were estimated only at 15000 at this time by Capt. Wade, and the strength of the train troops under the Sikh Durbār's direct control at 50,000.

But the British political agent is clever enough also to visualise that "the discipline and the taste which their officers have imbibed, from intercourse with the Europeans, for European customs and dress, have also conduced to affect a change in their former character which has greatly weakened their prejudices and disposed them to view with *less dislike foreign interference to support the successor of the Mahārājā in the integrity of his possessions.*"

Discussing the claims of the various contenders for power, Wade notes with satisfaction that "of the Sikh Sardārs, who once formed the component part of the nation whether raised by Ranjit Singh or contemporary with him in the possession of power, none now remains whose opposition is dreaded. Hari Singh Nalwā was the last of the former class and the late Ahluwāliā chief (Fateh Singh) of the latter."

Analysing the strength and support of each contender for power, Capt. Wade estimates that the force under Jam. Khushāl Singh numbers only 3000, and under the Rājā of Jammu (Gulāb Singh) a mere 2000, but their troops are "not only ill-paid but disaffected." "The Jamādār's wealth and possessions and extensive Jāgirs are on the left bank (British side) of the Satluj. He has no hold on Panjāb and is hated by the Sikhs. He would most likely in his own interest side with the legitimate heir to the throne and though "his influence is increased by the fact of his nephew, Gen. Tej Singh, having the command of one of the Mahārājā's divisions of infantry, to which a large portion of artillery and a portion of cavalry is attached, the other divisions are commanded by young Sikh officers raised to distinction by His Highness." As to the Rājās of Jammu, "there is no natural sympathy between them and the Sikhs and so they employ none but the Dogras and other tribes of the mountains to defend their country in the hills," irrespective of the fact that "they owed their present positions to the personal favours and protection of His Highness."*

Inspite of the earlier anti-British postures of the Dogrā brothers, Wade has "learnt on good authority that Rājā Gulāb Singh is anxious

* Ibid

to open a separate communication wiih the British Govt. for the integrity of *his* country in the hills". Kharak Singh, though "lacking both energy and intellect," is preferred to others (because he apart from being the nominee of Ranjit will lean more on their support of which the British had ample proof before-hand, as referred to before). Kanwar Sher Singh is also not dismissed out of account, because he "has lately betrayed the strongest desire to conciliate oui Govt. with a view to provide for his future interest."† Thus, the British, though in treaty-bound for "eternal friendship" with the Sikh empire, as may be seen from the above correspondence, were not mere disinterested or neutral spectators. Right from the days of the rise of the Sikh power during the Misal period, several secret agents of the British had travelled, in disguise or under cover, (George Forster in the guise of a Muslim merchant as early as 1782-83) to get as much information about the Sikh people and their country as possible. After taking the Cis-Satluj Sikh states under their wings in 1809, Lord Hastings acquired the Simla Hills in 1816, and Lord Amherest made it the summer capital of the Indian empire twelve years later, about 1200 miles away from Calcutta "when one-way travel to the new capital by boats and buggies took four to five months." At Ferozepur (1838), Lord Auckland suggested to Mahārājā Ranjit Singh to have a British resident at Lahore. This was, of course, refused, but the British soon thereafter established a military cantonment at Ferozepur, besides the Simlā hills, Ludhiānā, Ambālā, Rupar, Derā Dun, Meerut and Delhi.

What the Dogras (bent upon seizing the throne for themselves) and their opposing party at the Lāhore Durbar, the Sandhānwālias, besides the nominal Sikh monarch, did to each other and to the Sikh State will be made clear as gruesome events one succeding the other with lightening speed unfold themselves.

Kharak Singh ascended the throne immediately on the demise of his illustrious father, though his coronation was performed about two months later (Sept 1, 1839). Although Dhian Singh, the Prime Minister, had pledged ostensibly unstinted loyalty to him, he did not trust the new ruler to protect his interests. He also secured the support of the other Sardārs to ask the Mahārājā the very next morning to take an oath on the Guru Granth that their *Jāgirs* would be kept intact. This the Mahārājā did, without any hesitation. But,

† Ibid

this also made the Prime Minister's bonafides suspect in the eyes of the Mahārājā, who ordered Diwan Dinā Nāth that it was not necessary anylonger to route all correspondence throught the Prime Minister to the King. Day by day, Dhian Singh was becoming overbearing and rude to the new master who had, also inorder to clip his wings, appointed a near-relation of his favourite wife, Ishar Kaur, a person called Chet Singh Bājwā (about 20 years of age) as his principal adviser on political affairs. This irked Dhian Singh not a little, and hardened his attitude towards Kharak Singh even more. This resulted in the Mahārājā banning the entry of the Prime Minister in his *Zenāna* (or private chambers), a privilege he had enjoyed for long during the earlier regime. On July 20, 1840, it was reported that "Rājā Goolaub Singh is removing from the fort of Mināwar and from other forts in the Mināwar district lakhs of property and money to Jammu". "The Mahārājā abused him for this theft of public money in the open court against which Dhian Singh protested, saying, "confiscate all his property, but why abuse and degrade him ?"

All this cut him to the quick and he started circulating rumours in the city, and among the army, that Kharak Singh was in secret correspondence with the British and had not only agreed to acknowledge their surpremacy, but also to part with six annas in a rupee (3/8 ths) of the state revenues in favour of the British. This naturally created a sensation and the army became restive. Dhian Singh played his cards deftly. He enlisted the support of Mahārāni Chand Kaur, queen of Kharak Singh. He also invited Prince Nau Nihāl Singh to Lāhore from Peshāwar (where he was posted as Governor and had not been allowed earlier even to attend his grandfather's funeral or his father's coronation in the interest of duty !) On his arrival, Dhian Singh summoned a secret council of eleven which was attended by Mahārāni Chand Kaur, Kanwar Nau Nihāl Singh, the four Sandhānwalia Sardārs (Attar Singh, Kehar Singh, Lehna Singh and Kanwar Sher Singh) besides the three Dogrā chiefs—himself, his son (Rājā Hira Singh) and Rāi Kesari Singh of Jammu as representative of Gulāb Singh. Lāl Singh and Alexander Gardner were the two neutrals.

Dhian Singh placed before this august assembly some secret (though forged) communications, bearing the royal seal, said to have been sent by Chet Singh to the British. Spade-work had already been completed behind the scenes. So the decision was unanimously taken that Kharak Singh should be deprived of his executive powers, Chet Singh should be assassinated and Kanwar Nau Nihāl Singh take the place of his father.

Kharak Singh had hardly ruled three months when two hours before day-break of Oct 9, 1839, all the conspirators marched on the Lāhore fort which housed both the Mahārājā and his confidant, Chet Singh Bājwā. Two guards resisted at the main gate. They were cut to pieces. A personal attendant tried to obstruct their passage, but he too was shot dead by Dhian Singh. Hearing the sound of gun-fire, Chet Singh hid himslf in a *Khawāb-gāh* (secret chamber), but was found out and dragged before the Mahārājā and a dagger plunged into his heart by the Dogra Prime Minister, and inspite of the pathetic entreaties of himself and Kharak Singh to spare his life, stabbed continuously till he died. The Mahārājā was taken into custody and confined in his own palace inside the Lāhori gate. Nau Nihāl Singh took over the control (at the age of eighteen and a half), though Kharak Singh still remained the titular head of state and all important papers needed his assent and bore his signatures. It is on record that especially in regard to economy and general management, the two differed strongly, but there is no evidence to infer that the Prince went out of the way either to insult or over-rule the final decision of the King solong as he lived. It is Mahārājā Kharak Singh who, inspite of the reservations of his son and the principal courtiers not to permit the return passage of the British from Kābul through the Panjāb, ordered that whatever the expense to the state "their alliance admitted of such expense".* This was eleven days after Nau Nihāl Singh took over the administration.‡

Almost all European writers are unanimous in their views that had Nau Nihāl Singh, instead of his father, assumed power after Ranjit Singh, the Sikh state would have instead of disintegrating seen new heights of glory and "he (Nau Nihāl Singh) would have found an

* Panjāb Akhbār, Oct 19-20, 1839

‡ On July, 15, 1840, the Kanwar attended on the Mahārājā, presented him Rs. 1100/-& asked about his health. (Panjāb intelligence, July 1840).

ample field for his ambition in Sind, in Afghānistān, and beyond the Hindukush, and he might, perhaps, at last have boasted that the inroads of Mahmud (of Ghazni) and of Taimur had been fully avenged by the aroused peasants of India."† This is so, because Nau Nihāl Singh, the apple of Ranjit's eye, in whose hands the Mahārājā himself trusted the Sikh empire would become the pride of all Asia, was extremely popular with the army, "for he had been a soldier from his boyhood, was of brave and indomintable spirit, united at the same time to great caution, discretion and forethought".‡ However, why the old lion didnot choose him as a successor is another mystery and adds one more lost opportunity to the "might have beens" of Sikh history.

Though he was put in authority through the active help of Dhian Singh, Naunihāl Singh distrusted his benefactors's intentions. He therefore so balanced his Cabinet of six (consisting of Dhian Singh, Faqir Aziz-ud-din, Jamādār Khushal Singh, Bhāi Rām Singh, Lahnā Singh Majithia, and Ajit Singh Sandhānwaliā) that no particular faction would have ascendancy over the other. He attended the military parades regularly in order to bring him closer to the soldiery who amply responded to his love for them. His features and disposition bore a striking resemblance to those of his illustrious grandfather and this endeared him also to the people at large. Rājā Gulāb Singh had not paid the revenues of the state for some time. An expedition was sent out against him and the arrears realised. Cantoments were established ringing the Rājā of Jammu's territories at Siālkot, Mandi, Kāngrā and Poonchh. He humbled the Rājā of Mandi who had raised the standard of revolt and took him prisoner. The British Govt. was asked to replace Capt. Wade as political agent at Lāhore, as he was indulging in court intrigues, playing one party against the other. He was soon recalled and his place taken over by Mr. Clerk. The Governor-General also tried to avail of this consfused state of affairs and,on the pretext of congratulating Kharak Singh on his assumption of power, tried to extract a promise that the British troops under Lord Keane returning from Ghazni might be allowed passage through the Panjāb, which concession Ranjit had earlier refused to countenance. The concession was given but a

† Cunningham:History of the Sikhs, P. 209.

‡ M'gregor, History of the Sikhs, part II, p. 5.

difficult route via D.I. Khān was suggested, avoiding Lāhore, and taking a firm promise that never would the British troops cross the territories of the Sikh Kingdom again. The Governor-General resented this condition, but had to agree to it.

Meantime, Kharak Singh languished in his confinement, entrusted to the care of quacks, who the more they tried to cure his mysterious malady, the worse his situation became.† It is said, Dhian Singh held them in his trust and they ministered slow poison to the King-emperor† which resulted in his death nine months later (Nov. 5, 1840) at the age of thirty-eight. So much were the ears of the son poisoned by the stories circulated about the vile curses Kharak Singh was said to be showering upon him, that as time passed, Naunihāl Singh visited his father but rarely, and then too bitter quarrels ensued between the two in which insults and abuse were freely traded. A day before his demise, Kharak Singh received his son (some say this was Naunihāl's only visit to his ailing father) but it made no difference to the attitude of each to the other. Both came out of it more bruised in spirit and soul. When Kharak Singh died, Naunihāl Singh heard the news on his hunting ground nearby through the booming of guns announcing the royal death, and he became the *de-jure* monarch of the state. "But the same day that dazzled him with a crown also deprived him of life."

After Mahārājā Kharak Singh's cremation was over the same day, (with two of his *rānis* and eleven of his maids performing *Sati* along with him), * Kanwar Naunihāl Singh accompanied by Miān Udham Singh, son of Rājā Gulāb Singh, started out on his return journey to the fort, on foot, followed by courtiers and other distinguished mourners. Naunihāl, visibly shaken with grief, was holding the hands of Mian Udham Singh. As they entered the Roshni gate, the beam-stones and tiles of the archway suddenly crashed upon their heads. Udham Singh died on the spot, but Naunihāl Singh was still breathing when he was extracted out of the debris, though his

---

† Carmychael Smyth says small doses of white lead, *Safedā Kaskaree,* were ministered to him in wine. (*Reigning Family of Lāhore*, P. 33).

* This was done according to eye-witness European accounts under compulsion. The junior (Hindu) *Rānis* refused to mount the funeral pyre, but were literally dragged to it under orders of Dhian Singh. When asked to bless the new Mahārājā, they instead cursed him and Dhian Singh for this gruesome treatment meted out to them.

head had sustained some injury and his left arm was fractured. He was immediately put in a palanquin (how and from where it appeared suddenly is still a mystery) and carried to the fort, escorted personally by the Prime Minister. He asked for water, but according to Smyth, it was refused. The earlier head injury was minor (equal in circumference to a rupee), but when the door was opened and his death finally announced, the floor was splattered with blood ! All European eye-witness accounts like those of Gardner and Smyth make it obvious that the Dogrā Prime Minister was responsible for this heinous crime (though Dr. Honiberger says "the crime might have been committed by the supporters of Kharak Singh and Chet Singh, but who these supporters were after the death of both, we are not told). Says Cunningham, "It is not positively known that the Rājās of Jammu thus designed to remove Nau Nihāl Singh, but it is difficult to acquit them of crime, and it is certain that they were capable of it." According to Latif, Sardār Lahnā Singh Majithiā attempted to follow the palanquin, but Dhian Singh stopped him. Other Sardārs also tried to follow, but were prevented by the Prime Minister from entering the fort, the gates of which were at once closed. "In vain did Mahārani Chand Kaur beat her head against the gates, but was not allowed to see her beloved and only child." Nor was his wife, Nānaki, permitted to attend upon him. Some of the modern historians like Dr. Hari Rām Guptā have tried to absolve the Dogrā chief by attributing this tragic happenning to an accident, as perhaps, according to them, to the booming of guns on that day, the old archway may have been shaken to the foundations ! But that it should fall only on Naunihāl Singh who was the first to pass though it seems to indicate that even this accident had the prevision to plan its occurrence to the right person at the right time ! To the question that if it is was planned by Dhian Singh, why he should have sacrificed the life of his dear nephew alongwith Naunihāl Singh, the answer is that according to the protocol, it was never imagined (nor could it be so organised) that the two would walk back together. To attribute the accident to the curses of the *Satis* is to make such major events of history dependent upon superstitions. Dr. Gupta himself in the illuminating introduction to his well-edited newsletters, "*Panjab on the eve of the first Sikh War*", emphasises the Dogrā family's conspiracy to usurp the Sikh throne. Says he:- "The perusal of these news-letters discloses a well laid-out plot to seize the Sikh empire, on the part of the Jammu rājās, in particular by Rājā

Gulāb Singh. During the later years of Mahārājā Ranjit Singh's rule, Rājā Dhian Singh, the Prime Minister, had almost become a dictator. He was not prepared to stand any reduction in his powers and wished to rule as the sole master"... He supports Sir Lepal Griffin in his assertion that "Dhian Singh had a still dearer ambition than this. His eldest son, Hirā Singh, had been brought up like the the Mahārāja's (Ranjit Singh's) own child, and as such was regarded by the Khālsā army. Was it then too bold an ambition to hope that some day he might rule the Panjāb as king, with Dhian Singh, his father, as his chief adviser". In fact, according to Cunningham, "Mahārāni Chand Kaur expressed a wish to formally adopt Hirā Singh as her son and thus add to his claim for the throne." If most of the important courtiers who were too terrified to speak the truth kept silent, it only proves the guilt of the Dogrā chief. Otherwise, they would have spoken in defence of their chief, who was being accused by one and all of this deliberate murder, of not one but two Kings in little less than one and a half years. The statement of only one courtier, Diwān Rattan Chand, that the prince's brain was crushed, makes it all the more suspicious, as the others didnot speak out at all. Dr. Honiberger was an employee of the state and had everything to gain by pleasing his new master than those never to return by saying that "there was no hope" of recovery of Naunihāi Singh. If Dhian Singh had nothing to hide, why did he not allow in anyone, not even the prince's mother and wife, except a few chosen hillmen, his aides, himself and two of his own confidants. According to Gardner, they battered the young prince to death. This may be true, "for two of them who knew too much about it were murdered, the other two fled to the British India and one was never heard of again."

According to Mohd Latif, "two hours before the Sardārs who had waited at the gates outside were informed that there was no reason to apprehend danger; that the prince would in all likelihood shortly recover, as he had received but a slight wound, which having caused a severe shock to the brain, had rendered him unconscious for the time being, that he required a short repose, and his rest should not be disturbed."

Two hours later, Chand Kaur was informed that his son was dead. But if she wanted to occupy the throne herself, Dhian Singh would render every assistance, provided she followed what she was instructed by him to do. She was not to announce the death of her son nor mourn her loss publicly or make any fuss about it. And so the death of this promising and youthful monarch on whom the whole Khālsā had pinned their hopes, was kept a closely-guarded secret for three days.

In the interval, Prince Sher Singh was invited by the Prime Minister to hasten to the capital. It is only after he arrived that the death of the illustrious Prince was announced. He was cremated close to the spot where his grandsire had been consigned to the flames. Two of his young handsome widows burnt themselves alive with him. And thus the dream ended like a dream.

And now Dhiān Singh showed himself in his true colours. He refused to honour his word to Rāni Chand Kaur. His suspicion was that the Mahārāni's faction and that of the Sandhānwālias were not favourably disposed towards him. "She is a woman after all," he pleaded with the Sardārs and they heartily agreed. A woman is a woman after all, even to the sons of Gobind who had raised womanhood along with men to new heights of dignity and power. But she proved too shrewd for the wily Prime Minister. She summoned Sardār Attar Singh Sandhānwālia from Hardwār and won over the affection of the Hindus through liberal charities to the Brāhmins. She also let it be known that the wife of Nau-Nihāl, Rāni Gilwālan (or Sāhib Kaur) was pregnant and that she would act only as the regent if a male issue was born to her. But if it was a female, she would accept Kanwar Sher Singh, the nominee of Dhian Singh, as the monarch. Meanwhile, he should agree to work as the Vice-President of the Council of Regency, and so, by common consent, Rāni Chand Kaur became Regent to the Prince (?) yet to be born with a Council of four to govern the State. Those included in the Council were: Rājā Dhian Singh, Attar Singh Sandhānwāliā, Gurmukh Singh Giani, Sardār Lehnā Singh Majithia and Diwān Dinā Nāth. But the internal frictions were so acute that the Council could hardly function in harmony even for a month. Kanwar Sher Singh retired to his Jāgir

---

* And yet, Mohd Latif disbelieves any plot and asserts that it was a sort of a divine vengeance visiting on this "monstrous" Prince. What monsterities had been committed by one who died at the age of 20, crowned with glory as a warrior, Governor and later as the administrator of the rāj are however left unstated. Possibly, the fact that he headed the armies which conquered Kābul or ruled over the Muslim Pathānland successfully is too much to stomach even for a historian like Mohammad Latif !

at Batālā, and Dhian Singh took leave of absence to live in Jammu. It was, however, so organised by the Dogrā brothers that while Rājā Gulab Singh and Hira Singh offered full support to the Mahārāni's cause, Dhian Singh and Suchet Singh played on the side of Sher Singh, whom the forces also liked as a brilliant warrior and administrator. Dhian Singh during his leave of absence was keeping himself fully posted with the happenings in the capital, and the confusion prevailing there. Hardly a month had passed that he invited Kanwar Sher Singh, from Mukerian to Lāhore, where he was also to join him. Sher Singh came with 300 horsemen and halted at the Shālimār gardens, their appointed rendezvous. But Dhian Singh didnot turn up. Sher Singh's confidants whispered into his ears that Dhian Singh was only making use of the prince and that his real sympathies lay with his son, Hira Singh, and brother, Gulāb Singh, who had openly sided with Mahārāni. Convinced of this, Sher Singh tried to negotiate through his aide, Jawālā Singh, directly with the Khālsā army, which had of late assumed a decisive role in view of the confused and shifting loyalties of the rulers and the courtiers. When they who are charged with ruling the destinies of nations make their state a market-place of low intrigue, sycophancy, and change of colours to promote nothing but self-interest, no one can accuse a disciplined force like the army to plunge into the arena of politics, howsoever disastrous this course and how much worse its consequences.

Every party that came to power promised *ināms* and better salary to the soldiers. The power of every kind of state ultimately rests on force. Hence, it was natural that the decisive role in a period of transition and confusion should also turn their heads. They elected their own *Panches* (like any trade union of the present times) to negotiate terms with every faction bidding for power. What is worse, the officers were kept out of the elective posts. The Khālsā, when they were also suitably trained and armed, couldnot resist the temptation of having a free play for their democratic propensities infused in their minds and hearts by the Guru. Democracy (a highly disciplined way of collective assertion) was for a time abused and degenerated into anarchy and free-for-all. When, however, the times are such, even angels turn into monsters. There is no choice left for them if they want to survive.

Kanwar Sher Singh met the *Panches* at Budhu-Kā-Āvā * outside Lāhore. The *Panches* welcomed the move. The soldiers were promised increased salaries. Meanwhile,those in power didnot lag behind,and the forces guarding the city of Lāhore and the fort were flooded with *ināms*. According to Sita Ram Kohli, (*Sunset of the Sikh Empire*, P. 36), the Rāni sent Ajit Singh Sandhānwāliā post-haste to Ludhiānā to meet the Governor-General's Agent, Mr. Clerk, and promised Kashmir or one fourth of Panjāb's revenues to the British for speedy help. The army, however, joined Kanwar Sher Singh in large numbers and with a force of 70,000 and 200 guns, he attacked the city, on Jan I4, 1841, at sundown. Before the night was over, Sher Singh had established his control over Lāhore. Gen. Ventura, with his force of 6500, took no time to pledge his allegiance, so did Col. Dhaunkal Singh and other officers and well-known warriors. Gulāb Singh distributed about Rs. 2 lakhs to the forces inside the fort and on an oath on the Qurān or Gangājali, Muslim and Hindu battalions were by him bound to his command. Unless he would so wish, the gates of the fort had not to be opened to the forces of Sher Singh and the soldiers would fight to the bitter end. Firing was resorted to from the ramparts of the fort, but a wall of the fort was breached by the surrounding force, though inside the fort they met with much resistance, resulting in large-scale bloodshed.† To avoid further carnage, Mahārāni Chand Kaur sued for peace and agreed to vacate the fort alongwith

---

* The place is sanctified by the story connected with Guru Arjun having blessed the brick-kiln (Āvā) of Bhāi Budhu, his devotee, who was suffering loss in business on account of incessant rains. But on a faqir, who had been refused food at his house, cursing him at the same time, the Guru too had to retract his blessings saying "your profits would remain, but the bricks will not be baked. Such is the power of the poor in the house of God". In 1939, the Sikh National college was built on this site.

† Why the Sikh soldiers deserted the cause of Rāni Chand Kaur was not only that she was a woman, but also because of Gulāb Singh having espoused her cause, and also because of the widespread rumours that like Kharak Singh, she had promised Kashmir and 3/8ths of the state-revenues to the British for their help which she was seeking to keep herself in power. Sher Singh had a much cleaner record. He had fought Sayyad Ahmad Brelvi and finally annihilated his forces. As successful Governor of Kashmir (when his forces had marched on Ladākh and occupied it), he was very popular with the forces at the young age of 33. From being a Francophile, he had now become an Anglophile in his habits, and was therefore acceptable to the English as well. His intelligence was favourably commented upon by Lord Auckland's sister.

Gulāb Singh, Hirā Singh and the Sandhiānwālias, and Kanwar Sher Singh agreed to grant safe and unmolested passage, without search of any kind, to the Mahārāni. He offered a *jāgir* worth Rs. 9 lakhs to her and agreed also to grant pardon to the civilian members and soldiers of her faction. The *jāgir* was, however, asked for in the vicinity of Jammu, for Rājā Gulāb Singh was to manage its affairs (!) When Gulāb Singh vacated the fort and left for Jammu, he took alongwith him about Rs. 80 lakhs worth of cash, gold and jewels from the state treasury, conveyed in 16 bullock carts and 500 horses on the pretext that these were the Rāni's personal effects left in his custody ! † Sardārs Attar Singh and Ajit Singh Sandhānwālia fled to British territory, and Lehnā Singh was taken into custody. Sher Singh treated Chānd Kaur with great courtesy and she also received him with affection and esteem. *Koh-i-Nur* was presented to him by Missar Beli Ram in her presence.

Meantime, Dhian Singh also arrived on the scene and expressed great jubilation over the outcome. The Mahārājā ascended the throne on Jan. 27, 1841, with Dhiān Singh as his Prime Minister. The officers of the army got a pay-raise of Rs. 10 to 15 per month. The soldiers also received the monthly increase of Rs. 2/- which cost the treasury about a crore of rupees.‡ Six months later, hearing

† According to Sir Lepal Griffln it is with this money that Gulāb Singh later purchased Kashmir from the British in 1846. Sardār K. M. Pannikar, in his *Founding of the Kashmir state* confirms that the 16 bullock-carts contained silver & gold coins and the 500 horsemen each had a bagful of gold mohurs with him.

‡ It is said by several historians that they became so insolent that they took law into their own hands, indulged in loot and killed some of their accountants (for misappropriation of their wages) and their officers (for bad manners or pro-English proclivities) ! They would leave station without permission. They wanted their cfficers also to be changed according to their wishes. Some of the Brahmin Sikh high officials, notably Gen. Tej Singh and his uncle Khushāl Singh, were so afraid that they got voluntarily confined to their homes. Sardārs Lehnā Singh Majithiā, who sided with the Rāni, suffered a similar humiliation. They killed several European officers of the Khālsā army, including Gen. Foulkes and Major Ford. Some of them had to be specially protected, including Gen. Ventura. Avitabile wanted to go back to Europe. The Governor of Kashmir, Mihan Singh, was murdered, so also Sobhā Singh, commander of the Gobindgarh fort at Amritsar. But this phase was soon over, and the *Panches* enforced strict discipline in their ranks and severely punished any breach of it.

of the reports of an expedition of the ruler of Bāltistān against Ladākh, a part of the Sikh kingdom, Sher Singh sent out a large force of 13000 under the command of notable Generals like Meehan Singh, Zorawār Singh, Dhian Singh and Gulāb Singh who not only defeated Ahmad Shāh, the ruler of Bāltistān, but marched right upto Lhāsā, the capital of Tibet, besides capturing little Tibet, Rohtaku, Gāru, the Mansarovar lake and the source of Indus and Satluj. A treaty was signed, however, with Tibet & China & the Sikh forces withdrew from Lhāsā.*

After a while, Sher Singh, intent on burying the internal schism for all times, sent word to the Mahārāni through the venerable Bābā Bikram Singh Bedi that he was willing to marry her. But, she responded that it was too early after the death of her husband and son to enter into a wedlock and that some time should be allowed to lapse. The Mahārājā appreciated her feelings. Later, a date was fixed for the marriage but a week before the appointed date, Gulāb Singh worked so cleverly on the fears of her brother, Chandā Singh Kanaihyā of Fatehgarh, that he came running to his sister to implore her to desist from this course which, he said, the Mahārājā was adopting to finish her off. Gulāb Singh was mortally afraid that if this union fructified, he would be asked to surrender both the Rāni's *jāgir* and the vast treasures he had cornered in her name. The Rāni succumbed to the pressure of her brother and refused to solemnise the marriage. She also left the fort, on his advice, and went to stay in a separate *haveli* in the city.

This advice had also come from Gulāb Singh who wanted to separate the two, so that there may be no further scope for the

* Extracts from the treaty signed between the Sikh kingdom and its officials and the plenipotentiaries of China and Tibet in Asuj of Samvat 1899 (1842 A.D.) may be of interest to the reader :—

"Now that in the presence of God, the ill feeling created by war has been fully removed from the hearts and no complaints now remain (on either side), there will be never on any account in future while the world lasts, any deviation even by the hair's breadth or any breach in the alliance, friendship and unity between the King of the world (Sher Singh) Shri Khālsāji Sāhib, Sri Mahārājā Sāhib Bahādur (Gulāb Singh) and the Khāgān (emperor) of Chinā and the Lāmā Guru Sāhib of Lhāsā. We shall remain in possession of the limits of the boundaries of Ladākh and the neighbourhood subordinate to it, in accordanee with the old customs and there shall be no transgression and no interference in the country beyond the old-established frontiers," etc. As Gulab Singh was fighting on behalf of the Sikh Kingdom, his name in the treaty seems to be a later interpolation.

Mahārājā to influence the life of the Mahārāni if she stayed within the fort. Telling her that it would be in her interest to remove all her old maid-servants, Gulāb Singh got them replaced by four hill-women of his confidence and choice. They had been heavily bribed by Dhian Singh to put an end to the Rāni's life as soon as the word was given to them. One day, Rāni Chand Kaur complained of headache. The maids gave her a sherbet of sorts to drink. This was mixed with poison. After one or two sips, she could not bear its bitter taste any more, and went to bed. When she had begun to dose is her bed about midnight (June 11, 1842), they struck her head with a grindstone so hard that her skull was crushed and she fell dead. To avoid any leakage of the principal perpetrators of this dastardly crime, instead of punishing them with death, Dhian Singh ordered that their tongues be cut off ! (According to Latif, they were put to death also later in the day). Mahārājā Sher Singh was out on tour and the news was conveyed to him, at Sialkot, five days later. No one benefitted more from this gruesome tragedy than did Gulāb Singh.* He appropriated the vast treasure if not also the *Jāgir* of the deceased.

Now the British also tried to play their part. Their political agent at Ludhiānā, Mr. Clark, came twice to Amritsar and Lāhore in February and April to prevail upon the Mahārājā to accede to their wishes, and advised him to release Lahnā Singh Sandhānwāliā from prison and permit the other two Sandhānwāliā chiefs Attar Singh and Ajit Singh, to return to the Panjāb. The Mahārājā carried out his wishes and made them his trusted counsellors. Their *Jāgirs* were restored. Their guns, forts, elephants and horses etc. worth about Rs. 40 lakhs were also handed over to them by the Sikh kingdom. Both the British and the Sandhānwāliās secured the guarantee of Bābā Bikram Singh Bedi for their good behaviour. Ajit Singh laid down his sword at the Mahārājā's feet in the open court and said with folded

---

* According to Dr. Hari Ram Guptā, all the three - Sher Singh, Dhian Singh and Gulāb Singh—were accomplices to this murder, Sher Singh because of her intrigues against her, Dhiān Singh because of her proximity to his rivals, the Sandhānwāliās, and Gulāb Singh because he wanted to appropriate her property. He is also of the opinion that the plot was master-minded by Dhiān Singh personally, that arsenic was given to her in a drink by the maids at his instance on June 12, and her skull was smashed with a grindstone by the maids.

(*Panjāb on the Eve of First Sikh War*, P. 39).

hands that unless the King himself would offer it back to him, he would not wear it. The Mahārājā, much moved by their show of loyalty and considering that after all they were the consin brothers of his father and served him loyally in high positions, placed his arms on his head saying, "you are a part of our blood. We have nothing against you."

Possibly, as Cunningham suggests (p. 231), the Mahārājā also needed a counter-weight against the all-powerful Jammu rājās. Ajit Singh, therefore, became his boon companion. His opinions and those of the other Sandhānwāliā Sardārs were given preference over the others. This was too much for Dhian Singh to stomach. He, therefore, worked on them assiduously to rouse both their ambition and fears against the Mahārājā who, he said, was planning their destruction. The Sandhānwāliās, Ajit Singh and his uncle Lehnā Singh, were also simultaneously working on the credulous mind of the Mahārājā that the grand Vizier was conspiring to assassinate him. The Mahārājā who had seen three of his prodecessors—Kharak Singh, Naunihal Singh and Chand Kaur—done to death at the Prime Minister's hands could not but believe in it. In one of his weak moments, finding him dead drunk, the Sandhānwāliās got the warrants of Dhian Singh's death signed by the Mahārājā.

The wily intriguers showed these warrants to Dhian Singh immediately thereafter, and enlisted his support to put an end to the Mahārājā's life. On September 15, 1843, when the Mahārājā was out to Shāh Balāwal, accompanied by only two persons, Diwān Dinā Nāth and his personal bodyguard, Ajit Singh and Lahnā Singh showed up there at the head of 150 horse and 300 infantry. Ajit Singh induced the Mahārājā to inspect a regiment he had newly raised and while making as if an offering of a new carbine to him, pulled the trigger and plunged several shots into the Mahārājā's manly chest. He later cut his head off with his own sword. His son, Kanwar Partap Singh, hardly 12, who was located in a garden nearby, fell at Lehnā Singh's feet, crying "Uncle, spare my life, I will be your slave." But the heartless ruffian cut the young handsome prince also to pieces.

Now, they all proceeded along to meet Dhian Singh. They showed him two severed heads of Mahārājā Sher Singh and Kanwar Partāp Singh. The Prime Minister was numb with fear. They asked him to accompany them to the citadel of the fort to proclaim Dalip

Singh as the new King. As if to confabulate with him on some secret mission, Lahnā Singh took Dhian Singh aside, thus separating him from his men. And without giving him a moment's chance of escape or resistance, shot him dead. The arch-conspirator had been caught in the coils of his own conspiracy. Nemesis had at last overtaken all his wily schemes.

The news of the triple murder spread like wild fire. The soldiers' minds were roused to a new frenzy especially by Hira Singh, son of the deceased Prime Minister. He collected the troops at Budhu-Kā-Avā.

Both Generals Avitabile and Court had promised him their support. So had Gen. Ventura. Before the Sardārs and the *panches* of the army, he bared his chest and said :—"I'm now fatherless and alone. We have served the Khālsā rāj with utmost loyalty and risen to these positions by dint of our chivalry and sacrifice. But, this was not the reward we sought. Attar Singh Sandhānwāliā had been with the British lately and had offered them six annas in a rupee (3/8ths) out of the Panjāb revenues. Can you trust such a man? I am now at your mercy. Either kill me or give me your support." He offered an increase of Rs. 3/- for every soldier. Every one present there agreed to fight on his side. Hira Singh stormed the fort, and killed Lehnā Singh. Ajit Singh tried to escape but was captured and shot. Their headquarters at Rājā Sānsi were raised to the ground. Missar Beli Rām, his brother Rām Kishan and Bhai Gurmukh Singh who were not friendly to the Dogras, were seized and placed in the custody of Sheikh Imam-ud-din who had them secretly murdered.

Dalip Singh was proclaimed the Mahārājā (Sept 1843) at the age of 5, with Rājā Hira Singh, 25, becoming his Prime Minister and Rāni Jindan, Dalip's mother, the Regent.† However, it was Hirā Singh

† Rāni Jindan (or Jind Kaur) was the daughter of Sardār Mannā Singh Aulakh (of village Chachar(in the district of Gujrānwālā), a Kumedān (commandant) incharge of the Mahārājā's kennels. Her beauty attracted her to Ranjit Singh to whom she was married according to Sikh rites, in 1835. All sorts of stories were given currency by her detractors, notably the British writers and political agents, who called her a concubine, a reputed wife, a dancing girl etc. of dissolute character, voluptuous and lusty whose professed lovers after Ranjit Singh were identified as Suchet Singh, Rāi Kesari Singh, Rājā Lāl Singh and so on. As if by a conspiracy, every English historian (and following them some modern Hindu and Sikh scribes as well who like these juicy tell-tale stories like chopsticks) have called all of Ranjit Singh's

who was all-powerful. And he was under the sinister influence of a Brāhmin soothsayar, Pandit Jallā, his tutor and guardian from an early age. Nothing moved which Jallā did not approve. Such was his power that a saying became current :

Upper Allā
te heth Jallā

i.e. "God above and Jallā below (control the destinies of the nation)." Hirā Singh had been a great favourite of Ranjit Singh. He was treated by the Mahārājā as his own son He was honoured with the title of Rājā when he was only thirteen. Alongwith two holymen, Bhāi Rām Singh and Gobind Rām, he alone was offered a chair in the presence of the Mahārājā while his father, the Prime Minister, stood behind the throne, with joined palms. It is said, for a time Ranjit Singh would keep Rs. 500/- each night under the boy's pillow to be distributed next morning as charity. Hira Singh did not live with his wives who were at Jammu in the care of Gulāb Singh, but offered separate land in Lāhore to build his mansions. This place came to be known as Hirā mandi (which in the British days became a favourite haunt of the dancing girls and still is). He was respected and loved by the soldiers due to these special favours. But, he lacked both will and experience and behaved like a reckless, spoilt child. He would make promises, but never keep them. When the soldiers became restive over any issue, he would assure them "he was the slave of the Khālsā," that "he was a Sikh and had nothing to do with the Dogrās," but would do only what later his own whim or Jallhā's-fancy or envy would dictate.

F. N. Contd.

sons illegitimate. They are described as idiots, of weak intellect, drunkards and sexual maniacs. "Kharak Singh, (legitimate or illegimate, by a wife or a slave girl) was of a weak intellect." (Griffin, Ranjit Singh, 108), "Tārā Singh was purchased from a chintz-weaver and the other (Sher Singh) the off-spring of a slave-girl" (Ibid, 107)." "Tārā Singh was an idiot," "Sher Singh was handsome, brave but stupid" (Ibid, 108). "Jindān was the reputed mother of Dhulip Singh. A menial servant, named Gulu, was generally accepted as his father." (Ibid, 109). Cunningham repeats these stories, all concoted by the jealous *feringis* and circulated by the rival parties in the Darbār as it advanced their own selfish interests. The sons are all accepted by Ranjit Singh as his own, offered *Jāgirs* and highest positions of authority in the realm. They are also accepted by the British as legitimate heirs when they are in power. But, nothing is left to chance to denigrate them when either they are dead, or fallen from power, or no more wanted or necessary.

Himself the product of the Mahārājā's munificence and large-heartedness, he acted in a most vicious and cruel manner in respect of anyone who crossed his way, or whom he suspected of enmity or jealousy prompted him to remove out of the way. With the family of Missar Beli Ram (whom he imprisoned but whom the army wanted released) he was especially cruel. He imposed fines of of Rs. 5 lakhs on Beli Ram and 10 lakhs on his old venerable father, Diwān Chand. He insulted and humiliated Jamādār Khushāl Singh till he died of a broken heart in mid-1844. Fond of sycophancy, he raised Imamuddin, murderer of Bhāi Gurmukh Singh and Missar Beli Rām, to the position of Governor of Jullunder-Doab and his father that of Kashmir. The Multān Governor, Sāwan Mal, who was extremely popular among the Muslim peasantry and gentry alike, he tried to denigrate. His *Jāgir* was nibbled at, and hostile elements roused and encouraged against him till he was assassinated. He pursued Prince Kashmirā Singh and Sardār Attar Singh Sandhānwaliā who had to take refuge with Bhāi Bir Singh, a highly-revered Sikh Saint across the Satluj. Bir Singh's haunt at Naurangābād was attacked with full force, calling it a refuge of traitors to the raj, and both the prince and Bhāi Bir Singh were killed, alongwith several hundreds of their followers. The Sikh soldiers were filled with great remorse for killing so noble a soul and they became restless. Hira Singh offered them money to perform obsequies for the holy man and by treating them to rumours that as the British were planning to attack the Panjāb, unity in the Sikh ranks was essential at that crucial moment.

Shām Singh Attāriwālā, the noble patriot, was never consulted in anything. In fact, he was in mortal dread for his personal safety and Lahnā Singh Mājithiā was obliged to go on a pilgrimage. He assuaged their feeling for the moment, but never desisted from the course he had adopted of removing or making ineffectual through assassination, neglect or humiliation the Sikh Sardārs who had the good of the rāj at heart.

Hirā Singh was not content with the removal of almost all his rivals. His ambition was to take over the entire state. Early in 1844, Gulāb Singh had suggested to him as much.* Asking his own estates to be enlarged so as to encompass Kashmir and Hazārā,

---

* *Panjāb on Eve of first Sikh War*, Guptā, (P. 61).

Peshāwar, D.I. Khān and Multān, besides Jammu and the salt-mines over which he already had firm control, he advised Hira Singh "to declare himself Mahārājā of the Panjāb, take Suchet Singh, his uncle, as Prime Minister, Rāi Kesri Singh as the Commander-in-chief and Pandit Jalla as the manager of his estates at Jasrota and the town-duties of Lāhore and Amritsar."

According to Sir Lepel Griffin (who wrote his works after the British had occupied Panjāb and transferred Kashmir to Gulāb Singh) "there are perhaps no characters in Panjāb history more repulsive than Rājās Dhyan Singh and Gulāb Singh, their splendid talents and undoubted bravery only render more conspicuous their atrocious cruelty, their treachery, their avarice, and their unscrupulous ambition." But let it not be said that the son of the grand Vizier at any time lacked any of his father's typical characteristics.

Hirā Singh ordered "that the property in the Tohākhānā be sent in large quantities to Jammoo. The hill troops were gradually increased in Lāhore. They were placed incharge of the magazine and the fort. So great was the suspicion of the army being dispersed all over the country and replaced at Lahore by the Dogrā troops that the military *Panchāyats* examined every little request of the Durbār with caution and circumspection and would not allow a single regiment to leave Lāhore without being statisfied of its dire necessity. Muslims and Purbias were recuited while the Sikh officers were discharged on flimsy grounds. Hira Singh had ordered (Jan 10, 1844) that "the affairs of Kashmir be managed by Gulāb Singh alone, and Rājā Gulāb Singh saw to it that only half of the revenue of the valley went to Lāhore and the other half to Jammu. But for the watchful eye of the Sikh army, Gilgit and Ladākh, Hazārā and Multān also would have been transferred to him, as was his demand at this time, besides the extension of licence for the salt-mines upto the Indus. Rājā Suchet Singh, his uncle, who developed differences with him and particularly with Jallā (whom the Sikhs hated but could not dispense with) was charged with supporting or giving refuge to some of Hirā Singh's enemies including Beli Ram, Chattar Singh Attāriwālā, Fateh Khan Tiwānā etc. He came ultimately to Lāhore on the advice of Gulāb Singh to patch up differences. But Jallā through a horoscopic prediction convinced Hirā Singh that this was a conspiracy to do him to death, of which Suchet Singh had no intention whatsoever. But he was attacked in his place of halt and murdered.

As would be seen, the Dogrā brothers' greatest enemy at the court was Pandit Jallā. He was also the greatest confidant of Hirā Singh. Jallā's family was imprisoned and starved in a Jammu prison by Gulāb Singh and later expelled. On their way to their new refuge, they were attacked and thirty of them killed by his force. With Hirā Singh also the differences were growing not so much (as was advertised) over Gulāb Singh's inability or unwillingness to remit revenues regularly, but over the division of the estates of his late father (whose two sons other than Hirā Singh were under the care of Gulāb Singh) and of Suchet Singh (who being childless had adopted Gulāb Singh's son as heir, bequething him all his properties. Thus, all these properties were infact coming to Gulāb Singh.)

Some European writers, like Michael Smyth and Richmond, are of the opinion that inwardly Hirā Singh and Gulāb Singh had a joint plan and the differences were kept up in the open only to mislead the unwary. They quarrelled and then they made up soon thereafter. Gulāb Singh encouraged the disaffected and unruly elements in the Sikh kingdom, and also negotiated peace with Hira Singh on their behalf as well as his own. But when he demanded the dismissal of Jallā, it was not acceptable to Hirā Singh.

Jallā had not only exasperated Gulāb Singh, but also the entire populace and the army. The Mahārāni's brother, Jawāhar Singh, he treated with contempt. He was rude and insolent in his behaviour to the tallest in the land and his pen would deprive the old veterans of their means of livelihood. But when he openly attacked the character of Rāni Jindān, she appealed to the army *Panches* to save her honour from the two wretches. The *Panches* were inflamed on hearing this and assured her full support. But before they could strike, Hirā Singh invited Gulāb Singh to help him out of this critical situation. He despatched a force of 700 Dogrā soldiers to attack the Sikh army in defence of Hirā Singh. This the Khālsā couldnot bear and decided to capture both Hirā Singh and Jallā. Sensing danger, they tried to flee to Jammu but were overtaken and killed. Jawāhar Singh, the brother of the Mahārāni, was appointed Prime Minister and Lāl Singh, her favourite courtier (some say her paramour), his principal adviser.

Taking advantage of the confusion prevailing at the Sikh Court, Gulāb Singh, the Dogrā Governor of Jammu, tried to declare his independence. The Sikh forces, therefore, marched upon him. Gulāb Singh surrendered without a fight, paid four lakhs as a tribute and looted it, as the satisfied army was marching back to Lāhore. The troops returned and severely punished the Dogrā forces. This time, Gulāb Singh promised to pay a tribute of 35 lakhs (5 lakhs only in cash), protested his loyalty in most abject terms, offering even his sword and shield to the Khālsā and accompanying them to Lāhore. Here, he was suspected of murdering Lāl Singh and imprisoned. But, he secured his release on a promise to pay 68 lakhs as fine (Rs. 27 lakhs in cash, and the rest, like usual, to remain a mere promise). The moment he was back to Jammu, he again started negotiations with the British and inciting the tribals and others to rebel against the Sikh Kingdom.

In the meantime, Prince Peshāwarā Singh had raised a standard of revolt first at Sialkot and then by seeking the help of the Afghāns. He was, however, captured near Attock and murdered, though he had been promised safe escort to Lāhore by Sardār Chattar Singh Attāriwāla, whose daughter was engaged to Dalip Singh.

The murder of Peshāwārā Singh was laid by the troops at the door of the Mahārāni's brother, Jawāhar Singh.

Jawāhar Singh had made himself thoroughly unpopular otherwise too, by his vengeful behaviour, insolence and his reputed moves either to flee to the British territory alongwith the young Mahārājā or to write to the British to take the Punjāb under their protection. He was invited, on Sept 21, 1845, to answer these charges before the *Panches* of the army. Mortally afraid, he took the young Mahārājā alongwith him on an elephant. He was asked to relieve himself of the royal cargo. He tried to plead his case, but in vain. A party of soldiers advanced and put the Vizier to death by a discharge of musketry. This naturally made the Rāni furious and it is said she vowed vengeance on the army. For a time, no one came forward to accept the high office of Prime Minister. Strangely enough, Gulāb Singh was invited to take it up, inspite of what inequities he had committed before, but he declined the honour. For some time, the Queen Mother attended the court herself. Ultimately early in Nov. 1845, Rājā Lāl Singh was nominated Prime Minister and Tej Singh was confirmed as the Commander-in-chief. The course downhill was now complete.

CHAPTER XXII

THE ANGLO-SIKH WARS

So much has been written both by the British and Sikh historians on the causes of the Anglo-Sikh wars † that one is constrained to believe that the British provoked the war, and the Sikhs hit back in self-defence. We have already referred to the military moves of the British authorities even on the eve of the Amritsar Treaty (1809), that if the Mahārājā would not accede to limit his empire to the Satluj, he may be challenged to a war. We have also alluded to such reports and messages exchanged between the British agents at Ludhiānā and the Governor-General on the eve of Ranjit's death and even before, which leaves no one in doubt that the British were only waiting for a suitable opportunity to attack the Panjāb physically, or by creating or helping to create disaffection and anarchy in order to place a convenient monarch on the throne of

† Notable documentations in this behalf are those of Dr Gandā Singh in his "*Correspondence Relating to the Anglo-Sikh Wars*", Dr. Hari Ram Gupta's "*Panjāb on tha eve of the first Sikh war,*" Cunningham's "History of the Sikhs", an eye-witness account of the first Sikh war and several others. Correspondence between the British agents at Ludhiānā and the Governor General has been thrown open to the public and can be studied at the Govt. of India Archives in New Delhi or the India office, London, the British Museum, the Record office at Lāhore and the Panjāb Archives at Patiālā. Several Memoirs (like those of Alexander Gardner and Carmichael Smyth) biographies (such as those of Henry Lawrence, Major Broadfoot, Viscount Gough, Lord Hardinge and Lord Ellenborough) and the reports published in the Calcutta Review, Panjāb Akhbār, and the British Press in those days leave no one in doubt as to the British having provoked the war and attacked first.

the Panjāb. Sayyad Ahmed Brelvi's major recruitment for a Jehād (holy war) against the Sikh rule came from the British territories without their trying in any way to thwart the fanaticism of these Muslim "holy warriors" against their ally and friend who never took advantage of their weakness at any time (as for instance at the time of their initial reverses during the Anglo-Nepalese war (1816-18) or when, in the first Burma war, their immense losses led to the fall of their prestige). Ranjit ignored the appeal of Bhonsle for help in 1820. He didnot consent to form an alliance against them with Nepal in 1834. He helped them actively in their designs on Afghānistān and did nothing to frustrate their attempts for the annexation of Sind and Baluchistān which by the treaty of Amritsar, the Sikhs had every right to claim or conquer. They never harboured or encouraged any force inimical to the British interests and in the event of a European incursion through the Panjāb, the Sikhs had taken upon themselves the responsibility of halting the advance, with their own might and resources. At no time during the pendency of the Amritsar treaty did Ranjit Singh or any of his successors give any cause to the British for its non-compliance, inspite of the British having occupied Ferozepur,* and confiscated Rājā Suchet Singh's treasures after his death (which the Lāhore Darbār legitimately claimed as its own).† Above all, they tried to deny facilities on the

* Before 1835, the over-all sovereignty of Ranjit Singh was recognised over Ferozepur, only 40 miles away from Lāhore across the Satluj. But the British needed it from the military point of view and so they occupied it in 1835 upon the death of Sardārni Lachhman Kaur, the nominal ruler, dying issueless, and converted it into a military station in 1838, while the Mahārājā was still alive, ostensibly for the purpose of making it an assembling point for the British army which was to march on Khurāsān. But later it was used against the Sikhs.

† The treasure Suchet Singh left behind at Ferozepur was estimated at Rs. 15 lakhs. It was secretly deposited by him at this place for the purpose of offering it to the British as a loan during the Afghān war. Money had been raised from the Cis-Satluj Sikh states by the British for the same purpose and Suchet Singh did not want to be left behind. Hirā Singh, then Prime Minister, claimed this money for the Sikh Durbār, protesting that it belonged to one of their subjects, dying issueless, and secondly that as he died as a rebel against his sovereign, his assets should accrue to the Sikh state, the more so when no one else claimed them in the British territories. But, the British wanted the Panjāb rāj to plead their case in a British court or that both Rājās Gulāb Singh and Hirā Singh should write to the British Govt. disclaiming any right to it as heirs. But, both Gulāb Singh and Suchet Singh's widow, who had adopted the son of Gulāb Singh, Mian Phinā, did not agree for

ground to the agents of the Sikh rāj to patrol and collect revenues from their territories across the Satluj, which by treaty-rights they were obligated to do. It is true that it was stipulated in the Treaty of Amritsar that "the rājā will never maintain in the territory occupied by him and his dependents on the left bank of the river Satluj (i.e. the British side) more troops than are necessary for the internal duties of that territory", but his rights to the administration of these areas were duly recognised. Ultimately, this is what was challenged by the British and a war ensued.

It is not wholly true that the Sikh forces had become unmanagable and the rulers in their own interest plunged them into a mortal combat with a powerful enemy inorder to break their back and to secure their personal interests through a prior arrangement with the British. It is no doubt true that the Khālsā army had become all-powerful. They suspected the pretentions of their rulers. The *Panchayats* could over-rule their officers. They had come to consider themselves as the *Sarbat Khālsā*, or the repository of power of that mystic entity called the Sikh Commonwealth, and issued orders under its own seal-Akāl Sahai-(God be our refuge), though the British refused to acknowledge such communications. But according to all available evidence (mostly European) they were actuated by nothing but patriotic motives and were a highly organised and disciplined force, and not a rabble out on a rampage. They would enforce their command on their own ranks with much more severity than on the others.* They were

F. N. Contd.

good reason, and this money was later adjusted against the price agreed to be paid by Gulāb Singh for the acquisition of Kashmir after the first Sikh War. Suchet Singh's total assets after his death were of the value of 2 crores.

* "The soldiery began to talk of themselves as *Panth Khālsāgi* (ji) (or as the *Sarbat Khālsā*, the body of the elect). But inspite of their having finished off Jawāhar Singh, made captive the formidable chief of Jammu (Gulāb Singh), reduced to submission the powerful Governor of Multān, put down the rebellion of one recognised as the brother of the Mahārājā (Peshāwarā Singh), and contrived to keep the famed Afghāns in check at Peshāwar and along the frontier, they were satisfied with Rāni Jindān holding regular court, and reposed confidence in the integrity of the chief accountant, Dinā Nāth, the paymaster Bhagat Rām and Nuruddin. Rājā Lāl Singh was nominated Prime Minister and Tej Singh confirmed as the Commander-in-chief" (Cunningham pp. 245-48) with their approval. This shows that the troops realised the importance of the civilian authority. Sir Henry Hardinge wrote (Sept 30, 1845) to the authorities in London that "it

receiving twice the wages of the East India Company soldiers. (In fact, their emoluments were the envy of the soldiers of the East India Company and they mutinied at several places (as in Sind and Ferozepur) to secure the same benefits as were enjoyed by the Sikh soldiers.

Were it not so, after the death of Ranjit Singh, when occasions were offered by the British and the Lāhore Durbar for a decisive show-down, the army would not have held its hand. To cite a few instances: when on July 23, 1839, it was reported to Mahārājā Kkarak Singh that Diwān Sāwan Mal, Governor of Multān, had refused to sell any food-grains to the British officers (possibly these were being sold without his permission) a royal command (Aug. 19) was issued to him "not to raise any objection." Mahārājā Ranjit Singh had refused to allow passage to the British troops through his territory on their way to Kābul on a joint expedition, but one of his successors waived this injunction and permitted the British troops to pass through the territory of Panjāb (avoiding Lahore however) on their way back, to save them both expense and hazards of a tortuous journey. Neither expense to the Sikh state was considered a sufficient ground (inspite of the protests of the treasury), nor the agitated mood of the court and the Sikh army, to rescind the orders. All the arrangements with the British were carried out both by the Lahore Durbar and the Sikhs army, in letter and spirit, of the Tripartite Treaty (1838) on Afghānistān.

When two years after the occupation of Kābul, the British envoy was murdered (Dec 23, 1841) and a punitive force was sought to be organised by the British to retrieve their prestige, the Sikhs under Mahārājā Sher Singh contributed 15000 troops (as against 6000 stipulated) to force through the Khyber Pass, by taking to a more hazardous and longer route for themselves and dividing the hostile Afghān forces into two and defeating them, for which Lord Ellenborough, Governor General (April 19, 1842), instructed his agent at Lāhore "to offer his congratulations on this occasion, so honourable to the Sikh arms."

But at the same time, the British were assembling a third army of reserve at Ferozepur "to keep the Sikhs in check." On Oct 1841, the Calcutta newspapers published alarming reports about the British

F. N, Contd.
was a democratic revolution so successfully accomplished by the Sikh army" and "their chiefs would exert all their efforts to compel the British Govt. to fight them inorder to save their personal interests."

plans to conquer the Panjāb "inorder to restore peace and order" (in the independent Sikh kingdom !) While Gulāb Singh was sent across the Indus by Mahārājā Sher Singh to help the British army advancing against Kābul, he was contacted by Henry Lawrence (Jan. 1842) and offered a consideration both for him and his brother, Rājā Dhian Singh, the grand Vizier, "in return for their aid to conquer Panjāb." "We need such men as the Rājāh and Gen. Avitabile, and should bind them to us by the only tie they recognise—self-interest." "Any other Sirdārs helping us cordially be (also) specially and separately treated for." Apart from Kashmir, "even with additions", Raja Goolab Singh "was to be assisted to get possession of the valley of Jallalābād and Peshāwar (a Sikh territory !)."* Later on, secret confabulations also took place between the Poorbia General, Tej Singh and Sardār Lāl Singh, the Vizier, to betray the cause of their state in return for ample rewards.

Contacts were established with Gen. Ventura, early in 1843, and he therefore, "kept the British informed of the developments in his state." He was always friendly with Sher Singh and according to Lord Ellenborough's letter of May 11, 1843 it was "he who had advised Sher Singh to finish off Dhian Singh." "The break up of the Panjāb will probably begin with (this) murder." On Oct 20, 1843, depending on his report, Lord Ellenborough wrote to Her Majesty the Queen of England that "the events at Lāhore will bring first the plains and later the hills under our protection or control." Messages were exchanged by Broadfoot with Diwān Moolraj of Multān to rebel.

Ajit Singh Sandhānwāliā was given asylum in the British territory and later the Mahārājā (Sher Singh) persuaded to accept him back with results which soon became obvious. He assassinated him, his son and also his Prime Minister !

Writes Col. Hugh Cook :—

"The British had watched the development in the Panjāb with considerable misgivings, particularly after the Sikhs had made an

---

* *Biography of Henry Lawrence by Sir Herbert Edwards* (pp. 326-27) as quoted in *Private correspondence Relating to the Anglo-Sikh Wars*. Gulāb Singh's agent, Sheo Dutt, met Maj. Broadfoot in Aug 1845 and assured him that his master would "cause the hillmen to revolt against the Sikhs and submit to the British and if so desired he could assemble 40,000 troops from the hills." (SC 25, Oct 1845, Maj. Broadfoot to Currie).

incursion into Tibet in 1841, which showed the aggressive spirit of the Khālsā. Lord Ellenborough, the Governor General, was convinced that war was bound to come. When the British invaded and annexed Sind in 1843, there was more fuel for anti-British sentiments, since the Sikhs themselves had ambitions in that direction." But the writer has integrity enough to observe that the Sikhs, "for want of a united leadership," didnot open a second front either at the time of the British invasion of Sind in 1843 or a year later when the British were engaged in a war with the Marāthās at Gwalior. However, the British were incensed and alarmed over the Sikh incursions into Tibet and had been convinced even at the highest level that the war with them was inevitable !

Sir Henry Hardinge, the new Governor General, allowed a garrison (at Ferozepur) and at Ludhiānā and Ambālā, their strength was "virtually doubled" (1844). "He arranged for Maj. Broadfoot to establish supply-dumps at twenty-mile intervals between Meerut and Ferozepur. These measures didnot go unnoticed by the Sikhs. There must have been talk in messes of the prospect of invading the Panjāb (and) relayed across the Satluj (to the Sikhs)." *

While recognising the "good account of the Sikh Govt. (during the Afghān war) and the desirability "of maintaining its existence in the Panjāb, the Duke of Wellington yet was anxious that "if we are to maintain our positions in Afghānistān, we ought to have Peshāwar (a Sikh territory), the Khyber Pass, Jallālābād and the passes between that post and Kābul."†

Later, when the British left Afghānistan after its conquest by the Allied forces, the Sikh Govt. was encouraged by Lord Ellenborough to occupy Jallālābād "so that their strength at home is considerably reduced" and they fall an easy prey in the Panjāb. "The State of Panjāb is therefore under my foot,"* he claimed. But the Sikhs refused to take the bait, though His Lordship chose "to be

* *The Sikh Wars*, by H. Cooke pp. 21-22.

† Letter to Lord Fitzgerald, London, April 6, 1842. It was suggested to Ranjit Singh as well as to his successors that Peshāwar be transferred to Dost Mohammad, then to Shāh Shujā, then again to Dost Mohd., then to Gulāb Singh and, last, the British wanted to occupy it themselves as well to maintain their position in Afghānistān !

most courteous and liberal to both parties (at the Sikh Court) and to wait till I am called in." *

Boats were ordered to be prepared at Bombay in 1844-45, to form a bridge on the Satluj for the crossing over of the British troops into the Sikh country. These were despatched to Ferozepur in the autumn of 1845. The troops in Sind were being equipped to march on Multān. Major Broadfoot who had succeeded as agent of the British for the Sikh affairs, has left no one in doubt through his own correspondence with the British authorities at this time that they were out for war on any pretext. Otherwise, there was no reason why he should have declared the Cis-Satluj possessions of the Panjāb Govt. to be under British protection, equally with Patiālā etc, and also to be liable to escheat on the death or deposition of Dalip Singh.

These views were, however, not announced to the Sikh kingdom but this is how Maj. Broadfoot enforced these views first by the display of force in the affairs of the Sodhis of Ānandpur and then by asking a small Sikh force which had gone across the Satluj to Kapura, a Panjāb possession, to relieve the mounted police there, to re-cross the river. And as they hesitated, they were fired at. According to Cunningham, only the extreme patience and circumspection of the Sikh commandant saved the situation. In the summer of 1845, some Sikh horsemen from Multān crosssd into the undefined borderland of Sind, in pursuit of some marauders and the British troops were immediately put on alert. "Two Sikh villages near Ludhiānā were placed under sequestration on the plea that criminals concealed in them had not been surrendered."

But the Sikhs were not prepared for war. Nor according to M'gregor was Rāni Jindān (though she is not free of blame). "Many of the Sikh Sardars diapproved and objected". According to Sir Henry Hardinge (Sept 30, 1845), "while they (the army) declared that they desired peace, there was a strong party clamouring for war." And who constituted this strong clamorous party to go to battle with the British? None others but "Lāl Singh and Tej Singh (who) urged them on to war." And Gulāb Singh, their faithful ally, was not to lag behind. All

* Lord Ellenborough to the Duke of Wellington, Simla, Oct 18, 1842. While conveying through the Panjāb in April 1841 the family of Shāh Shujā, Broadfoot had picked up a fight with the escort provided by the Lāhore Durbār, and while at Peshāwar called upon the Afghān population to rise and aid him against the troops of their Govt." (Cunningham: History of the Sikhs, P. 215).

the three, as has been said, were in league with the British and incited the troops for their own selfish reasons. And when the attack was launched, all the doubting and dissenting Sardārs were "patriotic enough to join the Khālsā."

It is said, Rāni Jindān was equally (if not exlusively) responsible for teaching her own army a lesson by provoking it to attack the British. And this because she was unhinged by the murder of her lecherous and intriguing brother, Jawāhar Singh. Were it so, she would not have elicited the whole-hearted sympathy of the troops which she did. Lord Hardinge himself pays a tribute to "her spirit and energy," saying, "she appears before the troops and the public and has laid aside her debaucheries with her veil." It is the intriguers at her court who led her on to a disastrous course, though her sense of judgement and quality of leadership cannot be appreciated on this account. *

That the traitorous men had been bought over by the British beforehand does not, in any way, mitigate the original sin of giving highest positions of authority to men who had proved time and again to be of doubtful character. They were all mercenaries and soldiers of fortune and without background of loyalty to *any* cause, or being sticklers for morality or decency in public life. They had become formidable chieftains in a decade or two, amassing colossal hoards, irregular armies, Jāgirs, awards and titles. If they tried to protect their self-interests anyhow, even at the expense of their nation, (whose ethos indeed they had never imbibed and of which they were not even an integral part for any length of time), the fault lies not so much in them as in those who put them on the pedestal of power, forgave their treasonable conduct time and again (as in the case of Gulāb Singh), of the low intrigues of Lāl Singh and Tej Singh (and the rapacity and rudeness of Jāmādar Khushal Singh, his uncle, through whom he rose in the favour of the Durbār.) These facts were not unknown to the rulers or the army. Strangely enough, those who were reputed to be anti-British like the Dogra Brothers, later turned out to be their best

* Dr. B. S. Nijjar, Director, Panjāb State Archives, however, blames Rāni Jind Kaur for inviting the British, basing his argument on the now popular ballad of Shāh Mohd, that becoming unhinged on account of her brother's death, she wanted to break the back of the Khālsā army by inciting the troops to war. Says he: "It was the Queen's personality which brought about a succession of events which weakened and disintegrated the Sikh empire beyond redemption. It is Rāni Jindān who can be held solely responsible for the downfall of the Khālsā." (Mahārāni Jind Kaur, P. 50)

allies (and, secretly, had all along been, as we shall see later on). So did those like Tej Singh and Lal Singh, who according to the highest British authorities like Sir Henry Hardinge, the Governor General, egged the army on to war. They were the first to betray the interests of their nation. It has often happened in history that they who incite the innocent, peace-loving people to fight whom they call the "enemies" of the nation, turn out to be the agents of the self-same enemy, and they who plead for reason and commonsense in times of crisis are dubbed traitors and cowards, though they are the only sure and stable friends of the nation. This trait has played such a havoc in India's history (more particularly Sikh history) that one can only exclaim with Cassius:—"The fault, dear Brutus, is not in our stars but in ourselves, that we are underlings."

The rest of the story is now easy to narrate when its nemesis is inherent and glaringly apparent in its very crude inception.

Though Cunningham is considered to be the most dependable of writers on the Anglo-Sikh affairs and he considers many of the above provocations of the British a sufficient cause for the Sikhs to strike in self-defence, (especially when their authority was being treated with indifference or contempt), he is also willing to point out that "the initiative (for war) was taken by the Sikhs who, by an overt act broke a solemn treaty, and invaded the territories of allies." * He is "certain" the English people had all along been sincerely desirous of living at peace with the Panjāb, and that they were not prepared at this time for a final show-down (inspite of the provocations).

And this inspite of the secret wishes they harboured of one day annexing the Panjāb. According to him, the leaders at the top also became traitorous because "the authority of the army began to predominate and this threatened the territorial chiefs and the adventurers

---

* A most significant fact which no Sikh historian has cared to study or highlight is that Mahārājā Dalip Singh in his petition (for the increase in his emoluments dated London, March 29, 1882) to the British Secy of State confirms this view. Say he:—"At the succession to the throne of the Panjāb by your humble petitioner, then of extremely tender age, the country was in an extremely disorganised state and the soldiery mutinous, and the Sikh army, without receiving any provocation, invaded the British territories and was completely routed and dispersed etc. (Foreign Deptt., Secret). This was at a time when he had become highly critical of the British, had met and lived with his mother (1860-63) and should have known better now at the age of 44. This fact must have been confirmed to him by his mother no less than by others whom he met or read or corresponded with.

in the employ of the government". Thus, according to him, it is not as if the British were the only villain of the piece. The Sikh soldiers too appeared to have lost self-control through lack of leadership. The contemporary account of the poet Shah Mohammed in his ballad *Jang Singhan te farangian*, (which duly records the superb bravery of the Sikh soldiers and the treachery of the officers like Tej Singh and Lāl Singh) also blames Rāni Jindān for her inglorious part in precipitating the crisis, the British unwillingness for war and the Sikh army's determination to challenge the feringi on the battlefield. In such a confused situation, when men lose grip of the situation and their future seems to lie only in the past, men as well as nations plunge into a desparate, even if meaningless and suicidal struggle, and end up receiving the worst of both the worlds.*

Possibly, the patriotic Sardārs could have exerted their considerable influence to a better purpose, or Rāni Jindān (assuming that she was sincere in her protestations) could have exercised her sovereign right to hold back the vicious enthusiasm of the army. Or the army could have assessed its own potentialities better, in view of the divided national counsels and the depleted treasury (there were only 95 lakhs in the state treasuries at Lāhore and Amritsar at this time, though there was much more money kept in the hills which the Govt. could not possibly lay their hands upon in times of crisis), due mostly to their own never-ending demands. It has been suggested that they were elated by the British defeat and humiliation in Afghānistān only a brief while ago. But, it seems, an inexorable fate was driving them on to a sure disaster, led (or misled) as they were by treachery and deceit. Still they declared (on Sept. 26) (Maj. Broadfoot to Govt of India) that "they would march only if the British troops marched from their stations to Ludhiānā and Ferozepur," which the British unfortunately did, amassing over 40,000 troops on the Panjāb border. Now, there was no choice but to take the enemy on.

The Sikh forces started crossing the Satluj between Hari-Ke-Pattan and Kasur on Dec 13, 1845, after the Governor-

---

* India's border-war with China in 1960-62 (on the inisistence of India's Opposition Parties), when China couldnot have wished & hoped for anything better and was provoking India persistently, and Pākistān's war with us (in 1971) depending more on assistance from abroad than their own strength are recent instances of how nations, without adequate power or preparations losing patience, before time, can lead to abject humiliation or total defeat.

General issued a proclamation of war (a few hours after, according to British sources.†) However, George Campbell points out (Memoirs, P. 78) that "though the Sikhs did cross the river, they entrenched themselves only in their own territory" (across the river). 60,000 men with 150 pieces of artillery comprised the Sikh force, according to British observers. The British force at Ferozepur was about eight thousand at this time, but for some mysterious reason it was not attacked. Tej Singh and Lal Singh both assured the local British authorities of their "secret and efficient goodwill to keep safe their own positions" at the hands of "the grateful conquerors." They therefore prevailed upon the Khālsā not to grapple with an insignificant British force, but keep itself in readiness to take on a more magnificent body to exalt their fame and to kill or capture the person of the Governor-General himself ! On the other hand, Lāl Singh wrote to the political Agent, Capt. Nicholson, at Ferozepur:- "I have crossed with the Sikh army. You know my friendship for the British. Tell me what to do"? Nicholson replied:- "Do not attack Ferozepur. Halt as many days as you can, and then march towards the Governor-General." What is more, Tej Singh knew (as his forces didnot) that "much of the artillery muni-

---

† According to Cunningham, the Sikh army crossed on the 11th. But Sir Henry Hardinge, Governor General, wrote to the Secret Committee (Dec 31, 1845) that upto the 12th, "no Sikh aggression had been committed and no artillery moved down to the river." On the 13th, he received "precise information" that "the Sikh army had crossed the Satledge (Satluj) and was concentrating in great force on the left bank of the river." He is quick to add, however, that the British force from Umbāllā had been in movement three days (before). According to Cust, who accompanied the force, they had started out on Dec 6 i.e. a week earlier.

Meantime, the Lāhore Durbār was asked by Maj. Broadfoot through the Sikh *Vakil* at Ludhiānā to explain their war-like preparations. But the reply was never wanted or awaited, and the *Vakil* was thrown out of Ludhiānā at a few hours' notice.

That all was set by the British for war is clear from the other contemporary accounts of British sources. Says Carmichael Smyth :— "Neither the Sikhs made an unprovoked attack, nor we acted towards them with great forbearance. To assert that the bridge of boats brought from Bombay was not a *causa belli* but merely a defensive measure is absurd; besides, the Sikhs had a translation of Sir Charles Napieer's speech stating that we were going to war with them. Who departed from the rules of friendship. I'm definitely of the opinion that we did."

The British Governor-General was himself stung by conscience. Says Cust :— "Dec. 18. I rode behind the Governor General and we sat under a tree to await the infantry. The Governor-General remarked, "Will the people of England consider this an actual invasion of the Frontier and justification of war?"

tion had been tampered with and rendered useless." "Had he (Tej Singh) attacked," writes Ludlow (British India, ii, 142) "our garrison of 8000 men would have been destroyed and the victorious 60,000 would have fallen on Sir Hardinge who had then but 8,000. So utterly unprepared were we that even this treachery of one of our enemies scarcely sufficed to save us." Here the advice of Nicholson to divide the Sikh army into two and then to further scatter it in various directions was also accepted by these wily men, so that both wings were destroyed by the British, one by one.

But the soldiers, however misled, were also animated by the spirit of a holy war being waged in defence of "the Commonwealth of Gobind". The speed with which they brought the heavy guns and abundance of grain across the large river, the way they distributed their various arms and occupied positions of vantage elicited the praise of everyone who witnessed their unbounded zeal for the cause which every Sikh considered to be his own. "He would work as a labourer as well as carry a musket; he would drag guns, drive bullocks, lead camels and load and unload boats with cheerful alacrity." But they were losing time and giving its advantage wholly to their avowed enemy.

On Dec. 18, arrived the British forces from Ludhiānā and Ambālā at Mudki, 20 miles from Ferozepur, and headed by Lāl Singh a Sikh detachment, barely 3000 strong, fell upon them. According to a premeditated plan, he abandoned them in the middle of the campaign "to fight as their undirected valour might prompt." The result, however, was undecisive and three days later in the evening of Dec. 21, only an hour before sunset, Sir Hugh Gough attacked the Sikh forces at Ferozeshahr, about 10 miles from Mudki, where both sides were equally matched and eight to ten thousand strong.

But such was the fierceness of the Sikh response to the British fire that "battalion after battalion was hurled back with shattered ranks". "The resistance met was wholly unexpected and there was complete confusion in the British army." "On that memorable night, the English were hardly masters of the ground on which they stood, they had no reserve at hand, while the enemy had fallen back upon a second army and could renew the fight with increased numbers". So much was the consternation that the Gov. General wrote a highly critical letter to Sir Robert Peel, on advice from London, asking for the removal of the Commander-in-chief, General Gough, and Hardinge himself, a great soldier, took over the command relegating the C-INC to the second position. Despair hung over the British army. A retreat towards Ferozepur was indeed ordered by the Adjutant General, Capt. Lumbey. Others counselled an unconditional surrender, there being no chance of success whatsoever. Robert Cust says "our affairs were so desparate that the Gov. Gen. ordered all papers be destroyed and wrote that "if the morning attack failed, all will be over." On the morning of Dec. 22, "the second wing of the Sikh army approached in battle-array and the wearied and famished Englishmen saw before them a desparate, and perhaps a useless struggle." This reserve was, however, commanded by Tej Singh, the arch-traitor. He delayed the action till Lāl Singh's forces were everywhere put to flight and till his enemies had rallied their ranks. And when the fight actually was joined, the traitor fled the battle-field, inflicting a defeat on his brave soldiers "just when the artillery ammunition of the English had failed" "when a portion of their force was retuning upon Ferozepur", and "when no exertions could have prevented the remainder from retreating likewise if the Sikhs had boldly pressed forward." And yet the loss suffered in a single day of battle by the British was 694 killed and 1721 wounded. Among the killed was also the notorious Maj Broadfoot, who had contributed so much to the unleashing of the war. Among the Sikhs, 1782 men laid down their lives. But, those left behind were elated in spirit and determined to fight to a successful finish. The traitors, therefore, wanted to give more time to the British to prepare themselves. It was a month later (Jan 21) that Ranjodh Singh Majithia crossed the Satluj and intercepted and miserably mauled a British force at Badowāl, proceeding towards Ludhiana. "But he was the first to fly and basely quit the field leaving his brave followers to conquer or lose", when he failed to take advantage of his excellent manoeuvre and allowed the British to be reinforced for a fierce attack. And yet, "the far-famed British soldiers were nowhere near succeeding, and the British sepoys glanced furtively at one another, or looked towards the east, their home. There was prospect ahead only of struggle, not triumph." "The Governor-General and the Commander-in-chief (both present on the scenes of the major battles) "trembled for the safety of their seige train and convoys of ammunition" without which they could not wage the struggle for long. "Tej Singh and Lāl Singh shrank within themselves" and Gulāb Singh, now back as a Minister and leader, arrived in Lāhore on Jan 27 to be at "service" of the Khālsā, his masters.

According to Gen. Sir Hope Grant, (Life, ed. H. Knollys, p. 72) "Sir Henry Hardinge thought it was all up and gave his sword, a present from the Duke of Wellington and which once belonged to Napolean, and his Star of the Bath to his son, with direction to proceed to Ferozepur, remarking that if the day was lost, he must fall." Only if the Sikhs would have attacked that fateful night ! Just at this time, the General-General issued a proclamation (Dec 25) that "whosover will defect to them, will be suitably rewarded and granted a pension."

Sir Harry Smith, the hero of Waterloo, in a small skirmish at Aliwāl (Jan 28) did gain the upper hand, to boost somewhat the morale of the British after their grievous losses at Badowāl but, this was a battle more "of imagination, and none of the participants knew about it till it was published in a British document as one of India's marathons." On the other hand, Hugh Cooke says in his *Sikh Wars* that as the defendants at Aliwāl were Dogrā irregulars, who did not seem to have much heart in fighting, the Hicks' Brigade carried Aliwāl with little difficulty with a total loss of 580 men.

Lāl Singh had played his full part. Now was the turn of Tej Singh and Gulāb Singh. Gulāb Singh opened negotiations with the British. The latter intimated that they were ready to acknowledge Sikh sovereignty at Lahore after the (Sikh) army was disbanded, "but the Rājā declared his inability to deal with the troops."

"So an understanding was reached", according to Cunningham, "that the Sikh army should be attacked by the English and that when beaten, it should be abandoned by its own Govt, and further that the passage of the Sutluj should be unopposed and the road to the Capital laid open to the victors" (p. 279). "It was under such circumstances of discreet policy and shameless treason," writes the same author, "that the battle of Sobraon was fought, a situation according to Murray, "unparalleled in the history of ancient or modern warfare." ‡

"Valuable information was offered by Lál Singh to the Governor General encamped at Ferozepur and waiting for the arrival of heavy guns." Possibly, the plan of war was supplied to His Excellency on a silver platter. Gulāb Singh had stopped supplies of rations and the

‡ History of India, p. 713, as quoted by Gandā Singh in his "Private correspondence Relating to Anglo-Sikh wars" (P. 98)

soldiers, "living for three days on a ration of parched gram and raw carrots", sent a deputation to Rāni Jindan at Lahore to protest. The Rāni said, the rations were being supplied, as also gunpowder & shots.

The deputationists protested that it was not so. Thereupon, this reckless woman flew into a rage and flinging at them her *dopatta* (woman's headgear) to shame them roared: -"Wear this, you cowards. I'll go in your (man's) trousers and fight myself". Much humbled & crest-fallen, they shouted with one voice: "We'll fight for our King, we'll die for his kingdom and Khālsāji".*

Gulāb Singh garrisoned Lāhore with his own hillmen and sent out the Sikh soldiers to war with the English which had already been settled against them. As if this was not enough, they were asked not to attack the English until he arrived. And he was clever enough to evade his departure from Lāhore as long as it was necessary for the British.

There was, however, one man among these treacherous men & women who had heard about the secret goings-on, and who was determined not to get his nation betrayed and defeated in shame. His name was Shām Singh Attāriwālā, whose daughter was married to Ranjit's grandson, the late Naunihāl Singh but, who was living in isolation, afraid of his life at the hands of the intriguers in the court of Lahore. Draped in the mourning white, head to foot, with a flowing grey beard and lustrous eyes in a massive countenance, he vowed to God, swearing on the Holy Granth, in the full view of his troops, not to return alive if not victory but defeat was in store for his nation. And God bless his soul that he fulfilled every word of it.

As pre-arranged, Feb 10 (1846) was the day fixed by the British for an assault on the Sikhs. But when three successive attacks of the English were repulsed by the Sikh warriors with stunning losses to the enemy, Tej Singh, the Commander-in-chief and Lāl Singh, the grand Vizier, fled the battle-field, leaving the leaderless army to take care of itself.

Riding a white mare, this man of pure heart, Shām Singh Attāriwālā, called upon the devoted followers of Guru Gobind Singh to make a frontal attack and pierce through the enemy's ranks to prevent their advance. They did so with all their fury and good heart. Not one was saved. And the noble Sardār of Attariwālā,

---

*Ibid p., 98.

with seven bullets lodged in his illustrions body fell dead, his mortal frame lying in a heap where the dead heroes lay thickest. It was left to a Muslim bard, Shāh Mohd, or the British Governor-General to pay rich tributes to the supreme valour exhibited by the leaderless Sikh army at Sobraon. Says His Lordship :-"Policy precluded me publicly recording my sentiments on the splendid gallantry of our fallen foe, or to record the acts of heroism displayed not only individually but also collectively, by the Sikh Sardars and the army, and I declare were it not from a deep conviction that my country's good required the sacrifice, I could have wept to have witnessed the fatal slaughter of so devoted a body of men."

Tej Singh, on the other hand, destroyed the pontoon bridge on the Satluj after crossing it, and planted ten guns on the Sikh side of the river to slaughter any of his troops crossing back alive. Not unnaturally, the Sikh losses were not less than 3,125 killed, (though the British claimed to have destroyed five to ten thousand Sikhs in this battle, only the descendants of 3125 men claimed a pension). All the 67 Sikh guns were also lost. The total British casualties were 320 killed and 2063 wounded. Victory again was converted into a shamelss defeat. However, as Cunningham movingly points out, "no Sikh offered to submit and no son of Govind asked for quarter." A point to be noted is that not a single battle was fought within the Panjāb kingdom and a fight in a small area across the Satluj in the British territory or the Sikh enclaves, decided the fate of the Sikh empire. The same night (Feb. 10-11), the British forces at Atāri, near Ferozepur, were ordered to cross into the Panjāb. No opposition, as pre-arranged, was offered to their entry into Lāhore. On Feb. 20, they had occupied the capital city.

The Governor-General wanted the Sikh Sovereign to submit formally. Even this was arranged and when he arrived in Kasur on Feb. 18, "he was received coldly and no salutes were fired." But when he formally submitted, he was shown the courtesy and dignity of a Sovereign.

On March 9, 1846, a 16-article treaty was signed at Lāhore by both parties, (a) transferring Jullundur—Doab to the British dominions, (b) ceding the entire hill-country between the Beas and the Indus, including Kashmir and Hazārā, in favour of the British in lieu of war damages assessed at Rs. one and a half crore, Rs. 50 lakhs to be paid in cash to the British from the Sikh treasury on or before the signing of the treaty, and Rs. one crore to be paid by Gulāb Singh in lieu of his being recognised as the independent ruler of the territories to be assigned to him in consideration of the "services" rendered by him to bring about the restoration of relations between the Sikhs and the British. (d) The Sikh army to be reduced to 25 battalions of infantry (800 each) and 12000 cavalry. (e) All the 36 guns used in the war against the British to be surrendered and all mutinous troops to be disbanded. (f) British troops to be allowed free passage whenever necessary through the Panjāb. (g) No British, European or American to be employed by the Sikh kingdom without the permission of the British Govt. (h) No change to be affected in the limits of the "Lāhore state" (thus denying both war and negotiated peace to an independent kingdom). (A treaty was also signed on March. 16 at Amritsar, the very place where Ranjit 39 years ago had laid the foundation of his friendship with the British, transferring Kashmir to Gulab Singh.) (i) No interference in the internal administration by the British, save "in furtherance of the interests of the Lāhore Durbār."*

Another treaty was signed two days later (a) guaranteeing bona-fide rights of the jāgirdārs during the reorganisation of the Sikh army, (b) to keep a British force at Lāhore for a maximum period of one year, with full possession of the fort and the city, "to protect the person of the Mahārājā and the inhabitants."

Besides the Mahārājā, then seven and a half years old, the treaties were signed by seven others, Bhāi Rām Singh, Lāl Singh, Tej Singh, Chattar Singh Attāriwālā, Ranjor (Ranjodh) Singh Majithia, Diwān Dinā Nath and Fakir Aziz-ud-din.

---

* A soldier, Col. Hugh Cook, writing on the *Sikh Wars* recently (after, as he claims, the study of all available records at regimental HQs, the Archives, the British Museum and the India office as well as personal impressions of the descendants of tbe British regiments involved) has this to say of the Sikhs soldiers and generals:— "The Sikh army proved itself as a first-class fighting machine, but it was not well-led. The personal bravery of the regimental officers and men was beyond question. The efficiency of the artillery (officered by Muslims) came as a complete surprise to the British. Tactically, the Sikhs showed a predilection for fighting on the defensive, and although to some degree they went through the motions of an attack, they in fact never launched themselves at the British. It is certainly difficult to see how, with active cavalry-partrolling, they could have allowed (Gen.) Littler to slip away from Ferozepur." While saying that the accusation of treachery against Tej Tingh and Lāl Singh "is not proven," he does admit that

It is not that the British were averse to taking over the Panjāb in one sweep. They were inhibited only by their commitments in the vast empire they had built up in the rest of India. Men were just not available for garrison duty. Moreover, the back of the Sikhs was not yet broken. Their army was to be reorganised and reduced, but who was to take charge of the spirit of the Khālsā, which though badly bruised, was seething with discontent and may, it was feared, be bent upon revenge.

John Lawrence was appointed Commissioner of Jullundur-Doāb. Kashmir was joined to Jammu and given over to Gulāb Singh in exchange for Rs. 75 lakhs only through a separate treaty (15 lakhs out of it was adjusted against Suchet Singh's treasures held by the British which earlier they had refused to surrender to the Sikh kingdom.) "Rāni Jindān sent Diwān Dina Nāth, Fakir Azi-zuddin and Bhāi Rām Singh to Henry Lawrence to protest saying if this transfer (of Kashmir to Gulab Singh) was given effect to, she would appeal direct to Queen Victoria, but this intervention had no effect." *

Lāl Singh was re-appointed Prime Minister, but he was bitter that his treachery was not amply rewarded like that of Gulāb Singh. So he instructed Imamuddin, the Governor of Kashmir, to resist its surrender to Gulāb Singh, but this intrigue cost the wily grand Vizier his position. Imamuddin betrayed his master to Henry Lawrence, who had gone personally with 10,000 Sikh troops to help the take-over.

F. N. Contd.

they had little enthusiasm for the cause for which they were fighting. Both of them were more in sympathy with the Durbār than with the *Khālsā* (army)."

He adds:-- "The Sikhs certainly missed an opportunity of using their cavalry towards the British supply-bases in those early days...Ranjoor (Ranjodh) Singh (inspite of his drive) showed hesitancy at Badowāl... Why the Sikhs deliberately chose to fight twice with a river at their back must remain a mystery."

But he hits the nail on the head when he concludes:— "The tragedy for the soldiers of the Khālsā was to have to go into battle with a Govt. which more than half hoped for its defeat and with ineffective leaders who did not believe in the cause they were fighting for" (Pp. 103-105). "At Ferozeshah, as the Viceroy remarked, the fate of India trembled in the balance and indeed had Tej Singh chosen to launch an attack with any determination on the second morning, the hard-won victory might well have ended in defeat."

* K.M. Pānnikar, Founding of the Kashmir state, P. 98.

Lāl Singh was tried, found guilty and on Dec 4, 1846, he was banished from the realm and all his *jāgirs* forfeited. The traitor had met his nemesis.

Tej Singh also tried to negotiate an independent dominion for himself, but was rebuffed by the British. Over the rest of the year, the Lāhore Durbār cut down the strength of the Sikh forces, and nothing was done in violation of the treaties imposed upon them. But when the time came for the departure of the British in Dec. 1846, they put pressure on the Sardārs (many of whom were already in their confidence) to request the Governor-General that the British forces stay in the Panjāb till the maturity of Mahārājā Dalip Singh (in 1854).

Every semblance of a request originating from the Durbār itself for the continuation of the British occupation was kept up, as the Governor General had desired in his communications to Currie, now his political aide in the Panjāb. Three months earlier, Rāni Jindān herself is stated to have pressed for their continuous stay, "on any conditions" in the interest of "her own life and that of the Mahārājā."* Gulāb Singh was also negotiating for this kind of settlement ‡

* Cf. a similar situation in the Marāthā history:— "When Bāji Rāo, an utterly worthless man ascended to the gaddi of the Peshwā, it led to a civil war among the Marāthā chiefs, Scindia and Holkar fought for control of the state and Bāji Rāo sought the help of the English. He signed the treaty of Bassein (1802) and bound himself to maintain a British force in his dominion and to render himself subsidiary to the English. This treaty made the English supreme over the Deccan," (Dr. Tārā Chand, *History of India*, P. 248).

‡ Sardār K. M. Pannikar (he was titled Sardār while in the employ of Patiālā) one-time Prime Minister of Kashmir (and later India's Ambassador to China) who is the greatest defender of Gulāb Singh's under-hand dealings with his Sikh masters (see his *Founding of the Kashmir state*) admits all the same that (i) in mid-Jan, 1841, "When he (Gulāb Singh) left the fort (at Lāhore) (after being defeated by Mahārājā Sher Singh), he carried away with him the accumulated treasures of Ranjit Singh which were there, including 16 cart-loads of silver coins and 500 horsemen each carrying a bagful of gold mohurs" (p. 48). (2) When, on Jan 19, 1842, the British forces were returning beaten from Kābul, Gulāb Singh helped them out "when all hope of Sikh cooperation with the British had come to an end." (p. 50). The British envoy at Lāhore, Maj. Henry Lawrence, had asked him to disband the mutinous Sikh battalions but he told him :— "Sikhs had already borne him ill-will enough and that he would not be supported in measures of coercion." (P.51). He (Gulāb Singh) therefore "set out quietly to undermine the opposition of the Sikhs." (p. 52). (3) When the Sikhs (for good reason) still hesitated to

Therefore, another treaty was signed at Bhairowāl on Dec. 16, 1846 in order to "give aid and assistance to maintain the administration of the Lāhore state during the minority of Mahārājā Dulleep Singh." Through this wonderful instrument, not only a British force (whose strength was to be determined by the Governor-General) was to be kept in the Panjāb, but a British officer with an efficient establishment was to be appointed at Lāhore "with full authority to direct and control all matters in every department of the state." Rāni Jindan was dismissed as Regent (what a price to pay for the continuation of a foreign power for the protection of herself and her son's throne !), and pensioned off (for 1½ lakhs per year). A Council of Regency (comprising Tej Singh, Sher singh Attāriwālā. Diwān Dinā Nāth, Fakir Nuruddin, Ranjore (Ranjodh) Singh Majithia, (Bhai) Nidhān Singh, Attar Singh Kaleawāllā (Kalianwālā) and, Shamsher Singh Sindhānwāliā,was also constituted under the British Resident who was to have full authority "to direct and control the duties of every department". Henry Lawrence was appointed Resident by the Governor

---

F. N. Contd.

help any more in the Kābul campaign, Maj. Lawrence suggested that a consideration should be offered to him (Gulāb Singh) and the (Jammu) Rajāhs secured in their territory even with additions (P. 54), like the valley of Jalālābād and Peshāwar (the latter was Sikh territory then). (Vide letter of Lawrence to Clark, Jan. 30,1842). (4) The British Govt. sent an appreciative *Kharitā* to him (April 3, 1842) through Mr. Clark saying.— "The fruit of long-sown friendship between us which was concealed for a long time (!) has now come to light." Adds Pānnikar:— "The basis of friendship between Henry Lawrence and Gulāb Singh was thus well and truly laid (in 1842 !)" (p. 55) (5) After Hirā Singh's death (Dec. 1844), his property was confiscated by the Lāhore Durbār. But Gulāb Singh appropriated it. Rāni Jindān sent Lālā Rattan Chand and Bābā Mian Singh to Gulāb Singh to demand its possession and (also) to pay a fine of Rs. 3 crores for his contumacious conduct." *But, he did not obey the royal command.* (6) According to Lord Hardinge, "Gulāb Singh took no part against the British" (during the first Anglo-Sikh war) but "tendered his allegiance on condition of being confirmed in the possession of his own territories." Lord Hardinge says, "not a single hill-soldier fired a shot against us". "They had their own interests to attend to, which required that the Sikh state should be weakened and that the hills should be separated from the plains." (p. 102). To reason out that Gulāb Singh fell out with the Sikh kingdom only after his brothers' and nephew's death, is thus not borne out by facts. All of them were alive when he carted away to Jammu the treasures of Ranjit Singh on the pretext of being given "safe passage" (after his defeat), or when the friendship between him and Henry Lawrence was "well & truly laid" (in his own interest and at the cost of the Sikh kingdom, his masters).

General. The subjugation of the Sikh rāj was now complete. They couldn't be subjected to more humiliation. Seeing what was going to be her fate, Rāni Jindān tried to scuttle the treaty, but now it was too late. And, let it be said to the credit of British diplomacy (or the sheer cowardice coupled with self-interest of the Sardārs) that not one of them protested (except perhaps in whispers or, within the walled security of their households). And no less than fifty two of them had been called to endorse the scheme to convert the sovereign Panjāb into a protectorate of the British! It was Lord Harding's wish "to annex the Panjāb without the inconvenience of another fight or more expense" in human sacrifice and money. And it was duly fulfilled.

A few months later, Tej Singh was made a Rājā. Dalip Singh was asked to apply the saffron mark (*tikka*) on his traitorous forehead in the open court (Aug 7, 1847), but he refused, possibly under instructions from his mother. Atleast Lawrence blamed it upon her. She was ordered by him to be confined to the Samman burj of the Lāhore fort, the very place where Ranjit had once challenged Shāh Zamān of Kābul. She protested, but no one cared. Later, she was charged (falsely) with a conspiracy to murder Tej Singh, though the charge was never pressed. However, she was removed from Lāhore and incarcerated in the Sheikhupurā fort on Aug. 20, 1847. She appealed to the Governor-General through Jiwan Singh, a *Vakil* of hers, but the Sāhib who met him (Jan 2, 1848) referred the appeal back to the Resident at Lāhore, who took no notice of it.

In 1847, occurred the incident of Multān. The Sikh Governor, Mool Rāj, son of Sāwan Mal, was asked to pay Rs. 30 lakhs as succession fee. He expressed his inability. Troops were sent against him but were repulsed. The Resident, however, confirmed him, as he was, like his late father, a very just officer. But, his contribution in revenue was increased from about Rs. 20 lakhs to 25 lakhs at the first renewal of office and Rs. 30 lakhs at the second renewal. But alongwith it, the prosperous district of Jhang was taken from him and placed in charge of Bhagwān Singh, the brother of Vizier Lāl Singh. All this was too much for him to take and he resigned his job on Dec. 18, 1847.

A new British Governor-General, Lord Dalhousie, 36, had by now replaced the old warrior, Lord Hardinge. A new Resident—Frederick Currie—was appointed at Lāhore (March 6, 1848) as Lawrence had taken leave of absence. He sent out two British officers (Vans Agnew and Anderson) to help the handing over of the charge to Kāhan Singh Mann, the newly-appointed Governor. They arrived in Multān on April 18. Moolrāj handed over the fort gracefully and without any resistance. But, when they were coming out, the horse of Moolrāj bolted and he sped away. A soldier, Amir Chand, who was kicked by Agnew's horse flew into a rage and struck Agnew with a spear, throwing him off his horse. Sardār Kāhan Singh, however, safely escorted him to his residence. Anderson who was following Agnew was also wounded in a brush with the local troops. Moolraj, it appears, had no hand in this, but the troops who loved him (whether Mohammedan, Hindu or Sikh) were certainly exercised over his humiliating exit. The Muslims swore on the Quran and the others on the Guru Granth to stand by Moolrāj and went over to his residence imploring him to lead their rebellion against the *feringis*. Even the mother of Moolrāj joined the insurgents. The escort that came from Lāhore with the British officers also walked over to their side. Some fire was exchanged between the two sides and a Sikh was killed by a shot coming from the side of the Idgah, where the wounded British officers were lodged. This further provoked the Sikh troops and they murdered both the British officers three days later (April 21).

Currie alerted Lt. Edwardes, Asstt. Political Agent and General Courtlandt of the Sikh Service at Bannu. By mid-June, at the head of his Durbār troops, both old and newly-raised, together with their new ally the Nawāb of Bahāwalpur, Edwardes was within four miles of Multān, after defeating the Multān insurgents at Kineyri.

Meanwhile, a 4000-strong contingent sent by the Lāhore Durbār under Rājā Sher Singh, son of Sardār Chattar Singh, Attāriwālā., also arrived in Multān for their assistance (Aug. 18 and 19). But here the idea was to let upheaval become more widespread to justify the total annexation of the Panjāb. The rebellion indeed was against the Sikh kingdom and so all assistance was rendered by the Lāhore Durbar to enforce its decisions and restore order in the realm.

However, discontent was allowed to be deliberately spread throughout the Panjāb. The British Commander-in-chief when asked to proceed towards Multān pleaded that it was too hot for his troops to fight! Meantime, Sardār Chattar Singh Attāriwālā, Governor of Hazārā, was being humiliated by his British advisor, Capt. James

Abbot. All of the Sardār's activities were suspect in his eyes. He instigated the Muslims of Hazārā "in the name of their murdered parents," to rebel aganinst his chief. He promised three years' remission of land-revenue if the Sikhs were driven out. He raised new levies (without the permission of the Sikh Govt) who surrounded Chattar Singh at Haripur where he was camping. His officers refused to obey him unless his orders were supported by Capt. Abbot.* In self-defence, he killed Col. Canora, an American officer of the Sikh force, who tried to attack him. Blaming Rāni Jindān (then in prison) for Moolrāj's insurrection, she was removed from the Panjāb (May 15, 1848) to Banāras (without a trial or even conveying to her any charges) and confined there. This added further fuel to the fire.†

The old veteran, Chattar Singh, whose daughter was engaged to Dalip Singh, pressed the British authorities to permit him to solemnise an early marriage, but a reply was always evaded. He let it be known that if this was not to happen within a year, he wanted to be relieved of his office and permitted to proceed on a pilgrimage for two years. Sher Singh, who was a great friend of the British and had initially helped Edwardes to contain the rebellion at Multān even at the risk of incurring the displeasure of the *Panth* at large, and blowing one of his rebellious soldiers, Soodan Singh, from the mouth of a cannon, called upon Edwardes at Multan to press his father's requests who forwarded them with a sympathetic note to the Governor-General. The latter, however, rebuffed him. Meantime, Chattar Singh's *jāgir* was confiscated on a false charge of killing Col. Canora and when he offered to resign, his resignation was not acceped. He, therefore, left his job, without permission, and raised a standard of revolt. Not unnaturally under the circumstances, his son, Rājā Sher Singh, also joined him. ‡

* The district town of Abbotābād was built & named after this arch-intriguer & an indisciplined bully.

† Even Dost Mohd. Khān, Amir of Kābul protested. "Such treatment is objectionable to all creeds and both high and low prefer death (to it)." (Panjáb papers, 1847-49, P. 512, as quoted in *Private correspondence relating to Anglo-Sikh wars*).

‡ What hastened this move on the part of Sher Singh was that Moolrāj was so suspicious of Sher Singh's motives (due to his pro-British proclivities and actions in the past) that he would not allow him or his troops to enter the city and made them camp outside just north of the fort. He kept his guns trained on his men. Under such circumstances, there was no choice for him but to march out (Oct 9) towards the Chenāb to join his father's forces.

Rājā Sher Singh issued an appeal (Sept 15, 1848) to all Sikhs to join hands with him in view of the "oppression, tyranny and undue violence with which the *feringis* have treated the widow of the great Mahārāja Ranjeet Singh, the mother of the people, and the cruelty they have shown towards the people of the country." Chattar Singh organised successful revolts in Bannu and Peshāwar (Oct 20 and 24, 1848), attacked and took over the fort of Attock (Jan 3, 1849) and proceeded towards Jehlum to join forces with those of Sher Singh.* Most of the troops of Chattar Singh incidentally consisted of the Pathān levies. The British Commander, Herbert, who tried to stop their halt at Attock saw his force of Mohammedan garrison rebel against him, and he was forced to surrender. George Lawrence, another British Commander, who took refuge with a Pathān chief at Peshāwar was handed over to Chattar Singh ! But, even now, at best it was an insurrection by the two Sikh chiefs against their own sovereign (even though his Govt. was controlled by the British). The Lāhore Durbār had nothing to do with either the rebellion at

---

* Another notable hero who joined them was Bhāi Mahārāj Singh, a very pious person, who was incharge of the Derā of Bhāi Bir Singh of Naurangābād. He had been falsely implicated in a conspiracy to murder the British Resident at Lāhore on April 21, 1847, and many of his followers arrested. He, with a band of about 1000 soldiers marched towards Multān, but as differences soon arose between him and Moolrāj, he marched out to join Chattar Singh's forces, reaching Rāwalpindi and from there back, via Pothohār and Dhani, to Rāmnagar, preaching hatred against the *feringis*. After Rāmnagar, he accompanied the rebel-force to Rasul and thereafter fought at Chilliānwālā and Gujrāt. After the defeat at Gujrāt, he escaped again to Rāwalpindi and tried to prevail upon the other rebel-chiefs to give another battle to the British at Rāwalpindi or Panjā Sāhib. But they did not agree, and the entire rebel-force of 16000 surrendered, possibly because the Durbār's official sympathy was not with them. But, Mahārāj Singh refused to surrender and decided to rally the Khālsā to his banner. He even tried to abduct the Mahārājā but failed. He contacted the Sikh chiefs in Doāba and beyond the Satluj, the Bedis and Sodhis, the hill-chiefs, the ruler of Afghānistān and the chiefs of Peshāwar. His men infiltrated into the regular Durbār forces as well. A day for launching the attack at the Hoshiārpur and Jullundur Contonments was fixed (Jan 3, 1850). But, while he was touring the Jullundur-Doab, he was arrested in a sugar-cane field, six days earlier, put in chains, and sent to Calcutta. From here, he was deported to Singāpore (May 15, 1850), where he was kept in a sealed cabin. After 3 years of solitary confinement, he became blind and in another 3 years, he was merely a bundle of bones. Even a walk in the fresh air was not allowed to him. On July 5, 1866, he breathed his last. He had lived like a hero. He also died like one.

Multān or in the north-west. But Lord Dalhousie took advantage of it and declared at Calcutta on Oct 5, 1849:—

"Unwarned by precedents, uninfluenced by example, the Sikh nation had called for war and on my word, Sir, they shall have it with a vengeance." In the words of his Lordship this was the "crisis I have for months been looking for." (Letter to Currie, Oct 8).

The British Resident was puzzled to receive the Governor-General's official communication of Oct 3 that "the Governor General-in-council considers the state of Lāhore to be, to all intents and purposes, directly at war with the British Govt." And yet they were still administering the same state in the name of the Sikh Mahārājā not one of whose Council of Regency (except Sher Singh) had acted in any manner which could be construed as an act of war. Even the pretence of making a formal decaration of war was dispensed with. Still the British forces under the Commander-in-chief, Lord Gough, could only move in with the British troops in mid-November. Even then, Lord Gough didnot know (Nov 15) "whether we were at war or peace, or who is it we are fighting—the Durbār or against it." (Life and campaigns of Viscount Gough, ii, 178). But he moved on towards the Chenāb on whose right bank Sher Singh's forces had taken positions. Still, he launched no major attack till Jan. 13. In earlier skirmishes of the advance guards with Sher Singh's troops (Nov 22) on the left bank of the Satluj, the British had suffered heavy casualties, including their commander, Brig Gen. Cureton, being killed. Possibly, that is what made Lord Gough wait a little longer. He was also hoping for Multān to fall which didn't happen. But, before Sher Singh's forces could be reinforced by his father's, an attack became essential and this was launched on Jan 13 at Cheliānwālā, in the district of Gujrāt.

It was one of the bloodiest battles of the Sikh wars. So bitter was the contest that no one knew who had won or lost. The British losses in a single half day of the battle were 2331 men killed and six guns captured.* When the news reached London, "the nation was

* While the British accuse the Sikhs of having killed their wounded in the darkness of the night, they also admit that the Sikhs returned two privates of the 9th. Lancers who had got lost in the jungle and had been captured, after the battle. Sher Singh also allowed a Lieutenant, named Bowrie, captured in Derājāt to visit his campatriots on parole just as his father, Chattar Singh, had allowed George Lawence to go to Lāhore. This kind of humane treatment was unheard of during wars till then.

stricken with profound emotion..."A nation used to long series of successes in India, felt that our fame and influence had undergone a heavy blow," and the blame was laid at the door of the venerable Lord Gough for bad tactics. There was cry for his immediate replacement by Sir Charles Napier. Even the hero of Waterloo, the Duke of Wellington, then 80 years old, volunteered to go to India and fight the Sikhs, if need be. Lord Dalhousie thought Gough had lost self-confidence, otherwise "no British army ever fought a great battle with less odds or with greater appliances and means of victory." "Such a mass of men, fierce and untamed even in their dying struggle, who fought like lions and ran right on the bayonets and struck on their assailants when they were transfixed," was the first experience for the British to encounter in all of their Indian campaigns.

For one whole month, the British forces could not dislodge the Sikhs from their entrenched positions. They were so demoralised that the Commander-in-chief decided to wait till fresh reinforcements under Gen. Whish could arrive from Multān. By now,Chattar Singh had joined his son's forces alongwith an Afghān contingent of 3000, led by a son of Dost Mohd. Khān, once their arch-enemy.

To the good luck of the British, Multān had by now fallen (Jan 22) and Moolrāj taken prisoner. He was tried at Calcutta and sentenced to death. But the death-sentence was commuted to life-imprisonment. Because of ill-heath, he was removed from Fort William to Banāras, but on the way, the young hero died (Aug 11) at the age of 36. The victory here should have been considered to be that of the Lāhore Durbar against a rebellious chief, but the British construed it as their victory against the Sikh Kingdom ! Lord Dalhousie was bent upon its annexation, though his envoy at Lāhore, Henry Lawrence, was protesting. "I did think it was unjust. I now think it is impolitic" (Feb 1849).

Another and final battle was fought at Gujrāt (Feb. 21, 1849). Here, the forces of father and son, Chattar Singh and Sher Singh, were defeated. The British had lost only 5 officers and 91 other ranks and 24 officers and 646 other ranks wounded. 53 of the Sikh guns were captured and they started retreating. They were pursued upto Rāwalpindi where they sued for peace with 16000 of their men still intact. Possibly, their hope that there would be a general uprising of the Sikhs or that the Lāhore Durbār would come to their rescue didnot materialise, and thus isolated, they decided to surrender on March 10. Four days later, at Mānkiālā, near Rāwalpindi, they formally laid down their arms in a piognant ceremony. Heroes of many battles, their eyes filled with tears and throats choked with emotion, they would take their sword in a final embrace, kiss it with all the passion their hearts could muster and lay it down saying, "we shall take it up again."† And, there was an unnamed Sikh hero who, it is said, refused to surrender the Sikh standard, and escaped to Kābul saying to his anguished conscience:—"We have lost the war for the time-being, but let us not let down or surrender our flag."

The Governor-General had, as has been said, decided upon the annexation of the Panjāb, even though the opinion in London was divided. Henry Lawrence, inspite of his own reservations, made a clean job of it. He told the Council of Regency not to protest and assured them of the continuance of their honours and *Jāgirs*. They were persuaded to prevail upon the young Mahārājā, then 11 years old, also to follow suit. A proclamation of the Governor-General was read out by Henry Elliot on March 29, 1849, at the Lāhore fort, blaming the Sikhs for unleashing the "war" and for "violating their pledges" and praising the British who had "faithfully kept their word and all obligations imposed by treaties upon them !"*

---

†Both Chattar Singh and Sher Singh were tried and imprisoned in Allahabād. Their wives were granted a small pension. In summer, they were not allowed even to sleep in the open. Sher Singh's family was later allowed to join him. After some time, they were taken to Calcutta. Their allowance was increased to Rs. 500/ p.m. each, and some compensation was paid also for the confiscated and auctioned property. On June 22, 1855, they were allowed to proceed on a pilgrimage to Jagan Nāth Puri. But, broken completely in health due to hard prison-life, the father died on Jan 18, 1856 and the son two years later (7 May, 1858). But, their names will remain inscribed in gold in the annals of India's struggle for freedom.

* Col. Hugh Cooke, who has written the story of the Sikh wars (1975) wholly from the British point of view and more especially to justify the war-tactics of Lord Gough (who was seriously criticised for his recklessness for inflicting such heavy losses on his army) and to glorify the heroism of various units of the British army participating in those wars, cannot yet justify the British stand on the so- called Second Sikh War and the annexation of the Panjāb as a result thereof. He says:— "The first (war) was a much more clear-cut affair than the second. It was fought by the British against the Sikh nation as a whole, and it started with a formal declaration of war against the Lāhore Govt., when the Khālsā invaded British India. The second grew out of an internal rebellion, which was not in the first place anti-British and in which British troops were not initially employed. Indeed the actual time at which the war started cannot be irrefutably fixed...It was no formal declaration of war with the Sikh nation, in theory the British were still

A treaty was signed with the British by the Mahārājā, (Rājā) Tej Singh, (Rājā) Dinā Nath, (Bhāi) Nidhān Singh, (Fakir) Noor-ud-din, Gundur Singh (agent of Sardār Sher Singh Sadhānwāliā) and Lāl Singh (agent and son of) Attar Singh Kaleanwālā, surrendering for ever the sovereignty of the Panjāb to the British and agreeing to the confiscation of all property of the Sikh kingdom (in lieu of war expenses and so-called debts), handing over of the *Koh-i-Nur* to the Queen of England in return for a life-pension of not more than Rs. 5 lakhs per year and the retention of title of the Mahārājā for Dalip Singh if he remained loyal and obedient to the British Govt. and remained in a place to be chosen by his new masters.

Thus ended the Panjāb as a sovereign state on April 5,1849. *

F. N. Contd.

suppressing a revolt against the authorities in Lāhore whom they were supporting... It was noteworthy too that the newly-raised regiments of Sikh local infantry remained loyal to the British and were actually used on operations.

"It will always be a moot point whether Mulrāj's rebellion could have been contained. (Herbert) Edwardes, who was nearest to the scene of trouble, maintained that it could, had the British authorities reacted more promptly. (However), Edwardes himself admitted that in the long-term it was better the events took the course they did, for the spirit of the Khālsā was still very much alive and like the phonenix would be sure to rise again."

So, the idea was not to quell a so-called rebellion against the British, but to take over the Panjāb anyhow ! Cooke thinks it was just as well, for had it been delayed till 1857, "the temptation for the men of the Khālsā to make common cause with the mutineers would then have been well nigh irresistible."

* To dispel any idea of the British particularly being grabby or less than morally just in relation to the Panjāb's annexation, the story of all their conquests in Hindustān would be a great revelation and of deep interest and value to the readers.. The British had landed in Surat (now in Gujarāt) and opened a small trading company there through petty concessions obtained from the Moghal emperor. On receipt of gifts in 1608 from James I of Great Britain, through Capt. Hawkins, worth 25000 gold pieces, Jahāngir granted them some trade-concessions on the western coast. In 1639, the site of Madrās was granted to another Briton, Mr. Day, where they built the fort of St. George. In 1690, they acquired a swampy area in Bengāl and founded Calcutta on its site, and built a fort called Fort William. The year Bandā Bahādur was executed (1716) after building the first Sikh Empire, they were still struggling for a few more trade-concessions from Farukh-Siyar. Upto 1757, they had held only the rights of Diwāni (against payment of a fixed sum to the Govt. of the Moghal king). In this year, they fought the Battle of Plassey with Siraj-ud-Daulā, the semi-autonomous Governor of Bengāl. With a small force of 800 European and 2200 Indians, Clive, then a young officer at Madrās, pounced upon the Nawāb's motley army of 50,000. He

F. N. Contd.

knew his cause was hopeless. Therefore, he purchased Mir Jāffar, the Nawāb's Commander, and helped by the Hindu bankers (led by a Sikh, called Omi Chand) all of whom he betrayed soon thereafter—through diplomacy and force (as with the Nawāb) or fraud (as with Omi Chand) who claimed a five percent share in the treasury then worth forty million, but who was confronted with a revised and distorted treaty to deprive him of his share, Bengāl fell into Clive's lap (which then included also Bihār and Orissā). In a hundred years thereafter, trade was only a pretext and it was the British diplomacy, agreements to protect the rulers and then to tear them up, playing of one ruler against another, the usurpation of the independent but protected states through lack of male progeny, the whole of India became their dominion. How could the Sikhs escape this systematic and well-planned advance ? Solong as they were occupied with suppressing revolts in their own colonies, like the United States or fighting France under Napolean and after him both Russia and France, they could not attend to the Indian affairs with the thoroughness of their diplomacy and the power of their arms. But, once they were free from their European embroilments, India could hardly resist their advance, no matter what tricks or tactics it involved.

However, the system of Govt. and the philosophy of life which they introduced afterwards remains a model and a challenge even after they have left our shores. And that is where they excelled over all previous imperialistic regimes.

CHAPTER XXIII

END OF THE DYNASTY

As we have seen, Mahārāni Jindān had been removed from power and pensioned off by the illegal and ill-conceived treaty of Bhairowāl (Dec, 16, 1846). This was made an indispensable condition by Lord Hardinge for any future arrangements with the Sikh kingdom. Three months later, she was implicated in a conspiracy to murder the British Resident at Lahore.* She had obviously no hand in it. She was certainly mature enough to realise that killing the British envoy who had his hands on her entire administration and whose forces had occupied Lāhore and the fort and all the Sikh regiments moved to out-stations (ostensibly with her own consent and the entire Court), she could hardly gain anything by such half-baked and childish pranks. It was no use being a nuisance without being a danger. But, the event came handy to the British authorities and they isolated her completely. No one of the courtiers was allowed to see her. She could not visit her estates at Dalipgarh alongwith her

* Known as "Premā conspiracy" (Premā was an ex-A.D.C. of Gulāb Singh), Premā and Lāl Singh Adālti were to lead the attack. One or two Sikh regiments were also implicated, alongwith Bhāi Budh Singh and Munshi Butā Singh, attendants of Rāni Jindān. The murder of Henry Lawrence was to take place on 21 April, 1847, in the Shālimār gardens, at Lāhore. The scheme leaked out and a reign of terror was let loose by the British Resident. Bhāi Mahārāj Singh, Saint of Naurangābād, was also implicated in it. The conspiracy failed, and those supposed to be involved in it were severely punished. Mahārāj Singh, however, could not be captured at this time.

son. Later, some correspondence of Mulrāj, pledging loyalty to her, was intercepted through a maid-servant and when next year, Mulraj revolted, it was used against her. When Mahārājā Dalip Singh refused in the open court to anoint the forehead of Tej Singh (17 Aug. 1847) with a *tikka*, on his being granted the title of "Rājā", the British Resident saw the cunning hand of the Queen-Mother behind it. Her pension was reduced to one third (Rs. 4000/- per month) and she was imprisoned in the Shiekhupura fort.

The Governor-General's wish that "the power of the Sikh Govt. should not only be defeated but subverted and their dynasty abolished," had begun to prevail. Henry Lawrence's views that the Sikh state should stand as a buffer against both Russia and Afghānistān and conciliated when estranged had already been brushed aside, and as a true and dedicated civil servant, he could not but carry out the wishes of his masters.

Her communication in Panjābi (from Bibi Sāhib to Lāran (Lawrence) Sāhib, the Acting Resident) from the Samman Burj of the Lāhore fort, where she was first confined to the Zenānā, is full of fury, though the grievances enumerated are more personal than political. In it, she said *inter alia*, "I had entrusted my head to your care. You have trodden it under the feet of the traitors.

"You should have instituted an enquiry...you ought not to have acted upon what the traitors told you.

"You have paid no regard to the friendship of the great Mahārājā (Ranjit Singh), have not remained true to your treaties and agreements and caused me to be disgraced.

"Rājā Lāl Singh was faithful to me. You turned him out (of the Panjāb). We then never said anything to you. We thought as the Sāhib was himself with us, we had no fear of anyone.

"If you donot administer justice, we shall appeal to (your) authorities in London. Even the allowance of 1½ lakhs has not been paid to me. I have sold my ornaments to defray the expenses of Rs 51,000 over the past four months.

"The Mahārājā came to me today and wept bitterly for a long time. He said Bishan Singh and Gulāb Singh had been frightening him. If something happened to him through fright, what shall I do ? He was told by you to reside in Shālimār. He had wept bitterly when he heard this.

"The treatment meted out to us has not been given to any other ruling house. Why do you take the possession of the kingdom by underhand means? Why don't you do so openly? On the one hand, you make a show of friendship and then you put us in prison? Preseve three or four traitors, and put the whole of the Panjāb to the sword." In another letter from the Sheikhupura fort, to where she was removed, she wailed that *she was in no need of the kingdom*, "only donot separate me from my son. He is too young to take care of himself. I'll send him to Lāhore when you hold the Durbār and myself also come only then, not before."

In yet another communication from Sheikhupurā, she repeated her last request, in reply to a note from Henry Lawrence that the Mahārājā was being well looked-after and was happy. "Crying, he was torn away from me and his mother dragged out by the hair. The treatment you have given me is not meted out even to the murderers," she wrote back in reply.

Inspite of her pathetic state which evokes profound sympathy, it is a pity that she still trusts Lāl Singh, the arch traitor, (and allegedly her lover), does not care for the restoration of the kingdom but only of her son to her, even though according to the British Resident, "every seditious intriguer who was displeased with the present order of things looked upto the Queen Mother as the head of state."

For about 9 months, she remained in the Sheikhupura fort (20 Aug. 1847 to 16 May, 1848). Believing or feigning that she was still intriguing with the rebellious elements outside, her allowance was reduced to one-third (Rs. 4000/-P.M) and all communications with the outside world cut off. She was warned that if any suspicion arose due to her conduct within the fort, she would be removed from the Panjāb. She was firmly told that her son would never be entrusted to her care.

It was believed that she had tried to instigate a few officers in the Capital to capture the Lāhore fort, and sent out secret messages for a simultaneous rising in Peshāwar, Ferozepur, Jammu and Mukerian. General Kāhan Singh and Bhāis Gangā Rām and Tulsi Rām, (besides many others) were implicated in this conspiracy and arrested on May 8, 1848. The last-named turning an approver was released and the other two hanged. Some of the conspirators escaped to join Mul Rāj in Multān. Some letters were also seized purporting to be in Jindān's hand to incriminate her in both the conspiracy and the rising in Multān. She was, therefore, banished to Banāras, on May 16, and confined there. Her allowance was reduced to Rs. 1000/- per month, though her considerable jewellery was restored to her.

Five months later (Oct 12), she employed a British lawyer, Newmarch, to appeal to the Governor-General asking for reasons for her ill-treatment and for a petty increase of atleast Rs. 250/- per month in her allowance. But the petition was turned down !

She wrote an appreciative letter to Rājā Sher Singh for his chivalry and patriotism, and called upon him to drive out the *Malechhas* (the untouchable *feringis*), and to encourage the Hindustānese as much as possible (to join the revolt). This letter again leaked out (or was it planted ?) and the Mahārāni removed to the fort of Chunār (in Bihār). But, she started observing purdah so that her face may not be seen by anyone, and she be recognised only by voice. This was a ruse played inorder to escape from the prison, which she did on April 15, 1849, replacing herself by a maid-servant. She escaped to Nepāl via Patna, (in the garb of a holy pilgrim or a *Bairāgan*), using every conceivable device not to be identified on the way, and suffering every kind of privation. Her jewellery left behind at Banāras was confiscated, though some precious stones she did carry on her person. On 29 April, 1849, she asked for asylum in Nepāl which was granted. It is here that she learnt that the Panjāb had been taken over by the British and the Mahārājā, though safe, was deposed.

The British authorities seem not to have pressed for her extradition. Only when a reception was organised for her by the King of Nepāl on 8 March, 1850, the British Resident protested, and the King cancelled the engagement. She wrote letters from here to other Sikh prisoners in Allāhābād (Butā Singh and Rājā Sher Singh). This being known, she was asked by Nepāl not to indulge in anti-British activities. She tried to escape to Kashmir where Gulāb Singh is reported to have consented to receive her. But this too got known by the British and they warned her not to enter British territory. She later contacted her son, who was then in London, but he too was cautious in his promises. However, after 1857, the British Govt. itself relented and allowed her to proceed to London. Her frozen assets were also given back to her. Her pension was increased to Rs, 2500/- P.M. She consented, in writing, to these terms and in April 1861, left for London alongwith Dalip Singh who had come to take her there. She arrived in London in July and died two years later nearly blinded and broken in body and spirit. She wore only a Panjābi dress while in England, and willed that her ashes be strewn on an Indian river. This wish of hers was carrried out by her son and the river Godāvri had the honour to receive them and wash them away to mingle with the infinity of the Indian seas.

The Fate of Dalip Singh

Mahārājā Dalip Singh was about 11 years of age when he was deposed. He was removed from the Panjāb to Fatehgarh, in U.P., immediately on the signing of the treaty of annexation (April 5, 1849). Here he was placed under the charge of Sir John Login of Bengāl Army. Under his influence, the young Mahārājā embraced Christianity two years later and was taken to England (1854) to reside at Suffolk, near London, permanently, as an English squire and landlord. Rāni Jindān, then a refugee in Nepāl, kept in touch with him, through secret communications, which however became public in 1856. Her wish to join her son in England became widely known. Naturally, the reply that she received from her son after the publication of this news in the Urdu Press was couched in a very cautions language. India was then seething with discontent. Dalip Singh had asked his mother not to depend upon him for her travel to England but try through the court of Nepal. He also told her discreetly:-"Whatever you do, do very cautiously and carefully, without getting me into any scruple". But after the part played by the Sikhs in the Mutiny of 1857, he was allowed to proceed to India to bring her to London (1860). When he arrived in Calcutta in Jan 1861, Sikh soldiers returning from the Chinese war made a wild demonstration of affection and loyalty before his hotel. This unnerved the British anthorities and they requested Dalip Singh to hasten back to England which he did. But, this event must have convinced him of the esteem in which his house was still held by the Sikhs. His mother is reputed to have exerted quite a favourable influence upon him so as to arouse his patriotic feelings to a white heat. But, as we shall see, this seems to have borne little fruit, or possibly, the story is blown out of proportions.*

* Queen Victoria had showered much affection on him, treating him almost as part of her family and becoming a God-mother of his eldest son, but the British Govt and the Govt. of India treated him with little consideration, especially in regard to his highly just financial demands, which had made him desparate.

In 1864, Dalip Singh came to India to cast the remains of his dead mother* on the waters of the Panjāb, but he was not allowed to enter the state (though in Bombay he was received with a 22-gun salute) and so he had to change his programme and staying in Bombay for a month, he entrusted her ashes to the lap of the river Godāvri.* On his way back, he married at Alexendria (Egypt) Bambā Muller, daughter of a German merchant and an Abyssinian mother.†

For about 20 years thereafter, he fought his legal battles in London. From the records now available in the India office, London, and the Archives of India, New Delhi, which contain much useful information about Dalip Singh (some of it in his own hands)

* According to Mahān Kosh (p. 1565), she died on Aug 1, 1863 and was cremated at Näsik in India a year later and that some of her ashes later were brought to Lāhore by her daughter, Bambā Sutherland, in 1926, and after a prayer offered by Sardār Harbans Singh of Attāri, they were buried next to the Samādhi of Mahārājā Ranjit Singh at Lāhore.

† She bore him three sons—Victor Dalip Singh (born 1866), Fredrick Dalip Singh (born 1886) and Albert Edward Dalip Singh (born 1879), and three daughters Bambā Jindān, (born 1869) Katherine (born 1871) and Sophia Alexandra (born 1874). They all died issueless. Bambā Jindān Dalip Singh married on Englishman, Dr. Sutherland. Both settled down at Lāhore where she died on March 10, 1957. Victor held a commission in the 1st. Royal Dragoons and married a daughter of the Earl of Coventry. Fredrick was educated at Eton, Cambridge, and took a tripos in History and later also his M. A. He too held a commission and saw service in France during the first world wàr (1914-1918). He was interested in Archaeology. But none of them has left an outstanding mark in any field. In fact, one of his daughters, Sophia Dalip Singh, writing to a Sikh acquaintance (Santokh Singh Ahluwāliā of Amritsar) reprimanded him for reminding her of her past. She writes: "Now, a bit of advice: it is very nice of you to feel so loyal to the memory of your late king (the Mahārājā), but you know things and times and circumstances have now so utterly changed that I think for your own sake, you would do well to try to forget old history." (June 2, 1936).

"Of course," she writes, "I take an interest in Sikhism but living in this country, one does not get much opportunity of hearing anything about it." (Ibid)

Writing six years later to the same address (6 Sept, 1942) when the Second World War was on, she bitterly criticised the national movement which was then raging in full fury.— "I cannot think the Congress people can be so shortsighted... I think the Mahātmā has really got too old for his leadership and anyhow his passive movement was never any good for this wicked world." "It would be bad day for them (Indians) if Britain didnot win." (July 16, 1940). Of course, all of Dalip's children remained and died as good Christians.

one thing is certain.* Whatever his private thoughts and motives, he had, after tendering many representations and legal notices to the British authorities finally despaired of his kingdom being restored to him by his bountiful guardians through legal means. He was, therefore, left with no choice but fight only for his rights to his private estates at Gujranwālā, to the salt-mines in Pind Dādan Khān, to an increase in his pension or to get a one-time ex-gratia grant of £ 2,50,000/- He had turned down an offer of £ 50,000/- "with disdain." Undoubtedly, he had been given initially a grant of £ 1,05,000 (with interest !) to buy an estate in London. By an Act of Parliament (1882), he was also granted a loan of another £ 60,000/- (mercifully, interest-free this time !) but the interest he had to pay on the earlier mortgages and and the insurance premium reduced his pension almost by half. If he asked for a Court of inquiry, alongwith his other above-mentioned demands (vide Governor General's note dated 19 Feb. 1886), it was to settle his "outstandings of the pension" and "just claims (of increase in pension and compensation for the loss of "private" jewellery and other estates in the Panjāb.) Torn from his people, whose views he could neither influence nor gauge, and deprived of resources, despair had not unnaturally overtaken him. However much he protested that his loyalty to the British Government "remained unshaken" (in his interview with Lord Kimberley, Secy of State, on the eve of his departure for India dated March 30,1886), and telling the Viceroy at Simla (Telegram from Aden, April 22, 1886) that the word "disloyal" should not be used in relation to him in any context, he was neither trusted, nor accomodated. He even volunteerd to get himself recruited in the British army in India in the event of their impending war with Russia (Secy of state to Governor General, April 1885). The Govt of India, however, were averse to his joining the Army, due to their own reasons. In his letter to the Secy of State (Jan 16,1886), he tried to disabuse the British mind about his kingly pretensions and stated clearly:- "*I donot aspire to be reinstated on the throne of the Panjāb* " And yet a paltry sum was not offered him to live in less than poor circumstances. He went so far as to deprecate the rising at Multān in 1848, and wrote with approval of the defeat

* Dr. Gandā Singh has lately published this material in his "*Mahārājā Dalip Singh Correspondence*" (Pbi. Univ. Patiālā).

inflicted on the rebels at Chillianiwālā and Gujrāt (Ibid), though for the same reason he said also that the treaty of annexation was unjust and illegal. However, he made no political claims as a result of this unjust and illegal treaty (possibly, he might have thought, it was imprudent or premature before he knew his strength). His grievance, therefore, was that whereas the *Koh-i-Nur* was mentioned clearly in the Treaty of Annexation (1849) to be handed over to the British Queen, no other jewels or personal property were mentioned therein, and these, therefore, should be restored to him.

He left nothing to chance and blamed the Sikh army for "indiscipline" and "unprovoked" attack on the British in the first Sikh war, and said unashamedly that if (after the first Sikh war) he was restored to the throne, "it was in consideration of my extreme youth and the friendship which existed between my father and his kind neighbours." (Petition to Secy of State, 29 March 1882).

He went further and admitted :- "*The Council of Regency finding that it was impossible to carry on the Govt. of your humble petitioner during his minority appealed to the British authorities for assistance, and Lord Hardinge after stipulating that the British Resident at Lahore should have full powers to control any Govt. department entered into the Bhyrowal treaty.*" (Ibid).

He is equally willing to concede that "*had the Panjāb been annexed to the British dominions after the dispersion of the Sikh army across the Satluj, your humble petitioner would not have a word to say,*" (Ibid), but because the British Govt. had chosen to become his guardians,they had betrayed the trust by delaying operations against the rebels in Multān and thus giving disloyal elements a a chance for a more widespread uprising to find a justification for the annexation of the Panjāb. But he does not for that reason denounce that illegal treaty, nor asks for the restoration of his throne. He even takes credit for the part played by the Sikhs in the mutiny of 1857. Says he :-"As my subjects, the Sikh army, had ten years previously given the English much trouble, so did they in 1857 take a noble revenge on their former foes (i.e. the Moghals) by being instrumental in preserving for the English their Indian empire during the memorable mutiny of that year (and again in Sudan in 1885).

He also sends the Secy of State a chapter from the *Sau-Sākhi* (a book of false prophecies) which had predicted, according to him, "that Gooroo Gobind Singh had been re-born in him, as it was prophesied that he would take his next birth in the house of a Sikh who would marry a Musalman woman (i.e. Ranjit Singh) and his name would be Deep Singh (corrupted form of Dalip Singh), that this man would be persecuted and land in extreme poverty, would live abroad and his children would be Englishmen, that he will join a war between *Buchoo* and *Dultoo* (i.e. the Russian bear and the English bulldog) and on defeat will retire to an unnamed village where self-knowledge will be revealed to him at this time. The *feringis* will "sell" their lands and the Gooroo's *Snakes* (i.e. disciples) would dominate under Deep Singh and his progeny, for three generations, from Calcutta to the Indus. (*Des Bech Kar Jaen feringi, tab gājegā mor bhujangi*)" etc. But, nothing worked, neither vainglorious threats, nor appeals to law or to good conscience. The "London Times" editorially derided his pretentions and demands (Aug. 31, 1882).

Knowing his political fate to be sealed, he decided to go back to India, and appealed to his countrymen (March 25, 1886), especially Sikhs, to forgive him. He made the following moving proclamation to his people :-

"It was not my intention ever to return to reside in India, but Sutgooroo who governs all destiny and is more powerful than I, his erring creature, has caused circumstances to be so brought about that, against my will, I am compelled to quit England, inorder to occupy a humble sphere in India. I submit to His Will, being persuaded that whatever is for the best will happen.

" *I, now, therefore, beg forgiveness of you, Khālsājee, the pure, for having forsaken the faith of my ancestors for a foreign religion, but I was very young when I embraced Christianity.*

"*It is my fond desire on reaching Bombay to take the Pahul again and I sincerely hope for your prayers to the Sutgooroo on that solemn occasion. But in returning to the faith of my ancestors, you must clearly understand, Khālsājee, that I have no intention of conforming to the errors introduced into Sikhism by those who were not true Sikhs such, for instance, as the wretched caste-observances, or abstinence from meat and drinks, which Sutgooroo has ordained should be received with thankfulness by all mankind, but to worship the pure and beautiful tenets of Bābā Nānak and obey the commands of Gooroo Gobind Singh.*

"I am compelled to write this to you because I am not permitted to visit you in the Panjāb, as I had much hoped to do. Truly, a noble reward for my unwavering loyalty to the Empress of India. But, Sutgooroo's Will be done. With Wah Gooroo ji Ki Fateh.

I remain,

My most beloved countrymen,
your flesh and blood
Dhulip Singh.

Among the common people, the excitement was indeed great.* A Bengāli had widely distributed in the Panjāb in connection with Surrendra Nāth Bannerjee's case a leaflet, ending with the words "*Mahārājā Daleep Singh Ki Jai.*" There were rumours of unrest among the Sikhs in the British army. But the Sikh chiefs and nobles of the Panjāb, now secure in their *Jāgirs* and enjoying them in the peaceful atmosphere created by the British rāj, refused to countenance their king †. In a communication to the Viceroy, Lord Dufferin (1884-88) they had said as much. Mr. Gladstone, the liberal Prime Minis-

* Foreign Deptt., Secret, Internal, 1886.

† He got in touch with Thākur Singh Sandhānwāliā, a cousin of his, and son of Lahnā Singh (the murderer of Mahārājā Sher Singh and Partāp Singh), sometime in 1883. He too had been fighting for his *Jāgir* and having been removed from the post of the E.A.C. had become anti-British. The Mahārājā also was fighting at this time for the restoration of his father's personal estates in the Panjāb. Thākar Singh was invited to England by him and he met the Mahārājā there late in 1884. When he came back, he offered prayers on his behalf at various Gurdwārās, includiug the Golden Temple, Amritsar, and propagated his cause, contacting also the Kookās. In March 1886, when Dalip Singh left for India, he asked permission of the Govt for the Sandhānwāliā to meet him in Bombay, but being stopped on the way, the two met at Aden, where Dalip Singh took Pāhual at his hands. On his return, Thākar Singh did not go to the Panjāb but slipped into Pondicherry, a French possession, and kept propagating the Mahārājā's cause. He was appointed "Prime Minister" by Dalip Singh on 10 Jan. 1887 through a letter from Paris! But he died a few months later (Aug 18, 1887) at Pondicherry. In 1873, it was through his efforts that a big Sikh gathering had collected at Amritsar to launch a Singh Sabhā movement to purge Sikhism of extraneous influences (and also to secure the firm allegiance of the Sikhs to the British rāj, though Sandhānwāliā personally was opposed to this part of the Singh Sabhā's programme),

ter of England had also stated that "it was our weakness and our calamity that we have not been able to give India the benefits and blessings of free institutions." It was during this period that the Indian National Congress was born (1885) and Lord Rippon (1880-84) had introduced the local self Govt. at the tehsil and the district levels. The crude and vicious methods of his predecsser, Lord Lytton, had been abandoned and there was a great ferment of new ideas sweeping the land.

The Kookās too, though they had become very anti-British in their sentiments (especially over the murder of their compatriots by the authorities and deportation of Bābā Rām Singh in 1872) had sent out their agents to Russia and Nepal and desired passionately the rāj of the *feringis* to be destroyed, did not support Dalip Singh's cause. Wrote Bābā Rām Singh, their leader, from jail in Rangoon :—"*If Dalip Singh comes, treat him as a stranger. He who has eaten the cow, of what benefit will he be to us ?*"*

Inspite of all this, Dalip Singh did proceed to India, but he was served with a prohibitory order at Cairo not to proceed beyond Aden.† He complied with the order, but at Aden, he also took *Pāhul* (May 25, 1886) at the hands of Thākar Singh Sandhānwāliā and four others (Roor Singh, Jawand Singh and two more Sikhs who, travelling by another boat, had halted at Aden at the same time). The very next day, Thākar Singh was asked by the authorities to return to India, which he both obeyed and flouted, as on his way back, he slipped surreptitiously into Pondicherry, then a French possession, to propagate the cause of Dalip Singh for another two years before his death (Aug. 18, 1887). Dalip Singh was obliged also to send his wife and 6 children back to England.

---

* Kukian di Vithia by Ganda Singh, p. 234. But the Viceroy had warned the Secretary of State (15 & 17 Aug. 1883) that the Kookas were especially very enthused over his projected visit to Panjab which should be prevented. The Kookas had also sent a deputation to Bombay to receive him. One of the Kooka subas is said to have established his contact with Dalip Singh in Moscow, though no proof is available.

† It is stated (*Vide* the Singh Sabhā movement, by Dr. Jagjit Singh, son of the venerable Bhāi Mohan Singh Vaid of Tarn Tāran, pp. 59-60) that it is because of the representations of the Sikh Sardārs that he had been asked not to proceed beyond Aden. This may be true, as the representation made in this behalf two years later (Nov 16, 1888, when Dalip Singh was in Russia) called him a "false pretender backed by Russian intrigue," and said, "they would die for their sovereign Empress and never receive him as their ruler." Their views were too well-known to Govt, even before. In their addresses to Lord Dufferin in 1887 and 88 they had made their position amply clear.

Before he left Aden, he addressed a letter to the "*Times of India* " (published on June 30, 1886) in which he expressed not only his dignified anger, but also great nerve wholly becoming the son of Ranjit Singh:-

He wrote inter-alia, "Although I am a naturalised Englishman, yet I was arrested at Aden without a warrant, one having been issued since I re-embraced Sikhism while staying at Aden. The tax-payer of India no doubt will be glad to hear that I've resigned the miserable stipend paid to me, under that iniquitous treaty of annexation, which was extorted from me by my Guardian when I was a minor, thus setting aside that illegal document entirely."

He made several proclamations, one "to the brother princes of Hindustan" and another to the people of India" to contribute for nine months a **paisa** (copper coin) each, to his war-chest, always assuring them that Russia would support him! On his victory, he said, he would (i) release all prisoners of the British (ii) restore throne to all dispossessed princes and (iii) run the Govt. through democratic elections, (iv) cow-killing will be prohibited and Muslims given pecuniary compensation for this. (v) Public debt will be repudiated and railways and telgraph lines confiscated. (vi) Private debts whose interest exceeds five percent shall be abolished etc.

He signed his proclamation and letters to British MPs as "Lawful Sovereign of the Sikh Nation", also as "Sovereign and Guru of the Sikh Nation", "Implacable foe of the British" etc.

According to British sources, he was in Paris on June 23, 1886, which shows he started back from Aden soon after his initiation into the Sikh faith and stayed there a year or more. On Jan 10, 1887, he appointed Sardar Thakar Singh his "Prime Minister" in exile, and sent him also the Royal Seal! Thakar Singh, however, died soon thereafter (Aug 18). From Paris, he travelled for the first time to Moscow a year later, where we hear of him through an editorial published in the Moscow Gazette (5th to 17th Sept., 1887). As reported to home authorities by the British Ambassador to Russia, the article points out, "how Dalip Singh was cheated of his kingdom. He was not allowed to be educated at Cambridge or Oxford for fear of developing his mind. Finding that no justice can be obtained from England, he finally threw himself into the arms of Russia. He had decided to break off all relations with England and to settle in Russia. We welcome him with the conviction that he will find among us all the sympathy which his fate demands." But, the Russian Ambassador in Paris had warned his Govt. not to come into his affairs to annoy England whom he wanted to "blackmail" to extract more money from its Govt.!

So, nothing concrete emerged out of this new association. He could neither obtain Russian citizenship nor even an interview with the Czar. He lived on

Rs. 80/- a month in a private home, and provided for himself by selling his jewellery and royal dressess. While in Russia, "he lived in a very retired and quiet way with a "Madame",* visiting only few Russian families during his stay of over a year.

Greatly dismayed, he returned to Paris (Nov 3, 1888), heart-broken. Deprived of the means of livelihood, his pension and family estates+ and jewels confiscated, his mother dead in his lap, humiliated and in deep frustration, his people removed far from him, the Sardars estranged if not also inimical, and betrayed by circumstances and the states on which he leaned, he was attacked by paralysis in July 1890 and lay dead, one night, in his apartment in the Grand Hotel of Paris, (Oct. 22, 1893). He was buried a week later on his estate in Suffolk, England, and still lies there in the cold comfort of an indifferent (or just) eternity.

---

* An English girl, about 20, reports the British Ambassador, after a few days. His wife had died on Sept. 18, 1887 and he was only courting her at this time and married her later on May 21, 1889 in Paris. He had two issues from her, and the second wife, (Miss) A.D. Wetherill, outlived him. These two - both girls - died childless.

\+ According to Mahan Kosh (p. 1873), he apologised to the Queen and his pension was restored. The British records corroborate this, as also Queen Victoria meeting him in his illness at Paris. (See Queen Victoria's Maharaja, by Alexender and Anand, Pp. 277-300). It is a pity that after his own and his mother's experience of the British "guardianship", Dalip Singh now wanted another foreign power (whose character and intentions were wholly unknown to him) to support him. It has been well said that "if you want to fight a great power, you should be more powerful; if you need to negotiate peace, you should be still more powerful." There is no pity or sympathy or the sense of moral good and wrong, in the domain of politics. A weaker nation, or party tied to the apron-strings of a bigger power, has only to thank itself, if it is taken over by its protector and guardian to serve not the interests of the ward, but its own. History is full of such examples. Mr. Subhash Bose's seeking help of the unknown Axis Powers and how they ill-treated him during Second World War is an instance in point.

CHAPTER XXIV

1857

On the taking over of the Panjāb, the Sikh army had by and large been demobilised, but land-revenue was reduced by 25 per cent. Those Sardārs who had not taken part in the rebellion against them were confirmed in their *Jāgirs*, though all *Jāgirs* offered for loyal military service by the Sikh Court after the reign of Mahārājā Sher Singh were resumed. The families which were too important to be ignored, even if hostile earlier, were also placated, though some like Mulrāj and Bhāi Mahārāj Singh and the Attāriwālās were tried for sedition outside the Panjāb and punished and their *Jāgirs* and endowments confiscated, or drasticully reduced. Bābā Bikram Singh Bedi, son of the venerable Bābā Sāhib Singh Bedi, however, who fought in the so-called second Sikh war and surrendered near Rāwalpindi was not allowed to visit Unā, his headquarters. His *Jāgirs* were also resumed and he died in penury, at Amritsar, though he was earlier offered a small pension which he refused with contempt.*

* Bābā Bikram Singh Bedi was asked, after the first Sikh war, to surrender his guns and the fort at Unā in the distt of Hoshiarpur. He refused to do so and organised a rebellion in the hills. Defeated, he joined the ranks of Sher Singh and Chattar Singh Attāriwālā and fought during what has come to be known as the Second Sikh war. Along with others, he too surrendered after the defeat, for he was over-ruled in his opinion that another war be fought with the British. He died in Amritsar in 1863.

The British authorities had appointed a Board of three—Henry Lawrence (Army and Political): his brother John Lawrence (Revenue) and another civilian: Charless Manson, (Law and Justice) to administer the Panjāb. Henry was bitter over the way the Panjāb was annexed on a false pretext of a local rebellion and had sent in his resignation, but the Governor-General did not like a man of his experience and wide sympathies to deny his services to the Govt. So, he was appointed President of the Board, even though his brother and the other members did not much favour his views which were sympathetic to the Sikhs. Other British aides were, however, intelligent, dedicated and not-too-unbalanced in their judgements. Inspite of the opinion of Sir Charles Napier, the Commander-in-Chief, who wanted to rule the Panjāb as a military dictatorship, Henry prevailed upon the Govt. to give them the benefits of a civilian rule.

Not that any unnecessary mercy was shown. 8000 people were jailed in the very first year All the forts of the Sikh chiefs were demolished, except for those necessary far the British forces of occupation. About 1,20,000 arms were surrendered by the people. About 40,000 of soldiers were dismissed and either went back to their traditional occupation of agriculture or became a problem for law and order as dacoits and cut-throats. The latter class was, however, soon suppressed.

But, what is most remarkable, some of the best Sikh forces were retained in service. A Panjāb force was assiduously built, consisting solely of Sikhs, though the recruitment was confined to the Jat Sikhs and the Khatris and the untouchables excluded, so as to divide the Sikh people right down the middle. In the Frontier Guards also, about a thousand choice Sikh soldiers were recruited. Ten percent Sikhs were also recruited in the 15C00-strong police force. The Grand Trunk Road from Lāhore to Peshāwar was repaired and put in good shape, and all along the 500-mile frontier with Afghānistān, fortified posts were established. Law and order were strictly enforced and the British code of criminal procedure promulgated.

Several kinds of duties were abolished including octroi. Dacoity was ended The existing four provinces were split up into 7 commissionerships, and 25 districts, and the officer incharge of the district made both a collector and judicial-cum-administrative authority. Devolution of authority was introduced, but officers strictly instructed not to impinge upon local customs ad institutions. An order was issued on March 21, 1847, by Henry Lawrence forbidding British subjects from entering any Sikh temple with shoes on. Cow killing was also forbidden in the city of Amritsar. "The Sikhs were not to be molested or interfered with."

Agriculture was especially promoted. In four years' time (1849-53), the results of the peaceable policy had become obvious and the Board abolished. Henry Lawrence took over as Chief Commissioner of the Panjāb. During the next five years (1852-58), he almost won over the hearts of the subject people through his liberality of outlook, balance, integrity, hard work and understanding. He restored confiscated Jāgirs, including those attached to the Sikh temples. The soldiers' right to their hereditary lands was also restored. During three successive years (1854-56), the crops were extremely good. An extensive network of canals was undertaken and, besides roads, even a railway line from Lāhore to Multān was surveyed and completed in 1859. *Begār* (forced labour) and *Sati* were abolished. Widow re-marriage was legalised.

A department of Public Instruction was opened in 1855, and primary education spread widely at state expense, even though in the Panjāb through the efforts of the Sikh kingdom, literacy was far more widespread than in other provinces. Old *madarsas* and *maktibs* were continued and endowed. Persian was retained as the language of records to be replaced by Urdu in due course, which became the medium of instruction for boys and the language of administration and justice at the lower levels. Urdu had been introduced earlier in the U.P., and as the court munshis and school teachers were brought largely from there (and this pandered also to Muslim sentiment), Urdu gradually dug in its toes in the foreign soil of the Panjāb. The Persian script and vocabulary were already known to the educated elite. When later, as a counterweight to them, Bengāli Bābus were brought in, they having been subjected much earlier to English domination, English became the language of higher courts and higher learning and administration . A Civil Procedure Code was first evolved during this period in the Panjāb and later applied to other provinces. The Rule of Law was established. It was a great change after the post-Ranjit Singh anarchy, in which leaders destroyed both themselves and the people they ruled.

To assuage further the Sikh feelings, orders were issued by the Governor-General that all Sikhs entering the British army should receive the *Pāhul* and observe stricly the code of Sikh conduct. (*) Later (12 Aug, 1857), the Governor-General also asked the Chief Commissioner of the Panjāb to explore the possibility of translating into English the Sikh Scripture at Govt. expense in consultation with the Sikh authorities. Inspite of all these soothing gestures, as we shall see, the British were careful not to trust or lean heavily on a particular community, to raise mixed regiments, and to play, if need be, one against the other.†

Suddenly, on May 11, 1857, news was received at Lāhore that the Hindustāni sepoys at Meerut had mutinied.‡ The next day, the news was widespread that the mutineers had captured Delhi. John Lawrence was at Rāwalpindi at this time and it was Sir Robert Montgomery, his aide at Lāhore, who handled the situation in such a masterly manner that, without firing a shot, the possibility of any trouble was scotched. No panic was shown and a ball-room dance was organised for the evening. Next morning (May 13), a military parade was held and inspite of the grave risk involved (with only one British battalion on hand), the English commander disarmed the three Indian companies. The fort and the arsenal at Lāhore were

* G.G's despatch to Secret Committee, No. 29 of 1851.

† "The Chief Commissioner (of Panjāb) apprehends however that the real lesson we should learn from the past misfortunes is to trust no race in particular, to mix races in our native army, to maintain that army within the lowest number and to keep it in thorough subordination and discipline."

(Richard Temple, Secy to C.C., Pb, to G. F. E. Admonstone, Secy to Governor-General, Sept. 8, 1858)

‡ The immediate cause of the Sepoy mutiny was the greased cartridge. The official records of the inquiry later held at Dum Dum revealed, that though the Govt had ordered sheep's lard, the contractor (a Bengāli Brahmin) had supplied the cheaper stuff (the pig's lard and cow's fat) to lubricate the paper-parcels of the cartridges which the soldiers had to bite inorder to remove the paper-cover and load the cartridge in the breach loader. This was considered to be the wily trick of the *feringi* to corrupt the religion of both Hindus and Muslims and became an extremely sensitive and explosive issue. The Indian soldiers were also disaffected by low wages, one tenth of what the British soldiers received. Their promotions were blocked after they had reached the level of the Subēdār Major or Risāldār. Their *gora* (English) officers treated them with scant attention. And the dispossessed princes, Zamindārs, nobles and theologians who were depived of authority and possessions by various laws passed by the Company took advantage of it. The Moghal emperor, a virtual pensioner of the British at this time, was also shown little respect which he and his courtiers resented deeply.

taken control of by the British soldiers. Next day, the same scene was satisfactorily repeated at Amritsar and the fort of Gobindgarh taken over. About 13, 000 soldiers, mostly Hindustānis, were disarmed by July-end.

Inspite of it, local disturbances did take place at Phillaur, Ludhiānā, Ambālā, Thānesar, Multān, Siālkot, Hoti-Mardān, Peshāwar and particularly at Ferozepur, but these were confined mostly to the Poorbiä soldiers and were soon quelled.

It is a near miracle how with the British force of merely 10,500 against 58000 natives in the Panjāb, the British exhibited neither undue alarm nor let the situation at anytime go out of hand. On the one hand, it was due to the healing touch of a single individual, Henry Lawrence, whose superb leadership saved a very explosive situation and on the other, the policies pursued were so humane that excess was never committed and laws were equally applied to all, irrespective of creed or caste, and custom and religion not blantantly interfered with and security of life, honour and property came to be recognised as the *sine qua non* of good government.

In a period of four extermely anxious months for the British, they raised eighteen new regiments and mostly Sikhs and Muslims were recruited to them. They all remained loyal and, as we shall see, for good reason. The Panjāb became not only the sword-arm, but also the main base of supply to the British forces in Delhi. The Cis-Satluj Sikh states, being treaty-bound, helped with 17000 soldiers, some of the Princes, like the Mahārājā of Patiala, leading personally their troops in Delhi. The British won and the old feudal order and the medieval outlook turned into the new modern age of science, democracy and humanism. As Sir Jādu Nāth Sarkār has pointed out "It was not a fight for freedom; it was, in fact, king-cobra Superstition's last bite before its head was smashed. It was not a rising of the people for political self-determination, but a conspiracy of mercenery soldiers (only of the north Indian army) to prevent the cunning destruction of their 'religion'."‡ In its name, horrible atrocities were committed by the mutineers on the British civilians (including women and children, especially at Lucknow, Kānpur and Allāhābād) and the British, not to be left behind, retaliated with a brutality that is unknown in their history.

---

‡ *Hindustān Standard,* Calcutta, Pujā Annual issue, 1956.

It seems strange to many ill-informed outsiders why the Sikhs having lost their independence only seven years ago, were not sympathetic to the mutineers and actively joined the cause of the *feringi*, their erstwhile enemy. This is because, as Dr. Tārā Chand rightly says:—"On the whole, the rising of 1857 was an attempt—the last attempt—of the medieval order to halt the process of dissolution, and to recover its lost status...It was a general movement of the traditional elite of the Muslims and the Hindus–Princes, landlords, soldiers, scholars and thelogians (Pandits and Maulvis)." "The emperor of Delhi, the king of Oudh, some Nawābs and (Peshwās) and Rājās (and Rānis), (all disaffected due to dispossession or curtailment of their own authority), talukdārs and Zamindārs, the soldiers, Pathāns (Walayatis), Mughals, Rājputs and Brāhmins of North India and the Maulvis who were members of this order, comprised the main body of the rebels.*" Thus it was neither a fight for independence for the whole people of India as such, nor it could be, as the idea of the Indian nationhood was yet unknown to our people.

Was not His Majesty the Moghal emperor himself living under British protection since 1803 ? Bahādur Shāh was also drawing a pension of one lakh rupees from the British. If he was reduced to a non-entity due to the inherent weaknesses of the later-Moghal rule, their internecine warfare, intrigues, fanaticism and open discrimination against others, piling up one humiliation upon them after another, who was responsible for it, if not the holders of authority at Delhi? According to Maulānā A.K. Azād, Bahādur Shāh was "a mere puppet, who had neither the army, nor the treasure, nor influence." Did he at any time before consider the people as whole to be his people ? Was an alliance at any time tried to be forged by the Moghal kings with the two other fighting and dominant powers of India—the Marāthās and the Sikhs ? Of course, the sympathies of the Marāthās were enlisted by Shāh Alam to fight the Sikhs and they in turn asked for the British help against the Sikhs to save the king's territories across the Jamuna late in the 18th century. It is the British who refused to intervene.‡ Earlier, help was sought time

* "History of the Freedom Movement in India," Vol 2, P. 43

‡ P.N. Bhalla, *East India Company's policy towards the Sikhs* (Panjāb, past an Present, Oct 1970, Pp. 276-77)

and again from the Afghāns against both the Marāthās and the Sikhs by the Moghal kings, and ultimately British protection was sought also to escape their wrath. Now, when the 82-year old decrepit and dying King's throne was in jeopardy, why should he have been saved by any patriotic element in the country, simply because he was issuing pathetic and conciliatory appeals, dictated by distress and helpessness than by the exigencies of high policy or a wounded conscience. And, had he not, together with the Nawāb of Jhajjar, helped the British during the Anglo-Sikh wars ? In fact, it was neither nationalism nor even communalim that determined each party's attitude to the other. It was plain and simple opportunism and self-interest of the leaders. Muslims, Hindus and others all were fighting on both sides of the fence.*

---

* Maulānā Abul Kalam Azād in his excellent introduction to the Government of India publication (1857) states the case in its true historical perspective. Says he, inter-alia:-

(1) The course of the trial (of the Moghal king) made it clear that the uprising was as much a surprise to Bahādur Shāh as to the British.

(2) The whole episode was unplannded by anyone. Ali Naqi Khān, Wazir of Oudh, who is credited with master-minding the uprising in his state was in fact a traitor to the cause. It was through him that Gen. Outram, the British Resident, had persuaded the King of Oudh to relinquish his kingdom "voluntarily" and he was promised a huge reward.

(3) The agents of Nānā Sāhib, the Peshwā, (Munshi Azimullah and Rango Bāpuji) are also credited with having visited Turkey on their way back from London (where they had gone to ask for the same amount of pension for their master as was paid to Bāji Rāo, his predecessor), and having met Omar Pāshā on the battlefield of Crimea. Rango Bāpuji had also appealed in London against Lord Dalhousie's decision for the merger of Satārā in British India. Inspite of these facts, according to Azād, there is no evidence of their any overt connection with the uprising in India.

(4) The Rāni of Jhānsi, Lakshmi Bai, fought to the end, but she too was prepared till the last for a compromise if her right to adoption was accepted by the British. And these were the only important leaders of the mutiny.

According to Azād, the factors leading to the munity were:

(1) The trading East India Company upto now were acting only as the licensees and agents of the Moghal Govt. or their governors. They presented them addresses, gifts, nazrānās etc, but now suddenly after several humiliations offered to Bahādur Shāh and the seizure of Oudh, soldiers and the feudal lords (whom they dispossessed to deal directly with the ryots) as much as their dependendents felt the British had become rulers, without due authority, and not certainly by conquest. They had also minted their own currency recently, without authority. [next page]

Again, as pointed out by Sir Vincent Smith, the total military strength of the Company at this time was 2,38,000 of whom only 38,000 were Europeans. The Bengal army consisted of 1,51,000 of whom nearly 23,000 were Europeans (out of these 13,000 were in the Panjāb). How many of these Poorbias, Muslims, Brahmins and Rajputs rebelled aginst the British, or took advantage of the acute crisis in which they had, indeed, landed? Since 1806, there had been no mutiny in Madras, or, the presidency of Bombay. The fact also should not be missed that the armies which fought against the Sikhs along with the British resulting in the annexation of the Panjāb were north-Indian Poorbias, who were now in revolt to uphold their caste-superstitions. When they became the force of occupation on behalf of the British in the Panjāb, they looked down upon the Sikhs, due to their own pride of caste. The Poorbias never took the Sikhs into confidence for the mutiny they had planned. Should the Sikhs have gone to their rescue, when, they sincerely believed, as Sir Jadu

---

F. N. Contd.

(2) The large number of soldiers of the Bengāl army was from Oudh and once the sovereignty of their ruler was jeopardised, they felt infuriated.

(3) Inspite of the weakness of Bahādur Shāh, his inability to lead, his dependence upon the British, his power and authority limited only to the Red fort of Delhi (and not even to the city of Delhi), he had become a symbol of unity because of the people's regard for Akbar and Shāh Jahān whose direct descendent he was and whom people had come to consider one of their own (and not a foreign king). (Here Maulānā Azād has become unduly sentimental. The people remembered the intrigues, the killings, the tyrannies and the weaknesses of the Moghal authority for the last hundered and fifty years more since Aurangzeb than what Akbar or Shāh Jahān had accomplished before them).

(4) The people had become sick of a hundred-year association with the East India Company's domination through trickeries and frauds. "The "cartridge affair" was only an excuse. Azād is very right when he says that the mutiny failed because (i) The leaders of the revolt could never agree. They were mutually jealous and intrigued against each other. When Bakht Khān went out to fight at Delhi, they gave him little or no support. The Lucknow Residency was surrounded by the mutineers for long but not attacked, as the soldiers feared once they succeeded, the Begum of Oudh will have no use for them ! (ii) Most of the leaders took part only for personal reasons and not for any national cause. (iii) The masses followed their selfish leaders but lent their support only to the winning side, most of the time remaining mere spectators. Tāntia Tope, when defeated, went to Madhya Pardesh and Narmada, his own country, to continue the fight. But no village there would even give him shelter and a professed friend finally betrayed him when he was asleep.

Nath rightly points out, (that the soldiers in rebellion) were "made a cat's paw by the dispossessed dynasties in a gamble for recovering their thrones."* They were all the time negotiating terms (including the Rāni of Jhānsi, the ruler of Oudh, the Moghal king and the Peshwa—all leaders of the rebellion) to secure their own rights, but being outwitted by the British, they took advantage of the Sepoy mutiny. In fact, even the Moghal emperor was a prisoner in the hands of the mutineering soldiers and danced to whatever tune they called.

According to Sir Vincent A. Smith, "the bastion of British strength was not only Panjāb, but also Bengal. *In Bengal, there was no danger, in the Panjab the situation was saved.*"†

Thus, unreserved help flowed not only from the Panjāb, but also from Bengāl. The whole of Southern and Western India, or the quarter million Indian army, mostly comprising soldiers of Indian origin, also stood by the British. Now-a-days, it is being re-discovered as a war of "liberation." but at that time no one knew "who was fighting this war and for whose liberation ?" According to Maulana Abul Kalam Azad (Intr. 1857, P. viii), Bahādur Shah had become a prisoner of circumstances. That is how the revolution had exhausted itself by September, 1857, and Bahādur Shah capitulated on promise of his life. The Rāni of Jhānsi was killed a little later (June 20, 1858). Nānā Sāhib and Bakht Khān of Delhi disappeared and Tantia Tope was executed. The Moghal emperor was tried and banished to Rangoon to die there in the confines of a jail. The two sons of Bahādur Shah were shot dead by Maj. Hodson, and their bodies displayed for three days at the same spot in Chāndni Chowk where once lay exposed the unclaimed body of Guru Tegh Bahādur on the orders of Bahadur Shah's wily ancestor, Aurangzeb. Full advantage was taken by the supposed "prophecy" of the ninth Sikh Guru on the eve of his execution that due to the tyrannies of the house of Aurangzeb, the Moghal throne would eventually pass into the hands of the *feringis* from the West, who would, alongwith his followers, avenge his innocent murder@. Advantage was also taken of a (fake)

(*) *Hindustān stanpard*, Calcutta, Pujā Annual, 1956. † Oxford, History of India, P. 669

@ Maj. W.S.R. Hodson, *Twelve years of a soldier's life in India* ed. by G. H. Hodson (2nd ed,. London 1859), as quoted by S. Malik in an arlicle on "Panjāb and the Mutiny" in the Journal of Indian History, Aug. 72.

poster on the walls of Delhi purporting to be the Moghal emperor's proclamation that "wherever a Sikh is found, he should be put to death."

After the mutiny was quelled, * a new revolutionary era dawned for India. Even Karl Marx supports this view in no uncertain terms.‡

* As a reward for help, Patiālā was offered the territories of the Nārnaul division, Nabhā was awarded a part of Jhajjar and Jind the area of Dādri. Delhi was attached to the Panjāb. Six turbulent districts from the North-Western province were also joined to the Panjāb. Thus, the Panjāb now spread out from Delhi to Peshāwar, divided into 32 districts. In 1901, six frontier districts were detached and converted into the N.W.F.P. (North West Frontier Province). The Chief commissioner of the Panjāb became a Lt. Governor. John Lawrence was later promoted Viceroy of India (1864-69).

‡ Writing two articles in 1853 in the NEW YORK "Daily Tribune" on the "British Rule in India," and "*The Future Results of British Rule in India*", Karl Marx remarks:—

"We must not forget that these idyllic village-communities, inoffensive though they may appear, had always been the solid foundation of Oriental despotism, that they restrained the human mind within the smallest possible compass, making it the unresisting tool of superstition, enslaving it beneath traditional values, depriving it of all grandeur and historial energies...Concentrating on some miserable patch of land, (they) quietly witnessed the ruin of empires, the perpetuation of unspeakable cruelties, the massacre of the populations of large towns, and rendered murder itself a religious rite in Hindustān...Contaminated by distinctions of caste and slavery, they subjugated man to external circumstances instead of elevating man to the sovereign of circumstances (and) brought about a brutalising worship of nature. Man fell down on his knees in adoration of *Kanuman* (Hanumān), the monkey, and Sabbala, the cow."

"With the result that India was never ruled by her sons, and her history became a chronicle of foreign invasions and foreign domination." According to Marx, even in the nineteenth century, "the choice lay between industrial, liberal and bourgeois British and under-developed, autocratic Russia", for which reason he prefers British rule in India, "whose level of economic development guarantees the integration of India within the world market and universalisation of European culture." "The major British contribution has been the introduction of industrial production which ended the social stagnation of traditional Indian society." The introduction of private property, "which even in an alienated form points the way towards emancipation" was also a British contribution according to Marx, "which when fully developed, has no choice but to be abolished." "The British rule integrated India into universal history. Those who came to India to exploit eventually became dependent on her development and well-being." Writing in 1846, in his "*Poverty of Philosophy*," he had emphasised that "the rising standard of living of British worker was achieved only at the expense of the horribly low wages paid in India." Writing a little after the Indian Mutiny, he said "atleast since the Revolt,

The Govt. was taken over directly by the British Crown and Parliament from the East India Company's trading and tired hands. The geographical unity of India had already been almost achieved by Dalhousie. Whatever remained to unify the vast land was completed after the Mutiny (the idea of India's oneness earlier lived in the religious imagination and emotions of the Hindus only). A new political and economic nation was born—the Indian nation. English education and modern thought and science (why call them western, asks J.N. Sarkār, and cloud the issues ?) were planted on a firm pedestal. Three universities of Calcuttā, Madrās and Bombay were created in 1857 itself. The Indians beat the British in their intellectual game, and soon Indian scholars and litterateurs, scientists and surgeeons, legal and professional lumanaries, experts in international intercourse, joint stock companies and banking and, above all, noble patriots wedded to the cause of democratic freedoms for the entire people of India filled the nation's stage. The new laws built on Roman jurisprudence, and interpreted impartially by a judiciary independent of the executive, a civil service recruited by, but not dependent for its livelihood or even its views on the executive, which should change in accordance with the wishes of the people; a professional middle class bubbling with new modern ideas and not tied down to the past like the old feudal chiefs or their satraps or serfs on the land; a Press free to criticise the Govt of the day and to inform and lead public opinion; besides modern science and technology all brought to India an entirely new outlook and methods of organising the society on secular, and politico-economic lines, cutting across the antiquated ideas of caste, creed, region or even religion. The whole country was made one, and travel made not only safe but became a

---

F. N. Contd.

the British expenditure in India is so heavy as to make the continuing British rule economically prohibitive. India costs Britain more than the income it brings her," (which did not prove true later on, but the essentials in Marx's thesis cannot be disputed).

He adds prophetically:—

"The political unity of India, imposed by the British sword, will now be strengthend by the electric telegraph. The native army, organised and drilled by the British drill-sergeant, was the *sine-qua-non* of Indian self-emancipation, and of India ceasing to be the prey of the foreign intruder. The free press is a new and powerful agent of reconstruction. From the Indian native, reluctantly, and sparingly educated at Calcutta under British superintendence, a fresh class is springing up, endowed with requirements of government and imbued with European science. That once fabulous country will thus be actually annexed to the Western world .."

means of luxury, through the network of roads and railways. That Her Majesty's Opposition should have a place as honourable in society as the Govt. was unheard of in India's tradition-bound *mai-bāp* and authoritarian society. "Tea-plantation, textile mills, irrigation canals, coal-mining and other forms of economic development advanced so fast that agriculture ceased to be the precarious single means of the people's livelihood. Immense amounts of capital were poured into India from John Lawrence's Viceroyalty onwards. Agriculture also progressed and cotton-cultivation multiplied four-fold (in quantity and ten fold in price) during the boom caused by the American civil war (1861-65)."

The British now had no one to suppress but only to awaken, educate and employ in useful avocations. New cities sprang up due to industrialisation and internationalisation of commerce, and age-old caste and credal barriers started breaking down by a colossal movement of men and women seeking new avenues of prosperity throughout this great and vast land, of whose inexhaustible potentialities men were made aware with each passing decade.

More and more laws were passed and enforced, to save the peasant from the money-lender, the lawful citizen from the thug and the cut-throat and what is most, the woman from the centuries-old thraldom and the possessive rapacity of man so that she, along with her children, became individual persons in their own right.

The more the English education and with it the modern ideas spread, the more the English Govt. was subjected to political unrest and agitation. A new class of civilised political animals was born who established their claim to leadership not with the sword or open rapine and loot, but through superior argument, civility of manner and sense of self-less sacrifice and service to the society.

What is most, the onslaught of Christianity threw a challenge to the old religions and superstitons either to fight their claim to survival or go under. A new interpretation of the old religious norms and cultural mores became inevitable. India was nolonger an island which it was a mortal religious sin for her sons to leave, even to travel across the high seas. India was now a part of the whole wide world and could nologer shut herself in, or live apart and alone. No compromise was possible between the present and the past, for the future that beckoned was far more glorious and rewarding than both.

And no matter how much they tried, the British could not stem the onsurge of new ideas and processes that they had themselves unleashed. Even if it was in the interest of *their* own empire that they did so; educating people in *their* own thought to make rapport with the subject peoples possible and easy; creating heavy industry, for labour was cheap here and prices of commodities could be pegged and imports and exports could both be regulated by laws made in *their* own interest by themselves: creating clerks and *bābus* and higher civil servants to run their *own* Govt; building railways and canals for their *own* capitalist profits; founding cities in order to attract entrepreneurs and labour from all over the country for *their* own benefit and larger taxes; giving liberty to people to express even opposing views, in order to gauge the working of their minds and to caution themselves and avert danger in time to their *own* lives and interests; enforcing laws uniformly and honouring life and property to contain unrest against *themselves*—all this is conceded. But once you train a man how to fight for you, if he starts eventually fighting for himself and turns you out with the weapons you have yourself provided him with, you cannot blame him. And this is what happened. The total success of the British empire in the Mutiny sowed also the seeds of its destruction in due course, by the weapons the British had themselves placed in the hands of the Indians.

Whether if the British wouldnot have entered upon the scene, the same kind of fundamental transformation would have occurred is a moot point. Historians point to Japān in this context, but not to China. India was governed by the Moghals for two centuries before, but they had heard only of force, fate and fraud governing the destinies of nations, not of an industrial revolution, or of sea-power, of scientific discoveries or international commerce or intercourse. They conquered with force and ended up with palace-intrigues. They may have built a few marvellous buildings but not a new man or a new society in which every one could participate, except on their terms. No wonder, the Marāthās fought them with their own weapons, but not to change the society, only masters. For instance, although Brahmins had treated the Marāthās, including Chhatarpati Shivājee, as outcastes, it is the Brahmins who under the Marāthā Kings invariably became the all-powerful Peshwas. The Sikhs fought for a far better ideal, but their dazzling successes in war,though they brought in their train a new kind of political unity and humanistic outlook of life, yet degenerated into what had brought ruin to the Moghals—internecine warfare and palace-intrigue, easy morals and conscience, a confusion of both the religious idea and the political state and so the dream ended how it had to end. It gave good heart to the people for a time, but it did not enlarge enough their minds, nor made them fit instruments to face the challenges of the new world which had taken birth atleast a century before they ever came to know of it ! *

It is not that the Sikhs at large had reconciled to their fate merely because of the efficient and lawful administration of the British Govt. or the new avenues of education and economic activity they were opening up. No amount of efficiency or peaceful existence or respect for legal rights by a foreign power can be a substitute for freedom, though free-men, if they indulge in or invite anarchy, have only to thank themselves if they invite an authoritarian rule (as after the excesses of the French Revolution) or lose their freedom, and common people prefer a safer and lawful (even foreign) domination to an independent but an unsure and unstable society.† After all, this is how the Afghāns followed by the Moghals had initially filled the vacuum in the history of our own nation.

The Mutiny had been suppressed and the Moghal and the Poorbia tyrannies against the Sikhs wholly avenged, with their active cooperation, but the fire in the hearts of Sikhs to strike for their freedom once again under propitious circumstances was not yet dead. When-

---

* If we look dispassionately at life, we realise that not all that is strange and foreign leads to unproductive results. Life is *given* to us, as are early education and upbringing by our parents. All wives are foreign initially. All languages are foreign and all peoples to the countries they inhabit now, including Sanskrit and the Aryan inhabitants, not only the Americans and the South Americans, or the Europeans and others. Colossal movements of men and women have occured in history to displace the aborigines and the Red Indians to give a fresh lease and meaning to life. All religions and all new ideas are fiercely resisted when they are born. But their acceptance follows and the results, though not every time so intended, transform peoples and societies and a new man and a new civilisation are born.

† Writes Vincent Simth:—"Something is lost in a corporate personality every time a nation loses its independence. The modern spirit had to come to the Panjāb with all its meterial benefits and spiritual unrest. But if it had come by free action of a reforming party within, rather than by compulsion of an alien rule, the conversion would have been more complete in the long run, though it might have been slower in the beginning. Much that later happened in the Panjāb might then have been avoided, *including the division of India.* The Sikhs by their own folly threw away the first chance of a Panjāb organically intergrated into a healthy plural society, Dalhousie by his over-confidence the second." (*Oxford History of India*, P. 619).

ever, therefore, they found an occasion, they hit the British as hard as they could.

That is why the British were very cautious in dealing with the Sikhs. 10th Panjab Regt. had revolted (Aug 1858) at D. I.Khān, and a majority of the Sikhs of this regiment were involved in it. They were arrested and punished. Still, writing to the Mily Secy to the Chief Commissioner at Murree (date Sept 1, 1858) Brig. Gen. N. B. Chamberlain, commandant of the irregular force at D.I. Khan, reported that "the spirit of the troops is no longer what it was. There is a spirit of restlesseness and an eager desire to know what is happening in Hindustān and a readiness to believe any report to our prejudice and we no longer command the sympathy of the Sikhs as a body. Indeed, it may be affirmed that they have commenced to think a revolt possible and to calculate the chances of success. And were it not for the counterpoise afforded by the trans-Indus and Panjābi Mohammedans and other classes which help to constitute the corps...I consider it quite possible that a most dangerous combination might now be at work throughout. the troops ready to burst out at the first opportunity." However, in another letter (dated 8 sept., 1858), it was conceded (Richard Temple, Secy to C. C., Panjāb to Secy to Governor General) that even if mixed regiments were raised, they could also combine under favourable circumstances and therefore no single class could be exclusively depended upon, and that "the key and sensitive and more powerful wings (like the artillery) be kept with the British soldiers only."

It was reported by G. Wilson from Fatehgarh to G. F. Edmonston at Allahabad (April 16, 1858) that "a body of Sikhs, about 400, from different regiments is reported to have reached Bareilley, from Lucknow, with their arms," and asking if he could try negotiations with them and dissuade them from joining Nānā Sāhib's forces. According to the same source, both *Azān* and cow-killing had been prohibited by Nānā Sāhib and the Muslims in Bareilley were prepared to fight Nānā if he prevented the *Azān* (Muslim call to prayer). A similar mistake in Delhi, like the bolstering of Bahādur Shāh by Muslim fanatics as the only rightful heir to the Moghal throne, cost the cause of the rebels any sympathy they had for them as a whole.

As a result of alarming reports from military commanders about the restlessness among Sikh forces in British employ, much panic was caused to the rulers. The Rājās of Patiālā, Nābhā and Jind were addressed urgent communications to be on the alert, and censor the entire mail received by the friends and relations of the Sikh army personnel recruited even from their areas. They dutifully warned "every *lambardār*, *tehsildār* and *thānedār* (Aug. 1858) to ascertain what conversation was going on among them and to send in daily reports, and to seize any man whom there may be reason to suspect, to maintain secret espionage on families and friends of the soldiers in the employ of the British." The Rājā of Nābhā issued orders that no soldier, coming on leave was to see his family or relations "without orders from me."

The Mahārājā of Patiālā went a step further. He reminded the Chief Commissioner (Aug 19,1858) that "on the commencement of the Mutiny last year, when large levies of Sikhs were raised, to all European officers I've seen or spoken I expressed whatever sentiments I entertained on the subject. I maintain that opinion even now." According to Richard Temple, Secy to C. C., Panjāb, vide his letter to G. F. Edmonstone, Secy to Governor General, dated 8 Sept, 1858, "Patiala had told the Chief Commissioner that the Panjāb troops should on no account exceed one-third the whole of our native soldiers." The Rājā of Jind had told them that "they (the Sikh soldiers) who rebelled aginst and killed their own rulers, how could they care more for the British ? His own troops, he said, had mutinied against him twice recently, and he had no security that they would not do so again." Says Richrad Temple in the same letter:—"It was from a full conviction of such dangers that the Chief Commissioner (of Panjāb) from the first raised no more Panjābi troops than appeard absolutely necessary to enable us to maintain the struggle. He even preferred to run the risk of an internal commotion (in Panjāb) to adding to Panjābi troops. And, even after that event, his plan was only to commence raising a second corps when the first had actually marched to Hindustān."

He notes with pleasure that out of a total of 51,000 Panjābi soldiers, only 15,000 were Sikhs and probably the purely Sikh soldiers in the Bengāl presidency did not exceed 22000 (out of a total of 1,51,000), and emphasises the apprehensions of the Panjāb Chief Commissioner that "we should learn from past misfortunes and to trust no race in particular, to mix races in the native forces, to maintain that army within the lowest number and keep it in our thorough subordination and discipline."

There is thus this other equally relevant side to the Sikh support to the British during the Mutiny, which has to be kept in view. Their patriotism was not dead, nor their spirits subdued. Only they did not and could not fight for the continuance of a now tottering and wholly emaciated Moghal regime against which they had fought for over two centuries or for the restoration of feudal rights to the disinherited Princes of unsure character and sympathies, or a soldiery run wild over "pig and cow" business, or for an Indian nation which at that time existed only on the British political maps, and not in the minds of the Indians themselves.

CHAPTER XXV

REVIVAL OR REGENERATION ?

It is the traditional habit of an old society taken unawares by a cataclysmic change either to become indifferent to it and take refuge in renunciation, or to denounce it as unauthorised, uncalled for and wholly unnecessary and therefore to be fought not so much in its essentials, but in its outlines. The Sikh response was no different. They too started out on an inner search, and the re-discovery of the basics of their religion which they believed had been corrupted by the resurgence of Brāhminism during the hey-days of their empire. And, now, the onslaught of Christianity, patronised by the new rulers, was further corroding their sources of moral and spiritual heritage. It is the first, they thought, which was responsible even for their political downfall, and the second that would deprive them of not only numbers but also pride in what they considered to be their glorious history and tradition. Dalip Singh, their king, had been converted, so also a wing of the family of the Kapurthalā rulers. The neo-Sikhs converted during Ranjit Singh's period were fast merging back into their ancient faith—Hinduism. The faith, therefore, was to be resurrected in its pristine purity, as they understood it. Their strength was daily being reduced,* and fears were openly being expressed that the future of the Sikhs lay only in their past.

*Although the population of the Panjāb had never been enumerated scientifically so far, it was felt that population of the Sikhs had decreased from one crore to 18 lakhs in 1881, (Vide *Singh Sabhā Lahr* by Dr. Jagjit Singh, P, 7). This is a fantas-

Three powerful movements of reform ensued. However, this paradox no historian of the Sikhs has highlighted, that the inspiration for all these came from or the control of these movements passed into the hands of either *Sahjdhāri* Sikhs, or recent converts to Sikhism from Hinduism. The Nirankāri movement was initiated by Bābā Dyāl and strengthened by Bābā Rattan Chand (or Bābā Rattā). The Nāmdhāri Bābā Rām Singh was the disciple of Bābā Bālak Singh of Hazro (Campbellpore) who was in turn inspired by Bhagat Jawāharmal of Rāwalpindi. The Singh Sabhā movement initially was inspired and controlled by Bābā Khem Singh Bedi (who discarded nothing that was Hindu in origin) and the Akāli movement, which was the most dynamic of all, was dominated from 1920 to 1962 by Master Tārā Singh, a Hindu convert from Sikhism. All of them were Khatris and came from the North-West of Panjāb.

The first in the series was the Nirankāri movement, which inculcated faith in the one Formless Lord (Nirankār) and declared as taboo all rituals, smacking of Brahminism and lately introduced into the Sikh society by Mahārājā (Ranjit Singh), followed by his courtiers and subjects. The movement was started by a devout Malhotrā Khatri Sahjdhāri Sikh, Bābā Dyāl,* (1783-1855 A.D.) during the reign of Ranjit Singh himself. They rejected idolatory and Hindu rituals and according to the Ludhiānā Mission report (1855) "they even gave abuse to the cow and did not either burn or bury their dead to distinguish them equally from Hindus and Muslims (and Christians) but consigned them to the river, which offended the

F.N. Contd.

tic exaggeration. The actual Sikh population, according the first census of 1881 was a little over 18 lakhs and in 1921, after the peaceful conditions of 40 years only 31 lakhs, making a total of not more 10 percent in 1881 and 8 percent 40 years later. The total Panjāb population in 1857 was estimated to be 53 lakhs, when the total population of India was believed to be about 15 crores. In the beginning of the Sikh rule their number was not more than 10 percent, which taking a most liberal view, may have risen three times over, but the Sikhs were still a minority, as the Sikhs didnot believe in proselytisation through any bait or pressure during the 80 years of their rule or at any other time.

* His father, Rām Sahāi, was a banker who had shifted from Kābul to Peshawar late in the eighteenth century. Bābā Dyāl was born here. His mother, Ladiki, was the grand-daughter of Bhāi Bhagwān Singh who is said to have worked as treasurer to Guru Gobind Singh. Dyāl ji learnt Persian and Panjābi early in life and imbibed Sikh tenets through his mother, his father having died early.

orthodox Hindus who brought a court case against them." They emphasised the tenets, as enshrined in the Sikh Scriptures, particularly meditation of the one God and rejection of the belief in gods and godesses, rituals and superstitions. Bābā Dyāl settled at Rāwalpindi, early in the nineteenth century, and instead of leaning on the offerings of the devout, started a grocer's shop to earn his living. He started imparting regular religious instruction. As was the injunction of Guru Gobind Singh, he fought especially against people setting themselves up as Gurus, and gave a new slogan to the people :—

"*Japo Piārio Dhan Nirankār : Jo dehdhāri, sabhē Khuār.*" (Meditate on the one Formless God, O dears, for the humans who claim to be Gurus, will all be reduced to the dust). Opposition was natural in such a case. Even a court case was brought against him during the early period of the British rule in the Panjāb. On his marrying during what was considered to be the "inauspicious" month and organising a *bhoj* (dinner) on the day of a devotee's death (when for 13 days, according to the Hindu belief, all food from the deceased's house is polluted) he was boycotted and thrown out of the Gurdwārā where he preached. He built another one instead, and died in 1855 a much honoured Saint.

His son, Darbārā Singh, succeeded him. He introduced the ceremony of the *Anand* marriage (which was later passed into law in 1909) without dowry or considerations of caste * Their present leader is Bābā Gurbakhsh Singh, son of the late Bābā Harā Singh (died 1972) and their Headquarters, after the partition of the country, are in Chandigarh. The President of this organisation is another

* The *Anand* Marriage ceremony consists of the bride and the groom circumambulating round the Sikh holy book four times, (instead of seven times around fire, as among the Hindus). As the reader (Granthi) reads out, one by one, the four stanzas of a composition by Guru Rām Dās (in Rāga Suhi) called *Lāwān* (lit. breaking away) from the Guru Granth Sāhib, the couple stand up with joined palms before the Granth. Then, as the musicians recite the composition, they take a walk round the Holy Altar, and after the fourth round is completed, the marriage is solemnised. All this can happen in a private home or a Gurudwārā and the ceremony conducted by any male or female, there being no priestly class among the Sikhs.

distinguished Sikh, Dr. Mān Singh Nirankāri, a well-known eye-surgeon of Amritsar.*

The other, and politically far more dynamic upsurge was the Nāmdhāri movement, also called the *Kooka* movement (so called because the devotees shout and scream—*Kook*—when they are in ecstacy) Its inspiration came from Bhagat Jawāhar Mal of Rāwalpindi who initiated Bābā Bālak Singh (1799-1862), of Hazro, near Campellpore in West Panjāb.

It is by him that the far better known Bābā Rām Singh, a soldier in Ranjit Singh's army, who abandoned soldiering during the post-Ranjit anarchy (1841) to meditate upon God's Name (or Nām, from which the word Nām-Dhāri, or believer in the Name, is derived) was initiated. Due to the intense piety of the revered Bābā, many people flocked to his path, especially the carpenter-class (besides the Jats and the untouchables and even some Brahmins and Muslims) from which he himself hailed. He made his village, Bhaini (now known as Bhaini Sāhib) his headquarters, and kept a shop for the upkeep of his family (wife, mother and daughter). After the loss of the Sikh empire, he preached the Sikh gospel with much vigour both to fight the onslaught of Christianity and also the evil political and cultural effects of foreign rule, and asked the people to desist from English education and cultural mores (dress and liqour and meat)

* The 1978 controversy regarding what is the known as the *Sant Nirankāri* movement has nothing to do, in its present form, with the original movement. It is a break-away movement from the original source in the thirtees of the present century, and believes in having a living Guru (the third in successian being Bābā Gurbachan Singh with his affluent and highly fortified headquarters in Delhi). The earlier two were Avtār Singh, the father of the present chief, and Bootā Singh (1883-1944), his mentor, who all hailed from West Panjāb. They left the parent movement due to personal and dietary (not doctrinal) reasons. They did not gather much following before 1947, when they came to Delhi as refugees, but from then on, attracted a large number of men and women in distress, especially from West Panjāb. Upto recently (accordingly to their own memorandum to the Delhi. Education Board, case No. 6 of 1977, under the Delhi Education Act 73), they claimed to be a part of the Sikh minority. A decade ago, they used to instal the Sikh Holy Book in their congregations, but later, on objections from the orthodox Sikhs (in view of their belief in Gurudom), they abandoned the practice. They still make the Sikh Scripture their main source of inspiration, but have lately started misinterpreting and even corrupting its compositions to fit in with their own improvised doctrines. Their gurus still keep a Sikh form, but instead of Sikh baptism, they administer foot-wash (*Charnamrit*) to their followers.

and even the post office and the railway train !* But he made several departures from the original path of Guru Gobind Singh. His followers were asked to wear spotless white and round (not conical) turbans. They boycotted even tap-water as the water-taps were supposed to be lined with animal skin ! His belief in the tell-tale *Sau-Sākhi* encouraged him also to preach against the British rāj, for which he was interned in his village (Bhaini Sāhib) and his followers arrested at various places and punished. This continued from 1863 to 1870. The orthodox Sikhs, however, became estranged from him and refused to offer prayers on his behalf at Anandpur and the Akāl Takht at Amritsar, though he was offered the usual robe of honour at the Golden Temple when he visited it. This made him bitter, but he did not relax on his mission. His devotees, however, much against his wishes, it appears, started committing excesses in their new-found zeal, especially against idol-worship and cow killing. Their hatred of cow-killing and Muslims became so intense that it led to the murder, in cold blood, of some Muslim butchers in Amritsar (1871). Cow-killing was forbidden in this sacred city by the British (following the Sikh practice) but of late it had started again and the *kookās* wouldn't suffer it. Some people were hanged, others sentenced for life. The Deputy Commissioner of Ludhiānā, without due inquiry, got 65 Nāmdhāris at Malerkotlā blown from the mouth of the cannon as the Kookas had killed a few butchers at Malerkotla. A few others were hanged, or sent to the Andamans.

---

* Why the Bābā was exercised, alongwith several other notable reformers like Swāmi Dayanand, founder of the Āryā Samāj and the leaders of the Singh Sabha movement, over the activities of the Christian missionaries is possibly because of their active programme for conversion. Dr. Gandā Singh, the well-known Sikh historian, has, however, put the whole thing in its proper perspective. Says he : "India owes a deep debt of gratitude to Christian missionaries for the light of religion and education that they brought to many parts of this country and for the social and political awakening in the masses that came in their wake. But for the services of hundreds of devoted souls and the tons of money that the foreign Christian missions have poured into the land of Bhārat, millions of people of the depressed classes, now forming a respectable portion of the Indian population, would still have been rotting as condmned untouchables. It was the foreign Christian missionaries who first lit the torch of renaissance in India by the introduction of scientific knowledge." (Autobiography of Bhagat Lakshman Singh, intr. xii-xiii). It may be of interest to note that some of best-known and respected Sikh religious teachers, political leaders and intellectual giants studied at the

Bābā Rām Singh, who had no hand in it, but whose activities were constantly being watched (he had sent a mission to Nepāl and Hyderā-bād) could not escape the British wrath and he was deported (Jan. 18, 1872) to Rangoon, where he breathed his last in jail (Nov. 29, 1884), with the name of God on his pious lips.

But his unswerving devotion to God, his crusading spirit and the heroic sacrifices of his followers (for whatever cause) made his essentially socio-religious movement a dynamic political force in those days. However, though his letters from the Rangoon jail to his various devotees (now published) make no claim whatever to his being a living Guru, or an *Avtār* (incarnation of God, or a successor to Guru Gobind Singh), his followers accepted him as such, as time passed. For instance, Bābā Rām Singh in his letters from the Rangoon jail calls himself a mere *raptiā* (reporter) (of the Guru's message) and denies any claim to Guruship. In a letter from the Rangoon jail to Bhai Gurjit Singh and five others, on the eve of Dalip Singh's visit to India, he says :—"The Guru of Gurus is Granth Sāhib, the Word as Guru. Consider this as the whole truth." But his followers' belief in his being an incarnation of God or a successor of Guru Gobind Singh, together with their insistence on vegetarianism and a separate kitchen, certain Brahminic rites (like *havan*) at the time of marriage (which, of course, became very simplified and cheap, no dowry being allowed), their violently anti-Muslim and anti-Christian stance, and the discarding of the sword for the rosary, broke them off from the mainstream of Sikh religious and social ethos. Inspite of

---

F.N. Contd.

Christian schools, including the veteran leader, Māster Tārā Singh (who got converted to Sikhism while yet a student at the Mission school at Rāwal-pindi). Bhāi Jodh Singh, the Sikh savant (later Vice-chancellor of the Panjābi university), Bhāi Vir Singh and Prof. Puran Singh, both poets and philosophers, were also the products of the Mission Schools. The former also became, like Master Tārā Singh, a convert to Sikhism while yet a student at the school. The bee-line that the Indians of every community (and especially among the leading lights in every line), still make forty years after our independence before the Christian Public schools is a matter for anyone to verify.

The Gurmukhi type was first got manufactured by the Christian missionaries and the first Panjabi work in the Gurmukhi script was the Christian Bible published at Sirampur and presented to Māhārājā Ranjit Singh (1835). The first grammar in Panjābi and the first English-Panjabi dictionary were also the creations of the Christian missionaries.

this and though they did not look upon the Sikh Scripture, the Granth Sāhib, as Guru, as most Sikhs believe, they yet recite, interpret and meditate upon only this Scripture or the Book of the Tenth King. They have now abandoned their opposition to western education, dress (except for their turban), tap-water, separate kitchen etc. except for the most orthodox circles whose number is very limited. Their devotion to their faith is, however, very profound, though they take only an extremely limited interest in the affairs of the Sikhs as a whole.

As has been said, Bābā Rām Singh referred in many letters (and earlier his discourses) to the *Sau-Sākhi* and other such tell-tale futuristic stories about the possible exit of the British in the eighties of the ninteenth century. This made his followers suspect in the eyes of the Govt. who kept a close watch on their activities. This, on the one hand, led to much oppression and on the other divided his ranks which made him very miserable. The orthodox also called his Sikhs "*tankhāhias*" (the erring ones), but he took all this with good heart and asked his followers to ignore these insults and hardships, and to meditate on and appeal to God for His mercy. Before his arrest, he appointed *Subās* (agents) in various places, like the *masands* of old, to look after the welfare of his growing community. One of them, Gurbachan Singh, even went to Russia to seek the Russian support for his country's independence when over three hundred thousands of the Kookās, he assured the Russian authorities at Tāshkent, would also rebel. But, nothing came of it. It only added to their troubles.

In the papers relating to the *Kookā* sect, the Govt. account details the following leading features of the doctrines of Bābā Rām Singh. ' He abolishes all distinctions of caste among Sikhs; advocates indiscriminate marriage of all classes; enjoins the marriage of widows; enjoins abstinence from liquor and drugs; but advocates much too-free-intercourse between the sexes; men and women rave together at his meetings; and thousands of women and young girls have joined the sect; he exhorts his disciples to be cleanly and truth-telling. One of his maxims says, it is well that every man carries his staff and they all do. The Granth is their only accepted volume. The brotherhood may be known by the tie of their *pagris, Sidhā pag*, by a watchword, and by a necklace of knots made in a white woollen cord to represent beads and which are worn by all the community."

The same source credits him with the conviction that "Gobind Singh's Grantha is the only true one, written by inspiration. Gobind Singh is the only Guru. Idol-worship is insulting to God."

Except for the charge of immorality, which is false, the rest was a true statement about the preachings of the venerable Bābāji. A strict moral code was observed by his followers, as is apparent from their history. As for ravings of men and women in his congregations, it was only in a state of real (or feigned) ecstacy that some of his devotees did so, like the Sufis and the whirling Dervishes. To this day, inspite of doctrinal differences, they remain an honoured sect of the Sikh community, like the *Nirmalās* and the *Udāsis*.*

Another revivalist movement was launched immediately after the deportation of Bābā Rām Singh (1872). It was far more widespread and accepted whole-heartedly by the Sikh orthodoxy and was known as the Singh Sabhā movement. Its first meeting convened by Sardār Thākar Singh Sandhānwālia was held at Amritsar (1873) which was attended by a large number of Sikh scholars, *pujāris* (custodians of Gurdwārās), *Udāsis* and Nirmalās and the Sikh chiefs and nobles. Gyani Gian Singh of Amritsar became its first Secretary. Its object was also to combat the onslaught of Christianity† and later also of Ārya Samāj and to purge the community of extraneous, notably Brahmanic influences. The first Singh Sabhā was founded at

---

*Bābā Rām Singh was succeeded in the Nāmdhāri leadership by his brother, Bābā Hari Singh ((alias Budh Singh) who also remained interned in his village for 20 years. He was succeeded by his son, Bābā Partāp Singh, also a very noble soul who participated actively, alongwith thousands of his followers, in the freedom movement led by Gāndhiji and Jawāharlāl Nehru. The present incumbent is Bābā Jagjit Singh, who mainly now-a-days manages his vast landed property at Sirsā (Hissār), his following having considerably dwindled. They have two main centres abroad—in Bangkok (Thailand) and Nairobi (East Africa). They are mostly in business or industry.

† The Christians were initially known in the Panjāb as Qurānis (i.e. untouchables, like the Muslims), as the early recruits to Christianity as to Islām were from the lowest Hindu caste, or *chuhrās* (scavengers). Later, some well-known families like those of Kapurthalā, led by Rājā Sir Harnām Singh, embraced Christianity. His daughter, Rāj Kumāri Amrit Kaur, became an inmate of Gāndhi's *ashram* & later our Health Minister. The family, however, stuck to Sikh names. Another Sikh who became a famous Christian mystic was Sādhu Sunder Singh of Patiālā who saw visions of Jesus Christ & was much honoured by the world Christian community.

Amritsar. * Seven years later, a General Singh Sabhā was formed which became an affiliating and controlling body for the other Singh Sabhās. Its ideals were (a) to propagate the Guru's Mission in its pristine purity; (b) to do away with the Brahmanic rituals which had creeped into the Sikh society; (c) to publish books; (d) to hold discussions and debates of scholars of doctrine and to make translations of the sacred works, more paricularly the Sikh Scriptures and to sift the life-stories of the Gurus made current by the *Janam Sākhis* or other Sikh or European writers; (e) to inculcate pride in the Sikh youth in their tradition and history; and (f) to propagate the cause of the Panjābi language by opening schools and publishing books, journals and newspapers. Those who were known to be against Sikh religion, or were ex-communicated or had become apostates or were disloyal to the British Govt. were not to be enlisted as members. But, if they asked for forgiveness, they could enrol themselves as its constituents. High British officials could, however, become members, and men of other religions too, if they were well-disposed towards the Sikh community.

Members were forbidden to hear or speak against other religions, or to oppose the Govt.

After the Singh Sabhā of Amritsar, a Singh Sabhā was formed on Nov. 2, 1879 at Lahore with Bhāi Gurmukh Singh, a Professor at the Oriental College, Lāhore, as its Secretary.

Through the efforts of Prof. Gurmukh Singh, Panjābi teaching was introduced in the Oriental College, Lāhore from 1877, under Bhāi Harsā Singh. Later, the Lāhore Singh Sabhā added much to

---

* A regular *Kathā* (religious discourse) was organised from this time at Manji Sāhib, just outside the precincts of the Golden Temple, Amritsar. Gyāni Sardul Singh initiated the debate on the birth-date of Guru Nānak which he considered to be in April. A *Gurmat Granth Parchārak* Sabhā was founded here in 1885 to investigate the life-stories of the Gurus and fix a standard edition of the Dasam Granth. The debates in which the top Gyānis of the times participated, lasted over two years (1895-1897) and a report was prepared about the genuineness or otherwise of the various compositions of the *Dasam Granth,* but no use seems to have been made of it uptodate nor its contents published. Other pamphlets published under its auspices were *Gurpurab Parkāsh, Gursikhān de nit-nem, Sadd Sidhānt, Gurumat Sidhānt, Guru Bilās of Kavi Sukhā Singh, Gur-Parnāli, Yātra Sri Hazoor Sāhib, Gurparb Karan di Vidhi,* etc., which sifted the Sikh doctrines and practices and presented the lives of the Gurus in a new light.

its strength by the acquisition of two veteran preachers of the Ārya Samāj.* Bhāi Jawāhar Singh, a railway official, and the first

---

* The Ārya Samāj was founded by Swāmi Dayānand (1824-1883) for the first time in Bombay on April 10, 1875. Born in a village belonging to the Rājā of Morvi in Kathiawār (now part of Gujarat State), the Swami ji refused during his life-time to divulge either his name or parentage. It is only after his death in 1883 that it was known that he was the son of a Brahmin, Ambā Shankar, a well-to-do banker and worshipper of Shiva and that his original name was Mul Shankar.

He left his home at the age of 21, abandoning the world to seek salvation, and refusing marriage. His first spiritual experience came to him at the age of 14, "when he saw mice running over the image of Shiva and defiling it." Seeing this, he revolted against idol-worship. The resolve to abandon the world was hastened in his sensitive mind by the death of his sister "which filled him with profound grief."

For about 18 years (1845 to 1863), he wandered about as a Sanyāsi learning the Truth from various sources. He was first influenced by Vedānta and was convinced of the identity of the Soul and the Oversoul. He was initiated into the *Brahmacharya* order and given the name of Sudha Chaitanya (pure consciousness). Later he entered the highest order of Sanyasis and was called Dayānand Saraswati. But, he soon abandoned Vedānta and opted for Yoga (or Sankhya-Yoga) on meeting with a blind Sikh Veda-learned Udāsi Guru, Vrijanand, at Mathurā. He agreed to teach him on the condition that "he should throw away all modern Sanskrit books". "This condition was fufilled," and he learnt to interpret the Veda in terms of *Sankhya-yoga*, rejecting both Paurānic and Vedāntic Hinduism in which a large majority of the Hindus and Europeans (including Max Mueller, Dr. S. Radhakrishnan, Sri Aurobindo and Swami Vivekanand) to this day interpret their sacred Scriptures.

For another 20 years (1863 to 1883), is the period of his ministry. He preached at Hardwār and Banaras, Bombay and Poona, Calcuttā and Lāhore where he reached last (1877) but left the largest following behind. For sometime, he tried partnership with the Theosophical Society (1878-81), but "a split took place on the question of the personality of God." He also came into contact with the leaders of Brahmo Samaj, like Debander Nāth Tagore and Keshub Chander Sen, Sir Sayyad Ahmad of reformed Islām, and Christian missionaries like Dr. T. J. Scott. A union was envisaged between the Brahmo Samāj, the Prārthanā Samāj and the Āryā Samāj but except for a brief three-year temporary liaison with the Theosophical Society, no other union came about.

It was in the Panjāb, however, that he found the ground fertile among the middle-class, educated city Hindus, mainly on account of their Sikh background, who wanted a religion which could meet the attacks of Christianity over idol-worship, caste, the world as Māyā, and the "looseness" of the faith. He preached against idolatory and caste and emphasised man's commitment to the world outside and illumination within, through meditation, on the one Formless God as enjoined, according to him, by the Veda. His appeal was immediate and profound. The othodox Sanātanist section opposed him bitterly, but the Sikhs, especially of the Singh Sabhā section, welcomed him with open arms and he oftentimes spoke from their platform. Some of his mission's early preachers and office-bearers in the Panjāb were also Sikhs like Dit Rām (later Gyāni Dit Singh) and Bhāi Jawāhar Singh Kapur (to become the first Secretary of both the Singh Sabhā and the Aryā Samāj at Lāhore).

But the publication of the *Satyārath Parkāṣh* (containing his views on society and religion) changed all this. In this book, all prophets of religion, their philosophy and practices were reviled, and Sikhism also didnot escape his wrath. Guru Nānak was called an ignorant "dambhi" (pretender) and this the Sikhs could not suffer. His preachers started converting Sikhs back to the fold of Hinduism in the name of *Shudhi* (Purification) alongwith Muslims, Buddhists and Charistians. Even Jains and Kabir-panthis were not spared. This created new tensions in the society. Their emphasis on Hindi and Sanskrit, to the exclusion even of the mother tongue, and their invective against other religions led to such socio-political results that their bitter fruits we have not yet wholly ceased to reap.

There was nothing particulary objectionable in his 10-point instruction :- (1) God is one. (2) He is all knowledge, infinite and Unborn, and all-pervading, unchanging, immortal, almighty, and yet just and merciful. To him, all worship is due. (3) Vedas are books of true knowledge. (4) One should accept truth and reject untruth. (5) Only virtuous deeds should be done. (6) Do good to the world and improve its material and spiritual conditions. (7) Treat everyone with love, justice and due regard to his merits. (8) Dispel ignorance and impart knowledge. (9) One's own good is not enough; do good to others also. (10) In personal matters, one may act with freedom but should curb one's ego if the society's good so demands. But, in practice, it took a different shape.

That all knowledge, including all scientific discoveries, are already and finally hinted at in the revealed Vedas, became too much to take. That all religions not conforming to the Veda are fake and invective be poured on their head and their votaries be reconverted to the true (Aryan) faith, negatived the 10-point code. Max Mueller called Swāmij's interpretation of the Veda "the most incredible one." His *Niyoga* doctrine (extra-marital relation of married men or women eleven times with different persons, in certain conditions, such as barrenness or sickness of a woman or long absence or impotence of man, or if a woman gets girls only etc) was severely criticised by the neo-reformists and not only the Christians and others. Several murders took place in the early years and several agitations later to increase tensions over religious, political or linguistic issues between the Aryā Samāj and others. Swāmi ji himself was also poisoned to death (1883) by a courtesan of the Hindu ruler of Jodhpur whose easy morals he had gone there to reform.

Secretary of the Lāhore Ārya Samāj) and Dit Rām, who was converted to Sikhism and became widely known as Dit Singh Gyani. Another reason for their popularity was their sincerity of belief in the true doctrine of the Gurus, their sense of mission and the zeal with which they set about their task. They started a Panjābi weekly, the *Gurmukhi Akhbār* (Nov. 10, 1880), to propagate the cause of Panjābi and disseminate news about the welfare of the community. A monthly magazine, called "*Vidyārak*", was issued about a year later (Oct. 1881) to interpret the Guru's Word. propagate the lives of the Sikh Gurus and the Sikh code of social and moral conduct, and to apprise the community about its progress in education, etc. This was edited by Gurmukh Singh. An Urdu weekly, called the "Khālsā Gazette" was also later published as also a Panjābi-English dictionary by Mayyā Singh.

F. N. Contd.

The Swāmiji, however, shook the Hindu society out of its lethargy, superstition and casteism for a whole half-century (1875-1925), throwing up such stalwarts as L. Lajpat Rāi (politician though no statesman as he turned violently anti-Muslim), Mahātma Hans Rāi (education), Lālā Hardyāl (academic revolutionary), L. Harkishan Lal (Economics), Dr. G. C. Nārang (historian) and the line of such illustrious social lumanaries in not yet ended. Mr. Charan Singh, the acknowleged Jāt leader of North India, was the Prime Minister of India (1979). Mr. Mehar Chand Mahajan was the Chief Justice of India and Mr. Suraj Bhan, former Vice-Chancellor of Panjab University, did a yeoman's service in the field of modern education.

But the over-all impress on modern Hindu Society and as a whole in the field of religion has been far more marked in the case of Sri Ramakrishna, Sri Aurobindo Ghosh and others, apart from Mahātmā Gāndhi who is a class by himself. Swāmiji's emphasis on rejection more than on acceptance and accretion which had kept afloat the Hindu ethos for several millennia ultimately led to the failure and undoing of the Samāj. Hinduism as a "fixed," Aryā religion like Islām and Christianity, failed to negate and evercome its entire catholic past.

The Aryā Samāj later split into two factions—the college party (meat-eating and dedicated to modern education, banking and industry) and the (vegetarian) Gurukul party (emphasising traditional instruction and life-style). The former has been responsible for spreading a network of schools and colleges in the Panjāb and a little outside as well. Their number never large (in 1901, they were 92000), is now fast

* The efforts of Bhāi Gurmukh Singh enlisted the sympathy and support of such influential Sikh personalities as (Sir) Bābā Khem Singh Bedi, (Sir) Attar Singh, Rais of Bhadaur, the Rājā Sāhib of Nābhā, the Rājā Sāhib of Faridkot,

Inspired by the new wave, Gyān Singh, a Nirmalā Sikh, prepared and published in Panjābi *Twārikh Guru Khālsā* and *Panth Parkāsh* (a history of the Sikhs in prose and verse) and, Pandit Tārā Singh Narotam, the first-ever dictionary in Panjābi of the Guru Granth Sāhib.

Bhāi Kaur Singh and Bhāi Vir Singh* founded the Khālsā Tract Society.

For some time, the two Singh Sabhās at Lāhore and Amritsar worked harmoniously with each other. The one at Lāhore had in fact got itself affiliated to the parent-body at Amritsar and a common general committee had been formed in 1880 and a common charter of programme, as detailed before, was issued. The ideals and functions of the two were also the same. In 1883, the parent affiliating body at Amritsar came to be known as *Khālsā Diwān*. Both had presented a common address to the Viceroy, Lord Rippon, in November of the same year at Lāhore. In 1882, they had jointly made a strong representation signed by thousands of Sikhs to Mr. Hunter, President of the Education Commission at Simlā, to introduce Panjābi in the Gurmukhi characters in the primary village schools. Many schools were founded by common efforts. Later, a common representation was made to the Panjāb Governor seeking his patronage to

---

F. N. Contd.

Sardār Jagat Singh, pleader, Diwān Bootā Singh, Sardār Mihān Singh, Sardār Mehar Singh Chāwlā, Dr. Jai Singh, and many others.

A net-work of Singh Sabhās spread throughout the country and soon 115 such centres were opened in the Panjāb.

* Bhāi Vir Singh (1872-1956), the Saint-poet, served the movement powerfully through his weekly organ, "*The Khālsā Samāchār*", and the numerous pamphlets (later published also in book-form), a *Kosh* (dictionary in Panjābi of the Guru Granth's vocabulary); an edited version of the *Gur Partāp Surya Granth or Suraj Parkāsh* (of Bhāi Santokh Singh), various novels on the themes of Sikh-Moghal struggle (though never as to arouse anti-Muslim feeling like Sundri, Bijai Singh, Satwant Kaur) or on Sikh doctrine like Bābā Naudh Singh and books of poems especially *Rānā Surat Singh, Lahrān de hār, Bijlian de-hār etc.* He also brought the poet Puran Singh (1882-1931), who had turned a Vedantist *Sanyāsin* in Japan, where he was studying industrial chemistry, back to the Sikh fold and inspired him on the same lines. He in his masterly poetic and prose creations has even excelled the master, as in *Khulē Maidān* and *Khulē Lekh*.

establish a Sikh college at Lāhore or Amritsar.* But, as time passed, fundamental differences came to the surface over doctrinal matters.

Bābā Khem Singh Bedi,† supported by Rājā Bikram Singh of Faridkot and a few other notables, encouraged his worship as a guru. This was opposed vigorously by Bhāi Gurmukh Singh and Bhāi Dit Singh, both belonging to the Lāhore Singh Sabhā.

They decried the efforts of the Bābā to merge the Sikh entity into Hinduism by reviving Brāhmanic rituals and caste, and

---

* A Khālsā college was set up in Amritsar in 1892 under almost British patronage and management. It remained the premier Sikh institution for half a century thereafter. The fight for transfer of management and staff from European to Sikh hands became a part of the country's struggle for freedom. Now-a-days, the Sikhs manage 88 colleges, mostly in Panjab, besides hundreds of high schools. Most of the students are, however, not Sikh, and in the recruitment of staff also no discrimination is practised against non-Sikhs. They have about 20 colleges outside the Panjāb, as in Bombay, Madrās, Delhi etc., though the partisan way in which some of them are managed leaves much to be desired. The staff is divided as much as the managements into factions and this leads often to bitter feuds and frequent change of hands, amidst shameless slogan-shouting and blackmail, and even litigation. The Hindu (particularly Samāj) institutions are comparatively better-run, though the Christian institutions in this respect are the best-managed, better even than the Govt-run institutions.

† Born in 1832, in the house of S. Attar Singh Bedi, at Una, (in the distt. of Hoshiārpur) and a great grandson of Bābā Sāhib Singh Bedi, he was a great friend of the British Govt. His Jāgir was, therefore, continued after the annexation of the Panjāb. In 1857 too, he was of much use to the Govt. and was later awarded large tracts of land in the district of Montgomery. Through his mistionary activities, he gathered a large following in Pothohār (which even extended right upto Kābul) and made Kallar in the distt of Rawalpindi his Head-quarters. However, his worship as Guru was opposed by the orthodox Sikhs. But his acceptance of the Brahmanic ritual also endeared him to the Hindus among whom he attracted a large following as well. He opened many women's educational institutions, though female education was not much encouraged in those days. He helped develop the newly-formed district of Montgomery. Due to his vast influence, he was knighted and was nominated member of the Council of States. He died in 1904, leaving four sons, including (Sir) Bābā Gurbakhsh Singh of Kallar. Their progeny have been extremely successful as colonisers, especially in Montgomery. Some of them like Tikkā Surinder Singh for a time also performed missionary duties; others who like Tikkā Jagjit Singh and Kanwar Mahinder Singh Bedi, sons of another brother, Bābā Hardit Singh, joined judicial or administrative services rose to high positions in Government. But, the new generation seems to have lost interest in the Sikh missionary activities,

even idol-worship (in the precincts of the golden temple) against which even the new revivalist movements among the Hindus themselves were bitterly opposed. Differences arose also over integrating the new converts from any religion, including Islām, and the untouchable classes, as the Gurus had enjoined. To this, strong objection was taken by the Amritsar party, led by Bābā Khem Singh and Rājā Bikram Singh.

Being very loyal to the British Govt., they were supported by all those who tried to be in the good books of the *feringis*. With the result that, in 1886, a separate body called the Lāhore Khālsā Diwān came into being, under Sir Attar Singh of Bhadaur. Matters came to a head, and at a meeting of the supporters of Bābā Khem Singh Bedi from all over the Panjāb, which met in Faridkot in 1887, a resolution was passed that "unless Bhāi Gurmukh Singh* begged forgiveness, he should be kept away from the Singh Sabhā and the Khālsā Diwān." This was signed by Bābā Khem Singh, Bābā Sumer Singh, Mahant of Patnā, Rājā Sāhib of Faridkot,‡ Bābā Ude Singh (an employee of Faridkot) and Bhāi Sant Singh Gyāni of Kapurthalā etc. Later, it was got endorsed by the Singh Sabhā of Amritsar on which were appended the signatures, among others, of Sardār Kāhan Singh Majithiā, Dr. Charan Singh (father

* Born in a family of modest means, Bhāi Gurmukh Singh, after graduation, joined as an Asstt. Professor at the Oriental College, Lāhore, but spent most of his time in the propagation of his religion, shorn of superstition and ritual and purged of extraneous influences. He was the soul of the Singh Sabhā movement, and started the first Panjābi weekly and monthly. He fought against the onslaught of Christianity as much as Brahmanism and met the attacks of the Āryā Samāj through argument and discussion. But when he trod on the toes of the powerful vested interests of certain leaders of his own community in the interests of the true doctrine, he wae ex-communicated. He died on Sept. 24, 1898.

‡ Rājā Bikram Singh of Faridkot (1842-1892) was a great supporter of the Singh Sabhā movement. But his name will be remembered more for the material help he gave for the first complete translation in Panjābi of the Sikh Scripture. He collected over five years a bevy of well-known Gyānis from all over. The persons who contributed to this work were Mahant Sumer Singh of Patnā, Giāni Badan Singh of Amritsar, Giāni Sant Singh of Kapurthalā, Pt. Bālak Rām, Pt. Hamir Singh and Ladhā Singh. But, differences of opinion were so violent that it cuuld not be published during the life time of Rājā Bikram Singh. Known as *Faridkoti Teekā*, it is, however, a very involved translation, the translated version becoming often times more difficult to follow than the original script. The enlightenment of modern scholarship being not available in those days, the translation leans heavily on the Vedāntic inspiration of the traditional Gyānis.

of Bhāi Vir Singh) and Bhāi Sardul Singh Gyāni as well. The last-named as well as Bhāi Sant Singh Gyāni were well-known traditional interpreters of the Sikh Scriptures.

A virulent campaign was started against Bhāi Gurmukh Singh for no other fault than that he wanted to see his faith purged of contradictory (and vicious) outside influences, an objective to further which the whole movement had been started. But, it appears, the feudal Sardārs as well as the religion-hawking Bābās, both, were scared out of their wits by the growing popularity of Professor Gurmukh Singh at their cost. Their vested interests were endangered if they allowed him (or Dit Singh)* to propagate any more the true doctrines of the faith.

A *Hukamnāmā* was, therefore, got issued from the *Akāl Takht* at Amritsar (the highest seat of Sikh religious authority), which was under the control of the loyalists and the traditionalists, to ex-communicate Bhāi Gurmukh Singh, and to forbid his *Ardāsā* (prayerful offerings) being accepted at the *Akāl Takht* or in any Gurdwārā. Anyone flouting this injunction was warned that he too would be dealt with similarly.

It was dated 18 March, 1887, just about the time Mahārājā Dalip Singh had left Paris for Russia. Later, from Russia on June 20, 1889, he had appealed to his community to contribute one anna each (1/16th of a rupee) and the others one paisa (1/64th a rupee) to his war-chest for the re-conquest of the Panjāb, but he

---

* Son of a weaver and a Rāmdāsiā (Ravi-dāsiā or a leather-dresser) by birth, he was born in 1853 in village Anandpur-Kalaur in the state of Patiālā. Fond of learning, he left home to study with a Gulābdāsiā Sādhu, Sant Gurbakhsh Singh, and mastered grammar, Vedant, prosody etc. at a very young age. He also learnt Urdu. At first, he preached Vedānt and later the gospel of Ārya Samāj. After a time, he learnt Panjābi so well that he was employed in the Oriential College for its teaching, and inspired by Prof. Gurmukh Singh, devoted his whole time to the propagation of the Sikh faith. He wrote over two dozen books and pamphlets to dispel ignorance about the religion and history of his new faith. He wielded a very powerful pen and met forcefully the attacks of the Āryā Samāj. He edited the "*Khālsā*", a Panjābi weekly, for many years and shook the community out of its sloth and obscurantism. He died in 1901. Funds were sought to be raised to set up a memorial for him, but due to the paucity of response, (or of enthusiasm as time passed) a small sum only could be set apart to offer a prize in his name for a thesis on Sikh history and religion at the Khālsā college, Amritsar. The author had the honour of receiving this prize in 1933 at the age of 15.

was rebuffed by the same Sardārs.* But, as has been said, Bhāi Gurmukh Singh and his associates, however, set up a separate Khālsā Diwān at Lāhore with Sardār (Sir) Attar Singh of Bhadaur, as President, Bhāi Jawāhar Singh Kapur, its trustee, Sardār Dharam Singh of Gharjākh (Gujrānwālā) as Vice-President and Prof. Gurmukh Singh as General Secretary. The venerable Bhāi Dit Singh (then editor of the *Khālsā*) also stood by him. Most of the Singh Sabhās also supported the Lāhore Diwān. Bhāi Gurmukh Singh didnot lose heart and worked ceaselossly for another ten years till his death (Sept. 28, 1898).

Gyāni Dit Singh published extracts from his drama called "*Swapan Nātak*" (the dream play) in a four-page supplement to his paper on April 16,1887. This was considered to be a veiled attack on Bābā Khem Singh and his main supporter, the Rājā Sāhib of Faridkot. Bābā Ude Singh, a protege of Faridkot, took the matter to the court where Gyāni Dit Singh was fined Rs. 51/- for defamation, but was later acquitted by the Sessions court. Such was the confusion that the four seats of Sikh authority (at Amritsar, Patnā, Anandpur Sāhib and Nānder) also stood by Bābā Khem Singh. Gyāni Dit Singh (though supported by Bhāi Kāhan Singh of Nābhā, Sir Attar Singh of Bhadaur and the Mahārājā of Nabha) was equally condemned for his advocacy of the true Sikh cause, and was abandoned both by fortune and friends. He died a broken-hearted man on June 17, 1901.

* On Nov. 16,1888, a Sikh deputation called on the Viceroy, Lord Dufferin, in the Govt. House, Lāhore. It consisted of the representatives of the Khālsā Diwān, Amritsar, and the Singh Sabhās of Lāhore, Siālkot, Ferozepur, Tarn Tāran, Hoshiārpur, Ludhiānā, Patiālā, Ambālā, Simlā, Jullundur, Quettā etc. Detailing the "severe trials the Sikhs have passed through with success, 'they denied to recognise the pretentions of Dhuleep Singh." They even said, "comparing their present conditions with those under the Sikh rulers they have found that they are better treated by the English." They called Dhuleep Singh, "backed by Russian intrigue a false pretender" and pledged that they would die for their sovereign Empress, but they would never receive him (Dhuleep) as their ruler."

In reply to Dalip Singh's appeal for aid, the Sikhs of Gujrānwālā, his father's birth-place, speaking in the name of the whole *Khālsā Panth* wrote back to him on Oct 30,1889. They denounced not only his activities but also of Ranjit Singh "who had promoted the interests more of the Dogrās, Muslims and Hindus" than those of the Sikhs ! They also warned him to desist from his rebellion against the British, " otherwise no one will support you. Go back and ask forgiveness of the Queen, the Empress of India. Donot write to us any more if you cannot change you ways."

And it is the very people who were enjoying the *Jāgirs* given them by Mahārājā Ranjit Singh that were continued under the British !

As has been stated before, the British Governor General, Lord Canning, even in the midst of the Mutiny of 1857, had asked the Chief Commissioner of the Panjāb to get translated the Sikh Scripture into English. But, it was not till 1870 that a German missionary, Dr. Ernest Trumpp* could be found competent and willing enough to undertake the herculean task of rendering into a foreign tongue the 1430 pages of this religious classic, bristling with numerous hurdles, not only doctrinal (over which differences were acute) but also linguistic, as the Granth is not written in a single language or over a brief period of time. Denied the benefits of modern research and scholarship, no traditional Gyāni (whose help he sought) was of much assistance to him either.

The Govt. of India endowed Dr. Trumpp liberally for over seven years at Lāhore but, in 1877, he gave up in despair, after having completed only one-fourth of the Granth's trnslation. Though he called it "the treasury of the old Hindui dialects, he could "hardly expect many readers to be attracted to its study the less so as Sikhism is a waning religion." To cover up his own inefficiency in language studies and deficiencies in comparative religious scholarship, he called the Granth "incoherent and shallow in the extreme and couched in dark and perplexing language in order to cover these defects". The missionary in him had won over the pioneer and the seeker.

The British Govt. published this work, which at most places was so literally rendered as to make the superb poetic origial look ridiculous in translation, if not also unidiomatic – Sanskrit words were taken as of Persian or Arabic origin and vice-versa. No attempt was made to understand the profound religious spirit informing the

* Born in 1823, at Ilsfield, Wartemberg (Germany), he was educated at the University of Tubingen. In 1848, he passed the Theological examinations. He visited France, Italy and England in his quest for linguistic studies. In England, he privately taught Latin and German, but came back to Germany to enter the service of the German Missionary Society. In 1854, he visited Karāchi, to carry out linguistic researches. Here he also learnt Sindhi, Hindi and Sanskrit. He did not keep good health here, and after a year he went back to Europe. He visited Palestine for a brief time where he learnt Arabic. In 1862, he procceded to Peshāwar to learn Pashto and Persian for a year and a half. Later, he was appointed to the Chair of Semitic languages and Literature at the University of Munich. In 1883, he became blind and died in 1885.

Scriptures throughout. Contradictions were pointed out, but not resolved through deeper study and analysis. The Grammar of the Granth was then not available, nor an attempt was made by Trumpp to evolve one, after a serious research. Uncritically, the vocabulary and concepts were related to the ancient Hindu or Muslim doctrines and no effort was spared to denigrate a living, modern religion or its votaries. Therefore, the large-scale and fierce protest it evoked due to the hurt its publication had caused to the entire community, forced the Govt. to withdraw its circulation.

But, it also alerted the Sikhs not to take the modern world for granted. If they would not do the job themselves in order to project their true image, they could not accuse others if they misunderstood or misinterpreted both their religion and history. Much scholarship, literary craftsmanship and creative mind, as well as missionary zeal and ample means were necessary to accomplish this task. The Sikhs who were fighting at this time for their mere survival, were now confronted with the task of justifying their need to exist at all, as an independent religion.

After hectic search for a European scholar, Bhāi Gurmukh Singh presuaded in 1882, Mr. Max Arthur Macauliffe, an Irishman, then of the Indian Civil Service, and working as a Divisional Judge, to undertake the task on behalf of the Sikh community. Full support, both financial and moral, was promised him by the Khālsā Diwān and the Sikh princes. The Mahārājā of Nabhā spared the services of the venerable Sikh savant, Bhāi Kāhan Singh, his aide, (and later his Foreign Minister) to help Mr. Macauliffe understand the true import of the Guru's Word and to teach him Panjābi and Sikh lore. These were the days when the oldest Janam Sākhi (or the life-story of Guru Nānak), was discovered at the India

---

* Bhāi Kāhan Singh (1861-1938), a great scholar of Panjābi, Persian & Sanskrit and with good knowledge of English, was a formidable force in the Sikh religious affairs for half a century. His "*Gurmat Parbhākar*" (1898) and "*Gurmat Sudhākar* (1898) (quotations and commentary) and "*Ham Hindu Nahin*"(1897) (we are not Hindus) gave a new turn to the understanding of the Sikh faith in the true Singh Sabhā tradition. His four-volume Encyclopeadia of Sikh Religion (called *Gur Shabd Ratnakār Mahān Kosh*) (1930) is a work of high scholarship, research and dedication. His influence on Macauliffe and the Tikkā Sāhib (Ripudaman Singh) of Nābha of whom he was a tutor was very pronounced. He was titled by the British Govt. Mr. Macauliffe, as a token of gratitude for his assistance, bequeathed the copyright of his work to him,

office, London (which was a gift to them from an Oriental scholar, Mr. Colebrooke) and published at Lāhore and later at Amritsar. In 1893, Macauliffe resigned his job and over a period of 15 years, helped not only by Bhāi Kāhan Singh but also by other traditional well-known interpreters of the Sikh Scriptures, like Bhāis Dit Singh, Hazārā Singh, Sardul Singh and Sant Singh, completed his great work which was published under the title of "Sikh Religion" by the Oxford University Press, in 1909, in six volumes. However, these volumes contained only the life stories of the Sikh Gurus (and the *Bhaktas* whose work is included in the Adi Granth), based mostly on traditional sources and without an attempt at any critical analysis or careful historical research. The attempt to translate the Guru Granth in its entirety was also abandoned by Macauliffe, as it led to too much of contention and discord, both among the Gyānis and the then leaders of the community, mostly belonging to the Khālsā Diwān, Amritsar. Mr. Macauliffe, therefore, contented himself with translating only such passages which were relevant to the study of the life histories of the Gurus. The Sikhs at large were satisfied with the monumental efforts of Mr. Macauliffe, but his work neither answered the challenges of the modern times, nor the demands of modern scholarship. Still, his work, being the first of its kind and accepted by the Sikhs of those days commanded immense respect, more especially because it came from a European, and compensated the Sikhs for the hurt earlier caused by Dr. Trumpp and the Govt. of India, which had subsidised him and published his work.

But, it was attacked by others as too sectarian and parochial, meant to tear the Hindus from the Sikhs. Others criticised it as being too traditional and couched in an archaic language. Others that it had invented or circulated unauthorised stories in order to inculcate loyalist tendencies among the Sikhs towards the British Govt. But such, indeed, always is the lot of the pioneers.

Mr. Macauliffe was initially much lauded and boosted by Govt. as well as the Sikhs, but he died broken-hearted, forsaken at the hands of both. His lot, therefore, was no better on his death (see below) than that of Bhāi Gurmukh Singh or Dit Singh, the two other pioneers of Sikh resurgence and revival. *

* The Panjāb Govt. had recommended a measly award of £ 1000/—(Rs. 13000/—) to him. Lord Morley, the Secy of State, reduced it to Rs. 5000/—. Mr. Macauliffe rejected the offer. He said he had spent about Rs. 2 lakhs on the project from

There were several other movements of reform in the country, like the all-embracing Brahmo Samāj and the atheistic Dev Samāj, but their influence was minimal, except for the fact that a scion of the Majithia family, Sardār Dyāl Singh (son of Sardār Lehnā Singh Majithiā and who took a leading part also in the nationalist movement) became an adherent of the Brahmo Samāj and gave away to them his money in Trust to found an English language newspaper, The Tribune, a college and a Library, all at Lāhore. The rise of the Rāmākrisha Mission in Bengal, so powerfully advocated by Swāmi Vivekānanda abroad as well as in India (he also came to the Panjāb), of the Theosophical Society (which, under Alcott and Annie-Besant with its HQs in Adyar, Madras, attracted an influential section of the Hindu intelligentsia) left the Sikhs unaffected by and large. However, the esoteric Radhasoami Satsang, founded at Beas (Amritsar) by Bābā Jaimāl Singh, but reinforced and strengthened by Bābā Sāwan Singh and the present head, Mahārāj Charan Singh, during the three quarters of the present century, and based on a mystic interpretation mainly of the Guru-Granth, has continued to attract both a large number of the Sikh masses and the select intelligentsia, besides the Hindus and a section

F.N. Contd.

his own resources. It appears from Macauliffe's letter to Bhagat Lakshman Singh (Sept. 7, 1912) that a lobby had started working against him (and the Sikhs) in the Govt. The Govt. was possibly annoyed over the rising anti-British agitation among the Sikhs. The Sikh princes behaved in an equally stingey manner. What is worse, the Sikh Educational Conference, presided over by Sir Sunder Singh Majithiā at Rāwalpindi, refused to pass a resolution endorsing or appreciaring his work, due to some personal pique (Macauliffe, according to Bhagat Lakshman Singh, who wept as he narrated this story to the author in 1940, had written a parody about the great Sardārs of Amritsar, on account of their apathy towards his work). Bhagat Lakshman Singh quoted Mr. Macauliffe as saying that as the Chief Khālsa Diwān wanted itself to get the Adi Granth translated into English, they had become jealous of Mr. Macauliffe's efforts. But when he died (March 15, 1913) the same Sikh Conference held at Ambālā that year after some opposition, passed a resolution appreciating his great services to the cause of Sikh religion ! But when Bhagat Lakshman Singh appealed for funds to raise a suitabl memorial in his honour, only a small sum of Rs. 3245/—could be collected and with its interest a "Macauliffe Memorial gold medal" was instituted to be awarded each year to the best student in Sikh theology and history at the Khālsā College, Amritsar, which was unclaimed by Sikh scholars for long years. The present author received this medal at the age of 16 (in 1934), while an intermediate student at this great Sikh institution.

of other religious adherents as well from both within India and abroad.*

With the death of the most influential workers of the Singh Sabhā, like Sir Attar Singh of Bhadaur (1896), Bhāi Gurmukh Singh, (1898), Rājā Bikram Singh of Faridkot (1898) and Bhāi Dit Singh (1901), the leadership of the Sikhs, both religious and secular, came into the hands of the Chief Khālsā Diwān, founded at Amritsar on No. 10, 1901, but it was not till a year later that it was given a constitution. Its first function was held on Oct 30, 1902. Only 29 Singh Sabhās got themselves affiliated to it and with 47 other nominated members, they constituted the new body and the Khālsā Diwān at Lāhore became extinct by 1904 and its spokesman, *The Khālsā*, stopped publication a year later. Its first President was Bhāi Sāhib Arjan Singh of Bāgrian, high priest of the Phulkian states, and its Secretary, Sardār (later Sir) Sunder Singh Majithiā. It was duly registered on July 9, 1904.

This body, powerfully supported by the ceaseless flow of Bhāi Vir Singh's zealous pen, the organisational ability of Sardār Tarlochan

---

* There are at present over 300 Rādhāsoami centres of the Beas Satsang in India and over 200 abroad. Thousands of people gather to hear their chrismatic Master, Mahārāj Charan Singh (born 1915), a lawyer and an agriculturist by profession, expound to them,through his moving discourses in their own chaste mother-tongue, how to get out of the shackles of their past Karma which is the source of their pain in this very life. Their technique is to concentrate on the Third Eye, midway between the two eye-brows, and not on any other of the six *Chakaras* (or lower centres of energy). They repeat the name of God (*Simran*), especially his True name ((*Sat-Nām*) rather than his derivative names, contemplate the Master's presence ((*Dhyan*) and seek to "hear" the Unstruck Melody (*Anhad Dhun*, within themselves. This enables them to vacate the lower pulls of the body and to enter into the fourth state of *Sahja and Anand* (Poise and Bliss).
The movement is extremely well-organised to receive and feed multitudes who muster to hear their revered Master in meditative silence for hours together. Being extremely solicitious of other faiths, they disparage no one and try to concentrate on their esoteric essence as the Muslim Sufis and the Sikh and Hindu Saints do. They are strict vegetarians and teetotallers and keep out of politics of every kind. They have now nothing to do with the Rādhāsoamis of the Dyāl Bagh, Agrā, though their first Master, a professional soldier, was initiated into the order by them. The Beas Satsang is also called *Sant-Mat* (or the Way of the Saints) and its Masters have invariably worn the Sikh form. The Rādhā Soami cult has nothing to do with the Krishna worship. Rādhā stands for the human soul and Soāmi for the Oversoul into which it has to merge. Good, honest, creative living is emphasised in the household and withdrawal from the world is not encouraged.

Singh, an economist, (who founded the Panjāb and Sind Bank at Amritsar which now has 500 branches all over India mostly opened after the Partition under the progressive chairmanship of Sardār Inderjeet Singh), the zeal and dedicated scholarship of Bhāi Jodh Singh, the patriotic fervour of Sardār Harbans Singh Attariwālā and many others led the Sikhs atleast for two decades (1901-1920) as their unchallenged organisation. Its Sikh Educational Conference (founded 1908), through its annual conferences spread a network of modern education among the Sikhs. A Khālsā College was founded at Amritsar, in 1892, under British management (and supported by the Sikh States), but through the inspiration of the leaders of both the Khālsā Diwāns at Lāhore and Amritsar, also passed into their hands after an agitation, as time passed.

Their political loyalties were basically with the British Govt., though their leaders, especially after the 1907 agrarian agitation of the Sikhs under Ajit Singh, as we shall see later on, were never wholly trusted. Nor was their own agitation for the transfer of the control of the Khālsā College, Amritsar, to Sikh hands taken to kindly by the Govt. However, what Rājā Rām Mohan Roy on the one hand and Sir Sayyad Ahmad on the other did for the spread of liberal education coupled with religious instruction and fight for communal rights for Hindus and Muslims respectively, the trio (Sir Sunder Singh,‡ Bhāi Vir Singh and Bhāi Jodh Singh)† accomplished for the Sikhs in the two decades before the Akāli movement of the twenties,

‡ Born 1872, and belonging to the well-known Majithiā family which had served during the Sikh regime with distinction, this rich land-owner & sugar baron was a great force in Sikh affairs for about forty years (1901—1941). He was a member of the Panjāb & Imperial Councils for long & a Minister in Panjāb till his death (1941) for about two decades. He was leader of the Chief Khālsā Diwān & its President for many years. He later built a Khālsā Nationalist Party in 1935 & fought general elections in 1937 on its ticket.

† Born 1882, at Ghungrilā (distt. Rawalpindi), Bhāi Jodh Singh, Professor of Mathematics and Sikh Divinity, later became the Principal of the Khālsā College, Amritsar and the first Vice-Chancellor of the Panjabi University, Patiālā. His written contribution is confined to his excellent *expose* of the Guru's doctrine in *Gurmat Nirnaya, Bhagat Bāni* etc. only, but he was deeply involved otherwise also in Sikh religious affairs (as an orthodox) and in political affairs (as a moderate). He was titled bot' 'he British and Congress Govts., and was an eminent member of the Panjāb His solid crusading work for the spread of Sikhism and Panjābi lang esteemed.

when the leadership of the Sikhs passed into the hands of the Akālis who bacame for another twenty years the firm allies of the nationalist movement led by Gāndhi and Nehru. Earlier, the Government had taken a keen interest in the movement of Sikh revival. The Panjāb Governor's aide, Sir Robert Egerton (later himself Governor) became a patron of the Lāhore Singh Sabhā in 1876. And on Oct 23, 1890, the Viceroy, Lord Lansdowne, had said publicly at Patiālā:—"The Govt. of India is sympathetic to this (Singh Sabhā) movement". But, by 1905, this honeymoon was over. The Govt. had become suspicious of the Sikhs and transferred their sympathies, as we shall see, to the Muslims in an unmistakable manner.

CHAPTER XXVI

THE SIKHS FIGHT FOR INDIA'S FREEDOM

(1900—1947)

After the Mutiny of 1857, the consolidation of the British rāj in India was complete, But, the Govt. of India had no worthwhile means to improve the economic lot of the people. The famines of the Panjāb (1861), Orissā (1865), South India (1876-77), Kashmir (1878), and the severest of all which spread throughout India from 1896 to 1900 took a huge toll of life. Unless therefore some developmental projects were initiated at Government's own initiative even by raising public loans, the governance of the country was neither profitable nor possible. It is comparatively easy to conquer a country, but harder by far to keep it after a time, without the goodwill of the people at large.

Agriculture, unless more canals were dug, was becoming static and even unproductive. The rising population in times of peace couldnot simply be wiped out through recurring famines and diseases like cholera, plague, tubercolosis, malaria and small-pox. The cash-crops, while bringing in more money, reduced the availability of food. The near duty-free English cloth yielded high profits for Lancashire, but impoverished the rural India where ninety percent of the people lived. The growing indigenous textile mills also justly felt discriminated against. The unification of the country led to the abolition of internal tolls, thus reducing appreciably the incomes of both the central and the provincial governments.

In the first millineum of the Christian era, Indians had ventured out not only to propagate their religion and culture, but also to colonise, especially in South East Asia, Indo-China and Indonesia. But, with the coming of the Afghāns and the Moghals, the resistance and the fight for survival had consumed all their energy and resources, and such was now the dread of venturing out that it became a religious curse to travel overseas for a people who once traded with Greece and Rome, the Arab world and Africa, Central Asia and China, and even with South America. All that was now a past story. With the abolition of slavery by an Act of British Parliament, early in the nineteenth century, and the refusal of the African slaves to work as free labour, indentured labour (on contract for five to seven years) was recruited (from 1837 onwards to 1915) from Bihar and eastern U.P. to work on the sugar-farms of their British masters in Mauritius, Fiji, Trinidad, Jamaica and British Guiana or to work otherwise as labourers, petty contractors and clerks in South Africa (paricularly Natāl), Kenya, Uganda, Tanzania, Malāyā, Singapore and Hongkong. Their working and living conditions were miserable, their wages low. they couldont carry their families along, thus creating bitterness in their minds as much as among their people back home. The South Indians, mostly Tamils, ventured out to nearby Malaya (mostly as labourers on rubber estates) and Singapore. So also the Sikhs. They went out either as carpenters, masons or clerks as in East Africa or as policemen or watchmen as in Malaya, Hongkong and Singapore. The Gujaratis and Sindhis set out on their own as small traders or bankers. About 3.5 million Indians had settled abroad in about a century (1837-1915). The Sikhs also started settling down as farm-hands on the Pacific Coast of America and Canada, mostly around California and Vancouver.

They not only wrote back about their own humiliating plight, but also about the dignity of a free people, and even more more about the affluence of the West, built mostly on the economic exploitation of their colonies in Asia, Africa and Latin America, through manipulation of tariffs, discriminatory laws, and condemning the colonies to a low level of agricultural economy inorder to promote their own industrial and military growth. But, the internal economic tensions and rivalries between the industrial giants of the West, particularly between Germany and England and America, and England and Russia and England and France, were also being brought to light for the first time in India. And the example of Japan, which had no raw materials of its own like coal, iron-ore or cotton, competing with the West in industry and the Western war-machine,was being quoted again and again. And, had not Japan, an Asian country, defeated a mighty European power, Russia, in 1904-1905 ?

The more the liberal education and ideas of the West spead through the efforts of Govt., and the various denominational communities, particularly Christians, Arya Samājists and the Sikhs, the more the discontent spread. The University of the Panjāb was also founded in 1882. An Arts college (Mayo School of Art) and a Panjāb Chiefs' College for the instruction of the sons of the feudal gentry had also been started. The Indian Press had begun to voice the grievances of the people (though newspapers published even in Calcutta were not more than 600 to 1000 copies in circulation.) The Indian elite clamoured for the political rights for their people, under their own leadership. Inspite of the passage of the Indian Councils Act of 1861 (which was applied to the Panjab only in 1897), and Lord Rippon's efforts to hand over municipal administration largely to Indian hands, the Indian National Congress, (founded in 1885 by an Englishman, A. O. Hume) became an ever-growing platform for the Indians to register their protest against the growing distress and unemployment among the rural areas and the discrimination against Indian industry. The monopoly of higher civil services by the British was also a thorn in the side of the educated elite. The protest against the denial in India of the political rights guaranteed at home was gathering more and more momentum. Also the transfer of the mechanised wing of the army and the higher military posts to Indians (then the close preserve of the British) was being more and more pressed.

After fifty years (and in some cases one hundred and fifty years as in Eastern, Southern and Western India) of the rule of the British, the glamorous veneer of the colonial masters had worn off. They had, instead of their earlier paternal attitude, become overbearing, distant, arrogant, unconcerned and even insulting in their behaviour.

At first, the Muslims felt deeply aggrieved over the success of the British in 1857, as they thought it was their (Muslim) empire which had been brought to a close. The privileged Muslims and Zamindārs and their numerous hangers-on, including religious leaders, and men of learning, had been deprived of their power and position. They had neither taken kindly to industry, nor to education, their ancestral occupations being either land-owning or army. The doors of the Army were almost closed on them, except in the Panjāb, where they had stood loyal to the British Govt. The Hindus, particularly the educated Hindus of Bengāl and Madrās, had come to monopolise all the junior civil services, displacing the privileged position of the Muslims at the imperial capital, which was Calcutta even after the Mutiny, till it was transferred in 1912 to Delhi. But, as the Hindus took to Western education and social and religious reformers like Rām Mohan Roy, Dibander Nāth Tagore, Surendra Nath Bannerjee, Rama Krishna Parmhansa and Vivekānanda shook them out of their lethargy, Bengal, followed by the industrialised Bombay and Poonā (once the seat of the Marāthā power) and the commercial Gujarāti classes (who suffered in competition with the West both in their internal and external trade), started having reservations about the imperial rule. And they took the lead in Home Rule agitations. The Presidencies of Bengāl and Bombay became the nerve-centres of the revolutionary political change, alongwith artistic, spiritual and educational movements. The abolition of *Sattee* and *Thugee* was now not enough, nor the laws about widow remarriage. The establishment of High Courts had made justice very costly and cumbersome and it was the richer and tougher clients who benefitted from them or the lawyers, well-versed in the art of wearing down the prosecution or the defence. The introduction of the new system of medicine, more reliable but also far more expensive, led to the emergence of an affluent class of medical consultants and physicians. To these two—the lawyers and the doctors—their easy and abundant money brought political ambition in its wake, to the detriment of the old ruling class of feudal landlords.

The British had to look around for support, and they came to the conclusion, as any colonial power would in similar circumstances, that on the one hand the Panjāb should be made more affluent and dependable being now the sword-arm of India, and secondly the distrust of the Muslims, who had settled down completely in the ways of peace and loyalty, should be abandoned and they should be encouraged to fight the growing menace of what practically seemed to be Hindu nationalism, though the fight was conducted in the name of all Indians.

The Sikhs had to be placated similarly, if they contiuned to toe the British line. If not, they should also be sacrificed in view of their limited numbers and their concentration only in the Central districts of the Panjāb.

So, while a network of telegraph and railways was spread out in the whole country, including the Panjāb, attention was paid even more to the reclamation of arid lands in this border state. Between 1878, and 1918, the irrigated area increased four-fold. In 1861, the upper Bāri Doāb canal was inaugurated to bring agricultural affluence to the Central districts of Amritsar and Lahore. In 1870, work was started on the Sirhind canal and this 3700 mile-long network was completed in 1882. In 1871, the Western Jamna canal started irrigating the districts of Rohtak, Hissār, Karnāl, and Ambālā, the home of the war-like Hindu Jāts, who were the leaders of the 1857 mutiny. In 1892, a million new acres were brought under the plough with the canals taken out from the Chenāb. The waters of Jehlum were similarly harnessed and the desert of Thal was reclaimed which included Shahpur and Sargodha. From 1905 to 1915, the prosperous district of Montgomery, like Lyallpur before since 1892, (both named after the British Governors of the Panjāb) came into being, through the digging of more canals, and by feeding the waters of the Rāvi with those of the Jehlum and the Chenāb.

The outlay of 70-lakh Pounds Sterling on the last project was more than compensated. The yearly revenue-yield was about one third of the investments. The Panjāb became not only the sword-arm but also the granary of India. Food began to be exported for the first time. The Panjāb exported during 1920-21 about 13 crores worth of foodgrains. 5000 miles of railways were laid, and six river-beds spanned. The Sikhs of the district of Ludhiana, Amritsar and particularly of Ferozepur (the main recruiting centres for the army) were persuaded to settle on these lands, alloted at nominal costs of 6 to 9 rupees per acre or free upto 16 acres. Lands were available in any measure, even upto 500 acres, the costs being only Rs. 10 to 20 per acre, depending upon its location. Most of the Jāts, who profitted from this bonanza, were from the Mālwā region. The price of land rose about forty times in a few years. The Sikhs also formed about 25% of the Indian army from the Panjāb (50% being Muslims). By the time of the first world war (1914-18), this proportion became stabilised at the All-India level. Most of the recruits were Jāts and as they owned the newly-broken lands also, they became a privileged class among the Sikhs. The Jāts who were considered low-born and uncouth pariahs, alongwith the untouchables (with jokes abounding about their ignorance, crudity and ferocity) as is evident from the story of Shivajee, (no Brāhmin was prepared to apply *tilak* on his forehead or read out the Vedas at the time of his coronation, as he was the son of a farmer), due to the revolution of Guru Gobind Singh had become the pride of the whole nation. Even the untouchable Sikh Mazhabis (scavengers) were also recruited to the army, and they proved their mettle on the battlefield. The *chamārs* (carters of carrion) had also abandoned their old professions and either became helpers on the farms and in the households or recruited themselves as soldiers. This gave them a new standing in society. After all, the majority of the Sikhs who had fought under Guru Gobind Singh and Bandā Bahādur were also men of the lower castes and their first King, Sardār Jassā Singh was an Ahluwāliā, or a Kalāi (distiller) by ancestory, then considered to be not a very respectable profession. Unless human dignity and social pride of an individual is guaranteed by a society, no amount of economic affluence or political authority can bring him the spiritual fulfilment and inner confidence in the meaning of human birth.

But, the new economic revolution on the farms being confined only to the privileged classes, created new stresses in the society. Land became so expensive that it became beyond the reach of the actual tiller of the soil. More and more people became tenants of land or the landless labour working on the farms without owning them. The yields on the farms brought in its train gradual increases in the land-revenue (to be paid in cash) and farm inputs. Life became a little more easy and luxurious (with the drink-habit thrown in for a good measure or opium as in the districts of Ferozepur and Ludhiana). With the 'nose' (symbolic of Jāt honour) to be kept, a "battle of noses" in the villages ruined the peasantry, spending recklessly on marriages and other ceremonies. There was no way out but to borrow from the village Baniā (usurer) who was only too willing to lend at excessive rates of interest, mortgaging land, houses, cattle and even household goods of the farmer, who being assured of good crops never cared for these nice little calculations which he left to the care of the good old *Sāhukār*.

As no income tax was levied on farm-incomes, the differences in income and life-style between the neo-rich land-owing farmers and their tenants, the actual tillers, grew proportionately. The banking facilities were neither provided nor sought for by the farmer and surplus money in the hands of the rich was either spent recklessly on ceremonies and high living or buried underground, as of old. Expensive and long drawn-out litigation over land-ownership and increasing crime over *zar* (money) *zoru* (woman) and *zamin* (land), all symbols of prestige, ruined the peasantry and enriched the lawyers or the court officials. Women being fewer than men among the Jāts (due to their ancestral habit of female infanticide) now became the prime object of possession and money changed hands to "buy" or procure women at any expense or by any means. Murder to possess a woman or land became an object of pride. So also, as time passed, the murder of the extortionist village *bania.* The rampant corruption in the police force, the revenue office and the lower courts, ended the illusions of the lawfulness of the Govt. The Govt., alarmed at this social distress, enacted the Land Alienation Act (1900), to protect the farmer from the usurer. His land, cattle or household goods could no longer be attached to satisfy his debts. But, another clause which separated permanently the Jāt from the so-called non-agriculturist castes (Khatris, Aroras, Banias and to some extent Brahmins etc., even if they owned lands and lived off them), forbade the latter to buy land from the former (except by permission of authority which was seldom given). The army service had already been reserved for the Jāt. A Jāt money-lender was protected, but not a Khatri landlord. The revolution that the Gurus had brought about over a period of four centuries was now put in reverse gear and undone by the good old Lord Curzon with a single stroke of the pen. It did not affect the Hindu Jats, nor the Muslims so much as the Sikhs. The Hindu observed the caste meticulously anyhow, the Muslim did not (except on the basis of status). But the Sikhs, all of whose Gurus came from the Khatris, and some of the best commercial and intellectual classes, were divided all along the line. The matrimonial alliances, already rare, became rarer still, new tensions were formed and fostered by vested interests, political rivalries were born and hardened and even after independence we are still reaping their bitter fruits. The Jāt Hindus and Muslims forged a common political platform with the Jāt Sikhs, against non-Jat Hindus, Sikhs and Scheduled castes, though the last three combined numerically made a formidable force. (In the present Panjāb, they constitute about 70%).

The Govt. also faulted in another way. From 1887, the famine-ridden areas of the East Panjāb (now Haryana) were mostly negelcted, the main emphasis being on the development of the Muslim West Panjāb, in whose prosperity the Sikh Jāt participated only through migration and uprooting from the ancestral homes, thus further reducing their numerical strength in the Central regions. The Co-operative Credit Societies Act, passed in 1904, to advance credit on lower rate of interest, also helped only the richer and the well-educated landlords; also the opening of agricultural colleges for research and model-farms for demonstrations.

The partition of Bengal, in 1905, separating the Muslim-majority area from the Hindu-dominated region, including Calcutta, added fuel to the fire. The desire was to keep in check the rising tide of Indian nationalism in Bengal and to insulate the Muslims against it. In Bombay, the moderate politics (of petitions and prayers) led by Ranade, Gokhale and Dadabhoy Nāroji was giving place to Tilak's dynamic slogan: "*Swarāj is our birth right, and we shall have it.*" In the Panjāb, the Colonisation Act (1907), which increased both the land-revenue and the water rates in the canal-irrigated areas, was the last straw on the camel's back. The price-rise, unprecedented during the last 50 years, also made a significant contribution. The Panjāb, which was the last to fall to the British, was also the first to rise against them in full fury.

Riots started in protest at Lāhore and Rāwalpindi. Agrarian unrest was the primary cause which led to the famous song of Bānkē Dyāl :—"*pagri sambhāl Jatā, pagri sambhāl oē. Lut liā māl terā hālon behāl oē* ("Assemble your turban, the symbol of your honour, O Jāts, for all your wealth has been drained by the *feringi* to your ruin.) The leaders of the movement were Sardār Ajit Singh, a Jāt of Lyallpur, and Lālā Lājpat Rāi, a lawyer of Lāhore. Both were expelled on May 9, 1907, from the country, under an old Bengāl Regulation Act of 1818, and imprisoned in Mandlay (Burmā). Both were released two years later. Ajit Singh left for abroad in 1909 and landed in Rio-de Jeneru (Angentina) travelling via Irān, Paris, Geneva etc. In 1914, he aligned himself with the Ghadar (Revolutionary) party of San-Francisco (U. S.A.). Lālā Lājpat Rāi, alongwith Bhāi Parmānand, a descendant of Bhāi Mati Das (and then a Professor at the D.A.V. College, Lāhore), organised the students and other youths in a revolutionary movement in India.

Bhāi Parmānand was sentenced to death in 1915, for his alleged part in the Lāhore riots of the same year, but this sentence was later commuted. Another academically highly brilliant Panjābi, Lālā Hardyāl, M.A., a student of the Gurukal Kāngri and later in England (who was considered to be a mathematical wizard and had a prodigious memory) left his studies to join Lālā Lājpat Rāi at Lāhore, in 1908. Later in the same year, he again left for Europe and started a paper, *Bande Mātram*, from England. He visited India again in 1910, founded a Bhārat Naujwān (youth) Sabhā (Association) along with Dinā Nāth, a Panjābi, and Chatterjee, a Bengāli. Entrusting the work of the Sabhā to Lālā Amir Chand, a Panjābi teacher of Delhi, he left for California in 1911, and became the literary spokesman of the Sikh settlers who were busy consolidating their own *Ghadar* (Revolutionary) Party there.* There were by this time about 16,000 Indians settled in California, and 4000 in Canada (most of them being Sikhs and ex-soldiers). In the beginning, they went in either as students or worked to earn as farmhands, especially as fruit pickers, on a daily wage of one to 1½ dollar (Rs. 3 to Rs. 4½). The American Govt., supported by their industry, encouraged this immigration. Some American industrialists had put up free hostels for them and also offered them scholarships or work in their factories. Having themselves won their freedom from the British, they were sympathetic to Indian aspirations also. The Press published Indian grievances and the visits of Swāmi Vivekānand from Bengāl and Swāmi Rām Tirath from the Panjāb had further deepened their interest in the high culture and spiritual literature of India, to which they had already been introduced by their Philosophers like Emerson, Walt Whitman and Thoreau.

---

* Tārak Nāth Dās, a Bengāli student, had started publishing, since 1909, his monthly magazine "*Free India*" managed by a patriotic exile from Bengāl, Surinder Mohan Bose. In 1909, he founded the "East India Association." In 1911, Mr. G.D. Kumar, a native of Bannu, and a teacher of Urdu and Hindi, migrated from Canada to settle in Seattle (Washingoton state) and joined the editorial staff of *Ghadar* (San-Francisco.)

On his illness, Lālā Hardyal was invited to edit the paper. He came in March 1913, along with Bhāi Parmānand and the Hindi Associations upto now scattered in three different places in the Oregon, Califorina and Washington states were headquartered in San Francisco. The earlier aims of industrial and agriculture development and education and ending of foreign exploitation in India gave place to one single aim of ending foreign rule through violent means and the formation of the *Ghadar* (Revolutionary) Party in America. The preachings of Lokmanya Tilak in Bombay, Lālā Lajpat Rai and Ajit Singh in Panjāb and the writings and speeches of Aurobindo Ghosh in Bengāl also turned the tide in favour of violence. The onset of

The *Ghadar party* (originally known as Hindu Association of the Pacific Coast) came into being at Astoria (Oregon), on April 21, 1913, through the efforts of the Oregon-based Bhāi (later Bābā) Sohan Singh Bhaknā, Bhāi Harnām Singh Tundilāt, Bhāi Udham Singh and Bhāi Ishar Singh, Pt. Kānshi Ram, & Lālā Rām Rakhā, with the help of the philosopher-litterateur, Lālā Hardyāl, Bhāi Parmānand, the revolutionary, and Mr. Jitendra Nāth "Lahiri", a post-graduate student from Calcuttā at the Berkeley University, California, and Mr. Barkatullāh. A *Ghadar Āshram* (also called *Yugantar Āshram*) was founded in San Francisco. Bhāis Jawālā Singh, Wasākhā Singh, Santokh Singh, Jagat Rām, Rur Singh and Kartār Singh (Latālā) also expressed their willingness to join. Kartār Singh Sarābhā, a student from the Panjāb, who was persuading the students on his own to strike for freedom, also joined in. A weekly journal, "*Ghadar*" (Revolutlon) was brought out on Nov. 1, 1913.

Headquartered in San-Francisco, the main aim of the organisation was to end British rule in India, through an armed revolution and to set up "a republican Govt. based on liberty and equality." Elected committees of Indian workers were affiliated to the Association. These were to be formed in every factory and gang. The subscription was one dollar a month. Religious discussions were banned, religion being considered strictly a personal affair. And in the matter of diet, no restrictions were to be enjoined, this also being a matter of habit. On an appeal being made for volunteers prepared to sacrifiee everything for the cause of the country, the first youngman to volunteer was Kartār Singh Sarābhā. And though there were only eight others to follow, the movement for revolutionary activities had begun.

To be called a Canadian or an American Sikh became in those days (and also much later) a badge of honour. Such a one was unmistakably considered to be wholly dedicated to the cause of India's revolution.

Branches were soon opened not only in America and Canada, but also in Shanghāi, Honkong, Phillipines, Thāiland (Siam) and

---

F. N. Contd.

recession in America and the increasing disputes (sometimes violent) between the American and Indian workers also led to a reappraisal of their earlier attitude. The Chinese and Japanese immigrants were helped by their countries' consulates but there was no one to protest on behalf of the Indians.

Pānāmā, where a considerable number of Panjābis (mostly Sikhs) had lately migrated.

Panjābi poems, written by Bhāi Bhagwān Singh, a Granthi at Hongkong who later shifted to Vancouver and from there to San-Francisco, inflamed the passions as nothing else could. Other popular poets also followed in his wake. One of the poems headed "*kill or die,*" reads :—

"*Let us kill the Whites; kill the wicked and tyrannous European. Do not leave any trace of him. Extirpate the whole nation.*

Set fire to all the churches. Kill European men as well as women. Show no mercy whatever. Flay them alive so that they remember for ages.

Fill the rivers with their dead. We'll even go to England shouting, 'Kill, kill, kill'".*

Training in arms was given to the select revolutionaries. But the resources were extremely limited. Hardly $ 10,000 a year were collected from all over the world, but mostly from America and Canada. But when came the time for the purchase of arms and their transportation to India, the immigrants helped out generously.

Three other factors, all wholly unexpected, happened at this time. One was the *Kāmāgātā Māru* episode to fire the imagination of the revolutionary youth everywhere and to inscribe on their minds a sense of deep hurt to their national pride. The other was the coming of the First World War (1914-1918) atleast 4 years earlier than the Ghadarites had visualised. Thirdly, the entire Indian leadership—Tilak, Gokhle, Gāndhi, Bipin Pal, Lājpat Rāi, had opted for total cooperation with the British. While the *Kāmāgātā Māru* episode inspired them to greater and earlier action against the British, the other two factors (besides some more reasons which we shall presently refer to) actively hindered and frustrated their plans.

The *Kāmāgātā Māru* was the name of the Japanese ship, which was chartered by Sardār (later known as Bābā) Gurdit Singh, a contractor from Sarhāli (Amritsar district) of the Punjāb, then working in Malāyā. The growing unemployment at home and the favourable (though highly exaggerated) reports reaching the Panjāb of high incomes earned by the immigrants in Canada and U.S.A.

* *The Role of the Ghadar Party,* by G.S. Deol, Pp. 75-76

persuaded many young persons in the Panjāb and the Panjābis in S. E. Asia and Hongkong still struggling to plant their feet abroad to migrate to Canada, a part of the British Commonwealth. Unfortunately for them, however, the Canadian Govt. under pressure possibly of the British Govt. (who saw in the immigrants a potential threat to their security both on account of the reports they sent back home of the far higher standards of living, and the need to bring about similar conditions in India under a Govt. of their own) changed the laws for entry into Canada. On May 9, 1910, the Canadian Govt. passed an Act making it lawful for the Canadian authorities to prevent the entry of any Asian into Canada. But the measure was directed solely against India. Next year (1911), 11,000 Chinese and about 3,000 Japanese were admitted into Canada as immigrants, but only one Indian. Indians protested to the Canadian Prime Minister and also agitated in London, but to no result. Two Societies, the "*Khālsā Diwān Society*" and the "United India League," were foremost in this agitation. Their joint deputation visited London, in May, 1913, but it did not move the British authorities.

To further tighten the regulations against the Indians, the Canadian law also provided that unless a ship came direct from the country of origin of the passenger and each passenger had, besides a ticket, cash worth $200 on his person, he would not be allowed entry. Indians could procure the money somehow, but they had no vessel sailing to Canada direct or under India's own flag. Bābā Gurdit Singh was approached by the Panjābis in Hongkong and also the immigrants in Canāda (who wanted to help their relations and friends to migrate) to charter a ship which he did at Hongkong. A concern known as "*Guru Nānak Steamship Company*" was registered with Gurdit Singh as its Mg. Director. He at first tried to charter the ship from Calcutta itself, but permission was refused by the Govt., so he had no option but to proceed to Hongkong. Here, he received expert legal advice in writing to the effect that there was no ban on the Indians travelling from there to Vancouver as potential immigrants. But soon thereafter, Bābā Gurdit Singh was arrested, his house searched, but nothing incriminating being found, he was released. However, this scared some of the would-be immigrants and instead of 500, the total capacity of the ship, Bābā Gurdit Singh could only get 376 passengers on board the ship, leaving Hongkong on April 4, 1914. The ship reached Vancouver (Canādā) on May 22, picking up passengers from Shanghāi, Moji (Jāpān) (where passengers from Manila also joined them) and Yokāhāmā (Jāpān).

But they were refused permission to land on Canadian soil by the immigration authorities. Everyone had fulfilled all the regulations then prevailing. About fifty of them were preachers, students or traders who were exempted from these regulations. Even they were not allowed to land. The ship was refused permission even to load or unload its cargo. Permission to seek legal advice or to meet their countrymen who had come to receive them at the port was also refused. Some Canadian immigrants formed a Shore Committee, & lodged a test case of Mansā Singh in the court, but it was dismissed. The Charter of the company was transferred to Indian settlers in Canada. They even paid the last instalment of $ 22000/-. But the question was not legal : there were political forces working behind the scene. The passengers on board fell short of provisions, medicines and even water. But, they were not allowed to buy them at the port. Gurdit Singh sent a wire to the King of England, after which certain facilities were allowed. Their cases, however, were decided against them, except in the case of Dr. Raghunāth, who brought the police against his own countrymen!* And so there was no choice but to return back home. But when they asked for provisions for the return-journey, even this request was not accepted on which they refused to set sail and locked up their Captain in his cabin.

The Canadian authorities sent out a boatload of policemen to surround the ship. They fired at the passengers without warning and the passengers, hungry and roused to anger, hit back with lumps of coal. The police later alleged that they had also been fired at. But while some of the policemen received minor injuries, one of the passengers had a pistol bullet lodged in his body. Another two or three were also hurt. They were willing to leave, but not without provisions, otherwise they said they would prefer to die.

* Another man working for the police was a Sikh, Belā Singh. an aide of William Hopkinson of the police deptt. The latter is said to have asked for a bribe from Bābā Gurdit Singh which he refused to pay. Hopkinson, therefore, became more bitter against his enterprise and thwarted every effort at a compromise. Two of the companions of Belā Singh were murdered, and three months after the departure of the ship, Hopkinson was also assasinated by Mewā Singh, a Sikh priest in Vancouver. Mewā Singh was hanged on Jan 11, 1915. His day of martyrdom is celebrated by Sikhs all over Canada to this day.

The Indians in Vancouver were naturally deeply agitated and resolved in a meeting at the Gurdwara that "if the ship was fired at, they would set fire to the city of Vancouver." On this, the Canadian Govt. changed its mind and stocked the ship with provisions for the return journey.

After being in the Canadian waters for 2 months, the ship *Kamāgātā Māru* sailed back (July 23) on its return journey to Calcuttā. Before they reached home, however, the revolutionaries of the Ghadar party, notably Bhāi Bhagwān Singh, had got them provided with 270 pistols at Yokohama, through Bābā Sohan Singh Bhaknā, who had also fired them with a new revolutionary zeal to strike for the country's freedom when back home. This fact getting known, the British authorities did not allow them to stop over at Hongkong or Singāpore. The ship moored at the Budge-Budge docks, 17 miles from Calcutta, on the forenoon of Sept 29.

The First World War having broken out (July 28), the Govt. didnot want to take any chances. The passengers had been thoroughly searched two days earlier at Kalpi, and all arms taken possession of, except those which were carefully concealed by the passengers. A special train was waiting for them to be taken to the Panjāb, but the proud Sikh men, though beaten, were not the ones to go back to their homes crestfallen and humiliated by defeat. They wanted to stay at Calcuttā to earn some money to be able to keep face with their families and co-villagers in the Panjāb. They, therefore, set out, in a procession, carrying the Sikh Holy Book and singing devotional hymns. The passengers were asked to return to the ship or board the train. But only six persons got into the train. Over 300 refused to obey this unjust and illegal order in their own land, and marched on. The police opened fire and eighteen innocent and travel-weary passengers fell dead. Some of the passengers attacked the police and killed three of their number. Thirty of them, including Bābā Gurdit Singh, escaped in the confusion that followed. Others were tracked down and arrested, tried and sentenced to various terms of imprisonment. Bābā Gurdit Singh offered himself for arrest, seven years later, in a large Sikh gathering at Nankānā Sāhib, having beaten all the resources of the police and the British Govt. Some of escapees joined the Ghadar workers in India.

This had roused the ire of the masses as much as of the nationalist forces in the country. But due to the onset of the war, no one was willing to strike on their behalf, except through mild public protests.

The Ghadarites who also timed their revolutionary activities in this period came to nothing. But, they made an honest and a determined effort to liberate their country, however innocent they were in their study of world-history and the forces at work against them at that time. They collected money, purchased arms, enlisted the sympathy of the German Consulates in the U.S.A. (and later also Kābul) and sent out bands of dedicated and idealistic youngmen like Sohan Singh Bhaknā, Kartār Singh Sarābhā, Parmā-nand of Jhānsi and others. They were fired by the patriotic feeling instilled in them by Barkatullāh, Giani Bhagwān Singh and Pt. Rām Chand. Most of them came with the sole idea of sacrifice for the honour of their motherland and its people. Their number, according to Lord Hārdinge, was no less than 7000. And, a large majority was of the immigrants from the Panjāb. A majority of them had seen army-life before and knew key-men in the armed forces in their state. It is here they first wanted to create a model revolution for others to follow, though the idea also was to create a "Free State of Kāshmir" alongwith it, by 1925, as it was thought feasible for the Muslim majority there to rebel against their Hindu ruler. But, Kāshmir could not claim their attention when they landed in India and they concentrated only on the Panjāb.

The Govt. was, however, closely watching their activities. They nabbed men of suspicious antecedents at the port of disembarkation itself. According to Sir Michael O' Dwyer, in four years' time (1914-1918), "out of the 8000 returning Indians, 4000 were interned and over 2500 restricted to their villages."*

However, as has been said, the revolt misfired. The reasons were many. Some of these were : the dates fixed for the outbreak of the revolt were changed frequently. The first date was Nov. 15, 1914, but the arms had not arrived. The contact men in various centres of the army either changed their minds, or contact couldnot be established with them at the given time as at the Mianmir

---

**The Role of the Ghadar Party* by G.S. Deol, P. 106.

(Lāhore) Cantonment to provide leadership. The leadership was too loud-mouthed and their activities were mostly an open book known to the police. Informers had been planted among them by the Govt. Disaffection was sought to be created in various centres like Tarn Tāran, Jullundur, Ferozepur, Ludhiana, Hoshiarpur, etc. but their efforts were not co-ordinated. The Govt. treasury was sought to be looted at Ferozeshah (the place where the Sikh army was treacherously led to defeat), but it misfired. Dacoities created a scare among the law-abiding citizens. Except for a few killings of policemen, lambadārs, Zaildārs, and police informers, the fire didnot spread out far. Even the support of the student community (except at Ludhiana) could not be enlisted, though Sant Randhir Singh of Nārangwal (Ludhiana) did get them the support of some villagers of his district. Dr. Mathra Singh tried to create a stir among the Afridi tribes, and Nidhan Singh in the areas of Rawalpindi, Jehlum and the vicinity of Peshawar. Soldiers were approached (besides in the Panjāb) at Meerut, Kanpur, Allāhābād, Banāras and Lucknow. But little success was achieved. Besides the import of arms from U.S.A. by surreptitious means, arms and bombs were sought to be manufactured in India also, but the schemes always leaked out and were frustrated.

Suspected men in the affected army units were arrested, and so also the leading revolutionaries. They were implicated in several conspiracy cases—at Lāhore (180 men), Banāras (14) and even abroad as at Mandalay (17) Chicāgo (4) and San Francisco (35, of whom 18 were Gremans and Americans for violating America's neutrality and for carrying war-preparations on American soil against the British Govt. in India). In India some of them were sentenced to death, and most transported for life. Some were given various terms of imprisonment or their properties confiscated. Abroad, it was either fines or jail terms, or both.

Among the twelve who were hanged in India were a 17-year-old lad, named Kartār Singh of Sarābhā (Ludhiānā), Dr. Mathra Singh and Jawand Singh. Among those who were transported for life to the Andāmāns were Sant Randhir Singh (whose pious life of religious devotion has stirred thousands of his followers), Sohan Singh Bhaknā, President of the Ghadar party and Jawālā Singh and Kesar Singh, Vice-Presidents. The last three were arrested on landing in India. Thus, the movement was deprived of leadership.

Denied a mass base, lack of central direction and cohesion, lack of sympathy on the part of national leadership (all dedicated to war-effort), the onset of a World War (in which Britain could take no chances and even their high-handedness could pass as justice in the cause of internal peace), lack of secrecy, the active hostility of Sikh leadership (the Chief Khālsā Diwān disowned them, calling them "mischief makers") and idealism not grounded in fact caused the movement to fail. Violence succeeds only when it is superior to the adversary's in tactics and strategy as well as arms, or when the whole mass is aroused against an established authority. Here, both these elements were lacking. However, the episode left a trail of heroism and sacrifice behind, and roused the political consciousness of the masses. India could nolonger be taken for granted either by the British, or by its own moderate leaders.

As has been stated, every Indian leader of consequence had supported the British in the World War. Lokmaniyā Tilak had been in the forefront of the struggle for freedom, *by any means*, and had boldly declared as early as 1894, "Swārāj is our birth-right and we shall have it." His *Ganpati Pujā* (like the *Kāli Pooja* in Bengāl) had led to the display of mass drill and learning of several arts of fighting with the only weapons Indians were left with—lāthis and knives. After his failure in 1905, alongwith Lājpat Rāi in London to persuade the British Govt. for a quicker transfer of power, within the Commonwealth, he had openly advocated violence. He was charged with sedition and transported for six years to Māndlay in 1908. Released on June 17, 1914, on the eve of the World War, "he wholeheartedly supported the war-effort."

Mr. M.K. Gandhi (later known as Mahātmā Gāndhi and father of the Indian nation), a Barrister-at-law, had left India to practise in South Africa and had heroically fought also for Indian settler's human rights there, evolving the technique of non-violent, passive resistance in the process (under the influence of Leo. Tolstoy of Russia and Thoreau of America). Inspite of his differences with the Govt. of India, he had helped the British in the Boer War in South Africa and enlisted himself as a volunteer and won a medal for distinguished service. When the Great War was declared, he was in London. He petitioned the British Govt. through the Secy of State for India, Lord Crewe, along with 55 other Indians (including Mrs. Sarojini Naidu and his own wife) offering their unqualified services to the British Govt. The Govt. showed hesitancy, but due to Gandhi's persistence, he was recruited as a nursing orderly in London itself. Inspite of his weak health for having developed pleurisy, he worked ceaselessly for the cause till he was forced to leave for India on grounds of health. While in London, Mrs. Naidu and Mrs. Kasturbā Gāndhi stitched uniforms for the British troops as their contribution to the war-effort.

The Indian National Congress (already in the hands of moderates like Gopāl Krishan Gokhalē) which met at Madrās, in Dec. 1914, had the pavillion decorated with the portraits of their Imperial Majesties and the Royal Arms. The Governor of Madrās, Lord Pentland, who appeared for a time at the Congress, was lustily cheered. The Congress also passed a resolution in total support of the war effort. Lālā Lājpat Rāi, then considered a fire-brand, was also speaking and acting in a similar vein.

The attitude of the leadership towards the Govt. can be gauged by the wording of the petition Gāndhi himself had drafted and sent to the Secy. of State. It said, they wanted to place their services at the disposal of the authorities *"as an earnest of our desire to share the responsibilities of membership of the great empire if we could share its privileges."** The annulment of Bengāl partition at the time of the Imperial Durbar at Delhi in 1912 had also soothed the Bengāli sentiment.

Thus, the moderation and cooperative attitude of the Sikh leaders of those times towards the British Govt. should be read in this context.

The Panjāb had in fact (along with Bengāl, though due to different immediate reasons) taken to political agitation far ahead of the other states. When Mr. Gokhalē visited Amritsar in 1907, the students of the Khālsā college (then wholly British-managed) drove his carriage, yoking it to their bodies, instead of the horses which were taken off. In 1909, Sir Curzon Willie was murdered in London by a Panjābi. We have already alluded to the Ghadar movement, launched mostly by the Panjābi Sikh youths in the United States and in India. Such was the climate among Sikhs that even the moderates among Sikhs had become suspect in the eyes of the Govt. The C. I. D. in its confidential report to the Govt. had asked the Govt. to beware

---

* *Mahātmā*, Vol 1, P. 153.

of Bhāi Vir Singh, Bhāi Jodh Singh, S. Tarlochan Singh and S. Harbans Singh Attariwālā together with Sardār (later Sir) Sunder Singh Majithiā. It strongly cautioned the Govt. against their activities and even charged them with preaching "sedition," through the *Parchāraks* (missionaries) employed by the Chief Khālsā Diwān. * The charge was that they talked of the Sikhs as a *qaum* (nation) and placed the facts of the past sacrifices and struggles of their community before the people through their speeches, writings and other activities cloaked as "religious," or what has also been called "patriotic orthodoxy." They also called for more "sacrifice" and "struggle" if their nation was to forge ahead. They were spreading "Sikh" education alongwith western knowledge and the greatest crime of all, they wanted their premier Sikh educational institution, the Khālsā college at Amritsar, to pass from British management to that of the Sikhs themselves!

However, when the war ended, late in 1918, the hopes raised by the British and their Allies, notably the United States, that the war against Germany was being waged for the freedom of all peoples, were belied.

Already, through the Minto-Morley Reforms of 1909, the British had enlarged somewhat the sphere of Indian participation in the Govt. But, while the Muslims got separate electorates (the right to choose their representation), and weightage, both at the Centre and in the states, where they were in a minority, the Sikh representations for similar concessions for the Sikhs (made mostly by the Chief Chālsā Diwān) to the Lt. Governor of Panjāb (and forwarded to the Govt. General by him with his own strong recommendations) were taken no notice of. The Muslims had built up their own platform, the All India Muslim League in 1906 (encouraged in every way by the British Govt.) After the Āghā Khān-led deputation met the Governor General in Simla the same year, and the acceptance and incorporation of their demands in the Reforms of 1909, nationalist India was scared into coming to a permanent political settlement with them, on their terms, as soon as possible. The partition of Bengāl in 1905 on communal lines (though annuled after a violent agitation for

* "(Sir) Sunder Singh's constant companions are such men as Trilochan Singh, and Vir Singh, Jodh Singh & others. The disloyalty of these men is notorious & admitted on all hands." (Secret C.I.D. Memo, 1911 by D. Petrie):

7 years, though Bihar and Orrissa also were separated alongwith Assām to form different provinces) had further deepened their anxieties. In 1916, therefore, a Hindu-Muslim pact was hammered out at Lucknow, between the Congress and the Muslim League, which conceded separate electorates to the Muslims and half of the total seats in Panjāb (on population basis) and weightage in the other provinces where they were in a minority. One-third seats were assured them at the Centre also (against 25% of their population). But no Sikh was either invited to this conference, nor their views given any attention. They had, therefore, no choice but to fight their political battles alone.

After the announcement of the Secy. of State, Mr. Montagu (Aug. 20, 1917) that Indians would be "associated increasingly in every branch of administration, and self-governing institutions gradually developed with a view to progressive realisation of responsible government," the Sikhs also submitted, three months later, a representation to the Viceroy for a one-third share in the Panjāb Council.

Their past political status and the present educational advance, their services in the war and their contribution to Panjāb's economy were made major bases of their demand, besides the arguments on which the Muslim demands had been conceded, namely, that numbers alone in the Indian conditions, if pressed to the logical conclusion, would result in the communal domination of one religious community over another, with disastrous results to the cultural, economic and political rights of the minorities.

It is unfortunate that when the issue of the Montague-Chelmsford reforms in which separate electorates had been given to the Sikhs as well, was debated in the joint committee of the Panjāb Council, out of eight members (2 being Sikhs) the two Hindu representatives sided with the Muslims to throw out their just and equitable demand, proposed by Sardār Gajjan Singh (especially when voting-rights were themselves determined on the basis of property and education). A similar fate met their resolution (moved by Sir Sunder Singh) in the Imperial legislative Council at Delhi. They received about 18 percent seats in the Panjāb Council (17 out of 93), three seats (out of 145) in the Central Assembly and one in the Council of States (out of 60).

A system of Diarchy was also introduced with only a few subjects like Agriculture, Education, Revenus, Local Self-Govt. and Public Health and Works being transferred to Indian members and these also being subject to the Governor's veto. The all-important Home and Finance and Law and Justice remained in British hands in the provinces. At the Centre, the Govt. had even a firmer control on Finance and customs, besides of course, Foreign Affairs, Home and Defence.

But, all this paled into insignificance before what happened a few months later. India had contributed 12 lakh men (8 lakh combatants) and 100 crore rupees outright and 25 to 30 crores every year to prosecute the war. Utmost loyalty had been pledged aad shown throughout the war. No violent, or even passive agitation was encouraged or initiated by any nationalist section throughout the country. A Hindu-Muslim constitutional accord had been forged at Lucknow (1916) to answer any charge of division in Indian ranks, or India's unwillingness or inability to rule its own destiny. But no promise was made as to when India was going finally to be self governing, even like any other "dominion" within the British Commonwealth. The bold and halting statement of Lord Montagu of "progressive and gradual" advance towards Self-Govt. left many nationalist hearts cold, if not also suspicious. The Govt. took 5 years in its deliberations (atleast three in detailed discussions) and this is what it had produced—a rat dug out of a mountain. The liberal moderates "who saw in British officials their opponents but in British institutions their hope and who preached moderation in agitation and cooperation in action" were now thrown aside. Tilak and Gokhale were both dead. And a new era of Gandhian passive resistance and non-cooperation dawned upon India.

It is of interest to note that almost all of these leaders were either trained in British law or medicine (Gandhi, the two Nehrus, Dr Ansari, S. Kharak Singh, Sarat Chandra Bose, Rajendra Prasad, Sardar Patel etc. or as in the case of several others, including Aurobindo Ghosh, Surindra Nath Bennerjee, and Subhash Chandra Bose, they had successfully competed for entry into the British Civil Service in London, and abandoned it to take up the higher cause of service of India, the Mother.) Macalauy's note of 1833 for educating Indians in the western liberal tradition and arts and sciences (as against the traditional education advocated by other Englishmen and Indians) had resulted in what it led to in Europe—Revolution in defence of man's freedom.

The Marxist Revolution of 1917 in Russia (now called the Union of Soviet Socialist Republics) added a new dimension to what had inspired the Indian revolutionaries so far—the French and the American revolutions of the late eighteenth century, and the lives of Garibaldi, Mazinni and Bismarck. Now, D'Valera of Ireland and Kemal Ataturk of Turkey, both fighting against the British had become, besides Lenin, the avowed enemy of all types of colonialism, their new sources of inspiration.

The Great War ended in Nov. 1918. The Govt. had, as was natural during the war, armed itself with a Defence of India Act to put anyone in prison, without trial, on mere suspicion of any act prejudicial to the security of the state. It irked nationalist opinion, but they suffered it during the war. The Govt. was anxious to arm itself with more powers to curb terrorist activities, especially in the Panjāb and Bengāl. A committee of inquiry was appointed under an English judge, Sir Sydney Rowlatt, who collected much evidence to support the Government's fears and the need to further strengthen the law in this behalf. The publication of the report on the proposed reforms took a year more to become law, while the two Rowlatt Bills were passed into law within a few weeks, in March 1919, as the Defence of India Act was soon to lapse on the termination of hostilities. The provincial Governments were given the powers to intern any person, and the judges were allowed to try political offences without a jury in specific cases. Every non-official member of the Imperial Lagislative Concil voted against this draconian measure, in times af peace, but the nominated votes saw the bills through. The war had inflated prices, thrown the economy out of gear, the soldiers (most of them from the Panjab, 80,000 being Sikhs) were being demobilised *en-masse*, the deportations and hangings of the *Ghadar* party workers during the war-years (most of whom were Sikhs in the prime of their youth), the mishandling of the Rakābganj offair in Delhi (to which we shall refer later) all had contributed their share to excite the wrath of the people, particulary in the Panjāb.

Gandhi, who till now was a devoted citizen of the British Empire, had hoped that his country's total commitment to the cause of war would result in the transfer of substantial power to Indian hands. President Wilson's 14-point Charter (annouced in 1918) to be implemented after the war (which included the right of self-determination for all peoples) had further strengthened the nationalist sentiment in this behalf. But, instead, what India got was more distrust and more lawless laws. Both Tilak and Gokhale were dead. And the mantle now fell on Gandhi, who, sensing the agitated mood of the people, gave a call for *Satyāgraha* to oppose these tyrannous Acts.

On March 30, 1919, there was a complete *hartāl* (suspension of business) at Amritsar, which passed off peacefully, though in several other parts of India, the police had to open fire to disperse crowds. On April 9, two popular Panjāb leaders, Dr S.D. Kitchlew and Dr. Satyāpāl, were arrested and detained. The people rose in angry protest and attacked two British banks and killed their white managers. On April 11, Brig. Gen. Edward Harry Dyer arrived in Amritsar and occupied the city. He banned all public meetings. But the people were determined to organise one to protest against the detention of their leaders and the passage of the Rowlatt Acts. On April 13, the birthday of the Khālsā, when men and women had gathered in the holy city from far and near, a large unarmed crowd (including women and children) assembled at the Jallianwālā Bagh, near the Golden Temple. Gen. Dyer soon arrived on the scene, blocked the only avenue of exit from this private enclosure, and trained his machine-guns on them and went on firing "till all his ammunition was exhausted." 309 persons were killed and three times as many were brutally wounded.* People rose like wounded tigers and went on a rampage, cutting telegraph wires, removing fish-plates on the railway tracks, setting post offices and other Govt. buildings on fire. European life became unsafe. The Govt. declared Martial Law in principal towns—Amritsar, Lāhore, Gujrāt, Gujrānwālā and Lyallpur. A reign of terror was let loose. Where an English woman was murdered in an Amritsar street, men and women were made to crawl to their homes. Students, besides respectable leaders, were flogged and made to report to the police four times in the day.

* Though Gen. Dyer is generally considered to be the only man responsible for this tragedy, recent statements made by the survivors (e.g. of Mr. Daulat Rām of village Megharwal, distt. Hoshiārpur, who retired two decades ago as an Agent of the Allahabād Bank) show that Col. Smith, the Civil Surgeon and Rev. Mackenzie, a missionary, goaded the Govt. in a meeting of British officials at Amritsar to teach the Indians a lesson after a few Europeans had been killed by an Indian mob. They demanded the bombardment of the Amritsar city. It was Mr. G. A. Wathen, the British Principal of the Khālsā College, Amritsar, who protested that if any harm came to the Golden Temple, the Sikh soldiers would rebel. It is this warning that made Gen. Dyer desist from a worse crime. ("Times of India" April 19, 1979). Wathen saved his students also in many ways & otherwise too helped them to find employment with Govt. throughout his tenure. His name is still cherished by his old students. it may also be mentioned that most of the soldiers who fired at Jallianwala obeying Gen. Dyer's Command, were Indians,

India had been suitably rewarded for her services in defence of the British *rāj*! The Panjāb had become the nerve-centre of India's new upsurge for freedom, and a place of pilgrimage for everyone who believed in this country's free destiny.

Large-scale arrests followed. Summary trials were held and men sentented to death or given long terms of impmisonment. Community fines were levied on the villages and aerial bombing resorted to, as at Gujrānwālā. Those who refused to open shops at Lāhore were warned with death.

The Indian National Congress held its annual session at Amritsar in Dec. 1919, attended by of all those most of whom from now on till the attainment of freedom were to lead and guide its fortunes: Gāndhi*, Moti Lāl Nehru, Bābā Kharak Singh, Sardul Singh Caveeshar, Madan Mohan Malviya (patriot, Hindu Sanātanist leader and founder of Banaras Hindu University), Jawaharlal Nehru, the Ali Bros, Dr. M.A. Ansāri, C.F. Andrews, C.R. Dās, Hakim Ajmal Khān, Lajpat Rai (a lawyer turned politican who was the only Panjābi ever to become President of the Indian National Congress) and others. Dr. Rabindra Nath Tagore, the Nobel Laureate of Bengāl, returned his title of kinghthood in protest. A mighty wave against everything foreign (especially British) swept the land. The Panjāb gave Gandhi a slogan: complete independence, and a plan of action: *Satyagraha*. It gave him and the new leadership also an immediate cause to agitate, and fired the whole country with an enthusiasm for their liberation as nothing else had done before. From now on, there was no looking back.

Whatever was left out was completed by the British decision to abolish the Muslim institution of Caliphate in Turkey. The Muslims had for ages looked upon the Sultān of Turkey as the Caliph (Khalifā or religious head) of the entire Islamic world. Turkey had sided with Germany in the first World War, and been defeated. The Turkish empire was dismembered. And now the Sultān was to lose

* Mahātmā Gandhi (1869-1948) was born in Porbandar in Gujarāt (which state also gave this country many other illustrious leaders, like Swāmi Dyanand, Mohd Ali Jinnāh, Vallabbhāi Patel and Morārji Desāi), practised for a time as a successful barrister in S. Africa, but drifted into politics there for the protection of Indian rights in that oppressive land of apartheid. Later he became the virtual dictator of the National Congress in India and led the country to freedom mainly through non-volent means. *Swadeshi*, however, was not Gāndhi's contribution. It was earlier tried by the Kookās and by Bengāl agitators successfully long before Gandhi.

his symbolic headship of the Muslim religious world as well. The Indian Muslims felt equally humiliated. And Gāndhi and the Congress took up the Muslim cause as their own. The British had brought a complete Hindu-Muslim unity over this issue as well.

The Sikhs who had, like Gāndhiji before, looked upon the British rāj as a blessing in disguise, now started looking towards Gāndhi and more particularly towards Jawāharlāl Nehru and Subhāsh Chandra Bose, the rising star of Bengāl, as their future leaders and deliverers. They had suffered the most, both in the Ghadar movement and during the war (in men killed as well as demobilised). In the Jallianwala Bāgh tragedy, it was their lot to shed more blood. And soon thereafter, they launched the Gurdwārā Reform movement (popularly known as the Akāli movement), which though initially aimed at purging the Sikh shrines of the corrupt practices of their hereditary custodians, (†) ended up in politicalising the masses against the Govt, and making the Sikhs the vanguard of the freedom movement. The age of the loyalists, however well-intentioned, was over, and an All-India Central Sikh League, wedded to freedom as well as fight for Sikh rights, was born. A

† Such was the vicious character of these people that just when the whole country had risen in defence of ths Jalliānwālā Bagh martyrs, the custodian of the Golden Temple, Rur Singh, offered a Robe of honour to Sir Michael O'Dwyer, Governor of the Panjab, who had supported Gen. Dyer to the hilt. The General himself was also offered a Kirpān (Sword of Honour) and it was quoted in the British Parliament by Lord Finlay that he had been made a Sikh (through such honour). The biographer of Dyer, Ian Colin, supports the view *(Life of Gen Dyer, P. 201)* that he was invested with five *Kakhās* (Sikh symbols), but the dialogue between him and Rur Singh published on the same page shows that he took it very lightly. He objected that as a British officer he could not grow his hair long. The custodians said, "We will let you off it." Then he raised another objection, "But I cannot give up smoking." When told that this he must do, he said that he promised to reduce smoking by one cigaratte a year! Bhai Jodh Singh, personally in the know of these affairs, disclaims any knowledge of it. On the face of it the story looks ridiculous. He was honoured but not converted. Master Tārā Singh also makes no mention of it in his Autobiography. Dyer, after the Hunter Inquiry, was dismissed. Churchill criticised him severely, though a fund, of about £25000, was also raised for his defence by a British newspaper, and he was presented also with a golden sword. Sir Michael was, however, shot dead by a Sikh, Udham Singh, in London, in 1940. He was hanged, but in 1976, the Congress regime in the Panjāb brought his ashes from London as a national hero, and after carrying them in decorative processions throughout the Panjāb, cast them into the Satluj river at Kiratpur-.

meeting was held at Lahore in 1920 under the auspices of the Sikh League, presided over by Bābā Kharak Singh, and attended among others. by Mahātmā Gāndhi.

A resolution of non-cooperation with the Govt. was passed, inspite of opposition by the loyalist forces. What is even more, the question of Rakābganj Gurdwārā, at Delhi (see below) was re-opened in the light of the new mood of anger sweeping through the entire land.

Since 1912, India's capital had been transferred from Calcutta to Delhi. The British Viceroy's lodge was being built in the village of Raisina where also stood a memorial, called Rakābganj, to the eternal memory of Guru Teg Bahādur's martyrdom. On the advice of the architects, the Govt. demolished the boundary-wall of the Gurdwārā in 1914, inorder to straighten a road leading to the Viceroy's lodge. This had spread great resentment in the community, but though protests were lodged, no agitation ensued due to the onset of the war. But, the Sikhs now decided to send out a *Shahidi Jathā*, (Martyrs' Band) of 100, led by Sardār Sardul Singh Caveeshar, to Delhi to restore the demolished wall. 700 volunteers came forward, including some Hindus and Muslims. Fearing widespread agitation, the Govt. immediately rebuilt the wall, and the agitation was called off. This success gave a new morale to the Sikhs to fight for the restoration of all historic shrines to the control of the community.

The first shot was fired on Oct. 12,1920, at the Jalliāṇwālā Bāgh, where a Sikh religious Diwān was held, attended among others by Bāwā Harkishan Singh, Prof Tejā Singh (both professors of English literature at the Khālsā College, Amritsar) and Jathedār Kartār Singh Jhabbar (who became famous for his sacrifices in the Akāli movement in the early days). The Jalliāṇwālā Bāgh massacre and the reign of terror that followed were still fresh in the minds of the people. That the Custodian of the Golden Temple had honoured both the murderer and his stubbron supporter, rankled in their hearts. Many so-called untouchables were administered *Pāhul* in this meeting and, alongwith the whole congregation,they moved towards the Golden Temple to offer prayers on behalf of the un-touchables. There was heated argument. Ultimately, it was decided to consult the Holy Book. It was agreed that everyone should follow, on whatever verse the Guru Granth Sāhib was opened. When the verse was read out, the entire congregation was filled with immense joy, as the Guru's Word said :-

"God forgives even those who are without merit,
And assembles them all in His Skirt,
And Ferries them across through the Guru's Boat".

(Sorath, M. 3)

The priests had no option but to accept the offerings of all devotees of whatever caste. Seeing this, the Pujāris at the Akāl Takht fled in panic never to return. The Akālis occupied the vacant seats of authority. The Deputy Commissioner, Amritsar, also bowed before the inevitable, and constituted a committcee of eight (all reformists) to take the legal control of the two shrines. Thus came into being the Akāli movement, wholly unplanned, but resulting in not only success in its immediate aims, but also in far wider political spheres as well in those stirring times.

On Nov. 15 and 16, 1920, a representative meeting of the Sikhs was called at Amritsar through a *Hukamnāmā* (edict) issued from the Akāl Takht, and as a consequence, a committee of 175 was constituted to take control of and manage the Sikh historic Gurdwārās* throughout the Panjāb. It was given the name of Shiromani Gurdwārā Parbhandhak Committee (S.G.P.C. for short). An executive committee was also elected and another one to frame a constitution. It was duly registered later on 30 April 1921, after fresh elections of the body, with 20 per cent nominations.

The new committee held its first meeting on Aug. 27, 1921. Many Gurdwārās* had come under the local communities' control after a brief agitation, even before the committee came into being, as at Bābē-di-Ber in Siālkot (Oct. 7, 1920) and Panjā Sāhib at Hassan Abdāl, (20 Nov. 1920), Gurdwārā Bhāi Jogā Singh at Peshawār and Kharā Saudā at Nankānā Sāhib (27 Dec. 1920).

* A Gurdwārā (lit. Guru's Door) is not merely a place of worship for Sikhs,but also offers them refuge and food, free of charge It is also a community welfare Centre and many are associated with the sacred memory of the Gurus. The Golden Temple played a most notable part in the Sikh struggle for freedom,as did the *Akāl Takhat* in pre-Ranjit Singh times,for the get-together of the entire *Panth* to deliberate on matters of war and peace. Every one is free to visit, reside in or feed himself free in the Sikh Gurdwārās. They now-a-days run many schools and colleges, hospitals and orphanages etc. also.

A great tragedy, however, occured at Panjā Sāhib later. On 29 Oct. 1922, when a railway train was passing through here, carrying Akāli prisoners and was not scheduled to stop at this railway station, the Sikhs lay on the railway track and after two of them—Partāp Singh and Karam Singh—were crushed to death,the train stopped and the Sikhs fed them as they were reported to be hungry. The Jathā consisting of military pensioners was being conveyed to the Attock Jail.

On Jan. 24, 1921, the SGPC's political wing,the Shiromani Akāli Dal,* also came into being after a meeting at Amritsar.

But, when the Akālis wanted to capture the historic Gurdwārā at Tarn Tāran, they were attacked by the *Pujāris* (custodians). Two Sikhs were killed and 17 injured. 18 *Pujāris* were also wounded in the scuffle. But, the control of the Gurdwārā was taken over by the community. On Jan. 31, the Akālis took possession of *Guru Kā Bāgh*, near Amritsar, through an agreement with the Custodian, but he later backed out.

The movement thus far had been more or less peaceful. The custodians,seeing the mood of the devotees and the surcharged political atmosphere, did not resist for long. But, Mahant Narain Dās, custodian of Nankānā Sāhib, the birth-place Guru Nānak, thought differently. He had too much to lose—the vast *Jāgirs* attached to the Sikh temple, besides the huge offerings of the devout. His corruption and low morality, however, had by now become widely known. Fearing the Sikh wrath against him, he started collecting bad characters and armed them with guns and other lethal weapons. The S.G P.C. had decided to hold a large Sikh gathering there on March 4 to 6, 1921, to put pressure on the Mahant to mend his ways, but before this could happen, a *Jathā* of 150 Sikhs, led by Bhāi Lachhman Singh of Dhārowāl had reached Nankānā Sāhib about a fortnight earlier (Feb. 20), with a view to a peaceful visit to the holy shrine. As they entered the precincts of the inner sanctuary, the doors were suddenly shut on them and the congregation squatting on the floor and engaged in hymn-singing was indiscrimirately fired at, or attacked with the swords and cutlasses and spears by the ruffians. They were cut into pieces, sprinkled with kerosene oil and burnt to ashes. The leader, Lachhman Singh, was tied to a tree and burnt alive. Another Sikh, Dalip Singh who came to dissuade the Mahant from this cruel slaughter, was also shot dead.

This tragedy shook the community to its every depths. The Governor and other officials and ministers reached the spot next morning. The control of the Gurdwārā was handed over to a seven-man committee consisting of Sardār Kartār Singh Jhabbar, S. Amar Singh, editor "Sher-i-Panjāb" of Lāhore*, and others.

In the beginning of March, Mahātmā Gandhi, L. Lajpat Rāi and the Ali Brothers also visited Nankānā Sāhib and made fiery speeches, asking for a boycott of all court proceedings launched by Govt. in this behalf. The S.G.P.C. appealed to all Sikhs to protest against this heinous crime by wearing a black head-gear (turbans and *dopattās*) as a sign of mourning. This has been a distinctive badge since then of the Akāli* Sikhs (though they now-a-days also sport a blue turban after the traditional Nihangs). The Govt. was alarmed at the political turn being given to a religious movement, arrested many leading Sikh agitators and sentenced them to long terms of imprisonment. Sardār Kartār Singh Jhabbar was sentenced to 18 years, Tārā Singh Thethar to 11 years, and Teja Singh Bhuchar to 9 years.‡ The moderates among the Sikhs led by Bhāi Jodh Singh, Sardār Harbans

---

* S. Amar Singh was a very powerful writer of Urdu poetry and prose. He also wrote excellent satire and humour. A notable speaker and a great devotee of the Guru, he later fell out with Master Tārā Singh and joined hands with Bābā Kharak Singh and Giāni Sher Singh.

† The word Akāli is derived from *Akāl* (the timeless, or deathless God). It is not an order initiated by the Tenth Master, as is generally believed. The word got currency only during Ranjit Singh's period in reference to Akāli Phoolā Singh Nihang, his free-lance general and custodian of the *Akāl Takht*. The name *Akāli* also became identified with his blue robes and head-gear. As he was a death-daring warrior and a highly respected religious leader, his appellation was borrowed by the neo-Akālis in the twenties. Now-a-days, they are a wholly Sikh political party in the Panjāb, distinguised by their blue or black turbans. They mix up religion with politics or separate the two as it suits their convenience. (See later).

‡"It must be noted here that the call for agitation at Nankānā Sāhib on the part of the S.G.P.C., had not yet been given. The *Panth* was yet to meet there a fortnight later, to advise the Mahant "to mend his ways." Bhāi Lachhman Singh had in fact been warned by the SGPC through a letter received by him on the way, not to proceed there immediately. But one member of the *Jathā*, Tahal Singh, insisted that he having performed the *Ardāsā* (prayer in the form of a pledge) would not hold back. Others thereupon also followed suit and all were murdered. This is the result of taking action without deliberation by individuals leaving no option for leadership but to plunge the whole community into a struggle to upkeep their honour." (Master Tārā Singh, Autobiography, PP. 53-54).

Singh Attāriwālā (even when they were supported by such fiery youths as Sardār Kartār Singh Jhabbar) were not heeded in their plea that the court proceedings should be pursued vigorously so that the culprits could be brought to book. (Later, however, Mahant Narain Dās was sentenced to life-imprisonment and some of his associates who took active part in the killing, hanged). Bābā Kartār Singh Bedi, son of Sir Bābā Khem Singh, who supported him, was forgiven only on his making a pilgrimage to the holy shrine on naked feet from Amritsar to Nankānā Sāhib.

After this incident, the Govt. seems to have become an active party ranged totally against the Akāli agitation. They appointed their own Custodian for the Golden Temple, Amritsar, Capt. Bahādur Singh, and took away the keys of the *Toshā-Khānā* (Treasury-cum-museum) of the Temple (Nov 7, 1921). Bahādur Singh resigned after a few days and no one could be found by Govt. to take his place. The Sikhs held protest meetings all over the Panjāb. The Govt. arrested the leaders indiscriminately. Ultimately, seeing the wave of anger mounting in the community, the Deputy Commissioner came personally to deliver the keys to Sardār Kharak Singh, then President of the S.G P.C., only about three months later (Jan 19, 1922) in an open meeting, as was insisted upon by the Sikhs. All the persons arrested, including Sardār Kharak Singh and Māster Tārā Singh, in this connection, were also unconditionally released. Hearing this, Mahātmā Gandhi was so excited that he sent the following congratulatory telegram the same day to Sardār Kharak Singh :— "*The first decisive battle for independence won. Congratulations.*"

But only a month after, the Govt. again started arresting Sikh leaders, either for wearing a *kirpān* (ritual-sword) longer in size than nine inches (which by an order had been forbidden), for wearing a black turban (which had become a symbol of protest among Sikhs), or their unwillingness to pay for the punitive posts established in several mutinous villages.

A few months later, Sunder Dās, the Mahant of *Guru-Kā-Bāgh* (in the Ajnālā tehsil, 15 miles from Amritsar) went back on his pledged word and tore the agreement he had made earlier with the S.G.P.C., handing over the control of the shrine and the *Bāgh* (lit. garden, but which was now only a piece of land growing prickly *Kikar* trees) attached to it. The Sikhs used to cut wood from this *Bāgh* for use in the community-kitchen (*langar*) there. But when on

August 8, 1922, five Sikhs went there to collect wood, they were all arrested,on the report of the *Mahant* to the police,for their trespass. Possibly, the Govt. policy had changed by now and they wanted to teach the agitating Akālis a lesson.

The English Superintendent of police, Mr. S.G.M. Beaty, arrived on the scene on Aug 17.*

Many Sikh leaders and workers were arrested and charged with incitement to unlawful activities. Seeing this change of atmosphere, the SGPC intensified its agitation and started sending out (from Aug. 31) *Jathās* of 100, everyday, to the Guru-Kā-Bāgh, the first one entirely composed of ex-Army veterans and led by Subedār Amar Singh. They were all arrested. But after this, the policy of arrests was abandoned and cruel beating of the *Satyāgrahis* started. They were clubbed mercilessly by the police, dragged by the hair and thrown in mud. The Sikh volunteers would assemble the wounded, take them back to the hospitals at Amritsar, and a fresh round would start the next morning. Even when some agitators, all peaceful to a fault, and suffering assaults, insults and humiliations with the name of God on their lips, were killed in the process or rendered unconscious, or received permanent injuries, the *Satyāgrahis* did not either decrease in number or in zeal. In fact, there was a competition among various regions to be the first in the line of martyrs. The whole of India was stirred to its depths. This was a new experiment for the world. A war-like people, wholly loyal to Govt. until recently, suffering peacefully and without demur for a cause they all considered just and lawful ! There was now nolonger any question here of Khatri or Jāt, touchable or untouchable. All were pressing forward, in an unending stream, prepared to cast themselves into the crucible of fire, without asking "why". The Hindus were stirred by their unique example of sacrifice, without any thought of counter-violence or vengeance, as much as the Muslims.

But the one man who was excited the most and wrote most appreciatively of it was Mahātmā Gāndhi. He was being justified in his programme and tactics from a wholly unexpected quarter and in a situation not at all of his own making. He was getting, without any

* Beaty who became notorious as a Sikh-baiter and who inflicted many cruelties on the Sikh volunteers was after the end of the Akāli movement murdered by a Babbar Akāli in the state of Patiālā.

effort, recruits for the agitations for a far wider cause he had yet to launch. Maulānā Zafar Ali Khān, editor of "Zamindār" of Lāhore, wrote powerful poems in defence of the Akāli struggle. Hakim Ajmal Khān and Dr. M. A. Ansāri* came personally to witness the struggle and express their wholehearted solidarity with it. The Congress passed resolutions congratulating the Akālis on the "unexampled bravery of the Akālis who had set a great and noble example of non-violence for the benefit of the whole nation." Neither money was ever in need of asking, nor doctors, or sympathisers. The great nationalist leader (he became President of the Indian National Congress) and a great Hindu, Pt. Madan Mohan Mālviyā, came and declared at Amritsar : "I cannot resist asking every Hindu home to have atleast one male child initiated into the fold of the Khālsā.‡ What I see here before my eyes is nothing short of a miracle in our whole history." Mr. C. F. Andrews, the noble Christian missionary and a friend of India's freedom, was saying :—"It was a sight which I never wish to see again, a sight incredible to an Englishman. There were four Akāli

---

* Both belonged to Delhi, became the President of the Indian National Congress and played a most patriotic part in our struggle for freedom. Dr. Ansāri was the practitioner of modern medicine and Hakim Ajmal Khān of *Ayurvedic* and *Unāni* systems. (He was the founder of the Hindustāni Dawākhānā in Delhi). Both were extremely rich, but sacrificed much for the national cause.

‡ However, when the untouchables, led by Dr. B.R. Ambedkar, declared that though the Sikhs had nothing materially to offer them as against Muslims and Christians, they had opted for the Sikh faith inorder that they may not go out of the Hindu culture altogether, both Malviyāji and, what is worse, even Mahātmā Gāndhi publicly opposed this move. Gandhi refused to extend the benefits enjoyed by the untouchables under the Poonā pact if they turned Sikhs ! "This will create a Hindu-Muslim-Sikh problem throughout India," he said, "instead of only Hindu-Muslim problem." Ambedkar couldnot give up those privileges at that time (1934-35) but turned a Buddhist later on, with his 7 million followers, [illegible] are still struggling for the rights granted to Harijans (Gandhi's name for untouchables) under the Constitution of free India, but they have not been successful so far. (For details, see *Master Tārā Singh, Sangharsh te Jiwan*, PP. 173-188).

Ambedkar, a Barrister, writer and debator of great brilliance, became a crusader for the rights of the untouchables. He became very anti-Hindu after his being shunned even in his professional work as a lawyer by the caste Hindus and leaving one service after another under their pressure. He became anti-Gāndhi & pro-British also, but it was on Gāndhi's insistence that he was introduced into the Govt of India after freedom as Minister of Law. He drafted and piloted free India's democratic Constitution which is a great tribute to his wide knowledge and sympathies.

Sikhs with black turbans facing a band of about a dozen policemen, including two English officers.

"Their hands were placed together in prayer. Then an Englishman, without a provocation, lunged forward the head of his lāthi, bound with brass, and struck the Sikh at the collar-bone with great force. He fell to the ground, rolled over and slowly got up once more to face the same punishment, till he was laid prostrate by repeated blows. Others were knocked out more quickly. It was brutal in the extreme. I saw with my own eyes one of these policemen kick in the stomach a Sikh who stood helplessly before him. I wanted to cry and rush forward. But then I saw a police sepoy stamping with his foot an Akāli Sikh hurled to the ground and lying prostrate.. And more and more. The brutality and inhumanity of the whole scene was indescribably increased by the fact that the men who were hit were praying to God and had taken a vow (at the Golden Temple) to remain silent and peaceful in word and deed ... I saw no act, or look of defiance. It was a true martyrdom, a true act of faith...There is something far greater in this than a mere dispute over land and property. A new heroism, (and this on the part of these notable warriors who had served in our campaigns in France, in Flanders, in Messopatamia and East Africa) learnt through suffering has arisen in the land It reminded me of the shadow of the Cross."*

And, it was at this time (as mentioned by Andrews) that a golden hawk (believed to be the *Guru-kā-Bāz*) always accompanied the *jathās* bothways daily in their rendezvous with death. The Sikhs believed that the Guru (Gobind Singh, the lord of the white hawk), through this gesture, had sanctified and approved of their heroic struggle.† When nothing availed, Sir Gangā Rām, the executive engineer at Lāhore and a great philanthropist, came forward to take on lease the disputed property from the Mahant (Oct 17) and handed it over to the SGPC. About 5600 persons arrested in the campaign were also released in May 1923.

---

* For a fuller account, the reader may consult Prof. Ruchi Ram Sahni (then a trustee of the "Tribune," who was an eye-witness) in his book "*Struggle for Reform in Sikh Shrines*."

† *Struggle for reform in Sikh Shrines*, by R. R. Sahni, Appendix, pages 176-188.

The Akālis used this triumph to launch upon a *Kār Sevā* (the removal of sediment from the sacred tank of the Golden Temple). Hundreds of thousands of people, princes as much as peasants, participated in it. It was a rare sight to see—men and women, draped in rich silken robes or white, homespun wear, carrying overloaded iron-baskets of mud on their heads, dripping all over their bodies and they carrying through this labour of love, chanting in unison the Word of the Gurus, lost to themselves and the world around them. This communal service lent a new sense of unity and pride to the Sikh people. They had given a unique example of sacrifice. Now they were becoming a model of dedicated service to the whole nation.

Though it appeared calm was about to prevail, on the pretext of the long-standing Patiālā-Nābhā dispute, the Sikh Mahārājā of Nābhā (who was favourably disposed towards the nationalist forces and used to speak to highlight India's problems in the Imperial Council much to the embarassment of the Govt., and who after the Nankānā tragedy even sported a black turban in response to the Akālis' call) was suddenly deposed on July 9, 1923, and externed to Derā Doon. Under Govt. pressure, he had indeed written out in his own hand :— "I relinquish the throne of my own accord." But, the Sikhs could see through the real reasons. And a wholly religious agitation took on political overtones.

On September 9, they observed a Protest Day, and resolved that they would put the Sikh Mahārājā back on his throne, whatever the cost. On Oct. 12, the Govt. declared both the Akāli Dal and the SGPC illegal bodies, and arrested all the sixty members of their executive committees. A case was launched against them "for waging war against the king," which continued for three years. This added fuel to the fire. Protest meetings followed by more arrests and prosecutions became the order of the day throughout the Panjāb. Within the state of Nābhā, Sikhs were arrested in an open protest meeting held at the Gurdwārā Gangsar, Jaito (17 miles from Bhatindā).

To pray for the success of the Sikh cause, an *Akhand Pāth* (continuous reading of the Sikh Scripture) was initiated by the Sikhs of this place. The state POLICE FORCIBLY REMOVED THE READER, a 15-year old lad, Niranjan Singh Gyani from the Holy Altar, and substituted him by their own man. This was considered sacrilegous and the movement gathered a new momentum. To re-assert the sanctity of the Sikh ritual, small bands of Sikhs (25 each) started pouring into Jaito. They were arrested, beaten and then let off. But to put more force into it, the strength of the *jathā* was increased to 500 which first started out on its journey on Feb 9, 1924, on foot, on the auspicious day of *Basant Panchmi* (the spring-festival). They reached Jaito on Feb 21, 1924. The police took no chances and started indiscriminate firing in the air from the fort. When it did not deter the members of the advancing *jathā*, they were machine-gunned and 27000 rounds fired. Many were killed, (40 to 50 is the estimated number) and the majority (about 300) were injured, either by gun-shots or being trampled later by the Police horses' shodden hoofs. The others were arrested. Some 25 of them were prosecuted for assault on the police (though the Sikhs were wholly unarmed) and given long jail-terms. A huge crowd which had assembled by now was also cruelly beaten by the police. Barrister Saifuddin Kitchlew, Panjāb Congress leader who had come to inquire into the situation, was also arrested. The whole country infact seemed involved. Mr. M.A. Jinnāh was the mover, along with Pt. Madan Mohan Mālviyā and 45 others, of a motion in the Central Assembly censuring the Govt. over the firing. The motion was disallowed, but the sympathy of the nation had been unmistakably expressed.

Another *jathā* of 500 followed from Amritsar, on Feb 28, and reached Jaito on March 14. They were met there by Pt. Madan Mohan Mālviyā on whose advice they offered arrest. Seventeen such *jathās* who came one after the other, were similarly arrested and jailed.

On July 9, 1925, a Gurdwārā Act was passed by the Panjāb Council, mainly drafted by Bhāi Jodh Singh, then a prominent member of the Council, (with the consent and support of the Akāli leaders in jail). It was enacted without opposition, thus finally transferring the legal control of all historic Gurdwārās of the Panjāb into the hands of the S.G.P.C. *

* This body is now-a-days elected, every five years, through the direct vote of all Sikh men and women, elections being conducted under Govt. auspices. (The latest elections were held on March 31, 1979, however, after 14 years). The definition of a Sikh as given in the Act is :— "He who believes in the ten Sikh Gurus and the Guru Granth Sahib and has no other religion." This thus included the *Sahjdhāris* in the voting list. A bill for an All-India Gurdwaras Act has recently been drafted on behalf of the S.G.P.C. by a very able and competent Sikh, Sardār

The *Akhand Pāth* at Jaito was allowed to be resumed, though the Mahārājā of Nābhā could not be restored to the throne. He himself had weakened his case by his earlier strong disapproval of the Akāli agitation in his behalf. (But when it was abandoned, he accused the Akālis of betrayal. Gāndhi also refused to take up his cause for the same reason).

Pandit Jawāhar Lāl Nehru,* and Mr. K. Santhānam, (journalist and patriot from Madrās) who came to make inquiries also were arrested (and later released). But apart from the sacrifices, deaths, fines, jail terms, and loss of limbs and businesses made during this movement, the spirit of supreme dedication, self-denial and togetherness shown by the Sikhs (and lauded and supported by the whole Indian nation which also got a new experience and a new line of guidance in its struggle for freedom) had put this hitherto sword-arm of India in the front line of civil resisters,‡ willing to court martydom for a good cause without retaliation or regret. Sikhs were never the same again, nor was the nation at large.†

F. N. Contd.

Harbans Singh, ex-Chief Justice of Panjāb. It is, however, upto the Central Govt. to enact it or not.

* Jawaharlāl Nehru (1889-1964) the first Prime Minister of India, played a heroic role in our struggle for freedom, Born in the rich family of an extremely successful lawyer, he himself did his M.Sc. at Cambridge and was called to the Bar in England. But he never practised Law and after his illustrious father, Moti Lāl Nehru, became a trusted lieutenant of Gāndhi. Socialist, democratic and secular to the core, he often differed with his master (see, *Letters* published by Asia Pub House) but ultimately it was he whom Gandhi nominated as his political heir and successor. Their home in Allāhābād became the HQs of the Indian National Congress and Nehru suffered Jail-terms for a total of 9 years. His policy of non-alignment, of industrialisation and secular democracy as Prime Minister have put the country on the world-map. Such was his love for the minorities, particularly Muslims, that Patel used to say :— "Jawaharlāl is the only nationalist Muslim in the country."

‡ Between 1922-25, an extremist movement wedded to violence also arose among the Sikh repatriates from abroad. This was known as the *Babbar Akāli* movement. They killed many loyalists and informers of the police in the Doaba region. Many armed encounters were held with the police. They were either hanged or transported to Andamans for life, or offered other sentences. The main Akāli movement, though somewhat sympathetic to it, kept aloof from it by and large.

† According to Akāli estimates, 40,000 Sikhs were imprisoned and 500 killed. But, more impartial and authoritative sources claim that about 30,000 Sikhs courted arrest in the Akāli agitation and 400 were killed. Confiscated pensions of military

The Results

The main fruitful result of the Akāli movement was the politicalisation of the entire Sikh community right down to its rural roots. The honeymoon with the Govt. was over. The loyalists abandoned the political (and even social) field in panic. There was now a complete and wholly appreciative understanding of the Sikh ethos throughout the country. Their none-too-happy image as a war-like people gave way to their being the dedicated and peaceful warriors of God, spiritually awakened, highly catholic and cooperative in outlook, ready to dare and die for all good causes (and not only their own) which brought the whole country glory and honour.

It threw up a class of middle class leadership (initially well-educated) which could think and act in behalf of the larger issues and bring this small, though highly purposive and dynamic community, into the mainstream of national life. Its history and spiritual ethos had now become an inseparable part of the national heritage.

If nothing else would have been gained, this one single gain was enough. It is no small or unworthy task to illumine a people's glorious but forgotten and at best half-understood past in terms of the present. The Sikh people had become the worthy instruments of the national struggle for freedom and their victorious, non-violent struggle assured for them a certain political and social future. The name of a Sikh had become a symbol to conjure with.

But, as the historic Gurdwārās with their large offerings came into the hands of the S.G.P.C. to be elected by adult Sikh franchise, a wholly new experiment in the whole history of religious endowments, it led to new stresses in the Sikh society. The S.G.P.C. was looked upon as "a state within a state," a Parliament of the Sikhs,

---

F. N. Contd.

personnel, participating in the movement and fines on others amounted to about Rs. 15 lakhs. Some papers in sympathy with the movement had to pay large securities which were later forfeited. (For details, see *Akāli Morchian Dā Itihās,* by Sohan Singh Josh ; *"Struggle for Reform in Sikh Shrines,* by R.R. Sahni; *Some Confidential papers of the Akāli movement* by Dr. Ganda Singh; the *Akāli Movement* by Mohinder Singh; *Akāli Lahar* by Giani Partap Singh and *Akālis, past and Present,* by K.C. Gulāti, records in the national Archives (1921-25) and debates of the Pb. Legislative Council etc. Master Tārā Singh's Autobiography (Master Tārā Singh, *Jiwan to Sangharsh*) is the most useful of all, as it gives the background and the weaknesses of the movement as well, in a very dispassionate manner.

supported as it was by popular sanctions, renewed after every five years. It also became a ladder for political ascendancy and success (*) and hence also an arena of intrigue, manipulation, pushing and jostling for power, and, most of all, the pressing into service of the Gurdwārā platform for vague political objectives and personal glory.

This gave a great set-back to religious and moral education for which purpose indeed the Gurdwārā Reform movement had been launched. New-fangled ideas of self-gratification overcame the ideals of self-denial, service and spiritual illumination of the people.

The Hindus of the Panjāb who had stood by the Sikhs and generously supported their agitation with money and sympathy (whenever funds were lacking, even Gāndhiji was approached) but the suits filed against the Mahants (who were Hindu in form) and the removal of idols from the precincts of the Sikh temples led to Hindu-Sikh tension as well. On both sides, the church had become property and had to be fought for and defended in the name of Hindu or Sikh religion.

The income, never large (even now at 100 million rupees annually or so, most of it spent on administration and upkeep of the temples, and equal only to a medium-scale industry's), however, made the new Akāli custodians politically more formidable from now on. And, as political slogans continued to be changed, the spiritual instruction gave way to political fanaticism, exclusiveness and the re-birth of ritualism (the more profitable, the better) and the dream

* No one has written better on this facet of the Akāli movement than one of its outstanding leaders, Master Tārā Singh. He writes in his Autobiography, "Our victory in the *morcha* (agitation) to obtain the keys of the Toshākānā had puffed up our ego sky-high. Our *Jathās* would travel any class by train without a ticket. We started insulting British officers without cause. Such fire was being emitted in speeches as led later to irresponsibility and indiscipline among our ranks. Everybody became a law unto himself. If the Govt. would not have come down upon us with a heavy hand, to unite us once again in the face of danger, our victory had finished us off. Tall talk, egoism and each for himself led to mutual quarrels and distrust. It is my firm conviction that he who cannot contain himself after a victory will lose in the end, also he who is demoralised by defeat. Initially the Akāli movement had raised the level of our character. Now, it was all over. I ask you:— *O Sikhs*, donot listen to those who say 'politics is built on strife and falsehood.' Our (Sikh) politics can only be based on the highest values of our religion." (PP. 58-59)

of the regeneration of the *Panth* continued, as time passed, to take a back seat. Though every section of Sikh opinion had participated in the movement, Akālis (as organised in the Akāli Dal) took the sole credit for it, ran its own tickets and turned nationalists and religiously-inclined people out of the Sikh religious platform.* Caste, faction and region became more important than religion. Compromise was affected with the Communists, but not with the nationalist Sikhs. The religious platform became a springboard for political ascendancy in the Panjāb.

At first, the leadership was divided into "Acceptors" and "Non-acceptors" of the Gurdwārā Act of 1925. The Bill was drafted and passed with the total concurrence of the Sikh leaders inside the jail. Whenever the Govt. hesitated, pressure was brought to bear on them through the Congress and other non-Sikh platforms.† But, when the Govt. asked the Sikh leadership (foolishly, or possibly with the knowledge that this would divide them) to commit in writing, that they would faithfully work the Act as a condition of their being released, the extremists (led by Bābā Kharak Singh, Sardār Mangal Singh‡ Sardār Sohan Singh Josh@ Master Tārā Singh*.

---

* For instance, no one out of the Sikh Savants who contributed, as no one else did, to enrich Sikh literature or conduct missionary activities like Bhāi Vir Singh, Bhai Jodh Singh, Prof. Tejā Singh, Dr. Gandā Singh, Prof. Sāhib Singh, Bhāi Kāhan Singh (of Nābhā), Bāwā Harkrishan Singh etc. was over nominated to the S.G.P.C., though a provision for nomination has always been there in the Act.

† Please see Gandā Singh's "Some Confidential papers of the Akāli movement," published by the S.G.P.C. itself (1965).

‡ Sardār Mangal Singh (Gill) of Ludhiānā played a notable part in the Akāli and Congress movements. It is he who started the *Hindustān Times* in Delhi, but due to financial losses transferred its ownership to Pt. M.M. Malviya etc after a year. He was a member of the Moti Lāl Nehru Committee which drafted the first Constitution of free India. Later, he was a member of the Central Assembly where alongwith Sardār Sant Singh, Advocate of Lyallpur, he fought for nationalist causes with great ability and zest. He was also editor of *Akāli* at Lāhore.

@ Sardār Sohan Singh Josh turned a Communist revoluntionary and was implicated in the Merrut conspiracy case. He was also a legislator in the Panjāb, but became a wholetime CPI worker and member of their politbureau. He and many other workers of both Marxist parties of the Panjāb (C.P.I. and C.P.M.) are Sikhs. The universities and industrial workers and farmhands have especially been influenced by their propaganda in favour of Marxism.

* Master Tārā Singh (1885-1967), born in Haryāl (Rāwalpindi distt.) was a convert from Hinduism while yet a student, his earlier name being Nānak Chand.

etc.) refused to give any written undertaking. Others like Sardār Bahādur Mehtāb Singh and Gyani Sher Singh, who thought it was their moral duty to work an Act passed at their own behest, did so, and were scandalised as pro-Govt. toadies, inspite of their dedicated service of long years and their incarceration and sacrifices. Mehtāb Singh, an affluent Barrister, had resigned his Vice-Presidentship of the Panjāb Legislative Council and otherwise also had suffered imprisonment and great financial loss. Gyāni Sher Singh, the blind Sikh missionary, became the political rival of Master Tārā Singh and built his own Akāli Dal joined by Sardār Bahādur Mehtāb Singh. Hence their Party derisively was called the "Sardār Bahādur Party."

The extremists were also released soon thereafter and worked the Act even more zealously (in fact, they defeated and drove the others completely out), but it led to a schism, which was exploited by Mahārājā Bhupindra Singh of Patiālā, for his own reasons (he helped the other party led by Gyāni Sher Singh generously) besides the Govt., and resurrected the loyalists (inspite of their own timidity and inability in view of the general atmosphere) as a force once again to reckon with, under the Akāli label, or as the Khālsā Nationalist party which both were patronised later by Sardār Kharak Singh as well.

The intelligentsia was completely isolated and took to civil or military service, business, professions or farming, but not to politics, which was falling more and more into the hands of the caste

---

F. N. Contd.

He did his B.A. and took a teachers' training certificate, and became Headmaster of the Lyallpur Khālsā High School on a pittance of Rs. 15/-per mansem, which shows his high idealism at an early age. He dominated Sikh politics for over forty years (1920-60). He graduated from the Khālsā College, Amritsar. and was a student of Bhāi Jodh Singh who helped him get a scholarship through Sir Sunder Singh, later his arch political foe. He edited a newspaper in Urdu, *Parbhāt* & also in Panjābi *Akāli & Jāthedār* & wrote two excellent novels, *Prem Lagan* and *Bābā Tegā Singh*. It is a pity that his abundant literary talent (his humour and banter, his contagious optimism, his delineation of character at its best and worst, his love of idealism and faith in high moral values, besides his love of life in all its manifestations, and the natural flow of his language and ideas, as exhibited here and other places, on politics and religion) were sacrificed to his deep involvement in politics. Basically, they reveal a very human person, full of compassion for all life and a penchant for reason, balance and compromise.

and faction-ridden (mostly illiterate) damagogues.* Even Sardār Kharak Singh, the President of the S. G. P. C. and the Akālī Dal, who had brought such signal honour and glory to the Sikh movement, fell a prey to these machinations and resigned from both offices never to return.† After this, for a decade and a half

---

* Master Tārā Singh in his *Autobiography* (*Jiwan te Sangharsh*) endorses the statement that the victory of the Akālis in the Gurdwāra Reform movement turned their heads. "*Burchhāgardi* (gangsterism) prevailed" (P. 77). "If even a small section of Sikh opinion is not able to identify the gangsters and self-seeking *chaudharies*, there is a grave danger to the future of the *Panth*." (P. 78). "Our leaders committed many mistakes during the Akāli movement. I will not go into details, nor blame many people. I will name only two persons, Sarmukh Singh Jhabāl (a man of great influence, character, and many other high qualities, but highly irresponsible) and Gopal Singh Qaumi. I had started the Nāhhā agitation and was in jail and was being prosecuted, but I was not in favour of a *morchā*, on this question. These two gentlemen were very enthusiastic and created an atmosphere in which they left no scope for us to think coolly and dispassionately. But when the things went out of their hands, they tried to retrace their steps publicly, and came to ask my opinion in jail. I said 'a General who leads to the uncalled-for slaughter of his forces, commits suicide to save his conscience and honour. So should you. This silenced them." (P. 86)

† Master Tārā Singh, however, gives different reasons for the quittal of Bābā Kharak Singh (1868-1963). This Ahluwāliā Sardār, a lawyer by profession and son of a rich contractor of Sialkot, Rai Bahādur Sardār Hari Singh, suffered much for the Sikh cause and was known as the *betāj bādshāh* (uncrowned king) of the Sikhs. But, sāys Tārā Singh :— "After the Nehru Report (1928) was rejected by the Sikhs and was not accepted by the British either, the Congress also withdrew it next year & passed a resolution that "no constitution would be acceptable to the Congress, which would not satisfy the Muslims, Sikhs and other minorities." This satisfied us, but Bābāji was nolonger for cooperation with the Congress, unless the Sikh colour was added to the Congress flag. When this was done, he objected that yellow and not ochre was the Sikh colour. And such objections went on multiplying till he resigned both offices." (Autobiography, Page. 111)

Another and more serious objection of Bābāji, however, was that the Congress had accepted the "dominion status" instead of complete idnependence as their goal. The Congress at Lāhore (1929) accepted the latter alternative, but Bābāji thereafter took no part either in the Congress or the Akāli movement and even helped their adversaries among the Sikhs through his Central Akāli Dal, of which he remained President for long. It appears he had become sick of the intrigues for power and opportunism. For a time, he was also President of the Panjāb Congress. Inspite of his differences, he was held in high esteem by nationalist forces for his integrity, fearlessness in the face of danger & courage of convictions. In 1951, Nehru said of him :— "I do not see any body in the country today who

(1925-1939), the Akālis, however, earned a great reputation for themselves as the dedicated soldiers of India's freedom. They became the most militant wing of the Indian National Congress and participated in every *Satyāgraha* movement led by Māhatmā Gāndhi, contributing far more in men and material than their numbers warranted. Out of those who were sent to the gallows or were offered life-imprisonments and deported to the Andamans, over eighty percent were Sikhs. The name of Sardār Bhagat Singh, the revolutionary, became a household word. His daring and supreme sacrifice of life (1931) inspired and boosted the sagging morale of every youth throughout the country. Māster Tārā Singh, on hearing of the firing on the brave non-violent Pathāns at Peshāwar (10 May, 1930) led a *Jathā* of 100 Sikhs to offer *Satyāgraha* there and was arrested alongwith others. "The Sikhs and Pathāns are sons of the same motherland, and if any such impression prevails that they are enemies, the Sikhs will wash it off by mingling their blood with that of the Pathāns", he declared with great emotion.

Sardār Kharak Singh discarded his clothes throughout his prison-term (1922-27) in the Derā Ghazi Khān jail, when the jail authorities insisted on the Congressmen removing their headgear (the Gāndhi caps) and the Sikhs not donning a black turban. Though the restriction on the black turban was soon removed, Bābā Kharak Singh refused to wear clothes in sympathy with Congressmen. In the Hindu-Muslim riots of 1923 and later in 1928 at Kohāt, the Sikhs always were on the side of the victims and nursed the wounded and helped liberally the families of the dead.

In 1937, on the eve of the first General Elections, leading to provincial autonomy, a joint Akali-Congress ticket was evolved. No one of the two was to oppose the candidate of the other, as both, after the elections, were to form part of a single Opposition. Such was the bonhomie that the Congress acquiesced, under strong Akāli pressure, to leave the seat of Bābā Gurdit Singh (Congress) of the Kāmā Gātā Māru fame open for contest by a neo-Akali, Partap Singh Kairon (later to become the formidable Congress

---

F. N. Contd.

can be compared in courage, bravery and truthfulness with Bābā Kharak Singh." Gandhiji, Sardār Patel & Morārji Desai paid similar tributes on various occasions.

Chief Minister of Panjab), who trounced his adversary, much to the discomfiture of the Indian National Congress.*

But when the Great War started in 1939, a new chapter was opened in the history of the Panjāb and Sikh politics.

* Two significant events took place during these years (1930-37). One was the formation of the Gur-Sewak Sadha by 5 Sikh intellectuals led by Prof. Teja Singh which prepared a new edition of the Adi Granth in which, for the first time, words were separated one from the other, according to fixed rules of grammar, and their renderings given in easy Panjābi. The second event was the convening of the Sarb-Sampardaya-Sikh Conference at Bhaini Sāhib, in (1934) in which all Sikh sects participated on equal terms and doctrinal differences were not allowed to stand in the way.

CHAPTER XXVII

THE RISE OF MUSLIM NATIONALISM

(1940 – 1945)

It has already been indicated that the more the nationalist movement grew, the more the British die-hards tried for division among the Hindus and Muslims. After 1857, the Muslims were the aggrieved and the distrusted party, having been deprived of their privileged position in India. They became sullen and isolated, though it appears odd, because neither the Afghāns nor the Moghals ever trusted or promoted the Indian Muslims either in their civil or military establishment, which were manned in the higher ranks almost exclusively by their own kith & kin, race or place of origin.
However, as nationalist sentiment grew in Bengāl and Mahārāshtra, and the Indian National Congress grew in strength and clamoured for total *Swarāj* (as Tilak did, though he identified it with Shivāji's *Swarāj* and hearkened back to the past, thus creating distrust among the Muslims, while Gokhale looked towards the future and wanted to build *Swarāj* on the democratic Parliamentary lines of the West and was soon isolated, being too moderate), the Hindus who led these movements, being better educated, came to be distusted more and more. The Muslims were encouraged to state their claim initially for a share in the pie, but later not only to ask for more but to fight for it in the streets, now under one pretext, now under another.

Even before Sir Sayyad Ahmad Khān (the namesake of another Sayyad Ahmad Khān, who had proclaimed a *Jehād* against the

Sikhs in the 1820s) had opened the Aligarh Muslim college in 1875, to impart western education (alongwith instruction in religion) to Muslims, British writers (some in the imperial Civil Service) had begun to write about the Muslim rights, and the wrongs being perpetrated on them. Sir William Hunter, a civil servant, in his book "*The Indian Musalmān*" (1871) in its last chapter had discussed threadbare the "*Wrongs of the Mohammedans under British Rule*". In 1882, Sir Sayyad advocated separate electorates for the Muslims in the municipal elections, introduced by Lord Rippon. In 1887, he made renewed pleas to the Muslims to remain uninvolved in the Congress party's pleas for a quicker introduction of the western-style Parliamentary bodies. He said, the Hindus being caste-ridden, this system was unsuited to Indian conditions. In 1905, Bengāl was divided by Lord Curzon on the basis of Hindu and Muslim. In 1906, the All India Muslim League was formed and its deputation, led by His Highness the Āghā Khān*, had assured for the Muslims not only separate electorates in the forthcoming Minto-Morley Reforms (1909), but also weightage in the provinces and at the Centre where they were in a minority.

Wilfred Scawen Blunt in his "India under Ripon, a private Diary" (1909) got so far, while in Calcuttā, as to outline pretty clearly the Pakistān demand of the future. He said the sub-continent should have two separate Governments, a Muslim one in the North and a Hindu one in the South. Mr. M. A. Jinnāh later quoted John Bright as having suggested as early as 1858, "the impossiblity of a unitary Govt. in India." Amir Ali's "*Spirit of Islām*" (1887) and poet Hāli's *Mussadas* also pointed in the same direction.

Not that the Muslim grievances were not genuine. They really were. They were (though mostly for their own reasons) far behind in education, commerce and industry. Their only two occupations on land, or in the civil and military services during the Moghal regime,

---

* The Āghā Khān (it is his religious title, not his name), the fabulously-rich spiritual leader of the Khojā Muslims is of Turkish origin, with a large Muslim following in India, East Africa, U.K. and elsewhere. Living in Paris or Geneva, in the true western style, the successive Āghā Khāns have through the monies collected from the community spread education and employment among their sect on an unprecedented scale. They have also taken keen interest in Muslim political affairs and the spread of Islām in modern idiom.

were nolonger available to them. They were wholly demoralised after 1857. But, the worst part is that their claims were never understood in the right spirit, nor the wrongs righted in good time by their fellow-countrymen,who constituted the majority people, and who also had outstripped them in almost all fields of human endeavour.

What is even more unpardonable is the writings and religious activities of Hindus, concentrating more on rousing anti-Muslim feelings than otherwise. The excesses of some Muslim rulers of India like Aurangzeb, or marauders from abroad like Nādir Shāh and Ahmed Shāh Abdāli and Muslims generally and their duels with the Hindus were highlighted in such a way, as in the novels of Bankim Chandar Chatterjee (e.g. in the "Anand Math," which also gave us the patriotic song of "*Bandē Mātram*" but which was opposed by the Muslims for the anti-Muslim context in which it was uttered in the text), that it generated anti-Muslim feelings.

The attacks on Islām by Aryā Samāj, their campaigns for *Shudhi* (re-conversion of Muslims), the Hindu clamour for ban on cow-slaughter, Gāndhi's own resolve to fast unto death to save the "erring daughter of a friend" (Motilāl Nehru) from marrying a Muslim and Lokmānya Tilak making *Ganpati Pujā* etc. as part of the nationalist ritual, hearkening back to the Hindu, particularly anti-Muslim past, as under Shivāji, hurt and alienated the Muslim sentiment from the Hindus. Lālā Lājpat Rāi in his last days talked of separating Hindu areas from the Muslim ones, thus preceding Mr. Jinnah by many years. Gāndhi himself identified *Swarajya* with *Rām Rājyā*. Whatever it might have meant to him, it meant a revivalist rāj to the others. The Lucknow Pact (of 1916) tried to retrieve the position by granting both weightage and separate electorates to the Muslims. Also, the powerful and unqualified support given by the Congress under Gandhiji to the Khilāfat movement (1919-1922)* brought together

* The Muslims of India resented not only the dismemberment of the Turkish empire after Turkey's defeat in the first World War, but also the abolition of the institution of *Khilāfat* through which the Turkish Sultān exercised his authority as the religious head of Muslims everywhere. Muslims in India were in an open rebellion and the Gandhi-led Congress also joined hands with them. Muslims were called upon to resign all Govt. jobs, pay no taxes, return all titles, boycott British institutions, including schools and courts and British goods. Thousands courted arrest and thousands even left India to live in Afghānistān. The song "*Mērē Maulā bulā lo madinē Mujhē, yahān Hind men dengē na Jeenē mujhē*" (O Allāh call me to thy home in Medina, for they will not let me live in India).

the Muslims and Hindus as never before. But, it hurt the nationalitst cause more by mixing up religion with politics. And, then, when Kemāl Ataturk, the new President in his wisdom declared Turkey to be a Secular Republic, and finally abolished Caliphate in 1924,"as a decadant and medieval institution," the Muslims and Hindus both felt cheated. And the Hindu-Muslim riots which immediately preceded and followed it, could be the only result of this sentimental unity of the people without a unity of purpose. However, it did bring into the Congress fold such stalwarts as Maulānā Abul Kalām Azād (the Meccā-born interpreter of the Qurān and a powerful writer and speaker of Urdu later to become President of the Congress), Dr. M.A. Ansāri, Hakim Ajmal Khān, the Khān Bros of North-West Frontier* together with their valiant Pathān followers, and the Ali Brothers., but the general Muslim sentiment stood apart and away from the nationalist cause, not because they wanted the eternal continuance of the British rule, but because even their modest demands were misinterpreted and not met on time. Bargaining became a respectable

---

F. N. Contd.
became current in these very days.
The Afghān Muslim Govt., however, barred their entry into the Afghan territory. Later Kemāl Atāturk abolished Caliphāte. The Muslims of India knew only then that common religion could not create common political or economic interests. But, they forgot the lesson too soon, much to their detriment.

* Of the Muslims who suffered most for the nationalist cause, the names of two illustrious brothers, Khān Abdul Ghaffār Khān and Dr. Khān Sāhib of the Frontier province, are the more famous. Born in a rich land-owning Pathān family of Utmānzai, near Peshāwar, Ghaffār Khān became such a dedicated follower of Gāndhi that he was known as the *Frontier Gāndhi*. He preached non-violence to the war-like Pathāns with such staggering success that his entire people, inspite of much suffering, came to the Congress fold. Dr. Khān, the elder brother, and trained in medicine in England, became the Congress Chief Minister in the N. W. F. P. He was murdered by a Muslim after Pakistān came into being, when he had taken over as Chief Minister of West Pakistān. Ghaffār Khān (also known as Badshāh-Khān, or the King of Khāns) was incarcerated in Pakistāni Jails for [illegible] lived in Kabul, fighting in his nineties for an independent Pathanland as he did not believe in the communal politics of Pakistan. He died in 1987.

His son, Wali Khān, is still the leader of the Opposition. But, while accepting Pakistān, the Congress leaders abandoned the Pathāns to their fate or to a plebiscite whose verdict they knew would go against them in the changed circumstances. They boycotted the plebiscite and yet the negative vote Pakistān received from the Pathāns was nearly equal to the vote favouring the merger of NWFP in Pākistān. (49.57%).

word, so also Muslim communalism and exclusiveness. It was a perversity of fact to call inconsequential a just (though seemingly exaggerated) demand of a minority, (then about 80 million strong) with a political history and religious cohesion which had once swept through the world from China to Spain,and led to the establishment of the Indian and Turkish empires for atleast 500 years and had introduced new discoveries in mathematics, medicine and astronomy, besides architecture, cultural mores, and culinary and decorative arts. To dismiss their pride and their humiliation, both, as of no consequence, was the height of majority egotism. It was neither nationalism nor humanism; it was plain and simple opportunism.

Otherwise, at no time did the Muslims before 1939, ever clamour for separation or political rights outside of India. Mr. Mohammad Ali Jinnāh, hardly a Muslim by orthodox standards, was born of a Hindu (Bhātiā) mother, knew no Urdu or Arabic, had never studied or read the Qurān, and is reported also to be not averse to egg-and-bacon for his breakfast or a strong drink before dinner. He had married a Pārsi girl in an unorthodox way, was educated in London as a Barrister and was long reputed to be an ambassador of Hindu-Muslim unity. Of course, he did not like mass-politics of Gāndhi in the atmosphere of caste, regional, religious and tribal pulls among an illiterate electorate. He did not believe (perhaps rightly) in the "Inner Voice" of Gandhiji in political affairs, which changed so often at his convenience, his political fasts, strikes, *dharnas* and mass agitations to force concessions out of the Govt., instead of through argument and debate, especially when the idea of the Indian National Congress also was to evolve a civilised democratic society on the western model. According to Durgadas (From *Curzon to Nehru*, pp. 169-174), Sir Fazli Hussain, Premier of Panjāb (died 1936), after the announcement of the Communal Award in 1932,was prepared to thwart Jinnah's rise to absolute leadership of Muslims and cooperate with the Congress over the issue of complete freedom. In fact, Mr. Jinnah's withdrawal from politics after the Round Table Conference (1930-31) was on account of the fact that he was the least heard among the Muslim leaders, esp. of the Muslim-majority provinces. And when he came back on the scene from London, (where he had started his practice) on the eve on 1937 elections, the Congress hailed his re-entry, sick as they were of the titled Muslim gentry which played to the British tune. I[illegible]s Jinnah who had said in the Legislative Assembly, in 1925: "I am a nationalist first, nationalist second, nationalist last."

What is more significant is that the Muslim representaives at the All-Parties Conference at Lucknow (Aug 28-31, 1928) had agreed to the Nehru Report (1928), envisaging joint electorates with reservation of seats for the Muslims, on the basis of population only where they were in a minority, but with a right to contest more seats (which concession was denied to the Sikhs in the Panjāb). No reduction of Muslim majority in Panjab was envisaged, however, (though no reservation for them or any other community was conceded either.)*

No less a person than Maulānā Abul Kalām Azād (in his *India Wins Freedom*, p. 15) accuses his own party, the Indian National Congress, of having hurt the national interests grievously by not agreeing, on time, even to the trivial Muslim demands which ultimately led to the national disaster of partition. For instance, almost all Muslim seats had been won in 1937 in the U. P. by the Muslim League. They wanted only two seats in the Cabinet, where their influence, outside the Muslim-majority provinces, was the greatest. But according to Azād, Jawāharlāl Nehru offered only one seat to the Muslims. The Congress also insisted that all League members join the Congress and disband their provincial Parliamentary Board. K. F. Nariman, the nationalist leader, was ignored for the Chief Ministership of Bombay in the same year for the reason that he belonged to the minority Pārsi community. "Even if it is not

---

* Though the Panjāb leaders (including Maulānā Zafar Ali Khān, Dr. S.D. Kitchlew, Dr. Mohd Ālam, Dr. Satyapal, S. Sardul Singh Caveeshar etc.) all agreed to this. the Akālis were very sore, that while in the Muslim-majority provinces like the Panjāb, the Muslims will offer no reservations to non-Muslims, they would enjoy this privilege wherever they were in a minority. Mr. Jinnah (see later) made different proposals but was isolated by Muslims themselves. Master Tārā Singh and his rival, Gyani Sher Singh, both appended a statement to this Panjāb settlement, and called for elections by proportional representation and not through single-member constituencies. They upheld separate electorates with weightage for minorities and even opposed adult franchise as "premature" and "not practicable" "though we shall not make a grievance of it." Later, the Akāli conference at Lāhore (1929) rejected the report outright. The British Govt. also took no notice of it and formed their own Commission under Sir John Simon to tour India and make recommendations. The Muslims also backed out at the Round Table Conferences held later in London, for they were getting a better deal from the British.

true," says Azād, "it is difficult to disprove such an allegation." His appeal against this discrimination was rejected both by Gāndhiji and Nehru, under the influence of Vallabhbhāi Patel, and P.D. Tandon (both President of the Congress at one time or another). (A similar situation arose after the 1952 elecltions. Partap Singh Kairon commanded the majority of the Congress support in the Panjāb Assembly, but belonging to the Sikh minority, he had to give way to Bhim Sen Sachar on the insistence of Maulāna Azād himself !)

Otherwise, when the small pamphlet on Pākistān entitled *NOW OR NEVER* by Rahmat Ali, a Combridge student, was distributed in the Central Assembly, in 1935, according to Sri Parkasha (himself then a Congress Member of the Assembly) the man who laughed it out most was Mohammad Ali Jinnāh.*

In 1930, Dr. Mohd, Iqbāl's presidential address to the Muslim League at Allahabad, spelling out the creation of a "*Muslim India within India*" consisting of only the North-Western provinces, was never taken seriously either by Jinnāh or any other Muslim of note. At no time during his membership of the Central Assembly did Jinnāh ever dissociate himself (nor did his followers, who held the balance) from any nationalist cause,proposed by the Swarāj Party led by Moti Lāl Nehru. Even when Jinnāh opposed the Nehru Report, he only asked for 30% seats reserved through communal electorates at the Centre, weightage in the minority provinces and on population basis where they were in a majority. He was, however, outvoted by other Muslims present there. At the three Round Table conferences in London (1930-31), the Muslim leaders, including Mr. Jinnāh, Sir Mohd. Shafi and others talked only of safeguards for their community, separate electorates, weightage and so on, but never about Pākistān, not even as a bad joke. Jinnāh's Muslim League had won only 2 seats in the Panjāb (out of 175 in 1937) and a Unionist Ministry, wholly opposed to his organisation, under Sir Sikandar Hayat Khān, came to power. So also in Bengāl, where Muslims under the banner of the Proja Krishak Party of Fazal-ul-Haq took up the reigns of office. It is a pity that the Congress opposed both, and sat in the opposition, thus leaving no choice for Sir Sikandar Hayat and Fazul-ul-Haq but to join the Muslim League, in due course. In the other states, where the Congress swept the

---

* ***Pakistān, birth and early days*, P. 2.**

polls, the League-led Muslims became the sole Opposition. (When C. R. Dās proposed as President of the Calcutta corporation that 60% Muslims be recruited to its offices till their numerical strength in the population was represented in civil services, there was so much furore against him that he had to throw up his hands in despair).

The Federal part of the Govt. of India Act (which also brought the Indian states into the federal structure for the first time and gave India a unitary govt. in essence, though federal in form), was boycotted by the Congress, as the powers reserved by the Crown over Finance, Defence and Foreign Affairs were not transferred to popular hands and the nominated members from princely states were feared to tilt the balance against the nationalist cause of freedom. The federal Constitution had been hammered out after three successive Round Table conferences in London, & many unity conferences at home and was acceptable to the Muslims (though the League under Jinnāh later joined hands with the Congress for his own reasons to reject it), the Indian states and other minorities like the Scheduled Castes. If the Congress would only have worked it for a time, the country's history would have been written out completely differently. After all, the Congress did accept office in the provinces, inspite of the Veto of the British Governor, after taking a promise that the Governors would use it only on certain specified occasions like the breakdown of law and order, war or blatant injustice to a minority. And let it be said to their credit that they never used it even once. Similar assurances could have been extracted for the Centre as well. But, this was never to happen.

And then came the World War (1939-44). The Congress (unwisely) quit office in the provinces also, and started an individual Satyagraha (1940), inspite of the fact thst Maulānā Azād, then Congress President, and Jawāhar Lāl Nehru were both for participation in the war-effort if the British would declare Dominion Status as India's goal to be achieved after the war, and transferred its substance now. But Gandhiji was so dead set against any war, and for an executive wholly responsible to the Central Assembly here and now, that the invitation of the Viceroy to Maulānā Azād for talks (1940) was ignored. The Pirpur Report on the "misdeeds" of the Congress Govts. in relation to the Muslims inflamed the Muslim passions as never before. This was a chance which the British die-hards also could not afford to miss. They formed Govts at the Centre and the states with the help of the Muslim sympathisers of the League on a public assurance by the Viceroy (Aug 1940) that though the political goal for India continued to be Dominion Status, no constitutional advance will be made without the concurrence of the Muslims.

Other independent elements and Ambedkar's Scheduled Castes also joined in. Sir Sikandar Hyāt Khan, Premier of the Panjab (inspite of his "Hands off the Panjab" call to Mr. Jinnah in the Panjab Assembly), and Fazal-ul-Haq, Premier of Bengal, (who had quarelled with Jinnah publicly and criticised his authoritarian attitude) both joined the Muslim League , under British pressure, and in their own interest, the League having been recognised by British Govt. as virtually the sole spokesman of the Muslims, soon after the following resolution was passed at the annual session of the A. I. Muslim League held at Lahore and presided over by Mr. M. A. Jinnah in 1940 :—

"Resolved that no constitutional plan would be acceptable in this country or acceptable to the Muslims, unless geographically contiguous units are demarcated into regions which should be so constituted with such territorial adjustments as may be necessary in which Muslims are numerically in a majority, as in the north-western and north-eastern zone of India should be grouped to constitute independent states in which the constituent units shall be autonomous and sovereign."

Pakistan was born through our own calculated folly and now there was no looking back.

Now we come back to our story.

The more the talk of transfer of power took place, the more the Sikhs felt agitated about their political future. They had cast their lot with the Congress but they had been by-passed and ignored at the time of the Hindu-Muslim pact signed at Lucknow (1916). Their viewspoint went also unheeded in the preparation of the Nehru Report (1928). The Muslims had been given a statutory majority in the Panjab, though with joint electorates. The concessions offered them (reservation with right to contest other seats) in the other provinces were not accorded to the Sikhs in the Panjab on the same basis inorder not to disturb the wafer-thin Muslim majority. This led to widespread discontent against the Congress, and a session of the Central Sikh League held at Lahore the next year (1929) and presided over by Bābā Kharak Singh made the historic annual session of the Congress presided over by Jawāhar Lāl Nehru look pale in comparison. It was at this historic session held on the banks of the Rāvi, that a resolution was passed by the Congress and a pledge taken that the Congress would accept nothing short of *Purana Swārāj* (complete independence).*

The Govt. sent out a wholly British-constituted Reforms Commission under Sir John Simon, to tour India. This was boycotted, and at Lāhore, a demonstration led by L. Lajpat Rai against it, was severely cane-charged which resulted after a few days in the death of that well-known patriot and leader. His murder was avenged by Sardār Bhagat Singh, a nephew of Sardār Ajit Singh, the revolutionary (referred to before). He also threw a bomb in the Central Assembly at Delhi. Bhagat Singh was tried and hanged (alongwith his two companions, Sukhdev and Raj Guru) at the Lahore Central Jail on March 23, 1931, at the young age of 23.†

This highly charged the atmosphere. Three Round Table conferences were held at London (1930-31) but without any result. The Sikh representation was hand-picked by the Government, ignoring the Akāli Dal as well as the Congress Sikhs. The Congress agreed to be ultimately represented by Mahātmā Gāndhi. The Muslims were represented by Mr. Jinnah as well as the titled Muslim gentry from the Panjāb and elsewhere. The Akālis made it known that they disowned and wholly dissociated with the activities of the Sikh representatives. In this atmosphere of hostility and disavowal, they did whatever best they could. The two Sikh representatives chosen by the British Govt. were : Sardār Ujjal Singh (he later became Parliamentary Secretary to Sir Sikandar Hayat, a Congress Finance Minister in Panjab and Governor of Madras after freedom) was a leading businessman and a moderate political leader of Lāhore, who presented the Sikh case with ability and integrity. The other was

* The Nehru report only had asked for "Dominion Status" within a year, but this demand was rejected by the Govt., and hence the irrevocable demand for complete independence was made officially for the first time. Bābā Kharak Singh, the Sikh leader, had also rejected the report mainly on this ground.

† In 1975, his mother was honoured as Panjāb Mātā (Mother of Panjābis) by the Congress Govt.

Sardar Sampuran Singh, Barrister, later to become the leader of the Congress legislature party in the Panjab.

They supported joint electorates with reservation of seats, demanded 30% seats for the Sikhs, but they could not secure in the Communal Award (1932) announced by Lord Ramsay Macdonald, the British Prime Minister, more than 19 percent seats, with the Muslims assured their communal majority in the Panjab. Separate electrorates to them were, however, offered alongwith the Muslims and the Untouchables. The Congress had earlier at their session at Lahore (1929) and Karachi (1931) passed resolutions saying, that "no Constitution would be acceptable to the Congress which does not satisfy the Muslims, the Sikhs and the other minorities," but when it came to the crunch, the Sikhs felt lost, and were left to fend for themselves.

Mahātmā Gāndhi went on a fast unto death over the Communal Award, offering separate electorates to the Harijans (as he chose to call the untouchable Hindus) and Dr. B. R. Ambedkar, their leader, yielded to public pressure in scrapping separate electorates for them. Gāndhi through what is known as the Poona Pact made with Dr. Ambedkar (1932), agreed to the reservation of seats for them on the basis of population with their right also to contest other general (Hindu) seats. This saved the untouchables for the Hindu fold, otherwise it was feared that they and the Muslims combining might turn the tables on Caste Hindus, and might even quit the Hindu fold, in due course, for which Ambedkar had been agitating all along. He did turn a Buddhist later (possibly, he wanted to be integrated with a world-community) together with a large number of his followers, though he had earlier toyed with the idea of turning a Sikh. But the Sikhs neither handled him with care, nor conducted their own missionary activities with any sophistication or aplomb. But even more then this, Mahātmā Gāndhi of revered memory scuttled the move. He refused to extend the concessions allowed to the Harijans under the Poona Pact if they changed from Hindusm to any other religion, including Sikhism.

Master Tārā Singh who was then interned at Shahdarā near Lāhore, called a meeting of Sikh leaders there and made a threatening gesture, saying :—"Here we reject the Communal Award, totally, with contempt. It is a blatant Muslim rāj inflicted upon us against which our forefathers have fought for two centuries. We will fight against this to the finish. If we don't, let the Guru curse and abandon us. If the Guru does not help, we will abandon him."

Hard words indeed, but spoken more in anger and passion than after due deliberation. For, soon thereafter, the great Master and his Akālis were confabulating with the Congress for the division of seats for elections to the Panjab Assembly under the same Communal Award. The Congress-Akāli combination won the majority of the Sikh seats (18 out of 32) the rest going to the Sikh Nationalist Party under Sir Sundar Singh Majithia or independents who joined hands with the rural-oriented Unionist Party of Sir Sikandar Hayāt, the Premier, and Sir Chhotu Ram, a Jāt leader from Haryana.*

Some time earlier (May 1935), the premier Sikh institution, in the Panjāb, the Khālsā college, Amritsar, was rocked by a 21-day students' strike†. Though it was resolved through the intervention of Bābā Kharak Singh (who upheld the authorities' case against the students), it resulted in a most unexpected manner. The younger brother of Master Tārā Singh, Professor Niranjan Singh, well-known teacher of Chemistry and a reputed nationalist, was thrown out of the college alongwith four others (one of these being the supporter all along of the authorities, but dismissed as he was a self-proclaimed Marxist and wrote pornographic literature !)

The strike had been launched earlier in defence of Prof. Niranjan Singh. A scurrilous pamphlet written against him, and ascribed to Master Sunder Singh Lyallpuri, one-time Akāli leader, and editor-

* One of the worst episodes of this period is the Shahidganj agitation (1934-35). At a place in Lāhore where the Sikhs were tortured to death in the 18th century and was known as Shahidganj (see part I), and which was a sacred spot for the Sikhs, a mosque had been erected by the Muslims which was sought to be demolished by the Sikhs. It led to a great and long agitation by the Muslims. The matter was litigated. The Sikhs won the case both in the High Court and the Privy Council. But, it left a trail of bitterness between the two communities.

† With the cause becoming wider—i.e. Nationalist Vs. loyalist, the strike was led by the present writer, who was later honoured by his election as the Panjāb President of the All India Students Federation (1937-1938). The strike brought almost all the veteran Congress and Akāli leaders into its orbit as sympathisers and active helpers, like Master Tārā Singh, S. Sohan Singh Josh, the Khān Bros, Dr. S.D. Kitchlew, Diwān Chaman Lāl, Bar-at-Law, Fredā and B.P.L. Bedi, Bābā Sohan Singh Bhaknā and others. Even Jawāharlāl Nehru wrote to the writer a letter of sympathy and appreciation, and the entire nationalist press supported it wholeheartedly.

founder of the "Akāli", (but it was believed, inspired and sponsored by others), was distributed among the students engendering great moral indignation and resentment among the teachers and students alike. The Principal disowned the pamphlet, and said he would support Niranjan Singh if he took the matter to the court. But, it appeared later that the show-down was for higher—and different—stakes.

As the removal of the Principal, Bhai Jodh Singh, the veteran religious teacher and educationist (due, it was revealed later, to an earlier family feud among the two) had also been included in the students' demands, after his rustication of four students, including a nephew of Tārā Singh, the agitation became politically motivated: nationalist versus loyalist, the students supporting the former and the Govt. and its supporters, (including Sir Sikandar Hayat Khan, the Panjab Premier, Sir Sundar Singh Majithia, the President of the College committee, and other Sikh notables on the management and also belonging to the same moderate political persuation) supporting the Principal.

The agitation ended, but the cleavage between the two Sikh factions widened. Tārā Singh took it as a personal insult and looked around for friends who could help him establish another Sikh institution of higher learning at Lahore to rehabilitate both his brother and his own reputation as the acknowledged leader of the Sikhs.

And, this brought to the scene the late Sardār Baldev Singh of ever-green memory, the then richest Sikh industrialist of Tātā-Nagar (Bihār), hailing originally from the village Dumnā of the Ropar District in the Panjāb. He agreed to pay the full cost of raising the new Sikh institution at Lāhore and entered and dominated Sikh politics ever thereafter, first as a protege of Master Tārā Singh but later as his mentor and master. Mahātmā Gāndhi also had many industrialists, like the Birlā Bros, to support him. They contributed large funds to his many causes, but they never were allowed to influence his politics (except from the background and that too under his over-all direction), but the Sikh phenomenon had a flavour and a compulsion of its own. It was the purse of the rich that dictated the later political events.

It is not that Tārā Singh had abandoned his sense of integrity which he kept throughout his lifetime. He was earlier reported to have torn a blank cheque sent him by the Mahārājā of Patiālā (against whose misrule and other moral failings he was agitating) in the presence of his emissaries. (Later he compromised with him). He did not ask or seriously manouvere for any position for himself or his family throughout his life. His personal character was unimpeachable. He lived most of the time in deliberate poverty. He many a time took a stand publicly against Baldev Singh, and with all the fury he was capable of, and yet ultimately it was he who had to yield, not his nominee. Was it only good manners, or a moral obligation to a generous friend, expediency, helplessness created by outside circumstances, an effort somehow to keep his party afloat, or what? No one can tell.

However, from now on, a different Akāli Party emerged on the scene. Shortly after the outbreak of the Great War, late in 1939, Master Tārā Singh wrote to Maulanā Āzād (Aug 9, 1940), with a copy of his letter to Mahātmā Gāndhi, seeking advice for his community which was anxious to help materially in the war-effort, "as this was the only way to strengthen India's war-machine and industry." He wanted also "to offer one lakh recruits to the British in case of their settlement with the Congress over the larger issue of freedom." "Even if the Congress started a civil disobedience movement," he said, "you can count on my full sympathy and support but the Congress should do nothing to obstruct strengthening of our army and our industry which the British were now obliged to undertake in their own interest." "Otherwise I want you to understand my position and that of my community clearly, namely, that it wants seriously to help the war-effort." Gāndhi who was thinking of launching a *Satyāgraha* to take advantage of the war-situation (inspite of serious reservations expressed by Nehru and Azād) was in no mood to listen to this kind of logic. He hit back furiously through a letter which said:—

Sevagram
Aug. 16, 1940

Dear Sardarji,

I am glad you have sent me a copy of your letter to Maulana Sahib. As I have told you, in my opinion, you have nothing in common with the Congress nor the Congress with you. You believe in the rule of the sword, the Congress does not. You have all the time 'my community' in mind. The Congress has no community but the whole nation. Your civil disobedience is surely a branch of violence. I am quite clear in my mind that being in the Congress you weaken 'your community' and weaken the Congress. With your mentality, you have to offer your services to the British Govt. unconditionally and look to it for the protection of the rights of "your community." You donot suppose for one moment that the British will take your recruits on your conditions. They would commit suicide if they did. You have to be either fully nationalist or frankly communal and therefore dependent upon the British or other foreign power.

This is the considered opinion of one who loves you and the Sikhs as he loves himself and in reality more. For I have ceased to love myself.

Yours faithfully

(M.K. Gandhi)*

Harijan (29-9-1940)

The Gujrānwālā District Congress Committee wrote to Pt. Jawāharlāl Nehru not to allow the Akāli-Congress rift to widen, but Nehru also echoed the same sentiments as Gāndhiji had done before. He replied:—"It is not possible for anyone or any group at this critical moment to have it both ways and gain the favour both of the British Govt. and the national movement at the same time." (Hindustān Times, Oct 17, 1940).

Master Tārā Singh felt deeply hurt, and so were the Sikhs at large. With Partāp Singh Kairon (later Congress Chief Minister), Ishar Singh Majhail, (later Minister in Panjāb as a Congressman), Darshan Singh Pheruman, (later congress M.P.) Gurmukh Singh Musāfir, (later M.P. and Congress Chief Minister of Panjāb for a brief while) and S. Baldev Singh as special invitees, a resolution was passed

* Gāndhiji had another grievance against the Sikhs as well at this time. In the election to the office of Congress President, Panjāb had all voted for Shri Subhāsh Chandra Bose against the nominee of Gāndhiji, Pattabhi Sitāramaiyyā, who lost heavily. Gāndhi called it his "personal defeat" and never forgave those who had acted against his wishes. Bose had to quit the Congress, form a new militant Party—the Forward Bloc—was detained in his house in Calcuttā on the declaration of the war, but escaped to West Germany via Kābul, in the disguise of a Pathān. There, he joined hands with the Axis Powers, formed his own Govt. of free India and later headed the I.N.A. and died soon after in a plane-crash. Sardul Singh Caveeshar, great patriot & once member of the Congress Working Committee, succeeded him.

unanimously by the Akāli Dal Working Committee (Sept. 29, 1940), supporting Master Tārā Singh's stand for the defence of India during war-years and expressed its anger over Mahātmā Gāndhi's uncalled-for remarks about the Sikhs. This shows that their case had not been properly understood. They had insisted that in no case would they abandon the cause of the country's freedom, would join all movements of Satyāgraha launched for this purpose, even during the war, and will never join hands at any price with its enemies. But they wanted their historic role in the army not to be jeopardised, nor their political future left hanging in the air when freedom came to the rest of the country.

The Congress Sikhs, it may be noted, flocked to Gandhiji's standard in sizeable numbers in the "Quit India" movement of 1942. Only the die-hard Akālis (led by Master Tārā Singh among the leaders) kept aloof, and encouraged recruitment to the armed forces. Already, after the Akāli movement (1920-25), the British had reduced the Sikh strength in the army from 20% to 13%, inspite of the fact that out of 20 military crosses won by India, 15 came to the Sikhs. The Sikhs feared (and justly) that if after the war, there was a transfer of power to two independent states—India and Pakistān—they would at best be either torn into two equal and insignificant halves, or at worst thrown into Pākistān to suffer parmanently at the hands of an avowedly communal state. A fight was, therefore, inevitable between the parties and their added strength in the army (as the well-known Hindu leaders like Dr. Moonje, Dr. Shyāma Prosad Mookerjee, later founder of the Jan Sangh and Vir Sāvarkar, once an arch-revolutionary, were clamouring at this time) would be of great advantage to them.

However, grievous mistakes were also committed in pushing forth crudely this programme. Inspite of the Congress Ministeries' resignation in 1939 in seven provinces, and the "Quit India" movement of 1942, the Hindu youths were flocking no less to the army, (though the Muslims were taking the lead). Even if they wished not to be left out in this race for their traditional share in the armed services, the Sikh leaders could have left this task to other hands and not compromised their own stand, as the Communists and the Royists (followers of M. N. Roy) had done for their own reasons. But they not only identified themselves led by the venerable Master Tārā Singh with the cause of the war, which could be justified and even appreciated, but what is worse and was wholly unnecessary, if not also politically dangerous, they allowed S. Baldev Singh (or he allowed himself) to join the Unionist Govt. in 1942*, (though the Akāli legislators continued to be a part of the Congress Opposition in Panjāb as well !).

And, with or without tne approval of Master Tārā Singh, his trusted and able representative, Sardār Ajit Singh Sarhadi, an Advocate with a high reputation for integrity, joined the minority Govt. of the Muslim League in the N. W.F.P. (Dr. Khān Sāhib, the great Pathān leader of the majorty Congress Party in the legislature then being in jail). This created suspicion about Akāli intentions not only in the minds of the nationalist circles throughout India, but also there was a vertical split in their own ranks, though Master Tārā Singh was not true to himself when he disowned any responsibility for it. He said "Ajit Singh accepted Ministership on his own responsibility and against my advice", but he also added:—"I still have faith in his *bona fides*." However, patriots of old standing like Gurmukh Singh Musāfir (later M.P. and Chief Minister of Panjab) Ishar Singh Majhail, (later Minister), Udham Singh Nāgokē, (later M.P.) Sohan Singh Jalal Usman (later Minister), Darshan Singh Pheruman (later M.P.) of the Akāli Party and many others courted arrest at the call of the Congress. Sardār Partāp Singh Kairon and Sardār Sardul Singh Caveeshar, Master Mota Singh, Sardār Gopal Singh Qaumi etc. had already opted for the Congress. Master Tārā Singh, however, claims in his Autobiography that though the Akalis were helping the war-effort, they had, with his knowledge and concurrence, also been allowed freedom to join the individual Satyāgraha and the Quit India

* It was publicised that Baldev Singh had joined the Unionist Govt. as an independent, even though he was elected on the Akāli ticket, with the help of the Congress. His pact with Sikandar Hyāt brought little dividends to the Sikhs except for the ridiculous sum of Rs. 20,000/- being set apart for the promotion of of Gurmukhi & (b) Jhatkā meat being allowed to Sikh prisoners in Jail from then on ! It was also said that 20% seats in the services will be reserved for the Sikhs in the Panjāb, but this promise was never kept. On the other hand, Sir Sikandar Hayāt's secret police implicated the Sikh leaders, including Tārā Singh, in a bomb outrage on the Kālkā-Simlā highway in which some British officers were killed. "It is on account of the impartiality of the British investigators that we were saved," says Tārā Singh (Autobiography, P. 193). However, the Akālis, rushing through an amended Gurdwārā Bill with the help of Unionist votes, got their hold over the S. G.P. C. further strengthened and increased its resources manyfold through greater contributions therafter from the local Gurdwārā Committees.

movement launched by the Congress. *

The British Govt. sent Sir Stafford Cripps (Socialist member of the War Cabinet and leader of the House of Commons) to India in 1942 to see if a compromise with the Indian leaders could be achieved. The American President, Roosevelt, was also pressing hard for this; so was China's Generalismo, Chiang Kai Shek, both partners of Britain in the war. But the two major parties, the Congress and the Muslim League, both rejected his offer, the Congress because of the limited authority offered in respect of Defence, the Viceroy's veto and the vague terms in which power was sought to be transferred after the war, and the League because after the Congress rejection it was no use accepting it, even though the Muslims had almost been given a veto over India's independence. † A Constituent Assembly was agreed to, but its terms of reference could be construed either way. There could be a united India with a much weakened centre, or there could be a division between India and Pakistan, for the provinces (i.e. the Muslim-majority ones) had been given the right to stay out and join later, if they thought fit. Moreover, the Congress demanded the transfer of effective power here and now, which was not conceded. As for the Sikhs, they had nothing to choose. They were either to become mere non-entities in a united India, or totally wiped out (unless they submitted willingly to a permanent communal subjugation in Pakistan.)

The Rajaji formula presented to Jinnah (July, 1944) with the blessings of Gandhiji and the Gandhi-Jinnah talks thereafter, left no

*The dichotomy in the minds of the Sikh leaders is best exemplified by the behaviour of S. Sampuran Singh, leader of the Congress Assembly Party in the Panjab. He too offered *Satyagraha,* but when the trying Magistrate questioned him on whether he would disapprove of his community offering recruits to the army, he said he would not. He was fined one *ānnā* (four *paisās*) and on his refusal to pay even this fine, the Magistrate paid it out of his own pocket, and released him!

† The Viceroy, Lord Linlithgow, had, in Aug 1940, said publicly that the British Govt. could not contemplate the transfer of power "to any system of Govt. whose authority is directly denied by large and powerful elements in India's national life." Mr. Churchill, while sending out Sir Stafford Cripps to India said as much in the House of Commons on March II, 1942:- "He (Cripps) will strive to procure the necessary measure of assent not only from the Hindu majority, but also from those great minorities among whom the Muslims are the most numerous and on many grounds pre-eminent." With these assurances in his pocket, why should Mr. Jinnah have compromised with the Congress or the Sikhs?.

one in doubt that Pakistan or a variation of it was round the corner.† Rajaji had even announced that if the people of the Panjab and Bengal couldnot reconcile their differences, they should be left out and the rest of India granted freedom by the British ! Nothing could bewilder and antagonise the Sikhs more. There was now no one (not even Gandhi) to look upto.

The Muslims, if they had been generous and far-sighted, should have also foreseen the result of their intransigence with regard to the Sikhs. They demanded weightage in the minority provinces on a scale which they would ridicule in the case of Sikhs. Themselves they had gradually come to consider as a "nation," with its own "polity, jurisprudence, social behaviour, religion, customs, personal law, language, history etc. having nothing in common with the Hindus," but when the Sikhs wanted the same criteria of "religion, history, polity, language, custom and social behaviour" as being distinct from the Muslims to be applied in their case, they would call them obstructionists and intransigent, "Hindus in their bearded disguise," or at best "a sub-nation" condemned to slavery for all times. As virtual rulers of the Panjāb, since 1920, they would try to grab as many posts in the Govt. as possible, but the Sikhs they would deprive of their due. Sir Fazal-i-Hussain's son, Azim Hussain, his biographer, has written about an offer by a Sikh educationist (who was denied a lecturer's post at the Govt. college, Lāhore) to turn Muslim, if that would add to his merits and said his father was wholly non-communal and merit was the only criterion with him.* But the fact that the letter was written by a first class first postgraduate who later occupied high posts in Sikh educational institutions, shows to what length the new Muslim rulers could go even with their limited powers in the days of the Dyarchy (1920-36) and with the veto of the British Governor still hanging over their heads!

---

† Rājāji (Sri Rajgopalachari, Gandhi's confidant and well-known Congress leader, whose daughter was married to Gandhi's son) and Gandhiji had conceded that after the demarcation of Muslim majority areas, they would have the freedom through a plebiscite or such like means to become independent states, but the Muslim League should also agree in advance that they would enter into a treaty with the rest of India over such subjects as defence, commerce and communications. Mr. Jinnah wanted only the commitment for Pakistān, himself refusing to commit anything in advance.

**Fazl-i-Hussain*, a Political biography, p. 370

The Hindus in the Panjāb, on the other hand, had fared no better with the Sikhs at this time. They helped them unresevedly during the Akāli movement, but when it came to the possession of a disputed Gurdwārā property, they stood by the hereditary custodians who were Hindu in form & customs. They who, through the Aryā Samāj and Brahmo Samaj condemned idolatory, considered it an anti-Hindu act, if some idols were removed from the precincts of a Sikh temple. On a complaint by the Panjāb Hindus, even Mahatmā Gāndhi called for a Sikh explanation over this (vide Secret Correspondence relating to Akali Movement). On the one hand, the Sikhs were considered to be an inalienable part of the Hindus, but in no Hindu educational institution or bank or any other Hindu-sponsored social activity could a Sikh face ever be seen. Even into the institutions, run wholly with the money of Sardār Dyāl Singh Majithia, the Brahmo and later Hindu Trustees would never welcome a Sikh. This attitude was exploited by worthies like Giani Kartār Singh.*

And now, a tirade was launched against them by the powerful Hindu (mainly Aryā-Samāj) owned Press that the Sikhs were out for a communal state of their own, following the lead of the Muslim League. Even when the secheme of "Āzād Panjab" was launched in 1944, by the Akāli Dal, as a reaction to Rājāji's proposals for Pakistan, (the major Hindu-Sikh areas from the Chenab to Delhi being detached from the Panjab and constituted into a separate state within India) the Hindus of the Panjāb opposed it tooth and nail. If distrust was sown also in the minds of the Sikhs at this time

* Giani Kartar Singh, a half-educated Jāt of Lyallpur but an untiring worker with a keen memory and a flair for detail, became during the forties, an Akāli leader and legislator of some consequence, rising to the position of President of the Akāli Dal in 1947. Unorthodox in his views on politics, he would shift his stand without any qualms of conscience, no matter what hurt ultimately it caused the community at large. Being poorly-clad, shabby in his looks, exclusive in his outlook and having abandoned his home, he created the impression of dedication and poverty. He helped small individuals in their petty affairs to create a wide circle of grateful followers. But all this he used later to project himself and his political future. For a time in the thirties, he was with the Congress and once courted arrest in the *Satyagraha* also. But in the forties he hobnobbed with the British and the Muslim League, and putting forward extremist views on Sikh rāj etc., he became well-known as a "true" spokeman of the Sikh orthodoxy. He was advertised as a *faqir* who was unmindful of his personal comforts or political position.

about them, the blame doesnot entirely lie with the Sikhs.*

The war was still on. Britain had been cruelly bombed and half-evacuated. France, Holland, Belgium, Norway, Denmark, Check-oslavakia, the whole of eastern Europe, except for central and eastern Russia had fallen to the onslaught of Nazi Germany. In 1941-42, the Japanese were advancing menacingly towards India. All the countries surrounding India in the east—Indo-China, Malaya, Singapore, Thailand, Burma etc. had fallen to them, one by one. Out of the 90,000 surrendering Indian soldiers at Singapore, about 20,000 (mostly Sikhs) had formed an Indian National Army (I.N.A.) under Captain (later promoted General by his National Army), Mohan Singh, inorder to fight the battle in behalf of the country's freedom under Japanese over-all direction and control. The Japanese treated the remaining prisoners of war cruelly, about 11000 of them died of starvation, disease or murder. Later, differences cropped up with the Japanese and Mohan Singh and his top aides were arrested. Mr. Subhas Chandra Bose had by

F. N. Contd.

However, on the first opportunity after the transfer of power, he ditched his community and party, both, to become an anathema to sensitive minds. Master Tara Singh, his patron and political guru, thus describes his role and character :—"Gianiji has many qualities but his greatest drawback is partisanship. He would create a split anywhere the goes, and capture himself the organisation, and make helpless opportunists of even well-meaning people. He builds his power thus, but loses his trust. His sharpness has been the cause of his undoing. He pretended his love for the Panth to me, *but* would help Sardar Patel to split our rank and even to get us arrested. He created his own Akāli Dal (against the official one). How far shall I write of all his defects? I will only be creating more misunderstanding and lead myself into the ditch" (Autobiography, pp. 248-50).Inorder to become a Minister for a time in the Panjab, "the Giani played one faction against the other and created much bad blood both against himself and the community." He died a lonely man, after a nervous breakdown in 1974 in a Patiālā hospital.

* The All India Sikh Students Federation brought into being (1944) through the efforts of S. Sarup Singh (later leader of the Opposition in the Panjab legislature), S. Amar Singh Ambālvi, Advocate, Dr. J.S. Neki etc and inaugurated at Gujrānwālā by the present writer, did much to publicise the Sikh cause in this behalf. Their conference held next year at Lyallpur and attended by all Sikh leaders of note (it was presided over by this writer) concretised the Sikh demands for the first time.

this time taken over and reorganised the Indian National Army.* The Congress had, under Gandhiji, launched, on Aug 9, 1942, a "Quit India" Movement, in which for the first time, the Congress had given the slogan:- "Do or die." Which meant in effect that no means, including violent, should be spared to damage the supply-line of the Govt's war effort and to harass and embarass them. This was done with a vengeance.

On the other hand, the British had been, under the compulsions of war, obliged to expand the peace-time strength of the army from 1,15,000 to over 2 million. The Indian industry which was upto now confined by and large to textiles greatly expanded, so as to include vast expansions of steel, cement, bauxite (to produce aluminium) and mica production. The arms industry was also considerably expanded though not in the more sophisticated lines. However, the Indian army was mechanised as never before, and training given to Indians in the Air force and the Navy stood the country later in good stead. The Govt. had to increase the expansion of money and Britian's war-debts payable to India in pound-sterlings, increased to Rs. 1800 crores during the war years. The new boom also led to inflation, bribery and corruption on a vast scale and hoarding and black marketing thrived as never before. Due to the loss of Burma in war (the main supplier of rice) there was a large-scale famine in Bengal, in 1943, which cost about a million human lives.

Gandhi, on the other hand, was trying his own thesis. He had written a letter to Hitler to desist from war (which was never acknowledged). But, when he asked Briain publicly and repeated it in an interview with the Viceroy to throw away their arms and

* Two conferences, one held in Tokyo, (March, 1942) and the other in Bangkok (June, 1942), attended by the Japanese, the I.N.A. leaders and Rāsh Bihāri Bose, the Indian revolutionary settled in Tokyo, tried to enunciate the goal of complete freedom, "free from foreign domination of whatever nature," but the Japanese didnot react kindly to it. Differences became acute and Gen. Mohan Singh and his associates were arrested. Rāsh Bihāri also withdrew from the movement. In June 1943, Shri Subāsh Chandra Bose became the supremo of the I.N.A. and with his HQs in Rangoon, some engagements were fought on the Indo-Burma border early in 1944. An "Azād Hind Govt" with the Andamans and Nicobar islands as their teritory was also formed under Bose, now popularly known as *Netāji* (or The Leader). After about three months, the I.N.A. resistance collapsed, though with small total losses (1500 killed out of 20,000) in all their engagements. (From

fight non-violently, (which he said, was "a nobler and braver way,") if their country was occupied, the Viceroy, Lord Wavell, even refused the usual courtesy of asking his Secretary to escort the Mahātmā to his car. When Gandhiji mentioned the fact of this discourtesy to Maulana Azad, the latter remarked that the Viceroy must have been so stunned by his extraordinary and novel suggestion that he must have lost all sense of time and space!

After the failure of the Cripps Mission (1942),and the slackening of the "Quit India" movement, but the Japanese still threatening at the door, Lord Wavell was asked by the War Cabinet under Winston Churchill to make one more attempt to break the deadlock. And thus ensued the Simla Conference held in June, 1945, in which the Viceroy announced the Govt's intention to transfer all departments, except Defence, to Indian hands, but himself keeping the veto. The British had insisted, and the Congress agreed, that the caste Hindus share equal power (40%) with the Muslims in Central executive, the balance of 20% going to Scheduled castes, Sikhs and Christians. But the talks broke down, as the Congress insisted that they must include at least one Muslim in their quota, and that not all the Muslim seats will be alloted to the Muslim League which insisted on being the sole representative of the Musalmans. The Viceroy also supported the Congress stand. At this conference, the Sikhs were represented by Master Tara Singh. While the Congress

---

F. N. Contd.

the viewpoint of those who did not join the INA, Maj Gen. Gurbakhsh Singh's Autobiography in Panjābi is a reliable document). The Japanese offered them little air or artillery support. A year later (Jan 45), another attempt was made, but in about four months, this too came to a miserable end. Mr. S. C. Bose flew to Tokyo and died in a plane-crash. After the war, the British released Mohan Singh and his other companions, Col. Niranjan Singh Gill etc. on the intenvention of Master Tārā Singh, but tried to courtmartial G.S. Dhillon, Shāh Nawāz and Sahgal. However, they too were released due to the wide sympathy their cause had aroused but very few of them were taken back in the army, for their having broken their "oath of allegiance." The Congress Govt. under Nehru agreed with the British C.IN-C and the Viceroy in this. Nehru called their action "misguided." After about 5 years of popular support, the I.N.A. became a part of history, the top leaders joining the National Congress and the others retiring or pursuing agriculture or business. Col. Niranjan Singh Gill was appointed Ambassador abroad and Gen. Mohan Singh and Gen. Shah Nawāz became MPs (the latter also a Minister). (For details, see Gen. Mohan Singh's "*A soldier's fight for freedom*)."

and the League were asked to submit 15 names each (5 from each list were to be selected by the Viceroy), the Sikh and the Scheduled caste leader, Shivaraj, had to submit three names each, out of which one was to be selected by the Viceroy. Master Tara Singh was said to have given his own name *thrice*, but then it was Baldev Singh, not Tara Singh, who had been selected. Something had happend in between to the wondernment of the latter.*

By now, the Japanese had surrendered, being atom-bombed by the United States, and Lord Wavell, the Viceroy, ordered the general elections in the winter of 1945-46. The League swept the polls in the Panjāb (and Bengal), bagging almost all Muslim seats, though in the Panjab, it still lacked a clear over-all majority and lost in the Pathanland, the N. W. F. P., to the Congress. Sir Sikandar Hayat was dead (1943) and his place taken over by Sir Khizar Hayat Tiwana, Muslim Unionist opposed to the League. He again formed a Govt in the Panjab with the help of the Congress and the Akālis (who had secured 2/3rd of the Sikh seats, 1/3 going to Congress Sikhs).

The widespread sympathy of all India over the trial of the I.N.A., the Indian Naval Mutiny of 1946, besides the cruel shattering of Britain's economy, but most of all, the success of the Labour Party at the polls in Britain, all induced the British to send

* Writes Wavell, "In the afternoon, (June 27, 1945), Baldev Singh came to see me. He has two of the Congress (ex-Premiers) Kher (of Bombay) and Sinha (of Bihar) staying with him. He said the Panjab would be quite satisfied if they had Sikh and Panjābi Mussulmān (in the Executive Council)." (Wavell, *The Viceroy's Journal*, p. 148). It may be mentioned that in the list of invitees to the conference, it was only Master Tārā Singh who was to represent Sikh interests. (Others were premiers or ex-premiers of provinces, leaders of the Congress, League and National and European parties in the Central Assembly, Maulana Azad, President of the National Congress, Mr. M. A. Jinnah, Mahatma Gandhi (who was present in Simla but didnot participate officially in the Conference) and Rāo Bahādur Shiva Rāj, (representative of the Scheduled castes).

Again: "(July 6). Master Tārā Singh came to inform me that at the insistence of his Committee, he had placed his own name at the head of the Sikh nominees (the other two names were complete duds). This may be awkward since Tārā Singh would be a poor member of Council (P. 152), (The anti-Tārā Singh lobby had done its home-work by now). [More] a Cabinet Mission in April, 1946, with full authority, to discuss, finally, the terms of the transfer of power to Indian hands. This mission consisted of the top members of the new Socialist Government : Lord Pathic Lawrence (leader), Sir Stafford Cripps and Mr. A. V. Alexander.

(July 9), "Khizar (Hayāt Khan, Premier of the Panjāb)...knew all about Tārā Singh's list, which he described as Tārā Singh and two dummies, that (Sir) Dātār Singh, though honest and capable would not be acceptable to Sikhs, as he belonged to a non-agriculturist tribe and was not an Akāli (p. 153). (Possibly, Sir Dātār's name, he being an agricultural expert, was suggested by the Viceroy).

Earlier on May 12, the Mahārajā of Patiālā had called on Wavell. "Patiālā was chiefly concerned with the Sikhs. He said they were hopelessly divided (Akāli, Congress, Communist etc) and had no leader or outstanding personality and usually came to him in difficulty. It is probably undersirable for H. H. to play with Sikh politics, but he thought they would inevitably consult him..." (P. 266).

Wavell adds significantly :—"I could only say (to Patiālā) that I thought the Sikhs, if they played their cards well, could exercise an influence in the Panjāb far beyond their numbers. But they donot usually play well and are too fond of cheating (this I did not say to H.H.)"—(Ibid). Lord Wavell, however, does not spell out anywhere what kind of play he expected from the Sikhs, except that along with some other British die-hards, he too perhaps wanted them to cast their lot with Pākistān and get some weightage etc., remaining however a statutory minority under the rule of a permanent communal majority of Muslims, an eventuality they never relished for good historical reasons.

CHAPTER XXVIII

THE TRANSFER OF POWER

(1946—1947)

It is well-known that the Cabinet Mission, after several meetings with the leaders of the Congress, the Muslim League and the Sikhs (the three principal parties recognised in the White Paper of the British Govt.) issued on May 16, 1946, a statement envisaging a confederal scheme for India, giving Defence, Foreign Affairs and Communications to the Centre and all other powers to the states. It also stipulated the grouping of the states into three sections—A, B, and C—the entire Muslim-dominated Panjab, N.W.F.P. and Sind forming one group; Assam and Bengal the other and the rest (mostly Hindu) forming the third group, thus giving more than Mr. Jinnah could ever dream of. Pakistan was not formally conceded, but it was also stipulated that if after ten years' interval, the scheme didnot work, it could be changed or scrapped and the groups thereafter were free to secede from the Centre. In fact, Mr. Jinnah had been given a decade's opportunity to consolidade his hold over the North-Western and Eastern India, and not much notice was taken of the Sikh demand which was presented by the Sikh delegation, headed by Master Tārā Singh, to the Cabinet Mission (sec below), though the Sikhs were recognised as the third party, besides Hindus & Muslims for the transfer of power.

As there is still a good deal of confusion and controversy in regard to the role of the Sikh representatives, a thorough sifting of the available data is necessary. In the first place, the thesis built on bāzār gossip that the British were wanting to create an independent Sikh State and that the Akalis got cold feet at the crucial moment, is patently absurd and false. So also that Baldev Singh was responsible for this, or that the Sikh case was not well put before the Mission by Tārā Singh and others. A canard has also been spread by a half-wit that Mr. Jinnah was willing to concede a Sikh Homeland but a letter conveying the "Sikh" consent was not delivered to him by the emissary and so the Sikh State didnot come through ! *

As Master Tārā Singh has himself pointed out there are many such braggarts and nitwits, especially among the Sikhs, who always try to sow suspicion about everyone and every event, talk tall and big, and then leave the people in the cold, themselves being unable and also unworthy either to lead or to suffer for any cause. *

First, let us take the testimony of Lord Wavell, then Viceroy, who had the opportunity and the authority to discuss every matter with the then leaders of public opinion. Says he:—"Baldev Singh came (Feb. 11, 1947). He discussed the political situation and said that Jinnah did not want a settlement. He had discussions with him in London but had got nowhere, and Jinnah offered no assurances to the Sikhs even if they supported Pākistān." †

That the British Govt. were equally helpless is stated clearly by Sir Stafford Cripps in the statement he made in the British Parliament (July 18, 1946). He said, "What the Sikhs demand is some special treatment analogous to that given to the Muslims. The Sikhs, however, are a much smaller community, 5½ million against 90 million Muslims and are not geographically situated so that any area...can be carved out in which they find themselves in a majority."

---

* One such "intellectual", the late Kapur Singh (dismissed from the I. C. S., for corruption, in 1958) has written many such totally false stories to dupe the unwary in a pamphlet called "Sachi Sakhi", highly critical of every Sikh leader from Ranjit Singh to Tara Singh and Baldev Singh (for what he calls their "anti-Sikh activities"), and introduced the latter two to a few well-known astrologers of Delhi and Hoshiarpur and for decade and a half they guided the Sikh polity in no uncertain terms. Not that the Hindu political leaders lag behind in this tantaric pastime. They launched India's freedom at midnight (Aug. 14-15) due to astrological reasons, but then it is a part of their cultural heritage. The Sikh Gurus had denounced belief in future-telling & auspicious & inauspicious days.

However, as we shall see later, the Cabinet Mission did propose to S. Baldev Singh the creation of a Sikh Homeland (consisting of what is almost the present Panjab) with an option to join either India or Pakistan, but it was rejected by him as being "too small" and deman, ding the dividing line in the West between the two Panjabs to be drawn at the river Chenab, which the Cabinet Mission couldnot sell to Mr. Jinnah, by any chance, at that point of time.

In fact, as a solution to the Panjab's communal problem (after the Cripps Mission had clearly enunciated in 1942 that the British Govt. was prepared to agree upon a new independent Constitution for the Muslim provinces not acceding to the Indian Union which in fact accepted the thesis of Pakistan), *the S. G. P. C. in their Memorandum of March 31,1942, had themselves suggested the river Rāvi to be the boundary between the two Panjabs.* Said the Memorandum, inter-alia:—"The Sikhs cannot attain their rightful position or can effectively protect their interests unless the Panjab is redistributed into two provinces with the River Ravi as the boundary between them." (For full text, see *Partition of the Panjab*, Kirpal Singh, 15-22). (Of course, the distsrict of Lahore was to be included in the Jullundur and Ambala divisions along with Amritsar and Gurdaspur). Master Tara Singh in his letter to Cripps (May 1,1942) had also made it amply clear that the "Sikhs and Hindus donot want to go out of India. Why should they be forced to secede against their wishes ?"

As has been stated, Mr. C. Rajgopalachari, the veteran Congress leader, had in 1944 offered to Mr. Jinnah (with the blessings of Gandhiji) a Commission to demarcate "contiguous districts in the North-West and East of India wherein the Muslim population is in the absolute majority," and to give them the right of "self-determination." Mahatma Gandhi in his own letter to Mr. Jinnah (Sept. 24,1944) conceded as much and said, "if such Muslim-dominated areas wanted to form a separate state they would, after ascertaining the wishes of the people by a direct vote of the adult population or some equivalent method be allowed to do so, after India is free from foreign domination." Mr. Jinnah didnot agree mainly because he could not accept the provinces of these boundaries "maimed and mutilated beyond redemption which would leave us only with the husk." And, he did not want to accept a post - dated cheque !

According to V. P. Menon, Master Tara Singh had declared at Simla that "he was prepared to accept Pakistan if Mr. Jinnah should agree to a Sikhs state " (*Transfer of Power*, P. 312), but Mr. Jinnah never responded. In their statement of May 16, 1946, the Cabinet Mission had rejected the plea for Pakistan saying "the setting up of a separate sovereign state of Pakistan on the lines claimed by the Muslim League would not solve the communal problem, nor can we see any justification for including within a sovereign Pakistan those districts of the Panjab and of Bengal and Assam in which the population is predominaltly non-Muslim. Every argument that can be used in favour of Pakistan can equally in our view be used in favour of the exclusion of the Non-Muslim areas from Pakistan. This point would particularly affect the position of the Sikhs." * What they suggested, however, in the formation of the groups and the compulsory inclusion in it of the large Hindu and Sikh minorities belied the verbal sympathy of the Cabinet Mission.

Mahatma Gandhi reacted against it violently. Writing in the *Harijan (*May 20,1946*)*, he asked in bitter anguish:—"Are the Sikhs for whom the Panjab is the only home in India to consider themselves against their will as part of a Section which takes in Sind, Baluchisstan and the Frontier province ?" † The Working Committee of the Congress also disapproved of this logic. Speaking in Noakhali, (Dec. 15,1946), Gandhiji advised Mr. Bardoloi, Chief Minister of Assam:- "Do not go into the Sections if you donot want it. I have the same advice for the Sikhs though their position is more difficult being a community within a province. But, I feel, every individual has a right to act for himself." *Gandhi went further and said:·"Let those who*

---

* "*Wavell: the Viceroy's Journal,*" Appendix II. While the Congress by and large, including Nehru and Gandhi, could not see why if the Cabinet Mission had felt as strongly about the Sikh case, they had thrown them into Muslim-dominated groupswithout any means of escape and both Nehru and Gāndhi reinterpreted the plan to mean that no one would be pushed into the groups against their wishes, Maulānā Azād didnot agree with them. "By reinterpreting the Cabinet Mission plan, Jawaharlāl made the League suspicious and they decided on a final break up. The mistake of 1946 proved even more costly than the mistake in 1937 (of refusing to induct two Muslim Leaguers in the U.P. Cabinet). (*India Wins freedom*, P. 162).

Left to Āzād, therfore, he would have taken no notice of the Sikh fears and protests in this behalf.

† "*The Mahatama,*" Vol 7, P. 286.

want to secede from the Constituent Assembly and the Groups B & C like the Sikhs, Assam, N. W. F. P. and may be, Baluchistan, do so. Let the rest frame their own Constitutions, including Congress for section A". *

This was the time for action when the Akali Sikhs also had decided to boycott the Constituent Assembly and refused to take their seat in the interim Govt. in view of "the Cabinet Mission's proposals being unjust and gravely detrimental to the interests of the Sikhs". They had also constituted an All Party 10-man Panthic Board, under Col. Niranjan Singh Gill of the I. N. A., for resistance "against this permanent subjection to a statutory communal majority in the Panjab." But after a little thunder and pledge-taking at Amritsar (June 9 and 10, 1946) not to accept this unholy conspiracy, and to fight against it to the bitter end, and refusing permission to Baldev Singh to join the interim Govt. (June 17),they withdrew their earlier reservations and entered both the Constituent Assembly and the Cabinet at the Centre, only two months later (Aug. 14,1946), though the Muslim League had boycotted both (the League also later joined the interim Govt. though they continued their boycott of the Constituent Assemebly.) The letters of protest from Baldev Singh and Master Tara Singh to the Secretary of State had elicited no worthwhile response, and the latter also advised them to enter the Constituent Assembly, and to safegurad their interests in the free India's Constitution for which the Congress leaders offered their own ample assurances through the A. I. C. C. in their meeting held at Delhi, on Jan 5,1947.

After the declaration of Pākistān, (Jun 3, 1947) Gandhi changed

---

* Ibid. pp. 298, 307. And yet Gandhi changed his stand so often that no one knew where he stood. When the Congress Working Committee passed a resolution (March 8, 1946) that the prevailing situation "would necessitate a division of the Panjāb into two provinces" (Muslim and non-Muslim), Gāndhi protested in his letter to Nehru (March 20) that "the Committee had (without consulting him) suggested the partition of the province on the basis of Community and two-Nation theory." He thought he had been humiliated and badly let down by his followers, (Durgadas, From Curzon to Nehru, P. 239). He himself had offered "self-determination to the Muslim-dominated areas on the basis of adult franchise in 1944, but continued to stress that he was against Pākistān ! He also supported at the A. I C C. meeting (15 June, 1947) the Mountbatten plan of Partition in no uncertain terms. It is not without significance that he had said :—"Consistency is the hobgoblin of fools!" Really!

his stand and asked the Hindu and Sikh minorities to stay put within Pakistan, inspite of the cruelties, murders and humiliations heaped upon them day after day. But inspite of Gandhi, the Congress under Nehru and Patel stood by the Sikhs, however, when the question of partitioning the Panjab came to the fore on the creation of Pakistan, to which the Congress had to agree in the face of a virtual civil war that was unleashed by the Muslim League first in Calcutta on Aug 16, 1946 and later in Noakhali (East Bengal) and worst of all in West Panjab from March 1947 onwards.

To suggest that if Master Tārā Singh, the Akali Leader, would not have unsheathed his sword at Lahore on March 2.1947, after Pakistan had become a near reality and torn the Muslim League flag, neither the Muslims would have been provoked to violence against the Hindus and Sikhs, nor the door to settlement with the League barred. But, as Tara Singh himself says in his Autobiography-"There was no League flag around for me to tear up. And I never drew the sword. I only shouted alongwith other Akali legislators *Pakistan Murdabad*, (Death to Pakistan), when I saw a large crowd of Muslim Leaguers advancing towards our indoor meeting place and screaming:—"*Pakistan Zindabad*," (Long live Pakistan). Mian Iftikhar-ud-din (once President of the Panjab Congress who had then joined the League) intervened and persuaded the League crowd to disperse, and so no showdown took place."

Master Tara Singh met Mr. Jinnah personally at Lāhore and later in Delhi before and during the Cabinet Mission's arrival, but always drew a blank.

It is true that, a few years earlier, Mr. Jinnah realising that the dream of Pakistan could not mature without his satisfying the Sikhs was said to be content with a Pakistan constituted of areas where Muslims were 65% or more in population. In 1942, according to Master Tārā Singh, a message was sent by Mr. Jinnah through Raja Maheshwar Dyāl to the Birlā House, New Delhi, where important Hindu and Sikh leaders had gathered (including Master Tārā Singh and Dr. Sir Gokal Chand Narang of the Panjab). Thiswise Lāhore, Gujranwālā, Sheikhupurā, Lyallpur, and Montgomery would possibly have formed part of the new East Punjāb state. Jinnah had warned, however, that should this offer of his be leaked out prematurely before its acceptance by Hindus and Sikhs, he would denounce it. But this is what happened. Dr. Narang wanted to consult Goswami Ganesh Dutt, President of the Hindu Mahasabha in the Panjab, but on hearing of the proposal, he rejected it outright, though the Sikhs persisted and giving it the name of "Azad Panjāb" (Free Panjāb) started propagating it, with the blessings of Sri C. Rajgopalachari, the venerable Congress leader of the South. But, the Panjab Hindus felt this would be like conceding Pakistan willingly, and opposed it vehemently through their press and platform. And the scheme remained still-born.

The present writer met Mr. Jinnah twice in May and in July 1946 at New Delhi. He also gave him in mid-May a two-page (unsigned) letter from Giani Kartar Singh, in the presence of his Secy., Mr. Khurshid Ahmad (later President of the so-called Azad Kashmir), detailing Sikh demands in the event of Pakistan being conceded. The demands inter-alia were:- (1) There will be constituted a province from Chenab to Sonepat in which the Hindus & Sikhs from other areas would also be allowed to congregate. It will have the right of secession. (2) Pakistan will have a democratic constitution with freedom of religion, culture, expresion & conscience to all its constituents. (3) Sikhs and Hindus each will get 25%, Muslims will have only 40%, and other minorities 10% of seats in the Pakistan legislature & Cabinet. (4) The Pak army will not have less than 30% of Sikhs & 30% of Hindus & others. The office of Commander-in-Chief will rotate between Sikhs and Muslims. (5) If the President of Pakistan is a Muslim, the Prime Minister will be Hindu or Sikh, and vice-versa. (6) No law will be passed in respect of any community without the approval of 3/4th of the legislators of the community concerned. But Mr. Jinnah didnot give the document even a moment's thought. (†) Ian Stephens, then editor of the "Statesman" of Calcutta

---

† The document should be lying in the Pākistān archives, or in Mr. Jinnah's personal library in Pākistān.

When in July, 1946, Giani Kartār Singh met him along with the present writer, Jinnāh told him the better way would be first to break the Khizar Ministry and for the Akālis to join the Muslim League Govt. in Panjāb. He was not prepared to commit himself on anything else, before this happened. It was, however, a clever move on his part to commit the Sikhs to the Muslim League and Pākistān without the League committing anything to the Sikhs in advance. Such a move would have jeopardised the future of the Sikhs completely, closing all other options to them which they later exercised to their advantage, and got the Panjāb partitioned to save as many of them from communal domination as possible, with the help of the Congress.

& New Delhi,who knew the minds of the all those who mattered on the political scene, confirms this. "The Akalis' move, however, according to this writer's information was unavailing. They failed to get what they considered a clear response. Need Mr. Jinnah had been so unbending?" (*Pākistan*, P. 140).

Sikh leaders of all shades of opinion (Akāli, Congress, Sikh princes, Moderates, Communists etc.) were consulted before presenting the Sikh case to the Cabinet Mission. It took about a whole month of deliberations for the present writer to draft and re-draft the representation and to argue it out in the leaders' meetings. Ultimately, it was unanimously resolved that the Sikhs should press for a federal India, with 40% of seats each to the two major Communities at the centre, (as had earlier been agreed to at Simla), the balance being divided among the other minorities, including the Scheduled Castes, Sikhs, Christians and Pārsis. A similar arrangement should be made in the Panjāb for the Sikhs and Hindus, with Muslim statutory majority being reduced to 40% or so. If, however, India was to be divided, the Sikhs would demand an independent sovereign Sikh state *with its own Constituent Assembly*. A resolution to this effect was also passed by the SGPC, supported, among others, by S. Swaran Singh (later Congress Minister).

About two hours before the Sikh leader, Master Tara Singh, was scheduled to meet the Cabinet Mission (on April 4), Billy Short, an aid of the Cabinet Mission) called on Master Tara Singh. It was later known he had come to ask the Sikh leader to leave their case to the good sense of the British Govt, by saying that they didnot want to stand in the way of an over-all Hindu-Muslim settlement! Sardar Baldev Singh also joined these talks which lasted only about half an hour. The Sikh leaders, however, did not take the bait, though they were not a little disheartened that without even giving them a hearing, the Cabine Mission had taken their case to be of little consequence and wanted them to withdraw totally from the political scene leaving their future to be determined by others as their "good sense" might dictate !

As Māster Tārā Singh wrote later in his Autobiography :—"Our case, we knew, was weak on three counts : (a) We had made the plea for an independent Sikh state contingent on Pākistān coming into being. Many thought we were not serious and put forward this plea only as a counter-argument against Pakistan. (b) Those Hindus who supported us in the demand were not at all themselves willing to concede this demand. They used it only as an argument against Mr. Jinnah. (c) The Sikhs were divided in the Panjab legislature into Akali (23) and Congress (10). (b) Above all, there were not more than two *tehsils* (Tarn Tāran and Moga) with Sikh majority, and these two were also not contiguous ! If the position were as it is today with a Sikh majority in the Panjabi-speaking state, there was nothing to stop us from pressing our demand home. We were very strong then politically. But, we didnot know then (a strange admission on the part of a political leader) that Israel had come into being with a minority population which was converted into a majority through immigration, both legal and illegal."

Inspite of it, the Sikh case was presented to the Cabinet Mission, as supported by the whole Panth. Dr. G. Adhikari, the Communist leader, had also through a pamphlet pleaded for a "Sikh Homeland," though his party soon withdrew it, for unstated reasons.

Only one Sikh representative, Tārā Singh, had been invited, but three went to argue the case. The other two, Giani Kartar Singh and S. Harnām Singh Advocate, who had escorted the Sikh leader to the Mission's meeting-roomin the Rashtrapati Bhavan in New Delhi in his car. jumped out of the vehicle as soon as thev saw Billy Short, whom they all knew, coming out to receive them. "Could we also, could we," both mumbled jointly. And the wily Billy, who knew the Akali penchant for disorganisation, invited all the three in.

According to V. P. Menon, a close confidant of the Viceroy and his Constitutional Advisor, the three Sikh leaders struck each a different tune. Possibly, they wanted to impress or sought to project themselves on the world stage at this historic time. But whatever the difference in wordings (and Giani knew only a smattering of English), they empasised their bewilderment at population being the sole criterion for a future constitutional settlement. The past history of the Sikhs, their role and strength in the army, their contribution (40% of land revenue and water rates to Panjāb's economy) all were brushed aside even by the British who had always pampered them for a century for these very reasons. Even their anxiety for the Sikh historic shrines to be left in Pakistan was taken no notice of except casually. Says Menon:-"The case of the Sikh community was presented by Tara Singh, Giani Kartar Singh and Harnam Singh as well as by Baldev Singh. The first three were interviewed together, though each had his own individaual view to put forward. The

Mission wanted particularly to know whether, if given the choice, the Sikh communtiy would prefer the transfer of power to a single body, or to more than one body; if to more than one body then which one would they wish to join and if such a thing were practical and could be arranged, would the Sikh wish to have a separate autonomous state of their own ?"

"Master Tara Singh said that he stood for a united India and for some sort of coalition Govt. of all communities. The Hindus and Muslims were not united and should remain antagonistic for some time; in that situation, the Sikhs in a united India would have some kind of a bargaining power. If India were divided, the Sikhs would come under the majority of one community or the other. In that case, they would prefer a separate independent Sikh State with the right to federate either with Hindustan or Pakistan.

"Giani Kartar Singh said that the Sikhs would feel unsafe in either a united India or in Pakistan. They should have a province of their own, where they would be in a dominant, or almost dominant, position. In reply to Sir Stafford Cripps, Giani suggested Jullundur and Lahore Divisions together with Hissar, Karnal, Ambala and Simla districts and Montgomery and Lyallpur districts to form such a province !

"Harnam Singh was opposed to the partition of India. It would be a prey to foreign invasions and there could be no safeguard except in an independent Sikh state. He advocated an increased representation of Sikhs in the proposed Constitution-making body and pleaded for a separate one for Sikhs, if there were to be more than one Constitution-making body."

This shows that it is not that the Sikh leaders by any chance didnot put forth their case clearly and faithfully. Only, they being nowhere in a majority, could not plead forcefully for a state of their own.

Baldev Singh (who met the Cabinet Mission later separately) said, "unless given special protection it would be impossible for Sikhs to exist." "Asked by Cripps specifically as to how Khālistān could be formed, he replied that it would be the Panjab, excluding Multan and Rawalpindi divisions, with an approximate boundary along Chenab river......But the Sikhs favoured a united India. He wanted safeguards for minorities. If the Muslims should agree to 45% in the Panjāb, instead of 57%, and the balance divided among Hindus and Sikhs, Sikh interests would be protected." *

It is within the knowledge of the present writer that Cripps thereafter became more specific and asked Baldev Singh if the areas in the Panjab in which no community predominated (including the Sikh states of Patiala, Nabha, Faridkot, Jind and Kapurthala) were constituted into a separate state and this be designated as a "Sikh Homeland" with special privileges for the Sikhs and with a right to join either India or Pakistan, how would he react to it, Baldev replied "it is too small for our growth and aspirations. It leaves the canal areas out, also our major shrines. My people will not touch it." It is a pity that such an offer (the best in the circumstances which the Sikhs later took 20 years to fight for) was rejected out of hand, without even discussing its possibilities or making it a basis for further elaborations and discussions. It is a further pity that when the same day, Baldev informed some of his trusted colleagues of this offer, no one took it up, nor took him to task for rejecting it without proper deliberation. Possibly, no one was willing to take the resposibility of excluding any area in which the Sikhs had their stake. But, this was not the way of statesmanship nor leadership of any kind.†

* The invitation to Sardār Baldev Singh, then a Minister in the Panjāb Cabinet, to meet the Cabinet Mission came as a complete surprise to the Sikh leadership. Early in March 1946 at a small conclave of the Sikh leaders at Lāhore(which was attended by the present writer), Master Tārā Singh asked him pointedly as to whom is he going to represent? Baldev replied shyly:—"The other minorities, not the Sikhs." No one, however, took his reply seriously. He had secured this invitation though the Panjāb Governor and Malik Khizar Hayāt Khān who, along with Lord Wavell, then Viceroy of India, did not trust Tārā Singh, though they had no choice but to invite him also. On the other hand, the Sikh leaders telegraphically informed Sir Jogendra Singh, a very sophisticated man of learning from a rich land-owning background,and then a respectable member of the Viceroy's Executive Council,not to see any of the Govt. dignitaries or the Cabinet Mission, even informally, and he was kept scruplously out of all negotiations, though Patiālā was occasionally consulted informally but kept out of inner councils, he being credited with an ambition to take over the leadership of the community, which he later indeed tried to do through his *Panthic Darbār* but failed.

† This and related matters about the period (46-47) are discussed threadbare in about 20 articles the author contributed to the "Civil & Military Gazette", Lahore, titled *"A Sikh View Point"*. Replies to them were published by a Muslim spokesman in the same prestigious English-language daily.

When Mr. Jinnah saw there was no way out for him or his party (inspite of all the killings his League had committed to terrify the Hindus and Sikhs), he accepted the "maimed and vivisected Panjāb and Bengāl" which he had resisted for so long with all his might. Only a month before (April 30, 1947) Jinnah accepted the partition of the Panjāb, he had warned: "The proposal for partition of Bengāl and Panjāb was a sinister move actuated by spite and bitterness...If Panjāb and Bengāl were partitioned, all the other provinces would have to be cut up in a similar way." (*Transfer of Power*, V. P. Menon 360-61). On March 9, Pt. Nehru had written to the Viceroy enclosing copies of the Congress resolution passed in this behalf. The Viceroy forwarded this resolution with a letter to the Secretory of State and the June 3 statement of the Viceroy was the result. But, the Sikh leaders in their anxiety to displease no section of opinion among themselves, left the decision of their political future for others to take. It is a God's blessing, however, that the Sikh demand for partitioning the Panjāb after Pākistān was declared, was accepted by the British in their own declaration of June 3,1947 (a sure hint for which they had given in their earlier statement of May 16,1946 as well), and the Congress supported and infact initiated it with all their heart as the only way out to tear apart from Pākistān as much of the territory and resources for the Hindus and Sikhs as possible. If either of these two parties, British or Congress, would have resisted the Sikh demand, the story of the Sikhs would have been written differently. After all, there were serious suggestions made earlier and also at the Round Table Conference by the British officials, notably Sir Geoffrey Corbet, Secy of the Indian delegation, that the Ambālā Division be detached from the Panjāb to give the Muslims in the rest of the province a voting power of 68%. This would have sealed the fate of the Sikhs as a poitical force for ever. Sind had been detached from Bombay on the same basis, giving the Muslims another majority state. Whenever the Congress also talked of reorganising the provinces on a linguistic basis, in respect of the Panjāb, they only meant, according to Pattabhi Sitaramiyya, the official historian of the Congress and later its President, the detachment of the Ambālā division from it and nothing more. At no time before this, had any party wanting a settlement with the Muslims (the British, the Congress, the Panjab Hindus or any other), ever countenanced the detachment of the predominantly Sikh areas from the Panjāb to be formed into a new state to give the

Sikhs also a chance for self-experssion, though the other two communities together even in that area would have outstripped the Sikhs by atleast 15%, but no single community would have dictated to the other.* A scheme to detach Multān and Rāwalpindi divisions from the Panjāb (but excluding Montgomery and Lyallpur) proposed by the Sikh delegation to the Round Table Conference, (which later formed the basis of *Azād Panjāb* in 1944) was not taken seriously at all by any party—Congress, Muslim League or the British.

At his Press Conference held in the Central Hall of Parliament, on June 4,1947, Lord Mountbatten, the Viceroy, on being questioned persistently by the present writer confessed that it was on the recommendation of the Congress that he had agreed at all to the Sikh demand for the partition of the Panjāb (and consequently also of Bengāl). And though the price that the Sikhs had to pay in terms of both bloodletting and property was colossal, it gave them also a chance for the first time in their whole history of 500 years to congregate together in a contiguous area, a possibility that had eluded them for centuries. †

*The decision to settle the refugees from Lyallpur, Montgomery, Lāhore, Sheikhupura etc. in the East Panjāb from where their forefathers had migrated (and thus incidentally to make the Central Panjāb a Sikh-majority area) was taken by the Panjab Cabinet on Sept 16, 1947, under the premiership of Dr. Gopi Chand Bhargava. Governor C.L. Trivedi who presided over this meeting of officials and Ministers (which included Tarlok Singh I.C.S. and Swaran Singh, then Home Minister) said as much, though the others pointed out that there was no other option open to them. Mr. Tarlok Singh became Commissioner of rural and Mr. M. S. Randhāwā, ICS, of urban rehabilitation and both these patriotic and able officers did a yeoman's job to create the foundations of a Sikh-dominated Panjābi-speaking state, though this may have been only the effect of what they did and not their deliberate intention.

† The present writer, then editor of the English-language weekly of Delhi, the Liberator, was the only Sikh invited to this Press Conference, and he took full advantage of it through persistent questioning to elicit some extremely useful information from Lord Mountbatten who, in his broadcast statement on June 3, 1947, had spelt out the Muslim-majority districts expected to be included in Pākistān as being Lāhore, Gujrānwālā, Sialkot, Sheikhupurā, and Gurdāspur, besides the Rāwalpindi and Multān divisions, which included the canal-colonies of the Sikhs in Lyallpur and Montgomery.

Question :—Your Lordship stated in your broadcast that the ultimate boundaries will be settled by a Boundary Commission and will almost certainly not be identical with those which have been provisionally adopted. Didn't your Lordship have in mind certain factors other than the question of majority population of a certain community?

Answer:—I put that in for the simple reason that in the district of Gurdāspur in the the Panjāb where the population is 50.4% Muslim and 49.6% non-Muslim with a difference of 0.8%, you will atonce see that it is unlikely that the Boundary Commission will throw the whole of the district in the Muslim-majority areas (i.e. Pākistān). (This commitment at this stage not only saved most of the Gurdāspur district for India, but gave it the only road-link to Kashmir).

Question: You said (in your broadcast) that in the matter of the division of the Panjāb, "other factors" will also be taken into consideration. What are those "other factors?"

Answer :—What I said was we could not expect the present (Labour) Govt. in England to partition any province on the basis of private property. It was for the Indians themselves to decide.

(Many more questions were fired at him about the sacred Sikh shrines, the possibility of creating a Sikh enclave around Nankānā Sāhib so as to include Lyallpur and Montgomery (which had a Sikh majority, though it was not contiguous to other Sikh areas, on the analogy of the proposed East Pākistān etc., but to all of them H.E.'s replies were :)

"Every time you ask me whether I'm going to decide a question for you, I say "no". If you put the same question in a second and third way, I'll still say my answer is "no." I am quite sincere when I say that you have got to make up your own mind."

Question : What the Sikhs asked for was the division of the Panjāb, not their own division into two. What provision have you made to preserve their integrity?

Answer : The people who asked for the partition (of the Panjāb) were the Sikhs. The Congress took up their request. I have done what the Sikhs requested me to do through the Congress.

Question: If the Sikhs are uprooted from where they have 70% property, worth 700 crores, will they not become paupers? There could be an organised exchange of population etc.

Answer:—Look, if that was what you wanted, why did you not put your resolution in that form ? Why did you not make a request that you wanted to be divided into Muslim and non-Muslim property areas? You've got what you've asked for. (When I pleaded more and solicited his own sympathy and support, H.E. said) "Believe me, I want to help you." At the end of the Conference, he repeated again "I am really sincere in my desire to help the Sikhs." According to "Partition of Punjāb" (Pp. 79.82), Lord Mountbatten kept his word. The Award of the Boundary Commission was delayed for upto two days even after independence, in order to get clearance from London for his recommendations of certain areas and canal head-works in the Ferozepur district transferred to East Panjāb. Justice Mohd. Munir

The Muslim League had accepted the Cabinent Mission's plan, of May 16, 19, 1946, but later reversed their stand, mainly because the Congress refused to coerce the Hindu and Sikh minorities to join the Muslim-dominated groups, and Nehru had declared that the Constituent Assembly could frame any kind of Constitution as it was sovereign. Jinnah said he would boycott the Constituent Assembly and not join the interim Govt. either. Mr. Nehru thereupon was invited to form a wholly Congress Govt. at the Centre. The League protested vehemently against it and called upon the Muslims to observe a"Direct Action Day" on Aug. 16, on which day the city of Calcutta witnessed a virtual holocaust. The Muslim League volunteers under the inspiration and guidance of the Bengāl Chief Minister, Shahid Suhrawardy, unleashed a reign of wholesale killings and terror upon the inncent Hindus. Mr. Jinnah, who had threatened on July 27 at the Bombay meeting of the League Council that "today we have forged a pistol and are in a position to use it," had proved true to his word. Earlier at a convention of the Muslim Legislators held at Delhi in April (even before the Cabinet Mission had enunciated its proposals), Sir Feroze Khan Noon, Muslim League leader of the Panjāb, had thundered:-"If we find we have to fight Great Britain for placing us under one Certral Hindu Rāj, then the havoc which Muslims will play

---

F. N. Contd.

who was arguing the Muslim case before the Boundary Commission was categorical that Mr. Radcliffe had told him that Ferozepur, Zirā and Fāzilkā were going to Pākistān. Ferozepur tehsil had 55% Muslim population & Zira 65.2%, though Fāzilkā had only 43% Muslim population. Under these arrangements, the Ferozpur canal Headworks would also have gone to Pākistān & no choice left for Bikāner state, depending upon water from this Canal system, but to accede to Pākistān. A map, supplied two days in advance to Governor Jenkins of Panjāb by Abel, Secy. to Viceroy, also included Ferozepur & Zirā in Pākistān but in the final award, these were included in India. Pakistān believed Lord Mountbatten was reponsible for it. He helped also as head of the Partition Council in the rescue and rehabilitation of Hindu and Sikh refugees and his noble wife, Edwina Mountbatten, did a yeoman's job in rescuring women abducted in Pākistān. Within three months, peace was restored in the whole sub-continent. It is a great tribute to his administrative skill, sense of dedication to duty and high moral values. India still cherishes his friendship. In Britain also he has helped many Indian causes. (For details, see *Time only to Look forward*, Nicholas Kay, London, 1949, Chapter I)

will put to shame what Chengiz Khān and Halāku did in the past." (Incidentally, this meeting was also attended by Giani Kartār Singh as a distinguished guest). And what happened in Calcutta for the five nightmarish days (Aug 16 to 20) with at least 5000 killed and 15000 injured, with extensive properties burnt and looted, created a reign of terror throughout the country. Reprisals against the Muslims followed in the Hindu-dominated state of Bihar to be avenged soon after by the Muslims (Oct. 1946) in the Noakhali distt. of East Bengāl on a scale unprecendented in our history, not only in killings and forcible conversions and marriages, but the abductions and rape of the womenfolk of the Hindus, who constituted only 20% of the population of this district.*

Mr. Jinnah had stated clearly in Bombay on Sept 11 that "the Hindu India must choose between Pākistān and civil war." Answering a question, he had even called for an exchange of minority populations, though he never seriously discussed with the Sikhs or others when they tried to probe him further on the issue through the press. Gāndhiji resisted this move and went straight to Noakhali to restore peace. However, no League leader or newspaper ever condemned these horrors. But, the worst was yet to come, and this was to be in the Panjāb.

It began in December 1946, in the Hazārā district of the N. W. F. P., and spread to the rural areas of Rāwalpindi and Jehlum

---

* A deputation of East Bengāl Hindus waited on Giani Kartār Singh in Delhi after the Noākhali riots and implored him to depute some intelligent Sikh missionaries to visit East Bengāl. "Millions at this stage of crisis are ready to flock to your faith," they said. When the deputation left, this writer expressed his great excitement and joy over the unprecendented possibilities of this mission. The Giani was totally unmoved, and said in his usual hoarse, elongated and unconcerned voice:—"This will only add to our problems. Even if we become 20 million, there is going to be only one Central Minister and that we already have in Sardār Baldev Singh!"

Another amusing thing he did was to send a two-man Sikh delegation to England (consisting of "Professor" Gangā Singh, who used to harangue village audiences in Panjāb & didnot know even basic English or had any sense of politics & *Mr.* M. S. Dhupia, (Secy. of a New Delhi club) to mobilise British support for the Sikh Cause in the United Kingdom, after the formation of Pākistān had been announced or June 3, 1947. Gangā Singh soon after abjured his faith and Mr. Dhupia was left alone to use his organising talents to collect & lead a small procession of Sikh fortune-tellers through the streets of London in protest!

in the month of March 1947, immediately after the resignation of the Coalition Ministry, under Sir Khizar Hayāt Khān on March 2, under strong Muslim League pressure and the colossal private armies it had raised in the shape of Khāksārs and the Muslim Guards which were banned for a time (on Jan. 24, 1947). But so much was the furore raised against this order, through demonstrations and open defiance of the law, that the order had to be rescinded, and the Govt itself resigned on March 2, leaving the field free for the Muslim League to play havoc with the life and property of the Hindus and Sikhs in the Panjāb. The League celebrated this day as a "Victory Day." The next day, the Governor invited the Muslim League party to form a Govt. But, as they didnot command the majority, they expressed their inability to do so, and the British Governor, Sir Evan Jenkins, took over the administration in his own hands. Heartily stung on their failure to form the Govt., the League volunteers went on a rampage and resorted to stabbing and killing of Hindus and Sikhs. On March 6, both Amritsar and Multān were in the grip of panic. Much property was set upon fire. And what happened in the rural areas of the Rāwalpindi division in this month and after, makes description of all the horrors perpetrated impossible to narrate. The unashamed brutality, the cold murders of people gathered in the Sikh temples or in the community homes, the parading of naked women in public streets, the mass rape of young girls, the abductions, the total destruction and looting of property, the forcible conversions, the mass suicides of non-Muslim women to escape dishonour, the dashing of children to the ground, make one's blood curdle at the level of inhumanity to which the Muslim League sympathisers had succumbed. Multān, Campellpore, Jhelum, and Sargodha, were attacked next, where the Muslim population was overwhelmingly large, ranging from eighty to ninety percent.

Master Tārā Singh's home in village Haryāl (in the district of Rāwalpindi) was raised to the ground and the site slapped with shoes and ploughed over.

The police, mainly Muslim, watched helplessly on the sidelines, or actively supported the Muslim mobs. The British officers in the districts thought it was none of their business any longer to intervene. Let the Hindus and the Muslims sort it out among themselves as best as they could! Inspite of Mr. Jinnah's speech, on the birth of Pākistān assuring minorities full democratic rights, had not Governor Mudie of West Panjab written to him as the Governor-General of Pākistān : "I donot care how the Sikhs cross the border. The great thing is to get rid of them as soon as possible."

After the announcement on June 3,1947 of the Mountbatten Plan for the division of the country into India and Pākistān on the basis mainly of religious persuation (though "other factors" also had to be considered) and the appointment of the Boundary Commission under Sir Cyril Radcliffe* to demarcate areas into Muslim and non-Muslim, the fire spread to other Muslim-dominated areas of the West Panjab as well. Though this was the only alternative before the Sikhs—the division of the Panjāb—it was cruel to leave the historic Sikh shrines (besides 700 crores worth of property) and half of the Sikhs in Pākistān. Master Tārā Singh immediately (June 12) rejected it as also the Akāli Dal and the Panthic Board, but on June 4, i. e. a week earlier, S. Baldev Singh had declared over the A. I. Radio : "It doesnot please everybody, not the Sikhs anyway, but it certainly is something worthwhile. It is not a compromise but a settlement. Let's take it at that". The Sikh leadership, through divided counsel, had thus compromised their stand. And, from mid-June, serious trouble also started in Lāhore, to be followed in Gujrānwālā, Wazirābād, Sheikhupura, Sialkot, Lyallpur and in fact where not ? In Sheikhupura alone, over 22000 people were killed, and this ten days after Pākistān had come into being. Arson and stabbing, abductions of the young girls, and looting of movables were resorted to on an extensive scale to put terror into the hearts of the non-Muslims, to abandon their ancetoral homes and flee to India. Since March 1947, a huge Hindu-Sikh exodus from the North-West had already started to take shelter in Patiālā, Ludhiānā

* Justice Teja Singh and Justice Mehar Chand Mahājan were members of this Commission. They argued the case of non-Muslims ably but were over-ruled. However, the decision of the Cammission was delayed upto two days after independence (Aug 15) and this gave hope to many not to leave their homes before this. This created an awful situation after the Pakistān Govt took over, though the interval also is believed to have been responsible for some last-minute changes in the Award (as stated earlier) to the advantage of the Sikhs.

and other Sikh centres in the East Panjāb. And by the date announced for independence of the two dominions (Aug. 15, 1947), it had become a huge, unannounced, primodial flood. Hundreds of thousands of people, men, women and children, trekking on foot, with a few belongings stacked in their bullock-carts, hungry and half-naked, leaving their dying or dead behind, were marching towards an India they had never seen or known before. Even the trucks and trains carrying refugees were brutally attacked on the way by the ruffians. One train steamed into the Amritsar station from Pākistān, all blood and stinking bones and torn limbs, but not a sign of life.

This total contempt for non-Muslim life could not fail to inflame the people of the East Panjāb and the Sikh States, and retaliation started in full fury everywhere from early August. No pains were spared to pay the Muslim Leaguers in their own coin : blood for blood, loot for loot, though abductions, conversions and rape were rare occurences. And thus within about three months of the birth of Pākistān, with about half a million killed on both sides, five million Muslims,mostly from East Panjāb, and as many Hindus and Sikhs from West Pākistān, trekked to their new homelands which consisted mostly of refugee camps, distant relations. railway platforms, tunnels, holes, bridges, culverts and open streets. Thc Sikhs of the Panjāb had paid full price and more for the freedom of the country and their own ruin. But thanks to their resilience, determination and faith in their great destiny, they again rose from the ashes to become once again the pride and envy of the whole nation.

CHAPTER XXIX

THE ERA OF HOPE

(1948-78)

No one who visits the Panjāb today will fail to notice the remarkable transformation that has taken place in this border state whose economy and social life lay shattered without any visible sign of resurrection, only 40 years ago. It is a tribute to the inherent vitality of the Panjābis as a people, Sikhs especially. They rehabilitated themselves, without much material help from the Govt., even better than before. Those who were once millionaires worked as day-labourers, pulled rickshaws, hawked wares, ploughed barren lands, put up small workshops on the roadside, but not one begged for alms. In five years, all refugee camps were abolished, as no one was willing to live in them any longer. The biggest dam of Asia, the Bhākrā Nangal, was constructed in record time. The newest capital of the world, designed by the most modern architect of the times, Le Carbousier, and called Chandigarh (lit. the fortress of the Hindu goddess of war, Chandi) was built in the foothills of the Shivālik range. In small-scale industry, Panjāb led the whole country. And in agriculture, virtually a green revolution took place. The deficit areas of the East Panjāb became the granary of the whole country. Sixty per cent of the Central

Govt wheat pool and 50% of the rice stocks are contributed today solely by the Panjāb. India's chronic dependence for import of food and consequent loss of colossal amounts of foreign exchange besides loss of prestige (that an overwhelmingly agricultural country cannot even feed itself), is now a thing of the past. We've now started exporting and even hoarding food. The highest yield in wheat per acre in the whole world is in the district of Ludhiana. A white revolution (a buffalow or two in milk in every home) is round the corner. Chandigarh is the largest banking centre of all India. The age expectancy has risen to 65 (against the all-India average of 47). It was only 32 in 1947. And with the mechanisation of agriculture and liberal application of fertilisers, the new seeds yield four times bigger crops. The Panjāb's per-capita income today is the highest in the country (over 400 American dollars). Of the country's nearly 40 per cent living below the poverty-line, the fewest live in the Panjāb. India produces the third largest number of trained technicians, physicians, scientists and engineers after the U. S. A. and U. S. S. R. That Panjāb claims a fair share of these can be seen from the fact that over two million Panjābis, mostly trained at home, are now either settled or work abroad, and through their remittances, not only add to the all-round prosperity of their state, but also bolster the foreign exchange reserves (now estimated at six billion U. S. Dollars) to reinforce her economic credibility. The Panjāb could become the California of India (and even better) if their requests for generating more power and water were not thwarted by every succeeding Govt. at the Centre, time and again. Or, if they were not denied a fair proportion of the Central resources merely on the plea that they were doing better than others: or more heavy industry were allocated to this region.* These are the legitimate demands whose denial leads to friction, ill-will and much bad blood and generates extremist demands for

* India today ranks 9th among the industrialised countries of the world. While it didnot produce even needles in 1947, today India builds ships, aeroplanes, heavy electricals, railway engines, machine tools, tanks, electronic equipment, watches, motor cars, trucks and buses, fertilisers and whole steel, cement and textile plants etc. But the concentration of industries is mostly in the eastern, western or southern regions of India. Panjab's share is still only 2%.

separation, or decentralisation of Govt. of India's powers so as to limit their activities only to Defence, Foreign Affairs and Communication etc. It is a danger signal which the Govt. of India (whatever its texture or composition) must heed in good time.

"Every land of plenty", says a survey of independent *India Today* (March 16, 1979) "exercises its anachronisms. While the Panjābis have the highest per capita consumption of milk in the country, they also consume the most liqour. In 1956-57, the state consumed four crore (forty million) litres of alcohol, today, inspite of Haryana being carved out as a separate state, Panjāb's consumption of liqour (70 per cent of which is country-made spirit) has shot upto 29 crore (290 million) litres, highest not only in India but also in South East Asia and greater than most Scandanavian countries. (Here is a field rich for social work, as the Panjābis would not submit easily to the dictates of the state laws in this behalf).

"*And yet the irony is heightened by the corresponding figures in crime which are the lowest in the country*," adds the commentator. "How the Panjābis starting from a scratch have built up a powerful new society is not the story of a few stray farmers, businessmen or administrators. It is a collective account of enterprise and gusty endeavour, of sheer skill and resilience furthered by a deep adherence to the basic tenets of Sikhism. What other reason could there be? That Panjāb which has the same soil and water conditions as Uttar Pardesh or Bihār should far outstrip these states and have to feed them?"* And Panjāb is not the

* Of the many Chief Ministers of the Panjāb after independence, the name of its main architect, Partāp Singh of village Kairon (once member of the Congress Working Committee and well-known freedom fighter) has passed into a legend. Giani Zail Singh (of Faridkot) the only non-Jat Sikh leader of the States' Peoples'movement not only built on his base, but also extended it. He particularly gave his attention to the revival of Panjāb's cultural and religious heritage. Hans Rāj Sharma, as his Finance Minister, husbanded cleverly the resources of the state. Justice Gurnam Singh got little time, but elicited much respect as a level-headed statesman who softened communal frictions in the state, against his earlier extremist statements, and activities. Sardar Parkāsh Singh of village Bādal (Farid Kot), Akāli premier (1977-79) concentrated on rural integrated programmes and extension of inputs and infrastructures for better agriculture and industry.

land of the Kulaks by any chance but only small and medium self-cultivating farmers, sixty per cent of whom own less then five acres. Thanks again to Sikhism, an egilatarian society is taking shape, secular to the core, welcoming innovation, self-help and adventure, not addicted by and large to caste or karma, astrology and auspicious days, and of what to eat and wear, and loving life in all its fury and fantasy. * It is thus not surprising that the Panjābi Sikh man or woman is perhaps the handsomest and the most healthy and vigorous of our people.

Out of nearly 30 years, the Congress party ruled the Panjab for over 25 (upto March 1977). The progress registered in these years has been phenomenal. A few figures ;

(1) As against 3.1 million tonnes of food production, 28 years ago, today ('87-'88) the state produces 6 times more of foodgrains. The productivity in wheat is 1881 kgs per hectare as against the all-India average of 821 kgs; in rice 2897 kgs against 1108 and 374 kgs of cotton as against 142 kgs of all India average. Rice production has risen 300 per cent during the last ten years, and sugarcane by 50 per cent.

(2) The Panjāb Agriculture University, Ludhiana, has developed more than 70 new varieties of seeds, leading to a revolution in the production of not only wheat, but also rice and cotton.

(3) The Panjāb farmer owns every fifth tractor and every fourth tubewell in the country. He also applies the maximum fertilisers—70 kgs a hectare to 20 for the whole country.

And all this when the Bank rates of interest have gone upto 18% and the facilities are denied to the small farmers, when electric supply is erratic, when there are curbs on the use of canal water, when floods ravage the crops every third year, when the glut in production (as in the case of cotton, sugarcane and potatoes) leads to distress sales. One result of massive technical education has been the migration and settlement abroad of about two million Sikhs. One more reason for this has been the near total neglect of the aspirations of the intellectuals, no matter what the colour of the regime in the Panjāb.

Outside the Panjāb, a first-rate intellectual, Prof. Gurmukh Nihāl Singh, M. Sc (London) created a great name for integrity & efficient administration as Chief Minister of Delhi (1953-57).

* Attention must be paid to the crusading work in this behalf done by the late Sardār Gurbakash Singh (died 1977), editor of the Panjābi monthly "Preet-Lari" and founder of the *Preet* (love) movment with its HQs in Preet-Nagar, near Amritsar. His remarkable writings shook the people, Sikhs especially (as he wrote in Panjābi) out of their age-old superstitions, reinterpreting their past, and givin them a glimpse of the new scientific, secular world. His influence was widespread inspite of his own leanings towards agnosticism and Marxism.

When all this is said, a historian cannot also overlook the fears and aspirations of a people which can be legitimately satisfied but are not, and lead to a sense of frustration,violence and extremist talk.

When freedom came, the Sikhs were the most depressed of all the Indian people. They had been split into two, with the other (and more prosperous) half rendered penniless and without a home or sure means of livelihood. There was no one to welcome them outside the Panjāb. They tried to settle on vacant and arid lands as in the Tarái area of the U.P. but when their lands bloomed with smiling crops, all sorts of laws were passed to deprive them of their hard-earned labours. Gāndhiji in his prayer meetings cruelly censured their habits and cultural mores, creating much disaffection against their entry into Delhi and Western U.P. They had indeed asked for a separate state in the event of the Muslim state of Pākistān being conceded, but had now abandoned that slogan for good. Master Tārā Singh declared this publicly:—, "It is the enemies of Sikhs who are raising this slogan; now we only want to rehabilitate our uprooted race." * But, the Sikhs had become suspect for having harboured this wish once, no matter under what circumstances. Had not Bengāl led by Sri Sarat Chadra Bose, Shahid Suhrawardy and Fazalul Haq

---

* Pandit J.L. Nehru told a deputation of Panjāb Hindus on Sept. 20, 1947 :— "Master Tārā Singh met me yesterday. He protested vehemently against any idea of Khālistān and said the Sikhs being a small section of the people of India would not pick any quarrel with them. They wished to remain citizens of India and live with the Hindus as brothers." (*India, from Curzon to Nehru,* by Durgādās, P. 269). But Gandhi's diatribes against the Sikhs, as they entered this country as refugees, were in total contrast to the sympathy and support he had given them earlier in 1946 after the Cabinet Mission's Statement of May 16. It was a cruel and malicious maligning of a whole people in distress. "He advised the Sikhs (and Hindus) not to retaliate and die at the hands of their Muslim brethren. They would not only save Hinduism and Islam but also serve India and save the world," (*Mahatma,* Vol VII, P. 371 record of a prayer meeting, April 7, 1947). "They should resist Pākistān being forced on them with the incomparable weapon of *Satyagraha.*" (Ibid, P. 374). "Years ago, I had said at Nankānā Sahib, 'Sikhs have given proof of their martial valour. But the consummation of Guru Gobind Singh's ideal will be reached only when they substitute for the *Kirpans* the sword of the spirit or non-violence." (The Mahātmā didnot offer this advice when Kashmir was attacked a little later). Moreover, this was a time when Sikhs were being butchered in Rāwalpindi etc., and no retaliation on their part had yet started. Instead of offering this advice to the Muslims, he advised Sikhs to suffer as best as they could.

tried to carve an independent unified Bengāl outside of India and Pākistān ? Had not Gāndhiji himself called upon the Sikhs to stay out of the Constituent Assembly and the Groups, if they so wished ? Had not the venerable Pt. Jawaharlal himself said in 1946, "if the Sikhs too wanted an area where they could breathe the air of freedom, let them have it." Had not Gāndhiji after assuring the Hindu and Sikh minorities that "Pākistān would only be built on his dead body," agreed to it while he was still very much alive, and tried to consolidate its economy and polity by pressurising the Indian Govt. to release funds in their favour and by asking the minorities, inspite of widespread arson and killings, not to move out of Pākistān ? Didnot Rajgopalachiar concede the demand of Pākistān, in 1944, and Gāndhiji himself supported him ? Why were the Sikhs alone made a

---

F.N. Contd.

Again, on June 28 1947, "he adjured them in a prayer meeting to shed their drink habit and luxurious habits of Sikh women." (Certainly the moral norms of Sikh women were no worse than those of others, including the Mahātmā's own Ashram (See, *Freedom at Midnight*, Vikās, Pp. 66-69). As for drinking habit of Sikh men, were they the only ones in the country at this time to indulge in this habit ? And, then, where was the occasion and how was it relevant to the issue of Partition?

After violence erupted in Delhi and Panjāb, he said: "Let Hindus and Sikhs invite back the Muslims driven out of their homes. Transfer of millions of Hindus and Sikhs and Muslims is unthinkable. The wrong of Pākistān will be undone by the right of a resolute non-transfer of population." (*Mahatmā*, Vol VIII, P. 123). Again: "The Sikhs brandished their swords and frightened the Muslim residents to vacate their houses (in Delhi). Sikhs were given to drinking. They sold *Kabābs* in the Chāndni Chowk where even Muslims didn't, to the annoyance of Hindus." (Nov 19, Mahatmā, p. 194).

But, he defended Sardār Patel, who had criticised the Muslim League's vandalism and said if Nehru didnot agree with him,he would sack him." (Ibid P. 252). What double standards!

And when he went on his last fast on Jan. 12, 1948 and criticised the Hindus also for having joined hands with the Sikhs in the uprooting of Muslims in Delhi, Patel, after listening to his plaint "got up without a word," according to Maulānā Āzād. "I stopped him. He shouted back, 'What is the use of of my staying ? Gandhiji is not prepared to listen to me. He seems determined to blacken the name of the Hindus before the whole world. If this is his attitude, I have no use for him." (*India Wins Freedom*, page 217). A little over fortnight later, he was murdered by a Hindu fanatic. But, he had created against the Sikhs a kind of public opinion throughout the world which they have still to live down.

target of attack? Even when the present writer waited upon Gāndhiji (in June 1947), to seek his help for a Panjābi-speaking state being carved out of what was soon going to be East Panjāb, his first sharp reaction was:—"But you are then asking for a Sikh State." When told that no single community would be in a majority in this state (the Muslims, had not yet migrated to Pākistān), he immediately calmed down and said:—"If this be so, bring me a blue-print. I shall speak to the others." But, his offer was never taken up by the Sikhs with any seriousness, because he had changed his mind soon after the riots and the wholesale migrations of the minorities from the two Panjābs.

Gāndhi was assasinated (Jan. 30, 1948) by a Hindu fanatic and a member of the para-military R.S S.S. which was banned immediately thereafter. * Kashmir had been attacked by Pākistān four months earlier, first through the Pathān irregulars and later by their regular forces. It was Gāndhi's first test on the home-ground of his creed of non-violence. When the Govt. asked for his opinion, he took no time to acquiesce "for it was," he said, "a defensive war." The Sikhs showed their mettle and pariotism once again and the forces personally led by the Mahārājā of Patiala and Lt. Gen. Kulwant Singh soon were on the verge of breaking into Pākistān, when the new Muslim state sued for peace through the U.N., and a cease-fire was arranged. By this time, Pākistān had already occupied one-third of Kashmir's territory which they refused to vacate, inspite of their pledged word, and the U.N's insistence, without which a plebiscite of the whole state (to which both parties had also agreed) couldnot be organised under the aupices of the U.N. Sheikh Abdullah, the acknowledged leader of Kashmir as much as the Muslim population of this predominantly Muslim state, and Muslim officers and men of the Indian army, proved their loyalty and commitment to India, thus cementing with their blood the foundations of a truly secular state in this country. This was a triumph of both Gāndhi and Nehru and the most

* Founded by a Marāthā Brahmin, Dr. Hedgewār in 1925, and succeeded in 1940 by M. S. Golwalkar for Hindu "cultural" regeneration, it has adopted an anti-Muslim and anti-minority stance since its inception. Though spread throughout North India, its leadership has always remained with Marāthā Brahmins. Its iron discipline, secret confabulations and military parades and drills leave no one in doubt as to its methods and aims for achieving power. The Jan Sangh is its political wing. But the real power is in the hands of the R. S. S. S.

glorious chapter of our free history. Kashmir today, integrated fully with India, is contributing its full share in promoting the democratic and secular outlook in this complex land of great variety of race, religion and culture, and sharing fully the benefits of her great economic progress under an atmosphere of democratic freedoms granted equally to all her citizens.

The Sikhs, finding the climate for secularism asserting itself decisively, also decided on March 16, 1948, to merge their political entity finally in the Congress. The Akālī leadership under Giani Kartar Singh also declared that the Akāli Dal will henceforth confine itself to religious and cultural uplift of the Sikhs. However, such was the demoralisation or confusion in their ranks that even the resolution for merger with the Congress was not publicised in its original form which contained their demand for a Panjābi-speaking state for the first time ! *

This annoyed the Sikh masses as much as the other secular forces who wanted the East Panjāb, alongwith the rest of the country, to be redistributed on the basis of language. And taking advantage of it, Master Tārā Singh revived the Akāli Dal as a political party and ran his own ticket at the 1951 elections. He was defeated, but he

* The present writer drafted and moved the resolution. It was adopted unanimously in the presence of almost all Sikh leaders of note : Master Tārā Singh, S. Baldev Singh, Giani Kartār Singh, S. Swaran Singh, S. Hukam Singh, S. Ishar Singh, Majhail, S. Ajit Singh Sarhadi, S. Sarup Singh, S. Amar Singh Ambālvi, S. Dalip Singh Kang, S, Joginder Singh Mann, S. Bhupinder Singh Mann, S. Udham Singh Nāgoke, etc. It said. "As the Congress is pledged to create linguistic states and the creation of a Panjābi-speaking state will fulfil wholly the aspirations of the Sikhs as well as of all secular-minded Panjābis, this meeting unanimously calls upon the Akāli members of the Panjāb legislature to merge in the Congress Party in order to strengthen the secular forces, especially after the assasination of Mahātmā Gandhi at the hands of a member of an avowedly communal organisation." But when the resolution was published next morning, all references to the Panjābi-speaking state had been omitted (under instructions from S. Baldev Singh and his associates). This writer put the record straight by getting the original resolution published in the Press. It was never contradicted. It only shows our two faces on all fronts at most times.

succeeded in arousing the passions of the Sikhs against both the Akāli leadership in the Congress camp and the Congress itself.

Sensing amply the feelings of the Sikhs for political self-expres-sision, Sardar Vallabhbhai Patel,* then Home Minster and incharge of Indian States Deptt. created a Sikh-majority state in the heart of the East Panjāb, called P. E. P. S. U. (Patiālā and East Panjāb States Union) in May, 1948, comprising of the erstwhile Sikh states of Patiālā, Nābhā, Jind, Kapurthala and Faridkot, with the Mahārājā of Patiālā as the Rājparmukh (Head of state). But, Patiālā's bid to take over the leadership of all Sikhs, through his newly-constituted *Panthic Darbār* and many mistakes of the Central Govt. under the directions of Sardār Patel and his nominees, especially U.N. Rao, the administrator appointed after the dismissal of S. Gian Singh Rārewālā, an able administrator and well-beloved of his co-religionists, widened the gulf between the Akālis and the Congress, inspite of the fact that the Congress Sikhs swept the polls in 1952, both for Parliament and the State Assembly, both in PEPSU and Panjāb. A Congress Ministry came into being in PEPSU for a while, under Col. Raghubir Singh. For some time it was led also by Babu Brish Bhān, a lawyer and an old stalwart of the Praja Mandal movement and this made the Akālis doubly sore. They had been deprived of hegemony even in the Sikh-dominated state and a Hindu made its premier !

During this period (1948-1956), Master Tārā Singh launched many campaigns. In one of them, he won a signal victory† and for

* Sardār Vallabhāi Patel, a lawyer of Gujarāt, and a farmer by birth and aptitude (being tough and forthright) was given a quick lift by Gāndhiji for his great organisational abilities. (He was given the apellation of Sardār for the same reason by Gāndhi). According to Maulānā Āzād, his entire position in the country and Congress (he rose to be its President) was due to Gāndhi's patronage. He was an orthodox Hindu, much favouring the R. S. S. S. and also the Akāli Dal for a time, on the eve of Partition, when he also supplied them arms & money and had a great hold over the Congress organisation. The Muslims didnot like him and gradually he was distrusted by others as well. His differences with Nehru were acute, though he was his Deputy Prime Minister till his death (1950), over secularism, socialism, policy towards Tibet and China and Communism in general. His work for the integration of Indian states would always he cherished. His other brother, Vithalbhāi Patel, was a Speaker of the Central Assembly before 1947.

† It is a pity this concession has not been offered to other communities, though they remain equally backward after conversion. The question of imposing Sanskrit and Hindi (as against Hindustāni written in Roman) as an all-India

which other minorities (like Muslims, Christians and Buddhists are still fighting). This was in relation to similar concessions being granted to four Sikh Scheduled castes as were allowed by the Constitution to their Hindu counterparts. Tārā Singh had threatened, true to his line,* a fast unto death over this issue and Patel, the iron man of India, succumbed. Though apparently contradicting the basic Sikh doctrine of castelessness, it also saved the so-called lower castes among the Sikhs (Mazhabis, Rāmdāsias etc) from reverting back to Hinduism. Such is the power of caste in our country that the social realities take precedence over the doctrines of the faith ! Inspite of their public postures, the Sikh society refuses to integrate fully its converts from lower castes, though in matters of entry and employment in the Sikh temples and their acceptance as priests and musicians and in the community kitchens is now widespread. But inter-caste marriages and their acceptance as social equals by the rich Sikh peasantry, especially in the villages, is still a far cry, though cruelty to, or inhuman aggression against them is not at all a common occurence, as in the Hindu-dominated villages elsewhere in India.

But the main grievance remained: the Sikhs had no place under the sun where their political and cultural expression was possible. The Southern states had been reorganised on the basis of language, but this principle was not applied to North India. Even their mother-tongue, Panjābi, was denied the status of a state language, mainly because the Panjāb Hindus for political reasons opted for Hindi, both at the Census and in the schools. A scheme called the *Sachar Formula* (so-called, because Mr. Bhim Sen Sachar was then the Chief Minister of Panjāb) was evolved in the early years of freedom by which the study of both Panjābi and Hindi became com-

F.N. Contd.

language, or reservation of seats for Muslims with joint electorates as in the case of Harijans, as proposed by Āzād and opposed by Patel, are points which irked the Muslims.

*Master Tārā Singh had a purpose behind this "permanent revolution." He told the author:—"Unless I keep my turbulent followers occupied by one agitation or another, they either fall apart and quarrel among themselves or try to pull the leadership down." To hold the Sikhs, under one's charge, he said, "one needs to live and act as dangerously as to keep the throne of Afghānistān." Possibly, he

pulsory after the third primary stage, but the choice of the medium of instruction was left to the parents, the Hindus thus freely opting for Hindi and Sikhs for Panjābi. This divided the two communities further apart. Even the academic world got divided on communal lines. In 1949, the Panjāb University, dominated as it was by the Arya Samāj elements, also decided that Panjābi could not be considered a "fit" medium of instruction, even if the Sikhs would (as they did) agree to both Nāgri and Gurmukhi as its scripts. And this added fuel to the fire. The Panjāb became a battle-ground over the language issue.

After many agitations launched by the Akāli Dal, a compromise called the Regional Formula, was finally accepted* by all parties in

---

never settled any issue finally for his people for the same reason. When told that his deputy, Sant Fateh Singh, had virtually replaced him by his "genuine fast" for 18 days (1961), he threw up his hands in despair and said :—"Only Sikhs could have done it. A Sikh Havildar once got a Victoria Cross for his personal bravery: the British only promoted him Jemādar. Left to the Sikhs, they would have made him Commander-in-Chief, and one day the hero would have staked this whole army in a reckless campaign and got them all destroyed."

* The Akālis had demonstrated their mass support unmistakably among the Sikhs and the Congress was out for a final settlement. It is yet beyond any reasonable man's wits why at this time the Akāli leaders accepted the Regional Formula instead of pressing their demand of a Panjābi-speaking state and even disbanded their party as a political organisation. The only available explanation is the nearness of the general elections which the Akāli nominees could win, due to joint electorates, only with the help of the Congress. This experiment has been tried so often by the Akālis that at times it becomes hard indeed to distinguish who is an Akāli and who a Congressman among the Sikhs. They have changed their political & personal loyalty so often that even in a country,where change of political parties is notoriously widespread, the Akālis possibly have built a record. There is hardly a Sikh of note who later found himself either as a Congress legislator, Minister or other office-bearer who didnot trek from the Akāli party to the Congress. The pity is that when they quit their offices and get back to the Akāli Dal, (as most do) they leave no expletive unused to downgrade the Congress, or those who stick to it as "agents of the Hindus" and worse. Some Sikh journalists have also made it their profession to denigrate others for their consistent loyalty to the national causes, themselves later becoming the worst kind of stooges and sycophants of the very people & ideals they criticised before in the severest posible terms.

1956. The Panjāb was divided into two regions—Panjābi and Hindi, and certain cultural and other minor affairs transferred to their authority, though these subjects numbered 14. But, this makeshift and wholly artificial arrangement never worked (nor was allowed to, by the dominant party) thus adding strength to the movement for a separate Panjābi state. Though Panjābi became the sole medium in the Panjābi region, and was to be compulsorily taught in the Hindi region as well (and vice-versa) the Hindus never opted for it. It was not introduced for administration even at the district level! On the other hand, a pro-Hindi agitation was launched by the Hindus, virulent and aggressive in the extreme.

Jawāharlal Nehru, the Prime Minister of India, a great friend of the minorities, and the powerful Chief Minister of Panjāb, Sardār Partāp Singh Kairon (1956-64) both stood against it, as the demand took on more and more of communal overtones, thanks to the fact that the language issue had cleaved the Panjāb on purely communal lines. However, due to the bonhomie and social nearness of the Hindus and Sikhs and the all-embracing outlook of the Sikh faith, no untoward incident ever took place which might have disfigured our history as it happened in Assam, between Bengālis and Assamese, or in Mahārāshtrā between the Marāthās and the Gujarātis, or the Marāthās and the Southern people settled in Bombay. There was tension (some times acute, especially in the cities), but no fear of life, property or honour of any non-Sikh being attacked was ever entertained by anyone. And life on the countryside had a quiet and even flow.

It was a grievous mistake, however, not to have fought for this wholly democratic slogan from a common platform of all Panjābis, rather than make it a wholly Sikh issue, however helpless the Sikhs had been rendered due to the near total Hindu preference for Hindi. The Akālis soon learnt to their cost the bitter-or sweet-lesson, that the moment they came into power (and this was three times after the creation of the new Panjāb), they had every time to bring the Jan Sangh (the main militant Hindu organisation opposed to their demands) into their Government in the interest of communal harmony! Why could this be not done by the Akālis in respect of the more secular forces in their fight for a very just cause, remains a mystery.

This led also to another unfortunate result. The Akālis time and again made compromises with the Congress, entered legislatures as Congress nominees, and then on the eve of the next poll, went back to their parent organisation. Twice (in 1948 and 1956), they dissolved the Akāli Dal as a political party and then revived it as soon as they found it more convenient, a wholly opportunistic game, unworthy of a people whose intergrity and respect for the plighted word has won for the Sikhs a great name throughout history. It led also to a wholly spurious charge being levelled against the Sikhs that they or atleast a powerful minority among them wanted an independent, sovereign, Sikh state on the analogy of Pākistān, & not a Panjābi-speaking state, thus casting doubt on their basic loyalty to their motherland.

Another offshoot of this confusion was the use of the Sikh religious shrines for political propaganda, fasts and *morchās*. The Sikhs have always fought their political battles in the open. The Gurdwārās have been their source of inspiration and get-together, and resolutions (*Gurmattās*) were passed on matters of state only when it was not possible to do so anywhere else, as under the Moghal and Afghān regimes.

This confusion of ideals led to the neglect of the spiritual education of the people, the fight for political power, manipulation and partisan ends taking precedence over it. Only time will tell how much our spiritual regeneration has suffered thereby.

A new (and wholly unknown factor) entered our political life as well. This was the weapon of fasting, popularised by Gāndhiji with his Jaina tradition for political ends. According to the Sikh doctrine, it is nothing but a sacrilege and a suicide. But, the Sikhs too took to it with a vengeance.

Master Tārā Singh was ousted from Presidentship of the S.G.P.C. in Oct. 1958, by an unknown Congressman, Prem Singh Lāllpurā (now he is an Akāli), mainly through the machinations of Giāni Kartar Singh, then a Minister in the Panjāb Govt, and the 22 members nominated from PEPSU, as a result of its recent merger in the Panjāb. Tārā Singh decided to fast unto death at Delhi, charging the Govt. with "gross interference in the Sikh religious affairs." However, the calamity was averted through a letter the present writer brought from Pt. Jawaharlal Nehru to soothe the injured feelings of the venerable old Sikh Chief. Pandit Nehru, after stating that he was equally against Gāndhi's several fasts for political purposes, that he had no interest in the Gurdwārā affairs and could discuss with him how best every semblance of Govt's connection with them could be abolished (including elections conducted under Govt. auspices etc.), expressed his "sincere apologies" if he had by any chance hurt the Akali Chief's feelings. Thereupon, Master Tārā Singh abandoned his resolve to fast. (*) A year later, he won a resounding victory at the elections to the S.G.P.C. and was re-installed its President (March 1960).

Immediately thereafter, he launched once again an agitation for a Panjabi-speaking state. He was arrested on May 24 and lodged in the Dharamsālā Jail. In his absence, his Vice-President, Sant Fateh Singh (a pious but an unknown and uneducated entity in his fifties and hailing from the Bikaner state where he was the high priest of a temple at *Buddha Johar*, who had suddenly been catapulted into this high position by his Chief for his saintly and self-sacrificing nature) went on a fast unto death over this issue in the holy precincts of the Golden Temple at Amritsar, on Dec. 18, 1960, after the failure of his six-month old agitation. Passions rose high and there was fear that if the Saint died (which was very likely), there would be bloodshed in the state (which was unlikely), or atleast the majority of the Sikhs would be permanently estranged from the Govt. Early in January, 1961, a two-man deputation, consisting of Master Tārā Singh's younger brother, Principal Niranjan Singh and the present writer, approached Shri J.P. Narayan, to get Master Tārā Singh released from the Dharamsālā jail. J.P. called on Mr. Nehru & Master Tārā Singh was released two days later. He flew to Bhāvnagar to get some assurances from Pt. Jawāharlāl Nehru (who had gone there to attend the annual session of the Indian National Congress) inorder that the fast of Sant Fateh Singh may be ended, without breaking his solemn vow.

* Master Tārā Singh was so moved by this letter that he refused to divulge to the press (inspite of their insistent protests) the first paragragh of the letter in which the Prime Minister of India had expressed his "sincere apologies." Later, he told the present writer:—"Jawāharlāl has shown his greatness by saying that he apologises to me, should I be so mean as to publicise this to the press ?" Master Tārā Singh had a streak of high idealism in him and he was essentially a man of compromise, if his and his people's self-respect were not hurt.

Though Pt. Jawāharlāl Nehru refused to offer any assurances at that time, better counsels prevailed later on and as soon as Master Tārā Singh landed back disappointed in Delhi, Mr. Nehru had declared that "it is not out of any discrimination against the Panjāb or distrust of the Sikhs that the process of forming a linguistic state was not possible..." that "Panjābi was essentially the dominant language" of the Panjab state, common to both Hindus and Sikhs, though it is not possible to accept the principle of purely linguistic states in the case of Panjāb. He was convinced that in the case of its (Panjāb's) division, "it will be harmful to the Panjāb, to the Sikhs as well as Hindus and to the whole of India." Possibly, he feared communalism accentuating as a result of it, which proved true later on.

As for Fateh Singh's vow, Mr. Nehru said, "Oaths are not taken with regard to some legal aspect or statutory way of looking at things, but about the substance of things. And, therefore, what I have stated should be quite enough for Sant Fateh Singh to meet his difficulty and give up his fast."

Master Tārā Singh was satisfied at this statement. One doesnot know why? Perhaps he thought atleast the Govt had conceded Panjābi being the dominant language of Panjāb, in the teeth of Hindu opposition. The Govt. could also not turn round and claim "victory" for itself, as having humiliated or trounced its Akāli opponents without yielding any substantial ground. Be that as it may, he telephoned Sant Fateh Singh to immediately abandon his fast. The Sant did so, but the people at large thought he had "broken a solemn vow", taken in public, before the Guru Granth Sāhib, and thus betrayed their trust. Master Tārā Singh's leadership was also under attack. It was said, as Tārā Singh feared he himself would have to undergo a similar ordeal, if Fateh Singh died, he had advised his second-in-command to abandon his fast, without achieving anything. He was heckled at public meetings and shunned privately. In the meantime, interested people gathered round Sant Fateh Singh to build him up as a rival to his chief. He himself was not averse to it and in his several meetings with the Prime Minister later, whenever the question of final responsibility came up, he never mentioned even once the name of Master Tārā Singh as either being his chief, or one with whom the political negotiations should be conducted or clinched. In fact, he insisted that he was the only one who mattered in regard to all Sikh affairs!

This not unnaturally unnerved Tārā Singh, the hero of many battles, now laid low by an ungrateful deputy, just because he could fast tenaciously for a few days more than others! Stung by jealousy and loss of esteem more than any other reason, it appears, Master Tārā Singh also decided to go on a fast unto death over the issue of a "Panjābi-speaking state" on Aug. 15, 1961. But, when the Govt did not budge (one, because the Govt. was convinced through secret reports that the great leader would somehow outlive his "fast unto death", but also because they wanted to end this procession of fasts over political issues once for all), Master Tārā Singh climbed down, on the assurance by Govt. through the Mahārājā of Patiālā, Malik Hardit Singh, ICS etc. to appoint a Commission to look into Sikh grievances. Master Tārā Singh was happy to get out of his self-inflicted ordeal (Oct 2), but not so his militant followers. They accused him of bad faith and of breaking a solemn vow without achieving the desired result. Tārā Singh offered himself, in the traditional Sikh way, for a punishment at the hands of the devout. The *Pānj Pyārās* (the five select religious devotees) imposed upon him (and also upon Sant Fateh Singh) the age-old puhishment for the erring Sikhs-cleaning the shoes of the Sikh congregations for a few days. A high-powered Commission was appointed by Govt. to go into Sikh grievances, but Tārā Singh decided to boycott it, after asking for its constitution. * At the 1962 elections, both factions were badly trounced by the Congress, though Fateh Singh got the upper hand among the Akāli winners.

---

* The Commission, presided over by Mr. S.R. Das, former Chief Justice of India and consisting of Mr M. C. Chagla, former Chief Justice of Bombay (and once Secretary to Mr M. A. Jinnah) and Sir C. P. Ramaswamy Aiyer (once Diwan of Travancore who had declared his state's Independence in 1947) was the best which could be constituted to hear the case of Sikh grievances. But, Master Tārā Singh chose to boycott it because certain names suggested by him had not been accepted for the Commission by the Govt. This was a strange plea, the accuser also wanting a Judge of his own choice !

Inorder that the Sikh case may not go by default, about 50 Sikh intellectuals, inculding MPs and MLAs, met in New Delhi and requested the present writer to present the Sikh case before the Commission. This was done, and eight cases of obvious discrimination were listed in our Memorandum, especially in regard to Punjābi language, the treatment of Sikh farmers in the Tarāi region of UP, absence of heavy industry in Panjāb, atc. It is a traversity of facts to suggest that no cases

Sant Fateh Singh, however, was now being shown more respect and given a better hearing by the Sikhs for his having undertaken a "geniune" fast and abandoned it only on his Chief's intervention, and not on his own! A new leadership threatened the community for a brief decade. Two of Tārā Singh's main supporters, Justice Gurnām Singh and Lachhman Singh Gill, a rich Delhi Contractor (both to become Chief Ministers later) deserted him. (Later, they deserted each other also). Māster Tārā Singh went into eclipse. Sant Fateh Singh and his men captured the S. G. P. C. and formed their own Akāli Dal. Mr. Nehru died on May 27, 1964. Sardār Partāp Singh, the powerful Panjāb Chief Minister bitterly opposed to communal politics, was deposed soon after, for charges of corruption brought against him by Master Tārā Singh and others. A year later, he was murdered due to personal enmity. Mr. Shāstri, the new Prime Minister, appointed a Parliamentary Committee, on the eve of the Indo-Pak war of the same year (1965) † under the chairmanship of its much-esteemed Speaker, Sardār Hukam Singh, a former President of the Akāli Dal but now a member of the Congress Party. This committee's unanimous recommendation favouring a linguistic division of the Panjāb had not even reached the Govt, when the Congress Working Committee, on the initiative of the succeeding Prime Minister, Mrs. Indira Gandhi, (daughter of Jawāharlāl Nehru) resolved with an overwhelming majority on March 2, 1966, that "out of the existing state of Panjāb a state with Panjabi as the state language be formed."* A Commission was appointed under justice J.C. Shāh to demarcate the linguistic areas, and through a majority report, the Commission recommended to

of discrimination had been listed in this Memorandum. As for the Panjābi-speaking State, it was asserted that this was a discrimination against the whole Panjabi people, and not only against the Sikhs.

† Tributes must be paid in this context to two outstanding Sikh Generals, Lt. Gen. Harbakhsh Singh who as Corps commander, contrary to the advice of the top brass to retire the Indian forces to Beās, took a decision to fight the war on the enemy ground and won the 18-day war for India, and Air Marshal Arjan Singh, whose force knocked out the enemy's air power to their surprise and bewilderment.

* Shri Morarji Desai was the one of three members to oppose this resolution, the other two being Dr. Rām Subhāg Singh (of Bihār) and Biju Patnāyak (of Orissa), The Act passed in Parliament allowed to the Panjāb an area of over 50,000 Sq. kilometres and a population of I, 12,00,000 of which 55% were Sikhs. The population has now increased 1½ times and the Sikh population became 13 millon (1981) which is over 60%.

Govt. the separation of areas which now constitute the Panjāb, except for Kharar tehsil, which the majority of the Commission wanted excluded, but which the Govt. of India wisely decided to include in the new state (as in this case happily they believed the Census fignres to be false).

However, the division was very unfair, unjust and even communally motivated. It didnot demarcate the Panjābi-speaking areas from the Hindi-speaking ones. It only separated the Sikh-dominated areas from the Hindu-populated lands. This writer, then a Member of Parliament, protested vehemenly against it to the Prime Minister (see Appendix VII) as well as in the Rājya Sabha. The whole thing appeared ridiculous. Even the capital city of Chandigarh and the Kharar tehsil, both of which are 90% Panjābi,speaking (except for migratory labour) were not allocated to Panjāb on the spurious plea that more candidates at the matriculation stage from the city of Chandigarh took up Hindi as their medium of examination,and that in the Kharar tehsil, 52% people were Hindi-speaking. Similarly, Kāngrā, which was 90%Panjabi-speaking in 1951 and had declared itself overwhelmingly Hindi-speaking ten years later (due to communal reasons) was attached to Himāchal Pardesh. Several other Panjābi-speaking areas right upto Karnāl in Haryānā and Simla in Himāchal Pardesh would have come to the Panjāb under any fair linguistic division. The industrial belt of Panjāb built by Panjābis at Faridābad near Delhi, not being contiguous to the Panjābi-speaking areas, was alloted to Haryana. But, as unfortunately the fight for the new Panjāb was waged from a "Sikh" platform, to satisfy "Sikh" aspirations, the Commission divided the Panjāb into Hindu and Sikh with a vengeance. A confusion of command was created over the dams, the headworks of canals etc., and even the division of river-waters became a communal rather than a national issue. Only two major institutions were kept intact and not divided on a communal basis--the Panjāb and Haryana High Court and the lunatic asylum in Amritsar !

However, the fears generated widely and held earlier of a Sikh communal state emerging on our North-Western borders have been belied so far. The same people who were ranged as if in a death-battle against each other—the Akālis and the Jan Sangh—joined hands to fight the secular forces which had, inspite of their earlier reservations, brought into being the new state ! The Panjāb has grievances (and genuine ones, as already pointed out earlier in this chapter) and these must be redressed in good time before we land ourselves in a worse communal situation which seems to be developing now-a-days in this border state. If Chandigarh has been alloted to the Panjāb by another award of Mr. Indira Gāndhi (1970), there is no reason for some other productive areas as of Fazilkā and Abohar being transferred in a barter-deal to Haryānā as a compensation, the moreso when the Central Govt has agreed also to pay for the building of a new Capital city for Haryānā. If Panjāb seeks more water, electricity or control over its canal head-works to regulate water-supply, why create tensions over it by inciting their neighbours to stake their claims over them as well? Why not allocate a few major industries and more funds for development to the Panjāb in proportion to their economic progress and potentialities rather than starve them of these for registering progress earlier and better than others? The Akāli Govt., thinking that more propitious days had dawned for them, tried in 1977-78, to reopen Mrs. Gāndhi's award on Chandigarh, the Bhākhrā Nangal dam, the canal head-works and the early clearance of the new dams etc., but the reply of the Desai Govt at the Centre was the same:- "Get the concurrence of the other states involved." Their plea for more autonomy and funds was rebuffed even more severely! Every Central Govt. has to remain in the Centre of things and look to the needs of every state, but why punish the more progressive ones, or play one against the other?

Of the 22 years since its inception in 1966, the new Panjāb has been governed by the Congress for 12 years. The Akālis had constituted Governments thrice, but none lasted more than 18 months, more due to their own factional fights than the machinations of others. Sardār Lachhman Singh Gill defected with 14 of his followers from the Akāli party to result in the downfall of the first Akāli Ministry (1966) under Justice Gurnām Singh. He sought the support of the Congress who (unwisely) stood by him without sharing power. All his men became Ministers.* He even tried to arrest Sant Fateh Singh, and his lieutenant, Sant Chanan Singh. Later, Gurnām

* Lachhman Singh Gill tried to arrest Sant Chanan Singh, then President of S.G. P. C. against whom a criminal case was launched for missappropriation of Gurdwārā funds. To evade arrest, both he and his chief, Sant Fateh Singh, took refuge at the *Akāl Takhat*, adjoining the Golden Temple at Amritsar. It is a strange coincidence that on the day Gill defected (Now 22, 1967), Māster Tārā Singh died in Amritsar, the head of a party he had tried both to integrate and bring to power in a Sikh-dominated state and to see it riven by faction and feud and falling to

Singh became Chief Minister again (1969) to quit the same sordid way (1970). Seven years later, (1977) for exceptional reasons which swept the Congress off its seats of power, throughout north India, (whether due to the proclamation of Emergency on June 25, 1975, by the Congress Govt. as a result of which 45000 Akālis courted arrest or forced sterilisations or suspension of Civil liberties for 19 months etc), the Akālis for the fiirst time in their history won a decisive majority both in Parliament and in the State legislature. But, inorder to gain a seat in the Central Cabinet, they had to make an alliance with the all-India Jantā Party. In the Panjāb also, to win the confidence of the Hindu minority, a coalition had to be forged by them with the Panjāb Jantā Party which consisted mostly of the old Jan Sangh in that region. The Akāli Party realised perhaps that the need for not only a minority but also for every state to build an all-India outlook and alliance is paramount in our country, both to promote economic health and the political stability of the individual state or community. And whatever the complexion of the Central Govt., it must keep all of them under their equal control. Otherwise, there will be no Centre, only a circumference let loose into an endless void. This they have to do both to keep this complex & vast country together, and on the other hand to meet external challenges & internal upheavals & tyranny over hapless minorities or under-privileged sections. And in Govt. as in human affairs, straight lines running parallel to each other never to meet, never work or produce any creative results. And, is it not ironical that the very people who shout against the Centre & cry for decentralisation

F. N. Contd.

pieces due to its inherent contradictions. Lachhman Singh Gill introduced Panjābi, however, at the Secretariat level for the first time to please Sikh sentiments. But, his tenure was cut short six months later, and the budget he presented had to be "passed" with the help of the police but without the help of the legislature. The new mid-term elections of 1969 put an Akāli-Jan Sangh combine in the Govt. again under Gurnām Singh, who tried to arrest his rival, Lachhman Singh Gill, on criminal charges of corruption etc. But the man died too soon to fall into the hands of his determined rivals. Gurnām Singh also did not last longer than 18 months, mainly due to S. Darshan Singh Pherumān (once a staunch Congress M.P. turned a Swatantarite), undertaking a fast unto death, over the issue of Chandigarh and other Panjābi areas being included in the Panjāb. He was a sincere old man and died at the age of 85 after going through his cruel ordeal for 74 days (Oct. 27 1969). Soon thereafter, Sant Fateh Singh also announced another fast for Jan. 26 1970, and self-immolation of himself and five others on Feb. 1. However, Mrs.

of power become virtual autocrats themselves, in their own provincial or local spheres ? The emergence of an independent Muslim Pākistān has accentuated ten-fold the problems of the Muslims. They were offered 40% of seats in the Central Govt. equal to the Caste Hindus as late as in 1946, and with the help of the other minorities in the Govt., and their own and the Sikh strength in the army (around 60 percent), they could acquire a position of such prestige, if not also of such domination, that the whole of India would have felt its certain impact. With the historic dynamism and the egalitrianism of Islām, what is it that they would not have achieved, especially in a secular state, mostly populated by the all-embracing race of Hindus, their

---

F, N. Contd.

Gandhi intervened and gave her award (see text). The Congress and the CPI. were against its acceptance at the All-parties Conference convened by the [illegible] but Sant Chanan Singh intervened, to save the life of his chief and pleaded for its acceptance. However, a resolution was unanimously passed not to transfer Fazilkā and Abohar to Haryānā in return for Chandigarh and also to restore the control over the Bhakrā Nāngal complex to the Panjāb. Gurnām Singh also threatened that his Ministry was in danger if the award was not accepted. (Earlier in December, 1966 on a verbal assurance by S. Hukam Singh, the Sant had broken his fast over this very issue, without achieving anything). Fateh Singh broke his fast once again amidst great controversy. Differences between Gurnām and Fateh Singh became acute, especially over the Sant's Akāli nominations to the Rajya Sabha, without reference to the Chief Minister. Gurnām Singh helped his own nominee—Bhupinder Singh Giani against J. Santokh Singh of Delhi (both later became pro-Congress), the Sant's nominee—and this led to a revolt by the Akali and Jan Sangh members against him. He was ousted from power and after founding his own Gurnām Singh Akāli Dal for a time and fighting the Sant, he left the political field and was appointed High Commissioner to Australia by Mrs. Gandhi. A few days later, this brilliant and able man died in a plane-crash. Sant Fateh Singh also could not play any major role thereafter, his party having been routed in the new general election in 1972. He died broken-hearted on Nov. 23, 1972, and his main lieutenant, Sant Chanan Singh a fortnight later. But his sincerity of conviction and his fight for a Panjābi-speaking state on more rational lines will always be cherished.

Though the Akālis came back to power under S. Parkāsh Singh Bādal in the State (1977) and in the S.G.P.C. (1979) with a massive mandate, under S. Gurcharan Singh Tohra, MP, they were riven by faction and feud, based mainly on personalities, though this is the bane of the whole country at present, and not only of a particular state or a community or party. Their representatives, however, during the two years (1977-79) did not participate on any issue in Parliament!

leaders by and large deeply wedded to secularism and democracy. And where are they now ? East Pākistān torn from West Pākistān, and both in an economic and political shambles and social unheavals of a kind whose results are too staggering to contemplate. Life is unsafe, political stability is not to be found, nor democratic freedoms of any kind for men or women. There has been little industrial advance, and once the granary of all India, Pākistān is now obliged to import foodgrains. Once the sworn enemies of the Panjābi language, their mother tongue, they are now fighting (unsuccessfully) for it as against Urdu, which they now consider alien, but which till recently had become their virtual lingua-franca. As the "Times of India" has recently commented, "The haven for liberation has been turned into a prison-house." And as a result of creating Pākistān, of the demoralised, half-educated, economically backward and leaderless Indian Muslims (80 millions of them), the less sald the better,

In this climate of depression and oppression around us, one hopes the Sikhs, averse as they have been throughout history to any kind of suppression or oppression, including their own, would ponder over their future with more calmness than they hitherto have. Their doctrine (as enunciated in earlier pages) is so liberating, democratic to the core, all-inclusive, secular in outlook, egalitarian, casteless, dividing not man from man on the basis of colour, religion or nationality or political or economic outlook, has a future as perhaps no other religious community has. Only it must be given a field free from fear, anxiety or domination. This they already have, more or less, surrounded as they are by the great religion of the Hindus, who with all their social and spiritual aberrations are yet the best buy in this part of the world, and with whom their religious and cultural affinities (besides the common politico-economic aspirations) are the deepest. India is the largest home-market for their produce, and Hindus are the only community to date to offer them the largest number of recruits to their faith. The two have throughout history stood together, and one hopes and prays that they will in future too.

The talk of total independence is alluring; the Sikhs are competent both to create and sustain an independent, sovereign state for a time, but today the world has become so small and therefore so interdependent that the small states can only invite a kind of instability (or anarchy) whose ultimate end is not freedom, but subjection to a super-power or to become a battle-ground for two or three of them. This is happening before us, all around in Asia, Africa and Latin America. Let us beware lest we Sikhs too fall a prey to the talk of wild-eyed soothsayers and the self-assured prophets of doom. They are not our friends; they only echo "His Master's Voice" from somewhere abroad. We should also realise well in time that politics built on religion destroys both. Politics will be built in a free, democratic society on the basis of socio-economic policies and even men of the same religious persuation will organise themselves, politically, in accordance with their different socio-economic convictions. And one should not be surprised if sickened by obscurantist forces & tyranny, the people of Pākistān & Bangladesh* once again of they own free choice, join hands with India in a federal or confederal set-up.

A great responsibility devolves on the Panjāb Hindus in this context. Their press leaves no stone unturned even now first to create problems, e. g. over the issue of mother-tongue (which they still try to bypass, if not disown), and support their co-religionists in other states for reasons other then rational, even at the expense of their own state merely to put the Sikhs in the wrong.

Then, when the Sikhs protest, they are dubbed "communal", and the Govt. warned of their doubtful loyalty. This is what does not allow the vicious circle to break. If they really are anxious to see their state grow, in which they too have a vital stake, industry and commerce still being in their hands by and large, they must not rub the Sikhs on the wrong side time and again, both for the interest of the country and of themselves. The Sikhs also should know that if the Panjab or north Indian Hindus donot play fair with them at times, they could muster the support of the entire South and East of India to their side, where there is ample sympathy and appreciation for them, especially with regard to more financial powers for the states and over the question of language. As for religious and cultural questions of an all-India nature, joint fronts could be built with the other

* The successful war in Bangladesh (1971) again brought two Sikh heroes in the forefront-Lt. Gen. Jagjit Singh Arora who accepted surrender of the Pak forces and (what is much less known) Maj Gen. Sujān Singh Ubān, whose death-daring gueril'a fighters had played havoc with the enemy's lines of communications before the Indian army's entry into East Pākistān. It is a saga of chivalry worthy of entering our folklore. President Mujib commended his part personally to Mrs. Gandhi, who called him "The back-bone" of the Bangladesh war.

minorities, who would welcome not only the cooperation but the leadership of the Sikhs for obvions reasons.

CHAPTER XXX

THE TROUBLED DECADE

(1978-1988)

So much has happened during the last ten years that one never knows how and in which way is the destiny of the Sikhs to find its moorings. The mixing of religion with politics by the Akālis has exhibited its results in all its ugliness and horror. Senseless violence and unethical fundamentalism have shaken both the country's secular and democratic structure and cast a vicious suspicion over the whole glorious past of the Sikhs, including their own integrity and faithfulness to the nation, for whose freedom, safety and oneness, their contribution through the ages, including the present century, has far exceeded their limited numbers. The ruling Party at the Centre did not lag behind in playing politics with a grim and tragic situation, resulting in a mess which has now become the nation's nightmare.

Since November 1973 the orthodox Sikhs led by the Akali Dal, had started preaching vigorously against neó(Sant) Nirankāris as heretics, and calling upon all devotees not to have any dealings with them in the matters of religious beliefs. Though occasional protest meetings were held here and there against them, the Congress Govt. in the Punjāb, then under the stewardship of Giani Zail Singh, did not let the anti-Nirankari feelings get out of hand. Instead, Giani Zail Singh had enlisted the sympathy of the orthodox Sikh masses by several acts, such as the building of Guru Gobind Singh Marg all along the path the great Guru and his forces had taken, in their fight against the Moghals, and leading a huge procession through it, in a spirit of thanks-giving and devotion, which even surprised and overtook the Akālis, and earned him the title of "Mahān Singh" (The Great Sikh), at Anandpur Sāhib, at the hands of its Akāli management! He kept the 45000 Akāli prisoners in jail, during the emergency (1975-76), in excellent cheer, providing them with all the facilities they needed, and even taking care of the families of those who asked for help! He instituted a

Commission under Justice Chhangāni against Parkāsh Singh Bādal, ex-C.M., and after securing a clear verdict against him, refused to prosecute him! It is said, half the Akāli MLAs and Jathedārs were on his payroll, and his confidants and informers. He avoided confrontation with them, under all circumstances, and kept most of them in good humour.

As has been stated before, the Akālis came to power in the Panjāb, in May 1977, and they built a coalition Government with the Janata and Jan Sangh, though they had been fighting against the latter's communal policies all through. The Central Govt. had also been taken over by the Janata-Jan Sangh – Lok Dal combine, and the Akāli anxiety to find a representation there, (S. Surjit Singh Barnālā became the Agriculture Minister), left them with little option but to forge a similar coalition Govt. in the Panjāb, under the Chief Ministership of S. Parkāsh Singh Bādal, an amiable and soft-spoken graduate Jāt Sikh from the Village Bādal (Faridkot), and once a protege of Sant Fateh Singh, and respected, alike by Hindus and Sikhs, having a wholly non-sectarian outlook.

The Akāli-Jan Sangh Govt. ran successfully for a year or so, when differences started surfacing among the Akālis and, on charges of alleged corruption, Sukhjinder Singh, a former Deputy Superintendent of Police, and Education Minister in the Bādal Govt. was dismissed from his office, thus sowing seeds of suspicion and disintegration among the Akāli Legislature Party, as well as in the Shiromani Akāli Dal, their parent political body. Sukhjinder Singh thereafter opted for an extremist, fundamentalist posture, backed by Jathedār Gurcharan Singh Tohrā, an ill-educated but otherwise shrewd and manipulative President of the SGPC, who, also being a Jat, himself was a candidate for the Chief Ministership!

Meantime, on the Baisākhi day of 1978, (April 13), the neo-Nirankāris wanted to hold their annual session at Amritsar, and, due, it is said, to the Jan Sangh pressure on the Akāli Govt., they allowed this session to be held on a day when large masses of orthodox Sikhs gather at Amritsar to have a dip in the holy tank, and visit the Hari Mandir to pay their homage. When they heard of the Nirankāri conclave in their holiest city, the Orthodox Sikhs got inflamed and, led by one Fauja Singh, an Agricultural Inspector of the Govt., and belonging to the Akhand Kirtani Jathā (a religious body of devout followers of Sant Bhāi Randhir Singh, patriot and Sikh fundamentalist preacher from Ludhiānā), they marched on the venue of the Nirankāri conference, after holding a huge Diwān (congregation) at Manji Sāhib, in the

Golden Temple complex, "pledging not to allow the Nirankāris to foul the sacred Sikh atmosphere of Amritsar."

A new though comparatively little-known Jāt Sikh preacher, (Sant) Jarnail Singh Bhindranwālā, (who had been nominated head of what is called the Damdami Taksāl at Chowk Mehta, near Amritsar,* on the death, by accident, of Sant Kartar Singh, its head, on Aug 3, 1977), and was preaching Sikh fundamentalism in the Panjāb villages, also joined them, threatening menacingly before the agitated Sikh congregation at Manji Sāhib : "We will not allow the Nirankāri convention to be held here. We shall march there to cut them to pieces".+ The Nirankāris were holding their session only two miles away.

The 300-old Sikh procession was neither stopped by the police, nor the Nirankāri "Guru", Gurbachan Singh, warned in advance of the impending danger. It is said, Fauja Singh advanced towards the Baba manacingly, naked sword in hand, "with which he attacked him".+ " The Baba's bodyguard shot him dead."+ Confusion prevailed, and it became a free-for-all. Twelve Sikhs and three Nirankāris lost their lives. The Bābā was escorted by the Panjāb police to the safety of his Delhi home and a criminal suit lodged against him, for the murder of 12 Sikhs, who had become "martyrs" by then. Fearing partiality in a Punjāb Court, the Bābā got his case transferred to Karnāl, in Haryana, where he was aquitted honourably, a year later. The Akāli Government never filed an appeal against the Judgement in a higher Court!

Meanwhile, Sant Bhindrānwālā had emerged a hero to the Sikh masses. Fauja Singh' s widow, Bibi Amarjit Kaur, who later built her own terrorist outfit, called the Babbar Khālsā, (in addition to her heading the Akhand Kirtani Jatha) to avenge her husband' s murder, however, accused Bhindrānwālā of having got her husband murdered, due to jealousy, himself having cowardly slipped away from the scene, to save his skin, even before the procession reached the Nirankāri Convention!

In September, 1978 the Jathedar of the Akal Takhat issued a Hukumnāmā against the neo-Nirankaris and called for their total social boycott by the Sikhs. It is said, in order to make some political capital out of it, the Panjāb Congress Party, then led by Giani Zail Singh also tried to embarrass and if possible, defeat the Akāli Communal politics by exploiting Bhindranwālā's

* Damdami Taksāl is said to derive its origin from Damdamā Sāhib (in Bhatinda), which Guru Gobind Singh had blessed, during his stay there, as "Guru's Kāshi". Its first head was Bābā Deep Singh, the martyr. The Taksāl (lit. mint) concentrates on teaching the Guru's Word to the young Sikhs, as well as Code of Conduct for orthodox Sikhs

\+ "Amritsar", by Mark Tully and Satish Jacob, BBC correspondents in Delhi

.fundamentalist appeal, and pitching him against them. Meantime, another organisation, called the Dal Khālsā, was also brought into being on April 13, 1978, by certain hot heads at Chandigarh "with the avowed object of demanding a sovereign Sikh state". These two organisations fought the Akālis, a year later, at the SGPC elections, but the Bhindrānwālā-supported candidates won only 4 out of 140 seats. The later "solemn" declarations of the Sant that he was not interested in any office, political or religious, thus proved to be an eye-wash. Later, he helped to success some Congress candidates also at the Assembly polls, as well.

In July 1979, the Janata Party broke up at the Centre and the Jāt leader, Charan Singh, took over as Prime Minister, overthrowing Morārji Desai, with the active support of Mrs. Indira Gandhi's Congress (I) Party, which was then in the Opposition. A month later, they too parted company, and the Parliament was dissolved for new general elections to be held six months later. This not unnaturally bewildered and un-nerved the Akāli ruling Party in the Panjāb as well, as the outcome of the new Parliamentary elections (1980) had gone overwhelmingly in favour of Mrs. Indira Gandhi's Congress(I) Party*, with the Akālis badly trounced in these elections. This almost resulted in panic in their ranks, as they feared that the Panjāb legislature would be dissolved and fresh elections held, for which they were not prepared. Their infighting, high corruption and the Sikhs' disenchantment with their performance on the economic as well as cultural and religious fronts, had prepared the ground for their total rout, at the Assembly polls.

It may be stated here that neither over more autonomy for the state, nor Chandigarh, the capital city, nor over allocation of more river waters to Panjāb or the construction of Satluj- Yamuna link canal, which later became the major grounds for a battle royal, were ever raised by the Akālis during their entire tenure ! This had also disgusted the Sikhs with the Akāli politics.

And now they tried seriously to walk into the Congress camp and sent word to Mrs. Gandhi (Mr. Sukhjinder Singh leading the campaign)+ that he, with his 35 other followers and sympathisers would break away from the Akāli legislature Party, in the Panjāb Assembly, if the Congress members

---

* Mrs. Gandhi, in order to win the elections, enlisted the help even of the rank communalists, like the Imām of Delhi's Jāma Masjid, Abdullah Bokhāri, by agreeing, in writing, to his 22 demands the fire-eating Mullah had placed before her! Later, he fell out with her, as he felt he was not consulted on Muslim names for the Central Cabinet! Earlier, the Janata Party had also exploited his communal appeal.

One wonders why the Akālis did not strike a deal with her at this time of her need to win the polls, at all costs.

+ The present writer is personally aware of these confabulations.

supported them to make up a majority. Mrs. Gandhi, however, refused the offer and dissolved the Assembly. In the fresh elections, her Party won a resounding victory and a Congress Ministry came into being, early in 1980, led by a confirmed secular Sikh, S. Darbara Singh, as Chief Minister. One wonders, if Mrs. Gandhi's was the right decision (advised as she was by Giani Zail Singh, then Home Minister of India) to refuse the Akāli breakaway group's solemn offer. This would have exposed the Akāli opportunism, as it would have given them some opportunity to re-think their communal politics. But that was not to be .

The Akālis, though beaten at the hustings, had quite some fire left in them. Howsoever divided into Tohrā-Sukhjinder versus Bādal factions, the powerful religious platform with its vast resources in men and money, the SGPC, was still in their grip. They also made a bid to capture the Delhi Gurdwārā Parbandhak Committee, an equally powerful body with resources matching those of the SGPC, but failed. At the 1980 elections, they won a majority of seats but were outwitted by the Congress Sikhs, winning over four of their number "for a consideration" ! Thus the Akālis both won and lost the game ! The Congress picked on Jathedār Santokh Singh, an illiterate, pugnacious braggart, who had sided with Mrs. Gandhi during the Emergency and during her days of wilderness, (1977-79), as President of the new set-up. He had been President of the Delhi Gurdwārā Committee a decade before also , as a protege first of Master Tārā Singh and then of Sant Fateh Singh, both Akāli leaders violently opposed to the Congress. He had given quite some hard time to the Congress during his earlier regime. Therefore, in order to get rid of his authority, finally , over the Delhi Gurdwārās, the Parliament had passed, in 1972, an unusual bill, amending the Delhi Gurdwārā Act and stipulating that, henceforth, no one who is not a matriculate or a Gyāni (a degree in Panjābi), would be eligible for any office in the Delhi Gurdwārā Committee. But such is the manipulative politics of our land that the same bill was re-amended, in 1980, to delete this clause, in order to facilitate Santokh Singh to preside over the Gurdwārā Committee, once again!

This hurt the Akāli Dal even more than their rout at the Assembly polls. They had been cheated of the fruits of a democratic election and they vowed to avenge it. Tohra told the present writer as much : "They have denied us our dues even in our religious establishment, and they will soon have a "Dharamyudha" (Holy war) on their hands". And, he proved true to his word, only a year later!

The Akālis were already on the lookout for instances of "religious interference" on the part of the ruling Party, and here was a fool-proof case to support their contention!

Sant Jarnail Singh Bhindrānwālā, with his new-found, widespread popularity, was also looking out for a cause to capture the leadership of the Sikhs. The attack on the Nirankāri Convention had passed into history. So, something more spectacular was needed. This was offered to him, as if on a platter, by the gruesome assassination of the Nirankāri Chief, Bābā Gurbachan Singh, on 24 April, 1980, by a Sikh, (later alleged to be one Ranjit Singh, a 35-year old Sikh carpenter, working for a time for the Bābā's household, and earlier a close confidant of Sant Bhindrānwālā). Strong suspicion was naturally roused against Bhindrānwālā, as he had declared publicly that "whosoever had performed these "great feats" deserved to be honoured at the Akāl Takht. If they came to me, I'll weigh them up in gold![+] He had also been haranguing the audiences in Panjāb against the Akāli Government having first allowed a Nirankāri Convention at Amritsar, on a Baisākhi day, and then allowing the Nirankāri Chief to flee, after the murder of 12 devout Sikhs. He also accused the Akālis of having got the criminal case against him transferred from a Panjāb Court to Haryānā and not even appealing to the High Court against his acquittal in the Session's Court.

Bhindrānwālā feared arrest, and so took sanctuary in the Serāi Guru Rām Dās,just outside the complex of the Golden Temple, Amritsar. But, soon, the Home Minister of India told Parliament that Bhindrānwālā personally was not involved in the murder. On 9 September,1980, came another dastardly murder, that of Lālā Jagat Narain, Proprietor-editor of "Hind Samāchār, a widely-circulated Urdu daily, published from Jullundur. The Lālā was not only supporting the Nirankāri cause, but opposing, all through, the Panjābi language being adopted as medium of instruction in Hindu Schools, or as an official language of Panjāb. He had led a virtual crusade in 1951, and in 1961, for Hindus of Panjāb to declare at the Census Hindi and not Panjābi, as their mother tongue.[*] He was writing scurrilouly not only against "Khālistān"

+ "India Today", New Delhi (April 30, 1983) makes this quotation from Bhindrānwālā, repeated many times by him, in respect of all the murderers of eminent Hindus, like Jagat Narain, and Nirankāris like Bābā Gurbachan Singh

The strong disavowal of their mother-tongue, Panjābi, the preachings of the powerful Ārya Samāj Press against the Sikhs generally, and every demand which helped the Panjāb's cause laid the foundations of a deep spiritual cleavage between the Hindus

and the Anandpur Sāhib resolution (see Appendix), but also cast aspersions on the loyalty of the majority of the Sikhs, and wanted extreme measures taken against them. Bhindrānwālā spoke frequently against him.*

The suspicion was strong that Bhindrānwālā had a hand in this murder. So, warrants of his arrest were issued, but these could not be served on him at Chando-Kalān in Haryana, where he had gone to preach. Somehow, he got scent of this, and escaped as hurriedly as he could to his headquarters at Chowk Mehta. The critics of Govt. allege that the escape was made possible by the Home Minister, Giani Zail Singh, asking the Haryānā Chief Minister, not to arrest him, and even to escort him to safety ! But the copies of the Sikh sacred writings he was carrying in his van were left behind, and set on fire by a Haryānā Hindu mob. Bhindrānwālā never forgave the Govt. or the Hindus for this sacrilege.

When the Panjāb Chief Minister sent the police at Chowk Mehta to arrest him, he sent word that he would offer himself for arrest, voluntarily, on Sept. 20, after he had addressed a religious congregation. The Police, fearing violence, had no choice but to agree. But, when Bhindrānwālā addressed the huge concourse that had gathered to listen to him on that day, he charged the whole atmosphere with anger and frenzy, with his fiery speech. A very important pro-Congress person, who had gone all the way from Delhi to support his cause also made a wild anti-Govt. speech, thundering that, "if the Govt. touch even a hair of Sant Bhindrānwālā, the Sikhs will set the Panjāb on fire". His name was Jathédār Santokh Singh, President of the Delhi Gurdwāra Parbandhak Committee! The Jathédār was playing on both sides, assuring Bhindrānwālā all help of the Govt., as well as his own, to build him up as the "Supremo" of the Sikhs against the wily Akālis, and bring Mrs. Gandhi to his feet, and on the other hand assuring Mrs. Gandhi that he would bring Bhindrānwālā to her camp and fight the Akālis with his active help in the interest of her Party!

---

and Sikhs, and divided them into two political entities. A common Panjābi ethos remained still-born.

* It may be of interest to note that the Akāli Supremo, Master Tara Singh, inspite of his acute differences with Lālā Jagat Narain, helped him, through his Akāli legislators, to win a seat in the Rajya Sabha, the Upper House of Parliament! He collaborated with him also in presenting a Memorandum to the Dās Commission, charging Partāp Singh Kairon with high corruption and getting him dismissed as Chief Minister of Panjāb!

Violence against the Police followed the arrest of the Sant, and, eleven persons lay dead on the spot. Sporadic violence also broke out in other places as well, mostly aimed at Hindus. Some Govt. and railway property was also damaged. Bombs were hurled at the police headquarters in Patiala and Tāran Tāran. Amritsar and Jullundur also witnessed gruesome scenes, warning the Govt. as well as the people that a new violent volcano had, or was about to burst, on the scene. Bhindrānwālā was taken to Ferozepur jail, but he was honourably released in less than a month (Oct.14), and the Home Minister told Parliament that Bhindrānwālā was innocent.*

To celebrate this victory, Bhindrānwālā came to Delhi, with about a hundred of his followers, most of them carrying unlicensed guns. He was taken out in a huge procession and honoured by the Delhi Gurdwārā Parbhandak Committee, led by Jathedār Santokh Singh. Later, he went to Bombay and was received by the Sikhs with great fanfare and large sums contributed to his Fund, ostensibly for *prachār* (propagation of the faith), but used by him ultimately for more sinister purposes. Soon after, Jathedār Santokh Singh, his main supporter in Delhi, himself was murdered by a colleague (Dec 21,1981), and the only preacher who made the obituary speech at the condolence meeting in his memory at Delhi was no other than Sant Bhindrānwālā !

As violence increased against the police and the Hindus, the Congress Govt felt suspicious of Bhindrānwālā's real motives, and so estrangement between the two became deeper and deeper, the more so after his killer gangs went on a rampage against the Hindus in Panjāb. This was the time when the Akālis foolishly wooed him back to their camp!

At this point of time, Bhindrānwālā was leading a *morcha* (agitation) against tobacco being sold in the holy city of Amritsar. This had enthused the Sikh masses, as smoking of tobacco is a religious taboo among them. The Akāli Dal decided to lead this agitation in cooperation with him, and also to agitate several other unsettled issues to gain a foothold in the people's sympathies.

---

* It has been suggested by several political parties and scribes that the Home Minister wanted to use him both against Darbārā Singh, his arch-rival in Panjāb politics, as well as against the Akālis! Darbārā Singh, on the other hand, isolated, it is said, all the Congress workers owing allegiance to Giani Zail Singh! He also placed on the table of the Panjāb Assembly the findings of the Akāli-appointed Justice Gurdev Singh Commission, which had accused Giani Zail Singh, then Home Minister of India, of corruption!

Early in March, 1981, a mild stir was created by an address delivered by an expatriate, Mr. Gangā Singh Dhillon, who headed the Nanakānā Sāhib Foundation at Washington, (a wholly religious body, though of little consequence), at the fifty-fourth annual All- India Sikh Educational Conference, convened at Chandigarh (March 14, 1981), by the politically moderate and generally pro-Government Chief Khālsā Diwān. How this unheard-of Sikh expatriate "leader" came to be invited to be the Chairman of a Sikh Educational Conference in India, was a matter of deep surprise to every one, the more so when he declared in his address unequivocally that "the Sikhs are a nation"! The Conference dutifully also asked the Khālsā Dewān "to take appropriate measures"!* Soon after, a split occured in the Conference. By a majority vote, the resolution was withdrawn but the self-proclaimed friendship of Ganga Singh Dhillon with Gen. Mohammed Zia, President of Pākistān, made the move look even more sinister.+

A month later, (April 15,1981), the SGPC passed a similar resolution, without any provocation, that the "Sikhs are a nation", and that the Govt. of India should settle their long-standing grievances, so that they could also "breathe the air of freedom", as the Congress leadership had pledged to do,time and again, during India's struggle for freedom, in which the Sikhs had played a most noted and worthy part. The resolution, written in Panjābi, had used the generic word "qaum", which could be interpreted either way-- community or nation, but it alerted the Govt. that this sudden outburst was not without significance. On 26 July, 1981, a huge Sikh Convention was called by the Akāli Dal at Gurdwārā Manji Sāhib, just outside the Golden Temple, Amritsar, where a charter of 45 demands (later reduced to 15) was read out, as the minimum demands of the Panth , (See Appendix), by Sant Longowāl. These were presented to Mrs. Indira Gandhi, on Oct. 16, 1981, by the Akāli Dal. Not much notice seems to have been taken of them,except the first demand for the release of Bhindrānwālā (whom the Akālis now wanted to oblige and seriously take over). It was perhaps to give teeth to these demands that the "Sikhs are a nation" thesis was suddenly propounded by the SGPC. Another meeting was held with the Prime Minister in April, 1982, but without any result.

The demands were divided into two categories -- religious and political. The main religious demands included the granting of the Holy City status to Amritsar, like Hardwār, Banāras and Kurukshetra, and banning the sale of liquor, meat and tobacco in the city; the relaying by the Govt. - run All India

* The Tribune, Chandigarh, March 15, 1981.

\+ In an interview with the "Tribune", Dhillon said :– "I fail to understand why there is so much hue and cry. 'Qaum' is not a community. It is a nation. 'Firqa' is a community. Sikh are a nation, not a community. (March 15, 1981).

Radio of Kirtan (devotional music) for three hours from the Golden Temple; the naming of the Frontier Mail as "Golden Temple Express", and the right to carry Kirpān (ritual sword) , on the airlines (Kirpān had been banned on national airliners, following the hijacking of an Indian Airline's plane, by some Sikh youths, on September 29,1981, demanding release of Bhindrānwālā and threatening the passengers' lives with Kirpāns, though the threat was never carried out).* An All India Gurdwārā Act was also demanded.

The major political demands were the same as enunciated in the Anandpur Sāhib resolution of 1973 (and revised in 1978)+ namely (i) the granting of more powers to the Panjāb State, thus limiting the Central Govt's powers to only Defence, Foreign Affairs, Currency and Communications (ii) the Transfer of chandigarh and other Panjābi-speaking areas to Panjāb. (iii) the re-allocation of the waters of Panjāb's rivers -- Ravi and Beas - between Haryānā, Punjāb and Rājasthān, so as to increase Panjāb's share. The Govt. was also asked to stop the work of the Satluj-Yamuna link canal, as the waters were needed by the Panjāb farmers.

As has been said before, these demands, howsoever genuine, were never pressed during the Akāli regime. Only the waters' issue was referred to the Supreme Court of India by the Akāli Govt, which, very unwisely, the Congress Govt. under S. Darbārā Singh, was asked by the Centre to withdraw! One wonders why a verdict of the highest Court of the land was thus avoided. It gave substance to the Akāli charge that their case, legally, was so fool-proof, that the Central Govt was afraid of any adjudication even by the highest Court of law in the land!

The case of Chandigarh, a wholly Punjābi-speaking City, had also been made a bone of contention between Haryānā and Punjāb, without any valid reason. Again, the Akālis were not the only Party pressing for more financial and other powers for the states. The demand had been voiced also by Tāmil Nadu, Karnātaka, West Bengāl, Andhrā, etc. There was nothing secessionist in asking for local authority to be able to build more agro-based industries, like sugar and textile mills, or fruit and vegetable-processing plants, while the Panjāb farmer was being made to sell his cotton, sugarcane, fruits, at distress prices. Panjāb's surplus fruits and vegetables could also be processed and preserved for export, much to their advantage. But, the licence-giving

---

* The hijackers were arrested at Lahore, in Pakistan, and lodged in a jail but never tried, nor repatriated to India, inspite of the protest of the Indian Govt. They are still there even after seven years (1988).

\+ See Appendix for details.

authority lay with the Central Govt., who doled out industries to various states, in accordance with their own fluctuating political needs! Panjāb had received only two percent share in heavy industry, ever since independence, and 66% of the Bank credits in Panjāb (as against 33%, as stipulated by the Reserve Bank of India) were being spent elsewhere in India. This irked every succeeding Government of the Panjāb, Congress or Akāli, but only the Akālis agitated for it.

The Green revolution having exhausted its possibilities, in the late seventies, the distress among the Panjāb farmers, especially their growing — and educated — children was spreading rapidly. Due to new land-laws, the rich peasants had been wiped out. The holdings, now limited by new laws to a bare 18 acres, per family of five, were being redistributed among their offspring, thus reducing 65% of the holdings to five acres or less, per family.* Corruption at every level of the administration was eating into the morale of the people, and justice had become not only costly, but longdrawn and scarce. Only the man with a long purse and infinite patience could secure it, even if that. Landless labourers were growing, and there was a craze for migration to the Gulf countries, and even to more distant lands, like the U.K., USA and Canada, thus depriving the Panjāb of enterpreneurs, professionals, labour and middle technicians.

The labour shortage was being made up by seasonal immigrants from Bihār and Rājasthān, going upto half a million each year, thus creating further social tensions, the labour being generally Hindi-speaking Hindus, and working for much less wages, to the detriment of the Panjābi labour. The liberal education being imparted at the Universities, increased educated unemployment even more. Over two million Sikhs had migrated abroad, since independence. The stories of their affluence (actual or feigned), accentuated the distress in the Panjāb. The gulf between the rich industrialists (mostly city-dwelling Hindus) and the middle class Sikh peasantry (who had to sell their produce to, and borrow money from, the village Hindu Bania) increased, day by day. This could be a grist to any political party's mill. The Akālis got most of the recruits for their morchas and Bhindrānwālā for his terrorist outfit, out of these elements — educated unemployed, marginal farmers, and landless labourers, some of whom had also become professional killers and smugglers. The Congress was indentified with the rich

* Some of the bigger landlords however flouted the land-laws with impunity and, with the active connivance of the administration, got their vast lands parcelled out in fictitious names, including their distant relations, servants, minors, and even cats and dogs, and buffaloes, horses and cows! This negatived the Government's intention, by and large, to distribute the surplus land among the Harijans and the landless, thus increasing social tensions. Prolonged Court cases further exasperated the under-privileged sections.

professional Hindu Bania, or the rich Sikh, though the Akāli leadership was even more in the hands of the rich farmers or affluent Sikh industrialists and professionals or religious zealots hungering for political power. But impressions, once deeply ingrained, die hard. The lowest strata joined the two Communist Parties, mainly comprising of industrial labour, and the landless, though they were led there also by the well-to-do and educated,city-bred, professionals — teachers, doctors, lawyers and professional agitators etc.

The economic distress or disparities, if tackled on a joint Party basis from an economic platform, might assuredly have brought fruitful results, becoming near impossible for the Central Govt. to refuse just concessions. The territorial and the waters' issues could have been resolved, through mutual give - and - take, between Haryānā and Panjāb, rather than being made Sikh, communal or one - Party issues, to be adjudicated upon always by the Central Government.

But the Akālis opted for immediate and easy solutions, and coloured every demand with a religious overtone, coupled with ongoing violence against their whole history. And, the results were disastrous. However, it must be understood that the agitation had nothing to do, except marginally, with the so-called threat to the Sikh identity or the Akālis' desire to bring or keep more people to the orthodox Sikh faith. The aims were wholly political, (not even economic), otherwise violence against the police or the Hindus would make no sense whatsoever. If anything, these crude tactics unnerved, isolated and subjected about 5 million of the (mostly non-Jat) Sikhs, settled outside the Panjāb, generally highly prosperous, to such ugly pressures that numerous young Sikhs discarded the outer symbols of their faith than bring other people into their fold! As time passed, the Sikhs in the Panjāb also were sickened by the grim atmosphere and became apprehensive of their future in their home-state as well!

Mrs. Gandhi, however, had a taste of the Akāli frenzy, during the Emergency she had proclaimed in 1975. In no other part of the country did so many people protest against it with that vehemence and consistency. About 45000 of them had been put in jail in the Panjāb alone. Sant Harchand Singh of village Longowāl (in Sangrur distt), a Sikh preacher of modest, hand-spun education, and once an Akāli MLA (though he never spoke a word throughout his tenure as a legislator), had leapt into fame as the acknowledged leader of this movement. He was now the President of the Akāli Dal. Soft-spoken and amiable of disposition and peaceful of intention, he influenced the Sikh masses, as no one else at that point of time could. The Akālis of every faction stood by him, though they quarelled often enough among themselves, and some of them, like G.S. Tohrā, conspired against his authority secretly as well. Tohrā often times played the Bhindrānwālā card against him, or scared both to isolate Bādal, his arch political rival.

So, Mrs. Gandhi tried to adopt a conciliatory attitude. She sent various emissaries to the Akālis saying, she was not averse to agreeing to almost all of their religious demands. As for Chandigarh, Mrs. Gandhi stood by her award of 1970. "Take Chandigarh and in compensation, hand over the cotton-producing belt of Abohar and Fazilka to Haryānā," even though these areas were not contiguous to Haryānā and needed a hundred square miles of a corridor to connect the two! Unfortunately, the Akālis had weakened their case by accepting this Award, in 1970, through their then Chief Minister, Justice Gurnām Singh, and Sant Chanan Singh, then President of the SGPC, in order to save the life of their leader, Sant Fateh Singh, who had gone on a fast unto death, over this issue. It is the Congress and the Communists who had protested against it. But, the Akālis had now different ideas.

As far as the re-allocation of waters to the Panjāb, Mrs. Gandhi showed her readiness to withdraw the previous agreement reached between the Central Govt. and the Congress Govt. of Haryana and Panjāb, on Dec. 31, 1981, and refer the matter to a Tribunal, headed by a Supreme Court Judge. This was, however, subject to the Akālis agreeing to complete the Satluj-Yamuna link-canal, as early as possible, to provide more water to Haryānā. The Akālis, during their regime, had, in fact, accepted Rs. one crore (ten million) for the digging of the canal from the Janta-led Government of Haryānā.!

But, now, they changed their tune altogether, and instead launched a *morcha*, at Kapuri, in the Patiala district. On May 24, a "Nehar Roko" (stop the canal) agitation was launched, under the leadership of Sant Harchand Singh Longowāl. This soon fizzled out, for lack of response from the Sikhs, but the work on the link-canal also got obstructed for a while, though for other reasons. Fearing trouble, not many labourers would offer themselves for work, nor many farmers allow their farms to be acquired for the digging of the canal in the expectation of better prices later, from the Government.

After this, a "RASTA ROKO" (Stop Traffic) agitation was launched, followed by "Rail Roko" (stop the trains) agitation. On Aug 4, 1982, the Morcha "dictator", Longowāl, announced a *"Dharam-Yudh"* (or Holy war) against the Govt. Thousands of Akālis courted arrest. The jails were overflowing with the prisoners, with the result that some of them had to be "jailed" in the open! The "Morcha" was by and large peaceful, except for a few untoward incidents. Twice, the Indian Airlines planes were hijacked again (Aug 4 and Aug. 20, 1982). In both attempts, the hijackers were not allowed to land at Lahore (Pākistān), and had to fly back to Amritsar. In the first case, the lone hijacker was arrested and, in the other case, killed by the police. The "Roko" agitations also produced little effect on the Govt. But, the atmosphere became very surcharged. At a railway crossing (Sept 11), a bus carrying Akāli prisoners collided with a train and 34 of them were crushed to death. The Akālis charged the Govt. with their deliberate murder, and feelings of the masses were roused to a pitch heat. The Akāli dead were termed "martyrs" and a Gurdwārā called "Takkar Sāhib" (The 'Collision Sāhib' Gurdwārā) was constructed in their memory on the spot where they fell!

Acts of violence now increased further against the Nirankāris as well as the Police and the Hindus. Bombs were used as much as guns. At the time Sant Longowāl launched the *"Dharam-Yudh"* (Holy war), Bhindrānwālā was conducting his own *morcha* against the arrest of Bhai Amrik Singh, President of the All India Sikh Students' Federation and son of his predecessor, and others of his persuation. He, however, came to Amritsar and joined the Akāli *morcha* staying at the Golden Temple Rest House (Sarāi Guru Rām Dās). Soon after, the Chief Minister, Darbārā Singh, was attacked with hand grenades, though he escaped unhurt, but 18 others, including the Education Minister, received injuries. The bomb blasts and explosions now increased in frequency, notably at Amritsar, Jullunder, Ludhiānā and various other towns, where the Hindus were in a majority.

In November/December, 1982, was to be held the ASIAD,or Asian games, in New-Delhi, in which athletic teams from all over Asia had to participate. The Govt. of India had spent vast sums on this major international event, in building various gymnasiums, over-bridges, swimming pools etc., and was anxious to see its venture (criticised by the Opposition as an extravaganza) succeed. The Akālis had threatened to disrupt it, and the Govt.. of India, in panic, asked Mr. Bhajan Lāl (once a Janata Chief Minister of Haryānā who walked over, wholesale, with all his Janata legislators, to the Congress, on Mrs. Gandhi's victory in 1980), to block the way of the Akāli protestors from Panjāb, who had to pass through Haryānā to reach Delhi.

But before this, twice, in Nov. 1982, Mrs. Gandhi tried for a rapproachment, once through S. Swaran Singh, her former Cabinet Colleague, and a little later through Capt. Amrinder Singh, a Congress M.P., (later he resigned to join the Akālis) and son and heir of the ex-Maharaja of Patiala. But both times, the negotiations came to nothing. S. Harkishan Singh Surjit, Communist M. P., and an advisor of Mr. Tohrā (who himself was a Communist Party card-holder once), and Mr. Amrinder Singh blamed Mrs. Gandhi for having backed out of her commitments, at the last moment, though her Cabinet colleagues (Mr. Shiv Shanker, Mr. R. Venkataraman, later our President, & Mr. P. C. Sethi, Home Minister) and the Akāli negotiators (Tohrā, Balwant, Ravi Inder Singh, Badāl & Editor R. S. Bhatia) had agreed.* Mrs. Gāndhi's version was that the Akālis were fighting for higher stakes and could not control violence and hence were not interested in a settlement. Also, that they were shifty and changed their stand too often!

Mr. Bhajan Lāl, out to please his new masters at Delhi, took his job seriously, and let alone the Akālis (who got cold feet, seeing Govt's fool-proof security arrangements), the Haryānā Police searched and even insulted every Sikh, including the high military personnel, taking that road by car, bus or motor-cycle. The Asiad passed off peacefully, but the humiliation of the Sikhs at the hands of the Haryānā police sank into the psyche of the whole community, and gave a new impetus to the flagging Akāli agitation and especially to violence against the police, Hindus, Nirankāris and Sikhs belonging to the Congress or considered to be Govt. agents or spies. A Sikh D. I. G. of the Police, Mr. A. S. Atwāl, on a visit to the golden temple was shot dead (April 25, 1983*) . Bank-looting and robberies became almost a weekly occurrence. Fish plates on the railway lines were removed to cause rail derailments and disruption of traffic. One night, 22 railway stations were attacked simultaneously. Several buses were stopped on the way, and Hindu commuters separated and killed.

In Haryānā, counter-violence also took place against the Sikhs at some places, But the Central Govt. dismissed its own Party Govt. in Punjāb (Oct 6, 1983). The violence in Haryānā was soon contained, but Panjāb was declared a "Disturbed Area" the same day, giving unlimited powers to the police of arrest, detention for a year without trial and institution of Special Courts etc, to handle the fast-deteriorating situation. This did not, however, stop the killings. The more the police and the para-military forces acted against the terrorists and their sympathisers, the more the terrorists of various hues went on a killing-spree, justifying it on the ground that through false encounters, the security forces were finishing the Sikh youth of the Panjāb recklessly -- a charge never proved to be true.

---

* In most of these and other negotiations, Mr. P.C. Alexender, Principal Secretary to Prime Minister, Rao Sahib Krishnaswami, Cabinet Secretary and Mr. T.N. Chaturvedi, Home Secretary, also participated. Mr. Narsimha Rao and Mr. Pranab Mookerjee, Union Ministers, also took part in several of them. Early in 1983, Mr. Rajiv Gandhi, M.P. & then Gen. Secretary of the Congress Party also shared in the deliberations.

* He had been warned by Govt. not to go there, as he was a "wanted" man by Bhindrānwālā, having been responsible for successful operations against his men. But, he ignored the Govt. advice.

It is, however, a fact that the killings were directed mainly by Bhindrānwālā personally. All the killer-gangs like Dal Khālsā, Bhindrānwālā Tigers, the Dashmesh Regiment, the A. I. Sikh Students' Federation, Khālistān Commando Force and the National Council of Khālistān -- all wedded to the slogan of Khālistān -- (or an independent Sikh state, whose geography, economy or means of defence they refused to define), owed allegiance to him, except for Babbar Khālsā and the Akāli youth federation, which protected Sant Longowāl and his men from their onslaughts (see later) ! The National Council of Khālistān was based in Great Britain with a medical doctor, Jagjit Singh Chauhān (once Finance Minister in the Lachhman Singh Gill defectors' Ministry, which, as stated in the last chapter, was initially supported by the Congress and after six months voted out) as its self-proclaimed President. From his talks with this writer, it appeared he had some personal grouses to settle with the Congress, his main charge being that his career as an Akāli had been finished by the Congress, on false promises, and he later badly let down, and left in the lurch ! Others were out for adventure and loot, also animated by a feeling that they were serving a "good cause" and defending their minority community, against the "tyranny" and "injustice" of the majority, which failed to see season. But the Sikhs, at large, neither condoned violence, nor the idea of "Khālistān". However, even the best of them could not speak out their minds, as the whole families of their detractors were being wiped out by the terrorist gangs.*

Not that there were no differences among the various Akāli groups and their sympathisers. They fought against each other, within the precincts of the Golden Temple, and sometimes killed each other. Sant Harchand Singh had become scared of Bhindranwālā so much that the two did not meet for six months, and as has been said, even enlisted the support of the Babbar Khālsā to protect him. An Akāli youth Federation was also brought into being by him to counter the growing influence of the All - India Sikh Students' Federation, under Bhai Amrik Singh, which was wholly at the command of Bhindrānwālā and was spearheading the killings, along with what was called Dashmesh Regiment.

---

* The speeches made by Bhindrāwālā and his interviews to the Press revealed his mind clearly. "A Sikh without arms is naked, a lamb led to slaughter. Buy motor cycles, guns and repay the traitors in the same coin". (International Herald Tribune, April 24, 1984). "The Sikhs are a separate nation. They must have a special status in the Union, like Jammu & Kashmir". (The Week", March 27 to April 2, 1984). " I ask them – the British Sikhs – to join the fight for our independence as a separate nation". (Daily Mail, London, April 12, 1984). In a recorded speech, he told a select gathering in the Golden Temple complex, "It comes to 35, not even 100. Divide 55 crores, then each Sikh gets only 35 Hindus (to kill), and not even 36th. How do you say you are weak?"

Bhindrānwālā tried desparately either to become the President of the SGPC, or the head of the Akāl Takhat. He gradually and secretly sought to win over the members of the SGPC. But when the final head-count was taken by his men, according to Gyāni Kirpal Singh, Jathedār of the Akāl Takhat, not more than 15 owed any sort of allegiance to him! Mr. Tohrā was too shrewd a manipulator to be taken off-guard. So, he got Bhindrānwālā to swear before a huge Sikh Congregation (13 April 1983) that he would " never accept any office, and also stand behind Sant Longowāl to conduct the *morcha* under his leadership"! Tohrā warned both Longowāl & Bhindrānwālā that a Congress - Akāli coalition Govt. was in the offing, under the leadership of Bādal, and unless they stood together, all their interests would be sold out by the rich farmers and political manipulators! This argument did work for a time.

As the fear of Bhindrānwālā being arrested or killed was constantly in the air, he left the Sarāi and occupied the Akāl Takhat (Dec. 15, 1983). The Jathedār of the Akāl Takhat, Giani Kirpāl Singh, protested that no Guru even had made the Akāl Takhat his place of residence and that it would be a sacrilege. But, he was over-ruled by Tohrā. Fights had also ensued between the Babbar Khālsā and Bhindrānwālā 's men at the Sarāi, and this, added Tohra, had left no choice for Bhindrānwālā but to seek sanctuary at the Akāl Takhat ! When asked, after the **"Operation Blue Star "**, why had he not made a public issue of it, Jathedār Kirpāl Singh said :- **"Asān Marnā si ? (Did you want us to be killed ?)".***

Indeed, such was the terror of Bhindrānwālā that no one even in the police or the Judiciary dared cross his path. Any act of injustice by these agencies, if reported to Bhindrānwālā, got redressed within 24 hours, after he telephoned or sent word through a special messenger to do the job, as he dictated, or else . .

The "Kār Sevā " (Community works) or "Langar" (Community Kitchen) trucks, which brought provisions for the Temple from outside, or materials for construction, could not be searched by the police or other forces, and sophisticated arms were smuggled from within the country as well as

* In several 1985-86 issues of the monthly Punjabi Journal, "Gyān Amrit" of Amritsar, earlier edited by Giani Partāp Singh, ex- Jathedār of the Akāl Takhat and after his murder, by Dr. Mān Singh Nirankāri, several verbatim interviews of Giani Kirpāl Singh are given, revealing the true mind of Bhindrānwālā and his relations with other leaders and Akāli-groups. They also reveal the inner working of the Akāli Dal, the manipulations and intrigues, the cowardice and lack of principles of the Akāli leadership and even of the High Priests.

Pākistān, into the Temple complex, including light machine-guns, sten guns, mortars, rifles, revolvers and pistols, anti-tank weapons, mines, explosives, a grenade-manufacturing plant, etc. Large quantities of these and their ammunition were recovered from the Complex after "Operation Blue Star" (See below)".

Money was no problem either. It flowed from all over, including UK, USA and Canada, & other countries, besides Pākistān, and almost all the major Sikh Centres in India. Gold, Silver and even precious stones were also either contributed or looted. The Golden Temple complex, besides the Akāl Takhat, were fortified against any attack by the police or the army, under the direction of an able Sikh General, cashiered (but later acquitted by the Court) Shāhbeg Singh, who had earned a name for himself in the Bangladesh war as a guerilla fighter. He wanted to wreak his own vengeance.

Fiery Sikhs abroad formed their Dals and Jathās on the analogy of those back home, collected money from the unwary, smuggled Sikh "refugees" into foreign countries, against colossal fees, sold forged passports and fake "Khālistāni" stamps and currency notes. For many, it had become big business, with a little of chivalry and adventure also thrown in, in the "service" of the Sikh Panth. Every killer-gang was flush with funds and those who did the "job" were handsomely rewarded. Some of the big-time terrorists were, it is said, heavily insured by international agencies ! Several rapes were ascribed to them, and also that they settled their long-standing private and family feuds in the process!

Mrs. Gandhi, however, kept the doors of negotiations open. Many meetings -- both secret and open -- were held with the Akāli leadership, in 1981-82, but more in 1983 and particularly in April - May, 1984. Most of the religious demands were unilaterally accepted by her, going personally to Gurdwārā Banglā Sāhib, in New Delhi (Feb. 1983), and making an announcement, amidst loud shouts of **"Sat Sri Akāl "**, the Sikh war - cry. She agreed for the relay of "Kirtan" from the Golden Temple from the All India Radio Jullundur, for one hour in the morning and half an hour in the evening, a concession not granted to any other religious community in India. (The Akālis, however, made a grievance of it, saying they wanted the broadcast time to be increased twice over!) The demand for carrying the Kirpan on the aeroplanes had already been accepted, this being a constitutional guarantee, under Article (25) of India's Constitution. She also announced that within a radius of 300 metres of the Golden Temple, no permission would be accorded for the sale of tobacco, meat or liquor.(The Akālis wanted the whole city of Amritsar to be covered, which the Govt. said was impossible).

Why the Akālis had included the ban on meat in their demands, still eludes anyone's imagination, as meat is not forbidden to the Sikhs, and more liquor is consumed, per capita, in Panjāb, than even the Scandanavian countries. Some of the top-ranking Akāli leaders also do not hesitate to warm themselves up with spirituous drinks (occasionally, even in jail !), nor fail to distribute it among their supporters, even during the Gurdwārā polls! And why was a ban not recommended on hashish & opium which the Nihangs used freely& some Akāli leaders traded in, or smuggled from Pākistān ?

In 1984, the last meeting was held by Govt. representatives on 26 May, with G. S. Tohrā and S. S. Barnālā, but, as we shall see, failed to clinch the issue.

One of the primary reasons for the failure of Political talks was the raging violence in the Panjāb, which the Govt. insisted, must end. The Akālis repudiated any responsibility for it, and either accused the Govt. of creating conditions which inevitably led to violence or blamed the anti-social elements, whom the Govt. could not control, and which was ultimately the job of the Govt. to do ! When asked to issue a "Hukamnāmā" (religious edict) form the Akāl Takhat that any Sikh, indulging in violence, will be ex-communicated, the Akāli reply was that they could not blame only the Sikhs for acts which others in the Sikh garb, notably from Pākistān, may be committing ! When told to prevent storing of sophisticated, unlicensed arms within the Temple, the Akālis said it was for the Govt. to stop their inflow from outside. In any case, they said, they knew nothing about it (a statement which was patently false)! Pākistān also had tried to influence the course of events in Panjāb in no uncertain terms, and inflamed the Jathās, going on a pilgrimage to the Gurdwārās in Pākistān, through propaganda in favour of Khālistān. They also supplied arms, money and training and gave them sanctuary, without fail, smuggled in Muslim soldiers, dressed as Sikhs, to help the terrorists in Indian Panjāb, but the ground had been prepared by the Akāli agitation itself. If Pākistān took advantage of it, or sought to take its revenge for losing Bangladesh, through Indian arms, or to destabilise India's granary and the sword-arm which Panjāb had become, once again, their role was subsidiary to those who were bent upon, within the country, to disrupt peace in the Panjāb to serve their narrow political ends.

As has been said, even confirmed smugglers and habitual cut-throats and Naxalites had joined their ranks, for their own reasons. Smuggling has been an "honourable" and much sought-after occupation in the Panjāb's border districts, especially for heroin, which brought exceptionally rich dividends, besides arms. The Naxalites, mostly educated Sikhs & others wedded to anarchy, had, in their earlier attempts failed to bring about an economic revolution in Panjāb, inspite of their large-scale violence. On being ruthlessly curbed by the state, they assumed the new garb of Sikh fundamentalism and took to loot and killings for "Khālistān".

And, what a pity that all the political ingenuity of this great and civilised nation could not produce a permanent solution to minor territorial and economic demands, within the law and the Constitution of India. Why couldn't a machinery, like the Privy Council in England, or a statutory inter-state body be evolved to adjudicate upon inter-state or Centre-state disputes, within a reasonable time-frame, instead of politicalising every issue and settling it, in accordance with the political needs of the ruling Party or whims of the political top-brass, in Delhi !

On the other hand, whatever reasons the Akālis trotted forth for their inability to stop violence, the real reason was that they were mortally afraid of Bhindrānwālā, who fired all the shots and controlled all the gun-running. A regular hit-list had been prepared by him of the Police personnel, who allegedly either killed his men in encounters, or tortured them in jail. The Hindu militants now organised under the banner of "Shiv Sena" etc. (and even other innocents travelling by bus, or plying rickshaws, or out for a morning walk, or exercising on a playground etc) and members of the Congress (I) and the sympathisers of the Govt. called "spies", or those who criticised Bhindrānwālā , were all put on the everchanging hitlist and finished, one by one.

S. Harbans Singh Manchandā, the President of the Gurdwārā Parbandhak Committee, Delhi, was assassinated in the heart of New Delhi (March 28, 1984), in broad daylight. Dr. V. N. Tiwāri, professor of Pānjābi at the Panjāb University and a nominated M. P., was done to death at his Chandigarh residence (3 April 1984). On May 10, a former Jathedār of the Akāl Takhat, 85-year-old, venerable Giani Partāp Singh, and a staunch critic of Bhindrānwālā, was murdered in Amritsar. Romesh Chanḍra, son of lala Jagat Narain, was butchered on May 12. Harbaṇs Lal Khanna, a BJP leader and an ex-MLA, was done to death on April 2, 1984. So also Bachan Singh, a Deputy Superintendent of Police, in Amritsar. Several Sikh granthis and Hindu Mahants were also killed. The Panjāb had become a virtual slaughter house. The killing of Surinder Singh Sodhi (April 14), a protege of Bhindrānwālā, by one Baljit Kaur, an associate of Longowāl, further heightened the intra-Party tussle among the two (now warring) groups. Baljit kaur was tortured and brutally killed soon after, and her mangled body thrown out of the temple, stuffed in a gunny bag! Life had become dirt cheap inspite of Pānjab having been declared a "Disturbed area" and draconian powers given to the police!

Meantime, the Golden Temple and the Akāl Takhat were being fortified, as never before in Sikh history. Though Govt. had declared time and again (even in Parliament) that the police or the Army would, under no circumstances, enter the Temple, the insiders feared the attack any time, and did not want to be caught napping.

Mrs. Gandhi was being accused by the Opposition and, secretly even by her own partymen, of having lost the nerve to govern the country. The Government's critics even charged her publicly of wooing the Hindu vote, en bloc, by not resolving the Sikh question, and thus deliberately prolonging the agony of the Panjāb and the nation ! She, therefore, had convened eight meetings of the leaders of the Opposition late in January, 1983, and early in February of that year, along with the Akāli and Govt. representatives, to thrash out a consensus formula, but these had come to nothing. Early in February 1984, two more such meetings were held, but to no effect. Meantime, the Akālis themselves were scared by the turn events were taking and their authority passing into the hands of a lone crusader, Bhindrānwālā, thus isolating the entire Akāli leadership and making them irrelevant on the political scene.

They, therefore, hit upon another plan, one to attract public notoriety throughout India, and two, to appear to the Sikh masses even more extremist in their outlook than Bhindrānwālā. Tohrā had also told Mrs. Gandhi that if his plan succeeded, Bhindrānwālā may also fall in line. This was the amendment of Article 25, explanation 2, of the Indian Constitution.* This related in fact to the temple entry of Harijans (or Untouchables, whether

---

* Article 25 reads as follows :
(1) Subject to public order, morality and health and to the other provisions of this part, all persons are equally entitled to freedom of conscience, and the right freely to profess, practise and propagate religion.
(2) Nothing in this article shall affect the operation of an existing law or prevent the State from making any law –
(a) regulating or restricting any economic, financial, political or other secular activity which may be associated with religious practice;
(b) providing for social welfare and reform or the throwing open of Hindu religious institutions of a public character to all classes and sections of Hindus.

Explanation I – The wearing and carrying of Kirpāns shall be deemed to be included in the profession of the Sikh religion.
Explanation II – In sub-clause (b) of clause (2), the reference to Hindus shall be construed as including a reference to persons professing the Sikh, Jain or Buddhist religion, and the reference to Hindu religious institutions shall be construed accordingly.

Hindu, Sikh or Buddhist) into the Hindu, Sikh and Buddhist temples. Moreover, this was the only Article, under which the Govt could enact any All India Gurdwārā Act, on which the Akālis had set their heart. It is under this Article that Sikhs were permitted to carry kirpāns, and their separate identity certified. But, the Akālis thought otherwise.

Their contention was that this Article compromised the identity of the Sikhs as a separate faith. If so, why had no protest been lodged for the last forty years, and why no Sikh member of the Constituent Assembly had protested against it at the time the Constitution was being framed? But, the Akālis interpret or misinterpret even their own history and Scriptures only in accordance with their ever-changing political needs and compulsions!

This demand was not a part of the 45 demands originally formulated by the Akāli Dal. However, the die was cast. A virulent agitation was launched. April 24 to 31,1984, was declared by Longowāl to be observed as "Panth Azād" (Free Panth) week. The only person among the Akālis to oppose this move was the only non-jat among the Akāli hierarchy, Mr. Balwant Singh, a former Block Development Officer with the Punjāb Govt.. and once a Congress MLA, (defecting later to the Akālis to become their Finance Minister-cum-industrialist-businessman), who, with his newly acquired affluence, had also developed the ambition to become the next Chief Minister! He had kept himself out of the main agitation, by and large, and never courted imprisonment, devoting his entire time and energy to his ever-expanding businesses. He had kept both the Akālis and the Congress in good humour, and kept the line of negotiations open. But he was over-ruled by Tohrā, who had other ideas. He wanted to involve Bādal, his main rival for Chief Ministership, in extremist postures, to destroy his non-sectarian image among the Hindus, and secondly to please Bhindrānwālā with the consolation prize of "Sikh independent identity" being recognised by government. He also wanted the Sikh masses, now worked into a frenzy, to accept him as their saviour, and thus to destroy Longowāl's diplomatic and moderate image as well. Longowāl fell for the bait. So did Mrs. Gandhi.*

---

* The present writer wrote two articles as Chairman of the High-powered Commission on Minorities, in the "Times of India" (March 15, 16, 1984), detailing the genesis of the Sikh problem and suggesting a political way out, and not to treat it solely as a law-and-order problem. These had a very healthy effect on both sides. But when he wrote an "Open letter to Longowāl" (March 31, 1984) in the "Hindustan Times", and pleaded with the Akālis over the TV the next day to desist from amending Sec. 25, in their own interest, he was put on Bhindrānwālā's hit-list, and extra police protection given to him !

The agitation was inaugrated in late April, 1984 from the Gurdwārā Banglā Sāhib in New Delhi, a Congress stronghold, by Bādal, by tearing a page of the Constitution, on which Section 25 was inscribed, and burning it. This was to be repeated by the Akālis all over the country. Bādal and Tohrā along with several thousand Akāli workers, were arrested and put in jail, but Mrs. Gandhi was not averse to considering this what later turned out to be a non-issue (for nothing was heard of it, later on) sympathetically. Tohrā wanted a separate "Sikh personal Law " also to be codified, mainly to deprive the married daughters from a share of the ancestral property, and the right of second or third marriage, without obtaining divorce of the other wives! Up to 1954, there was no restriction on the number of marriages by Hindu or Sikh males, and only the male heirs could inherit their ancestral property. But, in that year, the Hindu Marriage and Succession Codes were revised by Parliament, at the instance of Pt. Nehru, in the teeth of the Orthodox Hindu Opposition, including that of President Rajendra Prasad, to bring the rights of property and divorce to Hindu women (which included Sikh women). The Sikh and other Jats resented this, for fear of further sub-dividing their lands. Also custom had sanctioned more than one marriage to Hindu and Sikh males. But it was now being denied. It may be mentioned that ever since their birth to date, Sikhs have been governed by the Hindu customary laws, in marriage and inheritance.

Already, Mrs. Gandhi had held several secret and open negotiations with the Akāli leaders, but failed. However, she made a last-minute try, once again, and called in Tohrā, Bādal and Barnālā, (now out of jail), on May 26.

This meeting was necessitated by the entire Indian Press screaming against Sikh perfidy — (all Sikhs were unfortunately identified with Akālis) — and disloyalty to the Constitution of India. The Opposition parties in Parliament had joined hands with the ruling Congress to decry this sinister move of tearing the Sikhs from the Hindu Society (which offered them almost all their converts), to drive the Hindus out of Panjāb and to break away the border state from the rest of India into an independent political unity. Moreover, in May 1984, there were more murders of Hindus and attacks on Hindu temples and industrial and commercial establishments than ever before. Sikh Granthis, village headmen and police personnel also continued to be attacked.

Government offices were burnt down in several places. Hand-grenades and bombs became the order of the day. The Hindus had also retaliated at certain places as in Patiala, where they burnt a copy of the Sikh Scripture (May 31), but such incidents only added fuel to the fire.

The Akālis were also becoming desperate, and had given a call to the Panjāb farmers, from June 1, to withhold their wheat-stocks from reaching the market for sale, to refuse to pay taxes, and to non-cooperate with the Govt. in all other ways. A massive demonstration was also to be held at Amritsar on that day, in support of the Akāli demands. Sensing that the situation might go out of hand, Mrs. Gandhi was persuaded to part with Chandigarh, with only Fāzilkā town being handed over to Haryānā, or to refer the issue of both Chandigarh and Hindi areas in Panjāb to a Commission; to appoint another Commission under a Supreme Court judge for adjudication of river-waters; and to accept in whatever way legal and Sikh opinion might desire to amend Section 25 (Explanation II). Tohrā was happy and thought he had won the day. He rushed to Amritsar by a special plane, provided by Govt, and met Bhindrānwālā. According to reliable sources, Tohra was strongly rebuffed by the militant leader. "You want to sell me for your own chair! I will not touch this settlement. We have all vowed either to get the Anandpur Sāhib resolution accepted, in toto, or die fighting. Go, and tell your Delhi masters and your cowardly Bādal and Longowāl that I shall not be duped or bought over." Tohrā threatened to throw him out of the Akāl Takhat, but the threat did not work. At that point of time, it just couldn't. Bhindrānwālā was too strongly entrenched in his fortress, and was prepared for the worst. Taken by shock and surprise, Tohrā went straight to Mr. B.D. Pāndē, Governor of the Panjāb, and told him he had failed." The Govt. could take whatever action they wanted to meet with the menacing situation," he said.

On June 2, Mrs. Gandhi appealed, once again, over the TV network, for the Akālis to withdraw their agitation, to "shed hatred and not blood," and accept the terms of the settlement already offered to them, and which she spelt out again in her broadcast. She spoke feelingly about Sikh contribution to India's economy, defence and integrity as also their "shining contribution" to the freedom struggle. "The life of Guru Nānak Dev symbolised tolerance. The moral of Guru Granth Sāhib is truth and kindliness. The great Gurus taught love and brotherhood."

She added :– "Sikhism itself was born as a faith to bring together people of different religions. Let not a miniscule minority among the Sikhs be allowed to trample under foot civilised norms for which Sikhism is well-known, and to tarnish the image of a brave and patriotic community. If any misgivings or doubts remain, let's sit round the table and find a solution. This is the democratic way."

But, the appeal had no effect whatever on the agitators. The killings continued unabated, the killers later taking shelter in the Golden Temple complex. The Govt., therefore, decided to clear the temple of the anti-social elements with the use of force. The army attacked the Golden Temple on June 5, 1984, with at least a force of 1000 men and officers, under the overall command of Maj. Gen. K.S. Brār, R.S. Dyāl and Sunderji (later to become the C-IN-C of the Indian Army replacing Gen. A.S.Vaidya,who held the post at the time of the Operation). It was called "Operation Blue Star". Such secrecy was maintained about the assault, that up to the time of the operation, even the Sikh President of India, Giani Zail Singh (July 1982-July 1987), was not taken into confidence.

An alternative to starve the inmates to death, or surrender, was duly considered by the Army top-brass, but fearing a general Sikh uprising in Panjāb, and surrounding the Golden Temple during the siege period, made them scary, and the plan was given up. However, the army personnel were strictly instructed not to fire at the Golden Temple, whatever the provocation. June 3 being the day of Guru Arjan Dev's martyrdom, pilgrims had also gathered in the Sarāi and in the Parikarmā in large numbers. But, on constant warnings being given by the army over the loudspeakers, from June 5, to keep away from the Temple during operations, only about three thousand people, including a few women, remained inside, before the assault. Some of these included the Gurdwāra Sewādārs (custodians), who remained to protect the sanctity of the Temple, and keep the religious services going uninterruptedly. Bhindrānwālā's men had taken positions on all sides of the Parikarmā (marble-walk around the temple) besides the Akāl Takhat which was highly fortified. Many of Bhindrānwālā's followers, including Maj. Gen. J.S. Bhullar, fled to safety and crossed over to Pākistān.*

Rājput, Dogra, Muslim ana Madrāsi companies were mainly employed by the army, together with some Sikhs, though the command was under the overall charge of Sikh commanders, some of them like Gen. Dyal extremely devoted to their faith. A Muslim, Lt. Col. Issar Khan, led the battalion inside the Temple! (The Temple's foundation stone was also laid by a Muslim!). "We went in with humility in our hearts and prayers on our lips", says Gen. Sunderji. It was a most sensitive and treacherous role given to the army in peace time, for it could have, as it later did have, cataclysmic repercussions, both political and social, on the nation. The Indian army is itself a very religious army and the Hindu respect for Sikh temples is no less than that of the Sikhs. But no one had ever invaded or any armyman or police in uniform entered the Golden Temple in its 400-year old history, or dared to commit

---

* Bhullar later surfaced in New York, took over the Secretariat of the militant World Sikh Organisation of USA, which came into being on July 31, 1984, but later, disgusted with internal ıanglings, deserted them to settle elsewhere in Europe. Later, he came to India and offered himself for arrest.

sacrilege, except once in the later part of the 18th century, when Ahmad Shah Abdāli blew up the temple, with gun-powder, in 1762, and filled the tank with rubbish and the blood of kine. The Sikhs, two years later, had reconquered Amritsar and, with Afghāns in chains, the Temple was rebuilt with their forced labour, and the whole of Panjāb finally freed from the onslaughts of that scourge of Asia.+

Men had, therefore, to crawl towards the Akāl Takhat and up the narrow staircase of that building, unmindful of the casualties, which were heavy. Room to room engagement ensued. Suddenly, a devastating explosion occurred on the ground floor, causing immense noise and fire. The facade of the Akāl Takhat fell, with a stunning thud, and there was utter confusion among the fighting inmates. After a whole night and the next morning's hand-to-hand fight, the guns on both sides were silenced. 32 terrorists surrendered. The others were blown or cut to pieces, including Bhindrānwālā, Amrik Singh and Gen. Shahbeg Singh, who had master-minded the whole terrorist operation, with utmost precision and thoroughness.

The main operation was over by June 6, mid-day. But sporadic firing continued for another few days. According to Govt. estimates, 554 terrorists were killed and 121 wounded. The army casualties were 4 Officers, 4 JCOs and 84 other ranks and about 300 seriously injured, including 15 officers. Those captured by the army included 1592 from the Golden Temple and about 3000 from other Gurdwārās in the Panjāb, where operations were simultaneously conducted, including the historic Gurdwārā of Dukh Niwāran Sāhib at Patiala. According to Government's information, cash over Rs. 30 lakhs (3 million) was recovered, besides 41 machine guns, 432 rifles (303), and a large quantity of 12 bore guns * (343), self-loading rifles (98), mines

+ Mrs. Gandhi told the present writer three months later, that the decision was most painful for her to take. She kept awake for three nights thereafter, in remorse, being herself a religious person, and even having married her much-beloved younger son, Sanjay, in a Sikh family. She said, one of the major reasons of the assault was not merely the fear of a Sikh resurrection from June 1, the day appointed by Longowāl to start total non-cooperation with Govt, but also the warning given by certain reliable and friendly diplomatic sources, (possibly Moscow), that in the first week of June, three border districts (Amritsar, Gurdāspur and Ferozepur) will declare themselves an independent Sikh State (Khālistān), and be recognised immediately by some nations (including some western nations, China and Pākistān)! This later turned out to be a wrong and motivated information.

(128), revolvers, pistols, assorted rifles, anti-tank weapon (RPG-2), and large quantities of ammunition. (Even Pākistāni currency worth over a lakh and a quarter rupees also fell into the hands of the army!) A grenade-manufacturing plant and a sten-gun parts manufacturing shop were also discovered, within the Temple complex!

Naval divers were employed to recover arms and dead bodies from the sacred tank, and the air-force helicopters and planes were also utilised to move troops and gather vital information.

But, the damage caused to the holy Akal Takhat by explosive materials (or through tank-firing ?) was too hard to bear. The whole facade had collapsed, but for the Kothā Sāhib (the Holy chamber), where the Guru Granth Sahib is kept and carried in a solemn procession from the main Temple in the early hours of the morning, with great ceremony.

However, priceless paintings in the interior chambers were smoked out or destroyed. So also a part of the Toshakhānā treasures, including a part of the gold-threaded canopy, gifted by Mahārājā Ranjit Singh. The Art Museum and various precious manuscripts of the Guru Granth Sahib were also destroyed. Why they could not be saved has never been explained.

When three days later (June 9), the Sikh President of India, visited the Temple, the stink of the dead hundreds had not yet died down. The Akāl Takhat's front portion looked like a hollow, vacant shell. The Parikarmaā's marble-floors were just a rubble. And he wept.

He was not the only one to be shocked to tears. The Sikhs all over were in mourning, as were most of their countrymen, both on what a grim tragedy had been enacted by the Sikh killer-gangs, and what an extremist Sikh Party, hungry to grab political power, by any means, had done to the whole chivalrous history of the Sikhs! The Indian people were also amazed and shocked as to what a democratic Govt. had done to stake the stability of the whole nation, over trivial issues, which they refused to resolve, in time, for their own political reasons!

This was our first serious test in democratic functioning on the home ground, and on both counts, we failed miserably. A nation that had won her independence, through a non-violent struggle and preached its gospel throughout the world, could settle none of its internal problems except through violence!

The Government intelligence, it appears, had also failed dismally to gauge how well Bhindrānwālā's men had built up their fortifications, and what kind of ammunition and equipment they had! They did not even have the full layout of the Temple, nor any knowledge of its numerous bylanes and underground tunnels and pathways for escape! The military Commanders admitted as much later, as the para-military and the Police forces had admitted their failure earlier, to check the inflow of sophisticated arms into the Temple!

Why was Bhindrānwālā not captured, nor his killer-gangs nabbed when they were much more vulnerable, and went in and out of the Temple, at will, committing every conceivable crime. Why didn't the police enter the Temple on the murder of their D.I.G., A.S. Atwāl, when Bhindrānwālā had not yet occupied the Akāl Takhat. Why was Bhindrānwālā released from prison at all? Why was he not arrested when he was touring Delhi, Bombay, or other parts of Panjāb and Haryānā, or living in the Sarāi outside the Temple-complex? These questions have not been answered, either by the "White Paper on Panjab" issued by the Govt. after the "Operation Blue Star", (June 20), nor by any Govt. dignitary.

The Army's explanation that they feared insurrection of the Panjāb Sikhs, if they laid seige to the Temple which, according to them, would anyhow have failed, as the insurgents were well-provided with foodgrains and water, also appears to be rather facile, as four years later, in "Operation Black Thunder" (May 12-18, 1988), the Panjāb police laid siege to the Temple, and without entering the Temple or firing an extra shot, got the surrender of all the (about 150) terrorists hiding there, alongwith their arms! The fear of insurrection also proved to be premature and imaginary, as no insurrection ever took place! And the threat of non-cooperation also did not materialise!

However, the decision, taken in panic, and executed with lightening speed, cost the army many of its Jawans and officers, though under the most extreme provocation, no bullet was fired at the Golden Temple, even when several of those who swam to the Temple to take up positions there, were shot and killed in cold blood.

A 36-hour curfew had already been declared, from 9 PM of June 3, which was extended selectively. All roads leading to Amritsar were closed for traffic or any other movement of men or materials from June 1. Army assisted the police in cordoning off the Golden Temple complex. The Temple Complex is closed-in, on all sides, except for numerous but narrow by-lanes and underground tunnels of which, as has been said, only the defenders were aware, but the army was not! The expert military training given to the rebels made such deadly impact on the army that they could proceed towards the Akāl Takhat, facing the main Temple, only by inches, even if that. The terrorists were firing from a number of machine gun positions and hurling grenades, lighting them with match-sticks. Machine-gun firing came from the main Temple as well, but the army was forbidden to fire back in that direction.

"The Akāl Takhat had been fortified as well as any dug out position of a modern army. Starting from the basement upwards, gun placements had been planned out and sited at every level, including the door-level, window-level, the roof-ventilators on the first floor, and the two upper storeys. They had cut holes in the walls and the marble facade, like a pill box for the positioning of weapons".

As has been said before, the firing was so heavy that the army Jawans and officers were being slaughtered, without respite. Tanks were, therefore, hurriedly brought in, but these were also silenced by the anti-tank weapons.

After a bitter fight, lasting about 15 hours, Bhindrānwālā* and his gang were dead, but leaving almost the entire Sikh community aflame with anger, and call for revenge, not so much for the "martyrdom" of a few hundreds of the marauding zealots, but the indignity and humiliation and loss of pride on account of the grievous damage suffered by the holiest of their shrines, which even the British had dared not touch even in the days of the Martial Law in 1919., when the British authorities were bent upon "teaching the Sikhs a lesson". . .

But, the question why had Bhindranwālā, professedly a devout Sikh, not quitted the holy shrine and fought, if he so wanted, outside its premises, so as to guard and preserve its sanctity from being invaded, especially on June 4 or 5, when he knew full well that the attack on the Temple was inevitable, and he was being constantly warned by the army over the loudspeakers, that this was going to happen, unless he surrendered.

After all, when a similar situation had arisen in Jan. 1848, when some armed Nihangs had occupied the "burjis" (towers) of the Golden Temple, with the intent of capturing its custodianship, and the Khālsā Durbār, under Maharajā Dalip Singh, had sent in an army detachment to clear them by force, the Nihangs immediately surrendered, saying "we do not want the holiest of

---

* Bhindrānwālā left behind his wife, Pritam Kaur, and two sons, Inderjit Singh (9) & Ishar Singh (12). Both are studying at school, at present, and now live in their ancestral village, Rodē (Faridkot), with their grandfather, Bābā Joginder Singh.

our shrines to become a battle ground!" No Guru before had ever done so, nor any Sikh hero, even in the worst days of their persecution, with no place for them anywhere to hide their heads. Did Bhindrānwālā and his "dedicated" men enact this tragedy, in order to provoke the Govt. to do their worst, and thus to leave behind a trail of bitterness and fear among the entire world Sikh community that their religion was not safe in the hands of any Indian Govt? In the eyes of his supporters, he may have become a "martyr" (the highest honour a Sikh craves), but he had wiped out the honour, the dignity and the 500-year-old history of togetherness built by the Gurus and the Sikh heroes with their blood.

And, now, where were the other heroes of the Akāli battle for Sikh "survival"and "glory" -- Tohra,* Bādal and Longowāl? Tohrā and Longowāl, "by prior arrangement with the Govt.," had dared not venture into the Temple complex during "Operation Blue Star", and had hid themselves in the Sarāi outside. When the army surrounded the Sarāi, and called for their surrender, in the early hours of June 6, both Tohra and Longowāl came out, with their hands uplifted, and handed themselves over to Gen. R. S. Dyāl, who put them in an army vehicle. Following them, several hundreds of others, trapped in the Temple Rest House, also followed suit. Some of the extremists seeing this shamefaced cowardice on the part of their "heroes", threw flaming bombs at them, thus killing many, and creating a panic in the surrendering "soldiers of the faith". But, the twosome -- Longowal and Tohrā, -- were escorted to an air-conditioned Govt. Rest House! On the way, Tohra asked Gen. R. S. Dyāl, " if their life would be spared". Dyāl laughed in his sleeves at their bravery and sense of chivalry, but assured them that they would not only be safe, but provided with an air-conditioned room in the Amritsar Rest House, which he himself was occupying!+

After all, these were the Sikh heroes who had left their comrades back in the Temple, to face the army bullets, abandoning both their sense of shame and chivalry, to save their own skins! Bādal was tucked away in the heavily-guarded safety of his village, and surfaced only after over a week, (June 10) at Chandigarh, saying casually he had heard of the "Operation Blue Star" over the Radio, but due to the curfew imposed on the entire Panjāb and the fact that he was in a state of utmost shock, he could not move out of his village! Of

* The Panjabi monthly "Qaumi Ekta" in its various issues of 1986-87 thoroughly exposed the nefarious role of Mr. Tohra in this sordid drama. The articles were written by the editor R.S. Bhatia, once Gen. Secy of the Akāli Dal.

\+ This was told to the present writer by Gen. Dyāl himself. That prior arrangements with the Govt. had been made by them "for their security and safe surrender" is borne out by military intelligence.

course, he made vehement protests against the Government's "treachery" and "perfidy" and pledged to "fight" against it, "by all means". He was also duly arrested, like others of his ilk-Sukhjinder, Talwandi, Barnālā and others, who had been mopped up earlier and put in jail. This was also the best way to protect them from the mounting public wrath! Only Balwant Singh, the prime negotiator and businessman, neither offered himself for arrest nor was nabbed by Govt! He was kept out by the Akālis, all through the morcha days, to keep conciliation proceedings going with the Govt., in order that they leap back to power, through some kind of face-saving device and manipulation! Senseless "chivalry" on the part of some, and wild slogan - mongering to rouse passions of the innocent Sikh masses on the other, had cost the Sikhs all that they had built, assiduously, over the centuries! Perhaps, such was the Will of the Guru that the wily braggarts and religious exploiters be hoisted with their own petard!*

The Govt. was now as anxious as the Sikhs to restore the sanctity and the solemn ritual (Maryādā) of the Golden Temple, and to repair the damage to the Akāl Takhat, the Parikarmā and its other surrounding buildings and the Darshani Deori, as early as possible. The ritual was started with the head Granthi of the Temple, Giani Sāhib Singh, and the Jathedār of the Akāl Takhat, Giani Kirpāl Singh, agreeing to conduct the services. They also made statements over the Television, giving less than factual statements, over the damage suffered by the holy precincts. They had escaped to safety, on the eve of the operations, leaving the sanctity and the ritual to any laymen, who cared to continue and preserve them! Mortally afraid of their lives, they had never dared Bhindrānwālā or his gang from polluting the holy precincts, which was indeed their prerogative and duty.

Soon after the President's visit to the Temple, he made a passionate broadcast over the TV (June 17) "with a heart heavy with the deep wounds of the past happenings", and expressed his "distress" over the tragedy, but he also said, "before we are swayed by emotions, we should go into the background of these events, look at the present and reflect on the future". "All that had happened", he said, "took place, with impunity, against the teachings of the

---

* The Akāli M.Ps & MLAs resigned their seats, in protest, but on the refusal of the authorities to accept them, these worthies continued to keep their subsidised official residences in Delhi and Chandigarh, and later also collected their salaries and other allowances, for not attending the legislative bodies! Earlier, Jathedār Jagdev Singh Talwandi had refused to resign the Presidentship of the Akāli Dal, unless he was nominated by his Party to the Rājya Sabha (which was agreed to)! Tohra had agreed to vacate the Presidentship of the SGPC, after a tenure of 14 years, if similarly rewarded. But when he became an M.P., he refused to give up the other, more prestigious and lucrativee, job!

Sikh Gurus, despite repeated appeals. With the result that the Gurdwārās meant for our spiritual upliftment, passed into the hands of a few terrorists. The SGPC lost its control and it became difficult for devotees to visit their holy shrines."

While saying this, he also held responsible those in authority in Panjāb of "laxity" and "carelessness" in controlling a fast deteriorating situation. He also blamed the terrorists and those who supported them "to divide our country and violate the sanctity of our shrines", "storing arms and using them against the State, instead of coming out and offering themselves for arrest and trial". "When no other alternative was left, the Panjāb (sic) Govt. had to send in the security forces. On the appeals of the army, two Sikh leaders offered themselves for arrest, as did many others who thought they had nothing to do with that fight (!) How the terrorists took hold of the Temple complex and acquired such dangerous and foreign weapons, and what role the foreign powers had in this, is being inquired into. All this testifies to there being a deep-rooted conspiracy".+

He deprecated the call that Sikhs in Govt. positions, especially in the army, should resign. "Does religion, which means duty, sanction this?", he asked. "Once, one has taken an oath in the name of the Guru and does not abide by it, it is nothing short of cowardice and being led astray. Therefore, I am thankful to those who performed their duties honestly and loyally". He talked of the common bonds of ancestry as between Hindus and Sikhs. "It is our duty to see that our Motherland does not suffer. We are all the children of *Bhārat Mātā* (Mother India) and all religions have nurtured in its lap. It is our bounden duty to foster unity among all our countrymen, as was the call of the Gurus".

This was the hour of glory for India's worthy President, who had risen above his personal sentiments (which were undoubtedly deeply hurt) and sectarian prejudices and pulls, and speak as the upholder and guardian of India's secular Constitution. If, as was the ever-mounting pressure on him on behalf of the Sikhs especially, he would have chosen to resign, he would have not only betrayed the trust reposed in him by the nation, but also belie the whole Sikh history and tradition, to stand up against the marauders and despoilers of the sanctity of the holy temples, no matter what their faith.

However, what happened later created much misgiving and bad blood between the Prime Minister and the President.

+ Unfortunately, the "White Paper on Panjāb", issued by Govt. three days later, made no mention whatever of the foreign hand — Pākistān, China or the CIA! Why? The reasons have never been told.

A few days after the President visited the Temple, Mrs. Gandhi also paid a visit (June 12) and offered prayers at the Hari Mandir and made her offerings, in all solemnity, and in a spirit both of remorse and thanksgiving. She ordered the Akāl Takhat to be re-built and restored to its original glory, before the Temple complex could be handed over by the Army to the SGPC. The Akāli Jathedārs tried to scuttle this move, saying they would not allow any Govt. functionary to raise the Akāl Takhat structure again! This must be done, they protested, with the approval of the SGPC (most of whose members were in jail), by the Sikh *Sangats* themselves, after a due ceremony, through *Kār Sewa* (voluntary communal service), and not by hired labour! Also, that under the Gurdwārā Act, no one other than the SGPC could handle any kind of construction in the sacred premises. But, these were treacherous times, and technical niceties had to be set aside.

As it was feared (and rightly) that the Akāl Takhat will be allowed by the SGPC to remain as it is, to remind and inflame the future generations of the depredation and desecration caused to the highest seat of Sikh spiritual authority by the Govt., (they would never state its genesis, nor the terrorist role in it), Mrs. Gandhi instructed Sardar Buta Singh, then her Minister of Public Works, to undertake the task and finish it, at the earliest possible time, no matter what the cost, but built as per the old design and decoration, in every sensitive detail.

S. Buta Singh at first tried to negotiate with the High Priests and the various well-known Sikh Saints to undertake the job, but when the settlement was well in sight, the Jathedārs repudiated it. The Saints, led by Bābā Kharak Singh, insisted that unless there was unanimity of opinion among all sections, they would not participate or preside over the reconstruction of the Akāl Takhat! Politics had again overtaken a religious and pious duty!

S. Buta Singh undertook the job (July 17), supervised by Nihang Santa Singh, (see later) and carried it out with devotion, thoroughness and speed, so as to finish the work in less than three months. Anyone, who saw the reconstructed building, admired the beauty and grandeur of the new structure. No pains were spared, nor expense. Experts were invited even from abroad, and renowned engineers, architects, artisans and artists of various kinds were pressed into service, from all over India, to leave nothing to chance. The old weapons of Guru Hargobind (damaged or twisted due to fire) were sensitively repaired and rehabilitated. So also the Pālki Sāhib (the palanquin to carry the Sikh scriptures). The dome was gilded like before ((Forty kilos of gold were used, it is said). Estimates vary, but eight to ten crores (80-100 million) of rupees were spent by Govt., who had made it a point of prestige to restore what had been despoiled through the army or the terrorist action. Only, the

400-year old paintings on the walls and beneath the dome were destroyed and could not be restored. But, the sacred work was initiated with due ceremony and ritual, as sanctioned by the Sikh tradition. The prayers were led by several well-known Sikh Saints.

Violence had practically stopped in the Panjāb, but the Sikhs in the army felt highly agitated and about 1500 of them, belonging to the Panjāb Regimental Centre at Rāmgarh (in Bihār) and about 600 of the 9th Sikh Regiment at Gangānagar in Rājasthan deserted their barracks, with their arms. At Rāmgarh, the seat of the largest uprising, they killed their Commandant, Brig. S.C. Puri, and several civilians and policemen on the way to Amritsar. They were, however, overpowered and arrested. 35 of them were killed on the way. Three other small mutinies also took place, one in Jammu, the other just outside Bombay and the third at Pune. The total number involved was not more than 3,000. The vast majority of the Sikhs in the army (97%) stood loyal to the Government. (According to well-informed sources, the Sikhs still constitute between 10% to 12% of the Indian army,and 7 to 8% of the Navy and Airforce. The number of Army officers is even larger. To insinuate, as the Akālis did, that they had been reduced to two percent in the army was patently absurd and false.)

A point over which the nationalist Sikhs erred grievously, was the reviving of the now-defunct institution of "*Sarbat Khalsa* (representatives of the whole Sikh people) at Amritsar, Aug.11,'84 under the tutelage of Nihang Santa Singh,who called himself the head of the Buddha Dal(the veterans' army) and *Chalta Phirta Takhat* " (the ever - Revolving seat of spiritual authority) ! Earlier, his position as a religious leader of sorts was recognised even by the SGPC. He claimed his "spiritual descent" from Akāli Phoola Singh, the famous general of Ranjit Singh and once Jathédār of Akāl Takhat. But now he was abused as a hemp-bibbing braggart, who with his 300-strong Nihang *Fauj* (called Guru-ki-Lādli Fauj, or the Guru's very own beloved army) was allegedly being paid a lakh of rupees or more, per day, by Govt. to supervise the sacred works. His life was also threatened by the extremists. He was warned by the High priests that he may be ex-communicated. But he stood his ground firmly, and even castigated the Akāli priests and Jathedārs, saying, "where were these worthies when Bhindrānwālā had usurped their authority? Why did they not speak out or stand up against him? Anyway, who are they

* Sarbat Khālsā was first convened in 1748 at the Akāl Tākhat to combine the forces of the various Sikh Dals to fight the Afghāns, led by Ahmad Shah Abdāli. The last time, it was called was in 1764, to attack Lāhore, against the same enemy. NEVER again was this kind of gathering ever heard of.

but the paid employees of the SGPC, who have lost all moral authority to criticise anyone, anymore".

Mostly the Congress Sikhs, the Nāmdharis and the Nihangs attended this function, which anyhow made an impressive show, and revealed to the world that the Sikhs' heart was still sound. The congregation was convened to secure religious sanctions for the rebuilding of the Akāl Takhat. Why this revival of a defunct institution should have been necessary for the nationalist Sikhs, is beyond many reasonable people's comprehension. They were doing a noble job to soothe the hurt of the Sikh community and should have gone on with the job, without any fanfare or entering upon treacherous religious ground. But this also cut the ground from under the Akāli feet that no Sikh dare oppose them, on their own ground. The fact that the Jathedār of Takhat Patna Sahib, Bhai Man Singh, presided over the function was taken no notice of, by the Akālis.

And, as S. Buta Singh, an ex-Akāli M.P., (now in the Congress) was the political force behind this show, he too became an object of severe criticism. His caste — Mazhbi or Sweeper's — also became a butt of ridicule, the Mazhbis being considered the lowest of the low in the Jāt estimation! The entire Gurdwārā Reform movement, resulting in the formation of the SGPC, had started, as it has been stated before, over a Mazhbi Sikh being prevented from making an offering at the Golden Temple, in 1920! But, by now, even the Akālis had forgotten this, as also the valiant fight of the Sikh Gurus against caste. It was now politics that determined their attitude towards caste.

The Akāli-appointed Jathedārs of various Takhats (within the Panjāb) gathered together* in a *Sarbat Khālsā* at Amritsar, (Sept 2) and declared Giani Zail Singh and Sardār Buta Singh *"Tankhāhiyas"* (or Renegades) which virtually meant their ex-communication from the Sikh fraternity, unless they apologised and accepted the punishment given to them.+ The five head

* It must be noted that the heads of the two Takhats — at Patna Sāhib and Nanded Sāhib (outside the Panjāb) and opposed to the Akāli Jathedārs' doings) — were never consulted by the Akāli Jathedārs of Sri Akāl Takhat, Sri Keshgarh (Anandpur) and Sri Damdama Sahib (Bhatinda) (all in the Panjab) against all Sikh traditions. Their places were filled by the granthis of the Golden Temple and the Akāl Takhat! It may also be noted that, originally, there were only four Takhats and the fifth one at Damdama (Bhatinda) was added in 1965, by the SGPC, at the instance of Sant Fateh Singh, for political reasons!

\+ This "punishment" (or Act of Penance) generally consists of cleaning the shoes of the Sangat, in a Gurdwara, or of utensils of the community-kitchen (Guru ka langar).

priests had already declared Nihang Santa Singh a Tankhāhiya, on July 22, five days after he had started rebuilding the Akāl Takhat, a punishment he treated with contempt.

This was the worst-ever demonstration of the Akāli priests to mix religion with politics. Were the Govt. functionaries as well as the armed forces to function where the Sikh affairs were concerned, under the fiat of the Akāl Takhat? Ever under Ranjit Singh, such a stance was never adopted by the Nihang custodians of the Akāl Takhat, under Akāli Phoola Singh, who was never allowed to interfere in the matters of the state and indeed died fighting for it. The neo-Akālis did not realise how far-reaching could be the consequences for the Sikhs themselves of such a dangerous move ?*

---

recitation of the Guru's Word more often, and offering of Parsād to a temple. A small fine may also be imposed. Almost all Sikh leaders of the present century had to undergo this punishment!

* The five head-priests (Jathedārs) of the five Takhats at this time were : Giani Kirpāl Singh (Akāl Takhat), Giani Harchanan Singh Mahalon (Keshgarh, Anandpur); Giani Lakhā Singh (Damdamā Sahib), Giani Mān Singh (Patna Sahib) & Giani Joginder Singh Moni (Hazoor Sahib, Nanded). But the last two were never invited by the Panjābi office holders, and their places filled by Giani Sāhib Singh (Head Granthi, Golden Temple) and Giani Puran Singh (Head Granthi, Akāl Takhat), without any authority or precedent.

S. Buta Singh tried every nerve to involve the SGPC representatives, outside jail, like S. Parkāsh Singh Majithia, S. Atma Singh, Vice-President, S. Major Singh Uboke, Gen. Secy., S. Bhān Singh, Office-Secretary, S. Abnāshi Singh, incharge library, Dr. Baldev Singh Brār, etc. (The last two were later murdered by the militants). On 16 June 1984, the Head Priests passed a unanimous resolution, entrusting the Kār Sewā to Sant Harbans Singh of Delhi and Sant Karnail Singh. Both, however, backed out (See later). The Head Priests were denounced by the SGPC representatives as being "unauthorised" to take any such decision. The SGPC representatives assured S. Buta Singh that they would permit the 85-year Sant Baba Kharak Singh of Amritsar or some other Saints, approved by them, to start the Kār Sewā. But after making promises, they all backed out, except for S. Atmā Singh, and no resolution could be passed by the SGPC! Baba Harbans Singh, a Sikh Saint, highly revered for his piety and service of the various historic Gurdwaras, who was initially named by Sant Baba Kharak Singh to do the job, on account of his own old age, also later backed out, saying "unless the military was withdrawn from Panjāb, no Kār Sewā could be held. Also, they all needed the approval of the SGPC!" Sant Baba Narain Singh, Kaleranwale, and four other highly-respected Sikh divines, however, led the prayers before the reconstruction of the Akāl Takhat was taken in hand. But, the idea of the Akālis was to make a political capital out of it, rather than restore the Takhat to its original glory. It may be mentioned, however, that the Head Priests of the three Takhats in Panjāb and the two Granthis, above-mentioned,

The Jathedārs also announced that they would lead a *Shahidi Jathā* (Martyrs' band) on Oct. 1, to rescue their Gurdwārās from the control of the army. Five days before this (Sept 25), however, the Govt. handed over the Temple management, including the newly-built Akāl Takhat, to the SGPC representatives. The "Singh Sāhibān" (as the five Takhat Jathedārs are called) washed the whole Parikarmā (now reconstructed) and the renovated Akāl Takhat, with milk, and accepted these and other structures, after solemn prayers, in a spirit of thanksgiving. Before the handing over, the President of India spoke to a select Sikh gathering in front of the Akāl Takhat and made a moving speech of "forget and forgive". "It is not the victory of anyone. It is the defeat and the victory of all of us ", he said. He prayed for "sincere forgiveness of the Gurus for the unfortunate incidents of the past," though the President's spokesmen later clarified that by these words, he had not apologised to the High Priests, he only asked for forgiveness for "everyone" involved in the tragedy from the Gurus!

The President had also, through his secret emissaries, worked overtime to convince the Jathedārs that he was never "consulted" over the military operations, that he was a "constitutional" head, and it was the Home Ministry, whose officials acted and signed in his name and behalf! For this and "some other undefined reasons," the Jathedārs let the President off their hook, and excused him the same day (Sep. 25), as the Temple was handed over to them. But they never forgave S. Buta Singh, or Nihang Santa Singh. The Prime Minister, it appears, did not like the President to climb down before the Sikh religious ministers, so abjectly, and also to isolate Buta Singh especially, to suffer the ignonimity of ex-communication alone, along with Santa Singh. The distance between them started growing, and their relations were never the same again. The man who on the eve of his Presidency had said, "I'd even sweep the floor for Mrs. Gandhi", had now left Mrs. Gandhi to fend for herself before the Sikhs! The Gyaniji had rubbed his own guilt in this whole drama off his conscience!

Sikhs all over the world held huge protest-demonstrations, many a time attacking the Indian Embassies and Consulates. The BBC, and the British and American newspapers gave wide publicity to the Sikh anger. Even Dr. J. S. Chauhān, head of the "Khālistān Council", was allowed to broadcast over the British Radio (channel 4) that "Mrs Gandhi's end was now near, and that whosoever killed her would be rewarded by the British Sikhs with a lakh and a half pounds sterling!" A militant Sikh organisation of the West was formed

were later dismissed unceremoniously by a Sarbat Khālsā convened by the militants on Jan 26, 1986, and the reconstructed Akāl Takhat demolished to be rebuilt (It is still under construction after 2 years (1988).

on 31 July, 1984, at New York, with Mr. Didār Singh Bains of Yuba City, a multi-millionaire farmer, as President, and Maj. Gen. G. S. Bhullar, its General Secretary. Mr. Gangā Singh Dhillon became its Executive member, though Chauhān was scrupulously kept out. They all talked of violence and more violence against the Indian state -- and of Khālistān. Efforts were made to bring the Sikh question also before the United Nations, though these did not succeed.

The Panjāb newspapers and correspondents were under strict censorship. No foreigner was allowed to visit the Panjāb. So, rumours flew around that Sikh youths were being massacred by Govt. in a general genocide. Nothing was farther from the truth. The entire Indian Press and public opinion, including the Parliament and the Opposition parties, supported by and large the Govt. action.

In such a surcharged atmosphere, however, two of the most trusted Sikh body-guards of Mrs. Gandhi assassinated her, on the morning of Oct. 31, 1984, at her official residence in New Delhi. The whole country was plunged into a mood of deep shock and anger over this gruesome tragedy. That two of her own most trusted bodyguards -- Satwant Singh and Beant Singh -- should have committed this crime, heightened the trauma of the people at large.*

She was, besides bringing honour to the country in the councils of the world, had transformed the country's economy. It is during her regime that the Green revolution swept through the Panjāb. It was she who, in the teeth of the Hindu Opposition in the Panjāb,and in the face of her illustrious father's total rejection of the very concept, had brought a Panjābi-speaking State, with Sikh majority, into being. Her 15-point programme for the minorities' uplift was her signal contribution to bring security and self-confidence to the Indian minorities. She loved and respected the Sikhs for their valour, integrity and total loyalty to the nation. To be butchered at the hands of two of them, made the vast number of her supporters all over the country as well as the Hindu masses generally, go berserk.

---

* It is said, a few days before, the Govt's intelligence had warned that Beant Singh looked suspect in their eyes and should be removed from guard-duty. When the file was presented to Mrs. Gandhi, she refused to do so, saying:– "What kind of secularism shall we defend in our country, if a Sikh, merely on suspicion, is removed from a sensitive post?" She trusted Beant implicitly, though Mr. Rajiv Gandhi had become suspicious of his attitude and movements and told Mrs. Gandhi so. Beant Singh's ex-nurse wife, and once a Christian now called Bimal Kaur Khalsa, entered politics, fought election to the Panjāb Assembly (1985), but lost with a small margin.

One need not comment on the confusion and cowardice shown by the huge commando force, specially maintained at the Prime Minister's residence to guard her person. As bullets were successively being pumped into her slender body, unprotected by armour, they are said to have scattered, hélter skelter, in all directions, killing in the process Beant Singh and injuring Satwant, the two persons whose evidence was vital for any prosecution later on! And where did her other "dedicated" staff, which shadowed her all through her waking hours, disappear at this crucial moment rather than jump between her and the sizzling bullets, no one would ever know. Even the Ambulance driver was missing and the Prime Minister of the country was carried, almost dead, and profusely bleeding, to a Govt. hospital, in a taxi, without any warning, to find the doctors missing! And why were the findings of a high-powered Commission under Justice Thakkar appointed later by the Govt. to inquire into this most heinous tragedy, not made public, also remains a mystery!

The President of India was on a visit abroad. Mrs. Gandhi's only surviving son and heir, 40-year old, Rajiv Gandhi, was in West Bengāl. (Sanjay Gandhi, her other and politically more active son, had died in a plane-crash in 1980). Both came rushing the same evening. The President went straight from the airport to pay his last homage to his mentor and leader, Indira Gandhi, lying dead at the Medical Institute in New Delhi. But, such was the mob fury that his car was stoned! For the next five days, Sikh life was secure no where -- on the roads, in their homes, shops, temples, -- railway trains anywhere.

Atleast three thousand Sikhs (2733, according to official estimates) were butchered in most heinous circumstances, burnt alive or cut into pieces, tortured and occasionally their women gang-raped, their property looted or burnt. -- in New Delhi, Kānpur, Bukāro, even Coimbatore in South India. The most massacres, however, occurred in New Delhi, where the police looked on helplessly, and nothing worked.

Peace was, however, restored within four days. The Delhi Governor, Mr. P. G. Gavai, IAS(Retd), was sacked and replaced by the then Home Secretary, Mr. M. M. Wali. He did an excellent job, encouraged by the new Prime Minister, Rajiv Gandhi, who had been sworn in by the President the same day (Oct. 31). The P. M. personally toured the riot-affected areas, in the dead of night, even while his mother's body lay, dead and cold, waiting to be cremated. He appealed to the people, in the name of his dead mother, to desist from violence "which will disgrace and shame our country and help only its enemies". Liberal compensations were paid for losses, widows offered new flats, orphans given freeships in schools. But not many killers were arrested or prosecuted, and this continued to be a running sore with the Sikh community. The Delhi Gudwārā Committee offered modest pensions to about 1200 widows. State Governments, led by the Govt. of Goa (which contributed a million rupees) and philanthropists, including many Hindus, made large contributions to rehabilitate the refugees. The civil liberties' Unions took up their cause vociferously, in all conceivable forums of the nation. But, the Sikhs outside the Panjāb were shaken to their roots. For the first time in the history of free India, they had become vulnerable, and if not fear, then anxiety and uncertainty about their future filled their minds and hearts (and still does). A Commission appointed under Justice Mishra of the Supreme Court called these riots "one of the blackest spots of free India's history". "The identification of every Sikh with the two assassins is an unpardonable mistake," Mishra said, and added:- "If the assassins instead of being Sikhs were Hindus, would our countrymen have behaved the same way? If not, there was no justification for the riots."

New elections were soon held, in December, 1984. And Rajiv Gandhi came out victorious, with a staggering majority for his Congress (I) Party in Parliament, as well as the Legislative Assemblies of the States. Only elections to the Panjāb were withheld, for the time being.

The new Prime Minister had set Panjāb as number one item on his agenda. He released, early in 1985, most of the top Akāli leaders, then in jail, against whom the charge of waging war against the State was also withdrawn. These included Tohrā, Longowāl, Bādal, Barnālā and a few other top-notchers.

Secret negotiations were carried on, through the newly-appointed Governor, Arjun Singh, former Chief Minister of Madhya Pradesh, and a very suave, diplomatic and understanding negotiator. Alongside of it, an Anti-Terrorist Bill was rushed through Parliament (May 20, 1985) to meet the growing violence by more stringent measures and giving vast powers to the police. In Delhi (May 10 and 11), 20 bomb blasts killed 45 people at the hands of the terrorists. They also continued to hit targets of their choice in the capital city, as well as elsewhere, though no conflagration occurred as a result of these mishaps. The idea was to scuttle any compromise with the Govt. This happened many times before and after as well. No sooner a settlement was in the offing, killings of Hindus somewhere or the other would postpone or scuttle it. On June 11, 1985, an Air-India plane on its flight from Canada to Bombay exploded in mid-air, near Ireland, and all the 329 passengers, including the Sikh co-pilot and several Sikh passengers and an eminent Indian Scientist, Nayudama, were killed. This was also blamed on them.

However, on July 24, 1985, the Rajiv-Longowāl Accord was signed to the great relief and joy of the whole nation. It was sprung on the people, including the President of India and the Sikh Ministers at the Centre, as a complete surprise, as none of the Sikh Congress leaders were taken into confidence and strictest secrecy was maintained throughout.

Soon thereafter, elections to the Panjāb Assembly were announced. But, meantime, another gruesome tragedy overtook the Panjāb. About a month later on Aug. 20, Sant Longowāl was shot dead at a large public meeting, which he was addressing in his native village. This sent shock-waves throughout the country, but the people of the Panjāb, Sikhs particularly, kept their cool and no repercussions took place.

Acute differences surfaced among the Akālis on the eve of elections. Bādal and Tohrā had not been consulted at any stage, before arriving at a settlement. Longowāl, Barnālā and Balwant Singh alone took part in the negotiations with the Governor and only Longowāl, in the presence of the other two, signed the Accord with the Prime Minister. Longowāl tried to placate Bādal and on the morning of his murder, it seemed, Bādal had fallen in. But, later, it turned out to be a vain hope.

The Akālis won a resounding victory — 73 seats out of 117, and formed a Ministry under Sardar Surjit Singh Barnālā, a soft-spoken lawyer from Sangrur, and once a Central Minister during the Janata regime. But Bādal was

RAJIV-LONGOWAL ACCORD

JULY 24, 1985

Memorandum of Settlement

Following is the text of the memorandum of settlement.

1. Compensation to innocent persons killed.

1.1 Along with *ex gratia* payment to those innocent killed in agitation or any action after 1-8-1982 compensation for property damaged will also be paid.

2. Army recruitment.

2.1 All citizens of the country have the right to enroll in the army and merit will remain in the criterion for selection.

3. Enquiry into November incidents.

3.1 The jurisdiction of Mr. Justice Ranganath Mishra Commission enquiring into the November riots of Delhi would be extended to cover the disturbances at Bokaro and Kanpur also.

4. Rehabilitation of those discharged from the army.

4.1 For all those discharged, efforts will be made to rehabilitate and provide gainful employment.

5. All India Gurdwara Act.

5.1 The Government of India agrees to consider the formulation of an all India gurudwara bill. Legislation will be brought forward for this purpose in consultation with Shiromani Akali Dal, others concerned and after fulfilling all relevant constitutional requirements.

6. Disposal of pending cases.

6.1 The notifications applying the Armed Forces Special Powers Act to Punjab will be withdrawn.

Existing special courts will try only cases relating to the following types of offences (a) Waging war (b) Hijacking.

6.2 All other cases will be transferred to ordinary courts and enabling legislation if needed will be brought forward in this session of Parliament.

7. Territorial claims.

7.1 The capital project area of Chandigarh will go to Punjab. Some adjoining areas which were previously part of Hindi or the Punjabi regions were included in the Union Territory. With the capital region going to Punjab the areas which were added to the Union Territory from the Punjabi region of the erstwhile state of Punjab will be transferred to Punjab and those from Hindi region to Haryana. The entire Sukhna lake will be kept as part of the Chandigarh and will thus go to Punjab.

7.2 It had always been maintained by Mrs. Indira Gandhi that when Chandigarh is to go to Punjab some Hindi-speaking territories in Punjab will go to Haryana. A commission will be constituted to determine the specific Hindi-speaking areas of Punjab which should go to Haryana, in lieu of Chandigarh.

The principle of contiguity and linguistic affinity with a village as a unit will be the basis of such determination. The Commission will be required to give its findings by 21st December, 1985, and these will be binding on both sides. The work of the commission will be limited to this aspect and will be distinct from the general boundary claims which the other commission referred to in para 7.4 will handle.

7.3 The actual transfer of Chandigarh to Punjab and areas in lieu thereof to Haryana will take place simultaneously on 26th January, 1986.

7.4 There are other claims and counter-claims for requirement of the existing Punjab-Haryana boundaries. The government will appoint another commission to consider these matters and give findings. Such findings will be binding on the concerned states. The terms of reference will be based on a village as a unit, linguistic affinity and contiguity.

8. Centre-State relations.

8.1 Shiromani Akali Dal states that the Anandpur Sahib resolution is entirely within the framework of the Indian Constitution, that it attempts to define the concept of Centre-State relations in a manner which may bring out the true federal characteristics of our unitary Constitution, and that the purpose of the resolution is to provide greater autonomy to the state with a view to strengthening the unity and integrity of the country, since unity in diversity forms the corner-stone of our national entity.

8.2 In view of the above, the Anandpur Sahib resolution insofar as it deals with Centre-State relations, stands referred to the Sarkaria Commission.

9. Sharing of river waters.

9.1 The farmers of Punjab, Haryana and Rajasthan will continue to get water not less than what they are using from the Ravi-Beas system as on 1-7-1985. Waters used for consumptive purposes will also remain uneffected. Quantum of usage claimed shall be verified by the tribunal referred to in para 9.2 below.

9.2 The claims of Punjab and Haryana regarding the shares in their remaining waters will be referred for adjudication to a tribunal to be presided over by a Supreme Court judge. The decision of this tribunal will be rendered within six months and would be binding on both parties. All legal and constitutional steps required in this respect be taken expeditiously.

9.3 The construction of the SYL canal shall continue. The canal shall be completed by 15th August, 1986.

10. Representation of minorities.

10.1Existing instructions regarding protection of interests of minorities will be recirculated to the state chief ministers (PM will write to all chief Ministers).

11. Promotion of Punjabi Language.

11.1 The Central Government may take some steps for the promotion of the Punjabi language.

This settlement brings to an end a period of confrontation and ushers in an era of amity, goodwill and co-operation, which will promote and strengthen the unity and integrity of India.

totally ignored and not accommodated, as his stature demanded, even as a Deputy Chief Minister, as Balwant Singh, an ally of Barnālā and now number two in the Cabinet, stood firmly in the way. This turned out to be fatal for the Party, which soon broke up into two. 28 legislators walked out of the Party over the issue of Barnālā having sent the police again to the Golden Temple (April 30, 1986)* to rescue it from the terrorists, who had once again taken positions there, passed resolutions favouring Khālistān (April 29), and murders, outside, started mounting. (Barnālā was later declared "Tankhāhiya" and ex-communicated by Rāgi Darshan Singh, the new "acting" Jathēdār of the Akāl Takhat). The respite between the period of Accord (July 20, 1985 and Jan. 26, 1986, when Chandigarh had to be transferred to Panjab and wasn't) was now ended. The rift in the legislative Party also caused a cleavage in the Akāli Dal and a new Akāli Party, the United Akāli Dal, came into being, with Bābā Joginder Singh, father of Bhindrānwālā, as acting President, and Mr. Simranjit Singh Mānn, then in jail, who had resigned his high rank in the Indian Police Service after "Operation Blue Star", as the permanent President. The militant All-India Sikh Students' Federation was also split into two — Gurjit and Manjit factions! There was now a single-point programme of the new Akāli Dal :– "Turn Barnālā out of the party and Govt., and we shall settle, not otherwise". The wheel had come full circle.

Mr. Barnālā strived his every nerve to curb terrorism, but couldn't. His new Police Chief, Mr. Julius Ribeiro,also left nothing to chance and finished, as he claimed, about half of the hard-core terrorists, numbering, according to him, only about one hundred or so, but the ferocity of attacks on civilians, buses, village headmen, Congressmen and Communists, and indeed whosoever the terrorists imagined stood in their way, or criticised them, or created a public agitation of awareness against their activities was gunned down. Even Ribeiro was attacked in his official residence at Jullundur, and hardly escaped being killed, though both he and his wife were grievously hurt. Ribeiro was the person who had saved Sikh lives after Mrs. Gandhi's assassination, throughout Maharashtra, where he was then the D.G. of Police! Not one life was lost.

There was no shortage of sophisticated arms, nor money nor training. Pakistān provided all of these and even provided fire-cover in the border areas, where killings were the most frequent and persistent. India protested, often

---

* This was done, as a sequel to the declaration of Khālistān by the Sarbat Khālsā, convened by the militants, on April 29. A similar resolution was passed by them on Jan 26, 1986, from which date the militants had taken control of the Temple complex.

enough, but Pākistān always denied the charge. Proofs were given, but taken no notice of.

As has been said, a Sarbat Khālsā" was convened by the militants on Jan 26, 1986 at the Akāl Takhat, and a resolution for "Khālistān" passed. It was repeated on April 29, by the Panthic Committee of five militants formed earlier on Jan 26.* The ten-page resolution said its capital would be Delhi and its boundaries announced "later". (In 1988, the whole of India, minus Kashmir, was declared to be the territory of Khālistān) ! However, it was stated that though state religion would be Sikhism, non-Sikhs will have equality of status and opportunity!. The militants took over the control of all historic Gurdwaras in Panjāb from Jan. 26, 1986.

Abroad particularly in the UK, USA and Canada, militants took over almost all the Gurdwārās, collected enormous funds, sent large amounts, secretly, to the militant organisations back home, and appropriated the rest, often-times, for their personal use! Whosoever opposed them openly was either threatened into silence, or murdered. Private military training schools were already there in the USA, and the Sikh extremists took training in Guerilla warfare, at heavy fees. Killer-gangs started prowling for their quarry all over. Rājiv Gandhi had become the prime target all over Western Europe and north America, and several Sikhs were charged with conspiracy to assassinate him, and, after trial, four of them were sentenced to long years of imprisonment in America. But, the Panjāb killers were either given refugee status abroad, or not repatriated, when demanded by the Government of India. The Govt. of India alerted the Govts. particularly of the U.K., Canada and the U.S.A., and threatened to cool off relations, if Indian interests abroad were not duly protected, or export of terrorism from these countries to Panjāb was not halted.

At first, these Govts pleaded their inability, quoting their own democratic laws and procedures, but ultimately started falling in line, fearing a strong commercial backlash in a fast-developing India. The moderate nationalist Sikhs also gradually started asserting themselves more vociferously, and things came to near normal in 1988. The only demands now voiced all over were : (i) the implementation of the Rajiv-Longowāl Accord; (ii) Release or trial of all Sikh prisoners & full rehabilitation of Sikh deserters from the army and (iii) trial of those guilty of violence against Sikhs in 1984, in Delhi and elsewhere.

---

* The five-member Committee consisted of Gurbachan Singh Manochhal, Wasan Singh Zaffarwāl, Dhannā Singh, Gurdev Singh and Aroor Singh. They were all militants. Their names went on changing.

One of the leaders of a killer-gang in Panjab, wanted by the police in India and now a citizen of Canada is said to be worth over a million dollars in property. He declared to a Canadian Court in 1986 that he was unemployed and lived on Govt. doles!

The Govt., it seemed, was sympathetic to these demands, but somehow dragged its feet now for this, nor for that political compulsion. However, mercy was shown to about 2400 out of 2700 deserters from the army and they were duly rehabilitated, or taken back into service. Some Sikh prisoners were released from the Jodhpur Jail, early in 1988, but over 300 still languish there, after over four years, without trial! This seems totally unfair, according to all democratic norms. They should have been either tried or released. Against all of them is a single charge : waging war against the State.

A Commission under Justice Rangānāth Misra was appointed to go into the Nov 1984 anti-Sikh riots in Delhi and elsewhere. He adjudicated that these were not organised, but spontaneous, although he named 18 persons, some of them known Congressmen of Delhi, as guilty, and asked for their prosecution which was not done. He also asked for the appointment of two high-powered Committees by Govt. to go further into the sworn charges against over 2000 persons,but this too was not pursued seriously,though as has been said before, much Govt. effort went into the relief and rehabilitation of the victims or their dependents. "This was one of the darkest tragedies of the free India, " The Commission commented and was in no way justified, whatever the provocation!

On Aug. 10, 1986, a little over one year after his retirement, Gen. A.S. Vaidya, who was the C-IN-C at the time of "Operation Blue Star" was gunned down at far off Pune, in an open street, in broad daylight, in spite of the heavy security provided to him.

Mr. Barnālā was lauded and boosted on all hands, during his tenure as Chief Minister. Though his Party was reduced to a minority, due to their split, he was supported by the Congress to see that he was not voted out. In Feb. 1987, the President of India, in his address to Parliament, paid him a handsome compliment — an unusual and unprecedented step — for "exemplary courage" in upholding the values of secularism. The Prime Minister also commended his fight both against extremism and for standing upto the religious authorities in Amritsar, in fighting terrorism. He had appointed over 100 Sikh ex-soldiers to guard the Parikarmaā of the Golden Temple, so that the holy complex never again became the meeting point of the terrorists. According to him, he had given employment to over 10,000 youngmen, during his brief tenure. He had, as has been said, sent in the police force to drive the terrorists out of the sacred spot on April 30, 1986 which caused a split in his Party, led by Bādal, Sukhjinder and Capt. Amrinder Singh who became the leader of the new break-away legislature group. Surprisingly, Mr. Tohrā, while still in jail, also got elected again, in Nov. 1986, as President of the SGPC, in the teeth of Barnālā's opposition, as the

Govt. refused to influence the Committee's 15 members from outside the Panjāb in his favour. They all cast their votes for Tohrā!

Another *Sarbat Khālsā* was called (Jan 26, 1987) by the militant leader, Gurdev Singh, who had by now appointed himself head of the Akāl Takhat. A Panthic Committee of five which had been constituted by the extremists* earlier, on Jan 26, 1986 (when the Sarbat Khālsā was first convened by them) was reconstituted. The Convention dismissed the earlier SGPC- appointed Jathedārs and nominated people of their own persuasion and choice as heads of the Akāl Takhat, the Golden Temple and other historic Gurdwārās. Most of them were in jail. But ad-hoc acting functionaries were also nominated by them. Akāli Ministers were asked to resign forthwith. A resolution favouring "Khālistan" was passed again. In a gathering of about 25000 to 30000 Sikhs, the national flag was burnt and a Khālistāni flag hoisted.** The resurrection of a defunct institution – the Sarbat Khālsā -- by the Congress Sikhs had now boomeranged on them!

A renowned Sikh musician, Prof. Darshan Singh, who was highly critical of the Govt., was made the Acting head of the Akāl Takhat, by *Sarbat Khālsā* and Bhāi Jasbir Singh Rodē, then in Jail, who had fled to Dubai after making fiery speeches in Pākistān, in defence of Khālistān, and being allegedly involved in a plane-hijacking, as the permanent head! He also happened to be the nephew of Bhindrānwālā. Others appointed to these high seats of spiritual authority belonged also to a similar militant and secessionist category. The SGPC was "dissolved", through a Gurmattā (resolution), and Tohra and Bādal were virtually declared *Tankhahiyās* (without naming them) for having betrayed the Panthic interests !+

An unsuccessful attempt was also made on the life of the new Prime Minister on Oct.2, by a Sikh at Rāj Ghāt, in New Delhi, where he had gone to pay homage to the memory of Mahātmā Gāndhi on his birthday.

Meantime, the extremists, led by Tohra, had demolished the newly-constructed building of the Akāl Takhat and started re-erecting it, through

* It consisted of Wāsan Singh Zafarwāl, Gurbachan Singh Manochhal, Gurdev Singh, Ude Singh and Subeg Singh, though these names continued to change often enough and many a time kept secret, most of them living in Pākistān and coming and going from and to India, as the opportunity dictated. They were all well-known militants.

** "Times of India", Jan. 28, 1987.

\+ "The Sikh high priests were directed to summon the so-called 'Sikh leadership" so that they could be punished with ex-communication for the desecration of the Sikh religious places." (ibid)

* The assailant, a middle-aged Sikh, Karamjit Singh, later told the Delhi Court (where he is still under trial) that he had tried to kill the P.M.," as a revenge for a dear friend of his having been murdered during the Nov 1984 riots in Delhi. (The Tribune, July 27, 1988)

Kār Sewā . Vast funds were collected for the purpose and part of it even misappropriated by the militants to buy arms, or by other Akālis to line their own pockets. The building is not yet complete, though over two years have passed. But then, politics in India knows little morality or cares for public funds or even public sentiments!

Prof. Darshan Singh declared Mr. Barnālā a Tankhāhiyā (Feb. 9, 1987), on his refusal to join the United Akāli Dal, as enjoined by the Acting Chief of the Takhat. Virulent propaganda was launched against him. But, the revered Rāgi had soon to quit the post, in disgust, when too much was demanded of him by the Panthic Committee, including his public commitment to Khālistān ! Now, he knew where he had landed, and soon quit his post, to seek the refuge of his home, near Chandigarh!*

As violence escalated, Barnālā's minority Govt. could no longer be supported by the Congress. Moreover;corruption had escalated so much at all levels, particularly the ministerial level, that people were full of disgust.

---

* When asked if he would again like to accept that post, if offered by the SGPC, he said, "The sanctity of religious places has been terribly undermined by those very persons who were supposed to uphold the dignity and high traditions of the Panth. Such persons were nothing but pure and simple self-seekers." (Hindustan Times, July 14, 1988). Later, when Bhai Jasbir Singh Rodē was released, early in 1988, and was installed the Jathedār of the Akāl Takhat, (March 9), he was supported by Govt. to negotiate peace with their unofficial emissary, Muni Sushil Kumar, respected head of a Jain sect in Delhi. Rodē was accepted by the Panthic Committee, whose nominee he was and even approved of by the SGPC, at a special meting (March 9). At first, he talked of "Puran Azādi" (complete independence) "in religious and social matters", but when he started saying "The Sikhs could settle within the framework of the Constitution of India", he was dubbed by the Panthic Committee as a "Sarkāri Jathedār" (or a Govt. agent)! To his relief, he was arrested again, on other charges (May 12), and the SGPC also removed him, and appointed another — their own — Jathedār Harcharan Singh of Delhi, a businessman and a protege of Badāl, though he was still in jail (May 30). An acting head was also appointed, thus making the head of the Akāl Takhat a shuttle-cock! Normally, the Jathedārs of the Takhats are appointed for life, unless incapacitated by illness or charged with moral turpitude. Their choice is unanimous by the SGPC, and their salaries are never advertised, but offered, in sealed envelopes, as *bheta* (offering), not as wages. But, recent events have made them helpless pawns in the Akāli or militants' race for power. Rode speaking to "Statesman", in an interview (July 19, 1988) in the Amritsar Central jail, blamed both the UAD and the Central Govt. for his present fate, but also said :– "he was trying and wanted the militants to settle with the Govt. and get at least as much as the Govt. was willing to give". He wanted a Kashmir-type settlement, though thought that the struggle for Khālistān could also continue! He agreed that at the time of operation "Black Thunder" (May 12-18), "a large number of criminals and extortionists were indulging in all sorts of crimes, including murder". Later, Darshan Singh Ragi again was appointed Jathedar, by SGPC.

Mr. Barnālā was, therefore, unceremoniously dismissed (May 11, 1987), the State again placed under the President's rule, with Mr. S.S. Ray, former Union Minister and once Chief Minister of West Bengal, who was responsible for tackling successfully the Naxalite rebellion in his State, as Governor (April 1, 1986).

During the last eight years, (1980-88), the Punjāb had had numerous Governors, some of them like Mr. B.A. Pāndé, former Cabinet Secretary and able Administrator, leaving in disgust, or others transferred as soon as they were appointed — former Union Minister, Mr. Chenna Reddy, former C.M. of Andhra Pradesh, Mr. A.P. Sharma, former Union Minister and Labour Leader, Mr. K.T. Satārāwālā, former Secretary with the Central Govt. and later transferred as Ambassador after a year, Nawāb Mohammad Amin Khān, ex-Nawāb of Lohāru, Mr. Arjun Singh, Mr. S.D. Sharma, former Central Minister and now our Vice-President. Some of them were very reluctant to come or stay for long, but were persuaded to do so. But, Mr. Ray has devoted all his sympathies and his energies to the onerous task that lies ahead of him and is yet not finished.

Mr. Arjun Singh had taken his job first reluctantly, but then very seriously, and had created a good niche for himself for getting the Rajiv-Longowāl accord signed. But, immediately after the Panjāb elections, he was taken to the Centre for Party work and later inducted into the Union Cabinet, to leave again to become the Chief Minister of Madhya Pradesh!

The first-ever Sikh President of India,+ Giani Zail Singh, retired as President of India, on July 25, 1987, in the midst of a raging controversy. He claimed (through a letter to the P.M., which somehow leaked out to the Press) that he had been totally ignored by the young Prime Minister, never imparted vital information even when he asked for it, and even the courtesy of the Prime Minister calling on him or briefing him on the matters of State, every week, had been honoured more in its breach. It was feared that he might dismiss the Prime Minister (a wholly unconstitutional idea, when the P.M. had a majority in the Lok Sabha) "for not upholding the Constitution", or allow some private individuals to prosecute him on charges of alleged "corruption", over some defence equipment deals. But, ultimately, wiser counsels prevailed, and the show-down was averted. But, it left a trail of extreme bitterness behind. Why was Giani Zail Singh so bitter, and why was he attacked even in Parliament by Congressmen that he was harbouring terrorists, have never been explained. Had it anything to do with the President

+ It was during Mrs. Gandhi's regime (1966-1984) that two Muslims and one Sikh became the President of India, a Sikh became Speaker of Parliament twice. or held the positions of Home Minister, Defence Minister, External Affairs Minister etc. One Sikh has always been Governer of a State. Twice, a Sikh headed the Air Force

seeking too much to meddle in Panjāb affairs, or for apologising to the Sikh head priests? No one knows.*

Mr. Barnālā blamed the non-implementation of the Accord as one of the main factors for his failure to contain violence. The people of the Panjāb also became sullen and suspicious, as one Commission after another gave awards on Chandigarh as well as on River waters, which were unacceptable to any Party in the Panjāb. The Akālis charged that the Central Government was not sincere. The Government charged that it is the Akālis who had asked for the Commissions, under Supreme Court judges, to be appointed for adjudication on disputed issues, and had agreed to accept their awards as "binding on both parties". Why were they not accepting them now?

Chandigarh is a Punjabi town. It was built for the new Panjāb as its capital. It should have been transferred to the Panjāb, without any compensation, as was Bombay to Maharashtra & Madrās to Tāmil Nadu. But it was not, & made a bone of contention between Panjāb & Haryana. According to the new Accord, a Commission had to be appointed to adjudicate on which contiguous, Hindi-speaking areas, (with village as unit) be transferred to Haryana, in lieu thereof, & Chandigarh transferred to Panjāb on Jan. 26, 1986.

According to one Commission, under Justice K.K. Mathew, no Hindi areas in Panjāb could be demarcated by him, except for Abohar & Fazilka, but these were not contiguous to Haryana! So, another Commission under Justice E.S. Venkataramiah, appointed on April 2, 1986, determined that some

---

* It was seriously suggested by an influential section of the Press, and some Govt. sympathisers, that the Government consider seriously the President being impeached, over allegedly divulging state secrets, and on other unspecified counts, but the Govt. held its hand. It had no majority in the Upper House and 2/3rd majority was necessary, in both Houses of Parliament, to carry such a resolution through. But more than that, they wanted first to try every other avenue to both satisfy and warn the President of the dire consequences, if he took any unconstitutional step. He was told in clear terms that he couldn't do "anything", except on the advice of his Cabinet. Happily, some friendly mediators defused the crisis, which threatened to continue right upto the last day of his tenure (July 25, 1987). Several opposition Parties, including some members of the ruling Party, tried defections in the Congress Parliamentary Party, and to renominate the President for a second-term election, if the latter would dismiss the Prime Minister, but the move failed. To soothe his sentiments, a Minister, K.K. Tiwāri, who had spoken against the President in Parliament, was dismissed by the Prime Minister. (A year later, he was rehabilitated!) However, some in the press also even warned the President not to forget that he was very vulnerable as a Sikh, in the context of the prevailing Panjāb situation! If so, why was he made the President in the first instance?

70,000 acres of land, adjascent to Haryānā, should be given by Panjāb to its neighbour, in lieu of Chandigarh, (though he too couldn't identify them, except for 45,000 acres of 30 Hindi-speaking villages.) But this acreage he found "inadequate", & so he said, 25000 more of Panjābi-speaking acres must also be awarded to Haryānā! However, he could not identify any such contiguous area. For this, another Commission, under Justice D.A. Desai, was appointed on June 20, 1986 to determine the specific areas, within 24 hours! He, however, threw up his hands in despair!

The Akālis, however, protested they could offer only 45000 acres of the Hindi-speaking contiguous area, but not the rest, as it was Panjābi-speaking! They refused to build a capital elsewhere, as at Ranjitgarh, for which they could demand a staggering sum of over Rs. 300 to 400 crores from the Central Govt., as Haryana was promised. Why was none of the alternatives acceptable to the Akālis, passes one's wits. Also, why the Govt. could not persuade Haryana to accept money from the Panjāb Govt., in lieu of 25000 extra acres, if the full quota of 70,000 acres had to be transferred to Haryānā, anyhow.

So also in the case of the re-distribution of the waters of the Panjāb rivers, Justice Erādi was appointed, whose decisions (May 1987) were too wide of the mark, and beyond his terms of reference, according to the Akālis, which they could not accept! A little more give-and-take between the two neighbouring states could, however, resolve the issue for the time being, or the issue could be kept pending, till more propitious times, as the Panjāb was authorised, till a new settlement was arrived at, to draw the quantity of waters, as they were doing at present.

Through better management and brick-lining of the mud-canals, which have water-logged a good part of Panjāb's territory, existing waters could be better harnessed. The long-awaited Thein Dam, with a huge capacity for irrigation and for generating more power, is now vigorously being implemented, and some heavy industry, like the 300-crore rail coach factory at Kapurthala, has started functioning. More processing industries are in the pipeline, and over a dozen new spinning and sugar mills have come up during the last two years in the Panjāb. By diversifying agriculture so as to produce more of oil-seeds, fruits and vegetables, rather than get stuck with wheat and rice, may revolutionise Panjāb's agricultural economy. Already, a buffalow or two to each landless family is creating a milk revolution on the countryside. But, most of the best-quality rice is not allowed to be exported, nor the processing of the ever-increasing yield of cotton, fruits and vegetables allowed. "Give us more jobs", says the Panjāb Governor, "and we shall finish terrorism". He may be very right.

However, the militants have not been silenced, nor has Pākistān desisted from arming and training them or giving them sanctuary. Killings continue unabated, every day, without respite, though the SGPC for once has apologised to the community for their sordid deeds — and their helplessness!

A very heartening event, however, was the surrounding of the Golden Temple by the Panjāb Police, under its new Director General, Mr. K.P.S. Gill, a Sikh, on May 12 to 18, 1988 and flushing out about 150 terrorists, many of them hardcore, alongwith their arms, by starving them to exasperation.* This is known as "Operation Black Thunder". The entire Sikh community welcomed it, and even cooperated in surrendering the buildings, surrounding the Temple, on due compensation, so that the terrorists do not find any refuge therein hereafter!

Another very welcome sign of the Panjāb scene is that in none of the 12,200 villages of the Punjāb, where the Sikhs are in a majority, has a single Hindu-Sikh riot occurred, nor in any of the over five score of Panjābi towns, big and small, where the Hindus predominate.** The agricultural output has been increasing, year by year, and Panjāb capita income is still the highest. Panjāb continues to provide 60 to 65 per cent of wheat and as much of rice to the Central Pool, each year.

Only if peace returns and violence is ended, through political action, not merely by tackling it as a law-and-order problem, will the Panjāb once again attain the leadership of the rest of India. Religion should be divorced, finally, from politics, in the interest of both, if any lessons are to be learnt from the turmoil of the past decade, and full attention paid to the economic distress of the under-privileged sections of our Society. That will be a fitting tribute to the Sikh Gurus' humanistic teachings as well.

*During these operations, 33 decomposed bodies were recovered from the debris (out of 36 reported killed) within the Golden Temple complex. These persons were murdered by the terrorists, calling them "spies" and "informers" of Govt., and thrown on the debris of the demolished Akal Takhat, pitilessly, to decompose and stink there! One of the terrorists, caught in this Operation, Bhān Singh confessed he was incharge of the torture Chamber in the Temple Complex. He had killed five persons while torturing them. He smeared his victims' wounds with salt, after beating them senseless, and branding them with red hot iron. "He also raped women in the Complex." Another, Nirvair Singh, had crossed over to Pākistān and alongwith others, jailed at Faisalābad (earlier Lyallpur). They tried to flee, but while scaling the Jail walls, they were shot at and seven of them were killed. He had thus no choice but take up arms, as bidden and trained by Pākistān, and indulge in killings, in Panjab. No one knows where has the 40-kilo gold disappeared after the demolition of the Akal Takhat, in 1986 and how have Rs. 5.8 crores looted from the Banks disposed off?" ("Sunday", Calkcuta, July 24, 1988)

** The present writer brought this fact forcefully to the notice of the Prime Minister, on May 28, 1988, when he called a meeting of some intellectuals, to discuss the Panjab situation.

As for the Panjābi language, which became the basis for the creation of a Panjābi-speaking State, the less said the better. Original Panjābi works of the highest merit do not sell, except as text books. There is no Publishing House to publish Panjābi books. The Panjāb Govt. and the Academies encourage only the left-overs, and the left-outs among writers, for whatever reason. And the pre-eminence of English prevails, both at the Secretariat and in the Schools and the Universities. Eminent writers of Panjābi have taken to writing in English, or get their works translated into that or other languages.

As for Sikh political and religious identity, for whose "preservation" the Akāli Dal ostensibly came into being, over sixty years ago, both have a very unsure future, if the present trends are not arrested in time. Already, a considerable number of Sikh youngmen and women have slowly but surely started discarding their faith, outside the Panjāb, due to fear of the future. The older generation is full of anxiety and is easily black-mailed by the militant Hindus, organised in the "Shiv Sena" of Bombay and the BJP, all over northern India. To pursue the chimera of a land-locked Khālistān (without any minerals or metals and its river-sources locked up in Himāchal Pradesh and any virgin land lying in Haryana or elsewhere), will be to commit both political and religious *hara-kiri*. The vast potential and resources of India will be denied to them and, sand-watched between India and Pākistān,both hostile it will only make a tiny Khālistān the cockpit of international intrigue and warfare.

A historian can only warn. The guidance must come from the intelligent and honest Sikh leadership. The world is changing faster than ever before, with our whole ancient norms, institutions, religious habits and antiquated methods of work and technology under attack. If we shall not overtake the events, the events will overtake us, to our detriment. Time stays still for none, and history never forgives.

APPENDIX I

List of 45 Demands of the Akāli Dal submitted to the Government in September, 1981

A. RELIGIOUS

1. Interference in religious affairs of Sikhs.
2. No endeavours by the Government for Sikh control over the management of Gurdwārās in Pakistan.
3. Apathy towards safety of life and property of Sikhs settled abroad and in other States of India.
4. Forcible occupation of the Delhi Gurdwārās in 1971.
5. Applying Land Ceiling Act to Gurudwārās in Haryānā.
6. Failure to name any train as Golden Temple Express, while 15 trains have been named after other religious places.
7. Delay in awarding Holy City status to Amritsar.
8. Not permitting installation of a transmitter in the Golden Temple.
9. Not enacting the All India Gurdwārās Act.
10. Not recognising SGPC as the only representative institution of the Sikhs.
11. Usurping the SGPC's authority in the field of sending pilgrims to Pakistan.
12. Interfering in the Sikh tenets and violating the sanctity of Sikh traditions.
13. Illegal and forcible occupation of Delhi Gurdwārās with the help of the police.
14. Restrictions on carrying of 'Kirpāns' (swords) by Sikhs in the National Airlines.

B. POLITICAL

1. Violation of the assurance given to Sikhs for an autonomous region and instead declaring Sikhs as criminals.
2. Ban on 'Punjabi Subā' slogan.
3. Keeping out Chandigarh and other Punjabi speaking areas out of Punjāb and taking away control of water head works and river water distribution.
4. Denial of internal autonomy to the State.
5. Toppling of Akali Governments through illegal corrupt practices.
6. Denial of second language status to Punjabi in neighbouring States.
7. Expressing lack of confidence in Punjabis and disarming them by withdrawing licensed arms.
8. Rejecting the Anandpur Sahib Resolution and following a policy of divide and rule by inciting communal tensions.

ECONOMIC

1. Reduction in the recruitment quota of Sikhs in armed forces from 20 per cent to 2 per cent.
2. Nationalising of the Punjab & Sind Bank.
3. Failure to establish a dry port at Amritsar.
4. Grant of minimum central aid to Punjab.
5. Concentration of economic power in the hands of 5 per cent people.
6. Economic exploitation of Punjab.
7. Increase in prices.
8. Paucity of heavy industries in Punjab.
9. Eviction of Punjabi farmers from Uttar Pradesh.
10. Fixation of land ceiling at 7 hectares, but no ceiling on urban property.

11. Not introducing group insurance scheme in Punjab.
12. Denial of loans to farmers at the rates given to industrialists.
13. Non-remunerative prices for agricultural produce.
14. Procuring agricultural produce at cheap rates but selling the same to consumers at higher prices.
15. Failure to safeguard the rights of Harijans and other weaker sections.
16. Non-payment of compensation to the victims of Indo-Pak wars in Punjab.
17. Non-payment of unemployment allowance.
18. Linking of production to the price index.
19. Denial of facilities to farmers and workers under the Employment Insurance Scheme.
20. Forcible acquisition of urban agricultural land at cheap rates.
21. Ban on the sale of rural land within the 5 Kms. radius of the corporation limits.

D. SOCIAL

1. Non-recognition of the Sikh Personal Law.
2. Projecting Sikhs in improper way in films and TV etc., encouraging anti-Sikh literature and not giving sufficient time for coverage of Sikh literature on Radio/TV.

APPENDIX II

Revised List of 15 Demands submitted by the Akali Dal to Government in October, 1981

RELIGIOUS DEMANDS

1. Unconditional release of Sant Jarnail Singh Bhindranwale and judicial enquiry with regard to Police action in connection with Delhi Rally (September 7), Chowk Mehta and Chando Kalan.
2. Removal of alleged Government high-handedness in the management of Delhi Gurdwaras, holding of democratic elections after removal of forcible control by "one of Government's stooges".
3. Restoration of the SGPC's right to send pilgrim parties to Pakistan and deploy sewadars for the maintenance of local Sikh shrines.
4. Permission to Sikhs travelling by air to wear kirpans in domestic and international flights.
5. An All India Gurdwaras Act should be passed.
6. Grant of holy city status to Amritsar on the pattern of Hardwar, Kurukshetra and Kashi.
7. Installation of "Harimandir Radio" at Golden Temple, Amritsar to relay kirtan.
8. Renaming Flying Mail as Harimandir Express.

POLITICAL, ECONOMIC AND CULTURAL DEMANDS

9. As per the Anandpur Sahib Resolution, the S.A. Dal is firmly convinced that progress of States would entail prosperity of the Centre, for which suitable amendments should be made in the Constitution to give more rights and provincial autonomy to States. The Centre should retain Foreign Affairs, Defence, Currency and Communications (including means of transport), while the remaining portfolios should be with the States. Besides, the Sikhs should enjoy special rights as a nation.
10. Merger of Punjabi-speaking areas and Chandigarh into Punjab.
11. Handing over of dams and headworks in the State to Punjab and re-distribution of river waters as per national and international rules.

12. Second language status to Punjabi language in Haryana, Delhi, Himachal Pradesh and Rajasthan.

13. Stoppage to uprooting of Punjabi farmers from Terai area of U.P.

14. Setting up of a dry port at Amritsar.

15. A licence should be granted for a New Bank in place of the Punjab and Sind Bank, which should be under Sikh control and remunerative price should be fixed for agricultural products by linking it to the index of industrial production.

APPENDIX III

The Anandpur Sahib Resolution

FOREWORD

The Shiromani Akali Dal undoubtedly is a great organisation, whose coming into existence has been a matter of pride for the Sikhs. Its entire history is a glorious record of struggles and agitations, victories and achievements of which it can be justly proud. The past record of the party vouchsafes that whosoever has ever tried to confront it, he did have to perish ultimately. The most momentous part played by it in the Freedom Struggle of the country would ever form an indelible part of history written in letters of gold.

Shiromani Akali Dal has been guiding the Sikhs according to exigencies of the situation for their rights and for a respectable status in the set-up of the country. Its objective has been exaltation of the Sikh Panth and for the achievement of this lofty ideal, Shiromani Akali Dal has been adopting different and varied means.

Keeping in view the anti-Sikh policies of the Congress government and the political, social and economic conditions prevailing in the country, the Shiromani Akali Dal has decided to redraw the aims and objectives of the Sikh Panth and to give a more vigorous lead for their achievements so that by so doing it may serve the larger interests of the Panth, the Punjab, as also the Country and thus live upto the expectations of the Sikhs.

For such a purpose, a sub-committee of the Sikh intellectuals and thinkers was formed by the Shiromani Akali Dal at a meeting of its Working Committee, held on 11.12.1972 to draw up the draft of a 'Policy-Programme', with the General Secretary of the Party, S. Surjit Singh Barnala, as its Chairman, and S. Gurcharan Singh Tohra, M.P., President, Shiromani Gurdwara Parbandhak Committee, Jathedar Jiwan Singh Umraanangal, S. Gurmit Singh, ex-minister, Dr Bhagat Singh, ex-minister, S. Balwant Singh, ex-Finance Minister, S. Gian Singh Rarewala, S. Prem Singh Lalpura, S. Jaswinder Singh Brar, General Secretary, Shiromani Akal Dal, S. Bhag Singh, Ex-M.L.A., Major General Gurbux Singh Badhni and S. Amar Singh Ambalvi Advocate, as its members.

This Sub-Committee had eleven sittings beginning with the first at Amritsar, on 23.12.1972. Most of the meetings were held at Chandigarh for its peaceful and congenial atmosphere.

All the members of the sub-committee evinced keen interest in its working and engaged themselves in very interesting and useful discussions which were a treat to watch and partake of. A unanimous report was ultimately drawn up after very close deliberations on each and every aspect of the matters and more subtle of their aspects. Actuated by feelings of love for the Sikh Panth, more of its eminent Army Generals, Legal experts, Doctors, Political thinkers, experienced politicians and religious leaders joined together to lend their helping hands to draw up this plan for a more glorious future of the Panth. During their discussions a very happy balance of love for the Panth and the Country was all too evident, as also the keenness to safeguard the interests of the Sikhs and the Country.

When the meticulously drawn up report of S. Surjit Singh sub-committee was presented in the meeting of the working committee of Shiromani Akali Dal held at Shri Anandpur Sahib, the sacred and historic seat of the Tenth Lord, it was approved, after close discussions extending over two days, for placing it before the General House.

This draft is, therefore, being sent to you to enable you to study it in depth so that the meeting of the General House may be benefitted by your valued opinion.

With Panthic Love and regards.

Office of
Shiromani Akali Dal,
Sri Amritsar,
1.8.1977.

Yours humbly,
Ajmer Singh,
Secretary,
Shiromani Akali Dal

The Resolutions

adopted, in the light of the Anandpur Sahib Resolution, at the open session of the 18th All India Akali Conference held at Ludhiana on 28-29 October, 1978 under the Presidentship of Jathedar Jagdev Singh Talwandi are as under:

Resolution No. 1

Moved by S. Gurcharan Singh Tohra, President Shiromani Gurdwara Parbandhak Committee and endorsed by S. Parkash Singh Badal, Chief Minister, Punjab.

The Shiromani Akali Dal realizes that India is a federal and republican geographical entity of different languages, religions and cultures. To safeguard the fundamental rights of the religious and linguistic minorities, to fulfil the demands of the democratic traditions and to pave the way for economic progress, it has become imperative that the Indian constitutional infrastructure should be given a real federal shape by redefining the central and state relations and rights on the lines of the aforesaid principles and objectives.

The concept of total revolution given by Lok Naik, Sh. Jaya Parkash Narain, is also based upon the progressive decentralization of powers. The climax of the process of centralization of powers of the states through repeated amendments of the Constitution during the Congress regime came before the countrymen in the form of the Emergency, when all fundamental rights of all citizens were usurped. It was then that the programme of decentralization of powers ever advocated by Shiromani Akali Dal was openly accepted and adopted by other political parties including Janata Party, C.P.I.(M), A.D.M.K. etc.

Shiromani Akali Dal has ever stood firm on this principle and that is why after very careful considerations it unanimously adopted a resolution to this effect first at all India Akali Conference, Batala, then at Sri Anandpur Sahib which has endorsed the principle of State autonomy in keeping with the concept of Federalism.

As such, the Shiromani Akali Dal emphatically urges upon the Janata Government to take cognizance of the different linguistic and cultural sections, religious minorities as also the voice of millions of people and recast the constitutional structure of the country on real and meaningful federal principles to obviate the possibility of any danger to National unity and the integrity of the Country and further, to enable the states to play a useful role for the progress and prosperity of the Indian people in their respective areas by the meaningful exercise of their powers.

Resolution No. 2

The momentous meeting of the Shiromani Akali Dal calls upon the Govt. of India to examine carefully the long tale of the excesses, wrongs, illegal actions committed by the previous Congress government, more particularly during Emergency, and try to find an early solution to the following problems:

(a) Chandigarh originally raised as a Capital for Punjab should be handed over to Punjab.

(b) The long-standing demand of the Shiromani Akali Dal for the merger in Punjab of the Punjabi-speaking areas, to be identified by linguistic experts with village as a unit, should be conceded.

(c) The control of Head Works should continue to be vested in Punjab and, if need be, the Reorganization Act should be amended.

(d) The arbitrary and unjust Award given by Mrs Indira Gandhi during the Emergency on the distribution of Ravi-Beas waters should be revised on the universally accepted norms and principles, thereby justice be done to Punjab.

(e) Keeping in view the special aptitude and material qualities of the Sikhs, the present ratio of their strength in Army should be maintained.

(f) The excesses being committed on the settlers in the Tarai region of U.P. in the name of Land Reforms should be vacated by making suitable amendments in the ceiling Law on the Central guidelines.

Resolution No. 3

(Economic Policy Resolution)

The chief sources of inspiration of the economic policies and programme of the Shiromani Akali Dal are the secular, democratic and socialistic concepts of Sri Guru Nanak Dev and Sri Guru Gobind Singh Ji. Our Economic programme is based on three basic principles:

(a) Dignity of Labour.

(b) An economic and social structure which provides for the uplift of the poor and depressed sections of society.

(c) Unabated opposition to concentration of economic and political power in the hands of the capitalists.

While drafting its economic policies and programme, the Shiromani Akali Dal in its historic Anandpur Sahib resolution has laid particular stress on the need to break the monopolistic hold of the capitalists foisted on the Indian economy by 30 years of Congress rule in India. This capitalist hold enabled the Central government to assume all powers in its hands after the manner of Mughal Imperialism. This was bound to thwart the economic progress of the states and injure the social and economic interests of the people. The Shiromani Akali Dal once again reiterates the Sikh way of life by resolving to fulfil the holy words of Guru Nanak Dev:

"He alone realizes the True Path who labours honestly and shares the ruits of that Labour".

This way of life is based upon three basic principles:

(i) Doing honest labour.

(ii) Sharing the fruits of this labour, and

(iii) Meditation on the Lord's Name.

The Shiromani Akali Dal calls upon the Central and the State government to eradicate unemployment during the next ten years. While pursuing this aim, special emphasis should be laid on ameliorating the lot of the weaker sections, Scheduled and depressed classes, workers, landless and poor farmers and urban poor. Minimum wages should be fixed for them all.

The Shiromani Akali Dal urges upon the Punjab Government to draw up such an economic plan for the State as would turn it into the leading province during the next ten years, by raising per capita income to Rs. 3,000/- and by generating an economic growth rate of 7% per annum as against 4% at National level.

The Shiromani Akali Dal gives first priority to the redrafting of the taxation structure in such a way that the burden of taxation is shifted from the poor to the richer classes and an equitable distribution of National income is ensured.

The main plank of the economic programme of the Shiromani Akali Dal is to enable the economically weaker sections of the Society to share the fruits of National income.

The Shiromani Akali Dal calls upon the Central Government to make an international air-field at Amritsar which should also enjoy the facilities of a dry port. Similarly, a Stock Exchange should be opened at Ludhiana to accelerate the process of industrialization and economic growth in the State. The Shiromani Akali Dal also desires that suitable amendments should be made in the Foreign Exchange rules for free exchange of foreign currencies and thereby removing the difficulties being faced by the Indian emigrants.

The Shiromani Akali Dal emphatically urges upon the Indian Government to bring a parity between the prices of the agricultural produce and that of the industrial raw materials so that the discrimination against such states which lack these materials may be removed.

The Shiromani Akali Dal demands that the exploitation of the producers of the cash crops like cotton, sugarcane, oil seeds etc. at the hands of the traders should be stopped forthwith and for such a purpose arrangements for the purchase of these crops by the government, at remunerative prices, should be made. Besides, effective steps should be taken by the government for the purchase of cotton through the Cotton Corporation.

The Shiromani Akali Dal strongly feels that the most pressing National problem is the need to ameliorate the lot of millions of exploited persons belonging to the scheduled classes. For such a purpose the Shiromani Akali Dal calls upon the Central and State Governments to earmark special funds. Besides, the State Governments should allot sufficient funds in their respective budgets for giving free residential plots both in the urban and rural areas to the scheduled castes.

The Shiromani Akali Dal also calls for the rapid diversification of farming. The shortcomings in the Land Reforms Laws should be removed, rapid industrialization of the State ensured, the credit facilities for the medium industries expanded and unemployment allowance given to those who are unemployed. For remunerative farming, perceptible reduction should be made in the prices of farm machinery like tractors, tubewells as also the inputs etc.

Resolution No. 4

This huge session of the Shiromani Akali Dal regrets the discrimination to which the Punjabi language is being subjected in the adjoining States of Himachal, Haryana, Delhi and Jammu and Kashmir etc. It is its firm demand that in accordance with the Nehru Language Formula, the neighbouring States of Punjab should be 'given second' language status to the Punjabi language because a fairly large sections of their respective population are Punjabi speaking.

Resolution No. 5

The meeting regrets that against the 'claims' of the refugees who had migrated to Jammu and Kashmir as a result of the partition of the country, no compensation has been provided to them even after such a long time and these unfortunate refugees are rotting in the camps ever since then.

This Akali Dal Session, therefore, forcefully demands that their claims should be soon settled and immediate steps should be taken to rehabilitate them even if it involves an amendment in section 370.

Resolution No. 6

The 18th session of the All India Akali Conference takes strong exception to the discrimination to which the minorities in other states are being subjected and the way in which their interests are being ignored.

As such, it demands that injustice against the Sikhs in other states should be vacated and proper representation should be given to them in the government service, local bodies & state legislatures, through nomination, if need be.

Resolution No. 7

The 18th session of the All India Akali Conference notes with satisfaction that mechanization of farming in the country has led to increase in the farm yield and as a result the country is heading towards self-sufficiency.

However, the session feels that poor farmers are unable to take to mechanization because of the enormity of the cost involved.

As such, the Shiromani Akali Dal urges upon the Government of India to abolish the excise duty on tractors,so that with the decrease in their prices,the ordinary farmers may also be able to avail of farm machinery and contribute to the growth of gross agricultural produce of the country.

Resolution No. 8

The meeting of the Shiromani Akali Dal appeals to the Central and State governments to pay particular attention to the poor and labouring classes and demands that besides making suitable amendments in the Minimum Wages Act, suitable legal steps should be taken to improve the economic lot of the labouring class, to enable it to lead a respectable life and play a useful role in the rapid industrialization of the country.

Resolution 9

This session seeks permission from the Government of India to instal a broadcasting station at Golden Temple, Amritsar, for the relay of 'Gurbani Kirtan' for the spiritual satisfaction of those Sikhs who are living in foreign lands.

The session wishes to make it clear that the entire cost of the proposed Broadcasting Project would be borne by the Khalsa Panth and its over-all control shall vest with the Indian Government. We have every hope that the government would have no hesitation in conceding this demand after due consideration.

Resolution No. 10

The huge Session of the Shiromani Akali Dal strongly urges upon the Government of India to make necessary amendments in the following enactments for the benefit of the agricultural classes who have toiled hard for the larger National interests:

1. By suitable amendments in the relevant clause of the Hindu Succession Act, a woman should be given rights of inheritance in the properties of her father-in-law instead of the father's.

2. The agricultural lands of the farmers should be completely exempted from the Wealth Tax and the Estate Duty.

Resolution No. 11

The vast Session of the Shiromani Akali Dal strongly impresses upon the Government of India that keeping in view the economic backwardness of the scheduled and non-scheduled castes, provisions proportionate to their population should be made in the budget for utilization for their welfare. A special ministry should be created at the Centre as a practical measure to render justice to them on the basis of reservation.

The Session also calls upon the government that in keeping with the settlement already, no discrimination should be made between the Sikh and Hindu Harijans in any part of the country.

Resolution No. 12

The Congress government is called upon to vacate the gross injustice, discrimination done to Punjab in the distribution of Ravi-Beas waters. The Central Government must also give approval for the immediate establishment of six sugar and four textile mills in Punjab, so that the state may be able to implement its agro-industrial policy.+

+ The Janata Govt. (1977-79) under Morarji Desai took no notice of these resolutions. In fact, a meeting of Chief Ministers called by the Panjab C.M., Badal, was scuttled by Mr. Desai, for giving more powers to the states.

APPENDIX IV

'Operation Blue Star'

Major General Kuldip Singh Brar was given the assignment — 'Operation Blue Star' — of flushing out the terrorists from the Golden Temple with a categorical instruction to cause no damage to Harmandir Sahib. Here below is his press statement giving a full account of the operations :

" I was asked to flush out the extremists from the Golden Temple with instructions to cause no damage to Harmandir Sahib and to avoid as much as possible any damage to Akal Takhat. I was to use minimum force for achieving this objective to avoid bloodshed. I was also to try and prevent internecine fighting between the Bhindranwale and the Longowal followers. This was the broad mission assigned to me.

The very ideas of forcibly entering the Golden Temple shocked me. Therefore, I thought : Was there any other means to enter the Golden Temple? Two ideas struck me. The first was: Would it be possible to lay siege around the Golden Temple complex and compel the terrorists to come out by starving them?

From the military point, it was impossible. Because no amount of troops could have cordoned off the whole complex which is very closely built and has passages underneath. Besides, the buildings around the complex were also in the firm control of extremists. Therefore, the effective sealing off the Golden Temple was doubtful.

Secondly, there was a huge amount of foodgrain stock and war-like arms and ammunitions inside the complex. Then, there was the Sarovar which could have provided water to the extremists. Therefore, idea of starving them and forcing them out too was almost impossible. We also knew that they had plans to incite people to come to the Golden Temple to help and support them. This would have prevented any effective action to flush the terrorists out. Therefore, with great sadness in my heart,I came to the conclusion that there was no other way but to enter the Golden Temple.

The first condition that we lay down for ourselves was that we would cause no damage to the Harmandir Sahib at any cost. I warned my troops that even under extreme provocations from the terrorists, the troops would not fire towards the Harmandir Sahib. But there was every danger from the extremists. Those who were using the Golden Temple for murders and robberies could have done anything. When they could use the Akal Takhat for such purposes, they would even not desist from damaging the Harmandir Sahib, I thought. I felt that it could not be ruled out. I requested my corps commander to take devout soldiers for the task. We had planned to swim to reach the corners of Harmandir Sahib.

Our next important task was to reach the Akāl Takhat. The terrorists had put up sandbag defences at every terrace. Therefore, any plan to clear the extremists out of the Akal Takhat without causing any damage to it was almost impossible. Nevertheless, I requested the corps commander that he should see that the troops in the initial stage forbid even rifle or automatic firing. Secondly, I suggested him to use tank search lights which are so powerful that it leaves a man almost blind. I also suggested to use non-lethal police gas and about 100 canisters of the gas with 200 gas masks were made available to the troops. The intention was to go in the Akal Takhat area using the non-lethal gas to incapacitate the extremists. We had also planned to enter the Akāl Takhat using only stungrenades, which are nothing but fire crackers that produce a blast. We had planned to use stungrenade, because it would have caused no structural damage to the Akāl Takhat.

I had also planned to send a party of fire extinguishers just behind the stungrenade party in order to extinguish any fire the stungrenade might cause to the Akal Takhat area.

The operation began on 5th June evening. First, some of the stalls, which were overlooking the main temple entrance, had to be eliminated in a parallel operation. It was done slowly on the 5th evening. That very evening, I had to launch a parallel operation to secure the Hotel Temple View and to secure the Akhara view. I also had to remove the top portion of both observation towers, and the top portion of the water tank, because these were very heavily fortified with machineguns and they would not have permitted any movement of my troops, even if we had approached the area from which we were to launch.

As far as the other buildings under extremist occupation were concerned, I decided to leave them alone. I did not have the resources to deal with them, but I did have to put up cordon all along the Golden Temple complex with an infantry battalion and equipment from paramilitary forces. The idea of cordon was to prevent any extremists from getting away from the Golden Temple complex in small bits, because it was possible for some of them to step out of the building.

As far as fortification was concerned, the roof tops, the first floor, the second floor, the ground floor, and all parts and buildings of the temple complex were heavily fortified. They had bunkers, they had fire trenches and they had converted all doors and windows into fixed defences. I realised that even the approach to the Golden Temple complex would mean heavy casualties. In fact, the temple was fortified into an impregnable bastion.

In addition to fortification in three tiers — the top, middle and the bottom — the extremists had also defences in the basement. From the basement, the extremists emerged from the manholes. They go round to cover verandah through these manholes, open fire at my troops, went back to these manholes and re-emerged into a room some 50 metres away to get into action again. They also used staircases from the ground floor and the top floor and fired on our position. They even used the main staircase of the main entrance. To reach the Parikrama, one had to climb some steps and in this part were concealed fire positions on either side of the staircase. Even before the operation really got on the way, I saw several casualties on the staircase without realising who was firing at us.

The Akāl Takhat, as brought out earlier, is offset. But eventually it was discovered that it had a machinegun bunker at ground level. Troop movement from any direction came under very heavy fire from the Akāl Takhat.

As we tried to enter the Harmandir Sahib complex, the extremists fired at us from all openings coming out of the Harmandir Sahib. We had kept our force in reserve on the southern side. I had isolated the area on the eastern side and I had taken only one infantry battalion for this entire complex and because basically this was the complex which houses pilgrims and innocent people. But in this part also there were militants.

The Babar Khālsā men, who where very well-equipped, were in this area. By isolating this area from the main complex, we were able to achieve the aim and at the same time by the use of minimum force, with just one infantry battalion, we were able to secure this area with minimum damage and loss to extremists' lives.

Longowāl and Tohrā when surrounded gave themselves up. They did not put up any fight. But the extremists, who were in this area and had lodged themselves on the top of the building, did fight with our troops. They fired on us from all directions. We suffered heavy casualties in this area. But eventually when they found they were outnumbered, they gave in.

However, in the main temple complex we received pitched battle. Our progress towards the Akal Takhat was extremely slow. My commandos, who were to lead the infantry and to reach the Akāl Takhat at the earliest, started suffering heavy casualties. The battalion which was earmarked from both sides of the main entrance suffered very heavily. Twenty troops died and 60 were injured in between the right gate of the main entrance and the left gate of the main entrance. I realised that it was difficult for this battalion to progress operations any further. A part of the terrorists was on the ground floor level and unless they were forced to go to the first floor or to the roof top, it was difficult to bring the situation under control. Besides, until the extremists would remain on the ground floor, we would suffer heavy casualties.

In spite of heavy odds against them, my commandos had to take control of this area. I must give credit to the battalion commander, a very dashing soldier, Lt Col Issrar Khan who rallied strength together and worked his way out. As commandos reached the entrance area of the Akāl Takhat, the terrorists hiding in manholes started suffering casualties. Now the extremists from the top started lobbing grenades on the troops. The grenades they used were deadly, and inflicted heavy casualties on us. However, the commando battalion did succeed in getting into this particular area.

Now the commando task was to work their way towards the Akāl Takhat. When they attempted to move further, they came under extremely heavy fire and opposition from the extremists. Consequently, they were not able to make much headway. The commandos had the toughest deal heading for the Akāl Takhat and they had to get into the scaling ground at the earliest. In this scaling ground, they suffered very heavy casualties. But they had to move on. There was no way out to retreat. There was no way of getting back. I asked them to either take a lodgement on top and press on towards the Akāl Takhat. I was coming at this stage from across on the southern side. So I was coming from the Harmandir Sahib side and fire was coming from the Akāl Takhat direction. Now my officers were asking for permission to return fire. Returning fire would have meant taking Harmandir Sahib in the line of fire. Therefore, a very difficult order had to be given to them that they will not return fire on anything which will endanger Harmandir Sahib. A very tall order which my troops cared to ensure. Similarly, when the commandos and the troops came under heavy fire from the Akāl Takhat, I once again received a request that we would now have to fire towards Harmandir Sahib. Once again they were told not to do this at any cost. At this stage, the two companies were kept in reserve. The two were under the command of Brigadier Dewan, a Vir Chakra decorated officer. He was given the task to somehow link up with the commandos who were already suffering heavy casualties. I must say he did a splendid job. The reinforcement eased pressure on the commandos and as a collective measure, the troops managed to close into the Akāl Takhat.

Now came the situation when the extremists became desperate and started extremely heavy firing from every side. The forces, trying to close into Akāl Takhat, were engulfed in the firing. Obviously, troops suffered very heavy casualties at this stage. Now I had no other alternative but to move armoured carrier, known as Scot which moves on wheels, hoping that it would have psychological effect on the extremists. I had thought once the extremists would see it, they would give up the pitched battle. On the contrary, the armed personnel carrier was knocked out of action by anti-tank weapons, fired by the extremists from the Akāl Takhat. I realised that the Akāl Takhat was not only fortified with machineguns, rifles and all sorts of other weapons, but also with anti-tank weapons. Now a tank was brought to scare the terrorists. Even this failed to have any effect on them. The terrorists continued to fire on us.

However, around 4.30 a.m. on 6 June, 30 soldiers managed to get into the Akāl Takhat. The battle continued for another two hours and the extremists fought to the last man. Ultimately, the firing stopped. When we reached the basement of Akāl Takhat we found the bodies of Bhindranwale, Amrik Singh and Shahbeg Singh. Bhindranwale was earlier on the second floor of the Akāl Takhat. He first came down to the first floor and then to the basement where he died.

APPENDIX V

POPULATION OF SIKHS IN INDIA (1981)

India/State/ Union Territory	No. of House-holds	Sikhs Persons	Males	Females
INDIA*	2,105,790	13,078,146	6,957,891	6,120,255
STATES				
1. Andhra Pradesh	3,147	16,222	9,582	6,640
2. Bihar	11,581	77,704	42,253	35,451
3. Gujarat	4,386	22,438	12,233	10,205
4. Haryana	121,513	802,230	425,097	377,133
5. Himachal Pradesh	10,524	52,209	28,116	24,09
6. Jammu & Kashmir	22,507	133,675	70,652	63,023
7. Karnataka	1,264	6,401	3,745	2,656
8. Kerala	260	1,295	834	461
9. Madhya Pradesh	24,142	143,020	77,524	65,496
10. Maharashtra	20,522	107,255	58,145	49,110
11. Manipur	170	992	634	358
12. Meghalaya	321	1,674	855	819
13. Nagaland	107	743	531	212
14. Orissa	2,619	14,270	7,806	6,464

15. Punjab	1,618,484	10,199,141	5,419,277	4,779,864
16. Rajasthan	82,664	492,818	260,906	231,912
17. Sikkim	88,	322	209	113
18. Tamil Nadu	382	4,395	2,546	1,849
19. Tripura	32	285	223	62
20. Uttar Pradesh	77,551	458,647	245,569	213,078
21. West Bengal	9,274	49,054	28,428	20,62

UNION TERRIORIES

1. Andaman and Nicobar Islands	234	991	543	448
2. Arunachal Pradesh	307	1,231	711	520
3. Chandigarh	19,914	95,370	51,639	43,731
4. Dadra & Nagar Haveli	3	11	5	6
5. Delhi	73,020	393,921	208,507	185,414
6. Goa, Daman & Diu	237	1,380	928	452
7. Lakshadweep		—	—	—
8. Mizoram	41	421	376	45
9. Pondicherry	6	31	17	14

* Excludes Assam

NOTE :

1. The total population of India in 1981 was a little over 66 crore (Males were about 34 crores and females 32 crores), the females thus being two crores less.

2. The Hindu population (including SCs) was 54 crores, (28 crores males & 26 crores females, a difference of 2 crores)

3. The Muslim population was $7\frac{1}{2}$ crores (Males: 3 crores and 90 lakhs and females 3 crores and 65 lakhs, a difference of 25 lakhs. How could they have four wives each, as was advertised)

4. The Christians were one crore & 61 lakhs (Males : 81 lakhs, and females 80 lakhs, a difference of only one lakh)

5. The Sikhs were one crore, 30 lakhs (Male : 69 lakhs and female 61 lakhs, a difference of 8 lakhs).

6. The increase in population during the past ten years (71-81) was Hindus, including Harijans (30%), Muslims (50%), Christians (16%) and Sikhs (55%).

APPENDIX VI

The Sikh Code of Conduct

(Rahitnāmās)

(These injunctions, some of which are ascribed to the Tenth Master or the devout Sikhs, who are reported to have taken instruction from him personally, though there are several versions of them extant, by and large, reflect the Sikh moral & social code as understood by the orthodox in the 18th century).

---

1. If one sees a hungry, naked or a needy man, one must share one's earnings with him, these being God's gifts. If one could be of use to another, due to the Guru's Grace, one must tarry not, and even at the cost of one's own time and work, one must satisfy his needs. Thiswise the Guru is pleased.
2. One must not pain another and be sweet of tongue, and if someone speaks ill of him, he must not take it to heart.
3. If some misfortune befalls a Sikh, then the others should be ready to sacrifice their all for his sake. Thiswise, they will have the reward of fulfilment as true men of faith. Such consideration be shown to each other as the Sikh shows to the Guru.
4. The greatest virtue is that one must not resort to falsehood. A man should not cohabit with another's woman, a married woman should not look with favour upon another man. And one must not fall a prey to greed, undue attachment and slander.
5. If a person repairs to to the congregation of the Khālsā, then five Sikhs should go out to receive him and seat him in their midst with due courtesies.

6. If someone seeks to talk to the Guru, then, he should read out the Guru's Word and be fulfilled in every way. And if he seeks to have the Guru's Vision, then he should repair to wheresoever the holy Khalsa is assembled. If he views them with faith and due reverence, he will forsure see therein the Vision of the Guru.

7. All food is sacred, for it is God's gift. But food from two types of persons one must avoid, firstly of him who has turned his back upon the Guru, and secondly of the one who claims that it is through his generosity (and not through the Guru's Grace) that another has eaten at his table.

8. One must spend less than one's income. The spendthrifts will come to grief in the end.

9. One must not be addicted to any intoxicant, for it makes one indolent and lazy, and one can neither attend to work nor worship and one is induced to sin and to seek out such pleasures which ultimately lead to sin.

10. If one is to adjudge on a dispute, then one must keep faith with God. Neither due to popular pressure nor for one's own interest or greed one should ever favour one's own side, class or creed. He who does so will be punished grievously in the end.

11. One should speak not the language of pride, nor slander or backbite, nor betray another's trust, nor ridicule or laugh at another, for this leads to great pain in the end.

12. A ruler should do justice, awake ever to the fear of God and see that no one is pained in his dominions. The ruler should apply the same standards of justice to himself as he applies to the others.

13. In one's business one must be clean, have one word and not another, and should deceive no one. Work of every kind-high, middle or low—is the highest form of worship. And nothing equals a man who along with his work dedicates himself to God.

14. Whatever work one does, should be based on righteousness. The noblest work is trade, followed by agriculture. And if one must serve, one must go in for soldiering, but remain detached and be content with what he receives as his due wages. And whenever he is sent out to fight, he should fight as a hero and if there is loot, he should not participate in it and submit ever to the Will of God.

15. One should not incur any debts and if one must, the debt should be repaid without a demand being made and till all repayment is made,one must not indulge in pleasures nor wear scents.
16. The Sikh-Khālsā should have belief only in the one God and no incarnations of Him nor any false Gurus who will set themselves up as such.
17. If a person dies, his relations and friends should submit to the Will of God and indulge not in wailing and eat food as usual on that day and sleep on the bed.

(Extracts from "Prem Sumārag" ascribed to Guru Gobind Singh)

II

Some more Injunctions

1. A Sikh of the Guru should consider the mouth of the poor to be the Guru's treasury.
2. One should not gamble, nor steal or rob, nor indulge in sex perversities.
3. One must invoke the blessings of God in the beginning of each task.
4. The only addiction one must have is food. One must bear arms and show not one's back on the field of battle.
5. One should not hesitate in forgiving.
6. The Guru's Sikh should not drink spirituous drinks, for these turn one's mind.
7. On the death of a person, only God's Word should be recited on the occasion and the sacred food *(Karāh Parsād)* distributed.
8. The Guru's Sikh shouid not wear the sacred thread nor the frontal mark, nor close-crop one's hair (as the Hindus do on someone's death), nor worship at a graveyard, tomb, or mosque, nor accept the authority of the Mullahs or Qāzis, etc.,
9. One should not live on the income of a *Dharamsālā* (Sikh Gurdwara or temple), nor become a *Pir* or a *Masand.*
10. The Khālsā should remain distinct both from the Hindus and the Muslims.

(Rahitnāmā ascribed to Bhai Ghaupā Singh, the male nurse of the Tenth Guru")

III

1. The Khālsā should obliterate the distinciion between the Hindu and the Musalmān.
2. The Khālsā is he who has dedicated his body, mind and riches to the Timeless Being *(Akāl Purukh)*
3. He who has deception in his heart will go to hell.
4. One must take due care of one's horse and one's arms.
5. He who is avaricious or denigrates food is fit only to be fined by the Congregation.

(Rahitnāmā ascribed to Bhai Daya Singh, one of the five beloved ones).

IV

1. Listen, O Nandlāl, these are the duties of a Sikh : to meditate on God, to share his earnings with others, to keep his body and mind clean, and to care for nought else.
2. Says Gobind Singh, "Listen, O Lālji (i.e. Nandlal), he who parts not with one-tenth of his income in the name of the Guru or lives by falsehood, him no one should trust".
3. He who keeps not his word, will be denied the refuge of God.
4. He who plays false with the Guru's treasury and thus deceives (the Guru), will be subject to the tortures of a thousand hells.

5, The Kāhlsā is he who slanders not.
The Khālsā is he who fights in the vanguard.
The Khālsā is he who looks not upon another's woman or riches.
The Khālsā is he who is imbued with the God's Name.
The Khālsā is he who is dedicated ever to the Guru.
The Khālsā is he who faces steel on his front (and not on his back).
The Khālsā is he who cares for the poor.
The Khālsā is he who destroys the evil-doers.

7. All men belong to God and so one must give pain to no one. For when men suffer, God's wrath is provoked.
8. Listen, O Nandlāl, with due attention, I have three facets—the Absolute, the Personal and the Guru's Word. Let this be clearly understood.

(Tankhāh-nāmā ascribed to Bhāi Nandlāl)

1. The foremost injunction is that one should be initiated into the Singh fold by being baptised with a double-edged dagger (*Khandē Ki Pāhul)*.
2. The Khālsā should deal not with one who is the killer of his daughter.
3. One must not taste the kosher-meat, nor smoke tobacco or opium, etc.
4. A Sikh must be versed in the Gurmukhi characters and other knowledge of every kind. He must also acquire it from wheresoever it is available.
5. One must not fall a prey to lust, wrath, greed or pride.
6. All the religions and ways of life that there are in the world, one must disparage not any of them.
7. One should not accept a bribe to do justice, nor bear false witness.

(*Rahatnāmā* ascribed to Bhai Dèsā Singh, a devout Sikh of Amritsar, who bases his argument on Nandlāl)

APPENDIX VII

Hukamnāmas

(Edicts or Letters of Command)

The publication, in 1967, of Guru Tegh Bahadur's, Guru Gobind Singh's and a few other extant *Hukamnāmās* of Mātā Sundri etc. by Dr. Ganda Singh, well-known Sikh historian, do not throw much historical light on the eventful life of the Gurus, except for the following Hukamnāmā of the Tenth Guru, dated October 2, 1707, which, in translation, would read as follows :

The Tenth Master

(10 Satguruji)

"To the entire congregation *(Sangat)* of Dhaul, you are my Khālsā. The Guru will protect you. Meditate on the Guru. Your human birth will be redeemed. We were received here by the King emperor and honoured with a robe *(Siro-pao*-lit. that which covers one from head to foot) and a jewelled dagger *(Dhukhdhuhki)** with Rupee Sixty thousand. Other tasks also are being accomplished by favour of the Guru. We are also returning to you in a few days. To the entire Commonwealth of the Khālsā my command is: keep unity in in your ranks. When we come to Kahlur (i.e. Anandpur), the entire Khālsā should come, armed, into our Presence. Send two *tolās* of gold worth Rs. 40 by draft *(hundi)*. If the messenger *(mewrā)* delays, turn him out of the congregation. Samvat 1764 (Virami), Katik 1."

Which shows that the Guru had the intention of going back to Anandpur after settling his affairs with Bahadur Shāh, the King-

* The word has also been rendered as 'scarf' or necklace.

emperor, and that there is no reason to believe that either he had accepted an employment with him or was frustrated with life which he deliberately ended by inviting vengeance against him by a Pathān. On the other hand, he had every intention to resume the fight if a settlement could not be reached. Bandā Bahādur was sent by him, therefore, not as a substitute for himself but as a leader of the vanguard to assemble the forces of the Khālsā and to await the Guru's instructions. Unfortunately, the Guru was assassinated in the meantime and Bandā had to take his own decisions.

Other *Hukamnāmās* of his mostly enjoin upon individuals and the *Sangats* of Dacca, Bhai Rupā, Bhai Rāmā (Patiala), Lucknow, Macchiwārā, Naushehrā Pannuan (Amritsar), Pattan Sheikh Farid, Dasua (Hoshiarpur), Patna, Pirāg (Priyag-Allahabad), Rupeena, Cholā, Khārā (U. P.), Banāras, etc., to send to the Guru gold, weapons, swords, shields, cloth and turbans, war-elephants, oxen, camels, spices, niwār, earthen water-jars (surāhis), talking birds, special pigeons, *cannons* and ammunition, etc.

On the one hand, this list reveals not only the military needs, but the aesthetic tastes of the Guru. On the other hand, as pointed out by Dr. Loehlin,* it throws light on the material conditions of the various *Sangats* and territories. The Dacca *Sangat*, for instance, is asked to send weapons, cloth and war-elephants, Banaras is to provide cloth, Patna spices, cloth and turbans, pigeons, birds and vessels, Lucknow cannons and their equipment, and Mālwā camels and oxen.

What is most important is, however, the Guru's insistence that the offerings are in no case to be sent through the *Masands*. The Sikhs are not to have any dealings with them nor to trust them. In the *Hukamnāmās* written in 1702, however, it was stated that those who were penitent may be accepted back in the fold. This answers the charge of those who like S. M. Latif aver that the Guru "threw several of them alive into the boiling oil."† Most of *Hukamnāmās* have their lines numbered to guard against interpolation. The Guru's love for the Sikhs is overwhelming. He calls them "my Khālsā, my Very Own, my Joy." The *Hukamnāmās* also reveal that the Guru's house was provided with every kind of need by the devout Sikhs and the messenger who brought the *Hukamnāmā* was shown utmost respect and rewarded for his labours, as the Guru himself often enjoins.

* "The Granth of Guru Govind Singh and the Khālsā Brotherhood" (1971) pp. 62-63.

† "A History of the Panjāb," P. 273.

One interesting feature of the *Hukamnāmās* is that the Guru, even after the birth of the Khālsā (1699), addresses both the orthodox (Singhs) and the unorthodox (Sahjhdāris) as "*tusi merā Khālsā ho*" (you are my Khālsā). The word Khālsā has however been employed by the earlier Gurus also, including Gurus Hargobind and Tegh Bahādur, in their *Hukamnāmās* in the sense of the Guru's exclusive spiritual charge as against *Sahlangs*, whose spiritual instruction was entrusted to the *Masands*.

APPENDIX VIII

Some Historical Writings of Guru Gobind Singh
Bachittar Natak
(or, the Wondrous drama)‡
Uttered by the Tenth Guru in Person

This is an autobiographical poem of historical significance, written by the Tenth Guru, and detailing his early life and struggles. The first four chapters reveal his concept of God not only as the Compassionate Being, but equally as the Destroyer of evil, the Holy Sword, the Retributor, the Avenger, whose justice is not only even-handed, but never-failing. And no incarnation of His, nor any Prophet is equal to His Majesty, all being subjeet to death and the ravages of Time. And He is not only Timeless, but All-powerful and the Creator, both of good circumstance and bad, and what avails man is not showmanship, but inner fulfilment.

CHAPTER I

I

Greetings with love and devotion to the Holy Sword.
May He Help me to bring this book to a successful end.

2

O Sword, O Conquerer of continents, O Vanquisher of the hosts of evil, O Embellisher of the brave in the field of battle, Thy Arms are unbreakable, Thy light refulgent, Thy Glory and Splendour dazzle like the sun.
O Happiness of the holy, O Crusher of evil intent, O Subduer of sin, I seek Thy refuge.
Victory, O Creator of the world, O our Deliverer, My Sustainer :
Victory, Victory, Victory to Thee.

‡This and other major works, considered authentic,of Guru Gobind Singh have been translated into English by the present author and published by the Panjābi University, Patiālā, under the title *"Thus spake the Tenth Master."*

CHAPTER II, III and IV

(The Autobiography)

In the Second, third and fourth chapters of the "*Bachittar Nātak,*" Guru Gobind Singh writes of his pedigree, tracing his lineage and that of Guru Nānak to Sri Rāmchandra. Bedis, he says, were those who were versed in the Vedas and Sodhis (like Guru Gobind) those who derived their lineage from Sanaudh, the King, who himself branched off from the Bedis. Though Guru Gobind Singh does not believe in Rama being the incarnation of God, or deathless, he is proud of his lineage from him. Similarly, though Krishna is not God for him, he writes about his beauty, his child-like pranks, his mastery of music and his chivalry in a most appreciative tone.

4.

In the house of the Bedis was born Nānak, the King of Kings, who brought joy to his followers and became their refuge, both here and in the Hereafter.

9

It was Nānak, the venerable, who was known as Angad.

Thereafter, it was Amar Dās who assumed the form of Rām Dās.

All this is known to men of faith, but the fools know not the Mystery.

II

Ram Dās, then, merged in God,
Appointing Arjun as the Guru.
And when Arjun ascended to the heavens,
He established Har Gobind in his Throne.

12.

When Har Gobind proceeded to the Abode of God,
It was Hari Rāi who was seated in his place.
After him came Hari Krishna, his son,
And then it was Tegh Bahādur who succeeded him.

13

It was for the sake of the sacred thread and the frontal-mark (of the Hindus)

That he performed a great act of chivalry.
To protect the holy, he offered all he had,
And, lo, he offered his head, but uttered not a sigh of regret.

14

He suffered martyrdom for the sake of religion.
His head he surrendered, but not his honour.*
God's men are, indeed, ashamod to act
Like showmen and perform tricks.%

15

Having broken the (body's) earthen pitcher on the head of the King of Delhi,† he departed to the world of God.
Nay, not one has performed the Deed that Tegh Bahādur had.
The whole world mourned his loss,
And cried, "Alas, Alas," but the domain of gods
Resounded with the shouts:
"Victory, Victory, Victory, be to the man of God."

CHAPTER VI

Now I relate my own story; how Lord God sent me in this world, while I was undergoing penances (for His sake).

On the mountain of Hem Kunda, at a place called *Sapt Sringa*, or the range of the seven peaks, where King Pandu (also) had suffered austerities.

There, I went through various kinds of penances, and dwelt on the All-death, the All-powerful God, so much that I became one with the Lord.

The Incomprehensible One was also worshipped by my father and mother who had imbibed His discipline in many ways to unite with Him.

The Lord-God was immensely pleased with their devotions and so He ordered me to be born in this dark age.

It was not my desire to take birth, for my mind was fixed on the Feet of God. But God remonstrated with me with great earnestness and spoke thus to this insignificant creature:

---

* Also translated as (i) God's secret, (ii) determination,

% The reference is to the demand of Emperor Auranzeb or his Qāzis to perform a miracle which the Guru refused to do, saying it was the work of mountebanks, not of men of God,

† The responsibility for his father's martyrdom is fixed decisively on the king of Delhi and no one else.

GOD'S UTTERANCE

"I establish thee as my Son, that thou spread My Path. Go, and instruct men in Righteousness and the Moral Law, and make people desist from evil."

THE POET'S UTTERANCE

I stood up, with joined palms, and bowing my head to Lord-God, I said, "Thy Path I shall spread only if Thou be at my back."

For this was I born into the world. I utter only how and what God uttered to me, for I am the enemy of no one.

He who calls me God will forsure burn in the fires of hell. For, I am only the Servant of God; yea, doubt not the veracity of this statement.

I am but the slave of the Supreme Being come to witness His Play. I tell the world only what my God said to me, for I will not be silenced through fear of the mortals.

I utter as is the instruction of my God, for I consider no one greater than Him. I'm pleased not with any religious garb, so, I shall sow the seeds of God, the Unaccountable One.

Nay, I worship not stones, nor am I attracted by sectarian coats. I utter only the name of the Infinite One and so attain unto the Supreme Being.

I wear not matted hair, nor ear-rings, nor have regard for any such ritual, and do only what God bids me do.

I repeat only the name of one God who fulfils us all at all places.

No, I utter not another's name, nor establish another God.

CHAPTER VII
THE POET'S BIRTH

When my father departed to the East, he went to all places of pilgrimage. When he reached Triveni (at Allahabad), for many days he distributed charities and did other meritorious acts.

There was I conceived and, later took birth in the city of Patna. Afterwards, I was taken to the Panjāb, where I was fondled and nursed with great affection and care.

My body was tended in every way, and I got instructed too in every branch of knowledge.

And when I was barely of the age to perform my religious and secular functions, my father left for the heavenly abode.

CHAPTER VIII

When I became a (Spiritual) sovereign, I tried to spread religion to the best of my ability. I hunted various games including bears, nilgaus and elk. Then I left my home and proceeded towards the city of Pauntā.

On the banks of the Kalindri, I refreshed and amused myself with many kinds of amusements. There, I killed many ferocious lions and nilgaus and elks.

Fateh Shāh, the King, became furious, and measured arms with me, without cause.

(And thereafter are given, in superb verse, descriptions of the battles of Bhangāni and Nadaun, the wars with Dilāwar Khān, Hussain Khān, Prince Muazzam (later Bahādur Shāh) etc., but all of them only upto the birth of the Khālsa (1699). The story of the later wars has not been recorded by the Guru.)*

* For their complete English translation, see the auther's "*Thus spake the Tenth Master.*"

APPENDIX IX

Victory be to the One Supreme Being whose Will ever prevails.

ZAFAR NĀMĀ

(or the Letter of Victory)

uttered in person by the Tenth Master

The Memorandum (to Aurangzeb)*

I have no faith in thy oaths,
Even though you bring in God as your witness.

I haven't even an iota of trust in thee,
For, all thy ministers and thy courtiers are liars.
He who puts faith in thy oath on the Qurān,
He, in the end, comes to ruin.

But, beware, that the insolent crow
Can lay not his hands upon one whose protection is *Humā* the "Bird of Heaven."

---

* This letter of defiance, comprising of III couplets, originally in Persian verse, was sent through special messengers by Guru Gobind Singh to Emperor Aurangzab, in the Deccan, shortly before the latter's death in 1707, detailing the atrocities and perfidies perpetrated on the Guru's house by his minions. The Guru by now had lost his four sons, two in a battle at Chamkaur and the other two having been bricked up alive (or executed) at Sirhind. His mother had died of shock. Most of his followers had either scattered or fallen on the battle-field. To hurl a letter of victory into the face of an imperial tyrant is to the eternal glory of this master-spirit.

The first twelve stanzas are an invocation and uttered in praise of God. The Guru's main grievance as expressed in this letter is that an oath taken on the Qurān by his enemies was broken by them and he was tricked into leaving the fort at Anandpur and engaging in battle against a huge host with only forty men at Chamkaur. The Guru's faith in moral principles even during a war is thus exemplified here, in no uncertain terms, which shows that he was no mere warrior, but principally the upholder of God's Moral Law.

It will be seen that the Guru accuses the king personally of the breach of an oath on the Qurān, which his general flouted (with or without his knowledge) but the Guru holds Aurangzeb himself responsible for it. Possibly, some written assurance by him was conveyed by the Qāzis to the Guru which was later never kept.

21

I had, perforce, to join battle with thy hosts,
and I too fought with the musket and arrows as best as I could.

22

When an affair is past every other remedy,
It is righteous, indeed, to unsheath the sword.

45

I know not that you, O man, were a perjurer,
And a worshiper of power, and a breaker of faith.

46

Nay, you keep no faith, nor mind Religion,
Nor you know God, nor believe in Mohammad.

47

He who observes the tenets of his faith,
He makes a promise but never to break it.

52

If your majesty were to be present here before me,
I would have with all my heart acquainted you with your treachery.
The written word and the verbal promise of your envoy,
Both. should have been fulfilled by you.

56

Thy promise was to honour thy Qāzi's word.
If that be true, then, you should come to me.

60

Come to me that we may converse with each other,
And I may utter some 'kind' words to you.

63

If He, My God, were to order me thus,
I'd with utmost pleasure present myself to you.

76

You are bound, indeed, by your word on the Qurān,
Let, therefore, the matter come to a good end, as is your promise.

78

What, if you have killed my four tender sons,
when I, like a coiled snake, remain behind.

79

It isn't brave to put out a few sparks,
And stir up fire to rage all the more.

81

When you and I will, both, repair to the Court of God,
You will bear witness to what you did unto me.

82

But, if you will forget even this,
Then, God on High will also forget you from His Mind.

85

I believe not that you know God,
Since from you have come only tyrannous acts.

94

You may be the king of kings, a brave warrior, of charitable disposition, ornament of the thrones of the world, and
master of the earth :
But, I protest, you know not the Religion of God.

106

You are proud of your empire and material possessions, while
I am proud of the Refuge of God, the Immortal.

109

If you are strong, torture not the weak,
And thus lay not the axe to thy empire.

110

If the One God is one's friend, what harm can the enemy do,
Even if he multiplies himself a hundred times.

APPENDIX X

Raj Karega Khalsa

BY DR. GANDA SINGH

(Professor Emiritus of History, Panjābi University, Patiālā)

The *Rāj Karēgā Khālsā* couplet is at times misunderstood and misconstrued. It has been dubbed as an innovation of the 'neo-Sikhs' of the Singh Sabha persuasion. The motive behind it in the pre-independence days was to create in the minds of British officials suspicions about the political aspirations of the Sikh community. And, now, it is, not unoften, misrepresented by anti-Sikh political parties as a communal demand against the popular Indian Government. Both are unhistorical misconstructions. The words of the couplet are clear. There is no ambiguity about what they mean. It says:

Rāj Karègā Khālsā, yāqi rahè nā koè,
Khwār hoè sabh milèngè bachè sarn jo hoē.

Which means:

> "The Khālsā shall rule, no hostile refractory shall exist. Frustrated, they shall all submit, and those who come in for shelter shall be protected."

Just as all other historical allusions in the Sikh prayer refer to past history, so does this couplet refer to the days of the later Mughal Emperors, Bahādur Shāh, Farrukh Siyar, etc. It is a composition of the first quarter of the eighteenth century. It forms a part of the *Tankhwāh-Nāmāh* of Bhāi Nand Lāl, who, after the death of Emperor Bahādur Shāh in 1712, returned to his home-town in Multān and died there. It was, evidently, first sung by the Khālsā during the days of Bandā Singh Bahādur (1710-16) who was the first Sikh political leader to declare the independence of his people in the Panjāb. Bahādur Shāh, the son and successor of Aurangzeb, not only then declared the Sikhs to be rebels, but also issued edicts to his faujdārs on December 10,1710, "to kill the disciples of Nānak (the Sikhs) wherever they were found : *Nānak prastān rā har ja kih ba-yaband ba-qatl rasānand (Ahkbār-i-Darbār-i-Muallā).*" This was repeated by Emperor Farrukh Siyar (1713-19) in almost the same words, given in the *Miftāh-ut-Tawārikh*, p. 39a. According to this order, the Sikhs were to be wiped out of existence wholesale. No trace of them was to be left in their own land, their birth-place, the land of their ancestors. This was a tyranny of the worst type. And no self-respecting son of the land, much less the Sikhs, could stand it, however great and numerous were the odds pitched against him. The Singhs of Guru Gobind Singh were not frightened by these edicts. They had been cast in a different mould and had received the baptism of the double-edged sword (*Khandē di Pāhul*). They knew the land was theirs and it was their right to live therein. They had only to assert this right. Tyranny has no long life, and tyrants perish under the weight of their own sins. It was only the question of time, and the Sikhs would come to their own. And they proved to be right. The Rāj of the Khālsā was established and they successfully broke the first sod in the ultimate conquest and independence of the Panjāb.

It was then when they were presecuted and done to death for aspiring to *rāj karo*, to rule in their homeland, that to keep up their spirits, with their minds strengthened by faith and emboldened by constant prayer, the Sikhs sang this couplet: Rāj Karegā Khālsā yāqi rahè nā koè. It is true that they had to suffer very heavily and had to make innumerable sacrifices for over half a century. But they knew their cause was right and success would ultimately be theirs. Throughout this period of waiting, they sang this couplet praying for the fulfilment of their aspirations. And when they became independent, they sang it in commemoration of their success and as a reminder of their promise of protection to those who sought it.

With the coming in of the British to the Punjab in 1846-49, the aspirations for Swarāj were once again revived, and with it the justification of the recitation of this couplet. The dread of the feringees suggested to some of loyalists, afraid of being listed as rebels, a compromise in giving to the word Khālsā an alternate meaning as 'pure'. They wished to convey to the rulers that the *Khālsā* had then no political ambitions or aspirations to rule in the country and that the couplet appended to their prayer only meant that the 'pure' shall rule.

It is not always correct, particularly in the context of this couplet, to translate the word *Khālsā* as 'pure' (derived, of course, *from khālis.*) Khālsā is, in fact, a technical term which in the days of Mughal administration meant "inalienable lands or revenues directly looked after or administered by the government or the king." Guru Gobind Singh applied this word specifically to those of the Sikhs whom he had baptized as Singhs, the lions. To them he gave the name of Khālsā, his own. "The term," wrote H H. Wilson in 1855 in his *Glossary of Judicial and Revenue Terms*, "has been of late familiar as the collective denomination of the Sikh Government and people." The recitation of the *Rāj Karegā Khālsa* has provided to the Sikh people with a source of inspiration and strength in their social and political undertakings in the past and shall always act as an incentive for them in the service of the country. With the blessing of God, India is now a free country. The old aspirations of the Sikhs have come to be fulfilled in the establishment of the People's Rāj, the Sovereign Democratic Republic of India, with equality of status and of opportunity to all sections of the people of the country.

In the psesent democratic set-up in India, the people of the country have to be educated in democratic principles of government to be able to organize themselves in groups and parties to take upon their shoulders, or to share with others, the burden of the governance of the country as and when they are called upon to do so. Like the majority group of the Hindus and the largest minority group of the Muslims, they are as well a group of people in the country and have a right to aspire to political power as a group by itself or in collaboration with others. They have for this purpose to educate the constituents of their group. The Sikh group can best be educated for the service of the country on the lines laid down and traditions set up by the great Gurus and heroes and martyrs whose glories are recounted in their prayer. The *Rāj karegā Khālsā* is an inseparable part of the Sikh prayer and of their past aspirations and traditions to serve their countrymen, and its recitation reminds them of their duties and responsibilities not only towards their own people but also towards the entire family of Mother India whose own flesh and blood they are.

April, 1973

[Panjāb, Past & Present]

APPENDIX XI

MIRI AND PIRI

Much confusion has been created in Sikh affairs lately by misinterpreting the Sikh ethos, as it evolved after the Sixth Guru, Hargobind, decided to wear two swords, one signifying "Miri" (secular power) and the other "Piri" (spiritual power). The unwary interpret it as the Guru's desire to combine religion with politics! If we look into Sikh history, scriptures and tradition carefully, this interpretation can not hold .

In the first place, according to Sikh traditional historians, like Bhai Santokh Singh, it was a chance occurrence. "Contrary to the earlier practice, when each succeeding Guru was offered a *'topi'* (cap) and *'seli'* (woollen cord) by his predecessor,while a devout Sikh anointed his fore-head with a saffron-mark *(tikka)*, Guru Hargobind ordained, after the martyrdom of his Guru-father, Arjun Dev, that he would like to deck himself with a sword."+ It so happened that Baba Budha put the sword on the wrong (i.e. the right) side of the Guru's body. Seeing this, the Guru said :– don't remove it from here. Let me wear another one on the right (i.e. the left) side, one denoting "Miri" and the other "Piri"!

Even if the choice was deliberate, as one would like to believe, the devout Sikhs resisted it. Bhai Gurdas, the great Sikh Savant, (already quoted in this context in Chapter X), wrote some strongly-worded verses against the new stance of the Guru's! "Earlier, the Kings came to pay homage to the Gurus, now our forts are attacked by the kings! The followers too find no peace, for the Guru is ever on the go, and is terrified by nothing" etc. (Vār 26, Pauri 24).

What is more, in his entire life-time, the Guru himself never staked a claim for statehood. In fact, when Jehāngir offered him his hand of friendship, he accepted it with good heart. If some skirmishes did take place later with the forces of Shah Jahān, the fight was never for Statehood, but for human equality. Indeed, none of the first five Gurus, for a whole century, ever

+ Mahān Kosh, P. 683. Paintings of Guru Nānak wearing a red round cap and a black woollen cord (Seli) wrapped round it can be seen in the Museums at Lahore and Chandigarh.

thought of or organised an armed rebellion against the State, with which their relations upto the time of Akbar were of the very best.

Even Guru Hargobind fought always in self-defence, and never kept a large, regular force, as his life-story testifies. This clearly reveals his intentions. Guru Hari Rai kept a cavalry of 2200, but never used it. Guru Hari Krishan died very young, but Guru Teg Bahādur never raised an army, though he participated actively in the welfare of the people in many ways.

If the idea of building the Akāl Takhat was to mix religion with politics, this could have been better served by using the Golden Temple itself as a platform also for agitating or discussing secular affairs. But, no Guru ever thought of it. Upto date, the tradition persists that no discourse (not even religious) is permitted within the precincts of the Hari-Mandir, and any such discussion must be held outside. To build the Akāl Takhat as a separate seat of secular power, only means that the Guru intended to separate religion and politics, and not mix the two. But, he also thereby emphasised that, henceforth, the Sikhs would not shirk even the use of arms to fight tyranny and to participate in, and not withdraw from, socio-political life. However, they had neither to dominate others, nor to be dominated or exploited by others. The age-old acceptance by the Hindus of the world as "Māyā" and "whosoever ruled over us is good enough" were thus discarded by the Sikhs for ever.

While Guru Hargobind wore two swords, no other Guru after him – not even the Tenth Master – did so. He wore arms and fought but not to create a State for his own religion, but one in which everyone was equal in religious hope as in secular welfare.

While Guru Gobind Singh fought many battles, at no time did he claim any reparations or territories as a result of his victories. In one of his verses, included in the Dasam Granth, he clearly separates religion from politics.

"Bābē ke Bābur ke Do-oo

Āp Karē Parmēshar So-oo

Duni Shāh in Ko Paichāno.

Deen Shāh un Ko anmāno.

Jo Bābē Ke Dām na, de hai.

'Tis te geh Bābur Ke lē hai."

(i.e. consider the House of the Bābā (Nānak) and the House of Bābur to be the creation of the self-same God. The one rules in the realm of the spirit, and the other in the realm of the secular world. But, whosoever pays not his tribute to the House of the Bābā, him the forces of Bābur seize and destroy. Which means that he who does not uphold the Moral Law, him the God destroys through the tyrannies of the worldly power).

The one complaint the Tenth Guru makes against Aurangzeb is not why he had won the throne of Hindustān, but why he ruled in the name and for the sake of a single religion and why, during warfare, he forsook the tenets even of that religion?(see, Zafarnāmā). Toynbee has well said, that the Sikhs fought the Moghals, with their own weapons, but as a determined minority in defence and for the sake of the majority. For, said Guru Gobind Singh, that even while fighting and playing politics, one should neither divide mankind into caste and community, nor flout God's Moral Law and a human civilised Code of Conduct. Otherwise, God in diverse ways punishes such transgressions invariably, and without fail. That, in reality, is the meaning of religion or Dharma upholding polity.

The point has also to be emphasised that Guru Gobind Singh invested the Adi Granth (containing purely spiritual instructions) with the Guruship, after him, and not his own Granth (which includes mostly war poetry or secular instructions)!

The Tenth Master extended his hand of friendship even to Aurangzeb, his persecutor, and was on the way to the Deccan to meet and settle with him the affairs of his house and his people (See, ZafarnBāmā.) But, the emperor died during this period and no meeting ever took place. But, the Guru helped his Sufi son, Bahādur Shah, in the war of succession, though the Sikhs under Bandā had to fight again with him a battle of life-and-death.

The Sikhs created for a time a state under Banda Bahādur (1710-17). They captured the Panjāb and the 12 Sikh Misals later ruled over the various parts for about three decades (1764-1799). Ranjit Singh later created a large empire in the north-west of India. But, the Church was always kept apart from the affairs of the State. At no time was a fiat (or a Hukamnāmā) ever issued by the Akāl Takhat, as to how to run the affairs of the State. Occasional get-togethers at the Akāl Takhat, of the Sikh Misals, as in 1748 and 1764, were only to forge unity among the warring chiefs, in order to put up a united front against the Afghān marauder, Ahmad Shāh Abdāli. As soon as the fight was over, each Misal ruled over its territory, unaided or dictated to by any edict from the Akāl Takhat. During the days of Ranjit Singh, the Akāl Takhat was never consulted in any matter of the state. Nor was anyone declared a *Tankhāhiya* (Renegade) for any political activity or lapse, an innovation introduced by the neo-Akalis, after the passage of the Gurdwara Act, 1925, to punish or embarass their political opponents.

If politics and religion are one for the Sikhs, why did the Akāli Dal, first in 1948 and then again in 1956, after a compromise with the Congress, an avowedly secular Party, convert the Dal into a purely "socio-cultural" body, having nothing to do with politics? Is it that they can play with the doctrines they consider sacred and inviolable the way political necessity dictates?

No Guru ever stayed at the Akāl Takhat, nor made it a battle-ground. No Sikh hero throughout history did so, nor even the neo-Akālis before 1983-84. In fact, neither the 7th, 8th, 9th and the Tenth Master, nor Bandā Bahādur, ever visited the Akāl Takhat or the Golden Temple. After the death of Bhai Mani Singh (1738), it is the *Udāsis* (Hindu in form, Sikh in belief) who became the Custodians of the Akāl Takhat as well as the Hari Mandir. The Nihangs controlled these shrines, during the period of Ranjit Singh and the British nominated, from 1850 to 1920, its own custodians. It was the misuse of the Takhat during the British period in issuing Hukamnāmās against Sikh patriots and in honouring tyrants like General Dyer that the Akāli movement was started in the nineteen twenties of this country.

Another very relevant point which all Sikhs must ponder is : Who are the Sikh Govt. functionaries answerable to, in their secular activities — the Govt. of the day, or the Akāl Takhat? Especially where, in discharge of his duty, a Sikh official of the Govt. may have to go even against the management of the Sikh Gurdwārās. If his first loyalty in such matters is to the Akāl Takhat, and not to the State of which he is an employee, and is under oath to protect its security and integrity, it will be hard indeed for any state apparatus to employ him.

The Bible forbids the mixing of religion with the affairs of the state. "Give unto Caesar what is Caesar's and unto God what is God's". But the successive Popes of Rome tried to combine in themselves the dual role of religious heads and secular affairs of the Christian States. The result was not only the division of the faith into Protestant and Catholic, but also wholesale massacres of one at the hands of the other. States fought with each other, no matter even if they belonged to the same faith. There is hardly a Christian State today which combines the two. If someone does, it is only in name, as in the United Kingdom.

The Muslims started combining the two, as the Prophet Mohammad himself was both the religious head as well as the secular ruler of his State. But, ultimately, they all broke up into nation-States and even fought with each other. It was Ataturk, who abolished the Caliphate in Turkey, in 1924, where the Sultān combined the two functions in his person. Pakistan couldn't stay together on the basis of a common faith.

And Sikhs fought with each other to death, when it came to grabbing power. Brother cut the throat of brother, one Misal of another, and even sought foreign protection against each other, as the Cis-Satluj Phulkiān States did, under the Moghals, the Afghāns and even the British.

And if the Sikhs must combine the two, what about the others who must live in their realm? Will they be deprived of their right of vote and other democratic privileges? And will the Sikhs agree to suffer the same fate both outside India, and even outside the Panjāb? Mahārāja Ranjit Singh abolished the "Gurmattā" system, introduced by the Sikh Misals for a time, and never called a *Sarbat Khālsā* for any matter whatsoever. That is how, though belonging to a minority faith, he ruled so successfully over an overwhelmingly non-Sikh (mostly Muslim) majority.

And will only the Sikhs be entitled to vote for the Sikh candidates at the polls? And will the Sikhs be allowed to join only a single Sikh (or, only a Sikh) political Party, and no other? And how shall we define a Sikh and what shall be the political and secular status of the unorthodox Sikh sects? And will there be a place for democracy in the Sikh polity? And, if democracy is to prevail, all arguments in favour of an exclusive Sikh polity fall to the ground.

Politics involves us in low intrigue, self-assertion, back-biting, hitting below the belt, opportunism, compromise of principles, conflict and war. Sikh Religion enjoins universal brotherhood, moral living, self-surrender, contemplation of the one God. "He who dominates over another is a fool, an indiscriminate wretch", says Guru Nānak. How can a true Sikh combine the two?

It is quite another thing to take up arms in defence of one's nation against foreign rule or aggression. But that each religious community, within a nation, should have its own distinct polity, or a nation-state, was never the intention of the Gurus. Otherwise, they would not have taken up arms against the Moghals, and the Sikhs later against the Afghāns, or migrated, en masse, from a Muslim Pākistān, as late as 1947!

APPENDIX XII

THE SIKH CONGREGATIONAL PRAYER

(This Prayer is recited after every service, morning and evening, at home as well as in congregations at the Temples. Its first six lines were composed by Guru Gobind Singh)

Having first remembered Lord the God, call on Guru Nānak.

And then on Guru Angad, Amar Dās and Rām Dās:

may they ever protect us.

Then call on Arjun and Hari Gobind and the holy Hari Rāi.

And then on Hari Krishna, seeing whom all one's sorrows are dispelled.

And then remember Tegh Bahādur, the ninth Guru, that the

nine Treasures come hastening to thy home.

O our Masters, be ye ever with us.

May the Tenth King, Guru Gobind Singh, be ever on our side.

And now turn your thoughts to the teachings of the

Guru Granth Sāhib, the Visible Embodiment of the Gurus, and

utter : "Glory be to God."

(All congregation answers) : "Wonderful Lord."

The four Sons,[2] the five Beloved ones,[3] the forty Saved ones,[4]

the martyrs, the true disciples, the contemplators of God, and

---

2 The martyred sons of Guru Gobind Singh.

3 Whom Guru Gobind first baptised.

4 Those who fell in the battle of Chamkaur. Some say it refers to those fallen near Khidrāna (later known as Mukatsar). They had first deserted the Guru and later returned to do battle and die. But their number could on no account be forty.

those who remained steadfast on the Path: remember their glorious deeds and utter : "Glory be to God."

(All) : "Wonderful Lord."

They who dwelt on God's Name, shared their earnings with others, wielded the sword on the battlefield, and distributed food in companionship, offered their heads at the altar of Dharma, were cut up limb by limb, were skinned or boiled* or sawn alive, but uttered not a sigh nor faltered in their faith, remember their glorious deeds, and utter: "Glory be to God."

(All) : "Wonderful Lord."

O great King, save us from the five sins — lust, wrath, greed, undue attachment and ego. O God, let us call on Thee alone, yea , Thee alone, and let the merit of this remembrance be happiness of all kinds. O God, wherever are the members of the holy Khālsā, extend Thy Protection and Mercy to them: let the Panth be ever victorious: let the Holy Sword be ever our Protector: Let the war-cry of the Khālsā resound through the world: "Glory be to God."

(All) : "Wonderful Lord.

O God, may Thy Sikhs be blest with the boon of faith, of discipline, of trust, of an awakened mind, and above all, the contemplation of Thy Name.

May the banners, the staying-places, the choirs of the Khālsā stay whole through the ages, and may Religion be ever victorious.

O God, let our minds be ever humble, our intellects exalted,

---

* The references are to the martyrdoms of Bhāi Mani Singh, Bhāi Tāru Singh, Bhāi Dayālā and Bhāi Mati Dāṣ, respectively.

and be Thou ever the Protector of our minds and our honour.

Utter, O Khālsā, "Glory be to God".

(All) : "Wonderful Lord."

Blest by the Guru, may our spirits be ever in the ascendent. O God, may the whole world be blest is Thy Will and Mercy.

APPENDIX XIII

DEBATE ON 'JALLIANWALA BAGH' IN THE HOUSE OF COMMONS

(JULY 8, 1920)

(In a country which fought for Independence through non-violence means, violence has become a way of life by the people as well as the State. The following debate will reveal how the British leaders reacted to the Jallianwala Bagh tragedy of April 13, 1919. Even Mr. Winston Churchill, deadly opposed to India's Independence and Congress leadership, could not defend this tragedy.)

Lord Edwin Montagu, Secretry of State for India, was the first to speak. He said that he understood the debate was to be confined to events in India and after consideration, he had decided that the best course for him to adopt would be to say as little as possible; it would only add to the controversy. He had expressed his views and those of the Government. The despatch by his Committee had been fully approved by the Cabinet and he had no wish to add or withdraw anything. The question, therefore, was whether Members would endorse the views of the Government, the Hunter Commitee, the Commander-in-Chief in India, the Government of India and the Army Council, or whether they wanted to censure them. The issue confronting the House was simple:

'If an officer justifies his conduct, no matter how gallant his conduct—and everybody knows how gallant General Dyer's record is -- by saying there was no question of undue severity, that if his means had been greater, the casualties would have been greater, and that the motive was to teach a moral lesson to the whole of the Punjab, I say without hesitation, and I would ask the Committee to contradict me if I am wrong, because the whole matter turns on this, that is a doctrine of terrorism.' If members agreed to that, then they justified every thing Dyer did. 'Once you are entitled to have regard neither to the intentions nor to the conduct of a particular gathering, but to shoot and to go on shooting with all the horrors that were involved in order to teach some - body else a lesson, you are embarking on terrorism to which there is no end.

'I say further that when you pass an order that all Indians must crawl past a particular place, when you pass an order to say that all Indians must forcibly or voluntarily salaam any officer of His Majesty the King, you are enforcing racial humiliation. I say, thirdly, that when you take selected school-boys from a school, guilty or innocent, and whip them publicly, when you put up a triangle where an outrage, which we all deplore and which all India deplores, has taken place, and whip people before they have been convicted, when you flog a wedding party, you are indulging in frightfulness and there is no other adequate word which could describe it. Are you going to keep your hold upon India by terrorism racial humiliation and subordination, and frightfulness, or are you going to rest it upon the growing good will of the people of your Indian empire? I believe that to be the whole question at isssue.'

"It was no good," he insisted, "for Parliament to introduce reforms if the administration on the spot did not recognize them. There is the other choice, to hold India by the sword, to recognize terrorism as part of the weapon, as part of your armament, to guard British honour and British life with callousness about Indian honour and Indian life." He reminded them that there had been thirty-seven instances of firing during the disturbances but only the shooting in the Jallianwala Bagh had been condemned. The great objection to terrorism and rule by force was that it was pursued without any regard to the people who suffered from it. And having tried it, you had to continue because of the increasing animosity of the people. There was an alternative to terrorism: the people of India could be led to free partnership in the Commonwealth.

"There is a theory abroad on the part of those who have criticized His Majesty's Government upon this issue that an Indian is tolerable so long as he will obey your orders, but if once he joins the educated classes, if once he thinks for himself, if once he takes advantage of the educational facilities which you have provided for him, if once he imbibes the ideas of individual liberty which are dear to the British people, why then you class him as an educated Indian and as an agitator. What a terrible and cynical verdict on the whole!"

(The House erupted into shouts of 'Shame', 'No', 'Withdraw' and 'What a terrible speech'.)

Montagu eventually managed to proceed and he insisted that if members wanted to adopt the democratic method of Government of India, then Dyer should be condemned.

Before he sat down he made an impassioned appeal. "I invite this House to choose, and I believe that the choice they make is fundamental to a continuance of the British Empire and vital to the continuation, permanent, I believe it can be, of the connection between this country and India."

When Mr. Winston Churchil rose to speak he was fully aware that the Government's survival was in jeopardy, for Mr.Carson MP, who had preceded him, had clearly commanded the support of several of its members. But he was not prepared to placate them. He believed Dyer had got off too lightly; he certainly had not been punished unfairly. (He was dismissed). The action taken in India and the decision of the Army Council, he stressed, was based on Dyer's first statement and not what he had said at the Hunter Committee.

Mr. Churchill said :-

"One tremendous fact stands out. I mean the slaughter of nearly four hundred persons and the wounding of probaly three or four times that number at the Jallianwala Bagh on 13 April. This is an episode which appears to me to be without precedent or parallel in the modern history of the British Empire. It is an event of entirely different order from any of those tragic occurrences which take place when troops are brought into collision with the civil population. It is an extraordinary event, a monstrous event, an event which stands in singular and sinister isolation."

Jallianwala Bagh had not saved India. 'Our reign in India or anywhere else had never rested on a basis of physical force alone, and it would be fatal to the British Empire to try to base ourselves only upon it.'

Speaking for himself, Churchill said that Dyer not only deserved loss of employment and censure, but disciplinary action. But as it appeared that his conduct had at the time been condoned, the Cabinet decided against further action.

There was a sullen silence from many whose loyalty he had hoped to command. Herbert Asquith, the former Prime Minister, tried to diffuse the atmosphere. Dyer may have been commended at the time but were his superior officer and the Lieutenant-Governor impartial judges? In the hectic circumstances surrounding the incident, they might have reached conclusions which subsequent reflection and investigation might not have justified. Bu purely on the merits of the case, he had not heard anything to impugn th correctness of the action taken by the various authorities later. People ha been shot down like sheep in a pen. "There has never been such an incident the whole annals of Anglo-Indian history, nor, I believe, in the history of o Empire."

The Labour Party view was put forward by Mr. B.G. Spoor, the Mem for Bishop Auckland, who said that two weeks previously at the Labour Pa Conference, a resolution had been passed calling for the recall of the Vice

the impeachment of Sir Michael O'Dwyer, and the trial of officers who had been censured and the repeal of repressive legislation. That resolution expressed more clearly the feelings of the people than the exhibition they had witnessed that evening.

Sir Edward Carson has said, 'Let us be fair to the British Officers . Yes, but also let them be fair to the hundreds of Indians who lost their lives and to the children who were bombed from the air by British officers. Amritsar was not an isolated event any more than General Dyer was an isolatd officer."

(Courtesy : "Amritsar" by Alfred Draper", Collins).

APPENDIX XIV

Some Correspondence

(About Sikh Religion, Literature & Polity)

Pennsylvania (USA)
June 15, 1971

Dear Dr. Gopal Singh,

Today your book, THE RELIGION OF THE SIKHS, has come and of course I have begun immediately to read it. Thank you very much indeed.

Even since I received your translation of the Sikh Scripture in India several years ago, as you remember, I have been interested in this religion. *It seems to me to be extraordinarily modern. It is both practical and mystical and* I understand now, atleast to some extent, the spirit which informs my Sikh friends and gives them their admirable qualities. Again my warm thanks and I remain,

Your Cordially
PEARL S. BUCK

Pearl S. Buck, the Nobel Laureate, called the author's English translation of the Guru Granth Sāhib "a superb piece of work," and said (1962) :

"Sri Guru Granth Sahib is a source-book, an expression of man's loneliness, his aspirations, his longings, his cry to God and his hunger for communication with that Being. I have studied the Scriptures of other great religions, but I donot find elsewhere the same power of appeal to the heart and mind as I find here in these volumes .... There is something strangely modern about these Scriptures ..... They speak to persons of any religion or of none. They speak for the human heart and the searching mind. One wonders what might have been produced if the ten founders of the Sikh religion had been acquainted with the findings of modern Science. Where would their quest for knowledge have led them, had Science been their means instead of religion. Perhaps in the same direction, for the most important revelation now being made by scientists is that their knowledge, as it opens one door after another to the many universes in eternal existence, affirms the essential unity of science and religion. It is impressive and significant that in the study of these Sikh Scriptures, we see this affirmation through the approach of the brilliant minds and deep searching hearts of men who are part of India. Through them we see a Beyond that belongs to us all. The result is a universal revelation."

2

London
9 December 1962

Dear Dr. Gopal Singh,

Following up my letter of 22 August, this is to let you know that I have now had the pleasure of studying your splenddid translation of the Guru Granth Sahib. May I congratulate you on having carried through this great and exacting piece of work ?

Before I had access to the Guru Granth Sahib only in extracts. To have the whole of it before me is a new experience. I have now got a grand impression of it that I would not have had without your work.

A non-Sikh naturally thinks in terms of the Sikh Scriptures' likeness to and difference from the Scriptures of other religions. In Qurān, we have a single voice. The Bible is a collection of separate books: it is a whole literature, not a single work. At the same time, as I see it, a single theme runs through the Bible: namely, God's practice of presenting challenges to human beings. The Guru Granth Sahib, like the Bible, is a work of many hands. On the other hand, it has much more unity than the Bible has. The theme here, if I have rightly understood it, is the joy of praising God. The voices are different but their theme is the same, so the effect we have is that of a choir singing variations on the same song.

I once had the good fortune to visit the Golden Temple at Amritsar and to listen to the uninterrupted chanting of the Guru Granth Sahib. The experience made a great impression on me: an impression of sincerity and whole-heartedness.

Thank you once again for your kindness and generosity in sending me your volumes. They are a possession that I value greatly, and I owe this to you.

Yours Sincerely
ARNOLD TOYNBEE

(Arnold Toynbee was a world renowned historian and scholar of world religions.)

3

Moscow
15 December 1964

Dear Dr. Gopal Singh,

I have not forgotten your meritable rendering into English of Sikh Scripture and the problem of its translation into Russian. Soviet indologists hold in high esteem your valuable contribution and have extensively used the same in their research work.

V. V. Balabushevich
Head of the Indian Deptt.
Academy of Sciences, USSR

4

Cambridge
Jan. 25, 1964

Dear Mr. Ienberg,

I have just received Dr. Gopal Singh's magnificent gift (the English translation of the Sikh Scripture). I knew too little about the Sikh community and its culture, and a glance through these volumes shows me how much I have been missing.

E. M. Forster

(E. M. Forster was a novelist of international repute and author of "A Passage to India" etc.)

5

Patiala
May 5, 1971

My Dear Gopal Singhji,

Kindly accept my thanks for a copy of your recent book, THE RELIGION OF THE SIKHS. Nothing gives one greater pleasure than to see a friend doing such useful service to the community. Your contribution to Sikh literature promises to last for centuries to come. Good luck to you—and Satguru's blessings.

Affectionately......GANDA SINGH

(Dr. Ganda Singh was the celebrated historian of the Panjāb))

6

Geneva
18 June, 1169

Dear Dr. Gopal Singh,

This is to express my deep appreciation for your inscribed book on Guru Nanak.

I am sure, the Christian community in India are greatly in your debt.

Sincerely Yours
Eugene C. Blake

(Mr. E. C. Blake was then the Secretary General of the World Council of Churches. In the letter, he is referring to the many initiatives the author took in behalf of the Christian community as M.P., as President of Inter-Religious organisation and Secretary General of the All-India National Solidarity Council etc, whenever the religious or cultural rights of the Christian minority were assailed in India. The World Assembly of the W.C.C. at Nairobi (1975) and Vancouver (1982) invited the author to speak on Sikhism & inter-religious dialogue. The late Pope Paul VI & Pope John Paul II also received & decorated him wlth medallions for the same reasons.

7

New Delhi
May 16, 1961

Dear Dr. Gopal Singh,

Your letter of May 14th. In the course of my talks with Sant Fateh Singh, I told him, as I had told him previously, that in my opinion the cutting up of the Punjāb State in any way and the formation of what is called the Punjābi Suba would be harmful to Punjāb, to India and more especially to the Sikhs. I could not therefore agree to it. But I have been anxious about developing Punjābi language and much has been done in this respect. If he had any further suggestions to make, we would be glad to consider them, as also any specific grievances of the Sikh community.

No reference was made in our talks by Sant Fateh Singh to any fast or any other threat. We parted in a friendly way.

Yours Sincerely
Jawāharlāl Nehru

(The author had written a personal letter to the then Prime Minister of India to settle the Sikh affairs in an amicable manner, after his talks with Sant Fateh Singh had broken down. He not only agreed to have discussions about the specific Sikh grievances but also about further growth of the Punjābi language. As would be seen, this is all he said later also after Sant Fateh Singh had gone on a fast followed by Māster Tārā Singh's.)

8

New Delhi
Nov. 25, 1962

Dear Dr. Gopal Singh,

Your letter of 24th November. I shall gladly meet Justice Gurnām Singh tomorrow, 26th November, at 11.30 A.M. in my office in External Affairs.

Yours Sincerely,
Jawāharlāl Nehru

(Justice Gurnām Singh, then leader of the Akāli Opposition in Panjāb Assembly, was not on good terms with the Prime Minister after the failure of his leaders' fasts leading to nothing. A stalemate had ensued and the Prime Minister, much embittered against Akālī leadership, had refused to interview any of them. The author broke this stalemate much to the advantage of the Sikhs, as after this meeting, the Prime Minister started re-thinking on the issue of the Panjābi-speaking state.)

9

Srinagar
May 20, 1962

My dear Dr. Gopal Singh,

Thank you for your letter of May 16th. I have read it with much interest.

It will be a good thing if the Gurdwārā administration is converted into a Trust. Personally, I think that the Gurdwārā Act as it is brings in the Govt. too much for its operation, in elections etc. This leads to complaints about governmental interference. Why should Govt. not step out of it and leave it to the Trust to arrange for elections etc. and keep it out of politics.

Yours Sincerely
Jawāharlāl Nehru

(The letter was in reply to the author drawing attention of the Prime Minister to the Sikh complaints of Govt. interference in Gurdwārā affairs. Later, on another representation to him by the author, he instructed Sardār Sawaran Singh, his Minister (who was going to Pākistān after the Chinese invasion of Oct. 1962 to hold negotiations about the Kashmir dispute),to talk to the Pākistān authorities about giving Nankānā Sāhib the status of the Vatican City. But the writer was told later by S. Swaran Singh that Mr. Z.A. Bhutto, then Foreign Minister of Pākistān, could not find time for this important issue !)

10

Prime Minister's House,
New Delhi
June 8, 1966

Dear Gopal Singhji,

I have your letter of June 7th and have noted your views.

Now that the Report has come in and the Commission was headed by an eminent judge, it becomes extremely difficult to deviate from it, except by mutual consent between the parties concerned.

With regards.

Yours Sincerely
Indira Gandhi

(This was in response to a protest the author had lodged with the Prime Minister over the highly unjust and arbitrary division of the Panjāb. He pleaded for her intervention to restore the Panjābi-speaking areas to Panjāb.)

11

Stockholm
June 14,1965

Dear Dr Singh,

His Majesty has had much pleasure in perusing your splendid work, Sri Guru Granth Sahib, in its four magnificent volumes as well as your beautiful book of poetry (The Unstruck Melody) having been recently informed that your name figures on the list of candidates for the Nobel Prize in Literature.

Yours Sincerely
C F. Palmstierna.
(Secy. to the King of Sweden)

12

In the name of God, Most Gracious, Most Merciful

Care of Collector. Madurai
6 June, 1967

My dear Shri Gopal Singhji,

May Peace of Allāh be upon you.

According to one of the sayings of Prophet Mohammad (May Peace by upon him) the biggest 'Jihad' is to speak a word of truth before a tyrant. The statement issued under your signature, urging the withdrawal of detention and all restrictions against me and my associates falls under this category. I congratulate you for upholding the cause of truth and justice so fearlessly in this all-surrounding darkness of deceit and hypocricy. It is needless for me to mention how highly grateful I feel to you for this gesture.

May God bless you.

I hope, you are doing well.

With Kindest Regards

Sheikh Mohammad Abdullah

(He later beeame Chief Minister of Kashmir once again (1975) till his death. The author secured the signatures of over 260 MPs for his release from detention & presented the petition to Mrs. Indira Gandhi, then Prime Minister. She was gracious enough to agree with the representation & Sheikh Sāhib was released immediately thereafter)

"The work that should have been accomplished long ago by the Sikh community or the Shiromani Gurdwārā Parbandhak Committee in view of its importance and need has been achieved, single-handed, by an illustrious son of the Guru. But as Sheikh Saadi has said:

"This glory one achieves not by the force of arms. It's on whom is God's Grace who attains to it."

A stupendous task, bristling with difficulties, has been achieved with success. Dr. Gopal Singh has written many works of high literary merit before also, but the English translation of the Guru Granth Sahib surpasses them all. The whole community should be proud of him. Fruitful indeed is the time that he has spent on this sacred work."

Māster Tārā Singh, (Akāli Leader)

INDEX